ON Science 10

Authors

Tom Dickinson
B.Sc., M.Sc., Ph.D.
Science Writer and Educator

Lois Edwards
Ph.D.
Science Writer

Nancy Flood
B.Sc., M.Sc., Ph.D.
Science Writer and Educator

Eric Grace
B.Sc., Ph.D.
Science Writer

Craig Jackson
B.Sc., B.Ed., D.Met.
Independent Learning Centre, TVO
Formerly of Kapuskasing
District High School

Michael Mazza
B.Sc.
Science Writer and Consultant

Jim Ross
B.Sc., B.Ed., M.Ed.
Science Writer and Consultant

Contributing Authors

Jenna Dunlop
Ph.D., M.B.A.
Science Writer

Katherine Hamilton
B.Sc., Ph.D.
Science Writer

Natasha Marko
B.Sc., M.Sc., M.A.
Science Writer

Jennifer Parrington
B.Sc., B.Ed.
York Region District School Board

Trudy L. Rising
M.Sc.
Science Writer and Consultant

Program Consultants

Tigist Amdemichael
B.Sc., B.A., B.Ed., M.Ed.
Toronto District School Board

Steve Bibla
B.Sc., B.Ed.
Toronto District School Board

Curriculum, Pedagogical, and STSE Consultant

Tigist Amdemichael

Assessment Consultant

Anu Arora
B.Sc. (Hons.), M.Sc., B.Ed.
Peel District School Board

Literacy and Environmental Education Consultant

Steve Bibla

Consultant

Leesa Blake
B.Sc., B.Ed., M.A.
Toronto District School Board

Trudy L. Rising

Aboriginal Consultants

Chris Craig
South Nation Conservation Authority
Member of the Algonquins of Pikwakanagan

Francis McDermott
Shabot Obaadjiwan Algonquin First Nation
Nibina Forestry

Differentiated Instruction Consultant

Jennifer Parrington
B.Sc., B.Ed.
York Region District School Board

ELL Consultants

Maureen Innes
B.A.
Nipissing University

Wendy Campbell
B.A., B.Ed.
Waterloo Region District School Board

Al Tordjman
B.A., B.Ed.
Waterloo Region District School Board

Advisors

Anjuli Ahooja
B.Sc. (Hons.), M.Sc., Ph.D.
Curriculum Chair, Science and Technology
Appleby College

Christina Clancy
B.Sc. (Hons.), M.Sc., B.Ed.
Dufferin-Peel Catholic District School Board

Lea Francis
B.Sc.F., Dip.RM., B.Ed.
York Region District School Board

Craig Jackson
B.Sc., B.Ed., D.Met.
Independent Learning Centre, TVO
Formerly of Kapuskasing District High School

Frank Mustoe
B.Sc., B.Ed., M.Ed., Ph.D.
Former Science Coordinator
University of Toronto Schools

Paul Passafiume
B.A.Sc., B.Ed.
York Region District School Board

Rob Smythe
B.Sc., B.Ed., M.Sc.(T)
Halton District School Board

NELSON

NELSON

ON Science 10

For more information contact Nelson Education Ltd., 1120 Birchmount Road, Toronto, Ontario M1K 5G4. Or you can visit our website at nelson.com.

Copyright © 2009, McGraw-Hill Ryerson Limited. All rights reserved. Excerpts from this publication may be reproduced under licence from Access Copyright (visit *accesscopyright.ca*), or with the express written permission of Nelson Education Ltd., or as permitted by law. Requests which fall outside of Access Copyright guidelines must be submitted online to cengage.com/permissions. Further questions about permissions can be emailed to permissionrequest@cengage.com.

ALL RIGHTS ARE OTHERWISE RESERVED. No part of this publication may be reproduced, stored in a retrieval system, or transmitted in any form or by any means, electronic, mechanic, photocopying, scanning, recording or otherwise, except as specifically authorized.

Every effort has been made to trace ownership of all copyrighted material and to secure permission from copyright holders. In the event of any question arising as to the use of any material, we will be pleased to make the necessary corrections in future printings.

The information and activities in this textbook have been carefully developed and reviewed by professionals to ensure safety and accuracy. However, the publisher shall not be liable for any damages resulting, in whole or in part, from the reader's use of the material. Although appropriate safety procedures are discussed in detail and highlighted throughout the textbook, the safety of students remains the responsibility of the classroom teacher, the principal, and the school board.

ISBN-13: 978-0-07-072222-4
ISBN-10: 0-07-072222-6

5 6 7 8 24 23 22 21

Printed and bound in Canada

PUBLISHER: Diane Wyman
PROJECT MANAGEMENT: Pronk&Associates (Jane McNulty)
DEVELOPMENTAL EDITING: Pronk&Associates (Michelle Anderson, Kathy Hamilton, Kris McCardel, Betty Robinson, Lauri Seidlitz)
MANAGING EDITOR: Crystal Shortt
SUPERVISING EDITOR: Jeanette McCurdy
COPY EDITORS: Linda Jenkins, Paula Pettitt-Townsend
PHOTO RESEARCH/PERMISSIONS: Pronk&Associates
ART BUYING: Pronk&Associates
REVIEW COORDINATORS: Jennifer Keay, Alexandra Savage-Ferr
EDITORIAL ASSISTANT: Michelle Malda
MANAGER, PRODUCTION SERVICES: Yolanda Pigden
PRODUCTION COORDINATOR: Paula Brown
SET-UP PHOTOGRAPHY: Dave Starrett
COVER/INTERIOR DESIGN: Pronk&Associates
ELECTRONIC PAGE MAKE-UP: Pronk&Associates

Acknowledgements

Pedagogical Reviewers

Nadia Camara
York Region District School Board
Richmond Hill, Ontario

Paul Carter
Peel District School Board
Brampton, Ontario

Erin Connelly
Ottawa Catholic School Board
Kanata, Ontario

Katy Farrow
Thames Valley District School Board
London, Ontario

Monica Franciosa
York Catholic District School Board
Richmond Hill, Ontario

Patricia Gaspar
York Region District School Board
King City, Ontario

Vijay Gulati
Toronto District School Board
Toronto, Ontario

John Hallett
Peel District School Board
Caledon, Ontario

Michele Laframboise
London District Catholic School Board
St. Thomas, Ontario

Annette Nelson-Szpak
Greater Essex County District
 School Board
Windsor, Ontario

Barbara Nixon-Ewing
Ontario Institute for Studies
 in Education
Seconded from Toronto District
 School Board
Toronto, Ontario

Clyde Ramlochan
Toronto District School Board
Toronto, Ontario

Sharon Ramlochan
Toronto District School Board
Toronto, Ontario

Kamla Kerry-Ann Reid
York Region District School Board
Unionville, Ontario

Mary Schroder
Dufferin-Peel Catholic District
 School Board
Mississauga, Ontario

Dr. Jane I. Smith
Simcoe County District School Board
Barrie, Ontario

Patricia Thomas
Ottawa-Carleton District School Board
Ottawa, Ontario

Frank Villella
Hamilton-Wentworth Catholic District
 School Board
Hamillton, Ontario

Accuracy Reviewers

Jenna Dunlop (Unit 1)
Ph.D, M.B.A
Science Writer
Toronto, Ontario

John Eix (Unit 2)
B.Sc. (Hons.), M.Ed. (Science Curriculum)
Retired
Upper Canada College
Toronto, Ontario

Irwin Talesnick (Unit 2)
B.A. (Physics and Chemistry), M.A.
 (Chemistry)
Professor Emeritus
Faculty of Education
Queen's University
Kingston, Ontario

Paul Delaney (Unit 3)
B.Sc. (Hons.), M.Sc.
Senior Lecturer, Dept. of Physics
 and Astronomy
Director, Division of Natural Science
York University
Toronto, Ontario

Harvey Shear (Unit 3)
Ph.D.
Professor, Dept. of Geography
University of Toronto
Mississauga, Ontario

Doug Roberts (Unit 4)
Ed.D., Ph.D. (Hon.)
Professor Emeritus, University of Calgary
Calgary, Alberta

T.J. Elgin Wolfe (Unit 4)
M.Ed.
Professor, Ontario Institute for Studies
 in Education
University of Toronto
Toronto, Ontario

Safety Reviewer

Peter Bloch
Toronto District School Board
Toronto, Ontario

Lab Testers

Leesa Blake
Toronto District School Board
Toronto, Ontario

Tanta Naus
Peel District School Board
Brampton, Ontario

Clyde Ramlochan
Toronto District School Board
Toronto, Ontario

Sharon Ramlochan
Toronto District School Board
Toronto, Ontario

Bias Reviewer

Bev McMorris
Retired Principal
Waterloo Region District School Board
Kitchener, Ontario

Literacy Reviewer

Joanie McCormick
Upper Grand District School Board
Fergus, Ontario

Special Features and Toolkit Writers

J. Randy Attwood
Nancy Christoffer
Jenna Dunlop
Laura Edlund
Patricia Gaspar
Eric Jandciu
Natasha Marko
Paul McNulty
Craig Saunders

Study Toolkit Writer

Kelly Stern

Unit Project Writers

Patricia Gaspar
Craig Jackson
Michael Lattner
Mary Kay Winter

Student Advisory Panel

The authors, editors, and publisher of *ON Science 10* extend special thanks to the students of Sinclair Secondary School in the Durham District School Board and St. Aloysius Gonzaga Secondary School in the Dufferin Peel Catholic School Board for their guidance in the development of this learning resource.

Set-up Photography

We are very grateful to Patricia Gaspar of King City Secondary School for her assistance in facilitating the set-up photography session.

Contents

Exploring ON Science 10 xii
Safety in your Science Classroom xiv

Unit 1 Tissues, Organs, and Systems of Living Things xviii

Get Ready for Unit 1 2

Chapter 1 Cells and More Cells 4
1.1 Studying the Structure of Cells 7
1.2 Genes: Answers and Questions 16
1.3 Cells from Cells 29
1.4 The Cell Cycle 40
Chapter 1 Summary 51
Chapter 1 Review 52

Chapter 2 Plants: From Cells to Systems 54
2.1 Plant Cells, Tissues, and Organs 57
2.2 Plant Organ Systems 70
Chapter 2 Summary 79
Chapter 2 Review 80

Chapter 3 Animals: From Cells to Systems 82
3.1 Cells and Tissues 85
3.2 Organs and Systems 93
3.3 Maintaining Healthy Systems 108
Chapter 3 Summary 121
Chapter 3 Review 122

Unit 1 Science at Work 124
Unit 1 Projects 126
Unit 1 Review 128

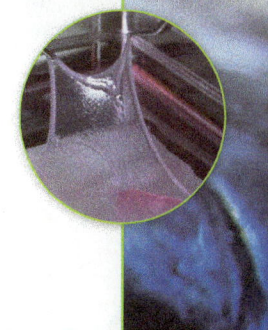

Unit 2 Chemical Reactions 132
Get Ready for Unit 2 134

Chapter 4 Developing Chemical Equations 136
4.1 Representing Ionic Compounds 139
4.2 Representing Molecular Compounds 152
4.3 Conservation of Mass and Chemical Equations 159
Chapter 4 Summary 173
Chapter 4 Review 174

Chapter 5 Classifying Chemical Reactions 176
5.1 Synthesis and Decomposition Reactions 179
5.2 Displacement Reactions... 190
5.3 Reactions and Environmental Issues 199
Chapter 5 Summary 213
Chapter 5 Review 214

Chapter 6 Acids and Bases 216
6.1 Identifying Acids and Bases 219
6.2 The pH Scale and Indicators 229
6.3 Reactions of Acids and Bases 236
Chapter 6 Summary 251
Chapter 6 Review 252

Unit 2 Science at Work 254
Unit 2 Projects... 256
Unit 2 Review 258

Unit 3 Climate Change ... 262
Get Ready for Unit 3 ... 264

Chapter 7 Earth's Climate System ... 266
7.1 Factors That Affect Climate Change ... 269
7.2 Describing Climates ... 279
7.3 Indicators and Effects of Climate Change ... 290
Chapter 7 Summary ... 305
Chapter 7 Review ... 306

Chapter 8 Dynamics of Climate Change ... 308
8.1 Energy Transfer in the Climate System ... 311
8.2 Greenhouse Gases and Human Activities ... 323
8.3 Cycling of Matter and the Climate System ... 333
Chapter 8 Summary ... 345
Chapter 8 Review ... 346

Chapter 9 Addressing Climate Change ... 348
9.1 Discovering Past Climates ... 351
9.2 Monitoring and Modelling Climate Change ... 360
9.3 Taking Action to Slow Climate Change ... 370
Chapter 9 Summary ... 385
Chapter 9 Review ... 386

Unit 3 Science at Work ... 388
Unit 3 Projects ... 390
Unit 3 Review ... 392

Unit 4 Light and Geometric Optics 396
Get Ready for Unit 4 398

Chapter 10 Light and Reflection 400
10.1 Sources and Nature of Light 403
10.2 Properties of Light and Reflection 411
10.3 Images in Concave Mirrors 419
10.4 Images in Convex Mirrors 431
Chapter 10 Summary 443
Chapter 10 Review 444

Chapter 11 Refraction 446
11.1 Refraction of Light 449
11.2 Partial Refraction and Total Internal Reflection 457
11.3 Optical Phenomena in Nature 468
Chapter 11 Summary 481
Chapter 11 Review 482

Chapter 12 Lenses and Lens Technologies 484
12.1 Characteristics of Lenses 487
12.2 Images Formed by Lenses 494
12.3 Lens Technologies and the Human Eye 502
Chapter 12 Summary 517
Chapter 12 Review 518

Unit 4 Science at Work 520
Unit 4 Projects 522
Unit 4 Review 524

Guide to the Toolkits and Appendices 528

Science Skills Toolkits 529

Math Skills Toolkits 552

Study Toolkits 560

Appendix A: Chemistry References 567

Appendix B: Properties of Common Substances 568

Appendix C: Numerical Answers and Answers to Practice Problems 570

Glossary 572

Index 579

Credits 586

Periodic Table 590

Activities, Investigations, and Features

Activities

1-1	Did You Get the Message?	5
1-2	To Test or Not to Test?	21
1-3	Modelling Mitosis	36
2-1	Observing Plant Growth	55
2-2	Inside a Leaf	62
2-3	The Flow of Phloem	71
3-1	More Than a Covering	83
3-2	Tissue Sleuth	89
3-3	Changing Your Pulse Rate	101
4-1	Making a Reaction Happen	137
4-2	Take My Electron–Please!	143
4-3	Electron, Anyone?	154
5-1	Foiled Again!	177
5-2	Building Up and Breaking Down	188
5-3	How Active Are the Non-Metals?	194
5-4	"Taking Care" of Toxic Materials	200
6-1	Cabbage Detector	217
6-2	Chemical Card Games	225
6-3	A Universal Rainbow	232
6-4	Air Pollution and Ontario's Lakes	244
7-1	Views on Climate Change	267
7-2	Modelling the Effects of Volcanoes on Climate	276
7-3	How to Make a Climatograph	281
7-4	Acidity and Coral Reefs	293
8-1	Modelling Balance in Systems	309
8-2	What Heats the Atmosphere?	315
8-3	Graphing Changes in Carbon Dioxide	329
8-4	Modelling Carbon Reservoirs	336
9-1	Who Is Responsible for Responding to Climate Change?	349
9-2	Analyzing Tree Rings	352
9-3	Pennies from Heaven	365
9-4	Talking the Talk, Walking the Walk	375
10-1	Glowing Slime	401
10-2	A Reflection Obstacle Course	414
10-3	Reflection from the Concave Surface of a Spoon	421
10-4	Reflection from the Convex Surface of a Spoon	434
11-1	The Re-appearing Coin	447
11-2	Investigating Properties of Light	459
11-3	The Fountain of Light	463
11-4	Apparent Depth	471
12-1	The Disappearing Finger	485
12-2	Hocus Focus	491

Investigations

1-A	Examining Cell Structures	46
1-B	Mitosis in Plant and Animal Cells	48
1-C	Does the Patient Have Cancer?	50
2-A	Transpiration in Different Plant Types	77
2-B	Modelling Water Transport in Plants	78
3-A	Heart Disease: Making the Public Aware	116
3-B	Frog Dissection	117
3-C	Who's Stubbing Out?	119
4-A	Monitoring Paper Recycling	169
4-B	Keep That Toothy Grin	170
4-C	Comparing the Masses of Reactants and Products	172
5-A	Evidence of Chemical Change	207
5-B	Synthesis and Decomposition Reactions	208
5-C	Displacement Reactions	210
5-D	Can Metals Be "Active"?	212
6-A	What Is Your Exposure to Acids and Bases?	247
6-B	The pH of Lakes Near Sudbury	248
6-C	Neutralizing an Acid with a Base	250
7-A	Specific Heat Capacity of Earth Materials	300
7-B	Comparing Ecoregions of Canada	302

7-C	Comparing the Effects of Climate Change on Vegetation in Canada **304**
8-A	Recognizing the Effects of El Niño and La Niña on Southern Canada **341**
8-B	Comparing Heat Absorption of Water and Soil . . . **343**
8-C	Modelling the Greenhouse Effect **344**
9-A	Understanding Ice-Core Data **382**
9-B	Evaluating the "Food Miles" Initiative **384**
10-A	Applying the Laws of Reflection **439**
10-B	Studying the Laws of Reflection **440**
10-C	Testing for Real and Virtual Images **442**
11-A	Investigating Refraction, from Air to Water **476**
11-B	Analyzing the Index of Refraction **477**
11-C	Saving Time **478**
11-D	Investing Total Internal Reflection in Water **480**
12-A	Image Characteristics of a Converging Lens **512**
12-B	I "Speye" **514**
12-C	Make a Simple Telescope **516**

Case Studies

Clones in the Kitchen **24**
Eliminating Wheat Rust with Transgenic Therapy **66**
Childhood Vaccinations: Weighing the Risks **110**
Green Chemistry **166**
Hydrogen: Fuel of the Future? **182**
Update on Acid Precipitation **240**
This Weather Is Making Me Sick! **294**
Overheating the Ocean's Forests **312**
Reduce, Re-use, Recycle, and Upgrade **378**
Saved by the Sun **428**
Protecting Your Eyes from UV Radiation **472**
Laser Eye Surgery: Shaping Vision **508**

Making a Difference

Ted Paranjothy **44**
Isdin Oke **68**
Jerri Clout **113**
Adrienne Duimering **166**
Nikhita Singh **205**
Simon Bild-Enkin **242**
BJ Bodnar **292**
P.J. Partington **328**
Jasmeet Sidhu **380**
Pénélope Robinson and Maude Briand-Lemay **415**
Michael Furdyk **463**
Kienan Marion **500**

National Geographic Features

Visualizing Microscopes **8**
Visualizing Acids in Nature **221**
Visualizing El Niño and La Niña **318**
Visualizing Bioluminescence **408**

Exploring ON Science 10

Solve a Puzzle, Find a Quote

Use the puzzle clues on these two pages to begin your journey through *ON Science 10*. (Do not write in this textbook.) When you are finished, the circled and numbered letters will help you discover a powerful quote by Marie Curie.

Marie Curie's pioneering work in the field of radioactivity included directing the world's first studies into the treatment of cancers using radioactivity. She was the first person ever to win two Nobel Prizes. **What idea inspired Marie Curie to attain such accomplishments?**

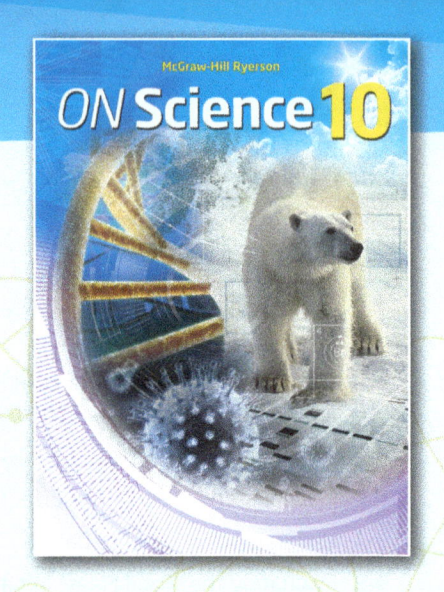

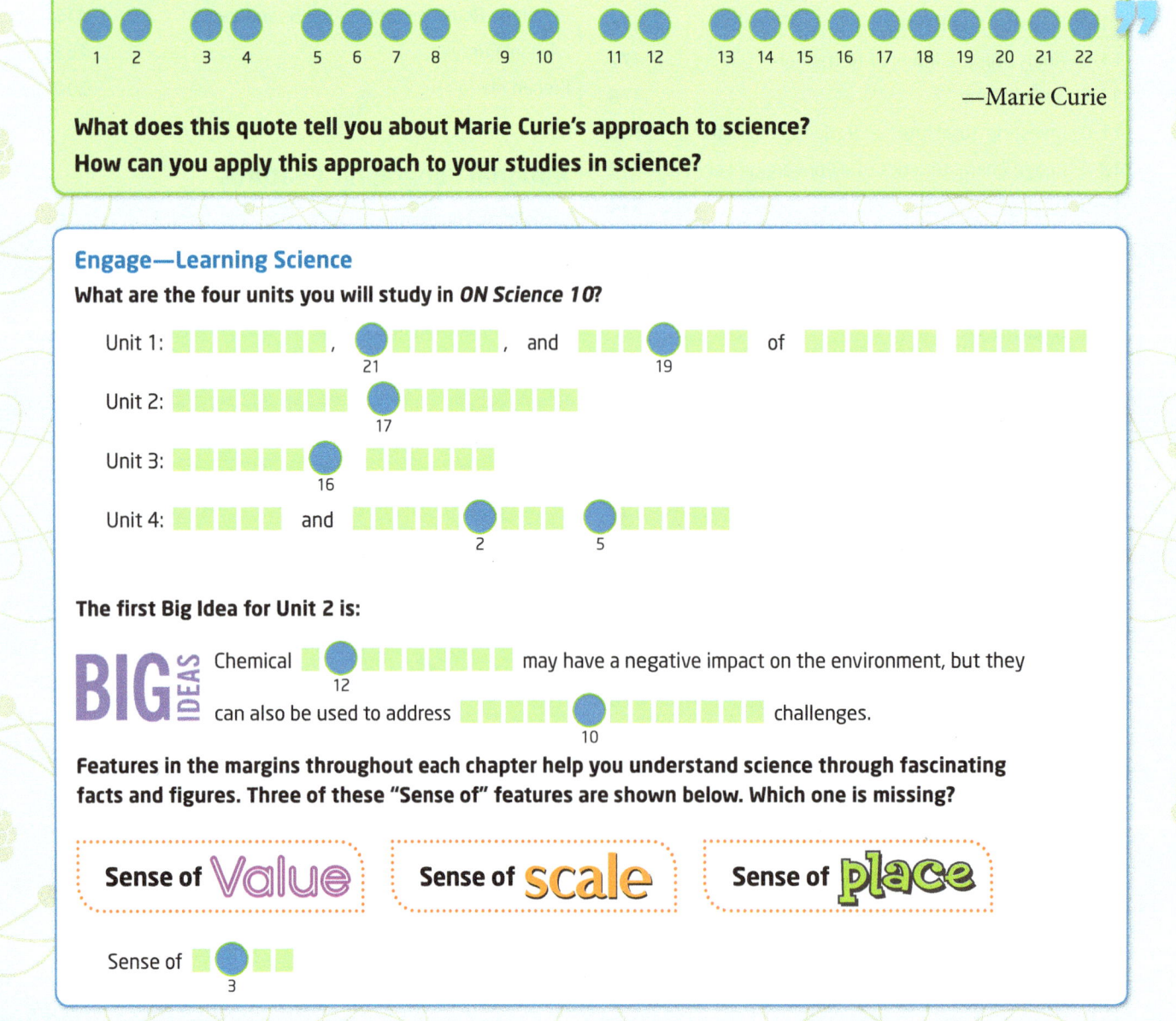

"**Nothing in life is to be feared.**
○ ○ ○ ○ ○ ○ ○ ○ ○ ○ ○ ○ ○ ○ ○ ○ ○ ○ ○ ○ ○ ○
1 2 3 4 5 6 7 8 9 10 11 12 13 14 15 16 17 18 19 20 21 22"

—Marie Curie

What does this quote tell you about Marie Curie's approach to science? How can you apply this approach to your studies in science?

Engage—Learning Science

What are the four units you will study in *ON Science 10*?

Unit 1: ●●●●●● , ●○●●●● , and ●●●○●●● of ●●●●●● ●●●●●●
                    21   19

Unit 2: ●●●●●●●○●●●●●●●●●
                    17

Unit 3: ●●●●●○●●●●● ●●●●●●
                 16

Unit 4: ●●●●● and ●●●●●○●● ○●●●●
                         2   5

The first Big Idea for Unit 2 is:

BIG IDEAS Chemical ●●●○●●●●●● may have a negative impact on the environment, but they
                              12
can also be used to address ●●●●●○●●●●●● challenges.
                                         10

Features in the margins throughout each chapter help you understand science through fascinating facts and figures. Three of these "Sense of" features are shown below. Which one is missing?

| Sense of **Value** | Sense of **scale** | Sense of **place** |

Sense of ●○●●
         3

xii NEL • Exploring ON Science 10

Explore—Doing Science

What does this safety icon mean?

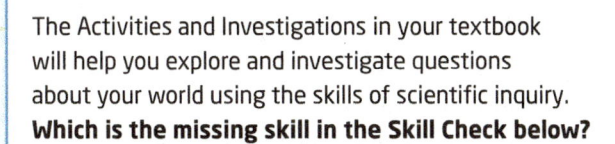

☐☐☐☐☐☐●☐☐☐☐☐☐
　　　　　7

The Activities and Investigations in your textbook will help you explore and investigate questions about your world using the skills of scientific inquiry. **Which is the missing skill in the Skill Check below?**

> **Skill Check**
> ✓ Initiating and Planning
> ✓ Performing and Recording
> ✓ Communicating

☐☐☐●☐☐☐ and
　　8
☐☐☐☐☐☐☐☐☐☐☐☐

Where would you look in this textbook to find out how to draw a pie graph?

☐☐☐☐ ☐☐☐☐☐☐● Toolkit 3
　　　　　　　18

Explain—Understanding Science

National Geographic features help you understand science through images. **What is the title of the National Geographic feature in Unit 2?**

Visualizing ☐☐☐☐●☐ in ☐●☐☐☐☐
　　　　　　　　4　　　　　　14

Learning how to understand and use science vocabulary is an important communication skill. **What is the second key term in Chapter 1?**

☐☐☐☐☐☐☐☐●☐☐
　　　　　　　20

Suppose you are looking for places in the book where a particular name or term is mentioned. **What part of this textbook can help you?**

The ☐☐●☐☐
　　　22

Extend—Applying Science

Every chapter has a Case Study feature that explores a specific real-world scientific topic or issue that relates to that chapter. Questions at the end of each Case Study challenge you to find out more about the topic. **What is the name of the Case Study in Chapter 4?**

☐☐☐☐☐ ☐☐●☐☐☐☐
　　　　　　1

In the Making a Difference feature, you will have the opportunity to read about young Canadians, most of them high school students, who have used the tools of scientific inquiry to positively influence their community, the environment, or some other facet of their lives. **Who is profiled in the Making a Difference feature in Chapter 1?**

☐☐☐ ☐☐☐☐●☐☐☐
　　　　　　6

Which prominent Canadian is profiled in the Science at Work feature at the end of Unit 3?

☐☐☐☐☐☐ ☐☐☐-☐●☐☐☐
　　　　　　　　　　13

Evaluate—Studying Science

What Study Toolkit strategy helps you alter your reading speed based on your purpose for reading?

☐☐☐☐, ☐☐☐☐, or ☐●☐☐
　　　　　　　　　　9

What chapter feature models the way you might solve a certain kind of problem?

☐☐☐☐☐☐ ☐☐☐●☐☐☐
　　　　　　　　11

If you wanted to check an answer to a Practice Problem, where would you look?

☐☐☐☐☐☐●☐ ☐
　　　　15

Safety in your Science Classroom

Become familiar with the following safety rules and procedures. It is up to you to use them and your teacher's instructions to make your activities and investigations in ON Science 10 safe and enjoyable. Your teacher will give you specific information about any other special safety rules that need to be used in your school.

1. **Working with your teacher …**
   - Listen carefully to any instructions your teacher gives you.
   - Inform your teacher if you have any allergies, medical conditions, or other physical problems that could affect your work in the science classroom. Tell your teacher if you wear contact lenses or a hearing aid.
   - Obtain your teacher's approval before beginning any activity you have designed for yourself.
   - Know the location and proper use of the nearest fire extinguisher, fire blanket, first-aid kit, and fire alarm.

2. **Starting an activity or investigation …**
   - Before starting an activity or investigation, read all of it. If you do not understand how to do a step, ask your teacher for help.
   - Be sure you have checked the safety icons and have read and understood the safety precautions.
   - Begin an activity or investigation only after your teacher tells you to start.

3. **Wearing protective clothing …**
   - When you are directed to do so, wear protective clothing, such as a lab apron and safety goggles. Always wear protective clothing when you are using materials that could pose a safety problem, such as unidentified substances, or when you are heating anything.
   - Tie back long hair, and avoid wearing scarves, ties, or long necklaces.

4. **Acting responsibly …**
   - Work carefully with a partner and make sure your work area is clear.
   - Handle equipment and materials carefully.
   - Make sure stools and chairs are resting securely on the floor.
   - If other students are doing something that you consider dangerous, report it to your teacher.

5. **Handling edible substances …**
   - Do not chew gum, eat, or drink in your science classroom.
   - Do not taste any substances or draw any material into a tube with your mouth.

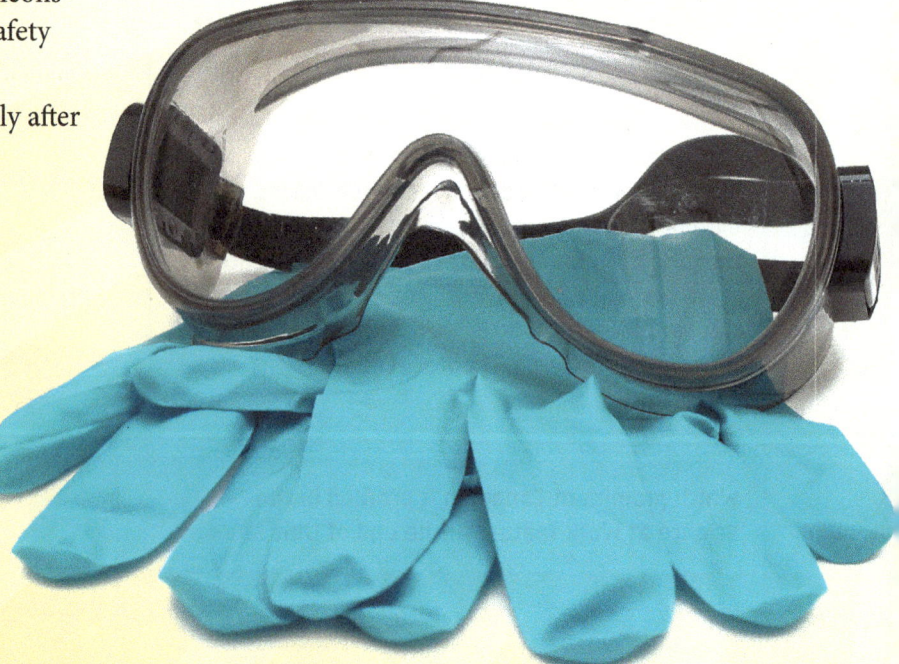

6. Working in a science classroom …

- Make sure you understand all safety labels on school materials or those you bring from home. Familiarize yourself, as well, with the WHMIS symbols and the special safety symbols used in this book, found on page xvii.
- When carrying equipment for an activity or investigation, hold it carefully. Carry only one object or container at a time.
- Be aware of others during activities and investigations. Make room for students who may be carrying equipment to their work stations.

7. Working with sharp objects …

- Always cut away from yourself and others when using a knife or razor blade.
- Always keep the pointed end of scissors or any pointed object facing away from yourself and others if you have to walk with such objects.
- If you notice sharp or jagged edges on any equipment, take special care with it and report it to your teacher.
- Dispose of broken glass as your teacher directs.

8. Working with electrical equipment …

- Make sure your hands are dry when touching electrical cords, plugs, or sockets.
- Pull the plug, not the cord, when unplugging electrical equipment.
- Report damaged equipment or frayed cords to your teacher.
- Place electrical cords where people will not trip over them.

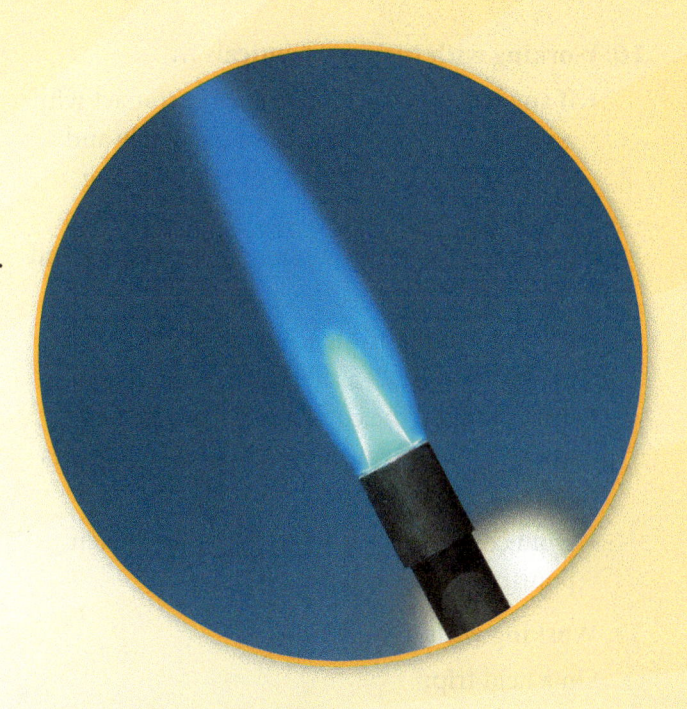

9. Working with heat …

- When heating an item, wear safety goggles and any other safety equipment that the text or your teacher advises.
- Always use heatproof containers.
- Point the open end of a container that is being heated away from yourself and others.
- Do not allow a container to boil dry.
- Handle hot objects carefully. Be especially careful with a hot plate that looks as though it has cooled down.
- If you use a Bunsen burner, make sure you understand fully how to light and use it safely.
- If you do receive a burn, inform your teacher, and apply cold water to the burned area immediately.

10. Working with various chemicals …
- If any part of your body comes in contact with a substance, wash the area immediately and thoroughly with water. If you get anything in your eyes, do not touch them. Wash them immediately and continuously for 15 min, and inform your teacher.
- Always handle substances carefully. If you are asked to smell a substance, never smell it directly. Hold the container slightly in front of and beneath your nose, and waft the fumes toward your nostrils.
- Hold containers away from your face when pouring liquids.

11. Working with living things …

On a field trip:
- Try not to disturb the area any more than is absolutely necessary.
- If you move something, do it carefully, and always replace it carefully.
- If you are asked to remove plant material, remove it gently, and take as little as possible.

In the classroom:
- Make sure that living creatures receive humane treatment while they are in your care.
- If possible, return living creatures to their natural environment when your work is complete.

12. Cleaning up in the science classroom …
- Clean up any spills, according to your teacher's instructions.
- Clean equipment before you put it away.
- Wash your hands thoroughly after doing an activity or an investigation.
- Dispose of materials as directed by your teacher. Never discard materials in the sink unless your teacher requests it.

13. Designing and building …
- Use tools safely to cut, join, and shape objects.
- Handle modelling clay correctly. Wash your hands after using modelling clay.
- Follow proper procedures when using mechanical systems and studying their operations.
- Use special care when observing and working with objects in motion.
- Do not use power equipment such as drills, sanders, saws, and lathes unless you have specialized training in handling such tools.

Safety Symbols

ON Science 10 Safety Symbols

The following safety symbols are used in *ON Science 10* to alert you to possible dangers. Be sure you understand each symbol used in an activity or investigation before you begin.

Disposal Alert
This symbol appears when care must be taken to dispose of materials properly.

Thermal Safety
This symbol appears as a reminder to use caution when handling hot objects.

Sharp Object Safety
This symbol appears when a danger of cuts or punctures caused by the use of sharp objects exists.

Electrical Safety
This symbol appears when care should be taken when using electrical equipment.

Skin Protection Safety
This symbol appears when use of caustic chemicals might irritate the skin or when contact with micro-organisms might transmit infection.

Clothing Protection Safety
A lab apron should be worn when this symbol appears.

Fire Safety
This symbol appears when care should be taken around open flames.

Eye Safety
This symbol appears when a danger to the eyes exists. Safety goggles should be worn when this symbol appears.

Instant Practice—Safety Symbols
Find four of the *ON Science 10* safety symbols in activities or investigations in this textbook. For each symbol, identify the possible dangers in the activity or investigation that the symbol refers to.

WHMIS Symbols

Look carefully at the WHMIS (Workplace Hazardous Materials Information System) safety symbols shown here. The WHMIS symbols are used throughout Canada to identify dangerous materials. Make certain you understand what these symbols mean. When you see these symbols on containers, use safety precautions.

- Compressed Gas
- Flammable and Combustible Material
- Oxidizing Material
- Corrosive Material
- Poisonous and Infectious Material Causing Immediate and Serious Toxic Effects
- Poisonous and Infectious Material Causing Other Toxic Effects
- Biohazardous Infectious Material
- Dangerously Reactive Material

Instant Practice—Safety Symbols
Hydrochloric acid is stored in containers. This solution is corrosive.

1. What symbol would you expect to see on a label for hydrochloric acid?
2. Describe the following.
   a. the risks illustrated by the symbol
   b. precautions someone would need to take when working with the solution
   c. where it could be safely stored
   d. first aid or emergency treatment
3. If you did not know the answer to part d., where would you find this information?

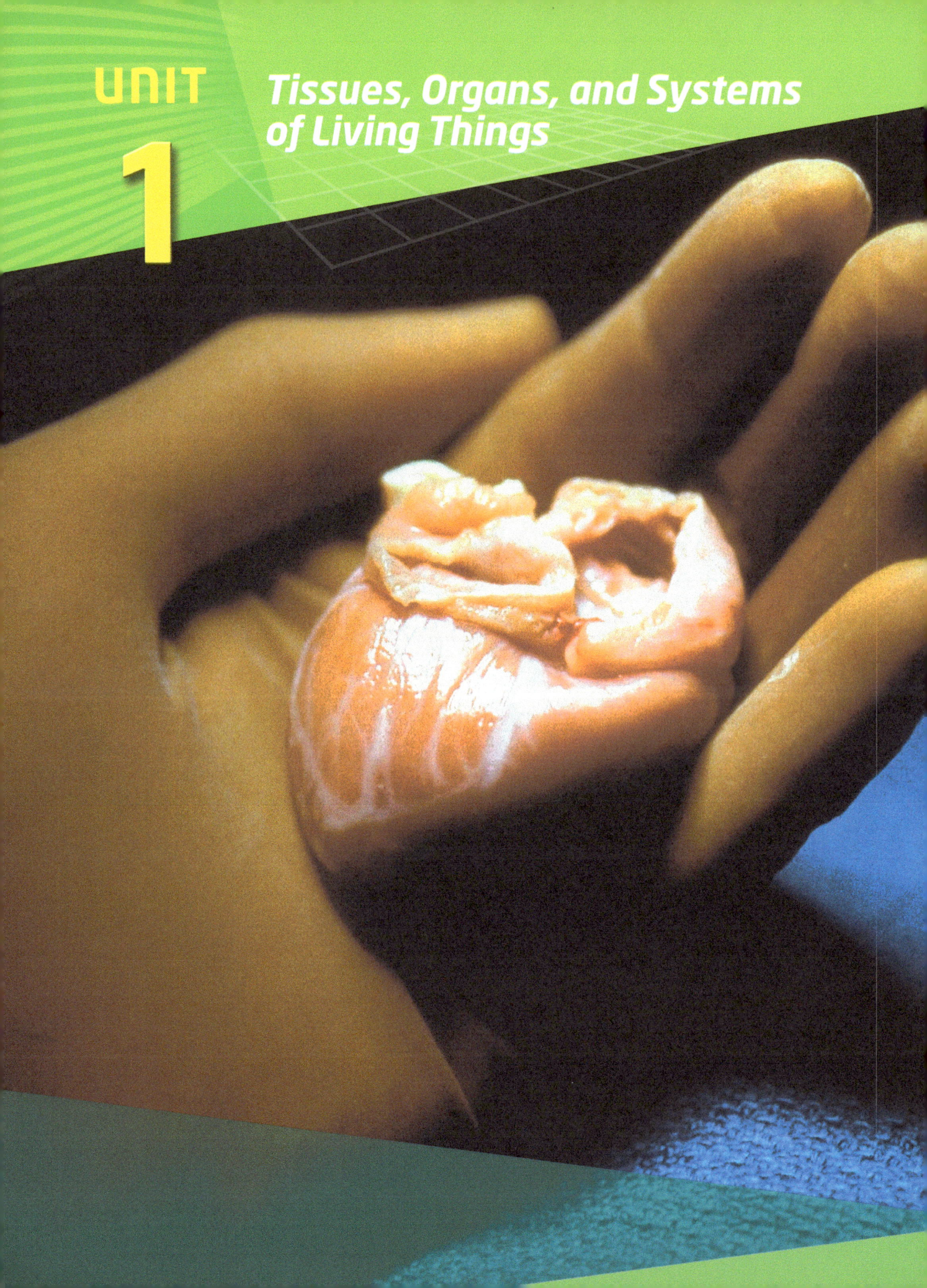

UNIT 1
Tissues, Organs, and Systems of Living Things

BIG IDEAS

- Developments in medicine and medical technology can have social and ethical implications.
- Plants and animals, including humans, are made of specialized cells, tissues, and organs that are organized into systems.

A pediatric heart surgeon's hand cradles an infant's tiny defective heart that is no bigger than a walnut. The 48-day-old patient, Dylan Stork, had a life-threatening heart defect. A heart transplant saved his life.

This baby was born with a defective heart, but some kinds of heart disease develop or worsen as a result of lifestyle choices. Research has shown that eating a balanced diet and getting plenty of exercise can help prevent heart disease. Research has also helped develop technologies to identify and treat heart problems. Fundraising events such as the Ride for Heart, shown here, help raise money for research into causes and treatment of heart disease while promoting healthy living.

In this unit, you will learn about cells, tissues, and organs and how they work together in systems in plants and in animals. You will also learn about technologies designed to diagnose, study, treat, and cure diseases affecting body systems.

What are some social and ethical issues related to human organ transplants?

Chapter 1
Cells and More Cells

Chapter 2
Plants: From Cells to Systems

Chapter 3
Animals: From Cells to Systems

Get Ready for Unit 1

Concept Check

1. Decide whether each statement about the cell theory is true or false. If a statement is false, rewrite it to make it true.

   a. The cell is the basic unit of life.

   b. Some cells come from pre-existing cells.

   c. All living things are made up of many cells.

2. Find the pond organism that is labelled A, and sketch it in your notebook. Identify and label the cell organelles listed below in your sketch. Then, below your sketch, state the function(s) of each of these organelles within the cell. (Note: Not all of these organelles will be present.)

   a. nucleus
   b. cell membrane
   c. cell wall
   d. vacuole
   e. mitochondria
   f. cytoplasm

3. In your notebook, write the number that matches each part of the microscope listed below.

   a. light source
   b. stage
   c. eyepiece
   d. objective lens

4. Diagrams A, B, and C show the process of diffusion. Describe what is happening in these diagrams using the following terms: *concentration*, *high*, *low*, *membrane*, *permeable*, *selectively*, and *solute*.

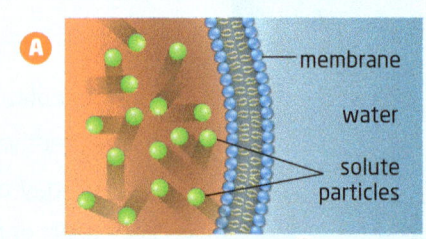

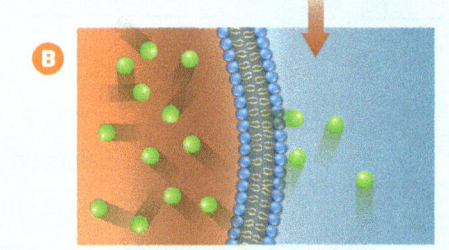

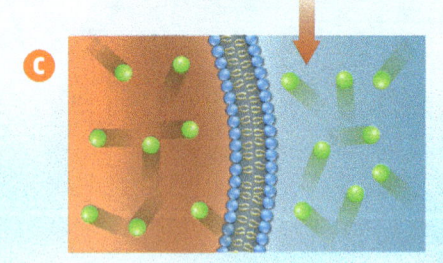

2 NEL • Unit 1 Sustainable Ecosystems

Inquiry Check

5. **Identify** In your notebook, list as many characteristics of unicellular and multicellular organisms as you can. Compare your list with a partner's list.

6. **Observe and Record Observations** Copy the following table in your notebook. Identify the organisms in the photographs on the previous page by completing the table. Explain your answers using the characteristics you listed in question 5 above.

Characteristics of Unicellular and Multicellular Organisms

Organism	Plant, Animal, or Protist?	Unicellular or Multicellular?	Observations
A			
B			
C			

Numeracy and Literacy Check

7. **Analyze** Bacterial cells replicate by splitting into two cells. When conditions are favourable (for example, when there is space and a food source), bacteria can divide every 20 min. This is called exponential growth. Use this table to answer the questions below.

Exponential Growth of Bacteria

Time (min)	Number of Bacteria
0	1
20	2
40	4
60	8

a. If conditions are favourable, how many bacterial cells will exist after 2 hours?

b. If conditions are favourable, how long will it take before the population of bacterial cells reaches 1000?

8. **Write** Use the words below to explain how multicellular organisms are structured.

> cells   organism   organ systems
> organs   tissues

Looking Ahead to the Unit 1 Projects

At the end of this unit, you will have an opportunity to apply what you have learned in an inquiry or research project. Read the Unit 1 Projects on pages 126-127. Start a project folder now (either paper or electronic). Store ideas, notes, news clippings, website addresses, and lists of materials that might help you to complete your project.

Inquiry Project
Investigate the phases of mitosis.

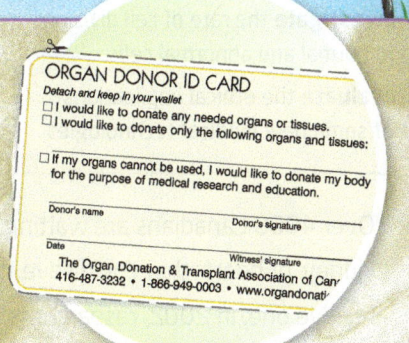

An Issue to Analyze
Research and form an opinion about organ donation.

Chapter 1   Cells and More Cells

What You Will Learn

In this chapter, you will learn how to...
- **describe** what all cells have in common, as well as differences between plant and animal cells
- **explain** the importance of mitosis for growth and repair
- **describe** the stages of the cell cycle and **relate** this cycle to the origins of cancer
- **explain** major cell technologies and related issues

Why It Matters

To prevent and treat diseases, doctors and researchers must first understand the normal structures and functions of the cells–and how cells make up the body.

Skills You Will Use

In this chapter, you will learn how to...
- **compare** plant and animal cells using microscopes and labelled biological diagrams
- **identify** the stages of mitosis in plant and animal cells
- **investigate** the rate of cell division in normal and abnormal cells
- **evaluate** the ethical implications of some new medical technologies

Over 4000 Canadians are waiting for an organ transplant–a liver, kidney, or heart–that could save their life. Fewer than half will receive one. In 2002, researchers used genetic engineering to produce the first four piglets that could potentially provide organs for humans. This was a major breakthrough because the human body normally rejects an organ from another species. How scientists achieved this will be discussed in Chapter 1, along with some of the ethical issues that have arisen from research in cell biology.

Activity 1-1

Did You Get the Message?

To be healthy, all organisms must have cells that function normally, sending messages to and from one another. Sometimes, these messages get "scrambled," disrupting normal functioning. In this activity, you will play the game "broken telephone" as a class. How do you think this game will simulate the transfer of messages from cell to cell?

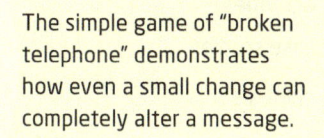

The simple game of "broken telephone" demonstrates how even a small change can completely alter a message.

Procedure

1. Your teacher will begin by whispering a message to a student so that no one else can hear. This student should then whisper the message to the next student, and so on until the message reaches the last person in the class. You are not allowed to repeat the message. The last person should write down what he or she heard.
2. Repeat step 1 with a second message.
3. Compare your teacher's original messages to what the last person wrote down.

Questions

1. How did the original and final messages compare? What might have caused the differences?
2. Was one message less scrambled at the end than the other? What might explain any differences?
3. How do you think this game might reflect what goes on inside your body?

Chapter 1 Cells and More Cells • NEL 5

Study Toolkit

These strategies will help you use this textbook to develop your understanding of science concepts and skills.
To find out more about these and other strategies, refer to the Study Toolkit Overview, which begins on page 560.

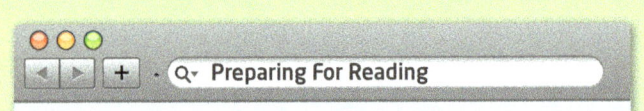

Preparing For Reading

Previewing Text Features

Before reading non-fiction text, preview the *features* of the text. Major text features include

- headings
- subheadings
- main body text

Other text features include

- definitions of key terms
- activities
- case studies
- sidebars

Some text features give you clues about the most important ideas in the text. For example, on the next page, you will see a box with the heading "Key Terms." These are the important terms you will learn in Section 1.1. Each key term is boldfaced when it first appears in the main body text, and it is defined in the margin on the same page. When studying for a test, use this feature to find important terms and concepts.

Use the Strategy

Turn to Section 1.2 in this chapter. Find the Key Terms box, and choose one term (other than *chromosome*). Find the page where the term is boldfaced, and record its definition.

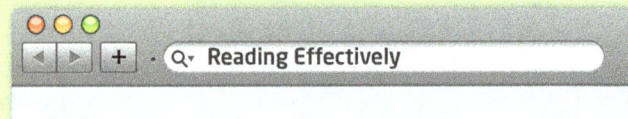

Reading Effectively

Visualizing

Visualizing means forming an image in your mind based on what you are reading. The table below shows how a reader might visualize the following text, which appears under the subheading "Protein Production" on page 18: "... some proteins help build parts of your body. Others are like couriers .... All of these various proteins get their 'orders' from DNA."

Steps for Visualizing While Reading

Steps	How I Form an Image in My Mind
1. Start with an image in the text that is familiar to you.	The words "get their orders" make me think about a supervisor talking to a group of workers, telling each worker what his or her job will be.
2. Look for details that make the image more accurate.	The examples "some proteins help build" and "others are like couriers" help me visualize the kinds of jobs that proteins do.
3. Once you have created the final image in your mind, make a sketch.	My sketch shows a strand of DNA giving one protein a hard hat and another protein a courier bag.

Use the Strategy

When reading the section titled "Mutations" on page 26, follow the steps in the table above.

Word Study

Word Families

Graphic organizers can help you remember the meanings of unfamiliar words. The graphic organizer on the right shows words that contain the word part *cyto*, meaning cell. Any word that contains this word part is related to cells. For example, *cytoskeleton* means a network that controls cell shape.

```
                cyto
     ┌───────┬────┴────┬────────┐
 cytoplasm  cytoskeleton  cytosol  cytokinesis
```

Use the Strategy

1. Draw a graphic organizer based on the word part *gene*. Find and record the definition of *gene* in Section 1.2.

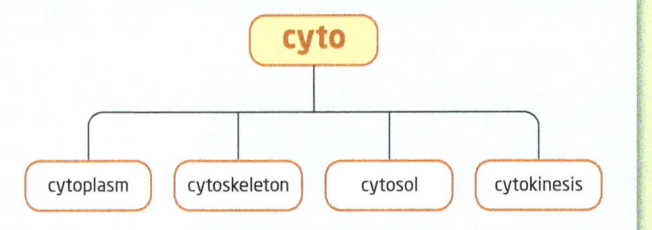

2. As you read the rest of the section, note any words that contain *gene* or *gen*, and add them to your graphic organizer. Write a definition of each word, relating it to the definition of *gene*.

6   NEL • Unit 1 Tissues, Organs, and Systems of Living Things

1.1 Studying the Structure of Cells

Key Terms
cell
microscopy
nucleus
organelle
micrograph
cytoplasm

Before the invention of microscopes in the 1660s, people had only a limited understanding of the human body and no knowledge of the microscopic world. For example, people had not yet seen their own blood **cells**, as shown in **Figure 1.1**, and had never seen the micro-organisms (such as bacteria) that cause many diseases. Therefore, they did not know that they could help to prevent diseases by disposing of sewage properly, sterilizing surgical instruments between operations, and washing their hands regularly. Most importantly, they did not know the importance of clean drinking water.

cell the smallest unit that can perform the functions of life

microscopy the science of using microscopes to view samples or objects

Microscopes and Human Health

In the 1860s and 1870s, compound microscopes were put to good use. Scientists and physicians around the world did experiments that paved the way for one of the biggest discoveries in medicine—that "germs" (viruses, many bacteria, and some other microscopic organisms) cause diseases. This discovery made it possible to introduce simple methods (such as hand washing and drinking clean water) to prevent many diseases, and thus increase the human life span. Since then, discoveries in **microscopy** continue to advance medical diagnosis and the treatment of diseases caused by micro-organisms and other illnesses, such as diabetes and cancer. In **Figure 1.2**, on pages 8 and 9, you can see a range of the microscopes used today.

Figure 1.1 Today's electron microscopes magnify objects thousands of times. These red blood cells, responsible for carrying oxygen to all the parts of your body, are magnified 4000 times.

NATIONAL GEOGRAPHIC
VISUALIZING MICROSCOPES

Figure 1.2

Microscopes give us a glimpse into a previously invisible world. Improvements have vastly increased their range of visibility, allowing researchers to study life at the molecular level. A selection of these powerful tools is shown here, along with their magnification powers.

▶ Up to 250×
LEEUWENHOEK MICROSCOPE Held by a modern researcher, this historic microscope allowed Leeuwenhoek to see clear images of tiny freshwater organisms that he called "beasties."

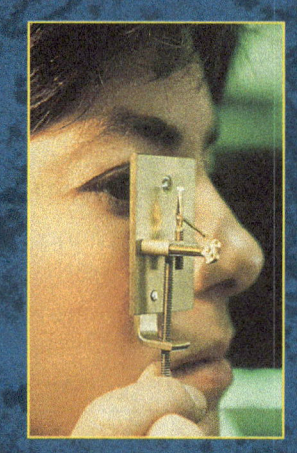

▼ Up to 2000× BRIGHTFIELD / DARKFIELD MICROSCOPE The light microscope is often called the brightfield microscope because the image is viewed against a bright background. A brightfield microscope is the tool most often used in laboratories to study cells. Placing a thin metal disc beneath the stage, between the light source and the objective lenses, converts a brightfield microscope to a darkfield microscope. The image seen using a darkfield microscope is bright against a dark background. This makes details more visible than with a brightfield microscope. Below are images of a paramecium, seen using both types of microscopes.

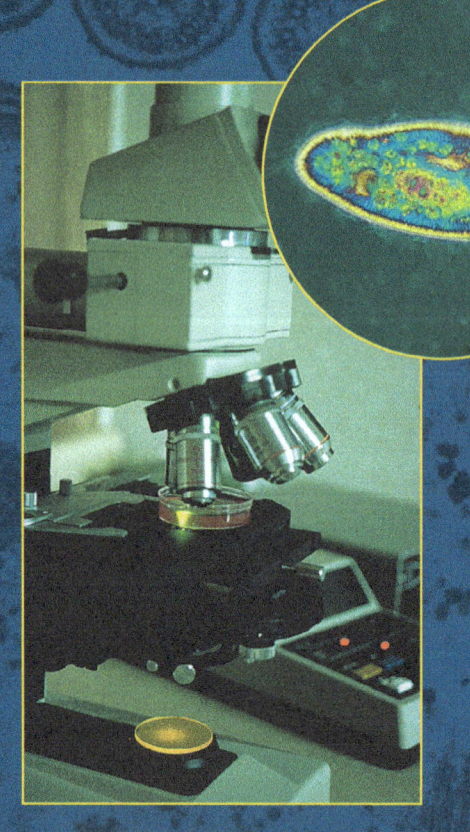

▲ Up to 1500× FLUORESCENCE MICROSCOPE This type of microscope requires that the specimen be treated with special fluorescent stains. When viewed through a fluorescence microscope, certain cell structures or types of substances glow, as seen in the image of a paramecium above.

8 NEL • Unit 1 Tissues, Organs, and Systems of Living Things

▶ **Up to 1 000 000×**
TRANSMISSION ELECTRON MICROSCOPE A TEM aims a beam of electrons through a specimen. Denser portions of the specimen allow fewer electrons to pass through and appear darker in the image. Organisms, such as the paramecium on the right, can only be seen when the image is photographed or shown on a monitor. A TEM can magnify hundreds of thousands of times.

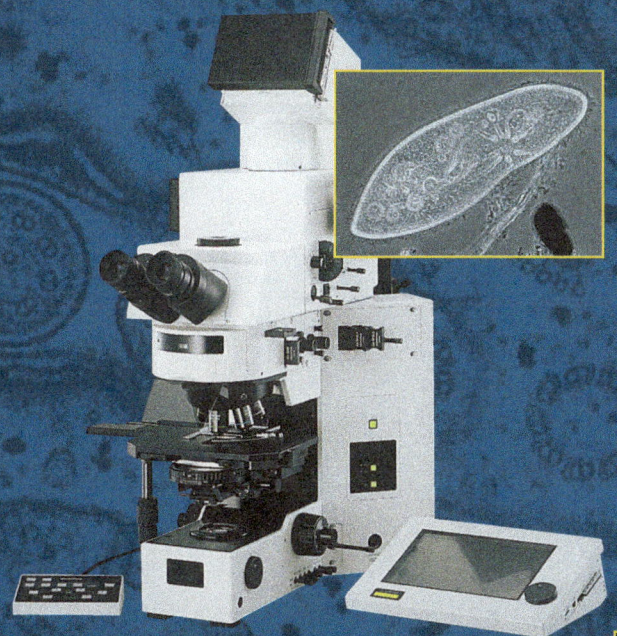

◀ **Up to 1500×** **PHASE-CONTRAST MICROSCOPE**
A phase-contrast microscope emphasizes slight differences in a specimen's capacity to bend light waves, thereby enhancing light and dark regions without the use of stains. This type of microscope is especially good for viewing living cells, like the paramecium above, on the left. The images from a phase-contrast microscope can only be seen when the specimen is photographed or shown on a monitor.

▶ **Up to 200 000×** **SCANNING ELECTRON MICROSCOPE** An SEM sweeps a beam of electrons over a specimen's surface, causing other electrons to be emitted from the specimen. SEMs produce realistic three-dimensional images, like the image of the paramecium on the right. SEM images can only be viewed as photographs or on a computer monitor, however. Here a researcher compares an SEM image with an enhanced image on a computer monitor.

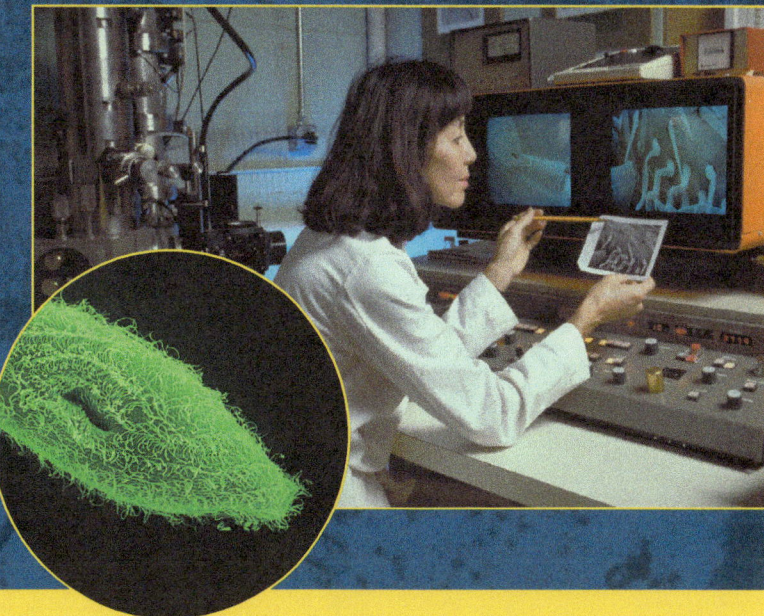

Cell Structure

Most of today's advances in the treatment of diseases would not be possible without an understanding of what happens inside cells. In turn, our understanding of cells would not be possible without advances in microscopy.

In 1665, English scientist Robert Hooke became the first person to study cells. Using a microscope he made himself, Hooke examined a piece of cork. There he saw a series of similar "pores" that he called cells because they reminded him of monks' living quarters in a monastery, which were called cells.

One of the first cell structures that scientists could see with early microscopes was the **nucleus**. The nucleus was usually the only cell **organelle** visible through light microscopes—it looked like a dark spot. Even cell membranes were not usually visible. Now, however, scientists know a great deal about the nucleus and cell membrane, what they are made of, and how they function. **Figure 1.3** shows a **micrograph** and diagram of a nucleus, while **Figure 1.4** allows you to compare the level of detail you can see in micrographs of cells as seen through a light microscope and through an electron microscope.

> **nucleus** the organelle that controls the cell's activities
>
> **organelle** a specialized structure in a cell
>
> **micrograph** a photograph taken with a microscope

typical animal cell

nucleolus makes ribosomes, which help to make proteins

nucleus

nuclear membrane protects the contents of the nucleus

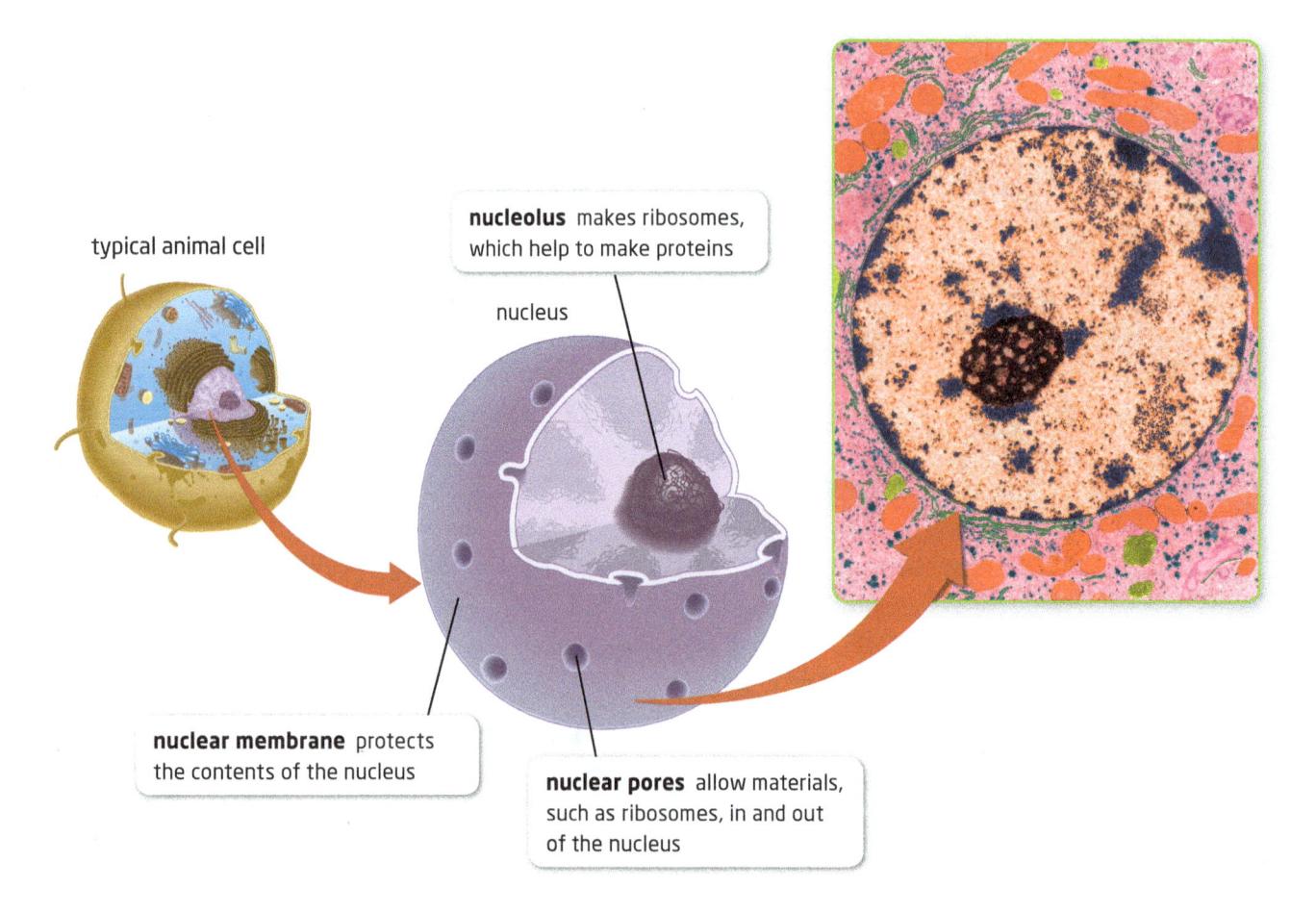

nuclear pores allow materials, such as ribosomes, in and out of the nucleus

Figure 1.3 Here you can see a diagram of a nucleus, as well as an electron micrograph of the nucleus in a human liver cell, magnified 2730 times.

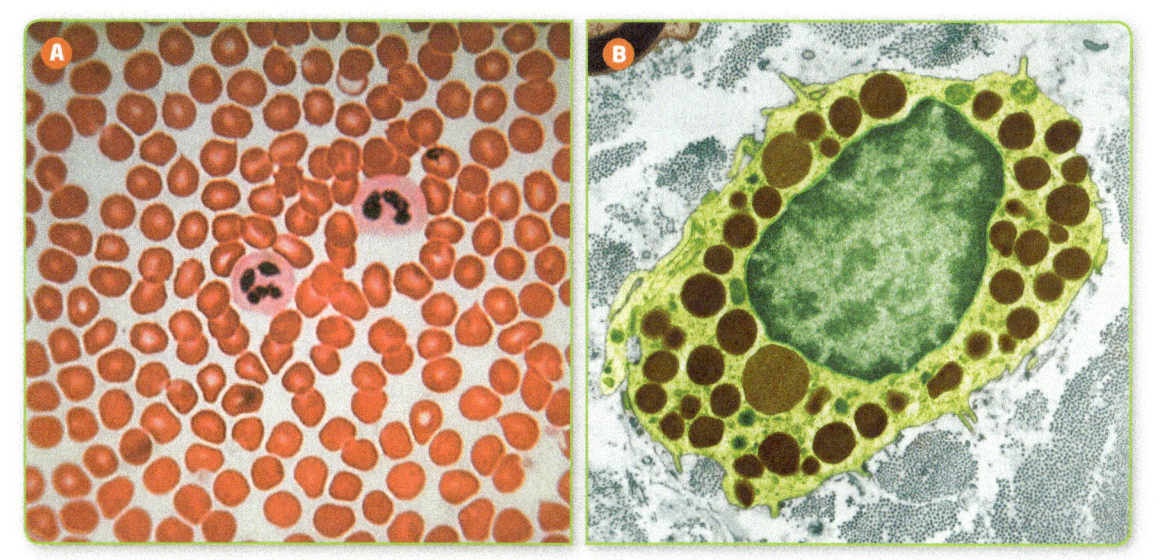

Figure 1.4 Micrograph **A** shows many red blood cells and two white blood cells, magnified 210 times by a light microscope. Micrograph **B** shows a single white blood cell, magnified 2500 times by an electron microscope. The nucleus of the cell is shown in green.

The Cell Theory

Largely based on what early microscopists observed, a theory of cells was developed in the mid-1800s. The cell theory is one of the most important developments in the study of biology. It has three main ideas:

1. All living organisms are made of one or more cells.
2. The cell is the basic organizational unit of life.
3. All cells come from pre-existing cells.

The first of these ideas is fairly easy to understand. The third idea refers to cell reproduction, which you will learn about in Section 1.3. The second idea means that to understand how living things function, you must know what is going on inside cells. In other words, all of an organism's body functions, such as eating, breathing, and eliminating waste, are designed to supply the needs of its cells. This section will help you understand the normal structure and function of cells. Later in this unit, you will learn more about how cells form the smallest unit of all living organisms. Some organisms, such as humans, are made of millions of cells, each with a specialized function.

Contents of the Cytoplasm

The fluid material between the cell membrane and the nucleus—the *cytosol*—is filled with many specialized organelles. Together, the cytosol and the organelles it contains are called the **cytoplasm**.

Sense of scale
If 1000 human body cells were lined up, they would be less than 2 cm long–about the width of a thumbnail.

cytoplasm the cytosol and organelles contained by the cell membrane

Chapter 1 Cells and More Cells • NEL 11

Animal and Plant Cell Organelles

The organelles of a cell are like the organs of a body—each plays a role in the proper functioning of the "body" that contains it. **Figures 1.5** and **1.6** illustrate typical animal and plant cells. Of course, not all plant and animal cells look exactly like those illustrated here. As you will see in this unit, there are many different kinds of cells, even within the same organism. Yet even cells with very different functions can have the same kinds of organelles.

As you study these diagrams, you may notice that a number of the organelles are involved in the production, storage, or transport of *proteins*. All cells in your body depend on proteins, which allow the cells to carry out the life processes that keep you healthy. Proteins are essential nutrients for the growth and repair of body tissues. You will learn more about proteins in the sections that follow.

Figure 1.5 This diagram and the micrograph below it show a typical animal cell. Just as cells in your body vary in structure and function, so do the organelles they contain. Cells that help a body move, for example, contain more mitochondria. Their need for the energy that comes from glucose is greater than that of other kinds of cells.

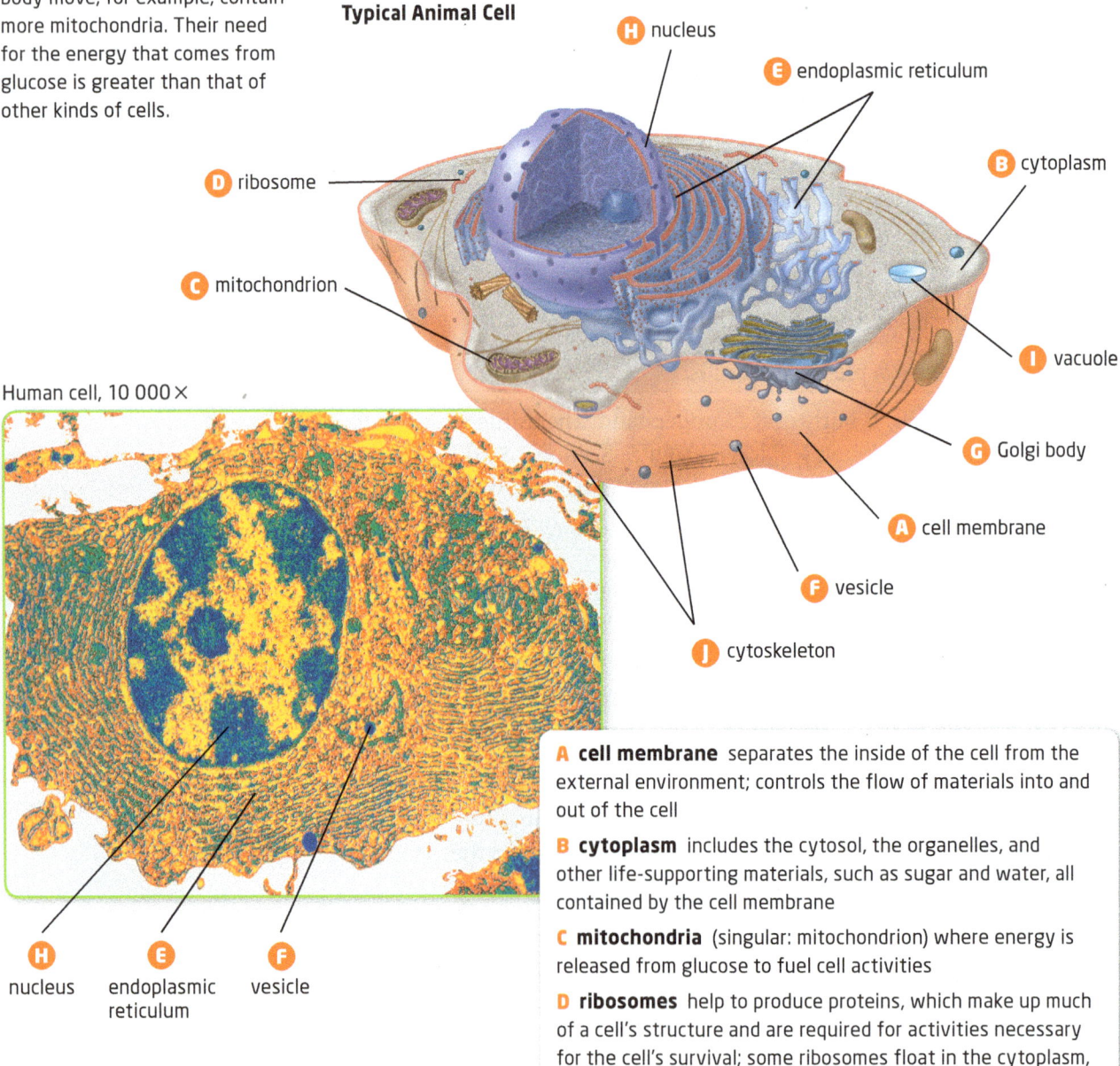

Typical Animal Cell

- **H** nucleus
- **E** endoplasmic reticulum
- **B** cytoplasm
- **D** ribosome
- **C** mitochondrion
- **I** vacuole
- **G** Golgi body
- **A** cell membrane
- **F** vesicle
- **J** cytoskeleton

Human cell, 10 000×

- **H** nucleus
- **E** endoplasmic reticulum
- **F** vesicle

A cell membrane separates the inside of the cell from the external environment; controls the flow of materials into and out of the cell

B cytoplasm includes the cytosol, the organelles, and other life-supporting materials, such as sugar and water, all contained by the cell membrane

C mitochondria (singular: mitochondrion) where energy is released from glucose to fuel cell activities

D ribosomes help to produce proteins, which make up much of a cell's structure and are required for activities necessary for the cell's survival; some ribosomes float in the cytoplasm, and others are attached to the endoplasmic reticulum

Typical Plant Cell

- F vesicle
- I vacuole
- L chloroplast
- J cytoskeleton
- H nucleus
- D ribosome
- E endoplasmic reticulum
- A cell membrane
- K cell wall
- B cytoplasm
- G Golgi body
- C mitochondrion

Suggested Investigation
Inquiry Investigation 1-A, Examining Cell Structures, on page 46

Go to **scienceontario** to find out more

Figure 1.6 This diagram and the micrograph below it show a typical plant cell. Like animal cells, plant cells vary in structure and function. For example, cells in the roots (and other non-green parts of the plant) usually have no chloroplasts. They do not need chloroplasts because they do not carry out photosynthesis.

Voodoo lily cell, 950×

- H nucleus
- C mitochondrion
- I vacuole
- K cell wall

E endoplasmic reticulum a network of membrane-covered channels that transport materials made in the cell; is connected to the nucleus

F vesicles membrane-covered sacs that transport and/or store materials inside the cell and sometimes help these materials cross the cell membrane to enter or exit the cell

G Golgi body sorts and packages proteins and other molecules for transport out of the cell

H nucleus controls all cell activities

I vacuoles contain water and other materials and are used to store or transport small molecules; plant cells tend to have one large vacuole; animal cells may have several smaller vacuoles

J cytoskeleton filaments and tubules that provide a framework for the cell, helping it maintain its structure and providing "tracks" along which vesicles and organelles can move

K cell wall a tough, rigid structure lying just outside a plant cell's membrane; provides support for the cell

L chloroplasts found only in plant cells; trap energy from the Sun to make glucose, which is broken down in the mitochondria to power cell activities (animals must get glucose from the food they eat)

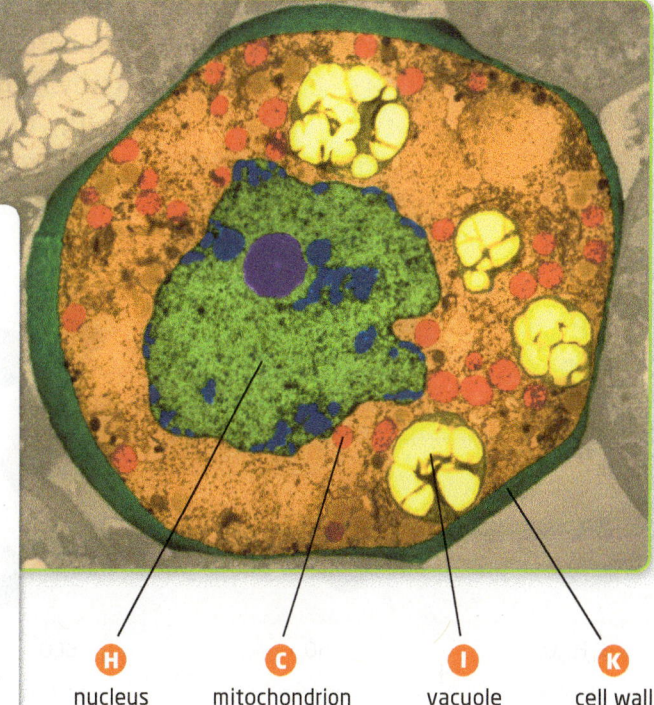

> **Learning Check**
>
> 1. Create a table to compare the organelles in plant and animals cells that are responsible for protein production, food storage, transportation of substances, and maintenance of the cell's structure.
>
> 2. Look back to **Figure 1.2** on pages 8 and 9. Name three types of microscopes and one feature that makes each unique.
>
> 3. What are the three main ideas in the cell theory?
>
> 4. What might be some disadvantages of electron microscopes? Specifically, why do you think you might not have electron microscopes in your school?

All Cells Use Energy

Some types of organelles are found in both plant and animal cells, while other types are found only in one or the other. For example, chloroplasts are found only in plant cells. Mitochondria, however, are found in both plant and animal cells—most cells cannot survive without the energy that mitochondria release from glucose. The process by which this occurs is common to most cells, and it is called cellular respiration.

Cellular respiration, shown in **Figure 1.7**, requires oxygen in order to occur. This is why we must breathe in air, which contains oxygen. As well as releasing energy, the process of cellular respiration produces carbon dioxide as a waste product. We get rid of carbon dioxide and water vapour when we breathe out.

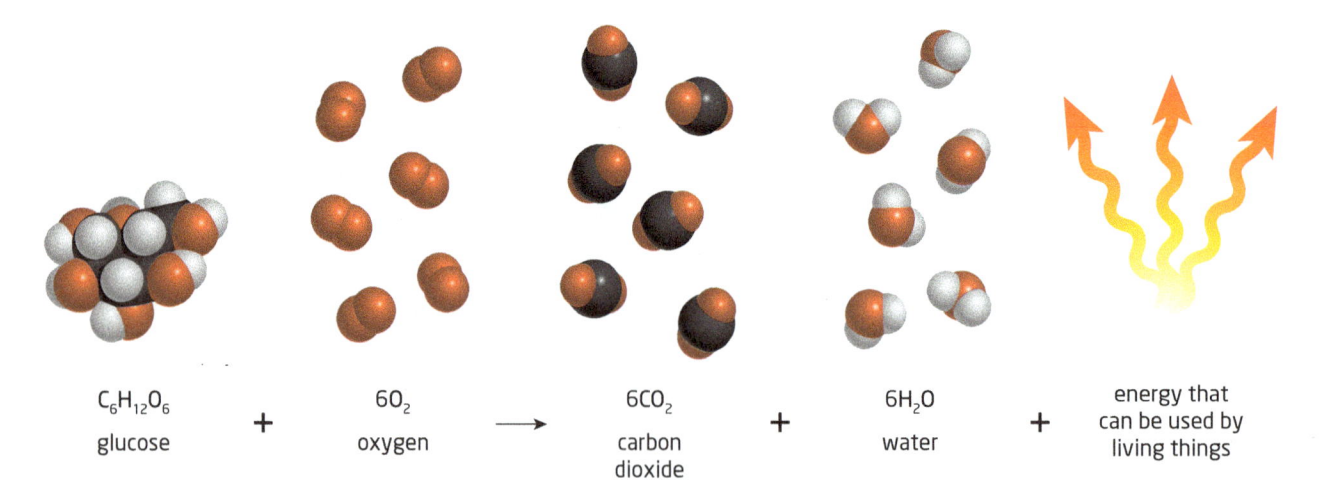

$C_6H_{12}O_6$ (glucose) + $6O_2$ (oxygen) → $6CO_2$ (carbon dioxide) + $6H_2O$ (water) + energy that can be used by living things

Figure 1.7 This is a very simplified version of the cellular respiration process. It shows the inputs and outputs. There are actually many steps between these inputs and outputs. For example, glucose gets broken down in a series of chemical reactions that release energy bit by bit.

Section 1.1 Review

Section Summary

- Developments in microscopy (microscope technology) have made it possible to look at the internal structures of cells.
- Cells contain a variety of organelles, each of which has its own structure and function. Some organelles are found in all cells, while others are found only in plant *or* animal cells.
- Advances in knowledge about cells have helped researchers find new ways to diagnose and treat diseases.

Review Questions

K/U 1. Why are electron microscopes more useful than light microscopes for looking at organelles?

K/U 2. Describe the functions of the following organelles: mitochondria, nucleolus, vacuole.

K/U 3. Examine the diagram on the right.
   a. Does the diagram show a plant cell or an animal cell?
   b. Which of the lettered structures helped you decide?
   c. What is this structure called?

C 4. Draw a Venn diagram to compare the cell wall and the cell membrane.

K/U 5. Using **Figures 1.5** and **1.6** as a reference, draw diagrams or create a table to compare plant and animal cells. Focus on which organelles or other features they share and which parts are only found in one of these types of cells.

C 6. Imagine that the cell is a factory and each of the organelles is a machine. Working in a small group, focus on one organelle. Create a diagram and a short statement to convince the factory president of the importance of your organelle. How is it essential to the operation of the factory? Combine the diagrams from all the groups into a class map of this cell factory.

A 7. The graph on the right provides data on the number of mitochondria in each of three cell types.
   a. Which cell type do you think requires the most food (in the form of the glucose it receives) for its functions?
   b. Why do you think skin cells have the least number of mitochondria of the three types of cells studied?

T/I 8. What do you think would happen to other forms of life on Earth if most or all of the plant life disappeared? Explain your answer in terms of what goes on inside cells.

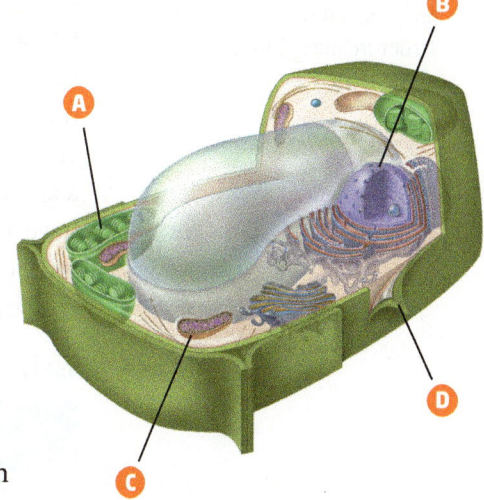

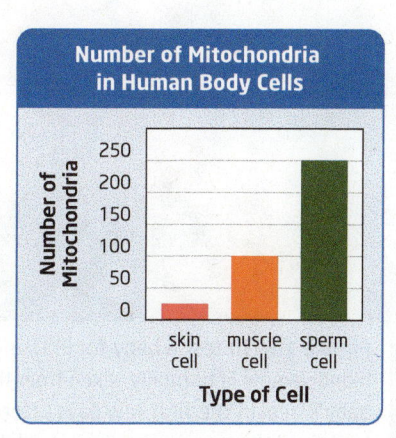

Key Terms
chromosome
DNA
gene
DNA screening
transgenic organism
cloning
mutation
mutagen

1.2 Genes: Answers and Questions

As shown in **Figure 1.8**, babies in Canada are normally tested soon after birth for a genetic condition known as PKU, the short form for phenylketonuria [pronounced fen-il-KEE-to-NU-ria]. If uncorrected, PKU can lead to severe brain damage. However, if diagnosed promptly, PKU can be corrected. Treatment includes following a diet very low in natural protein. (People with PKU must obtain their protein in a special liquid form.) Understanding what causes this condition involves knowing what happens deep within the cell—in the nucleus.

The Nucleus: Control Centre of the Cell

The nucleus contains the master set of instructions that determines what each cell will become, how it will function, and how long it will live before being replaced. These instructions are carried in **chromosomes**. Every plant and animal species has a specific number of chromosomes in the nucleus of each cell. In the cells of most plants and animals, chromosomes come in pairs—one of each pair comes from each parent when an egg and a sperm unite to produce a fertilized egg. Humans, for example, normally have 46 chromosomes in the nucleus of each body cell, 23 from the mother's egg and 23 from the father's sperm. As shown in **Table 1.1**, other species have their own specific number of chromosomes.

chromosome in a cell nucleus, a thread-like structure made mostly of DNA

Table 1.1 Comparison of Chromosome Numbers in Various Organisms' Cells

Organism	Chromosome Number (per cell)	Organism	Chromosome Number (per cell)
Human	46	Corn	20
Cow	60	Butterfly	80
Chicken	78	Fruit fly	8

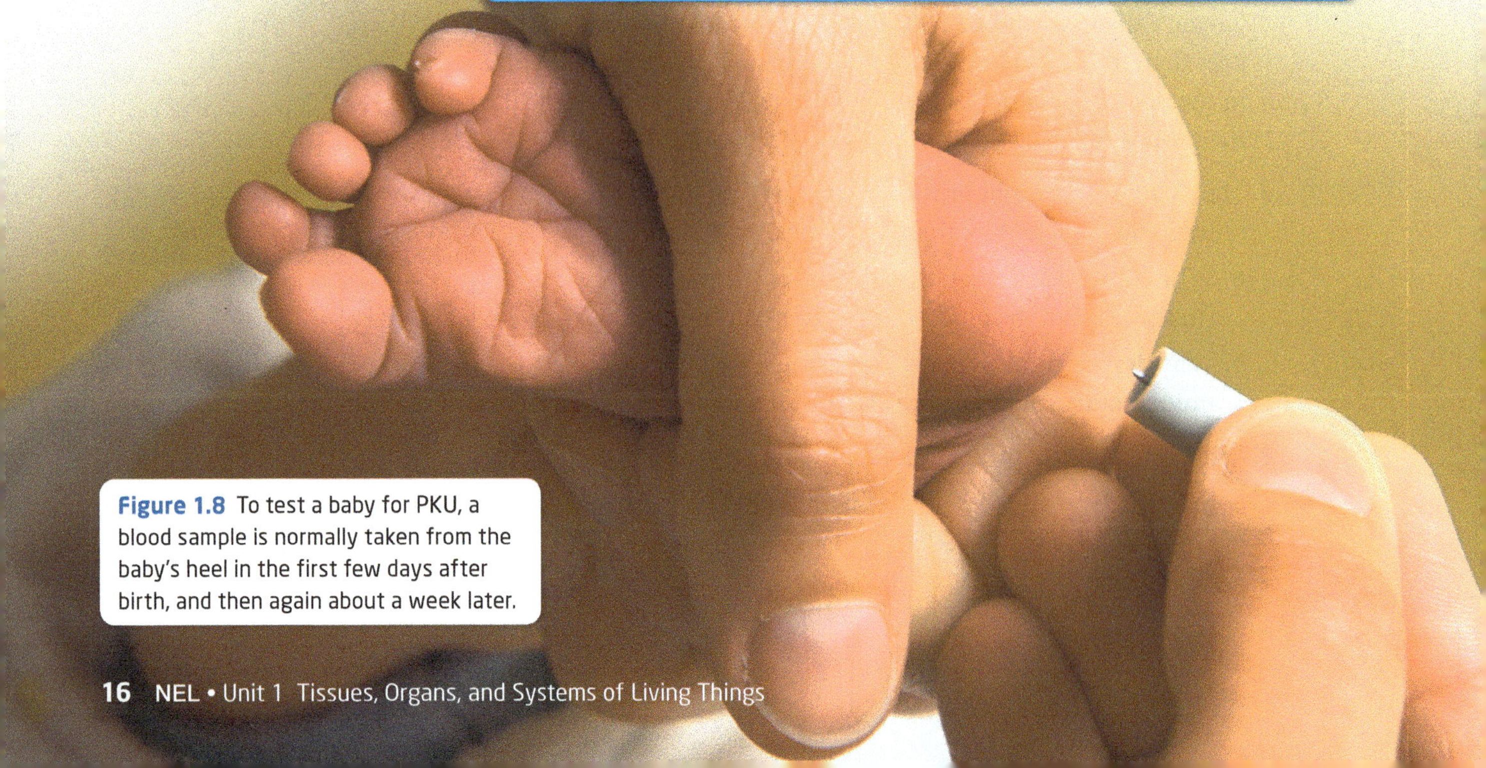

Figure 1.8 To test a baby for PKU, a blood sample is normally taken from the baby's heel in the first few days after birth, and then again about a week later.

The DNA Code

Chromosomes are made of a material called deoxyribonucleic acid (**DNA**). In fact, each chromosome consists of a single molecule of DNA, which is divided into segments called **genes**. Genes are located in specific places on the DNA molecule. Most genes provide instructions for making proteins. Thus, genes control the cell's activities, and much of its structure, by controlling what proteins are made and when.

In 1953, scientists James Watson and Francis Crick built upon the work of many other scientists to create a model of DNA like the one shown in **Figure 1.9**.

DNA material found in the cell nucleus that contains genetic information

gene a segment of DNA that controls protein production

A Each rung of a DNA molecule, along with the piece of the ladder's side to which the rung is attached, is a building-block molecule. Many of these building blocks strung together form a molecule of DNA.

C The order in which the A, T, C, and G building blocks are strung together is called the genetic code. The genetic code is different in every individual (except identical twins). This code is a "message" that determines the production of specific proteins, which combine to make the organism function.

adenine — thymine — cytosine — guanine

B There are four types of building-block molecules, which are usually represented by letters: A (for adenine), T (for thymine), C (for cytosine), and G (for guanine).

Figure 1.9 The twisted ladder shape of the Watson/Crick model of DNA is sometimes called a double helix.

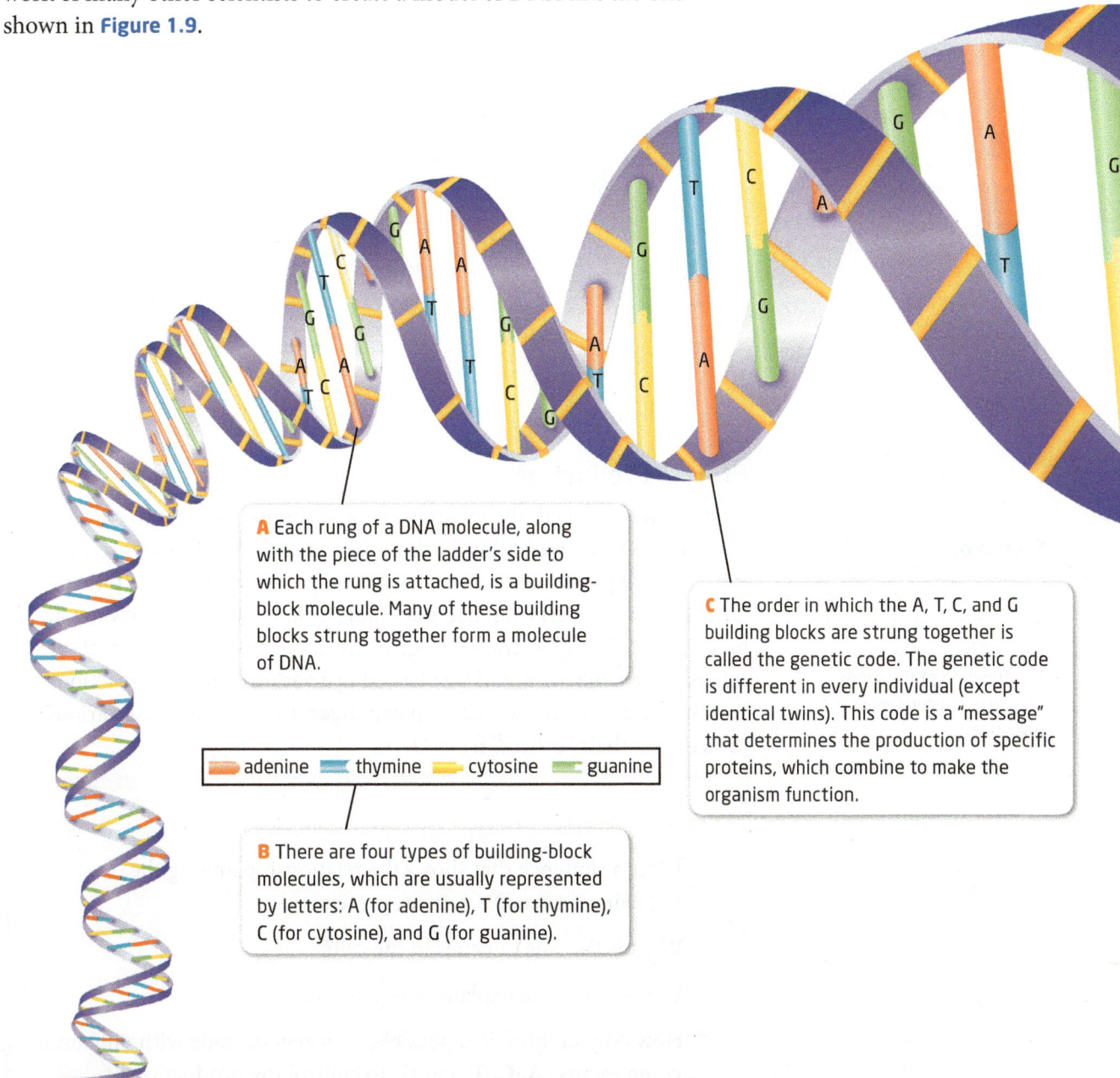

Chapter 1 Cells and More Cells • NEL 17

Why Is DNA Important?

As shown in **Figure 1.10**, a gene is a relatively small part of a DNA molecule. Each DNA molecule contains hundreds or thousands of genes. DNA controls many of your features, such as your hair and eye colour, and whether you can digest certain foods, such as milk. Your DNA exerts this control through genes—they determine what kinds of proteins your cells can make, and therefore how your body might function or look. Of course, your lifestyle choices, such as what and how much you eat and how much exercise you get, also play a role in how your body functions and looks.

Figure 1.10 This diagram shows a model of a section of a DNA molecule with three genes labelled. Genes vary in length, but each is probably thousands of building-block molecules long.

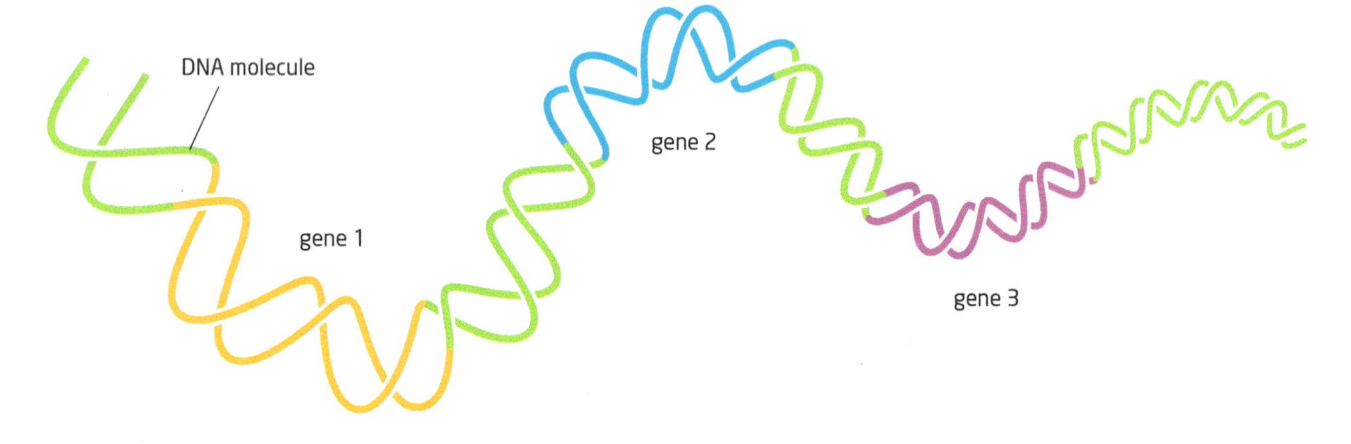

Protein Production

As you have just read, the job of genes, and thus of DNA, is to control the manufacture of proteins. Each protein is designed to do a specific job. For example, some proteins help build parts of your body. Others are like couriers, carrying materials short or long distances within your body. Some pick up or transfer signals from one body part to another. Still others, called enzymes, catalyze (speed up) various chemical reactions in your body, such as those that help you digest food. All of these various proteins get their "orders" from DNA.

Sense of scale

Our genes are estimated to represent only 3 percent of the DNA in our chromosomes. The function of the other 97 percent is currently unknown.

Learning Check

1. Write a sentence that shows the relationship among the following terms: DNA, gene, protein.
2. What is the role of genes in the cell?
3. Use **Figure 1.9** to explain how genes vary.
4. How do you think it is possible for a genetic code with only four components (A, C, T, and G) to control the production of thousands of different kinds of proteins? It might help to think of the building blocks as letters of an alphabet, and to remember that each gene is made of thousands of building blocks.

18 NEL • Unit 1 Tissues, Organs, and Systems of Living Things

DNA Screening

On page 16, you learned that babies are commonly tested for a genetic condition called PKU. Testing for the presence of genetic disorders is referred to as genetic screening, or **DNA screening**. Some types of genetic disorders can be observed by looking at a person's chromosomes.

Down syndrome is one of these disorders—it can even be detected in a fetus. Using a technique called amniocentesis, a needle is inserted through a pregnant woman's abdominal wall to withdraw a sample of fluid from the amniotic sac (which surrounds the growing fetus). Cells from the fetus are isolated, and a micrograph of the chromosomes in these cells is taken.

Although this micrograph, called a *karyotype*, cannot show errors in individual genes, it can show if a person has too many or too few chromosomes, or if any are broken. To diagnose Down syndrome, technicians look specifically at chromosome 21. Individuals with Down syndrome, such as the girl shown in **Figure 1.11**, have three of these chromosomes instead of the usual pair (two).

Testing for PKU

Other kinds of genetic conditions, such as PKU, can be detected by examining a blood sample. In such tests, the presence or absence of specific proteins in the blood can indicate whether a person's genes are functioning normally. If a certain protein is present at normal levels, the gene must be functioning properly. To test for PKU, for example, a baby's blood is examined for an enzyme needed to digest certain kinds of protein in foods. Without this enzyme, a substance called phenylalanine builds up in the baby's blood, with tragic consequences if uncorrected. Each year, one baby in 12 000 is born with PKU.

Testing for PKU is inexpensive compared to the costs of treating PKU if it is not detected early. Other types of genetic screening, however, are more expensive and the benefits may be less clear. For example, having certain genes may make a person *more likely* to get cancer or heart disease, but this does not mean that the person *will* get the disease. The person might lead a healthy lifestyle and be in little danger. Genetic information alone cannot provide *all* the answers.

> **DNA screening** the process of testing individuals to determine whether they have the gene or genes associated with certain genetic disorders

> **Study Toolkit**
> **Previewing Text Features**
> Notice the two heading styles on this page. What do these different styles tell you about the relationship between the information in each section?

Figure 1.11 This girl has Down syndrome, a genetic disorder resulting from having 47 chromosomes instead of 46. This extra chromosome leads to overproduction of certain proteins, which results in some physical and developmental disabilities.

Testing for Huntington Disease

A look at the case for and against genetic testing for Huntington disease reveals some of the ethical issues at stake in DNA screening. Huntington disease is a genetic disorder that affects nerve cells. Symptoms, which normally appear in a person's 40s, include loss of muscular control and brain function. The symptoms worsen for 15 years or so before the disease causes death.

Scientists have identified which gene causes this disease, which helps researchers such as Nancy Wexler, shown in **Figure 1.12**. Individuals have a 50 percent chance of having the gene that causes this disease if one of their parents has it. Someone who has the gene *will*, with certainty, develop the disease. Therefore, finding out if the gene is present in a person's body leads to a definite diagnosis.

Should Individuals at Risk Get Tested?

There is an ongoing debate about whether individuals at risk of Huntington disease (that is, people who have a parent with the disease) should get tested. Those against testing argue that diagnosing the disease can cause people needless emotional pain—since there is no cure, there is nothing they can do. Moreover, critics argue that testing is too expensive, especially since it will not save lives.

Those in favour of testing argue that having the test results—positive or negative—reduces the stress of uncertainty. In addition, knowing whether they do or do not have the gene might change many of a person's life decisions. If they test positive, for example, some people may choose not to have children (so they do not risk passing on the gene). However, even people who support the tests argue that the results must be kept strictly private so that individuals who test positive are not discriminated against.

Figure 1.12 Much research on Huntington disease has taken place in San Luis, an isolated village in Venezuela, where the gene is very common. One of the people leading research there is Nancy Wexler, whose mother had the disease. Here she stands in front of a chart she created to track the genes of a group of families from New York City.

Activity 1-2

To Test or Not to Test?

Globally, Huntington disease affects about seven in 100 000 people, although some locations have a higher incidence than others. Genetic testing for a disease like Huntington raises many complex ethical issues. What kinds of issues might these be?

Procedure

1. Choose the perspective of a stakeholder in the debate about testing for Huntington disease. Suggested roles include the following:
   - You are a 30-year-old who has one parent with the disease. You are wondering whether to be tested.
   - You have just tested positive for the disease. You have a two-year-old child.
   - You are the owner of an insurance company considering a new client's application.
   - You are an employer. Your company invests heavily in employee training and generally counts on people staying with your company for many years or even decades.
   - You are a government official in charge of public health care. You are looking for ways to control costs.
2. Make a list of points to support your opinion using this textbook and your own ideas. Prepare a summary statement of your position.
3. In your role, discuss the questions that follow in a small group.
4. Share your ideas as a class.

In your group, try to reach a consensus on each question.

Questions

1. Should employers or insurance companies be allowed to require people to test for Huntington disease, or should taking the test be a matter of personal choice? Explain your answer.
2. Should people be required to reveal a family history of Huntington to a potential employer or insurance company? Or should such a matter be private?
3. Should children with a risk of Huntington disease be allowed to have the test? Why or why not?
4. Should health-care professionals discourage people with a risk of Huntington from having children? Explain your answer.
5. Should individuals pay to be tested, or should the public health-care system pay? How might this decision affect access to the test?
6. Should all stakeholders have an equal voice in decisions about genetic testing for Huntington disease? Explain your answer.

DNA Screening in Canada

PKU, Down syndrome, and Huntington disease are not the only conditions that can be identified using DNA tests. For example, women can be screened for the presence of certain genes associated with breast cancer. Although only a small proportion of all breast cancers are due to genetic factors, the test could help women with the gene take preventative measures. Other conditions that can be determined with DNA screening include cystic fibrosis and spina bifida.

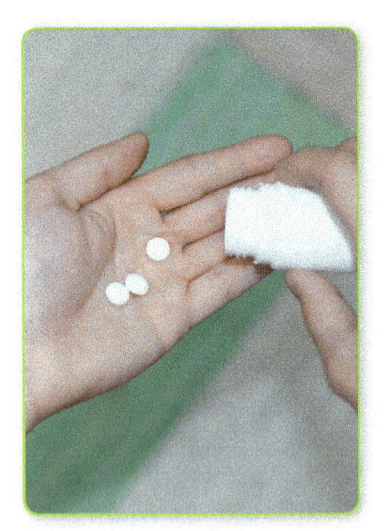

Figure 1.13 In 2007, the Food and Drug Administration in the United States approved Kuvan, a drug to treat PKU. For an adult, the annual cost of taking this drug might be as high as U.S. $200 000.

Ethical Issues and Drug Research

Much of the research into treatments for various diseases, including PKU and Huntington disease, is carried out by drug companies. Such research can be very costly and take years, if not decades. Once a company develops a drug that is effective and safe in lab conditions, it applies to carry out a clinical trial on humans. In Canada, approval for drug trials is given by Health Canada, a department of the federal government. The financial risks for a company involved in this type of research are very high, since the drug might not work as well outside the lab. As discussed in **Figure 1.13**, companies may try to recover the costs of research and development by putting a high price on their product.

Critics sometimes suggest that clinical trial results can be biased. Companies are sometimes accused of presenting their trial data as more positive than they really are. The ethical issues get even more troublesome if you think about what might happen if a company discovered an effective, but extremely expensive, cure for cancer or diabetes. Does the company own the cure and therefore have the right to sell or control it in any way it chooses? Or does the company have an ethical obligation to make life-saving cures available to everyone who needs them? These ethical questions are frequently debated by scientists, medical professionals, drug companies, and concerned members of the public.

Learning Check

5. What is a karyotype?
6. Describe two techniques used to screen a person's DNA.
7. How can having too little or too much of a certain protein cause problems for an organism?
8. Every container of diet soft drink that is sweetened with the chemical aspartame must have on its label a warning that it contains phenylalanine. Why do you think this warning is required?

Go to **scienceontario** to find out more

Altering Genes: Benefits and Controversies

The genetic code is universal. This means that the same four DNA building-block molecules (A, C, T, and G) produce the code for proteins in *all* types of organisms, including bacteria, plants, and animals. Theoretically, this means that the genetic code in one type of organism could be "read" by any other type of organism. If a particular gene could be transferred between two different types of organisms, one species could then make proteins usually made only by the other species.

In fact, scientists have been combining the DNA from different species for a number of years in a process called genetic engineering. The species whose genes are altered are often called genetically modified organisms (GMOs) or **transgenic organisms**.

transgenic organism an organism whose genetic information has been altered with the insertion of genes from another species

Transgenic Organisms

Table 1.2 shows some of the common kinds of transgenic organisms today. Many people see the manipulation of genes as a way to solve various problems. Others, however, worry about the effects of causing rapid change in species that have taken thousands, if not millions, of years to evolve. They feel that we know too little about the long-term consequences. For example, some people ask how GMO plants might affect the organisms (including humans) that eat them. Others worry about the effects of GMO plants on the ecosystem, especially if the GMO plants spread to new areas.

Some people ask whether transplanting organs from transgenic animals, such as the pigs you saw on page 4, is a good idea. They worry about various viruses that are carried in pigs without harming them, but that are not naturally found in humans. If these viruses moved with the transplanted organs, they could cause viral diseases that could spread quickly in the human population.

Table 1.2 The Uses of Some Genetically Modified Organisms

GMO Organism	Benefit	Example
Bacteria injected with human proteins are used for many medical treatments. Bacteria have a relatively simple genetic structure, so they were the first type of organism to be genetically modified. Here the bacteria *E. coli*, shown in magenta, has been genetically engineered to produce insulin, which is used to treat diabetes. Orange areas indicate insulin production sites on the bacteria.	Human proteins manufactured by bacteria are less likely to cause allergic reactions or diseases, compared with proteins obtained from other sources, such as animals or dead bodies.	
Many crops have had genes from bacteria or other plants inserted into their chromosomes. Corn, canola, wheat, cotton, and soy are just some of the crops for which farmers can buy GMO seed. Pictured here is a plot used to promote a company's GMO product.	Crops can be modified in this way to resist specific pests, to have a higher nutritional value, or to better withstand drought (lack of water) or cold.	
Some animals are injected with genes that code for a hormone that promotes growth. Here, Canadian scientist Robert Devlin holds up a 16-month-old GMO salmon on the left and a normal salmon on the right.	GMO animals injected with a growth hormone grow faster than non-GMO animals, increasing human food supplies.	

cloning the process of creating identical genetic copies of an organism

Go to **scienceontario** to find out more

Cloning

Cloning may be another solution to the problem of needing new organs or cells. Cloning is the process of producing identical offspring from genes, cells, or an entire organism.

Cloning has been used for centuries in its simplest form—by gardeners who have taken cuttings from a plant, rooted them, and thereby produced more plants that are exact copies of the parent plant. Then, in 1958, Fredrick Steward was able to grow a plant from a single carrot cell in a laboratory. **Figure 1.14** shows a simplified version of Steward's cloning experiment (**A**) as well as a process used to clone a mammal today (**B**).

A Steps in Cloning a Carrot

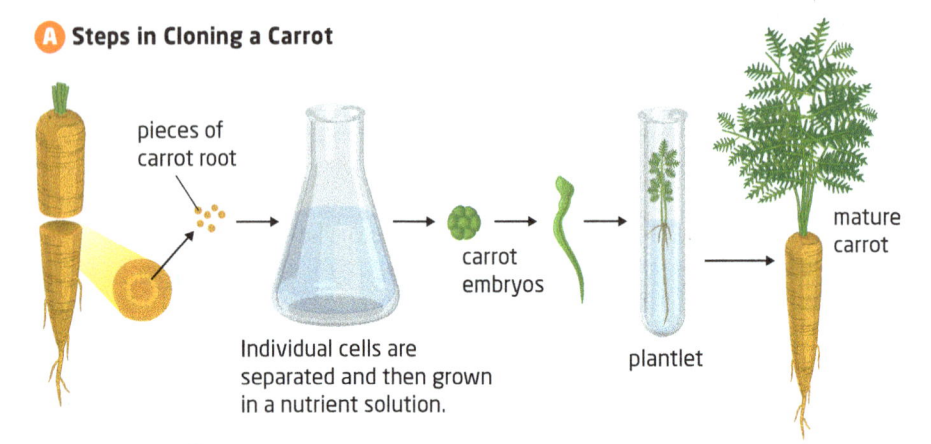

pieces of carrot root → Individual cells are separated and then grown in a nutrient solution. → carrot embryos → plantlet → mature carrot

Figure 1.14 In **A**, you can see the cloning process used by Fredrick Steward. In **B**, you can see a process used to clone a mammal, which was first accomplished in 1996.

STSE Case Study

Clones in the Kitchen

Why would we clone the animals we use for meat? The purpose of cloning, which is a type of biotechnology, is to produce genetic duplicates (copies) of animals that are considered superior in some way. That way, desirable traits that occurred naturally, such as higher quality meat, are passed along from generation to generation. Cloning animals benefits meat and milk producers because high-quality products mean higher profits.

Also, altering the genetic material from the donor animal before the animal is cloned provides more opportunities to incorporate benefits. For instance, cattle could be genetically engineered to better resist BSE (mad cow disease). However, animal cloning opponents are concerned about food safety. Few scientific studies have examined cloned meat, and livestock companies have done most of the research. Since these companies want positive results, some people believe their research may be biased.

Some studies show that even though cloned animals are genetic copies of the donors, they are not completely identical. For example, meat from some cloned animals has higher levels of fat compared with meat from the original donor animals.

Some meat and milk producers want to use cloned animals as a way to guarantee the quality of their products.

B Steps in Cloning a Mammal

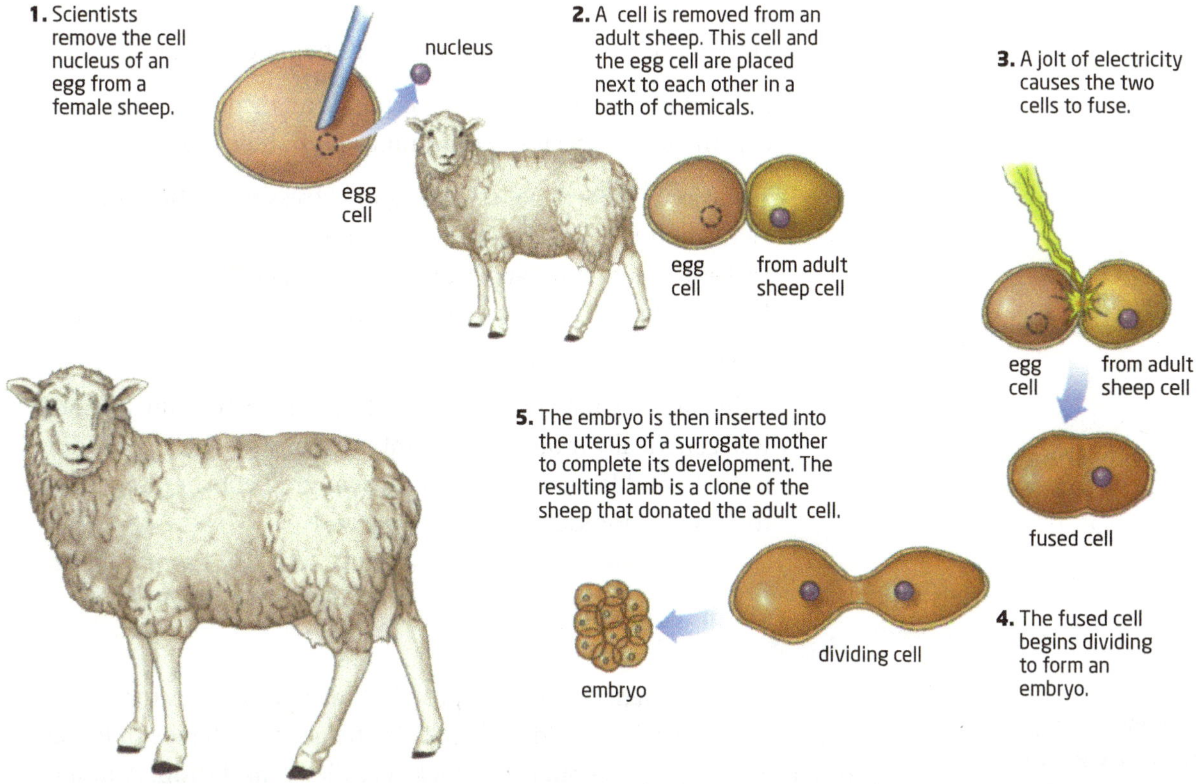

1. Scientists remove the cell nucleus of an egg from a female sheep.

2. A cell is removed from an adult sheep. This cell and the egg cell are placed next to each other in a bath of chemicals.

3. A jolt of electricity causes the two cells to fuse.

4. The fused cell begins dividing to form an embryo.

5. The embryo is then inserted into the uterus of a surrogate mother to complete its development. The resulting lamb is a clone of the sheep that donated the adult cell.

Furthermore, genetically *identical* animals are more prone to catch the diseases that animals around them have. That is, if a virus or other micro-organism infects one of these animals, it could easily infect a whole herd. In nature, a herd would include genetically *different* animals and would usually include some animals whose immune systems are better able to fight the disease.

Because we know so little about using cloned animals for food, Canada currently bans the sale of food from cloned animals or their offspring. Where do you stand on this issue?

Your Turn

1. Survey the other students in your class. Ask them, "If you eat meat, would you consider eating the meat of a cloned animal? Why or why not?" Calculate the percentage of "yes" and "no" answers you receive.

2. Suppose that Health Canada has decided to permit the sale of cloned meat. Identify your position on this issue. Provide three pieces of supporting evidence.

3. In a small group, brainstorm and record the positive and negative characteristics of cloned animals in a two-column table. In a brief report to the class, present your group's evaluation of whether animals should be cloned.

In 1996, a sheep named Dolly became the first mammal created from a cell of an adult sheep rather than from an egg. Dolly died at the age of six. Some people claim her life was shorter than normal because she was a cloned animal, while others argue that her death was completely natural.

> **Learning Check**
>
> 9. Why is the genetic code described as being universal?
>
> 10. In what way are organs from certain kinds of transgenic organisms potentially significant to human health?
>
> 11. Traditional Aboriginal ethical values stress protection for the rights of future generations, acceptance of human limitations, and a precautionary approach to new science and technology. How might such values affect someone's view on transgenic organisms or cloning?
>
> 12. Think about what you have eaten today. Do you think any of it was genetically modified, or contained any genetically modified ingredients? If so, what might those ingredients be? Look back to **Table 1.2** for ideas.

Mutations

As you have learned, the specific protein that a gene codes for depends on the order of the DNA building blocks in the gene. A change in the usual order of the A, C, T, G building blocks is called a **mutation**. A mutation in a gene can alter the structure of the protein it produces. Such a change can then affect how well the protein does its job. For example, people who have a condition called sickle cell anemia have a mutation in the gene that codes for hemoglobin, a type of protein in red blood cells. As discussed in **Figure 1.15**, the mutation changes the protein in such a way that it is less able to perform its function, which is to help the blood carry oxygen to body cells.

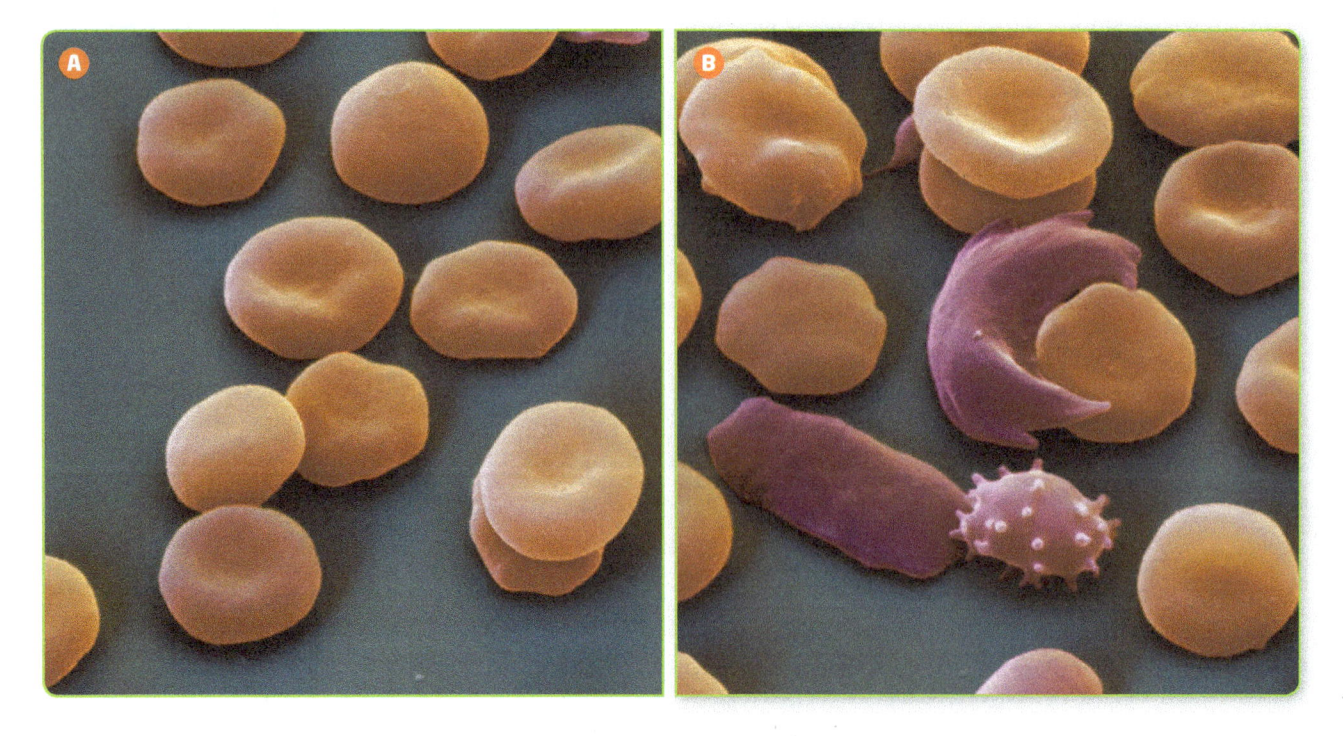

mutation a change in the DNA of an organism

Figure 1.15 A Normal red blood cells are disk-shaped. Their shape enables them to move easily through blood vessels. In **B**, you can see a C- or sickle-shaped red blood cell from someone who carries the sickle cell gene.

How Mutations Happen

The sequence of the A, C, T, and G building blocks in a DNA molecule can change for no particular reason. Often, however, mutations are caused by **mutagens**, forces or substances that physically damage DNA. Electromagnetic radiation, including X rays and UV rays (from the Sun) are mutagens. So are many chemicals, including mercury and the tar in cigarettes. As shown in **Figure 1.16**, some mutations occur in only one or a few of an organism's cells. Other mutations, however, affect cells (eggs and sperm) that are passed between generations. In other words, some mutations are inherited.

Not all mutations are harmful. Only part of a DNA molecule contains genes—the rest does not code for proteins. A mutation that occurs on a non-genetic part of a DNA molecule is not harmful, at least as far as scientists know. Even mutations that change proteins are not necessarily harmful. Some mutations, for example, might help an organism adapt to a particular environment, such as the mutations in bacteria that allow them to resist antibiotics. Other mutations may be neutral—neither causing a problem nor helping the organism. Whether the mutation is harmful or not may sometimes depend on an organism's environment. Do you think the mutation shown in **Figure 1.17** is beneficial, harmful, or neutral?

Could Science Correct Mutations?

Gene mutations are at least partly to blame for a variety of diseases. Research into gene therapy—correcting faulty genes—is ongoing. Researchers hope that gene therapy will one day be used to treat a variety of inherited diseases.

However, clinical trials on various forms of gene therapy have not yet had much success. People who participate in the experimental treatments often become sicker or die. Some people question whether this kind of research is even worth pursuing. For them, the issue is who decides what disorders should be corrected. For example, researchers have had some success using gene therapy for certain types of inherited blindness. Does the fact that this blindness can be "fixed" imply that these people are "broken"? Many people would disagree and argue that visually impaired people can live full, rich lives. Other questions include the following:

- Who gets access to treatments, and who pays for the treatments?
- Who funds research, and who owns or manages the resulting product or technology?
- How far should society go in using available technologies?

Some people believe these questions should be answered before gene therapy treatments are developed.

mutagen a substance or factor that can cause a mutation in DNA

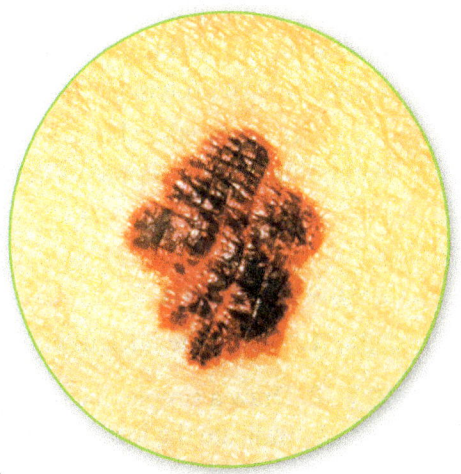

Figure 1.16 This photograph shows skin cells that have been mutated by UV radiation. This mutation would affect only the cells of this person; the mutation would not be passed on to the person's children.

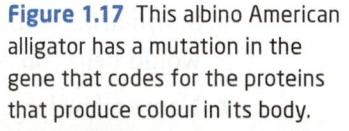

Figure 1.17 This albino American alligator has a mutation in the gene that codes for the proteins that produce colour in its body.

Section 1.2 Review

Section Summary

- The nucleus of a cell contains chromosomes, which are composed of DNA and divided into segments called genes. Genes control a cell's structure and function by controlling the production of proteins.
- There are many ethical issues related to technological developments in DNA screening, transgenic research, and clinical drug trials. Researchers often make progress faster than society's ability to make decisions on how to use such research.
- Mutations in genes change the structure and function of the proteins in the cells. Many, but not all, genetic mutations are harmful.

Review Questions

K/U 1. Why is the nucleus of a cell so important?

K/U 2. Draw a simple diagram of a portion of a DNA molecule, and indicate the location of a gene.

C 3. How does DNA screening have both positive and negative implications for society? Create a T-chart to summarize your answer.

A 4. How might researchers who work for pharmaceutical companies ensure that their clinical trials meet proper scientific standards?

C 5. As of 2007, 23 countries grew genetically modified crops. The table on the right shows the number of hectares of GMO crops in some of these countries.
   a. Graph the data using a bar graph.
   b. Summarize your results. What further information would help you compare the data?
   c. Name a few large countries that are not included in the table. Why do you think they are not included?

T/I 6. Researchers have calculated that, on average, each cigarette reduces a person's life by 5.5 min (as a result of the toxic chemicals in cigarettes, many of which are mutagens). If there are 20 cigarettes to a package and an individual smokes half a pack per day, how much will this individual's life have been reduced after one year?

A 7. Officials in charge of catching those who use illegal, performance-enhancing drugs in sport are concerned that, in the future, "gene doping" may become a problem. Suggest what this process might be and why athletes might try it.

K/U 8. What is a mutation? Would a mutation that caused a deer to be albino be beneficial, harmful, or neutral? If the deer lives in a zoo, would your answer change? Explain.

Use of GMO Crops*

Country	GMO Crops (hectares)
Argentina	19 101 000
Australia	100 000
Brazil	14 973 000
Canada	7 001 000
China	3 804 000
India	6 192 000
Mexico	100 000
Paraguay	2 590 000
Philippines	300 000
South Africa	1 781 000
Spain	100 000
Uruguay	486 000
United States	57 708 000

*Among countries with more than 90 000 hectares of GMO crops; rounded to the nearest thousand

Clive James/International Service for the Acquisition of Agri-Biotech Applications

1.3 Cells from Cells

Key Terms
cell division
mitosis
cytokinesis
DNA replication
prophase
metaphase
anaphase
telophase
cell plate

There are tens of thousands of different proteins in your body, and the types of proteins you have are determined by your genes. If a gene is missing or damaged, the protein it codes for may be missing or non-functioning. Thus, all 46 chromosomes you see in **Figure 1.18** are important.

Cell Reproduction

Cell reproduction is the process by which new cells are formed. An important difference between cell reproduction and the reproduction of a multicellular organism (one with a body consisting of many cells), however, is the number of "parents" involved. As you can see in **Figure 1.19**, when body cells and most single-celled organisms reproduce, there is only one parent: one cell divides to produce two new cells, which are called *daughter cells*. The two daughter cells are identical to each other and to their parent cell, at least in the genes they contain.

In sexual reproduction, two parents mate and the offspring receive half of their genes from each parent (one chromosome from each pair of chromosomes). Therefore, although offspring share genetic material and may look alike, they are not exactly the same. For example, not all of the kittens in a litter look the same. Each kitten receives half of its genes from each parent, but does not get exactly the same combination of genes as other kittens in the litter.

Figure 1.18 This karyotype shows the 46 chromosomes (magnified 1000 times) present in the nucleus of every cell in the body of a male human.

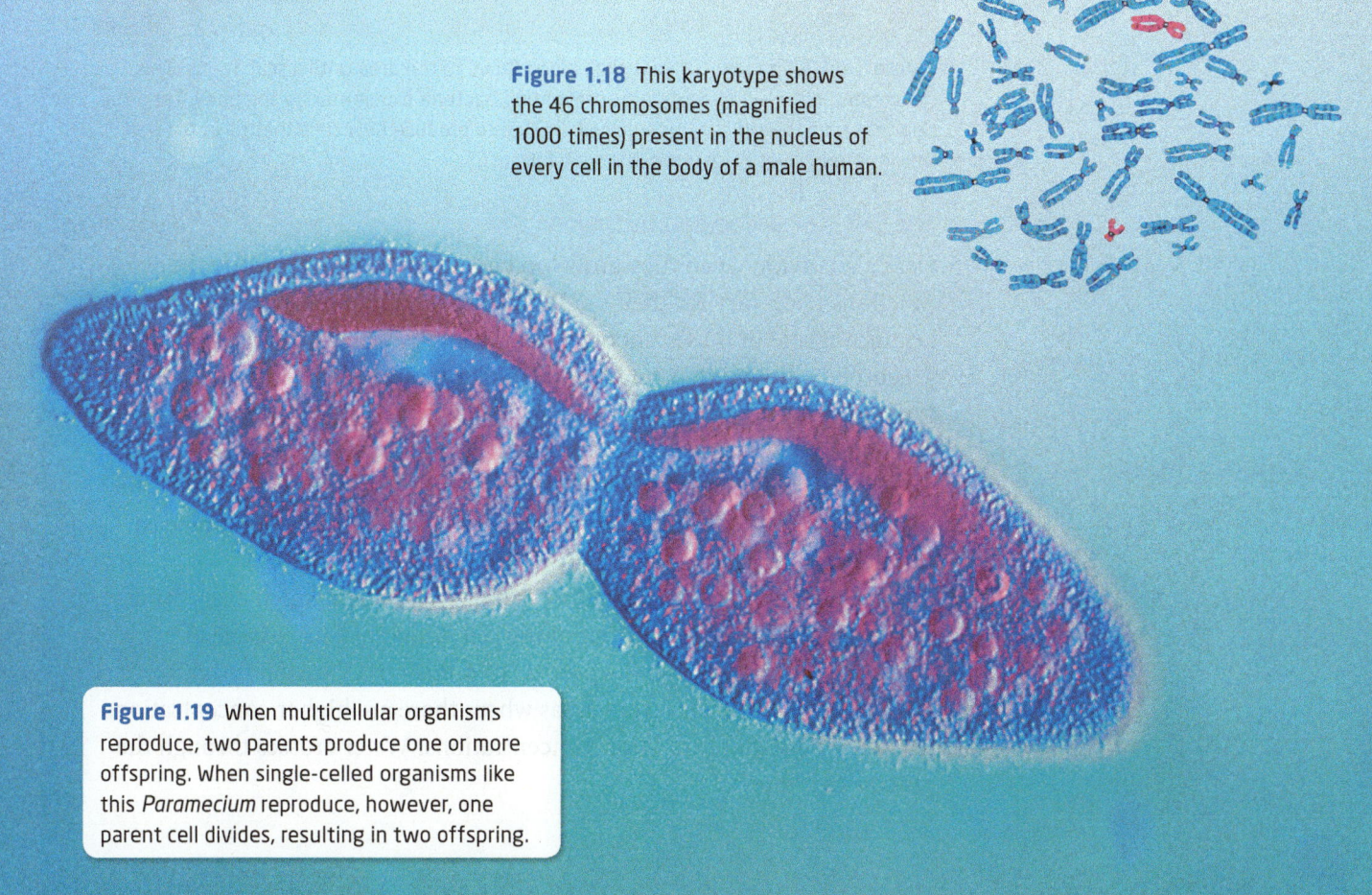

Figure 1.19 When multicellular organisms reproduce, two parents produce one or more offspring. When single-celled organisms like this *Paramecium* reproduce, however, one parent cell divides, resulting in two offspring.

Chapter 1 Cells and More Cells • NEL 29

cell division the process by which a parent cell divides into two daughter cells

Cell Division

The *Paramecium* shown in **Figure 1.19** has reproduced by dividing in two. In other words, it has undergone the process of **cell division**. For single-celled organisms, cell division is the main process by which individuals reproduce, and the population gets larger. For multicellular organisms, cell division is the process by which a fertilized egg (a single cell) becomes, eventually, an adult with millions of cells.

In multicellular organisms, cell division is also the process by which you replace lost or damaged cells, as you can see in **Figure 1.20**.

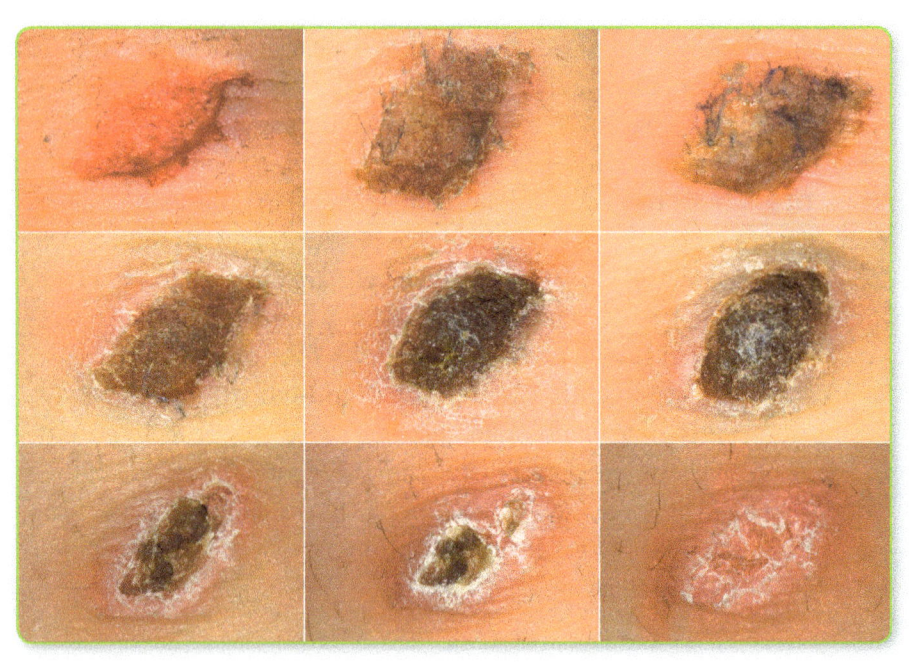

Figure 1.20 When you cut your skin, blood flows to the area until a scab forms. This scab restores the skin's continuity, preventing bacteria from entering the body. Then the skin cells underneath can undergo cell division to produce new cells that fill in the gap. Once the skin layer is restored, the scab falls off.

The Cell Membrane and Diffusion

Cells also divide when they grow too large to perform efficiently the functions necessary for their survival. The cell membrane plays a significant role in these functions. For example, when you eat food, it gets broken down into smaller and smaller molecules by your digestive system. These molecules—as well as the oxygen molecules in the air you inhale—then get delivered to every cell in your body. Once there, these substances must cross the cell membrane to get inside the cell, where they are needed. The cell's waste materials must also cross this membrane to exit the cell.

The cell membrane is, therefore, a barrier through which everything must pass on its way into or out of the cell. Much of this passage of materials occurs through the process of *diffusion*. Diffusion is the movement of molecules from areas where there are higher concentrations to areas where there are lower concentrations. Water crosses through the process of *osmosis*.

30 NEL • Unit 1 Tissues, Organs, and Systems of Living Things

Moving from High Concentrations to Low Concentrations

Like the membrane in the beaker shown in **Figure 1.21**, the cell membrane is permeable to certain substances; that is, these substances can cross the membrane. Materials that the cell needs (such as oxygen) diffuse across the membrane from outside the cell—where they are more concentrated—to the inside—where they are less concentrated. A cell membrane is referred to as selectively permeable because not all materials can cross it; some are kept out—or in.

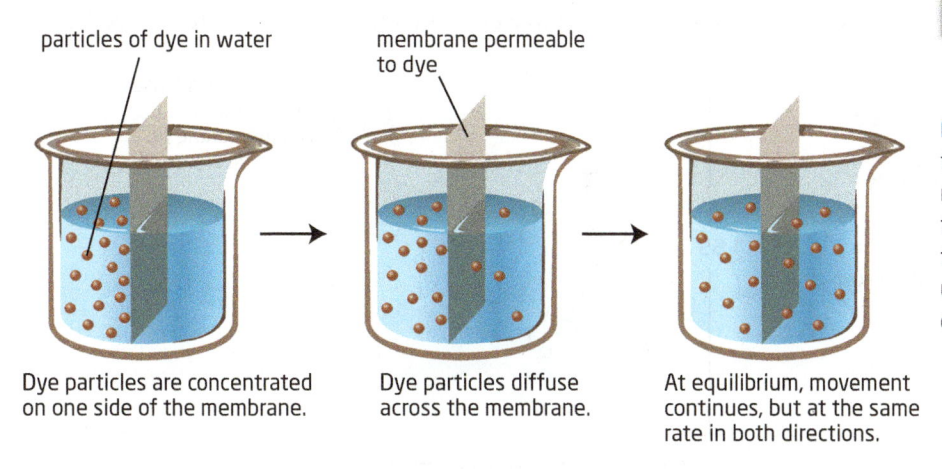

Study Toolkit

Visualizing When reading the text on this page, visualizing how molecules cross the cell membrane can help you understand and remember the process.

particles of dye in water

membrane permeable to dye

Dye particles are concentrated on one side of the membrane.

Dye particles diffuse across the membrane.

At equilibrium, movement continues, but at the same rate in both directions.

Figure 1.21 Diffusion occurs through a selectively permeable membrane. Dye particles diffuse from areas of high concentration to areas of low concentration until they reach a point of equilibrium.

Most cells are surrounded by solutions that contain water and dissolved nutrients and gases. Like other molecules, water moves from areas of greater concentration to areas of lesser concentration. In **Figure 1.22**, you can see how osmosis occurs over a cell membrane to equalize the number of water molecules inside and outside the cell.

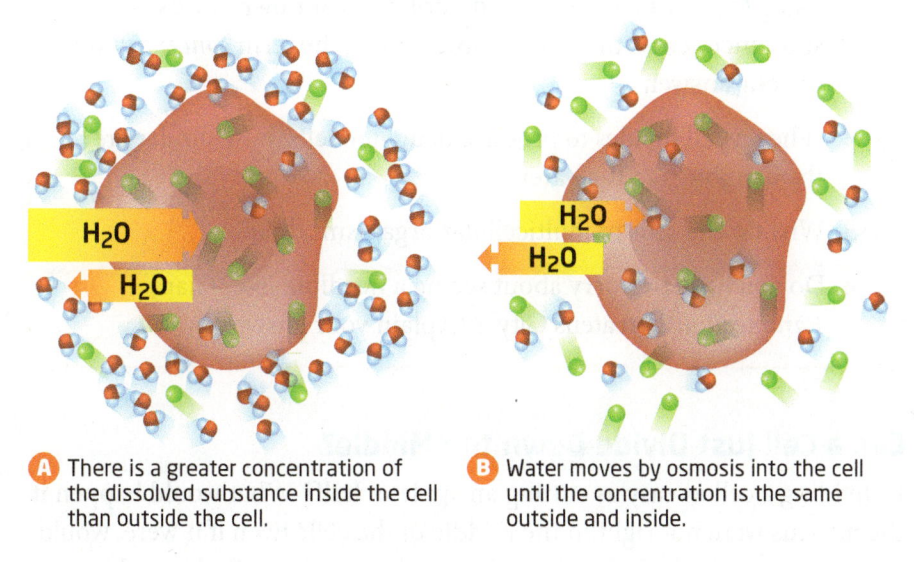

A There is a greater concentration of the dissolved substance inside the cell than outside the cell.

B Water moves by osmosis into the cell until the concentration is the same outside and inside.

water molecules

molecules of dissolved substance; cell membrane is impermeable to this molecule

Figure 1.22 In **A**, you can see that the dissolved substance is more concentrated inside than outside the cell. It cannot diffuse through the cell membrane. However, water is more concentrated outside than inside. In **B**, you can see that water passes through the membrane until the concentration of water molecules is the same on both sides of the membrane.

Growing Cells

The surface of the cell must be big enough to allow for the entry of all of the oxygen and nutrients needed by the cell's organelles, nucleus, and cytosol. As cells use these nutrients, they produce more organelles and cytosol and thus get bigger. As a result, their volume increases. And, with more organelles doing their jobs, the cell's need for supplies and its production of wastes increase.

Limiting Cell Size

Every cell faces the problem of needing enough surface area to service its volume. As something gets larger, the ratio of its surface area to its volume decreases. In other words, there is less surface area per unit of volume in a large organism than in a small organism. As suggested by **Figure 1.23**, a cell cannot get too big, or it will not have enough surface area for the passage of all the nutrients it needs and the wastes it produces. Therefore, when a cell reaches a certain size, it must divide to produce smaller cells. Each of these smaller cells will then have enough surface area to suit its needs.

Figure 1.23 If an amoeba were as big as a human, critical substances, such as oxygen, would take years to get through the cell's cytoplasm to reach the centre of the cell. This would be far too long. In the meantime, the nucleus and other organelles would not receive the nutrients they need to function.

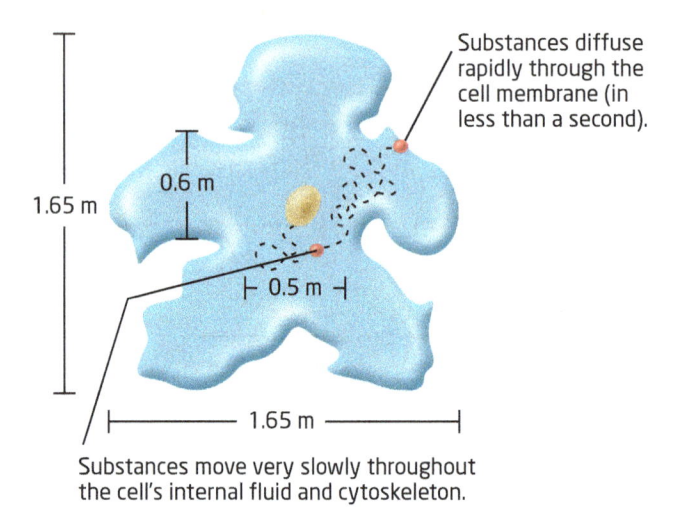

Substances diffuse rapidly through the cell membrane (in less than a second).

Substances move very slowly throughout the cell's internal fluid and cytoskeleton.

Learning Check

1. Using **Figures 1.21** and **1.22**, describe in your own words how substances cross the cell membrane. Use the term *concentration* in your answer.
2. When a cell divides to produce daughter cells, how similar are the daughters to the parent?
3. Why do the cells of multicellular organisms divide?
4. Do you have to worry about seeing a headline like "Giant *Paramecium* Threatens City"? Explain your answer.

Can a Cell Just Divide Down the Middle?

Is dividing a cell as easy as cutting an apple in half? What would happen if the nucleus were not right in the middle of the cell? Even if it were, would it work just to divide the total number of chromosomes in the nucleus in half? The contents of a cell, particularly its nucleus, are complicated. Each cell, therefore, has to take an organized approach to cell division—it cannot just break in two.

The nucleus contains the DNA, which is so important that the nucleus has its own multi-step division process, called **mitosis**. The cytoplasm divides by a different process, called **cytokinesis**.

mitosis the process by which the duplicated contents of the cell's nucleus divide into two equal parts

cytokinesis following mitosis, the separation of the two nuclei and cell contents into two daughter cells

Getting Ready for Mitosis

Recall that DNA is divided into segments called genes, each of which provides the instructions for making a different protein. Your body needs all of these proteins at one time or another—each plays a role in making up the structure of, or ensuring the proper functioning of, your body's many parts. Thus, every cell needs to have *all* the genes required to make these proteins. Although not every cell will end up making every protein, each starts out with the *potential* to do so.

Therefore, the parent cell cannot just divide its chromosomes equally between its two daughter cells when it divides. If this happened, each daughter cell would only have half the number of chromosomes its parent had and would be missing vital genes. In the case of human cells, each daughter cell produced through cell division needs a copy of all 46 chromosomes from its parent cell.

DNA Replication

A parent cell therefore makes a copy of every chromosome before it divides. It can then give one copy to each of the daughter cells. This copying process is called **DNA replication**. During replication, each chromosome is duplicated, although the two copies remain attached to each other, as shown in Figure 1.24.

Until the cell gets ready to divide, chromosomes are normally more like very long, loose threads. Each "thread" is actually a tightly twisted strand of DNA—the spiral "ladder" you saw in Figure 1.9. The chromosomes take on the thick, bulging look you see in Figure 1.24 just before the cell gets ready to divide. If you look closely at Figure 1.24A, you can see that each chromatid is composed of tightly bunched, threadlike material.

DNA replication is very precise. When copying errors occur, they are usually detected and fixed by special "proofreading" and repair proteins. At roughly the same time the DNA is replicated, an organelle called the *centrosome* also doubles, so that the cell has two copies. The centrosomes help to organize the tubules that make up the cytoskeleton. They play an important role in cell division, as you will see in the next section.

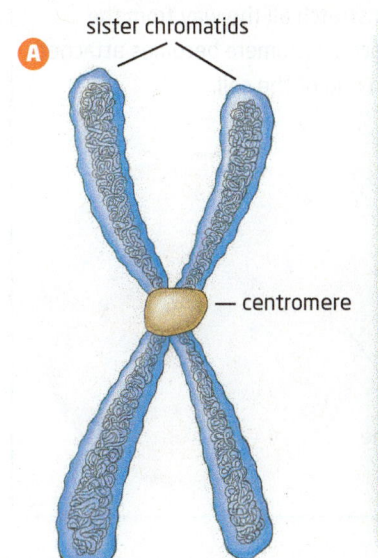

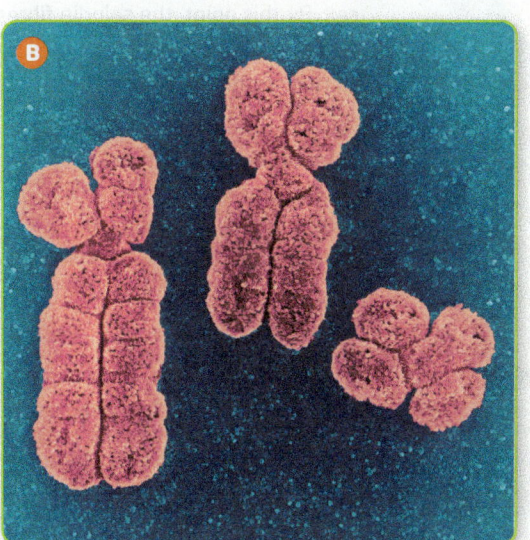

Study Toolkit

Word Families Creating a graphic organizer for words in this section that include the word part *phase* could help you understand and remember each word's definition.

DNA replication the process by which DNA is copied, creating sister chromatids joined at the centromere

---

Figure 1.24 During DNA replication, each chromosome is copied to produce two sister chromatids, attached at the centromere. The two sister chromatids shown in **A** are still one chromosome–but a replicated chromosome. In **B**, you can see a human chromosome, magnified 6100 times, that is ready to undergo mitosis.

Figure 1.25 The phases of mitosis in a typical animal cell are shown on pages 34 and 35. A micrograph of a cell in the process of mitosis is shown beside the diagram of the same phase.

The First Stage of Cell Division: Mitosis

Although some are longer and some are shorter, the average strand of human DNA is about 5 cm long. Yet 46 chromosomes can fit in the nucleus of a microscopic cell. This is only possible because each chromosome is incredibly thin. The diameter of each DNA molecule is just 2 nanometres (0.000 002 mm), so small that it can only be seen with an electron microscope. For most of a cell's life, its DNA is virtually invisible. This changes when the cell starts to divide through the process of mitosis, shown in **Figure 1.25**.

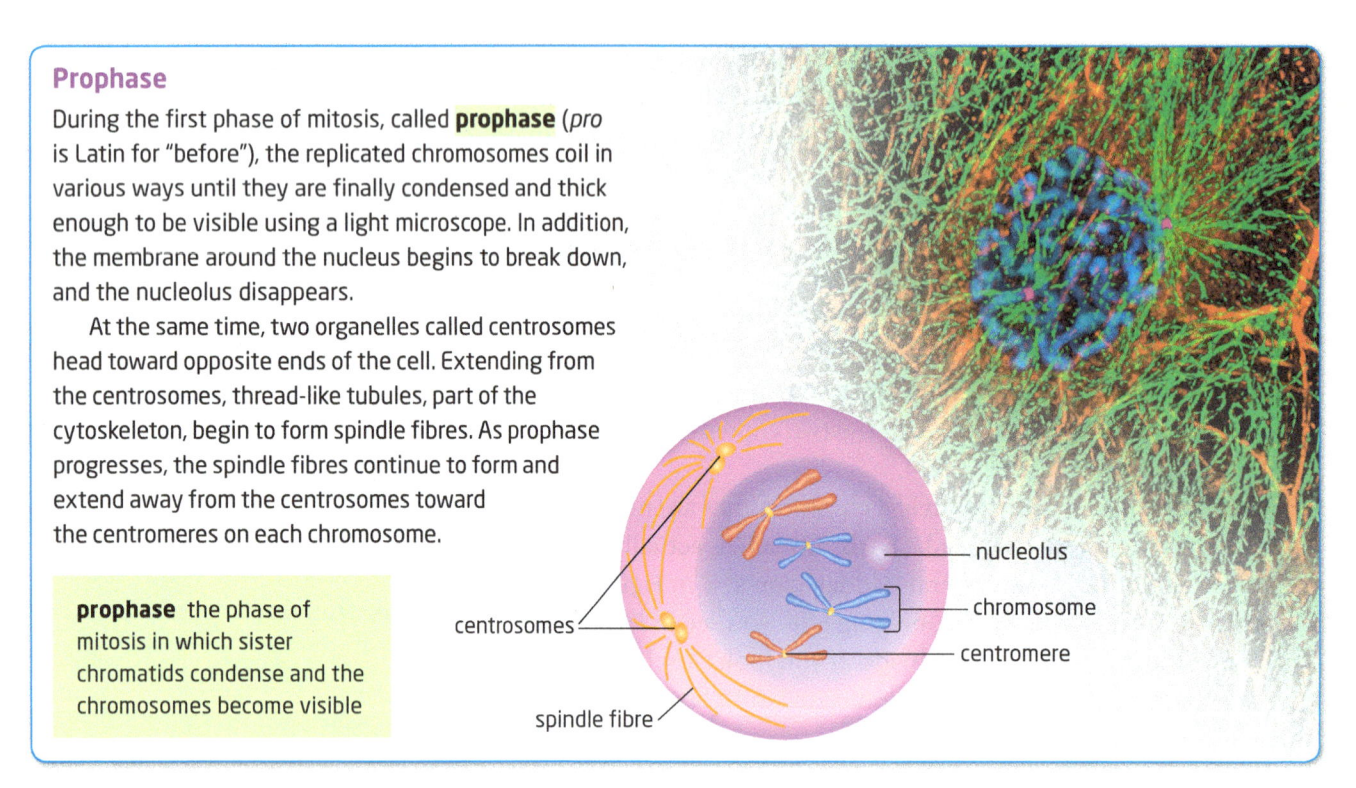

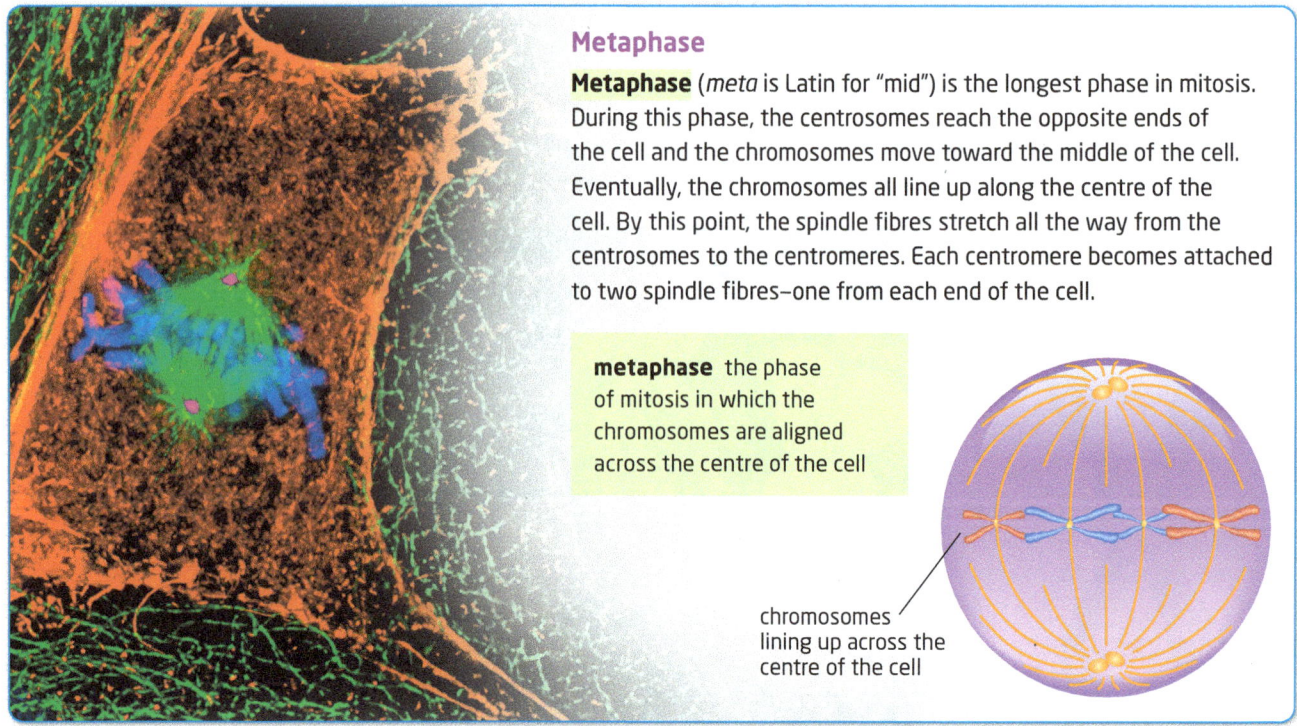

Prophase

During the first phase of mitosis, called **prophase** (*pro* is Latin for "before"), the replicated chromosomes coil in various ways until they are finally condensed and thick enough to be visible using a light microscope. In addition, the membrane around the nucleus begins to break down, and the nucleolus disappears.

At the same time, two organelles called centrosomes head toward opposite ends of the cell. Extending from the centrosomes, thread-like tubules, part of the cytoskeleton, begin to form spindle fibres. As prophase progresses, the spindle fibres continue to form and extend away from the centrosomes toward the centromeres on each chromosome.

prophase the phase of mitosis in which sister chromatids condense and the chromosomes become visible

Metaphase

Metaphase (*meta* is Latin for "mid") is the longest phase in mitosis. During this phase, the centrosomes reach the opposite ends of the cell and the chromosomes move toward the middle of the cell. Eventually, the chromosomes all line up along the centre of the cell. By this point, the spindle fibres stretch all the way from the centrosomes to the centromeres. Each centromere becomes attached to two spindle fibres–one from each end of the cell.

metaphase the phase of mitosis in which the chromosomes are aligned across the centre of the cell

34 NEL • Unit 1 Tissues, Organs, and Systems of Living Things

Anaphase

The next phase of mitosis, called anaphase (*ana* is Latin for "back"), is one of the shortest. In **anaphase**, the proteins holding the two chromatids together at the centromere break apart. The spindle fibres had been stretched like elastic bands between the chromosomes at the middle of the cell and the centrosomes at the opposite ends of the cell. Now the spindle fibres retract, each pulling a chromatid toward one end of the cell. Once the chromatids separate, each becomes a chromosome in its own right. At this point, the cell has twice as many chromosomes as usual.

anaphase the phase of mitosis in which the centromere splits apart and the chromatids are pulled to opposite sides of the cell by the spindle fibres

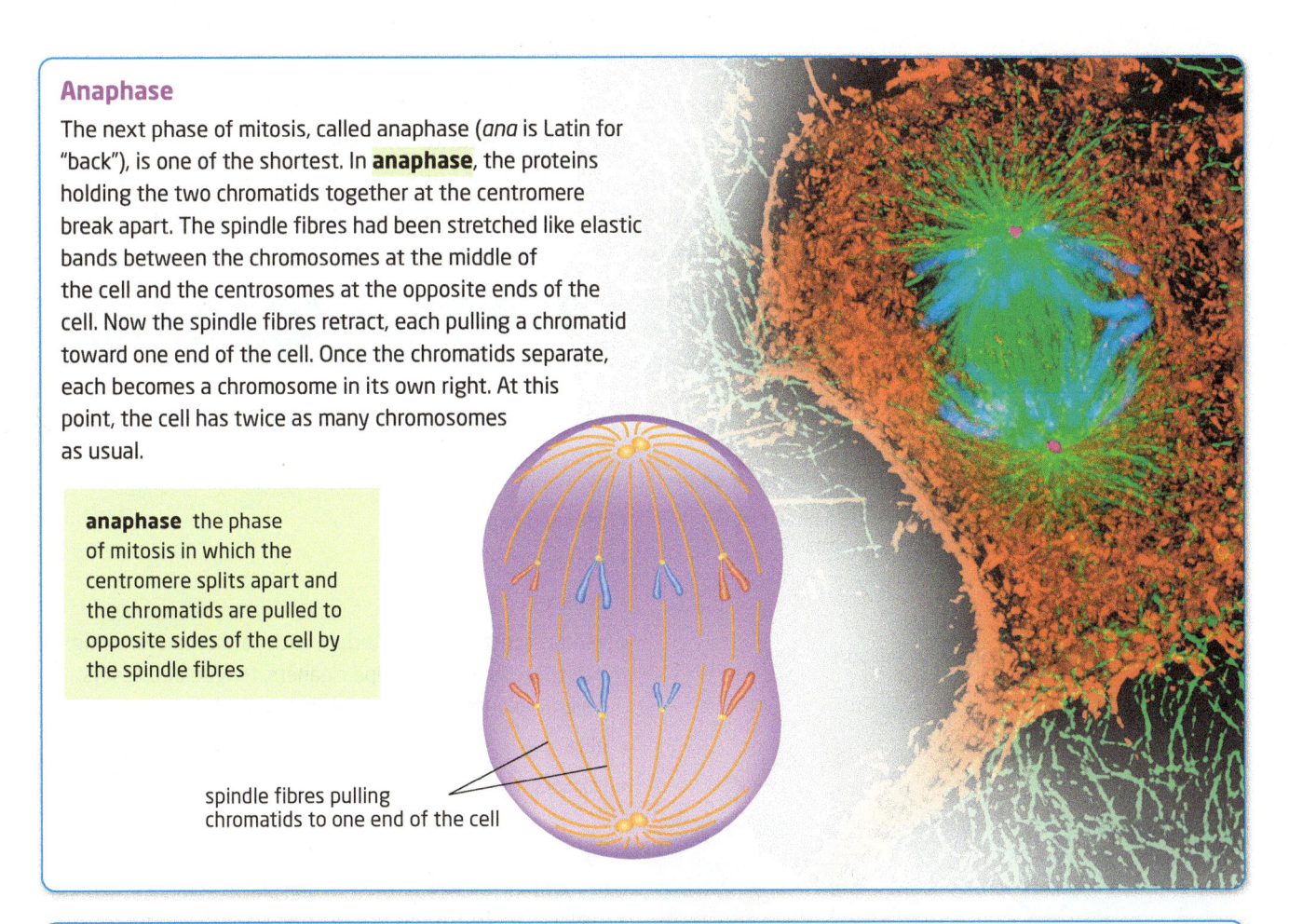

spindle fibres pulling chromatids to one end of the cell

Telophase

During **telophase** (*telos* means "end"), the spindle fibres start to disappear. Membranes form around two new daughter nuclei, one at each end of the cell. Within each nucleus, a nucleolus appears, and the chromosomes become less coiled and harder to see. Mitosis, the division of one nucleus into two identical nuclei, is now complete. The rest of the cell is ready to divide.

telophase the phase of mitosis in which two daughter nuclei are formed

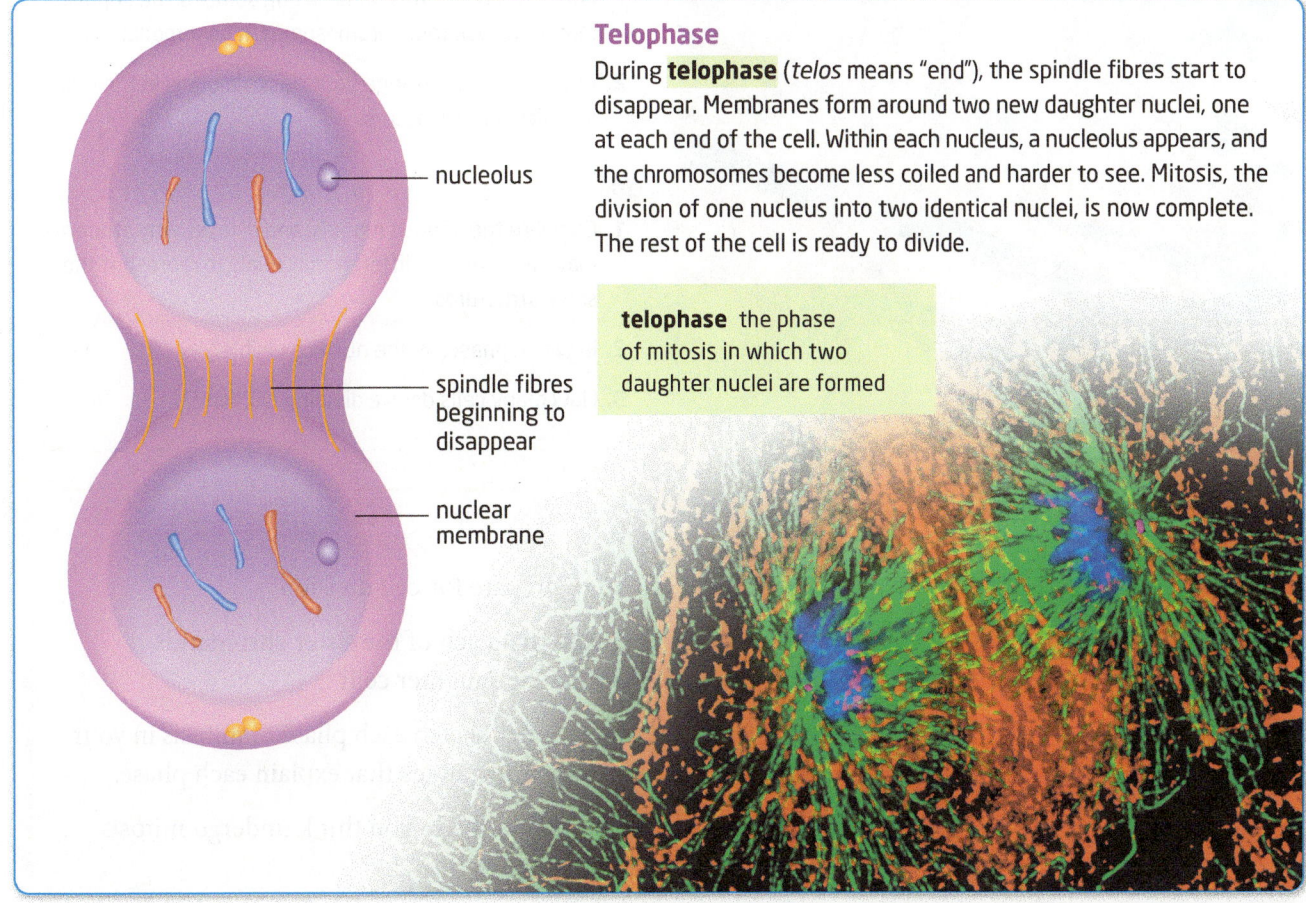

nucleolus

spindle fibres beginning to disappear

nuclear membrane

Go to **scienceontario** to find out more

Mitosis Is Continuous

Scientists—and students—use various strategies to make complicated ideas and processes easier to understand. One such strategy is to describe the process of mitosis as if it consists of a set of separate steps, as described on the previous pages. In reality, mitosis is continuous—there are no breaks between phases.

Activity 1-3

Modelling Mitosis

Understanding the process of mitosis can be easier if you make a model of it. What kinds of materials would best model the various parts of a cell during mitosis?

Safety Precaution

- Use caution when working with scissors.

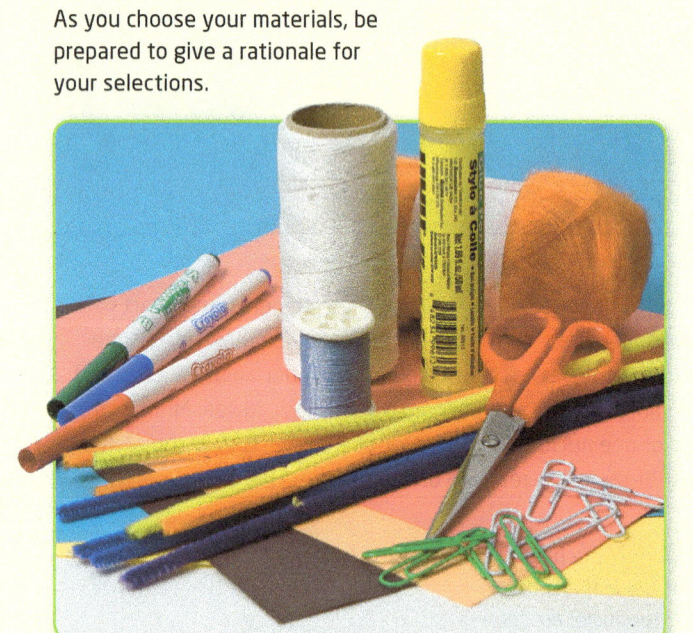

As you choose your materials, be prepared to give a rationale for your selections.

Materials
- coloured paper
- poster paper
- markers
- various construction materials, such as toothpicks, string, twist-ties, paper clips, pipe cleaners, tongue depressors, several colours of yarn, elastic bands, and thread
- glue
- scissors

Procedure

1. Your teacher will assign you one phase of mitosis. Make a model of this phase using some of the supplied materials. Use four chromosomes in your model.

2. When finished, arrange your class's models in the order in which mitosis occurs.

Questions

1. Compare the various models, and discuss why students may have chosen different materials to represent the same structures.

2. In which phases is the nucleus visible?

3. How many cells does a dividing cell form?

Suggested Investigation
Inquiry Investigation 1-B, Mitosis in Plant and Animal Cells, on page 48

Learning Check

5. What does a cell do to prepare for cell division?

6. What structures ensure that each of the sister chromatids becomes part of a different daughter cell?

7. Using **Figure 1.25** as a model, sketch each phase of mitosis in your notebook. Include point-form notes that explain each phase.

8. Which cells of the human body do you think undergo mitosis more frequently than other cells? Why?

The Second Stage in Cell Division: Cytokinesis

The division of the rest of the cell—the cytosol and organelles—usually begins before telophase is complete. **Figures 1.26** and **1.27** show the process for animals and plants.

Cytokinesis in Animal Cells

In animal cells, a ring of specialized proteins around the middle of the cell starts to contract. Like pulling the drawstrings on a bag, this contraction pinches the cell membrane until the parent cell is divided into two parts. Each daughter cell has a complete set of chromosomes in a nucleus and its own share of cytosol and organelles.

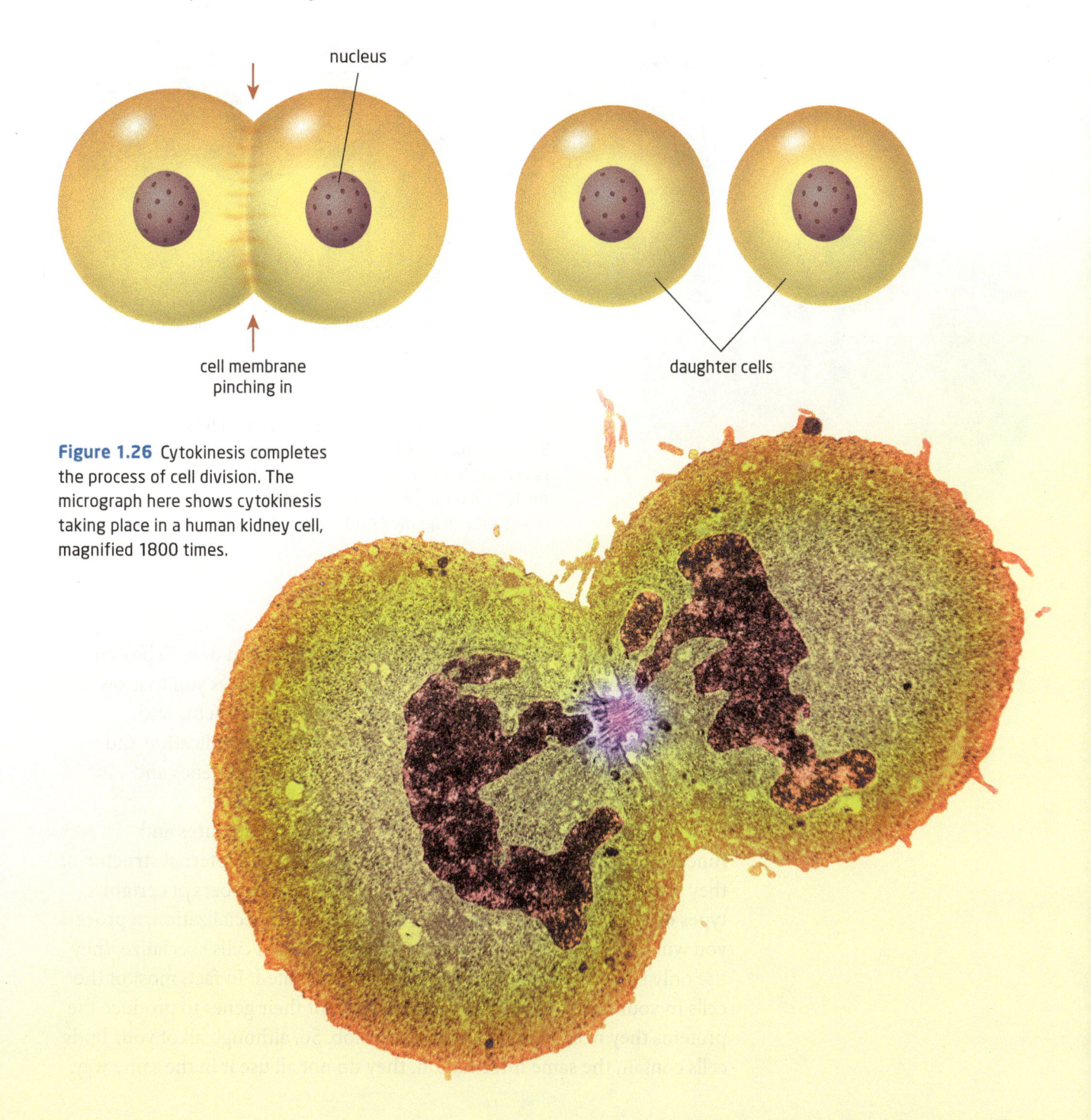

Figure 1.26 Cytokinesis completes the process of cell division. The micrograph here shows cytokinesis taking place in a human kidney cell, magnified 1800 times.

Chapter 1 Cells and More Cells • NEL

Cytokinesis in Plant Cells

The process of mitosis in plant cells is the same as in animal cells. However, in plant cells, the rigid cell wall makes it necessary for cytokinesis to be slightly different. In plant cells, the Golgi body starts to produce small vesicles. Each of these sacs carries the materials needed to form a new cell wall. The vesicles line up between the two new nuclei, forming a **cell plate**. The cell plate grows outward and joins the old cell wall. New cell walls are secreted on each side of the cell plate, dividing the cytoplasm into two. Then new cell membranes form inside the cell walls, and the division is complete.

> **cell plate** a structure that that helps to form the cell wall in the process of plant cell cytokinesis

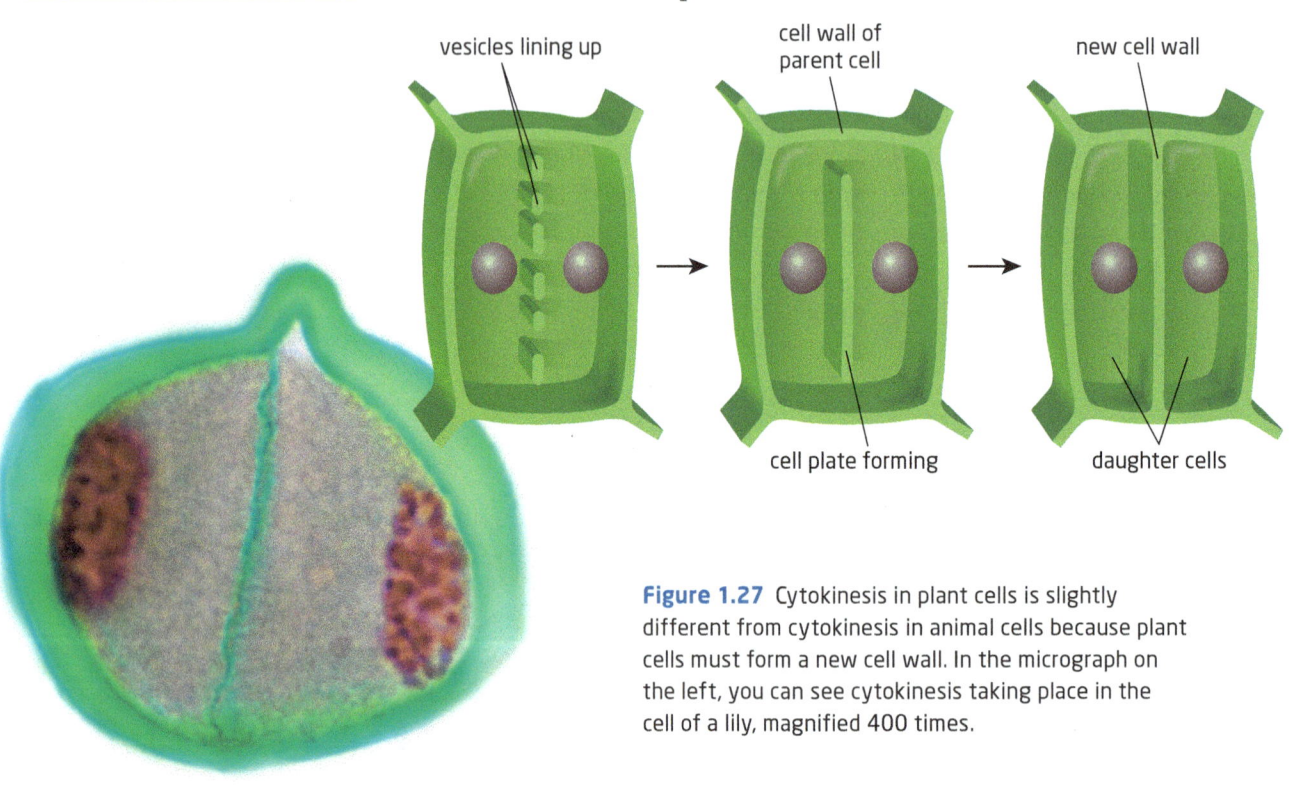

Figure 1.27 Cytokinesis in plant cells is slightly different from cytokinesis in animal cells because plant cells must form a new cell wall. In the micrograph on the left, you can see cytokinesis taking place in the cell of a lily, magnified 400 times.

The Same, but Different

You have seen that cell division produces two cells from one. Repeated over and over again, millions of times, this process allows you to grow from a single cell (after fertilization) into a multicellular fetus and finally into a full-sized human. The processes of DNA replication and mitosis ensure that each of your body cells has identical genes and can theoretically produce the same proteins.

Yet, you know that different cells have different structures and functions. Although all cells have the same basic set of internal structures, they make different proteins and contain different numbers of certain types of organelles. This happens as a result of cell specialization, a process you will learn more about in the next chapter. When cells specialize, they use only some of their genes—others are deactivated. In fact, most of the cells in your body use only about 10 percent of their genes to produce the proteins they need to do their particular job. So, although all of your body cells contain the same information, they do not all use it in the same way.

Section 1.3 Review

Section Summary

- When single-celled organisms and body cells of animals and plants divide, they form two identical daughter cells. For single-celled organisms, cell division results in population growth. For multicellular organisms, cell division allows individuals to grow or to replace lost or damaged cells.

- Cell division must be preceded by DNA replication so that each daughter cell gets the same DNA and genes as its parent cell.

- Cell division is a continuous process that involves two stages: mitosis, to divide the nucleus, and cytokinesis, to divide the cytoplasm.

Review Questions

K/U 1. Give as many reasons why cells divide as you can.

K/U 2. Compare prophase and telophase in mitosis.

C 3. Create a graphic organizer to summarize the essential activities during each phase of mitosis. Go to Study Toolkit 4 to see possible organizers you might choose.

C 4. How do the prefixes *pro-*, *meta-*, *ana-*, and *telo-* relate to what happens in each phase of mitosis? Look back to **Figure 1.25** for clues.

T/I 5. If there are 10 chromosomes in a particular cell at the start of prophase, how many will be present in the same cell at the end of anaphase, before cytokinesis has begun? How many will there be after cytokinesis has occurred?

C 6. Use diagrams to show the difference between cytokinesis in plants and animals.

K/U 7. You have been given the micrograph on the right. Describe the cell structures you see and what this tells you about the cell.

A 8. Biologists have noticed that within many groups of similar organisms, types that live farther north tend to be larger. For example, grey squirrels in Ontario and the northern United States are much larger than grey squirrels in the southern United States. Why do you think this might be?

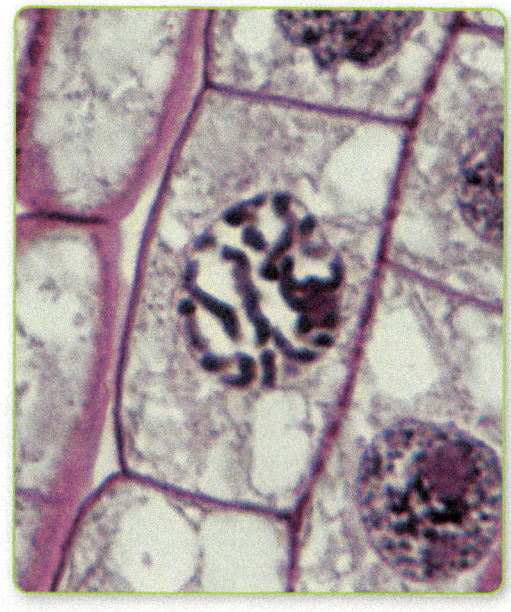

Onion root tip, 500×

Chapter 1 Cells and More Cells • NEL   39

Key Terms
interphase
cell cycle
cell cycle checkpoint
tumour
cancer

1.4 The Cell Cycle

As shown in **Table 1.3**, the life span of different types of cells varies widely. Some cells live a rough life, exposed to constant abrasion (rubbing) and chemicals that are sometimes toxic. This describes the experience of the cells that line your stomach, and those that make up your skin. They have short lifetimes compared with muscle cells, which last an average of 15 years. Nerve cells may last even longer. This means that cell division happens frequently in some parts of your body, but is a rare event in other parts.

Stages of the Cell Cycle

For your body to function properly, the cell division process must be carefully controlled. Some types of cells must be "encouraged" to divide, and others must be "encouraged" to remain as they are. This is the job of molecules, mostly proteins, that carry signals among cells, sharing information about various cells' abundance and health. These molecules control the cell cycle. As you can see in **Figure 1.28**, the **cell cycle**—the life cycle of a cell— consists of two main phases: cell division and **interphase**.

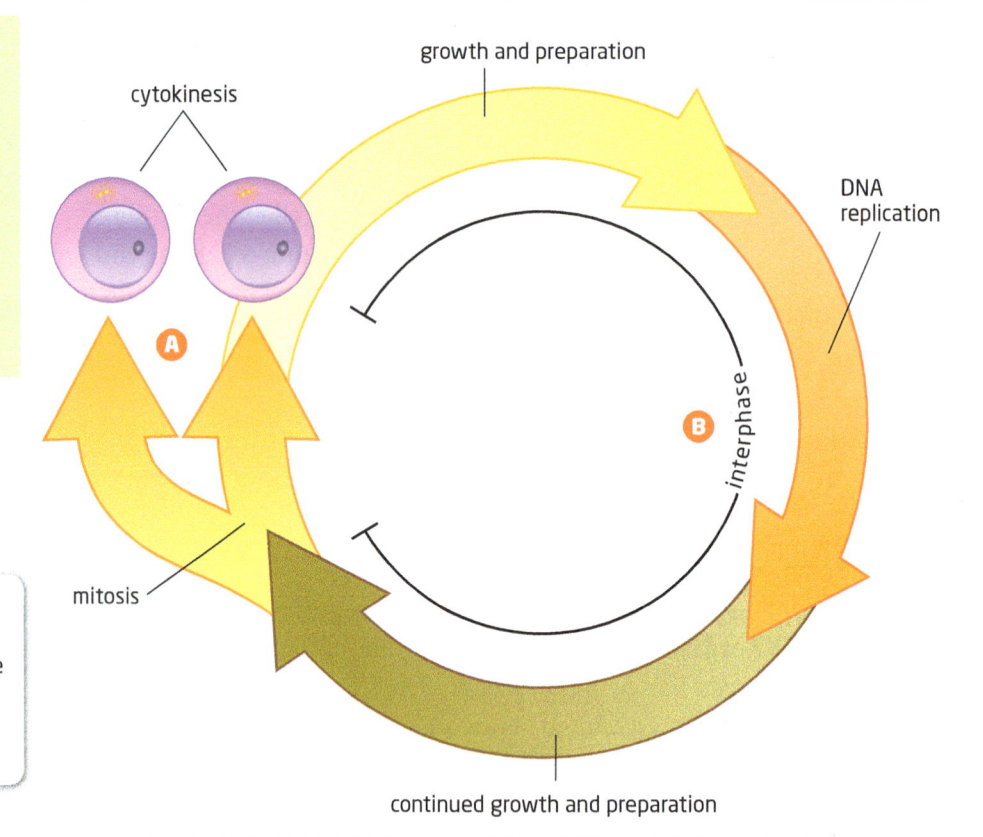

Table 1.3 Average Life Span of Various Human Body Cells

Type of Body Cell	Average Life Span
Brain	30-50 years
Red blood	120 days
Stomach lining	2 days
Liver	200 days
Intestine lining	3 days
Skin	20 days

interphase periods of growth in the life of a cell; consists of two growth stages and a stage of DNA replication

cell cycle a continuous sequence of cell growth and division, including the stages of interphase, mitosis, and cytokinesis

A Cell division First, the cell's nucleus divides into two parts during mitosis. Then, the two nuclei and cell contents divide into two daughter cells during cytokinesis.

Figure 1.28 The cell cycle for all cells consists of two main stages, but different types of cells spend different amounts of time in each stage.

B Interphase Cells do whatever activities they are designed to do, such as producing specific proteins. For example, a muscle cell might produce the proteins that allow muscles to contract. It also does the things that *all* cells do, such as taking in oxygen and glucose, releasing energy from glucose (cellular respiration), and removing wastes. In addition, DNA replicates in preparation for cell division. Before and after the DNA replicates are two periods during which the cell produces more organelles and grows larger.

40 NEL • Unit 1 Tissues, Organs, and Systems of Living Things

Checkpoints: Can This Cell Pass?

Controlling the timing and rate of cell division in different parts of a plant or animal is vital to normal growth and development. Too few or too many cells in any one body part can lead to serious problems. Although many details are not understood, scientists have a general picture of how the cell cycle is controlled in many cells.

Researchers have discovered that there are three main points at which the cell "checks" its growth. **Figure 1.29** shows how these **cell cycle checkpoints** work. At each checkpoint, specialized proteins act like stop signs. Unless they receive specific go-ahead signals, they will not let the cell cycle proceed. In general, cell division will not occur if

- there are not enough nutrients to support cell growth
- the DNA has not replicated
- the DNA is damaged

cell cycle checkpoints a point in the life of a cell when proteins determine whether cell division should or should not occur

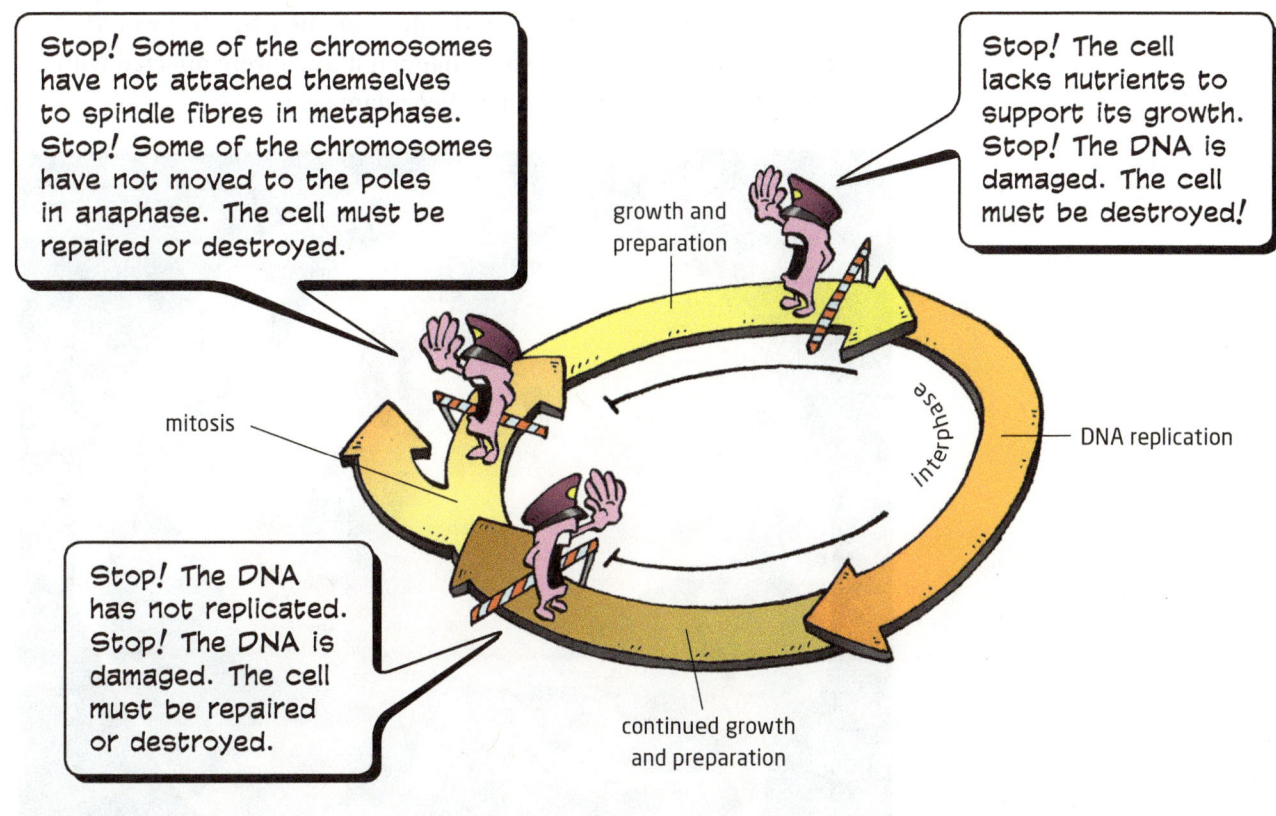

Stop! Some of the chromosomes have not attached themselves to spindle fibres in metaphase. Stop! Some of the chromosomes have not moved to the poles in anaphase. The cell must be repaired or destroyed.

Stop! The cell lacks nutrients to support its growth. Stop! The DNA is damaged. The cell must be destroyed!

Stop! The DNA has not replicated. Stop! The DNA is damaged. The cell must be repaired or destroyed.

Figure 1.29 Checkpoints in the cell cycle ensure that cell division occurs only when required.

For many cells, the first checkpoint after mitosis seems to be the most important. Many cells leave the cycle at this point, often just because more cells of that type are not required. The body does not need that cell to divide, so it does not receive a go-ahead signal. Cells that leave the cycle enter a non-dividing stage. Most cells in the human body—all muscle and nerve cells, for example—are in this stage.

Go to **scienceontario** to find out more

Cell Death

Some cells do not leave the cell cycle to become specialized—they leave the cell cycle because it is time for them to die. In some cases, this is because they have been damaged beyond repair, perhaps by physical forces or by exposure to toxic chemicals. The contents of the cells leak out, often irritating surrounding cells, causing swelling and redness in that body part.

Cell Suicide

Other cells carry out a kind of suicide. In this case, a cell breaks down in an organized way. Its contents are packaged and distributed so that other cells can use them. Scientists have learned that this type of death is pre-programmed into cells, determined by what are often called "suicide genes." These genes code for proteins whose job is to kill cells in specific situations. For example, as you can see in **Figure 1.30**, suicide genes are responsible for normal finger and toe development in human embryos.

Cells may also ensure their own death when their survival would be a threat to the organism. This would happen if a cell were infected with a virus, for example, or if its DNA had been damaged.

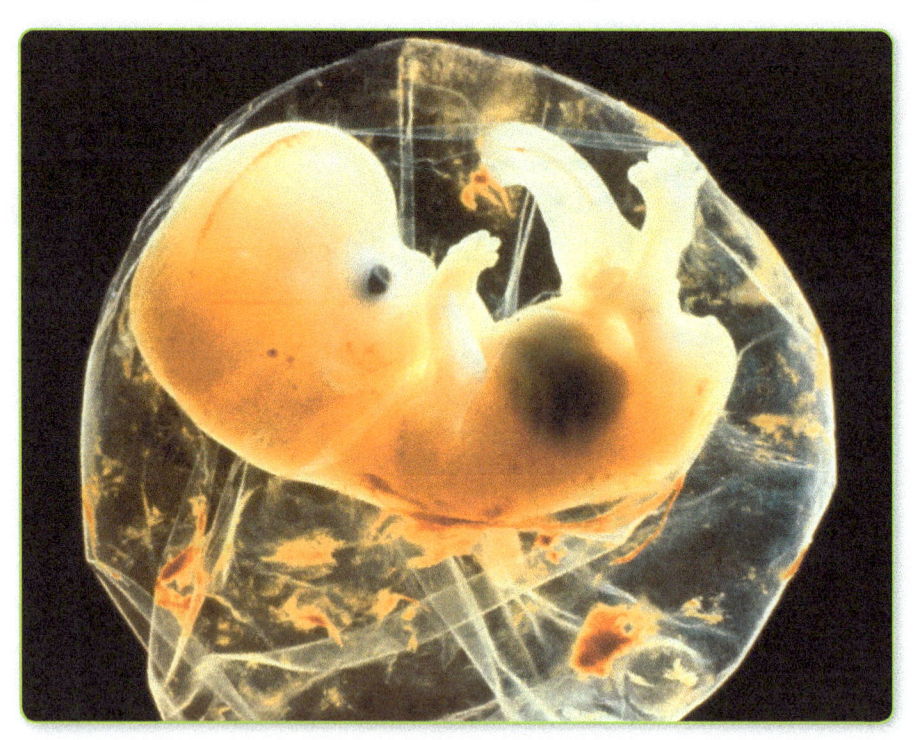

Figure 1.30 In various birds and mammals, the parts of the embryo that develop into hands and feet are solid at first. Separated fingers or toes are produced through the programmed death of the cells between the digits.

Cancer and the Cell Cycle

Some cells start out normally, but are then transformed so that they ignore the stop signs in the cell cycle. Instead of leaving the cell cycle to die, they divide repeatedly and excessively, forming a clump of cells called a **tumour**, which you can see in **Figure 1.31**.

tumour an abnormal clump or group of cells

Effects of Cancer on Other Tissues

These abnormal cells, with further mutations, can become **cancer**. Some cancers can spread to other body parts and continue dividing uncontrollably there. Tumours reduce the effectiveness of other body tissues. For example, the abnormal cancerous cells that are part of a lung tumour take up space in the lung that should be filled with normal cells performing normal lung functions. In addition, the abnormal cells use up nutrients that are needed by the normal cells.

> **cancer** cells with abnormal genetic material that are dividing uncontrollably and can spread to other body parts

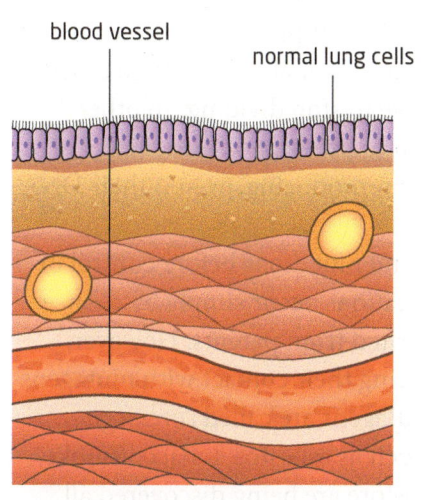

In healthy tissue, cell division is carefully controlled by chemical messages that pass from cell to cell.

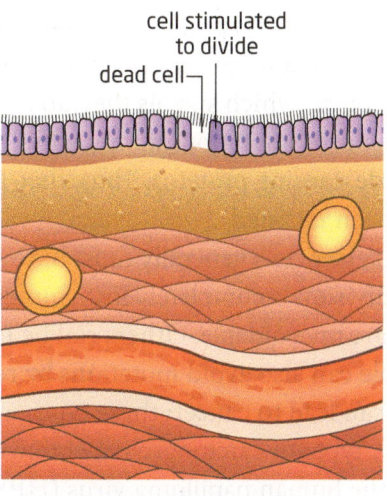

As cells mature and die, a normal part of the cell cycle, other cells are stimulated to divide and replace them.

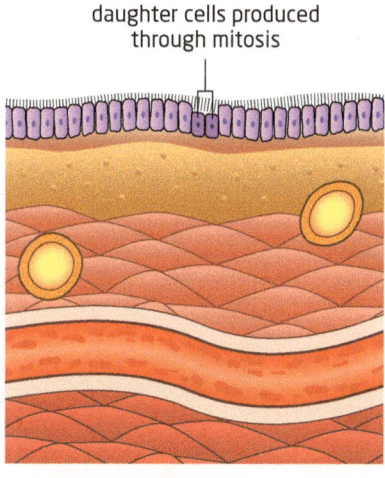

The rate of cell division is normally equal to the rate of cell death.

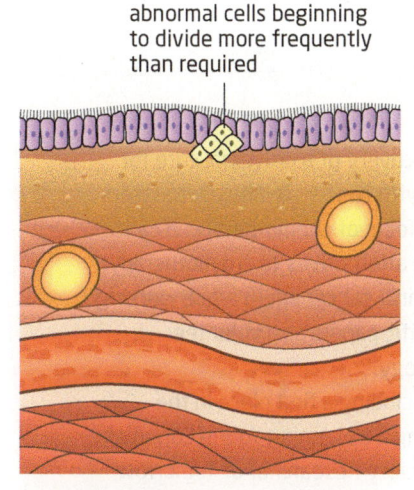

Sometimes cells lose the normal constraints on their rate of division. They begin to divide much more often and no longer function normally. All the cells that result from their division also divide uncontrollably, so the abnormal cells multiply rapidly.

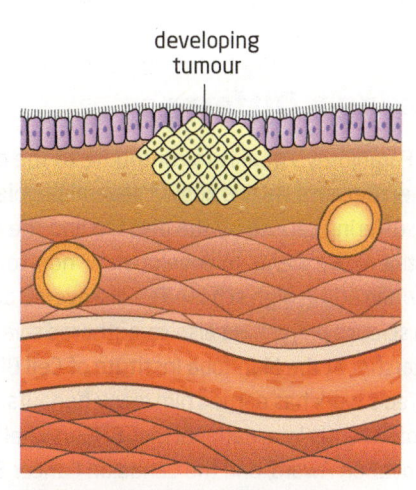

The mass of rapidly dividing cells grows to form a tumour. Further changes to the cells can produce cancer. The cancer cells invade and destroy neighbouring cells.

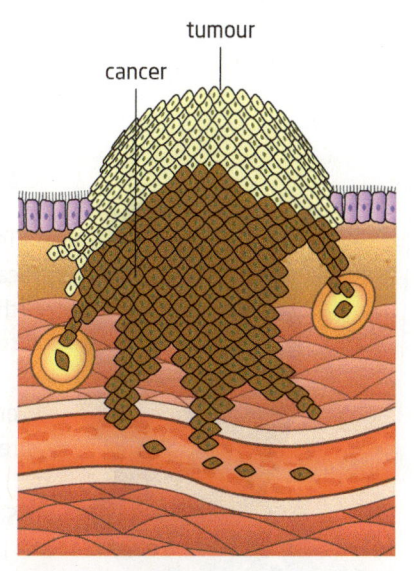

Eventually, some cancer cells may break away, move into the circulatory system, and spread to a new location in the body, where they again begin to divide uncontrollably.

Figure 1.31 Abnormal cell division is responsible for the development of tumours and cancer.

Go to **scienceontario** to find out more

> **Suggested Investigation.**
> Data Analysis Investigation 1-C, Does the Patient Have Cancer? on page 50

Losing Control

Most normal cells are attached to a surface while they divide. If a normal cell senses that it is not attached, it stops dividing. Many cancer cells, however, have a mutation that allows them to keep dividing even when they are not attached to a surface. This mutation encourages the abnormal cells in a tumour to spread. Still other cancer cells have mutations affecting the proteins that check and repair any errors made during DNA replication. These mutations, in turn, lead to more mutations.

Most normal cells can undergo 20 to 30 rounds of cell division. Any more divisions might result in mutated cells that might harm the organism. At this point, a normal cell carries out programmed suicide. However, many cancer cells have been found to make an enzyme called telomerase, which signals they do not have to stop dividing. In other cancer cells, mutations do not allow them to produce or recognize suicide-causing proteins. Thus, they keep reproducing, even if their DNA has been mutated.

Cancer cells generally must have several mutations before control of cell division is completely lost. Some mutations occur simply by chance and are unavoidable. Others can be inherited from parents. However, people can also avoid mutations by reducing their contact with mutagens that can lead to cancer; these types of mutagens are called *carcinogens*. Many types of carcinogens are known, such as asbestos, tobacco smoke, and the human papilloma virus (HPV). More are being discovered all the time. Cancer prevention—reducing gene mutations—is perhaps the best way to avoid cancer. However, cancer is a complex disease. Its causes are varied and our knowledge of how cells are changed by mutations is still far from complete. Cells still hold lots of secrets—enough to keep researchers busy for many years.

Making a Difference

Ted Paranjothy's goal is to contribute to the discovery of a universal cure for cancer. Because he has known several people with cancer, Ted has witnessed the suffering caused by the disease and the effects of chemotherapy, a cancer treatment. He wants to develop new, non-toxic alternatives to chemotherapy.

While still in high school, Ted discovered an anti-cancer agent while working on a science project. He also co-authored scientific papers as a volunteer researcher at the Manitoba Institute of Cell Biology.

Ted's work has earned him many honours, including a first place in the Sanofi-aventis International BioGENEius Challenge, a Manning Young Canadian Innovation Award, and the Canadian Cancer Society Researcher of Tomorrow Award. Ted has also volunteered with patients at a hospital and won an award for his community service. In 2007, Ted was named one of Canada's Top 20 Under 20. He attends the University of Manitoba and plans to become a physician-scientist, involved in both patient care and cancer research.

What could you do to help people with cancer in your community?

Section 1.4 Review

Section Summary

- Some cells live a long time, while others have a short life span, depending on where in the body they are found and the conditions they endure.
- The life of a cell, called the cell cycle, can be divided into two main stages: cell division and interphase. Interphase consists of two growth stages and a stage of DNA replication.
- Cell division is carefully controlled so that cells are produced only when needed. The control is exerted by proteins at checkpoints in the cell cycle. In cells that accumulate enough mutations, this control can be lost, which may lead to the development of cancer.

Review Questions

K/U 1. The micrograph on the right shows a cell undergoing mitosis.
   a. In what stage of mitosis is this cell?
   b. When cell division is complete, what cell cycle checkpoints will occur before the cell moves into interphase?

C 2. Using **Figures 1.28** and **1.29**, write a paragraph describing the life of a cell.

K/U 3. Give two examples of places in your body where you would find cells that live for a short time. Explain why.

K/U 4. Put the four photographs on the right in order, from the body part where cell division is happening most rapidly to the body part where cell division is happening least rapidly.

K/U 5. Describe three conditions during the cell cycle that determine whether the cycle will be allowed to continue.

A 6. Some treatments for cancer involve the use of drugs that specifically attack cells that are actively dividing. Why would this be effective for fighting cancerous cells?

C 7. Prepare a "Most Wanted" poster in which cancer cells are cast in the role of villains. Your poster needs to describe how to recognize these villains. What "cell crimes" do they commit?

C 8. Edward Abbey, an American writer and environmentalist, has stated, "Growth for the sake of growth is the ideology of the cancer cell." This quotation is often used by people who, like Abbey, worry about the negative effects that uncontrolled population and economic growth can have on the environment. Do you think this comparison to cancer makes sense? Explain your answer.

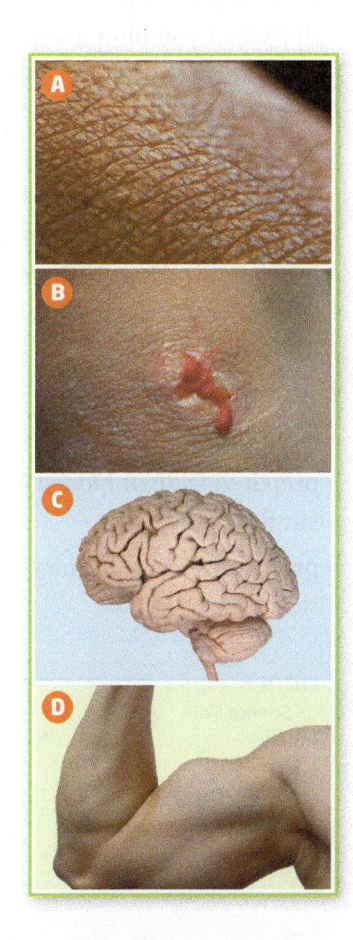

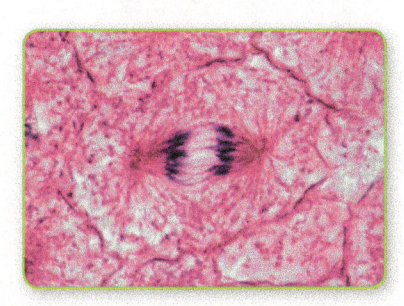

Cell undergoing mitosis, 450×

Inquiry Investigation 1-A

Skill Check

Initiating and Planning
✓ Performing and Recording
✓ Analyzing and Interpreting
✓ Communicating

Safety Precautions

- Be sure your hands are dry when you plug in or disconnect the cord of the microscope.
- The glass or plastic slides and cover slips used to mount specimens are fragile and can break easily. Handle them carefully to avoid getting a cut.

Materials

- compound microscope
- prepared slide of *Elodea* (or similar) leaf cells
- prepared slide of human skin cells

Science Skills
Go to **Science Skills Toolkit 8** for information about using a microscope and **Science Skills Toolkit 6** for information about making a labelled biological drawing.

Examining Cell Structures

The light microscopes used today in high school and university laboratories are based on the same principles as those used by Hooke and van Leeuwenhoek. For many years, scientists had to rely on light microscopes to make discoveries about the structure and functions of cells.

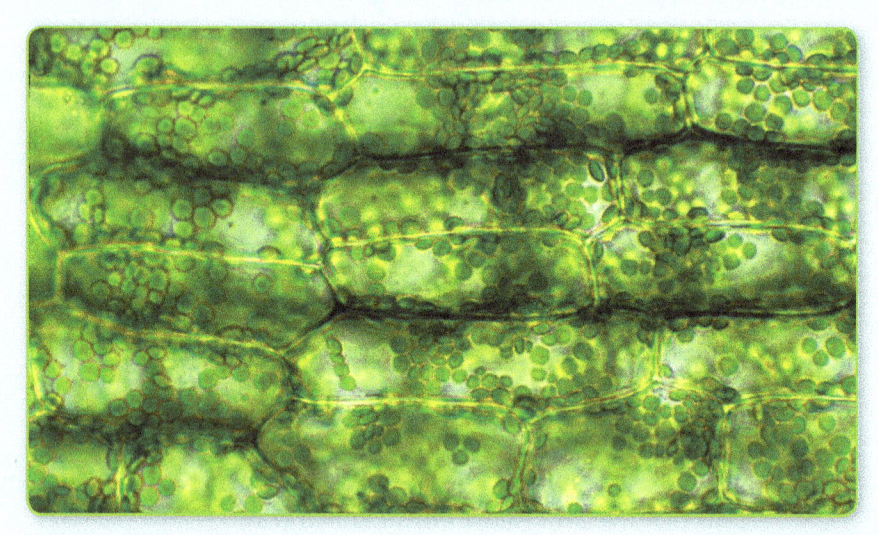

Elodea leaf cells, 160×

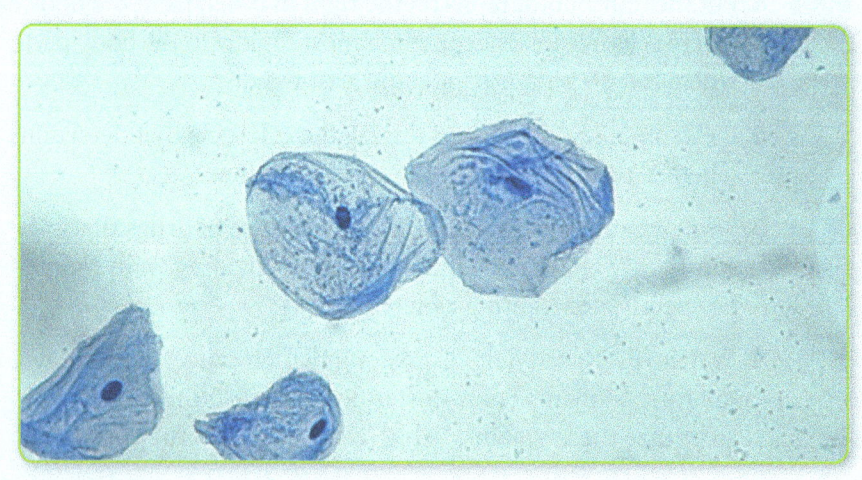

Human skin cells, 100×

Question

How do the cell structures of plants and animals differ?

Predictions

1. Predict what cell structures you will see in both the plant and animal cells.

2. Predict what cell structures you will see in only the plant cells or the animal cells.

Procedure

1. Set up a microscope.

2. Place the slide of the *Elodea* leaf cells on the microscope's viewing platform. Adjust the microscope on low power, and view the specimen. Do you see one cell, a few cells, or many cells?

3. Rotate the nosepiece until the medium power objective clicks into place. Again, adjust the microscope and view the specimen.

4. Repeat step 3 using the highest-power objective. Use extra caution when adjusting the focus. Even a slight turn of the fine-adjustment knob may crack the slide. Observe the specimen carefully. Is the entire specimen in focus at once, or do parts of it come in and out of focus as you adjust the knob? Make a proper biological drawing of one cell, remembering to include the magnification.

5. When you are done, turn the objective lenses so that the lowest power is again above the specimen and remove the slide from the stage.

6. Repeat steps 2 to 5 for the slide of human skin cells.

Analyze and Interpret

1. Consider the differences in what you see using the low, medium, and high-power objective lenses. Think about the level of detail you can see, the amount of the specimen that is visible (the whole specimen or a portion), and how much of the specimen you can focus on at once (without using the fine-adjustment knob). Which lens do you think gives you the best view of your specimens? Why?

2. Consult your drawings and recall the specimens under medium or high power, whichever you think gave you the clearest or most interesting view. Create a two-column table for each specimen. In the first column, write questions about what you see in the drawing. Your questions might start with phrases like "What is … ?" or "What does the _____ do?" These questions may be similar to questions asked by early microscopists.

3. In the second column of your table, answer your own questions as best you can. You are not expected to know all the answers.

Conclude and Communicate

4. Look back at the predictions you made at the beginning of this investigation. Did your observations support them? That is, what structures were you able to see inside the cells? How did the animal and plant cells differ?

5. Write a short statement that explains what you think you would need to improve your view of the contents of a cell.

Extend Your Inquiry and Research Skills

6. **Inquiry** How would the cell structures of other types of plants compare with the leaf cells you examined in this investigation? Use Science Skills Toolkit 8 to plan an investigation in which you make and examine your own slides of plant cells. If your teacher asks you to conduct your planned investigation, have it approved by your teacher before proceeding.

7. **Research** Research what other cell structures you can see in a human skin cell using an electron microscope. Do the following:
   a. List organelles that can be seen with the electron microscope that you could not see with the compound light microscope.
   b. Draw and label a magnified view of one organelle visible with the electron microscope.

Inquiry Investigation 1-B

Mitosis in Plant and Animal Cells

Plant and animal body cells reproduce by the process of mitosis. You will observe slides of the tip of an onion root and a whitefish embryo to see how mitosis in cells allows them to divide, producing new cells.

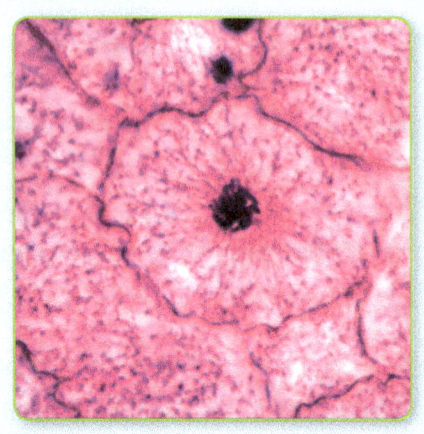

Skill Check

Initiating and Planning
✓ Performing and Recording
✓ Analyzing and Interpreting
Communicating

Safety Precautions

- Be sure your hands are dry when you plug in or disconnect the cord of the microscope.
- The glass or plastic slides and cover slips used to mount specimens are fragile and can break easily. Handle them carefully to avoid getting a cut.

Materials

- compound microscope
- prepared slide of an onion root tip
- prepared slide of a whitefish embryo

Science Skills
Go to **Science Skills Toolkit 8** for information about using a microscope and **Science Skills Toolkit 6** for information about making a labelled biological drawing.

Prophase: whitefish embryo, 450×

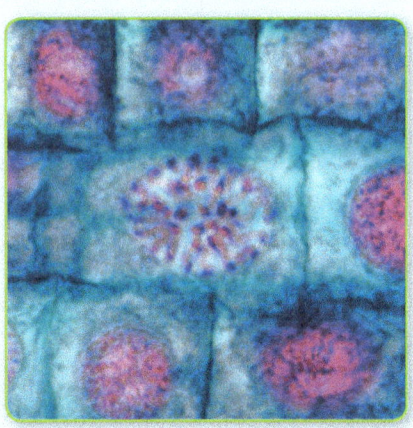

Prophase: onion root tip, 630×

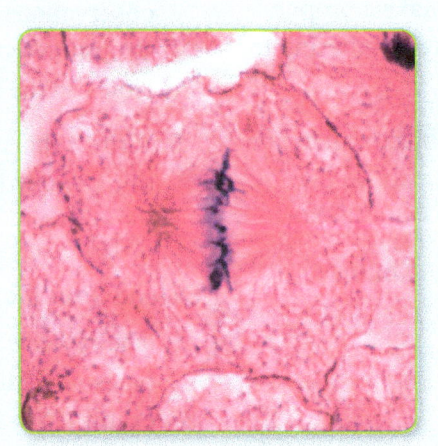

Metaphase: whitefish embryo, 450×

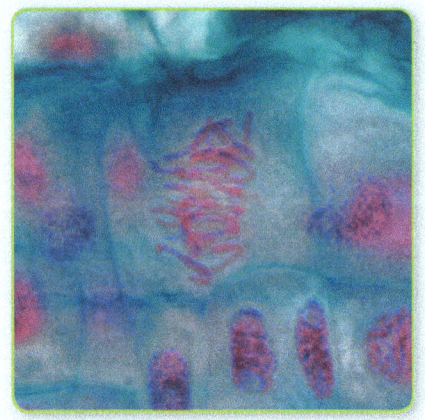

Metaphase: onion root tip, 630×

Question

How does mitosis produce new cells, and how is mitosis the same and different in plant and animal cells?

Procedure

1. Set up a microscope.
2. Set your microscope on low power, and examine the onion root tip. Focus the microscope, and move the slide until you can see the area just behind the root tip. Carefully turn the nosepiece to medium power, refocus, and then turn to high power and refocus. Be careful when adjusting the fine-adjustment knob at high power. Even slight turns can crack the slide.

48 NEL • Unit 1 Tissues, Organs, and Systems of Living Things

3. Use the photographs on page 48 to help you find a cell in prophase. While looking through the eyepiece of the microscope, you may have to gently move the slide to find a cell in prophase. Draw this cell, and label the parts of the cell you observe.

4. Repeat step 3 for metaphase, anaphase, and telophase.

5. Turn the microscope back to low power. Remove the slide of the onion root tip.

6. Place the whitefish embryo slide on the microscope stage under low power. Focus using low power, and find a region of dividing cells. Switch to medium power. If you need more detail, carefully switch to high power. Find a cell at prophase, and ensure that it is in the middle of your field of view. As with the onion root tip cell at this stage, draw what you see.

7. Repeat steps 3 and 4 using the whitefish embryo slide.

8. Return the nosepiece to low power. Remove the whitefish embryo slide from the microscope stage.

Analyze and Interpret

1. How do the cells in the region close to the end of the onion root tip compare to those farther back in the root tip? Compare the size of the cells, the number of cells undergoing mitosis, and the number cells in different phases of mitosis.

2. Look at your drawings of telophase from the root tip and whitefish embryo. How does the onion root tip cell look different from the whitefish embryo cells at this phase?

Conclude and Communicate

3. Infer why whitefish embryo cells and root-tip cells are used to study mitosis instead of cells in a human bone or plant leaf.

Extend Your Inquiry and Research Skills

4. **Inquiry** How do you think the tip of a live onion can be prepared so that you can observe it under a light microscope?

5. **Research** Research the stains that are used to view different organelles and any safety precautions or hazards associated with those stains.

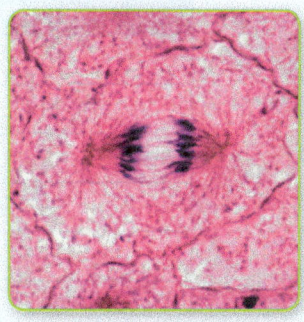

Anaphase: whitefish embryo

Anaphase: onion root tip

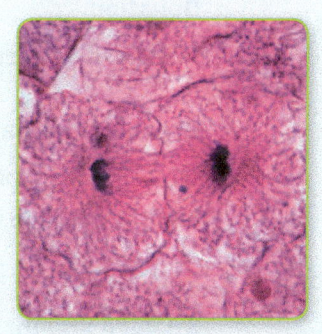

Telophase: whitefish embryo

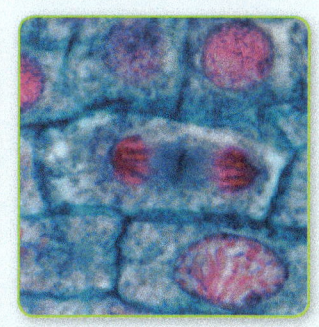

Telophase: onion root tip

Data Analysis Investigation 1-C

Skill Check

Initiating and Planning

Performing and Recording

✓ Analyzing and Interpreting

✓ Communicating

Does the Patient Have Cancer?

A physician supplied your laboratory with two samples of the same type of cells: one is normal, and the other is from a patient who may have a tumour. You were asked to culture the cells, record the cells' rates of division, and report back on any abnormalities. Your results are shown in the table below.

Number of Cells in Samples over Time

Time (days)	Normal Cells	Patient Sample
15	2	2
30	4	6
45	8	10
60	16	30
75	32	92
90	64	180

Question

What will you report back to the physician who requested the test?

Organize the Data

Draw a line graph showing the rate of cell division of normal cells and the patient's cells. Put time on the *x*-axis and population size on the *y*-axis.

Analyze and Interpret

1. Compare the rates of cell division in the patient sample and the normal sample. How would you interpret the graph?

Conclude and Communicate

2. Write a one- or two-sentence summary of your findings and your interpretation for the physician.

Extend Your Inquiry and Research Skills

3. **Inquiry** All cells, whether they are normal or cancerous, need energy. Cell division actually requires more energy than many other cell activities. Imagine that each cell in your sample needs two units of energy to divide.

    a. Compare the amount of energy used by the cells in each sample at 90 days.

    b. How might this energy requirement affect an individual who has a cancerous tumour?

Math Skills
Go to **Math Skills Toolkit 3** for information about making graphs.

Chapter 1 Summary

1.1 Studying the Structure of Cells
Key Concepts
- Developments in microscopy (microscope technology) have made it possible to look at the internal structures of cells.
- Cells contain a variety of organelles, each of which has its own structure and function. Some organelles are found in all cells, while others are found only in plant cells *or* animal cells.
- Advances in knowledge about cells have helped researchers find new ways to diagnose and treat diseases.

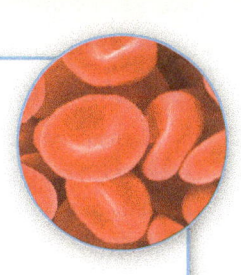

1.2 Genes: Answers and Questions
Key Concepts
- The nucleus of a cell contains chromosomes, which are composed of DNA and divided into segments called genes. Genes control a cell's structure and function by controlling the production of proteins.
- There are many ethical issues related to technological developments in DNA screening, transgenic research, and clinical drug trials. Researchers often make progress faster than society's ability to make decisions about how to use such research.
- Mutations in genes change the structure and function of the proteins in the cells. Many, but not all, genetic mutations are harmful.

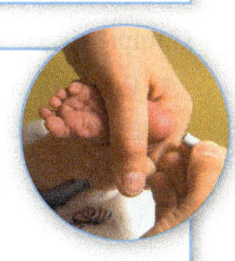

1.3 Cells from Cells
Key Concepts
- When single-celled organisms and body cells of animals and plants divide, they form two identical daughter cells. For single-celled organisms, cell division results in population growth. For multicellular organisms, cell division allows individuals to grow and to replace lost or damaged cells.
- Cell division must be preceded by DNA replication so that each daughter cell gets the same genes as its parent.
- Cell division is a continuous process that involves two stages: mitosis, to divide the nucleus, and cytokinesis, to divide the cytoplasm.

1.4 The Cell Cycle
Key Concepts
- Some cells live a long time, while others have a short life span, depending on where in the body they are found and the conditions they endure.
- The life of a cell, called the cell cycle, can be divided into two main stages: cell division and interphase. Interphase consists of two growth stages and a stage of DNA replication.
- Cell division is carefully controlled so that cells are produced only when needed. The control is exerted by proteins at checkpoints in the cell cycle. In cells that accumulate enough mutations, this control can be lost, which may lead to the development of cancer.

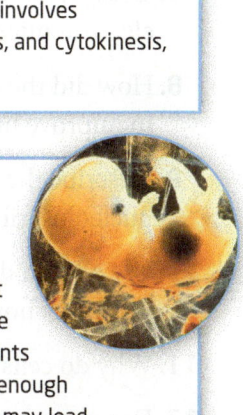

Chapter 1 Review

> **Make Your Own Summary**
>
> Summarize the key concepts of this chapter using a graphic organizer. The Chapter Summary on the previous page will help you identify the key concepts. Refer to Study Toolkit 4 on pages 565–566 to help you decide which graphic organizer to use.

Reviewing Key Terms

Complete each statement below using key terms.

1. The cytoplasm is composed of cytosol and _____. (1.1)
2. A(n) _____ is a photograph taken with a microscope. (1.1)
3. A chromosome consists of a single molecule of _____. (1.2)
4. A change in the usual order of a gene's A, C, T, and G building blocks is called a(n) _____. (1.2)
5. The material in the nucleus divides by a process called _____, whereas the rest of the cell divides by the process of _____. (1.3)
6. The _____ consists of interphase and cell division. (1.4)

Knowledge and Understanding K/U

7. Compare and contrast light microscopes and electron microscopes.
8. How did the invention of the microscope help to improve human health?
9. Describe the relationship between the nucleolus, ribosomes, and proteins.
10. Use a Venn diagram to compare chloroplasts and mitochondria.
11. Why do cells divide?
12. Draw and label a diagram to show metaphase in the process of mitosis. Include spindle fibres, centromeres, and centrosomes in your diagram.
13. What happens during interphase?
14. What is the function of spindle fibres?
15. Use these diagrams to answer the questions below.

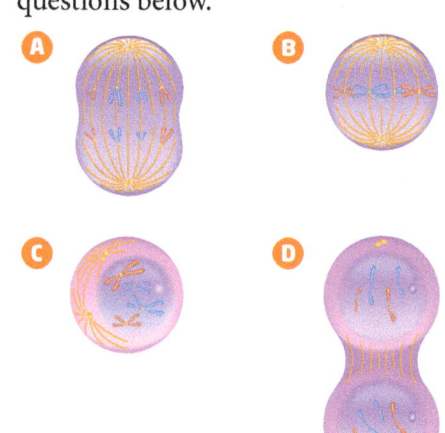

    A   B
    C   D

    a. Which diagram shows a cell in metaphase?
    b. Which diagram shows a cell with sister chromatids moving to opposite ends of the cell?
    c. Which diagram illustrates a cell in which a new nuclear membrane is forming?
    d. Which diagram shows a cell in anaphase?
    e. Write down the letters of the diagrams in the order in which they occur in mitosis.

16. Create a table that shows the benefits and drawbacks of genetically modified plants.
17. Cells have checkpoints to determine whether cell division should occur. Why are these checkpoints important?
18. Explain the difference between a tumour and cancer.
19. Why is the cell considered to be the basic unit of life?
20. How are the cells in your body identical?

Thinking and Investigation T/I

21. Herbicide-resistant plants are usually selected to resist specific herbicides. Why would it be an advantage for a company to produce both the genetically modified seed and the herbicide? That is, why would a company not necessarily want to develop a seed that would resist all herbicides?

22. Banana growers plant no seeds, yet banana plantations are filled with trees bearing bunches of fruit. How is this possible?

23. The table below shows the number of cells at each of the stages of the cell cycle that a student observed in a slide of a carrot root tip.

Number of Cells in Carrot Root Tip during Stages of the Cell Cycle

Cell Stage	Number of Cells
Interphase	82
Prophase	13
Metaphase	2
Anaphase	2
Telophase	5

a. If you know that it takes 800 min for a full cell cycle to take place, calculate the amount of time spent in each stage of the cell cycle.

Hint: To calculate the amount of time spent in prophase, for example, do the following:

$$\frac{\text{number of cells in prophase}}{\text{total number of cells viewed}} = \frac{\text{time spent in prophase}}{800 \text{ min (total time that cycle takes)}}$$

b. Why do you think so much time is spent in interphase?

c. Do you think the cell cycle for a cell in a leaf would be longer or shorter than the cell cycle for the cell in the carrot root tip? Explain your answer.

Communication C

24. **BIG IDEAS** Developments in medicine and medical technology can have social and ethical implications. Imagine that you are a journalist writing an article for the magazine *Ethics Today*. You have been asked to research and explain the social and ethical implications of a new technology related to medicine or biology. Suggested topics include using transgenic organisms to supply organs for transplant into humans, genetic screening for a specific disease, for-profit companies offering "personal genotyping" services, and cloning.

25. Chemicals that cause cancer are often called carcinogens. Explain the following statement: "All carcinogens are mutagens, but not all mutagens are carcinogens." Pick a particular carcinogen, and produce a pamphlet to educate people about it. Your pamphlet should include information such as what type of products contain it (for example, cleaning products), and what alternatives could be used instead.

26. Make a crossword puzzle that uses the key words from one of the sections of this chapter. Trade with someone who made a crossword puzzle using the key terms from another section, and see if you can solve each other's puzzles.

Application A

27. If a microscope were unavailable, you might be able to detect the existence of a micro-organism by its influence on the environment. Give examples of situations in which you could know that a microscopic organism was present, even if you could not see individuals of this species (that is, if you could not see its cells). Explain why you would know that the organism was there.

28. Your home has internal walls that divide it into rooms, just as most of the organelles inside a cell are separated from the cytoplasm by membranes. Compare the walls of a home with the membranes of organelles. What do they have in common, and what makes them different?

29. Explain why animals and plants are made of billions or trillions of microscopic cells rather than a few large cells.

30. Treatment for bladder cancer often involves chemotherapy, which uses chemicals to attack certain cells. Explain how each of the following methods of chemotherapy will interfere with the rapidly growing cancer cells. Remember what you have learned about the checkpoints in the cell cycle.

a. a chemical that blocks the replication of DNA

b. a chemical that prevents the formation of spindle fibres

Chapter 1 Cells and More Cells • NEL 53

Chapter 2: Plants: From Cells to Systems

What You Will Learn

In this chapter, you will learn how to...

- **explain** how plant cells specialize to form different kinds of plant tissues
- **explain** the links between specialized cells, tissues, organs, and systems in plants
- **describe** how plant organs work together to meet the needs of a plant

Why It Matters

Plants are essential for life on our planet. To protect this critical resource, we must understand how plant tissues, organs, and organ systems are formed, how they function, and how some plants are threatened by diseases.

Skills You Will Use

In this chapter, you will learn how to...

- **examine** and **draw** specialized plant tissues
- **investigate** how some plant tissues and organs work
- **research** a disease that threatens plant tissues and organs

Most of us only think about trees when they are threatened, such as by the forest fire that left this charred log. Yet we depend on trees and other green plants for everything from buildings and furniture to paper and railroad trestles. In fact, we depend on plants for life itself because they supply much of the oxygen we breathe and they form the basis of the food chains found on land and in the sea. In this chapter, you will explore how a fertilized egg in a centimetre-sized seed can become a tiny seedling and then a bean plant, rosebush, or maple tree.

Activity 2-1

Observing Plant Growth

What happens to the cells in a seed as the seed starts to grow? To find out, you will work on this activity as you study the chapter.

Materials
- seeds of pinto or kidney beans, soaked overnight
- small, clear plastic bag (wash for re-use after completing this activity) or small resealable plastic container
- paper towel
- water
- small container
- soil

Once soaked, your seed should split easily with your fingers. If not, let it soak another day.

Procedure

1. Carefully remove the seed coat from one of the seeds that has soaked overnight. Split it with your fingers, and record what you observe.

2. Moisten a paper towel, and place two or three other bean seeds on top. Fold the paper towel over the seeds, and place it in the plastic container. Observe the seeds each day for five days. Be sure to keep the paper towel moist throughout the experiment. Make a data table to record any changes you see.

3. On the fifth day, remove a bean seed that shows changes. Split it open, and record your observations in your data table.

4. Plant one of the other seedlings in a small container of soil. Add a little water to the soil every day for two weeks, and record what happens each day.

Questions

1. Using your knowledge of cell division, infer what happened to the seeds that were soaked in water overnight.

2. Make a hypothesis to explain the changes you saw after five days.

3. At the end of the chapter, explain what cellular and body processes occurred in the different areas of the seedling that you planted in the soil.

Study Toolkit

These strategies will help you use this textbook to develop your understanding of science concepts and skills. To find out more about these and other strategies, refer to the Study Toolkit Overview, which begins on page 560.

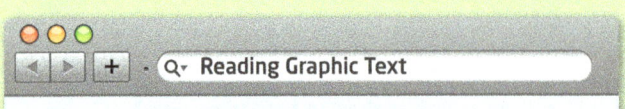

Reading Graphic Text

Interpreting Cross Sections

A cross section is a drawing that shows the inside of an object, as though you have sliced it open, either horizontally or vertically through its centre.

To interpret a cross section, first read the title or caption to find out what the cross section represents. Then visualize the object in three dimensions. For example, this cross section shows what you would see if you looked "down" at a root sliced in half horizontally.

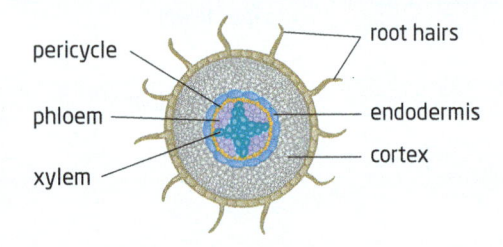

Labels: pericycle, phloem, xylem, root hairs, endodermis, cortex

Use the Strategy

Examine **Figure 2.10A** on page 64. Read the caption to find out what object is represented by the cross section. Which labelled parts of the object extend beyond what you can see in the cross section? Explain your reasoning.

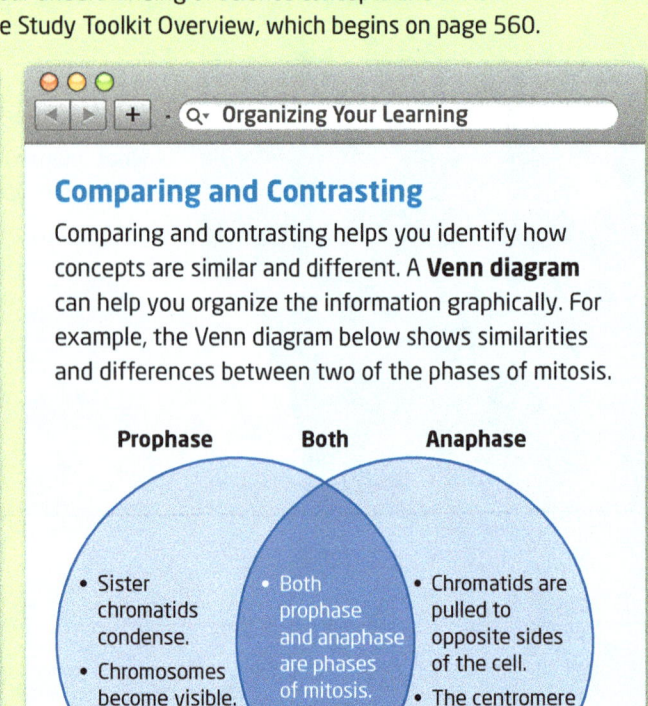

Organizing Your Learning

Comparing and Contrasting

Comparing and contrasting helps you identify how concepts are similar and different. A **Venn diagram** can help you organize the information graphically. For example, the Venn diagram below shows similarities and differences between two of the phases of mitosis.

Prophase
- Sister chromatids condense.
- Chromosomes become visible.

Both
- Both prophase and anaphase are phases of mitosis.

Anaphase
- Chromatids are pulled to opposite sides of the cell.
- The centromere splits apart.

Use the Strategy

Read the captions and labels for **Figure 2.3** on page 58. Make a Venn diagram to show the similarities and differences between xylem cells and phloem cells.

Word Study

Multiple Meanings

A word can have more than one meaning, depending on its context. The table below shows two words that you might have seen in an everyday, non-scientific context.

Use the Strategy

Write the everyday meaning of the word *tissue*. As you read this chapter, note its scientific meaning.

Everyday and Scientific Meanings of Words

Word	Everyday Meaning	Scientific Meaning (Biology)
cell	slang or short for *cellphone*	the smallest unit that can perform the functions of life
plate	a flat dish	a structure that forms between two plant cell nuclei

56 NEL • Unit 1 Tissues, Organs, and Systems of Living Things

2.1 Plant Cells, Tissues, and Organs

As shown in **Figure 2.1**, tree planters help to speed the process of regrowth in a forest that has been burned or logged. However, even if seedlings are not planted, seeds will be brought in naturally, either by the wind or by animals. How do these seeds change, turning into seedlings and finally adult trees? The answer lies in the processes of mitosis and **cell specialization**.

Cell Specialization

For many years, scientists wondered how the cells of a tiny seed specialize to become all the different parts of a plant. They knew that all body cells in an organism are produced through mitosis, which results in daughter cells with identical genetic information. Yet all cells are not identical, as you can see in **Figure 2.2**. At some point in their development, cells that start out being the same undergo **cell differentiation**, which results in cells specialized for different functions.

Cells are specialized according to the set of proteins they contain. Genes are responsible for producing proteins. Although all the cells in an organism contain all the same genes, not all genes are turned on in any given cell. One set of genes is turned on in one cell type and another set of genes is turned on in another cell type. The proteins produced in a cell determine the eventual function of that cell. The cell is then said to be specialized for a given task.

Figure 2.1 Many students work as tree planters during the summer months, often planting hundreds of seedlings each day.

> **Key Terms**
> cell specialization
> cell differentiation
> tissue
> organ
> meristematic cell
> transpiration
> gall

> **cell specialization** the process by which cells develop from similar cells into cells that have specific functions within a multicellular organism
>
> **cell differentiation** a stage of development of a living organism during which specialized cells form

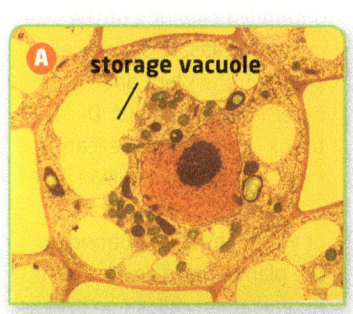

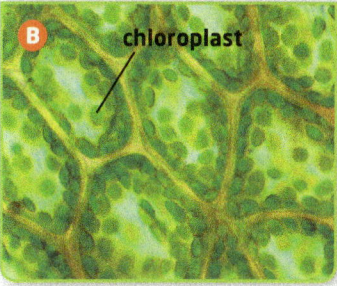

Figure 2.2 Differences between various specialized plant cells can be seen easily using a compound light microscope. **A** Cells that are specialized for storing energy usually have big storage vacuoles that take up most of the cell's inner space. **B** Cells that are specialized for photosynthesis are packed full of *chloroplasts*–the organelle where photosynthesis occurs.

Chapter 2 Plants: From Cells to Systems • NEL 57

tissue a cluster of similar cells that share the same specialized structure and function

organ a combination of several types of tissue working together to perform a specific function

meristematic cell an unspecialized plant cell that gives rise to a specific specialized cell

Specialized Cells and Tissues in Plants

A healthy plant is always growing and making new specialized cells—except when dormant during cold or very hot weather. Groups of specialized cells form **tissues**, and groups of tissues work together in **organs**, such as roots, stems, and leaves. Each plant organ performs critical tasks for a plant's survival.

What is responsible for this constant growth? Special cells, called **meristematic cells** or meristem, are responsible. Meristematic cells are undifferentiated cells that can form specialized cells in plants. These cells have also been called "permanent embryos" because of their lifelong ability to produce the cells that can become new tissues and organs in their part of a plant.

Meristematic cells are constantly producing more cells, which then become specialized. These cells combine to form the three types of tissues found in the body of a plant: dermal tissue, ground tissue, and vascular tissue, as shown in **Figure 2.3**. The cells in each of these tissues are specialized to perform specific tasks, such as photosynthesis or controlling gas exchange.

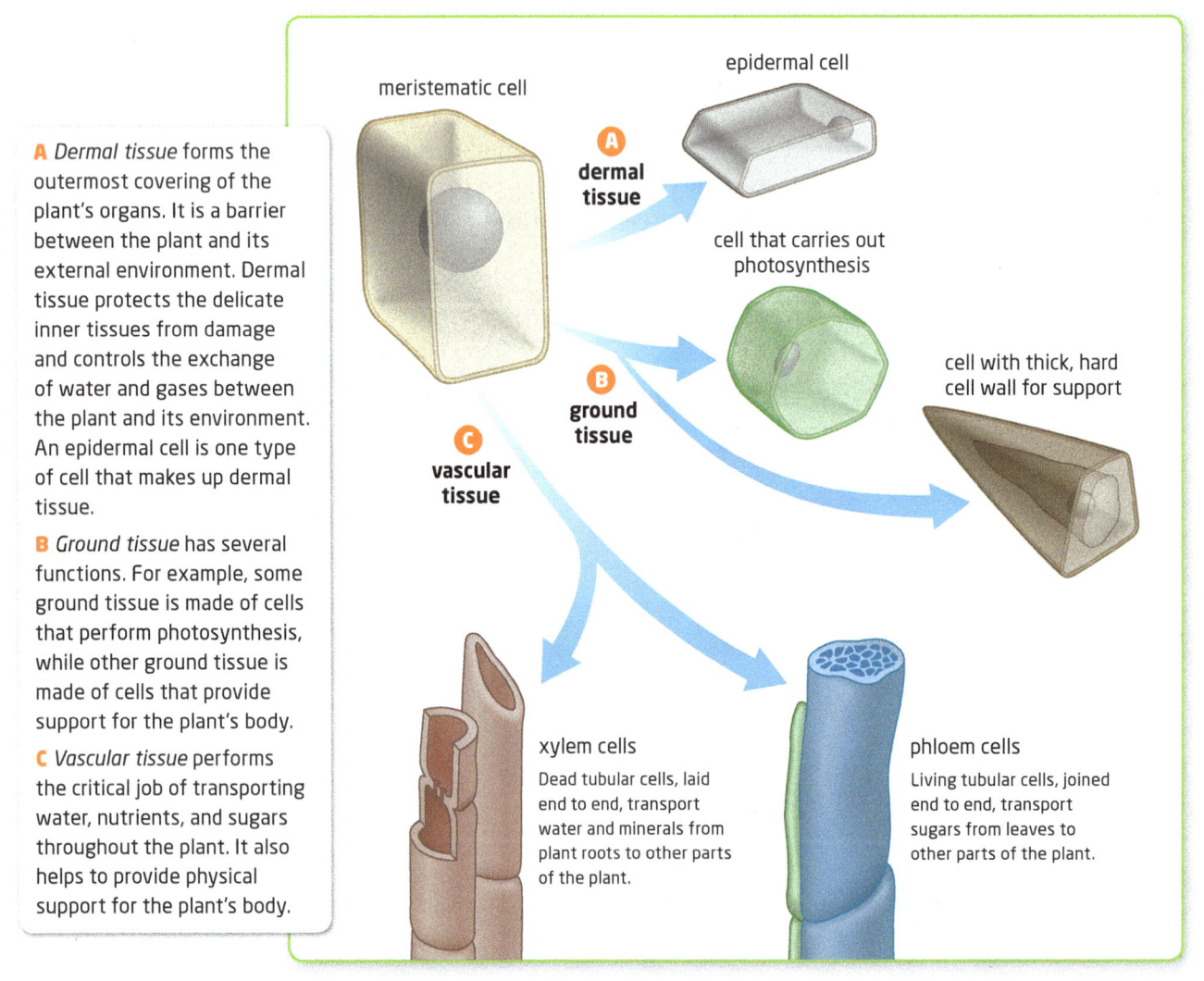

A *Dermal tissue* forms the outermost covering of the plant's organs. It is a barrier between the plant and its external environment. Dermal tissue protects the delicate inner tissues from damage and controls the exchange of water and gases between the plant and its environment. An epidermal cell is one type of cell that makes up dermal tissue.

B *Ground tissue* has several functions. For example, some ground tissue is made of cells that perform photosynthesis, while other ground tissue is made of cells that provide support for the plant's body.

C *Vascular tissue* performs the critical job of transporting water, nutrients, and sugars throughout the plant. It also helps to provide physical support for the plant's body.

xylem cells Dead tubular cells, laid end to end, transport water and minerals from plant roots to other parts of the plant.

phloem cells Living tubular cells, joined end to end, transport sugars from leaves to other parts of the plant.

Figure 2.3 Meristematic cells produce new cells that differentiate into the specialized cells that make up different plant tissues.

Repairing and Replacing Specialized Cells

The cells, tissues, and organs of multicellular animals, such as worms, fish, frogs, snakes, birds, and mammals are formed as the embryo develops. While some cells and tissues can be repaired and replaced, organs must last for an animal's lifetime.

Plants are different. In addition to forming new cells and tissues, plants form new organs periodically throughout their lives. For example, as leaves become less efficient with age, these light-collecting organs die and are replaced by new, more efficient leaves. Roots grow continuously, too, so there are always fresh roots to absorb water and minerals from the soil.

As shown in **Figure 2.4**, growing plants push upward, downward, and outward because of rapidly dividing meristematic cells (meristem) at the tips of roots and branches. Some produce cells specialized for leaves and flowers. A *bud* is a swelling of the stem that contains meristem for new, not yet developed, tissues in organs such as leaves and flowers. A plant's most active growth occurs near the *terminal bud*. The *lateral buds* are dormant (inactive), but they have the potential to produce new branches, leaves, and flowers.

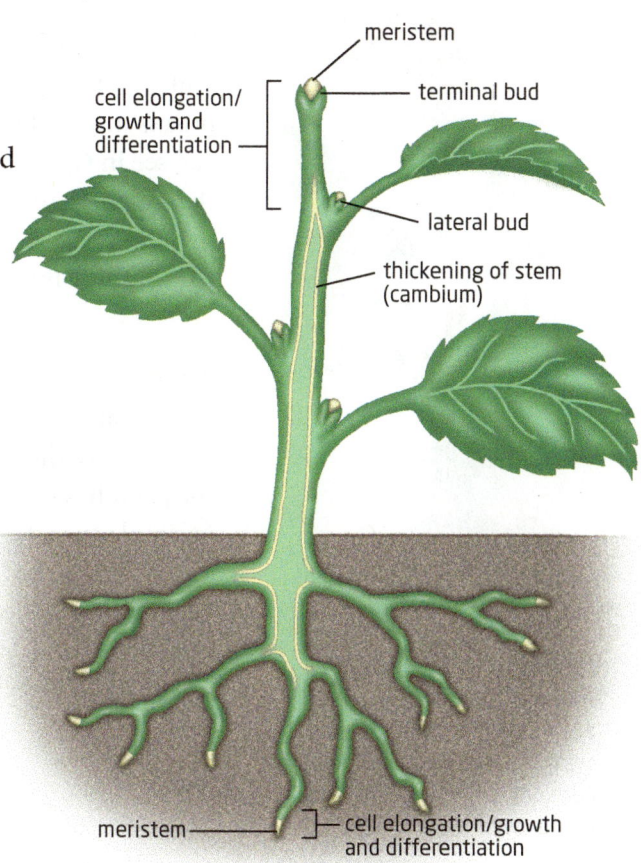

Growing Up or Branching Out

The cells in actively growing areas give off a chemical called *auxin* (a plant hormone), which controls the cells below and behind them. For example, **Figure 2.5** shows how cells at a plant's terminal bud produce auxin that inhibits, or holds back, the development of cells in lateral buds. The result is that plants tend to grow upward rather than outward. However, if you remove the tip of a plant (or if this is done naturally when a moose or deer nibbles its top branches) this "hold back" signal is removed. The plant will bush out at the lateral buds. If you replace the auxin lost from the tip, the control is restored, and the bushing out will stop.

Figure 2.4 Branches and roots grow because of dividing meristematic cells. A plant's stem becomes wider because of meristematic cells in a layer called the cambium.

Figure 2.5 Cells in the terminal bud produce the plant hormone auxin, which holds back growth in buds elsewhere in the plant.

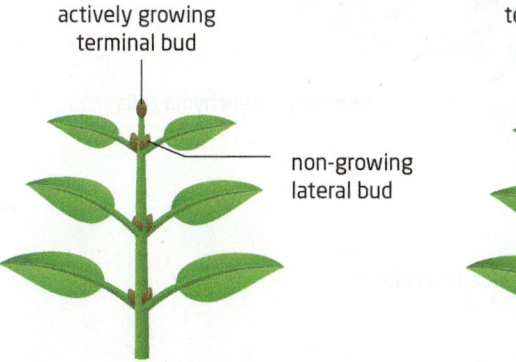

Auxin silences the expression of genes in lateral buds. The plant grows up more than out.

If the terminal bud is removed, there is no longer any auxin to inhibit lateral growth. Cells in the lateral buds begin to divide and specialize.

Tissues Working Together: Plant Organs

Different kinds of tissues combine to make up organs. You have many organs in your body, but flowering plants have only three or four. As you can see in **Figure 2.6**, three types of organs make up the body of a plant: the leaves, stem, and root. These organs make it possible for the plant to live and grow. A fourth organ is the reproductive organ, which, in many plants, is the flower.

The Leaf

A leaf's most important job is to provide a large surface area where photosynthesis can take place. Even leaves that look more like thin needles, like those on many coniferous trees, produce a large area because the plant has so many of them. If photosynthesis produces more glucose (a simple sugar) than the leaf needs, the excess is converted into starch and stored in the leaf. **Figure 2.7** shows the specialized cells of a leaf, which help this organ perform its most important functions.

Figure 2.6 This Gerber Daisy shows the four types of organs of a flowering plant: the root, the stem, the leaf, and the flower. Each organ performs specific functions.

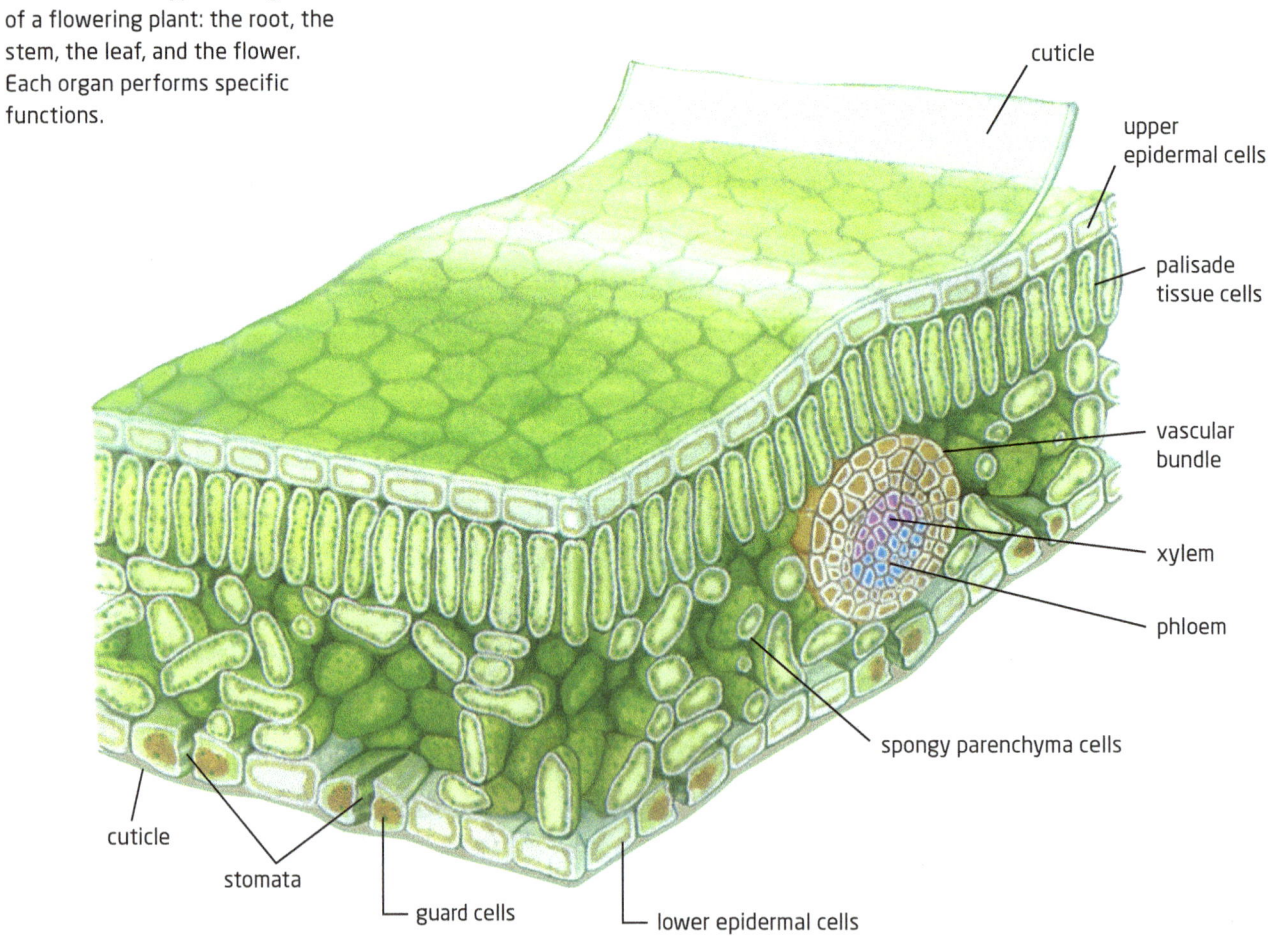

Figure 2.7 Many specialized cells work together to help a leaf perform photosynthesis.

60 NEL • Unit 1 Tissues, Organs, and Systems of Living Things

The Upper and Middle Leaf

The upper surfaces of a leaf is made of a sheet of dermal tissue called the epidermis. The cells of the epidermis secrete a waxy *cuticle* that helps reduce the amount of water that evaporates from the leaf's surface. The main function of the epidermis is protection, so these epidermal cells do not perform photosynthesis. The sunlight passes through them to the photosynthesizing cells.

Between the upper and lower surface of a leaf is *mesophyll* tissue. *Meso-* means middle. Mesophyll tissue consists of *palisade* tissue cells and *spongy parenchyma* cells. The palisade cells are specialized to perform most of the photosynthesis in the leaf. They are arranged in lines that resemble the long poles used in the walls, or palisades, of old fortresses—hence their name. The tops of these cells are arranged to meet the Sun's rays head on, so that the rays pass through the length of the cell. As the rays of light journey through the cell, they encounter the many chloroplasts, where photosynthesis takes place. These cells are very active, so they are packed with mitochondria, which perform cellular respiration.

Below the palisade cells is a layer of spongy parenchyma cells. Parenchyma cells are loosely packed to form a network with open spaces, like a sponge. The spaces contain the gases needed or produced by photosynthesis: water vapour, oxygen, and carbon dioxide.

The centre of the leaf contains xylem and phloem tissue arranged into *vascular bundles*. These vascular bundles form *veins* that dissect the interior of the leaf at regular intervals. At their tips, the vessels meet the open spaces in the parenchyma tissue. There, the xylem delivers water, in the form of water vapour, to the photosynthesizing cells, and the phloem picks up sugars that have been produced and delivers them to cells throughout the rest of the plant. The small branches of veins ensure that every cell in the leaf is close to a supply of water and *nutrients*, which are elements essential for the life of the plant.

The Lower Leaf Surface

The lower surface of the leaf is made of an epidermis that is critical for the exchange of gases between the leaf and the outside environment. To allow the gases to move in and out, *guard cells*, which you can see in **Figure 2.8**, are scattered across the lower surface of the leaf. These cells change their shape to control the opening and closing of pores in the leaf, which are called stomates or *stomata* (singular *stoma*). The stomata are connected to the open spaces in the spongy parenchyma cells. Guard cells and stomata play a significant role in **transpiration**. Carbon dioxide enters through these pores, and oxygen and water vapour exit through them.

> **Study Toolkit**
> **Multiple Meanings** Which terms on this page have an everyday meaning? How can these everyday meanings help you remember the scientific meanings?

> **Suggested Investigation**
> Plan Your Own Investigation 2-A, Transpiration in Different Plant Types, on page 77

transpiration the evaporation of water from leaves

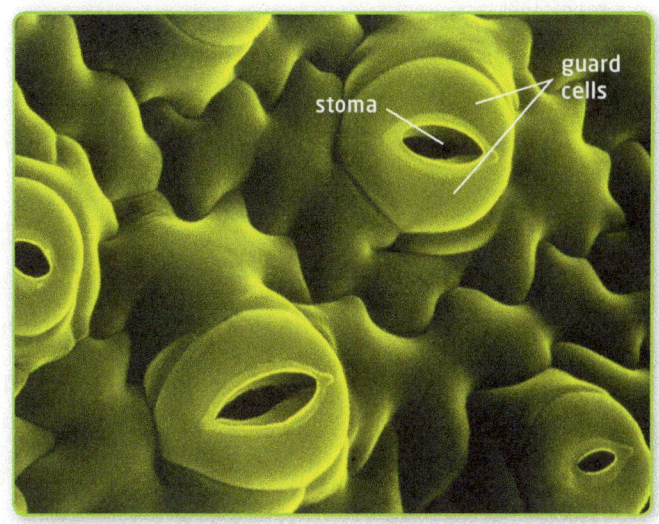

Figure 2.8 When guard cells fill with water, they take on a curved sausage shape and push the stomata open, as shown here. As the guard cells lose their water, they collapse and the stomata close, reducing water loss from the leaf.

Activity 2-2

Inside a Leaf

Use a microscope or microviewer to observe the specialized cells of leaves. What structures can you see?

Materials
- prepared slides of leaf cross sections
- compound light microscope or microviewer

Safety Precaution

- Handle microscope slides and cover slips carefully so they do not break and cut you.

Procedure

1. Place a prepared slide of a cross section of a leaf under the microscope. Examine the specimen under low power, and gradually increase the magnification as necessary.

2. Use the micrograph of stained cells above, on the right, to help you identify the following cell types and structures in each specimen:
   - epidermal cells
   - palisade cells
   - spongy parenchyma cells
   - stoma and guard cells
   - vascular cells

3. Describe the shape and arrangement of the cells in various tissues in the leaf. Explain how these shapes and arrangements relate to each tissue's functions.

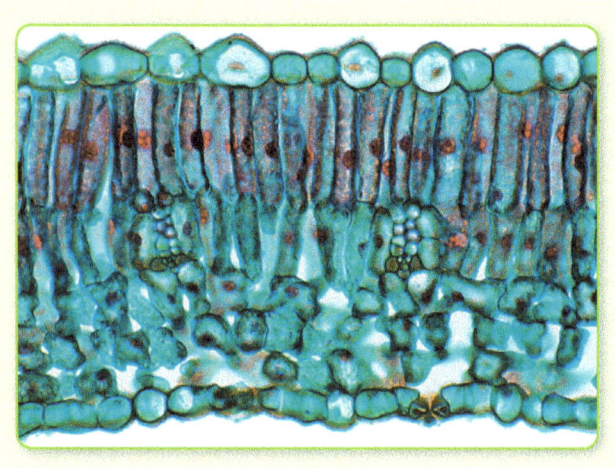

Lilac leaf cross section, 400×

Questions

1. On which part of the leaf did you observe the most stomata?

2. If you observed both open and closed stomata, describe the difference in the appearance of the guard cells in each case.

3. Explain how the shape and arrangement of each group of cells relate to the tissue's functions.

4. Explain how the arrangement of cells in the leaf contributes to the efficiency of photosynthesis.

Study Toolkit

Interpreting Cross Sections Visualize how a leaf would need to be cut to create the leaf cross section you see on this page. How does visualization help you understand how the cross section shows cellular organization in the leaf?

Learning Check

1. Describe what happens to a cell during cell differentiation.

2. Draw a diagram of a plant to show where you might find an example of each of the three types of plant tissues.

3. Draw and label a plant with four organs.

4. Based on the information in **Figure 2.5**, what advice would you give to a gardener who wants to grow bushier basil or oregano plants?

62 NEL • Unit 1 Tissues, Organs, and Systems of Living Things

Inside the Chloroplast: One of the Leaf's Organelles

As you are reading this page, specialized cells in the leaves of plants all over the world are doing what they do all day, every day there is light. In every cell with chloroplasts, photosynthesis is occurring. As shown in **Figure 2.9**, light energy from the Sun combines with carbon dioxide from the air and water from the soil to produce glucose. Glucose is a carbohydrate used by both plant and animal cells as a source of energy. Animals eat to acquire glucose and other food molecules, but most plants must make their own. Oxygen gas is a product of photosynthesis and, as you know, is essential for cellular respiration in both plants and animals.

Chloroplasts can change their shape and location in a cell to increase the amount of light they capture. They contain little sacs called *thylakoids*, which contain light-trapping chlorophyll molecules. This is the part of a chloroplast where photosynthesis occurs. Thylakoids are arranged in a stack called a *granum* (plural *grana*).

Figure 2.9 Chloroplasts are filled with grana, which are stacks of chlorophyll-containing thylakoids. Chlorophyll gives plants their green colour and allows the thylakoids to trap light energy from the Sun. This energy is used to fuel photosynthesis, the chemical reaction that produces glucose and oxygen.

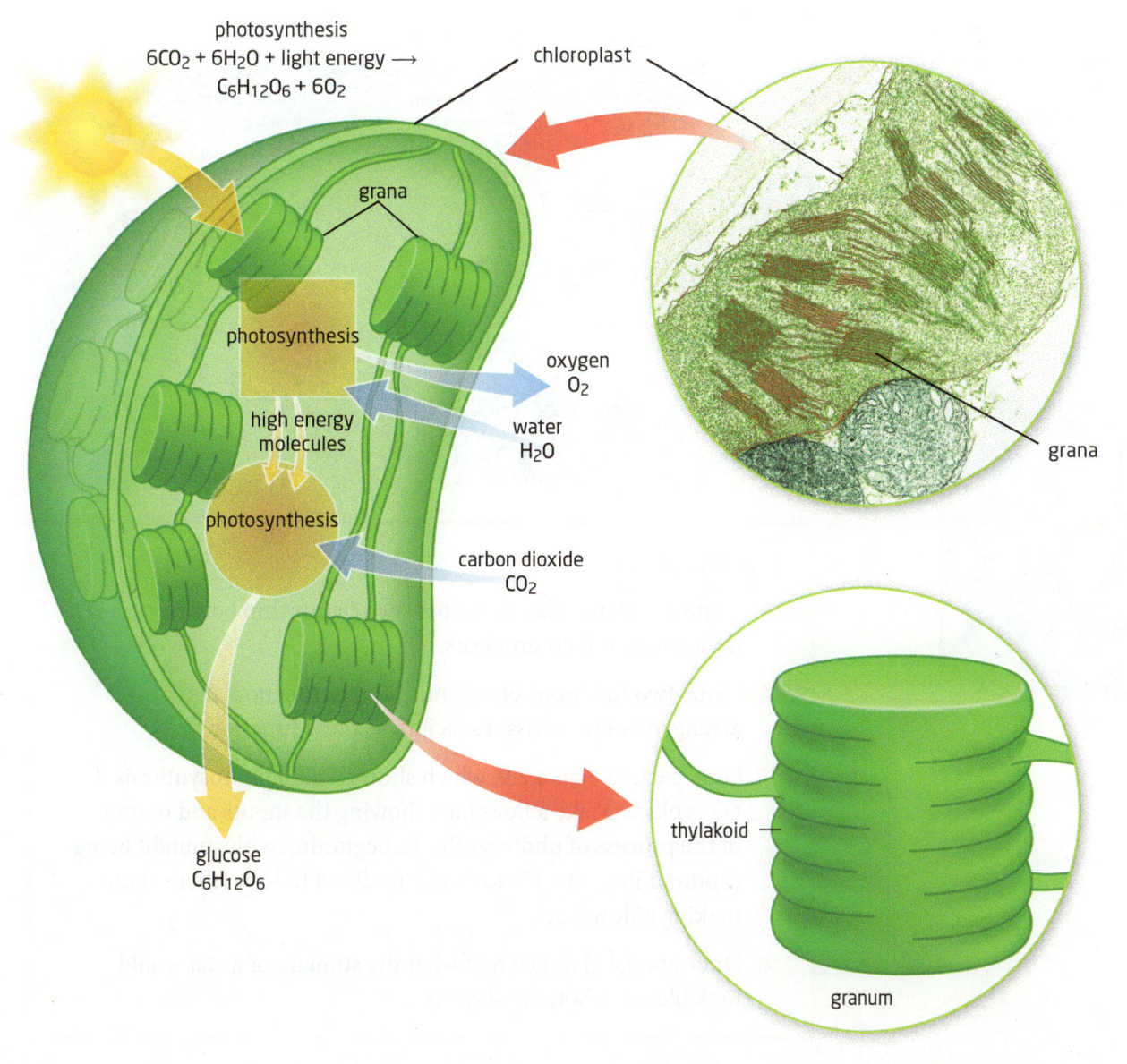

photosynthesis
$$6CO_2 + 6H_2O + \text{light energy} \longrightarrow C_6H_{12}O_6 + 6O_2$$

Chapter 2 Plants: From Cells to Systems • NEL

The Stem

A plant's stem has two main functions: physical support and transportation of water, nutrients, and sugars. Stems contain most of a plant's xylem tissue. As xylem cells grow, they form long, straw-like tubes, or vessels. The cells then die, but their thick cell walls remain behind, forming long fibrous "pipes" through which water can flow. The xylem vessels are hollow, so they provide a relatively easy passage through the plant. It has been calculated that water moves 10 billion times more easily through xylem than it would if it had to travel through cells filled with cytoplasm!

The dead xylem cells are fortified with a hard substance called lignin, which makes them strong, helping them keep the plant upright. Xylem vessels are grouped with phloem vessels in *vascular bundles*. This further strengthens the stem's ability to support the plant. Phloem tissue is also made of vertically stacked tubes. Their cell walls are porous, which allows materials to be exchanged between the phloem and the neighbouring cells. **Figure 2.10** shows the arrangement of xylem and phloem in a plant stem.

Figure 2.10 In **A**, you can see a cross section of a sunflower stem, magnified 25 times. In **B**, you can see how strands of xylem and phloem are grouped together in bundles that run the length of the stem.

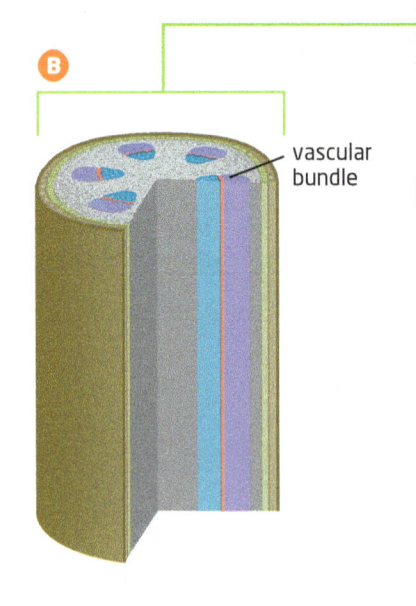

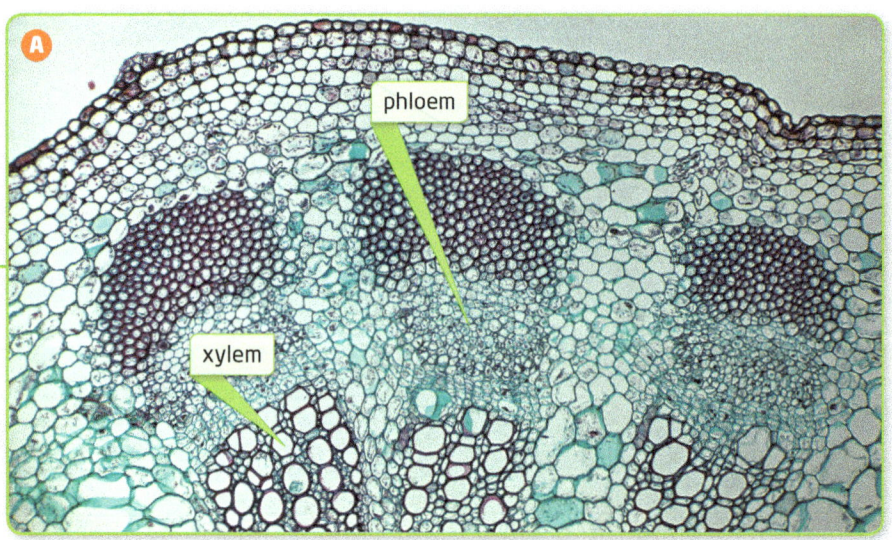

Learning Check

5. Write a sentence that describes the relationship between grana, thylakoids, and chloroplasts.

6. Name two functions of a stem, and describe how the arrangement of its tissues facilitates these functions.

7. Look back to **Figure 2.9**, which shows where photosynthesis takes place. Make a flowchart showing the inputs and outputs of the process of photosynthesis, beginning with sunlight being captured in grana. Go to Study Toolkit 4 to learn more about making a flowchart.

8. Draw and label a sketch of what the stomata of a leaf would look like on a hot, dry day.

The Roots

Roots anchor a plant to the ground and allow it to take up water and minerals from the soil. As shown in **Figure 2.11**, some roots also act as a plant's storage area. **Figure 2.12** shows a cross section of a root. The root hairs are the main site of water and mineral absorption. *Cortex* cells usually do not contain chlorophyll and can be used by the plant to store starch. There are lots of spaces between these cells, through which water and minerals can flow to the endodermis. The endodermis helps control the transport of minerals between the cortex and the vascular tissues. The *pericycle* is the layer of tissue that surrounds the phloem and xylem. It gives rise to branch roots. You will learn more about water movement in plant roots in Section 2.2.

Figure 2.11 Vegetables such as this beet use their roots to store extra energy supplies and mineral reserves for later use.

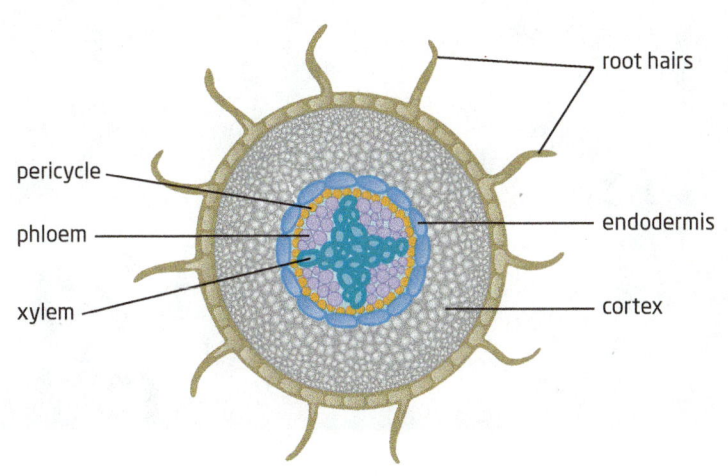

Figure 2.12 This cross section shows the structure of a typical root. Water and nutrients from the soil flow through the root's layers to the central vascular tissue. Then the water and nutrients are transported to the rest of the plant.

Types of Roots

Plants like dandelions have a *taproot*, one main root that grows larger and thicker than the rest, as shown in **Figure 2.13A**. The taproot allows the plant to reach far underground for water. The taproot anchors the plant firmly in the ground. In contrast, plants such as grasses have *fibrous roots* with branches that are all about the same size. Fibrous roots (shown in **Figure 2.13B**) spread out horizontally near the surface of the soil. They provide the plant with a large surface area over which water can be taken up from just under the surface of the soil. Fibrous roots also stabilize the soil and help to prevent erosion and landslides.

Figure 2.13 A Many common weeds, such as dandelions, have a large, main taproot. A taproot makes it hard to pull the entire plant from the ground, as many gardeners know! **B** Other plants, such as this yarrow, have fibrous roots, which are specialized to absorb water from near the surface of the soil.

Chapter 2 Plants: From Cells to Systems

Plants Under Attack

Plant tissues and organs can be attacked by *viruses*, just as animal tissues and organs can. More than 400 different viruses are known to infect plant cells, causing as many as 1000 plant diseases. Not all plant diseases are fatal or even harmful. For example, the beautiful Rembrandt tulips shown in **Figure 2.14** get their stripes from a virus that is transmitted from plant to plant. Other viruses, such as the tobacco mosaic virus (TMV) shown in **Figure 2.15**, are highly destructive, attacking the leaves of tomato, potato, pepper, and cucumber plants. TMV often lowers crop yields dramatically. Today, many anti-viral drugs are available to fight these viruses.

Figure 2.14 The virus that affects these flowers makes them attractive to humans.

Go to **scienceontario** to find out more

Figure 2.15 This research technician holds up a healthy tomato plant (on the left) and one infected with tobacco mosaic virus (on the right).

STSE Case Study

Eliminating Wheat Rust with Transgenic Therapy

Almost one third of the world's population relies on wheat as a primary source of food. Wheat is vulnerable, however, to several diseases and pathogens. The most common types belong to a group called rusts. Rust diseases are particularly damaging because they are easily carried by the wind from one area to another. As well, they mutate quickly and attack new, previously resistant varieties of wheat.

The rate of infestation by various kinds of rusts is growing. If long-term solutions are not found, the world may soon face global wheat shortages.

Brown rust, shown here, is a type of fungi that affects Canadian crops. It can reduce wheat harvests by up to 20 percent.

Traditional Treatments

Traditionally, wheat crops that were affected by fungal diseases were treated with fungicides. Although fungicides kill the fungi, they can also damage the wheat. Many types of wheat depend on a beneficial type of fungus called mycorrhizal [pronounced mi-cor-RI-zal] fungus. The tiny mycorrhizal fungus gets nutrients from the roots of the plant. In return, it converts nutrients, such as nitrogen, into usable forms, making the nutrients easier for the plant to absorb. When fungicides are used, they kill the mycorrhizal fungus along with the fungi that cause diseases. As a result, the plant may die.

Another strategy to fight rust diseases involves breeding wheat plants that carry rust-resistant genes with each other (selective breeding). Until recently, this strategy offered only a short-term solution, because rusts can mutate quickly and re-infect resistant wheat.

Plant Galls

Plant **galls**, as shown in **Figure 2.16**, are similar to tumours in animals. Like tumours, galls are produced by the abnormal growth of groups of cells. Plants produce galls in response to attacks by organisms such as insects, fungi, bacteria, and viruses. The attackers have a purpose—they use the plant's resources to support themselves or their offspring. For example, some types of insects lay their eggs in a specific kind of plant, such as an oak tree. Their larvae develop in a gall that grows in the tissue of the tree.

Insects promote the development of galls by injecting a chemical into a plant's tissues. This chemical interacts with the plant's fluids and alters which genes are turned on and off in the cells. The change stimulates the growth of a structure where young insects develop.

The most significant difference between plant galls and animal tumours is that galls do *not* normally spread to other tissues (as human tumours can, producing cancer). Gall growth is usually contained, and the effect on the plant is seldom fatal. Learning why these tumour-like growths do not spread may someday provide important information about how cancer in humans can be treated.

gall an abnormal growth of plant tissue caused by insects or micro-organisms

Figure 2.16 Galls often look as though they cause serious damage, but most do not harm the plant's normal functions.

A Genetic Solution?

Researchers in Australia recently discovered two genes that protect wheat against rust diseases. One gene, called Lr34, produces a protein that transports disease-fighting molecules throughout the plant cells. The other gene, called Yr36, triggers a resistance response, although scientists are not completely sure how this response occurs. As long as the rusts are not able to mutate, transferring these genes into non-resistant wheat plants may be the answer for protecting wheat crops around the world.

The spores of a rust are shown below, magnified 250 times. Rusts can interfere with the growth and health of plant tissues.

Your Turn

1. Identify different stakeholders (such as farmers, scientists, and people opposed or undecided about the benefits of GMO crops) who might be affected by the Australian research and the possible development of transgenic wheat. Describe the Australian research to a partner, from the point of view of one of the stakeholders.

2. Imagine that you are a scientist who is about to appear on a radio talk show to discuss GMO crops. What questions do you think you will be asked? What kinds of information would you want to find in order to prepare for the interview?

3. Research the benefits and risks of transgenic crops in terms of one of the following common crop diseases: stem rust, striped rust, black rust, or tobacco mosaic virus. Write a newspaper article to communicate your research. Imagine that your readers will be primarily from one of the stakeholder groups you identified in question 1.

The Reproductive Organ: The Flower

The flower is an organ that does not take part in the maintenance of the plant itself. Its task is reproduction. Although many plants do not produce flowers and can reproduce by other methods, flowering plants are abundant.

The different parts of the flower are really just specialized leaves. One set of these leaves is specialized to produce *pollen*, which manufactures sperm, while another set produces eggs. Most plants accomplish pollination with the assistance of the wind, or animals such as birds, bats, or insects, as shown in **Figure 2.17**. Through colour or scent, the flower attracts insects or other animals to the plant. Once there, these animals pick up pollen from the male parts of the flower. When they later visit another plant of the same type, they may transfer this pollen to the female parts of the second plant, setting the stage for *fertilization*. In some cases, they transfer pollen from a flower to the female parts of another flower on the same plant.

After the flower is pollinated, seeds are produced. The seeds are embedded in fruits. Here again, plant hormones are involved. A hormone called ethylene stimulates the ripening of fruits. As shown in **Figure 2.18**, companies use this knowledge to ship fruits, such as bananas and tomatoes, to markets all over the world.

Figure 2.17 Flowering plants require pollination in order to reproduce.

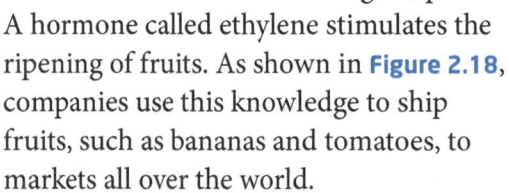

Go to **scienceontario** to find out more

Figure 2.18 Fruits such as bananas are often picked while still green. They can be shipped to customers, and ripened with ethylene gas (C_2H_4) once they reach their markets.

Making a Difference

In high school, Isdin Oke decided to test the effects of a compound that slows aging in plants. With help from a University of Guelph professor, Isdin and his classmate Colin Perkins exposed snapdragon flowers to 1-methylcyclopropene (1-MCP) and ethylene gas. 1-MCP is used to increase the shelf life of flowers, fruits, and vegetables. Isdin and Colin found that flowers exposed to 1-MCP aged at a much slower rate than flowers that were not exposed. They observed this effect even when the flowers were also exposed to the plant hormone ethylene, which stimulates aging. Their results could help scientists develop ways to prevent flowers from wilting and fresh produce from spoiling. Isdin and Colin took their project to the National Sanofi-Aventis Biotalent Challenge and earned gold at the 2008 Waterloo-Wellington Science and Engineering Fair. Isdin received a scholarship to the University of Guelph and is now studying nanoscience.

What are some possible social and economic benefits of slowing the aging of plants?

Section 2.1 Review

Section Summary

- Meristems produce cells that differentiate into specialized cells.
- New tissues and organs are produced from meristem in growing areas called buds.
- Plant tissues join together into four types of organs: the root, stem, leaf, and reproductive organ.
- Leaves provide a large surface area where photosynthesis takes place. Photosynthesis occurs inside chloroplasts, which are found in specialized cells in the leaf.
- Stems support the plant and transport water, nutrients, and sugars.
- Roots anchor the plant and take up minerals and water from the soil.
- Not all plants have flowers. In those that do, flowers are responsible for reproduction.

Review Questions

T/I 1. Could a plant live without meristem? Explain your answer.

K/U 2. Look back to **Figure 2.3**. Make a graphic organizer that shows the same information. Go to Study Toolkit 4 to learn more about graphic organizers.

K/U 3. Examine the diagram on the right.
   a. What two structures are labelled?
   b. When grouped together as shown, what are these structures called?
   c. What type of tissue are they?

C 4. Draw and label a plant to show the three organs that a plant needs to sustain its life, as well as a brief description of what each of these organs does.

T/I 5. On a leaf's surface, the epidermis is covered with cuticle. Explain why root epidermis is not covered with cuticle.

K/U 6. The epidermal cells of most leaves are transparent. Why is this adaptation beneficial to the plant?

A 7. Erosion, as shown in the photograph on the right, can be a major problem in many natural areas. What would you suggest planting to stabilize and renew an area that has washed away after a flood?

A 8. Scientists often have difficulty getting funding for their research. Why do you think tobacco mosaic virus was the first major plant virus whose structure was investigated?

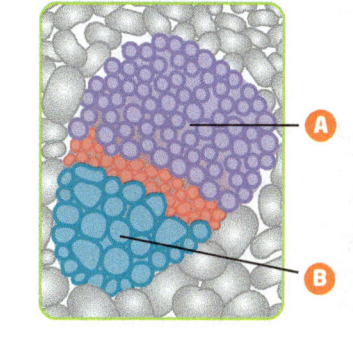

Key Terms

system
root system
shoot system

2.2 Plant Organ Systems

When you first look at a plant, such as the tree shown in **Figure 2.19**, it does not look alive in the dramatic way that many animals do. Yet a plant's stationary appearance is deceiving. Its internal structure is complex, with many interactions between its various organs. These organs, working together in **systems,** maintain a constant flow of fluids, nutrients, and hormones from one part of the plant to another.

The body of a typical plant is generally considered to have two main organ systems: the **root system** and the **shoot system**. These systems are shown in **Figure 2.20**.

- A plant's root system consists of all the roots that lie below the surface of the ground. The root system is responsible for taking in water and minerals from the soil. It is constantly growing to keep pace with the plant's increased demand for materials as it grows.
- The shoot system is responsible for supporting the plant, performing photosynthesis, and transporting water, nutrients, and sugars.

Sometimes flowers and their fruit are considered part of a separate system. However, as shown here, they are also considered part of the shoot system.

system in biology, a group of tissues and organs that perform specific functions

root system an organ system in a plant, which takes in water and minerals from the soil and transports these substances to the shoot system

shoot system an organ system in a plant, which supports the plant, performs photosynthesis, and transports sap

Figure 2.19 Trees like this enormous one from British Columbia's Carmanah Valley have traditionally held spiritual value for many First Nations people. Trees are often used in First Nations teaching metaphors to help people appreciate the place of humans in a healthy ecosystem.

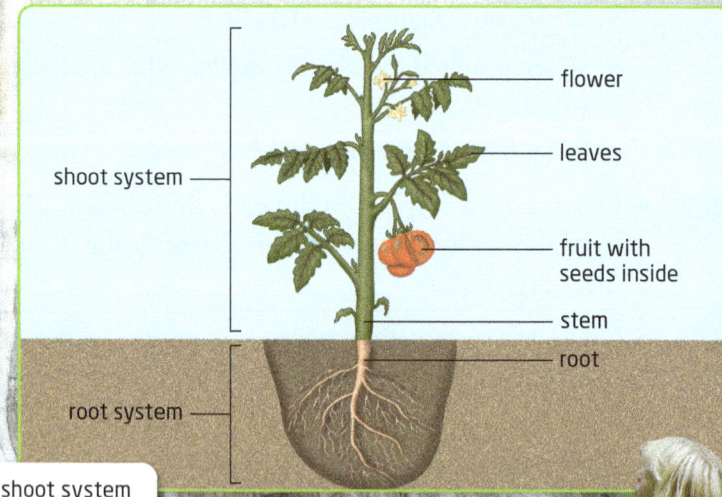

Figure 2.20 A plant's shoot system consists of organs above the ground, while its root system consists of organs below the ground.

70 NEL • Unit 1 Tissues, Organs, and Systems of Living Things

Systems Working Together

The root and shoot systems are connected by the flow of water, nutrients, and various hormones through vascular bundles that contain xylem and phloem. Maintaining this flow is essential for the plant's ability to survive.

- Xylem tissue takes care of moving water and minerals from the roots to other plant parts, including the leaves, where these materials are needed for photosynthesis.
- Phloem tissue moves the sugars produced by photosynthesis to other plant parts.

Unlike the cells in xylem, which die at maturity, the cells in phloem are alive. Therefore, xylem tissues do not use any of the plant's energy stores, but phloem tissues do. Phloem cells actively pump substances to where they are needed in the plant. For example, phloem tissue moves glucose from the leaves, where it is made, to parts of the plant where there is high demand for energy, such as the buds, and to places for storage, such as the roots.

> **Study Toolkit**
>
> **Comparing and Contrasting**
> What concepts on this page could you compare and contrast using a Venn diagram? Prepare a Venn diagram to make notes on one of these concepts.

Activity 2-3

The Flow of Phloem

What happens to a plant if the flow of materials in vascular tissue is interrupted? In 1686, an Italian scientist named Marcello Malpighi (1628–1694) investigated this question by removing a ring of phloem tissue from a tree. What do you think happened?

- ring of tree bark removed
- trunk is bulging above stripped ring

Procedure

1. Read the following account of Malpighi's experiment:

   In trees, phloem forms the layer of living tissue just beneath the bark. Xylem lies beneath the phloem. In his experiment, Malpighi peeled away a ring of bark and phloem from a tree. Shortly after the ring was removed, a swelling appeared in the bark of the tree immediately above the ring. Sweet-tasting fluid oozed out of this swelling. Although it appeared at first that Malpighi's experiment had not seriously damaged the tree, it died a few weeks later.

2. Using **Figure 2.10**, sketch a cross section of the tree stem in Malpighi's experiment.

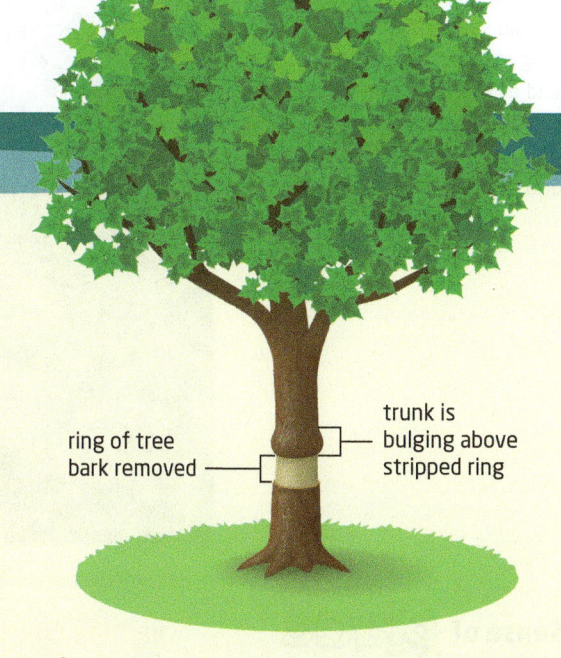

Questions

1. Use your sketch and your understanding of vascular bundles to analyze Malpighi's results.

2. What would his results have been if he had blocked transport in the xylem instead of the phloem?

3. The removal of a ring of tree bark and phloem is called girdling. Farmers with orchards of fruit trees sometimes girdle trees to produce sweeter fruit.

    a. Why does this practice increase sugar transport to the fruit?

    b. How do you think girdling affects the health of the tree?

Chapter 2 Plants: From Cells to Systems • NEL 71

Moving Water through the Systems

Water means everything to plants. Plants can survive without soil under certain circumstances, as shown in **Figure 2.21**, but they cannot survive without water. If there is too little water in the soil, nutrients cannot be taken up by the roots. This is because the nutrient molecules need to be dissolved in water in order to be absorbed and move up the xylem in the form of sap. As well, if the supply of water to the leaf is insufficient, photosynthesis cannot take place. Eventually, the plant would die.

However, too much water in the soil can also have a negative effect on plants. If the spaces between soil molecules are filled with water, there will not be enough room for oxygen. Under these conditions, the root cells will not get enough oxygen for cellular respiration. Keeping water balanced and moving through a plant is thus vitally important. This job requires the co-ordinated action of both the root and shoot systems.

Figure 2.21 You might not notice anything odd about the plants growing in this greenhouse. However, if you could look closely, you would see that they are growing in a nutrient solution instead of soil. This type of agriculture is called hydroponics, and it is now an important part of Ontario's agricultural economy.

Sense of place

Some plants live in areas where the soil is nutrient-poor, such as bogs. Many bog plants, including Venus fly traps and pitcher plants, get extra nutrients by catching and consuming insects or other organisms.

Learning Check

1. Under what conditions can plants survive without soil?
2. Sketch a diagram that shows a plant's organ systems. Label the organs involved in each system.
3. Some plants, such as beets and carrots, store food in their root systems. How do you think growing in nutrient-rich soil, with plenty of water and sunlight, would affect this type of plant?
4. Most authorities recommend that lawns receive only about 3 cm of water per week. Why would it be unwise to double or triple this amount?

Moving Through the Roots

Have you ever wondered how water gets from the soil to the top of a 30 m tree? It begins with water absorption in the roots. The structure of the root helps the plant absorb water and minerals from the soil. As shown in **Figure 2.22**, the epidermal cells of most types of roots grow small extensions of their cell membranes called *root hairs*, which expand the root's total surface area. As shown in **Figure 2.23**, nutrients and water are transported into the root by osmosis.

Then nutrients and water move toward the xylem at the centre of the root. The endodermis helps control the passage of water and minerals from the cortex to the vascular tissue. The water and nutrients are then pushed into the xylem vessels.

The Effect of Root Pressure on Water Movement

Once water from the roots reaches the xylem, how does it move upward, against the force of gravity, to reach the leaves at the top of a tall tree? Is it pushed from below, by root pressure, or pulled from above, as a result of transpiration?

Root pressure is created under certain conditions, such as at night when transpiration is low and when soil is very moist. As root cells bring minerals into the xylem, the mineral concentration in the xylem increases. This high concentration of minerals increases the tendency of water to diffuse into the root xylem by osmosis. As water flows in, root pressure builds in the xylem vessels. This pressure forces fluid up the xylem. Although root pressure can push water up the xylem, experiments have shown that root pressure is not enough to move water to the top of a tall tree, such as a giant redwood, and may only account for several meters of water movement up the xylem. A much more important factor acting on the movement of water through a plant is transpiration, which pulls water up from the roots.

Figure 2.22 Tiny root hairs, such as those on this radish seedling, extend off main roots and expand the surface area available for absorbing nutrients and water.

Figure 2.23 Water and nutrients enter the roots by osmosis and continue to move in, toward the centre of the root. The water and minerals can travel either through cells or through the spaces surrounding cells until they reach the endodermis. The endodermis is surrounded by a waxy, waterproof substance that prevents water from passing in between the cells of the endodermis. In order to pass into the vascular tissue, the water and minerals must pass through the semi-permeable cell membrane of the endodermis cells.

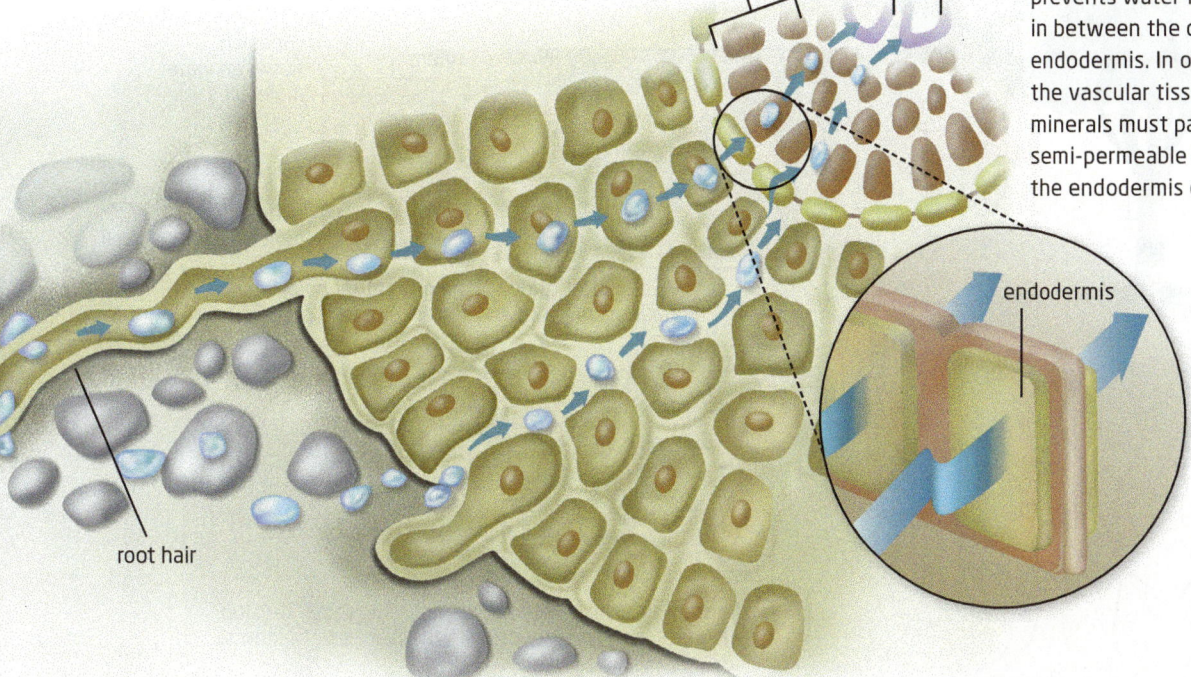

Chapter 2 Plants: From Cells to Systems • NEL   73

> **Suggested Investigation**
>
> Inquiry Investigation 2-B, Moving Nutrients Through the Stem, on page 78

The Pull from Above

Xylem tissue ends when it reaches the leaves. Here, liquid water turns into water vapour in the spaces between the spongy parenchyma cells in the middle of a leaf. Some of this water will be used during photosynthesis. However, much more of the water vapour will simply evaporate when stomata open to take in carbon dioxide and release oxygen. Transpiration makes room for more water from the xylem to move into the leaves, pulling the water column up.

As shown in **Figure 2.24**, transpiration, along with some of water's unique properties, moves water up the xylem. *Cohesion*, the ability of water molecules to cling to each other, holds the water column in the xylem together. Another property of water, *adhesion*, helps water fight the force of gravity. Adhesion is the tendency of water molecules to stick, or adhere, to certain surfaces, such as the wall of a xylem vessel. The clinging of water to the xylem walls helps to prevent the water from flowing back down to the roots.

The rate of transpiration is controlled by the amount of water vapour in the leaves. When the amount of water vapour is large, the guard cells open the stomata and water vapour moves out of the leaves. If the amount of water vapour is small, the guard cells relax and the stomata close.

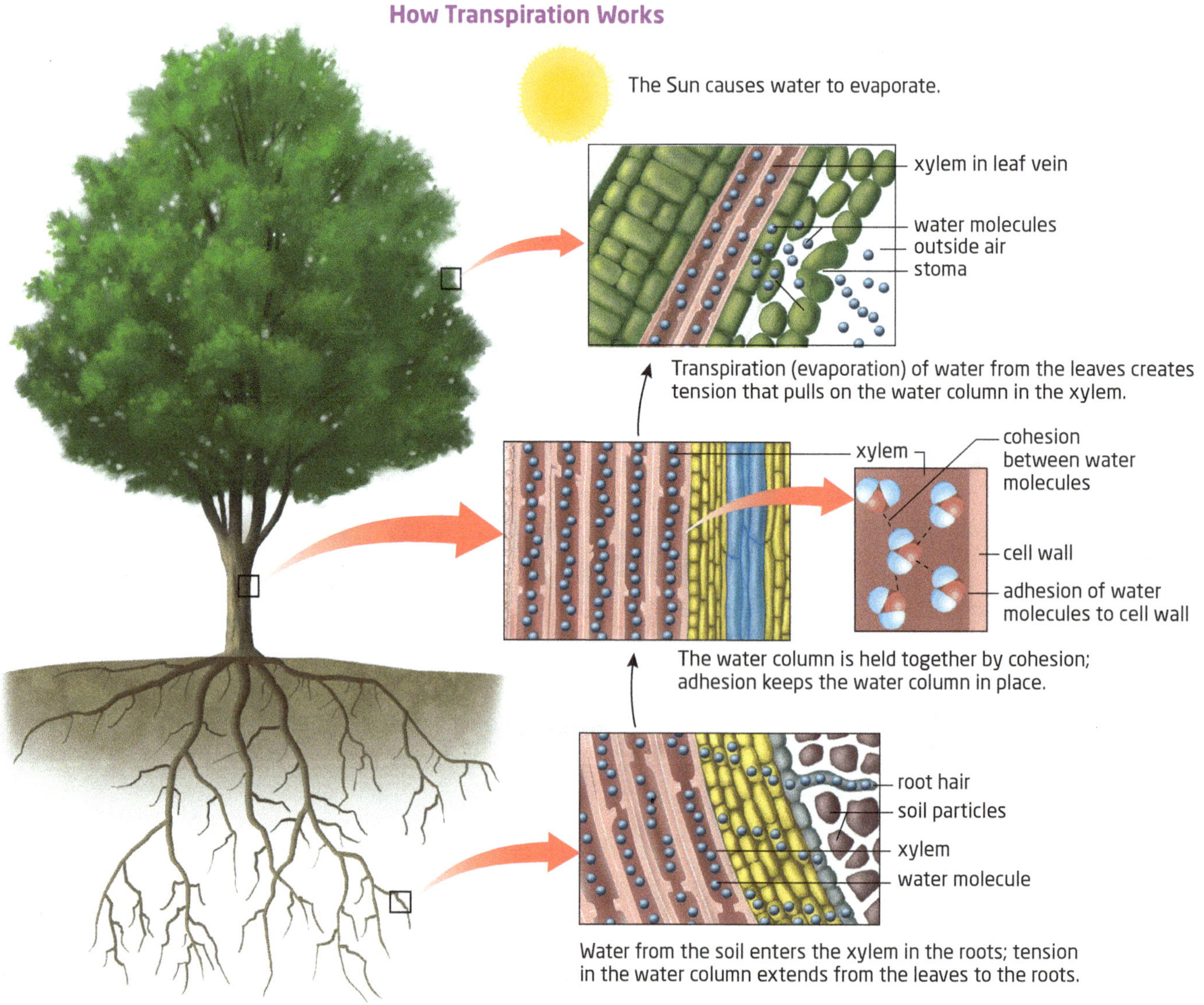

Figure 2.24 The process of transpiration pulls water in the xylem up toward the leaves.

How Transpiration Works

The Sun causes water to evaporate.

- xylem in leaf vein
- water molecules
- outside air
- stoma

Transpiration (evaporation) of water from the leaves creates tension that pulls on the water column in the xylem.

- xylem
- cohesion between water molecules
- cell wall
- adhesion of water molecules to cell wall

The water column is held together by cohesion; adhesion keeps the water column in place.

- root hair
- soil particles
- xylem
- water molecule

Water from the soil enters the xylem in the roots; tension in the water column extends from the leaves to the roots.

Moving Nutrients through the Systems

Photosynthesis produces a form of sugar called glucose. Once formed, the glucose is either used or it combines with other molecules to produce sucrose and other carbohydrates. Sucrose is soluble in water and is the main molecule distributed to other parts of the plant through the phloem. Sucrose that makes its way to the roots is usually chemically changed to starch and stored. When the stored starch is needed by other plant organs it must be removed from storage and transported back to them. However, starch cannot be transported through the stem. It is not soluble in water, so it must first be converted to sucrose, which then dissolves in water and is transported again as sap.

The Movement of Maple Sap

The process that provides us with maple syrup occurs during the spring. At this time, trees need to nourish the many buds that must divide and grow to produce leaves that can photosynthesize. **Figure 2.25** shows sap movement in a maple tree. The sap that flows upward from the roots through the phloem of maple trees in the spring contains large amounts of sucrose, which has been converted from starch. The sap moves through the phloem to where it is needed. Once the leaves have grown, they can make their own glucose through photosynthesis. In the summer and fall, as the leaves begin to produce more glucose than their cells require, the extra glucose is transported to other plant tissues or stored in the roots as starch.

Sense of Value

About one million litres of maple syrup are produced annually in Ontario. The province's maple industry is worth an estimated $15 000 000 a year.

Figure 2.25 This diagram shows the formation and use of maple sap in a maple tree. **A** In the spring, the flow of sucrose is mainly upward. **B** In the summer and fall, the flow is mostly downward, as the plant prepares for the winter.

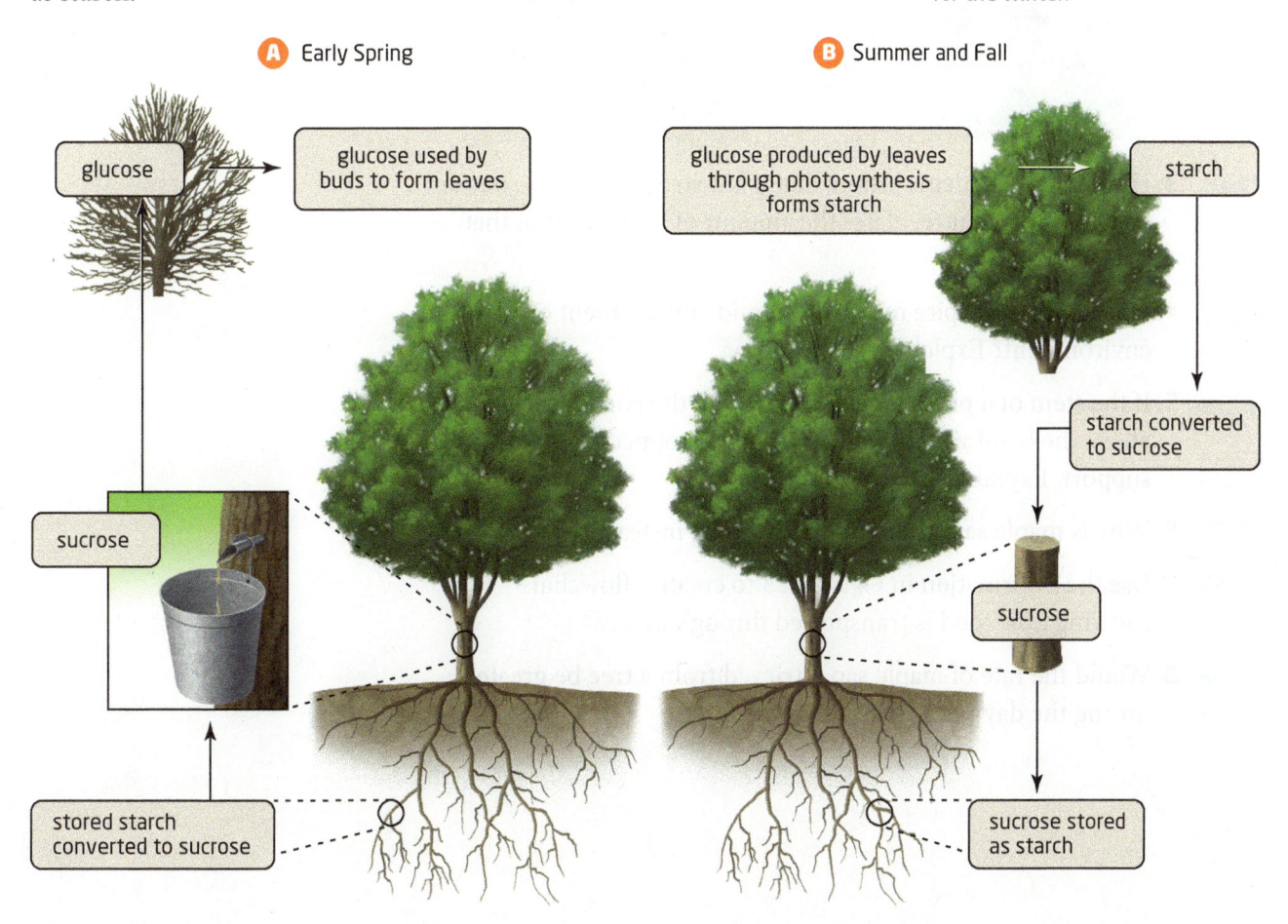

A Early Spring

- glucose
- glucose used by buds to form leaves
- sucrose
- stored starch converted to sucrose

B Summer and Fall

- glucose produced by leaves through photosynthesis forms starch
- starch
- starch converted to sucrose
- sucrose
- sucrose stored as starch

Chapter 2 Plants: From Cells to Systems • NEL 75

Section 2.2 Review

Section Summary

- Plants have two organ systems for sustaining life: the root system and the shoot system.
- The root system takes in water and nutrients from the soil and moves these substances to the stem.
- The shoot system supports the plant, performs photosynthesis, and transports water, nutrients, and sugars.
- Transpiration pulls water from the roots to the leaves through the xylem tissue. This pull is aided by two properties of water—cohesion and adhesion.
- Nutrients in the form of dissolved sucrose move through the plant in the phloem tissue. The sucrose is stored as starch if it is not needed immediately.

Review Questions

K/U 1. Compare and contrast the functions of the xylem and the phloem.

T/I 2. In which of the diagrams below will the leaves exert a stronger pull on water from the roots? Explain your answer.

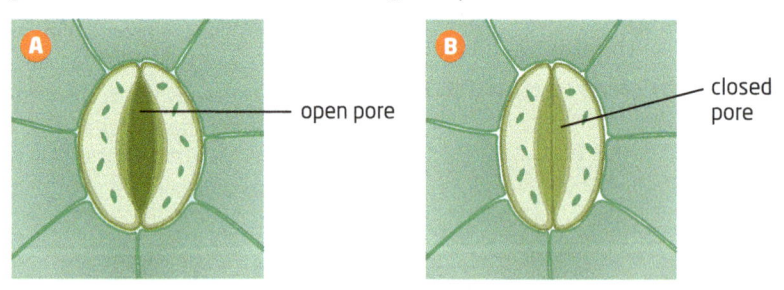

A — open pore
B — closed pore

T/I 3. How could you demonstrate that it is a structure on the bottom side of leaves that regulates the amount of transpiration that occurs in a plant?

A 4. Will a tulip transpire more in a humid environment or in a dry environment? Explain your reasoning.

A 5. If the stem of a plant is bent or snapped, the part of the plant above the bend will usually die, even if propped up with a support. Explain why.

K/U 6. Why is maple sap collected in the spring instead of in the fall?

C 7. Use the information in **Figure 2.25** to create a flowchart showing how food is transported through a tree.

A 8. Would the rate of maple sap retrieved from a tree be greater during the day or during the night? Why?

Plan Your Own Investigation 2-A

Skill Check
✓ Initiating and Planning
✓ Performing and Recording
✓ Analyzing and Interpreting
✓ Communicating

Safety Precautions

- Never eat or drink in the laboratory.
- Wash your hands with soap and water after you have completed this investigation.

Suggested Materials
- different kinds of small potted plants
- water
- clear plastic bags (large enough to fit over plants)
- measuring spoons or cups

Science Skills
Go to **Science Skills Toolkit 2** for information about designing an investigation.

Transpiration in Different Plant Types

Plan an investigation to compare the amount of transpiration that takes place in different types of plants.

Question
Is there a difference in the amount of transpiration in different types of plants?

Hypothesis
With your group members, formulate a hypothesis about how the structures of different types of plants will affect the amount they transpire.

Plan and Conduct
1. With your group, decide how you will test your hypothesis. Identify the dependent and independent variables.
2. Write a step-by-step outline for your procedure.
3. Prepare a data sheet for recording your data and notes.
4. Check your procedure with your teacher, and then perform your experiment.

Analyze and Interpret
1. Summarize the results of your experiment in a table.
2. Discuss your data with your group.
3. What can you infer about the difference in the amount of transpiration in different types of plants?
4. Do your data support your hypothesis? Explain why or why not.
5. Suggest one or two ways that your experiment could be improved.

Conclude and Communicate
6. How did the structure of the different plants affect the amount they transpired?

Extend Your Inquiry and Research Skills
7. **Inquiry** Design an experiment to test the effects of one or more environmental factors, such as daily temperature or seasonal rainfall, on the amount of transpiration in a plant.

Chapter 2 Plants: From Cells to Systems • NEL

Inquiry Investigation 2-B

Skill Check
✓ Initiating and Planning
✓ Performing and Recording
✓ Analyzing and Interpreting
✓ Communicating

Safety Precautions
- Never eat or drink in the laboratory.
- Handle sharp objects with care. Never cut an object held in your hand and cut with the blade moving away from you.

Materials
- three 100 mL beakers
- tap water
- medicine dropper
- 3 celery stalks, two with leaves on the end
- red food colouring
- small plastic bag
- elastic
- single-edged razor blade or sharp knife
- cutting board or other cutting surface

Moving Nutrients Through the Stem

In this investigation, you will determine what factors affect the movement of water through the stem of a plant.

Question
What factors affect the movement of water through stalks of celery?

Prediction
Predict whether water will move the fastest up a celery stalk with leaves, with leaves covered in a plastic bag, or without leaves.

Procedure
1. Identify the variables you will need to control for this investigation.
2. Cut the bottom off your three celery stalks. Make sure two of your stalks have lots of leaves. Remove all the leaves from the third stalk.
3. Cover the leaves of one of the stalks with a plastic bag, and secure the bag with an elastic.
4. Add water to three beakers, and add 2 to 3 drops of food colouring to the water in each beaker.
5. Place the bottom of each of the three stalks in separate beakers. Leave the beakers near a light source until the next day.
6. Remove the stalks from the beakers. Examine each one to observe how far up the stalk the coloured water has travelled.

Analyze and Interpret
1. Did your observations match your predictions? Explain.
2. What other forces influence the movement of water in a plant?
3. What other factors could you investigate?

Conclude and Communicate
4. Draw a labelled diagram to explain the movement of water in your three celery stalks.
5. What factors affect the movement of water in a celery stalk? What evidence supports your conclusion?

Extend Your Inquiry and Research Skills
6. **Inquiry** Use your findings to create a colourful bouquet from white carnations, Queen Anne's Lace, or other white flowers.

Chapter 2 Summary

2.1 Plant Cells, Tissues, and Organs

Key Concepts

- Meristems (groups of meristematic cells) produce cells that differentiate into specialized cells.
- New tissues and organs are produced from meristematic tissue in growing areas called buds.
- Plant tissues join together into four types of organs: the root, stem, leaf, and reproductive organ.
- Leaves provide a large surface area where photosynthesis takes place. Photosynthesis occurs inside chloroplasts, which are found in specialized cells in the leaf.
- Stems support the plant and transport water, nutrients, and sugars.
- Roots anchor the plant and take up minerals and water from the soil.
- Not all plants have flowers. In those that do, flowers are responsible for reproduction.

2.2 Plant Organ Systems

Key Concepts

- Plants have two organ systems for sustaining life: the root system and the shoot system.
- The root system takes in water and nutrients from the soil and moves these substances to the stem.
- The shoot system supports the plant, performs photosynthesis, and transports water, nutrients, and sugars.
- Water moves through the plant due to transpirational pull and root pressure, aided by two properties of water–cohesion and adhesion.
- Nutrients in the form of dissolved sucrose move through the plant in the phloem tissue. The sucrose is stored as starch if it is not needed immediately.

Chapter 2 Review

Make Your Own Summary

Summarize the key concepts of this chapter using a graphic organizer. The Chapter Summary on the previous page will help you identify the key concepts. Refer to Study Toolkit 4 on pages 565-566 to help you decide which graphic organizer to use.

Reviewing Key Terms

1. The _____ protects the inner tissues of the leaf. (2.1)

2. Specialized cells form during _____, which is a stage of development. (2.1)

3. _____ cells can give rise to various specialized cells in a plant. (2.1)

4. Roots, stems, and leaves are all plant _____. (2.1)

5. A plant _____ can be compared to a tumour in an animal. (2.1)

6. An organ _____ co-ordinates the functions of organs to do a complex job for an organism. (2.2)

7. Plants have two organ systems: the _____ system and the _____ system. (2.2)

Knowledge and Understanding K/U

8. How are new tissues and organs produced through the life of a plant?

9. Describe a function of auxin in plant growth.

10. Explain how a plant tissue differs from a plant organ.

11. Note whether each of the following is a cell (or part of a cell), tissue, organ, or system, and state its function.
    a. xylem vessel
    b. leaf
    c. fibrous roots
    d. epidermis
    e. root hair

12. Draw and label a diagram to show the function of the stomata and guard cells.

13. In your notebook, name the structures indicated in the stylized drawing of a leaf cross section below.

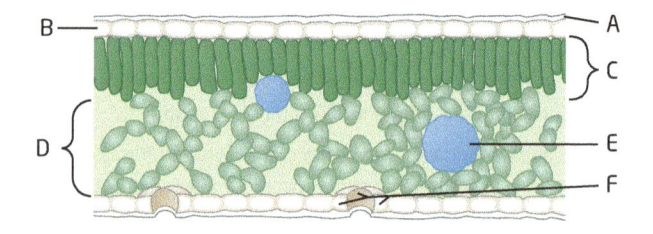

14. All plants must perform photosynthesis.
    a. What materials are needed for this process?
    b. Describe how the plant obtains these materials.

15. Explain how adhesion and cohesion affect the transport of water throughout a plant.

16. Using a Venn diagram, compare and contrast the two main types of roots and the environments in which you are likely to find them.

Thinking and Investigation T/I

17. Researchers wanted to know if certain environmental conditions would affect water loss from plants. They set up an investigation using three potted geranium plants. They placed plant 1 in a clear plastic bag, and they placed plant 2 in front of a fan. Plant 3 served as a control. Study the graph, and answer the questions that follow.

Rate of Water Loss

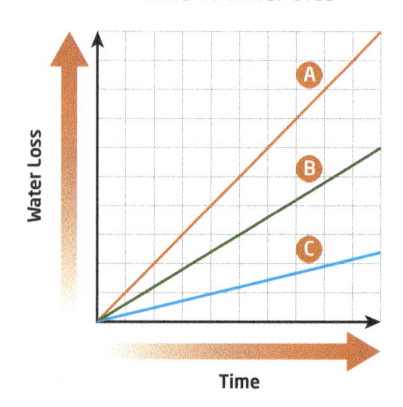

80   NEL • Unit 1 Tissues, Organs, and Systems of Living Things

a. Which line best represents each plant used in the investigation?

b. Do environmental conditions affect the rate of water loss in a plant? Write a conclusion for the experiment.

18. This graph shows the number of stomata in the leaves of daisies collected in four different provinces. In which province would you expect the least and the greatest amount of rainfall? Why?

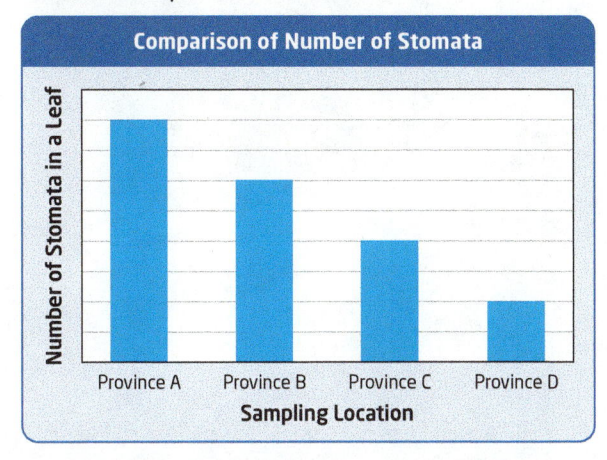

Comparison of Number of Stomata

(Bar graph showing Number of Stomata in a Leaf vs Sampling Location: Province A (highest), Province B, Province C, Province D (lowest))

19. If a houseplant outgrows its pot, it often wilts. Why?

20. Predict the results of an experiment in which a scientist compared the thickness of the cuticles of terrestrial plants that live in hot, dry areas to the thickness of cuticles of terrestrial plants that live in humid, rainy areas. Explain your reasoning.

21. What tissues do you think make up the fibrous "strings" in celery? How could you set up a simple experiment to find out what the function of the "strings" is?

Communication C

22. **BIG IDEAS** "Plants and animals, including humans, are made of specialized cells, tissues, and organs that are organized into systems." Use this statement as the caption for a diagram you create, using plants as the example.

23. Sketch a diagram to show how water and nutrients enter a plant, and how these substances are transported from the roots to the leaves. Write a description of the process, referring to your diagram.

24. Write an editorial column for your school newspaper, explaining why the school board should adopt a policy of only watering schoolyards in the cool of the night.

25. Describe the benefits and risks of a high rate of transpiration.

Application A

26. To be able to perform photosynthesis, cells need chloroplasts.

    a. Using this information, describe the difference between the cells specialized for photosynthesis and non-photosynthetic cells.

    b. How could you extend this information to determine which structures in a plant participate in photosynthesis?

27. Water usually does not carry much dissolved oxygen. How does this fact explain why plants can be killed by watering them too much?

28. A friend tells you that you can make an unripened peach ripen faster by putting it in a paper bag than by leaving it on a counter. Do you think your friend is correct? Explain your reasoning.

29. Why do you think farmers dry their grain before they store it?

30. Which diagram shows a method of watering a garden that makes the best use of the water? Explain your answer.

Chapter 2 Plants: From Cells to Systems • NEL 81

Chapter 3 Animals: From Cells to Systems

What You Will Learn

In this chapter, you will learn how to...

- **describe** how the cells of animals become specialized
- **explain** how unspecialized cells replace and repair damaged tissues
- **describe** how organs co-ordinate the actions of different tissues and work together in systems
- **assess** the impact of medical technologies and public health strategies on human health

Why It Matters

Over the years, human health has improved greatly due to advances in technologies that scientists use to study and understand the human body and how it functions.

Skills You Will Use

In this chapter, you will learn how to...

- **examine** and **draw** specialized animal tissues
- **investigate** a frog's body structure through dissection
- **research** the risk factors for heart disease

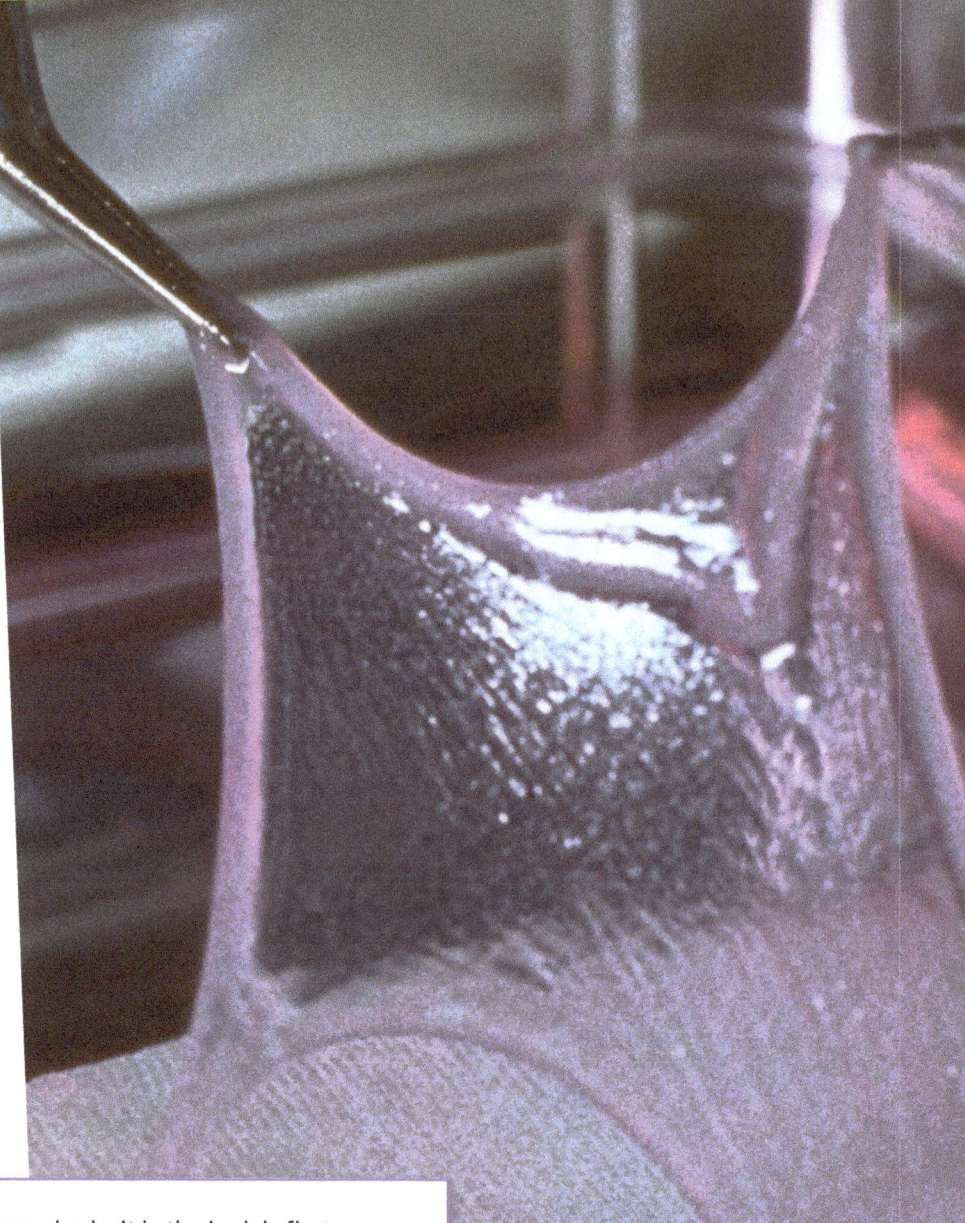

Skin is the largest organ in the human body. It is the body's first defence against infection and injury. In the past, people with severe burns had to have skin grafted from other parts of their body. However, if people were badly burned, they did not always have enough healthy skin left to graft. Such patients often died due to loss of fluids or infection. Medical specialists can clone new skin (shown here) from a tiny piece of the patient's unburned skin. This technique is one of many new medical technologies that are possible because of our understanding of how cells reproduce and form tissues and organs.

82 NEL • Unit 1 Tissues, Organs, and Systems of Living Things

Activity 3-1

More Than a Covering

The diagram below shows a highly magnified section of both layers of human skin, the epidermis and the dermis. In severe, third-degree burns, both layers are damaged. How well does cloned skin replace natural skin?

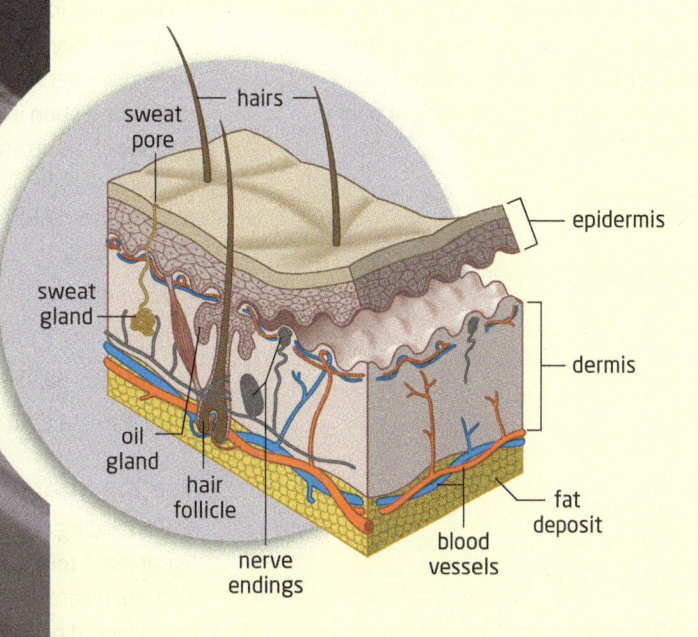

Procedure

Study the diagram. Based on what you see, record two hypotheses: one about the main functions of the dermis and one about the main functions of the epidermis. How are the cells in these layers specialized?
Hint: Observe both the appearance of the cells and the kinds of structures each skin layer contains.

Questions

1. Replacement skin created by cloning is not exactly the same as natural skin. Replacement skin lacks the specialized cells of the dermis. Why would this matter?

2. Explain the title of this activity.

3. Even though cloned skin cannot replace all of the abilities of human skin, why do you think using cloned skin to replace damaged skin is still valuable?

4. The epidermis is made of 25 to 30 layers of dead cells that are shed in the thousands every time you shower, shake hands, or scratch an itch. Explain how you think these cells are replaced by your body. After you have completed the chapter, improve your explanation with details you have learned.

Study Toolkit

These strategies will help you use this textbook to develop your understanding of science concepts and skills. To find out more about these and other strategies, refer to the Study Toolkit Overview, which begins on page 560.

Organizing Your Learning

Making Study Notes

Making study notes on a section of text will help you identify main ideas and state them in your own words. One approach is to change each heading within a section into a question, and then list details that answer the question. Be sure to use the key terms in your notes. Notes about Section 3.3 might begin like this:

> **Section 3.3:** How can humans maintain healthy body systems?
> - Various cultures have traditional treatments and cures for disease.
>   - **examples:** acupuncture, herbal remedies
> - Today's technologies allow doctors to perform surgeries without having to open up the body. This prevents infections that can cause death.
>   - **example:** Surgeons can use various forms of biophotonics, which are technologies using light. Includes endoscopy and surgical lasers

Use the Strategy

Read the first paragraph under the heading "Prenatal Care and Ultrasound" on page 109. After reading, follow the model above and make point-form study notes.

Reading Effectively

Asking Questions

While reading, stop to ask *who*, *what*, *when*, *where*, *why*, and *how* questions. Then continue reading to see if your questions are answered in the text.

When they are not, reread the text to see if you have misunderstood something or whether the answer to your question is not provided. This process helps you pay close attention to details in the text.

For example, questions you might ask while reading the "SARS" section on page 112 include the following:

- *What* is SARS?
- *How* is SARS treated?
- *Why* does SARS require a public health strategy?
- *Where* have SARS outbreaks occurred?

Use the Strategy

While reading the first two paragraphs on page 93, list at least four questions. As you read the rest of the section, record any answers you find. Follow up on unanswered questions with a partner.

Word Study

Word Origins

Some English words originated from words in ancient languages, such as Greek and Latin. Knowing the origin of a word may help you understand and remember it better. For example, the word *digestive* comes from the Latin *digerere*, meaning "to separate, divide, arrange." Knowing this might help you remember that the digestive system breaks food down into molecules that are either absorbed or eliminated.

Use the Strategy

The word *follicle* comes from the Latin word *folliculus*, meaning "little bag." Explain how knowing this word's origin can help you remember its current meaning.

3.1 Cells and Tissues

Key Terms
stem cell
embryonic stem cell

In a single-celled organism, such as the amoeba shown in **Figure 3.1**, the cell has to be able to do everything that is needed for the organism to survive. For example, the cell has to find food, break it down to release energy, respond to its environment, and eliminate wastes. Organelles in the amoeba, such as digestive vacuoles, perform these jobs. In more complex organisms, such as the whale in **Figure 3.1**, humans, and the plants you investigated in Chapter 2, these tasks are handled by *groups* of specialized cells.

What Factors Influence Cell Specialization in Animals?

Scientists estimate that there are between 75 and 100 trillion cells in the body of an adult human. Most of those cells are specialized to do certain tasks. Three main factors influence differentiation in animal cells:

- the contents of the cell's cytoplasm
- environmental conditions, such as temperature
- the influence of neighbouring cells

The Effect of Cytoplasm on Cell Specialization

Mitosis ensures that daughter cells receive identical sets of chromosomes. However, the contents of the cytoplasm may differ in each daughter cell. For example, one daughter cell may have more storage vacuoles than the other. Having more of these vacuoles will allow the cell to use more energy as it grows. Even when a human embryo is only a few hours old, the future of many of its cells—how they will specialize—has already been determined. This early specialization is partly because of differences in each cell's cytoplasm.

Figure 3.1 The amoeba on the left, shown at 200×, is about one hundredth of a millimetre long, while the blue whale below is over 30 m long. Despite their enormous size difference, both organisms solve the same basic challenges of life.

Chapter 3 Animals: From Cells to Systems • NEL

Figure 3.2 Siamese cats get their distinctive coat colour because only skin cells that experience cool temperatures during cell differentiation produce dark fur.

The Effect of Environmental Conditions on Cell Specialization

Cell specialization can also be affected by the environmental conditions a cell experiences as it develops. Such conditions include temperature and the presence or absence of certain nutrients. Differences in environmental conditions can also explain why cells with identical genes will develop differently. For example, in Siamese cats, only cells that develop at cool temperatures produce dark hair colours. Because the tips of the cat's feet, tail, ears, and nose are usually cooler than the rest of the body, the cat develops its distinctive dark "points," which can be seen in **Figure 3.2**.

The Effect of Neighbouring Cells on Cell Specialization

Nearby cells in the organism's body have one of the biggest influences on what a cell will become. When cells are close to one another, the substances produced by one cell can sometimes diffuse through a neighbouring cell's membrane. These substances can then change how the information in the DNA of the second cell gets expressed. For example, **Figure 3.3** shows where, in the developing embryo of a chick, neighbouring cells influence eye development in a specific location on the embryo.

Figure 3.3 The bluish area on this 12-day-old chick embryo shows where cells have already begun to differentiate into what will become an eye. This differentiation occurs, in part, through the influence of neighbouring cells.

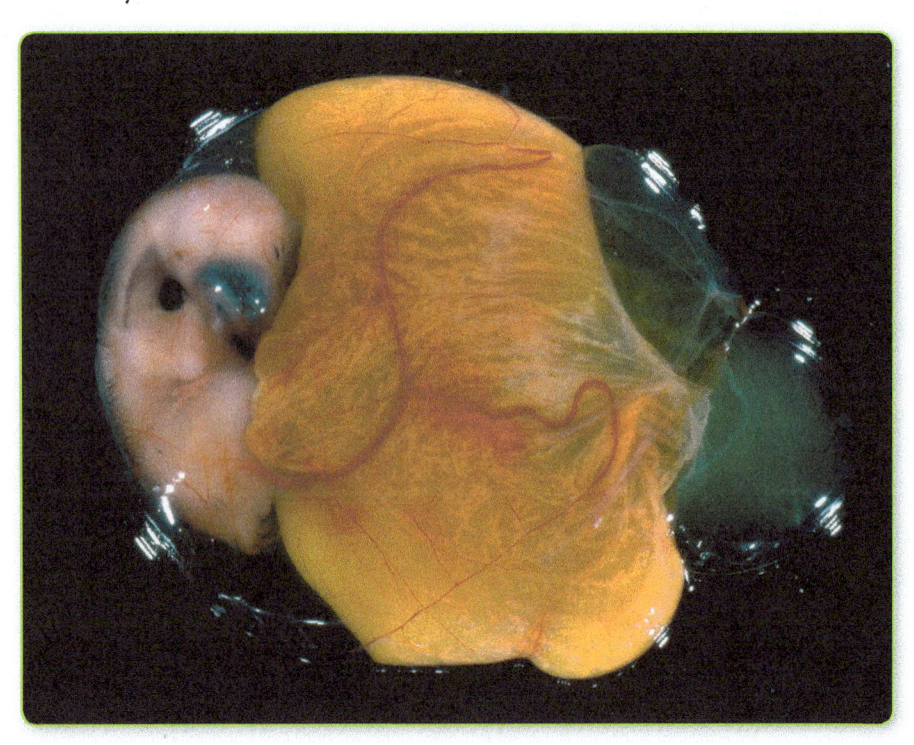

Why Abnormal Development Sometimes Occurs

Signals from the environment play an important role in normal development, and environmental factors are also often responsible when things go wrong, as shown in **Figure 3.4**.

Chemical contaminants in the environment have also been shown to trigger abnormal development. In humans, about 90 percent of problems in developing embryos can be traced to environmental factors, including a mother's exposure to harmful substances, such as heavy metals.

Figure 3.4 Development went off course in these leopard frogs. Biologists are unsure whether pollution, parasites, disease, or some other condition caused the deformities.

Similar Cell Conditions Form Similar Cells

As a cell matures, more of its genes get turned off or on by the effects of other cells or environmental conditions. One combination of active and inactive genes will produce a skeletal muscle cell. A different combination will produce a nerve cell. At some point, cells have had so many of their genes turned off that they stop dividing and live out their lives as mature, specialized cells. A muscle cell, for example, remains a muscle cell as long as it lives. It has left the cell cycle and no longer undergoes mitosis. It does not normally change to become a different type of cell.

Furthermore, cells that experience similar conditions—whether from the effects of other cells or environmental conditions such as temperature—become specialized to do similar jobs. Groups of similarly specialized cells form tissues.

Study Toolkit

Word Origins The word *striation* comes from a Modern Latin word meaning *strip* or *streak*. Look at the photograph of striated skeletal muscle on this page. How could word origin help you remember a feature of this muscle type?

Types of Tissues

It may surprise you to learn that although there are millions of different kinds of organisms on Earth, there are only a few different kinds of tissues. Animals—from worms to walruses—have four main tissues: *epithelial*, *muscle*, *nervous*, and *connective*. **Table 3.1** shows these major tissues, types of each, and how cross sections of them appear under a light microscope, each magnified about 250 or 300 times.

Table 3.1 Tissues in the Human Body

Tissue	Some Types	Appearance
Epithelial • line the surfaces of the body, both as a body covering and between internal organs • made of cells with strong connections between adjoining cell membranes, so they form a barrier	**Skin epithelia** • made of thin, flat cells that form sheets and act as a semi-permeable barrier between the inside and outside of a body	
	Columnar epithelia • made of columns of cells that line the small intestine (shown here), the stomach, and glands • may secrete mucus, have finger-like projections called cilia, and or absorb materials	
Muscle • designed to change their shape • act by shortening or lengthening	**Skeletal muscle** • made of cells that line up in the same direction, making the tissue look striped, or striated • attaches to bone, making it possible for the body to move • is found in limbs, like arms and legs, and places where the body needs support, such as around the lower abdomen and back	
	Smooth muscle • made of cells that are tapered at both ends and do not have a striated appearance • is found in blood vessels and the walls of internal organs like the esophagus and stomach • contracts more slowly than skeletal muscle, but its action can be sustained for a long time	
	Cardiac muscle • made of cells whose nuclei sometimes appear to be between cells • are branched and unevenly striated • contracts as a unit • found only in the heart	

88   NEL • Unit 1 Tissues, Organs, and Systems of Living Things

Table 3.1 continued

Tissue	Some Types	Appearance

Nervous
• made of cells called *neurons*, which have finger-like projections to receive and transfer signals
• coordinates body actions
	• are varied in their actions:
	  - some relay signals from the brain or spinal cord to muscles and glands
	  - others detect information from their environment (like the heat of a hot stove) and trigger the body's responses	

Connective • strengthens, supports, protects, binds, or connects cells and tissues • consists of cells in an extracellular matrix that can range from a liquid (in blood), to elastic materials that can stretch (in ligaments), to mineral deposits (in bone)	**Bone** • made of cells surrounded by calcium-hardened tissue through which blood vessels run • needed for movement, support, protection	
	Fat (adipose tissue) • made of large, tightly packed cells • found under the skin and around organs • needed for energy storage, padding and insulation	
	Blood • includes red blood cells, white blood cells, and platelets within a straw-coloured liquid matrix called plasma • transports nutrients and oxygen • clots when the skin is cut • attacks invaders such as bacteria and viruses	

Activity 3-2

Tissue Sleuth

In **Table 3.1**, you can see many examples of cells from different tissues in the human body. What characteristics differentiate each type of tissue?

Materials
- microviewer or compound microscope
- unidentified, prepared slides of various tissues from the human body

Procedure
1. Using a microviewer or a microscope, examine the tissue specimens provided.

2. Make a labelled biological drawing of a cell for each specimen. If you can, identify and label the cell membrane, cytoplasm, and nucleus, as well as any other structures you can see.

3. Use **Table 3.1** to identify the type of tissue shown in each specimen.

Questions
1. Briefly explain how the appearance of tissue, when magnified, gives you clues about the tissue's function and identity.

2. Write a short description below each of your drawings that states the function of that tissue in your body.

Sense of scale

No one has figured out precisely how many cells there are in a typical human body. Estimates range from 10 trillion to 100 trillion cells.

Learning Check

1. What is cell differentiation?
2. Create a web showing factors that affect cell specialization.
3. Name the four main types of animal tissues, and give examples of where they are found in the human body.
4. Skeletal muscle is also known as "voluntary" muscle, and smooth muscle as "involuntary" muscle. Explain why.

Stem Cells

As you learned in Chapter 2, plants have meristematic cells that remain unspecialized and continue dividing. Animals have similar cells, called **stem cells**. While an animal grows to adulthood, these stem cells perform a function similar to that of meristem cells—they produce more cells so the animal grows larger.

While animals like starfish and salamanders can regenerate some body parts, mammals can replace only small amounts of tissue, such as that needed for bone or skin repair. Human organs are formed in the embryo and the body cannot produce new ones.

As you can see in **Figure 3.5**, early in their development, human embryos have *totipotent* stem cells, which can become any kind of cell in the body. As the embryo develops, its stem cells become *pluripotent*. These stem cells are less versatile. They are capable of producing many, but not all types of cells. Late in development and after birth, people have only adult stem cells, which can produce only specific kinds of cells. For example, only skin stem cells can produce cells to repair skin, and only bone stem cells can repair bone.

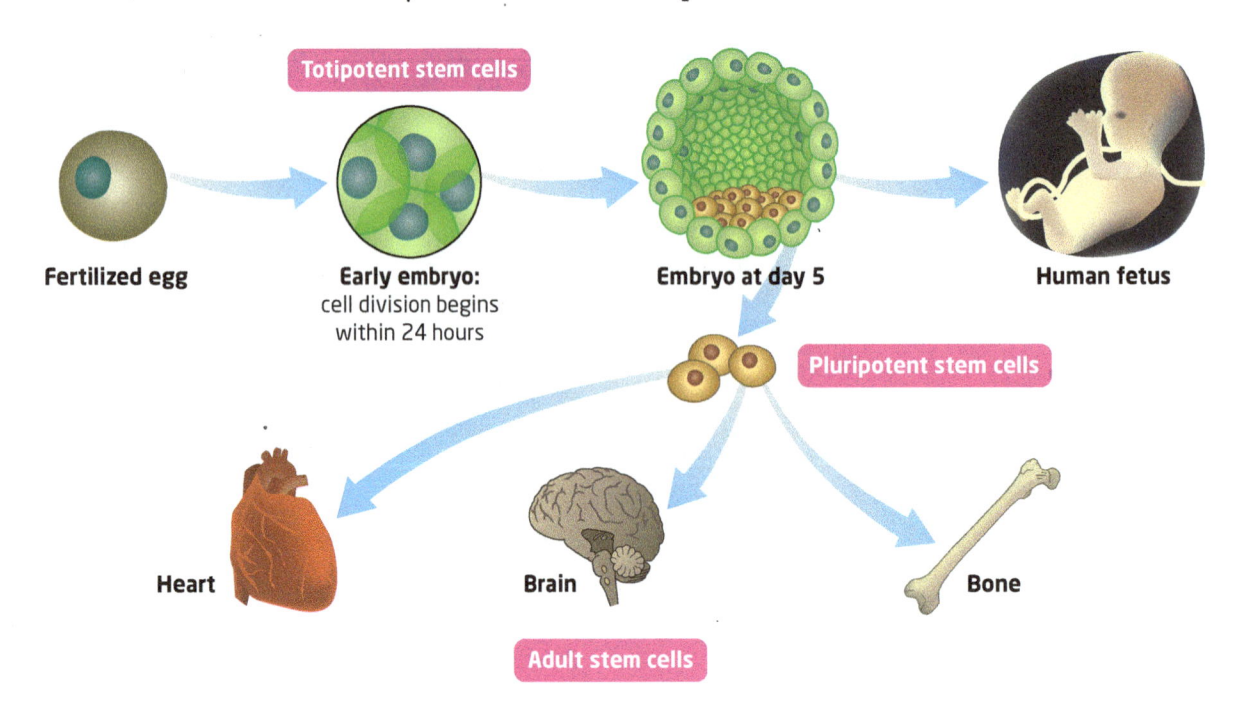

stem cell an unspecialized cell that can produce various specialized cells

Figure 3.5 Human stem cells become less versatile as they become more specialized.

Totipotent stem cells

Fertilized egg → Early embryo: cell division begins within 24 hours → Embryo at day 5 → Human fetus

Pluripotent stem cells

Heart — Brain — Bone

Adult stem cells

90 NEL • Unit 1 Tissues, Organs, and Systems of Living Things

The Medical Potential of Stem Cells

In 1968, two Canadian researchers, Dr. Ernest McCulloch and Dr. James Till, made an important discovery about the medical use of stem cells. The researchers showed that marrow transplanted from a healthy animal could restore blood cells in an animal that had undergone radiation therapy. Radiation, which can destroy rapidly dividing cells, is commonly used as a cancer treatment. Sometimes, radiation also destroys the patient's normal bone marrow cells. Then a bone marrow transplant is needed, as shown in **Figure 3.6**.

The Ethics of Using Embryonic Stem Cells

Embryonic stem cells are found in embryos that are very young—less than a week old. Under laboratory conditions, these totipotent stem cells are able to keep dividing for a year or even longer without ever differentiating. Embryonic stem cells are sometimes called "source" or "starter" cells because they can become any of the roughly 300 different types of human body tissue, making them valuable for research and medical treatments.

Despite the potential applications of embryonic stem cells, their use is not without problems. Scientists obtain these cells from eggs fertilized in vitro (outside the womb). Sources are usually unused embryos from fertility clinics. However, obtaining stem cells destroys the embryo. Some people consider this use to be taking a human life.

How might researchers avoid this problem? Recent studies have shown that some adult stem cells, such as those from the skin, can be transformed, or induced, into becoming pluripotent stem cells. However, most *induced pluripotent stem cells* are created using viruses, which could potentially damage the stem cells' DNA. As **Figure 3.7** shows, however, new research may soon offer a solution to this problem.

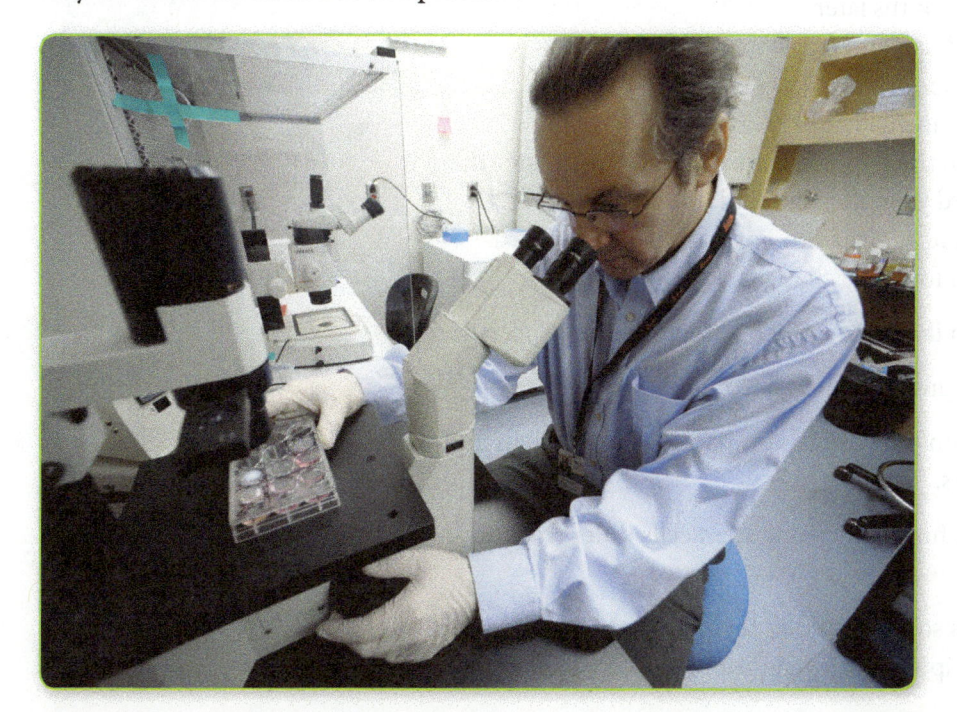

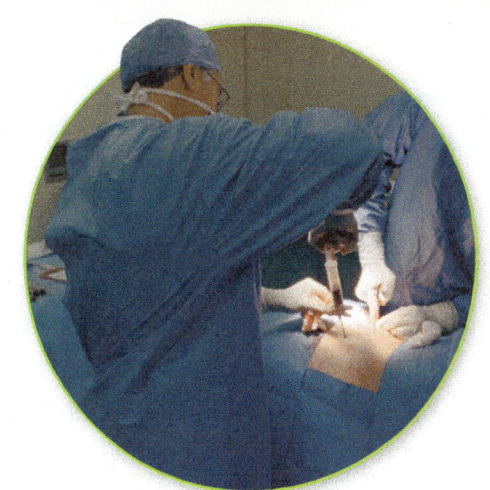

Figure 3.6 Traditional techniques used to harvest bone marrow for transplant (shown here) involve surgery. New techniques can harvest stem cells from a blood sample.

embryonic stem cell an unspecialized cell that can become any one of an organism's body cells

Go to **scienceontario** to find out more

Figure 3.7 In 2009, Andras Nagy (pictured here) and fellow researchers at Mount Sinai Hospital in Toronto successfully used DNA from a cabbage looper moth to induce pluripotent stem cells from adult skin cells. Unlike techniques that use viruses, this technique avoids the risk of damaging the stem cells' DNA.

Section 3.1 Review

Section Summary

- Cell specialization is influenced by the contents of an individual cell's cytoplasm, environmental factors such as temperature, and secretions from neighbouring cells.
- Animals have four main types of tissues: muscle, epithelial, connective, and nervous.
- Because stem cells have the potential to repair and replace damaged cells, they offer opportunities to develop new medical treatments. However, their use also raises some ethical questions.

Review Questions

C   **1.** Draw three types of specialized cells and state how their appearance relates to their function.

K/U   **2.** Match the images of tissues shown on the right to the correct function below.
   a. transports nutrients and oxygen
   b. transmits electrical signals
   c. covers the surface of the body
   d. assists in body movement

T/I   **3.** A toxic chemical was accidentally spilled by an industry into a river in early spring. A few months later, researchers retrieved fish and frogs with 20 times more abnormal growths than would normally be found. The next year, the growths were only 5 times greater than normal, and the third year after the spill, the number of abnormal growths had returned to normal levels. Provide a possible explanation for these changes.

A   **4.** What would happen if cells of a chick embryo did not specialize?

K/U   **5.** What features distinguish stem cells from other cells?

K/U   **6.** Create a table or Venn diagram to compare adult stem cells and embryonic stem cells.

C   **7.** Explain to a partner how embryonic stem cells differ from adult stem cells.

K/U   **8.** Why are researchers so interested in trying to induce adult stem cells to become pluripotent or even totipotent?

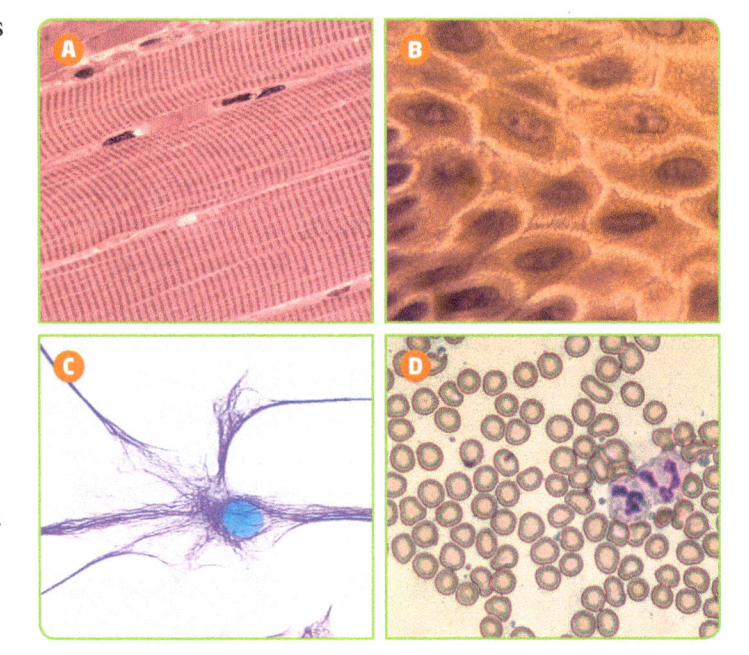

3.2 Organs and Systems

Key Terms
medical imaging technology

Unlike the glass catfish shown in **Figure 3.8**, most animals, including humans, do not have transparent skin. How, then, can we learn how the body functions and what is happening when it does not work as it should?

In earlier times, when a patient was ill, doctors sometimes performed exploratory surgery. This was the only way to look inside the body to try to see what was wrong. Today physicians can use a variety of **medical imaging technologies** instead. **Figure 3.9**, for example, shows the human body as viewed using some of the medical imaging technologies you will read about in this section.

medical imaging technology techniques used to form an image of a body's internal cells, tissues, and organs

Figure 3.8 In these glass catfishes, many organs are in plain sight because they have transparent skin.

Figure 3.9 This image of the human body was put together using several types of medical imaging technologies, as well as dissection and artwork.

Chapter 3 Animals: From Cells to Systems • NEL 93

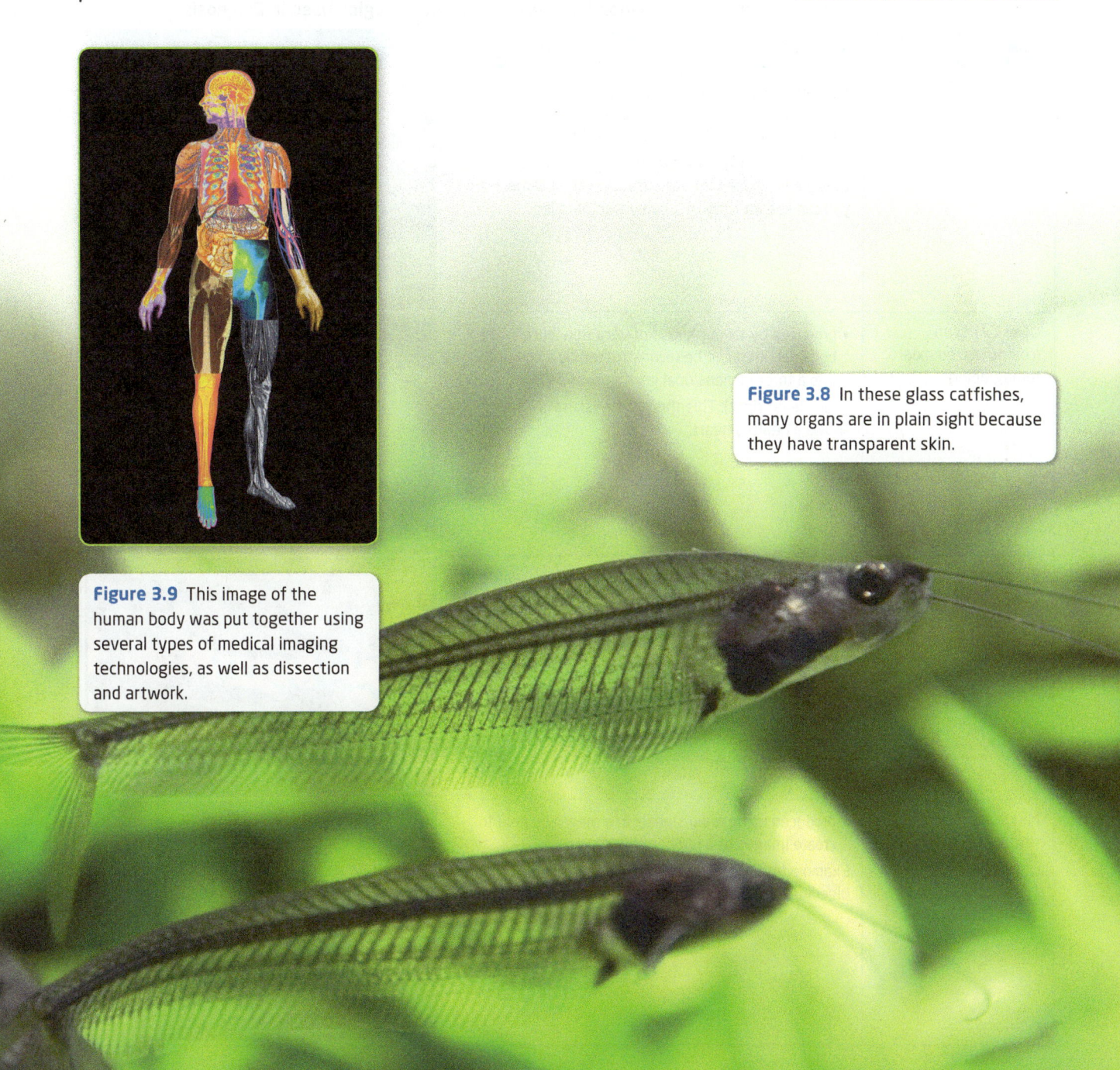

Which Technology Is Best?

Although physicians now have many ways to look inside the human body, their decision about which technology to use is not always straightforward. **Table 3.2** summarizes some of the main medical imaging technologies used today. A physician's decision about which technology to use often depends on a balance between wanting an accurate diagnosis for a reasonable cost, with as little negative impact (pain, anxiety, sickness) on the patient as possible. For example, an X ray is the most widely available technology, but details of organs like the brain are not visible. To diagnose a problem with brain functioning, specialists often start with instruments like a CT scanner, which you can see in **Figure 3.10**.

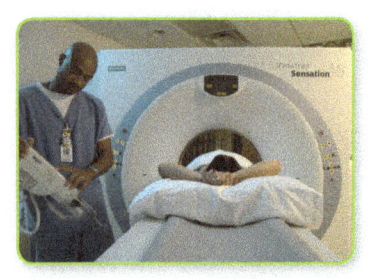

Figure 3.10 CT scans are an expensive, but accurate method used to diagnose heart disease, cancer, and various other diseases.

Table 3.2 Common Medical Imaging Technologies Used in Diagnosis

Type	Technology	Example
X ray	• produced by transmitting a wavelength of electromagnetic radiation through the body to expose photographic film on the other side Example (at right): X rays go through soft tissue, so they are best used for hard tissue, such as bone. Here you can see an X ray of a badly fractured leg.	
CT or CAT scan (computerized axial tomography)	• produced by taking X rays of very thin "slices" of a body part that can be reconstructed by a computer into a three-dimensional image Example (at right): This three-dimensional CT scan shows a healthy heart.	
Ultrasound (medical sonography)	• produced by directing high frequency sound waves at a part of the body, usually from a microphone attached to a computer • show real-time movement of body parts like the heart; useful for watching organ function Example (at right): This ultrasound image has been coloured to more clearly show blood flow through a neck artery. Blood flow is greatest when red and slowest when green.	
MRI scan (magnetic resonance imaging)	• produced using radio signals in a magnetic field to create images of body parts Example (at right): This MRI scan shows sites of bleeding in the brain, which has resulted in a stroke.	

94 NEL • Unit 1 Tissues, Organs, and Systems of Living Things

Advances in Diagnosis

Endoscopy, in which a tiny camera and a light attached to a flexible tube are inserted into the body, provides options for diagnosis as well as treatment. **Figure 3.11** shows two ways a stomach (gastric) ulcer might be diagnosed. An ulcer is a hole in the protective mucous lining of the stomach or intestine. This hole allows *gastric juices* to start digesting body tissue, causing a burning sensation and pain. Such ulcers are sometimes diagnosed using a barium X ray. The patient drinks a "barium milkshake" that, when X-rayed, shows the lining of the stomach and any ulcerations or tumours. However, since this technique uses radiation, other techniques, such as endoscopy, are sometimes preferred.

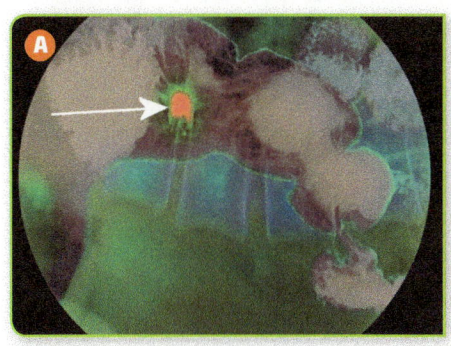

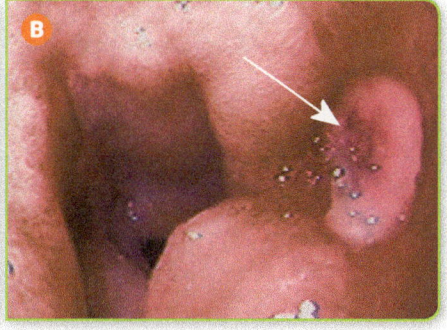

Figure 3.11 In **A**, you can see a barium X ray, which is a common means of diagnosing a stomach ulcer. In **B**, you can see an ulcer as seen through an endoscope. Endoscopy provides an alternative way to diagnose an ulcer without using radiation.

The Body's Organization: A Hierarchy

Advances in technology have also led to a better understanding of how bodies are organized and how various parts interact. For example, scientists know that organs, such as the heart, consist of several types of tissues working together to perform a task, such as pumping the blood throughout your body. As part of an organ system, the activities of different organs are co-ordinated to work together. In **Figure 3.12**, you can see that the body's cells are organized in a hierarchy, from cells to tissues, to organs, to systems.

The circulatory system moves blood throughout the human body.

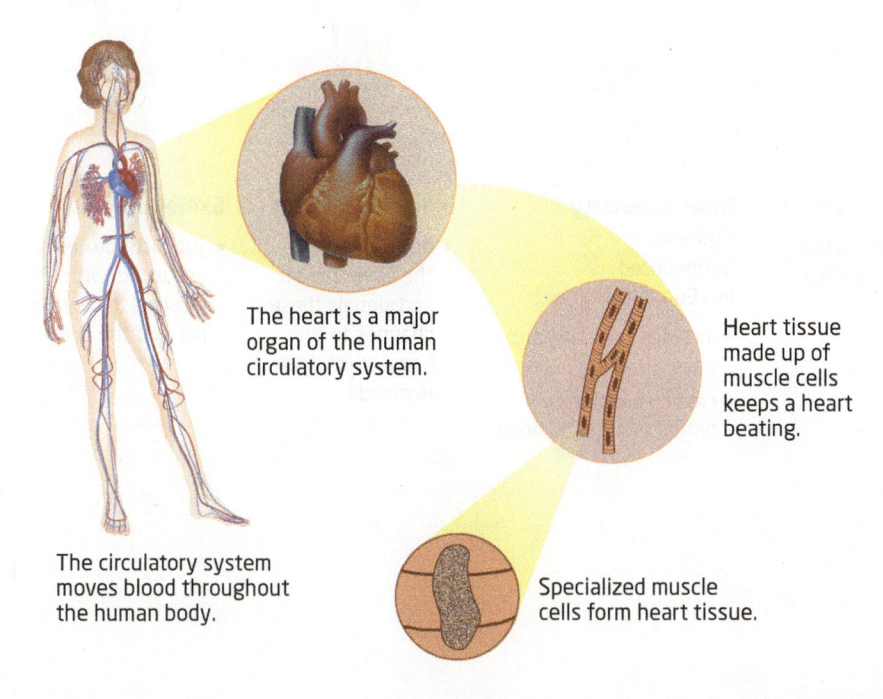

The heart is a major organ of the human circulatory system.

Heart tissue made up of muscle cells keeps a heart beating.

Specialized muscle cells form heart tissue.

Figure 3.12 Each system in the human body has a specific function. It accomplishes this function through the co-ordination of its organs. Each organ is made of tissues, which in turn are made of groupings of specialized cells.

Chapter 3 Animals: From Cells to Systems • NEL **95**

Human Organ Systems

Figure 3.13 The main functions of the human body to sustain life are accomplished by 11 organ systems working together.

As shown in **Figure 3.13**, the 11 organ systems of the human body keep you alive and healthy. In the rest of this section, you will focus on three of these systems—the digestive, respiratory, and circulatory systems—and how they interact in ways that are critical for survival.

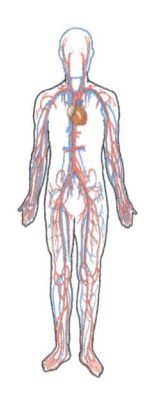

Circulatory System
- transports blood, nutrients, gases, and wastes

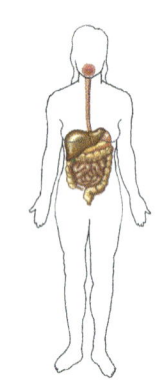

Digestive System
- takes in food and breaks it down
- absorbs nutrients
- removes solid waste from the body

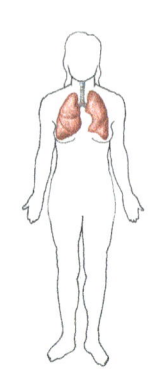

Respiratory System
- controls breathing
- exchanges gases in lungs

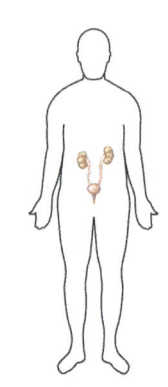

Excretory System
- removes liquid wastes from the body

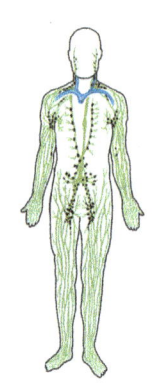

Immune System
- defends the body against infections

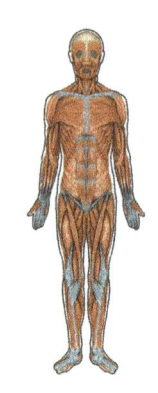

Muscular System
- works with the bones to move parts of the body

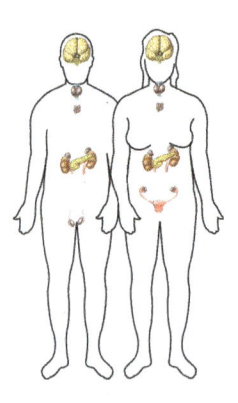

Endocrine System
- manufactures and releases hormones that act, along with the nervous system, to keep various body systems in balance

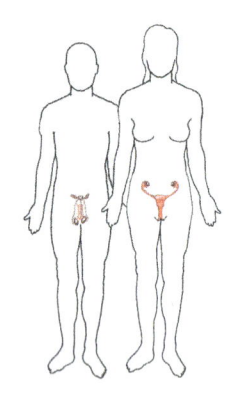

Reproductive System
- includes reproductive organs for producing offspring

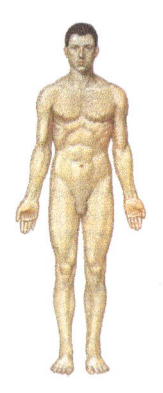

Integumentary System
[pronounced in-TEG-u-MEN-tar-ee]
- includes skin, hair, and nails
- creates a waterproof barrier around the body

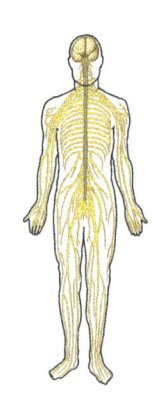

Nervous System
- detects changes in the environment and signals these changes to the body, which then responds

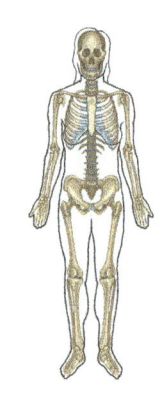

Skeletal System
- supports, protects, and works with muscles to move parts of the body

96 NEL • Unit 1 Tissues, Organs, and Systems of Living Things

Digestive system

As shown in **Figure 3.14**, organs forming the human digestive system mechanically and chemically break down food to produce nutrient molecules that the body's cells can absorb and use.

A

salivary glands
pharynx
esophagus
liver
duodenum
gall bladder
small intestine
tongue
stomach
pancreas
colon
rectum
anus

B

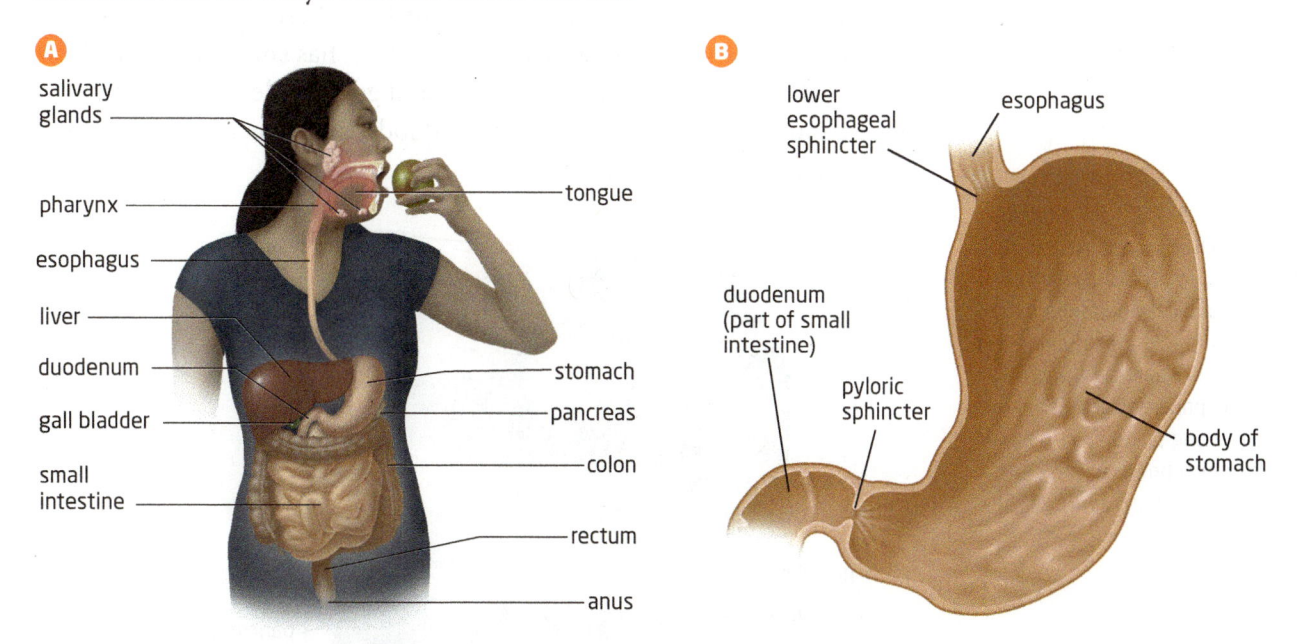

lower esophageal sphincter
esophagus
duodenum (part of small intestine)
pyloric sphincter
body of stomach

Figure 3.14 Diagram **A** shows the organs of the digestive system. On average, it takes 24 to 33 hours for each meal to complete its passage through the digestive tract. Diagram **B** shows the stomach, a major organ of the digestive system.

The Fate of a Meal

Digestion begins in the mouth, where the teeth begin the mechanical breakdown of food into smaller pieces. An enzyme in saliva, called amylase, starts the chemical breakdown. After the food is swallowed, it passes through the *pharynx* into a muscular tube called the *esophagus*. At this point, the food is in small chunks. The muscular walls of the esophagus contract and relax, pushing each chunk of food along until it gets to the stomach.

Gastric Juices Get to Work

In the stomach, the food chunks are surrounded by gastric juices that are secreted by the epithelial tissue that lines the stomach. These juices, which continue the chemical breakdown of the food, include hydrochloric acid and the enzyme pepsin. One of the reasons the gastric juices must be acidic is that pepsin, which breaks down protein, needs an acidic environment in which to function. The stomach lining also secretes *mucus*, which protects the stomach wall from breaking down in the presence of those protein-digesting juices.

Nerves in the stomach wall sense the presence of food and signal the stomach's muscle tissue to mix the contents, continuing the mechanical breakdown. Due to actions of the gastric juices and the churning of the stomach muscles, the partially digested food breaks down to a liquid.

> **Study Toolkit**
>
> **Making Study Notes** You can use the study notes model from page 84 for short sections of text as well as long. Practise the model using the section on gastric juices.

The Small Intestine

When the meal is fully mixed, a round muscle at the bottom of the stomach—called a *sphincter*—relaxes and some of the contents of the stomach are released into the *small intestine*. The first metre of the small intestine is called the *duodenum*, which is where most digestion takes place. This structure, shown in **Figure 3.15**, has small tubes called ducts that connect to the pancreas, liver, and gall bladder. These organs release more digestive enzymes into the duodenum, which completes the chemical breakdown of the food.

Figure 3.15 The liver produces bile, which is stored in the gall bladder. Bile breaks up globs of fat into small droplets. Pancreatic enzymes break the fat down into even smaller particles. Secretions from the pancreas are also critical for digesting proteins into amino acids, which body cells use to build new proteins.

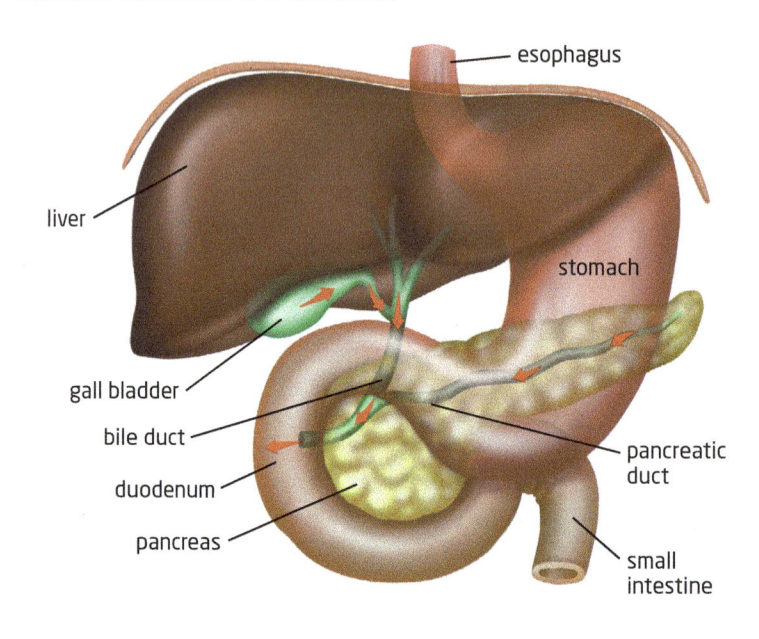

Sense of scale

Villi and microvilli increase the surface area of the small intestine dramatically. A simple tube of the same length would have an inner surface area of only 0.5 m². Instead, the specialized structure of the inner wall of the small intestine has an area of approximately 250 m²–the size of a volleyball court.

When the digested food moves into the remaining length of the small intestine, it is ready to be absorbed into the body. The small intestine is covered with millions of interior folds, called villi and microvilli. These villi, shown in **Figure 3.16**, maximizes the surface area over which nutrients and water can be absorbed into the bloodstream.

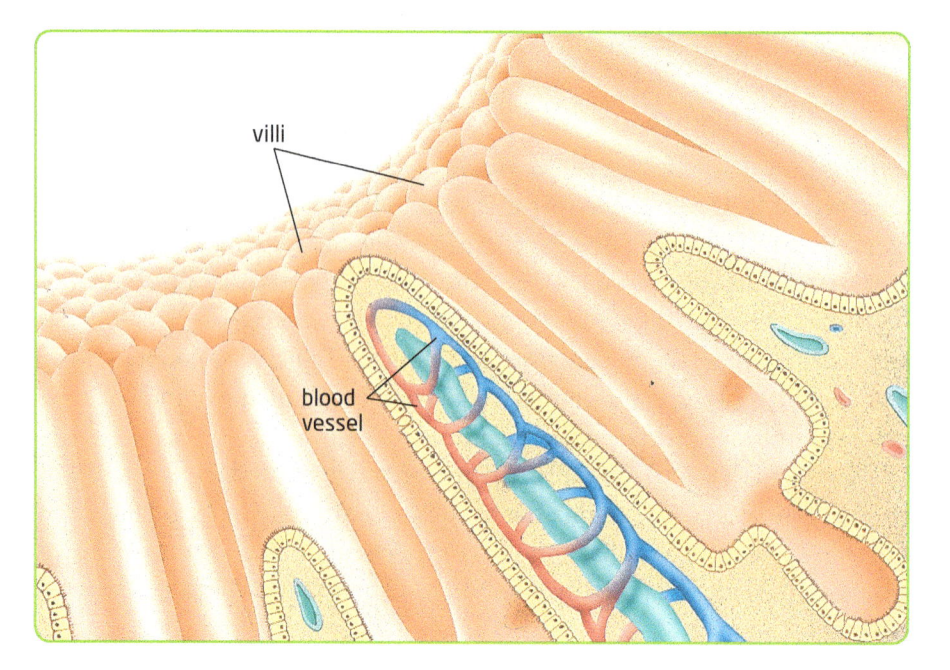

Figure 3.16 The small intestine is between 6 and 10 m long in an adult.

98 NEL • Unit 1 Tissues, Organs, and Systems of Living Things

The Large Intestine

The final organ in the digestive system is the *large intestine*, which includes the *colon*, *rectum*, and *anus*. In humans, the large intestine has a larger diameter and a shorter length than the small intestine. The large intestine's main functions are to absorb water, vitamins, and various salts from the digested food and to eliminate undigested food through the anus as feces. Most of the material in the cell walls of plants, for example, cannot be broken down in the human digestive system and must be eliminated. The large intestine also contains bacteria, such as those shown in **Figure 3.17**. These bacteria finish the process of breaking down food and also produce essential nutrients, such as vitamin K.

> **Learning Check**
>
> 1. What is an organ system?
> 2. In what ways are human organ systems similar to machines?
> 3. Look back to **Figure 3.12**. In your own words, or with a diagram or graphic organizer, explain how cells, organs, tissues, and systems are related.
> 4. Look back at the 11 body systems shown in **Figure 3.13**. Which system is not critical for the maintenance of the body? What is its function?

Figure 3.17 One species of bacteria, *Escherichia coli* (*E. coli*), is common in the large intestine. Most strains of *E. coli* cause no harm, and some benefit humans by taking up space and nutrients that might otherwise be inviting to dangerous bacteria. However, some types of *E. coli* can cause death in people with weakened immune systems.

The Excretory System

The digestive system is responsible for eliminating solid waste, but what about the body's liquid wastes? The excretory system, which you can see in **Figure 3.18**, takes care of these. Water and other materials absorbed through walls of the large intestine move into blood vessels. As blood passes through the kidneys, it is filtered and wastes are removed. As the blood is filtered, urine containing water and unneeded salts is formed. The urine is then stored in the bladder. When the bladder is full, the urine is flushed from the body.

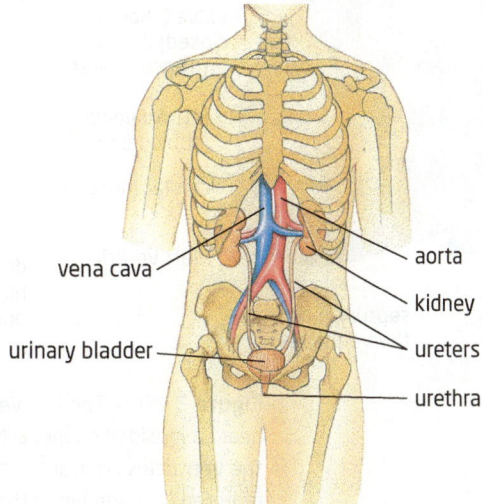

Figure 3.18 The excretory system eliminates liquid wastes from the body. To perform this task, the excretory system must interact with the digestive and circulatory systems.

Chapter 3 Animals: From Cells to Systems • NEL

Circulatory System

The circulatory system picks up and transports nutrients and oxygen to cells and carries wastes to the organs responsible for eliminating them from the body. **Figure 3.19** shows how the parts of the circulatory system branch throughout the body.

When the heart contracts, it produces pressure on the blood in the circulatory system. This pressure pushes blood through the body. Flexible flaps of tissue called *valves* are found throughout the circulatory system, including the heart and veins. They open when blood is pushed through them, and then close to prevent blood from flowing backward.

As **Figure 3.20** shows, the structure of the heart allows two separate paths through which the blood circulates. Blood that returns from the body is deoxygenated (has had its oxygen removed by body cells) and carries the body's carbon dioxide waste from cellular respiration. The first path the blood takes is therefore from the heart's right atrium to its right ventricle, which pumps the blood through the *pulmonary artery* to the lungs. There the blood eliminates carbon dioxide and picks up oxygen. This oxygenated blood then goes back to the heart, to its left atrium, and then to the left ventricle. From the left ventricle, it is pumped out through the *aorta*, a huge artery, to the rest of the body. Some of this blood goes to the heart itself, which, like all other organs, needs a constant supply of oxygenated blood in order to keep functioning.

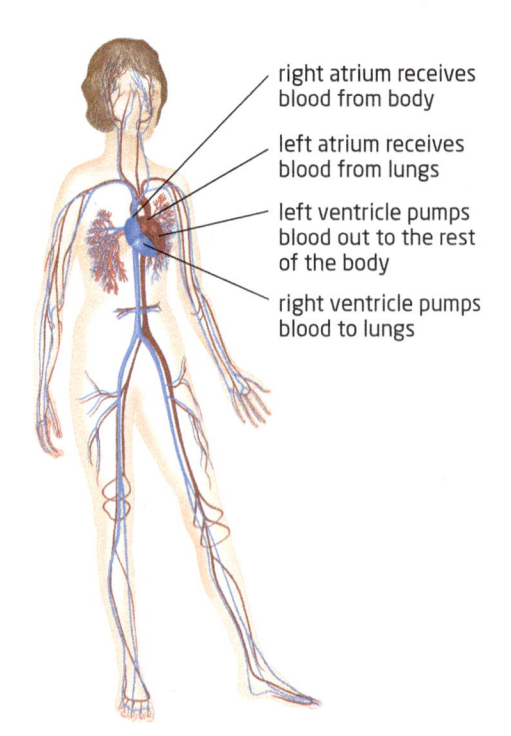

Figure 3.19 Arteries (shown in red) carry blood from the heart to all body parts. Veins (shown in blue) carry blood from body parts back to the heart. Along its pathways through the body, blood interacts with every other organ system.

- right atrium receives blood from body
- left atrium receives blood from lungs
- left ventricle pumps blood out to the rest of the body
- right ventricle pumps blood to lungs

A Heart Structure

- superior vena cava brings blood from the head and arms
- arteries
- right semilunar valve (shown closed) controls entrance to pulmonary artery
- right atrium
- right AV valve (shown open)
- right ventricle
- inferior vena cava brings blood from the trunk and legs
- aorta
- pulmonary artery carries blood to the lungs
- left atrium
- left semilunar valve (shown closed) controls entrance to aorta
- left AV valve (shown open)
- cardiac muscles
- left ventricle
- septum separates the ventricles

B Blood Flow in the Heart

- oxygenated blood to body
- deoxygenated blood to lungs
- oxygenated blood from lungs
- deoxygenated blood from body

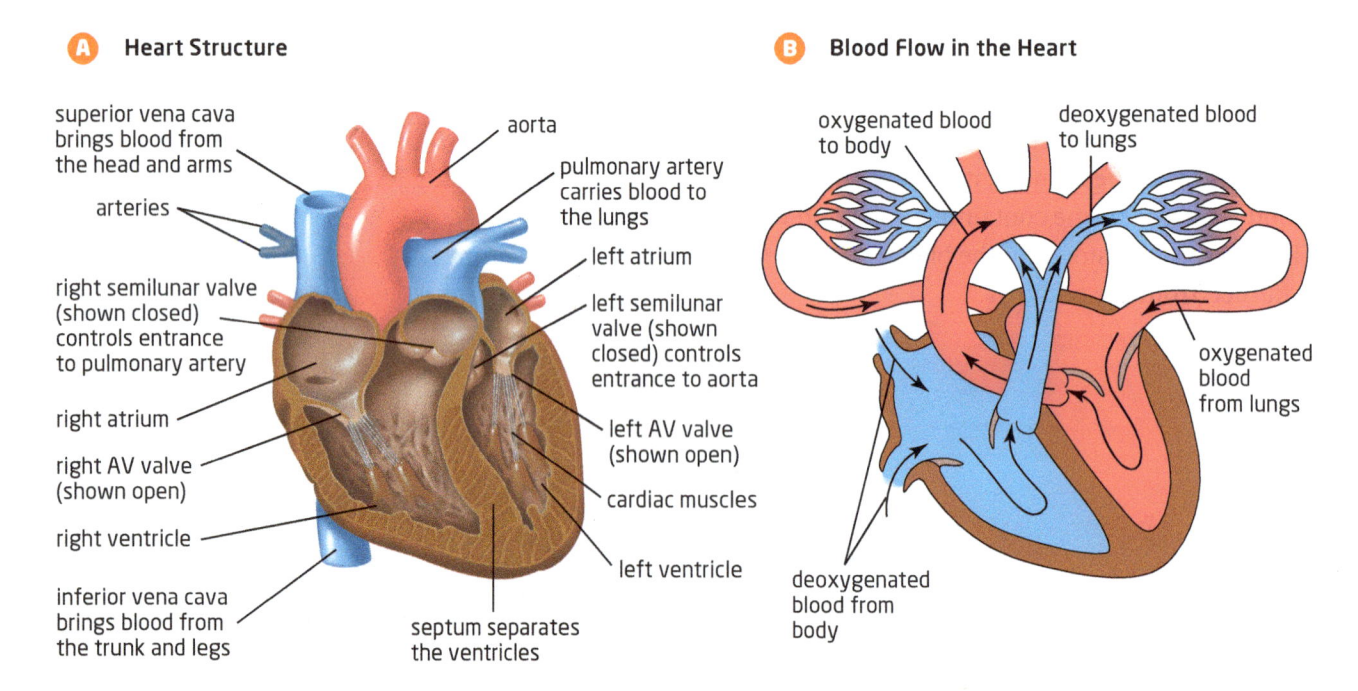

Figure 3.20 A The left ventricle is more muscular than the right, giving the heart a lopsided shape. **B** Note that the atria contract at the same time, and the ventricles contract at the same time. Thus, only two contractions are required to pump blood through all four chambers.

Same Task, Different Systems

All multicellular organisms have a way of getting oxygen to their cells. Some circulatory systems, like those of insects, are said to be *open*. They have one major vessel that empties oxygenated blood into parts of the body. In these places, cells are bathed in blood. Movements of body muscles take the blood back to be collected by the single vessel. In contrast, mammals and birds have a *closed* circulatory system—the blood stays in arteries and veins.

Fish have two-chambered hearts (one atrium and one ventricle), and amphibians have three-chambered hearts, as shown in **Figure 3.21**. The frog's heart has two atria, but only one ventricle. This means there is some mixing of oxygenated and deoxygenated blood, so some of the blood that is pumped back to the body has not passed through the lungs. However, the moist skin of frogs means that some oxygen diffuses directly through their skin, ensuring that their cells get enough oxygen.

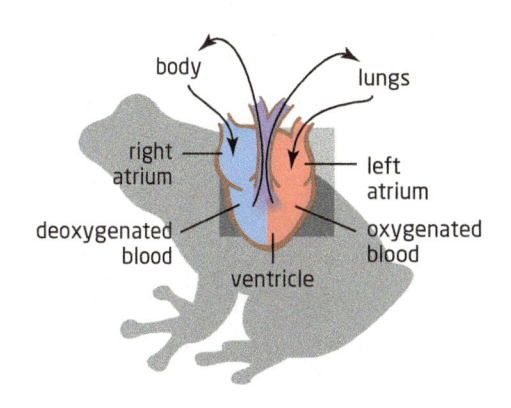

Figure 3.21 Amphibians like this frog have a three-chambered heart.

Activity 3-3

Changing Your Pulse Rate

Your pulse is produced by blood surging through your arteries each time your heart "beats." It is one indicator of how well your circulatory system is working. What factors affect the rate at which your heart pumps blood? Measure your pulse rate to find out.

Caution: Do not do this activity if you have any health problems that may put you at risk.

Materials
- watch or timer

Procedure
1. Locate one of your radial arteries, on the inside of your wrist in line with your thumb. Find your pulse using one or two fingers, not your thumb because your thumb has a pulse.
2. Using a watch or timer, count the number of pulses you feel in 15 s while you are sitting comfortably at rest. Multiply the number by 4 to obtain your pulse rate per minute. Record your results.
3. Stand up and run in place for 1 min. Immediately measure and record your pulse rate.
4. Rest for 2 min and measure and record your pulse rate again.

Questions
1. Using your results, explain the relationship between exercise and pulse rate. Suggest an explanation for this relationship.
2. Why is regular exercise good for your heart? What kind of heart tissue, in particular, would benefit from exercise?

Sense of scale

If the arteries, veins, and capillaries in your body were arranged end to end, they would stretch a distance of approximately 160 000 km.

Capillaries: Helping Systems Interact

Arteries and veins, shown in **Figure 3.22**, are connected by capillaries. Capillaries are extremely small, thin-walled blood vessels. They are only one epithelial cell thick! The areas where the branches of capillaries are close to one another are called capillary beds.

The capillaries bring blood into close contact with the tissues in organs throughout the body. For example, as you saw in **Figure 3.16**, capillaries bring blood into contact with the small intestine's villi and microvilli. There, blood picks up nutrients from digested food and delivers the nutrients to cells in the body. And as you will see on page 104, capillaries also bring the blood into close contact with tissue in the lungs, where it picks up oxygen. In every tissue of every organ in the human body, capillaries deliver blood that is rich in oxygen and nutrients. At the same time, blood in the capillaries picks up wastes from cells and transports them to the kidneys and lungs, where they are removed from the bloodstream.

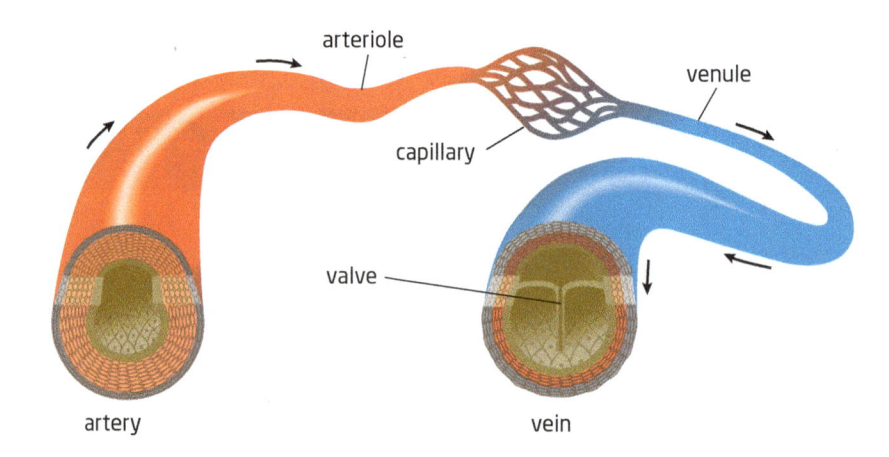

Figure 3.22 Veins are lined with valves that prevent the backflow of blood as it travels back to the heart. Veins have thinner walls than arteries, which have thicker, more muscular walls that expand when the heart contracts.

Heart Disease and Stroke

The delivery of blood is essential for the proper functioning of all of the other systems in the human body. Therefore, it is important that the heart works well. Unfortunately, there are an estimated 70 000 heart attacks each year in Canada, about 25 percent of which result in death.

The two most common causes of heart disease are hypertension (high blood pressure) and arteriosclerosis. Arteriosclerosis is a thickening of the walls of the arteries, which narrows the passageway for blood, as shown in **Figure 3.23**. Hypertension and arteriosclerosis can cause the formation of *blood clots*. If a blood clot breaks free, it may flow to a coronary artery and block a vessel, causing a *heart attack*. If the blood clot reaches the brain, it may block a vessel there, causing a *stroke*. When a stroke occurs, part of the brain is damaged due to oxygen deprivation. A type of surgery called angioplasty, shown in **Figure 3.24**, uses a balloon or laser to try to open clogged arteries.

Figure 3.23 An accumulation of cholesterol or other fatty substances–called plaque–can restrict blood flow through arteries.

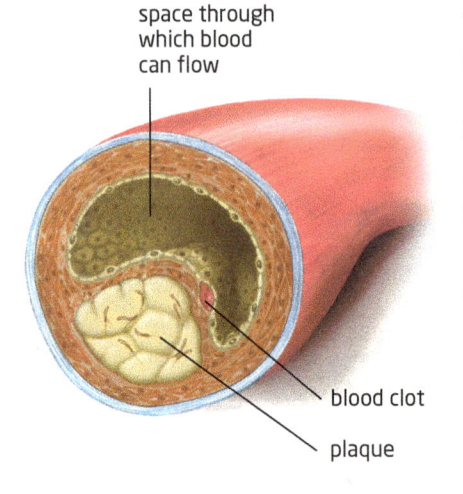

Figure 3.24 During an angioplasty, a surgeon inserts a plastic tube into an artery in an arm or leg and threads it all the way to the heart. When the tube reaches the blockage in the coronary artery, the surgeon inflates a balloon at the end of the tube to break up a clot or open up a vessel clogged with plaque. This procedure allows blood to pass through.

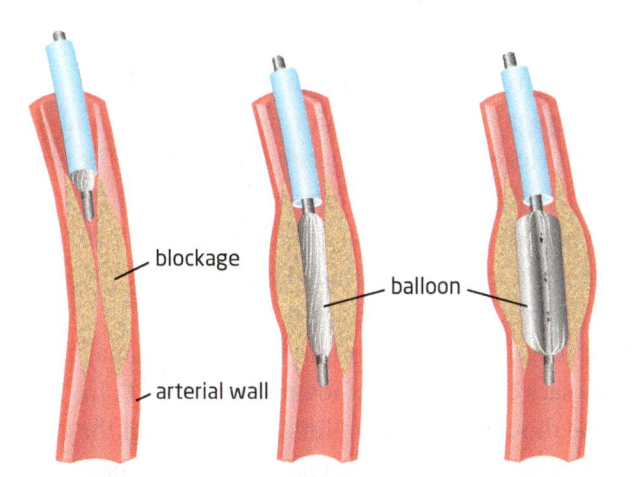

Suggested Investigation
Real World Investigation 3-A, Heart Disease: Making the Public Aware, on page 116

The Respiratory System

The organs of the respiratory system, shown in **Figure 3.25**, are responsible for the body's gas exchange, bringing oxygen into the body and getting rid of carbon dioxide. The respiratory system is connected to the circulatory system. One system could not do its work without the proper functioning of the other.

When you breathe, muscle contractions cause your rib cage to move up and out and your diaphragm to move down. This causes air to be pulled into your body through your nose or mouth. The air passes by epithelial cells that have microscopic, hair-like projections called *cilia*. These cells also secrete mucus. The mucus and cilia help keep foreign particles, such as dust and bacteria, out of your body.

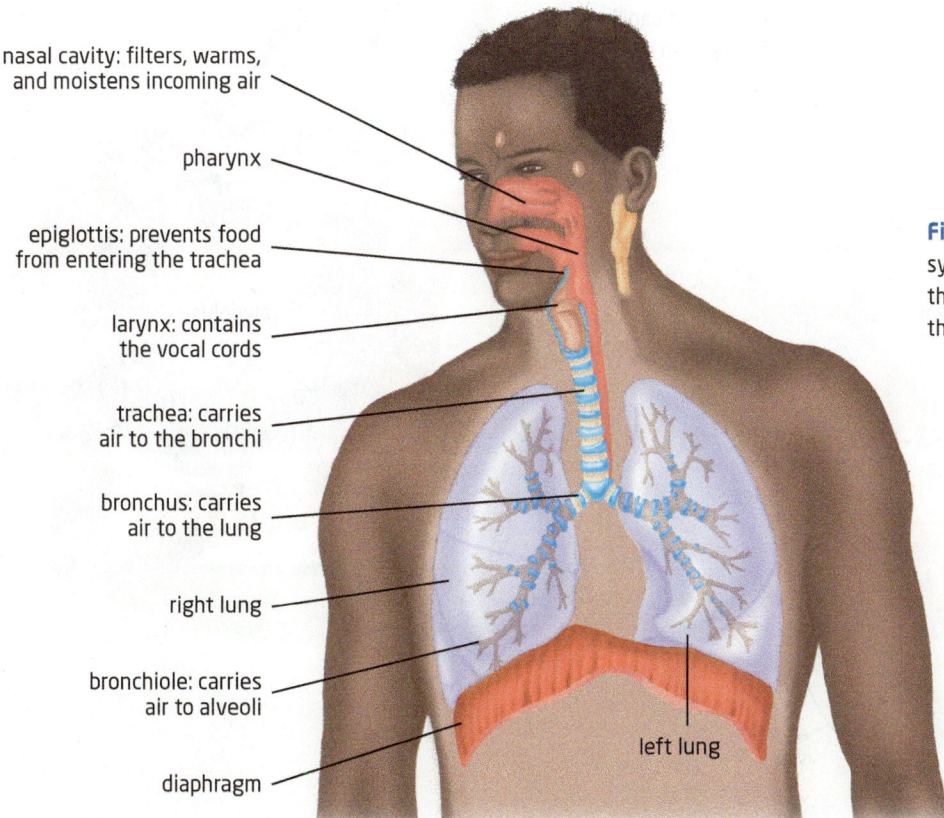

Figure 3.25 The respiratory system consists of the lungs and the airways that connect them to the outside world.

Chapter 3 Animals: From Cells to Systems • NEL   103

Through Smaller and Smaller Tubes

Once through the nasal passages and pharynx, the air moves into the *trachea*. A muscular flap, the epiglottis, opens so air can pass. When food is in the passage, the epiglottis closes so no food gets in the trachea. The air passes into branching tubes called the *bronchi* (singular bronchus). Each bronchus then continues to branch into smaller tubes called *bronchioles*. Muscle tissue in the walls of bronchioles allows the diameters of the tubes to contract or relax to control the amount of air entering the lung.

After entering the bronchioles, the air passes into increasingly smaller tubes until it ends up in tiny sacs called *alveoli*, shown in **Figure 3.26**. In the alveoli, the air is only one thousandth of a millimetre away from the bloodstream. This thin layer of epithelial tissue keeps most inhaled bacteria and viruses out of the bloodstream, but still allows gases to cross (oxygen out of the lungs and carbon dioxide back in).

Your red blood cells contain a protein called hemoglobin, which attaches to oxygen molecules. As shown in **Figure 3.26**, when deoxygenated red blood cells pass by the alveoli, the hemoglobin they contain causes them to pick up oxygen. The oxygenated blood then travels throughout the body, delivering its oxygen to cells that need it for cellular respiration.

When your chest muscles and diaphram relax, you exhale and the carbon dioxide in the alveoli is carried out of your body. Your body constantly monitors the amount of carbon dioxide being carried in the blood. When the level of carbon dioxide is too high, your breathing rate increases so this waste product can be eliminated more quickly.

> **Sense of place**
>
> People normally have around 13 kilopascals (kPa) of oxygen in their bloodstream. A person with 6 kPa is generally close to death. However, in 2009, a team of researchers at the top of Mount Everest (8850 m) were shocked to measure their oxygen levels at between 2.5 and 4 kPa.

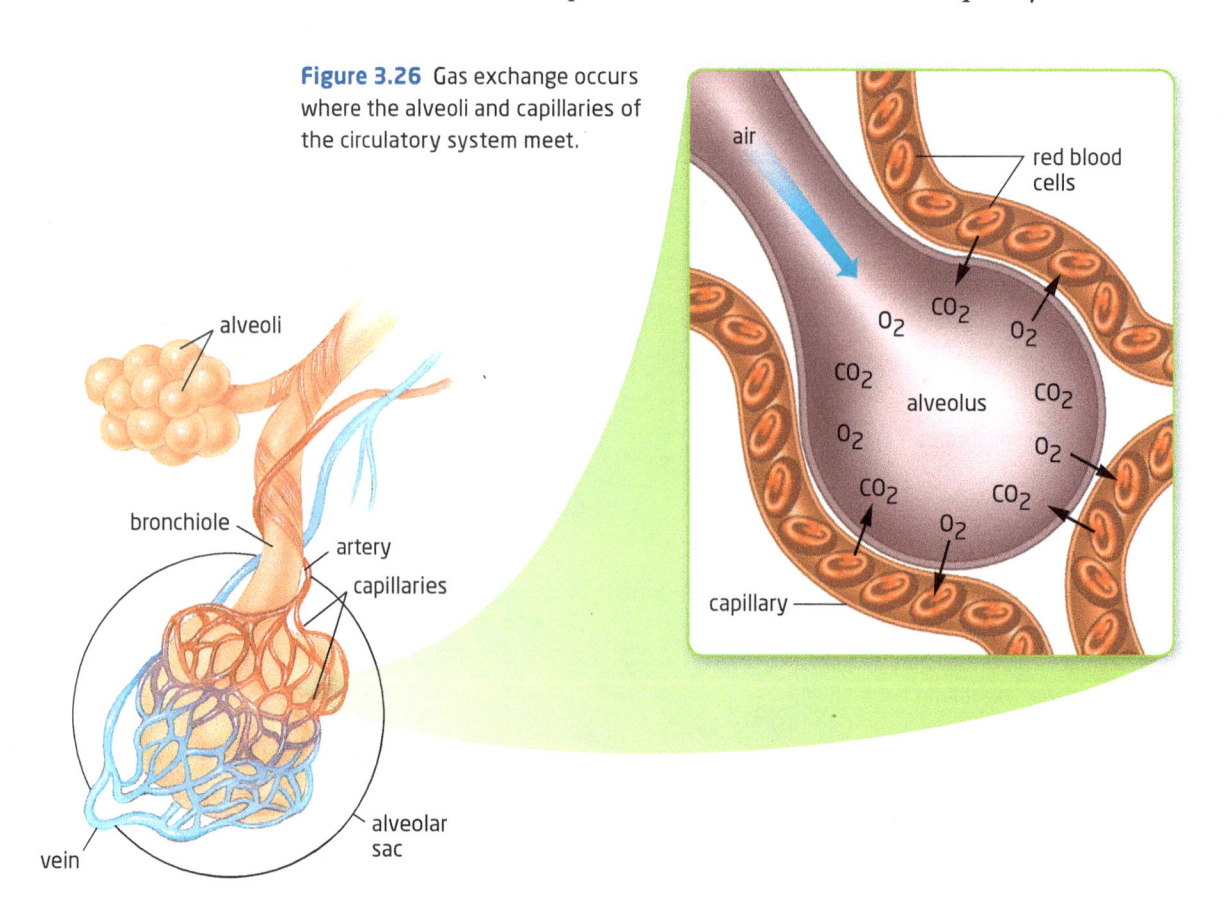

Figure 3.26 Gas exchange occurs where the alveoli and capillaries of the circulatory system meet.

104 NEL • Unit 1 Tissues, Organs, and Systems of Living Things

Diseases Related to Smoking

You probably know that smoking is not good for your health, but do you know why? One problem is that smoking damages the cilia, preventing them from sweeping foreign particles out on cells of the respiratory system. Another is that cigarette smoke is filled with more than 4000 chemicals, including over 40 that are known carcinogens. In addition, cigarette smoke has over 1000 times the level of carbon monoxide that is known to be harmful to human health. Cigarette smoke also contains tar, which accumulates in the lungs. Tar is responsible for many respiratory problems. People who smoke a pack of cigarettes a day absorb about 250 mL of tar into their lungs each year. **Figure 3.27** shows how lung tissue can be damaged by smoking.

> **Study Toolkit**
>
> **Asking Questions** Read the section "Diseases Related to Smoking" and write at least four who, what, when, where, why, and how questions. Reread the text to find answers, or do your own research.

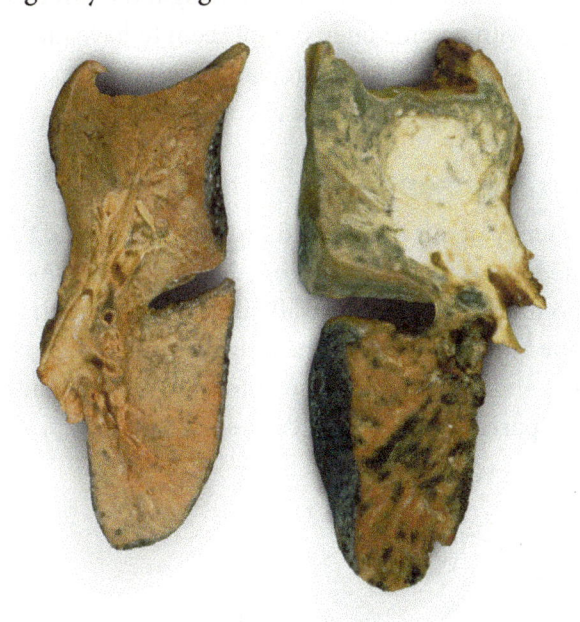

Figure 3.27 The cross section of the lung on the left looks mostly healthy, although some blackened tissue can be seen. This tissue may have been damaged by environmental conditions. The cross section on the right shows a lung destroyed by cancer. You can see a large white tumour and many black tar deposits due to cigarette smoking.

Other Gas Exchange Systems

Birds, many amphibians, reptiles, and other mammals have lungs just as humans do. Other animals, like the fish shown in **Figure 3.28**, have different ways to accomplish the same gas exchange function.

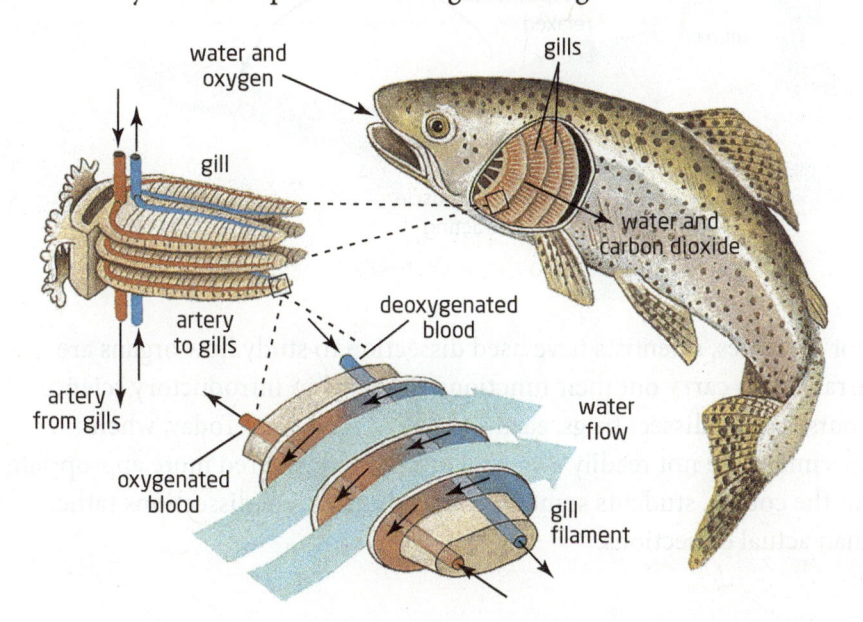

Figure 3.28 A fish draws water through its mouth and over its gills. As water passes over the gills, oxygen diffuses into the adjacent blood vessels. At the same time, carbon dioxide diffuses out.

> **Learning Check**
>
> 5. Draw and label a diagram showing the four chambers of the heart.
>
> 6. Examine **Figure 3.20** and the description of the parts of the heart and their functions. Why do you think the left side of the heart has stronger muscles than the right?
>
> 7. Describe the path air must take to reach the alveoli, where gas exchange takes place
>
> 8. Anemia is a fairly common condition in children, teens, and adult women. It usually results from having too few red blood cells. People with anemia often do not seem to have much energy. Use what you know about the circulatory system to explain why.

Anatomical Arrangements

Much of the efficiency of our organs and organ systems, and their ability to interact, is due to how they are positioned anatomically. As you have seen, the close contact between thin-walled capillaries and the villi of the small intestine and the alveoli of the lungs permits the movement of nutrients, oxygen, and wastes. This type of interaction happens in other systems and body parts as well, as you can see in **Figure 3.29**.

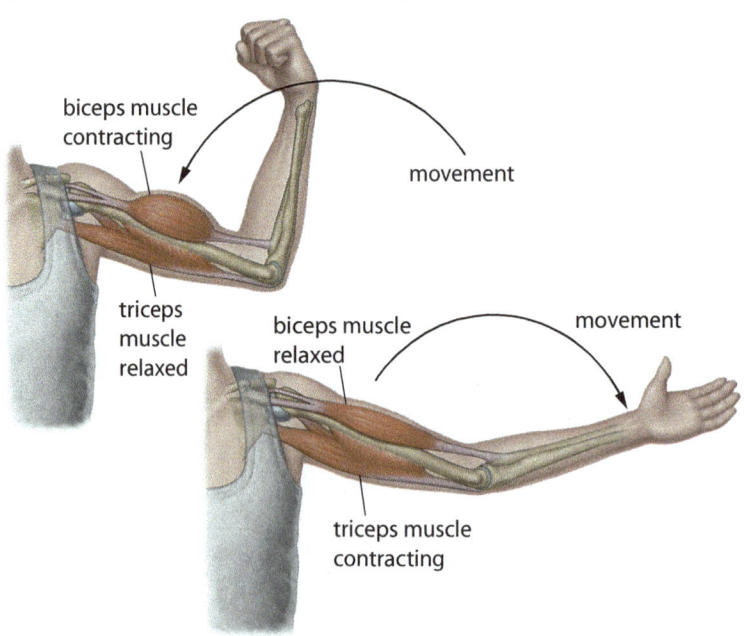

Figure 3.29 You can move because pairs of skeletal muscles work together with your body's bones. As shown here, when your bicep muscle contracts, it pulls the bone in your forearm up. When your bicep relaxes, the tricep muscle contracts and the forearm drops.

For centuries, scientists have used dissection to study how organs are arranged to carry out their functions. Students in introductory science courses often dissect frogs, earthworms, or fetal pigs. Today, when specimens are not readily available or if it is considered more appropriate for the course, students sometimes carry out virtual dissections rather than actual dissections.

Suggested Investigation
Inquiry Investigation 3-B, Frog Dissection, on page 117

106 NEL • Unit 1 Tissues, Organs, and Systems of Living Things

Section 3.2 Review

Section Summary

- The human body has 11 organ systems that interact with one another in order to perform the tasks necessary for survival and reproduction.
- The stomach is a major organ in the body's digestive system, which is responsible for taking in nutrients and breaking them down into a form that can be used by other cells in the body.
- The heart is a major organ in the body's circulatory system, which is responsible for moving gases, nutrients, and wastes in the body.
- The lungs are major organs in the body's respiratory system, which is responsible for gas exchange.

Review Questions

K/U 1. What features of the small intestine's structure help it accomplish its task?

T/I 2. In patients with cystic fibrosis, the duct joining the pancreas to the small intestine is often blocked. What effect might this have on digestion?

A 3. What do people mean when they talk about "food that went down the wrong way"?

K/U 4. Match the correct label to each letter on the diagram to the right.
   a. deoxygenated blood to lungs
   b. oxygenated blood to body
   c. oxygenated blood from lungs
   d. deoxygenated blood from body

T/I 5. At altitudes of 5500 m above sea level, the body has more difficulty functioning because there is less oxygen available to breathe. The highest city in the world is Wenzhuan, in the Himalayas, at an elevation of 5099 m above sea level. How does your knowledge of the circulatory and respiratory systems help you make a connection between these two facts?

K/U 6. Describe what happens in the alveoli.

T/I 7. Hyperventilation refers to breathing in and out deeply and rapidly. One effect of hyperventilation is to get rid of a large percentage of the carbon dioxide in your blood. A side effect is that your brain does not get enough oxygen, which may cause you to lose consciousness. Why might this occur?

C 8. Use cutouts or draw a diagram of the lungs, heart, and major blood vessels coming to and from them to show the relationships among these major organs. Using your cutouts or diagram, explain to a partner how blood gets to and from the lungs and what happens to the blood while it is in the lungs.

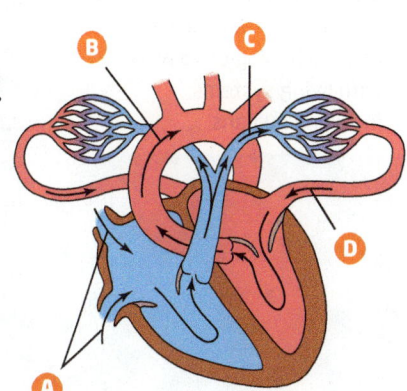

Key Terms
biophotonics
public health strategy
vaccination
cancer screening

3.3 Maintaining Healthy Systems

Throughout history, people from around the world have had ways to prevent and treat various diseases and conditions. For example, Chinese acupuncture has been used for centuries to treat ailments such as headaches and chronic pain. First Nations people in North America helped Europeans cure scurvy, a deficiency of Vitamin C, by giving them a tea made by boiling the bark of the white cedar. They also had many other medical treatments using various plants and herbs from their environment. Many traditional treatments, such as acupuncture, are now being studied by scientists.

Advances in Medical Technologies

Many of today's medical imaging technologies—examples of which you have seen in this chapter—have greatly advanced the diagnosis and treatment of disease. The human body has many ways to keep infection out, including its layer of skin. Opening the body for any reason, even in a sterile modern hospital, is best avoided.

Some of today's technologies, such as those that use **biophotonics**, have advanced a wide range of minimally invasive surgeries that result in fewer complications and less discomfort for patients than traditional surgeries, which often required large incisions. For example, endoscopy, which you saw used for diagnosis on page 95, can also be used to conduct surgeries as shown in **Figure 3.30**. Endoscopy is a form of biophotonics. Surgical lasers, as shown in **Figure 3.31**, are another form of biophotonics. Using lasers allows pinpoint accuracy for operations involving delicate tissue such as the eye.

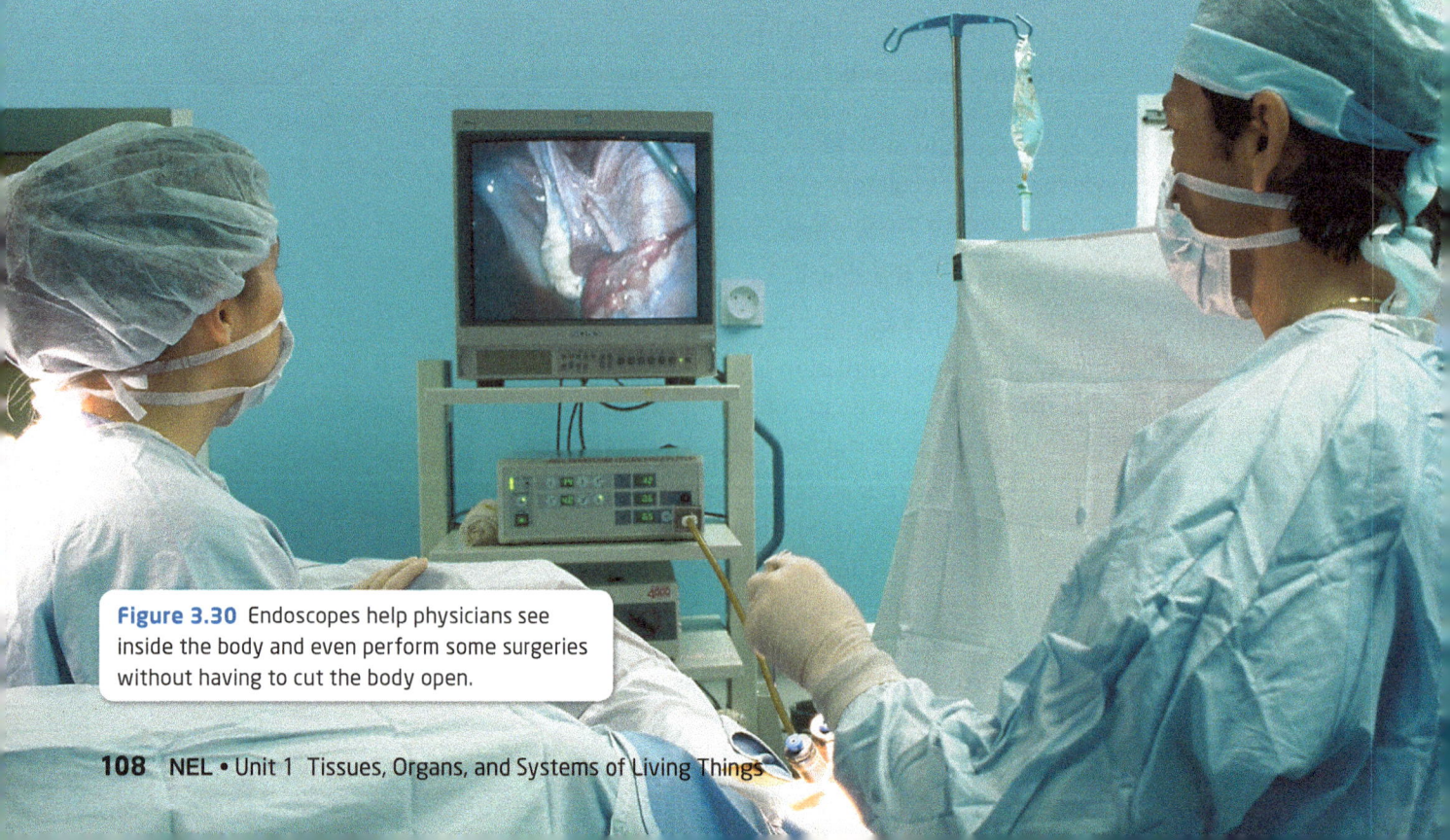

biophotonics all procedures and devices that use various light technologies to work with living systems, including humans

Figure 3.30 Endoscopes help physicians see inside the body and even perform some surgeries without having to cut the body open.

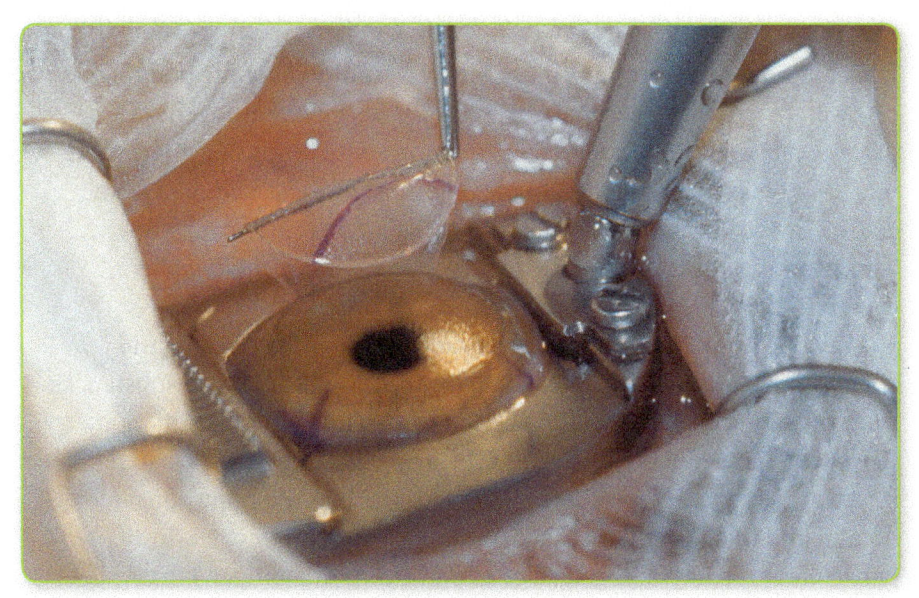

Figure 3.31 Using a high-energy carbon dioxide laser, eye surgeons can take a tiny slice off the front of the cornea. This form of eye surgery, a type of biophotonic technology, can correct a patient's near-sightedness.

Prenatal Care and Ultrasound

Prenatal care has also benefitted from advances in medical imaging technologies. Because sound waves do not penetrate deeply into tissues, they are generally considered safe, even for a developing fetus. Ultrasound is commonly used in the first few months of pregnancy to make sure a fetus's heart is beating normally and that it has its major organs. As you can see in **Figure 3.32**, it is also used to correct some abnormalities before birth.

Pregnant women are usually advised to avoid X rays and other kinds of diagnostic tests. Since there have been few studies on the long-term effects of the use of ultrasound, the medical community advises that ultrasound, like any other medical procedure, should be performed only when necessary.

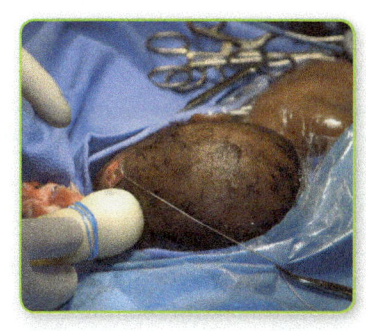

Figure 3.32 Ultrasound helps doctors perform amniocentesis, which you read about in Chapter 1, as well as surgeries. Here a surgeon holds an ultrasound probe to the scalp of a premature baby needing brain surgery.

Preventive Health Care

Preventive health care includes steps individuals can take to guard their own health, such as eating well and exercising regularly. It also includes **public health strategies**, which are co-ordinated efforts to reduce the incidence of various health problems. A public health strategy that has greatly improved human health is the use of **vaccinations** to control the spread of deadly diseases. For example, a worldwide vaccination program for smallpox has virtually eliminated the disease.

The last known naturally occurring case of smallpox was recorded in Somalia in 1977. The disease now exists only in samples stored in scientific labs. How this and other vaccination programs work is discussed in the next section.

public health strategy a co-ordinated effort to track, research, and reduce the incidence of specific health problems in a population

vaccination the process of giving a vaccine by mouth or injection to provide active immunity against a disease

Chapter 3 Animals: From Cells to Systems • NEL

Fighting Infectious Disease

Understanding vaccinations means understanding how the body fights disease. Infectious diseases are caused by *pathogens*. Pathogens are disease-causing agents such as viruses, and some kinds of bacteria and fungi. Organs such as your skin prevent most of these invaders from getting in your body. However, if a pathogen does enter your body, your immune system then tries to attack and destroy the invader, usually successfully.

The body's first response to an invader is to send a flow of fluid containing white blood cells called *phagocytes*, and dissolved substances from the blood to the site of the infection. This causes inflammation, a swelling and redness in the area. The job of the phagocytes is to fight infection, as seen in **Figure 3.33**. Any material that the body considers foreign and that stimulates this response is called an *antigen*. In particular, proteins on the surface of pathogens are antigens that trigger this response.

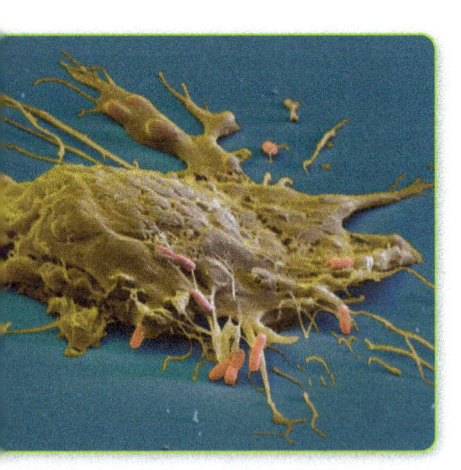

Figure 3.33 This photograph shows a white blood cell attacking *E. coli* bacteria, which are the small pink shapes.

STSE Case Study

Childhood Vaccinations: Weighing the Risks

Before the vaccine for measles became available, most children contracted the illness. Since then, it has been virtually eliminated in Canada. In 2004, there were only seven cases reported. Any new case of measles has been imported from another country, where the measles vaccine is not given to all citizens.

Vaccines act as antigens, prompting the immune system to produce antibodies. Once the body has produced the antibodies needed to fight a particular disease, the antibodies remain in the body, creating an immunity. Over the years, the antibodies continue to provide protection against stronger forms of the disease, which could be very dangerous.

A public health strategy of vaccinating children has greatly reduced the incidence of common diseases such as measles, mumps, and rubella. Canada's rubella vaccination program began in 1983. By 2004, the number of reported cases of rubella had dropped from 5300 to less than 30 cases per year, a decrease of 99.4 percent.

Concerns about Vaccinations

Some parents are concerned about vaccinating their children. Most common vaccines are produced in animal tissues, such as eggs. Some parents believe the vaccines are contaminated with animal diseases. In addition, some children have reactions to the injections. These reactions may involve minor side effects, such as redness and swelling at the site of the injection. However, more serious allergic reactions can also result. Due to these potential problems, some parents have chosen not to vaccinate their children. Many medical professionals are concerned that a decline in the vaccination rate could lead to a resurgence of potentially deadly diseases.

At this time, there is no accepted scientific evidence that childhood vaccines cause long-term health problems. Most members of the medical community agree that the benefits of getting the vaccines outweigh the risks.

A hundred years ago, many children died of diseases. Today, childhood vaccinations prevent many of these diseases.

Developing Antibodies

Bone marrow is another important part of the immune system. White blood cells and many other disease-fighting molecules are manufactured in the bone marrow. Among these molecules are specialized proteins called *antibodies*. Each antibody identifies and attaches to a specific antigen. This attachment either prevents the invader from infecting the rest of the body or signals to other parts of the immune system that this intruder needs to be destroyed.

> **Learning Check**
>
> 5. Give an example of the medical use of biophotonics.
> 6. What is a public health strategy?
> 7. You get a splinter stuck in your finger. Explain what happens as your body fights off the bacteria that have probably come through your skin along with the splinter.
> 8. Use an example of a specific disease to explain how vaccinations have affected human health.

Your Turn

1. Identify the different stakeholders affected by routine vaccinations. Write a statement describing the issues regarding vaccines from the viewpoint of each of the stakeholders.
2. Identify the kinds of information you think a public health strategy needs to communicate for it to be successful. Justify why you think these pieces of information are important.
3. Research one childhood disease for which there is now a vaccine. Write a pamphlet to inform the public about the disease and the vaccine. Make sure your pamphlet presents the kinds of information you identified in step 2. Include a list of answers to questions you expect people would ask.

Vaccines are produced in a sterile environment.

Common Vaccines in Canada

- diphtheria
- tetanus
- pertussis (whooping cough)
- polio
- Haemophilus influenzae type B (Hib)
- measles
- mumps
- rubella (MMR)
- hepatitis B
- chickenpox
- pneumococcal disease
- meningococcal disease
- influenza (flu)

Stopping the Spread of Disease

Many other infectious diseases do not have vaccinations available to control them. These diseases need to be controlled with different kinds of public health strategies, which are usually focussed on containing the spread of the disease. Three such diseases will be examined next: SARS, AIDS and the West Nile virus.

SARS

Go to **scienceontario** to find out more

In the spring of 2003, severe acute respiratory syndrome (SARS) entered Canada when a person who was infected in Hong Kong brought the virus back home to Toronto. SARS causes fluid to fill a patient's lungs, making it nearly impossible for the person to get enough oxygen. Because the SARS virus is readily transferred to others through the air, the disease quickly spread and caused a public health crisis in Ontario, as shown in **Figure 3.34**. By the end of an epidemic that lasted four months, the SARS virus had spread to 432 people, 44 of whom died.

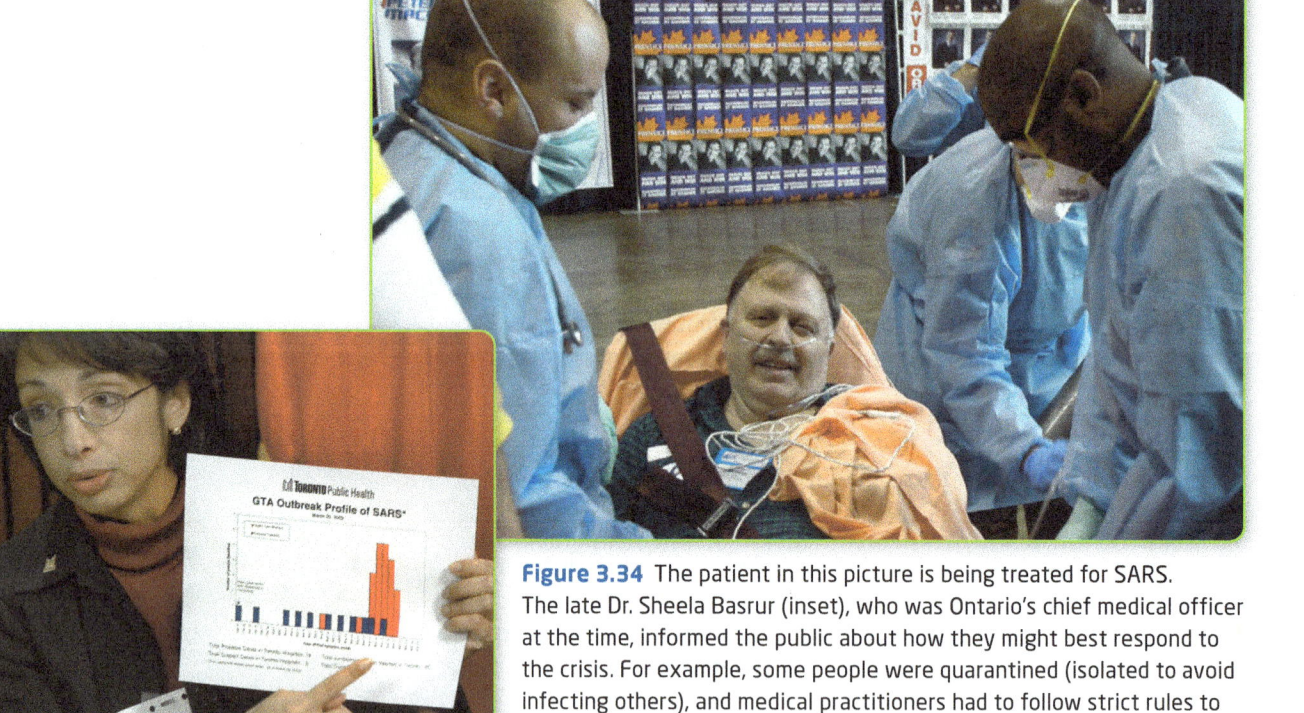

Figure 3.34 The patient in this picture is being treated for SARS. The late Dr. Sheela Basrur (inset), who was Ontario's chief medical officer at the time, informed the public about how they might best respond to the crisis. For example, some people were quarantined (isolated to avoid infecting others), and medical practitioners had to follow strict rules to prevent becoming infected.

AIDS

Acquired immunodeficiency syndrome, (AIDS) is caused by the human immunodeficiency virus (HIV), which attacks the immune system itself. This means that when other pathogens enter the body, the immune system is unable to mount an attack. HIV/AIDS has been directly responsible for the deaths of more than 25 million people worldwide. The federal government's strategy on HIV/AIDS includes keeping track of how many people have the disease. It also includes research, educational programs to prevent more people from acquiring HIV/AIDS, and help for people who have the disease.

Making a Difference

Jerri Clout is on a mission to help raise awareness about HIV/AIDS. At 13, the North Bay student became youth ambassador for Patrick4Life, an organization dedicated to educating people about how to prevent the transmission of HIV/AIDS. Patrick was a local youth who had hemophilia. He got HIV through a blood transfusion and died of AIDS at age 23. Jerri has been co-chair of the annual RUN/WALK for PATRICK for three years and helped design an HIV/AIDS pamphlet. In 2006, she founded Youth4Youth, an AIDS awareness organization. At the request of Ontario's Minister of Health, Jerri welcomed girls and women from around the world to the 2006 Worlds AIDS Conference in Toronto and attended the 2008 World AIDS Conference in Mexico City. In 2008, Jerri was named one of Canada's Top 20 Under 20 by Youth in Motion.

What could you do to raise HIV/AIDS awareness in your community?

West Nile Virus

Canada had its first case of West Nile virus in 2002. Although most people who get infected have no symptoms, a few become seriously ill or die. The Public Health Agency of Canada now co-ordinates a strategy to try to reduce people's exposure to the virus, as suggested in **Figure 3.35**. The strategy involves identifying the presence of the disease in various animals and, where it is present, informing local authorities. Local authorities may then use pesticides to reduce mosquito populations and provide educational programs to the public.

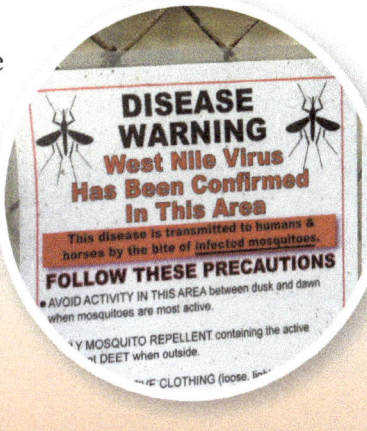

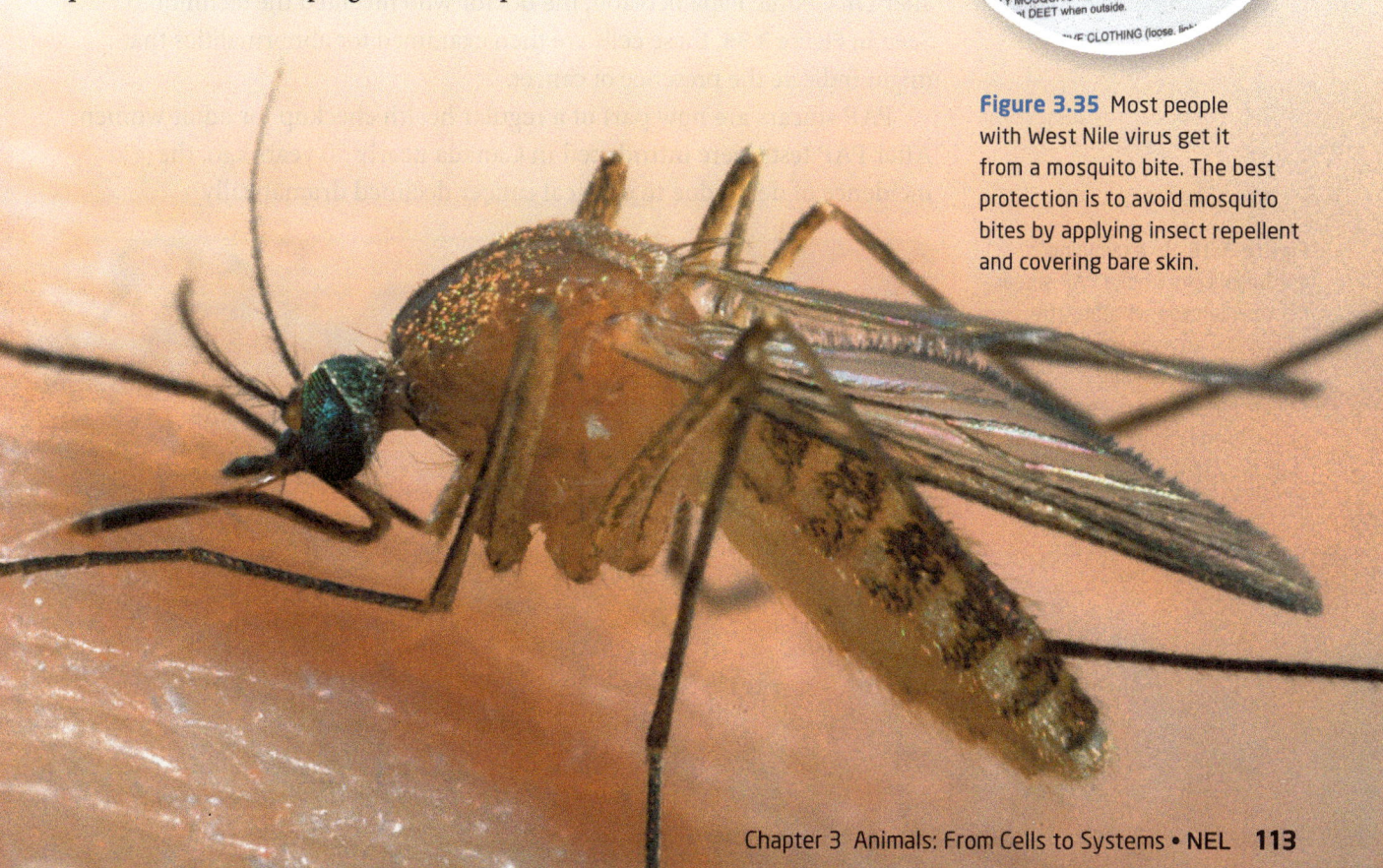

Figure 3.35 Most people with West Nile virus get it from a mosquito bite. The best protection is to avoid mosquito bites by applying insect repellent and covering bare skin.

Chapter 3 Animals: From Cells to Systems • NEL

Suggested Investigation

Data Analysis Investigation 3-C, Who's Stubbing Out?, on page 119

cancer screening tests used to detect cancer cells at an early stage of the disease so that it can be treated more effectively

Figure 3.36 By examining epithelial cells from a PAP smear, doctors can see whether the cells show any abnormalities. In this view, you can see a mass of cancerous cells with enlarged nuclei in the centre and normal cells around the edges.

Cancer Prevention

Not all public health strategies are directed at infectious diseases. For example, many public health strategies are directed at a non-infectious disease that two in five Canadians will get at some point in their lives: cancer.

In Chapter 1, you learned about carcinogens and how they can cause the mutations that lead to cancer. Clearly, then, one of the best ways to prevent cancer is to avoid the substances and situations that cause cells to mutate in this way. Many public health strategies encourage these preventive measures, such as not smoking cigarettes in order to avoid lung cancer and avoiding excessive exposure to the sun in order to avoid skin cancer.

However, some situations are not within a person's control. For example, for years, people had no idea that many houses and buildings contained asbestos insulation, which is now known to be carcinogenic. Programs are now in place to remove this insulation wherever it is discovered, but people lived with it for many years before the danger was recognized.

Screening for Cancer

Other causes of cancer are not known and therefore cannot be avoided. In these cases, **cancer screening** programs are the next line of defence. Discovering and treating cancer early in its development greatly increases a person's chances of survival. Depending on the type of cancer, early detection and treatment allows 65 to 95 percent of the individuals to survive.

Some cancer screening programs are done routinely as part of a person's annual physical checkup. For example, doctors remove a small sample of cells from a woman's cervix using a technique called a PAP smear (named after Dr. George Papanicolaou, the doctor who invented the technique). Seen in **Figure 3.36**, these cells are then examined for abnormalities that might indicate the presence of cancer.

PAP smears are now part of a regular health checkup for adult women. After PAP tests were introduced in Canada nearly 50 years ago, the incidence of death due to cervical cancer declined dramatically.

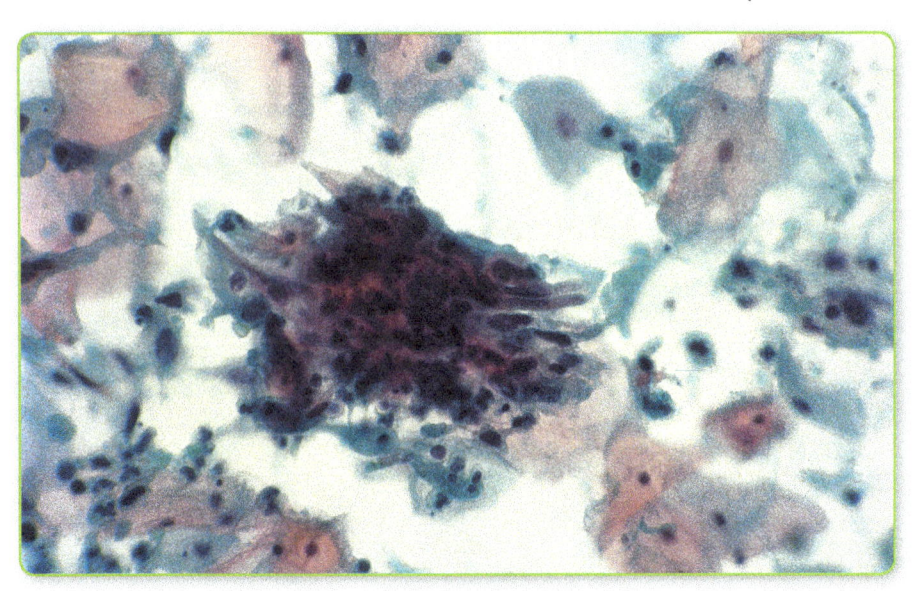

Section 3.3 Review

Section Summary

- Many technologies, such as ultrasound and various forms of biophotonics, have become important for diagnosing and treating abnormalities in tissues, organs, and systems.

- Public health strategies for a variety of diseases and conditions work to improve the health of Canadians by encouraging healthy lifestyle choices and other preventive measures.

Review Questions

A 1. Place the machines shown at the right in order from most to least likely to be used on a pregnant woman. Explain your reasoning.

K/U 2. Describe one tissue and one organ that are involved in your body's defence against pathogens.

T/I 3. A colonoscopy is done on people older than 50 to see if they have any growths on the walls of their colon. How do you think this procedure is done and why might these growths be a concern?

A 4. According to a 25-year study, obesity in Canadians between 12 and 17 years old increased from 3 percent in 1979 to 9 percent in 2004.

   a. What reasons can you give for why this occurred?

   b. Even at 9 percent, this is a fairly small proportion of the total population. Why would these data be so alarming to researchers?

K/U 5. How does a vaccination against a disease help to prevent it?

K/U 6. Give an example of how cancer screening has led to a reduction in cancer deaths.

K/U 7. Describe one public health strategy and explain how it tries to alter people's lifestyles.

T/I 8. Compare and contrast the two approaches to controlling disease: prevention and cure. Give some ways in which each is done in today's world.

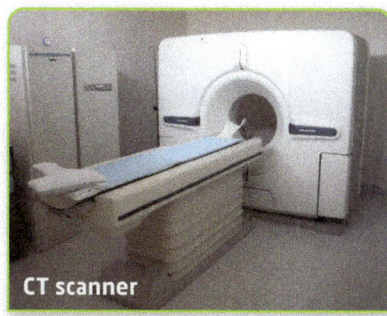

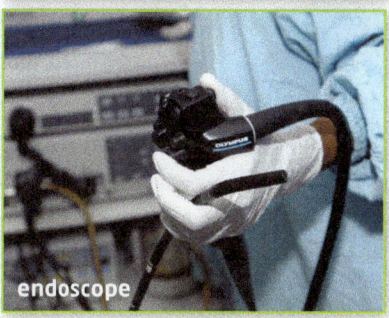

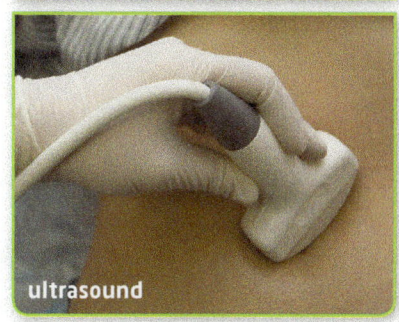

Real World Investigation 3-A

Skill Check

✓ Initiating and Planning
✓ Performing and Recording
✓ Analyzing and Interpreting
✓ Communicating

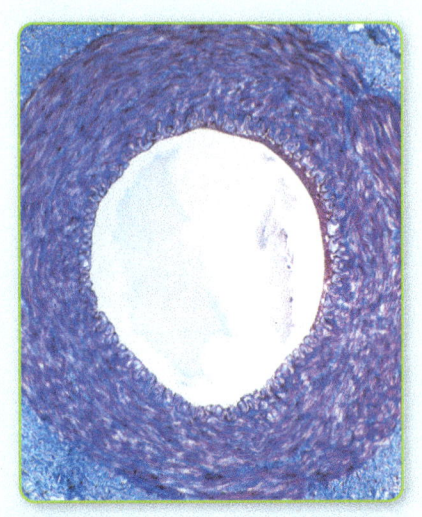

Heart Disease: Making the Public Aware

Imagine that the Heart and Stroke Foundation has decided to embark on a new public education campaign to inform people of the risk factors for acquiring cardiovascular disease. Your class has been asked to design educational materials for this campaign.

In a small group, research the risk factors for cardiovascular disease. As part of your research, find out what age group is most at risk for heart attacks and strokes. Consider whether this age group is the prime audience for your communication strategy.

Question

What are the risk factors for acquiring cardiovascular disease, and how can these risks be communicated to the public effectively?

Organize the Data

Summarize your research. What are the main risk factors for getting heart disease?

Analyze and Interpret

1. Decide what part of the population you will target for your campaign. Write a brief profile of that demographic, including their age, gender, education, lifestyle, and any other factors that may be significant for your campaign.

2. Decide on a method of communication that will best reach this audience (for example, television commercial, radio program, web site, printed pamphlet, podcast).

Conclude and Communicate

3. As a group, prepare an outline or storyboard for your product and have it approved by your teacher.

4. Complete your product and present it to the class.

5. Which medium did you think was most effective in conveying the information? Why?

6. What changes could you make in your own life to decrease your chances of acquiring heart disease?

Extend Your Inquiry and Research Skills

7. **Research** People who recover from heart attacks usually do so only if they receive immediate attention. What kind of attention must they receive?

This micrograph shows a cross section of a healthy artery.

This cross section shows an artery with inflammation due to arteriosclerosis. The black area at the center of the artery is the only space left for blood flow.

Inquiry Investigation 3-B

Skill Check

Initiating and Planning
✓ Performing and Recording
✓ Analyzing and Interpreting
✓ Communicating

Frog Dissection

Follow your teacher's instructions to perform a dissection of a frog, or observe a virtual dissection.

Question

How does the arrangement of a frog's organ systems facilitate their interactions?

Procedure

Part A: Making Incisions

1. Rinse the frog in water.
2. Place it in the dissection tray on its dorsal (back) side and pin its limbs to the tray.
3. Use forceps to lift the frog's skin between the rear legs. Use the scalpel to cut through the lifted skin in order to make the incisions noted in the diagram below. Take care to cut only the skin.

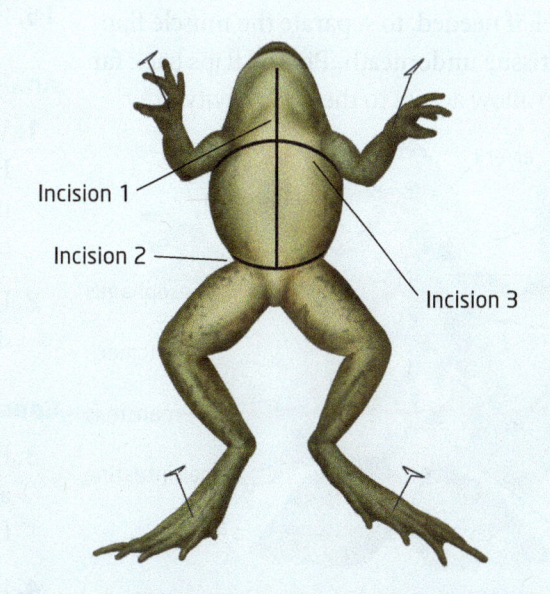

Safety Precautions

- Extreme care must be taken when using dissecting instruments, particularly scalpels. As much as possible, make cuts away from your body.
- The frogs are preserved in a chemical solution. Wear plastic gloves, goggles, and an apron at all times, and work in a well-ventilated area. If some of the chemical comes into contact with your skin, wash it off immediately.

Materials

- gloves, goggles, and lab apron
- preserved frog
- water
- dissection tray
- pins
- scissors
- forceps
- scalpel
- probe
- paper towels for clean up

4. Lift one flap of skin with the forceps. Use a scalpel to help separate the skin from the muscle layer below. Pin the flap to the dissection tray. Repeat with the second flap of skin.

5. Make a vertical incision through the abdominal muscle. Begin by using the forceps to lift the muscle layer between the rear legs of the frog. Make a small cut with the scalpel. Using the scissors, continue the incision up the midline to a point just below the front legs.

6. Use scissors to cut through the chest bones. When you reach the point just below the front legs, turn the scissor blades sideways so you only cut through the bones in the chest. Be careful not to cut too deeply or you might damage the heart or other internal organs. Stop when the scissors reach a point just below the frog's neck.

7. As you did with incisions 2 and 3, use the scalpel to make sideways incisions in the muscle. Again, be careful not to cut too deeply.

8. To separate the muscle flaps from the organs below, use the forceps to pull back and hold the muscle flaps. Use the scalpel to separate the muscle from the organ tissue. Pin the muscle flaps back far enough to allow easy access to the internal organs.

9. Use forceps to pick up the triangular flaps of skin and muscle just above the back legs. Use the scalpel, if needed, to separate the muscle flap from the tissue underneath. Pin the flaps back far enough to allow access to the body cavity.

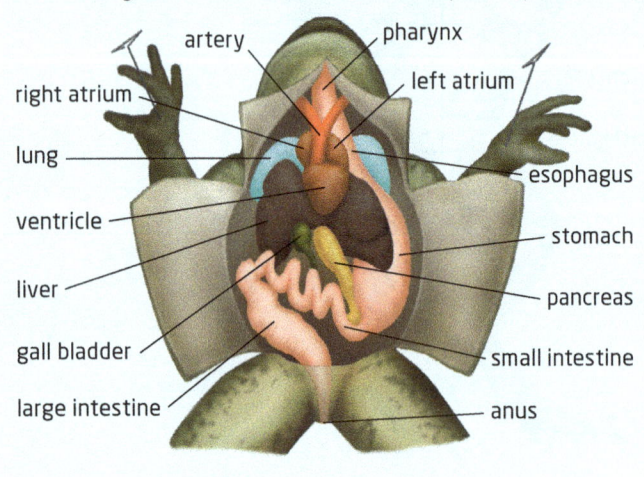

Internal organs of a frog

Part B: Internal Examination

10. The first organs you will see are the liver and heart. Draw and label them on a diagram of your frog.

11. The heart and liver cover the organs below them. Use the forceps and probe to pick up the liver and hold it to the side. Use the labelled diagram on this page to find the organs of the digestive system. Draw and label as many of these organs as you can see, from the mouth to the anus. Hint: The pancreas is a thin, yellowish ribbon.

12. Trace the path of blood vessels to and from the heart. The vessels going to and from the lungs may be hard to see. Notice that the frog has two atria, as humans do, but only one ventricle.

13. Observe how small arteries are attached to organs of the digestive system.

14. Dispose of your frog properly, according to your teacher's instructions.

15. Rinse and dry all equipment, including the dissecting tray.

16. Put the dissecting tray and tools away.

Analyze and Interpret

1. Where is the frog's heart compared to its lungs? How do the locations of these organs affect interactions between the frog's respiratory and circulatory systems?

2. Describe how the frog's circulatory and digestive systems are physically connected.

Conclude and Communicate

3. Explain why the interaction of the respiratory and circulatory systems is necessary for the frog's survival.

4. Draw and label a diagram to show blood flow into and out of the heart.

Extend Your Inquiry and Research Skills

5. **Inquiry** Cold-blooded animals, such as frogs, are able to deliver blood to their cells once their bodies warm up. Predict when you think frogs are likely to be most active.

Data Analysis Investigation 3-C

Skill Check

Initiating and Planning

Performing and Recording

✓ Analyzing and Interpreting

✓ Communicating

Who's Stubbing Out?

Physicians for a Smoke-Free Canada calls smoking "the leading cause of preventable death and illness in Canada" and "the most pressing public health concern in our country." The organization says Ontario's health-care costs due to tobacco use are enormous. For example, the cost of hospitalization due to active and passive (second-hand) smoking is more than $800 million a year. The cost of prescription drugs needed as a result of smoking is more than $500 million a year. Smoking has been clearly linked to diseases such as lung cancer, emphysema, and heart disease.

For years, dozens of public health initiatives have targeted smoking-related diseases. These initiatives have included four strategic directions:

- Protection: reducing the number of Canadians exposed to second-hand smoke
- Cessation: supporting and encouraging smokers to quit
- Prevention: preventing young people from taking up smoking
- Harm reduction: mandating changes to tobacco products to reduce their hazards

Specific initiatives have included legislation, media campaigns, pamphlets, posters, support groups, web site support, toll-free help lines, and other measures.

Are the initiatives successful? In this investigation, you will study smoking data for Ontario to identify trends.

You may have seen these kinds of warning labels from cigarette packages. The federal government requires them by law as part of its strategy to educate people about the dangers of smoking.

Prevalence of Smoking in Ontario
(percentage of the population from 1999 to 2005)

Age	1999	2000	2001	2002	2003	2004	2005
Total							
15–19	25	25	19	19	13*	16	17
20–24	34	28	31	29	29	21	24
25–44	29	28	21	24	22	22	26
45+	16	17	17	14	14	11	12
Male							
15–24	32	27	26	25	22*	21	23
25+	24	25	23	21	22	22	23
Female							
15–24	27	26	24	23	20*	16	18
25+	20	20	15	17	14*	10	14

* low sampling (six months of data)
Source: Physicians for a Smoke-Free Canada with data from the Canadian Tobacco Use Monitoring Survey

Question

Are rates of smoking decreasing?

Organize the Data

1. Draw a bar graph for the data shown for each age group in the total population for the years 1999 and 2005.
2. Draw a bar graph to compare the percentage of smokers among males and females for ages 15 to 24 in each of the seven years.
3. Draw a bar graph to compare the percentage of smokers among males and females for ages 25 and above in each of the seven years.

Analyze and Interpret

1. Were males or females of ages 15 to 24 more likely to smoke in 1999 or in 2005?

Conclude and Communicate

2. Does it appear that campaigns to reduce smoking over the years 1999 to 2005 were successful? What assumption do you have to make in order to draw this conclusion?
3. Would you say that the change in smoking rates during this time period was major or minor? Explain your answer.

Extend Your Inquiry and Research Skills

4. **Inquiry** Is there any evidence from the data that public health initiatives have targeted one group more than another? Explain.

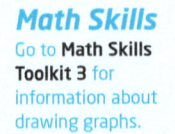

Math Skills
Go to **Math Skills Toolkit 3** for information about drawing graphs.

Your teacher may ask you to work on this investigation in a small group.

120 NEL • Unit 1 Tissues, Organs, and Systems of Living Things

Chapter 3 Summary

3.1 Cells and Tissues

Key Concepts

- Cell specialization is influenced by the contents of an individual cell's cytoplasm, environmental factors such as temperature, and secretions from neighbouring cells.
- Animals have four main types of tissues: muscle, epithelial, connective, and nervous.
- Because stem cells have the potential to repair and replace damaged cells, they offer opportunities to develop new medical treatments. However, their use also raises some ethical questions.

3.2 Organs and Systems

Key Concepts

- The human body has 11 organ systems that interact with one another in order to perform the tasks necessary for survival and reproduction.
- The stomach is a major organ in the body's digestive system, which is responsible for taking in nutrients and breaking them down into a form that can be used by other cells in the body.
- The heart is a major organ in the body's circulatory system, which is responsible for moving gases, nutrients, and wastes throughout the body.
- The lungs are major organs in the body's respiratory system, which is responsible for gas exchange.

3.3 Maintaining Healthy Systems

Key Concepts

- Many technologies, such as ultrasound and various forms of biophotonics, have become important for diagnosing and treating abnormalities in tissues, organs, and systems.
- Public health strategies for a variety of diseases and conditions work to improve the health of Canadians by encouraging healthy lifestyle choices and other preventive measures.

Chapter 3 Review

Make Your Own Summary

Summarize the key concepts of this chapter using a graphic organizer. The Chapter Summary on the previous page will help you identify key concepts. Refer to Study Toolkit 4 on pages 565-566 to help you decide which graphic organizer to use.

Reviewing Key Terms

Match each key term listed below to its definition.

- **a.** ultrasound
- **b.** muscle tissue
- **c.** epithelial tissue
- **d.** biophotonics
- **e.** stem cells
- **f.** cell differentiation
- **g.** nervous tissue

1. groups of cells that become specialized to act as a barrier (3.1)
2. the process of cells becoming specialized (3.1)
3. groups of cells that are specialized to change shape (3.1)
4. cells that maintain their ability to divide and produce new cells (3.1)
5. technology that uses sound waves to create an image of a body part (3.3)
6. groups of cells that are specialized to send electrical signals (3.1)
7. technology that uses light for advanced surgical procedures (3.3)

Knowledge and Understanding K/U

8. Give four levels of organization in the human body, from smallest to largest.
9. How are scientists working to decrease the controversy over using embryonic stem cells in research?
10. Draw a flowchart showing the following structures in the correct sequence for digestion:

    rectum   duodenum
    anus   stomach
    mouth   colon
    esophagus small intestine

11. What conditions can result in fluid accumulating in the lungs?
12. When people have pneumonia, their alveoli become inflamed and the air spaces within them become clogged. What symptoms would the patient show?
13. Where in your circulatory system do you think your blood pressure is highest? lowest? Justify your answer.
14. Name the three categories of blood vessels and the function of each.
15. Use the figure below to answer the following questions.

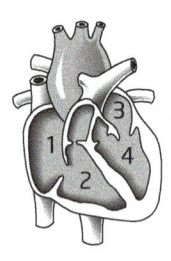

    a. Which heart chamber pumps blood to the lungs?
    b. Where does the blood go after leaving chamber 4?
    c. From which part of the body does chamber 3 receive blood?
    d. Does the vessel carrying blood into chamber 3 have oxygenated or deoxygenated blood?

16. Why are some tissues (such as in the lungs and small intestine) structured to increase surface area?
17. Give an example of two organ systems that interconnect or rely on each other to function.
18. Compare and contrast frog anatomy with human anatomy.
19. What type of blood cell is involved in fighting pathogens?
20. How does a vaccination work?
21. What is the main purpose of cancer screening?

122 NEL • Unit 1 Tissues, Organs, and Systems of Living Things

Thinking and Investigation T/I

22. Nerve cells have long, fibre-like projections, and red blood cells are thick and disk shaped. Explain how their differences in structure are related to the different functions they perform.

23. Childhood illnesses such as rheumatic fever can result in damage to the valves of the heart. The valves can accumulate scar tissue that makes them less flexible and unable to completely stop the backflow of blood in the heart. When this occurs, the heart often gets bigger. What tissues in the heart do you think might get bigger? Why do you think this would occur?

24. Examine the diagram below.

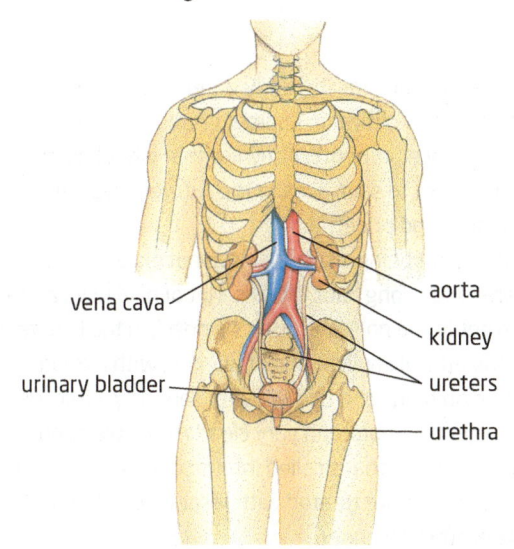

    a. What system is shown in this diagram?
    b. Why does the kidney have such large blood vessels going to and from it?

Communication C

25. **BIG IDEAS** Developments in medicine and medical technology can have social and ethical implications. For example, imagine that your local newspaper published a letter to the editor that argued that all research involving stem cells is unnecessary and unethical. Write a response to the editor in which you describe how stem cells are used in the body, acknowledge ethical concerns about the use of stem cells, and offer your opinion about whether the benefits outweigh the costs. Be sure to support your opinion with your knowledge of science.

26. A local hospital has started a fundraising campaign to buy new imaging equipment. A friend says his parents do not want to support the campaign because they supported a drive last year to buy a new X-ray machine. Discuss why this new fundraising campaign may still be needed.

27. **BIG IDEAS** Plants and animals, including humans, are made of specialized cells, tissues, and organs that are organized into systems. How can heart disease affect organs in other systems?

Application A

28. An elderly woman has just had her gall bladder removed. Describe the kind of diet you think she should follow.

29. In each of the situations below, hypothesize how you think the number of breaths you take per minute would compare with your breathing rate as you read this question. Give an explanation for your hypotheses.
    a. while sleeping
    b. while exercising
    c. while on top of Mt. Logan, Canada's highest mountain (elevation 5959 m)

30. Why do you think babies and young children might contract infectious diseases more frequently than teenagers do?

Science at Work

Canadians in Science

When cancer is diagnosed early, the odds that a patient will survive are often excellent. Unfortunately, many cancers are only diagnosed at advanced stages. Tedros Bezabeh, a senior research officer with Canada's National Research Council, is developing methods to detect cancer early and save lives. In one study, Tedros is using magnetic resonance spectroscopy to compare stool samples from healthy people with samples from patients with colorectal cancer, a cancer of the colon or rectum. He is trying to detect chemical changes that occur in colon cells when cancer is developing. He hopes this work will lead to the development of a non-invasive test to detect colorectal cancer at a very early stage.

In his research, Tedros Bezabeh applies magnetic resonance spectroscopy techniques to detect changes in human fluids and tissues. Magnetic resonance spectroscopy uses radio frequency waves to study the chemistry of tissues.

In Tedros Bezabeh's Words

I am working to develop new techniques for the early detection and better diagnosis of cancer. Early detection is critical in improving treatment outcomes and increasing survival rates in cancer patients. Knowing that what I do in the laboratory now can be used in clinics to save lives in the future gives me a special feeling of accomplishment and pride.

The most challenging thing about being a scientist is to not expect quick results. You have to be in there for the long haul. It takes a lot of hard work and a great deal of perseverance to get to the goal line, but it's worth it in the long term.

As researchers, we take the ethical implications of working with human subjects, and by extension human fluids and tissues, very seriously. First, we need to make sure that the subjects understand very clearly what we need them to do or why we need specimens—that's called informed consent. Research ethics boards ensure that our subjects are treated with respect and that our research is conducted in a safe, ethical manner.

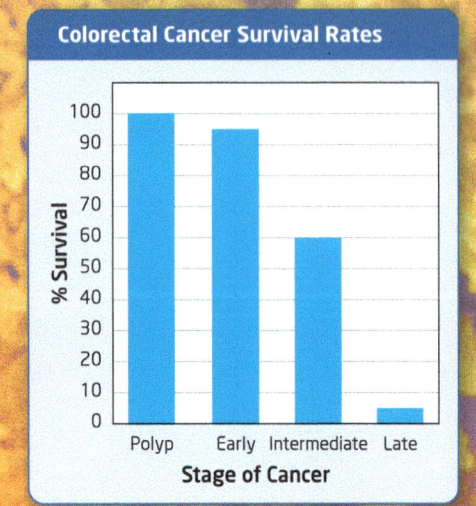

Colorectal Cancer Survival Rates

When colorectal cancer is diagnosed early, more than 90% of patients survive for at least five years. Unfortunately, only about one third of patients are diagnosed with colorectal cancer when it is still at an early stage. Polyps are benign tumours that can develop into colorectal cancer.

Biology at Work

The study of biology contributes to these careers, as well as many more.

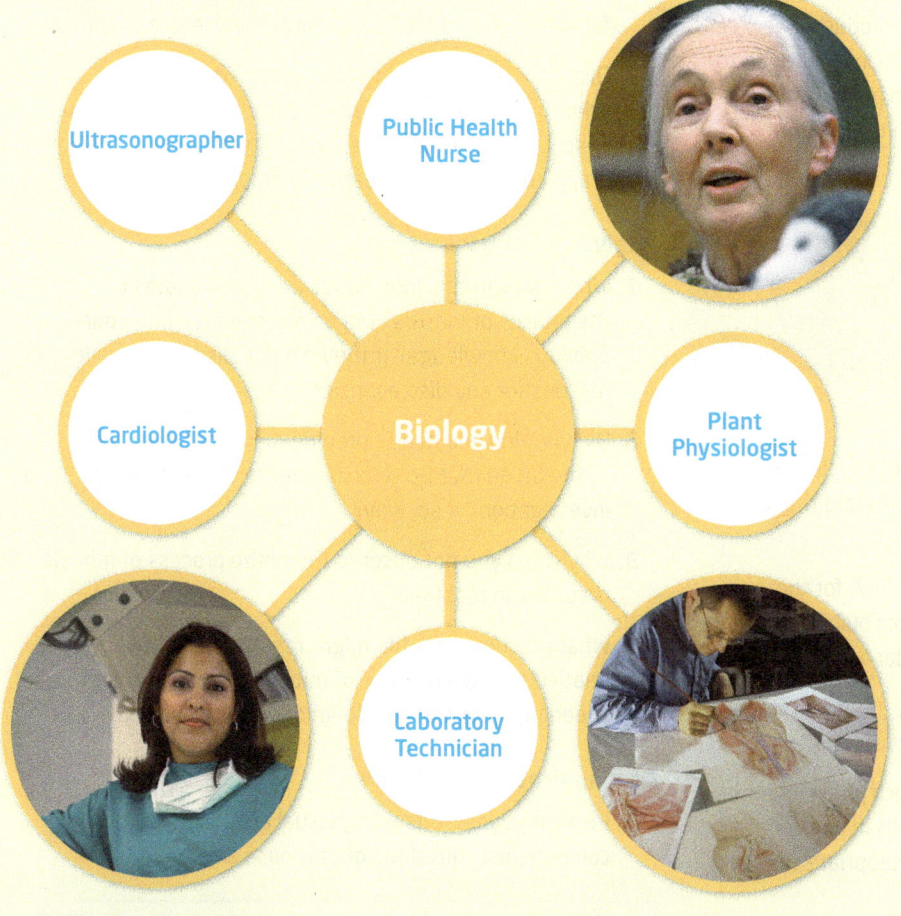

Bioethicist

Bioethicists study moral issues related to medicine and science. For example, a bioethicist may study the arguments for and against embryonic stem-cell research. Bioethicists work in hospitals and post-secondary institutions, where they help health-care workers and researchers make decisions about ethical dilemmas. They are also involved in developing policies in hospitals and in research settings that involve human or other animal subjects.

Medical Illustrator

Medical illustrators are artists who have a detailed knowledge of the structure and functions of the human body. They create illustrations and models for advertising, textbooks, and other teaching tools. They work for medical schools, research institutions, publishers, and companies that manufacture pharmaceuticals and medical devices.

Radiation Therapist

Radiation therapists work with other health-care workers to plan and administer treatment for cancer patients. They operate equipment that delivers high-energy radiation to tumour cells. They also help patients prepare and deal with the side effects of treatment.

Go to **scienceontario** to find out more

Over to You

1. Why do you think it is important that non-invasive tests be developed for the early detection of cancers? (An invasive test involves the cutting or removal of tissue from a patient, or the placement of a diagnostic instrument inside a patient's body.)

2. Why is informed consent important for research that involves human subjects?

3. A pharmaceutical company has designed a drug for patients with advanced colorectal cancer. The drug is new and has not been used on humans. What are the ethical arguments for and against administering this new drug to patients with advanced colorectal cancer?

4. Research a career involving biology that interests you. If you wish, you may choose a career from the list above. **What essential skills would you need for this career?**

Unit 1 Projects

Inquiry Project

Investigating Phases of Mitosis

In this unit, you learned how mitosis in cells allows them to divide their nuclear material equally, thus producing new cells. In this project, you will plan and conduct an investigation to examine the relative amount of time each phase of mitosis takes in the cells of actively growing onion root tips.

Inquiry Question
How can you confirm the relative amount of time each phase of mitosis takes in onion root tip cells?

Initiate and Plan

1. Using a visual format, describe the cell cycle in plants. Consider the various phases of mitosis and the time spent in each phase.
2. See Science Skills Toolkit 8, on page 547, for the technique of growing onion roots from bulbs and staining the root tip cells for observation under a microscope.
3. List the materials you will need, the steps in your procedure, and any safety precautions you should take.
4. Infer the relative amount of time each phase of mitosis takes by counting the number of cells in each phase. Decide how many cells would be appropriate to count for scientific validity.
5. Decide on a type of graph suitable for summarizing your data and illustrating relative amounts of time for each phase of mitosis.
6. Have your teacher approve your procedure before you begin.

Perform and Record

1. Conduct your investigation. Select an appropriate format, such as a table, to organize and record your data.
2. Display the data collected in a graph using appropriate scientific conventions. Write a summary statement that describes any trends or patterns you observe in the graph and record it beneath the graph.

Analyze and Interpret

1. What can you conclude about the relative rates of the phases of mitosis? Did your results confirm your previous knowledge? If they did not, discuss possible reasons for any discrepancies.
2. Did you find you had to prepare more than one slide of the onion root tip cells in order to complete your investigation? If so, why?
3. Why could you not observe the entire process of mitosis occurring in real time?
4. What practical benefits might result from knowing the relative time each phase of mitosis takes, and therefore speeding up or slowing down one of the phases?

Communicate Your Findings

5. Present your results using visual and written components, suited to your purpose and audience.

Assessment Criteria

Once you complete your project, ask yourself these questions. Did you...

- **K/U** describe the cell cycle in plants, including a description of mitosis?
- **T/I** describe an appropriate procedure?
- **T/I** identify in your procedure the number of cells required for scientific validity?
- **T/I** propose a conclusion that either confirms your prior knowledge or describes any possible reasons for discrepancies?
- **T/I** describe how you addressed challenges?
- **A** describe the practical benefits of knowing the relative times of each phase of mitosis?
- **C** organize the data collected using an appropriate format and scientific conventions?
- **C** display the data appropriately in a graph?

An Issue to Analyze

Organ Donation

Canada has one of the lowest organ donation rates in industrialized countries. In 2008, 4195 people were on the national waiting list for an organ or tissue transplant. Due to a lack of donors, 195 of those people died. For the past 15 years, the number of organ donations has held steady at approximately 400 donations per year. However, in this same amount of time, the population of Canada has increased by 4 000 000.

As a research scientist for the Ministry of Health, prepare a recommendation related to one medical technology that would be useful in supporting patients in need of a new organ, given the lack of organ donors available.

> **Issue**
> What are the issues related to medical technologies available to support people in need of organs?

Initiate and Plan

1. Select a medical technology used in treating people in need of new organs.

Perform and Record

2. Using electronic, print, and human sources, research the scientific and technical principles underlying the technology.

3. Brainstorm a list of the economic, political, and ethical issues related to the technology.

4. Consider the following questions to guide your research:
   - What are the risks of being a donor?
   - Does a donor have to be of the same race or ethnic group as the recipient?
   - How are recipients identified? Who chooses which person is a better candidate?
   - How are organs matched to a recipient?
   - How much money and time are being spent finding alternatives to organ donation?
   - Should people be required by law to sign an organ donor card?
   - How can we control the black-market sale of organs?

5. Select an appropriate graphic organizer to summarize your research.

Analyze and Interpret

1. Prepare a risk-benefit table outlining, from a variety of perspectives, the risks and benefits associated with the chosen medical technology.

2. Based on the risks and benefits, make a recommendation to the Ministry of Health on use of the technology as support for patients in need of organs.

3. If the technology is not appropriate support, propose other courses of action to consider.

Communicate Your Findings

4. Decide on an appropriate format to present your recommendation to the Ministry of Health.

> **Assessment Criteria**
>
> Once you complete your project, ask yourself these questions. Did you...
>
> - **K/U** describe the scientific and technical priniciples related to the medical technology?
> - **A** identify the economic, political, and ethical issues related to the technology?
> - **A** make a recommendation based on the risk-benefit analysis of whether or not the technology is appropriate for patients in need of organs?
> - **A** propose other courses of action if the technology is not appropriate?
> - **C** organize the research using an appropriate format and appropriate academic documentation?
> - **C** select a format for the recommendation that is appropriate for both audience and purpose?
> - **C** use scientific vocabulary appropriately?

Unit 1 Review

Connect to the BIG IDEAS

Use this bicycle wheel graphic organizer to connect what you have learned in this unit to the Big Ideas, found on page 1. Draw one bicycle wheel for each Big Idea and write the Big Idea in the centre. Between the spokes of the wheel, briefly describe six examples of that Big Idea.

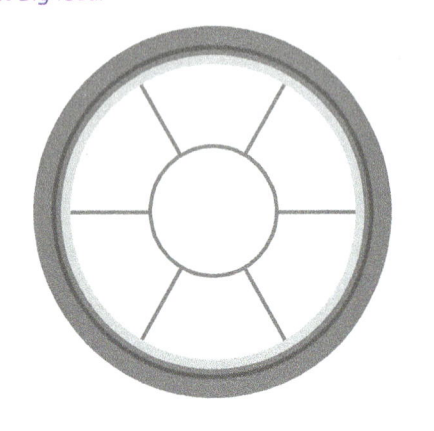

Knowledge and Understanding K/U

1. In which of the following organelles would you expect to find DNA?
   a. vacuole
   b. Golgi apparatus
   c. endoplasmic reticulum
   d. nucleus

2. Which of the following is *not* one of the main ideas in the cell theory?
   a. Living organisms are made of cells.
   b. Cells come from pre-existing cells.
   c. Cells are the basic organizational unit of life.
   d. All cells have a nucleus.

3. Which of the following is a list of types of plant tissues?
   a. dermal, vascular, connective
   b. dermal, vascular, chloroplasts
   c. dermal, vascular, ground
   d. ground, chloroplasts, grana

4. In which human organ would you expect to find *E. coli*?
   a. heart   c. intestine
   b. lung   d. brain

5. Which of the following organ systems is specialized to transport materials for use throughout the body?
   a. digestive system   c. endocrine system
   b. circulatory system   d. nervous system

6. Explain the meaning of the term *daughter cells*.

7. Using a specific example, describe how DNA screening is a valuable tool, but one that raises ethical issues.

8. Explain the meaning of the term *transgenic*.

9. Copy the following diagram into your notebook, and fill in the labels for the different parts of the cell cycle.

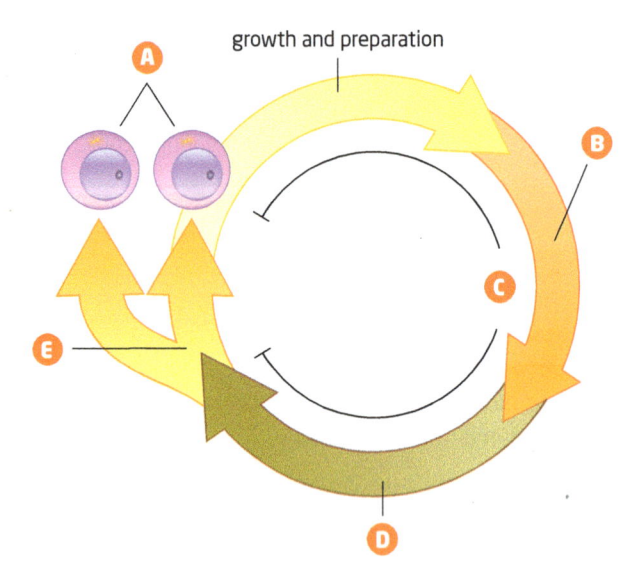

10. How is cell division related to cancer?

11. Explain the roles of cell division and cell specialization in plants and animals.

12. Explain how the early embryonic stem cells of animals differ from adult stem cells.

13. How is the arrangement of organs in the human digestive system suited to its main functions?

14. Describe one example of a public health strategy and its effect on human health.

Thinking and Investigation T/I

15. Some chemicals prevent the organization of spindle fibres.

  a. Predict the effect of one of these chemicals on cell division and growth.

  b. Design an investigation to test your prediction.

16. The specimens below were observed using a microscope. Identify each specimen, and list the evidence you used to make your identifications.

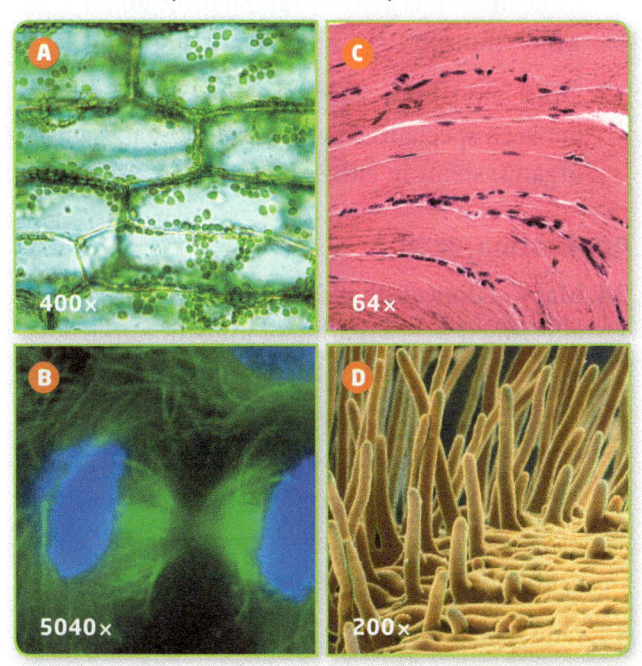

A 400×
B 5040×
C 64×
D 200×

17. Is it better to water plants in the evening or in the morning? Write a procedure for an investigation that would allow you to answer this question.

18. Despite having generously watered your indoor plants before you left on a short trip, you return home to find that their leaves have all wilted. Develop a hypothesis for why this has occurred, and suggest what you could do to correct the problem.

19. Which cell has the greater chance of survival: an amoeba in pond water or a cell that has been isolated from a multicellular plant and placed in pond water? Explain your reasoning.

20. A bacterium evades your body's defence mechanisms and begins to replicate. This bacterium replicates itself every 30 min. Calculate how many bacteria will be in your body after 8 h.

21. The Canadian government is funding a special five-year study to help determine the causes of heart disease among Canadians. The citizens of a small town in Ontario have agreed to participate in the study. You are in charge of designing the study. Your first task is to select one factor that you will focus on, such as diet or exercise. What part of the population will you study? What data will you need to collect? How will you obtain the data? What will your hypothesis be? Identify the independant and dependant variables, as well as the controls for your study. Give reasons for your choices and proposed course of action.

22. The graph below shows the rates of hospitalization due to asthma in Ontario between 1994 and 2001. From the data, can you conclude that asthma is declining in Ontario? Explain your answer.

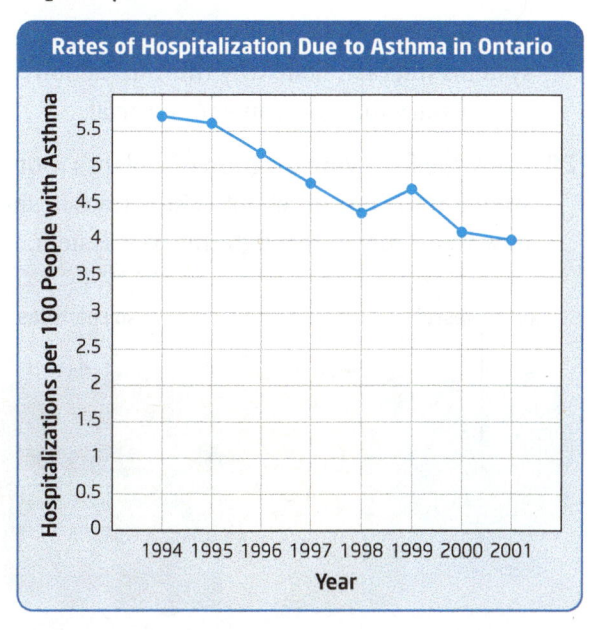

Rates of Hospitalization Due to Asthma in Ontario

Unit 1 Review

Communication C

23. Draw and label a diagram of a plant cell. Indicate the structures that make it different from an animal cell.

24. Biologist and science writer Lewis Thomas once compared Earth to a single cell. Make point-form notes about the ways in which you think this analogy works. Use this analogy to explain the structures and functions of a cell to a classmate.

25. Conduct research about one of the medical or other technological developments you have read about in this unit. Examples include medical imaging technologies, surgical techniques, transgenic organ transplants, cloning, and the use of stem cells in research. Create a poster promoting the benefits of this technology for human health.

26. Describe how a plant that is growing to be tall and spindly can be made to start branching out.

27. Make a table showing each of the major types of animal tissues and the main functions they carry out.

28. Give an example that illustrates how organ systems interact. State why this interaction is necessary for an organism's survival.

29. Copy the following diagram of a plant's root system into your notebook. Use arrows to show how water moves through this root system.

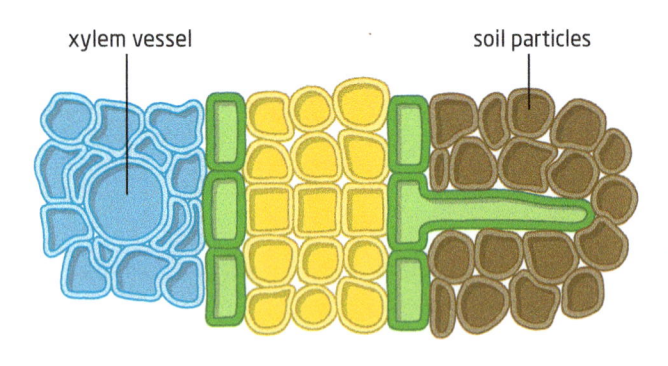

30. Create a diagram or flowchart explaining how a molecule of oxygen reaches a cell in your finger.

31. Write a newspaper-style editorial that addresses the following question: "Should the public health-care system continue to pay for individuals who acquire smoking-related illnesses?" Justify your response.

32. Draw and label a diagram to show the stomata on the underside of two leaves: one in which transpiration is actively taking place and one in which transpiration is not occurring.

33. Draw and label a diagram to explain the links between specialized cells, tissues, organs, and organ systems in either a plant or an animal.

Application A

34. Many chemicals that act as poisons work by affecting the functioning of mitochondria. Why do such poisons cause an organism to die?

35. Many genetic diseases can be detected using a blood test for the presence or absence of specific substances in the body. Explain why this kind of genetic test works, even though it does not examine the DNA itself.

36. One type of tree disease is caused by a fungus that plugs up the xylem cells in a tree's trunk. Why could this kill a tree?

37. Treatments for many types of cancer involve killing cells that divide rapidly using chemicals (chemotherapy) or radiation. These treatments often kill the cancer cells by causing mutations in them. Sometimes, however, the treatment of cancer can cause surrounding normal cells to become cancerous. Why might this occur?

38. West Nile Virus is carried by mosquitoes and can cause a disease that is fatal to those who contract it. One response to the risk of West Nile Virus is to spray pesticides (some of which can cause cancers) in and around water sources that contain mosquitoes. Discuss the pros and cons of this response. Research and summarize other methods of prevention

Literacy Test Prep

Read the selection below and answer the questions that follow it.

> If a blocked blood vessel prevents the blood supply from reaching the heart, heart cells die because they are robbed of oxygen. If too many heart cells die, the heart may stop working entirely. When this happens, a person typically experiences intense chest pains and has difficulty breathing. In such instances, the person has suffered a heart attack.
>
> Heart attacks can be fatal. If someone suffers a heart attack, it is important that medical treatment begins quickly. The most effective treatment can only be carried out in a hospital. Treatment for heart attack victims may involve the administration of drugs that break up blockages in blood vessels and surgical procedures that open up clogged arteries. The more quickly treatment is administered, the fewer the number of heart cells that will be damaged.
>
> Researchers at several Ontario universities are trying to find ways of using stem cells to replace cells that have been damaged by heart attacks. To avoid future heart problems, heart attack victims are usually encouraged to maintain a healthy diet and get regular exercise.

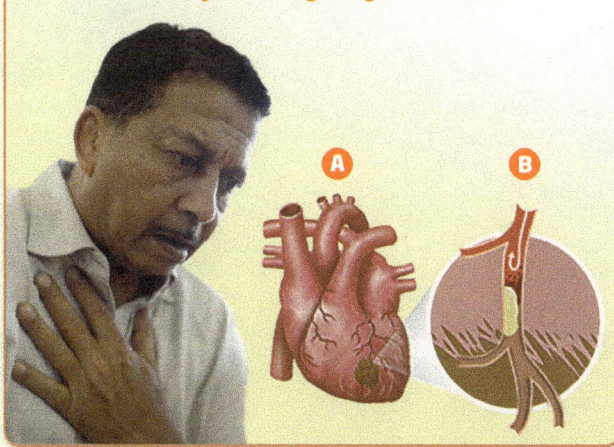

Multiple Choice

In your notebook, record the best or most correct answer.

39. According to the information in the first paragraph, a heart attack occurs when
   a. heart cells die due to a lack of oxygen
   b. a person has chest pains and trouble breathing
   c. plaque builds up in an artery
   d. a person eats poorly and does not exercise regularly

40. How are diagrams A and B related?
   a. A occurs before B occurs.
   b. B proves that A is accurate.
   c. B illustrates an inside view of what A illustrates.
   d. B illustrates how plaque builds up in blood vessels.

41. Researchers hope that stem cells can one day
   a. prevent heart attacks by supplying oxygen to heart cells
   b. repair heart tissue that has been damaged by heart attacks
   c. grow new hearts for transplant
   d. determine why some people are more likely than others to develop heart problems

42. The main idea of the second paragraph is that
   a. heart attacks can be fatal
   b. treatment for a heart attack may involve opening clogged arteries
   c. heart attack victims must be treated in a hospital as quickly as possible
   d. heart cells die during a heart attack

43. Which is the *best* inference you can make about the last sentence?
   a. A healthy diet and regular exercise can prevent the conditions that lead to heart attacks.
   b. People who have a poor diet and who do not exercise regularly are more likely to have a heart attack than other people.
   c. People who eat well and exercise regularly will not have a heart attack.
   d. Eating well and exercising regularly can repair muscle tissue that has been damaged by a heart attack.

Written Answer

44. Select appropriate information from this selection to write a paragraph beginning with the following statement: "The best cure for a heart attack is prevention."

UNIT 2
Chemical Reactions

BIG IDEAS

- Chemical reactions may have a negative impact on the environment, but they can also be used to address environmental challenges.
- Chemicals react with each other in predictable ways.

This river gets its astonishing red colour from nickel tailings—what is left after most of the nickel has been extracted from its ore. The colour comes from red, iron-containing compounds.

Sudbury, rich in nickel and other metals, supports industry that provides thousands of jobs and produces metal used to make countless useful items. But 100 years of metal processing has taken its toll on the area. By the late 1970s, over 100 000 ha of land in and around Sudbury had become barren due to pollution.

People in Sudbury have been working to reclaim this land. They have used one chemical—limestone—to help restore the soil to its natural levels of acidity. They have used other chemicals—fertilizers—to encourage the growth of trees and grass.

In this unit, you will learn how chemicals react. You will see how chemical reactions can result in useful products, while also sometimes damaging the environment. Chemical reactions, however, can also be used to reverse that damage.

What properties of limestone enable it to restore acidified soil?

Chapter 4
Developing Chemical Equations

Chapter 5
Classifying Chemical Reactions

Chapter 6
Acids and Bases

133

Get Ready for Unit 2

Concept Check

1. Complete each sentence with a word from the box below.

compound	ion	valence
element	metal	

   a. A(n) _____ is a pure substance that cannot be broken down further by physical or chemical means.

   b. A(n) _____ is a substance that can be broken down into elements by chemical means.

   c. Molecular compounds are formed when a non-metal bonds with a(n) _____.

   d. _____ electrons are those found in an atom's outermost occupied energy level.

   e. A(n) _____ is an atom that has lost or gained valence electrons.

2. Copy and complete the following table in your notebook.

   Facts about Subatomic Particles

	Electrons	Neutrons	Protons
Location		inside the nucleus	
Charge			positive (+)
Relative size	smallest of these particles		

3. Identify the information listed below for the element beryllium. Refer to the periodic table below.

   a. symbol
   b. name of group
   c. number of protons
   d. number of electrons
   e. atomic number
   f. number of neutrons in an isotope with a mass number of 9

4. Determine whether each statement below describes a physical property or a chemical property of an element. If the statement describes a physical property, indicate whether it is a qualitative property or a quantitative property.

   a. It is a pale yellow gas at room temperature.
   b. It can burn or etch glass permanently.
   c. Its density is 1.695 g/L.
   d. It explodes when it reacts with water.

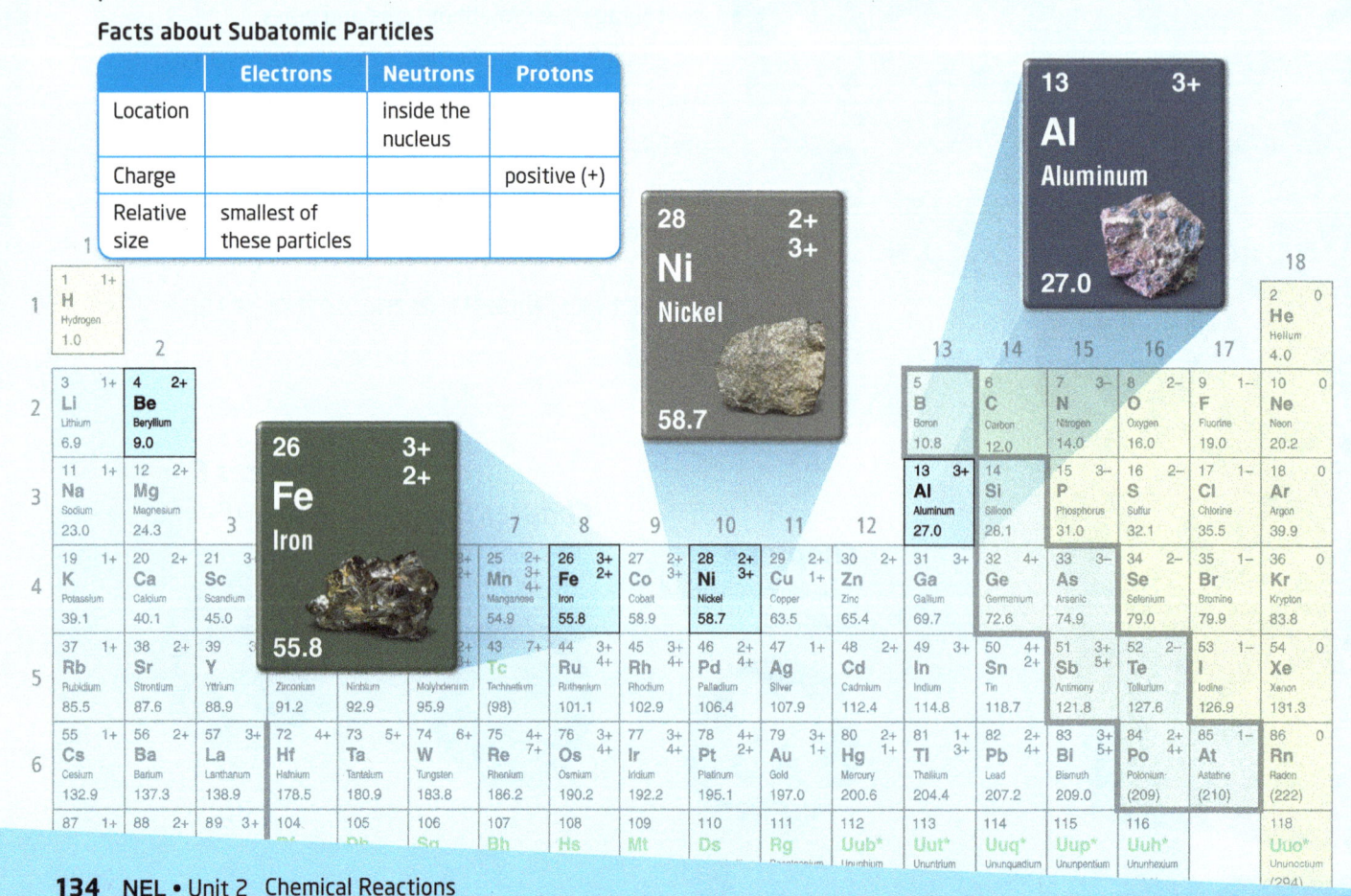

Inquiry Check

5. **Analyze** Bohr-Rutherford diagrams for two compounds, and their melting points and boiling points are shown below.

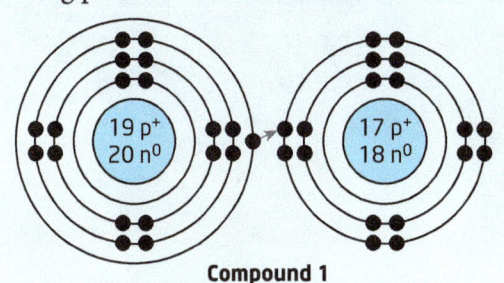

Compound 1
melting point = 775°C; boiling point = 1500°C

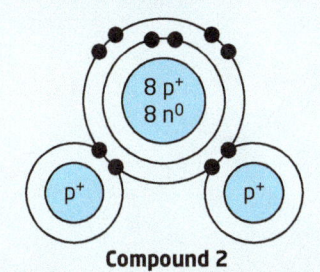

(19 p+, 20 n⁰) and (17 p+, 18 n⁰)

Compound 2
melting point = 0°C; boiling point = 100°C

(8 p+, 8 n⁰) with two p+

a. What elements are represented in compound 1 and compound 2?

b. Determine which diagram shows an ionic compound and which shows a molecular compound. Justify your answer.

c. Determine the chemical formulas and names for the compounds.

Numeracy and Literacy Check

6. **Balance Equations** During a chemical reaction, atoms cannot be created or destroyed. Consider the blue and yellow spheres below as atoms. Is this equation balanced? If not, what is missing from which side?

7. **Calculate** The densities of three metals are given in the table below.

Density of Three Metals

Name and Symbol	Density (g/cm³)
aluminum (Al)	2.7
iron (Fe)	7.9
nickel (Ni)	8.9

One of these metals has a mass of 10 g and a volume of 1.12 cm³. Determine the identity and atomic number of the metal. Show all your work.

8. **Write** Complete a 3, 2, 1 organizer using the text on page 133. Include three interesting facts, two questions that you have, and one key idea in your organizer.

Looking Ahead to the Unit 2 Projects

At the end of this unit, you will have an opportunity to apply what you have learned in an inquiry or research project. Read the Unit 2 Projects on pages 256–257. Start a project folder now (either paper or electronic). Store ideas, notes, news clippings, website addresses, and lists of materials that might help you to complete your project.

Inquiry Project
Extract metallic copper from copper(II) carbonate.

An Issue to Analyze
Form an opinion about the retrieval of gold from e-waste.

Chapter 4: Developing Chemical Equations

What You Will Learn

In this chapter, you will learn how to...

- **identify**, **name**, and **write** the formulas of ionic and molecular compounds
- **write** and **balance** chemical equations
- **describe** how balanced chemical equations demonstrate the law of conservation of mass

Why It Matters

A chemically literate society can make informed decisions about health issues and help to reduce our impact on the environment. A key part of chemical literacy is being able to interpret chemical names and formulas of compounds, as well as the reactions that chemicals undergo.

Skills You Will Use

In this chapter, you will learn how to...

- **investigate** the law of conservation of mass in chemical reactions
- **develop** chemical equations for reactions using appropriate symbols

Imagine what this crash test dummy would look like if an air bag had not been deployed on impact. Air bag inflation systems rely on a chemical reaction that, once triggered, rapidly produces a certain amount of gas. This gas inflates the air bag. The development of air bags is just one example of many technologies that rely on chemical reactions. Key to these applications is the ability to identify the best chemicals to generate the desired products in predictable amounts.

Activity 4-1

Making a Reaction Happen

For chemicals to react, they must come in contact. However, chemicals such as baking soda and citric acid do not appear to react when added together. Additional conditions must be present for a reaction to occur. What could one of these conditions be?

Safety Precautions

- Wear safety goggles and a lab apron.

Materials

- 1 L resealable plastic bag
- 2 scoops
- baking soda
- citric acid
- water

Reactions require the right conditions in order to occur.

Procedure

1. Make a data table using the headings "Before Mixing with Water" and "After Mixing with Water." Give your table a title.

2. Place one scoop of baking soda in one corner of a resealable plastic bag. Add one scoop of citric acid in the same corner of the bag. Observe the bag for signs of a chemical reaction, and record your observations.

3. Twist the corner of the bag that contains the baking soda and citric acid. This will keep them dry as you place several millilitres of water in the other corner of the bag.

4. Press the air out of the bag, and seal the bag.

5. Untwist the corner of the bag, and mix the water with the baking soda and citric acid. Record your observations.

Questions

1. What evidence that a reaction took place did you observe?

2. What one condition was required for the reaction to occur?

3. How would you expect the mass of the bag and its contents to compare before the reaction and after the reaction? Explain your reasoning.

Chapter 4 Developing Chemical Equations • NEL   137

Study Toolkit

These strategies will help you use this textbook to develop your understanding of science concepts and skills. To find out more about these and other strategies, refer to the Study Toolkit Overview, which begins on page 560.

Reading Effectively

Skim, Scan, or Study

As you read a chapter, the speed at which you read a section of text is determined by your *purpose* for reading. The table below shows three different purposes for reading, each with a different approach.

Purpose	Reading Approach
Preview text to get a general sense of what it contains.	Read quickly (skim).
Locate specific information.	Read somewhat quickly (scan).
Learn a new concept.	Read slowly (study).

Sometimes, you can determine the reading approach by the placement, treatment, or features of the text. For example, text that is placed at the beginning of a chapter or unit is often meant to stimulate interest and may not include important concepts. Text with several **boldfaced** words should probably be read slowly.

Use the Strategy

Choose the reading approach that you think should be used for each task below, and explain why.

1. Find the definition of the word *anion*.
2. Learn how to balance chemical equations.
3. Get a general idea about what Section 4.3 contains.

Now complete each task, and decide whether the reading approach you chose was appropriate.

Organizing Your Learning

Identifying the Main Idea and Details

To identify the main idea in a chapter, section, or paragraph, use these strategies:

- Pay attention to titles, headings, and subheadings.
- Skim the text and visuals to get a general sense of the content.
- Note any terms that are boldfaced, italicized, or highlighted.

Facts and examples in the text provide details that help to support the main idea. A **spider map**, like the one below, is a visual way to organize the main idea and the supporting details.

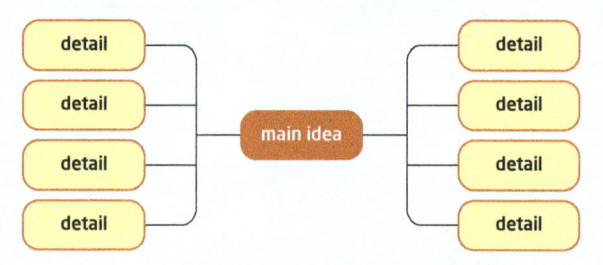

Use the Strategy

Examine the section titled "Naming Binary Ionic Compounds" on page 142. Then draw a spider map to show the main idea and the supporting details in this section. Compare your spider map with a classmate's spider map, and discuss how you decided what to include.

Word Study

Base Words

A base is a word part that may or may not have another word part (such as a prefix or a suffix) added to it. To identify the base of a word, find the smallest word (usually a noun or a verb) within it. For example, in the word *polyatomic*, the base word is *atom*. You can use the meaning of the base word to understand the longer word.

Use the Strategy

Think about the word *reactant*. What is the base of this word? Use this base word to predict the meaning of *reactant*. Use a dictionary, or the Glossary at the end of the textbook, to check your prediction.

4.1 Representing Ionic Compounds

Think about all the paper products you encounter in your daily life. Paper is used for countless purposes throughout our society. Even with current recycling initiatives, however, paper is often wasted and taken for granted.

Paper is made with fibres that can come from wood, plants, or recycled paper. Historically, paper manufacturing required a large supply of trees and energy, and produced large amounts of pollutants, as shown in **Figure 4.1**. Paper manufacturing is estimated to be the source of 50 percent of the waste that is dumped in Canada's waterways. Many **ionic compounds** are used to produce paper. More recently, stronger regulations and more effective recycling and treatment of waste materials have helped to reduce the environmental impact of paper manufacturing. The goal is to build zero-emission pulp and paper mills, in which all wastes are recovered. For example, ionic compounds such as sodium carbonate (Na_2CO_3) and calcium oxide (CaO) are used in the recovery of chemicals from the pulping process.

Key Terms
ionic compound
ion
cation
anion
valence electron
binary ionic compound
polyatomic ion
ternary compound

ionic compound a compound composed of oppositely charged ions

Suggested Investigation
Inquiry Investigation 4-A, Monitoring Paper Recycling, on page 169

Figure 4.1 This pulp and paper mill in Thunder Bay, Ontario, produces useful products. It also produces solid, liquid, and gas wastes.

Forming Ionic Compounds

Elements can combine to make ionic compounds when their atoms lose or gain electrons, becoming charged particles called **ions**. When atoms lose electrons, they form positively charged ions called **cations**. When atoms gain electrons, they form negatively charged ions called **anions**.

When an ionic compound forms, one or more electrons from one atom are transferred to another atom. An ionic bond forms between oppositely charged ions, creating a neutral compound. The loss and gain of electrons allows each atom to form a full outer energy level of electrons and, therefore, become more stable. Scientists often refer to this arrangement as a *stable octet*. This is because all noble gases, except helium, have eight electrons in their outer energy level. Recall that noble gases are the least reactive (most stable) elements.

The Periodic Table and Ion Formation

Ionic compounds are usually composed of the ions of a metal and one or more non-metals. As shown in **Figure 4.2**, metals are found on the left-hand side of the periodic table. They tend to lose electrons to form cations. Non-metals, except for hydrogen, are found on the right-hand side of the periodic table and tend to gain electrons to form anions.

Recall from your previous studies that there are patterns related to the arrangement of electrons in atoms in the periodic table. One important pattern involves the number of **valence electrons**—electrons in the outer energy level. **Figure 4.3** shows how elements in the same group have the same number of valence electrons. For example, all the elements in Group 1 have one valence electron, while all the elements in Group 17 have seven valence electrons. Valence electrons are involved in the chemical bonding between elements. Therefore, knowing the number of valence electrons helps you predict the formation of compounds, name the compounds that are formed, and write the chemical formulas for the compounds.

ion a charged particle formed from the loss or gain of one or more electrons

cation a positively charged ion

anion a negatively charged ion

valence electron an electron in the outermost occupied energy level

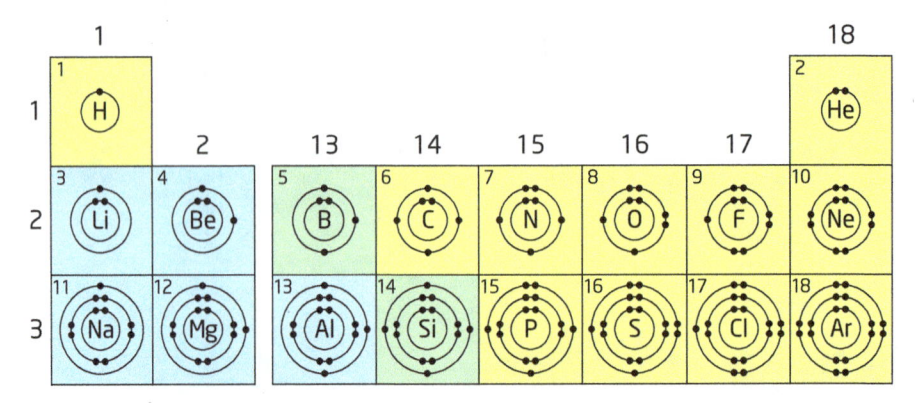

Figure 4.3 The atoms of the elements in each group share a common property: they all have the same number of valence electrons.

Figure 4.2 The periodic table includes information about the ion(s) that each element forms.

binary ionic compound a compound composed of a metal cation and a non-metal anion

Naming Binary Ionic Compounds

There are two ways to identify a compound: by its chemical name and by its chemical formula. An organization called the International Union of Pure and Applied Chemistry (IUPAC) develops rules for naming compounds so that scientists throughout the world can use the same names for the same compounds. The chemical names of all ionic compounds have two parts—one part for each type of ion. The following rules are used to name **binary ionic compounds**, which are composed of only two different elements:

Table 4.1 Examples of Names of Non-Metal Ions

Name	Symbol
fluoride	F^-
chloride	Cl^-
oxide	O^{2-}
sulfide	S^{2-}
nitride	N^{3-}
phosphide	P^{3-}

Rules for Naming Binary Ionic Compounds

1. The first part of the name *always* identifies the positive ion, which is the metal cation. Thus, this part of the name is the name of the metal.
2. The second part of the name *always* identifies the negative ion, which is the non-metal anion. The name of the non-metal ion always ends with the suffix *-ide*. Some examples are provided in **Table 4.1**.

A few names of simple ionic compounds, as well as the elements that form them, are given in **Table 4.2**. Notice the name of an ionic compound that you are very familiar with—sodium chloride, or table salt, shown in **Figure 4.4**.

Table 4.2 Examples of Names of Ionic Compounds

Elements in Ionic Compound	Name of Ionic Compound
magnesium and phosphorus	magnesium phosphide
sodium and chlorine	sodium chloride (table salt)
calcium and bromine	calcium bromide
aluminum and oxygen	aluminum oxide

Figure 4.4 Table salt is an ionic compound composed of sodium cations and chloride anions.

Learning Check

1. Why is knowing the number of valence electrons important in chemical bonding?
2. When naming a binary ionic compound, what suffix is used in the part of the name that represents the anion?
3. Write the names of the following binary ionic compounds.
    a. $MgBr_2$
    b. CaI_2
    c. Al_2O_3
    d. KCl
4. Why is it important to provide rules for naming compounds? Provide an example from your own life that illustrates your reason.

Determining the Chemical Formula for an Ionic Compound

A binary ionic compound forms when electrons are transferred from a metal to a non-metal. The number of electrons that are given up by the metal must equal the number of electrons that are gained by the non-metal.

For example, one electron is transferred from one sodium atom to one chlorine atom to form sodium chloride. Many binary ionic compounds, however, do not form in a 1:1 ratio of ions to achieve a stable octet of valence electrons. Examine the Bohr-Rutherford models in **Figure 4.5** to see the transfer of electrons between aluminum and chlorine atoms. The aluminum atom can give away its electrons only when there is just the right number of atoms to receive them. In this example, one atom of aluminum forms an ionic compound with three atoms of chlorine.

In the following activity, you will model the transfer of electrons between metal atoms and non-metal atoms and relate this to the chemical formulas for ionic compounds.

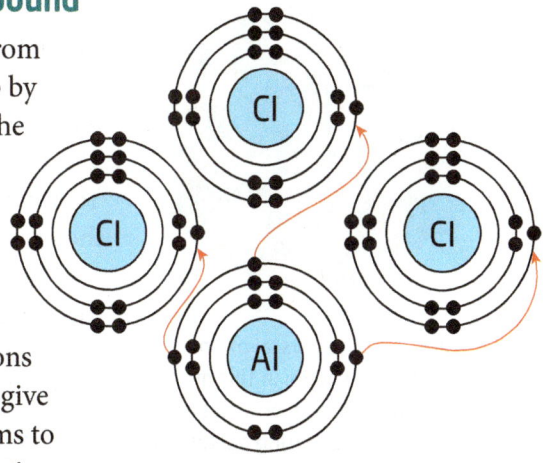

Figure 4.5 The three valence electrons of an aluminum atom can transfer over to three chlorine atoms, forming aluminum chloride.

Activity 4-2

Take My Electron–Please!

In this activity, you will use circular objects to represent electrons and to model the formation of ionic compounds. Based on what you know about ionic compounds, what must happen to the electrons?

Materials
- bag that contains small circular objects (such as washers or coloured paper reinforcements) to mimic valence electrons

Procedure

1. Make two columns on a sheet of paper. Write "Metal" as the heading for the first column and "Non-metal" as the heading for the second column. Near the top of the first column, write the symbol for the metal sodium. Near the top of the second column, write the symbol for the non-metal chlorine. Use the objects to represent electrons, and draw a Bohr-Rutherford model for each atom under the name of the element.

2. Move the "electrons" from the metal atom to the non-metal atom to model the transfer of electrons that occurs when the elements react to form an ionic compound. Examine the "electrons" around each symbol.

- If the metal has no "electrons" remaining in its original outer level and the non-metal now has eight "electrons" in its outer level, then the transfer is complete. If your model does not represent this, continue modelling electron transfer until it does.

3. Record the names of the elements and the ratio of the ions needed to complete the transfer of electrons. For sodium and chlorine, the ratio is 1:1.

4. Write the chemical formula for the binary ionic compound formed by writing the symbol for the metal followed by the symbol for the non-metal and using the numbers of ions in the ratio as subscripts. The chemical formula for the compound formed by sodium and chlorine is NaCl.

5. Repeat steps 1 to 4 for each of the following pairs of elements: (a) magnesium and fluorine, (b) lithium and nitrogen, and (c) aluminum and sulfur.

Questions

1. For each pair of elements, compare the total number of electrons lost by the metal atoms to the total number of electrons gained by the non-metal atoms. Describe the pattern, and explain why it must be so.

2. "An ion has a charge, but an ionic compound has no charge." Based on your models, what evidence supports this statement?

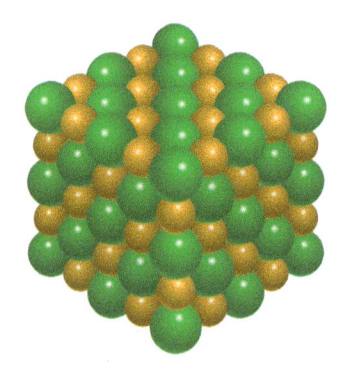

Figure 4.6 The crystal of an ionic solid, as shown in this model, is made up of many ions that are arranged in a repeating pattern in three dimensions.

Figure 4.7 By using models of the ions, as shown, the number of each ion needed for the compound to have a total charge of zero can be determined.

Determining Chemical Formulas for Binary Ionic Compounds

Recall that ionic compounds tend to be solid at room temperature and exist as *crystal lattices*. The ions in a crystal lattice are organized in a large repeating array, as shown in the model of sodium chloride in **Figure 4.6**. There are no individual particles of sodium chloride in the crystal. Therefore, to write the chemical formula for an ionic compound, you use the ratio of the ions that make up the crystal.

Figure 4.7 shows one way that you can determine the chemical formula for an ionic compound based on the name of the compound, knowledge of the valence electrons for each atom, and the ion charge that each atom forms. Since ionic compounds are neutral, the sum of the positive and negative charges from the ions must be zero. Therefore, the correct ratio of ions must be determined so that the net charge of the compound is zero.

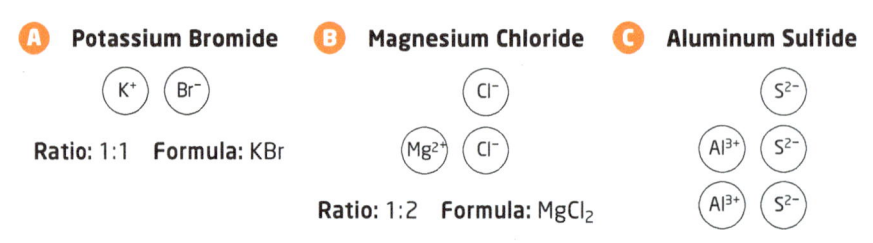

A Potassium Bromide
K^+ Br^-
Ratio: 1:1   Formula: KBr

B Magnesium Chloride
Mg^{2+} Cl^- Cl^-
Ratio: 1:2   Formula: $MgCl_2$

C Aluminum Sulfide
Al^{3+} Al^{3+} S^{2-} S^{2-} S^{2-}
Ratio: 2:3   Formula: Al_2S_3

The symbols and charges of several non-metal ions are shown in **Table 4.3**. Remember that the charge of each anion represents the number of electrons that the atom gains, which is related to the element's group in the periodic table. According to the same principles, the charge of each cation represents the number of electrons that the atom loses, which is related to the element's group in the periodic table. Therefore, it is important to understand the relationship between loss and gain of electrons and position of the element in the periodic table.

Once you have determined the ratio of ions, you can write the chemical formula by writing the symbol for the cation with a subscript to show how many cations are needed, followed by the symbol for the anion with a subscript to show how many anions are needed. If only one ion is needed, do not write a subscript—the subscript is understood to be the number 1.

Table 4.3 Charges and Symbols of Some Non-metal Ions

Symbol	Group	Electrons Gained
F^-	17	1
Cl^-	17	1
Br^-	17	1
O^{2-}	16	2
S^{2-}	16	2
N^{3-}	15	3
P^{3-}	15	3

Writing Chemical Formulas for Binary Ionic Compounds

The steps to follow when writing the chemical formula for a binary ionic compound from its name are summarized in **Table 4.4**. As you read through the steps, look at how each one applies to the examples in the table.

Table 4.4 How to Write the Chemical Formula for a Binary Ionic Compound

	Examples	
Steps	**Aluminum Fluoride**	**Magnesium Nitride**
1. Identify each ion and its charge.	aluminum: Al^{3+} fluoride: F^-	magnesium: Mg^{2+} nitride: N^{3-}
2. Determine the total positive charge and the total negative charge needed to equal zero.	$Al^{3+}: 3+ = 3+$ $F^-: 3(1-) = 3-$ $(3+) + (3-) = 0$	$Mg^{2+}: 3(2+) = 6+$ $N^{3-}: 2(3-) = 6-$ $(6+) + (6-) = 0$
3. Note the ratio of cations to anions.	$1Al^{3+}: 3F^-$	$3Mg^{2+}: 2N^{3-}$
4. Use subscripts to show the ratio of ions.	AlF_3	Mg_3N_2

Using the Cross-Over Method

Another way to determine the chemical formula for an ionic compound, which is also useful to check that a formula you have written has balanced charges, is to use the *cross-over method*.

- Write the ions beside each other.
- Take the amount of charge (ignoring the sign) from the cation and make this number the subscript for the anion in your formula.
- Take the amount of charge (again, ignoring the sign) from the anion and make this number the subscript for the cation in your formula.

The following example shows how to use the cross-over method to write the chemical formulas for two ionic compounds.

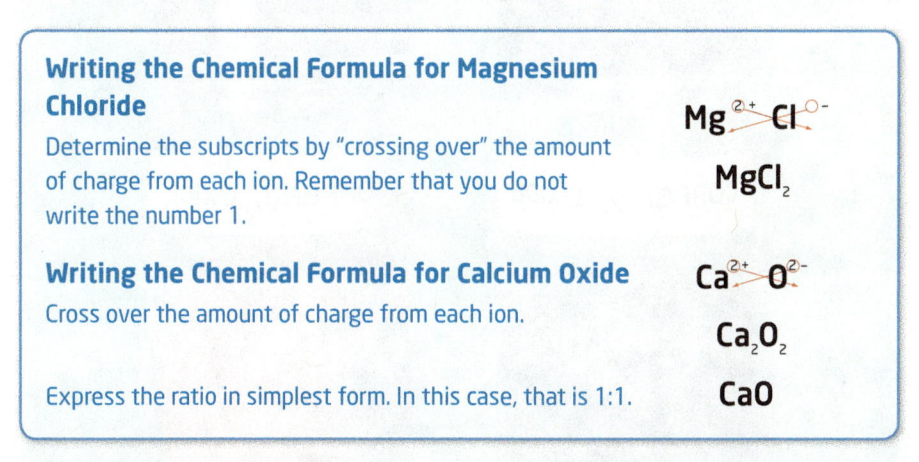

Study Toolkit

Skim, Scan, or Study
To help you determine how carefully you should read the material, identify the purpose of **Table 4.4**. Then describe a suitable reading approach, based on the options listed on page 138.

Writing the Chemical Formula for Magnesium Chloride

Determine the subscripts by "crossing over" the amount of charge from each ion. Remember that you do not write the number 1.

$Mg^{2+} \searrow Cl^-$

$MgCl_2$

Writing the Chemical Formula for Calcium Oxide

Cross over the amount of charge from each ion.

$Ca^{2+} \searrow O^{2-}$

Ca_2O_2

Express the ratio in simplest form. In this case, that is 1:1.

CaO

Learning Check

5. Describe what happens to aluminum's valence electrons in **Figure 4.5**.

6. Draw Bohr-Rutherford diagrams to show why $MgCl_2$ is the correct chemical formula for the ionic compound formed in a reaction between magnesium and chlorine.

7. Show how the total charge of the following compounds is zero.
   a. sodium oxide
   b. lithium nitride
   c. aluminum iodide
   d. barium phosphide

8. Write the chemical formula for each binary ionic compound.
   a. potassium sulfide
   b. lithium selenide
   c. zinc oxide
   d. rubidium bromide
   e. cesium sulfide
   f. strontium nitride

Multivalent Metals

You may have noticed that some metals have more than one ion charge listed in the periodic table. These elements, called *multivalent metals*, can form different ions, depending on the chemical reaction they undergo. For example, copper can form ions with a 1+ or 2+ charge, as shown in **Figure 4.8**. To distinguish between the ions, a Roman numeral is written after the name of the metal. For example, Cu^+ is written as copper(I), called "copper one." Cu^{2+} is written as copper(II), called "copper two." The charge of the most common ion that a multivalent metal forms is listed at the top of the element's box in the periodic table.

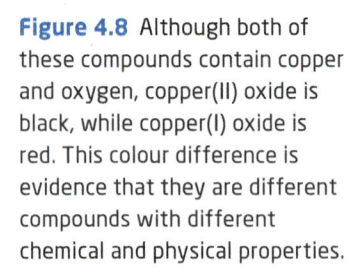

Figure 4.8 Although both of these compounds contain copper and oxygen, copper(II) oxide is black, while copper(I) oxide is red. This colour difference is evidence that they are different compounds with different chemical and physical properties.

Writing Chemical Formulas and Naming Ionic Compounds with a Multivalent Metal

To write the chemical formula for a compound that contains a multivalent ion, based on the name of the compound, the same steps that were used for binary ionic compounds apply (see Table 4.4 on page 145).

When naming a compound that contains a multivalent ion, you must include a Roman numeral to show which charge the ion has. Table 4.5 contains the symbols for Roman numerals that apply to multivalent ions. To determine this charge, you must work back from the charge of the anion, as shown in Table 4.6.

Table 4.5 Roman Numerals

Number	Roman Numeral
1	I
2	II
3	III
4	IV
5	V
6	VI
7	VII

Table 4.6 Naming an Ionic Compound That Contains a Multivalent Metal

Steps	Examples Cu_3N	Examples SnS_2
1. Identify the metal.	copper (Cu)	tin (Sn)
2. Verify that the metal can form more than one kind of ion by checking the periodic table.	Cu^+ and Cu^{2+}	Sn^{2+} and Sn^{4+}
3. Determine the ratio of the ions in the chemical formula.	3 copper:1 nitride	1 tin:2 sulfide
4. Note the charge of the anion.	3–	2–
5. The positive and negative charges must balance out so that the net charge is zero.	Total negative charge: 3– Total positive charge: 3+	Total negative charge: 4– Total positive charge: 4+
6. Determine what charge the metal ion must have to balance the anion.	$3(Cu^?) = 3+$ Therefore, the charge on the copper must be 1+.	$1(Sn^?) = 4+$ Therefore, the charge on the tin must be 4+.
7. Write the name of the metal ion.	The name of the metal ion is copper(I).	The name of the metal ion is tin(IV).
8. Write the name of the compound.	copper(I) nitride	tin(IV) sulfide

Using the Reverse of the Cross-Over Method

You can also use the reverse of the cross-over method to determine the charge of a multivalent metal ion. Be aware, however, that this method may result in an error unless you check that the charge of the anion is correct.

Determining the Name of FeO

Add the charge signs for each ion.

Fe⤫O

The charge of the oxide ion is not correct, which means that the subscripts were reduced.

Fe^+ O^-

The oxide ion should be O^{2-}. Therefore, double the charge of each ion. The iron ion is Fe^{2+}, so the name of FeO is iron(II) oxide.

Fe^{2+} O^{2-}

polyatomic ion an ion that is composed of more than one atom

ternary compound a compound composed of three different elements

Ionic Compounds with Polyatomic Ions

The beautiful shells in **Figure 4.9** are made from the ionic compound calcium carbonate. Notice that the name of this compound ends in *-ate*. The carbonate ion is composed of carbon and oxygen. An ion, such as carbonate, that is composed of more than one atom is a **polyatomic ion**. Because calcium carbonate contains the carbonate ion, it is composed of more than two elements: calcium, carbon, and oxygen. Therefore, calcium carbonate is *not* a binary compound. It is an example of a **ternary compound**. Like a binary compound, however, it is named by writing the name of the cation followed by the name of the anion.

Some common polyatomic ions that you will use in this course are listed in **Table 4.7**. Notice that the names of most of these ions end in *-ate* or *-ite*. There are three exceptions: ammonium, hydroxide, and peroxide. The ammonium ion is a cation. Therefore, when naming a compound that contains this ion, write its name first. The names *hydroxide* and *peroxide* end in *-ide*, like the names of the non-metal ions in **Table 4.1**. The name *hydroxide* tells you that there are two elements in the ion: hydrogen and oxygen. The name *peroxide* tells you that there are two oxygen atoms in the ion.

Table 4.7 Common Polyatomic Ions

1+ Charge	3− Charge	2− Charge	1− Charge
• ammonium, NH_4^+	• phosphate, PO_4^{3-} • phosphite, PO_3^{3-}	• carbonate, CO_3^{2-} • sulfate, SO_4^{2-} • sulfite, SO_3^{2-} • peroxide, O_2^{2-}	• hydrogen carbonate (bicarbonate), HCO_3^- • hydroxide, OH^- • nitrate, NO_3^- • nitrite, NO_2^- • chlorate, ClO_3^-

Figure 4.9 These shells are made from calcium carbonate—an ionic compound that is composed of a calcium ion and a carbonate ion. The carbonate ion is a polyatomic ion.

Writing Chemical Formulas for Compounds with a Polyatomic Ion

Calcium hydroxide is an ionic compound that is used in many products and processes. For example, it is an ingredient in making mortar and plaster for construction. **Figure 4.10** shows how to write the chemical formula for calcium hydroxide. The brackets are an important part of the formula. The hydroxide ion is composed of one hydrogen atom and one oxygen atom. The ratio of the ions in calcium hydroxide calls for two hydroxide ions, which would be a total of two hydrogen atoms and two oxygen atoms. If you write the formula *incorrectly* as $CaOH_2$, the subscript applies only to the hydrogen atom. You must use brackets to show that two whole hydroxide ions are in the formula. **Table 4.8** outlines the steps to follow when writing the chemical formula for a compound that contains polyatomic ions.

Calcium Hydroxide

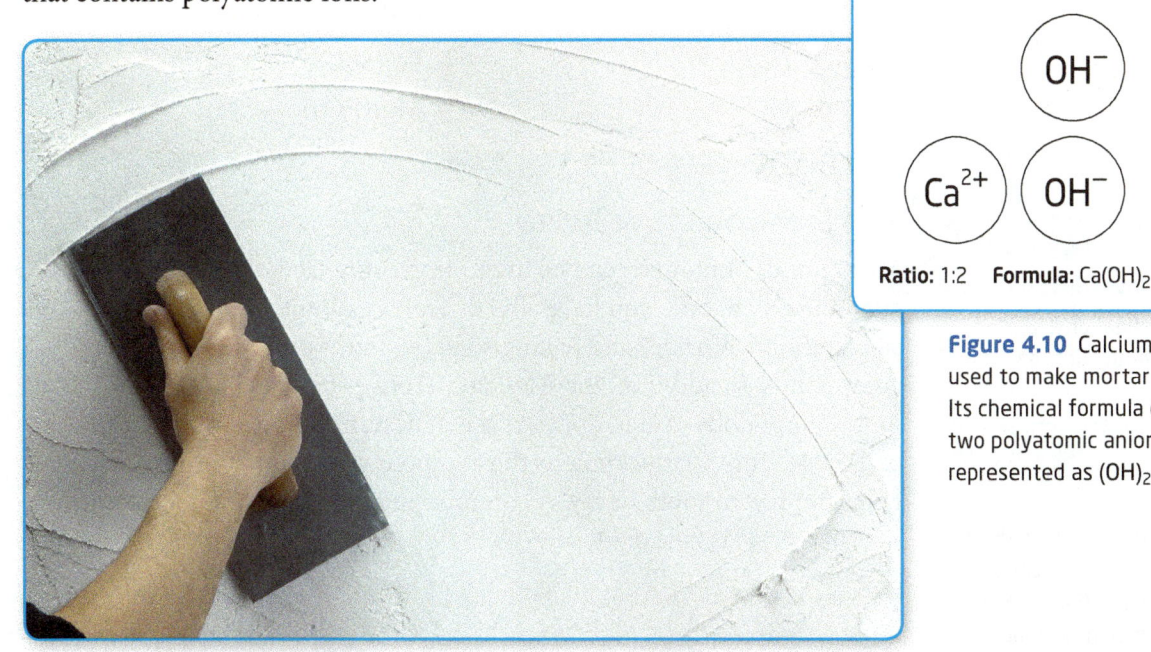

OH^- Ca^{2+} OH^-

Ratio: 1:2   Formula: $Ca(OH)_2$

Figure 4.10 Calcium hydroxide is used to make mortar and plaster. Its chemical formula contains two polyatomic anions, which is represented as $(OH)_2$

Table 4.8 How to Write the Chemical Formula for a Compound with a Polyatomic Ion

Steps	Examples Aluminum Carbonate (used as an antacid)	Ammonium Sulfate (used as a fertilizer)
1. Using the periodic table and a table of common polyatomic ions, identify each ion and its charge.	aluminum: Al^{3+} carbonate: CO_3^{2-}	ammonium: NH_4^+ sulfate: SO_4^{2-}
2. Determine the total positive charge and the total negative charge needed to equal zero.	Al^{3+}: 2(3+) = 6+ CO_3^{2-}: 3(2−) = 6− (6+) + (6−) = 0	NH_4^+: 2(1+) = 2+ SO_4^{2-}: 2− = 2− (2+) + (2−) = 0
3. Note the ratio of cations to anions.	2:3	2:1
4. Use subscripts to show the ratio of ions. Place the polyatomic ion in brackets if it needs a subscript.	$Al_2(CO_3)_3$	$(NH_4)_2SO_4$

Learning Check

9. Identify each of the following compounds as binary or ternary. Then write the chemical formula for each ionic compound.
   a. nickel(III) oxide
   b. copper(II) iodide
   c. tin(IV) nitride
   d. chromium (II) bromide
   e. iron(III) phosphide
   f. lithium hydroxide
   g. potassium sulfate
   h. ammonium phosphide
   i. barium nitrate
   j. cobalt(II) phosphate

10. Write the name of each ionic compound. Check for multivalent and polyatomic ions when naming.
    a. $AuCl_3$
    b. Sn_3P_4
    c. Cr_2O_3
    d. Ni_2S_3
    e. $(NH_4)_2S$
    f. CaF_2
    g. $Fe_2(SO_3)_3$
    h. $Mg_3(PO_3)_2$

Ionic Compounds at Home

Many ionic compounds can be found in most households. Some of these compounds are ones you have already learned about. For example, table salt (sodium chloride) and baking soda (sodium bicarbonate) are ionic compounds. In addition, there are numerous products that contain ionic compounds. Antacids contain magnesium hydroxide and calcium carbonate. Toothpaste contains the compound sodium fluoride, which helps to prevent tooth decay. A common ingredient in sunblocks, shown in **Figure 4.11**, is zinc oxide.

Suggested Investigation
Inquiry Investigation 4–B, Keep That Toothy Grin, on page 170

Figure 4.11 Ionic compounds are in numerous products, including many that you use. For example, a common ingredient in sunblocks and sunscreens is the ionic compound zinc oxide.

Section 4.1 Review

Section Summary

- Ionic compounds are composed of oppositely charged ions, called cations and anions.
- Solid ionic compounds are made up of repeating patterns of ions that occur in specific ratios. The chemical formula for an ionic compound shows the ratio of ions.
- Subscripts are used in the chemical formula for an ionic compound to show the ratio of ions needed to make the total charge zero.
- The name of an ionic compound contains the name of the cation followed by the name of the anion. For binary ionic compounds, the part that represents the anion always ends with the suffix -ide.
- When naming compounds with multivalent metals, a Roman numeral is used to indicate the ion form of the metal.
- Ternary ionic compounds contain polyatomic ions, which are composed of more than one atom. Polyatomic ions have specific names that are based on the group of atoms present.

Review Questions

K/U 1. Write the name of each ion.
   a. Cl^-
   b. SO_4^{2-}
   c. Mg^{2+}
   d. Cu^{2+}

K/U 2. Write the symbol of each ion.
   a. hydroxide ion
   b. sulfide ion
   c. aluminum ion
   d. chromium(III) ion

C 3. Draw a Bohr-Rutherford model to show how atoms of potassium and sulfur form a binary ionic compound. Clearly show the ratio of ions in the compound.

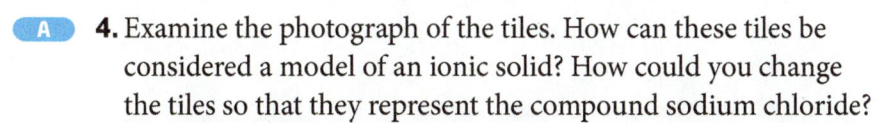

A 4. Examine the photograph of the tiles. How can these tiles be considered a model of an ionic solid? How could you change the tiles so that they represent the compound sodium chloride?

K/U 5. Name each ionic compound.
   a. Li_2CO_3
   b. NH_4NO_2
   c. CuO

K/U 6. Write the chemical formula for each ionic compound.
   a. magnesium nitride
   b. aluminum hydroxide
   c. tin(II) bromide
   d. nickel(II) sulfate

T/I 7. Describe the error in each chemical formula, and write the correct chemical formula for the compound.
   a. sodium phosphate, Na_3P
   b. calcium nitrate, $Ca(NO_3)_2$
   c. potassium sulfite, KSO_3

K/U 8. Using the periodic table in **Figure 4.2**, identify the possible ion charges for iron.

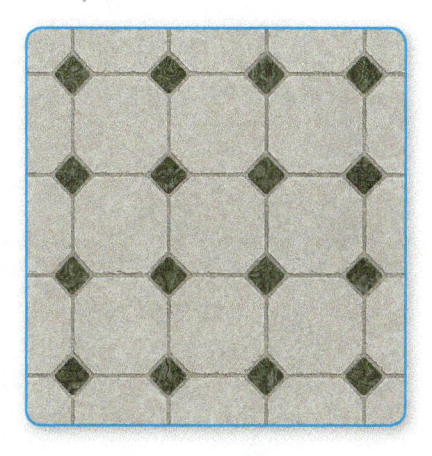

Key Terms
molecular compound
molecule
binary molecular compound

4.2 Representing Molecular Compounds

The chemical shown in **Figure 4.12**, named dihydrogen monoxide, is a molecular compound with many uses. For example, it is a key ingredient in most pesticides, it contributes to environmental hazards (such as acid rain, the greenhouse effect, and soil erosion), and it causes severe illness or death in either very low or very high concentrations in the body. Knowing these facts, a group of students voted in favour of banning dihydrogen monoxide. The students were missing a key piece of information, however. Dihydrogen monoxide is just another name for water!

This example illustrates how important it is to know the names and chemical formulas for compounds, so that you can make well-informed decisions about the chemicals you encounter every day at home, at school, at work, and in the environment.

Study Toolkit

Base Words What is the base of *molecular*? Use this word to predict the meaning of *molecular*. Use a dictionary or the Glossary at the end of this textbook to check your prediction.

Figure 4.12 What's in a name? Everything, when it comes to chemicals. You are continually exposed to this molecular compound, dihydrogen monoxide. Should you be worried?

Forming Molecular Compounds

Molecular compounds, also known as *covalent compounds,* are usually composed of two or more different non-metals. A molecular compound forms when atoms share a pair of electrons to form a covalent bond. In a covalent bond, the shared electrons are attracted to the nuclei of both atoms. This attraction holds the atoms together. Therefore, unlike electrons in an ionic compound, electrons in a molecular compound are not transferred between atoms, so the atoms remain uncharged. Nevertheless, the formation of a molecular compound is based on the same principle as the formation of an ionic compound: the stability that is associated with a full outer energy level of electrons. The Bohr-Rutherford model for water is shown in **Figure 4.13**. It demonstrates how the covalent bonding of each hydrogen atom to the oxygen atom produces filled outer energy levels for all three atoms.

> **molecular compound** a compound formed when atoms of two or more different elements share electrons

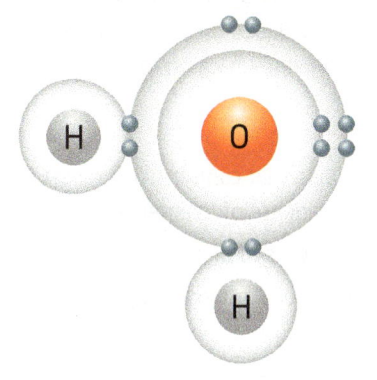

Figure 4.13 This Bohr-Rutherford model for water demonstrates how the atoms share electrons so that each atom has a full set of electrons in its outer energy level.

Molecules

In the last section, you saw that an ionic solid is composed of a repeating pattern of ions. In contrast, molecular compounds are composed of individual **molecules**. Each molecule, like the one shown in **Figure 4.14**, is composed of a set number of atoms of each element.

The term *molecule* is also used to describe two or more atoms of the same element that are joined by a covalent bond. Elements that exist in this form include H_2, N_2, O_2, Cl_2, Br_2, I_2, and F_2. Remember, however, that these molecules are not compounds because they contain only one kind of atom.

The following activity will give you a chance to model molecule formation.

> **molecule** a neutral particle composed of two or more atoms joined together by covalent bonds

Figure 4.14 Bubbles filled with carbon dioxide gas are escaping from this drink. The model of carbon dioxide gas shows that each molecule of carbon dioxide is composed of one carbon atom and two oxygen atoms.

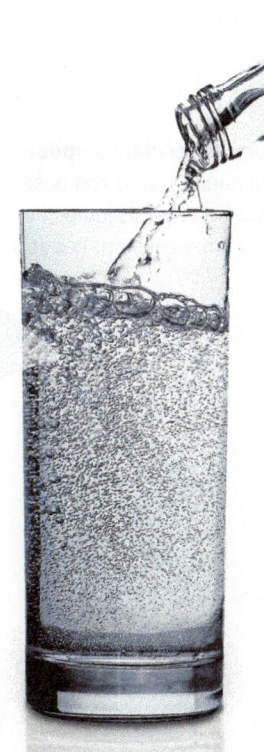

Chapter 4 Developing Chemical Equations • NEL 153

Activity 4-3

Electron, Anyone?

In this activity, you will use circular objects to represent electrons and model the formation of three molecular compounds: water (H_2O), ammonia (NH_3), and methane (CH_4). Based on what you know about molecular compounds, what must happen to the electrons between two atoms?

Materials

- bag that contains small rings (such as washers or coloured paper reinforcements)
- sheets of blank paper
- molecular modelling kit

Procedure

1. At the top of a sheet of paper, write the symbol for an atom of oxygen. Use the objects to represent electrons in a Bohr-Rutherford model of the atom. Write the symbol for the element as a representation of the nucleus. Examine your model, and determine how many electrons the oxygen atom would need to have a full set of eight electrons in its outer energy level.

2. For each electron that the oxygen atom needs, write one symbol for an atom of hydrogen. Use the objects to show the electrons in the hydrogen atoms. Draw arrows to connect the electrons that will be shared by the oxygen atom and each hydrogen atom.

3. Using the objects, show how electrons between the oxygen atom and each hydrogen atom are shared to form covalent bonds and full outer energy levels of electrons.

4. Use the molecular modelling kit to build a three-dimensional model of the molecule. Draw a sketch of your model, and label your sketch.

5. Repeat steps 1 to 4, using nitrogen instead of oxygen.

6. Repeat steps 1 to 4, using carbon instead of oxygen.

Questions

1. How many electrons are surrounding each hydrogen atom after each compound forms?

2. What is the total number of electrons in the outer level of the central atom in each molecule you modelled? How is this number related to the number of covalent bonds that can form?

3. Water, methane, and ammonia are older conventional names of the compounds modelled in this activity. Why do you think chemists sometimes continue to use an old name for a compound, rather than switching to a name that follows the official rules for naming compounds?

Naming Binary Molecular Compounds

binary molecular compound
a compound that is composed of two non-metals joined by one or more covalent bonds

The rules for naming **binary molecular compounds** ensure that the identity of each compound is absolutely clear. For example, the chemical name of the molecular compound *carbon dioxide* reveals two pieces of information. First, it tells you that the compound is composed of the elements carbon and oxygen. Second, it tells you that the ratio of carbon atoms to oxygen atoms is 1:2. The prefixes in the name show the number of atoms of each element in a molecule of the compound. Table 4.9 lists the common prefixes and their meanings.

Table 4.9 Prefixes Used in the Names of Binary Molecular Compounds

Prefix	Number	Prefix	Number
mono-	1	penta-	5
di-	2	hexa-	6
tri-	3	hepta-	7
tetra-	4	octa-	8

Using the Prefixes

The dark hazy smog in **Figure 4.15** is a common sight in some large cities. Many molecular compounds are present in smog, including several compounds that are composed of nitrogen and oxygen. The molecular compound nitrogen dioxide (NO_2) is one of these compounds. Its name reflects the fact that each molecule of the compound is composed of a single nitrogen atom bonded to two oxygen atoms. Two NO_2 molecules can join together to form a completely different compound, N_2O_4. This compound, dinitrogen tetroxide, has different properties and is used in rocket fuels. Notice that the subscripts are not reduced to the simplest whole number ratio because, unlike ionic compounds, a simplified ratio can result in a different molecular compound (for example, NO_2 and N_2O_4).

Table 4.10 shows the steps to follow when writing the name of a binary molecular compound based on its chemical formula. Two examples are given to illustrate the steps.

Sense of place

It is estimated that over 6000 Toronto residents visit hospitals each year due to health problems associated with exposure to air pollution or smog. In addition, exposure to air pollution costs the Toronto economy more than $150 million in health-care costs each year.

Table 4.10 Naming a Binary Molecular Compound

Steps	N_2O_4 (used as a rocket fuel)	BrCl (used to detect mercury in water)
1. Count the number of atoms of the first element in the chemical formula.	Number of nitrogen atoms: 2	Number of bromine atoms: 1
2. Write the appropriate prefix followed by the name of the element. Note that the prefix *mono-* is never used for the first element.	First part of name: dinitrogen	First part of name: bromine
3. Count the number of atoms of the second element in the chemical formula.	Number of oxygen atoms: 4	Number of chlorine atoms: 1
4. Write the appropriate prefix followed by the name of the element using the suffix *-ide*. If the prefix ends with *a* or *o*, this letter is dropped before *oxide*.	Second part of name: tetroxide Full name: dinitrogen tetroxide	Second part of name: monochloride Full name: bromine monochloride

Figure 4.15 Smog like this, which hangs over Toronto, contains the molecular compound NO_2, or nitrogen dioxide.

Figure 4.16 This herbicide is produced using the molecular compound phosphorus trichloride.

> **Learning Check**
>
> 1. What does a prefix in the name of a molecular compound tell you?
>
> 2. Write the name of each molecular compound.
>
>   a. CS_2 d. CCl_4
>
>   b. N_2O_3 e. PF_5
>
>   c. CO f. Si_2Br_6
>
> 3. Use a diagram to illustrate the meaning of each part of the name *diphosphorus pentoxide*.
>
> 4. Show how the prefixes that are used in the names of molecular compounds are also used in everyday language.

Writing Chemical Formulas for Binary Molecular Compounds

The prefixes that are used to name molecular compounds make it easy to infer their chemical formulas. To write the chemical formula for a binary molecular compound, simply write the symbols of the elements with the subscripts indicated by the prefixes, as outlined in **Table 4.11**. One of the examples in the table is phosphorus trichloride, a very toxic chemical that is used to make insecticides and herbicides, such as the one in **Figure 4.16**.

Table 4.11 Writing the Chemical Formula for a Binary Molecular Compound

Steps	Phosphorus Trichloride (used to make insecticide)	Disulfur Dinitride (used to synthesize other chemicals)
1. Write the chemical symbol of the first element.	First element in formula: P	First element in formula: S
2. Determine the number of atoms of the first element, based on the prefix. This number will appear in the final chemical formula. If there is no prefix for the first element, there is only one atom.	Number of phosphorus atoms: 1	Number of sulfur atoms: 2
3. Write the chemical symbol of the second element. Keep in mind that the ending *-ide* is not part of the element's name.	Second element in formula: Cl	Second element in formula: N
4. Determine the number of atoms of the second element, based on the prefix. This number will appear in the final chemical formula.	Number of chlorine atoms: 3	Number of nitrogen atoms: 2
5. Write the chemical formula for the compound, using the appropriate subscripts.	Formula: PCl_3	Formula: S_2N_2

Sample Problem: Writing the Chemical Formula for a Binary Molecular Compound

Problem
Write the chemical formula for dinitrogen pentoxide.

Solution
Step 1: Determine the chemical symbol for the first element.
- The symbol for nitrogen is N.

Step 2: Determine the number of atoms of the first element, based on its prefix in the name of the compound. This is the subscript for the first element in the chemical formula.
- The prefix used with nitrogen is *di-*, which means two. The subscript for nitrogen in the chemical formula is 2.

Step 3: Determine the chemical symbol for the second element.
- *Oxide* refers to the element oxygen, O.

Step 4: Determine the number of atoms of the second element, based on its prefix in the name of the compound. This is the subscript for the second element in the chemical formula.
- The prefix used with oxide is *pent-*, which means five. The subscript for oxygen in the chemical formula is 5.

Therefore, the chemical formula is N_2O_5.

Check Your Solution
Check that the correct elements are represented in the chemical formula. Then, check the subscripts. The prefix *di-* is used with nitrogen. Therefore, a 2 should be a subscript to the symbol for nitrogen. The prefix *penta-* is used with oxygen. Therefore, a 5 should be a subscript to the symbol for oxygen.

GRASP
Go to **Science Skills Toolkit 11** to learn about an alternative problem solving method.

Practice Problem

1. Write the chemical formula for each binary molecular compound.
   a. nitrogen trifluoride
   b. phosphorus tribromide
   c. nitrogen trihydride
   d. sulfur difluoride
   e. diphosphorus hexoxide
   f. carbon tetrachloride

Other Molecular Compounds

Binary molecular compounds make up only a small fraction of all molecular compounds. For example, octane, shown in **Figure 4.17**, is a compound that is a component of gasoline. There are special rules for naming such complex molecular compounds, and for writing their chemical formulas. You will learn these rules in later chemistry courses.

Figure 4.17 Octane has the chemical formula C_8H_{18}. Notice the prefix *oct-*. This prefix indicates that this compound contains eight carbon atoms.

Section 4.2 Review

Section Summary

- Molecular compounds form when atoms share electrons in covalent bonds.
- Prefixes are used in the name of a binary molecular compound to indicate the number of atoms of each element in a molecule of the compound.
- The chemical formula for a binary molecular compound shows the number of each atom in a molecule of the compound. The subscripts correspond to the prefixes in the name of the compound.
- Molecular compounds have important functions in energy generation and in the production of chemicals used by agricultural industries. Many molecular compounds, however, are environmental pollutants. Other molecular compounds can have negative consequences if they are not handled correctly.

Review Questions

C 1. Draw a Bohr-Rutherford model of a water molecule to show how the electrons in the outer energy level of the atoms are arranged.

K/U 2. When writing the name of a molecular compound, which part of the name ends in the suffix *-ide*?

K/U 3. Name each molecular compound.
   a. CO
   b. PCl_5
   c. N_2O_5

A 4. Suppose that you see the compounds carbon tetrahydride and nitrogen trihydride on an MSDS. What are these compounds more commonly known as?

C 5. Using a flowchart, write a set of rules for naming binary molecular compounds.

K/U 6. Write the chemical formula for each binary molecular compound.
   a. sulfur hexafluoride
   b. oxygen difluoride
   c. carbon tetrabromide

K/U 7. Examine the model on the right. Write the name and chemical formula for the compound represented.

T/I 8. "The subscripts in the chemical formula for a molecular compound are not always in the lowest ratio." Using what you have learned about naming binary molecular compounds, provide evidence that supports this statement.

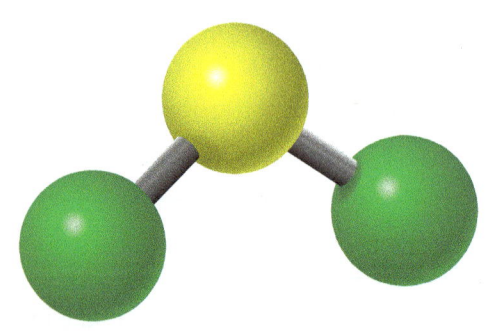

This model shows a molecule composed of one sulfur atom and two chlorine atoms.

158 NEL • Unit 2 Chemical Reactions

4.3 Conservation of Mass and Chemical Equations

Key Terms
reactant
product
chemical reaction
chemical equation
coefficient

In July 1992, there was a tragic fire in the Chemistry Department at the University of Western Ontario. The fire claimed the life of a student who was working in a chemistry lab. The cause of the accident was linked to the reaction between water and sodium metal. Water had contaminated a sample of alcohol, and sodium is very reactive with water, as shown in **Figure 4.18**. The reaction generated flammable hydrogen gas that ignited and caused an explosion.

During the clean-up of this accident, a second student was injured. Small pieces of sodium that had not completely reacted had been scattered by the explosion. A lab assistant apparently touched a piece of sodium with a wet paper towel, causing another reaction. This reaction occurred near a container of liquid waste that was giving off flammable vapours. The vapours ignited, and a second fire started. Accidents like these emphasize the importance of following safety procedures and having a thorough understanding of how chemicals react.

Figure 4.18 To avoid lab accidents, people who work with chemicals must follow safety precautions and understand how chemicals can react. This is especially important when handling potentially dangerous materials like this sodium metal, which is highly reactive with water.

reactant a pure substance that undergoes a chemical change

product a pure substance that is formed in a chemical change; the properties of the product are different from the properties of the reactants

chemical reaction a process in which new substances with new properties are formed

Suggested Investigation
Inquiry Investigation 4-C, Comparing the Masses of Reactants and Products, on page 172

Go to **scienceontario** to find out more

Figure 4.19 **A** Antoine and Marie-Anne Lavoisier were a successful scientific team. Marie-Anne translated scientific papers published in English into French for her husband and drew the instruments he used in his experiments. **B** Marie-Anne's sketches included the closed system apparatus that Lavoisier used for his experiments that demonstrated conservation of mass.

Conservation of Mass in Chemical Changes

You have learned that a chemical change involves the reaction of a substance to produce a new substance. A chemical change always involves the conversion of substances, called **reactants**, into other substances, called **products**. For example, in the reaction shown in the opener on the previous page, sodium and water are the reactants and hydrogen is one of the products. The properties of the products are different from the properties of the reactants, even though the products have the same atoms as the reactants. In a chemical reaction, atoms are conserved (they are neither created nor destroyed). The atoms, however, are rearranged to form new substances. A **chemical reaction** is one or more chemical changes that occur at the same time.

In the late 1700s, a French chemist named Antoine Lavoisier, shown in **Figure 4.19**, greatly advanced the study of chemistry. Lavoisier was very good at examining the work of other scientists and then performing his own experiments and composing an explanation of what he observed. One of his strengths as a researcher was his careful measurement of mass. He performed many experiments in which he carefully measured the mass of the reactants, performed a reaction in a closed container, and carefully measured the mass of the products. For example, he worked with mercury(II) oxide, which forms mercury and oxygen when heated. Time after time, his results were the same: the total mass of the reactants equalled the total mass of the products. He summarized his results in the *law of conservation of mass*.

> **Law of Conservation of Mass**
> In a chemical reaction, the total mass of the products is always the same as the total mass of the reactants.

Lavoisier's work allowed John Dalton to re-introduce the idea of atoms to the world in the early 1800s. Since atoms make up each reactant and product, Dalton suggested that each atom in the reactants is also present in the products.

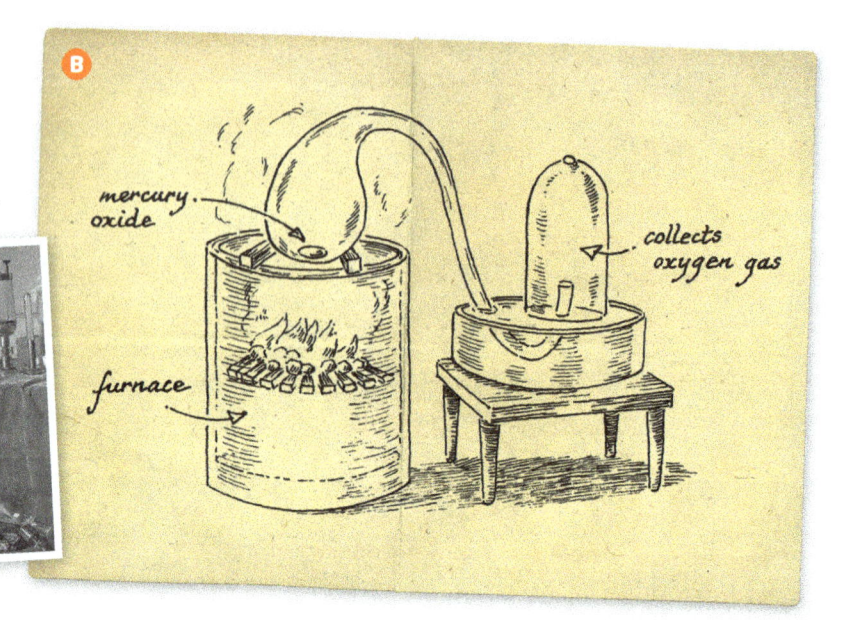

Figure 4.20 **A** A flame is used to ignite a mixture of hydrogen and oxygen. **B** Water forms, with a loud explosion.

Writing Chemical Equations

A **chemical equation** is used to represent a chemical reaction. For example, Figure 4.20 shows the reaction between oxygen and hydrogen in a balloon to produce water. There are three forms of chemical equations that we can use to represent this: a word equation, a skeleton equation, and a balanced chemical equation.

Word Equations In a *word equation*, the name of each reactant is written to the left of an arrow and the name of each product to the right of the arrow. A plus sign on the reactant side means *reacts with*. A plus sign on the product side means *and*. The arrow stands for *yields* or *reacts to produce*. The word equation for the reaction between hydrogen and oxygen is

$$\text{hydrogen} + \text{oxygen} \rightarrow \text{water}$$

Skeleton Equations A word equation shows the reactants and products of a reaction, but it does not provide information about the chemical composition of the substances. Replacing the words with chemical formulas produces a skeleton equation. The *skeleton equation* for the reaction between hydrogen and oxygen is

$$H_2 + O_2 \rightarrow H_2O$$

Balanced Chemical Equations Although the skeleton equation shows the composition of each substance in the reaction, it does not show the units of reactants that react and units of products produced. A *balanced chemical equation* demonstrates the law of conservation of mass, which requires the same number of atoms of each element to appear on both sides of a chemical equation. A **coefficient** is a number that is placed in front of a chemical formula in a balanced equation to show how many units of the substance are involved in the reaction. The balanced chemical equation for the reaction of hydrogen with oxygen is

$$2H_2 + O_2 \rightarrow 2H_2O$$

It is very important to remember that the only way to balance a chemical equation is to add coefficients. If you change a subscript, you will change the identity of the substance. For example, if you had tried to balance the skeleton equation above by adding 2 as a subscript to the oxygen in the chemical formula for water, the formula would become H_2O_2, which is the chemical formula for hydrogen peroxide.

> **chemical equation**
> a representation of what happens to the reactants and products during a chemical change

> **coefficient**
> a number that is placed in front of a chemical formula in a balanced chemical equation

Showing the State of a Substance

To complete a balanced chemical equation, the states of the reactants and products at the temperature of the reaction may be included. **Table 4.12** shows the abbreviations used to identify the states of substances in chemical equations. These are placed at the ends of the chemical formulas.

Table 4.12 Abbreviations for the States of Reactants and Products

State	Abbreviation	Example (at room temperature)
Solid	(s)	sodium chloride: $NaCl(s)$
Liquid	(ℓ)	water: $H_2O(\ell)$
Gas	(g)	hydrogen: $H_2(g)$
Aqueous solution	(aq)	aqueous sodium chloride solution: $NaCl(aq)$

Reactions in a Rebreather

To take amazing photographs and videos, underwater photographers often need to use a rebreather, as shown in **Figure 4.21**. A rebreather allows a photographer to rebreathe the air that has been exhaled, with some oxygen added in. One kind of rebreather prevents any exhaled gas from escaping, which prevents bubbles that might scare wildlife. The rebreather contains chemicals that react with the exhaled carbon dioxide and remove it from the recirculated air. The chemical reactions that are involved in a rebreather are shown below. Including the states of the reactants and products provides important information.

First, the carbon dioxide gas combines with liquid water to form an aqueous solution of carbonic acid, H_2CO_3.

$$CO_2(g) + H_2O(\ell) \rightarrow H_2CO_3(aq)$$

Next, the carbonic acid solution reacts with an aqueous solution of sodium hydroxide.

$$H_2CO_3(aq) + 2NaOH(aq) \rightarrow Na_2CO_3(aq) + 2H_2O(\ell)$$

Finally, the sodium carbonate reacts with calcium hydroxide, which results in the original atoms from carbon dioxide gas becoming part of solid calcium carbonate.

$$Ca(OH)_2(aq) + Na_2CO_3(aq) \rightarrow CaCO_3(s) + 2NaOH(aq)$$

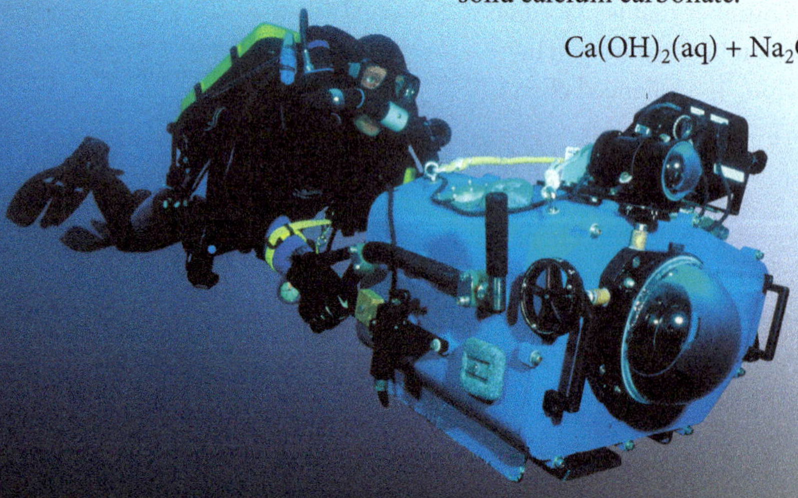

Study Toolkit

Identifying the Main idea and Details Examine the material on this page. Draw a spider map like the one on page 138 to show the main idea and supporting details of the text. Organizing the material in this way will help you to understand the important concepts.

Figure 4.21 This photographer is using a rebreather, which prevents bubbles that might ruin a terrific picture.

Balancing Chemical Equations

The steps below summarize how to use coefficients to balance chemical equations. The formation of water from hydrogen and oxygen is used to illustrate the steps.

How to Balance a Chemical Equation

1. $H_2(g) + O_2(g) \rightarrow H_2O(\ell)$

   In the skeleton equation, there is the same number of hydrogen atoms on both sides of the equation. There are more oxygen atoms in the reactants, however, than in the product.

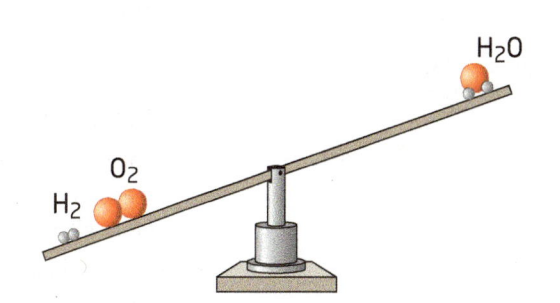

   Checking the Atom Balance

Element	Reactant	Product	Equal?
H	2	2	yes
O	2	1	no

2. $H_2(g) + O_2(g) \rightarrow 2H_2O(\ell)$

   Placing the coefficient 2 in front of H_2O causes the number of oxygen atoms on both sides of the equation to be the same. Because the coefficient applies to all the elements in the compound, however, it causes the number of hydrogen atoms in the product to increase to four.

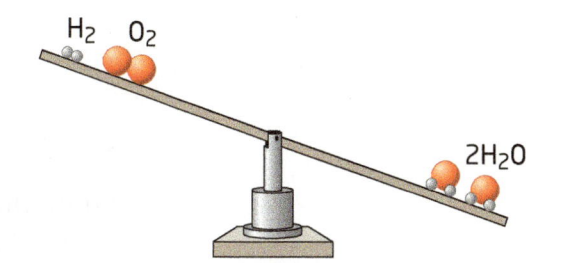

   Checking the Atom Balance

Element	Reactant	Product	Equal?
H	2	4	no
O	2	2	yes

3. $2H_2(g) + O_2(g) \rightarrow 2H_2O(\ell)$

   Placing the coefficient 2 in front of H_2 makes the number of hydrogen atoms on both sides of the equation equal again. The coefficient 2 applies only to H_2 on the left side because H_2 and O_2 are separate substances.

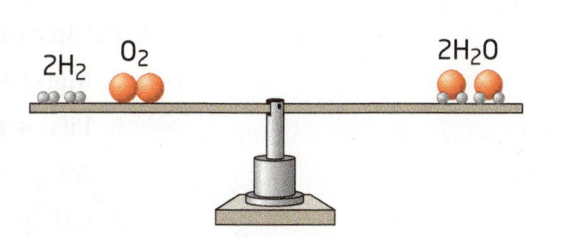

   Checking the Atom Balance

Element	Reactant	Product	Equal?
H	4	4	yes
O	2	2	yes

Approaches to Balancing Chemical Equations

When you are balancing a chemical equation, it is important to remember that every equation is different. The same approach does not work for every chemical equation. You should be systematic, however, in the approach you use. A few suggestions to help you get started are listed below.

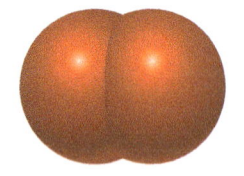

Figure 4.22 Oxygen exists as a diatomic molecule.

Tips for Balancing Chemical Equations

- Remember that these elements exist as diatomic molecules: hydrogen (H_2), nitrogen (N_2), fluorine (F_2), chlorine (Cl_2), bromine (Br_2), iodine (I_2), and oxygen (O_2), shown in **Figure 4.22**.
- Balance compounds first and elements last.
- Balance hydrogen and oxygen last. They often appear in more than one reactant or more than one product, so they are easier to balance after the other elements are balanced.
- If a polyatomic ion appears in both a reactant and a product, think of it as a single unit to balance the chemical equation faster.
- Once you think the chemical equation is balanced, do a final check by counting the atoms of each element one more time.
- If you go back and forth between two substances, using higher and higher coefficients, double-check each chemical formula. An incorrect chemical formula might be preventing you from balancing the chemical equation.

Learning Check

1. State three ways to represent a chemical reaction.
2. Why is the law of conservation of mass significant when writing chemical equations?
3. Determine the number of atoms of each element in the following.
   a. $2NaI$
   b. $3PCl_5$
   c. $2NaNO_3$
   d. $(NH_4)_2SO_4$
4. Balance each chemical equation.
   a. $Mg(s) + O_2(g) \rightarrow MgO(s)$
   b. $Li(s) + Br_2(g) \rightarrow LiBr(s)$
   c. $Al(s) + CuO(s) \rightarrow Al_2O_3(s) + Cu(s)$
   d. $CH_4(g) + O_2(g) \rightarrow CO_2(g) + H_2O(g)$
   e. $Al(s) + O_2(g) \rightarrow Al_2O_3(s)$
   f. $CaCl_2(aq) + AgNO_3(aq) \rightarrow AgCl(s) + Ca(NO_3)_2(aq)$
5. Describe an everyday activity that requires a balancing process, similar to that of balancing a chemical equation.

Writing Balanced Chemical Equations

As you practise writing and balancing chemical equations, keep in mind the tips you have learned. Study the Sample Problem below, which discusses the production of ammonia, shown in **Figure 4.23**. Then try the Practice Problems that follow.

Sample Problem: Writing a Balanced Chemical Equation

Problem
Ammonia, $NH_3(g)$, is produced from the reaction of nitrogen gas and hydrogen gas. Write a balanced chemical equation for this reaction.

Solution
Begin by writing a word equation.

Word equation: nitrogen + hydrogen → ammonia

Next, write a skeleton equation by writing the chemical formula for each substance. Remember that nitrogen and hydrogen are diatomic molecules.

Skeleton equation: $N_2 + H_2 \rightarrow NH_3$

Finally, balance the equation using coefficients. Show the states of the products and reactants, if the information is provided.

$$N_2(g) + 3H_2(g) \rightarrow 2NH_3(g)$$

Check Your Solution
Ensure that all chemical formulas are correct. Count the atoms of each element in the reactants and product to make sure the chemical equation is balanced.

Figure 4.23 Ammonia is an important fertilizer, and it is used in many household cleaners.

GRASP
Go to **Science Skills Toolkit 11** to learn about an alternative problem solving method.

Practice Problems

1. Write a word equation, a skeleton equation, and a balanced chemical equation for each chemical reaction. Include indications of state for all reactants and products in the balanced equation.

   a. A solid piece of magnesium reacts with oxygen gas to produce solid magnesium oxide.

   b. Iron reacts with oxygen to produce rust, Fe_2O_3.

   c. Nitrogen gas reacts with bromine gas to form gaseous nitrogen tribromide.

2. The combustion of methane gas, $CH_4(g)$, involves its reaction with oxygen to produce carbon dioxide gas and water vapour. Write the balanced chemical equation for this reaction.

Making a Difference

Adrienne Duimering was 14 years old when she saw statistics about fatal fires in Canada. Many of these fires could have been prevented. Adrienne wanted to know what products were available to help prevent fires. She discovered that fire retardants (chemicals used to fireproof flammable fabrics) can be expensive and toxic to the environment. Adrienne decided to investigate fire retardants for her 2007 Science Fair project. Her purpose was to find an inexpensive, environmentally friendly retardant. Adrienne tested the fire-retarding abilities of sodium bicarbonate (baking soda) and ammonium sulfate on common materials. She found that both compounds were effective fire retardants. Her project, "Fighting Flames Frugally," won a silver medal at the Canada Wide Science Fair. Adrienne has participated in the Vancouver Island Regional Science Fair since Grade 4. Her other projects have included investigations of the properties of insulators and ice-melters. Adrienne is now a Canada Wide Science Fair mentor and helps other students prepare for the competition.

Which products in your home could be replaced with safer, less expensive alternatives?

STSE Case Study

Green Chemistry

The development of new medicinal drugs has great benefits for humans and animals. The chemical reactions that are used to make these drugs, however, often involve many steps. These steps result in about 100 000 times more waste than the amount of drug produced, by mass. The waste can be harmful to the environment and expensive to dispose of.

Reduction of Waste with Green Chemistry

(Bar graph: Litres of Waste per 1000 kg of Emend® Produced. Before Green Chemistry: ~420 000; Using Green Chemistry: ~80 000.)

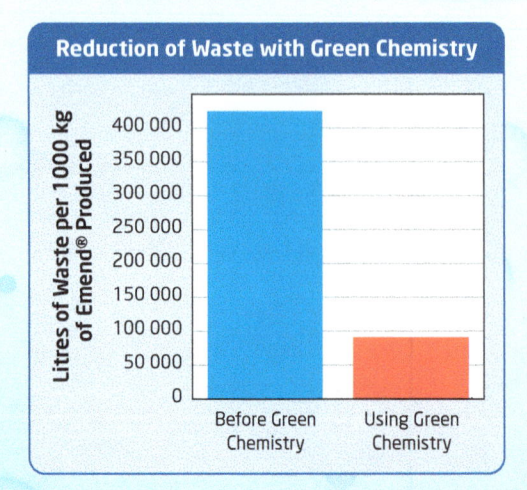

The new reaction produces 340 000 fewer litres of waste per 1000 kg of drug produced. This is a significant reduction in waste; 340 000 L of waste could fill more than 2000 average-sized bathtubs.

A relatively new field of chemistry, called green chemistry, focusses on designing reactions that produce less waste. These reactions can be used for drug manufacturing and other industrial processes. Green chemistry also focusses on reducing or eliminating toxic substances that are used in or produced by many chemical reactions.

Green Medicine

For example, Merck and Co., Inc. has developed a greener reaction for synthesizing its drug Emend®. Emend® is used to treat vomiting and nausea caused by chemotherapy. The new reaction is far more efficient than the original reaction. It uses smaller amounts of reactants, water, and energy, but results in twice as much of the desired product. It also involves fewer steps than the original reaction. In addition to the environmental benefits of the new reaction, the production costs have decreased.

In the past, chemists who were working to help the environment focussed on ways to clean up the toxic wastes that were produced by chemical processes. The aim of green chemistry is not to create these toxic wastes in the first place.

Practical Uses of the Conservation of Mass

The principles of the conservation of mass have many practical applications. Sometimes, a toxic chemical spill is cleaned up by adding another chemical, as shown in **Figure 4.24**. Care must be taken to make sure that all the toxic chemical has reacted and none remains. If the reactant that is used for the clean-up might also harm people or damage the environment, it is important to calculate the exact amount needed, so that none remains. Calculating the exact amount of a reactant relies on an understanding of the law of conservation of mass.

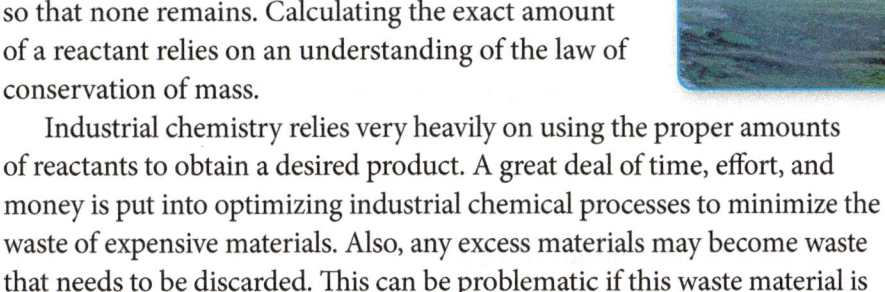

Industrial chemistry relies very heavily on using the proper amounts of reactants to obtain a desired product. A great deal of time, effort, and money is put into optimizing industrial chemical processes to minimize the waste of expensive materials. Also, any excess materials may become waste that needs to be discarded. This can be problematic if this waste material is at all toxic or harmful for the environment.

Figure 4.24 A chemical is being applied to an oil spill test tank to determine how efficient it is in breaking up the oil.

Your Turn

1. Conduct on-line research to identify the 12 principles of green chemistry.

2. Choose one principle of green chemistry. Explain how this principle helps to protect the environment.

3. Initially, a company has to spend time and money to make its manufacturing process greener. You are an environmental consultant who must convince chemical companies to switch to green chemistry. Prepare a presentation highlighting why green chemistry is worth the investment.

What Makes a Chemical Reaction Green?
Some of the principles of green chemistry include
- preventing waste
- using safer solvents
- using renewable raw materials
- ensuring that reactions are energy efficient

Atom economy (AE) is an important principle of green chemistry. Chemists design reactions to use as little of the reactants as possible to produce the greatest yield of the desired product, and thus reduce waste. They calculate percent atom economy using this equation.

$$\%AE = \left(\frac{\text{mass of final desired chemical compound}}{\text{sum of masses of all reactant compounds}} \right) \times 100\%$$

Section 4.3 Review

Section Summary

- The law of conservation of mass states that the total mass of the reactants must equal the total mass of the products in a chemical reaction.
- A chemical reaction can be represented by a word equation, in which the names of the reactants and products are shown, or by a skeleton equation, in which the chemical formulas of the reactants and products are shown.
- A balanced chemical equation has coefficients in front of the chemical formulas. The number of atoms of each element is the same in the reactants and the products.
- An understanding of the law of conservation of mass can be applied to the clean-up of hazardous materials and the manufacture of products, to reduce potential harm or waste.

Review Questions

1. A student carries out a reaction in which one product is a gas. If the student does not collect the gas, how will the mass of the reactants compare with the mass of the products? Explain.

2. The photograph on the right shows a piece of magnesium metal in a solution of hydrochloric acid, HCl(aq). A solution of magnesium chloride and a gas are produced. What element do you expect the gas to be? Explain your reasoning, using the law of conservation of mass.

3. How many atoms of each element are in the following?
   a. $2FeI_3$
   b. $3Ca(OH)_2$
   c. $3Ca(NO_3)_2$
   d. $3NH_4ClO_4$

4. Use a flowchart to describe how you would write a word equation to represent a chemical reaction.

5. What does an addition sign mean in a chemical equation?

6. What are the four abbreviations that are used to show the states of substances in chemical reactions?

7. State whether each chemical equation is balanced. If an equation is not balanced, identify the elements that are not balanced and then balance them.
   a. $Al(s) + 3F_2(g) \rightarrow 2AlF_3(s)$
   b. $Ca(OH)_2(aq) + 2HCl(aq) \rightarrow CaCl_2(aq) + H_2O(\ell)$
   c. $2C_2H_6(g) + 7O_2(g) \rightarrow 4CO_2(g) + 6H_2O(g)$
   d. $K_2SO_4(aq) + 2AgNO_3(aq) \rightarrow Ag_2SO_4(s) + KNO_3(aq)$

8. When solid sodium carbonate is heated, it changes into solid sodium oxide and carbon dioxide gas. Write the word equation, the skeleton equation, and the balanced chemical equation for this reaction.

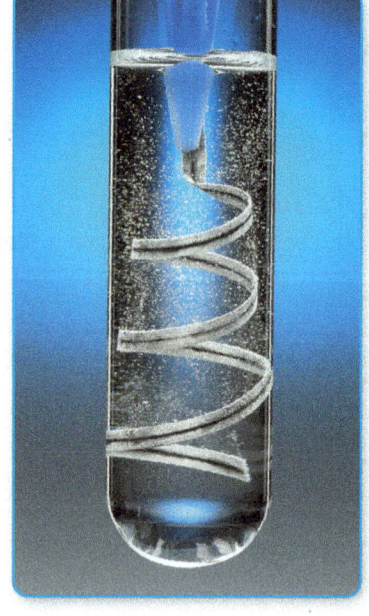

Magnesium reacts with aqueous hydrochloric acid.

Inquiry Investigation 4-A

Skill Check

Initiating and Planning
✓ Performing and Recording
✓ Analyzing and Interpreting
✓ Communicating

Safety Precautions

- Wear safety goggles, gloves, and a lab apron.
- The pulp material contains a small amount of chlorine bleach, which can harm skin. Avoid contact with skin, and wipe up any spills immediately.
- Use the dropping bottles with care. Do not spill the testing solutions.

Materials

- paper-pulp waste water
- 25 mL graduated cylinder
- 6 test tubes
- test-tube rack
- dropping bottles of testing solutions: potassium iodide/starch, silver nitrate, barium hydroxide, 0.5 mol/L sulfuric acid, and universal indicator

Substance	Observation
Cl_2	Dark blue
Cl^-	White precipitate
S^-	Black precipitate
SO_4^-	White precipitate
SO_3^-	Odour like burnt match
Acid	Orange/red
Base	Blue/purple

Monitoring Paper Recycling

For this investigation, imagine that you are an inspector at a paper recycling plant. You are responsible for monitoring pollutants that could be released.

Question

What by-products from the use of bleach are released into the waste water during the manufacture of recycled paper?

Procedure

1. Read the procedure. Prepare a data table with a row for each test you will perform. Give your table a title.

2. Your teacher will supply you with 50 mL of paper-pulp waste water. Put 5 mL of the waste water into each of six clean test tubes. Label each test tube according to the substance being tested. Perform the following tests to determine the presence of elements or ions in the waste water.
   - Chlorine: Add five drops of potassium iodide/starch solution.
   - Chloride ion: Add five drops of silver nitrate solution.
   - Sulfide ion: Add five drops of silver nitrate solution.
   - Sulfate ion: Add five drops of barium hydroxide solution.
   - Sulfite ion: Add 5 mL of 0.5 mol/L sulfuric acid.
   - Acid or base: Add five drops of universal indicator.

3. Dispose of all the materials as directed by your teacher.

Analyze and Interpret

1. What elements and ions are present in the waste water? Give evidence for each.

2. List any tests that gave negative results. Does this rule out the presence of these substances? Explain your reasoning.

Conclude and Communicate

3. Should the waste water be dumped into a river? Explain.

4. Is there an undesirable component to recycling? Explain.

Extend Your Inquiry and Research Skills

5. **Research** Modern paper mills have moved away from using chlorine as a bleaching agent. Research how these new processes are being used to solve the environmental challenges posed by chlorine.

Inquiry Investigation 4-B

Skill Check

Initiating and Planning
✓ Performing and Recording
✓ Analyzing and Interpreting
✓ Communicating

Safety Precautions

- Wear safety goggles and a lab apron.
- Wash your hands thoroughly at the end of each part of this investigation.
- Clean up any spills, and report them to your teacher immediately.
- Alert your teacher if you are allergic to eggs.

Materials

Part 1
- 2 different brands of toothpaste with fluoride
- permanent marker
- hard-boiled egg
- artist's paintbrush
- concentrated lemon juice
- cup or beaker

Materials

Part 2
- 2 different brands of teeth whitener strips
- permanent marker
- hard-boiled egg, stained

Keep That Toothy Grin

Your teeth are made of a compound called hydroxyapatite [pronounced hi-DRAHK-see-A-puh-tite], which is similar to the mineral compound found in eggshells. In this investigation, you will use eggshells to study the effectiveness of different toothpastes and teeth whiteners.

Part 1: Testing the Effectiveness of Toothpastes

The sodium fluoride in toothpaste undergoes a chemical reaction with hydroxyapatite in teeth to form a new compound, which resists food acids that cause tooth decay. In this part of the investigation, you will explore the effectiveness of two different toothpastes using an eggshell to represent teeth and lemon juice to represent food acids.

Question

Is one brand of toothpaste more effective at protecting teeth from acidic substances?

Procedure

1. Make a table like the one below. Give your table a title.

Section	Observations		
	Start	Day 1	Day 2
Control			
Toothpaste 1:			
Toothpaste 2:			

2. Choose two different brands of toothpaste, and record the names of these brands in your table.

3. Use a permanent marker to divide one egg into three sections. Put a small mark on two of the sections to indicate the brand of toothpaste applied. The third section will act as a control.

4. Use the paintbrush to brush the appropriate toothpaste on each of two sections of the egg. Be sure to apply a thin but complete coat to cover the shell.

5. Examine each section of the egg, and record your observations in your table.

6. Pour lemon juice into a cup or beaker. Carefully place the egg in the cup and ensure that the lemon juice covers all of the egg.

7. Place the cup in a location designated by your teacher, where it can sit undisturbed.

8. Examine the eggshell each day for several days. Record your observations in your table.

9. Clean up and dispose of the materials as instructed by your teacher.

Part 2: Testing the Effectiveness of Teeth Whitening Strips

Even though teeth may be strong, they may develop stains. In this part of the investigation, you will explore the effectiveness of two different teeth whitening products, again using an eggshell to represent teeth.

Question

Is one brand of teeth whitening strip more effective for removing stains from teeth?

Procedure

1. Make a table like the one below. Give your table a title.

Teeth Whitener	Observations		
	Start	Day 1	Day 2
Control			
Brand 1:			
Brand 2:			

2. Choose two different brands of teeth whitening strips, and record the names of these brands in your table.

3. Use a permanent marker to divide the egg into three sections. Put a small mark on two of the sections to indicate the brand of whitening strip applied. The third section will act as a control.

4. Examine each section of the egg, and record your observations in your table.

5. Apply each whitening strip to the appropriate section of the egg, according to the manufacturer's instructions.

6. Examine the egg each day for several days. Record your observations in your table.

Analyze and Interpret

1. Compare the untreated eggshell with the eggshell you treated with toothpaste in Part 1.

2. Compare the results obtained by the teeth whiteners in Part 2.

3. Identify unexpected variables that might have influenced your results for both experiments.

Conclude and Communicate

4. Identify which brand of toothpaste, if any, better protected the eggshell from decay.

5. Infer why it is a good idea to brush with fluoride toothpaste.

6. Identify which teeth whitener, if any, better removed the stains from the eggshell.

7. Would you expect teeth treated with a teeth whitener to remain stain-free? Explain.

Extend Your Inquiry and Research Skills

8. **Inquiry** Some toothpastes claim to whiten teeth, in addition to protecting them. Design an experiment to test this claim.

9. **Research** Gather information about different teeth whitening products for at-home use and for in-office use by dentists. Research, as a consumer, the factors that should be taken into account when considering these products.

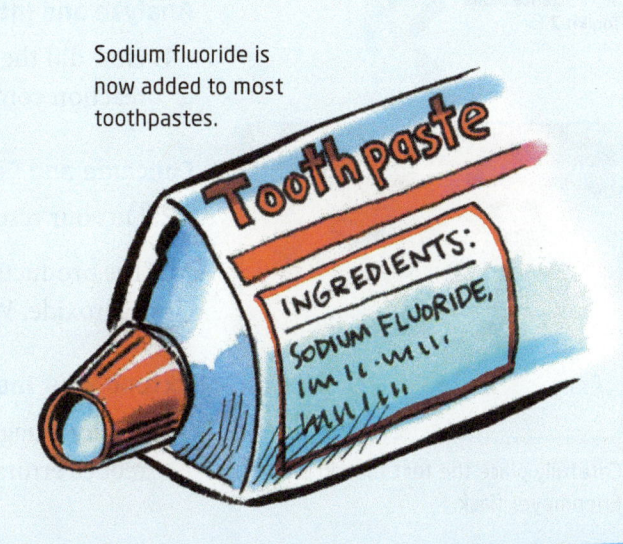

Sodium fluoride is now added to most toothpastes.

Inquiry Investigation 4-C

Skill Check

Initiating and Planning
✓ Performing and Recording
✓ Analyzing and Interpreting
✓ Communicating

Safety Precautions

- Wear safety goggles, gloves, and a lab apron.
- Rinse any spills with plenty of water, and report them to your teacher immediately.

Materials

- graduated cylinder
- 0.1 mol/L sodium hydroxide solution
- 200 mL Erlenmeyer flask
- 0.1 mol/L iron(III) nitrate solution
- small test tube
- stopper
- balance

Science Skills
Go to **Science Skills Toolkit 7** for information about creating data tables.

Carefully place the test tube in the Erlenmeyer flask.

Comparing the Masses of Reactants and Products

In this investigation, you will use Lavoisier's approach to investigate the law of conservation of mass.

Question

Do the masses of reactants and products in a reaction support the law of conservation of mass?

Procedure

1. Make a data table to record the masses and your observations of materials before and after the reaction. Give your table a title.
2. Using a graduated cylinder, measure 20 mL of sodium hydroxide solution. Pour the solution into the Erlenmeyer flask.
3. Pour iron(III) nitrate solution into the small test tube until the test tube is about half full.
4. Tilt the Erlenmeyer flask and carefully place the test tube inside. Do not let the solutions mix. Seal the flask with the stopper.
5. Determine the mass of the flask and its contents. Record your measurement, as well as the appearance of both solutions.
6. Tip the flask to allow the solutions to mix.
7. Measure the mass of the flask and its contents. Record the mass and appearance of the contents.
8. Dispose of the materials according to your teacher's instructions. Clean up your work area.

Analyze and Interpret

1. How did the mass of the reactants and glassware before the reaction compare with the mass after the reaction?

Conclude and Communicate

2. Do your results support the law of conservation of mass? Explain.
3. The products of the reaction are sodium nitrate and iron(III) hydroxide. Write a balanced chemical equation for the reaction.

Extend Your Inquiry and Research Skills

4. **Inquiry** Suggest ways to redesign the experiment in order to reduce errors.

Chapter 4 Summary

4.1 Representing Ionic Compounds

Key Concepts

- Ionic compounds are composed of oppositely charged ions, called cations and anions.
- Solid ionic compounds are made up of repeating patterns of ions that occur in specific ratios. The chemical formula for an ionic compound shows the ratio of ions.
- Subscripts are used in the chemical formula for an ionic compound to show the ratio of ions needed to make the total charge zero.
- The name of an ionic compound contains the name of the cation followed by the name of the anion. For binary ionic compounds, the part that represents the anion always ends with the suffix *-ide*.
- When naming compounds with multivalent metals, a Roman numeral is used to indicate the ion form of the metal.
- Ternary ionic compounds contain polyatomic ions, which are composed of more than one atom. Polyatomic ions have specific names that are based on the group of atoms present.

4.2 Representing Molecular Compounds

Key Concepts

- Molecular compounds form when atoms share electrons in covalent bonds.
- Prefixes are used in the name of a binary molecular compound to indicate the number of atoms of each element in a molecule of the compound.
- The chemical formula for a binary molecular compound shows the number of each atom in a molecule of the compound. The subscripts correspond to the prefixes in the name of the compound.
- Molecular compounds have important functions in energy generation and in the production of chemicals used by agricultural industries. Many molecular compounds, however, are environmental pollutants. Other molecular compounds can have negative consequences if they are not handled correctly.

4.3 Conservation of Mass and Chemical Equations

Key Concepts

- The law of conservation of mass states that the total mass of the reactants must equal the total mass of the products in a chemical reaction.
- A chemical reaction can be represented by a word equation, in which the names of the reactants and products are shown, or by a skeleton equation, in which the chemical formulas of the reactants and products are shown.
- A balanced chemical equation has coefficients in front of the chemical formulas. The number of atoms of each element is the same in the reactants and the products.
- An understanding of the law of conservation of mass can be applied to the clean-up of hazardous materials and the manufacture of products, to reduce potential harm or waste.

Chapter 4 Review

Make Your Own Summary

Summarize the key concepts in this chapter using a graphic organizer. The Chapter Summary on the previous page will help you identify the key concepts. Refer to Study Toolkit 4 on pages 565-566 to help you decide which graphic organizer to use.

Reviewing Key Terms

1. To balance a chemical equation, you place a(n) _____ before the chemical formula for one or more substances. (4.3)

2. A compound that is formed from a metal and a non-metal is likely a(n) _____. (4.1)

3. Two atoms can join together by sharing electrons in a(n) _____. (4.2)

4. The substances that are formed during a chemical reaction are called the _____. (4.3)

5. A(n) _____ forms as the result of the loss or gain of electrons. (4.1)

6. The starting materials in a chemical reaction are called the _____. (4.3)

7. A group of atoms that have an overall charge is a(n) _____. (4.1)

Knowledge and Understanding K/U

8. Each photograph represents a prefix that is used when naming binary molecular compounds. Identify the prefix and the number it represents.

   a. A support can be used for a camera.

   b. The shape of a stop sign is distinctive.

9. Identify the compound as ionic or molecular. Write the chemical formula for each compound.
   a. sodium sulfide
   b. carbon tetrachloride
   c. sulfur trioxide
   d. calcium carbonate
   e. phosphorus pentachloride
   f. ammonium phosphate
   g. aluminum sulfate
   h. copper(II) nitrite
   i. gold(III) fluoride

10. Identify the compound as ionic or molecular. Write the name of each compound.
    a. Cl_2O
    b. Li_2O
    c. K_3PO_4
    d. $Fe(OH)_2$
    e. $SnCl_4$
    f. FeI_3
    g. $Al_2(SO_4)_3$
    h. CO_2

11. List the total number of each type of atom in the following.
    a. $2H_2O + 2NaF$
    b. $3Br_2 + 2FeI_3$
    c. $Pb(NO_3)_2 + 2NaI$
    d. $2K_3PO_4 + 3(NH_4)_2SO_4$

12. Copy and balance each chemical equation.
    a. $Mg_3N_2(s) \rightarrow Mg(s) + N_2(g)$
    b. $Mn(s) + O_2(g) \rightarrow Mn_2O_3(s)$
    c. $CO_2(g) + H_2(g) \rightarrow CH_4(g) + H_2O(g)$
    d. $PbO(s) \rightarrow Pb(s) + O_2(g)$
    e. $C_2H_6(g) + O_2(g) \rightarrow CO_2(g) + H_2O(g)$
    f. $Cu(s) + AgNO_3(aq) \rightarrow Ag(s) + Cu(NO_3)_2(aq)$
    g. $C_3H_8(g) + O_2(g) \rightarrow CO_2(g) + H_2O(g)$
    h. $PbCl_4(aq) + K_3PO_4(aq) \rightarrow KCl(aq) + Pb_3(PO_4)_4(s)$

13. Write a word equation, a skeleton equation, and a balanced chemical equation for each of the following reactions. Indicate the states of the reactants and products in each balanced equation.

    a. Nitrogen gas and hydrogen gas react to form gaseous ammonia.
    b. When solid calcium carbonate is heated, it changes into a solid residue of calcium oxide and carbon dioxide gas.
    c. When aluminum metal is exposed to oxygen, a solid layer of aluminum oxide forms.
    d. Photosynthesis is the process in which plants use energy from the Sun to convert water and carbon dioxide gas into oxygen and glucose, $C_6H_{12}O_6$(aq).
    e. An aqueous solution of calcium chloride reacts with fluorine gas to form an aqueous solution of calcium fluoride and chlorine gas.
    f. Aqueous solutions of barium sulfate and sodium hydroxide react to form sodium sulfate in solution and solid barium hydroxide.
    g. Solid titanium metal is prepared by reacting gaseous titanium(IV) chloride with molten magnesium metal. Molten magnesium chloride is also produced.

Thinking and Investigation T/I

14. Explain why each chemical formula in a skeleton equation must be written correctly before you try to balance the equation.

15. A chemistry researcher determines the mass of a chemical in an opener container. After heating the chemical and container over a Bunsen burner, she determines that the mass of the container and chemical has increased. Based on the conservation of mass, provide an explanation for this observation.

16. Each of the following chemical equations is balanced, but it is incorrect in some other way. State what is incorrect, and then write the equation correctly.

    a. $NH_3 \rightarrow N + H_3$
    b. $2C + 2O_2 \rightarrow 2CO_2$

Communication C

17. Make a flowchart to show the steps involved in determining whether a binary compound is ionic or molecular, and the steps involved in writing the name of the compound.

18. **BIG IDEAS** Chemicals react with each other in predictable ways. Create a graphic organizer to summarize the key features of a word equation, a skeleton equation, and a balanced chemical equation. Be sure to include the advantages and disadvantages of each type of equation.

19. **BIG IDEAS** Chemical reactions may have a negative impact on the environment, but they can also be used to address environmental challenges. Discuss the meaning of the phrase "green chemistry" and how it is beneficial to the environment.

Application A

20. Magnesium burns in the presence of oxygen to form a solid compound.

    a. What is the name and chemical formula for the compound that is formed during the reaction between magnesium and oxygen?
    b. Write a balanced chemical equation for the reaction. Include the states of the substances involved.
    c. When 24 g of magnesium is burned, 40 g of product forms. How many grams of oxygen reacted? Explain why your calculation is valid.

21. Name an occupation that requires people to interpret chemical formulas for compounds. Discuss why you think this knowledge is required.

Chapter 5: Classifying Chemical Reactions

What You Will Learn

In this chapter, you will learn how to...

- **describe** evidence of chemical reactions
- **identify** reactants and products of four reaction types: synthesis, decomposition, single displacement, and double displacement
- **discuss** chemical reactions associated with key environmental concerns

Why It Matters

Reactions provide energy and produce products that you use, but they can also create environmental hazards through toxic by-products. An understanding of chemical reactions is key to minimizing hazards and to developing innovative products for society.

Skills You Will Use

In this chapter, you will learn how to...

- **identify** the evidence of a chemical reaction
- **develop** an activity series for metals
- **investigate** synthesis, decomposition, and displacement reactions

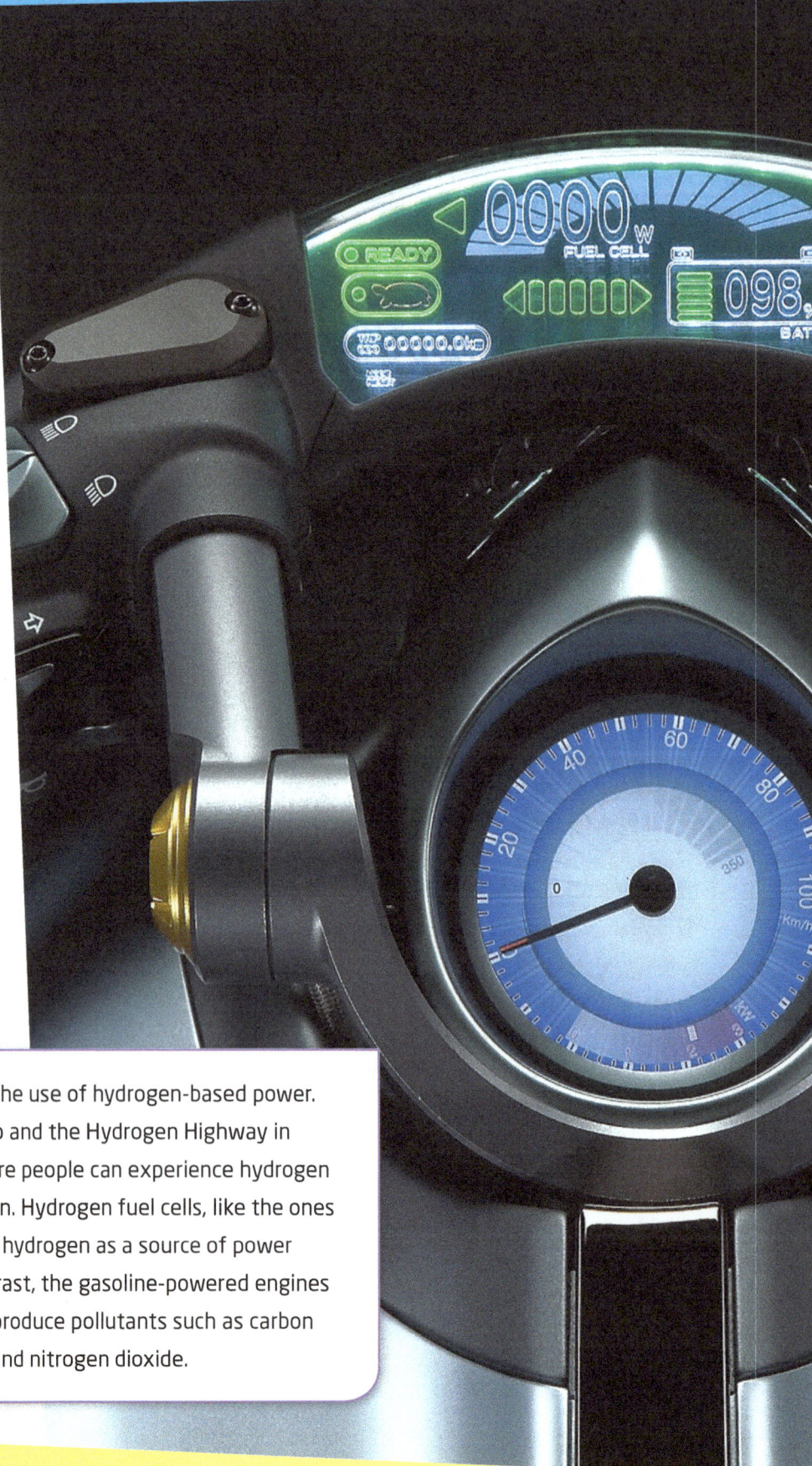

Canada is a leader in exploring the use of hydrogen-based power. The Hydrogen Village in Toronto and the Hydrogen Highway in British Columbia are places where people can experience hydrogen and fuel cell technology in action. Hydrogen fuel cells, like the ones that power this motorcycle, use hydrogen as a source of power and produce only water. In contrast, the gasoline-powered engines that are commonly used today produce pollutants such as carbon monoxide, nitrogen monoxide, and nitrogen dioxide.

Activity 5-1

Foiled Again!

As you know, mass is conserved during a reaction. In this activity, you will observe that some substances appear and others disappear. What is happening to the atoms and ions in the reaction between aluminum and a solution of copper ions and chloride ions?

Aluminum can undergo a reaction with aqueous copper(II) chloride.

Safety Precautions

- Wear safety goggles and a lab apron.
- The materials can become quite hot. Avoid touching the hot liquid or glass. Use a thermal glove.

Materials

- 50 mL of copper(II) chloride solution
- two 250 mL beakers
- aluminum foil
- water
- paper towel
- spoon or other hard object

Procedure

1. Read the procedure, and then create a table to record your observations. Give your table a title.

2. Your teacher will give you about 50 mL of copper(II) chloride solution in a beaker. Crumple a piece of aluminum foil into a ball. Record your observations of the starting materials in your table.

3. Place the foil ball in the solution.

4. When the reaction stops, record your observations of the materials as you allow everything to cool for a minute or so. Pour all the warm liquid into the second beaker, being careful to keep the solids in the first beaker. Rinse the residue out of the first beaker twice with cold water, and pour the rinse water into the second beaker. Dispose of the liquid as directed by your teacher.

5. Pour the residue onto a paper towel, and press out the remaining water. Examine the residue. Press a hard metal object onto the residue, and smear the residue along the paper. Record your observations.

Questions

1. What happened to the colour of the solution? Propose an explanation.

2. What happened to the aluminum? Propose an explanation.

Study Toolkit

These strategies will help you use this textbook to develop your understanding of science concepts and skills.
To find out more about these and other strategies, refer to the Study Toolkit Overview, which begins on page 560.

Organizing Your Learning

Identifying Cause and Effect

To identify cause-and-effect relationships when you are reading, look for words or phrases that are signals. For example, the phrase *was the result of* signals a cause-and-effect relationship. Other signal words and phrases include

- **Cause X** affects/produces/results in/causes **Effect Y**.
- … **Cause X**. As a result,/Therefore,/Consequently, **Effect Y**.
- **Effect Y** is a result of/is due to/occurs because of **Cause X**.

Use the Strategy

Read the section titled "Treating Car Exhaust" on page 200. Note three words or phrases that signal cause-and-effect relationships. Write short sentences like those above. Include the signals, and use your own words to fill in the causes and effects.

Reading Effectively

Monitoring Comprehension

As you read, stop periodically to check your comprehension. Place a small sticky note beside each chunk of text. Put a ✓ on the sticky note if you understand what you have just read, and put an ✗ if you do not. For each chunk of text that you *do* understand, restate the main idea. For each chunk of text that you *do not* understand, follow the steps below.

- Reread the chunk of text. Try to identify the part that is confusing you.
- If a word or term is confusing you, check the margin, the Glossary, or a dictionary for a definition.
- If a concept is confusing you, examine the visuals on the page to see if they can help you understand the concept.
- If a formula or definition is confusing you, look for examples in the text that might help you understand.

Use the Strategy

Read the material on the next page. Follow the strategy above to check your comprehension.

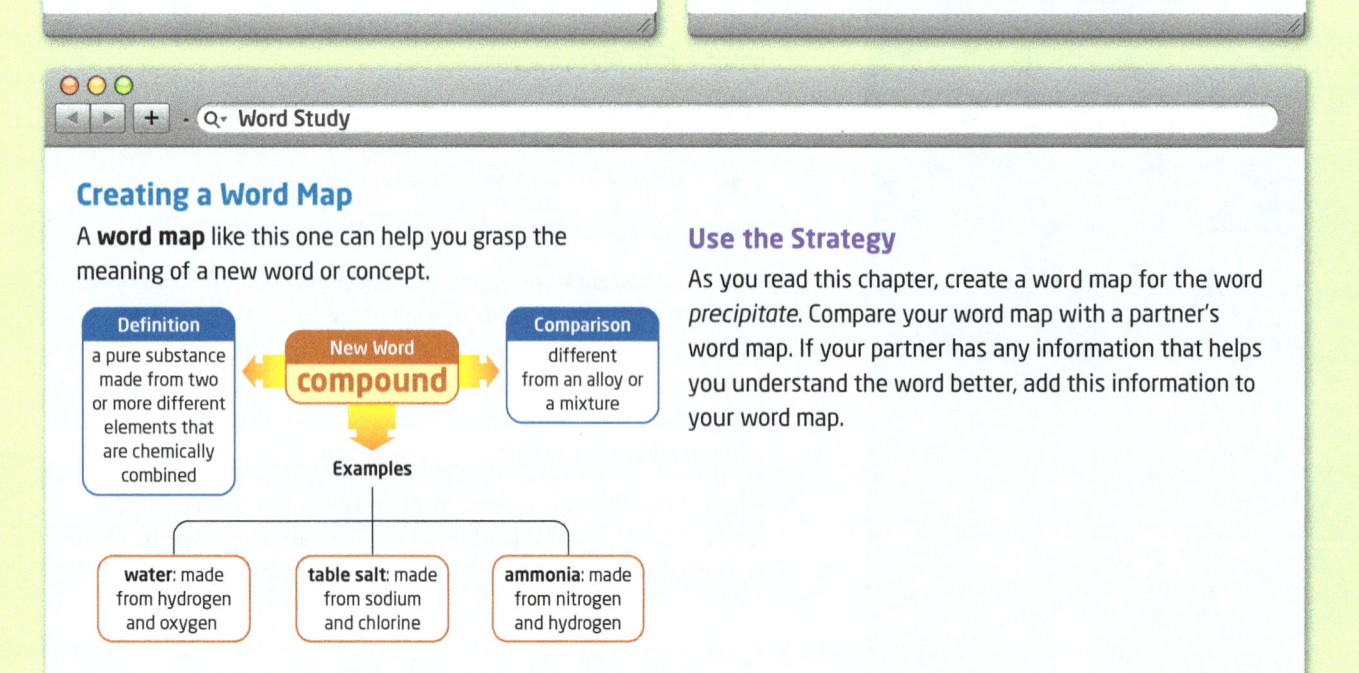

Word Study

Creating a Word Map

A **word map** like this one can help you grasp the meaning of a new word or concept.

Definition: a pure substance made from two or more different elements that are chemically combined

New Word: compound

Comparison: different from an alloy or a mixture

Examples:
- **water**: made from hydrogen and oxygen
- **table salt**: made from sodium and chlorine
- **ammonia**: made from nitrogen and hydrogen

Use the Strategy

As you read this chapter, create a word map for the word *precipitate*. Compare your word map with a partner's word map. If your partner has any information that helps you understand the word better, add this information to your word map.

5.1 Synthesis and Decomposition Reactions

Key Terms
precipitate
synthesis reaction
decomposition reaction

In 1988, while flying at an altitude of over 7 km, an airplane lost a large portion of its upper fuselage, shown in **Figure 5.1**. Investigators determined that a major contributing factor to this incident was metal corrosion.

In previous science studies, you may have learned that using road salt in winter has an unwanted side effect of promoting the corrosion of vehicles and other human-made structures. This particular type of corrosion involves the formation of rust. Scientifically, the chemical name for rust is iron(III) oxide, and the chemical formula is Fe_2O_3. Iron(III) oxide is produced, or synthesized, from the reaction between iron and oxygen. The balanced chemical equation for the formation of iron(III) oxide is

$$4Fe(s) + 3O_2(g) \rightarrow 2Fe_2O_3(s)$$

Both iron and steel (an alloy of iron, carbon, and other elements) are important components of numerous products that are damaged by rust. Therefore, understanding this reaction and developing ways to prevent rust and corrosion are important areas of scientific study.

Figure 5.1 Metal corrosion along a seam on the fuselage of this airplane weakened the panels. This contributed to the panels ripping apart while the airplane was in flight.

precipitate an insoluble solid formed in a chemical reaction

Suggested Investigation
Plan Your Own Investigation 5-A, Evidence of Chemical Change, on page 207

Evidence of Chemical Change

Studying chemical reactions involves looking closely at chemical changes. You are already familiar with a number of chemical changes. When wood in a campfire burns, a chemical change occurs. Photosynthesis, in which plants change water and carbon dioxide into glucose and oxygen, is also a chemical change. New substances are made in each of these processes. It is not always easy to tell if a new substance forms during a change. There are some clues, however, that you can use to tell if a chemical change has occurred. For example, a reaction might create a new product that is an insoluble solid, called a **precipitate**. This precipitate is a new substance and, therefore, is evidence that a chemical change has occurred. As shown in **Figure 5.2**, six clues that suggest a chemical change is occurring are formation of a gas, formation of a precipitate, change in colour, change in odour, change in temperature, and production of light.

Figure 5.2 Several pieces of evidence can point to the possibility of a chemical change. For example, a new product that is a gas or precipitate may form. Also, a change in colour, odour, or temperature, or light being emitted can indicate that a new substance has formed.

The formation of a gas

The formation of a precipitate and a change in colour

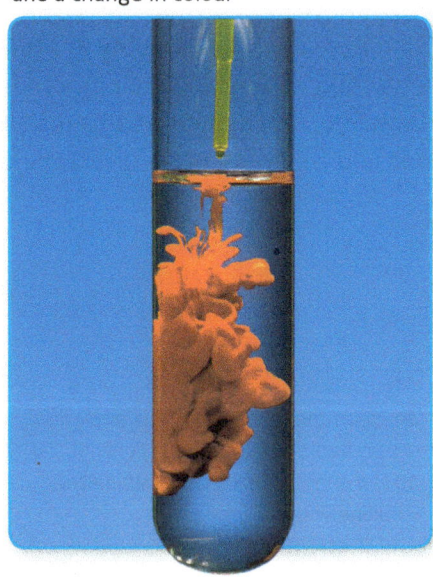

A change in odour

The production of light and heat

180 NEL • Unit 2 Chemical Reactions

Classifying Chemical Reactions

The new substances, or products, that form during chemical changes will depend on the type of chemical reaction occurring. Understanding the different types of chemical reactions will allow you to identify what products are most likely to form. Chemists classify chemical reactions into different categories. In this chapter, you will study four different types of reactions: synthesis, decomposition, single displacement, and double displacement. The name of each reaction provides a clue about how the reactants change into products.

As you learn about each of the four types of reactions presented in this chapter, be sure to note the reactants and the products formed. You might want to record what you learn using a graphic organizer. This will help you to recognize the reaction types and to make predictions about the products.

Synthesis Reactions

A **synthesis reaction** is a chemical reaction in which two or more reactants combine to form a new product. Synthesis reactions can be represented by a general chemical equation and pictorially as

$$A + B \rightarrow AB$$

synthesis reaction
a chemical reaction in which two or more reactants combine to produce a new product

This means that two or more reactants (A and B) combine to form one product (AB). The reactants may be any combination of elements and compounds, but the product will always be a compound.

Figure 5.3 shows a space shuttle blasting off. The incredible power of its main thruster is generated from a synthesis reaction. The reactants are liquid hydrogen and liquid oxygen, which combine to form water vapour. The balanced chemical equation for this reaction is

$$2H_2(\ell) + O_2(\ell) \rightarrow 2H_2O(g)$$

Recall that both oxygen and hydrogen exist as diatomic molecules. As discussed in Chapter 4, the other five that you should know are nitrogen (N_2), fluorine (F_2), bromine (Br_2), iodine (I_2), and chlorine (Cl_2). It is important to keep in mind that these elements exist as diatomic molecules, and that all of them except bromine and iodine are gases at room temperature. At room temperature, bromine is a liquid and iodine is a solid. This knowledge will be important when indicating states of reactants and products in chemical equations.

Figure 5.3 The synthesis reaction between hydrogen and oxygen helps to propel a space shuttle into orbit.

The Haber Process

One important product made by a synthesis reaction is ammonia, $NH_3(g)$. Ammonia is an important component in fertilizers. Nitrogen is essential to all living things. To optimize crop yields, farmers often supply nitrogen to their fields by applying fertilizers, as shown in **Figure 5.4**.

Ammonia also serves important roles in making paper, in extracting zinc and nickel from ores, in explosives, and in cleaning products.

Ammonia is the product of the synthesis reaction between the elements nitrogen and hydrogen. Fritz Haber, a German chemist, patented a process for performing this reaction in 1910. Chemists often refer to this reaction as the Haber process. The reaction is carried out under high temperature and pressure. The balanced chemical equation for this reaction is

$$N_2(g) + 3H_2(g) \rightarrow 2NH_3(g)$$

Figure 5.4 The synthesis of ammonia is an important industrial reaction. For example, ammonia and many compounds formed from it provide nitrogen in a form that plants can absorb.

STSE Case Study

Hydrogen: Fuel of the Future?

In North America, most of our transportation and industries rely on fossil fuels. Cars, trains, and airplanes run on petroleum products. Many power plants use oil, natural gas, and coal. A significant problem with this fossil fuel economy is that these fossil fuels, which took millions of years to form, are being depleted.

Hydrogen as a Fuel

Ballard Power Systems' response to this problem was to develop the first hydrogen fuel cell-powered transit bus for trial in Vancouver in 1993. BC Transit plans to continue its commitment to creating a zero-emissions transit system by showcasing the world's first demonstration fleet of hydrogen fuel cell buses at the 2010 Winter Olympics in Whistler.

Hydrogen is a plentiful element, and it is much cleaner to use than fossil fuels because it produces no greenhouse gas emissions. Hydrogen fuel cells produce electrical energy directly from the reaction between hydrogen and oxygen. Heat and water are the only by-products of fuel cells that use hydrogen.

However, hydrogen is usually bonded with other elements in compounds, such as water or natural gas. It takes energy to produce the chemical reactions that yield hydrogen from such compounds.

Because a hydrogen fuel cell produces no emissions, it is an environmentally friendly energy source.

Synthesis of Atmospheric Pollutants

Many atmospheric pollution problems, shown in **Figure 5.5**, are associated with synthesis reactions. For example, as discussed in Chapter 4, nitrogen gas in the atmosphere can react with oxygen to form a class of compounds called nitrogen oxides. These compounds are gases composed of differing proportions of nitrogen and oxygen. Chapter 8 includes a discussion of these greenhouse gases and their contribution to climate change.

A colourless molecular compound called nitrogen monoxide, NO(g), is initially formed in a reaction that is represented by the chemical equation

$$N_2(g) + O_2(g) \rightarrow 2NO(g)$$

The nitrogen monoxide can then undergo another synthesis reaction that produces a brown reactive gas called nitrogen dioxide, $NO_2(g)$. This reaction occurs according to the chemical equation

$$2NO(g) + O_2(g) \rightarrow 2NO_2(g)$$

Figure 5.5 The synthesis reaction between oxygen and nitrogen produces nitrogen dioxide, which contributes to the hazy appearance of smog.

Toronto's Hydrogen Village

A Hydrogen Village project is being developed in the Greater Toronto Area. This project has several goals. For example, it will strive to create commercial markets for hydrogen and fuel cell applications. It will provide information about the benefits of hydrogen and fuel cells. It will also encourage investment in, and development of, hydrogen and fuel cell technologies.

This hydrogen refuelling station is at Exhibition Place in Toronto.

Challenges Associated with Implementing a Hydrogen Economy

- It takes a large amount of energy to produce and transport hydrogen.
- It is costly to transport and store hydrogen.
- Hydrogen is a bulky gas to store and is highly flammable.
- Hydrogen fuelling stations are not readily available.

Your Turn

1. Based on this case study, list the benefits and challenges of a hydrogen economy. What problems must we solve before hydrogen fuel can be used extensively?

2. "One of the most urgent challenges of our generation is switching from a fossil fuel economy to a hydrogen fuel economy." Do you agree or disagree with this statement? Provide two reasons to support your position.

3. Choose a country that is part of the International Partnership for the Hydrogen Economy. Research what advances that country has made in the use of hydrogen as a fuel. Present your findings to the class.

Synthesizing Binary Ionic Compounds

Although products of chemical reactions are identified and studied experimentally, it is sometimes useful to determine the products that are most likely to form in a reaction. For the synthesis of binary ionic compounds composed of metals with one possible ion charge, you can use ion charges to determine the most likely product.

GRASP
Go to **Science Skills Toolkit 11** to learn about an alternative problem solving method.

Sample Problem: Making Binary Ionic Compounds with Univalent Metals

Problem
Complete and balance the following synthesis reaction.

$$Na(s) + Cl_2(g) \rightarrow$$

Solution

Step 1: This is a synthesis reaction. Therefore, the two reactants combine to form a single product.

Step 2: You can use the ion charges to determine the most likely product. Sodium has an ion charge of 1+, and chlorine has an ion charge of 1−.

Step 3: For the product to have a net charge of zero, it must be composed of a 1:1 ratio of sodium ions and chloride ions. Therefore, the product is NaCl. The cross-over method for determining the chemical formula is shown in the margin.

Cross-Over Method

Na⁺⟩⟨Cl⁻

NaCl

Step 4: The problem also asks for a balanced chemical equation for the reaction. First, write the skeleton equation.

$$Na(s) + Cl_2(g) \rightarrow NaCl(s)$$

Then, balance the equation using coefficients.

$$2Na(s) + Cl_2(g) \rightarrow 2NaCl(s)$$

Check Your Solution
First, check to make sure that the product consists of a combination of all the elements in the reactants. Then, make sure that the total sum of positive and negative ion charges gives a net charge of zero for the compound. Count the number of each type of atom in the final chemical equation to make sure the equation is balanced.

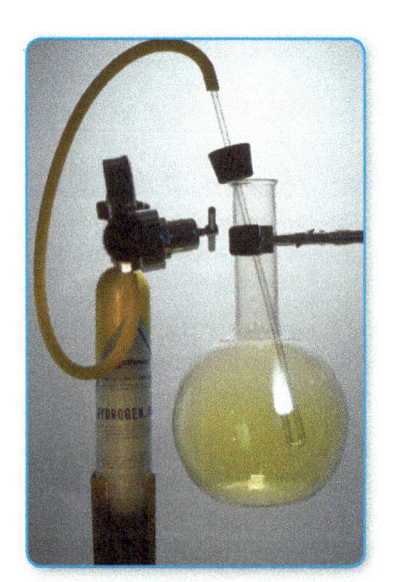

Figure 5.6 The hydrogen gas (in the tank) is ignited to provide an increase in temperature that is needed for the reaction with chlorine gas (in the flask) to occur.

Practice Problems

1. Complete and balance the following synthesis reactions.
   Note: All the products formed in these reactions are solids.

   a. $Ca(s) + N_2(g) \rightarrow$ **c.** $Cs(s) + P_4(s) \rightarrow$
   b. $K(s) + O_2(g) \rightarrow$ **d.** $Al(s) + F_2(g) \rightarrow$

2. Write a balanced chemical equation for the synthesis reaction between hydrogen gas and chlorine gas, shown in **Figure 5.6**. Note that the product is a gas.

> **Learning Check**
>
> 1. What is the general chemical equation for a synthesis reaction?
>
> 2. Predict the product that forms in the synthesis reaction between potassium metal and iodine gas. Provide the balanced chemical equation for the reaction. Explain your reasoning.
>
> 3. Determine whether each of the following chemical equations is a synthesis reaction.
>   a. $2Cr(s) + 3F_2(g) \rightarrow 2CrF_3(s)$
>   b. $2Al(s) + 3SnCl_2(aq) \rightarrow 2AlCl_3(aq) + 3Sn(s)$
>   c. $2Ti(s) + 3Cl_2(g) \rightarrow 2TiCl_3(s)$
>
> 4. Use your understanding of the term *synthesis* to infer the meanings of the terms *synthetic* and *synthesize*.

Decomposition Reactions

A **decomposition reaction** is a chemical reaction in which a compound breaks down into two or more products. Decomposition reactions can be represented by a general chemical equation and pictorially as

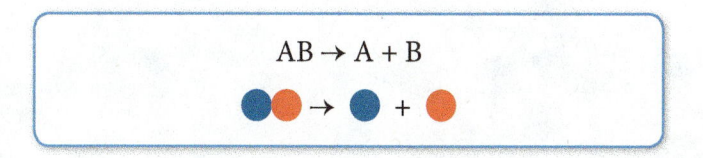

$$AB \rightarrow A + B$$

> **decomposition reaction**
> a chemical reaction in which a compound breaks down (decomposes) into two or more simpler compounds or elements

The products may be any combination of elements and compounds, but the reactant will always be a compound. A decomposition reaction is the reverse of a synthesis reaction.

An essential component in the development of hydrogen as a fuel source is the ability to produce sufficient amounts of hydrogen. One way that hydrogen gas is produced is through the decomposition of water. Electric current is used to break apart the bonds between the hydrogen and oxygen atoms to form the separate elements. The reaction is represented by the chemical equation

$$2H_2O(\ell) \rightarrow 2H_2(g) + O_2(g)$$

This process is referred to as the electrolysis of water. Almost 4 percent of the hydrogen gas used in the world is produced by decomposition of water. A laboratory demonstration of electrolysis is shown in **Figure 5.7**.

Figure 5.7 The electric current supplied by the battery provides the energy needed to decompose water into the elements hydrogen and oxygen.

Go to **scienceontario** to find out more

Decomposition Reactions and Explosives

The electrolysis of water is an example of a decomposition reaction that results in the production of elements. The tremendous forces associated with the explosion in **Figure 5.8** are the result of a decomposition reaction that produces several substances. Trinitrotoluene (TNT), $C_7H_5N_3O_6(s)$, is a commonly used explosive that decomposes into elements and compounds according to the chemical equation

$$2C_7H_5N_3O_6(s) \rightarrow 3N_2(g) + 5H_2O(g) + 7CO(g) + 7C(s)$$

Three of the products of the decomposition of TNT—nitrogen, water, and carbon monoxide—are gases. The formation and rapid expansion of these gases pushes material away from the blast site, producing the explosion.

Figure 5.8 Explosives, like the ones used in this coal mine blast, produce tremendous force to break apart rocks. They can occur as a result of the decomposition of a compound and the rapid heating and expansion of the gases that are produced.

Products Made in the Decomposition of Ionic Compounds

Just as you saw for synthesis reactions, it is sometimes useful to identify the products that are most likely to form in a decomposition reaction. For the purposes of this course, you will learn to determine the most likely products of decomposition reactions of ionic compounds that form elements. During the decomposition of an ionic compound, electrons transfer back to the atoms of the metal, and each element becomes electrically neutral. Read through the sample problem on the next page. Then practise writing the products in the decomposition of ionic compounds by completing the practice problems.

Sample Problem: Elements Formed from the Decomposition of Ionic Compounds

Problem

Complete and balance the following decomposition reaction.
$$AgCl(s) \rightarrow$$

Solution

Step 1: This is a decomposition reaction. Therefore, the reactant decomposes into the two elements that it is composed of—silver and chlorine.

Step 2: Silver is a metal and is represented as Ag(s). Chlorine is one example of a diatomic molecule, and it exists as a gas. Therefore, it must be represented as $Cl_2(g)$.

Step 3: The problem also asks for a balanced chemical equation for the reaction. First, write the skeleton equation.
$$AgCl(s) \rightarrow Ag(s) + Cl_2(g)$$
Then balance the equation using coefficients.
$$2AgCl(s) \rightarrow 2Ag(s) + Cl_2(g)$$

Check Your Solution

First, check to make sure that the product consists of the two elements present in the reactant. Then, if any of the products are diatomic molecules, ensure that they are represented correctly. Count the number of each type of atom in the final chemical equation to make sure that the equation is balanced.

Study Toolkit

Identifying Cause and Effect Examine the sample problem. Identify signal words and phrases that indicate a cause-and-effect relationship. Describe the relationship(s) you have identified.

GRASP

Go to **Science Skills Toolkit 11** to learn about an alternative problem solving method.

Practice Problems

1. Complete and balance the following decomposition reactions. **Note:** All metal products are solids, and any remaining products are gases.

   a. $AuCl_3(s) \rightarrow$
   b. $MgF_2(s) \rightarrow$
   c. $Li_2O(s) \rightarrow$
   d. $CsCl(s) \rightarrow$

2. Write the chemical equation for the decomposition of chromium(III) oxide into solid chromium and oxygen gas.

3. Many automobile airbags rely on decomposition of the compound sodium azide, NaN_3, to produce nitrogen gas that rapidly inflates the bag, shown in **Figure 5.9**. Sodium metal is also produced in the reaction. Write the balanced chemical equation for this decomposition reaction.

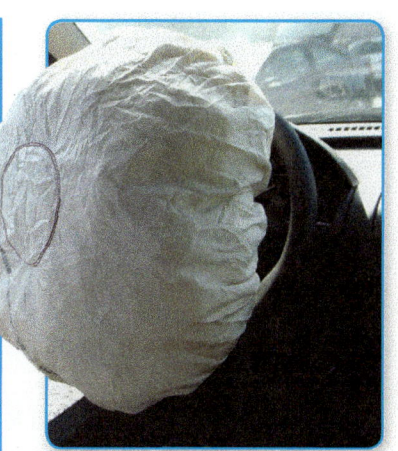

Figure 5.9 Airbag technology has relied on the decomposition of sodium azide. The reaction is triggered by an electrical impulse, and nitrogen gas is produced, which inflates the bag.

Activity 5-2

Building Up and Breaking Down

In this activity, you will practise several ways to represent a chemical reaction while analyzing the reactants and products of synthesis and decomposition reactions. How can models help you remember what is occurring in each type of reaction?

Materials
- molecular modelling kit

Procedure

1. Make a table with the following headings: Word Equation, Skeleton Equation, Model Equation, and Balanced Chemical Equation. Give your table a title.

2. Examine the reactions described below. Write a word equation and a skeleton equation for each reaction in your table.

   a. Hydrogen and oxygen react to form water, accompanied by the release of heat.

   b. When heated, calcium carbonate decomposes to form carbon dioxide and calcium oxide.

   c. Carbon and oxygen react to form carbon dioxide, producing heat.

3. In a group, use the molecular modelling kit to make a model of each substance. Once your models are made, arrange them into a skeleton equation for each reaction.

4. Balance each chemical equation by adding or removing whole models until the total number of each atom is the same in the reactants and products. In your table, draw a diagram to show the models you used.

5. Based on your work with the models, add coefficients to each skeleton equation to write balanced chemical equations in your table.

Questions

1. Which chemical equations represent a decomposition reaction? Explain your reasoning.

2. Which chemical equations represent a synthesis reaction? Explain your reasoning.

3. How has using models helped you understand what is occurring in each reaction?

Water contains hydrogen and oxygen.

Suggested Investigation

Inquiry Investigation 5-B, Synthesis and Decomposition Reactions, on page 208

Figure 5.10 This worker is standing inside a kiln that is used for heating calcium carbonate. Kilns are ovens used for heating or drying materials.

Synthesis and Decomposition in Construction

The next time you go out, look around and notice the many things that are made using concrete. A component of concrete is the ionic compound calcium oxide, CaO. Calcium oxide is made by decomposing another ionic compound, calcium carbonate, $CaCO_3$. The calcium carbonate is mined in the form of limestone. When calcium carbonate is heated in a kiln, shown in **Figure 5.10**, it decomposes into calcium oxide and carbon dioxide. The balanced chemical equation for the decomposition of calcium carbonate is

$$CaCO_3(s) \rightarrow CaO(s) + CO_2(g)$$

When needed to make mortar or plaster, the calcium oxide is combined with water in the synthesis reaction

$$CaO(s) + H_2O(\ell) \rightarrow Ca(OH)_2(aq)$$

The resulting mortar is watertight and has enough flexibility to help prevent cracks.

Section 5.1 Review

Section Summary

- Evidence of a chemical change may include one or more of the following: formation of a gas, formation of a precipitate, change in odour, change in colour, change in temperature, and production of light.
- During a synthesis reaction, two or more reactants combine to form one product. The general chemical equation for a synthesis reaction is A + B → AB. The reactants may be any combination of elements and compounds, but the product will always be a compound.
- During a decomposition reaction, a single reactant breaks down to form two or more products. The general chemical equation for a decomposition reaction is AB → A + B. The products may be any combination of elements and compounds, but the reactant will always be a compound.
- Examples of synthesis reactions include the formation of rust and production of ammonia. Important decomposition reactions include the electrolysis of water and the explosion of TNT.

Review Questions

K/U 1. Describe what happens during a synthesis reaction.

K/U 2. Provide an example of a synthesis reaction that has important industrial applications.

T/I 3. Describe the chemical reaction that is associated with the corrosion of the structure shown on the right. Write a balanced chemical equation for the reaction.

K/U 4. Describe what happens during a decomposition reaction.

A 5. Describe why the process shown in **Figure 5.7** on page 185 is considered a decomposition reaction. Write a balanced chemical equation for the reaction.

C 6. Use a drawing to demonstrate why synthesis reactions are considered the reverse of decomposition reactions.

K/U 7. Balance the following chemical equations, and identify each reaction as a synthesis reaction or a decomposition reaction. Provide an explanation for your choice.
   a. $Ca(s) + O_2(g) \rightarrow CaO(s)$
   b. $Ca(s) + S_8(s) \rightarrow CaS(s)$
   c. $CsCl(s) \rightarrow Cs(s) + Cl_2(g)$

K/U 8. Based on the reactants, determine the products that are most likely to form in the following reactions. Explain your reasoning. You do not need to indicate the states of the products.
   a. $Mg(s) + N_2(g) \rightarrow$
   b. $K_2O(s) \rightarrow$
   c. $Na(s) + Br_2(\ell) \rightarrow$

Chapter 5 Classifying Chemical Reactions • NEL   189

Key Terms

single displacement reaction

activity series

double displacement reaction

5.2 Displacement Reactions

Geologists think that the Sudbury Basin resulted from a meteorite impact that is the second largest known impact crater on Earth. Today, the Sudbury Basin has an oval shape and measures approximately 60 km long and 30 km wide. The largest deposits of nickel in the world are in the Sudbury region, shown in **Figure 5.11**. These deposits are the result of nickel-rich molten rock that rose through the cracks caused by the meteorite impact. These deposits make Canada the world's second largest producer of nickel. Most nickel is used to produce stainless steel.

In Sudbury, the mines produce nickel(II) sulfide, which must go through several processing steps before the metallic element is formed. The final step in one of the methods for recovering nickel involves reacting nickel(II) sulfide with oxygen. The oxygen takes the place of, or displaces, the sulfur from the compound. This is just one example of many important reactions that involve the displacement of elements to produce new compounds.

Figure 5.11 The nickel deposits in Sudbury are the result of a meteorite impact. Isolating the nickel relies on a series of chemical reactions that include the displacement of one element by another to form a new compound.

Single Displacement Reactions

In a **single displacement reaction**, a reactive element (a metal or a non-metal) and a compound react to produce another element and another compound. Therefore, it is a chemical reaction in which an element takes the place of, or displaces, another element in a compound. Single displacement reactions can be represented by general chemical equations and pictorially as

A + BC → AC + B (for a single displacement, where A is a metal)

and

A + BC → BA + C (for a single displacement, where A is a non-metal)

single displacement reaction a chemical reaction in which one element takes the place of another element in a compound

Study Toolkit

Monitoring Comprehension As you read through the material on this page, make note of points that you do not understand. Use the strategy on page 178 to help you understand the material.

The first equation represents a reaction involving a metal replacing another metal. The second equation represents a reaction involving a non-metal replacing another non-metal.

Recall that Activity 5-1 on page 177 involved placing aluminum foil into an aqueous solution of copper(II) chloride. The reaction that occurred was a single displacement reaction, which can be represented by the chemical equation

$$2Al(s) + 3CuCl_2(aq) \rightarrow 2AlCl_3(aq) + 3Cu(s)$$

The above reaction equation shows how the metals, coloured blue, behave. The aluminum displaces the copper to form an aqueous solution of aluminum chloride and a copper precipitate.

Displacing Metals with Metals

The reaction in **Figure 5.12** shows the result of placing a piece of copper wire into an aqueous solution of silver nitrate. Metallic silver forms on the surface of the wire. The solution turns blue because copper atoms from the wire turn into ions and dissolve into the solution. The copper displaces the silver from the compound silver nitrate in the solution. The balanced chemical equation for the reaction is

$$Cu(s) + 2AgNO_3(aq) \rightarrow Cu(NO_3)_2(aq) + 2Ag(s)$$

Notice that copper, a metal, displaced silver, also a metal, during the reaction. Because a metal forms positive ions, it must displace the positive ion from the compound so that a new ionic compound can form.

Figure 5.12 In the single displacement reaction between copper metal and aqueous silver nitrate, copper displaces the silver to produce a blue copper(II) nitrate solution and solid silver deposits.

activity series a list of elements organized according to their chemical reactivity; the most reactive element appears at the top and the least reactive element appears at the bottom

Activity Series

You might be wondering why the reaction described on the previous page does not go in reverse. Why does silver not simply displace the copper? The answer lies in the reactivity of the metals. You may recall from your study of the periodic table that alkali metals (the elements in Group 1) are described as the most reactive metals. So, not all metals are equally reactive. By trying many combinations of metals and compounds, scientists organized the metals based on their reactivity into an activity series.

An **activity series** is a list of elements organized according to their chemical reactivity. The most reactive element is at the top of the list, and the least reactive element is at the bottom. **Figure 5.13** shows the activity series for metals. A reactive metal will displace or replace a metal in a compound that is below it in the activity series. As you can see in **Figure 5.13**, copper appears above silver in the activity series, so copper can displace silver ions in an aqueous solution, but silver cannot displace copper ions in an aqueous solution. If you place a piece of silver into an aqueous solution of a copper compound, no reaction occurs.

Replacing Hydrogen with Metals

Notice that there is one element on the activity series of metals that is not a metal. This element is hydrogen. Because hydrogen ions can be positively charged, metals can take the place of hydrogen in compounds. The element formed in these single displacement reactions is hydrogen gas. In **Figure 5.14,** you can see the result of placing a piece of zinc metal into hydrochloric acid. (You will learn more about acids in the next chapter.) The balanced chemical equation for this reaction is

$$Zn(s) + 2HCl(aq) \rightarrow ZnCl_2(aq) + H_2(g)$$

Keep in mind that the metals above hydrogen in the activity series can replace hydrogen from an acid, but that the metals below hydrogen cannot.

Figure 5.13 This activity series for metals provides information about what displacement reactions will take place.

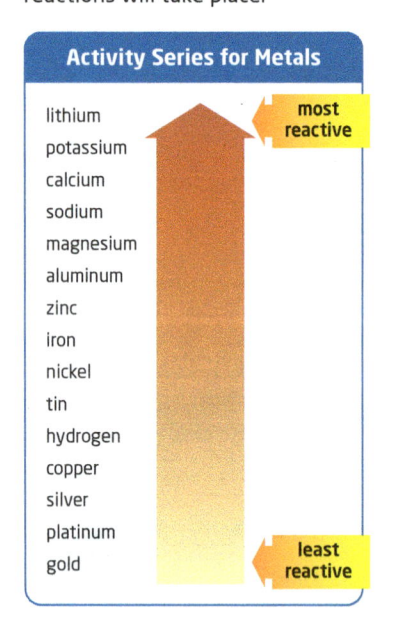

Activity Series for Metals

lithium — most reactive
potassium
calcium
sodium
magnesium
aluminum
zinc
iron
nickel
tin
hydrogen
copper
silver
platinum
gold — least reactive

Figure 5.14 Zinc displaces hydrogen from hydrochloric acid to produce zinc chloride and hydrogen gas.

HCl(aq)
Zn(s)
$H_2(g)$
$ZnCl_2(aq)$

Sample Problem: Predicting Products of a Single Displacement Reaction for Metals

Problem
Use the activity series to predict if the following single displacement reaction occurs. If so, complete and balance the chemical equation.

$$Al(s) + NiBr_3(aq) \rightarrow$$

Solution

Step 1: Aluminum is a metal and is higher in the activity series than nickel. Aluminum will replace nickel in the compound.

Step 2: In forming the new compound, the aluminum becomes Al^{3+}. The bromide ion remains Br^-. For the ionic compound formed from these two ions to have a net charge of zero, the product must be $AlBr_3$. The cross-over method for determining the chemical formula is shown in the margin.

Step 3: As a pure element, nickel is written as $Ni(s)$; nickel has no charge as a pure element.

Step 4: The problem also asks for a balanced chemical equation for the reaction. First, write the skeleton equation.

$$Al(s) + NiBr_3(aq) \rightarrow Ni(s) + AlBr_3(aq)$$

This also represents the balanced chemical equation.

Check Your Solution
First, ensure that the reacting metal, aluminum, is higher in the activity series than the metal in the reacting compound, nickel. Then check to make sure that the metals have been switched to produce a new metal product and a new compound. Ensure the compound product has the correct ratio of cations to anions, so it has a net charge of zero. Finally, count the number of each type of atom in the chemical equation to ensure it is balanced.

GRASP
Go to **Science Skills Toolkit 11** to learn about an alternative problem solving method.

Suggested Investigation
Data Analysis Investigation 5-D, Can Metals Be "Active"?, on page 212

Cross-Over Method

$Al^{3+} \quad Br^-$

$AlBr_3$

Practice Problems

1. Complete and balance the following single displacement reactions. If the reaction will not happen, based on the activity series, write "no reaction." **Note:** All metal products are solids, and products that are compounds are in aqueous solution.

   a. $SnCl_4(aq) + Al(s) \rightarrow$
   b. $CuF_2(aq) + Mg(s) \rightarrow$
   c. $Cu(s) + HCl(aq) \rightarrow$
   d. $Au(NO_3)_3(aq) + Ag(s) \rightarrow$
   e. $Al(s) + Fe_2O_3(s) \rightarrow$
   f. $Li(s) + HCl(aq) \rightarrow$

2. When magnesium metal is added to a blue copper(II) sulfate solution, the blue colour fades as colourless magnesium sulfate and brown pieces of copper form. Write a balanced chemical equation for this reaction, shown in **Figure 5.15**.

Figure 5.15 As magnesium metal reacts with an aqueous solution of copper(II) sulfate, copper metal forms.

Sense of scale

Activity series for halogens include only the first four halogens. Astatine, which is element number 85 and appears below iodine in the periodic table, is omitted because there is so little of it that studying it is difficult. Estimates place the amount of astatine in Earth's crust at less than 30 g–about the mass of four $2 coins.

Replacing Non-metals with Non-metals

The ion of a non-metal, such as a chloride ion, is negatively charged, so it can be replaced only with another non-metal. For example, in the reaction between fluorine and sodium iodide, fluorine replaces the iodine to produce iodine and sodium fluoride. The balanced chemical equation for the reaction is

$$F_2(g) + 2NaI(s) \rightarrow I_2(s) + 2NaF(s)$$

There is a separate activity series for non-metals. You can determine this activity series yourself by doing Activity 5-3. The activity series for non-metals works in the same way as the activity series for metals, with the most reactive element at the top of the list.

Activity 5-3

How Active Are the Non-Metals?

A scientist wished to determine the reactivity of five elements (oxygen, bromine, iodine, chlorine, and fluorine) in order from most active to least active. The scientist conducted six tests, putting one element and one compound together in each test. The results of six chemical tests based on the scientist's observations are expressed below as balanced chemical equations.

A. $Cl_2(g) + MgBr_2(aq) \rightarrow Br_2(\ell) + MgCl_2(aq)$

B. $I_2(s) + MgCl_2(aq) \rightarrow$ no reaction

C. $Br_2(\ell) + MgI_2(aq) \rightarrow I_2(s) + MgBr_2(aq)$

D. $2F_2(g) + 2MgO(aq) \rightarrow O_2(g) + 2MgF_2(aq)$

E. $O_2(g) + 2MgBr_2(aq) \rightarrow 2Br_2(\ell) + 2MgO(aq)$

F. $Cl_2(g) + MgO(aq) \rightarrow$ no reaction

Materials
- molecular modelling kit

Procedure

1. Make a table like the one below for each of the six equations. Give your table a title.

Balanced Chemical Equation	
Word Equation	
Model Equation	

2. Copy each balanced chemical equation into your table, and write the word equation beneath it. Use the molecular modelling kit to make a model of each substance in the equation. Draw a diagram of each model in your table.

3. Examine one equation, and infer which non-metal element was more active for that equation. Repeat for each equation.

Questions

1. What type of chemical reaction was the scientist studying?

2. Write the names of the five elements in a list, arranged from most active to least active.

3. Explain how you decided on the order of your list.

> **Learning Check**
>
> 1. What are two general chemical equations for single displacement reactions?
>
> 2. Classify each of the following chemical equations as representing a synthesis reaction, a decomposition reaction, or a single displacement reaction. Provide an explanation for your choice.
>   a. $2FeBr_3(s) \rightarrow 3Br_2(\ell) + 2Fe(s)$
>   b. $Au(NO_3)_3(aq) + 3Ag(s) \rightarrow Au(s) + 3AgNO_3(aq)$
>   c. $Br_2(\ell) + F_2(g) \rightarrow 2BrF(g)$
>
> 3. Draw a diagram that helps to illustrate the change that happens during a single displacement reaction.
>
> 4. Gold, silver, and platinum are found in nature as pure elements. Using the activity series, provide an explanation for this observation.

Suggested Investigation
Inquiry Investigation 5-C, Displacement Reactions, on page 210

Double Displacement Reactions

A **double displacement reaction** is a chemical reaction in which the positive ions of two compounds change places and form two new compounds. The reactants of a double displacement reaction are often aqueous solutions of ionic compounds. For the purposes of this chapter, you will only be studying the double displacement reactions of aqueous solutions that result in a precipitate as one of the products. Double displacement reactions can be represented by a general chemical equation and pictorially as

$$AB + CD \rightarrow AD + CB$$

double displacement reaction a chemical reaction in which the positive ions of two different compounds exchange places, resulting in the formation of two new compounds—one of which may be a precipitate

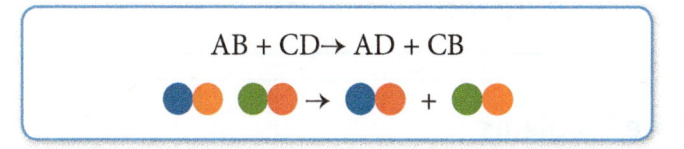

In this equation, A and C are cations and B and D are anions.

For example, as shown in **Figure 5.16,** when a colourless aqueous solution of silver nitrate, $AgNO_3(aq)$, is added to a yellow aqueous solution of potassium chromate, $K_2CrO_4(aq)$, a red precipitate, $Ag_2CrO_4(s)$, is formed. In a later science course, you will learn how to determine which products form precipitates and which combinations of compounds do not react by double displacement.

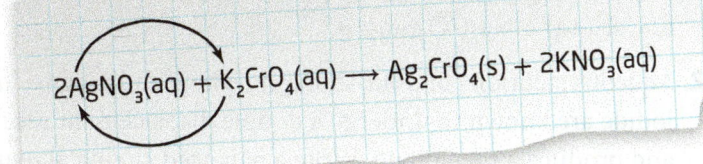

$$2AgNO_3(aq) + K_2CrO_4(aq) \rightarrow Ag_2CrO_4(s) + 2KNO_3(aq)$$

Figure 5.16 A red precipitate, $Ag_2CrO_4(s)$, forms when two ionic solutions, $AgNO_3(aq)$ and $K_2CrO_4(aq)$, undergo a double displacement reaction.

Sense of Value

Silver nitrate, AgNO$_3$(s), is a chemical that formed the basis of modern photography. The ability to produce an image on film was accomplished by incorporating this light-sensitive compound into an emulsion layer on film. Although most modern films now use silver halides, such as silver chloride, silver nitrate is still required. It is used as a reactant in the synthesis of the silver halide compounds.

Cross-Over Method

Ag⁺ Cl⁻

AgCl

Na⁺ NO$_3$⁻

NaNO$_3$

GRASP
Go to **Science Skills Toolkit 11** to learn about an alternative problem solving method.

Sample Problem: Predicting Products of Double Displacement Reactions

Problem
Complete and balance the following double displacement reaction. You do not need to predict the states of the products.

$$NaCl(aq) + AgNO_3(aq) \rightarrow$$

Solution
Step 1: This is a double displacement reaction. Therefore, the two cations in the reacting compounds switch places.

Step 2: Sodium and silver will displace each other to form two new compounds. Since both cations have a 1+ charge, the ratio of anions in each new compound does not change for this reaction. The cross-over method for determining the chemical formulas is shown in the margin.

Step 3: The problem also asks for a balanced chemical equation for the reaction. First, write the skeleton equation.

$$NaCl(aq) + AgNO_3(aq) \rightarrow AgCl + NaNO_3$$

This also represents the balanced chemical equation.

Check Your Solution
First, check to make sure that the sodium and silver cations have been switched to form two new ionic compounds. Then, check to make sure that each product has the correct ratio of cations to anions, so the ionic compounds have a net charge of zero. Finally, count the number of each type of atom in the chemical equation to ensure that it is balanced.

Practice Problems

1. The following are double displacement reactions that are experimentally known to produce precipitates. Complete and balance the chemical equations. You do not need to show the states of the products.

   a. $Pb(NO_3)_2(aq) + KI(aq) \rightarrow$

   b. $SrCl_2(aq) + Pb(NO_3)_2(aq) \rightarrow$

   c. $AlCl_3(aq) + CuNO_3(aq) \rightarrow$

   d. $KCl(aq) + AgNO_3(aq) \rightarrow$

   e. $CaI_2(aq) + Na_2CO_3(aq) \rightarrow$

2. Aqueous solutions of potassium phosphate and magnesium iodide are known to undergo a double displacement reaction and produce a precipitate. Write a balanced chemical equation for this reaction.

Chemical Reactions and Food Preservation

Sulfur dioxide has traditionally been used to preserve the light colour of certain dried fruits, such as dried apples, golden raisins, and dried apricots, shown in **Figure 5.17**. Sulfur dioxide gas is produced from an initial double displacement reaction, which is followed by a decomposition reaction. The balanced chemical equations for these reactions are

$$Na_2SO_3(aq) + 2HCl(aq) \rightarrow 2NaCl(aq) + H_2SO_3(aq)$$

$$H_2SO_3(aq) \rightarrow H_2O(\ell) + SO_2(g)$$

Sulfur dioxide gas is absorbed into the skin of the fruit. Without the sulfur dioxide, the fruit would darken and change flavour as it dried. When a package of dried fruit is first opened, residual sulfur dioxide gas and the smell of sulfur may be noticeable. Some individuals are allergic to sulfites or "sulfiting agents." This has prompted many companies that produce dried fruit to place a cautionary statement on the packaging to alert people about the presence of these agents in the food.

Figure 5.17 Sulfur dioxide is used to maintain the light colour of these apricots during the drying process.

Summary of Chemical Reaction Types

Table 5.1 summarizes the four types of chemical reactions that you have studied in this chapter. The characteristics will help you to identify each type of reaction and determine the products most likely to form.

Table 5.1 Summary of Chemical Reaction Types

Reaction Type	General Chemical Equation	Example	Characteristics
Synthesis	A + B → AB	$2H_2(g) + O_2(g) \rightarrow 2H_2O(g)$	Two reactants join to form a single compound.
Decomposition	AB → A + B	$2C_7H_5N_3O_6(s) \rightarrow 3N_2(g) + 5H_2O(g) + 7CO(g) + 7C(s)$	A single compound breaks apart into two or more products.
Single displacement	A + BC → AC + B A + BC → BA + C	$2Al(s) + 3CuCl_2(aq) \rightarrow 2AlCl_3(aq) + 3Cu(s)$ (metal displacement) $F_2(g) + 2NaI(s) \rightarrow I_2(s) + 2NaF(s)$ (non-metal displacement)	A reactive element takes the place of a less reactive element in a compound.
Double displacement (precipitate)	AB + CD → AD + BC	$NaCl(aq) + AgNO_3(aq) \rightarrow AgCl(s) + NaNO_3(aq)$	Two ionic compounds in a solution switch ions and form two new compounds, including a precipitate.

Chapter 5 Classifying Chemical Reactions • NEL 197

Section 5.2 Review

Section Summary

- In a single displacement reaction, a metal replaces the ion of a different metal, or a non-metal replaces the ion of a non-metal. The products are an element and a compound that differ from the reactants.
- An activity series is a list of elements arranged in order from the most reactive to the least reactive. For a single displacement reaction to happen, a more reactive element must replace the ion of a less reactive element.
- During a double displacement reaction between two compounds in aqueous solutions, the cations of the two compounds switch places to form two new compounds. For a certain type of double displacement reaction, one of the products is a precipitate.

Review Questions

K/U 1. Describe a single displacement reaction.

K/U 2. Using the activity series for metals in **Figure 5.13** on page 192, predict whether each of the following single displacement reactions will occur. If it will occur, complete the balanced chemical equation for the reaction.
   a. $Ca(s) + AgNO_3(aq) \rightarrow$
   b. $Cu(s) + ZnSO_4(aq) \rightarrow$
   c. $Al(s) + HCl(aq) \rightarrow$

A 3. Why would it be easier to recover silver from an aqueous solution than to recover lithium from the same solution?

K/U 4. Describe a double displacement reaction.

C 5. Make a Venn diagram to show the similarities and differences between single displacement reactions and double displacement reactions.

K/U 6. Classify each of the following as a single displacement or double displacement reaction. Predict the products of each reaction, and provide the complete balanced chemical equation. You do not need to indicate the states of the products.
   a. $Cl_2(g) + CsBr(aq) \rightarrow$
   b. $AgNO_3(aq) + Na_2CrO_4(aq) \rightarrow$
   c. $MgCl_2(aq) + AgNO_3(aq) \rightarrow$
   d. $F_2(g) + NaI(aq) \rightarrow$

T/I 7. The photograph on the right shows the reaction between a piece of aluminum wire and a solution of copper(II) sulfate. Identify the type of reaction that is occuring, and write a balanced chemical equation for the reaction. What is the brown solid that is forming on the surface of the wire?

A 8. As a result of a chemical spill, the water in a holding pond contains harmful levels of dissolved arsenate ions. Which type of reaction would be best to remove the ions? Explain.

5.3 Reactions and Environmental Issues

Key Terms
catalyst
leaching

An oil spill from a tanker that has run aground or from an inactive oil well makes the news because there is usually a very large area affected by the oil. As oil is released into water, it spreads over the surface in a very thin layer. A quick response is crucial for minimizing environmental harm. Oil is a mixture of many chemicals. As time passes after a spill, some of the chemicals evaporate, and the remaining chemicals become a thick, sticky mess. Cleaning up these spills involves several processes. These include initial containment, which can involve using special materials that absorb the oil, as shown in **Figure 5.18**. Subsequent steps can include using chemicals that help to break down the oil. An environmentally conscious approach includes using biological agents that hasten oil degradation. Chemical reactions that occur in the cells of these agents help to break down the molecules that make up oil into smaller, simpler, and less toxic molecules.

Thus, although chemical reactions can cause environmental issues, they can also be used to help solve environmental challenges. Begin investigating this idea by modelling a clean-up effort to remove toxic metals from a water supply in Activity 5-4.

Figure 5.18 These green pompoms are made of a special material that attracts and aborbs oil, while repelling water. Each pompom can absorb 25 times its mass in oil.

Activity 5-4

"Taking Care" of Toxic Materials

Many communities in Ontario have lead contamination in their drinking water. How can we get the lead out? In this activity, blue copper ions are used as a model for toxic lead. You will investigate one way of getting rid of a toxic material.

Safety Precautions

- Be careful with the materials. Avoid spills. If they do occur, clean them up immediately.

Materials

- 0.02 mol/L copper(II) chloride solution ("toxic" solution)
- 100 mL graduated cylinder
- two 250 mL beakers
- dropping bottle of saturated sodium phosphate
- dropping bottle of saturated copper(II) chloride

Procedure

1. Using a graduated cylinder, measure 100 mL of the "toxic" solution as accurately as you can. The blue copper ions represent toxic lead.

2. One drop at a time, add just enough sodium phosphate solution to the toxic solution to make the blue colour disappear. Record the number of drops that you added. Compare your number with your classmates' numbers.

3. Pour the clear, colourless liquid into another beaker. This represents the "clean" water. Place several drops of concentrated copper(II) chloride solution into your clean water to see if there is any excess phosphate present. If the solution turns blue, then there is no excess phosphate present.

Questions

1. A toxic metal can be removed from a solution in the form of an insoluble compound. What insoluble compound formed in this reaction?

2. Your toxic water originally contained copper ions and chloride ions. What remained in the water after you "cleaned" it?

3. Phosphate is a nutrient for plants that is often used in fertilizers. Phosphate can promote ecologically damaging algae blooms in rivers and lakes. What appears to happen when we clean up one chemical problem with another chemical?

Treating Car Exhaust

As shown in **Figure 5.19**, our society has come to rely heavily on the burning of fossil fuels for heating, energy production, and transportation. In a car's engine, gasoline burns and reacts with oxygen. The balanced chemical equation for the complete combustion of gasoline can be written as

$$2C_8H_{18}(\ell) + 25O_2(g) \rightarrow 16CO_2(g) + 18H_2O(g)$$

Unfortunately, conditions in an engine do not always provide the right conditions for complete combustion. Incomplete combustion, which occurs when there is not enough oxygen present, can produce poisonous carbon monoxide gas and carbon (soot). It can also cause unburned gasoline vapours to enter the exhaust.

Figure 5.19 Society's reliance on the burning of fossil fuels, such as gasoline, promotes chemical reactions that contribute to pollution.

Forming Nitrogen Oxides at High Temperatures

In addition to these potential pollutants, the exhaust includes a variety of nitrogen oxides, such as NO(g) and NO_2(g), which were discussed in Section 5.1. Although nitrogen gas is fairly non-reactive, the high temperatures present in an engine provide enough energy to break the bonds between the nitrogen atoms and allow nitrogen to undergo a synthesis reaction with oxygen gas in the air. If emitted, these compounds can contribute to smog and to the formation of ground level ozone O_3(g). The contribution of these greenhouse gases to climate change is discussed in Chapter 8.

Catalytic Converters

An important device for helping to reduce the harmful emissions in a car's exhaust is a catalytic converter, shown in **Figure 5.20**. All exhaust must pass through this device before it exits the vehicle. In the catalytic converter, atoms of precious metals, including platinum, palladium, and rhodium, act as catalysts to decompose the NO(g) and NO_2(g) back into the elements N_2(g) and O_2(g). A **catalyst** is a substance that makes a reaction happen faster and is not used up in the reaction. Catalytic converters also help to change the unburned gasoline into carbon dioxide and water.

catalyst a substance that increases the rate of a reaction and is regenerated at the end of the reaction

Study Toolkit

Creating a Word Map
Create a word map like the one on page 178 for the word *catalyst*. This will help you to understand and remember the meaning of this word.

Learning Check

1. How can chemical reactions be used to help clean up oil spills?
2. What chemicals does a catalytic converter help to break down?
3. What is the advantage of having a large surface area on a catalytic converter?
4. Why is it important to maintain a catalytic converter in good working order?

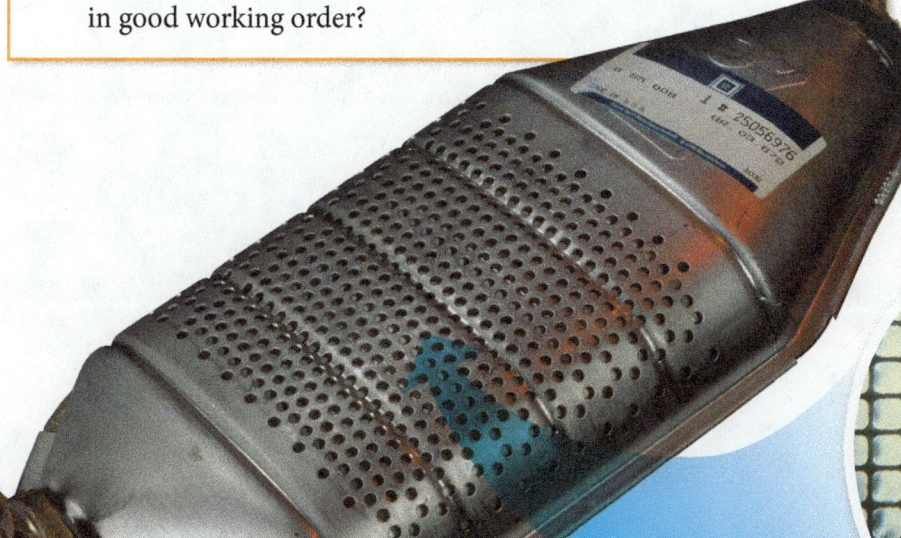

Figure 5.20 A ceramic material in the catalytic converter is coated with a thin layer of precious metals. The honeycomb shape provides a large surface area on which the reactions can occur.

Figure 5.21 Gold mining relies a great deal on chemistry. Even small pieces of gold are desirable.

Recovering Gold Using Cyanide and Zinc

Gold mining is an important part of the economy in Canada. Even small pieces of gold, shown in **Figure 5.21**, are desirable. The mining and recovery of gold relies on several reactions to separate small particles of gold from the rock, or ore, in which it is found. One method used to retrieve this gold involves reactions with cyanide ions, CN^-, and with zinc metal, Zn. Cyanide compounds are highly toxic, and even at low levels can be lethal. The use of cyanide compounds is strictly controlled, but there is a risk of cyanide ions being released into the environment. Researchers are investigating ways to use cyanide compounds more efficiently or to eliminate their use entirely.

Getting Gold Into an Aqueous Solution

In gold mining, the rock that makes up the gold ore is crushed into a fine powder to expose as much of the gold as possible. The powder is placed into carefully engineered piles, or heaps, as shown in **Figure 5.22**. When the heaps are sprayed with a sodium cyanide solution, NaCN(aq), the gold forms a soluble compound, $Na[Au(CN)_2]$(aq), according to the chemical equation

$$4Au(s) + 8NaCN(aq) + O_2(g) + 2H_2O(\ell) \rightarrow 4Na[Au(CN)_2](aq) + 4NaOH(aq)$$

The soluble compound containing gold is drained away from the ore. This process is referred to as **leaching**. As you can see, this reaction, like many reactions in industry and the environment, does not fit neatly into any of the four types of reactions you have learned about in this chapter.

leaching a technique used to extract a metal by dissolving the metal in an aqueous solution

Figure 5.22 Cyanide solution is applied to gold heaps like these, which are crushed gold ore. The soluble compound formed is drained away into ponds, which are also shown.

Getting Gold Out of the Solution

One way to recover the gold is to react the solution with zinc. Adding zinc powder to the solution displaces the gold and produces solid, metallic gold. The reaction occurs according to the chemical equation

$$2Na[Au(CN)_2](aq) + Zn(s) \rightarrow 2NaCN(aq) + Zn(CN)_2(aq) + 2Au(s)$$

Other chemicals, such as bromine and chlorine, can be used to leach gold. Some micro-organisms have also been used to remove gold biologically. However, cyanide ion leaching is still the most cost-effective method.

Cleaning and Disinfecting Pools

A cool pool on a warm day feels terrific, and a heated pool on a cool day feels really good. However, to keep pools safe, chemicals must be used to prevent the growth of bacteria and other organisms that could cause illness. The most common chemicals used for this purpose are chlorinating agents—chemicals that release chlorine when they are dissolved in water. The levels of these chemicals must be closely monitored, as shown in **Figure 5.23**. Just because a chemical is commonly used does not mean that the person using it can be careless. These chemicals have the potential to cause harm to anyone who does not use them properly.

Different types of chlorinating agents are not compatible with one another. Using the same scoop for both types or adding both types into a pool can result in an explosive mixture. Some of these chemicals are also corrosive, so contact with skin can cause chemical burns. Depending on the type of chemical and on how concentrated it is, damage can happen on contact. Before working around these chemicals, you should examine the Material Safety Data Sheet (MSDS) for each one. These sheets list hazards, safety precautions, and incompatibilities of chemicals, as well as treatment instructions in case of contact.

Sense of scale

The particles of gold that are recovered during the leaching process must be filtered from the solution using a very fine filter because the particles are generally less than 50 micrometres across. A micrometre, which is equal to 0.000 001 m, is so small that 1000 micrometres equal 1 millimetre.

Go to **scienceontario** to find out more

Figure 5.23 An understanding of pool chemistry is needed to monitor the levels of chlorine-based chemicals. These chemicals are used to keep pools clean and free of algae and bacteria.

> **Learning Check**
>
> 5. Why are cyanide compounds used in gold mining, even though less dangerous methods are available?
> 6. Make a comparison table to list some of the positive and negative effects of using cyanide compounds to recover gold.
> 7. What are the most common chemical agents that are used to prevent bacterial growth in swimming pools?
> 8. Why is it important to take safety precautions when working with pool chemicals?

Hazards in the Home

There are also chemicals in common products in your home, like those shown in **Figure 5.24**. These chemicals could put you at risk if you are not aware of the product warning labels and do not take the necessary precautions. You have already learned about WHMIS symbols and safety precautions in the laboratory, which are reviewed on pages xiv to xvii. Take a few minutes to read through this material. There is also a system of warning labels for consumer products, called the Hazardous Household Product Symbols, or HHPS. **Table 5.2** summarizes the HHPS warnings that are included on labels to warn consumers about possible harmful effects associated with exposure to a product or the type of container used.

It is important to pay close attention to warning labels—both at home and in the laboratory at school—and to know what the warning symbols mean and what precautions are required for safe handling of the materials.

Table 5.2 Hazardous Household Product Symbols (HHPS)

Symbol	Safety Precaution
Explosive 	This **container** can explode if it is heated or punctured. Flying pieces of metal or plastic can cause serious injuries, especially to the eyes.
Corrosive 	This **product** will burn skin or eyes on contact, or throat and stomach if swallowed.
Flammable 	This **product**, or its fumes, will catch fire easily if it is near heat, flames, or sparks.
Poison 	Licking, eating, drinking, or sometimes smelling this **product** will cause illness or death.

Figure 5.24 These common household cleaners contain chemicals that require precautions when using them.

204 NEL • Unit 2 Chemical Reactions

Bleach and Ammonia—A Toxic Combination

In addition to safety precautions for specific cleaning products, there are also dangers associated with mixing some products. For example, chemical reactions between bleach and ammonia can result in the production of toxic substances. The main active ingredient in household bleach is a compound called sodium hypochlorite, NaClO. When it is mixed with ammonia, NH_3, a reaction that produces chlorine gas can occur. This reaction is represented by the chemical equation

$$2NH_3(aq) + 2NaClO(aq) \rightarrow 2NaONH_3(aq) + Cl_2(g)$$

How dangerous is chlorine gas? It was used during World War I and World War II as a chemical weapon. When inhaled, chlorine is highly reactive with molecules in a person's respiratory system. This has the potential to cause considerable damage and, if exposure is too concentrated, death.

Two other reactions that can occur between ammonia and bleach are represented in the chemical equations below. Both reactions produce chemicals called chloramines—toxic compounds that contain both nitrogen and chlorine.

$$NH_3(aq) + 3NaClO(aq) \rightarrow 3NaOH(aq) + NCl_3(g)$$

$$NH_3(aq) + NaClO(aq) \rightarrow NaOH(aq) + NH_2Cl(g)$$

This further emphasizes the importance of reading warnings on labels and taking the suggested precautions. Warnings on a container of bleach are shown in **Figure 5.25**. Additional information about the safe use of products is often available on the websites of manufacturers and government agencies, such as Health Canada.

Figure 5.25 Proper safety precautions should be followed when handling bleach.

Making a Difference

In Grade 10, Nikhita Singh read a magazine article about water-repellant surfaces. She wondered if the scientific principles that cause water to repel could be used to reduce pesticide run-off.

Nikhita designed a science project to examine pesticides and run-off. Pesticide run-off often ends up in soil or water and can damage ecosystems. Nikhita tested variables such as the surface of different plant leaves, the type of pesticide, and the application method. Her results showed that it is possible to reduce pesticide run-off by up to 90 percent.

Nikhita completed her research in a laboratory supervised by researchers from the University of Western Ontario in London, Ontario. Nikhita took her project to the Intel International Science and Engineering Fair, the world's largest science competition for high school students. She won a third place award. In 2008, Nikhita was named one of Canada's Top 20 Under 20.

What do you think could be done in your community to reduce pesticide run-off?

Section 5.3 Review

Section Summary

- Catalytic converters are used to help combat pollutants from car exhausts. They act by decomposing nitrogen oxides in exhaust into the elements nitrogen and oxygen.
- The gold mining process relies a great deal on chemistry. Gold forms a soluble substance with cyanide ions. Zinc displaces the gold so that the metal can be recovered. The use of cyanide-containing chemicals, however, results in several environmental challenges.
- Bleach and other chlorine-based chemicals are used as disinfectants. Improper handling and mixing with other chemicals, such as ammonia, can result in reactions that produce toxic gases.
- Users of a product can find information about how to handle and use it safely by examining the safety precautions and symbols on the product's label. For laboratory and workplace products, WHMIS symbols are used. For consumer products, the HHPS system is used.

Review Questions

K/U 1. How can chemistry help to clean an oil spill and reduce its impact?

A 2. Oxygen gas is needed for the reaction in which gasoline is burned. If the formation of nitrogen oxides is an undesired additional reaction, why is nitrogen allowed into the reaction chamber?

A 3. When the prices of palladium and platinum are high, catalytic converters become an attractive target for thieves. When a catalytic converter is removed from a vehicle, what are the negative consequences for the owner? for the environment? What types of vehicles are most often the target of these thieves? Suggest what could be done to reduce the likelihood of catalytic converter theft.

K/U 4. Identify three environmental issues that relate to chemical reactions.

T/I 5. What does the WHMIS symbol shown on the right represent? Draw the equivalent symbol from the HHPS system.

This is a WHMIS symbol.

T/I 6. Describe where catalysts are placed on the catalytic converter shown in **Figure 5.20** on page 201. Explain why this is done.

K/U 7. What harmful gases are formed when bleach is mixed with ammonia?

C 8. Create a public service announcement (PSA) to inform your classmates about the safe use of a cleaning product of your choice. Some ideas for presenting your PSA include a pamphlet, podcast, or commercial. Include any HHPS and safety precautions that should be followed, and identify any substances that are incompatible with the cleaning product. List the sources where you found your information.

Plan Your Own Investigation 5-A

Skill Check
✓ Initiating and Planning
✓ Performing and Recording
✓ Analyzing and Interpreting
✓ Communicating

Safety Precautions

- Wear safety goggles, gloves, and a lab apron.
- Sulfuric acid can injure eyes and sensitive skin. Avoid contact.
- Do not touch materials with bare fingers. Use tongs or forceps.
- Clean up all spills immediately.

Suggested Materials
- MSDS for each material
- ammonium carbonate solution
- copper(II) carbonate solution
- magnesium
- sulfuric acid, dilute
- calcium hydroxide (saturated solution)
- universal indicator solution
- test tubes
- test-tube rack
- tongs
- scoop
- any other equipment suggested by your teacher

Science Skills
Go to Science Skills Toolkit 7 for information about creating data tables.

Evidence of Chemical Change

To know when a chemical reaction occurs, you need to know what clues to look for. There are a number of observations you can make that provide evidence of a chemical change.

Question
What types of evidence indicate that a chemical change is occurring?

Plan and Conduct

1. Plan a procedure that permits you to observe as many combinations among the five provided substances as possible. Design a table to record the results of all of your tests.

2. Review the MSDS for each material you intend to use. Write a plan for your investigation that includes the equipment you will use, the procedures (including safety precautions) you will follow, and the table in which you will record your observations. You must obtain your teacher's permission to perform your planned investigation before you begin.

3. Perform your approved procedure. Do not add additional steps without first informing your teacher and receiving the necessary permission. Be sure to make careful and complete records of your observations in your table.

4. Clean up your work area, and put all equipment away.

Analyze and Interpret

1. Examine your data, and list all evidence of a chemical change that you observed. Include any chemical tests that you applied.

Conclude and Communicate

2. Organize and communicate the results of all of your tests. You may use tables, diagrams, paragraphs, or other representations. Check your plan with your teacher before proceeding.

3. Analyze your observations, and infer what new substance or substances you think were formed in each reaction. Give reasons for your answers. Write a word equation for each reaction that you observed.

Extend Your Inquiry and Research Skills

4. **Inquiry** Propose two additional tests that would provide more evidence to support your identification of the new substances formed in this investigation.

Inquiry Investigation 5-B

Synthesis and Decomposition Reactions

Decomposition reactions and synthesis reactions are two types of chemical reactions that change one kind of matter into another kind of matter. In this investigation, you will observe both of these types of reactions. You will initially perform a decomposition reaction of hydrogen peroxide. The second reaction will be a synthesis reaction between iron and the oxygen that is generated in the first reaction.

Skill Check

Initiating and Planning
✓ Performing and Recording
✓ Analyzing and Interpreting
✓ Communicating

Safety Precautions

- Wear safety goggles and a lab apron.
- Burning iron becomes very hot. Be sure to wear thermal gloves.

Materials

- iron (steel wool, about 3 cm × 3 cm)
- 250 mL beaker
- 3% hydrogen peroxide solution
- yeast
- wire gauze pad
- tongs
- striker

Question

What is occurring to the elements and compounds involved in the synthesis and decomposition reactions that are carried out in this investigation?

Procedure

Decomposition Reaction

1. Add 60 mL of hydrogen peroxide to the beaker. Drop a pinch of yeast into the hydrogen peroxide, and cover the beaker with the wire gauze pad. Allow the reaction to proceed until it has slowed considerably, about 3 min.

Cover the beaker with a wire gauze pad immediately after adding yeast to the hydrogen peroxide.

Science Skills

Go to **Science Skills Toolkit 2** for information about generating questions to test experimentally.

208 NEL • Unit 2 Chemical Reactions

Synthesis Reaction

2. Working with a partner, obtain a small piece of steel wool. Fluff it up, so that you can see through the little fibres.

3. With your partner, carry out the following steps:

   - One partner grips the steel wool firmly in the tongs, while the other partner operates the striker to produce sparks that fall into the steel wool.
   - As soon as a spark begins to spread through the steel wool, slide the wire gauze pad to one side, just enough to insert the steel wool.
   - Plunge the burning steel wool into the oxygen gas, and slide the wire gauze pad back over to cover most of the beaker.
   - Hold the steel wool in the middle of the beaker, about 5 cm above the liquid.

Allow sparks to spread through the steel wool before placing it in the beaker.

4. Allow everything to cool. Clean up the glassware and your work area. Dispose of all materials as directed by your teacher.

Analyze and Interpret

1. The yeast acted as a catalyst in the decomposition reaction. What is a catalyst? Why was it used in this investigation?

2. The steel wool in this investigation was a source of iron. Write the chemical formulas for the reactants in the synthesis reaction you performed.

3. The blue-black, crumbly material left after the iron burned is a new substance, Fe_3O_4. Draw a diagram to illustrate the arrangement of the atoms in Fe_3O_4. Explain your thinking in one or two sentences.

Conclude and Communicate

4. Write a paragraph that describes the reactants and products in the reaction of hydrogen peroxide. Use appropriate drawings and a balanced chemical equation in your paragraph.

5. Draw a diagram to show how the atoms of iron and oxygen could become Fe_3O_4. Write a balanced chemical equation to match your diagram.

Extend Your Inquiry and Research Skills

6. **Inquiry** Identify another scientific question that you could investigate based on what you performed in this investigation.

7. **Research** The compound Fe_3O_4 is an example of a class of compounds called iron oxides. Research other examples of iron oxide compounds, and discuss their use in cosmetics.

Chapter 5 Classifying Chemical Reactions • NEL   209

Inquiry Investigation 5-C

Skill Check

Initiating and Planning
✓ Performing and Recording
✓ Analyzing and Interpreting
✓ Communicating

Safety Precautions

- Wear safety goggles, gloves, and a lab apron.
- Avoid skin contact with copper(II) sulfate dust and solution.
- Keep your work area clean. Wipe up any spills and inform your teacher immediately.

Materials

- 3 test tubes
- 3 rubber stoppers
- 15 cm of magnesium ribbon
- copper(II) sulfate crystals, fine
- calcium chloride
- sodium carbonate
- 30 mL of warm water

Displacement Reactions

You have learned about two types of displacement reactions: single displacement and double displacement. In this investigation, you will observe the reactants and products of three chemical reactions to determine which type of reaction is happening.

Question

How can you determine the type of displacement reaction that is occurring?

Procedure

1. Label three test tubes A, B, and C. Measure out 15 cm of magnesium ribbon, and coil it around a pencil.

2. To test tube A, add enough fine copper(II) sulfate crystals to just fill the rounded end of the test tube. To test tube B, add a similar amount of calcium chloride, $CaCl_2$. To test tube C, add the same amount of sodium carbonate, Na_2CO_3. Add only enough to fill the round part of the test tube!

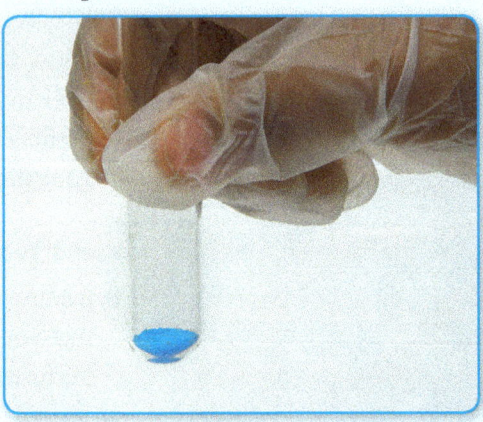

You only need to add enough of the copper(II) sulfate, shown here, and the other solids to fill the rounded bottom of each test tube.

3. Add 10 mL of warm water to each test tube. Place a rubber stopper onto each test tube. Agitate the test tubes safely to dissolve all the crystals.

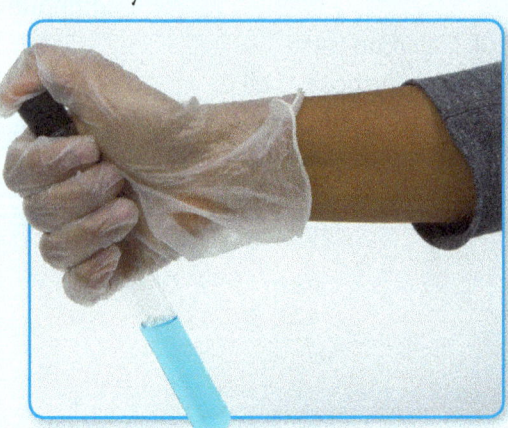

To shake the test tube safely, hold it as shown. Gentle shaking is all that is needed.

4. Add the coiled magnesium to test tube A. Record all of the changes that you observe.

5. Pour about 5 mL of the clear liquid from test tube A into test tube B. Record your observations.

6. Pour about 5 mL of the clear liquid from test tube A into test tube C. Record your observations.

7. Clean up your work area. Return the clean glassware to its place. Dispose of all materials as directed by your teacher.

Analyze and Interpret

1. When ionic crystals dissolve in water, they dissociate into ions. Name the ions in each solution before they react. Draw a particle diagram of each ion, and label each diagram with its chemical formula.

2. In your notebook, make a table like the one below. Write the names of the reactants for each test tube in the appropriate column. Give your table a title.

Test Tube	Reactants	Products	Reaction Type
A			
B			
C			

3. Based on your observations and the diagrams you drew in question 1, predict the products for each reaction, and write the names in the appropriate column in the table. Give reasons for your answers.

4. Identify the type of reaction you observed in each test tube, and write your answers in your table.

Conclude and Communicate

5. Write a word equation for each reaction that you observed.

6. Write a balanced chemical equation for each change that you observed.

7. Describe the differences in the reactants and products that helped you determine whether a displacement reaction is a single displacement or a double displacement. What was the evidence that suggested that each of the reactions had taken place?

Extend Your Inquiry and Research Skills

8. **Inquiry** How could the ability to test the products made in a chemical reaction be useful for identifying the type of reaction that has occured?

9. **Research** Identify a single displacement or double displacement reaction that has practical applications in society. Describe what those applications are. Research a reaction that you have not already studied in this chapter.

Chapter 5 Classifying Chemical Reactions • NEL   211

Data Analysis Investigation 5-D

Skill Check

Initiating and Planning

Performing and Recording

✓ Analyzing and Interpreting

✓ Communicating

Can Metals Be "Active"?

Gold never rusts. Iron, on the other hand, can rust in a few minutes. Iron is more active than gold. But what about the other metals? Each experimental observation for a series of reactions provides evidence of the relative activity of two metals. Based on this evidence, you can arrange the metals in an activity series.

Question

How can evidence from experimental observations be used to arrange metals into a list from most active to least active?

Analyze and Interpret

1. Study the observations for each of the reactions in the table below. Make a list of your interpretations of the results for each reaction.
2. Create a new table, organizing your interpretations to make a clear and convincing pattern.

Conclude and Communicate

3. Arrange the metals in a list from most active to least active.
4. Write a short paragraph to explain why you decided on the order of your list.

Extend Your Inquiry and Research Skills

5. **Inquiry** Provide skeleton and balanced chemical equations for the reactions that appear to occur, based on the observations in the table below.

Experimental Observations

Reactants	Observations
$Zn(s) + CuSO_4(aq)$	• solid copper metal forms • decrease in blue colour of solution
$Zn(s) + Pb(NO_3)_2(aq)$	• solid lead metal forms
$Pb(s) + AgNO_3(aq)$	• solid silver metal forms
$Pb(s) + ZnCl(aq)$	• no change
$Cu(s) + AgNO_3(aq)$	• solid silver metal forms • solution turns blue
$Cu(s) + Pb(NO_3)_2(aq)$	• no change
$Ag(s) + CuSO_4(aq)$	• no change
$Ag(s) + ZnCl(aq)$	• no change

Zinc metal in an aqueous solution of copper(II) sulfate will undergo a reaction.

Chapter 5 Summary

5.1 Synthesis and Decomposition Reactions

Key Concepts

- Evidence of a chemical change may include one or more of the following: formation of a gas, formation of a precipitate, change in odour, change in colour, change in temperature, and production of light.

- During a synthesis reaction, two or more reactants combine to form one product. The general chemical equation for a synthesis reaction is A + B → AB. The reactants may be any combination of elements and compounds, but the product will always be a compound. Examples of synthesis reactions include the formation of rust and the production of ammonia.

- During a decomposition reaction, a single reactant breaks down to form two or more products. The general chemical equation for a decomposition reaction is AB → A + B. The products may be any combination of elements and compounds, but the reactant will always be a compound. Important decomposition reactions include the electrolysis of water and the explosion of TNT.

5.2 Displacement Reactions

Key Concepts

- In a single displacement reaction, a metal replaces the ion of a different metal, or a non-metal replaces the ion of a non-metal. The products are an element and a compound that differ from the reactants.

- An activity series is a list of elements arranged in order from the most reactive to the least reactive. For a single displacement reaction to happen, a more reactive element must replace the ions of a less reactive element.

- During a double displacement reaction between two compounds in aqueous solutions, the cations of the two compounds switch places to form two new compounds. For a certain type of double displacement reaction, one of the products is a precipitate.

5.3 Reactions and Environmental Issues

Key Concepts

- Catalytic converters are used to help combat pollutants from car exhausts. They act by decomposing nitrogen oxides in exhaust into the elements nitrogen and oxygen.

- The gold mining process relies a great deal on chemistry. Gold forms a soluble substance with cyanide ions. Zinc displaces the gold so that the metal can be recovered. The use of cyanide containing chemicals, however, results in several environmental challenges.

- Bleach and other chlorine-based chemicals are used as disinfectants. Improper handling and mixing with other chemicals, such as ammonia, can result in reactions that produce toxic gases.

- Users of a product can find information on how to handle and use it safely by examining the safety precautions and symbols on the product's label. For laboratory and workplace materials, WHMIS symbols are used. For consumer products, the HHPS system is used.

Chapter 5 Review

> **Make Your Own Summary**
>
> Summarize the key concepts of this chapter using a graphic organizer. The Chapter Summary on the previous page will help you identify the key concepts. Refer to Study Toolkit 4 on pages 565-566 to help you decide which graphic organizer to use.

Reviewing Key Terms

1. An element taking the place of a less active element in a compound occurs during a _____. (5.2)

2. If a chemical reaction forms a single product from more than one reactant, the reaction is a _____. (5.1)

3. A substance that increases the rate of a chemical reaction but is not used up in the reaction is a _____. (5.3)

4. A single reactant breaks down into more than one product during a _____. (5.1)

5. A solid that forms during the reaction of two aqueous solutions is a _____. (5.1)

6. You can predict whether a single displacement reaction will occur by looking at a list of elements organized according to their chemical reactivity, known as an _____. (5.2)

7. A chemical reaction that involves the switching of ions between two compounds to form two new compounds is a _____. (5.2)

Knowledge and Understanding K/U

8. List six types of evidence of a chemical reaction.

9. What is the balanced chemical equation for the reaction that provides thrust to a space shuttle? What type of reaction is it?

10. Identify the type of reaction that is represented by each of the following chemical equations.
    a. $12KCl(aq) + Pb_3(PO_4)_4(aq) \rightarrow 3PbCl_4(s) + 4K_3PO_4(aq)$
    b. $MnI_4(s) \rightarrow Mn(s) + 2I_2(s)$
    c. $3Mg(s) + N_2(g) \rightarrow Mg_3N_2(s)$
    d. $Cu(s) + 2AgNO_3(aq) \rightarrow 2Ag(s) + Cu(NO_3)_2(aq)$
    e. $2NaClO_3(s) \rightarrow 2NaCl(s) + 3O_2(g)$
    f. $S_8(s) + 12O_2(g) \rightarrow 8SO_3(g)$

11. Identify all reaction types that fit each description below.
    a. includes at least one element as a reactant
    b. has a single substance as the reactant
    c. has only ionic compounds as reactants and products

12. Determine whether each of the following single displacement reactions will occur. If the reaction will occur, write the products and balance the chemical equation.
    a. $Li(s) + NaCl(aq) \rightarrow$
    b. $Al(s) + Cu(NO_3)_2(aq) \rightarrow$
    c. $Fe(s) + ZnCl_2(aq) \rightarrow$

13. For each of the following reactants, identify the type of reaction that will occur. Explain your reasoning.
    a. $Cl_2(g) + CaBr_2(aq) \rightarrow$
    b. $Li(s) + N_2(g) \rightarrow$
    c. $AgNO_3(aq) + NaCl(aq) \rightarrow$
    d. $PbO_2(s) \rightarrow$
    e. $Fe(ClO_4)_2(aq) + Al(s) \rightarrow$
    f. $Ba(NO_3)_2(aq) + MgSO_4(aq) \rightarrow$
    g. $BaCl_2(aq) + Na_2CrO_4(aq) \rightarrow$
    h. $Rb(s) + O_2(g) \rightarrow$
    i. $I_2(s) + CaBr_2(aq) \rightarrow$
    j. $Mg(s) + S_8(s) \rightarrow$

14. For each reaction in question 13, determine the products that are most likely to occur and write a balanced chemical equation. You do not need to indicate the states of the products. For any single displacement reaction that does not occur, write "no reaction."

15. Why is the formation of a precipitate an important piece of evidence of a double displacement reaction?

214 NEL • Unit 2 Chemical Reactions

Thinking and Investigation T/I

16. Examine the photograph and write a detailed description of the reaction that is taking place, including evidence of a reaction and what type of reaction it is likely to be.

A chemical reaction is taking place.

17. Gasoline is a fossil fuel that is a mixture of chemicals, many of which have the formula C_8H_{18}. When these chemicals burn, they react with oxygen gas to form carbon dioxide and water vapour. Write a balanced chemical equation for this reaction. Analyze the reactants and products of the reaction, and explain why it does not fit any of the four types of reactions covered in this chapter.

18. How would you classify the reaction in which zinc powder is used to recover gold? Which reaction type does this reaction most resemble? Explain your reasoning.

19. While cleaning the bathroom with different cleaning products, a friend complains of a strong irritating odour. What could have happened, and should your friend be concerned?

Communication C

20. Develop a method to model synthesis and decomposition reactions. Write an illustrated set of instructions to describe your model.

21. Analyze the safety and environmental issues related to the chemicals listed below. Using information sources such as MSDS and WHMIS, identify potential hazards, incompatible combinations, and safety precautions required when working with each chemical in a laboratory. Then research the safety precautions and warning labels used on consumer products that contain each chemical. Summarize your findings in the form of an information pamphlet for consumers.

  a. lye (often found in drain cleaners)

  b. ammonia (often used in window cleaners)

22. Describe when a single displacement reaction will not occur using a diagram of the activity series.

23. **BIG IDEAS** Chemicals react with each other in predictable ways. Create a flowchart that can be used to identify which of the four types of reactions a particular reaction is, when you are given only the reactants.

24. **BIG IDEAS** Chemical reactions may have a negative impact on the environment, but they can also be used to address environmental challenges. Suppose that you are a specialist in charge of deciding how to clean up an oil spill. You have the following options: let nature take its course, use biological agents, use a controlled burn, use chemicals to disperse the oil, and skim the oil off the surface.

Part of your job is to communicate your method(s) of choice to stakeholders. Research the benefits and drawbacks of each method, and describe the advantages and disadvantages that you would communicate to a coastal community that will be affected by the oil spill.

Application A

25. While working as a laboratory technician, you notice that the MSDS records are over five years old. What could you say to your manager to help convey the importance of maintaining up-to-date MSDS records?

26. Describe why it is important that the catalytic converter contain a catalyst rather than a material that would react with the compounds in a car's exhaust.

27. Large oil spills are often featured on the news and get a large amount of attention. Should there be a system to monitor much smaller spills? Explain.

Chapter 6   Acids and Bases

What You Will Learn

In this chapter, you will learn how to...

- **name** and **write** formulas for acids and bases
- **explain** how the pH scale is used to classify aqueous solutions as acidic, basic, or neutral
- **discuss** chemical reactions that involve acids and bases

Why It Matters

Acids and bases represent a very important class of chemicals. There are numerous examples of common substances that can be classified as acids or bases. The properties of acids and bases have been used throughout history to address many technological problems, and they have numerous industrial applications.

Skills You Will Use

In this chapter, you will learn how to...

- **classify** common substances as acidic, basic, or neutral
- **investigate** reactions between acids and bases

Canada is an exceptionally fortunate country, with almost 10 percent of its total area being covered by fresh water. Ontario is particularly privileged, with access to the Great Lakes. Unfortunately, the Great Lakes region and other areas in Ontario have been harmed from pollution. One particular source of this pollution is atmospheric, in the form of acid precipitation. Understanding the chemistry and properties of acids and bases has been an essential component to knowing the effects of acid precipitation and striving to counter these effects.

Activity 6-1

Cabbage Detector

Many common substances can be classified as acidic or basic. Some of these examples are from your kitchen. How can acidic and basic substances be detected based on their properties?

Safety Precautions

- Wear safety goggles and a lab apron.

Materials

- 10 mL of red cabbage juice
- 2 test tubes
- test-tube rack
- lemon juice
- "natural" or Ivory™ soap shavings

Using these materials, you can explore the properties of acids and bases.

Procedure

1. Obtain about 10 mL of red cabbage juice from your teacher.
2. Place a small amount of cabbage juice into each of two test tubes. Add enough so that the height of the juice in each tube is about 2 cm.
3. Squeeze a few drops of lemon juice, which is acidic, into the cabbage juice of one test tube. Record your observations.
4. Drop a flake of soap, which is basic, into the cabbage juice in the second test tube. Record your observations.
5. Add a flake of soap to the tube from step 3. Record what happens after adding the soap.

Questions

1. How many colour changes did you observe?
2. Are the changes that you observed chemical changes or physical changes? Explain your answer.
3. What do you think the red cabbage juice is doing?

Study Toolkit

These strategies will help you use this textbook to develop your understanding of science concepts and skills. To find out more about these and other strategies, refer to the Study Toolkit Overview, which begins on page 560.

Reading Graphic Text

Interpreting Tables

A table consists of cells organized into rows and columns. To interpret data in the cells of a table, scan the column or row headings and then look across the rows and down columns. For example, in the table below, the word *Blue* appears in the last row of the final column. The data can be interpreted as "Bromothymol blue changes from yellow to blue within a pH range of 6.0 to 7.6."

Indicator	Colour at Lower pH Values	pH Range in Which Colour Change Occurs	Colour Change as pH Increases
Methyl orange	Red	3.2–4.4	Yellow
Methyl red	Red	4.8–6.0	Yellow
Bromothymol blue	Yellow	6.0–7.6	Blue

Use the Strategy

1. Find **Table 6.5** on page 234. Cover the table, and read only the title. Based on the title, explain what kind of data you expect to see in the cells.

2. Read the column and row headings carefully. Explain what they mean.

3. Choose any cell in the table. Interpret the contents of the cell by writing a complete sentence.

Organizing Your Learning

Using Graphic Organizers

Summarizing ideas in a visual format can help you understand and remember them better. In a **graphic organizer**, different shapes are sometimes used to show how ideas are related. Lines and arrows are used to show cause-and-effect or sequence relationships. The main ideas in the section titled "Determining the pH of a Solution" are summarized in the graphic organizer below.

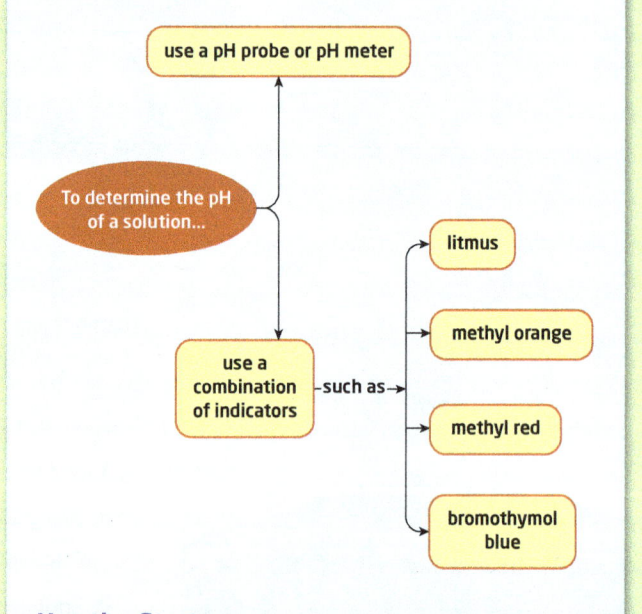

To determine the pH of a solution...
- use a pH probe or pH meter
- use a combination of indicators —such as→
  - litmus
  - methyl orange
  - methyl red
  - bromothymol blue

Use the Strategy

Turn to the subsection titled "Causes of Acid Precipitation" on page 239. Use a graphic organizer to summarize the text in this subsection.

Word Study

Word Parts

The names of compounds are formed by combining different word parts. Knowing what these word parts indicate can help you determine the elements that a compound contains. For example, *hydrofluoric acid* contains the word parts *hydro* (indicating hydrogen), *fluor* (indicating fluorine), and the ending *-ic acid*.

From these word parts, you can translate *hydrofluoric acid* into its elements: hydrogen and fluorine.

Use the Strategy

Identify the word parts in *hydrobromic acid* and *hydrochloric acid*. What two elements form each acid?

218 NEL • Unit 2 Chemical Reactions

6.1 Identifying Acids and Bases

Key Terms
acid
binary acid
oxoacid
base

In the previous chapters of this unit, you learned about compounds and different types of chemical reactions that they can undergo. In this chapter, two particular types of compounds—acids and bases—and the chemical reactions they undergo are discussed. As you will see, this includes a type of double displacement reaction that occurs between acids and bases.

Many of the substances that you encounter every day can be classified as acids or bases. Have you ever taken a bite of a grapefruit or other citrus fruit, like the lemon shown in **Figure 6.1**, and felt an immediate reaction? Perhaps your lips puckered and your cheeks pulled inward, or your eyes watered. This type of reaction is due to the presence of edible acids. The word *acid* comes from the Latin word *acidus*, which means "sour." In the case of citrus fruits, citric acid causes the sour taste that you are familiar with. Acids have been used for thousands of years. Vinegar is an acidic solution that is common to many household products. It was discovered centuries ago, during the fermentation of fruit juices to make wine.

One of the earliest known uses of bases is in making soaps. Nearly 5000 years ago, Babylonians made soap using chemicals in wood ash. Today, many modern household cleaning products are bases. Edible bases, which have a bitter taste, include baking soda and quinine in tonic water. Nevertheless, while some acids and bases are safe to eat, others are deadly and highly corrosive. Therefore, learning to identify acids and bases and how they react with each other is especially important.

Figure 6.1 The sour taste associated with lemons is due to a naturally occurring acid called citric acid.

acid a compound that produces hydrogen ions, H⁺(aq), when dissolved in water

Acids

An **acid** is often defined as a compound that produces hydrogen ions, $H^+(aq)$, when it dissolves in water. In future courses, you will expand on this definition as you learn additional ways to describe acids. Although some acids are safe to eat, such as citric acid and acetic acid (in vinegar), many other acids are not. Many acids are corrosive and will react with metals, so even though a sour taste is one property of acids, you should never taste an unknown chemical to try to identify it.

Forming Hydrogen Ions in Water

Aqueous solutions of acids conduct electric current because of the ions present in the solution. When an acid dissolves in water, it reacts with the water to form ions, in a process called *ionization*. For example, when hydrogen chloride gas is bubbled through and dissolved in water, as shown in **Figure 6.2**, it reacts with water to form ions, and then the hydrogen ions and chloride ions separate in solution.

$$HCl(aq) \rightarrow H^+(aq) + Cl^-(aq)$$

The chemistry of acids is a process that is carried out by numerous naturally occurring chemicals. **Figure 6.3**, on the opposite page, discusses just a few examples of the acids that can be found in nature and the effect that some of these acids can have.

Study Toolkit
Using Graphic Organizers
After reading this page, draw a graphic organizer like the one on page 218. This will help you to remember this information about acids.

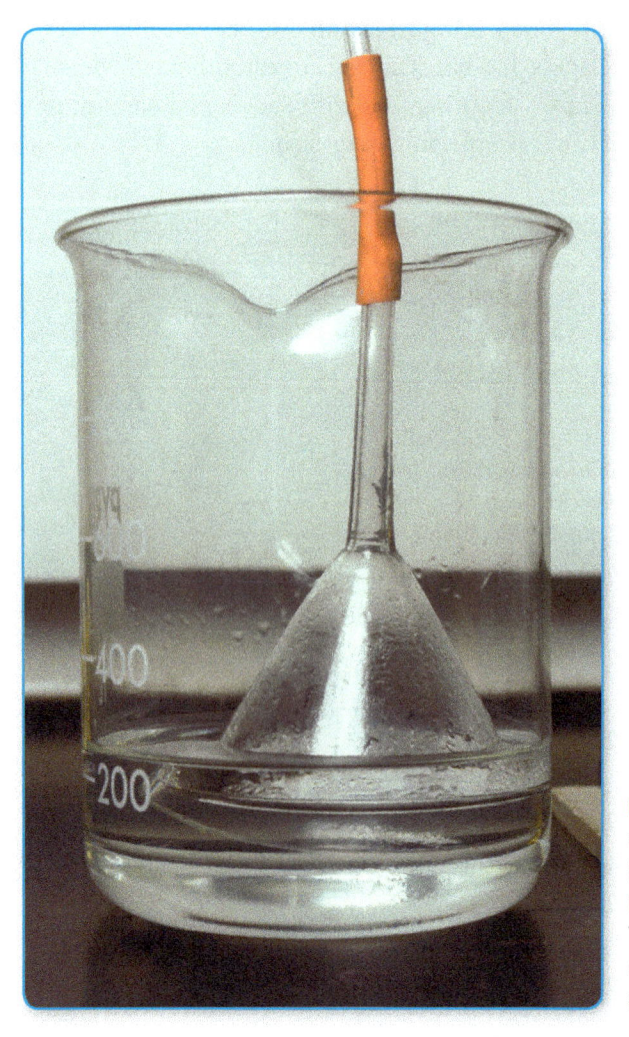

Figure 6.2 Hydrochloric acid, HCl(aq), forms when hydrogen chloride gas, HCl(g), is added to water. The resulting solution contains hydrogen ions and chloride ions.

NATIONAL GEOGRAPHIC
VISUALIZING ACIDS IN NATURE

Figure 6.3

From giant limestone structures to delicate flower petals, acids are at work in nature. All of the animals, plants, and rock formations you see here either produce their own acids or are affected by acids in the environment. In addition, many of the foods you eat are acidic, including lemons, peaches, and tomatoes.

◀ **WHIP SCORPION** The whip scorpion is also known as the vinegaroon because it smells like vinegar. In self-defence, the whip scorpion sprays a mist of acetic acid from glands near the rear of its abdomen. Acetic acid is the active ingredient of vinegar. The whip scorpion, which has no venom, is sometimes kept as a pet.

▲ **LIMESTONE CAVES** Carbon dioxide in the air dissolves in rainwater, forming carbonic acid. Therefore, rainwater is naturally acidic. Acidic water reacts with limestone, very slowly dissolving it. Over a long time, this process can carve large caverns in regions that have thick layers of limestone. In the caverns, some of the dissolved limestone can be deposited as solid rock again, forming twisted spires and flowing draperies of stone.

▲ **HYDRANGEA FLOWERS** Acids in soil determine whether some types of hydrangeas produce blue or pink flowers. In acidic soil, the plants produce blue flowers. In soils that are less acidic, the plants produce pink flowers.

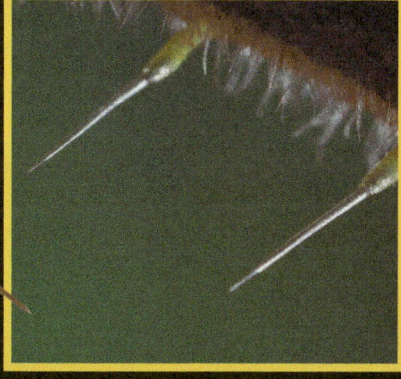

▲ **ANT AND NETTLE STINGS** When you are bitten by an ant or brush against the tiny hairs on a stinging nettle plant, you feel a stinging pain that comes in large part from formic acid. The acid dissolves the ends of the nerves in your skin, causing pain.

Chapter 6 Acids and Bases • NEL

Naming Acids

When naming acids, there are specific steps to follow according to the type of acid that is being named.

Naming Binary Acids

Binary acids are composed of two elements—hydrogen and a non-metal. For example, as just discussed, when the gas hydrogen chloride is dissolved in water, a binary acid, HCl(aq), is formed. **Table 6.1** lists chemical formulas, names, and uses of some binary acids. In addition to the names based on guidelines from the International Union of Pure and Applied Chemistry (IUPAC), the classical names for the acids are also provided. Since this classical system is still widely used, it is important to recognize these more conventional names. To name a binary acid according to the classical method,

1. Write the root of the non-metal name.
2. Add the prefix *hydro-* to the root name.
3. Add the ending *-ic acid* to the root name.

binary acid an acid composed of hydrogen and a non-metal

Table 6.1 Examples of Binary Acids

Chemical Formula in Solution	Classical Acid Name	IUPAC Name	Uses
HF(aq)	hydrofluoric acid	aqueous hydrogen fluoride	• manufacturing aluminum and uranium • etching glass
HCl(aq)	hydrochloric acid	aqueous hydrogen chloride	• producing plastic • processing metals
HBr(aq)	hydrobromic acid	aqueous hydrogen bromide	• extracting metal ore
HI(aq)	hydroiodic acid	aqueous hydrogen iodide	• taking part in chemical reactions to make other compounds

An application of acids in art is the production of etched glass, shown in **Figure 6.4**. This etching is the result of the highly corrosive property of hydrofluoric acid, HF(aq). The acid is so corrosive that it "eats away at" the glass.

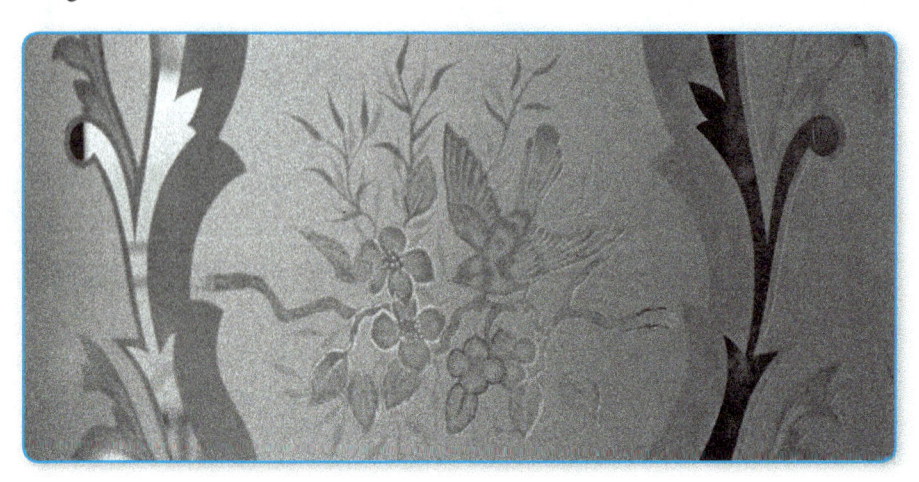

Figure 6.4 Hydrofluoric acid, HF(aq), is used to etch glass. Therefore, hydrofluoric acid cannot be stored in glass containers.

Naming Oxoacids

Oxoacids are composed of hydrogen, oxygen, and another element. For example, an acid can be formed with hydrogen and a polyatomic ion that contains oxygen. Examples of some common oxoacids are provided in **Table 6.2**. To name an oxoacid according to the classical method,

1. Write the name of the anion, without the -*ate* or -*ite* ending.
2. If the anion name ended in -*ate*, replace it with -*ic* at the end of the name
3. If the anion name ended in -*ite*, replace it with -*ous* at the end of the name
4. Add the word *acid*

Notice that the acid names for the compounds that are composed of sulfur use *sulfur-* as the root of the name rather than just *sulf-*. Acids that are composed of phosphorus are named in a similar way and use *phosphor-* as the root rather than *phosph-*. The extra syllable helps in the pronunciation of these names.

oxoacid an acid composed of hydrogen, oxygen, and another element

Table 6.2 Names of Acids That Contain Polyatomic Ions

Chemical Formula in Solution	Classical Acid Name	IUPAC Name	Uses
$H_2SO_4(aq)$	sulfuric acid	aqueous hydrogen sulfate	• in most car batteries • component of acid precipitation
$H_2SO_3(aq)$	sulfurous acid	aqueous hydrogen sulfite	• disinfecting and bleaching
$HNO_3(aq)$	nitric acid	aqueous hydrogen nitrate	• producing explosives and fertilizers
$H_3PO_4(aq)$	phosphoric acid	aqueous hydrogen phosphate	• making fertilizers, soaps, and detergents
$HClO_3(aq)$	chloric acid	aqueous hydrogen chlorate	• producing explosives and matches
$H_2CO_3(aq)$	carbonic acid	aqueous hydrogen carbonate	• occurs naturally in water • in carbonated drinks

Study Toolkit

Word Parts Look at the names of the acids in **Table 6.2**. Identify the word parts in each name. These indicate the ions that the acids are composed of. Knowing how to do this will help you to easily identify an acid.

Learning Check

1. What are three properties of acids?
2. What are two common uses of acids? Refer to **Tables 6.1** and **6.2**.
3. Write the name for each of the following acids.
   a. $HCl(aq)$
   b. $HF(aq)$
   c. $H_2SO_4(aq)$
   d. $H_3PO_4(aq)$
4. Name two products you use or foods you eat that contain acidic substances.

Writing Chemical Formulas for Acids

To write the chemical formula for an acid, first determine which anion to use in the formula. The periodic table is helpful for determining the symbol and charge for anions in binary acids, and **Table 4.7** on page 148 lists the chemical formulas and charges for polyatomic ions in other acids. Once you know what the anion is, combine it with enough hydrogen ions, H$^+$, so that the overall charge of the compound is zero.

GRASP
Go to **Science Skills Toolkit 11** to learn about an alternative problem solving method.

Sample Problem: Writing Chemical Formulas for Acids

Problem
What is the chemical formula for carbonic acid?

Solution
The problem asks you to determine the chemical formula for an acid.

Step 1: Determine if it is a binary acid or an acid containing a polyatomic ion.
- The name ends in *-ic acid* and does not begin with *hydro-*. This indicates that the acid is composed of a polyatomic ion that ends in *-ate*.

Step 2: Identify the chemical formula for the polyatomic ion, using **Table 4.7** on page 148.
- The formula for the carbonate ion is CO_3^{2-}.

Step 3: Determine how many H$^+$ ions are required so that the net charge of the acid is zero.
- Because each hydrogen ion has a 1+ charge, two hydrogen ions are needed to cancel the charge on the carbonate ion. The cross-over method for determining the chemical formula is shown in the margin.

The chemical formula for carbonic acid is H_2CO_3.

Cross-Over Method

$H^{+}(CO_3)^{2-}$

H_2CO_3

Check Your Solution
The name of the acid indicates that it contains a polyatomic ion, which is the carbonate ion. Since the carbonate ion has a charge of 2−, two hydrogen ions, H$^+$, make the overall charge of the compound zero.

Practice Problems

1. Write the chemical formula for hydrobromic acid. Then write the name and formula for the anion that forms.
2. Determine the chemical formulas for the following acids.
   - **a.** hydrochloric acid
   - **b.** nitric acid
   - **c.** hydrofluoric acid
   - **d.** sulfuric acid

Activity 6-2

Chemical Card Games

How well do you remember the names and chemical formulas of common acids? Play with other students to improve your knowledge. The objective is to match an ion formula to an acid name, or an ion name to an acid formula.

Materials
- set of chemical cards

Procedure

1. Play in groups of two to four students. One student should shuffle the chemical cards and deal four cards to each player. The rest of the deck is placed in the centre of the group.

2. Each player examines his or her cards and places any matching pairs, (for example, the formula NO_3^- and the name of the related acid) face-up on the table.

3. Player 1 draws a card from either the deck or a player's hand. If the player has a match, the matching pair is placed on the table. Play then passes to the next person. When all of the cards have been played, the player with the most matches wins.

Questions

1. Did you find that certain acid names or chemical formulas were easier to recognize than others? If so, explain why you think this occurred.

2. Determine a practical use for each acid that you identified.

Bases

Many **bases** are compounds that contain hydroxide ions, OH^-. Common household examples of bases include soap, baking soda, and remedies such as antacids, shown in **Figure 6.5**.

Although some bases are safe to consume or be in contact with, many bases are not. Some people mistakenly think that acids are dangerous and bases are not. This is false. Both acids and bases can cause severe chemical burns. So, even though a bitter taste and a slippery feel are properties of bases, you should *never* taste or touch an unknown chemical to try to identify it.

base a compound that forms hydroxide ions, $OH^-(aq)$, when dissolved in water

Figure 6.5 Many common household products contain bases.

Forming Hydroxide Ions in Water

Aqueous solutions of bases conduct electric current because of the ions in solution. When a base dissolves in water, the ions separate from one another and hydroxide ions are released into the water in a process called *dissociation*. For example, when sodium hydroxide dissolves in water, the ions separate in solution according to the chemical equation

$$NaOH(aq) \rightarrow Na^+(aq) + OH^-(aq)$$

Naming Bases

Since many bases are ionic compounds composed of metal ions and hydroxide ions, their names and chemical formulas are written following the same rules you learned for ionic compounds. Some bases also have a common name often found on consumer products. Table 6.3 lists the names, chemical formulas, and uses for several common bases.

Go to **scienceontario** to find out more

Table 6.3 Some Common Bases

Chemical Formula	Chemical Name	Common Name	Uses
NaOH	sodium hydroxide	lye, caustic soda	• in drain and oven cleaners • used to make paper, glass, and soap
Mg(OH)$_2$	magnesium hydroxide	Milk of Magnesia®	• in laxatives and antacids
Ca(OH)$_2$ (aq)	calcium hydroxide	lime water	• for soil and water treatment

Sodium Hydroxide in Industry

Sodium hydroxide is one of the most important chemicals in industry. The majority of sodium hydroxide is mass-produced by a method called the chlor-alkali process. The name of this process is based on the fact that sodium hydroxide is produced simultaneously with chlorine gas—another very important chemical in industry. The chlor-alkali process is composed of multiple reactions and involves the electrolysis of aqueous sodium chloride. The reactions can be summarized in the chemical equation in Figure 6.6.

Figure 6.6 Sodium hydroxide is mass-produced for industry by the chlor-alkali process. This procedure involves the electrolysis of aqueous sodium chloride and also produces chlorine gas, with hydrogen gas as a by-product.

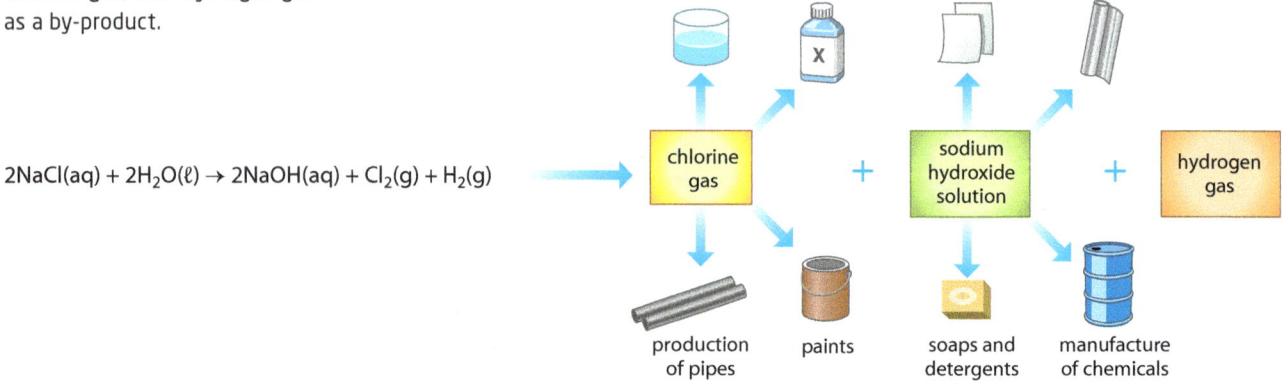

$$2NaCl(aq) + 2H_2O(\ell) \rightarrow 2NaOH(aq) + Cl_2(g) + H_2(g)$$

chlorine gas: purifying drinking water, medicines, production of pipes, paints

sodium hydroxide solution: paper production, soaps and detergents

hydrogen gas: aluminum production, manufacture of chemicals

226 NEL • Unit 2 Chemical Reactions

Writing Chemical Formulas for Bases

The principles for writing the chemical formula for a base are the same as those used for writing the chemical formula for an acid. To write the chemical formula for a base, you must make sure to include enough hydroxide ions in the formula so that the total charge of the compound is zero. Remember that the charge of the hydroxide ion is 1–, and the charge of the metal ions can be determined from the periodic table.

Sample Problem: Writing Chemical Formulas for Bases

Problem
What is the chemical formula for aqueous potassium hydroxide?

Solution
The problem asks you to determine the chemical formula for a base.

Step 1: Identify the cation and anion for the base.
- The name indicates that the anion is a hydroxide ion (OH$^-$) and the metal cation is potassium.

Step 2: Determine the ion charge of the cation.
- According to the periodic table, potassium has an ion charge of 1+ (K$^+$).

Step 3: Determine the correct subscripts for the chemical formula.
- For the compound to have a net charge of zero, there must be one hydroxide ion in the formula for each potassium cation. The cross-over method for determining the chemical formula is shown in the margin.

Therefore, the formula for aqueous potassium hydroxide is KOH(aq).

Check Your Solution
The name indicates that the compound is a base since it contains the word *hydroxide*. The name also indicates that the metal ion is potassium. Since the ion charge for potassium is 1+ and the charge for the hydroxide ion is 1–, addition of the charges in the formula KOH results in a net charge of zero.

GRASP
Go to **Science Skills Toolkit 11** to learn about an alternative problem solving method.

Cross-Over Method

K^{1+} OH^{1-}

KOH

Practice Problems

1. Write the chemical formula for an aqueous solution of sodium hydroxide. Then write the name and formula for the metal cation.
2. Determine the chemical formulas for the following bases (assume all are solids).
   - **a.** calcium hydroxide
   - **b.** aluminum hydroxide
   - **c.** beryllium hydroxide
   - **d.** lithium hydroxide
   - **e.** manganese(II) hydroxide
   - **f.** nickel(II) hydroxide

Sense of scale

Each year, over 65 million tonnes of sodium hydroxide are produced worldwide. Over 50 percent of that is consumed by China and the European Union. Canada consumes about 3 percent of the world's supply of sodium hydroxide.

Section 6.1 Review

Section Summary

- Acids are compounds that have a sour taste. When dissolved in water, they produce hydrogen ions, H^+(aq).
- Binary acids are composed of hydrogen and a non-metal. The name of a binary acid is written using the prefix *hydro-*, the root of the non-metal name, and the ending *-ic acid*.
- Oxoacids that form between hydrogen and polyatomic ions are named by replacing *-ate* with *-ic acid* and *-ite* with *-ous acid*.
- Bases are compounds that have a bitter taste. Many bases are ionic compounds that separate into metal ions and hydroxide ions, OH^-(aq), when dissolved in water.
- Since bases are ionic compounds, their names and chemical formulas are written following the same rules that are used for ionic compounds.

Review Questions

K/U 1. Describe the ions that form when an acid is dissolved in water.

C 2. Make a table that shows how the endings of acid names relate to the endings of the names of ions. Include an example of each.

A 3. What type of chemical in the grapefruit on the right provides it with its sour taste? Explain.

K/U 4. What are two properties of bases?

K/U 5. Write the name for each of the following.
   a. $Ca(OH)_2$(aq)
   b. H_3PO_3(aq)
   c. HF(aq)
   d. KOH(s)

K/U 6. Write the chemical formula for each of the following.
   a. phosphoric acid
   b. hydrobromic acid
   c. magnesium hydroxide
   d. aluminum hydroxide

T/I 7. Complete the following chemical equations to illustrate the ions in solution, and identify the compound as an acid or base.
   a. $HClO_3$(aq) →
   b. KOH(aq) →

T/I 8. You have been asked to organize the following aqueous solutions: HCl, NaOH, H_2SO_4, $Ca(OH)_2$, LiOH, and $HClO_3$. How would you group them? On what are you basing your decision?

6.2 The pH Scale and Indicators

Key Terms
pH scale
pH indicator

In May 2001, 49 people who attended a dance festival in Dauphin, Manitoba, became sick within a week. The evidence suggests that the source of the illness was the hotel pool. In Chapter 5, the use of chlorinating agents in pools was discussed as a method to help keep pools safe by killing organisms that could cause illness. Sodium hypochlorite, NaClO(s), is often added to pools to form hypochlorous acid, HClO(aq) in the water.

If the water contains too much acid, it might sting your eyes and it will react with substances in the concrete walls of the pool and in the mortar between the tiles. Therefore, a proper balance must be achieved. To maintain the proper acidity in the pool, the pool manager must regularly check the pH of the water, as shown in **Figure 6.7**. How acidic or basic a solution is can be described in terms of the pH. As you learned in the previous section, acids produce hydrogen ions when they dissolve in water. Hypochlorous acid is no different, and ions form according to the chemical equation

$$HClO(aq) \rightarrow H^+(aq) + ClO^-(aq)$$

Figure 6.7 This is a simple test kit to determine the pH of the water in the pool. A pH of 7.2 to 7.6 is ideal to keep the pool clean. Notice that this test kit also checks for proper levels of chlorine, which you have learned is also a common chemical used in pool maintenance.

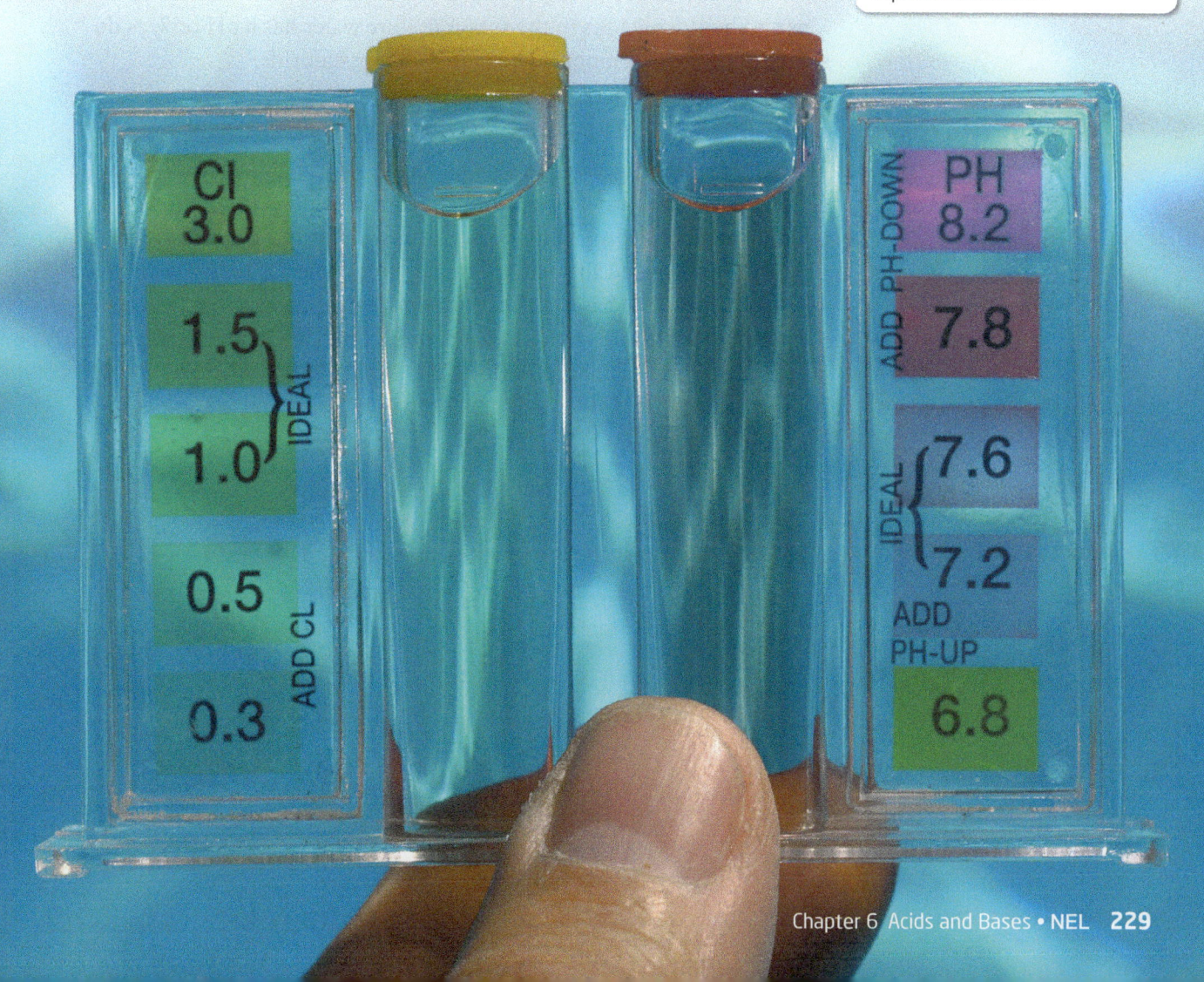

Chapter 6 Acids and Bases

pH scale a numerical scale ranging from 0 to 14 that is used to classify aqueous solutions as acidic, basic, or neutral

The pH Scale

Most common acids and bases form colourless solutions. Determining the pH of a solution can help you tell whether an unknown solution contains an acid, a base, or neither. The **pH scale** is a scale that typically ranges from 0 to 14, which is used to classify solutions as acidic, basic, or neutral. **Figure 6.8** shows the pH values of some common substances.

Acidic Solutions: pH < 7

Notice that acids have pH values below pH 7. This means there are many more hydrogen ions in the solution than hydroxide ions. The lower the pH, the more acidic the solution is. So, a lemon at pH 2 is more acidic than milk at pH 6. The pH of gastric fluids in the stomach is between 1 and 2.

Basic Solutions: pH > 7

On the other end of the scale, bases have pH values above pH 7. This means there are many more hydroxide ions in the solution than hydrogen ions. The higher the pH, the more basic the solution is. So, oven cleaner at pH 13 is more basic than eggs at pH 8.

Neutral Solutions: pH = 7

A solution that is neither acidic nor basic is neutral and falls in the middle of the pH scale at pH 7. This means there is the same number of hydrogen ions and hydroxide ions in the solution. Pure water has a pH of 7, as do solutions of some compounds, such as sodium chloride.

Differences in pH Values

The pH scale was suggested in 1909 by the Danish chemist Søren Sørenson as a more accurate way to describe acid concentrations in solutions. The concentration of hydrogen ions associated with a value on the pH scale differs from the value above it or below it by a power of 10. For example, a solution that is pH 4 has a concentration of hydrogen ions that is 10 times greater than in a solution that is pH 5, but is only one tenth as great as in a solution that is pH 3. So, a solution that is pH 3 has a concentration of hydrogen ions that is 100 times greater than in a solution that is pH 5.

Figure 6.8 pH values of common substances have a wide range.

Learning Check

1. A solution has a pH of 4. Is it acidic, basic, or neutral?
2. Summarize the pH values associated with acids, with bases, and with neutral solutions using a graphic organizer of your choice.
3. How much more concentrated are the hydrogen ions in a solution that is pH 7 than the hydrogen ions in a solution that is pH 10?
4. Why is it important that the pH of a swimming pool be carefully monitored?

Sense of Value

Litmus is derived from lichens, which are an important component of ecosystems in Canada. Lichens are the largest part of the winter diet of barren-ground caribou, and many Aboriginal peoples depend on lichens to see their herds through the winter. Some lichens are sensitive to certain air pollutants and can serve as early indicators of pollution problems.

Determining the pH of a Solution

There are several methods that can be used to determine the pH of a solution. The method chosen will depend on several factors, such as availability of equipment and how accurate the pH determination needs to be.

pH Meter

One way to determine the pH of a solution is to use an electronic pH meter or pH probe, as shown in **Figure 6.9**. These meters use the electrical properties of a solution to determine pH. By connecting a pH probe to a computer, changes of pH can be analyzed in real time.

Litmus Paper

Another way to determine pH is the use of indicators. A **pH indicator** is a chemical that is added in small amounts to a solution to visually show the acidity or basicity of the solution by changing colour at a particular pH or range of pH values.

An indicator that you might have used is litmus. Litmus solution is often dried onto thin paper strips and comes in red and blue. Using a strip of red litmus paper and a strip of blue litmus paper, you can determine whether a solution is acidic, basic, or neutral. Blue litmus paper turns red in an acidic solution and red litmus paper turns blue in a basic solution, as shown in **Figure 6.10**. In a neutral solution, neither type of litmus paper changes colour. However, using only litmus paper is not sufficient to precisely determine the pH of a solution.

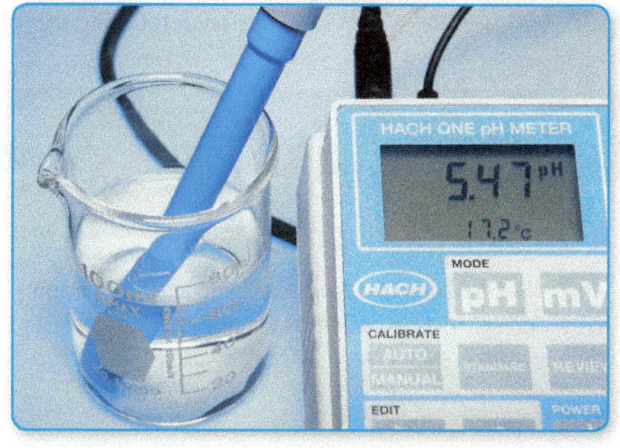

Figure 6.9 The pH meter shows that this solution has a pH of 5.47 and is acidic.

pH indicator a substance that changes colour to show the concentration of hydrogen ions (H^+) and hydroxide ions (OH^-) in a solution

Figure 6.10 This red litmus paper (centre) appears pink in an acidic solution (left) and blue to purple in a basic solution (right).

Figure 6.11 The colour of universal indicator changes through the colours of the spectrum from red to blue as pH increases. The changes in colour help to quickly identify the pH of a solution.

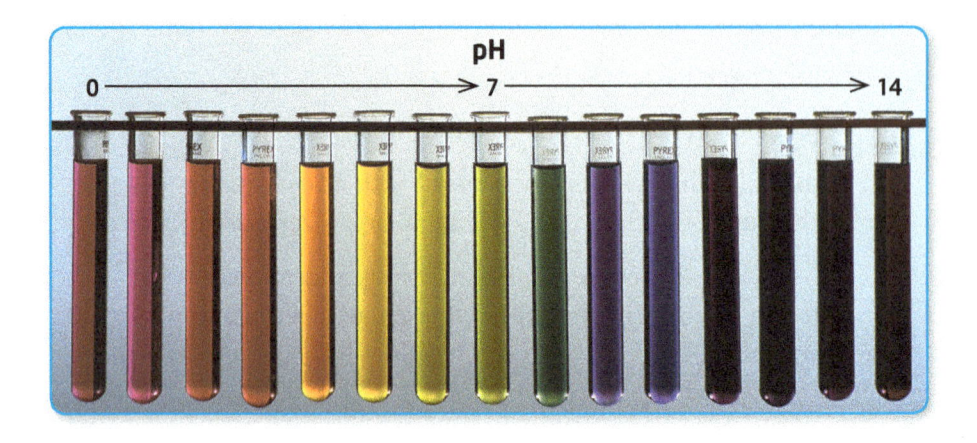

Figure 6.12 pH paper comes with a colour scale to compare colour changes and determine the pH.

Universal Indicator and pH Paper

To more accurately determine the pH of a solution, several indicators that cover the pH range between pH 0 and pH 14 must be used. Universal indicator is a mixture of several indicators that produce a different colour at different pH values, as shown in **Figure 6.11**. The pH paper shown in **Figure 6.12** is prepared by soaking strips of paper in universal indicator and then allowing them to dry. A drop of solution to be tested is placed on the pH paper. The resulting colour is compared against a colour chart to determine the pH of the solution.

Activity 6-3

A Universal Rainbow

When an acidic solution is combined with a basic solution, a reaction occurs that can be shown using an indicator. What identifies that a reaction is taking place?

Safety Precautions

- Wear safety goggles and a lab apron at all times.

Materials

- 2 test tubes
- test-tube rack
- marker or wax pencil
- 20 mL of 0.1 mol/L hydrochloric acid
- 20 mL of 0.1 mol/L sodium carbonate
- universal indicator
- plastic pipette

Procedure

1. Label two test tubes A and B. Put 10 mL of hydrochloric acid solution into test tube A, and 10 mL of sodium carbonate solution into test tube B. Both test tubes will be less than half full.

2. Add several drops of universal indicator to each of the test tubes.

3. Use the plastic pipette to gently transfer solution from test tube B into test tube A. Do not shake or stir the test tubes. Continue until all of the liquid has been transferred. Allow the test tube to sit for one minute, and then draw a diagram of the test tube.

4. If there is enough time, repeat this experiment, this time transferring liquid from test tube A to test tube B.

Questions

1. What signs of chemical change did you observe?
2. List the colours in order from top to bottom.
   a. How does the pH change from the top of the solution to the bottom?
   b. Classify the colours observed according to whether they represent an acidic or basic solution.

Other pH Indicators

Specific indicators can also be used, which change colour within a small range of pH values. A few common indicators and their colour changes are summarized in **Table 6.4** and shown in **Figure 6.13**. By testing a solution with several different indicators, you can more accurately determine the pH of a solution. For example, if a solution turns methyl orange to a yellow colour and causes methyl red to remain a red colour, then the solution must have a pH between 4.4 and 4.8.

Suggested Investigation

Plan Your Own Investigation 6-A, What Is Your Exposure to Acids and Bases?, on page 247

Table 6.4 Acid-Base Indicators

Indicator	pH Range in Which Colour Change Occurs	Colour Change as pH Increases
Methyl orange	3.2–4.4	red to yellow
Methyl red	4.8–6.0	red to yellow
Bromothymol blue	6.0–7.6	yellow to blue
Phenolphthalein	8.2–10.0	colourless to pink
Indigo carmine	11.2–13.0	blue to yellow

Go to **scienceontario** to find out more

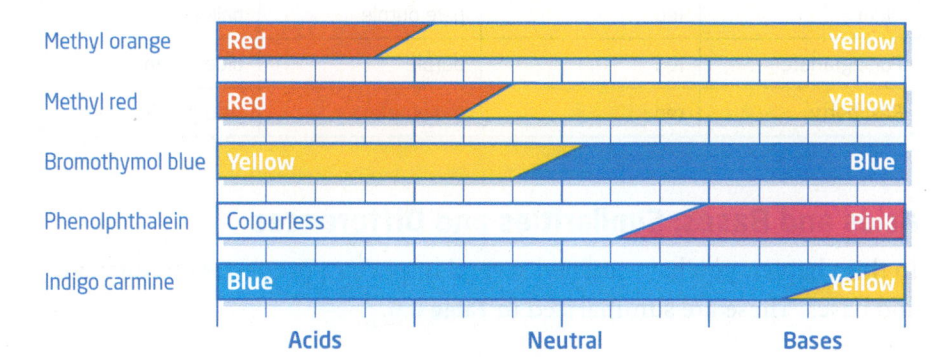

Figure 6.13 Various acid-base indicators change colour in different ranges of pH values.

Learning Check

5. What is a pH indicator?

6. A solution caused red litmus paper to turn blue. Was the solution acidic, neutral, or basic?

7. You suspect that a solution is slightly basic, and you want to perform one additional test to confirm your conclusion. Which indicators in **Figure 6.13** would be best to use? Why?

8. Write a proposal to persuade your school to buy universal indicator for use in science investigations instead of several individual indicators.

pH Indicators in Nature

In Activity 6-1, you noticed that the colour of the red cabbage juice changed when you added lemon juice or soap. The cabbage juice was an acid-base indicator that changed colour as you added acid (lemon juice) or base (soap). Additional substances that contain natural acid-base indicators are listed in **Table 6.5**. These include the pomegranate, shown in **Figure 6.14**.

Table 6.5 Acid-Base Indicators Extracted from Common Plants

Plant	Colour of Indicator		
	Acid	Neutral	Base
Apple	red	grey-purple	green
Blackberry	red	purple	blue-green
Blueberry	red	purple	blue
Cherry	red	red-purple	blue-green
Mountain cranberry	red	pale purple	pale green
Grape	red	purple	blue-green
Plum	red	pale purple	pale green
Pomegranate	red	purple	blue-green
Raspberry	red	red purple	pale green

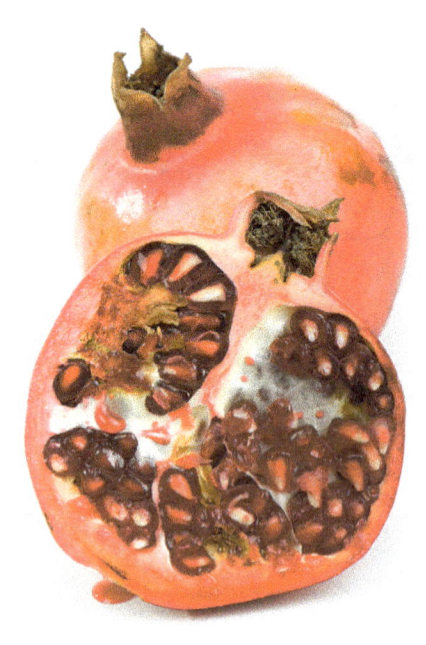

Figure 6.14 Extracts of some fruits, such as pomegranate, can act as pH indicators.

Acids and Bases: Similarities and Differences

In this chapter, you have learned several important properties about acids and bases. These are summarized in **Table 6.6**.

Table 6.6 Properties of Acids and Bases

Property	Acid	Base
Taste CAUTION: Never taste chemicals in the laboratory.	Acids taste sour.	Bases taste bitter.
Touch CAUTION: Never touch chemicals in the laboratory with your bare skin.	Many acids will burn your skin.	Bases feel slippery and many bases will burn your skin.
Indicator tests	Acids turn blue litmus paper red.	Bases turn red litmus paper blue.
Electrical conductivity	Solutions of acids conduct electricity.	Solutions of bases conduct electricity.
pH	The pH of acidic solutions is less than 7.	The pH of basic solutions is greater than 7.
Production of ions	Acids form hydrogen ions, H^+ (aq), when dissolved in water.	Bases form hydroxide ions, OH^- (aq), when dissolved in water.

Study Toolkit

Interpreting Tables
For **Table 6.6**, use the strategy outlined on page 218 for interpreting data in tables. What does the title of the table tell you about the content? What do the headings tell you about the information in each cell?

Learning how to efficiently interpret tables will help you obtain as much information from them as possible.

Section 6.2 Review

Section Summary

- The pH scale ranges from 0 to 14 and is used to classify an aqueous solution as acidic, basic, or neutral. Neutral solutions are pH 7. Acidic solutions have a pH less than 7. Basic solutions have a pH greater than 7.
- A change of 1 on the pH scale represents a change in the concentration of hydrogen ions in a solution by a factor of 10. The pH of a solution can be determined using pH indicators or an electronic pH probe.
- A pH indicator is a chemical that is added in small amounts to a solution to visually show the acidity or basicity of the solution by changing colours within a small range of pH values.
- Universal pH indicator and pH paper contain several indicators and can be used to determine the pH of a solution.

Review Questions

K/U 1. Is the mixture shown on the right acidic, basic, or neutral? Explain.

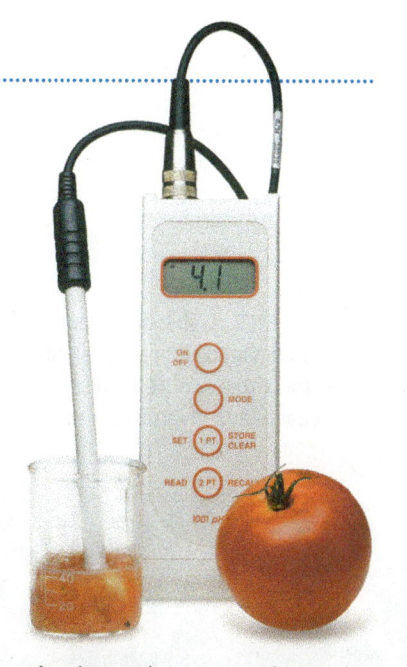

K/U 2. What are two methods that you can use to determine the pH of a solution?

C 3. Use a diagram to show how the concentration of hydrogen ions changes as pH increases.

K/U 4. Explain why both red and blue litmus paper must be used to determine that a solution is neutral.

A 5. Search your home for commonly used household products. In a table, record the product's name, describe its use, and identify it as an acidic or basic solution. What evidence can you provide to support your conclusions?

K/U 6. Name three examples of acid-base indicators found in nature.

T/I 7. Based on the information in **Table 6.4**, what indicator would you use to monitor the pH of a solution that you were changing from pH 7 to 9?

T/I 8. The data in the table below were recorded using different indicators to determine the pH of a solution. Based on these data, what is the best estimate for the pH of the solution? Explain your reasoning.

An electronic meter can be used to determine pH.

Colours of the Solution	
Indicator	Colour
Bromothymol blue	blue
Phenolphthalein	colourless
Indigo carmine	blue

Key Terms
neutralization
liming

6.3 Reactions of Acids and Bases

In 1971, astronauts from the United States trained near Sudbury, Ontario, for an Apollo mission to the Moon. This site was chosen because of the presence of rare rock formations called *shatter cones* that form from meteorite impacts. At the time, the land around Sudbury was quite desolate and barren, as shown in **Figure 6.15A**. This prompted many people to believe that the astronauts were training there because the land resembled the barren, lifeless surface of the Moon. Scientists determined that much of the damage to the environment was caused by acid precipitation, which was the result of gas emissions from local smelters. Smelters are industrial facilities in which metals are separated from ores.

The realization of the widespread damage caused by smelter emissions led the governments of Canada and the United States to agree to decrease the emissions. Principles of acid-base chemistry were applied to help counter the effects of acid precipitation. In addition, efforts such as tree planting initiatives by local communities and Aboriginal peoples have helped to improve the land around Sudbury, as shown in **Figure 6.15B**.

Figure 6.15 A The land around the Sudbury smelters was badly damaged from smelter emissions and acid precipitation. **B** Efforts that reduced emissions by 90 percent over the last 30 years have given the area a chance to recover.

Acid-Base Neutralization

When an acid and a base are mixed, they react and can neutralize each other. **Neutralization** is the reaction of an acid and a base to form a salt and water. For example, hydrochloric acid and sodium hydroxide react as shown in the balanced chemical equation

$$HCl(aq) + NaOH(aq) \rightarrow H_2O(\ell) + NaCl(aq)$$

You might recognize this type of reaction as a double displacement reaction in which the ions of the reactants switch places to form new compounds. The water forms as the hydrogen ions of the acid and the hydroxide ions of the base combine.

$$H^+(aq) + OH^-(aq) \rightarrow HOH(\ell)$$

The other ions join to form a salt. In this reaction, the salt formed is sodium chloride, or table salt. However, any ionic compound that is neither an acid nor a base can be called a salt. In most cases, the salt formed by a neutralization reaction is soluble in water and will not form a precipitate.

Whether the acid is added to the base or the base is added to the acid, the removal of both hydrogen ions and hydroxide ions from solution as they form molecules of water causes the pH of the mixture to approach 7. If the right amounts of acid and base react, the resulting solution will be neutral.

An Application of Neutralization: Antacids

The pits in the lining of your stomach, shown in **Figure 6.16**, secrete hydrochloric acid. This acid helps to break down food in the digestion process. A problem that many people suffer from is excess production of acid. This can result in heartburn, which includes a burning sensation in the stomach that can extend up through the chest area into the esophagus or throat. A common treatment for heartburn is the use of commercially available *antacids*. As their name implies, antacids are designed to neutralize the acid. They have an ingredient that is a base to help increase the pH of the gastric juices of the stomach. Common bases used in antacids are magnesium hydroxide and aluminum hydroxide.

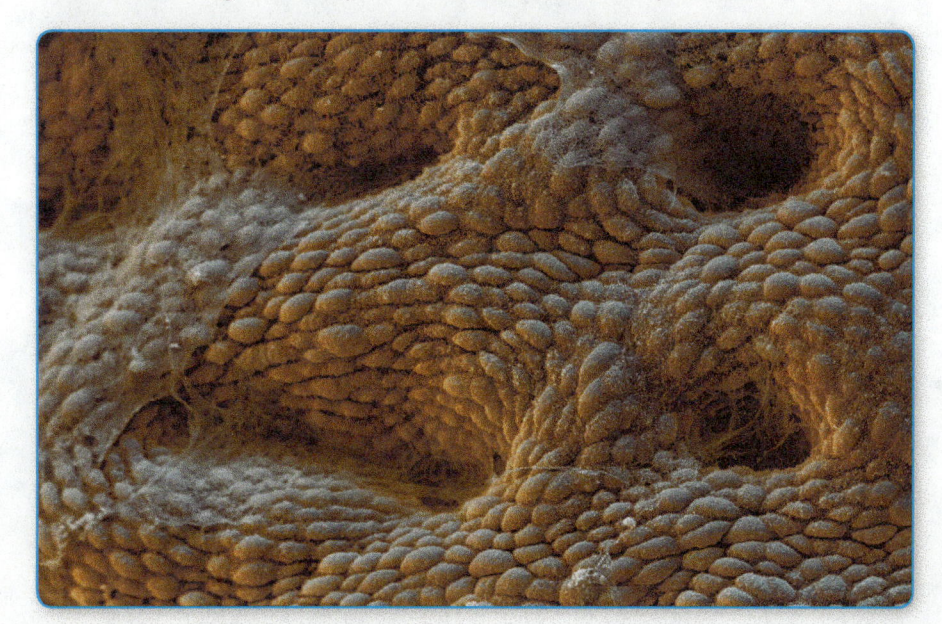

neutralization the reaction of an acid and a base to produce a salt and water

Suggested Investigation
Inquiry Investigation 6-C, Neutralizing an Acid with a Base, on page 250

Figure 6.16 This photograph of the lining of the stomach, at about 700 times magnification, was taken using an electron microscope. Acids are secreted into the stomach from gastric pits (dark holes). These acids are needed for digestion.

Neutralizing Acid Spills

In late March 2007, railroad tanker cars derailed, as shown in **Figure 6.17**. The accident spilled 150 000 litres of sulfuric acid into the Blanche River near Englehart, Ontario. An important step in the clean-up was adding a base, calcium hydroxide to the river to help neutralize the acid:

$$H_2SO_4(aq) + Ca(OH)_2(aq) \rightarrow CaSO_4(aq) + 2H_2O(\ell)$$

When an acid spill occurs, a quick response is critical. It is important to minimize the size of the spill by containing the spilled acid and stopping any leaks from containers such as overturned tankers. Neutralizing the acid and warning or evacuating people in the area helps to prevent injuries. Cleaning up the spill does not prevent harm to the environment, however. Following the spill near Englehart, dead fish washed up on the banks of the river as a result of acidic water.

> **Learning Check**
>
> 1. Define neutralization and give one example of a neutralization reaction.
> 2. Draw a graphic organizer that identifies the reactants and products of a neutralization reaction.
> 3. Why is neutralization important in cleaning up an acid spill?
> 4. With your teacher, examine the contents of the spill kit in your classroom laboratory. Which materials in the kit should be used if an acid spill occurs? if a base spill occurs? Explain how these materials work.

Figure 6.17 Sulfuric acid leaked from these tankers after they derailed near Englehart, Ontario. Residents in the area were warned not to use river water until the clean-up was complete.

Acid Precipitation

Rainwater is naturally acidic and normally has a pH of around 5.6. This acidity is the result of carbon dioxide in the air dissolving in and reacting with water to form carbonic acid:

$$CO_2(g) + H_2O(\ell) \rightarrow H_2CO_3(aq)$$

However, similar synthesis reactions of other non-metal oxides form additional acids, which lower the pH of rainwater even further.

Causes of Acid Precipitation

As you have already learned, the high temperature in a car's engine causes nitrogen and oxygen to react and form several oxides of nitrogen, represented as NO_x. These oxides can react with water to form acids. For example, nitrogen dioxide reacts with water to produce nitric acid:

$$NO_2(g) + H_2O(\ell) \rightarrow HNO_3(aq)$$

Catalytic converters help to decrease the amount of nitrogen oxides that enter the atmosphere, but do not eliminate the NO_x emissions completely. In Canada, the main source of NO_x emissions is the transportation sector. Since 1985, NO_x emissions have remained relatively constant.

Another major contributor to acid precipitation is sulfur oxides, represented as SO_x. Sources include industrial processes. For example, ores smelted in the Sudbury region contained sulfur, which forms sulfur dioxide during the smelting process. This gas is also produced during the combustion of fossil fuels that contain sulfur. Coal and natural gas contain some sulfur or sulfur compounds that can form sulfur dioxide when combusted.

$$S_8(s) + 8O_2(g) \rightarrow 8SO_2(g)$$

The sulfur dioxide can react with additional oxygen to form sulfur trioxide, which in turn can react with water to form sulfuric acid:

$$2SO_2(g) + O_2(g) \rightarrow 2SO_3(g)$$
$$SO_3(g) + H_2O(\ell) \rightarrow H_2SO_4(aq)$$

As you can see in **Figure 6.18**, more than 95 percent of sulfur dioxide emissions in Canada come from industrial sources and electric utilities. Under the initiation of the Canada-Wide Acid Rain Strategy and Eastern Canada Acid Rain programs, Canada experienced a reduction in sulfur dioxide emissions of approximately 50 percent.

Sense of place

In Canada's western Arctic, about a kilometre south of the Beaufort Sea, are the Smoking Hills. These sea cliffs contain carbon-rich shale and sulfur-rich pyrite that have been burning for centuries. Limestone in the area causes lakes to have a pH above 8.0. However, the acid precipitation that has resulted from the smoke from these hills has lowered the pH of some lakes to below 2.0.

Canadian SO_x Emissions in 2000

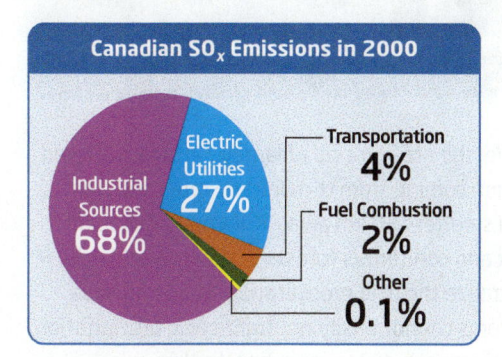

- Industrial Sources 68%
- Electric Utilities 27%
- Transportation 4%
- Fuel Combustion 2%
- Other 0.1%

Figure 6.18 The biggest potential for reducing SO_x emissions in Canada occurs in industrial plants and electric utilities.

Effects of Acid Precipitation

Eastern Canada is especially sensitive to the effects of acid precipitation. In provinces that are part of the Canadian Shield, such as Ontario, the soils and waterways lack a natural ability to fight the damage caused by acid precipitation. These areas contain mostly granite rock, which does not provide a natural source of basicity. Other areas, such as western Canada, contain more limestone-based rock, which does have a natural basicity. As a result, soils in these areas can help to neutralize the acid precipitation and, therefore, reduce its effects.

Effects of Abrupt Changes in Water pH

In some instances the change in pH of the lake or river water can be abrupt. The rushing waters of the snowmelt in **Figure 6.19** could hold a deadly dose of acid for fish in a nearby lake or stream. Mass fish kills can occur in the spring because acidic pollutants that have collected in the snow start to drain into these bodies of water. However, more often, fish gradually disappear from a lake or a stream as the environment slowly becomes less tolerable.

Figure 6.19 The spring snowmelt can carry a large amount of acid that had been trapped in the snow and ice. This can cause a sharp drop in pH in nearby lakes.

STSE Case Study

Update on Acid Precipitation

Scottish chemist Robert Angus Smith first described acid precipitation during the Industrial Revolution of the 19th century, when coal-powered factories that released huge amounts of pollution became common. Acid precipitation or, technically, "acid deposition" includes acidic rain, snow, sleet, hail, and fog. Acid precipitation comes from emissions from power plants, factories, motor vehicles, and even volcanoes. Acid precipitation affects terrestrial and freshwater ecosystems, in addition to human health.

Acid Precipitation in North America

In North America, scientists reported acid precipitation effects mainly in provinces east of Manitoba and in the northeastern United States. In general, the locations were downwind from major industrial polluters, and less able to neutralize acid precipitation naturally, compared to other locations.

For example, the area around Killarney, Ontario, suffered from air pollution coming from the United States and from Sudbury metal smelters 50 km away. Killarney's Canadian Shield bedrock and coniferous forests in shallow, acid soils could not neutralize the acid precipitation. Similarly, Nova Scotia ecosystems cannot easily neutralize acid precipitation, so some of its rivers can no longer support salmon.

Effects of Gradual Changes in Water pH

A healthy lake or stream can support a greater variety of organisms than an acidified one. **Table 6.7** shows the changes in lake organisms that occur as the water's pH decreases. As a lake or stream becomes more acidic, many types of tiny organisms start to disappear. These organisms are food sources for fish and other animals. In addition, as the pH decreases, fish have trouble reproducing. A decrease in fish populations affects animals that depend on fish as a food source. For example, populations of loons, shown in **Figure 6.20**, and other water birds decrease when there are not enough fish to support them.

Figure 6.20 An increase in the acidity of a lake can cause a decrease in water bird populations, such as loons.

Table 6.7 Changes to a Lake at Various pH Values

pH	Effects
6.0	• some insects, plankton, and crustaceans die
5.0	• large change in the variety of plankton • invasion by less desirable species of plankton and moss • loss of some fish populations
< 5.0	• few fish remain • land animals are affected by the loss of fish

Taking Action

Countries have taken action to reduce the effects of acid precipitation. For example, Canada and the United States signed the *Canada-U.S. Air Quality Agreement* in 1991. Canada also devised national pollution-reduction goals. Since then, Sudbury industries have reduced air pollution by 90 percent, and many lakes in the Killarney region are now less acidic and much healthier than before.

Since the signing of a 1991 agreement, many lakes in the Killarney region have undergone varying degrees of recovery.

Despite these efforts, some ecosystems are still receiving levels of acid precipitation that they cannot tolerate. And even ecosystems that get less acid precipitation may not simply rebound. Acid deposition may not be in the news a lot these days, but it is still a major environmental issue in many countries.

Your Turn

1. Identify the factors that contribute to acid deposition.
2. Research one technology for reducing air pollution and discuss it with a small group.
3. Research one of the following approaches for reducing the effects of acid deposition and present your information to the class:
   a. adding lime to acidic lakes in Sweden
   b. adding more acid-tolerant fish species to recovering Killarney, Ontario, lakes

Making a Difference

Simon Bild-Enkin has combined his interest in science and history to complete unique science fair projects. In Grade 10, he researched the effects of acid precipitation on historic buildings. Many buildings are made from limestone. Acid precipitation damages these buildings because limestone dissolves in acid. Simon investigated the effects of different concentrations of acid on limestone. He also tested the use of a protective coating of paraffin wax on the limestone. He found that higher concentrations of acid dissolved more limestone, and that a protective coating was helpful only if applied perfectly. Upon completing his experiments, Simon concluded that the best way to preserve buildings is to reduce the effects of acid precipitation by dealing with its causes.

Simon won third place at the Vancouver Island Regional Science Fair and presented his project at the 2007 Canada Wide Science Fair.

How could you contribute to initiatives to reduce the harmful effects of acid precipitation?

Reducing Emissions That Cause Acid Precipitation

Through a better understanding of the properties of chemicals and the reactions associated with them, scientists know more about acid precipitation and the problems it causes. Now, scientists are working to apply this understanding to help solve the environmental challenges caused by acid precipitation. One solution is to reduce the emissions that cause acid precipitation.

Sulfur oxides are a major contributor to acid precipitation. One way to reduce sulfur oxide emissions is to use *scrubbers* on smokestacks of industrial plants that burn coal in their furnaces, as shown in **Figure 6.21**. Nearly all sources of coal contain sulfur as a contaminant. When the coal burns, the sulfur contaminant also burns, forming sulfur dioxide (SO_2), as discussed on page 239.

Calcium carbonate ($CaCO_3$) is added to the coal and air as they enter the furnace. While the coal burns in air, it forms CO_2 and SO_2 gases. The $CaCO_3$ decomposes into CO_2 and CaO. Some of the SO_2 reacts with the CaO, forming calcium sulfite ($CaSO_3$). Unreacted SO_2 enters the wet scrubber, where a slurry of CaO in water is sprayed. Most of the remaining SO_2 reacts with the dissolved CaO, forming $CaSO_3$, which mixes with water to form a slurry that is discarded.

Figure 6.21 To reduce emissions that could form acid precipitation, sulfur dioxide is removed from exhaust gases through a reaction with calcium oxide that forms calcium sulfite.

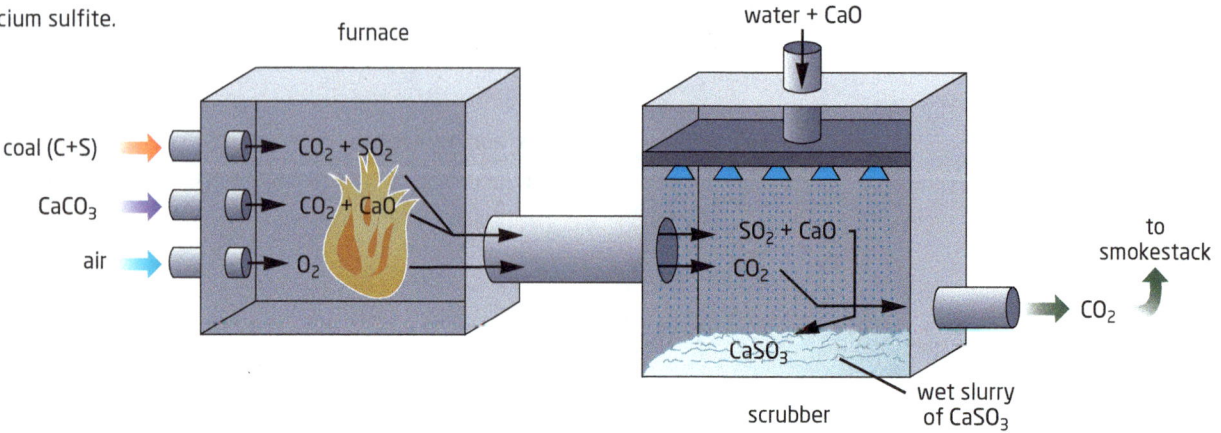

Renewing Acidified Lakes

Another way to address acid precipitation is to attempt to reverse its effects. For example, **Figure 6.22** shows a helicopter treating an acidic lake. The process, called **liming**, is like giving the lake a giant crushed antacid tablet. The calcium carbonate that is added to the lake is the active ingredient in many antacids. The calcium carbonate reacts with the acid and raises the pH of the water.

Effects of Liming on Lakes

Why isn't liming used to renew all lakes that have become too acidic? If liming a lake once could correct the problem for good, then it might be possible (over a long time and at great expense) to renew all acidic lakes. However, as long as acidic water continues to enter the lake, the pH will drop again and the lake will require additional treatments.

In addition, liming can cause problems. Adding limestone to a lake increases the calcium content of the water. Some species, such as the bog moss sphagnum and some types of insects, are sensitive to calcium levels. Preventing acid precipitation by using catalytic converters, scrubbers, and new technologies is a much better solution.

> **liming** the application of basic materials, typically lime-based, to renew acidified lakes and regions

> **Suggested Investigation**
> Real World Investigation 6-B, The pH of Lakes Near Sudbury, on page 248

Figure 6.22 Adding limestone to an acidic lake helps to renew the lake and raise its pH. However, if the source of the acid is not eliminated, treatments must be repeated at intervals to maintain the higher pH.

Learning Check

5. What is the pH of normal rainwater?
6. Based on the data in **Figure 6.18**, what percentage of SO_x emissions comes from industrial sources?
7. Make a drawing that shows the sources of gases that cause acid precipitation and identifies the technologies that are used to reduce each emission.
8. How is liming a lake similar to a doctor prescribing medicine for a patient?

Activity 6-4

Air Pollution and Ontario's Lakes

Gases produced by combustion in our cars, homes, and industries are released directly into Earth's atmosphere. What effect do these gases have on our lakes? In this activity, you will create some gases, observe their effect on Lake Erlenmeyer, and then attempt to neutralize the effect.

Safety Precautions

- Wear safety goggles and a lab apron.
- Be very careful with the open flame.

Materials

- water
- two 250 mL Erlenmeyer flasks
- universal indicator solution
- wooden safety match
- tongs
- stopper
- chalk dust

Procedure

1. Put about 50 mL of clean water into a 250 mL Erlenmeyer flask, and add 10 drops of universal indicator. This is flask A.

2. Working with a partner, one of you holds the second flask upside down. The other partner lights the match and, gripping it with tongs, places the lit end of the match into the flask. When the match head has finished flaring, remove the match and stopper the flask. You have trapped some gases from combustion. This is flask B.

3. Turn flask B right side up, open the stopper, and quickly pour the water and indicator from flask A into flask B. Replace the stopper, and shake gently for one minute.

4. Open the stopper, and add a generous pinch of chalk dust. Replace the stopper, shake vigorously, and let stand.

Questions

1. When the match head burns, sulfur, phosphorus, and carbon in the match head join with oxygen to form new chemical compounds. Propose some names for the gases produced.

2. What is the pH of the solution formed when the combustion products are dissolved in the water? What kind of solution must this be?

3. Crushed limestone or chalk, which are composed of calcium carbonate, is often added to acidified lakes to neutralize the acid. Does the addition of powdered chalk change the pH? Is this a fast or slow process?

Acid Leaching and Metals

Smelters, such as those at Sudbury, create acids as a by-product of the smelting process. However, acids are also an important part of refining metals. In Chapter 5, you learned how gold is leached from its ore using sodium cyanide. For other metals, such as copper and nickel, acids are used in the refinement process. The acid reacts with the metals and forms soluble compounds. The acidic solution containing the soluble metal salt is separated from the unwanted solid materials and the metals are later recovered from the solution. Although the properties of acids and of metals allow acid leaching to be used to extract these desirable metals from their ores, these same properties create environmental problems.

Toxic Metal Contamination and Clean-Up

At many mining sites, you can see tailings piles, such as those in **Figure 6.23**. Tailings are the materials, both solid and liquid, that are left after the desired product, such as copper, nickel, or gold, is removed from an ore. These piles are often stored in above-ground facilities, where they are exposed to air and water.

Sulfide compounds in the tailings can form acids as they react with water and oxygen. If not contained, the resulting acids could cause run-off that can harm the local environment. The acids can also leach metals from the tailings, which could contaminate the area around the tailings pile.

Acid leaching can actually be used to clean up soils that have been contaminated by toxic metals. A diagram of the process used is shown in **Figure 6.24**. The first step is to remove any solid metal pieces from the contaminated soil, which reduces the amount of acid needed to treat the soil. The metal removed can be sent to a smelter to be melted down. The soil is then treated with acid in order to leach out metal ions and any small pieces of metal. Once the metal has been dissolved in the acid, it is recovered through precipitation. Chemicals that form solid precipitates with the metal ions are added to the solution. After precipitation, the liquid component is recycled and used in the leaching process again, while the solid component that contains the metal is collected for appropriate disposal. Nevertheless, the process is expensive. Therefore, preventing contamination in the first place is the best solution to the problem.

Figure 6.23 The materials left over from the processing and recovery of a metal can be a source of pollution as a result of reactions of acids. These tailings piles are from a gold mine near Dawson, in the Yukon.

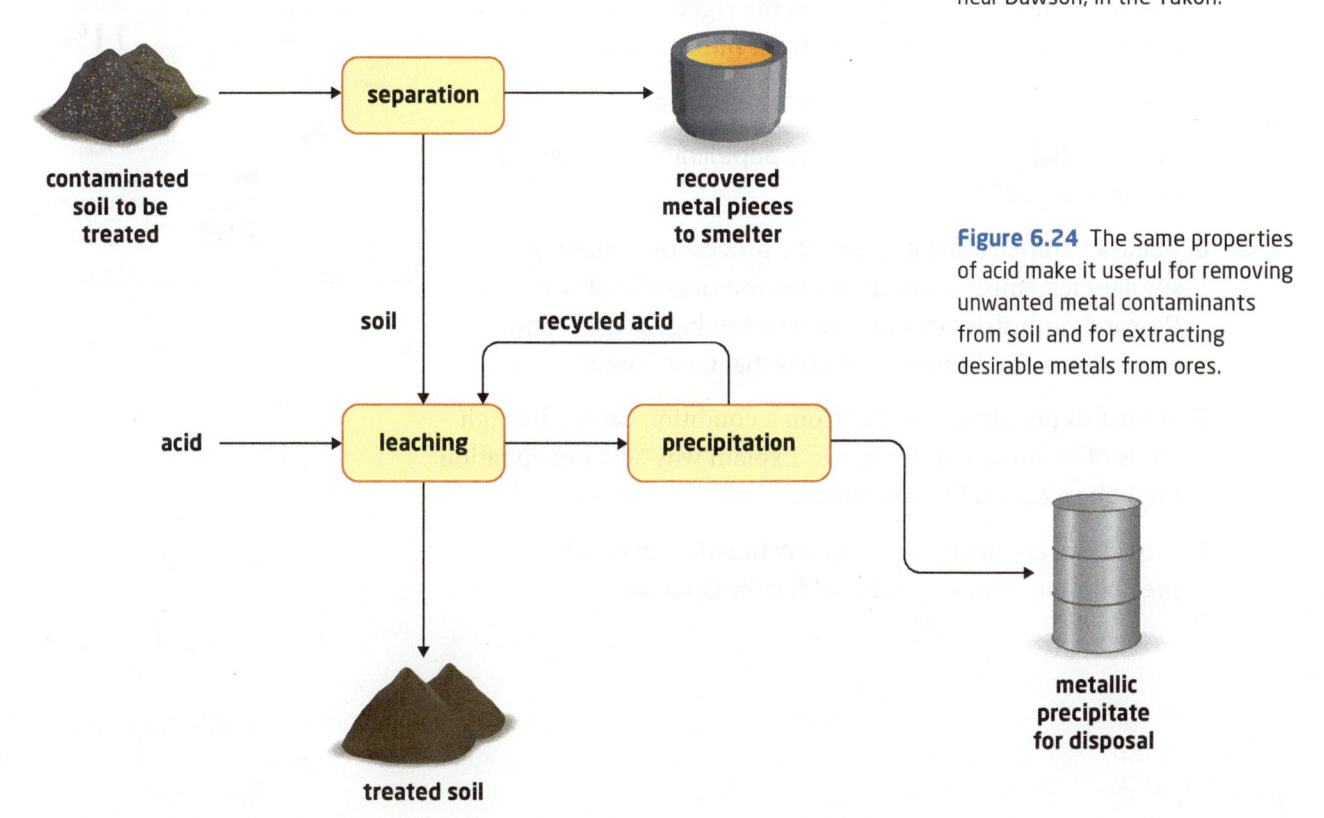

Figure 6.24 The same properties of acid make it useful for removing unwanted metal contaminants from soil and for extracting desirable metals from ores.

Chapter 6 Acids and Bases • NEL 245

Section 6.3 Review

Section Summary

- A neutralization reaction occurs when an acid and a base react to form water and a salt.
- Acid precipitation forms from non-metal oxides, such as the oxides of sulfur and of nitrogen. These oxides in the atmosphere react with water to form acids. Scrubbers are used to remove sulfur dioxide from exhaust gases.
- Acid precipitation can have detrimental effects, particularly on rivers and lakes. Renewing a lake involves adding limestone to the water to help neutralize the acid and raise the pH.
- The properties of acids make them useful for extracting metals from ores, but the process may contaminate an area. These same properties also mean that acids are useful for leaching toxic metals from contaminated soils.

Review Questions

K/U 1. Write a balanced chemical equation for the neutralization of sulfuric acid with potassium hydroxide. What is the name and chemical formula of the salt formed in this reaction?

K/U 2. When you have an upset stomach, you might take an antacid to feel better. Based on the properties of an antacid, explain why an antacid can be an effective remedy.

T/I 3. Describe how nitrogen oxides contribute to acid precipitation and name a technology that is used to reduce these emissions. Based on the data in the graph on the right, what percentage of nitrogen oxide emissions are from industrial sources?

K/U 4. What gas reacts with water to form sulfuric acid?

K/U 5. List two changes that occur in the populations of organisms in a lake at pH 5.0.

C 6. Make a pamphlet that explains the process of scrubbing smokestack emissions and the reactions associated with it. Research industries in which this technology is used, and suggest some additional industries that could use it.

A 7. Some fish populations suffer from a condition caused by high levels of aluminum in the water. Explain why acid precipitation might be a cause of this problem.

C 8. Provide an argument that counters the idea that acid precipitation is no longer a problem in Ontario.

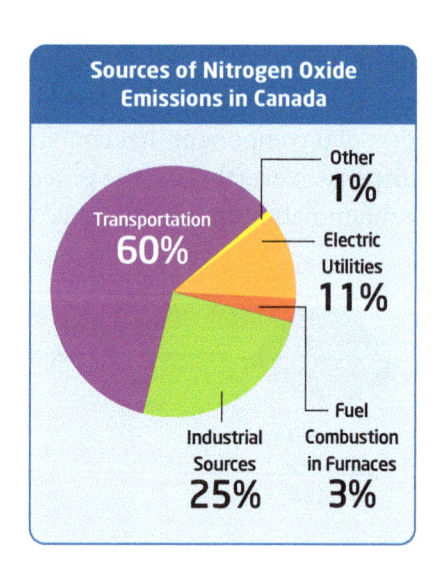

Sources of Nitrogen Oxide Emissions in Canada

- Transportation 60%
- Other 1%
- Electric Utilities 11%
- Fuel Combustion in Furnaces 3%
- Industrial Sources 25%

Plan Your Own Investigation 6-A

Skill Check
✓ Initiating and Planning
✓ Performing and Recording
✓ Analyzing and Interpreting
✓ Communicating

Safety Precautions

- Wear safety goggles and a lab apron.
- Use caution when handling substances of unknown pH.
- To avoid contaminating your samples, do not dip pH test strips into the substance to be tested. Instead, transfer a small amount of the material to be tested onto the pH strip.

Materials
- universal indicator or pH paper
- samples of foods, beverages, cosmetics, soaps, and cleaning materials
- other equipment, as needed, to perform tests

Science Skills
Go to **Science Skills Toolkit 7** for information about creating data tables.

What Is Your Exposure to Acids and Bases?

Every day, you are exposed to hundreds of acidic and basic substances. What are their pH values?

Question
How acidic or basic are substances in your everyday life?

Plan and Conduct

1. Your teacher will give you common household substances to investigate. Plan a procedure to identify the pH of each substance.
2. Design a table to record your measurements. Include a title for your table. Make sure you include enough headings and rows in your table to keep all your observations organized.
3. Have your teacher review your procedure and your data table. You must not begin your tests until your teacher has approved your procedure.
4. Perform your tests for the pH of the different substances.
5. Make complete notes for each test.
6. Share your results with your teacher, who will record them in a table on the board.
7. Clean up your work area, and discard any materials as directed by your teacher.

Analyze and Interpret

1. Examine your data table. Look for patterns you can use to group the substances according to pH values. What groupings of substances can you make? Explain what these groupings are based on.
2. Which acids and bases that you are frequently exposed to have the most extreme pH values? Which of these surprise you, and why?

Conclude and Communicate

3. How do you think the pH of a substance is related to how it is used in the home?

Extend Your Inquiry and Research Skills

4. **Inquiry** Design an investigation to use a pH meter to check the measurements that you made using pH paper.

Real World Investigation 6-B

Skill Check

Initiating and Planning

Performing and Recording

✓ Analyzing and Interpreting

✓ Communicating

The pH of Lakes Near Sudbury

Metals like nickel and copper have been mined in the Sudbury region since 1885. The processes associated with isolating these metals, however, have resulted in the release of sulfur dioxide into the atmosphere. By 1960, over 2×10^6 tonnes of SO_2 were being poured into the air each year. The sulfur dioxide mixed with rainwater and precipitated over wide areas as acid precipitation, leaving thousands of square kilometres with dead and dying lakes and forests. Today, the amount of SO_2 released has been greatly reduced, but about 3×10^5 tonnes are still released each year.

The data below show the mass of sulfur dioxide released from 1973 to 2006 in Sudbury and the pH of three nearby lakes. These lakes are shown on the map on the opposite page. In addition to reducing sulfur dioxide emissions to combat the effects of acid precipitation, two specific treatments have been done: limestone dust was added to Lohi Lake, and crushed limestone was applied to a large area surrounding Hannah Lake.

Math Skills
Go to **Math Skills Toolkit 3** for information about constructing graphs.

pH Data for Lakes Near Sudbury

Year	SO_2 (million tonnes)	Clearwater pH	Hannah pH	Lohi pH
1973	1.48	4.30	4.31	4.45
1975	1.42	4.30	5.33	6.12
1977	1.36	4.10	6.59	5.30
1979	0.50	4.40	7.05	4.70
1981	0.85	4.44	6.62	4.67
1983	0.54	4.57	6.91	4.74
1985	0.78	4.83	7.07	4.71
1987	0.73	4.74	7.15	4.68
1989	0.71	4.69	7.00	4.71
1991	0.64	4.96	7.17	5.00
1993	0.42	5.20	7.21	5.48
1995	0.25	5.52	7.16	6.21
1997	0.29	5.93	7.32	6.32
1999	0.30	6.18	7.44	6.38
2001	0.28	6.29	7.34	6.37
2003	0.30	6.41	7.20	6.40
2005	0.30	6.48	7.25	6.48
2006	0.30	6.61	7.31	6.37

Question

How effective have the methods been to reduce the acidity of lakes in the Sudbury region?

Prediction

Three separate approaches used to reduce the acidity of lakes in the Sudbury region were
- adding lime, a base, to the lakes to neutralize the acid
- adding lime to the soil around the lakes
- reducing sulfur dioxide emissions

Predict what you think has been the best approach to reducing the acidity of the lakes.

Organize the Data

1. Examine the data in the table. Decide how you will graph the data. Keep in mind that you will need to compare the data from year to year on your graphs. You also want to compare the amount of sulfur dioxide released with the pH of each lake, in addition to comparing the pH values of the different lakes.

2. Draw line graphs of the data, according to your decision in step 1.

3. Label your graphs thoroughly, including titles, axes, units, and any other information you need to communicate the data clearly.

Historically, lakes in the Sudbury area have been acidic.

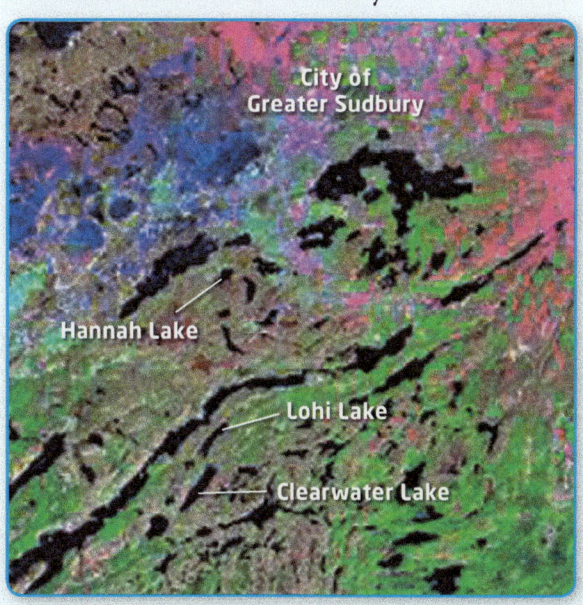

Analyze and Interpret

1. What was the pH values of the three lakes in 1973? Were they acidic, basic, or neutral?

2. Limestone dust was added to Lohi Lake once to neutralize the acid. In what year was the limestone added? Give reasons for your answer.

3. Crushed limestone was applied to a large area of barren watershed around Hannah Lake to provide soil for the planting of new trees. What effect did that have on the acidity of the lake? Explain your thinking.

4. Clearwater Lake was surrounded by barren watershed after the original trees and vegetation died. Nothing was added to relieve the acidity of the lake. What happened to the pH of Clearwater Lake? Why?

Conclude and Communicate

5. Which was the least effective action taken to reduce acidity? Explain.

6. Which lake showed the most improvement in pH level? Do you think the approach taken for that lake was cost-effective? Explain.

7. Which of the three approaches used will have the greatest overall effect? Explain.

Extend Your Inquiry and Research Skills

8. **Inquiry** There were two kinds of scrubbers built in Sudbury. Examine the graph, and try to determine which years those scrubbers came into operation. Explain your reasoning.

9. **Research** Search Internet or print resources to find the dates of any strikes in Sudbury by mine workers. What effect did the strikes have on sulfur dioxide emissions? What effect did the strikes have on acid levels in the lakes?

Inquiry Investigation 6-C

Skill Check

Initiating and Planning

✓ Performing and Recording

✓ Analyzing and Interpreting

✓ Communicating

Safety Precautions

- Wear safety goggles, gloves, and a lab apron.
- Clean up all spills immediately.

Materials

- two 25 mL graduated cylinders
- 0.1 mol/L hydrochloric acid
- 0.1 mol/L sodium hydroxide
- purple cabbage juice
- two 10 mL pipettes
- pipette bulb or pump
- two 100 mL beakers

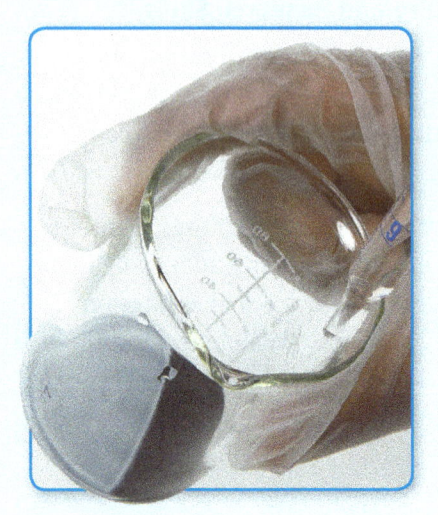

Slowly add sodium hydroxide to the cabbage juice and acid in the beaker.

Neutralizing an Acid with a Base

Antacids, lake renewal, and cleaning chemical spills rely on neutralization reactions between an acid and a base. In this investigation, you will explore acid-base neutralization.

Question

How do an acid and a base neutralize each other?

Procedure

1. Read the procedure, then prepare a table to record your results. Include a title for your table and the units of measurement in the headings.

2. Obtain about 25 mL of hydrochloric acid in one graduated cylinder, and 25 mL sodium hydroxide in the other. Read the volumes to one decimal place, and record the volumes on your table.

3. Add about 1 mL of purple cabbage juice to a beaker. The purple colour you see is the colour of a neutral solution. Use a pipette to transfer about 10 mL of hydrochloric acid to the beaker.

5. Use the second pipette to slowly transfer about 10 mL of sodium hydroxide solution to the beaker. Gently swirl the solution in the beaker as you make the addition. Stop adding the sodium hydroxide as soon as you see a colour change. Use some of the original cabbage juice as a guide for the purple colour that indicates neutrality.

6. Read the remaining volumes of hydrochloric acid and sodium hydroxide on the graduated cylinders, and record them in your table.

7. Calculate the volume of acid and base added in the reaction. Add this to your table.

Analyze and Interpret

1. Compare the quantity of base needed to neutralize the solution with the quantity of acid added. What do you notice?

Conclude and Communicate

2. Write a balanced chemical equation for the neutralization reaction that you observed.

Extend Your Inquiry and Research Skills

3. **Inquiry** If the experiment was repeated using sulfuric acid, H_2SO_4, what do you think would happen? With your teacher's approval, design and conduct an experiment to verify your prediction.

Chapter 6 Summary

6.1 Identifying Acids and Bases

Key Concepts

- Acids are compounds that have a sour taste. When dissolved in water, they produce hydrogen ions, $H^+(aq)$.
- Binary acids are composed of hydrogen and a non-metal. The name of a binary acid is written using the prefix *hydro-*, the root of the non-metal name, and the ending *-ic acid*.
- Oxoacids that form between hydrogen and polyatomic ions are named by replacing *-ate* with *-ic acid* and *-ite* with *-ous acid*.
- Bases are compounds that have a bitter taste. Many bases are ionic compounds that separate into metal ions and hydroxide ions, $OH^-(aq)$, when they dissolve in water.
- Since many bases are ionic compounds, their names and formulas are written following the same rules that are used for ionic compounds.

6.2 The pH Scale and Indicators

Key Concepts

- The pH scale ranges from 0 to 14 and is used to classify an aqueous solution as acidic, basic, or neutral. Neutral solutions are pH 7. Acidic solutions have a pH less than 7. Basic solutions have a pH greater than 7.
- A change of 1 on the pH scale represents a change in the concentration of hydrogen ions in a solution by a factor of 10. The pH of a solution can be determined using pH indicators or an electronic pH probe.
- A pH indicator is a chemical that is added in small amounts to a solution to visually show the acidity or basicity of the solution by changing colours within a small range of pH values.
- Universal pH indicator and pH paper contain several indicators and can be used to determine the pH of a solution.

6.3 Reactions of Acids and Bases

Key Concepts

- A neutralization reaction occurs when an acid and a base react to form water and a salt.
- Acid precipitation forms from non-metal oxides, such as the oxides of sulfur and of nitrogen. These oxides in the atmosphere react with water to form acids. Scrubbers are used to remove sulfur dioxide from exhaust gases.
- Acid precipitation can have detrimental effects, particularly on rivers and lakes. Renewing a lake involves adding limestone to the water to help neutralize the acid and raise the pH.
- The properties of acids make them useful for extracting metals from ores, but the process may contaminate an area. These same properties also mean that acids are useful for leaching toxic metals from contaminated soils.

Chapter 6 Review

Make Your Own Summary

Summarize the key concepts of this chapter using a graphic organizer. The Chapter Summary on the previous page will help you identify the key concepts. Refer to Study Toolkit 4 on pages 565-566 to help you decide which graphic organizer to use.

Reviewing Key Terms

Match each key term listed below to its definition.

- a. acid
- b. pH indicator
- c. pH scale
- d. base
- e. neutralization
- f. oxoacid
- g. binary acid

1. A compound that contains a hydroxide ion, OH^- (6.1)
2. A numerical scale that ranges from 0 to 14 and is used to classify aqueous solutions as acidic, basic, or neutral. (6.2)
3. A substance that produces hydrogen ions, $H^+(aq)$, when dissolved in water. (6.1)
4. An acid composed of hydrogen and a non-metal. (6.1)
5. A reaction of an acid and a base to produce a salt and water. (6.3)
6. A substance that changes colour to show the concentration of hydrogen ions (H^+) and hydroxide ions (OH^-) in a solution. (6.2)
7. An acid composed of hydrogen, oxygen, and another element. (6.1)

Knowledge and Understanding K/U

8. Identify each of the following compounds as an acid or a base. Then, write the name of each compound.
   - a. $HCl(aq)$
   - b. $Mg(OH)_2(aq)$
   - c. $H_3PO_4(aq)$
   - d. $LiOH(aq)$

9. Write the chemical formula for each of the following acids.
   - a. nitric acid
   - b. hydrobromic acid
   - c. sulfurous acid

10. How does the acidity of a solution change as its pH rises?

11. What do all indicators have in common?

12. What is the difference between universal indicator and litmus?

13. Why is it important to maintain water in a swimming pool at the correct pH?

14. What effect would each of the following changes likely have on acid precipitation in an area? Explain your reasoning.
    - a. removing catalytic converters from cars
    - b. removing sulfur from coal before burning the coal

15. Why should you never use taste to identify whether an unknown chemical is an acid or a base?

16. Write a balanced chemical equation for each of the following neutralization reactions.
    - a. hydrobromic acid + calcium hydroxide
    - b. lithium hydroxide + sulfurous acid
    - c. magnesium hydroxide + phosphoric acid

Thinking and Investigation T/I

17. Non-metal oxides are often called *acidic anhydrides*. Using a dictionary or other reference source, explain what this term means and why it is a correct description of these compounds.

18. The data in the table below were recorded during an investigation. Based on these data, what is the best estimate for the pH of the solution?

pH Indicator	Colour
Methyl orange	yellow
Bromothymol blue	blue
Phenolphthalein	pink

19. The data in the table were collected during an investigation of acids and bases. Decide whether each of the following solutions is acidic, basic, or neutral, based on the data collected.

Solution	Red Litmus Paper	Blue Litmus Paper
A	stays red	stays blue
B	turns blue	stays blue
C	stays red	turns red
D	turns blue	stays blue

20. The illustration below shows a step from an investigation in which a pH meter is being used to test a solution.

a. What type of solution is it? How can you tell?

b. Describe how red litmus paper and blue litmus paper would respond to this solution.

c. Should HCl(aq) or KOH(aq) be added to neutralize this solution? Explain your reasoning.

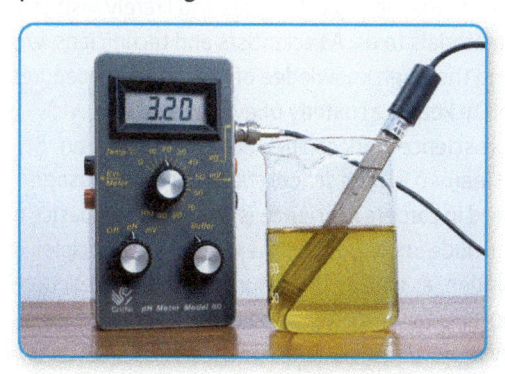

21. Why it is not correct to say that a solution is basic if it does not change the colour of blue litmus paper? What other result would be needed to support the conclusion that the solution is basic?

22. What kind of oxides form acids when they react with water? Give two examples to support your answer.

Communication

23. Use a graphic organizer to prepare a summary sheet on the instructions for writing the chemical formula for an acid from its name, and for writing the name of an acid from its chemical formula.

24. BIG IDEAS Chemicals react with each other in predictable ways. Using a diagram, show how acids and bases typically react, and define this type of reaction.

25. BIG IDEAS Chemical reactions may have a negative effect on the environment, but they can also be used to address environmental challenges. Explain how acid leaching is both helpful and harmful. Describe its importance to and effect on technology, society, and the environment.

Application

26. Which of these products turn blue litmus paper to red? Explain your reasoning.

27. Sulfuric acid is important in the manufacture of many different products. Use the Internet or other resource to determine at least 10 products or processes in which sulfuric acid plays a role. Display your findings using a graphic organizer.

28. Bacteria are used to make cheese (pH 5.5) and yogurt (pH 4.5) from milk (pH 6.5).

a. Which of these foods is most acidic?

b. How many times more acidic is the most acidic food compared with the least acidic food?

29. Research steps being taken by the government of Ontario to protect and renew the Great Lakes. What can you do to help?

Science at Work

Canadians in Science

When Dalia Bagby goes to work, she steps into a world where little things really do matter. Dalia is a scientist in the chemistry section of the Ontario Centre of Forensic Sciences (CFS). Police investigators routinely call on Dalia and her co-workers to examine materials—often only trace amounts of materials—collected at crime scenes. Dalia and her co-workers then prepare reports to detail their scientific findings. These reports can be entered as evidence during criminal court cases. Dalia has advanced degrees in chemistry from the University of Toronto and a keen interest in the justice system. She therefore considers the CFS to be the perfect work environment for her.

Dalia Bagby is a forensic scientist at the Ontario Centre of Forensic Sciences.

In Dalia Bagby's Words

It is rewarding to support investigative activities through impartial scientific analysis, although cases can be challenging at times. We often have little to work with. For example, a deliberately set fire may destroy much of the evidence that an ignitable liquid was used to fuel it. Glass fragments or paint chips from a hit-and-run accident may be the only clues about the type of vehicle involved.

Unlike what many popular television series portray about forensic science, my work almost always begins in the lab. My colleagues and I rarely visit crime scenes. Investigators bring materials to us. As scientists and technicians, we need solid analytical skills and thorough knowledge of laboratory procedures, especially procedures related to keeping custody of evidence.

As complex as my forensic science work can be, much of it is built on fundamental concepts that I learned in high school chemistry. My message to students who are interested in careers in science is to master the basics of core subjects. These basics include knowledge of the underlying principles of scientific inquiry and observation, as well as the nature of chemical reactions. This knowledge is even important for students who are not interested in careers in science. Chemistry is all around us. Something so fundamental to our world and everything in it should not be an enigma to anyone.

Dalia's work requires careful analysis of samples that are provided by police investigators.

Chemistry at Work

The study of chemistry contributes to these careers, as well as many more.

- Chemical Laboratory Technician
- Pharmaceutical Sales Representative
- Geochemist
- Chemistry
- Art Conservation Officer
- Technical Writer

Occupational Health and Safety Officer

Occupational health and safety officers help prevent injury and disease in the workplace. They evaluate safety policies, provide training to employees and develop strategies to reduce health and safety risks. The officers need knowledge of chemistry to understand the chemical hazards in a workplace.

Chef

Chefs manage the preparation of food in restaurants, hotels, and other locations. They often create new recipes and must understand how different food ingredients will react with one another.

Patent Agent

Patent agents help inventors to obtain certain legal rights, including an exclusive right for 20 years to make, use, or sell their inventions. Patent agents often have education and training in chemistry and other sciences. This helps them to better understand complex inventions that might include, for example, new chemical compositions, prescription drugs, and methods to make them.

Go to **scienceontario** to find out more

Over to You

1. In a small group, discuss how scientific investigation in a forensic sciences laboratory may differ from that at colleges and universities or in private industry.

2. Dalia Bagby states that she and her co-workers must follow procedures related to maintaining custody of evidence. What do you think some of these procedures might be?

3. In Ontario, the Centre of Forensic Sciences does not routinely analyze samples related to pollution and other environmental offences. Research and report on how the province of Ontario usually deals with these matters.

4. Research a career involving chemistry that interests you. If you wish, you may choose a career from the list above. **What essential skills would you need for this career?**

Science at Work • NEL 255

Unit 2 Projects

Inquiry Project

"Mining" Copper in the Laboratory

Canada is one of the leading producers of copper in the world. Because copper is a good conductor of electricity and heat, it is often used to make wire. When the ore is mined, it is processed to extract metallic copper, which is the form that is used to make wire and other products. In this project, you will use your knowledge of chemical reactions to recover the maximum amount of metallic copper from a copper compound.

> **Inquiry Question**
> How can you extract metallic copper from copper(II) carbonate?

Initiate and Plan

1. Create a graphic organizer of your choice, using both words and visuals, to summarize the most important skills and concepts you learned in each investigation in this unit. Exchange summaries with a partner. In what ways are the summaries similar? What additional information might you add to your summary to make it more comprehensive?

2. Formulate a hypothesis, using a series of possible chemical reactions that show how the maximum amount of metallic copper might be extracted from copper(II) carbonate. For each reaction, include a one-sentence explanation and a chemical word equation.

3. Develop a procedure to extract copper from copper(II) carbonate. Identify appropriate equipment and quantities of materials required.

4. Obtain approval from your teacher before carrying out your procedure.

Perform and Record

5. Record your data using an appropriate format. Begin by recording the initial mass of copper(II) carbonate.

6. Carry out your procedure, controlling the appropriate variables, adapting or extending your procedure as required, and using the equipment and materials safely, accurately, and effectively.

7. Measure the mass of the metallic copper you extracted.

Analyze and Interpret

1. Determine the mass of copper that could theoretically be extracted from the mass of copper(II) carbonate you used. Assume that approximately half of the mass of copper(II) carbonate is carbonate, and half is copper.

2. Write a conclusion, based on the evidence you gathered, to support or refute your initial hypothesis.

3. Identify possible sources of error in your procedure, and suggest improvements.

Communicate Your Findings

4. Make a poster to illustrate the steps in your procedure. Your poster should include a word equation and a balanced chemical equation for each step; any mathematical calculations you made; the types of chemical reactions involved.

> **Assessment Criteria**
>
> Once you complete your project, ask yourself these questions. Did you...
>
> - **K/U** identify the important skills and concepts you learned in each investigation in this unit?
> - **T/I** formulate an appropriate hypothesis?
> - **T/I** control appropriate variables and use equipment and materials safely, accurately, and effectively?
> - **T/I** determine the theoretical mass of copper that could be extracted from the mass of copper(II) sulfate you used?
> - **T/I** identify sources of error and make suggestions for improvements?
> - **C** organize your information in a clear and logical manner, appropriate for your purpose and audience?
> - **C** communicate using appropriate scientific vocabulary?

An Issue to Analyze

Urban Gold "Mining"

Nuggets of pure gold are occasionally found in nature, as they were in Yukon streams during the Gold Rush of the 1890s. Most of the world's supply of gold has come from mines, but many mines have run out of gold and closed down. In the last 30 years, however, as personal electronic devices have become increasingly popular, there is a new source of gold–recycled gold from e-waste.

Televisions, computers, cellphones, and other electronic and communications devices all contain gold because it is an excellent conductor of electricity and does not corrode. From 1 tonne of discarded cellphones, it is possible to recover 150 g of gold. In comparison, an average gold mine yields only 5 g of gold from 1 tonne of ore. Although "mining" e-waste for gold seems promising, there are consequences. In this project, you will research various perspectives on this issue and, based on your research, provide a recommendation to the Ontario Mining Association.

> **Issue**
> Is it worthwhile to "mine" e-waste for gold?

Initiate and Plan

1. Conduct research to investigate the possibility of retrieving gold from e-waste. Consider the following perspectives as you conduct your research:
   - scientific
   - technological
   - environmental
   - societal

   Also consider the perspectives of the stakeholders involved. Gather information from print, electronic, and human sources.

Perform and Record

2. Record and organize the information you gathered using a graphic organizer of your choice and an accepted form of academic documentation.

Analyze and Interpret

1. Analyze your research for bias and accuracy.
2. State your position on the issue of retrieving gold from e-waste. Explain your position.
3. Propose alternative courses of action if you concluded that retrieving gold from e-waste should not occur.

Communicate Your Findings

4. Present your position on this issue, using a format that allows for discussion and feedback, such as a podcast or a presentation. Include the research you used to support your position. Use appropriate scientific vocabulary.

Assessment Criteria

Once you complete your project, ask yourself these questions. Did you...

- **K/U** provide an accurate description of mining e-waste for gold?
- **A** clearly state your position on this issue, based on supporting evidence?
- **A** identify various perspectives and stakeholders?
- **A** propose alternative courses of action if you do not support mining e-waste for gold?
- **C** organize your research using an appropriate format and appropriate academic documentation?
- **C** present your final report using a format that is appropriate for both your purpose and audience?
- **C** communicate using appropriate scientific vocabulary?

Unit 2 Review

Connect to the Big Ideas

Use this bicycle wheel graphic organizer to connect what you have learned in this unit to the Big Ideas, found on page 133. Draw one bicycle wheel for each Big Idea and write the Big Idea in the centre. Between the spokes of the wheel, briefly describe six examples of that Big Idea.

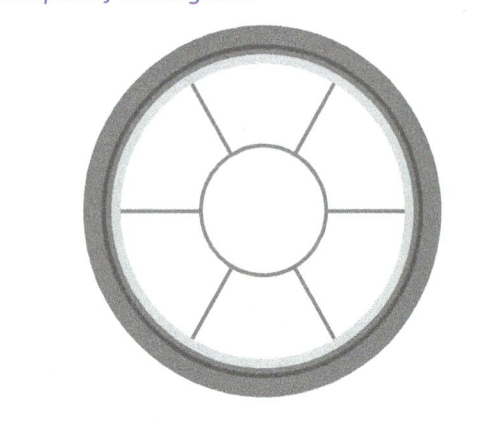

Knowledge and Understanding K/U

1. A student observed each of the following when conducting a chemical reaction. Identify the observation that does *not* represent evidence of a chemical change.
   a. The solution became hot.
   b. The solid reactant dissolved in the solvent when added to the flask.
   c. The solution became blue as the reaction proceeded.
   d. Oxygen gas formed, and bubbles came out of solution.

2. Which of the following is the correct chemical formula for dinitrogen tetroxide?
   a. NH_4O_6
   b. $2NO_2$
   c. N_2O_4
   d. N_2O_3

3. Which of the following is the correct name for $Ti(SO_4)_2$?
   a. titanium sulfite
   b. titanium(IV) sulfate
   c. titanium sulfate
   d. titanium(III) sulfite

4. Which of the following chemical formulas represents a total of 12 atoms of oxygen?
   a. $2Fe(NO_2)_3$
   b. $2Cr(NO_3)_3$
   c. $3Sn(SO_4)_2$
   d. $4Cu_3(PO_4)_2$

5. When the following chemical equation is balanced, what is the value of x?
   $$xCr + yO_2 \rightarrow zCr_2O_3$$
   a. 1
   b. 2
   c. 3
   d. 4

6. Explain why the law of conservation of mass is important for balancing chemical equations.

7. For each of the following, identify the type of reaction and balance the chemical equation.
   a. $S_8(s) + O_2(g) \rightarrow SO_2(g)$
   b. $HF(g) \rightarrow H_2(g) + F_2(g)$
   c. $H_2SO_4(aq) + NaOH(aq) \rightarrow Na_2SO_4(aq) + H_2O(\ell)$
   d. $Fe(NO_3)_3(aq) + KOH(aq) \rightarrow Fe(OH)_3(s) + KNO_3(aq)$
   e. $Al(s) + CuCl_2(aq) \rightarrow AlCl_3(aq) + Cu(s)$

8. Represent each of the following reactions using a word equation, a skeleton equation, and a balanced chemical equation. Include the states of the reactants and products.
   a. Freshly cut sodium reacts with oxygen gas in the air and forms solid sodium oxide.
   b. When a piece of magnesium ribbon is placed into a solution of copper(II) chloride, copper metal and a solution of magnesium chloride form.
   c. Solid magnesium oxide and carbon dioxide gas form when powdered magnesium carbonate is heated.
   d. When aqueous solutions of chromium(III) chloride and potassium hydroxide are mixed, a solution of potassium chloride and a precipitate of chromium(III) hydroxide form.
   e. Bubbles of hydrogen gas form when a piece of aluminum metal is placed in a solution of sulfuric acid. The resulting solution contains aluminum sulfate.

9. Identify the type of reaction in each part of question 8. Explain your reasoning.

10. What approximate pH value would you expect for each of the following?
    a. tomatoes
    b. oven cleaner
    c. milk

11. If the pH of a solution drops from 5 to 4, has the acidity increased or decreased? How much higher or lower has the concentration of hydrogen ions become?

12. What kind of substance is formed in addition to water, in an acid-base neutralization?

Thinking and Investigation T/I

13. When copper is heated in air, the solid product that is formed has a greater mass than the original copper. When calcium carbonate is heated in air, the solid product that is formed has less mass than the original calcium carbonate. Why is the mass of the solid product greater in one reaction but less in the other reaction?

14. Carbon monoxide, a poisonous gas, reacts slowly with oxygen to form carbon dioxide.
    a. Represent the chemical reaction described using a balanced chemical equation.
    b. In the presence of rhodium metal (Rh), this reaction occurs very quickly. What do you think the metal is doing?

Use the table below to answer questions 15 and 16.

pH Indicators

Indicator	Colour at Lower pH Values	pH Range in Which Colour Changes	Colour at Higher pH Values
Methyl orange	red	3.2–4.4	yellow
Methyl red	red	4.8–6.0	yellow
Phenolphthalein	colourless	8.2–10.0	pink

15. A solution causes methyl orange to be yellow and methyl red to be red. What is the range of pH values that this solution could be?

16. What is the colour of phenolphthalein in stomach acid?

17. A lifeguard comments that swimmers have been complaining that they have a burning sensation in their eyes burning after swimming. What two things would you suggest the lifeguard test for?

Communication C

18. Write a set of instructions on how to identify a binary compound as either an ionic compound or a molecular compound when the chemical formula is given. Write another set of instructions for when the name is given.

19. Create a graphic organizer showing what you know about the reactants and products of each type of chemical reaction that you have learned about this unit.

20. Make a diagram to show the emissions from an industrial plant that contribute to acid precipitation. Also show how scrubbers reduce these emissions. Include the reactions that are involved.

21. Would you be willing to pay slightly more for some products if it meant that manufacturers could reduce their pollution? How effective do you think this change would be in practice? Gather responses from your friends and family, and make a visual summary of your findings.

Unit 2 Review

Application A

22. Copper is widely used for water pipes. Suggest reasons for using copper rather than another metal, such as lead, zinc, or iron.

23. Water-soluble mercury compounds, such as mercury(II) nitrate, are particularly dangerous because they are easily spread through an ecosystem via waste water. One way to remove mercury(II) nitrate from waste water is to add sodium sulfate.
    a. Write the chemical formulas for mercury(II) nitrate and for sodium sulfate.
    b. Predict what type of reaction will occur based on the reactants. Write a balanced chemical equation for the reaction.
    c. Infer the state of the product that is composed of mercury. What would likely be the next step in the clean-up process?

24. Research the major sources of air pollution in your community. Is any of this pollution controlled in any way? What might be the human and economic costs for your community to clean up this pollution? Create a presentation aimed at your local town council.

25. In a train derailment, about one third of a tank of sulfuric acid leaked into a nearby lake. Once the spill had been contained and cleaned up, environmental scientists found that the pH of the lake was normal and had not changed at all. How could this have happened?

Use the table below to answer questions 26 to 28.

26. Analyze the data in the table below. What trend do you see in the emissions from each source?

27. A news agency reports that SO_x emissions from a particular source increased by nearly four times between 1990 and 1995.
    a. Which source is the report referring to?
    b. What questions could you ask to help you get a more complete picture of the situation?

28. Over the last 20 years, new regulations and technologies have been developed to help reduce SO_x emissions.
    a. Create a pie graph to represent the data in the table for 1985. Create a second pie graph to represent the data for 2005.
    b. Analyze the differences between your graphs, and write a summary of the changes you observe.

1985-2005 Historical SO_x Emissions for Canada (in tonnes)

Source	1985	1990	1995	2000	2005
Industrial	2 670 956	2 269 455	1 763 115	1 524 723	1 417 826
Non-industrial (fuel combustion and electrical power generation)	879 113	746 446	566 465	669 097	576 690
Air and ground transportation	172 873	181 828	150 472	122 446	110 409
Incineration	2 779	3 201	3 105	2 790	2 079
Miscellaneous	99	5	3	4	1
Agricultural/mining	4 503	4 401	2 740	1 691	1 712
Natural (forest fires and biological and geological sources)	200	138	549	158	89

Literacy Test Prep

Read the selection below and answer the questions that follow it.

Magnesium and its compounds have numerous applications in the world around you. If you have ever flown in a jet airplane, driven in a car, or enjoyed a fireworks display, magnesium has affected your life. In addition, magnesium is a nutrient that your body needs for performing life functions, such as releasing energy from food. Compounds such as magnesium oxide are used to make fertilizers and insulation for pipes, to refine sugar, and to treat waste water.

The diagram below shows how magnesium is obtained commercially from seawater, using a technique called the Dow process. The raw materials are seawater, sea shells, and hydrochloric acid. Examine the diagram, and use it to answer questions 29 to 34.

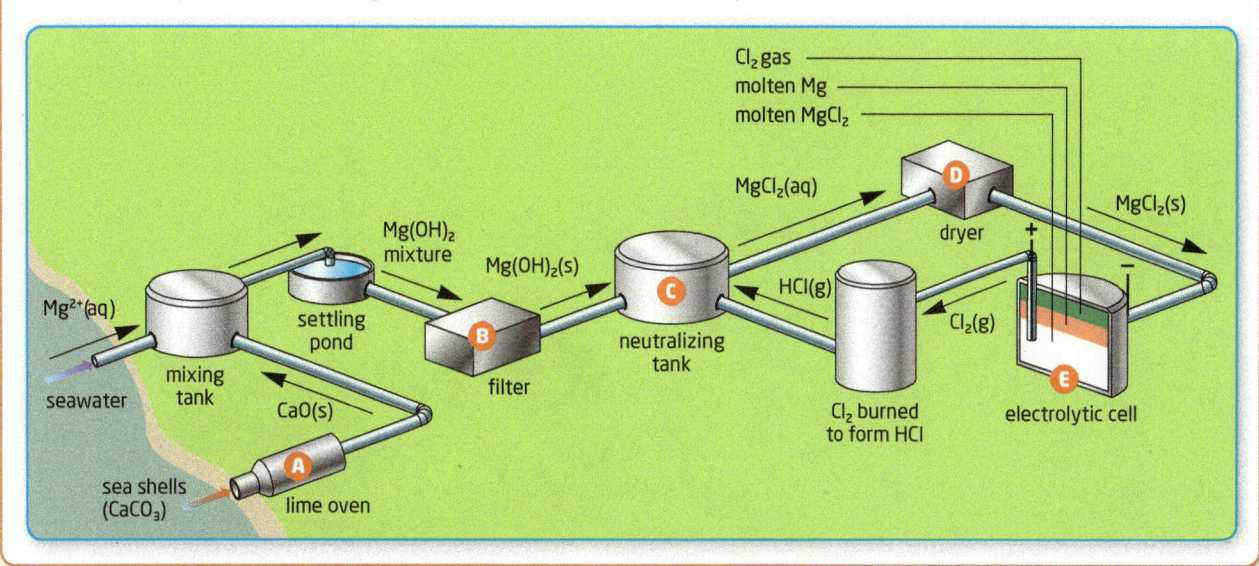

Multiple Choice

In your notebook, record the best or most correct answer.

29. Magnesium is obtained using a method called the
    a. seawater process
    b. Dow process
    c. magnesium process
    d. sea-shell technique

30. The raw materials that are used to obtain magnesium are
    a. magnesium chloride and calcium oxide
    b. sea shells, seawater, and chlorine gas
    c. sea shells and sodium hydroxide
    d. hydrochloric acid, seawater, and sea shells

31. Which chemical comes out of the neutralizing tank and is used for isolating magnesium?
    a. $MgCl_2(aq)$
    b. $MgCl_2(s)$
    c. $Mg(OH)_2(s)$
    d. $HCl(g)$

32. At which step in the diagram is magnesium metal obtained?
    a. E
    b. A
    c. C
    d. D

33. The purpose of the information in the first paragraph is to
    a. encourage the reader to buy magnesium
    b. provide a summary of how magnesium is produced
    c. inform the reader about the different uses of magnesium
    d. highlight the use of seawater in the production of magnesium

Written Answer

34. Summarize this selection. Include a main idea and one relevant point that supports it.

UNIT 3
Climate Change

BIG IDEAS

- People have the responsibility to assess their impact on climate change and to identify effective courses of action to reduce this impact.
- Earth's climate is dynamic and is the result of interacting systems and processes.
- Global climate change is influenced by both natural and human factors.
- Climate change affects living things and natural systems in a variety of ways.

Polar bears are powerful swimmers. But every year, they are forced to swim longer distances to find safety and food in their Arctic habitat. Polar bears live on large areas of sea ice over which they roam in search of prey. In recent years, sea ice has been melting and breaking up at higher rates than in the past—thus threatening the habitats of polar bears, seals, and other marine mammals.

Why are warmer temperatures causing Earth's ice cover to melt? In this unit, you will find answers to this question, and to many others related to global warming and climate change. You will learn about the causes and effects of climate change, both natural and human-made. You will also learn about individual, community, and government initiatives to slow down climate change in ways that will benefit the environment. One step in the right direction, shown here, is the switch to using energy-efficient technologies that do not rely on burning fossil fuels.

What strategies can individuals, communities, and governments use to address climate change?

Chapter 7
Earth's Climate System

Chapter 8
Dynamics of Climate Change

Chapter 9
Addressing Climate Change

Get Ready for Unit 3

Concept Check

1. Many human activities have an effect on the climate in a region. List as many climate-changing human activities as you can. Refer to the illustration below, and think about your prior knowledge as well.

2. Categorize each human activity you listed for question 1 as either negative (for example, raises global temperature or increases pollution) or positive (for example, lowers global temperature or reduces pollution). Record your answers in a T-chart. With a partner, brainstorm less-harmful alternatives to the activities you categorized as negative.

3. What do you know about carbon dioxide? In your notebook, create a concept map that illustrates the role carbon dioxide plays in the following processes: photosynthesis, cellular respiration, and global warming. Use linking words and/or explanations to describe the connections among the processes.

4. In your notebook, match each type of heat transfer listed in the box with its definition below.

   convection   radiation   conduction

   a. the emission or transmission of energy in the form of rays, waves, or particles
   b. the movement or transmission of energy by direct contact between molecules or substances
   c. the transfer of energy that occurs as a result of the movement of a fluid that has been warmed or cooled

5. Which types of heat transfer are occurring in the illustration below? Explain your answer.

264 NEL • Unit 3 Climate

Inquiry Check

6. **Analyze and Interpret** The following investigation was conducted by a student attempting to model one aspect of the greenhouse effect—that atmospheric carbon dioxide acts as a heat trap.

   i. Two identical glass jars were each filled with 500 mL of water that had a temperature of 2°C.
   ii. Both jars were sealed, and one was wrapped in a clear plastic bag.
   iii. Both jars were left in the Sun for one hour.
   iv. After one hour, the jars were opened and the temperature of the water in each glass jar was measured.

   a. Why did the student use a clear plastic bag? What did the plastic bag represent in terms of the greenhouse effect?
   b. What variables did the student control?
   c. List safety precautions that would be necessary for this procedure.
   d. How would you modify this procedure to more closely model the greenhouse effect?

Numeracy and Literacy Check

7. **Analyze** Use the graph to answer the questions.

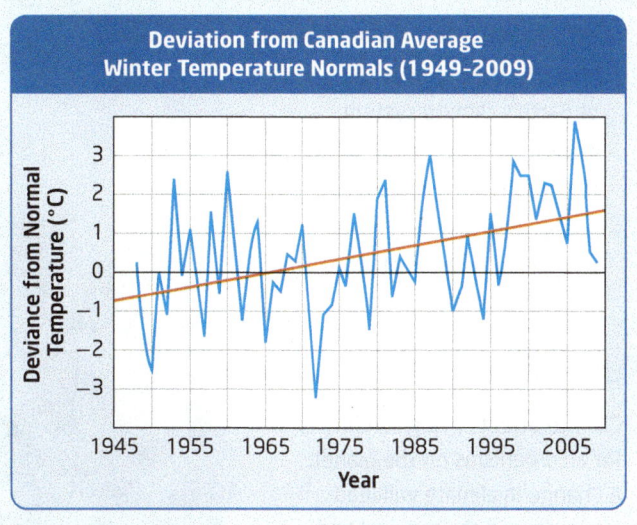

   Deviation from Canadian Average Winter Temperature Normals (1949–2009)

   a. What trend does the graph indicate is occurring in average winter temperatures in Canada?
   b. A line of best fit has been drawn in red to show the long-term trend. Using this line, determine the overall change in average temperature from 1950 to 2005.

8. **Write** Use a T-chart to list some possible positive and negative effects of climate change.

Looking Ahead to the Unit 3 Projects

At the end of this unit, you will have an opportunity to apply what you have learned in an inquiry or research project. Read the Unit 3 Projects on pages 390–391. Start a project folder now (either paper or electronic). Store ideas, notes, news clippings, website addresses, and lists of materials that might help you to complete your project.

Inquiry Project
Investigate how ground cover can help reduce the temperature near the Earth's surface.

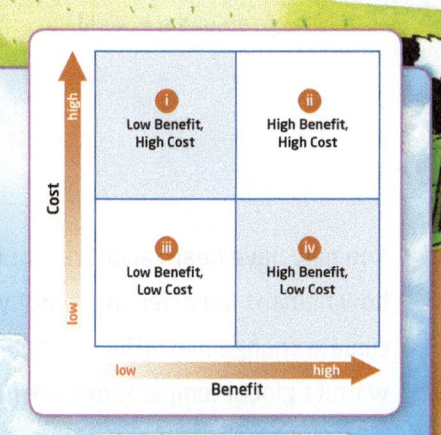

An Issue to Analyze
Perform a cost-benefit analysis of possible actions to deal with climate change.

Chapter 7   Earth's Climate System

What You Will Learn

In this chapter, you will learn how to...
- **identify** the principal components of Earth's climate system
- **describe** various tools and systems for classifying climates
- **analyze** effects of climate change on human activities and natural systems

Why It Matters

Climate affects living conditions for all organisms on the planet. A change in climate will lead to changes in the survival and distribution of many species, and to changes in human activities such as farming, fishing, and forestry.

Skills You Will Use

In this chapter, you will learn how to...
- **investigate** natural and human factors that affect climate change
- **assess** and **evaluate** tools and systems for studying climates
- **analyze** some of the effects of climate change around the world

You may have heard about recent changes to global climate and how humans are affecting it. But you may not realize how much climate change may affect human life in the future. For example, warmer global temperatures are reducing the area of the Arctic that is covered by ice. Aboriginal hunters in northern Canada rely on sea ice as important hunting grounds and travel routes. Their traditional way of life is threatened by changes in sea ice that result from global climate change.

Activity 7-1

Views on Climate Change

Many people say that human survival on Earth is in danger because of climate change. Other people say that only our lifestyles will change as we adapt to our changing planet. What do you think?

Earth's climate is changing.

Human activities affect climate.

Climate change is harmful to the planet.

Venn diagrams can be used to identify similarities and differences between subjects.

Materials
- chart paper
- markers or pens
- sticky notes
- stopwatch

Procedure

1. Working in pairs or in a small group, create a Venn diagram–like the one shown above–on the chart paper. Leave enough room in the overlapping sections for writing later.

2. Have a group member set the stopwatch for 10 min. Write down anything that you believe or have heard someone say about climate change on a sticky note.

3. With your group, decide where on the Venn diagram to put each of your thoughts. Set aside any comments that do not fit into these three categories.

4. Colour in the section of the Venn diagram that most closely matches your personal beliefs about climate change.

Questions

1. What are your overall views about climate change? What are the overall views of your group or class?

2. What information would you like to have in order to assess the validity of some of the statements or beliefs you have or have heard about climate change? Could any information make you change your beliefs about climate change? Explain why or why not.

Chapter 7 Earth's Climate System • NEL   267

Study Toolkit

These strategies will help you use this textbook to develop your understanding of science concepts and skills. To find out more about these and other strategies, refer to the Study Toolkit Overview, which begins on page 560.

Reading Graphic Text

Interpreting Climatographs

In a climatograph, a bar graph is combined with a line graph. Before interpreting a climatograph, read the title, the axis labels, and any accompanying text. Note the units of measurement and how the numbers are scaled. Then look for patterns in the shape of the line or in the clusters of bars. For example, the climatograph below shows that temperature and precipitation in Alert are highest during the summer.

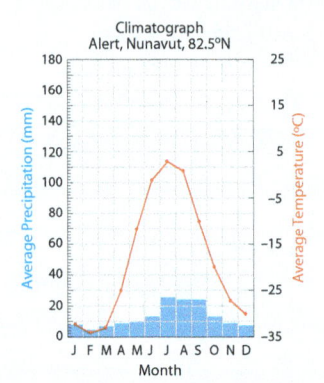

The tundra has a layer of permanently frozen soil, called permafrost. Plants grow close to the ground. Trees cannot survive because of the thin soil and lack of moisture.

Use the Strategy

Examine the climatograph for the desert biome on page 285. Identify and describe any relationships between the two sets of data. Write a sentence about average temperatures in the desert biome.

Reading Effectively

Making Inferences

Often, textual material does not contain *all* of the details about a topic. Some details or connections between ideas may be implied rather than stated explicitly. You need to make inferences by combining information in the text with your prior knowledge. For example, the table below shows one inference you could make about the text in the first column.

Information in Text	+ Prior Knowledge	= Inference
Air currents travel in fairly constant directions around the world. These air currents are known as prevailing winds.	When I watch the weather forecast for my area, I notice that weather systems often move into Canada from the southwestern United States.	The prevailing winds in North America generally blow from the southwest toward the northeast.

Use the Strategy

Read the first paragraph in the section titled "Winds Affect Precipitation" on page 274. Create a table like the one above, and make an inference about the movement of air masses.

Word Study

Word Origins

When you learn a new word, finding its *origin*, or the language it came from, can be helpful. For example, to better understand the meaning of *albedo*, find the word in a dictionary. You will probably see an entry that is similar to the one below.

albedo *noun* reflective power; *specifically*: the fraction of incident radiation (as light) that is reflected by a surface or body (such as the moon or a cloud) [from Late Latin, *whiteness*, from Latin *albus*]

The dictionary entry tells you that *albedo* comes from the Latin *albus*, meaning whiteness. This information might help you remember the meaning of *albedo*: the ratio of light that is reflected by a surface. It might also prompt you to think about related words, such as *albino* (an animal or a plant that has a very pale appearance) and *albatross* (a large white sea bird).

Use the Strategy

Find the Greek origin of the word *tectonic*. Explain how the Greek origin helps you understand the current meaning of the word.

268 NEL • Unit 3 Climate Change

7.1 Factors That Affect Climate Change

Earth is surrounded by a layer of gases called the **atmosphere**. Without this layer, days would be scorching hot and nights would be freezing cold. The condition of the atmosphere in a specific place at a specific time is known as *weather*. Weather describes factors such as wind, temperature, and the amount of moisture in the atmosphere.

In Canada, we experience patterns of weather in the cycle of seasons, with hot summers and cold winters. Countries on the equator, such as Ecuador and Indonesia, do not experience cold winters but may have cycles of wet seasons and dry seasons. The average conditions of the atmosphere over a period of several years over a large region are known as climate. The **climate** of Canada is very different from the climates of Ecuador and Indonesia.

Climates around the world have changed many times over the billions of years of Earth's history. For example, thousands of years ago, thick ice sheets covered most of Canada and a significant part of the United States, as shown in **Figure 7.1**. Today, evidence indicates that the climate is changing once more. In 1988, an international scientific panel was established to investigate the evidence and advise governments around the world about the effects that climate change could have on their citizens. This panel is called the Intergovernmental Panel on Climate Change, or IPCC. The IPCC studies and consults on causes and effects of climate change. These changes include the significant short-term and long-term changes in regional and global weather conditions.

> **Key Terms**
> atmosphere
> climate
> greenhouse effect
> hydrosphere
> albedo
> tectonic plate
> anthropogenic

> **atmosphere** a layer of gases that surrounds a planet or moon
>
> **climate** the characteristic pattern of weather conditions within a region, including temperature, wind velocity, precipitation, and other features, averaged over a long period of time

Figure 7.1 The blue line on **A** this map shows the boundary of the **B** glaciers that covered Canada between about 100 000 and 20 000 years ago.

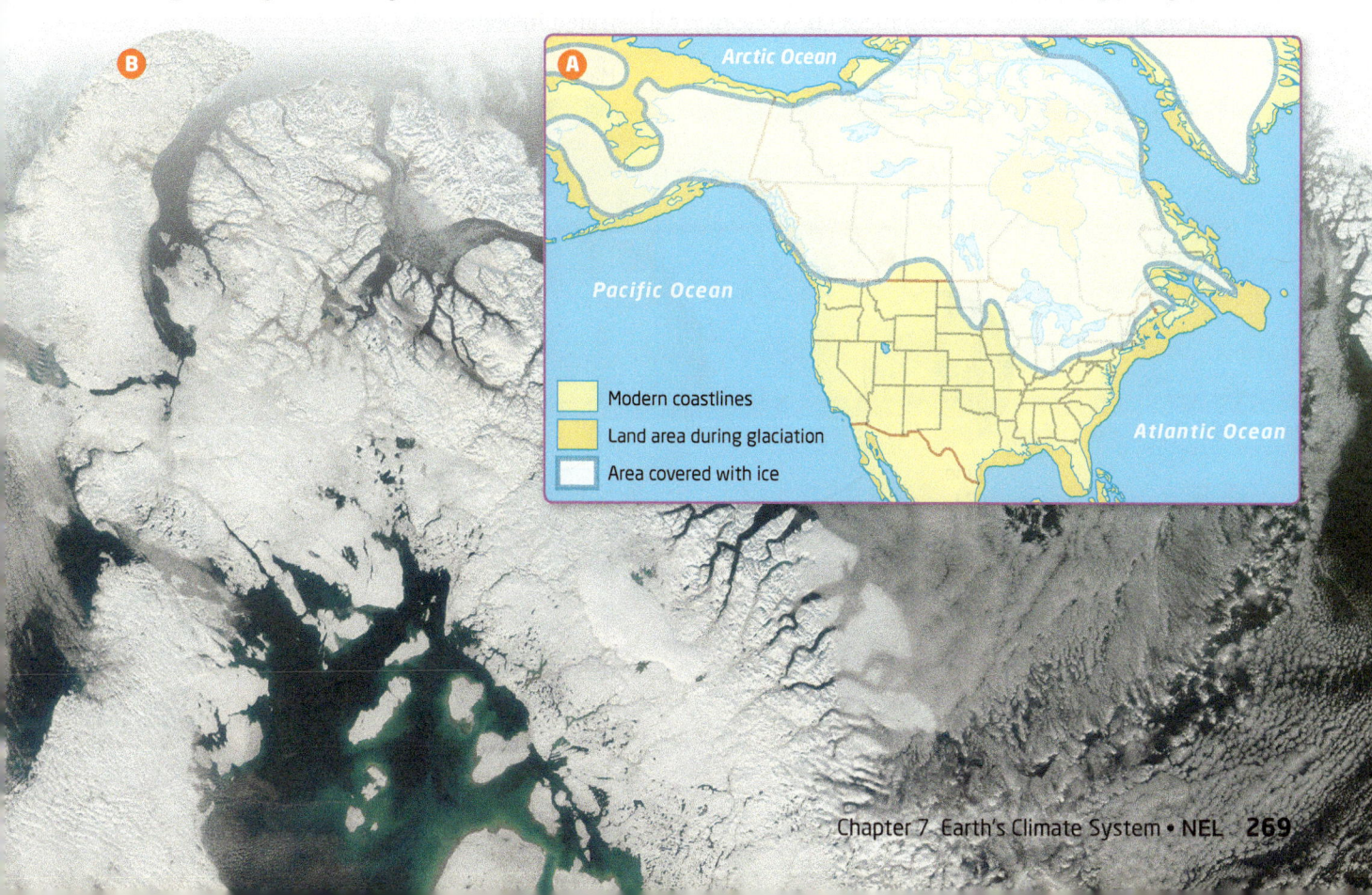

Chapter 7 Earth's Climate System • NEL 269

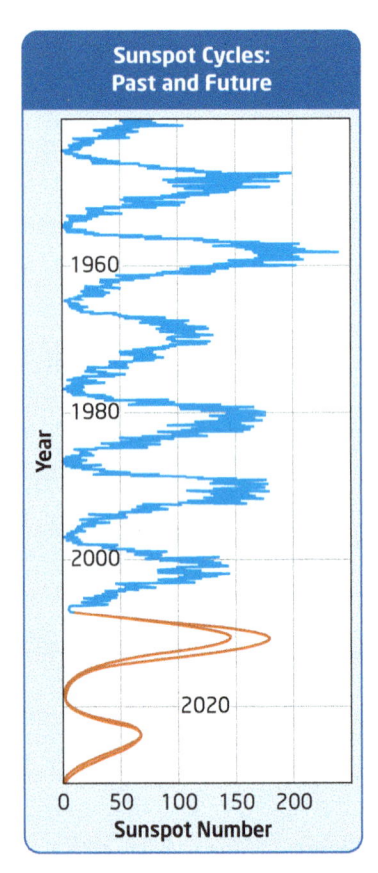

Figure 7.2 This graph shows how the number of sunspots changes over time. When the number of sunspots is high, the Sun emits higher amounts of solar radiation.

Earth and the Sun

Energy from the Sun is the single most important factor that affects climate on Earth. Solar energy travels through space as light and heat. The intensity of the energy that reaches Earth's surface affects the temperature of the air, water, and land on the planet. This heat produces the winds, rain, and other features of the climate. The amount of solar energy that reaches Earth's surface varies with changes in solar activity. The amount of solar energy also depends on the shape of the planet and on Earth's angle of tilt and orbit around the Sun.

Changes in Solar Activity

The Sun may appear unchanging, but the amount of radiation it produces varies. Measurements of solar radiation show that irregular fluctuations occur in the amount of energy produced by the Sun. In addition, a more regular solar cycle (or sunspot cycle) occurs approximately every 11 years, as shown in **Figure 7.2**. These solar variations differ by about 0.1 percent. Some scientists have proposed that variations in solar output have been the main cause of climate change in the past.

Movements of Earth in Space

Earth rotates (spins) once every 24 hours around its axis—an imaginary line running from the North Pole to the South Pole. While continuously rotating on its axis, Earth makes a year-long journey around the Sun. Throughout this path, or orbit, Earth remains in the same orbital plane, as though it were travelling on a flat surface. Earth's axis of rotation is tilted at an angle of about 23.5° from a line perpendicular to the orbital plane. The combination of Earth's annual orbit around the Sun and its tilted axis produces our seasons, as illustrated in **Figure 7.3**.

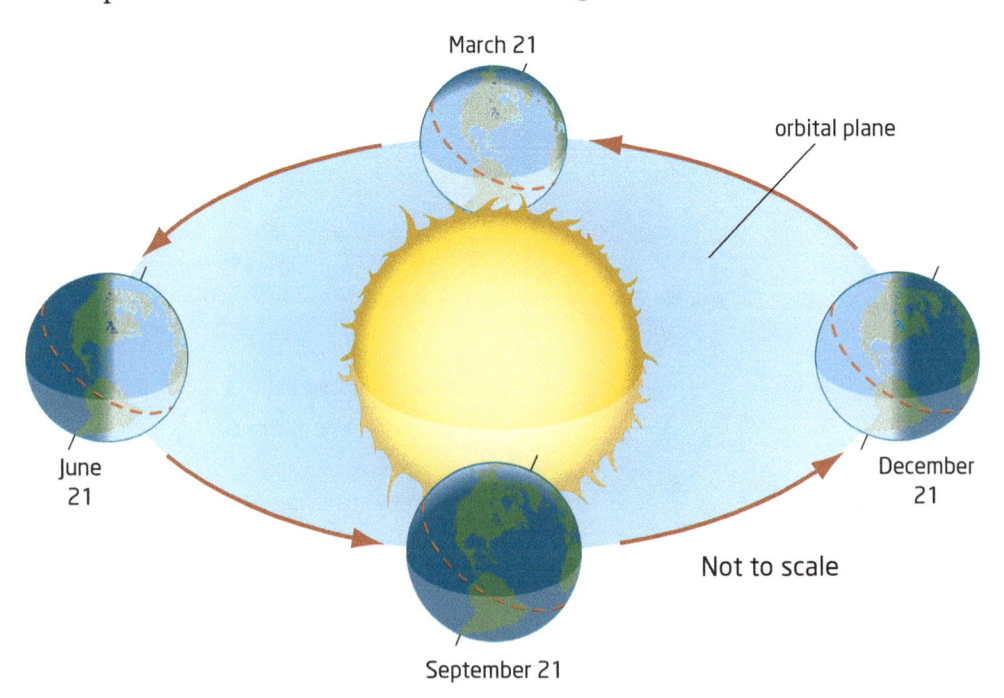

Figure 7.3 The positions of Earth in its orbit vary throughout a single year. The angle of sunlight on Earth's surface determines the seasons.

270 NEL • Unit 3 Climate Change

Changes in Earth's Rotation, Orbit, and Tilt

Throughout its history, Earth's orbit, tilt, and rotation have varied slightly in repeating cycles. In the early 1900s, a Serbian mathematician, Milutin Milankovic, calculated that these variations changed the amount and location of solar radiation reaching Earth. He proposed that these changes in solar intensity produced changes in the climate. This theory helps describe large patterns of climate change over a long time scale. However, it does not fully explain all of the recent changes that have been observed and measured using other evidence.

Eccentricity Due to the gravitational attraction of other planets in the solar system, Earth's orbit fluctuates slightly over a cycle of about 100 000 years. Its path around the Sun changes very slowly from being almost circular to being more elliptical, and then back again, as shown in **Figure 7.4**. When Earth's orbit is more elliptical, the planet receives much more solar radiation when it is nearest the Sun than it does when it is farthest from the Sun. When the orbit is more circular, the amount of solar radiation varies less throughout the year. These differences affect the length and intensity of the seasons.

Tilt The angle of Earth's tilt on its axis changes by approximately 2.4° over a period of about 41 000 years, as shown in **Figure 7.5**. The greater the tilt is, the greater the temperature differences are between summer and winter. Currently, Earth is tilted at about 23.44°, or roughly halfway between its extremes, and the angle is slowly decreasing.

Wobble The third factor in Milankovic's calculations of Earth's movements involves a change in the direction of the axis of rotation, known as *precession*, which is illustrated in **Figure 7.5**. Because Earth is not a perfect sphere, it wobbles slightly as it rotates on its axis. This wobble affects the amount and intensity of solar energy that is received by the northern and southern hemispheres at different times of the year. This variation determines whether the two hemispheres have similar contrasts between seasons, or whether one hemisphere has greater temperature differences between seasons than the other hemisphere does.

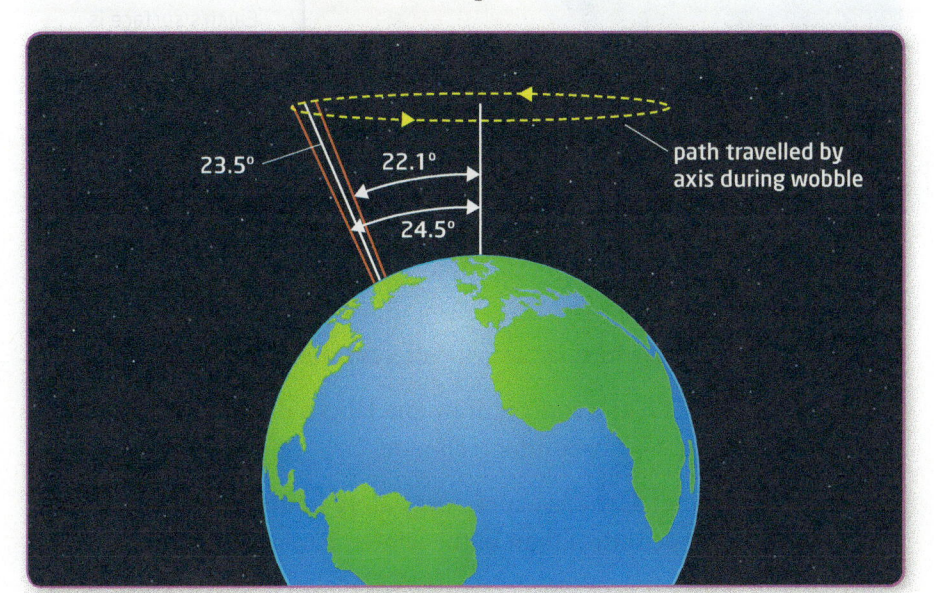

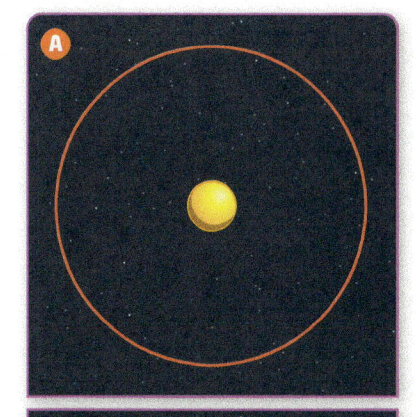

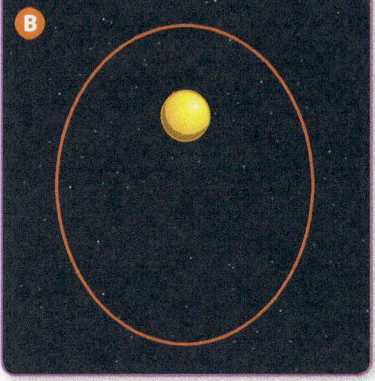

Figure 7.4 Over a period of about 100 000 years, Earth's path around the Sun changes from being **A** nearly circular, to being **B** slightly more elliptical, and back again.

Figure 7.5 Earth's angle of tilt varies between 22.1° and 24.5° from the perpendicular over a period of about 41 000 years. Precession varies cyclically over the course of about 26 000 years.

The Effect of Latitude on Climate and Seasons

Why is the climate in Ecuador hotter than the climate in Canada? The answer lies in the curved shape of Earth and in the different angles at which the Sun's rays strike the planet's surface. **Figure 7.6** illustrates the relationship between incoming solar rays and Earth's curvature.

Compare the amount of surface area illuminated by a ray of sunlight at the equator, by an identical ray at 45° south, and by a third ray at the North Pole. The Sun's rays striking the equator are perpendicular to Earth's surface. At latitude 45° south, the Sun's rays strike the surface at an angle. Because of this angle, the energy in the rays is spread over a larger area—nearly 1.5 times as large as the area on the equator. Therefore, each square metre of Earth's surface at latitude 45° absorbs only about two thirds as much energy as the same area absorbs at the equator. At the poles, a ray of sunlight is spread over an even larger area. Because each square metre receives less solar energy, the surface near the poles heats up much less than does the surface at the equator.

Figure 7.6 shows Earth as if it were not tilted relative to the Sun. If this were actually the case, average temperatures at different latitudes would remain the same throughout the year. Earth's tilt on its axis combined with its orbit creates the change of temperature with the seasons.

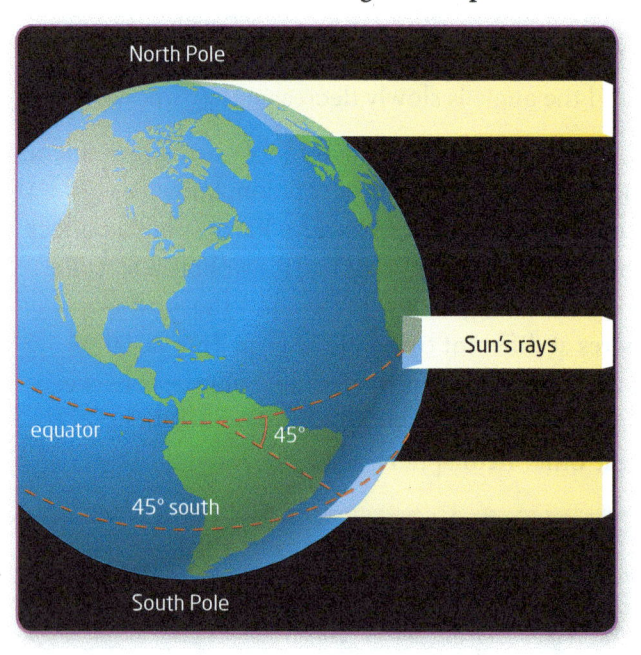

Figure 7.6 Because Earth's surface is curved, a beam of sunlight illuminates different-sized areas at different latitudes.

Learning Check

1. What is climate?
2. How do changes in solar activity affect climate?
3. Using **Figure 7.6** as a source, draw and label a diagram that illustrates how latitude affects climate.
4. In the summer, Canada experiences more hours of daylight and warmer temperatures than in the winter. Explain this difference.

How the Atmosphere Affects Climate

The atmosphere extends from Earth's surface up to about 560 km into space. It is composed mainly of the gases nitrogen (N_2) and oxygen (O_2), as well as water vapour (H_2O), very small concentrations of other gases, and particles of solids.

Earth's atmosphere absorbs thermal energy from the Sun and thermal energy that is emitted by Earth's surface. This process, called the **greenhouse effect**, is outlined in **Figure 7.7**. The greenhouse effect is a natural part of Earth's climate system. This process helps to keep Earth's temperature fluctuations within a certain range. Without this process, most of the solar energy reaching Earth would radiate back into space, and the average temperature at the planet's surface would be about 34°C lower than it is today.

greenhouse effect the natural warming caused when gases in Earth's atmosphere absorb thermal energy that is radiated by the Sun and Earth

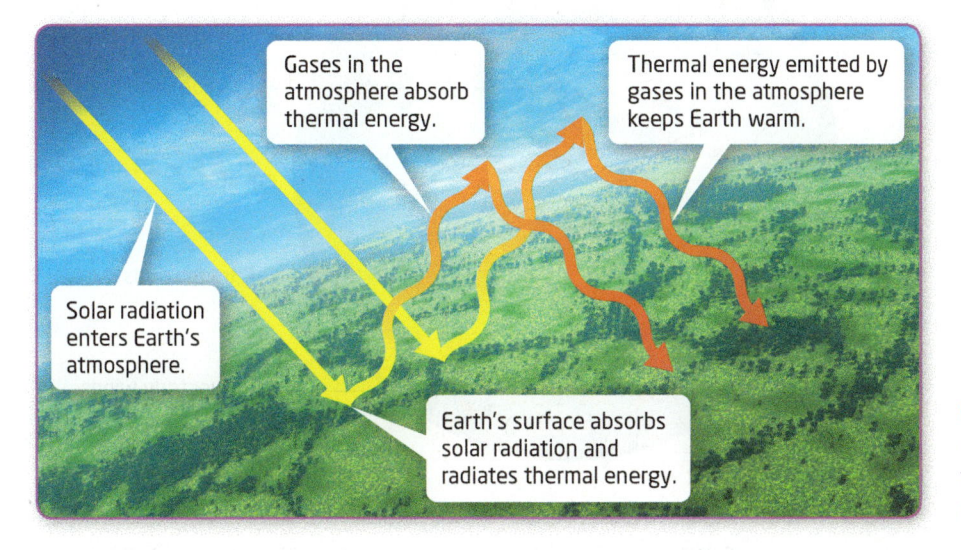

Figure 7.7 Earth's atmosphere retains energy from the Sun through a process known as the greenhouse effect.

Winds Disperse Energy through the Atmosphere

Wind is the movement of air from an area of high pressure to an area of lower pressure. All winds begin as a result of uneven heating of Earth's surface, as shown in **Figure 7.8**. This movement of air as wind transfers thermal energy around the world from warm areas to cooler areas. In addition, the movement of air affects ocean currents and precipitation patterns.

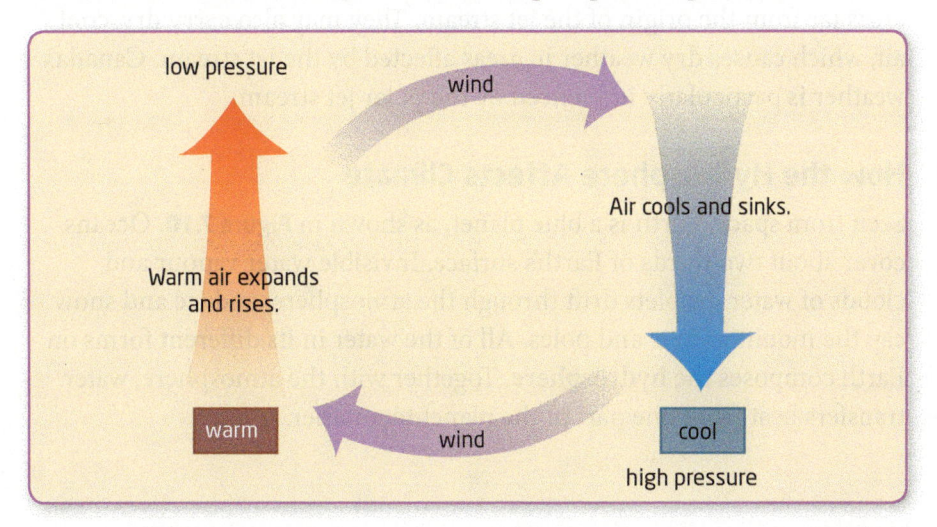

Figure 7.8 Air above warm areas expands and rises, while air above cooler areas sinks. These pressure differences create winds as air moves.

Winds Move Ocean Currents

The movement of currents at the surface of the oceans is driven by winds blowing over the water. You can see this effect if you blow gently across the surface of warm soup in a wide bowl. Energy from the moving air is transferred to the surface of the water, which causes the water to move. Because the oceans absorb energy from the Sun, the movement of the water results in the transfer of heat around Earth's surface. Winds blow in fairly constant directions around the world. These air currents are known as *prevailing winds*. A map of prevailing global wind patterns and ocean currents is shown in **Figure 7.9**.

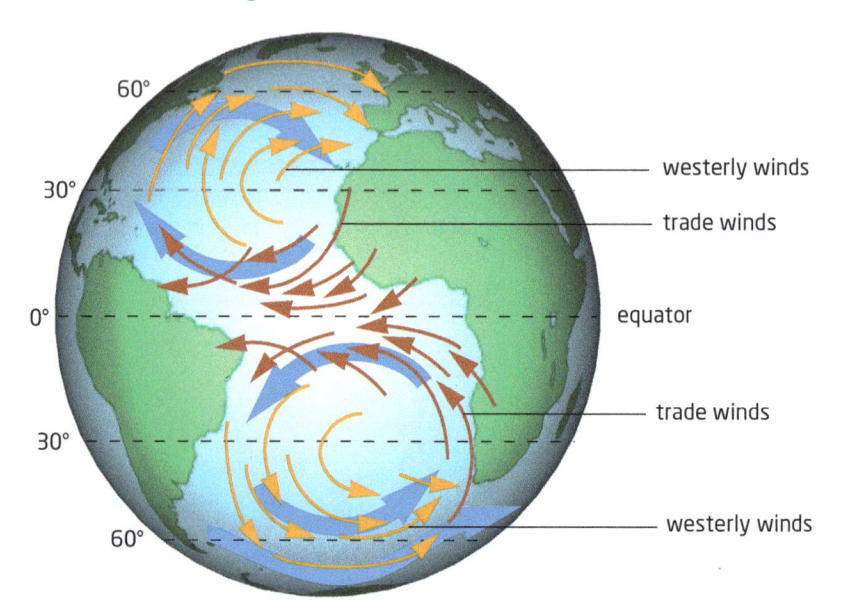

Figure 7.9 Winds (red and orange arrows) travel clockwise north of the equator and counterclockwise south of the equator. Ocean currents (blue arrows) move around the world in the same direction as the winds.

Winds Affect Precipitation

As air masses of different densities move across Earth's surface, they interact. When air masses meet, one air mass usually rises over the other. The rising air cools, and any water vapour in the air condenses to form precipitation.

Winds also affect precipitation through *jet streams*. Jet streams are high-altitude winds that travel long distances at very high speeds. These winds may carry warm, moist air, which can produce precipitation in areas far from the origin of the jet stream. They may also carry dry, cool air, which causes dry weather in areas affected by the jet stream. Canada's weather is particularly influenced by the polar jet stream.

How the Hydrosphere Affects Climate

Seen from space, Earth is a blue planet, as shown in **Figure 7.10**. Oceans cover about two thirds of Earth's surface. Invisible water vapour and clouds of water droplets drift through the atmosphere, and ice and snow cap the mountaintops and poles. All of the water in its different forms on Earth composes the **hydrosphere**. Together with the atmosphere, water transfers heat from one part of the planet to another.

hydrosphere the collective mass of water found on, under, and over the surface of Earth in the form of liquid water, ice, and water vapour

Figure 7.10 Earth's blue oceans absorb energy and transfer that energy around the planet's surface.

Oceans and Lakes Act as Heat Reservoirs

The oceans can hold much more heat than the atmosphere can. In fact, the top 2.3 metres of the world's oceans holds as much heat as all of the planet's air does. As a result, the oceans act as a "heat reservoir" that buffers temperature changes in the atmosphere.

Large bodies of water influence climate because water has a large specific heat capacity compared with other substances. *Specific heat capacity* is the amount of heat required to raise the temperature of one gram of a substance by one degree Celsius. Because water has a large specific heat capacity, a large quantity of energy is required to raise its temperature compared with the energy needed to change the temperature of land. As a result, the temperature of large bodies of water tends to change slowly and by small amounts. The temperature of land masses changes more quickly and by larger amounts.

Ice and Snow Reflect Heat

Because of their light colour, snow and ice reflect solar radiation. The fraction of energy that is reflected by a surface is known as **albedo**. The amount of energy reflected or absorbed depends largely on the colour of the surface. In general, light-coloured surfaces reflect energy, and dark surfaces absorb energy. The ocean surface reflects about 7 percent of solar energy. By contrast, a field covered by fresh snow, such as the one shown in **Figure 7.11**, can reflect as much as 80 to 90 percent of the solar energy that strikes it. Because of their large differences in albedo, the distribution of water, ice, and land on Earth's surface greatly affects the average global temperature.

How Moving Continents Affect Climate

Earth's outer layer is composed of massive pieces of solid rock known as **tectonic plates**. Earth has about 12 major plates that move at a rate of a few centimetres each year, carrying the continents with them. As a result, the shapes of the oceans and continents are always changing. The changing distribution of land and water affects patterns of air and water circulation and the transfer of thermal energy around the world. The formation of mountain chains also affects the pattern of wind and precipitation around the globe.

albedo the fraction of incident light or electromagnetic radiation that is reflected by the surface of an object, such as from Earth back into space; an object's ability to reflect sunlight

tectonic plate a piece of Earth's outer shell (the lithosphere) that moves around on the slowly flowing, underlying rock layer (the asthenosphere)

Suggested Investigation
Inquiry Investigation 7-A, Specific Heat Capacity of Earth Materials, on page 300

Figure 7.11 These corn fields in Canada reflect a great deal of solar energy during the winter. The white snow has a high albedo and reflects most of the sunlight that reaches the snow-covered ground.

Volcanic Eruptions

Another way in which plate movement affects climate is by producing volcanic activity. Most volcanoes are located at the boundaries of tectonic plates. In these areas, molten rock and gases from below Earth's crust rise up through cracks in the rock and spew into the air as volcanic eruptions. Scientists think that volcanic activity helped form the atmosphere at an early stage in Earth's history.

Volcanic eruptions, such as the one shown in **Figure 7.12**, spew ash and other particles into the atmosphere. These particles, called *aerosols*, reflect solar radiation and have a cooling effect on the global climate. They also scatter light and cause brilliantly red sunsets. This effect may last from a few years to several decades, until the particles are removed from the atmosphere by precipitation and settling. For example, the 1815 eruption of Tambora, in the Philippines, was followed by the "Year Without a Summer." On the other hand, some types of volcanic eruptions may raise global temperatures by releasing greenhouse gases.

Figure 7.12 Mount St. Helens, in Washington State, erupted in 1980 and sent 1 km³ of rock and dust into the air.

Activity 7-2

Modelling the Effects of Volcanoes on Climate

How does ash from a single volcanic eruption affect global climate? In this activity, you will model the process by which volcanic eruptions affect Earth's atmosphere.

Safety Precautions

- Exercise caution when using electrical devices and water in close proximity, to avoid electric shock.
- Clean up any spills or splashes immediately.

Materials
- overhead projector (or another light source)
- water
- small aquarium (5 L to 10 L)
- coffee creamer
- 5 mL measuring spoon

Procedure

1. Fill the aquarium with water and place it on the overhead projector. Plug the projector in and turn on its light. Darken the room.

2. Observe the colour of the water from the side of the aquarium, and the colour of the light that passes through the aquarium and hits the wall or screen.

3. Add 5 mL of coffee creamer to the water, stir, and observe again. Repeat until the liquid is translucent and more light is transmitted through the side of the aquarium than through the upper surface of the water.

4. Turn the room lights back on, unplug the overhead projector (or other light source), and empty the aquarium in the sink. Rinse it well and dry it before you put it away.

Questions

1. Describe how the colour of the transmitted light changed as the water was contaminated.

2. How does this activity model the effects of volcanic eruptions or meteorite impacts on the atmosphere?

3. What effect might this type of phenomenon have on global temperature?

Ash from volcanic eruptions scatters sunlight, which causes more vibrant sunsets than usual.

How Human Activity Affects Climate

Although solar variations, volcanic activity, moving continents, meteorites, and a wobbling planet have produced climate changes in the past, none of these causes can explain the warming trend that has occurred on Earth since the 1970s. There is growing evidence that the present change in climate is at least partly **anthropogenic** (caused by humans).

How can humans affect the climate? The main link is the effect human technology has on the atmosphere. For many centuries, a major source of energy used by people has been the burning of fossil fuels, such as coal, oil, and natural gas. In the late 1700s, a rapid increase occurred in the rate at which new machines were invented and new methods of transportation and manufacturing were adopted. All of these new inventions and processes demanded fossil fuels to power them. This period was called the *Industrial Revolution*.

From the 1700s to the present, technologies that burn fossil fuels grew and spread around the world. Trains, automobiles, ships, factories, aircraft, farming and mining equipment, home furnaces, and electricity generating stations are just some examples of technologies that use fossil fuels. When these fuels are burned to release energy, they release gases and other pollutants into the atmosphere as waste products, as shown in **Figure 7.13**. As the human use of fossil fuels has expanded, the concentration of these gases in the atmosphere has increased. Many of these gases affect the natural processes that produce the greenhouse effect. In Chapter 8, you will learn more about these processes and about the evidence for anthropogenic climate change.

> **anthropogenic** relating to or resulting from the influence of humans

> **Study Toolkit**
>
> **Word Origins** The term *anthropogenic* is rooted in the Greek terms *anthropos* (human, man) and *genes* (that which produces). How can this information help you remember the meaning of the term?

Figure 7.13 The burning of fossil fuels at this coal-fired plant on the St. Clair River near Sarnia, Ontario, releases gases and other pollutants into the atmosphere.

Section 7.1 Review

Section Summary

- Climate describes the standard weather conditions for a region at a given time of year, including expected temperatures, winds, precipitation, probability of storms, and hours of direct sunshine.
- The amount of energy that a location on the surface of Earth receives at any given time is determined by the angle of the Sun, which in turn depends on the latitude, time of year, and time of day.
- Winds, ocean currents, and the shape and size of continents affect climate.
- Earth reflects some of the solar energy that hits it back into space. The fraction of energy that is reflected by a surface is called albedo.
- Volcanic eruptions introduce gases and particles into the air that affect the reflection and absorption of energy from the Sun.
- Human activity affects climate by introducing particles and gases into the atmosphere that affect the absorption and transfer of energy from the Sun.

Review Questions

K/U 1. How is climate different from weather?

K/U 2. Use **Figures 7.3** and **7.6** to explain how energy from the Sun affects Earth's climate.

A 3. How do the specific heat capacities of water and rock explain why the climate in Toronto, Ontario, is more mild than the climate in Pierre, South Dakota?

T/I 4. How might the formation of mountain chains affect climate?

A 5. The graph on the right shows how temperature deviated from the global average temperature during the early 1990s. In June 1991, Mount Pinatubo erupted in the Philippines. How did this eruption affect global average temperature in the years following the eruption?

C 6. Create a diagram that illustrates the major factors that affect Earth's climate. Be sure to label each factor.

T/I 7. Which factor do you think has a stronger effect on climate, the atmosphere or the ocean? Explain your answer.

K/U 8. What human activity may be the cause of recent rises in global temperatures?

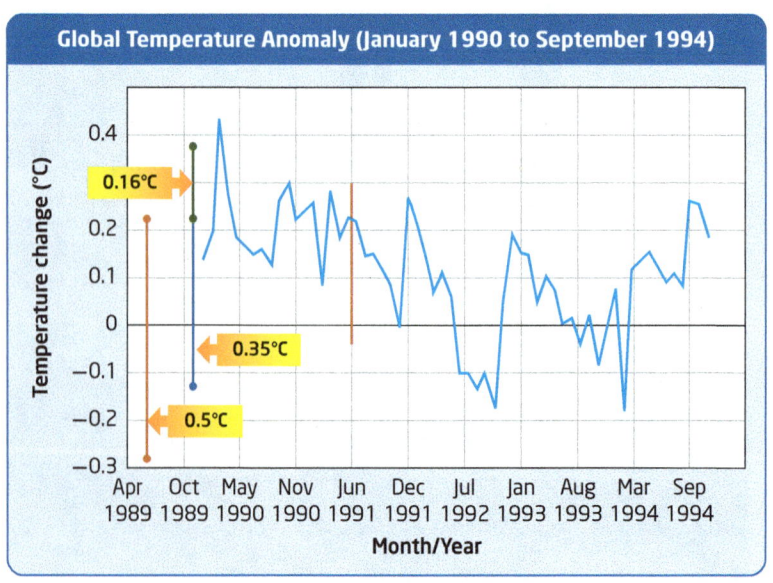

7.2 Describing Climates

Key Terms
climatograph
Köppen climate classification system
biome
ecozone
ecoregion

To measure how climate is changing, scientists must first describe and classify the range of climates that exist around the world today. The planet can be divided into regions that share similar weather conditions. These regions are commonly called *climate zones*.

More than two thousand years ago, the Greek scholar Aristotle classified three major climate zones on the planet, based on their increasing distance from the equator. Scientists use a similar broad classification today, as shown in **Figure 7.14**. The centre of the planet, between the Tropic of Cancer (about 23°26' north of the equator) and the Tropic of Capricorn (about 23°26' south of the equator), is classified as the *tropical zone*. In the tropical zone, temperature is relatively warm and varies little throughout the year. The areas between the North Pole and about 66°33' north (the Arctic Circle) and between the South Pole and 66°33' south are classified as *polar zones*. Polar zones are characterized by cold temperatures and by ice cover for much or all of the year. Between the polar and tropical zones lie the *temperate zones*. In Earth's temperate regions, temperature may vary greatly during the year, and many regions experience distinctly warm and cold seasons.

The unequal warming of Earth's surface explains why Earth has hot and cold climate zones as well as hot and cold seasons. Polar regions receive less intense sunlight than equatorial regions do. Therefore, polar regions are colder than equatorial regions.

Figure 7.14 Distance from the equator affects both average temperature and average precipitation, creating three types of broad climate zones.

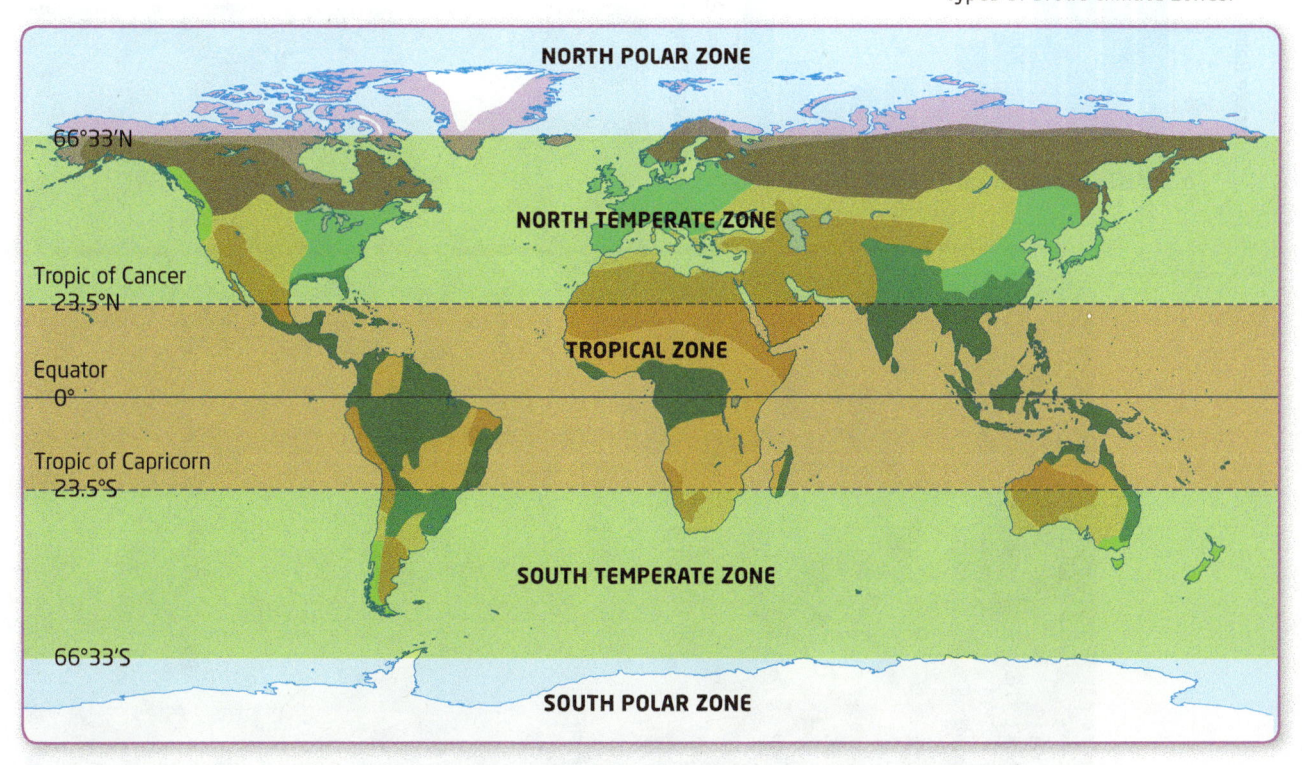

Chapter 7 Earth's Climate System • NEL   279

climatograph a graph of climate data for a specific region; the data are usually obtained over 30 years from observations made at local weather stations

Study Toolkit

Interpreting Climatographs
When examining **Figure 7.15**, remember that both temperature and precipitation are plotted on the y-axis of a climatograph. How do these climate features vary throughout the year in Manokwari, Indonesia?

Climatographs

To compare climates in different regions more precisely, scientists use a tool called a climatograph. A **climatograph** is a graph of climate data for a particular region based on average measurements taken over several years. A climatograph includes figures for average monthly temperature and an average of the total monthly precipitation.

For example, **Figure 7.15** shows a climatograph for Manokwari in Indonesia, a tropical rainforest region near the equator. The horizontal axis of the climatograph indicates the 12 months of the year. Temperature (in °C) is calibrated along the right vertical axis. Precipitation (in mm) is calibrated along the left vertical axis. This climatograph indicates that the average temperature in Manokwari remains close to 25°C throughout the year. Rainfall levels are high, with one wet season and one drier season in the year.

Climatographs are useful because they allow scientists to view how temperature and precipitation change throughout the year. These graphs also allow scientists to compare the weather patterns of different locations. For example, some locations have seasonal variations in temperature. Other regions have little variation in temperature, but they have wet and dry seasons. These variables can be used to classify and compare climates.

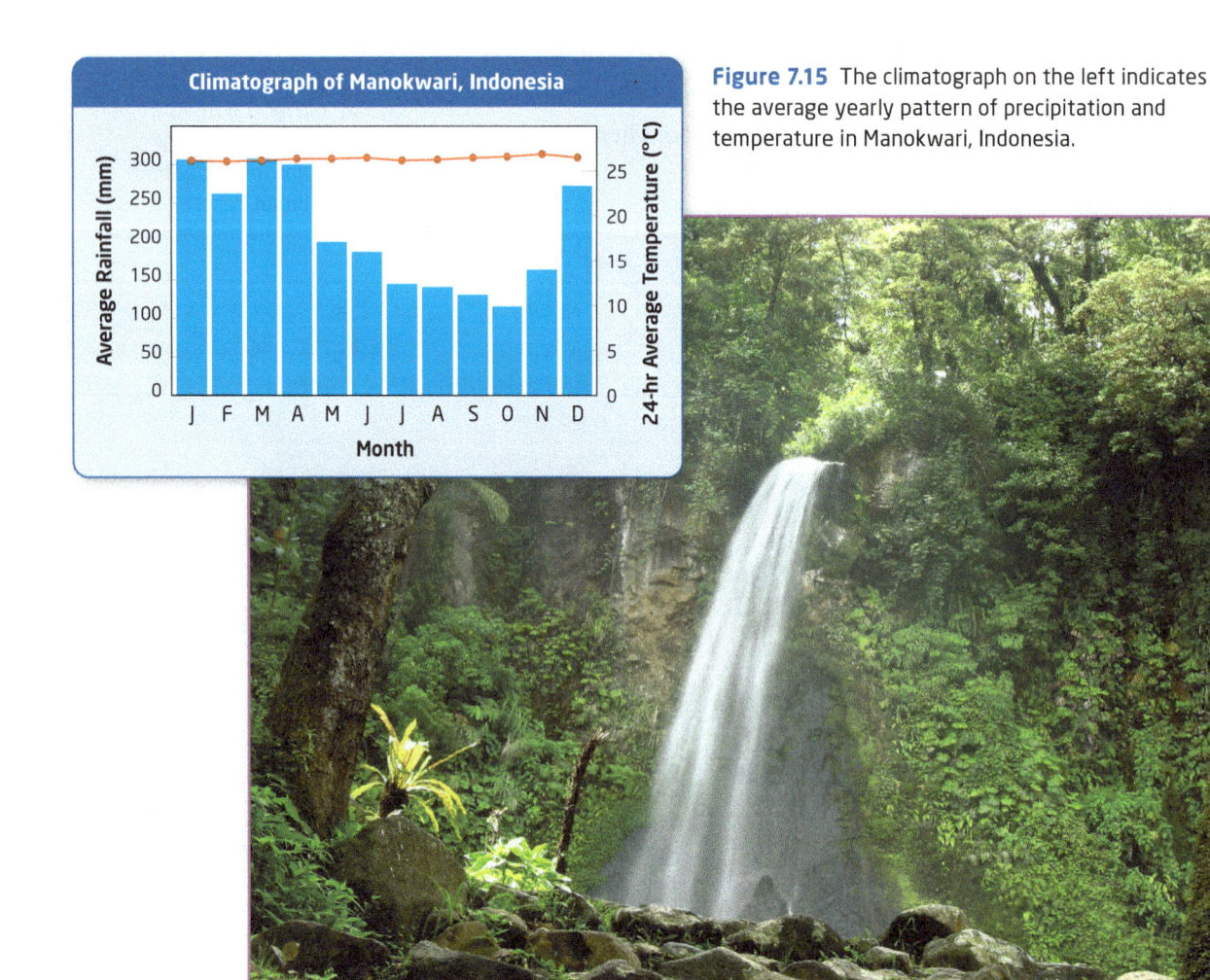

Figure 7.15 The climatograph on the left indicates the average yearly pattern of precipitation and temperature in Manokwari, Indonesia.

Activity 7-3

How to Make a Climatograph

How do scientists visually represent the climate of a particular region? In this activity, you will use climate data to make a climatograph like the one in **Figure 7.15**.

Materials
- coloured pencils (red and blue)
- graph paper
- ruler

Procedure

1. On a piece of graph paper, mark 12 intervals on the horizontal axis. Label each interval with the first letter of the month, starting with J for January, and label the axis "Month."

2. On the left vertical axis, mark nine intervals beginning at 0 and extending to 180. Each interval has a value of 20 mm. Label this axis "Average Precipitation (mm)."

3. Draw a second vertical axis for temperature on the right. On this axis, mark seven intervals beginning with −35°C and extending to 25°C. Each interval has a value of 10°C. Label this axis "Average Temperature (°C)."

4. Enter the data from the table for each month's average precipitation as a bar graph. Use a blue pencil to shade in the bars.

5. Enter the data from the table for each month's average temperature as a point in the middle of the space allocated for that month. Use a red pencil to draw a curve between the points.

6. Add a title to your climatograph.

Questions

1. Which month has the lowest average temperature?
2. Which month was the driest? Which month was the wettest?
3. Assume that a growing season must have average temperatures above +5°C. For how many months of the year can plants grow in this location?
4. Suppose each month's average temperature increased by 4°C. How long would the growing season be under these conditions?
5. Decide whether this climatograph better describes Thunder Bay, Ottawa, or Windsor, Ontario. Explain your reasoning.

Average Monthly Precipitation and Temperature for Location A

Month	Precipitation (mm)	Temperature (°C)
J	58	−10
F	59	−8
M	65	−2
A	69	6
M	76	13
J	77	18
J	88	21
A	92	19
S	83	14
O	75	8
N	86	1
D	83	−7

Classifying Climates

How would you describe the climate of southern Ontario? How would you compare its climate with that of Indonesia? Categorizing the abiotic and biotic components of a region allows scientists to more easily compare different parts of the world. Most climate classification systems involve creating and analyzing climatographs. The patterns in those climatographs help scientists classify regions of the world into groups by climate.

Köppen climate classification system
a method of identifying and describing climates based on observable features such as temperature ranges and rates of precipitation

Go to **scienceontario** to find out more

The Köppen Climate Classification System

During the early 20th century, a German climatologist named Wladimir Köppen (1846–1940) developed a system of classifying climates that is still in wide use today. The **Köppen climate classification system** divides the world into five major climate zones based on three factors:

- average monthly temperature
- average monthly precipitation
- average annual precipitation

Each zone can be further divided into subcategories based on seasonal patterns. **Table 7.1** summarizes the characteristics of the five major groups. Southern Ontario is in category D, and Indonesia is in category A.

The Köppen system is not perfect, and some scientists have modified the system to try to clarify overly broad categories. These modifications commonly involve subdividing the C category and the B category described in **Table 7.1**. In addition, some other systems, including the Trewartha climate classification system, redefine the climate groups to tie the categories more closely with the zones inhabited by specific groups of plants. For example, the Köppen system classifies the New England region of the United States the same as the regions around the Gulf of Mexico. The Trewartha system defines these regions as separate climates based on the type of vegetation in the regions.

Table 7.1 Köppen Climate Classification

Köppen's Category	Description
A. tropical moist climate	All months average above 18°C. Annual precipitation is greater than 1500 mm. There may be no dry season or a short dry season.
B. dry climate	Temperatures range from up to 40°C in summer to –40°C in winter. Precipitation is low during most of the year and is exceeded by potential evaporation and transpiration.
C. moist mid-latitude climate with mild winters	Warm to hot summers. The average temperature of the coldest month is above –3°C.
D. moist mid-latitude climate with cold winters	Warm to cool summers. The average temperature of the coldest month is below –3°C.
E. polar climate	Cool summers and extremely cold winters. The average temperature of the warmest month is below 10°C.

Biomes

If you map the distribution of climate zones around the world and then map the distribution of different types of natural vegetation, you will find that the two are closely matched. Every type of plant requires certain conditions of temperature and precipitation in order to grow. In addition, specific animals are adapted to survive in each landscape. Large regions that have similar types of climate and similar plants and animals are known as **biomes**.

Figure 7.16 shows the distribution of average annual precipitation and average annual temperature in eight major biomes found around the world. This classification system is useful because it indicates the interaction of climates with ecosystems. If the climate changes, then the distribution of plants and animals adapted to the climate will also change. For example, suppose you want to know what type of ecosystem is found where the average annual temperature is 25°C and the average annual precipitation is greater than 275 cm. Follow the data lines from each axis until the two lines intersect. The biome found in that type of climate is a tropical rainforest. Where the average annual temperature is 25°C but the average annual precipitation is less than 25 cm, the biome is a desert. Canada includes examples of all biomes except tropical rainforest.

> **biome** the largest division of the biosphere, that have includes large regions that have similar biotic components (such as plants and animals) and similar abiotic components (such as temperature and amount of rainfall)

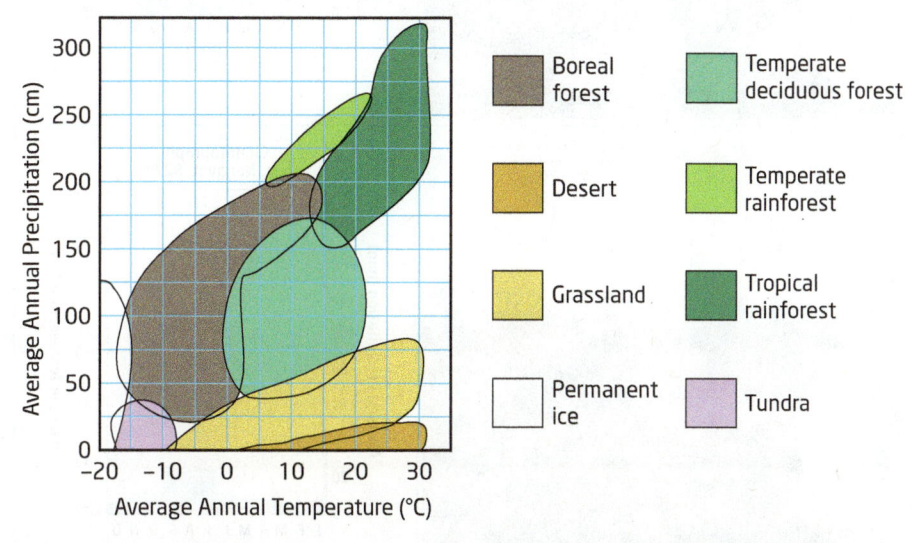

Figure 7.16 Average annual temperature and average annual precipitation of biomes can be graphed, and various biomes can be grouped together based on these factors.

Learning Check

1. Why are polar regions colder than tropical regions?
2. What two factors are plotted on a climatograph?
3. Create a Venn diagram to compare climates and biomes.
4. According to **Figure 7.16**, only one biome is characterized by receiving less than 25 cm of rain per year. What types of plants would you expect to find in that biome? Explain your answer.

Climate Zones and Biomes in Canada

Examples of seven of the world's eight major biomes can be found across Canada. The only biome that is not found in Canada is the tropical rainforest biome, for which you saw the climatograph at the beginning of this section. Because Canada is located north of 41°41' north latitude, it falls within the temperate and polar climate zones. Therefore, temperature in Canada never gets high enough for long enough to support tropical plants and animals. However, Canada supports biomes as varied as temperate rainforests, deserts, and permanent ice. Each biome in Canada is described in **Figure 7.17**. Can you identify the biome in which you live?

Figure 7.17 Canada contains all of the major biomes on Earth except tropical rainforest.

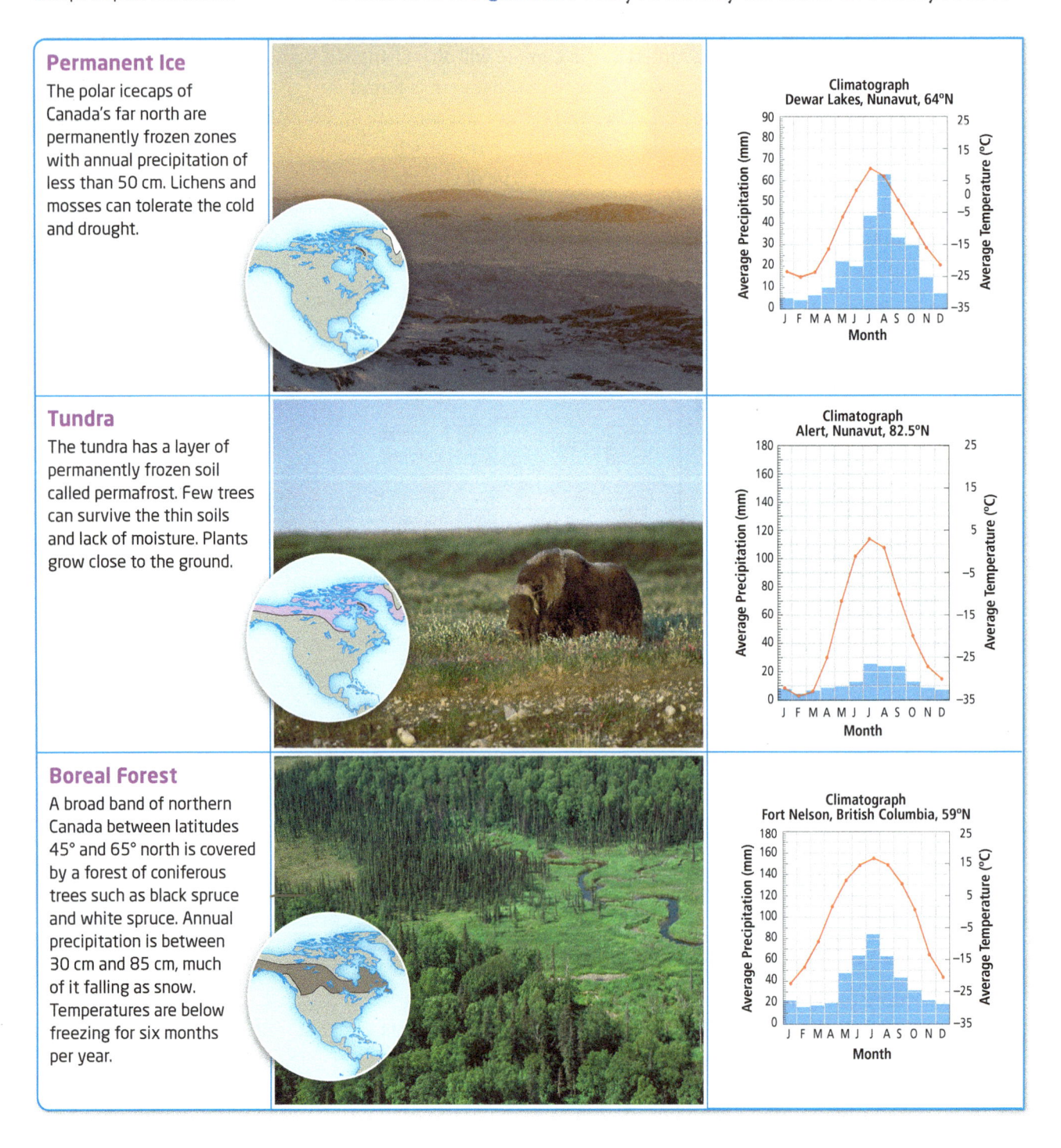

Permanent Ice
The polar icecaps of Canada's far north are permanently frozen zones with annual precipitation of less than 50 cm. Lichens and mosses can tolerate the cold and drought.

Climatograph: Dewar Lakes, Nunavut, 64°N

Tundra
The tundra has a layer of permanently frozen soil called permafrost. Few trees can survive the thin soils and lack of moisture. Plants grow close to the ground.

Climatograph: Alert, Nunavut, 82.5°N

Boreal Forest
A broad band of northern Canada between latitudes 45° and 65° north is covered by a forest of coniferous trees such as black spruce and white spruce. Annual precipitation is between 30 cm and 85 cm, much of it falling as snow. Temperatures are below freezing for six months per year.

Climatograph: Fort Nelson, British Columbia, 59°N

Temperate Deciduous Forest

Found mainly in eastern Canada, this zone has annual precipitation of 75 cm to 180 cm, distributed evenly throughout the year. Temperatures range from −30°C in winter to 30°C in summer. Maple, oak, and birch are typical trees in these forests.

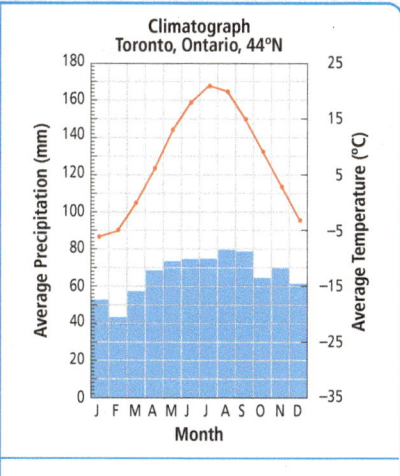

Temperate Rainforest

Coastal British Columbia is home to Canada's temperate rainforest, receiving more than 200 cm of precipitation per year. Average temperatures are mild, ranging from 5°C to 25°C. This climate produces very tall trees, such as Sitka spruce and Douglas fir.

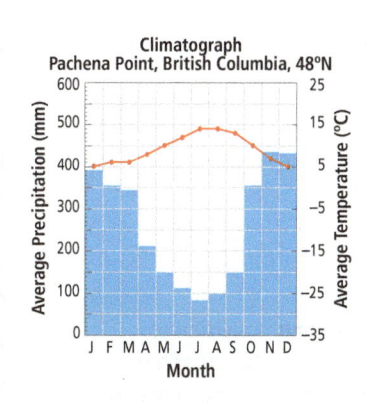

Grassland

The Canadian prairies have annual precipitation of 25 cm to 100 cm, with hot summers and cold winters. Limited rainfall restricts the growth of trees, and the typical vegetation is grasses with deep roots adapted for drought.

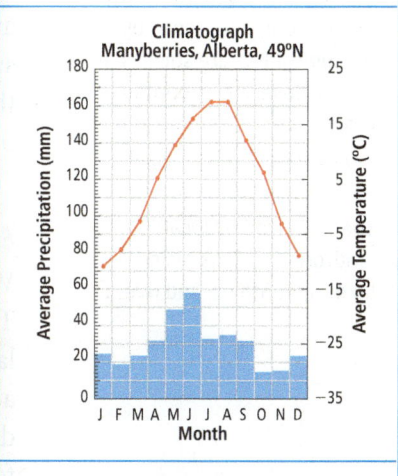

Desert

Canada's only desert zone is in southern British Columbia. It forms the northern end of the Great Basin Desert of the western United States. Rainfall is less than 25 cm annually. Plants have spiny leaves to conserve water and grow deep roots.

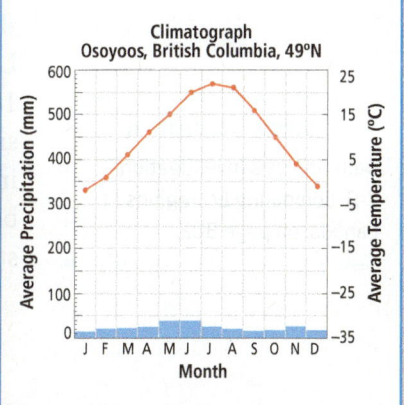

Chapter 7 Earth's Climate System • NEL 285

Go to **scienceontario** to find out more

Bioclimate Profiles

In the late 1980s, the Ontario government developed a new method of classifying climates at a glance by comparing temperature and moisture conditions in different locations over a period of several years. Graphs of climatic conditions and related factors are known as bioclimate profiles. They include such elements as

- minimum, maximum, and mean temperature
- probability of frost
- monthly total precipitation
- number of days with rain and days with snow
- water surplus and deficit

One goal for bioclimate profiles is to apply them to projected changes in climate. For example, researchers can compare bioclimate profiles of a particular region from the 1960s to 1990s with profiles from the 1990s to the present. This analysis will help governments and industries plan for such events as higher temperatures during crop growing seasons or increased demand for heating homes and buildings in winters.

Ecozones

Concerns about the effect of climate change on resource management led to the development of another classification system. That system combines climate with geology, landscape, soil, vegetation, wildlife, water, and human factors. This holistic approach classifies broad distinctive areas of land into **ecozones**. Like a biome, an ecozone is an area of Earth's surface that is characterized by particular climate features and living things. However, an ecozone is separated from neighbouring ecozones by a geological feature such as an ocean, desert, or mountain range. **Figure 7.18** shows the 15 ecozones that have been classified across Canada.

Ecoregions

Within each ecozone are smaller subdivisions known as **ecoregions**. These regions are characterized by local landforms such as plains, lakes, mountains, and rivers. Climatic conditions, wildlife, and human activities are affected by these features. Scientists have mapped 867 distinct ecoregions around the world. **Figure 7.18** shows the ecoregions found within Canada's boreal shield ecozone. In Ontario, the boreal shield ecozone contains many ecoregions, such as the LakeAbitibi and Lake Temagami ecoregions. Together, these two ecoregions cover about 18 percent of Ontario's land area. Although these ecoregions share many similar plant and animal species, white pine trees are far more common in the Lake Temagami Ecoregion. The minor climatic differences between these two ecoregions are important to conservationists who study the white pine populations.

---

ecozone a division of Earth's surface that has developed over a long period of time and is separated from neighbouring ecozones by a geological feature such as an ocean, desert, or mountain range

ecoregion a subdivision of an ecozone that is characterized by local landforms such as plains, lakes, mountains, and rivers

---

Suggested Investigation

Data Analysis Investigation 7-B, Comparing Ecoregions of Canada, on page 302

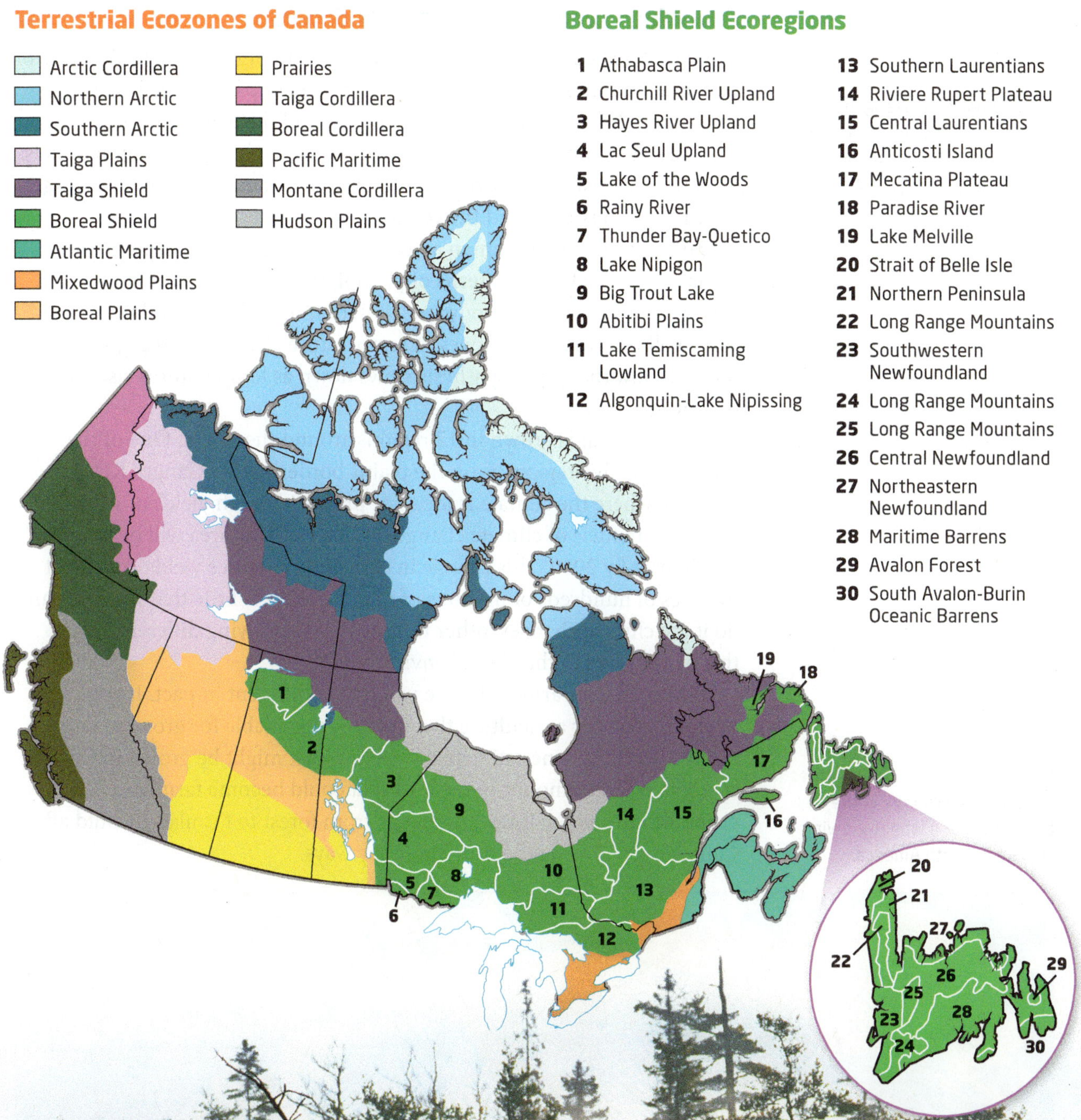

Terrestrial Ecozones of Canada

- Arctic Cordillera
- Northern Arctic
- Southern Arctic
- Taiga Plains
- Taiga Shield
- Boreal Shield
- Atlantic Maritime
- Mixedwood Plains
- Boreal Plains
- Prairies
- Taiga Cordillera
- Boreal Cordillera
- Pacific Maritime
- Montane Cordillera
- Hudson Plains

Boreal Shield Ecoregions

1. Athabasca Plain
2. Churchill River Upland
3. Hayes River Upland
4. Lac Seul Upland
5. Lake of the Woods
6. Rainy River
7. Thunder Bay-Quetico
8. Lake Nipigon
9. Big Trout Lake
10. Abitibi Plains
11. Lake Temiscaming Lowland
12. Algonquin-Lake Nipissing
13. Southern Laurentians
14. Riviere Rupert Plateau
15. Central Laurentians
16. Anticosti Island
17. Mecatina Plateau
18. Paradise River
19. Lake Melville
20. Strait of Belle Isle
21. Northern Peninsula
22. Long Range Mountains
23. Southwestern Newfoundland
24. Long Range Mountains
25. Long Range Mountains
26. Central Newfoundland
27. Northeastern Newfoundland
28. Maritime Barrens
29. Avalon Forest
30. South Avalon-Burin Oceanic Barrens

Figure 7.18 The boreal forest ecozone of Canada can be subdivided into many ecoregions. The forest shown here is located in northern Ontario.

Chapter 7 Earth's Climate System • NEL 287

Changing Climate, Changing Landscapes

Climate classification systems allow scientists to organize large amounts of information into smaller, simpler patterns. These patterns help scientists understand how and why climates vary around the world, and how climates affect other parts of the environment, such as plants and animals. Scientists can use this information to predict what effects climate change might have on society and the economy.

For example, some human activities, such as farming, depend on climate—especially on patterns of precipitation. With climate change, some regions will receive more precipitation than they do today and some will receive less. Changes in temperature also affect crop growth. Studies show that photosynthesis slows down as temperatures rise above optimum levels.

Today, wheat is grown in 12 regions around the world. One of the most productive regions is on the plains bordering the Ganges River in India, where the climate is ideal for producing high yields of wheat. However, models of climate change predict that this area will become much drier by 2050. This change in climate will reduce yields and affect the lives of hundreds of millions of people. There is little that farmers can do if the climate changes, other than switch to growing different crops that can survive in the altered environment.

In Canada, a warmer climate will have a different impact. It could open up areas for agriculture that are now unsuitable for growing crops. **Figure 7.19** shows one estimate of where wheat might be grown in Canada by 2050. A large amount of the area that could become farmland is currently covered by forest. A change from forest to farmland would affect Canada's economy and culture in many ways.

> **Suggested Investigation**
> Data Analysis Investigation 7-C, Comparing the Effects of Climate Change on Vegetation in Canada, on page 304

Figure 7.19 This map illustrates the projected change in the boundaries of a wheat-growing climate in North America.

Section 7.2 Review

Section Summary

- Climate zones can be classified based on latitude or on weather factors such as precipitation rates and temperature ranges.
- Climatographs are useful tools for studying and comparing climates.
- Climate classification systems categorize the abiotic and biotic components of a region and allow scientists to compare different parts of the world easily.
- Biomes are large regions that have similar types of organisms. Each biome is associated with a particular climate.
- Ecozones and ecoregions are subdivisions of biomes that can be used to compare the climate conditions in nearby or distant locations.
- Some human activities, such as farming, depend on climate. Changes in climate may cause people living in different parts of the world to change their lifestyles.

Review Questions

K/U 1. Into what three climate zones did ancient scientists divide Earth's surface?

K/U 2. What two benefits do climatographs have for scientists studying climate?

K/U 3. Why do scientists classify and compare climates?

C 4. Create a table similar to the one below that identifies five different ways to classify climates. In your table, include columns that describe the factors used to define categories and that identify advantages and disadvantages of each tool or system.

Advantages and Disadvantages of Climate Classification Systems

Tool/System	Description	Advantages	Disadvantages
Climatographs			
Köppen climate classification system			

K/U 5. What criticism have scientists had about the Köppen climate classification system?

A 6. If you were given only information about the monthly average temperature and monthly average precipitation of a region, what tools or systems could you use to identify and classify the climate of the region?

K/U 7. Use the maps in **Figure 7.17** and **Figure 7.18** to explain how the boreal forest biome is different from the boreal forest ecoregion.

T/I 8. If climate in Canada gets warmer, what will happen to the growing season of crops, and what effect could that change have on food supplies in Canada?

Key Terms
global warming
desertification
deforestation

7.3 Indicators and Effects of Climate Change

global warming an increase in global average temperature

The largest single indicator of climate change has been **global warming**—the increase in the average temperature of the atmosphere and oceans that has been measured over the past 100 years. The rate of increase has accelerated since the 1960s. This warming is an average for the entire planet, which means that some regions of Earth have experienced more warming than others and some have actually grown cooler during this period. The actual amount and rate of warming are also uncertain due to natural fluctuations from year to year and sources of bias resulting from where measurements have been taken. However, indirect indicators of warming, such as melting glaciers, support the evidence from direct measurements of temperature. In fact, all of the events or conditions described in this section are influenced or caused by changes in global temperatures.

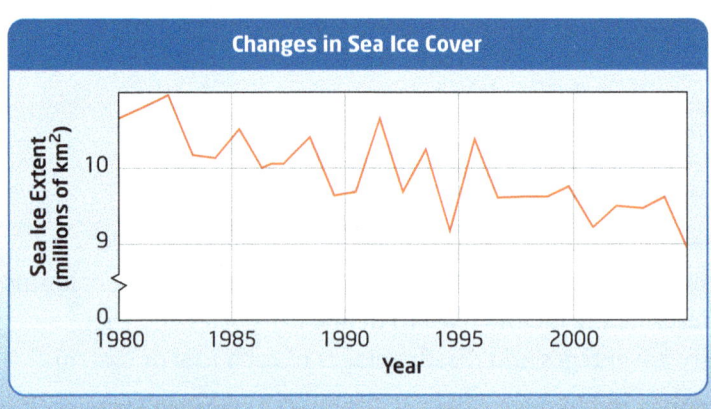

Changes in Sea Ice Cover

[Graph showing Sea Ice Extent (millions of km²) vs Year from 1980 to 2000, with values ranging from about 9 to 11]

Figure 7.20 The surface area of Arctic sea ice has been shrinking since the first satellite measurements in the late 1970s.

Changes in Polar and Glacial Ice

Satellite measurements have shown that large volumes of ice in Greenland and the Antarctic have been melting at higher rates in recent years, as shown in **Figure 7.20**. For example, the overall loss of mass in the West Antarctic ice sheet has been approximately 65 km^3 per year. That amount of melting releases enough water to raise sea levels by about 0.16 mm per year. The process that forms ice sheets is complex, and some ice sheets thicken while others grow thinner. However, the general trend has been to an overall shrinking of Earth's ice cover.

Impacts of Melting Ice

Apart from raising sea levels, melting ice affects the habitat of animals such as seals and polar bears. For example, polar bears such as the one shown in **Figure 7.21**, depend on large areas of sea ice over which they hunt their prey. As warmer temperatures melt sea ice and transform the arctic biome, polar bears in some parts of their range may be starving or ranging farther to find food. In 2007, the Wildlife Conservation Society (WCS) launched an initiative called "Warm Waters for Cool Bears." Under this initiative, landscape ecologists are studying satellite and weather data collected over 30 years to identify how sea-ice habitats are changing. This information will help scientists and policy makers decide what areas to protect as polar bear habitats.

The culture and lifestyle of Canada's Inuit population is closely tied to the environment of the Arctic and its wildlife. The traditional lifestyle of Inuit peoples involves travelling and hunting on sea ice. However, thinning and disappearing sea ice has made travelling treacherous and may make hunting for food or income more unpredictable. Political groups like the Inuit Circumpolar Council have expressed concern over the need to take action on global warming to reduce its impact on their communities. Programs, such as the Igliniit Project, have been initiated to record the weather conditions and observations made by Inuit hunters and travellers in an attempt to study how the ice is changing, and to gauge the effects of changing ice on Inuit communities.

Study Toolkit

Making Inferences A table like the one shown on page 268 can be used to organize information about causes and effects. Use this strategy to make an inference about how global warming affects polar bears.

Go to **scienceontario** to find out more

Figure 7.21 Every year, more polar bears die from starvation and from drowning as sea ice breaks up, forcing bears to swim longer distances to reach safety and food.

Making a Difference

BJ Bodnar developed a connection to nature while growing up on a farm. He uses this connection to inspire other people to confront climate change issues. When BJ was 14, he became the youngest member of the Saskatchewan Provincial Youth Advisory Committee and helped create Saskatchewan's Provincial Green Strategy. He has also served as Ambassador to the Al Gore Climate Change Symposium for Youth.

BJ has joined expeditions to the Canadian High Arctic, the Russian Arctic, and Antarctica. In 2008, BJ was named one of Canada's Top 20 Under 20 by Youth in Motion. He is studying political and international studies at the University of Saskatchewan.

If you were an advisor to the provincial government, what indicators of climate change would you focus on? Explain your answer.

Rising Sea Level and Ocean Acidity

Oceans are a major part of Earth's climate system, so any change in the oceans is a cause for concern. Climate scientists are especially concerned about sea level and ocean acidity. These indicators of climate change are described in **Table 7.2** on the next page.

The average sea level has risen between 10 and 15 cm over the past 100 years. Scientists project that the melting of ice in glaciers and icecaps outside of Greenland and Antarctica, including the approximately 150 000 km^2 of ice in Canada, could cause global sea levels to rise by 20 to 40 cm within the next 100 years. **Figure 7.22** shows which areas of the world would be submerged as sea level rises. However, the influence of tides, ocean currents, and prevailing winds will produce greater impacts in some areas and reduce impact in others.

As parts of the world's oceans become warmer, changes in ocean pH and in sea level have occurred. Research indicates that between 1751 and 2004, surface ocean pH dropped from approximately 8.25 to 8.14. Coral reefs that form in environments that are naturally high in carbon dioxide are poorly formed and are not as stable as those in waters that contain less dissolved carbon dioxide.

Figure 7.22 Rising sea level is likely a result of global warming. Many coastal areas and island nations would be flooded by relatively small changes in sea level.

Areas vulnerable to sea-level rise

Table 7.2 Effects of Climate Change on Earth's Oceans

Indicator	Cause	Effects
Rising sea level	About half of this increase is due to the observed melting of glaciers and icecaps. The other half is a result of the thermal expansion of seawater due to increased temperature.	As sea level rises, more land will be covered by water. Many of the world's largest cities are located in coastal regions, so large populations of people will be displaced by rising seas.
Rising ocean acidity	Scientists estimate that the oceans have absorbed about half of all carbon dioxide produced from fossil fuel emissions over the past 200 years. Some of the dissolved gas forms carbonic acid, which lowers the pH of the water. Lower pH means that the water is more acidic.	Rising acidity threatens the ability of corals and other organisms to build shells and hard skeletons and the ability of fish and plankton to reproduce. The success of commercial fishers who supply food to humans may also be affected, and low-lying islands and coastal areas would be more vulnerable to storms.

Activity 7-4

Acidity and Coral Reefs

How does ocean acidity affect living things? In this activity, you will model the effects of acidic ocean water on shells.

Safety Precautions

- Alert your teacher if you are allergic to eggs.
- Wash your hands thoroughly after handling acids.

Materials

- 3 glass jars or 50 mL beakers
- 20 mL water
- 20 mL vinegar
- 20 mL soft drink
- 3 pieces of chalk or eggshell
- graduated cylinder
- tongs

Procedure

1. Pour 20 mL of water into a glass jar. Pour 20 mL of vinegar into a second jar. Pour 20 mL of soft drink into a third jar.
2. Observe the surface of the pieces of chalk or eggshell. Record your observations.
3. Carefully place one piece of chalk or eggshell in each of the three glass jars. Observe and record any reactions.
4. Leave the chalk or eggshell in the jars overnight.

Eggshells contain calcium carbonate, and soft drinks are acidic.

5. The following day, use tongs to remove the chalk or eggshell from each jar.
6. Observe the surface of each piece of chalk. Record your observations.

Questions

1. What happened to the surface of the chalk or eggshell in each solution?
2. Which liquid has the highest acidity—water, vinegar, or soft drink? Explain your answer.
3. What effect would rising acidity have on the organisms that make shells from calcium carbonate?

Figure 7.23 Deer mice are carriers of hantavirus.

Climate and Health

Climate is closely connected with health—not only with the risk of disease and infections, but also the risk of injury or death due to extreme weather, such as heat waves, floods, tornadoes, lightning strikes, and snowstorms. Some of the most serious diseases that affect humans are carried by insects, rodents, birds, and other animals. For example, hantavirus is carried by mice, such as the deer mouse shown in **Figure 7.23**. Outbreaks of this infection—as well as of lyme disease, malaria, and plague—seem to increase during periods of higher temperatures. The risk of waterborne diseases also rises as climate change affects rainfall and temperature. Waterborne diseases are caused by microscopic organisms that live in water supplies.

Increasing temperatures affect the amount of dust in the air, the growth of mould, and the release of pollen by many plants. All of these substances may act as allergens and may trigger asthma attacks in some people. Scientists are researching how climate changes may contribute to an increase in the number of smog days in Ontario and elsewhere in Canada. As the air quality worsens, people who have allergies or other respiratory difficulties may have to reduce their outdoor activities. In addition, people who have respiratory problems may require medical attention, which increases health-care costs.

STSE Case Study

The Walkerton Water Tragedy

The largest waterborne multi-bacterial outbreak ever to occur in Canada happened in Walkerton, Ontario, in May of 2000. Unusually heavy rain fell for five days in a row, which caused the ground to become saturated. Run-off from a nearby farm entered one of the wells that supplied the town's drinking water. The run-off contained pathogens including *E. coli*. These pathogens made 2300 people seriously ill and killed seven people. The intense rain was the cause of the outbreak, but a number of problems combined to create the disaster. These problems included sloppy water testing and poor reporting by the workers at the water treatment facility.

Waterborne diseases are a significant health risk for humans around the world. These diseases, including giardiasis and cryptosporidiosis, occur when humans and other animals ingest bacteria, viruses, and other parasites by drinking contaminated water.

Heavy rains near farm pastures can carry protozoans and bacteria, such as the *E. coli* in the inset photo, from cow manure into drinking water supplies.

Changing Wind and Precipitation Patterns

Changes in heat distribution over Earth's surface have led to changes in wind patterns. The speed, frequency, and direction of winds over Earth's surface have fluctuated unpredictably for several years. Researchers believe that unusual wind patterns have helped increase the melting of ice in the Arctic.

High temperatures increase the rate of evaporation. When warm, moist air rises and cools in the upper atmosphere, it produces rain or snow. Since 1948, average annual temperatures across Ontario have increased by as much as 1.4°C. Average annual precipitation has also increased over this period, as shown in **Figure 7.24**. The total number of days per year on which precipitation falls has also increased. In the northern part of the province, a significant increase has occurred in the number of snowfalls and the quantity of snow during autumn.

Figure 7.24 The high Arctic has experienced the largest increase in precipitation since 1948, while regions of southwestern Canada have experienced little change in precipitation rates.

As Global Warming Increases
- precipitation and flooding increase
- run-off from streets and fields increases
- storm water systems and sewage systems overflow
- animal waste, fertilizers, and raw sewage can be diverted into drinking water reservoirs
- parasites flourish in drinking water
- waterborne disease increases

Improved Safety Net

The government responded to the Walkerton tragedy by increasing the safety measures around public drinking water. For example, water testing and inspection processes were improved. The training and licensing of water system workers were also improved and toughened. These changes and regulations have been strongly enforced.

However, more rigorous testing will not stop the water from becoming infected; the inspection process will merely alert officials if water does become contaminated. As long as the climate continues to change, our drinking water will be at risk of becoming infected.

Waterborne parasites may be spread far and wide when the micro-organisms get carried by flood waters.

Your Turn

1. What do communities need to do to prevent the spread of waterborne diseases due to increased precipitation and higher temperatures?

2. Consider the questions you would need answered if you were developing a public health strategy to prevent waterborne diseases. Create a list outlining the most important information that you would need.

3. Choose and research one of the following common waterborne diseases: cryptosporidiosis, E. coli infection, giardiasis, or cholera. Write a public service announcement (PSA) to inform the public about how climate change is affecting the nature and range of this disease.

Figure 7.25 Water shortage is a problem for many farmers. In 1988, drought caused Canada's total grain production to drop by nearly one third.

desertification the process by which land slowly dries out until little or no vegetation can survive and the land becomes a desert

Sense of scale

Between April 1998 and May 1999, a fall in the levels of the Great Lakes resulted in the loss of about 120 km³ of water from the system. That volume of water takes almost two years to flow over Niagara Falls.

Figure 7.26 When this street collapsed in Toronto in 2005, it damaged two high-pressure gas pipes, a drinking-water pipe, and telephone, hydro, and cable service lines that were buried beneath the road.

Desertification, Droughts, and Other Outcomes

An increase or decrease in precipitation affects the levels of reservoirs and ground water used for drinking water. Declines in precipitation can lead to **desertification**—the spread of deserts that have a reduced capacity to support life. Desertification may lead to famines as once-farmable land becomes unable to support crops. As average temperatures rise, crop losses from drought will increase, as shown in **Figure 7.25**.

According to some sources, about half of the nations in the world may experience water shortages by 2025. By 2050, nearly 75 percent of the world's population may be affected by the scarcity of fresh water. These shortages will affect not only countries in the dry, desert regions of the world, such as northern Africa and the Middle East, but also large parts of North America. However, experts think that new technologies and policy changes may help reduce the impact of these shortages. In addition, many water conservation efforts are in place to help conserve this important natural resource.

Storm Intensity and Frequency

In August 2005, an intense storm system moved across southwestern Ontario. Up to 153 mm of rain fell during a period of about four hours. By the time the storm had passed, it had caused more than $400 million in damage, including the damage shown in **Figure 7.26**. Every year, flooding, heavy rains, and strong winds cause extensive damage to buildings, bridges, and roads. Storms also disrupt electrical service and put people in physical danger.

Extreme storms remind people in a dramatic way of how climate affects our lives. Hurricanes are the most violent storms on Earth. They form over the tropical oceans during late summer and early fall when surface waters store the greatest amount of heat. The temperatures of the tropical waters where these tropical storms begin have increased by about 0.33°C since 1981. Over the same period, a statistically significant increase in the maximum wind speeds of the strongest hurricanes has occurred. In other words, the strongest storms have become stronger. These data are consistent with the hypothesis that warmer seas hold more energy to convert to hurricane-speed winds.

Learning Check

1. How have changes in winds affected the amount of polar ice?
2. How might desertification affect food supplies for humans?
3. Based on the information in **Figure 7.24**, how have precipitation rates changed in Ontario since 1948?
4. Create a flowchart that shows how rising global temperature affects the likelihood that Canadians may contract waterborne diseases.

Changing Biomes

As climate conditions change, the plants and animals that are adapted to a particular region may no longer be able to survive there. An international team of researchers recently studied the likely effects of climate change on biodiversity in six different regions around the world. The data showed that 15 to 35 percent of the 1103 species in the study were at risk of extinction by 2050. The scientists then extrapolated these results to the entire planet, including ocean ecosystems. The scientists concluded that more than one million species are threatened with extinction worldwide as a result of climate change. **Figure 7.27** summarizes some of the global impacts of climate change that you have read about in this section.

Figure 7.27 This map shows how climate change could affect all nations of the world.

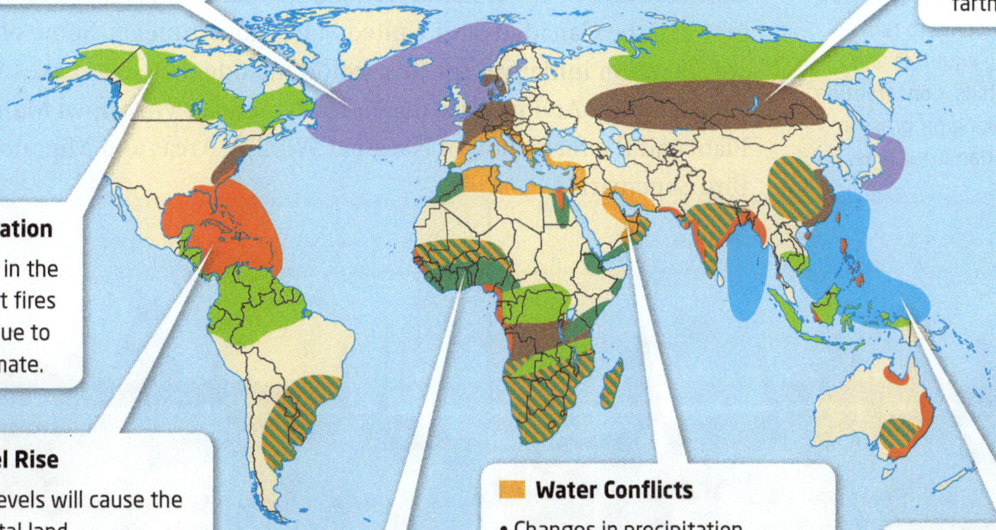

Main Fisheries Affected
- Changes in the food supply will affect international trade.

Greater Disease Risk
- Some diseases, such as malaria and other tropical diseases, will occur farther north.

Deforestation
- An increase in the risk of forest fires may occur due to a drying climate.

Sea-Level Rise
- Rising sea levels will cause the loss of coastal land.
- The potential for flood damage to low-lying coastal areas will increase.
- Large numbers of people will move away from affected areas.

Water Conflicts
- Changes in precipitation patterns will cause the demand for water to surpass the supply.

Decreasing Crop Yields
- Changes in agriculture and the food supply will affect international trade.

Increased Severity and Frequency of Tropical Storms
- Large numbers of people will move away from affected areas.

Chapter 7 Earth's Climate System • NEL 297

Figure 7.28 The brown trees in this photo were damaged by mountain pine beetles. The spread of this beetle has been directly linked to the warming climate.

deforestation the destruction of the world's forests through direct human activity, such as logging or slash-and-burn clearing for agriculture and grazing, and through the indirect effects of climate change, pollution, and acid rain

Figure 7.29 The Beverly Swamp, in southern Ontario, is a wetland habitat that is home to rare northern flying squirrels and grass-pink orchids. Conservation groups are making progress in protecting wetlands such as this one.

Deforestation

The removal of trees and forests from an area is known as **deforestation**. A shrinking forest area reduces the amount of carbon dioxide (CO_2) absorbed from the atmosphere by photosynthesis. Thus, loss of trees affects climate by increasing the amount of carbon dioxide in the air.

Deforestation may occur as a result of natural phenomena or human activities. For example, global warming may lead to hot, dry summers that provide ideal conditions for forest fires. In western Canada, infestations of mountain pine beetle have killed huge areas of forest, as shown in **Figure 7.28**. In parts of eastern Canada, forests have been damaged by air pollution and acid precipitation. In addition, humans may actively clear land of forests in order to use the wood or the land.

Canada's local, provincial, and national governments have implemented many programs to protect forests and to promote reforestation. For example, in 2006, the First Nations Forestry Council received $8.4 million to respond to the damage caused by mountain pine beetles. In addition to local and national programs, many private companies provide reforestation services.

Shrinking Wetlands–and Efforts to Save Them

Besides supplying water for human needs, freshwater ecosystems play an important role in regulating climate. Wetlands, such as the one shown in **Figure 7.29**, include marshes, bogs, fens, and swamps. These ecosystems store and filter water. They are also habitats for plants that remove carbon dioxide from the air, and for a variety of animals.

Lower water levels in the Great Lakes will dry out wetlands around the shoreline, reducing habitat for wetland species of plants and animals. Conservation of Great Lakes wetland habitats has required co-operation between the Canadian and United States governments. Some of the conservation initiatives for this region include the Great Lakes Wetlands Conservation Action Plan, the North American Waterfowl Management Plan, and the formation of National Wildlife Areas and Migratory Bird Sanctuaries.

Section 7.3 Review

Section Summary

- Global warming is the increase in the average temperature of the atmosphere and oceans over the past 100 years. It is the largest single indicator of recent climate change.
- As global temperature rises, polar icecaps are melting, which affects the lives of Arctic mammals, such as polar bears, and of traditional Inuit peoples of Canada.
- As atmospheric and ocean temperatures increase, sea level is rising. Rising sea level will affect large populations of humans who live on islands and along the coasts of the world's continents.
- As the global oceans absorb more carbon dioxide, the water becomes more acidic, which threatens coral reefs and oceanic food chains.
- Changes in wind and precipitation result from global warming. These changes may lead to water shortages throughout the world and possibly to more frequent and stronger storms.
- Climate change may affect the health of humans by increasing the incidence of certain diseases.
- Deforestation and desertification may result from higher temperatures and changes in precipitation.

Review Questions

K/U 1. What is the most important indicator of global climate change in recent years?

K/U 2. How does global warming affect sea level?

K/U 3. How might a warming climate affect human health?

C 4. The graph below shows the number of people who visited doctors for skin disorders between January 1967 and January 1971. Write a paragraph that summarizes the relationship between temperature, humidity, and the number of skin diseases reported during that timeframe.

K/U 5. Explain how an increase in average temperature might lead to an increase in precipitation in a region.

A 6. Why is a changing climate more of a threat to forests than to agricultural crops?

T/I 7. Is it reasonable to conclude that because the 2005 hurricane season produced a record number of storms and some of the strongest storms in history, global warming is causing an increase in the number and intensity of hurricanes? Explain your answer.

K/U 8. How does climate change affect the biodiversity of a region?

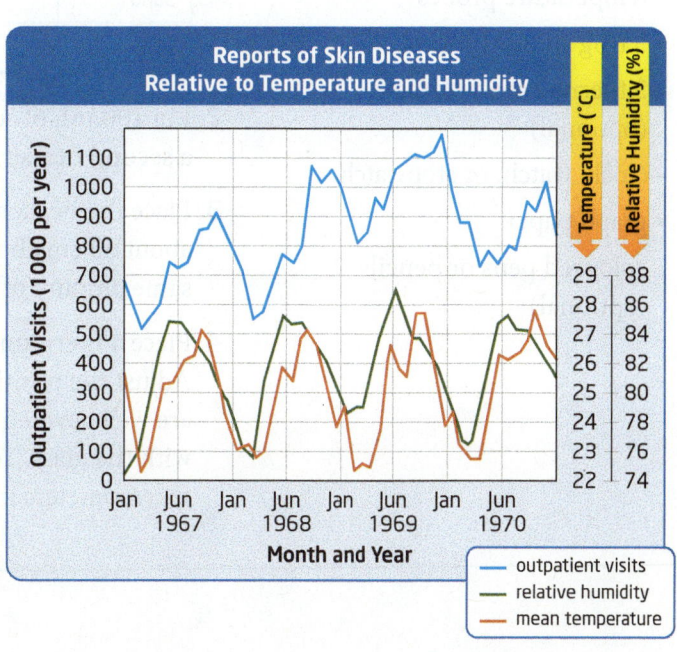

Reports of Skin Diseases Relative to Temperature and Humidity
- outpatient visits
- relative humidity
- mean temperature

Inquiry Investigation 7-A

Skill Check

Initiating and Planning

✓ Performing and Recording

✓ Analyzing and Interpreting

✓ Communicating

Safety Precautions

- Use caution when handling the lamp; the light bulb will become very hot.

Materials

- three 600 mL beakers
- scoopula
- 100 mL dark-coloured soil
- 100 mL light-coloured sand
- 100 mL cold water
- 100 W light bulb
- lamp or light bulb socket with clamp
- 3 thermometers or temperature probes
- 3 ring stands (optional)
- 3 thermometer clamps (optional)
- clock, watch, or stopwatch
- graph paper
- coloured pens or pencils (optional)

Specific Heat Capacity of Earth Materials

The amount of light reflected by different surfaces changes the amount of heat in the Earth system. In this investigation, you will use light to heat materials and test each material's specific heat capacity.

Question

How do different materials absorb and release electromagnetic radiation?

Procedure

1. In your notebook, draw two tables similar to the ones shown below. Give each table a title.

Table 1

Materials	Starting Time (min)	Starting Tempature (°C)	Warming Temperature at Each Minute (°C)
Soil			
Sand			
Water			

Table 2

Materials	Starting Time (min)	Starting Tempature (°C)	Cooling Temperature at Each Minute (°C)
Soil			
Sand			
Water			

2. Put 100 mL of soil in one of the beakers, 100 mL of sand in a second beaker, and 100 mL of water in the third beaker.

3. Place the beakers on a desk or workbench. Position the lamp about 30 cm above the beakers so that each receives about the same amount of light.

4. Place a thermometer or temperature probe in each beaker. Adjust the position of the thermometers or probes so that they are well covered by the material in the beakers but not in contact with the glass. You may use ring stands and clamps to keep the thermometers in place.

5. In your first data table, record the starting temperature of the material in each beaker.

6. Turn on the lamp and note the time (or start the stopwatch). Record the temperature for each beaker every minute for 10 min.

7. After 10 min, turn off the lamp. In your second data table, record the temperature for each beaker every minute for the next 10 min.

8. Clean up and put away the equipment you have used. Soil and sand should be collected for re-use and should not be placed in the trash or in drains.

9. Use the data from your tables to graph the heating and cooling of each of the materials. Use a different colour or symbol for each material.

Analyze and Interpret

1. Which material absorbed the most thermal energy in the first 10 min? Which material lost the most thermal energy in the last 10 min?

2. Identify any sources of error in this investigation.

Conclude and Communicate

3. a. Of the three materials you used, which would heat up the fastest on a sunny day?

   b. Which would take the longest to cool down at night?

4. How might the type of surface (such as dark rock, water, snow) in an area affect the temperature of the atmosphere above it?

Extend Your Inquiry and Research Skills

5. **Inquiry** Use 50 mL water to moisten the sand and the soil samples. Repeat the temperature measurements. What differences did you observe? How does water affect the rate at which the soil and sand heated up and cooled down?

6. **Research** Research the specific heat capacity of the following Earth materials: granite, water, ice, and asphalt. Predict which material would increase the temperature of the atmosphere above it most rapidly. Design an experiment to test your prediction.

Which material absorbs and releases heat most rapidly?

Data Analysis Investigation 7-B

Skill Check

Initiating and Planning

Performing and Recording

✓ Analyzing and Interpreting

✓ Communicating

Materials

- map of Canadian ecozones
- map of Ontario ecoregions

Comparing Ecoregions of Canada

Understanding local and global climate concerns starts with understanding your local climate. In this investigation, you will identify the ecoregion and ecozone in which you live. Then, you will compare that ecozone and ecoregion to other areas of Ontario and Canada.

Question

How do the ecoregions of Ontario compare to other ecoregions in Ontario and in Canada?

Analyze and Interpret

1. Look at the map of Canada's ecozones on page 287. Identify and record the ecozones that are found in Ontario.

2. Identify the ecozone in which you live.

3. How many ecoregions are located in Ontario? Describe the breakdown of ecoregions by ecozone.

4. Use the map on page 287 to identify the ecoregion in which you live.

5. The table on the next page summarizes the characteristics of each of Ontario's ecozones. Use the table to compare the boreal forest ecozone with the Hudson plains ecozone. Summarize how they are different and how they are the same.

6. Use a Venn diagram and the information in the table to summarize how the mixed-wood ecozone differs from the boreal forest ecozone.

This tree is part of the mixed-wood forest in Algonquin Park, Ontario.

302 NEL • Unit 3 Climate Change

Conclude and Communicate

7. Why have some of the ecozones not attracted much human habitation?

8. All of these ecozones are expected to become warmer and drier as climate changes. Compare how this change will affect life in the ecozones in Ontario.

9. Why is understanding the different ecoregions and ecozones of the world important? How do humans use this information?

Extend Your Inquiry and Research Skills

10. **Research** Some scientists predict that the ecozones of Canada will shift as a result of global warming. Research these predictions and create a map that shows how Canada's ecozones may be distributed in the future if current climate trends continue.

11. **Research** The location of major cities hasn't changed much in Ontario since humans began building permanent housing, but throughout world history cities have been founded and abandoned based on climate changes. Research this phenomenon and make a multimedia presentation that describes how a warmer, drier climate may affect where Ontario's big cities are likely to be located in 2100.

Characteristics of Ecozones in Canada

Ecozone in Ontario	Mean Temperatures and Location	Vegetation	Landscape	Defining Features
Hudson plains	• summer high +15°C or below • winter −30°C or below • on south edge of Hudson Bay	• scrub above the tree line • bushes, flowers, aquatic vegetation below the tree line	• flat, wet clay plains drained by many rivers • mostly swamps and bogs, some rocks	• endless black flies and mosquitoes • animals not used to human presence • this region is very lightly settled by humans
Boreal forest	• summer high below +20°C • winter low −20 to +40°C • north of a line from Sudbury to North Bay (the north half of the road map)	• primarily forest–mostly coniferous, some birch and beech • shrubs and grass	• flat, swampy clay plains with rivers in north • hilly with many lakes and rivers, but little soil in south	• most of the forest is second or third growth • large animals exist but are comfortable with human presence • settlements are areas near highways, on rivers for lumber and paper mills, or at mines
Mixed-wood forest	• summer high 15-25°C • winter low above −20°C • south of a line from Sudbury to North Bay (the south half of the road map)	• mixed coniferous and deciduous trees–maple, pine, originally oak • mostly logged and developed as farms or cities, though forest has reclaimed the northern portions	• thin soils and lots of lakes and rivers in north • well-drained, fertile soils in south with few rivers or lakes • gentle hills	• human population is not restricted to areas near major highways • little original vegetation remains • most large, native animals have been extirpated • farming is possible

Data Analysis Investigation 7-C

Skill Check

Initiating and Planning

Performing and Recording

✓ Analyzing and Interpreting

✓ Communicating

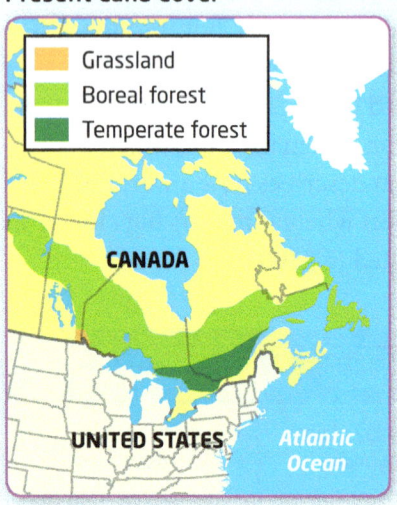

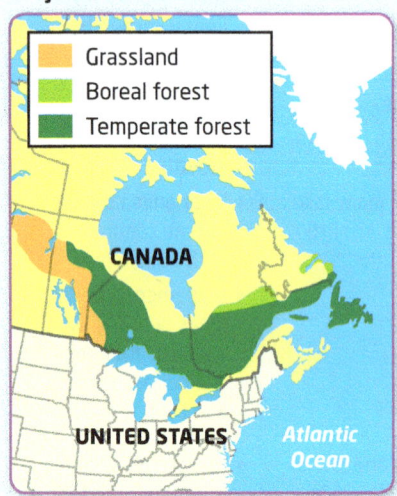

Comparing the Effects of Climate Change on Vegetation in Canada

Predictions made by climate scientists suggest that significant warming will occur in Canada over the next century as a result of global warming. How could this warming trend affect the living things in southern Canada? In this activity, you will evaluate the change in land cover that could occur in Ontario as a result of these climatic and ecological changes.

Organize the Data

1. Use the map labelled "Present Land Cover" to answer the following questions:
   a. Which vegetation zones are represented in Ontario?
   b. Which vegetation zone currently covers the largest area of the boreal shield?

2. Use the map labelled "Projected Land Cover in 100 Years" to answer the following questions:
   a. What vegetation zones do scientists predict will exist in Ontario a century from now?
   b. What vegetation zone is projected to cover the largest area of the boreal shield in 100 years?

Analyze and Interpret

1. Why didn't the boreal forest biome move northward in the second map?

2. What human activities may lead to the expansion of grasslands in western Canada?

Conclude and Communicate

3. The economy of communities in the boreal shield region is based heavily on natural resources. The forestry industry of Québec and Ontario produces nearly $20 billion in exports each year. How might the projected shift in vegetation affect this industry?

4. If all of Canada's vegetation zones shift northward as a result of climate change, how would the permanent ice biome be affected?

Extend Your Inquiry and Research Skills

5. **Inquiry** In the Niagara fruit belt in southern Ontario, farmers grow cherries, peaches, strawberries, and grapes for harvest in June through September. How do you think the projected shift in climate and vegetation will affect the Niagara fruit belt?

Present Land Cover

- Grassland
- Boreal forest
- Temperate forest

Projected Land Cover in 100 Years

- Grassland
- Boreal forest
- Temperate forest

Chapter 7 Summary

7.1 Factors That Affect Climate Change

Key Concepts

- Climate describes the standard weather conditions for a region at a given time of year, averaged over a long period of time. This includes expected temperatures, winds, precipitation, probability of storms, and hours of direct sunshine.
- The amount of energy that a location on the surface of Earth receives at any given time is determined by the angle of the Sun, which in turn depends on the latitude, time of year, and time of day.
- Winds, ocean currents, and the shape and size of continents affect climate.
- Earth reflects some of the solar energy that hits it back into space. The fraction of energy that is reflected by a surface is called albedo.
- Volcanic eruptions introduce gases and particles into the air that affect the reflection and absorption of energy from the Sun.
- Human activity affects climate by introducing particles and gases into the atmosphere that affect the absorption and transfer of energy from the Sun.

7.2 Describing Climates

Key Concepts

- Climate zones can be classified based on latitude or on weather factors such as precipitation rates and temperature ranges.
- Climatographs are useful tools for studying and comparing climates.
- Climate classification systems categorize the abiotic and biotic components of a region and allow scientists to compare different parts of the world easily.
- Biomes are large regions that have similar types of organisms. Each biome is associated with a particular climate.
- Ecozones and ecoregions are subdivisions of biomes and can be used to compare the climate conditions in nearby or distant locations.
- Some human activities, such as farming, depend on climate. Changes in climate may cause people living in different parts of the world to change their lifestyles.

7.3 Indicators and Effects of Climate Change

Key Concepts

- Global warming is the increase in the average temperature of the atmosphere and oceans over the past 100 years. It is the largest single indicator of recent climate change.
- As global temperature rises, polar icecaps are melting, which affects the lives of Arctic mammals, such as polar bears, and of traditional Inuit peoples of Canada.
- As atmospheric and ocean temperatures increase, sea level is rising. Rising sea level will affect large populations of humans who live on islands and along the coasts of the world's continents.
- As the global oceans absorb more carbon dioxide, the water becomes more acidic, which threatens coral reefs and oceanic food chains.
- Changes in wind and precipitation result from global warming. These changes may lead to water shortages throughout the world and possibly to more frequent and stronger storms.
- Climate change may affect the health of humans by increasing the incidence of certain diseases.
- Deforestation and desertification may result from higher temperatures and changes in precipitation.

Chapter 7 Review

Make Your Own Summary

Summarize the key concepts of this chapter using a graphic organizer. The Chapter Summary on the previous page will help you identify the key concepts. Refer to Study Toolkit 4 on pages 565-566 to help you decide which graphic organizer to use.

Reviewing Key Terms

1. The average conditions of the atmosphere in a region over an extended period of time can be described as that region's _____. (7.1)

2. The _____ describes how gases in Earth's atmosphere absorb and release heat. (7.1)

3. The movement of _____ affects the locations and shapes of continents and oceans. (7.1)

4. Some climate change may be _____, which means it is caused by human activity. (7.1)

5. The average monthly temperature and average monthly precipitation for a region can be plotted on a _____. (7.2)

6. A _____ is a region of Earth's surface that is characterized by specific biotic and abiotic characteristics. (7.2)

7. Ecozones can be subdivided into smaller areas called _____. (7.2)

8. _____ is an increase in the average temperature of the air and water for the entire planet. (7.3)

9. Droughts and long-term declines in precipitation may lead to _____. (7.3)

10. The destruction of forests, called _____, can be caused by natural or anthropogenic factors. (7.3)

Knowledge and Understanding K/U

11. What is the hydrosphere?

12. The graphic below shows two orbits around the Sun. Which orbit, the red or the yellow, provides Earth with more consistent intensity of energy throughout the year? Explain your choice.

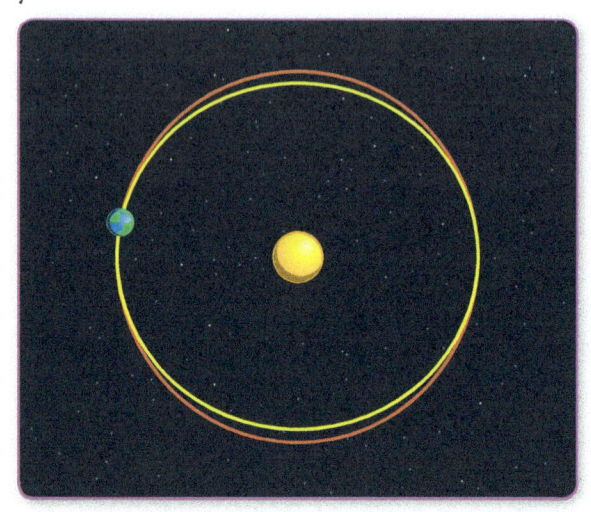

13. Summarize the greenhouse effect.

14. What causes the seasons?

15. List these events in order from fastest to slowest in terms of their ability to change the climate: change in ocean currents, formation of a mountain range, volcanic eruption, melting of a polar icecap.

16. About what percent of Earth's species are considered at risk of extinction due to climate change?

17. What is the value of climate classification systems such as the Köppen climate classification system?

18. How could the formation of a mountain range cause a desert to form?

19. How does Earth's albedo today differ from the albedo 20 000 years ago, during the last glacial period?

20. Explain why scientists do not classify climates based only on temperature records.

306 NEL • Unit 3 Climate Change

Thinking and Investigation T/I

21. How could decreases in precipitation cause water shortages around the world?

22. How can a volcanic eruption halfway around the world affect weather in Canada?

23. The graph below is a climatograph for Welland, Ontario. What does this graph tell you about the variation in monthly precipitation in Welland?

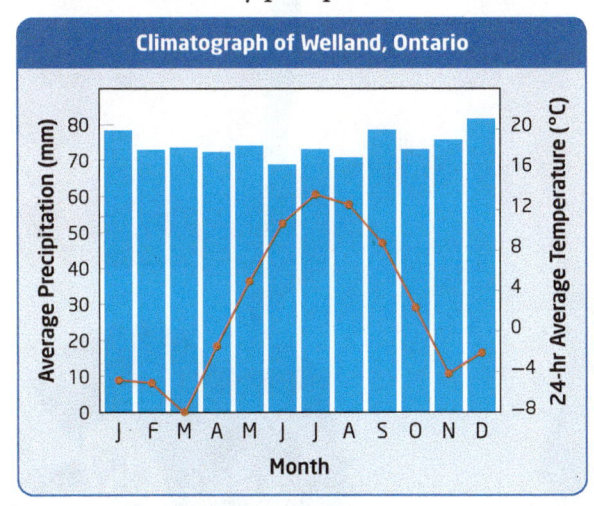

Climatograph of Welland, Ontario

24. How can the climate be predicted for 10 years in the future even if we don't know what the weather will be like in 10 days?

25. Other than the growing season of crops, what consequences are there to having a warmer climate in Canada?

Communication C

26. **BIG IDEAS** Earth's climate is dynamic and is the result of interacting systems and processes. Write a brief summary that describes how latitude, proximity to large bodies of water, and location of jet streams affect the climate of Ontario.

27. **BIG IDEAS** Global climate change is influenced by both natural and human factors. Create a table that describes how the following factors affect climate: solar activity; Earth's orbit, tilt, and rotation; latitude; winds; ocean currents; albedo; tectonic plate movement; and human activity. Include information about how each factor changes climate and how long each factor takes to affect climate. Give your table a title.

28. **BIG IDEAS** Climate change affects living things and natural systems in a variety of ways. Create a graphic novel that illustrates how global warming may affect polar bears and humans in Canada over the next 50 years.

29. **BIG IDEAS** People have the responsibility to assess their impact on climate change and to identify effective courses of action to reduce this impact. Create a multimedia presentation that explains how the actions of people in Ontario have contributed to anthropogenic climate change. Suggest courses of action that the people of Ontario could take to reduce their contribution to climate change.

30. Create a flowchart that shows how climate change can result in increasing incidence of waterborne diseases in humans.

Application A

31. How might snowier winters slow global warming?

32. An argument against taking action on climate change is that we do not know what changes would have taken place without us, so we cannot know what effect our actions are having on the environment. How can scientists tell which changes are created by human activities and which are not?

33. Describe how an increase in the number and intensity of hurricanes in the Atlantic Ocean could affect Ontario.

34. Why does a climatograph have scales on both the right and left sides?

35. Scientists agree that warmer oceans lead to stronger and more frequent storms. However, evidence suggests that a century-long hurricane cycle may explain the increased intensity and frequency of hurricanes in recent years. If this pattern does exist, how would the intensity and frequency of hurricanes change over the next few decades? Explain your answer.

Chapter 7 Earth's Climate System • NEL 307

Chapter 8 Dynamics of Climate Change

What You Will Learn

In this chapter, you will learn how to...

- **describe** and **explain** heat transfer in Earth's climate system
- **describe** the natural greenhouse effect and **distinguish** it from the anthropogenic greenhouse effect
- **describe** the principal sources and sinks of greenhouse gases

Why It Matters

Recent climate change has been driven by changes in Earth's atmosphere that have affected how heat is transferred through Earth's atmosphere and oceans. By recognizing how human activities alter these natural processes, we can understand how humans affect climate change and can act to reduce our impact.

Skills You Will Use

In this chapter, you will learn how to...

- **investigate** the effects of heat transfer within Earth's oceans and atmosphere
- **design** and **build** a model of the natural greenhouse effect

Every living thing on Earth is affected by climate, so even cows are becoming part of the solution! Cows and other livestock produce a lot of gas, which affects climate. By attaching tubes to the digestive tracts of cows, researchers hope to reduce the amount of these emissions. In this chapter, you will learn how natural processes transfer heat throughout Earth's surface. Then you will learn how human activities, such as agriculture, alter these natural processes.

Activity 8-1

Modelling Balance in Systems

How do changes in the balance of energy and matter affect climate? In this activity, you will use water to model the flow of matter and energy through a system.

Safety Precaution

Materials
- basin or tub
- plastic or paper cup
- 1 L of water
- pitcher
- ruler
- tool to make a hole

The amount of energy and matter that enters a system usually equals the amount that exits the system.

Procedure

1. Use a tool to poke a hole in the bottom of a plastic or paper cup.
2. Position the cup over a tub or basin.
3. Slowly pour 1 L of water into the cup. Observe what happens to the water, and record your observations.
4. Return the water to the pitcher.
5. Position the cup over the tub or basin again.
6. Pour the water into the cup as quickly as possible. Observe what happens to the water, and record your observations.

Questions

1. In step 3, you modelled a balanced system. How does the amount of energy or matter that enters the system relate to the amount of energy or matter that leaves the system?
2. In step 6, you modelled an unbalanced system. Identify all of the variables that could be changed to restore balance to the system.
3. How do you think changing the composition of the atmosphere could change the climate system?

Study Toolkit

These strategies will help you use this textbook to develop your understanding of science concepts and skills. To find out more about these and other strategies, refer to the Study Toolkit Overview, which begins on page 560.

Reading Effectively

Making Connections to Visuals

Visuals can clarify or expand on information in the text. Making connections to visuals will help you understand their purpose and meaning. For example, look at the photograph below (shown on page 328), and read the caption. Then think about answers to these questions:

1. What personal connections can I make to the visual, based on my prior knowledge?
2. What can I learn about the visual from the caption and the accompanying text?
3. What does the visual *not* show?

Vehicle exhaust is a direct source of greenhouse gases. It is also an indirect source of ground-level ozone.

Use the Strategy

With a partner, examine **Figure 8.19** on page 331. Discuss your answers to the questions above.

Word Study

Word Parts

To better understand long, unfamiliar words, break the words into parts. Combine the meanings of the parts to infer the definition of the unfamiliar word. For example, the word *interdependent* has the base word *depend* (to rely on), the prefix *inter-* (between or among), and the suffix *-ent* (in a state of). Combining the meanings of these word parts gives you the following definition of *interdependent*: in a state of relying on one another.

Use the Strategy

Break the word *chlorofluorocarbon* into parts. Determine what each word part means. Then combine the meanings of the word parts to infer a definition of the whole word. Use the context in which the word appears to check that your definition makes sense. Confirm your definition by using a dictionary or the Glossary at the end of this textbook.

Organizing Your Learning

Synthesizing

Synthesizing involves processing information from a variety of sources to gain a new understanding of a topic. Use sources such as this textbook, other books, your own prior knowledge, and different opinions (your own and other people's). Then combine all the information you gathered in an original way.

For example, you learned about climate change in Chapter 7. The **flowchart** on the right shows the process you might follow to synthesize your understanding of climate change.

Use the Strategy

Follow the steps in the flowchart to synthesize information about the main topic in Section 8.2.

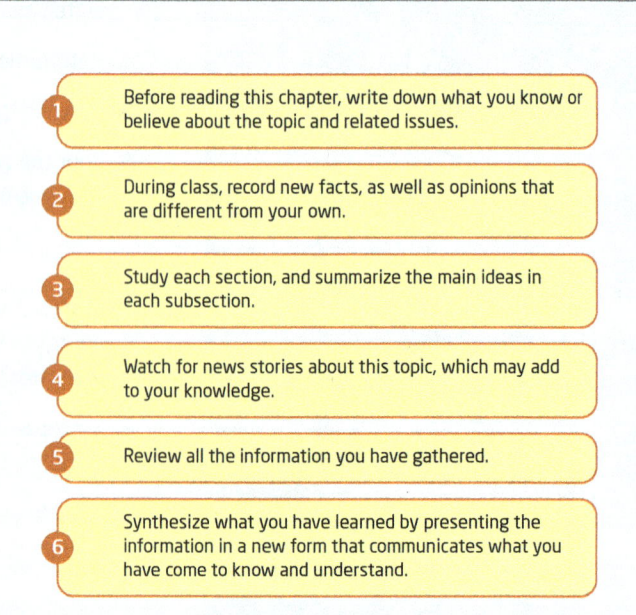

1. Before reading this chapter, write down what you know or believe about the topic and related issues.
2. During class, record new facts, as well as opinions that are different from your own.
3. Study each section, and summarize the main ideas in each subsection.
4. Watch for news stories about this topic, which may add to your knowledge.
5. Review all the information you have gathered.
6. Synthesize what you have learned by presenting the information in a new form that communicates what you have come to know and understand.

8.1 Energy Transfer in the Climate System

Key Terms
system
feedback loop
electromagnetic radiation
thermohaline circulation
energy budget

Earth's climate is a complex system. A **system** consists of a combination of parts that function as a whole. For example, your digestive system is made up of organs that work together to digest your food. Scientists further divide the systems they study into two major types: open systems and closed systems.

An *open system* is a system in which energy and matter cross the system's boundary. Your body is an open system, as shown in **Figure 8.1**. You take in food, water, and oxygen, and you release waste materials and heat.

A *closed system* is a system that allows energy but not matter to cross the system's boundary. The upper edge of the atmosphere marks the outer boundary of Earth's climate system. Although meteors bring small amounts of matter into Earth's climate system and hydrogen atoms sometimes escape Earth's atmosphere and move into space, Earth generally behaves like a closed system. Energy from the Sun continually flows into Earth's atmosphere and eventually passes back out into space. Nearly all the matter that forms the land, oceans, atmosphere, and living things on the planet remains within the system's boundary.

Earth maintains a temperature balance by radiating as much energy out into space as it absorbs from the Sun. Between the time solar energy is absorbed and the time it passes back into space, it produces wind, rain, ocean currents, fog, snow, and all of the other features of Earth's climate system.

system a group of interdependent parts that work together to form a single, functioning whole

Go to **scienceontario** to find out more

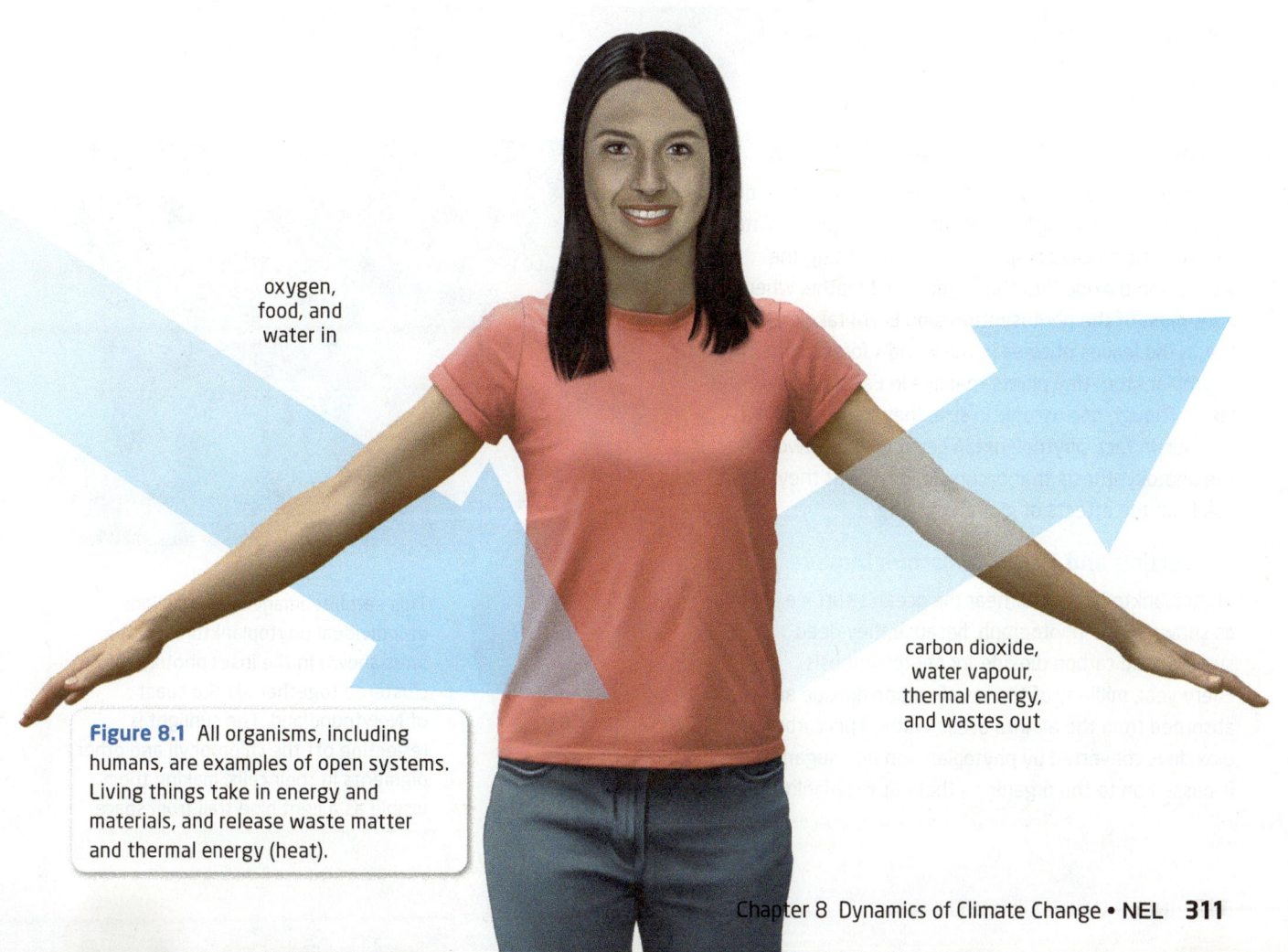

oxygen, food, and water in

carbon dioxide, water vapour, thermal energy, and wastes out

Figure 8.1 All organisms, including humans, are examples of open systems. Living things take in energy and materials, and release waste matter and thermal energy (heat).

Effects of Feedback Loops on the Earth System

feedback loop a process in which part of a system's output is returned, or fed back, to the input

As a closed system, Earth must constantly cycle the matter and energy within its boundary. Interactions among different forms of matter and energy in Earth's climate system often create feedback loops. A **feedback loop** is a process in which part of a system's output is returned (fed back) to the input. In Earth's climate system, many feedback loops affect the conditions of the atmosphere, ocean, and land.

Positive Feedback Loops

A *positive feedback loop* acts to increase the effects of the interacting parts. For example, the effect of melting ice on albedo, as shown in **Figure 8.2**, is a positive feedback loop. Because of positive feedback loops, small initial changes in climate can lead to larger and larger changes before the system as a whole achieves a new balance.

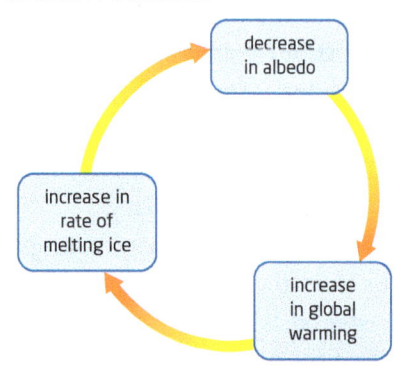

Figure 8.2 This diagram shows a positive feedback loop that involves rising temperatures, decreasing albedo, and melting polar and glacial ice.

decrease in albedo → increase in global warming → increase in rate of melting ice

STSE Case Study

Overheating the Ocean's Forests

It is a well-known fact that all living things on Earth depend on plants for survival. Why? Plants perform photosynthesis, which is the process responsible for converting the gas carbon dioxide into the oxygen we breathe. Where does most of the photosynthesis on Earth take place? Not in the leaves of trees in the world's forests, but in phytoplankton–tiny plants that live in Earth's oceans and lakes. Though microscopic in size, they are abundant in number. In fact, phytoplankton perform about two thirds of the photosynthesis that occurs on Earth. But they are at risk from the effects of global warming.

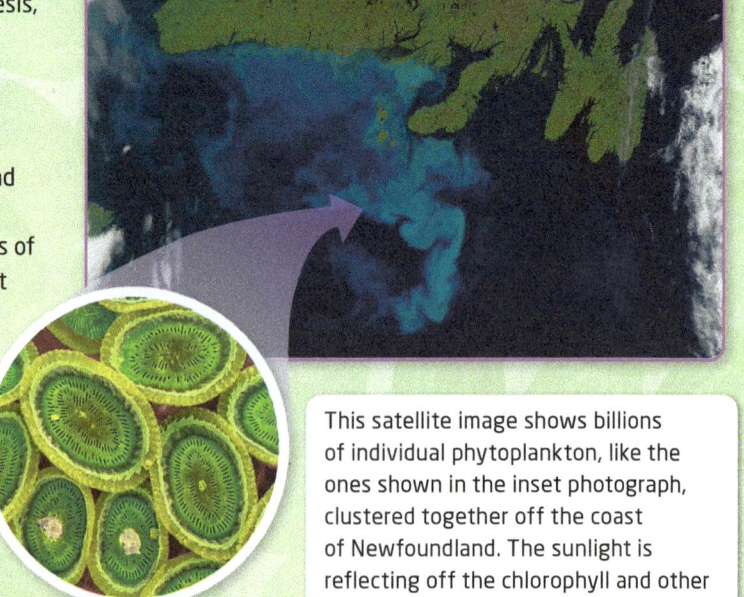

Converting and Trapping Carbon Dioxide

Phytoplankton live at or near the ocean's surface, as shown in the photograph, because they need sunlight and carbon dioxide for photosynthesis. Every year, millions of tonnes of carbon dioxide are absorbed from the air into ocean water. This carbon dioxide is converted by phytoplankton into sugars and is passed on to the organisms that eat the plankton.

This satellite image shows billions of individual phytoplankton, like the ones shown in the inset photograph, clustered together off the coast of Newfoundland. The sunlight is reflecting off the chlorophyll and other pigments in their cells, making them visible as a light blue trail from space.

Negative Feedback Loops

A *negative feedback loop* decreases the effects of the interacting parts and helps to maintain a system's equilibrium. In other words, the processes in a negative feedback loop act as checks and balances to prevent, slow, or reverse change in a system. For example, global warming increases the rate of evaporation of water. An increase in water vapour in the atmosphere creates more clouds. An increase in cloud cover increases albedo, which has a cooling effect. Therefore, although the feedback loop began with global warming, the net result of the feedback loop is a decrease in global average temperature. This process is shown in **Figure 8.3**.

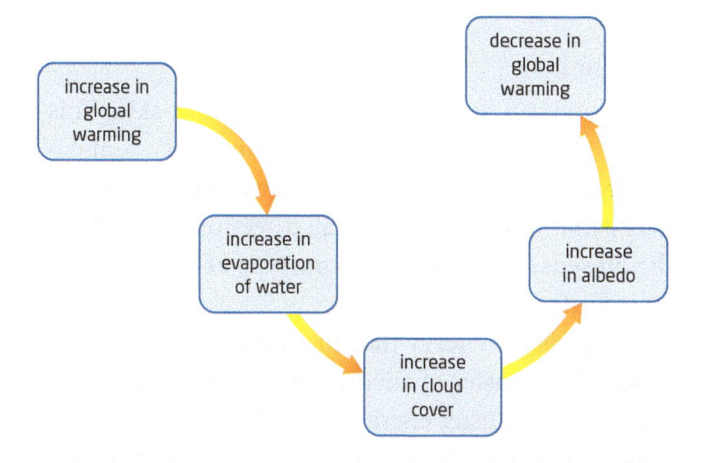

Figure 8.3 This diagram shows a negative feedback loop. It demonstrates how an increase in evaporation can reduce global warming.

When phytoplankton die, they sink to the bottom of the ocean, where the carbon that is inside their cells gets trapped. The larger the population of phytoplankton is, the more carbon will be removed from Earth's atmosphere.

Phytoplankton at Risk

Nutrient-rich water from the deep ocean comes to the surface through a process called upwelling. When warm surface waters do not move away from shore, upwelling cannot occur, and fewer nutrients reach the phytoplankton at the surface.

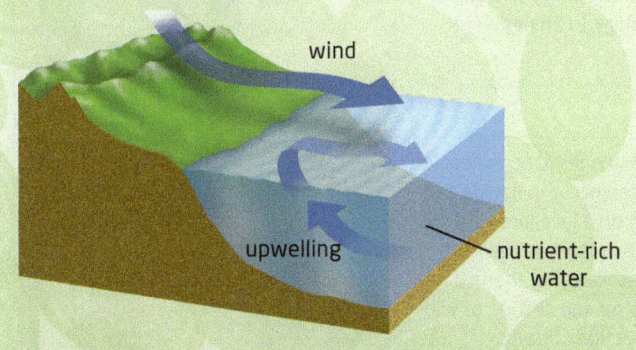

During upwelling, warm surface water moves away from shore and cold, nutrient-rich deep water rises to the surface.

Because fewer phytoplankton consume the carbon dioxide necessary for photosynthesis, they store less carbon. In turn, more carbon dioxide resides in Earth's atmosphere, which increases global warming. Increased global warming may continue to reduce the phytoplankton population.

Your Turn

1. Use the information in this article to construct a feedback-loop diagram that shows how global warming and phytoplankton are related. Explain whether it is a positive or negative feedback loop.

2. Brainstorm a list of possible economic and environmental consequences of reduced numbers of phytoplankton. Would the consequences affect only the area of the ocean in which the phytoplankton live, or would they affect a larger area? Explain your answer.

3. Research an ocean food web. Assess the impact of removing phytoplankton from this food web.

> **Learning Check**
>
> 1. Why is Earth considered a closed system?
> 2. Give an example of a negative feedback loop in the climate system.
> 3. Using an example, describe how a positive feedback loop affects a system.
> 4. Look at **Figure 8.1**. Use the diagram to describe a feedback loop that may happen in your body system to maintain your temperature balance.

Heating the Planet

On a sunny day, you can feel the sunlight warm your skin. This sunlight is responsible for the feedback loops in Earth's climate system. Solar energy travels 150 million kilometres through space as **electromagnetic radiation**, waves of energy that travel outward in all directions from their source. The warmth you sense on your skin is one type of electromagnetic radiation, called infrared radiation.

Thermal energy is the energy that an object has because of the motion of its molecules. The transfer of energy between objects is known as heat. Three main processes transfer energy through Earth's climate system: radiation, conduction, and convection. These processes are outlined in **Table 8.1**.

electromagnetic radiation energy that travels as waves that move outward in all directions from a source; includes infrared radiation, ultraviolet radiation, radio waves, X rays, gamma rays, and visible light

Table 8.1 Types of Energy Transfer

Type	Description	Example
Radiation	Radiation is the transfer of energy, including thermal energy, as electromagnetic radiation. Energy travels from the Sun to Earth as radiation, and heat travels from a fire to your body as radiation. All matter radiates some thermal energy—not only the Sun, but pebbles, bicycles, you, and even ice cubes. Because no matter is necessary to conduct radiation, this form of energy can travel through the vacuum of space. When radiation encounters matter, such as the atmosphere or your hand, it interacts with the matter. The matter may absorb the radiation, reflect it, or refract it.	
Conduction	Conduction is the transfer of thermal energy between two objects or substances that are in direct physical contact. The thermal energy always moves from a region of higher temperature to a region of lower temperature. For example, a hotplate conducts thermal energy to a skillet placed on it. In turn, the skillet conducts thermal energy to an egg.	
Convection	Convection is the transfer of thermal energy by highly energized molecules moving from one place to another. This movement can occur in liquids and gases, but not in solids. For example, when you turn on a lava lamp like the one shown to the right, a waxy substance at the bottom of the lamp is warmed by conduction. The wax expands and rises, carrying thermal energy by convection to the top of the lamp. The rising and sinking of wax bubbles create a pattern of circulation called a convection current.	

Energy Transfer in the Atmosphere

Land and water gain thermal energy by absorbing the Sun's short-wave radiation. As Earth's surface grows warmer, it converts some of its thermal energy into long-wave radiation. Earth emits (gives off) the long-wave radiation into the atmosphere, where it is absorbed by gases such as water vapour and carbon dioxide. This process heats the air and is the basis of the greenhouse effect. The transfer of thermal energy through the atmosphere drives the feedback loops that regulate Earth's climate.

After land and water have absorbed energy from the Sun, their molecules move more rapidly. Some of these molecules collide with air molecules and transfer thermal energy to the atmosphere by conduction. Air receives thermal energy in this way until the air reaches a temperature close to that of the ground or water it is next to.

When the lowest layer of air grows warmer, it expands and rises. As the warm air rises, cooler air descends and replaces it. In this way, thermal energy is continuously transferred to other regions of the atmosphere by convection. **Figure 8.4** summarizes the three ways in which the atmosphere is heated.

Figure 8.4 Conduction, convection, and radiation transfer heat in Earth's atmosphere.

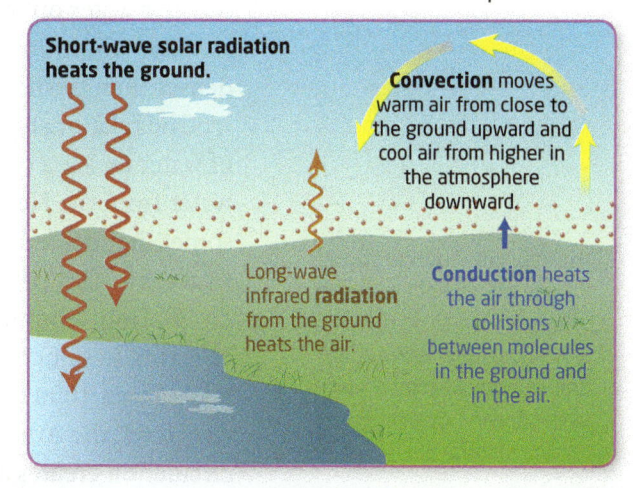

Short-wave solar radiation heats the ground.

Convection moves warm air from close to the ground upward and cool air from higher in the atmosphere downward.

Long-wave infrared **radiation** from the ground heats the air.

Conduction heats the air through collisions between molecules in the ground and in the air.

Activity 8-2

What Heats the Atmosphere?

How much solar energy reaches Earth's surface? In this activity, you will calculate the changes in temperature of the air and soil after a period of 1.0 h.

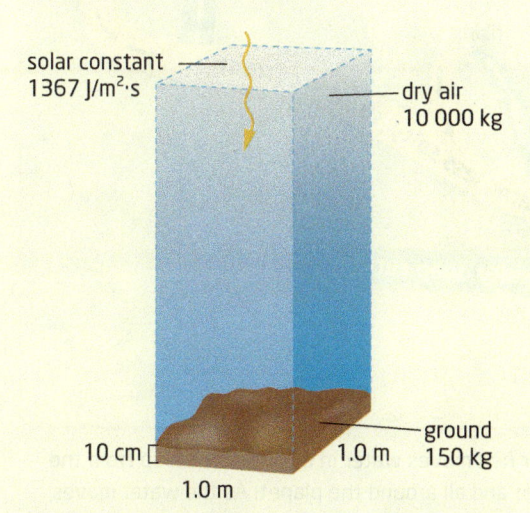

solar constant 1367 J/m²·s
dry air 10 000 kg
ground 150 kg
10 cm
1.0 m
1.0 m

This column of dry air has a specific heat capacity of 1.00 J/g·°C and a cross-sectional area of 1.0 m². The specific heat capacity of soil is 0.85 J/g·°C. Diagram not to scale.

Procedure

1. Calculate the amount of solar energy that reaches the column of air at the top of the atmosphere by multiplying the solar constant of 1367 J/m²·s, by 3600 s.

2. If the atmosphere absorbs 19 percent of the solar energy, how much energy does it absorb in 1.0 h?

3. If Earth's surface absorbs 51 percent of the solar energy, how much energy does it absorb in 1.0 h?

4. Use the equation $\Delta T = \dfrac{\text{heat absorbed}}{(\text{mass}) \times (\text{heat capacity})}$ to find the change in temperature for the air and the soil.

5. Calculate the temperature changes of (a) the air and (b) the soil. Use the heat capacities and masses provided in the diagram. Convert units where necessary.

Questions

1. Which heats Earth's atmosphere more: the Sun or Earth's surface?

2. How do you think your results would differ if the air were over water or ice instead of soil?

Chapter 8 Dynamics of Climate Change • NEL 315

Energy Transfer in the Oceans

The exchange of thermal energy between ocean currents and the atmosphere has a major influence on climates around the world and on climate change. In Chapter 7, you learned how uneven heating of the planet creates winds. Winds create currents of water that redistribute thermal energy at the ocean surface. Deeper, colder currents also move slowly along the ocean floor.

Like air masses, large masses of water can move vertically as well as horizontally. The density of water drives these vertical and horizontal movements. Cold water is dense, so it sinks to the ocean floor and pushes warmer water out of the way. The density of water also depends on salinity—the amount of dissolved salt the water contains. Salt water is denser than fresh water, so the salt water sinks.

The relationships between the temperature, salinity, and density of water create a continuous, twisting ocean current that mixes ocean water from the North Atlantic to the South Pacific oceans. This current, sometimes described as "the great ocean conveyor belt," is illustrated in **Figure 8.5**. This pattern of ocean circulation is known as **thermohaline circulation**, from the roots *thermo*, referring to temperature, and *haline*, referring to salt content. The entire journey of this ocean conveyor belt takes about 1000 to 1500 years. By mixing waters from the Arctic, the Antarctic, the Atlantic Ocean, and the Pacific Ocean, thermohaline circulation creates a global system of thermal energy distribution.

thermohaline circulation
a three-dimensional pattern of ocean circulation driven by wind, heat, and salinity that is an important component of the ocean-atmosphere climate system

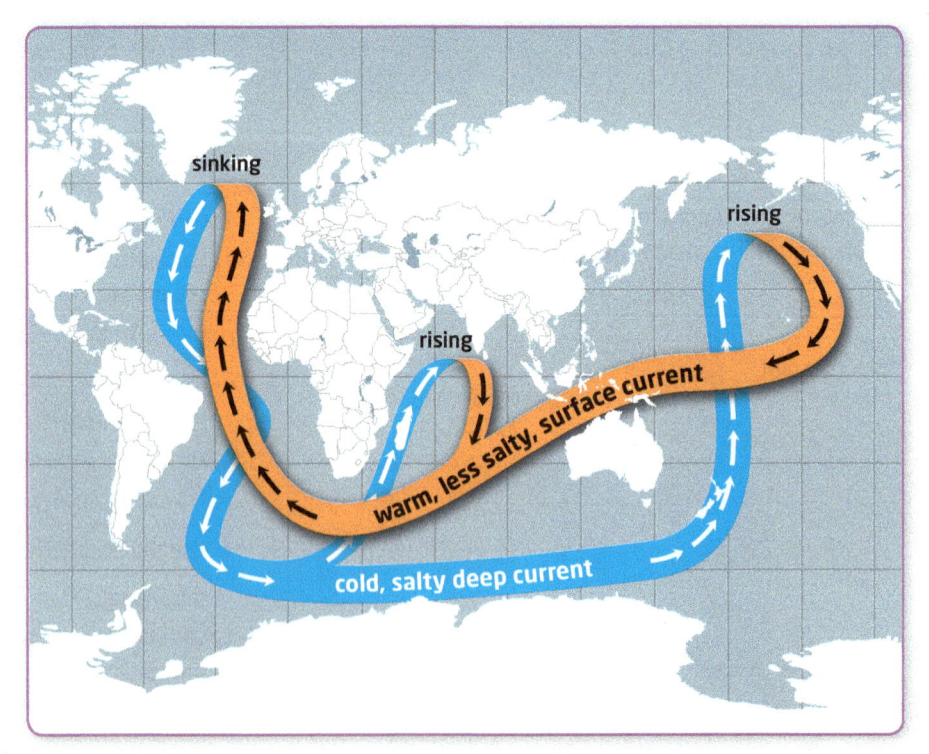

Figure 8.5 The *great ocean conveyor belt* moves water in a continuous loop from the surface of the ocean to the ocean floor and all around the planet. As the water moves, it carries thermal energy around Earth's surface.

Global Warming and Thermohaline Circulation

Climate scientists are concerned that global warming may disrupt the current pattern of thermohaline circulation by altering ocean salinity. Warming temperatures increase the rate at which ice melts, which can lead to an increase in fresh water that lowers salinity in northern oceans. At the same time, global warming increases the rate of evaporation, which can lead to an increase in salinity in tropical oceans. Thus, the polar water would become less dense and the tropical water would become more dense. As a result, the polar water would be less likely to sink toward the ocean floor, which is the main driving force for the thermohaline circulation system. Some studies suggest that these changes in water density will lead to a slowing of thermohaline circulation and will affect future transfer of thermal energy between the oceans and atmosphere.

Changes in ocean circulation patterns may have a negative effect on living things in the ocean by changing patterns of upwelling. Upwelling is the upward vertical motion of an ocean current. Upwelling brings nutrients from the sea floor into the surface currents. Areas where upwelling occurs are a rich source of food for marine organisms. If normal patterns of upwelling change, the survival of many marine species, such as the manta ray shown in **Figure 8.6**, may be at risk.

Figure 8.6 Manta rays, which can grow to a size of almost 8 m across, feed on the microscopic organisms that bloom where upwelling occurs.

> **Learning Check**
>
> 5. How is conduction different from convection?
>
> 6. The Sun provides energy to drive a number of processes on Earth. Identify one process driven by each type of heat transfer shown in **Figure 8.4**.
>
> 7. Compare the processes by which heat is transferred in the atmosphere and in the oceans.
>
> 8. Describe two methods by which heat could reach your hand if you held it above a hot stove.

Energy Transfer, El Niño, and La Niña

The importance of winds and ocean currents to global climate is most clearly seen when normal patterns of the ocean–atmosphere system are disrupted. A major disruption of this system happens every few years in the tropical Pacific during the events known as El Niño and La Niña. Both El Niño and La Niña are "sea-surface temperature anomalies." In other words, during both El Niño and La Niña, the temperature of the ocean surface in the Southern Pacific Ocean changes. These changes have dramatic effects on the transfer of thermal energy and, therefore, on climate change. These events are described in **Figure 8.7** on the next two pages.

> **Suggested Investigation**
>
> Real World Investigation 8-A, Recognizing the Effects of El Niño and La Niña on Southern Canada, on page 341

Chapter 8 Dynamics of Climate Change • NEL 317

NATIONAL GEOGRAPHIC
VISUALIZING EL NIÑO AND LA NIÑA

Figure 8.7

Weather in Canada can be affected by changes that occur thousands of kilometres away. Out in the middle of the Pacific Ocean, periodic warming and cooling of a huge mass of seawater–phenomena known as El Niño and La Niña, respectively–can impact weather across North America. During normal years (right), when neither El Niño nor La Niña is in effect, strong winds usually keep warm surface waters contained in the western Pacific while cooler water wells up to the surface in the eastern Pacific.

EL NIÑO During El Niño years, winds blowing west weaken and may even reverse. When this happens, warm waters in the western Pacific move eastward, preventing cold water from upwelling. This change can alter global weather patterns and trigger changes in precipitation and temperature across much of North America.

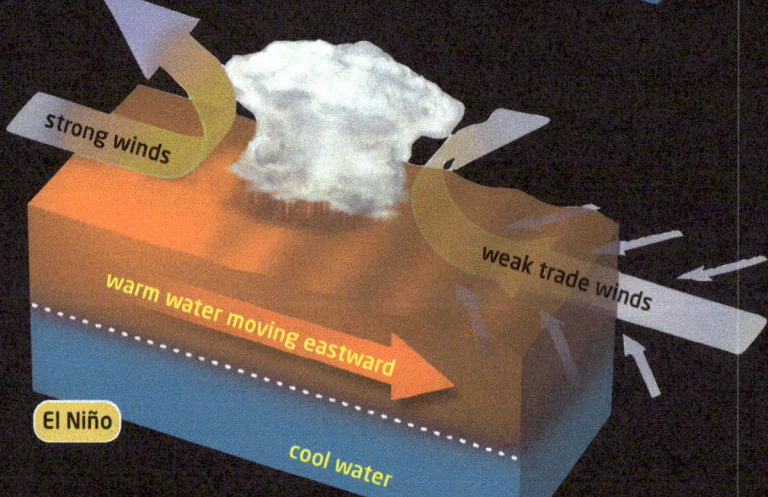

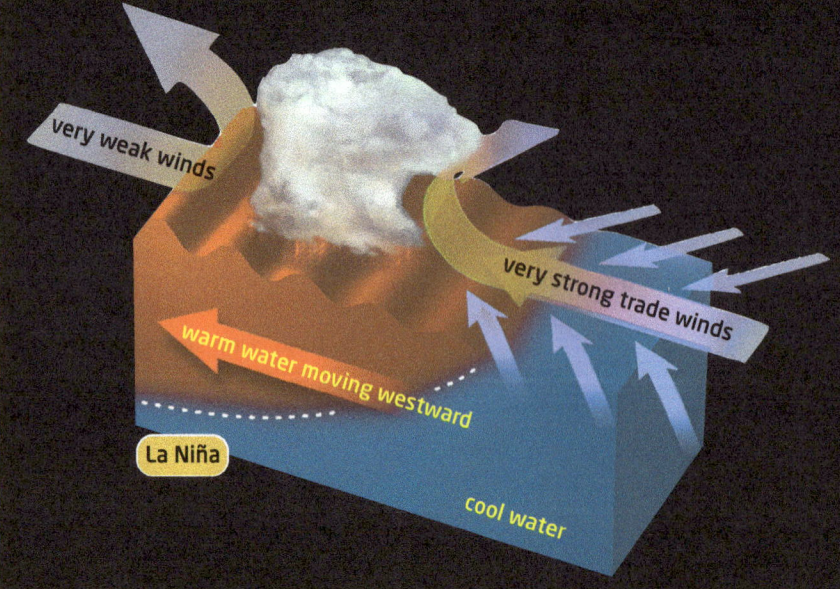

LA NIÑA During La Niña years, stronger-than-normal winds push warm Pacific waters farther west, toward Asia. Cold, deep-sea waters then well up strongly in the eastern Pacific, bringing cooler temperatures to northwestern North America.

318 NEL • Unit 3 Climate Change

El Niño

jet stream

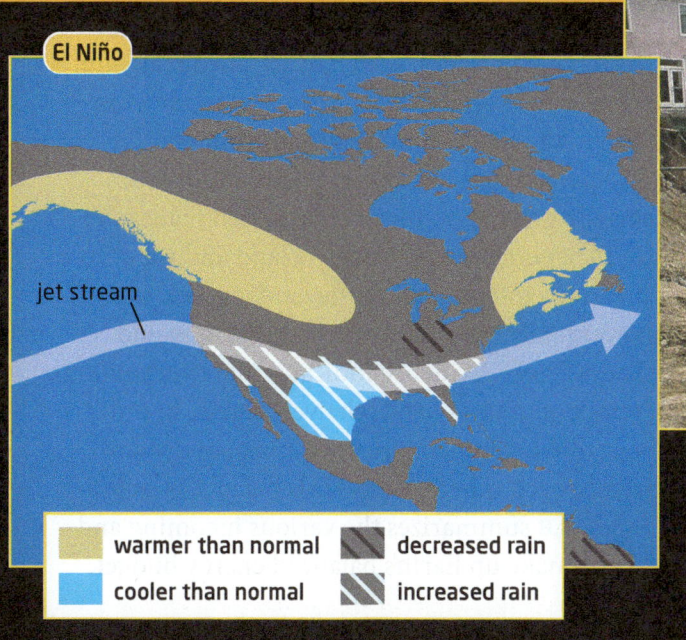

warmer than normal — decreased rain
cooler than normal — increased rain

Sun-warmed surface water spans the Pacific Ocean during El Niño years. Clouds form above the warm ocean, carrying moisture aloft. The jet stream, shown by the white arrow above, helps to bring some of this warm, moist air to the southern parts of North America.

▲ **LANDSLIDE** Heavy rains in California resulting from El Niño can lead to landslides. This upended house in Laguna Niguel, California, took a ride downhill during the El Niño storms of 1998.

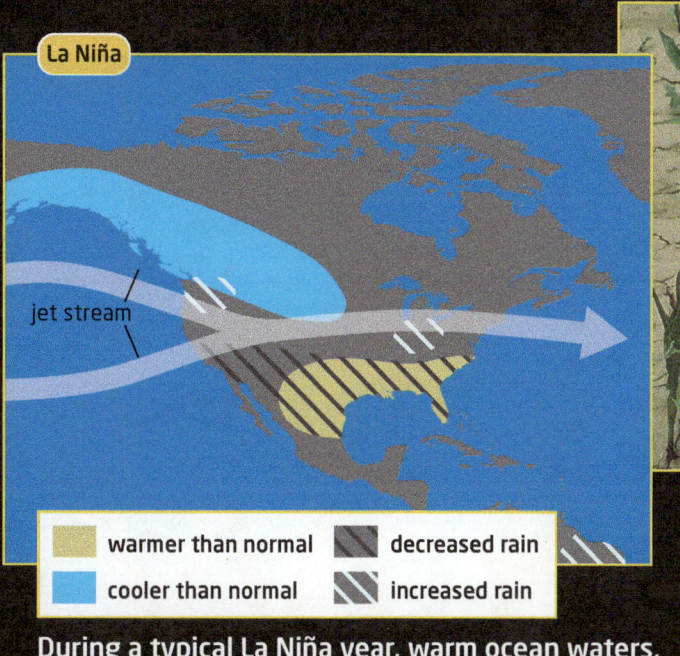

La Niña

jet stream

warmer than normal — decreased rain
cooler than normal — increased rain

During a typical La Niña year, warm ocean waters, clouds, and moisture are pushed away from North America. A weaker jet stream often brings cooler weather to the northern parts of the continent and hot, dry weather to southern areas.

▲ **PARCHED LAND** Some areas may experience drought conditions, like those that struck these cornfields during a La Niña summer.

Chapter 8 Dynamics of Climate Change • NEL 319

Suggested Investigation

Plan Your Own Investigation 8-B, Comparing Heat Absorption of Water and Soil, on page 343

Earth's Energy Budget

You have learned that incoming solar energy is absorbed by the land, water, and atmosphere and heats the planet. However, nearly a third of the solar energy that reaches Earth is not absorbed at all. It is reflected back into space by aerosols (suspended particles, such as dust, chemicals, and bacteria), by clouds, and by Earth's surface. **Table 8.2** summarizes what happens to incoming solar energy that enters Earth's atmosphere.

What happens to the 70 percent of solar energy that is absorbed? The thermal energy warms the ground, water, and air, which makes the planet's surface habitable. The energy moves from the land and water to the air and back through various interactions of the land, oceans, and atmosphere. It must also eventually leave the system, or Earth would continue to get warmer and warmer. Evidence indicates that over millions of years, Earth's average temperature has been relatively stable. In order to maintain a stable average global temperature, incoming energy and outgoing energy must balance each other exactly. This balance is called Earth's **energy budget**. **Figure 8.8** summarizes the various incoming and outgoing paths of energy that make up Earth's balanced energy budget.

energy budget a description of the total energy exchange within a system; a summary of how energy from the Sun enters, moves through, and leaves the Earth system

Go to **scienceontario** to find out more

Table 8.2 Reflection and Absorption of Solar Radiation

Reflection of Solar Radiation		Absorption of Solar Radiation	
• Aerosols in atmosphere	6%	• Gases in atmosphere	16%
• Clouds	20%	• Clouds	3%
• Surface	4%	• Surface	51%
Total reflected	30%	Total absorbed	70%

Study Toolkit

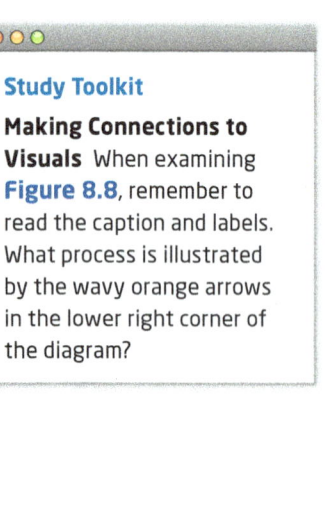

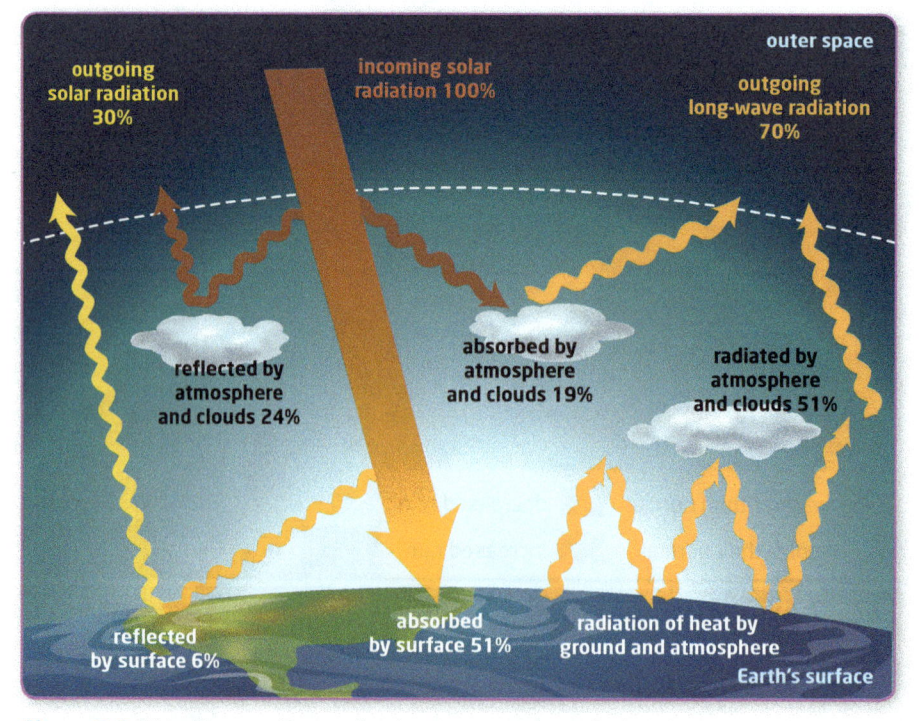

Making Connections to Visuals When examining **Figure 8.8**, remember to read the caption and labels. What process is illustrated by the wavy orange arrows in the lower right corner of the diagram?

Figure 8.8 This diagram shows what happens to solar radiation that enters Earth's atmosphere. Of the total incoming solar radiation, 30 percent is reflected and 70 percent is absorbed. All of the absorbed radiation is eventually radiated back into space.

- outgoing solar radiation 30%
- incoming solar radiation 100%
- outgoing long-wave radiation 70%
- reflected by atmosphere and clouds 24%
- absorbed by atmosphere and clouds 19%
- radiated by atmosphere and clouds 51%
- reflected by surface 6%
- absorbed by surface 51%
- radiation of heat by ground and atmosphere
- Earth's surface
- outer space

320 NEL • Unit 3 Climate Change

A 1979

B 2005

Changing Albedo and the Energy Budget

The biggest influences on Earth's albedo come from clouds, snow, and ice. A change in any of these factors can produce a change in the amount of energy in the atmosphere. For example, melting of glaciers and polar icecaps, as shown in **Figure 8.9**, will decrease the albedo of the surface and may warm the planet. On the other hand, an increase in cloud cover may increase albedo and cool the planet.

Since the late 1990s, NASA satellites have been observing the upper atmosphere by using sensors known as CERES, which is short for Clouds and the Earth's Radiant Energy System. One purpose of this research is to track changes in Earth's energy budget by monitoring changes in the overall amount of energy Earth reflects or emits. CERES researchers found that snow and ice cover in the Arctic declined from 2002 to 2005, as shown in **Figure 8.10**. Surprisingly, however, the albedo did not change during that time.

Scientists think that melting sea ice exposed a larger water surface to evaporation. A greater concentration of water vapour in the air led to increased cloud cover. The increased amount of energy reflected by white clouds matched the decreased amount of energy reflected by ice, keeping the polar albedo unchanged. This process is an example of a natural, negative feedback loop that acts to slow climate change and maintain Earth's current global temperature.

Figure 8.9 These satellite composite images show how the minimum area of the Arctic ocean that was covered by sea ice diminished between **A** 1979 and **B** 2005.

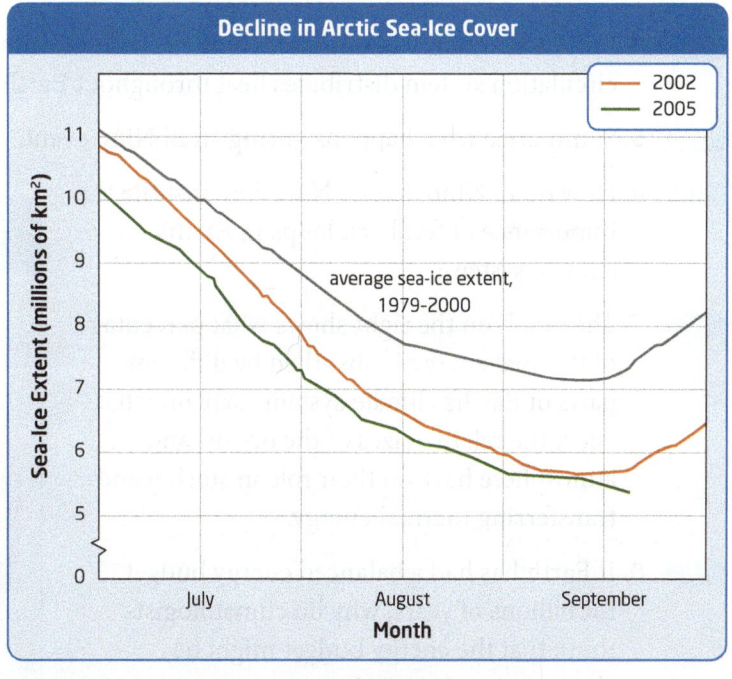

Figure 8.10 This graph shows the rate at which sea-ice cover above the Arctic Circle has declined over 20 years.

Section 8.1 Review

Section Summary

- Earth is a system of interrelated parts, including the atmosphere, hydrosphere, rocks, and living things.
- The interrelated processes in the Earth system form a variety of both positive and negative feedback loops, which affect the global climate system by increasing or decreasing the effects of climate change.
- The atmosphere redistributes heat, energy, and moisture around Earth's surface.
- Heat can be transferred by radiation, conduction, and convection.
- Earth's oceans transfer energy as water moves as a result of density differences that are caused by differences in the temperature and salinity of ocean water.
- El Niño and La Niña events are examples of the effects of heat transfer through the atmosphere and oceans.
- To maintain a stable average global temperature, incoming energy and outgoing energy must balance each other exactly. This balance is part of Earth's energy budget.

Review Questions

K/U 1. Identify four components of Earth's climate system.

A 2. One concern about global warming is that the polar icecaps will melt quickly and expose darker materials, such as rock and water, to sunlight. Ice and snow have a high albedo, but open water and rocks have a low albedo. Given the differences in albedo, describe the positive feedback loop that could occur as a result of the polar icecaps melting.

K/U 3. How is the energy that Earth absorbs different from the energy that Earth emits?

C 4. Draw a diagram that illustrates how the thermohaline circulation system distributes heat throughout Earth's surface.

K/U 5. Summarize what happens during an El Niño event.

T/I 6. How do El Niño and La Niña demonstrate the importance of feedback loops in Earth's climate system?

A 7. The graph on the right shows what percentage of thermal energy is absorbed by different parts of Earth's climate system. Explain what effect the relative sizes of the oceans and atmosphere have on their role in storing and transferring thermal energy.

T/I 8. If Earth has had a balanced energy budget for billions of years, why do climatologists think that the energy budget might be changing now?

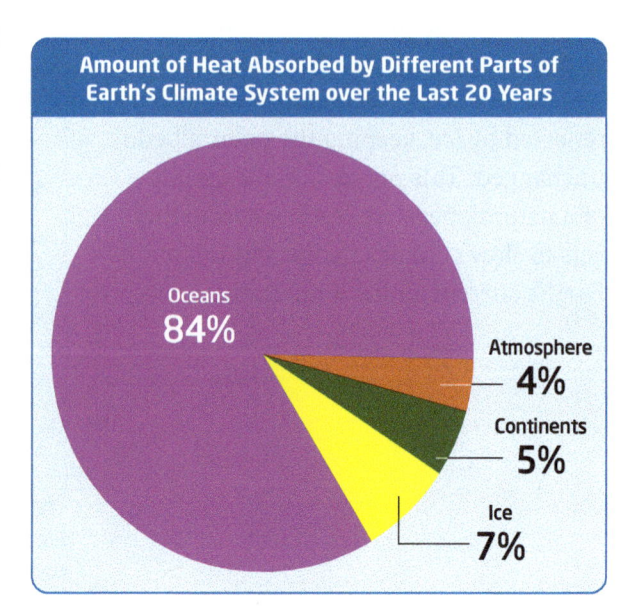

Amount of Heat Absorbed by Different Parts of Earth's Climate System over the Last 20 Years

- Oceans 84%
- Atmosphere 4%
- Continents 5%
- Ice 7%

8.2 Greenhouse Gases and Human Activities

The greenhouse effect is an important part of Earth's energy budget. Without the greenhouse effect, Earth would be too cold to support life as we know it. But just as the absence of greenhouse gases in the atmosphere would result in a much colder Earth, so an increase in greenhouse gases will produce a warmer Earth. In this section, you will explore the roles of various greenhouse gases in climate change and discover why human production of greenhouse gases is a cause for concern.

Key Terms
concentration
parts per million (ppm)
greenhouse gas
sink
ozone
chlorofluorocarbon (CFC)
anthropogenic greenhouse effect
global warming potential (GWP)

Concentrations of Gases in the Atmosphere

The measure of the amount of one substance within a mixture is called **concentration**. **Figure 8.11** shows an example of concentration in liquids. In 1958, researchers began to make frequent, regular measurements of concentrations of carbon dioxide (CO_2) in the atmosphere. These systematic measurements were the first direct indication that levels of greenhouse gases have been steadily increasing in recent decades.

The concentration of carbon dioxide in Earth's atmosphere increased from an average of about 315 parts per million in 1960 to about 370 parts per million in 2000. **Parts per million (ppm)** is a measure of the number of parts of one substance relative to one million parts of another substance. For example, 300 ppm of carbon dioxide in the atmosphere means that one million units of atmosphere contain 300 units of carbon dioxide plus 999 700 units of other atmospheric gases. **Table 8.3** describes units that are commonly used when measuring concentrations.

concentration the amount of a particular substance in a specific amount of another substance

parts per million (ppm) a unit of measurement that indicates the number of parts of a substance per million parts of another substance; for example, for salt water, 1000 ppm of salt means 1000 parts salt in 1 000 000 parts of pure water

Table 8.3 Measurements of Concentration

Measurement	Example
Parts per million (ppm)	1 mg per kg = 1 ppm
Parts per billion (ppb)	1 mg per tonne = 1 ppb
Parts per trillion (ppt)	1 mg per kilotonne = 1 ppt

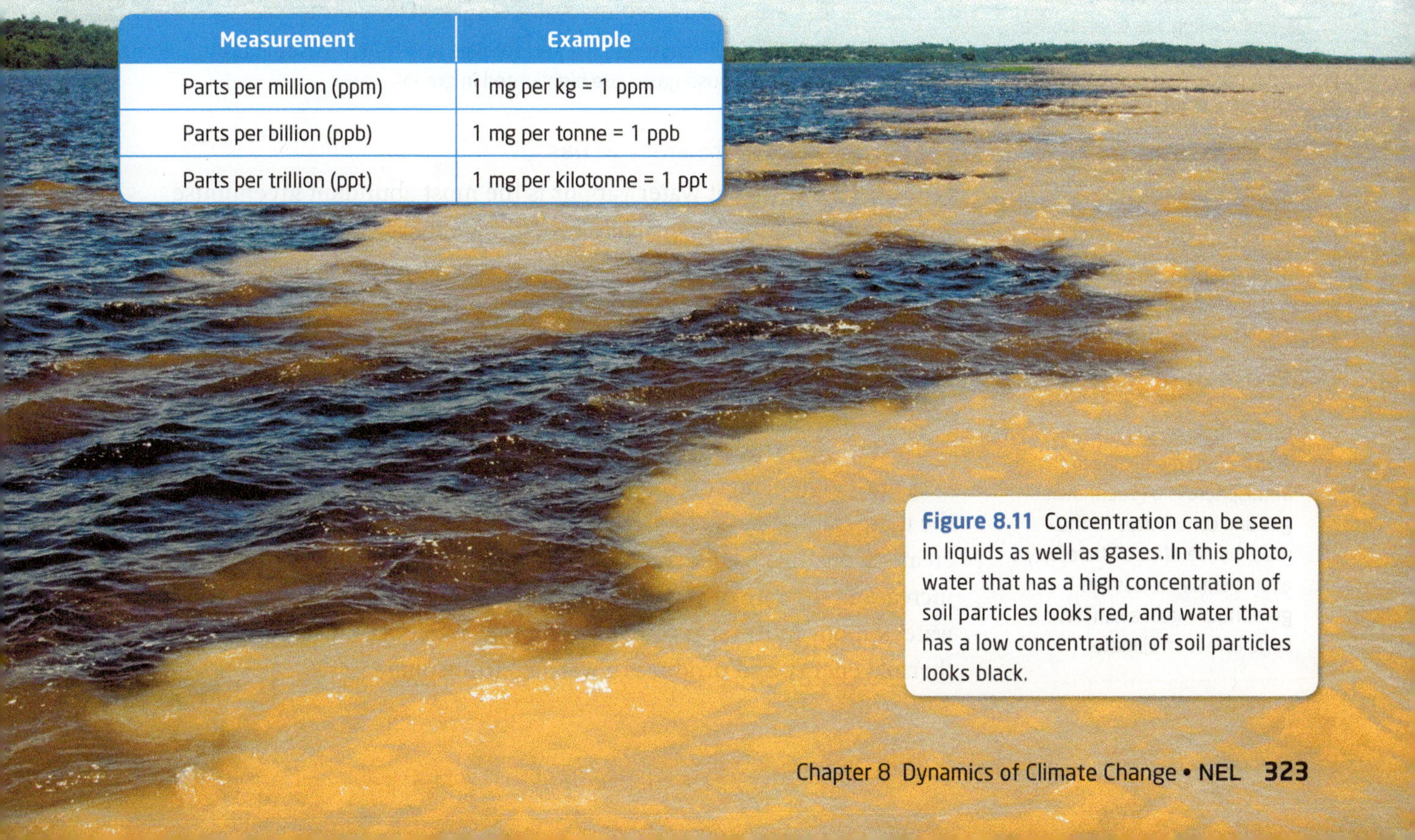

Figure 8.11 Concentration can be seen in liquids as well as gases. In this photo, water that has a high concentration of soil particles looks red, and water that has a low concentration of soil particles looks black.

greenhouse gas a gas in Earth's atmosphere that absorbs and prevents the escape of radiation as thermal energy; examples include carbon dioxide and methane

sink a process that removes greenhouse gases from the atmosphere

Greenhouse Gases and Global Warming

Ninety-nine percent of the atmosphere is made up of only two gases: nitrogen (N_2) and oxygen (O_2). However, neither of these two gases absorbs infrared radiation, and neither gas contributes to the greenhouse effect. Gases that absorb and re-emit infrared radiation are known as **greenhouse gases**. Molecules of the greenhouse gases all have three or more atoms each. Their molecular structure allows them to interact with radiation of different wavelengths. They produce a warming effect by absorbing and emitting energy. In **Figure 8.12** the gases highlighted in green show that carbon dioxide and water are the most abundant greenhouse gases in Earth's atmosphere.

The concentrations of many greenhouse gases have fluctuated throughout Earth's history. Processes that add greenhouse gases to the atmosphere are called *sources* of greenhouse gases. Processes that absorb greenhouse gases from the atmosphere are called **sinks**. Both sources and sinks can be natural or can be caused by human activities.

The Bulk Composition of Earth's Atmosphere

- Nitrogen gas 78%
- Oxygen 21%
- Argon 0.9%
- Other gases 0.1%

Percentages of "Other Gases" in the Atmosphere:
- Water vapour 1–4%
- Carbon dioxide 0.036%
- Neon 0.0018%
- Hydrogen 0.000 05%
- Helium 0.0005%
- Methane 0.000 17%
- Nitrous oxide 0.000 03%
- Ozone 0.000 004%

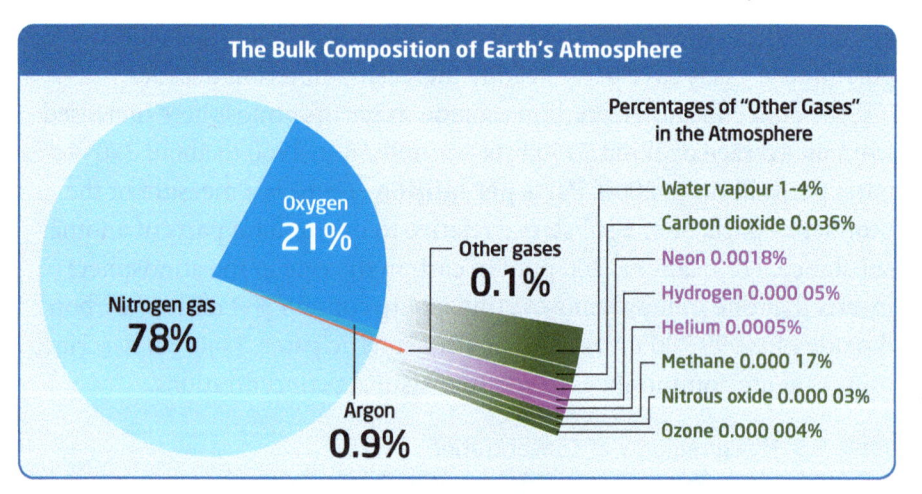

Figure 8.12 This pie graph illustrates the percentages of different gases in the atmosphere. The greenhouse gases are highlighted in green.

Suggested Investigation
Problem-Solving Investigation 8-C, Modelling the Greenhouse Effect, on page 344

Water Vapour as a Greenhouse Gas

Figure 8.12 shows that water vapour is the most abundant greenhouse gas in Earth's atmosphere. Scientists estimate that water vapour is responsible for between 65 and 85 percent of the greenhouse effect. However, water vapour is not added to or removed from the atmosphere in significant amounts by human activities. The concentration of water vapour in the atmosphere at any particular time is directly related to one factor—temperature.

Water vapour enters the atmosphere by evaporation. The rate of evaporation depends on the temperature of the air and oceans. The higher the temperature is, the higher the rate of evaporation is. This relationship creates a positive feedback loop. A warmer atmosphere leads to an increase in the rate of evaporation; increased evaporation leads to more water vapour in the atmosphere; and more water vapour absorbs more thermal energy and produces a warmer atmosphere.

Sense of scale
On average, only one in every 2000 molecules in the atmosphere is a greenhouse gas and contributes to the greenhouse effect. Therefore, even a small increase in greenhouse gases can have a large effect on climate.

Carbon Dioxide Sources and Sinks

The main natural source of atmospheric carbon dioxide (CO_2) is animal respiration. The main human source is combustion of fossil fuels. Carbon dioxide is removed from the atmosphere by plants when they convert it into stored carbon during photosynthesis. Because of this role, plants, such as those shown in **Figure 8.13**, are carbon sinks. Deforestation increases the amount of carbon dioxide in the atmosphere by clearing large areas of trees, which are important carbon sinks.

As you learned in Section 8.1, phytoplankton in the oceans also play a major role in the absorption and storage of carbon dioxide. Scientists estimate that the oceans currently absorb between 30 and 50 percent of the carbon dioxide produced by the burning of fossil fuels.

Interaction of Water Vapour and Carbon Dioxide

Because carbon dioxide and water vapour are both greenhouse gases, the effect of one is added to the effect of the other to form a positive feedback loop. For example, some scientists estimate that a doubling of carbon dioxide in the atmosphere would, by itself, warm Earth by about 1°C. However, this amount of warming would increase the rate of evaporation, and thus increase the amount of water vapour in the atmosphere. The additional warming effect of the water vapour would double the temperature increase to about 2°C. When other feedbacks are also added, such as a lowered albedo due to melting ice, the total warming from a doubling of carbon dioxide is raised to about 3°C.

The amplifying effect of water vapour also applies to atmospheric cooling. For example, in 1991 a massive eruption of Mount Pinatubo in the Philippines sent huge amounts of ash and greenhouse gases into the atmosphere, as shown in **Figure 8.14**. The particles suspended high in the atmosphere increased Earth's albedo, reflecting sunlight and cooling the planet for a period of several years. The cooling led to atmospheric drying, which caused the global temperature to drop even further.

Figure 8.13 Canada's forests, such as this one in northern Alberta, form an important carbon sink. They help to remove carbon dioxide from the atmosphere.

Figure 8.14 The white and grey plume in this satellite image is the column of ash and dust thrown into the air during the 1991 eruption of Mount Pinatubo in the Philippines. The brown area is the island of Luzon, which is about 225 km wide. This eruption cooled Earth's global average temperature by as much as 0.2°C for five years.

Sources of Methane

Methane (CH$_4$) is produced by bacteria that break down waste matter in oxygen-free environments. A major natural source of methane is wetlands (bogs and swamps), where large amounts of organic material decompose under water. Like wetlands, rice paddies also produce methane. Termites and cattle both produce methane during their normal digestive processes. Additional human sources include decomposing garbage in landfills, processing of coal and natural gas, and tanks of liquid manure from livestock production.

Scientists have suggested some unique ways to capture, or sequester, carbon from methane. One suggestion involves having cattle wear backpacks to capture the methane released from their digestive tract, as you saw at the beginning of this chapter. This methane could be collected for use as a fuel. Other scientists suggest that simply feeding cattle clover and alfalfa rather than corn and grain will reduce methane emissions by those animals by 25 percent. Some environmental activists have proposed a simple switch in human diets. These groups have started a campaign to convince people to stop eating beef and start eating camels and kangaroos, such as those shown in **Figure 8.15**. The digestive tracts of these animals do not produce the same greenhouse gases that the stomachs of cattle and sheep do.

Figure 8.15 Kangaroo meat is produced in Australia and New Zealand and shipped to markets around the world. The digestive systems of these animals produce almost no methane.

Learning Check

1. Why do scientists need to measure greenhouse gases in parts per million?
2. What does the word *sink* mean when used in the phrase *carbon sink*?
3. Create a flowchart that illustrates how water vapour and carbon dioxide interact to form a positive feedback loop.
4. What two human activities might cause methane to accumulate in the atmosphere?

Natural and Anthropogenic Sources of Nitrous Oxide

Most natural production of nitrous oxide (N_2O) comes from damp tropical soils and the oceans. Nitrous oxide also forms when nitrogen-rich compounds are broken down by bacteria. Human sources include chemical fertilizers, manure and sewage treatment, and vehicle exhausts.

Stratospheric Ozone: Earth's "Sunscreen"

Another greenhouse gas, called **ozone** (O_3), is composed of three atoms of oxygen. Ozone occurs naturally in the upper atmosphere at altitudes between 10 and 50 km. The ozone layer blocks harmful ultraviolet radiation from the Sun, preventing it from reaching Earth's surface. Ultraviolet radiation can cause skin cancers in humans and genetic damage in other organisms.

Ozone Depletion and the Ozone "Hole"

Since the 1970s, there has been a slow, steady decline in the total volume of ozone in the stratosphere. Beginning during the same period, an ozone "hole" has appeared over the Antarctic each year from September to December. The Antarctic ozone hole is shown in **Figure 8.16**. The ozone hole is not actually a hole; it is a large region in which ozone concentration is declining, which creates a thinning area in the stratospheric ozone layer. In this region, ozone levels have fallen to as little as one third of the concentration before 1970.

The main cause of ozone depletion is the addition to the atmosphere of human-made gases that contain chlorine. The depletion of the ozone layer results in an increase in the amount of ultraviolet light that reaches Earth's surface. However, scientists are also concerned by a positive feedback loop that results from the breakdown of stratospheric ozone. Because ozone acts as a greenhouse gas, reduced ozone levels will cause the stratosphere to cool. This cooling could lead to the formation of polar stratospheric clouds (PSCs). Within these clouds, chemical reactions result in the formation of free chlorine. The chlorine reacts with ozone and breaks apart the ozone, further reducing the amount of ozone in the stratosphere.

> **ozone** a greenhouse gas that is composed of three atoms of oxygen; it is commonly found in a concentrated layer in the stratosphere

September 1979   September 2007

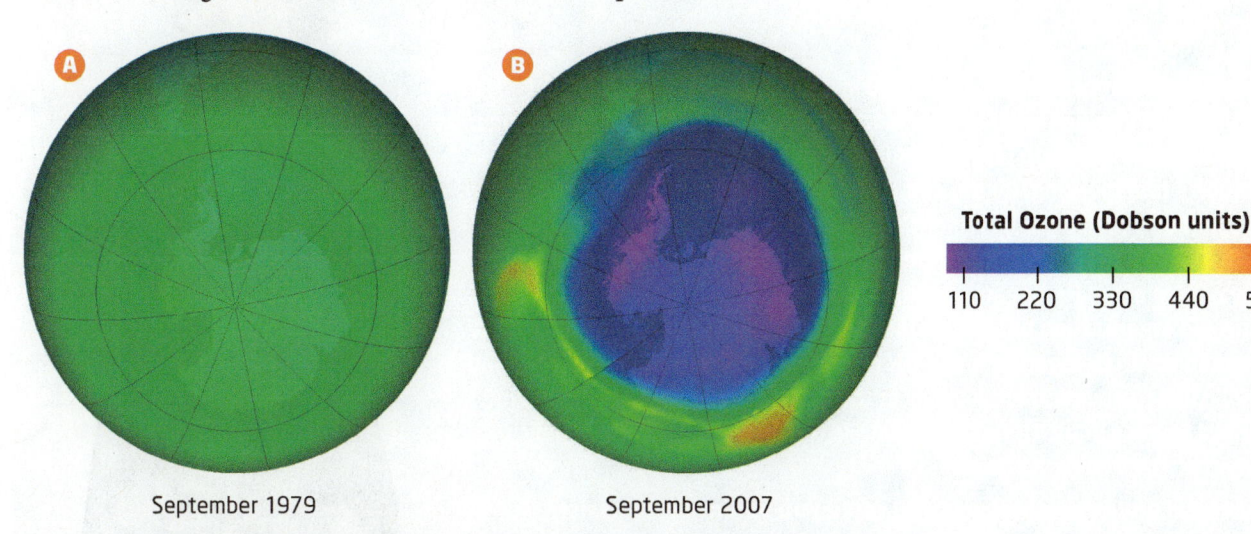

Figure 8.16 As the legend on the right shows, the concentration of ozone over Antarctica decreased between **A** 1979 and **B** 2007. The largest measurement recorded for the size of the ozone hole is 29.5 million km^2 – larger than the size of North America.

Figure 8.17 Vehicle exhaust is a direct source of greenhouse gases. It is also an indirect source of ground-level ozone.

Ground-Level Ozone

Ozone also occurs in the atmosphere near ground level as a smog-forming pollutant. This ozone is produced by a chemical reaction between sunlight and chemicals in vehicle exhaust—mainly hydrocarbons and nitrogen oxides—as shown in **Figure 8.17**. The greatest concentrations of polluting ozone are found over cities, but ozone can also be blown many kilometres from its source by winds. Ground-level ozone can cause damage to the lungs and heart, and produces cracks in rubber and plastic products. In addition, this greenhouse gas can trap thermal energy close to Earth's surface, which could contribute to global warming.

Halocarbons

The other greenhouse gases you have learned about have natural sources as well as being produced by humans. However, halocarbons are formed only by industrial processes—no natural source of these powerful greenhouse gases exists. *Halocarbons* are a large group of chemicals formed from carbon and one or more halogens, such as chlorine, fluorine, or iodine. Halocarbon molecules are more efficient than carbon dioxide at absorbing infrared radiation. Some of them are very stable and can remain in the atmosphere for thousands of years before they are broken down.

The best-known halocarbons are **chlorofluorocarbons (CFCs)**. Their main use is as solvents, cleaners, and coolants in refrigerators and air conditioners. As well as absorbing infrared radiation, CFCs break apart ozone molecules in the upper atmosphere. This reaction has led to depletion of the ozone layer and the formation of the ozone hole over the Antarctic. The use of CFCs has been banned in most developed nations since 1987. Because CFCs remain in the atmosphere for so long, however, they continue to damage the ozone layer.

chlorofluorocarbon (CFC) a human-made chemical compound that contains chlorine, fluorine, and carbon; when released into the atmosphere may cause depletion of the ozone layer

Making a Difference

P.J. Partington thinks people interested in working for the environment should just "jump right into it." That's what he did. He started volunteering with the Canadian Youth Climate Coalition after a friend invited him to the coalition's first meeting. By the end of the meeting, P.J. was co-ordinator of the coalition's policy group. A month later he was helping to organize the youth delegation to the 2006 United Nations climate negotiations in Nairobi, Kenya. Soon after, P.J. began working for TakingITGlobal, an international, youth-led organization based in Toronto. In 2008, he was responsible for the Canadian Youth Delegation to the UN climate negotiations in Poznan, Poland.

P.J. studied environmental policy at the London School of Economics and Political Science in the United Kingdom. He is now a climate change policy analyst at The Pembina Institute.

What local environmental group(s) could you volunteer to assist?
What value do you see in "just jumping in"?

The Anthropogenic Greenhouse Effect

Levels of carbon dioxide in the atmosphere have varied widely over the past 800 000 years. However, human activities have significantly increased the quantities of carbon dioxide and other greenhouse gases since about 1750, as shown in **Table 8.4**. Most of the increase in CO_2 has come from the burning of fossil fuels. Deforestation and agriculture have added carbon dioxide, methane, and nitrous oxide. Industrial activities have produced ground-level ozone, CFCs, and other pollutants that affect the climate system. The increase in global average temperature since the 1960s is likely due mainly to the increase in greenhouse gases produced by human activities. This result is known as the **anthropogenic greenhouse effect**.

anthropogenic greenhouse effect the increased capacity of the atmosphere to absorb and prevent the escape of thermal energy because of an increase in greenhouse gases introduced by human activities

Table 8.4 Greenhouse Gas Concentration Before and After the Industrial Revolution

Greenhouse Gas	Level Before 1750	Current Level	Increase Since 1750
carbon dioxide	280 ppm	384 ppm	104 ppm
methane	700 ppb	1745 ppb	1045 ppb
nitrous oxide	270 ppb	314 ppb	44 ppb
CFCs	0 ppt	533 ppt	553 ppt

Activity 8-3

Graphing Changes in Carbon Dioxide

What effect has the burning of fossil fuels had on global temperature? In this activity, you will track the amount of carbon dioxide in the atmosphere and the global temperature increase over time.

Materials
- graph paper
- coloured pencils or pens

Procedure

1. Use the data from the table to make the following three line graphs: year versus industrial carbon dioxide emissions, year versus carbon dioxide concentration in the atmosphere, year versus temperature increase since 1861.

2. Using a different colour, extend each of the line graphs to 2020. For help in creating your graph, refer to Math Skills Toolkit 3 on pages 555–558.

Questions

1. Describe the shape of each graph.

2. Describe the trends since 1861 for industrial carbon dioxide emissions, carbon dioxide concentration, and average global temperature increase.

3. "Human combustion of fossil fuels has resulted in rising global temperatures." How do the results of this activity affect your opinion about this statement?

Changes in Carbon Dioxide and Average Global Temperature

Year	Industrial CO_2 Emissions (gigatonnes)*	CO_2 Concentration (ppm per volume)	Temperature Increase Since 1861 (°C)
1861	0.67	285	0.00
1880	1.15	292	0.00
1900	2.63	298	0.05
1920	3.42	303	0.29
1940	4.95	307	0.46
1960	9.98	318	0.35
1980	20.72	340	0.41
2000	23.42	365	0.63

Source: Carbon Dioxide Information Analysis Center (CDIAC)
* 1 gigatonne = 1 billion tonnes

Go to **scienceontario** to find out more

> **Learning Check**
>
> 5. Identify five sources of nitrous oxide.
> 6. Use the data in **Table 8.4** to calculate the percentage increase in greenhouse gases since the Industrial Revolution. How is this increase related to climate change?
> 7. How do halocarbons and ozone interact to change the upper atmosphere?
> 8. Summarize the sources of the greenhouse gases that contribute to the anthropogenic greenhouse effect.

Comparing the Global Warming Potential of Greenhouse Gases

Which greenhouse gases should we be most concerned about? The contribution of a particular greenhouse gas to global warming depends on three things:

- the concentration of the gas in the atmosphere
- the ability of the gas to absorb heat
- the length of time the gas remains in the atmosphere

To help compare the relative impact of one greenhouse gas with that of another, scientists use a measure called **global warming potential (GWP)**. Carbon dioxide is assigned a GWP of 1. The warming effect of every other greenhouse gas is compared with the warming effect of the same mass of carbon dioxide over a specified period of time. **Table 8.5** compares the GWP of four major greenhouse gases. The table shows that methane is broken down in the atmosphere after about 12 years. However, since methane is able to absorb and emit more heat than carbon dioxide does, methane has a higher GWP.

Halocarbons account for less than 2 percent of all greenhouse gas emissions produced by human activities. But because they remain in the atmosphere almost indefinitely, concentrations of these gases will increase as long as emissions continue. Their ability to trap heat in the atmosphere over time can be thousands of times greater than that of carbon dioxide. Therefore, these gases are considered high GWP gases. Fortunately, many nations have banned the production and use of CFCs.

global warming potential (GWP) the ability of a substance to warm the atmosphere by absorbing thermal energy

Table 8.5 Global Warming Potential of Major Greenhouse Gases

Greenhouse Gas	Chemical Formula	Atmospheric Lifetime (years)	Global Warming Potential (GWP) over 100 Years
carbon dioxide	CO_2	variable	1
methane	CH_4	12	25
nitrous oxide	N_2O	115	298
chlorofluorocarbons (CFCs)	various	indefinite	4750–5310

Ways to Reduce Greenhouse Gas Production

Canada ranks among the top 10 nations in the world for the amount of greenhouse gases produced per person. You play a part in adding greenhouse gases to the atmosphere, even if you do not drive a vehicle. Almost one fifth of Canada's total greenhouse emissions come from people's homes. Here are some ways that you can help to reduce greenhouse gas production at home.

Conserve electricity Where do the electricity supplies to your home and school come from? Power plants that burn coal and other fossil fuels to generate electricity are a source of greenhouse gases. You can reduce emissions from power plants by reducing your use of electricity. For example, you can reduce emissions by using more energy-efficient light bulbs and appliances. **Figure 8.18** shows an energy-efficient compact fluorescent light bulb. You can also reduce your impact by the simple act of conserving energy. For example, turn off lights, televisions, computers, and other appliances when you are not using them.

Figure 8.18 Simply replacing incandescent light bulbs with fluorescent bulbs can prevent thousands of kilograms of carbon dioxide from ever being emitted.

Improve home-heating efficiency Most home furnaces and boilers burn oil or natural gas. Greenhouse gas production can be reduced by lowering the thermostat setting and improving insulation. Modern furnaces have improved energy efficiency compared with older furnaces, and they release lower amounts of greenhouse gases. Many building standards and codes are related to the energy efficiency of new structures. Some local and national programs also exist to help retrofit older buildings to make them more energy efficient.

Reduce, re-use, and recycle How does the garbage you throw out each week add to greenhouse gas emissions? First, producing all of the products you buy and use took energy. If you re-use and recycle items instead of throwing them out, as shown in **Figure 8.19**, you reduce the demand for energy to make more products. Second, garbage buried in a landfill produces methane, and garbage burned in an incinerator produces carbon dioxide. The less garbage you produce, the fewer greenhouse gases you produce.

Figure 8.19 Recycling programs help to reduce the amount of trash in landfills and the amount of greenhouse gases produced by companies that manufacture product packaging.

Chapter 8 Dynamics of Climate Change • NEL 331

Section 8.2 Review

Section Summary

- Earth emits thermal energy. Greenhouse gases in the atmosphere absorb this energy and radiate it in all directions. The thermal energy that returns to Earth gives rise to the greenhouse effect.
- Less than one gas molecule in a hundred is a greenhouse gas.
- The most common greenhouse gas is water vapour. Other major greenhouse gases include carbon dioxide, methane, ozone, nitrous oxides, and halocarbons.
- Human activities, such as agriculture and the burning of fossil fuels, are increasing the amounts of some of the greenhouse gases in the atmosphere.
- An increase in greenhouse gases has resulted in the anthropogenic greenhouse effect, which may be responsible for recent climate change.
- You can reduce your contribution of greenhouse gases by conserving electricity, improving home-heating efficiency, and minimizing waste as much as possible.

Review Questions

K/U 1. Why do scientists measure the concentration of gases in the atmosphere?

C 2. A friend says, "The greenhouse effect is a terrible thing because it is causing the world to heat up." Explain why this statement is inaccurate.

T/I 3. Water vapour is the most abundant greenhouse gas, but scientists are not attempting to limit the amount of water vapour created by humans. Why do you think this is so?

K/U 4. Identify three major anthropogenic sources of methane, and describe what is being done to minimize their impact.

K/U 5. What are chlorofluorocarbons, and what effect do they have on climate?

T/I 6. Sort the greenhouse gases into three categories: those made entirely by human activity, those that human activity has some effect on, and those that human activity has no significant effect on.

K/U 7. What three factors determine the global warming potential of different greenhouse gases?

A 8. The graph on the right shows the sources of greenhouse gases produced by Canadians. Assuming that the energy sector releases mainly carbon dioxide and the agriculture sector releases mainly methane, which source has the greatest global warming potential? Explain your answer.

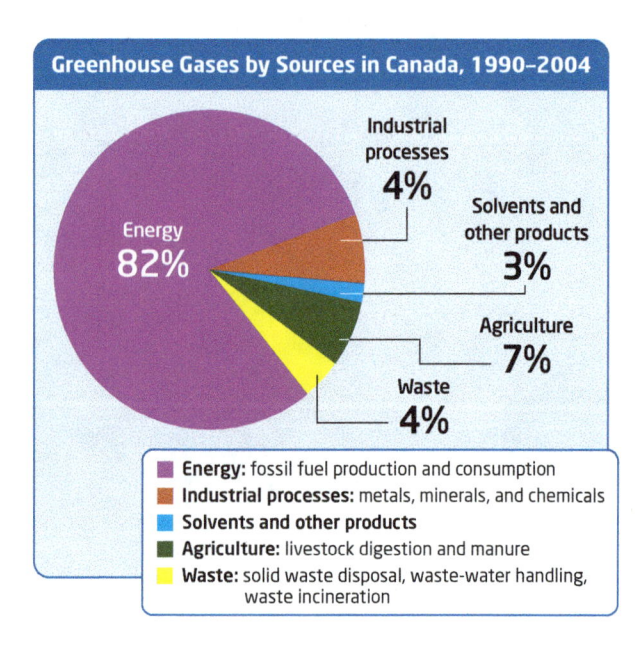

Greenhouse Gases by Sources in Canada, 1990–2004

- Energy: 82%
- Industrial processes: 4%
- Solvents and other products: 3%
- Agriculture: 7%
- Waste: 4%

- **Energy:** fossil fuel production and consumption
- **Industrial processes:** metals, minerals, and chemicals
- **Solvents and other products**
- **Agriculture:** livestock digestion and manure
- **Waste:** solid waste disposal, waste-water handling, waste incineration

8.3 Cycling of Matter and the Climate System

Key Terms
biogeochemical cycle
store
global carbon budget
nitrogen fixation

You have learned that Earth and its atmosphere behave as a closed system. This system contains a fixed amount of matter that cannot increase or decrease. However, you also know that the concentration of greenhouse gases in the atmosphere has been increasing. Where did these additional gases come from? The answer lies in natural cycles that transfer matter continuously among the atmosphere, land, water, and living things. An increase in matter in one part of the system is balanced by a decrease in matter in another part of the system. This circulation of matter is known as a **biogeochemical cycle**.

In a typical biogeochemical cycle, materials remain for a short or long period of time in part of the cycle before passing on to the next part of the cycle, as shown in **Figure 8.20**. Places where matter is stored for longer periods are known as **stores**. Stores are also commonly referred to as *reservoirs*. Usually, the cycle is in balance because the amount of material flowing into a store, such as the atmosphere, is nearly the same as the amount flowing out of the store. Human activities, such as coal mining and oil drilling, alter the balance of natural cycles by rapidly releasing large amounts of materials from stores, as illustrated in **Figure 8.20**. For example, burning fossil fuels releases carbon and nitrogen from stores underground and transfers them into the atmosphere. Disruptions of the carbon cycle and the nitrogen cycle by human activities have been a significant cause of recent climate change.

biogeochemical cycle a natural process that exchanges matter and energy between the abiotic environment to the biotic environment and back

store a part of a biogeochemical cycle in which matter or energy accumulates; also called a reservoir

Figure 8.20 Human activities can disrupt natural cycles. The purple arrows indicate human activities that affect natural processes, which are illustrated by the green arrows.

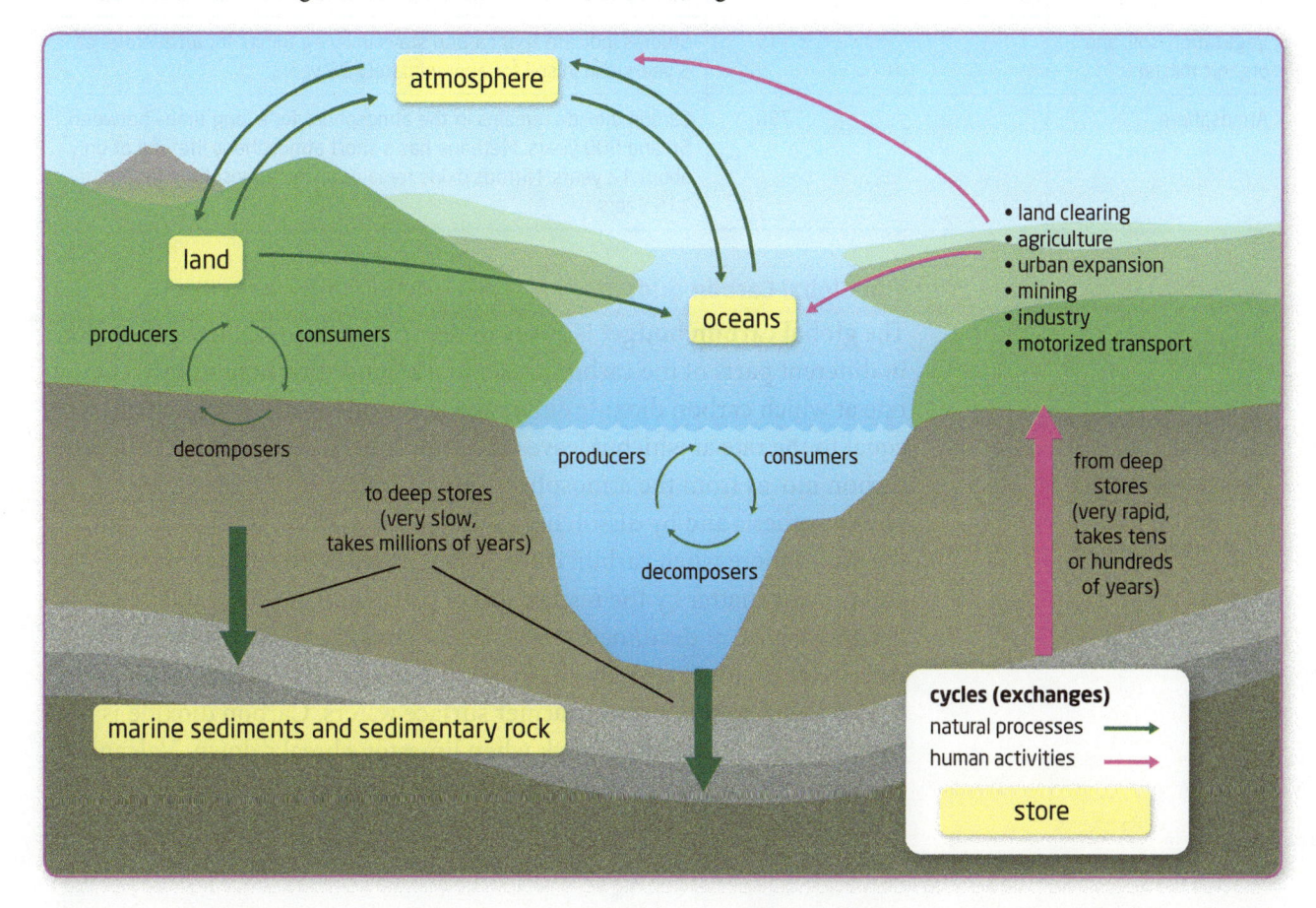

The Carbon Cycle and Climate Change

You already know that carbon dioxide is added naturally to the atmosphere by respiration and is removed from the atmosphere by photosynthesis. However, this balanced exchange of carbon compounds between living things and the atmosphere forms only one small part of the planet-wide carbon cycle, as shown in **Figure 8.21**. Carbon compounds are found in several stores on Earth, as shown in **Table 8.6**. These stores differ greatly in size and in the average length of time that carbon remains in each form. As you learned in Section 8.2, the gases carbon dioxide and methane contain carbon. Some rocks, such as limestone, and sediments on the sea floor contain solid forms of carbon, as do the bodies of living things. Carbon also exists as a solid in coal and as a liquid in oil. Carbon changes form as it moves through the carbon cycle; it can be a solid, a liquid, or a gas.

> **Study Toolkit**
>
> **Word Parts** Break the word *biogeochemical* into parts. Determine what each word part means. Then combine the meanings of the word parts to infer the definition of the whole word.

Table 8.6 Major Stores of Carbon on Earth

Store	Estimated amount of carbon (gigatonnes)	Residence time
Marine sediments and sedimentary rock	68 000 000 to 100 000 000	Carbon is trapped in these rocks for millions or billions of years.
Oceans	39 000	Much of the dissolved carbon may remain in the ocean for 500 to 1000 years as the cold, slow-moving, deep currents move along the ocean floor.
Fossil fuels (coal, oil, and gas)	3 300	Converted into fossil fuels, the carbon can not cycle back into the atmosphere or into living things for hundreds of millions of years.
Vegetation, soil, and organic matter	2 115	Studies indicate that carbon stays in living things for an average of 5 years and in soil for approximately 25 years.
Atmosphere	750	Carbon dioxide remains in the atmosphere for a long time—between 50 and 500 years. Methane has a short atmospheric lifetime of only about 12 years. Nitrous oxide remains in the atmosphere for about 115 years.

The Global Carbon Budget

The **global carbon budget** is a way of describing the exchanges of carbon in different parts of the carbon cycle. In a balanced carbon budget, the rate at which carbon dioxide enters the atmosphere is approximately equal to the rate at which it leaves the atmosphere. As **Figure 8.21** shows, carbon moves from the atmosphere into the other stores mainly by photosynthesis and by dissolving in the ocean. Carbon is released into the atmosphere when carbon dioxide is released from vegetation, soil, and organic matter by the respiration of plants and animals, and by the decomposition of dead matter by microorganisms. Carbon dioxide is released from fossil fuels by combustion. In the ocean, carbon dioxide comes out of solution from warmer surface waters. Carbon dioxide is released from sedimentary rock when limestone breaks down. Volcanic eruptions also release carbon dioxide into the atmosphere.

> **global carbon budget** the relative amounts of carbon in different stores; also an accounting of the exchanges (incomes and losses) of carbon between the stores of the carbon cycle

Vegetation, Soil, and Organic Matter On land, most carbon is stored in plants and animals and in decaying matter and organisms found in soils. Carbon atoms move into living things as animals eat or as plants take carbon dioxide from the air. Carbon moves out of living things as they respire and as cells are replaced with new cells.

The Atmosphere Carbon dioxide is released into the atmosphere from the top layers of the ocean and from the burning of fossil fuels. Carbon is stored in the atmosphere mainly as carbon dioxide, but is also present in methane and chlorofluorocarbons.

The Oceans Carbon dioxide from the atmosphere dissolves in the top layers of the ocean. The carbon remains dissolved in the water that sinks to form deep ocean currents.

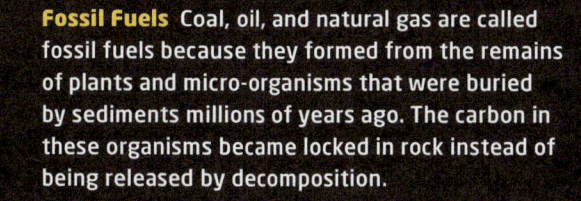

Marine Sediments and Sedimentary Rocks Marine animals, such as corals, clams, oysters, and mussels, use carbon to build their shells and other hard structures. Shells, sediments, and other materials build up in layers on the seabed and eventually harden to form sedimentary rocks, such as chalk and limestone.

Fossil Fuels Coal, oil, and natural gas are called fossil fuels because they formed from the remains of plants and micro-organisms that were buried by sediments millions of years ago. The carbon in these organisms became locked in rock instead of being released by decomposition.

Figure 8.21 The carbon cycle involves the movement of carbon between the oceans, atmosphere, rock, and living things on Earth. Changes in the balance of carbon in different carbon stores can result in climate change.

Activity 8-4

Modelling Carbon Stores

Which carbon store holds the most carbon? In this activity, you will use sticky notes to represent carbon that is stored in various stores.

Materials
- 10 yellow sticky notes
- 1 pink sticky note
- 1 blue sticky note
- 5 photographs

Rules
1 blue sticky note = 50 yellow sticky notes
1 pink sticky note = 100 000 yellow sticky notes

Procedure
1. Use the list of stores in the table to identify the carbon stores represented by each photograph. Identify the form that carbon takes in each store. Record your answers on each photograph.
2. Arrange the photographs in a circle on a table.
3. Use the information in the table to identify the number of sticky notes that belong in each store. Place the proper number of sticky notes on each photograph.

Questions
1. Which store holds the most carbon? How long does carbon remain in that store?
2. What factors affect how much carbon is in the fossil-fuels store? How would you model the recent change in the rate at which carbon remains in that store?
3. How does the thermohaline circulation pattern in the ocean affect the amount of carbon in the ocean?
4. Can you see any relationship between the amount of carbon in a store and the length of time that the carbon remains in the store?

Major Stores of Carbon on Earth Relative to the Atmosphere

Store	Relative Amount in Store
Rock and sediments	91 000–130 000
Oceans	52
Fossil fuels	4
Vegetation, soil, and organic matter	3
Atmosphere	1

How Human Activities Affect the Carbon Cycle

Human activities alter the carbon cycle by changing the relative amounts of carbon in each store and the length of time that carbon remains in each store. For example, carbon compounds are stored as fossil fuels for hundreds of millions of years. When humans burn fossil fuels, these carbon compounds are released into the atmosphere in much larger amounts and in a much shorter time period than they would be naturally. As a result, carbon compounds build up in the atmosphere, which leads to global warming.

When the amount of carbon dioxide in the atmosphere increases, the oceans begin to absorb additional carbon dioxide from the atmosphere. This process is part of a natural negative feedback loop that acts to maintain the amount of carbon dioxide in the atmosphere and, thus, the global average temperature. However, this absorption of carbon dioxide by the oceans causes the oceans to become warmer and more acidic, and their ability to absorb carbon dioxide is reduced. This imbalance could result in a positive feedback loop that accelerates the rate of global warming.

> **Learning Check**
>
> 1. What is the relationship between the terms *biogeochemical cycle* and *store*?
> 2. Identify the five carbon stores described in **Figure 8.21**.
> 3. Draw a time line that illustrates the relative amounts of time that a single carbon atom would spend in each reservoir if it were traced through the entire carbon cycle.
> 4. How does driving to school upset the global carbon budget?

The Nitrogen Cycle and Climate Change

Eighty percent of the atmosphere consists of nitrogen gas (N_2). In this form, nitrogen is very stable and non-reactive. However, nitrogen is used by living things in many physical processes. Before nitrogen can enter other parts of its cycle and be used by living things, it must be converted into a chemically reactive form such as ammonium (NH_4^+) or nitrate (NO_3^-). In these forms, and in gases such as nitrous oxide (N_2O), nitrogen plays a significant role in climate change.

Nitrogen Fixation

Because nitrogen gas is very stable, it takes large amounts of energy to split apart each molecule. The process that converts nitrogen gas into compounds that contain nitrate or ammonium is called **nitrogen fixation**. This process transfers nitrogen from the atmosphere to the land, water, and organisms. Three routes are responsible for most nitrogen fixation on the planet. The first two are natural and are shown in **Figure 8.22**. The third is exclusively a result of human activity.

In the early 20th century, a new industrial method called the Haber–Bosch process created a revolution in agriculture and had a major impact on the nitrogen cycle. The process uses high temperatures and pressures to combine nitrogen from the atmosphere with hydrogen to make ammonia (NH_3). The ammonia is used to manufacture nitrate fertilizers.

nitrogen fixation the process by which atmospheric nitrogen is changed into forms that can be used by plants and other organisms

Figure 8.22 **A** The extreme temperature at the edge of a lightning bolt allows nitrogen gas to bond with oxygen to form nitrates that living plants can use. **B** Bacteria in the roots of a pea plant convert nitrogen from the soil into a form of nitrogen that the plant can use.

How Humans Affect the Nitrogen Cycle

As shown in **Figure 8.23**, human activities have an impact on the functioning of the nitrogen cycle. In general, these human activities can be classified into three categories: addition of nitrogen to the land, addition of nitrogen to water, and addition of nitrogen to the atmosphere.

Figure 8.23 Human activities, such as industry and agriculture, alter the nitrogen cycle.

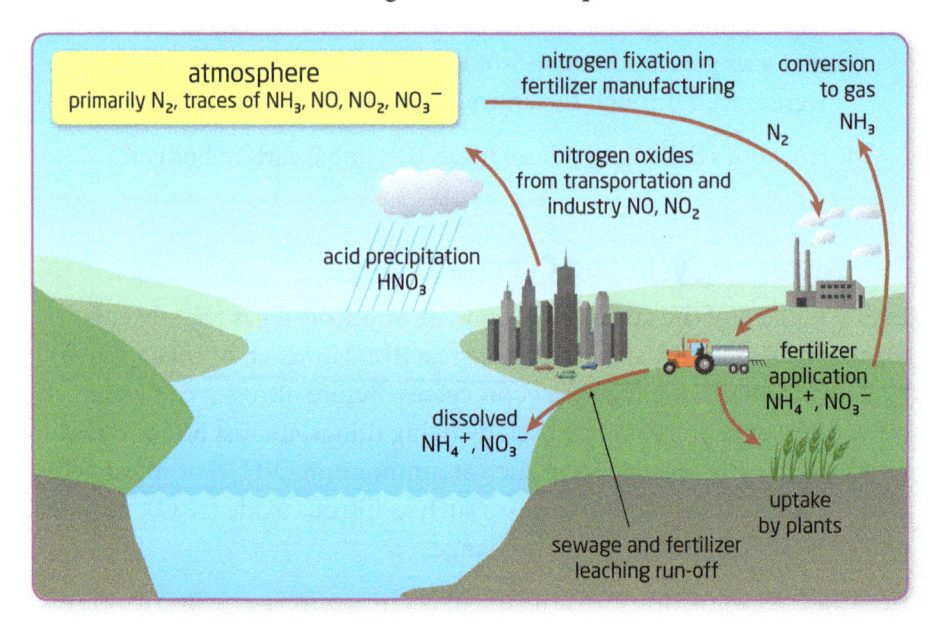

The Effect of Agriculture on the Nitrogen Cycle

Experts estimate that agricultural activities now account for as much as one half of all nitrogen fixation on Earth. Modern agriculture involves the use of manufactured fertilizers over a large area. Industrial processes manufacture over 100 million tonnes of nitrogen fertilizer per year. This fertilizer helps to grow crops that sustain about one third of Earth's population. But while artificial fertilizer helps to reduce starvation in some parts of the world, its overuse contributes to many environmental problems, including climate change.

Water Pollution and the Nitrogen Cycle

When farmers add more fertilizer to fields than their crops can take up, the excess nitrogen builds up in the soil. Rain and melting snow wash the nitrogen from the soil and carry it to nearby waterways. In streams and lakes, the nitrates cause rapid growth of algae and other water plants. Algal blooms clog waterways and deprive other aquatic organisms of oxygen. Nitrates in both surface water and ground water can also cause harm to human health, because nitrates in drinking water may lead to cancer.

At the mouths of rivers, massive quantities of fertilizers, sewage, and livestock waste pour into the ocean, creating *dead zones*. In these areas, algal blooms have created huge masses of dead algae. As the algae decompose, oxygen in the water is used up, making these areas unfit for all organisms that require oxygen. About 150 dead zones currently exist in the world's oceans, covering hundreds of thousands of square kilometres. In Canada, this problem is most noticeable in Québec and in Lake Winnipeg in Manitoba.

How Air Pollution Affects the Nitrogen Cycle

If you have ever been downwind of a large livestock farm, you may have caught a whiff of ammonia (NH_3) in the air. Ammonia reacts with other compounds in the air to form *smog*. Agriculture is also a source of the greehouse gas nitrous oxide (N_2O).

Millions of tonnes of nitrogen are added to the atmosphere every year from the combustion of fossil fuels in power plants and vehicles. Nitric oxide (NO) from vehicle exhaust is a common ingredient in smog and ground-level ozone. Reactive forms of nitrogen from these sources dissolve in moisture in the atmosphere to form nitric acid (HNO_3). This compound returns to Earth's surface in acid rain, which damages lakes, soil, vegetation, bridges, and buildings.

Reducing the Effect of Nitrogen on Climate Change

By reducing the amount of excess nitrogen produced and used by farms and other industries, climate scientists hope to reduce the amount of greenhouse gases that enter the atmosphere. Scientists have proposed several ways to reduce the amount of nitrogen-containing compounds in the air. These actions are outlined in **Table 8.7**. For example, in the midwestern United States, researchers have introduced a program to educate farmers about fertilizer use. The program encourages farmers to use the least amount of fertilizer possible. Participating farmers apply substantially less fertilizer to most of their land than they did previously. This decrease in fertilizer use decreases the excess nitrogen available for fixation. Because water that runs off the land and through rivers eventually reaches the oceans, this practice helps to reduce the size of dead zones in the area.

In Canada, the increased use of precision-farming techniques promises to reduce the amount of nitrogen-based fertilizers used by Canadian farmers in the future. In precision farming, farmers use satellites and geographic information systems to determine exact locations of areas that require fertilizers. Thus, the farmers can apply an appropriate amount of fertilizer to only the specific part of a field that requires fertilizer. This technique will reduce the amount of excess fertilizer that enters rivers, lakes, and oceans.

> **Study Toolkit**
>
> **Synthesizing** Use the flowchart on page 310 to explain how the use of nitrogen-rich fertilizers may lead to sea-level rise.

Table 8.7 Methods of Reducing Nitrogen Emissions

Course of Action	Estimated Maximum Reduction in Reactive Nitrogen Emissions
Controlling nitrogen oxide emissions from the burning of fossil fuels	25 billion kg/year
Increasing the efficiency of fertilizing crops	15 billion kg/year
Improving management of livestock	15 billion kg/year
Providing sewage treatment for half the world's urban population	5 billion kg/year

Section 8.3 Review

Section Summary

- Carbon and nitrogen cycle through living organisms quickly, but also have cycles that can store them in rocks for millions or billions of years.
- Carbon has five main stores: living things, oceans, rocks, fossil fuels, and the atmosphere.
- Human activities, such as the burning of fossil fuels, releases carbon dioxide into the atmosphere, which may result in climate change.
- Nitrogen fixation is the process by which atmospheric nitrogen is changed into forms that can be used by plants and other organisms. It can be done by lightning, by bacteria, or by industry.
- Human activities, especially the use of fertilizers for agriculture, have increased the amount of nitrogen in rivers, lakes, and oceans. This nitrogen causes algal blooms that result in dead zones in lakes and oceans.

Review Questions

K/U 1. Name the sinks in the carbon cycle.

K/U 2. Use **Table 8.6** and **Figure 8.21** to create a flowchart that shows how carbon compounds move between the different stores in the carbon cycle.

A 3. One proposal for dealing with carbon dioxide levels is to plant more trees. Why would this action be a good short-term solution but not necessarily a good long-term sink for carbon?

K/U 4. How are humans affecting the carbon cycle?

K/U 5. In what three ways is nitrogen gas changed into nitrogen molecules usable by living things?

T/I 6. The graph on the right shows the rates at which nitrogen fixation occurred as a result of human activities before 1850 and today. What is the total human-induced increase in nitrogen fixation in terragrams per year since 1850? What percentage increase in total nitrogen fixation has occurred since 1850?

T/I 7. Why might ponds near golf courses have more algae growing in them than pristine mountain ponds do?

C 8. Draw a diagram that illustrates how the carbon cycle and nitrogen cycle are linked.

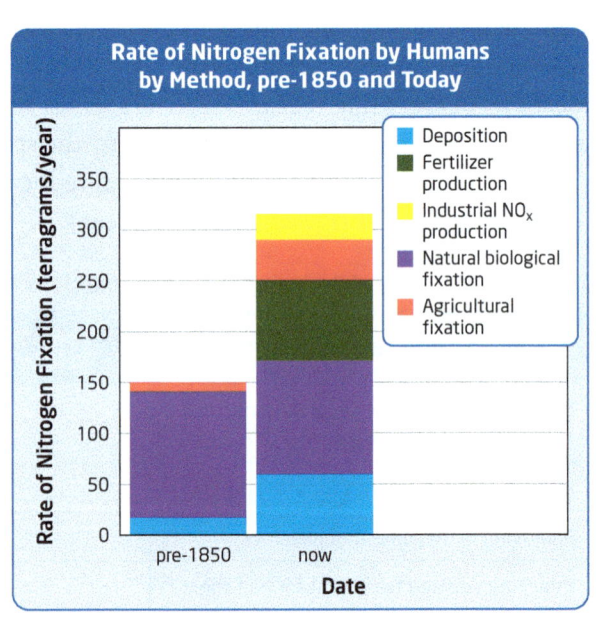

Real World Investigation 8-A

Skill Check

Initiating and Planning

✓ Performing and Recording
✓ Analyzing and Interpreting
✓ Communicating

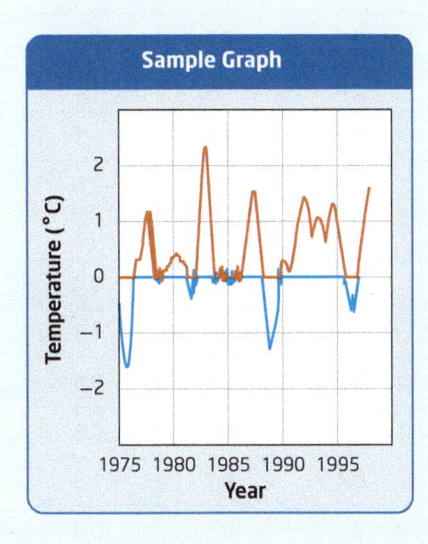

Recognizing the Effects of El Niño and La Niña on Southern Canada

You may have heard a lot of news reports about how El Niño and La Niña events have affected weather worldwide. But how can the temperature of the ocean surface affect the climate several thousands of miles away? In this investigation, you will look at the specific effects of these events on the weather in southern Canada.

Question

How do El Niño and La Niña events affect weather in Canada?

Materials

- graph paper
- coloured pencils (red and blue)

Sample Graph

Organize the Data

1. Construct a graph like the sample graph shown on the left by plotting the data from the table on the next page.
2. Use red to colour areas of the curve above the 0°C line, and blue to colour areas of the curve below the 0°C line.

Analyze and Interpret

1. During El Niño events, the surface temperature of the ocean is more than 0.5°C higher than average. In what years did El Niño occur?
2. During La Niña events, the surface temperature of the ocean is more than 0.5°C lower than average. In what years did La Niña occur?
3. Which years were "normal" (non-event) years?
4. Examine the graphs below. What do they show? Use these graphs to answer the questions on the following page.

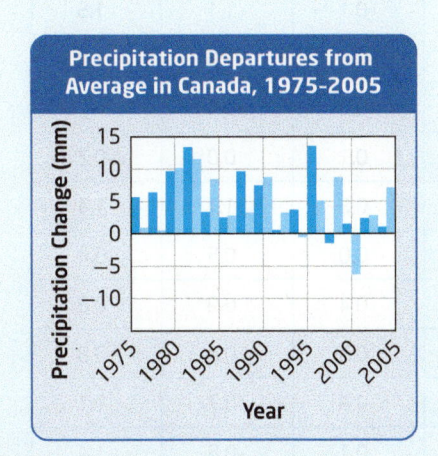

Precipitation Departures from Average in Canada, 1975–2005

Source: Environment Canada, 2003

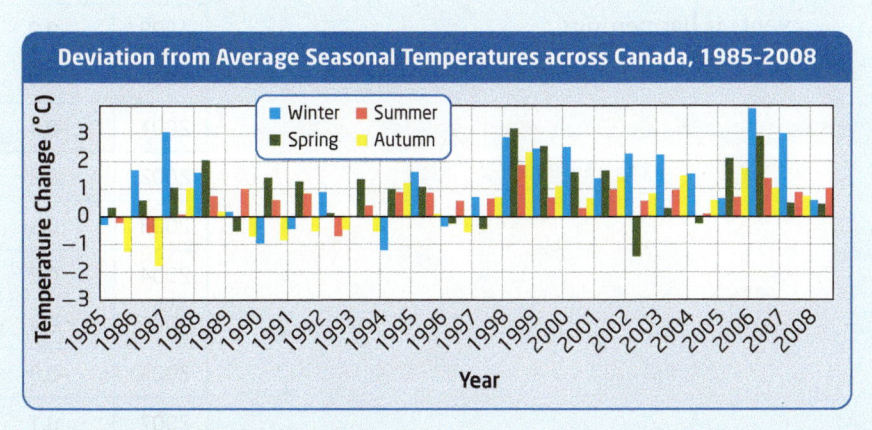

Deviation from Average Seasonal Temperatures across Canada, 1985–2008

Source: Environment Canada, 2006

5. What temperature and precipitation trends in southern Canada are related to El Niño events?

6. What temperature and precipitation trends in southern Canada are related to La Niña events?

7. Based on the pattern in your graph, in what year do you think the next El Niño is likely to occur?

Conclude and Communicate

8. Describe how an increase in the surface temperature of the South Pacific Ocean can affect air currents moving over Canada.

9. Research major winter weather events, floods, and droughts in Ontario. Which of these events coincide with El Niño or La Niña events?

10. Write a summary paragraph that explains how knowledge of El Niño and La Niña events can benefit residents of Ontario.

Extend Your Inquiry and Research Skills

11. **Research** Research the term ENSO (El Niño–Southern Oscillation) and explain why climatologists and meteorologists use this term instead of "El Niño."

12. **Research** Research information about sea-ice anomalies, and compare the area covered by sea ice to the occurrence of El Niño and La Niña. What relationship, if any, exists between the amount of sea ice and whether one of these events is happening?

Deviation from Normal Temperature in the Equatorial Pacific Ocean (°C)

Year	March	June	September	December
1977	0.3	0.4	0.5	0.8
1978	0.0	-0.3	-0.4	-0.1
1979	0.1	0.0	0.3	0.6
1980	0.3	0.3	-0.1	0.0
1981	-0.4	-0.3	-0.2	0.0
1982	0.2	0.7	1.5	2.3
1983	1.6	0.7	-0.5	-0.7
1984	-0.2	-0.4	-0.2	-1.1
1985	-0.8	-0.6	-0.6	-0.4
1986	-0.3	0.0	0.6	1.2
1987	1.2	1.2	1.6	1.1
1988	0.1	-1.3	-1.3	-2.0
1989	-1.2	-0.4	-0.4	-0.1
1990	0.3	0.2	0.3	0.4
1991	0.3	0.8	0.9	1.6
1992	1.5	0.9	-0.1	0.3
1993	0.5	0.7	0.3	0.3
1994	0.2	0.4	0.7	1.3
1995	0.6	0.1	-0.5	-0.8
1996	-0.5	-0.2	-0.1	-0.4
1997	-0.1	1.3	2.2	2.5
1998	1.4	-0.1	-1.1	-1.5
1999	-0.9	-0.8	-1.0	-1.7
2000	-1.0	-0.6	-0.4	-0.7
2001	-0.4	0.1	0.0	-0.2
2002	0.2	0.8	1.1	1.4
2003	0.5	0.0	0.5	0.4
2004	0.2	0.4	0.9	0.8
2005	0.4	0.5	0.2	-0.8
2006	-0.3	0.3	0.7	1.1
2007	0.1	-0.1	-0.8	-1.4

Plan Your Own Investigation 8-B

Skill Check
✓ Initiating and Planning
✓ Performing and Recording
✓ Analyzing and Interpreting
✓ Communicating

Safety Precautions

- Use heat-resistant gloves when touching the lamp.
- Do not let the lamp or its cord come in contact with the water.
- Ensure that the lamp is securely clamped.

Suggested Materials

- retort stand
- ruler
- 2 clear plastic containers
- overhead light with clamp
- 2 thermometers
- watch or clock
- water
- dark, dry soil
- masking tape

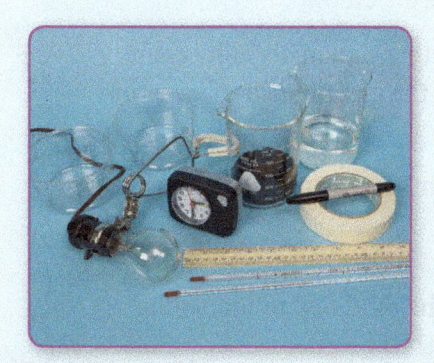

How do soil and water absorb heat differently?

Comparing Heat Absorption of Water and Soil

In this investigation, you will observe and analyze the temperature changes of soil and water when they absorb heat.

Question

How does the amount of heat absorbed by water differ from the amount of heat absorbed by soil?

Hypothesis

Formulate a hypothesis about the ability of soil and water to absorb and release heat.

Plan and Conduct

1. Develop and record your hypothesis.
2. List the steps you will need to take to test your hypothesis. Include in your plan how you will safely use your equipment to compare the rates of heat absorption and release by soil and water. If it is available, use probeware to measure temperature changes.
3. Have your teacher approve your investigation method.
4. Conduct your investigation.
5. Create line graphs to represent your data. Show the rate of heat absorption and heat release for both soil and water.

Analyze and Interpret

1. Which material do you think absorbed the most energy? Explain your reasoning.

Conclude and Communicate

2. Did your results support or contradict your hypothesis? Explain your answer.
3. Based on your findings, predict how a large body of water might influence the climate of a region.

Extend Your Inquiry and Research Skills

4. **Inquiry** Design an experiment to test the heat absorption of snow and ice. Use the results of your experiment to explain the effect that glaciers and icecaps have on the climates of nearby regions.

Chapter 8 Dynamics of Climate Change • NEL 343

Problem Solving Investigation 8-C

Skill Check
✓ Initiating and Planning
✓ Performing and Recording
✓ Analyzing and Interpreting
✓ Communicating

Safety Precautions

- Use caution when handling the lamp, since the light bulb will become very hot.

Suggested Materials

- 2 glass jars or transparent soft-drink bottles of the same size and shape
- light bulb socket with clamp
- 100 W light bulb
- ring stand with clamp
- 2 thermometers or temperature probes
- watch, stopwatch, or clock
- clear plastic wrap
- elastic band
- graph paper
- 2 small pieces of cardboard
- masking tape

Modelling the Greenhouse Effect

Earth would be uninhabitable by humans if not for the natural greenhouse effect. In this investigation, you will model the natural greenhouse effect.

Challenge
Design and build a model to simulate the natural greenhouse effect.

Design Criteria

1. You must use one container for a control and the other for the model simulating the greenhouse effect.
2. You need to use all of the materials listed to construct your model.
3. The control should be an open system, and the greenhouse effect container should model a closed system.
4. You must show a temperature difference between the control and the model after a 15 min trial.

Plan and Construct

1. Review the problem and materials. Decide how you will use the materials to model the greenhouse effect.
2. Have your teacher approve your plan.
3. Build your model and your control.
4. Conduct a 15 min trial, and observe and record your data.

Evaluate

1. Compare your temperature data from the model and the control.
2. In what ways was your model an accurate representation of the greenhouse effect? In what ways was your model an inaccurate representation of the greenhouse effect?
3. Share your design and results with a classmate. How could you refine your design to model the greenhouse effect more accurately?
4. Use your model to explain the anthropogenic greenhouse effect.

Extend Your Inquiry and Research Skills

5. **Inquiry** How could your design be modified to model the anthropogenic greenhouse effect?

Chapter 8 Summary

8.1 Energy Transfer in the Climate System

Key Concepts

- Earth is a system of interrelated parts, including the atmosphere, hydrosphere, rocks, and living things.
- The interrelated processes in the Earth system form a variety of both positive and negative feedback loops, which affect the global climate system by increasing or decreasing the effects of climate change.
- The atmosphere redistributes heat, energy, and moisture around Earth's surface.
- Heat can be transferred by radiation, conduction, and convection.
- Earth's oceans transfer energy as water moves as a result of density differences that are caused by differences in the temperature and salinity of ocean water.
- El Niño and La Niña events are examples of the effects of heat transfer through the atmosphere and oceans.
- To maintain a stable average global temperature, incoming energy and outgoing energy must balance each other exactly. This balance is part of Earth's energy budget.

8.2 Greenhouse Gases and Human Activities

Key Concepts

- Earth emits thermal energy. Greenhouse gases in the atmosphere absorb this energy and radiate it in all directions. The thermal energy that returns to Earth gives rise to the greenhouse effect.
- Less than one gas molecule in a hundred is a greenhouse gas.
- The most common greenhouse gas is water vapour. Other major greenhouse gases include carbon dioxide, methane, ozone, nitrous oxides, and halocarbons.
- Human activities, such as agriculture and the burning of fossil fuels, are increasing the amounts of some of the greenhouse gases in the atmosphere.
- An increase in greenhouse gases has resulted in the anthropogenic greenhouse effect, which may be responsible for recent climate change.
- You can reduce your contribution of greenhouse gases by conserving electricity, improving home-heating efficiency, and minimizing waste as much as possible.

8.3 Cycling of Matter and the Climate System

Key Concepts

- Carbon and nitrogen cycle through living organisms quickly, but also have cycles that can store them in rocks for millions or billions of years.
- Carbon has five main stores: living things, oceans, rocks, fossil fuels, and the atmosphere.
- Human activities, such as the burning of fossil fuels, releases carbon dioxide into the atmosphere, which may result in climate change.
- Nitrogen fixation is the process by which atmospheric nitrogen is changed into forms that can be used by plants and other organisms. It can be done by lightning, by bacteria, or by industry.
- Human activities, especially the use of fertilizers for agriculture, have increased the amount of nitrogen in rivers, lakes, and oceans. This nitrogen causes algal blooms that result in dead zones in lakes and oceans.

Chapter 8 Review

Make Your Own Summary

Summarize the key concepts of this chapter using a graphic organizer. The Chapter Summary on the previous page will help you identify the key concepts. Refer to Study Toolkit 4 on pages 565–566 to help you decide which graphic organizer to use.

Reviewing Key Terms

1. _____ can be measured in parts per million. (8.2)

2. Earth is an example of a closed _____. (8.1)

3. A(n) _____ describes the total energy exchange within a system. (8.1)

4. Because methane has a higher _____ than carbon dioxide, scientists are concerned about the increase in methane due to cattle. (8.2)

5. Through the process of _____, nitrogen is changed into forms that living things can use. (8.3)

6. Carbon dioxide, water vapour, and methane are all examples of _____. (8.2)

7. Energy and matter move through reservoirs in the Earth system as part of several _____. (8.3)

8. Matter can be stored in reservoirs, also called _____, for a few minutes to many million years. (8.2)

9. _____ may increase or decrease the effect of one small change on a biogeochemical cycle. (8.1)

Knowledge and Understanding K/U

10. What type of radiation do greenhouse gases allow to pass through the atmosphere? What type of radiation do greenhouse gases absorb?

11. How is an open system different from a closed system?

12. Why must scientists consider the global warming potential of different gases when recommending action to slow global warming?

13. Use the diagram below to explain what happens to most of the solar energy that enters the Earth system.

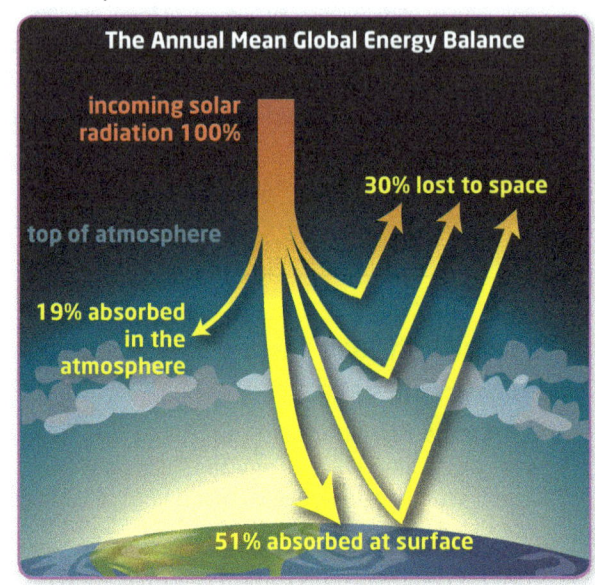

The Annual Mean Global Energy Balance
- incoming solar radiation 100%
- top of atmosphere
- 30% lost to space
- 19% absorbed in the atmosphere
- 51% absorbed at surface

14. Give an example of how energy is transferred by convection in the Earth system.

15. How does a decrease in albedo affect a positive feedback loop that begins with a rise in the global average temperature?

16. Is the feedback loop shown below a positive or negative feedback loop? Explain your answer.

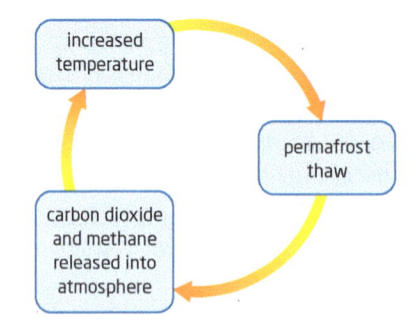

- increased temperature → permafrost thaw → carbon dioxide and methane released into atmosphere → (back to increased temperature)

17. How have humans caused imbalances in the nitrogen cycle?

18. What is the relationship between halocarbons and climate change?

19. How is Earth's natural greenhouse effect different from the anthropogenic greenhouse effect?

346 NEL • Unit 3 Climate Change

Thinking and Investigation T/I

20. Which would be more effective in reducing global warming: reducing methane levels to those of pre-industrial levels or reducing carbon dioxide levels to pre-industrial levels? Explain your choice.

21. How can El Niño, which occurs in the southern Pacific Ocean, affect weather in Canada?

22. Five hundred million years ago, carbon dioxide levels in the atmosphere were about 8000 ppm by volume. The current level is about 385 ppm by volume. Because Earth is a closed system and matter cannot be created or destroyed, what happened to the carbon?

23. The graph below shows carbon dioxide concentrations in Earth's atmosphere as measured at Mauna Loa, in Hawaii. Why do you think the concentration of carbon dioxide has a peak and a low point each year?

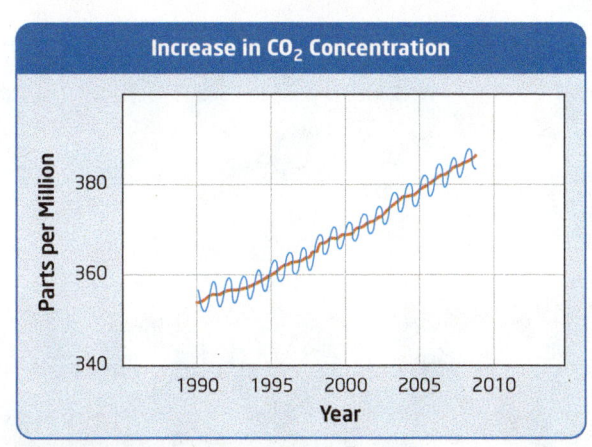

Increase in CO₂ Concentration

Communication C

24. **BIG IDEAS** Earth's climate is dynamic and is the result of interacting systems and processes. Create a model of an open system and a model of a closed system. Use your models to explain why Earth is a closed system.

25. **BIG IDEAS** Global climate change is influenced by both natural and human factors. Imagine that you have been asked to summarize the greenhouse effect for students in an elementary class. Write a paragraph that describes how the greenhouse effect regulates Earth's global temperature.

26. **BIG IDEAS** Climate change affects living things and natural systems in a variety of ways. Draw an example of a positive feedback loop for the melting of the Arctic icecap.

27. **BIG IDEAS** People have the responsibility to assess their impact on climate change and to identify effective courses of action to reduce this impact. Create a cartoon that illustrates one way in which people affect climate change. The cartoon should indicate how human activities affect climate change and how humans can adapt their lifestyles to reduce this impact.

Application A

28. Create a list of actions that you could take to limit greenhouse gas production.

29. One plan that has been suggested to counteract the greenhouse effect is to sprinkle iron dust over large patches of ocean, allowing algae to grow, die, and fall to the sea floor. Assess the benefits and drawbacks of this plan.

30. Why might a climate scientist be more concerned about an increase of 20 parts per billion of nitrous oxide in the atmosphere than an increase of 5000 parts per billion of carbon dioxide in the atmosphere?

31. A puddle of water lying in the sun on a black, paved road evaporates. Explain how convection, conduction, and radiation are involved in this process. Then explain how this process affects climate change.

32. Think about your everyday activities. Identify three of your activities that affect the nitrogen cycle and three of your activities that affect the carbon cycle. Then identify ways that you can reduce your personal impact on the nitrogen cycle and the carbon cycle.

Chapter 9
Addressing Climate Change

What You Will Learn

In this chapter, you will learn how to...
- **identify** the tools used to measure past and present climate change
- **investigate** how scientists predict future climate
- **describe** Canada's contribution to climate change

Why It Matters

How humans react to the changes in climate will affect the lives of future generations. However, we have to give up some conveniences in order to make global changes and avert potential climatic disasters.

Skills You Will Use

In this chapter, you will learn how to...
- **analyze** different sources of scientific data for evidence of climate change
- **assess** the effectiveness of programs and initiatives to address the issue of climate change
- **investigate** cause-and-effect relationships related to climate change

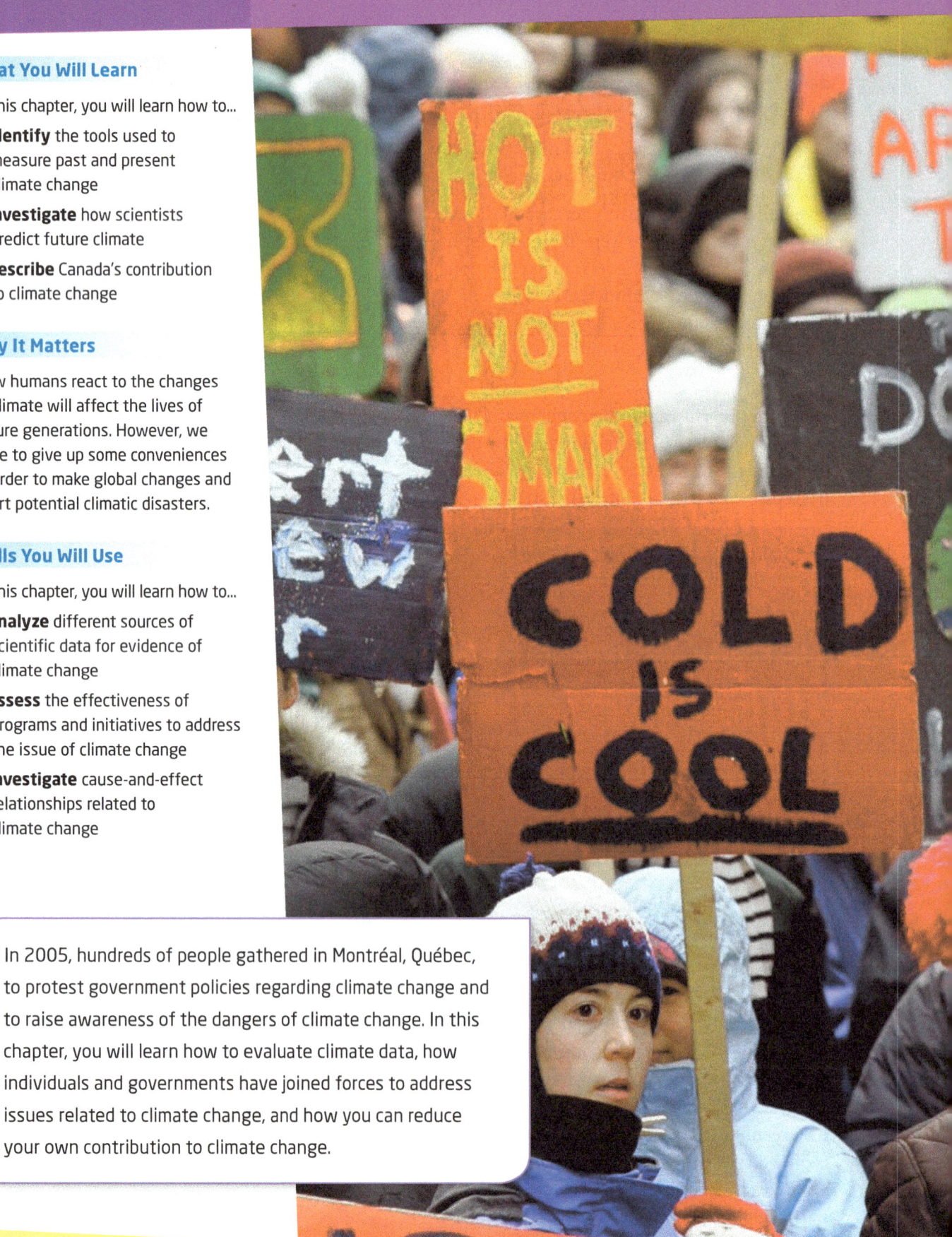

In 2005, hundreds of people gathered in Montréal, Québec, to protest government policies regarding climate change and to raise awareness of the dangers of climate change. In this chapter, you will learn how to evaluate climate data, how individuals and governments have joined forces to address issues related to climate change, and how you can reduce your own contribution to climate change.

Activity 9-1

Who Is Responsible for Responding to Climate Change?

The island nation of Kiribati is expected to be completely submerged before 2020 as a result of rising sea level. Because humans may have played a role in the rise of the sea level, how much should the global community be responsible for the effects on low-lying nations?

Kiribati's capital and largest city, South Tarawa

The island nation of Kiribati lies in the Pacific Ocean between Hawaii and Australia. Although the 32 islands that make up the nation of Kiribati are spread over an area of 3 500 000 km^2, their total land area is smaller than the island of Hawaii.

Procedure

1. Form groups of four people.
   a. One person will role-play an islander from Kiribati. This person will try to negotiate details related to a new home to which the 10 000 islanders can move.
   b. The other three group members will role-play government officials from Australia, Canada, and the United States. None of these nations wants to imply that they are responsible for the situation in Kiribati.

2. Take turns trying to negotiate a deal for resettling the people of Kiribati. Each person should have three chances to speak.

3. After everyone has spoken three times, write out your position on what should happen to the people of Kiribati and who should help.

Question

1. The people affected most by changing climate are often those who have contributed the least to that change. What is our responsibility to help these people deal with the situation that we helped create? Explain your answer.

Study Toolkit

These strategies will help you use this textbook to develop your understanding of science concepts and skills.
To find out more about these and other strategies, refer to the Study Toolkit Overview, which begins on page 560.

Organizing Your Learning

Identifying Cause and Effect

A **cause-and-effect map** can help you identify causal relationships. For example, examine this passage and the cause-and-effect map below it:

Most climate scientists agree that an increase in greenhouse gases is the largest single cause of current climate change. The main human causes of this increase are activities that produce air pollution and activities that reduce the ability of natural cycles to absorb greenhouse gases (such as cutting down forests).

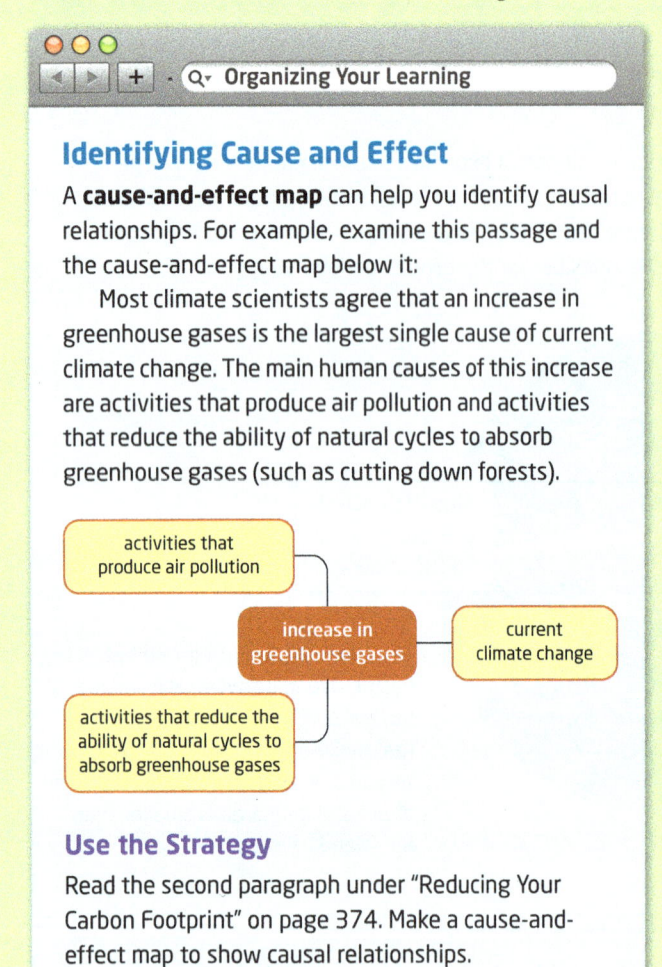

```
activities that                  
produce air pollution  ──┐        
                         ├── increase in ──── current
                         │   greenhouse gases   climate change
activities that reduce the │
ability of natural cycles to ──┘
absorb greenhouse gases
```

Use the Strategy

Read the second paragraph under "Reducing Your Carbon Footprint" on page 374. Make a cause-and-effect map to show causal relationships.

Word Study

Creating a Word Map

A **word map** can help you grasp the meaning of a new word or concept.

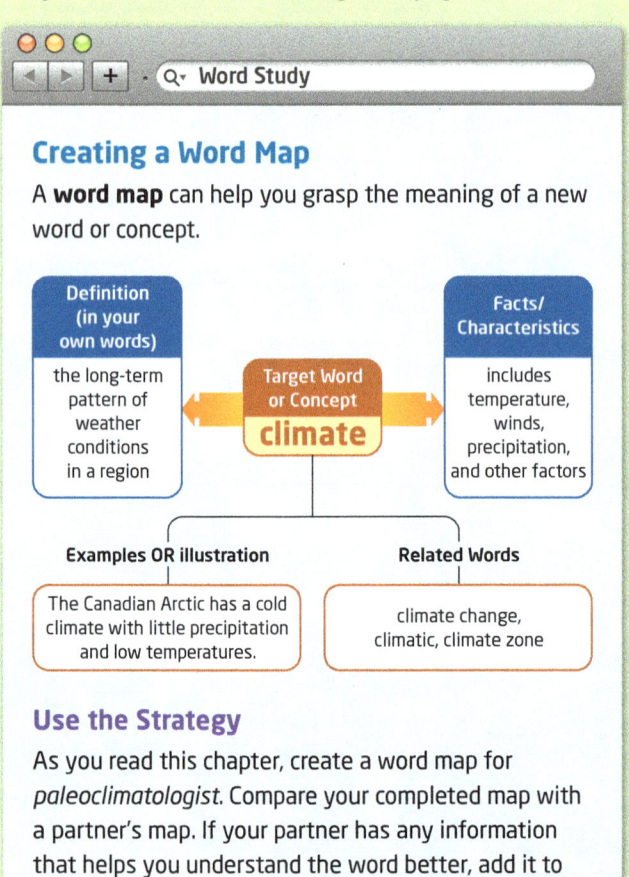

- **Definition (in your own words):** the long-term pattern of weather conditions in a region
- **Target Word or Concept:** climate
- **Facts/Characteristics:** includes temperature, winds, precipitation, and other factors
- **Examples OR illustration:** The Canadian Arctic has a cold climate with little precipitation and low temperatures.
- **Related Words:** climate change, climatic, climate zone

Use the Strategy

As you read this chapter, create a word map for *paleoclimatologist*. Compare your completed map with a partner's map. If your partner has any information that helps you understand the word better, add it to your word map.

Reading Effectively

Identifying the Main Ideas and Details

The title, headings, and subheadings of a chapter can help you identify and organize the main ideas and details, as shown in the example on the right.

Use the Strategy

Skim Chapter 9 and make an outline like the one on the right, using the title, the section headings, and at least two subheadings.

You can use outlines like this one to preview a chapter, and then use it to take notes to help prepare for a test.

Overall Main Idea:
Dynamics of Climate Change

Three influences on climate change:
- Energy Transfer in the Climate System
- Greenhouse Gases and Human Activities
- Cycling of Matter and the Climate System

Two biogeochemical cycles that affect climate:
- The Carbon Cycle
- The Nitrogen Cycle

9.1 Discovering Past Climates

People have been recording weather data for only a few hundred years. To learn about what Earth's climate was like more than a few centuries ago, scientists must get creative. People who study past climates are called **paleoclimatologists**. These scientists are interested in how Earth's climate system formed and has changed throughout Earth's history.

What Tree Rings Reveal About Past Climates

If you want to know what the weather was like 150 years ago, you could get the answer from an old tree. As trees grow, rings of new growth form within the trunk. Tree growth is affected by temperature and rainfall. The amount that a tree grows each season is indicated by the size and colour of the annual rings, which you can see in the cross section of the tree trunk in **Figure 9.1**.

A wide tree ring indicates wet and cool weather, which allows trees to grow rapidly. A thin ring is produced in dry and hot conditions, when tree growth is slower. A dark ring marks growth during late summer, and a light-coloured ring indicates growth during spring. Tree rings can also provide evidence of floods, droughts, insect attacks, and lightning strikes.

Living trees hold records of climate dating back no more than a few hundred years. Tree trunks from archaeological sites allow scientists to determine what climate was like a few thousand years ago.

Figure 9.1 Each cross section of a tree trunk shown here reveals dozens of rings. A tree grows an additional ring every year.

Key Terms
paleoclimatologist
ice core
isotope
sedimentary rock
fossil

paleoclimatologist a scientist who studies past climates on Earth

Ice Cores–Records of Past Climates

One of the most important sources of evidence used by paleoclimatologists lies buried deep in polar and glacial ice. The great ice sheets that cover most of Greenland and Antarctica have built up over hundreds of thousands of winters. Like tree rings, layers of snow and ice accumulate year after year. To uncover evidence of past climate conditions, scientists use a special drill, shown in **Figure 9.2A**, that penetrates deep into the layers to extract long, cylinder-shaped samples called **ice cores**, as shown in **Figure 9.2B**.

ice core a long cylinder of ice obtained by drilling into a glacier

The extent of the climate record obtained by drilling depends on the depth of the ice core. The European Project for Ice Coring in Antarctica (EPICA) obtained climate records from Antarctic ice that date back nearly 800 000 years. Drilling was completed in December 2004, reaching a final drilling depth of 3270 m. Data from this project are being compared with data from earlier research on ice cores extracted in Greenland by the Greenland Ice Core Project (GRIP). The comparison of ice from these two sites provides a more complete picture of natural climate variability around the globe than scientists have had before.

Activity 9-2

Analyzing Tree Rings

How can trees tell us about climate? In this activity, you will analyze tree growth rings for evidence of temperature changes and precipitation patterns.

Materials
- ruler
- pencil
- paper or notebook
- tree stump (sawn off) or other cross section of a tree

Procedure
1. Find the innermost ring of the tree. This is the oldest ring. Counting the rings from there to the edge of the tree stump gives you the tree's age. How old is your tree?
2. Measure and record the thickness of several rings near the centre and near the outer edge of your tree stump.
3. Record as many distinctive growth patterns or other markings as you can. For example, do you see three thick, dark rings in a row? Or a thin ring, a thin black line representing a forest fire, and a thick, black line?
4. Wash your hands after this activity.

The rings of a tree represent the growing conditions for each year of the tree's life.

Questions
1. How did the length of the growing seasons change as the tree aged? What was your evidence for this inference?
2. Compare your tree's growth pattern with those of two other students. Do you think the lives of your trees overlapped? Explain your answer.
3. Investigate the climate and major events (such as fires and insects that infest trees) over some of the lifetime of your tree. What relationships can you find between the tree rings and what happened when the tree was growing?

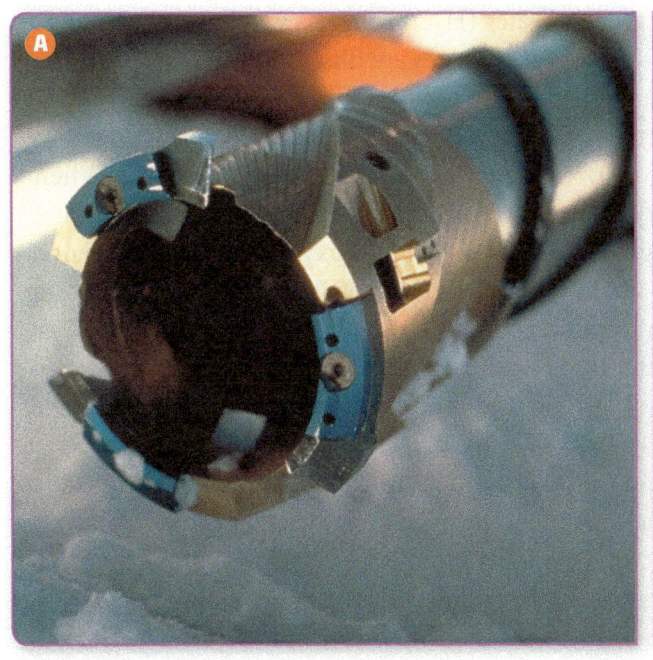

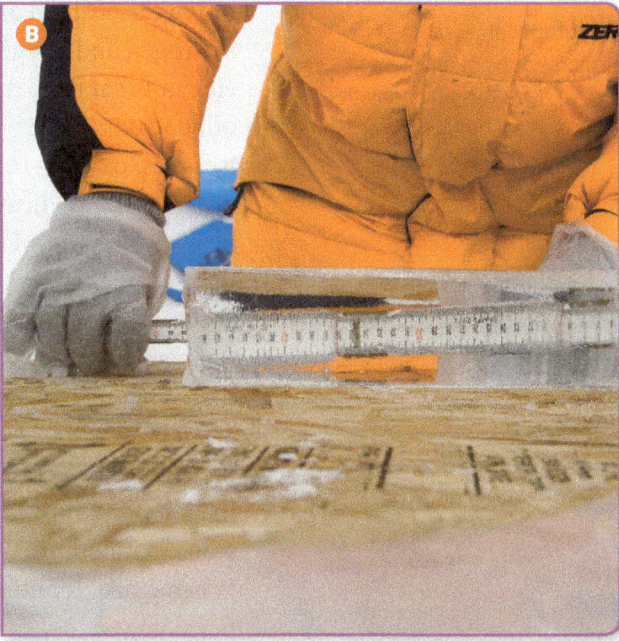

Evidence of Past Climates Obtained from Ice Cores

The ice that makes up ice cores is deposited annually when the summer melt is not enough to get rid of the previous winter's snow. The formation of glacial ice requires only a few hours of strong sunshine to cause the snow to form an airtight crust, even at –20°C or colder. Ice cores hold four types of clues frozen in time: the types of particles trapped in the ice, the size and shape of ice crystals, the composition of trapped air, and the composition of the water in the ice. Each clue remains trapped as a frozen record, until the ice melts.

1. Dissolved and particulate matter in the ice Dust, ashes, salts, plant pollen, and other matter drifting in the air are brought to Earth's surface when it rains or snows. Frozen samples of these materials give clues about events and conditions, such as volcanic eruptions, meteorite impacts, forest fires, and vegetation cover.

2. Physical characteristics of the ice Ice can occur in many forms—from snowflakes and hail to glaciers and pack ice. In each form, the ice is made up of crystals of frozen water that can vary greatly in size and shape. The physical characteristics of the ice crystals indicate the conditions of temperature and humidity at the time the ice crystals formed.

3. The composition of trapped air bubbles When water freezes, tiny air bubbles in the water may become trapped inside the ice. These pockets of air remain unchanged in the ice, providing time capsules of the atmospheric composition on the day when the ice formed. Analysis of the air locked inside ice cores at different depths gives scientists a record of changes in the atmospheric concentration of greenhouse gases over hundreds of thousands of years.

Figure 9.2 Scientists use **A** a special drill to obtain **B** ice cores. A drill can penetrate to a depth of 50 to 70 m in one day. This depth is equivalent to about 200 years of ice build-up.

Suggested Investigation

Data Analysis Investigation 9-A, Understanding Ice-Core Data, on page 382

isotope any of two or more forms of an element that have the same number of protons but a different number of neutrons (for example, deuterium is an isotope of hydrogen)

4. The composition of the ice Water (H₂O) contains varying proportions of hydrogen and oxygen isotopes. **Isotopes** are different atoms of a particular element that have the same number of protons but a different number of neutrons. For example, oxygen (O) has three naturally occurring isotopes, oxygen-16 (^{16}O), oxygen-17 (^{17}O), and oxygen-18 (^{18}O). When water contains "heavy" oxygen-18, the molecular weight of the water is heavier than the weight of water that contains oxygen-16. The difference in molecular weight affects the physical properties of the water, including the freezing point. Water that contains oxygen-18 freezes at a higher temperature than water that contains oxygen-16 does. In addition, water that contains oxygen-16 evaporates more quickly than water that contains oxygen-18 does.

The relative concentration of isotopes in different layers of ice indicates the temperature at the time the ice formed. Polar ice that forms when global temperature is high contains a higher percentage of oxygen-18. When global temperature is low, polar ice that forms contains a lower percentage of oxygen-18. This relationship is shown in **Figure 9.3**. Thus, different concentrations of isotopes in different layers of ice allow scientists to reconstruct temperature changes over many years.

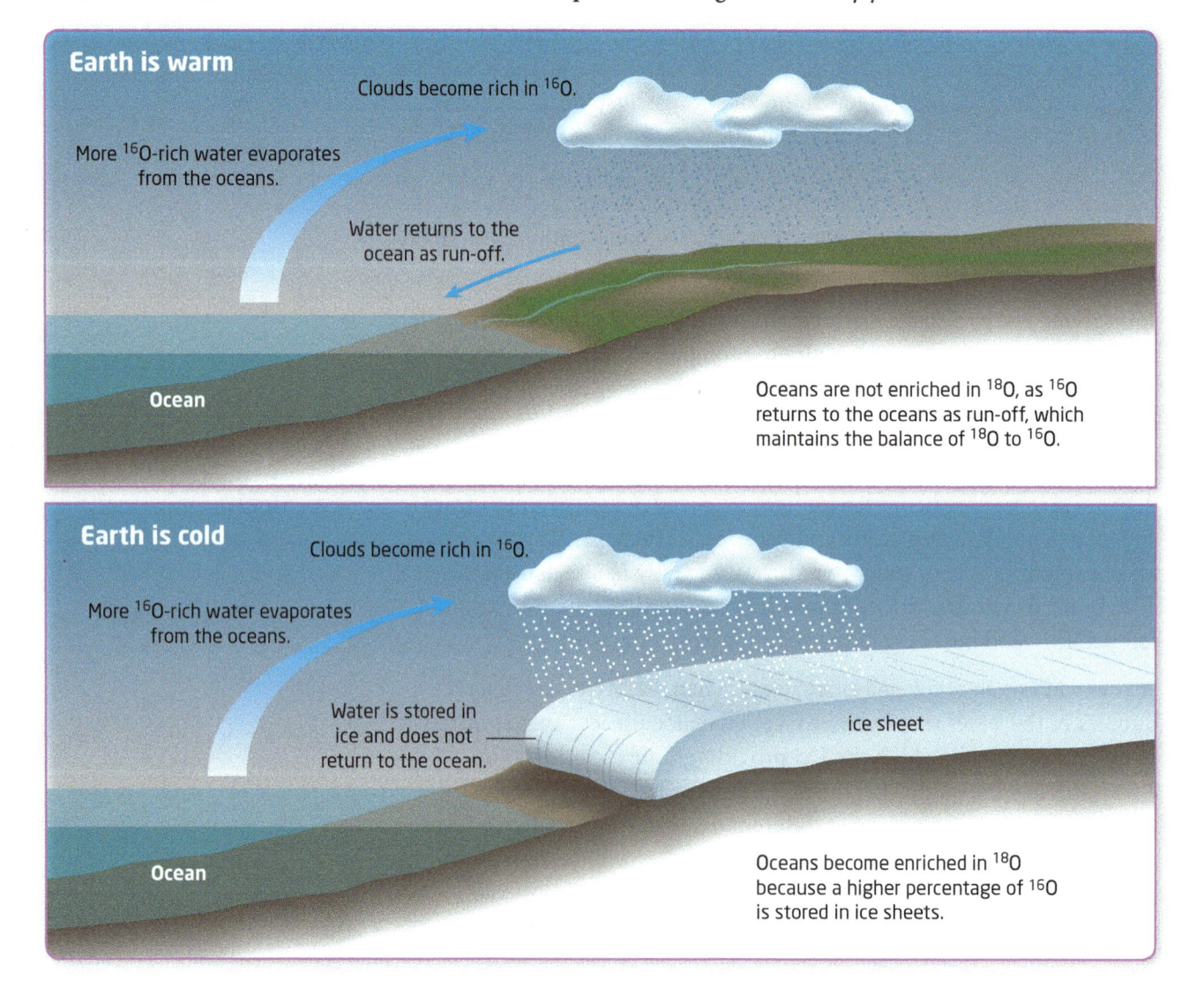

Figure 9.3 The amount of different oxygen isotopes in ice layers depends on global temperature changes.

Earth is warm
- Clouds become rich in ^{16}O.
- More ^{16}O-rich water evaporates from the oceans.
- Water returns to the ocean as run-off.
- Ocean
- Oceans are not enriched in ^{18}O, as ^{16}O returns to the oceans as run-off, which maintains the balance of ^{18}O to ^{16}O.

Earth is cold
- Clouds become rich in ^{16}O.
- More ^{16}O-rich water evaporates from the oceans.
- Water is stored in ice and does not return to the ocean.
- ice sheet
- Ocean
- Oceans become enriched in ^{18}O because a higher percentage of ^{16}O is stored in ice sheets.

How Scientists Determine Patterns of Past Climate Change

Chemical analyses of ice cores can be used to identify patterns of past climate change. For example, **Figure 9.4** shows carbon dioxide data that were gathered by studying the gas bubbles in ice cores. The data indicate that concentrations of carbon dioxide in the atmosphere have risen and fallen in a series of cycles over the past 650 000 years.

To estimate atmospheric temperatures in the past, scientists measure concentrations of hydrogen and oxygen isotopes in the ice from which the carbon dioxide data were obtained. The ratio of heavy water to light water in an ice core is directly related to temperature. According to the graph, carbon dioxide concentrations and temperatures are closely related. Does this connection prove that rising levels of carbon dioxide cause global warming? Or could global warming be caused by other factors that also lead to increasing concentrations of carbon dioxide? To answer these questions, scientists use computer models to determine how different variables determine different patterns of climate change.

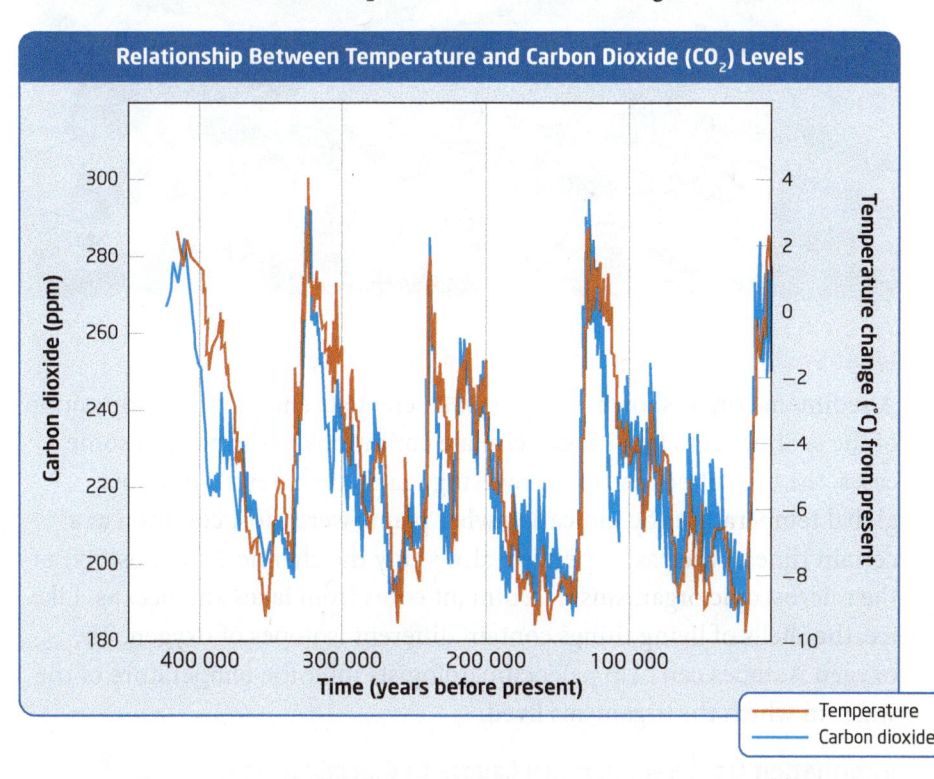

Figure 9.4 Changes in carbon dioxide concentration and temperatures can be graphed based on data from ice cores and sediment cores. The red line represents temperature, and the blue line indicates carbon dioxide levels.

Learning Check

1. How do paleoclimatologists use tree rings to study climate?
2. What four types of evidence do ice cores provide?
3. Based on the evidence provided in **Figure 9.4**, do you think increasing carbon dioxide in the atmosphere causes global warming? Explain your answer.
4. Draw a cause-and-effect map to summarize how oxygen isotopes in ice are related to global temperature.

sedimentary rock a type of rock that is formed by the deposition of sediment

Evidence of Past Climates from Sedimentary Rock

The oldest ice on Earth is less than one million years old. To obtain evidence of climates older than this, paleoclimatologists examine rocks. Every year, billions of tonnes of sediment (fragments of rock) wash from the land and accumulate in thick layers on ocean floors and lake beds. The hard parts of small sea creatures (such as diatoms, algae, and foraminifera) and pollen from flowering plants are preserved in these sediments. Over long periods of time, this deposited material becomes compressed and hardened into **sedimentary rock**, such as that shown in **Figure 9.5**.

Figure 9.5 Sedimentary rock results from the build-up of layers of sediment over long periods of time. Particles in each sedimentary layer hold clues to past climates.

What Sediment Cores from Lakes and Oceans Reveal

A sediment core is shown in **Figure 9.6**. Scientists analyze the composition of the sediments to learn about climate conditions in the past. In some cases, the type of pollen from flowering plants provides a clue about global temperatures by indicating what plants were most common at a certain time in the past. Scientists also study the chemical composition of the microscopic organisms in sediment cores from lakes and oceans. Like ice, the shells of living things contain different isotopes of oxygen. The oxygen isotopes can help paleoclimatologists infer the temperature of the water in which the organisms lived.

Information from Sedimentary Layers in Glacial Lakes

In some locations, sediment records in lakes reflect regularly repeating annual changes in sediment deposition. Annual sedimentary layers are called *varves*. Sedimentary layers in many glacial lakes provide a record of the seasonal changes in deposition that happen every year. In the summer months, thick deposits of coarse, light-coloured sediments form as meltwater washes sediment into the lakes. In the winter, when little new sediment is entering the lake, fine, dark-coloured sediments settle to the bottom of the lake. This pattern of light and dark layers can be used to measure the amount of sediment and the type of sediment that was deposited each year. In turn, paleoclimatologists can use this information to estimate rainfall and temperature patterns over a long period of time.

Figure 9.6 Scientists study the variations in chemical composition of sediment cores to estimate past climate patterns.

Evidence of Past Climates from Fossils and Preserved Organisms

The remains or traces of living things, called **fossils**, also provide valuable clues when paleoclimatologists reconstruct past climates. Fossils form when some part of an organism does not decay after the organism's death. The sediment formed by the remains of micro-organisms can be analyzed to obtain information about the composition of the oceans and atmosphere at the time the organisms lived.

Large fossils are also useful to paleoclimatologists. In some cases, bones, teeth, shells, and other hard parts of living things become fossils. In other cases, whole organisms are trapped in amber or are frozen in ice or permafrost. Even footprints, imprints of leaves, and fossilized dung provide information about the organisms that once lived in a region.

fossil the traces or remains of a once-living organism

What Paleoclimatologists Can Learn by Studying Fossils

The types and abundance of fossilized remains in each rock layer help scientists reconstruct the environment at the time the layer formed—including the climate. Because plants and animals are uniquely adapted to the environments in which they live, studying these fossils gives scientists clues about what environments were like thousands to millions of years ago. For example, alligators and palm trees are adapted to life in tropical regions. If fossils of alligators and palm trees were found on an Arctic island, scientists could infer that those Arctic islands once had a warm climate. An example of this use of fossils is shown in **Figure 9.7**.

Some fossils can provide very specific details about climates. When scientists study a fossilized coral reef, the amount and type of fish fossils tell the scientists much about the temperature and the depth of the water, because different species of fish survive in very specific water depths and temperatures.

Figure 9.7 This fossil is the remains of a fern from Earth's Cretaceous Period, which lasted from 145.5 million years ago to 65.5 million years ago. This type of fern grew in a warm, moist tropical climate that was very different from the ice-covered continent of Antarctica on which this fossil was found.

Sense of *time*

The oldest known sedimentary rock in the world was discovered in 2001 by a team of Canadian scientists on the eastern shore of Hudson Bay in northern Québec. The rock sample is 3.75 billion years old. That rock is about four fifths the age of Earth itself.

How Scientists Infer the Rate of Climate Change

The methods described in this section help scientists track climate change. But how long do these changes take to appear, and how long do they last? As you learned in Chapter 7, factors that affect climate act on different time scales. Tectonic plate movement takes millions of years. Orbital changes take several tens of thousands of years. Volcanic activity affects Earth's atmosphere within a day, and the effects can last for several years.

Sedimentary rocks, fossils, and ice cores indicate that climate has changed radically several times throughout Earth's history, as shown in **Figure 9.8**. In some cases, climate change took thousands to millions of years. However, evidence suggests that climate also changed abruptly several times in the past. For example, some ice cores taken from Greenland show increases in average temperature of up to 6°C in a few decades or less.

Scientists are still debating whether climate change is affected more by slow, gradual changes or by sudden, catastrophic changes. This question is at the centre of the controversy about whether humans can cause Earth's climate to change significantly. Recent evidence suggests that the climate shift that caused the last glacial period to end 11 000 years ago may have taken as few as three years to happen, even though the glaciers themselves took thousands of years to melt. A variety of evidence indicates that other ice ages in Earth's history resulted from slow, accumulated changes in the Earth system. However, most climatologists agree that humans are affecting the composition of Earth's atmosphere. This influence may increase or decrease the rate at which climate change progresses.

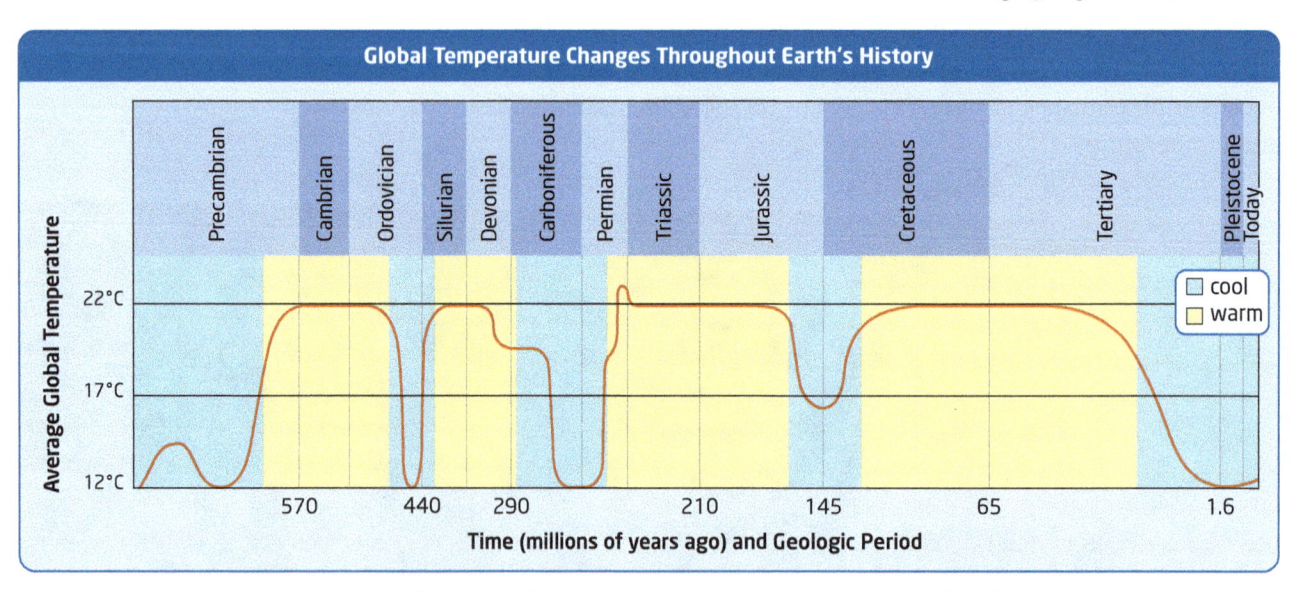

Figure 9.8 Evidence from sedimentary rocks and fossils indicates that before the most recent ice age, Earth experienced several major cooling periods.

Section 9.1 Review

Section Summary

- Paleoclimatologists reconstruct past climates by using the evidence that climate leaves behind in tree rings, ice, sedimentary rock, and fossils.
- Tree rings can provide evidence about growing conditions, such as temperature and precipitation, during the lifetime of the tree.
- Ice cores can provide information about global temperature and the composition of the atmosphere for thousands of years in the past.
- Scientists use chemical analyses of sediment cores from lakes and oceans to reconstruct past conditions of the atmosphere and the hydrosphere.
- Rocks can provide information about the conditions that existed when they formed.
- Fossils are remains of living things. Their distribution and characteristics provide clues about the climate at the time the organisms lived.

Review Questions

K/U 1. List four sources of evidence about past climates.

K/U 2. How do particles frozen in polar and glacial ice help paleoclimatologists reconstruct past climates?

K/U 3. Use the information in **Figure 9.3** to write a brief paragraph that explains how global temperature affects the ratio of oxygen-18 and oxygen-16 in the oceans and in glacial ice.

T/I 4. The diagram on this page shows a series of varves from a glacial lake. Dark layers indicate the winter deposition and light layers indicate summer deposition. How might you explain the difference in the thickness of layers in years 8 and 9?

T/I 5. Describe how the methods scientists use to study sediment cores to find out about past climate conditions are similar to the methods they use when studying ice cores.

A 6. What would finding fossils of tropical fish in sedimentary rock tell you about the climate conditions at the time that the rock formed?

C 7. Use a Venn diagram to compare information provided from tree rings to information provided from ice-core samples.

K/U 8. How can scientists produce graphs of atmospheric carbon dioxide levels for thousands of years in the past, when people have only been able to measure these levels for the last few decades?

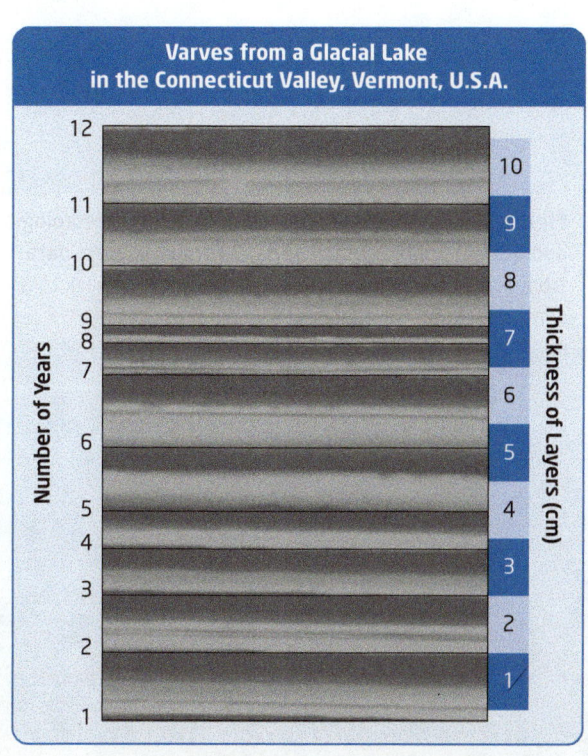

Key Terms
monitor
geostationary
climate model
general circulation model (GCM)
forcing agent

monitor to measure conditions systematically and repeatedly in order to track changes

9.2 Monitoring and Modelling Climate Change

Are oceans getting warmer? Are sea levels rising? To answer questions such as these, scientists need to collect accurate data over a long period of time. Making a consistent, long-term series of observations and measurements is known as **monitoring**. Monitoring is the only way to identify climate trends, such as an increase in average global temperature, reliably.

As well as having a long-term set of data, people who monitor climate change also need to know how the data were obtained. The way in which data are collected, and even the type of instruments used, can affect the reliability of the answers derived from the data. One method of obtaining data related to weather and ocean conditions is shown in **Figure 9.9**.

Improving Technology, Improving Data

Measurements of atmospheric temperature, humidity, precipitation, and other weather data have been collected for 200 years or more. These measurements provide a valuable baseline from which to measure changing weather patterns. However, records from meteorological stations may be somewhat misleading when used to study climate change. Most data were collected where such measurements were convenient, and observations may not have been performed or recorded systematically. Our scientific understanding of climate took a huge leap forward with the invention of technologies that can measure atmospheric changes from high above Earth's surface.

Figure 9.9 Scientists use buoys to monitor meteorologic and oceanographic data. A series of buoys collects data from across the oceans and radios information back to a central location for analysis.

Using Radar to Gather Weather and Climate Data

Meteorologists and climate scientists use radar data to forecast the weather and to estimate global average climate factors, such as humidity and precipitation. Radar systems take measurements by emitting short pulses of microwaves. The microwaves are reflected by water droplets and ice crystals in the atmosphere, as shown in **Figure 9.10**. Computers analyze the returning microwaves and generate an image of the clouds or precipitation based on the analysis. Because the microwave pulses spread out as they move away from the radar station, the radar images are more clear and accurate for areas closer to the radar station. Weather radar is used to track storms, because it can measure conditions that might wreck a weather balloon.

Figure 9.10 A radar instrument transmits short pulses of microwaves that move through the air until they strike an object, such as a raindrop or a snowflake. The object reflects some of the waves back to the radar instrument, thus communicating information about conditions in the atmosphere..

Climate Data from Weather Satellites

The ultimate step in monitoring Earth's climate came with the development of satellites that can measure climatic conditions over the entire planet. Records of Earth's temperature were first obtained from satellites in 1978. Today, hundreds of satellites orbiting Earth measure many different components of our climate system with great accuracy.

Two types of satellite are used to monitor climate:

- **Geostationary satellites** These satellites orbit Earth at the same speed as Earth rotates. Because of this similarity of speed, they remain above the same point on Earth at all times, appearing stationary to an observer on the ground. As a result, the satellites constantly monitor changes over one particular area of the planet.

- **Polar orbiting satellites** These satellites move north and south over the poles as Earth turns beneath them. One complete orbit takes just over 2 h. This type of satellite can monitor the entire planet in about 6 h.

Although satellites have been measuring variables related to Earth's atmosphere since the 1970s, most satellites have been designed for weather forecasting. Climate studies need measurements of subtle trends and changes that can take years to appear. This requirement led to the development of a new generation of instruments that are designed to help answer some of the unsolved questions about climate change.

geostationary describing a satellite that travels around Earth's equator at a speed that matches the speed of Earth's rotation so that the satellite remains in the same position relative to Earth's surface

Study Toolkit

Identifying the Main Idea and Details The headings in this section can be used to organize information about weather satellites. Make an outline to organize the main ideas and details about the satellites in the Earth Observing System.

The Earth Observing System (EOS)

In 1997, Canada, the United States, and Japan combined resources to launch the first of a series of satellites intended to make long-term observations of Earth's changing atmosphere, oceans, land, and ecosystems. This monitoring program is known as the Earth Observing System (EOS). By the end of 2008, more than 20 specialized satellites were in orbit as part of this program. Some of these satellites are illustrated in **Figure 9.11** and the functions of four of these satellites are summarized below.

Quick Scatterometer (*QuikSCAT*) This satellite measures the speed and direction of winds near the surface of the oceans in all types of weather. Scientists are using *QuikSCAT* to find out how winds and water interact to produce El Niño. The satellite also monitors changes in rainforest vegetation and changes in sea ice cover over the polar regions.

Terra This satellite carries five remote sensors to monitor heat emission and reflection from Earth, cloud cover, and pollution in the troposphere. *Terra* started collecting data in February 2000 and is designed to operate for more than 15 years.

Aura Named for the Latin word for air, *Aura* carries four instruments to monitor atmospheric chemistry and concentrations of greenhouse gases. This satellite, shown in **Figure 9.12**, measures ozone, water vapour, CFCs, methane, carbon monoxide, and nitrogen compounds. One significant indicator of climate change monitored by *Aura* is fluctuations in the size of the Antarctic ozone hole.

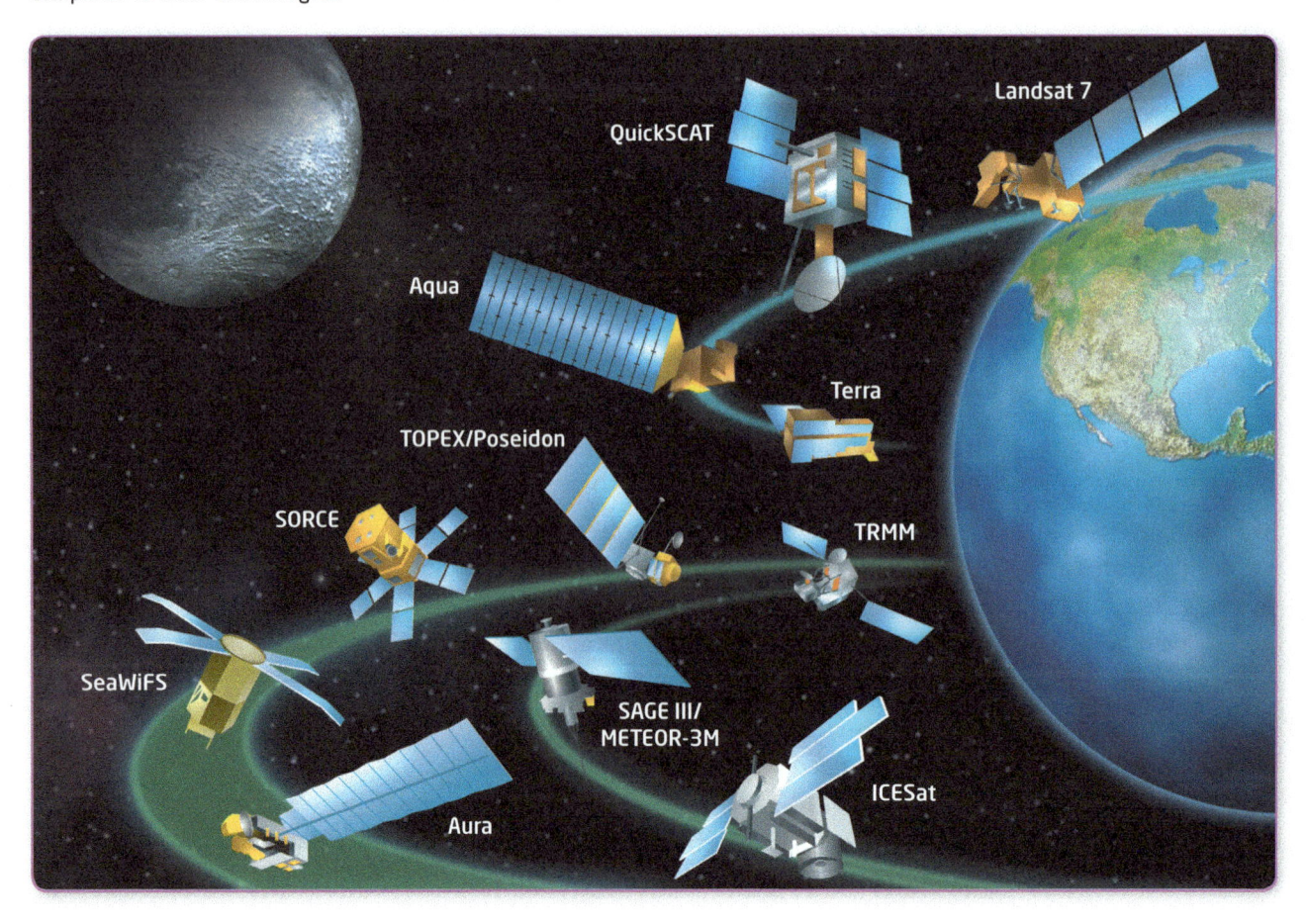

Figure 9.11 As satellite technology improved, older weather and climate satellites were replaced with new satellites that can perform more functions and collect more detailed data compared to older technologies.

Aqua Named for the Latin word for water, this satellite carries six instruments designed to study precipitation, evaporation, and the cycling of water. *Aqua* is shown in **Figure 9.13**. One of its instruments is the Atmospheric Infrared Sounder, or AIRS. It uses cutting-edge technology to accurately measure the amounts of water vapour and greenhouse gases in the atmosphere.

Measurements taken by AIRS over several years will give scientists their most precise picture to date of how water vapour is distributed over the planet in time and space. This information will help determine if global warming is causing the water cycle to accelerate. If Earth's water is moving through this cycle more quickly, more water vapour and clouds will appear in the atmosphere, and more precipitation will fall from the atmosphere at any particular time. Would an increase in global cloud cover lead to further warming, or to cooling, or to neither? Many unanswered questions can be resolved by analyzing new data from this satellite.

Figure 9.12 The *Aura* spacecraft monitors the Antarctic ozone hole.

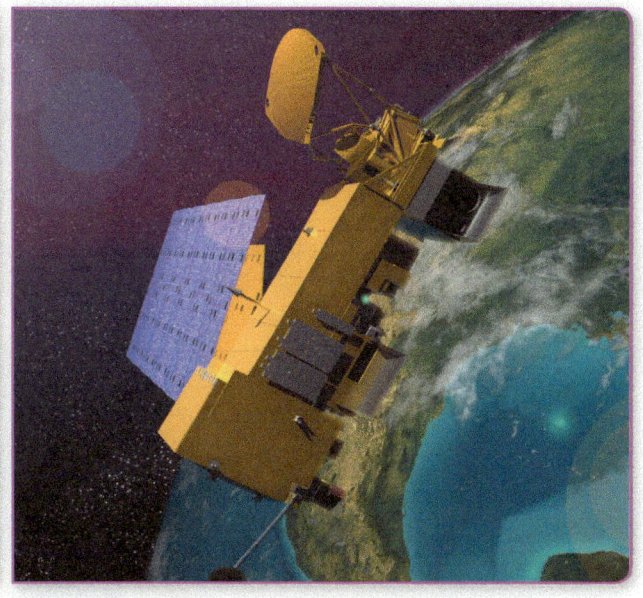

Figure 9.13 Every day, the *Aqua* satellite collects an amount of data equivalent to the data from more than 300 000 weather balloons.

Learning Check

1. Why is monitoring weather important in understanding climate change?
2. Use the illustration in **Figure 9.10** to create a flowchart that explains how radar is used to monitor weather and climate.
3. What major benefit results from monitoring weather by using satellites?
4. How is the mission of the *Terra* satellite different from the mission of the *Aqua* satellite?

Modelling Climates and Climate Change

Gathering accurate data is only the first step in understanding climate change. Equally important is the way in which the data are interpreted. To analyze and interpret data, scientists commonly use models, or representations of objects or systems. Examples of models include maps, miniatures, mathematical formulas, and computer programs.

Because of the size and complexity of Earth's climate system, scientists are unable to construct a physical model planet in their lab that would act like Earth. Therefore, scientists have to use observations of past climates and input the data into computers. Then, they use this information to see which climate features the model predicts well and which ones it does not.

Climate models are computer programs designed to analyze climate data and project how climate may change in the future. Data entered into a model include basic measurements such as global temperatures, polar ice cover, and carbon dioxide concentrations in the atmosphere. Mathematical formulas are applied to these figures based on studies of how different parts of the climate system interact.

Climate models used today link data about the atmosphere and oceans together into **general circulation models (GCMs)**, which are also known as global climate models. An example of a GCM is shown in **Figure 9.14**. These three-dimensional models represent how currents of water and air interact and move around the planet over specified periods of time.

climate model a mathematical or computer program that describes, simulates, and predicts the interactions of the atmosphere, oceans, land surface, and ice of Earth to simulate past, present, and future climate conditions

general circulation model (GCM) a complex computer program that uses mathematical equations to describe the physical processes of the atmosphere and to manipulate the variables that affect how the natural climate system works

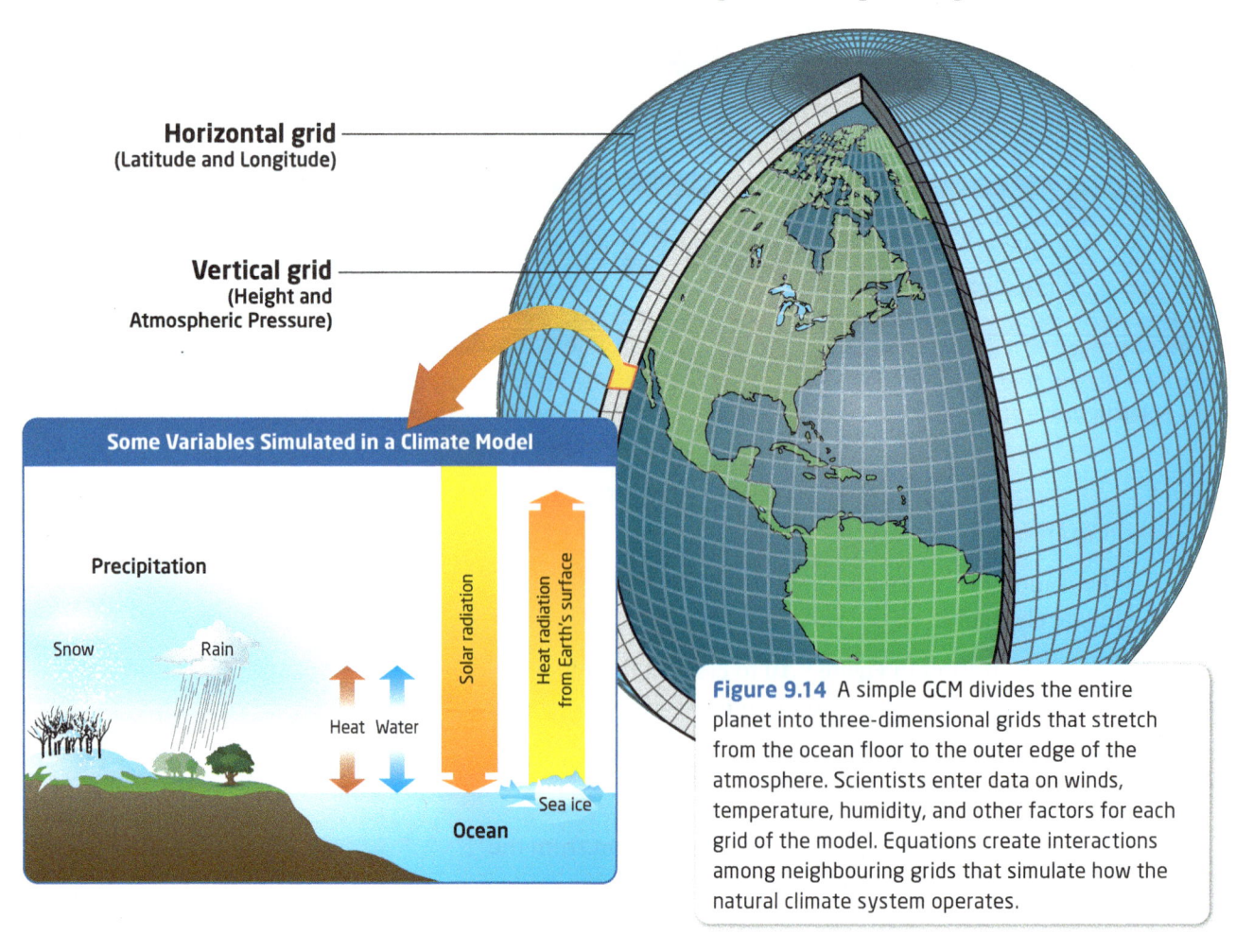

Figure 9.14 A simple GCM divides the entire planet into three-dimensional grids that stretch from the ocean floor to the outer edge of the atmosphere. Scientists enter data on winds, temperature, humidity, and other factors for each grid of the model. Equations create interactions among neighbouring grids that simulate how the natural climate system operates.

Activity 9-3

Pennies from Heaven

How does a computer model simulate interactions between the components of the climate system? In this activity, you will simulate a simple system by using pennies and a couple of rules for how they interact.

Materials
- about 200 pennies or other small markers
- large surface, such as a table

Procedure
1. On a piece of paper, create a square grid that has five rows and five columns.
2. Place a stack of three to eight pennies on each square in the grid. The pennies simulate water vapour, and the model shows how water enters and exits Earth's atmosphere.
3. Make a note of how many pennies are in each square of your grid. Label this diagram "Initial Conditions."
4. Move the pennies according to the rules on the right. After each round, record how many pennies are in each place in the grid. Repeat this step three times.

Rules
1. If a square has three or fewer pennies on it, remove a penny from each adjacent square.
2. If a square has four pennies on it, remove a penny from any adjacent square that has five or more pennies.
3. If a square has five pennies on it and the top one is tails up, do not remove any pennies except for those called for by the other rules. If a square has five pennies on it and the top one is heads up, move the top penny to an adjacent square.
4. If a square has six pennies on it, move one penny to an adjacent square that has four or fewer pennies on it.
5. If a square has seven or more pennies on it, move a penny to each adjacent square.

Questions
1. In which cells of your grid was water vapour content highest and lowest? Explain your answer.
2. How would you change this model to better simulate the movement of water vapour in the atmosphere?

Limitations and Sources of Uncertainty in Climate Models

In December 1961, a scientist named Edward Lorenz ran a weather and climate simulation on his computer. He then input the same data into another computer and got completely different results. He discovered the difference was that one computer carried calculations to six decimal places, while the other one carried them to only three decimal places. The differences in rounding were significant when solving some equations.

Improved accuracy in data and in models has produced "virtual climates" that closely match observations of climate in the real world. Despite scientists' growing understanding of the climate system, however, uncertainties remain. Uncertainties can result from several sources. The precision of the measurements taken of the variables in the system is one source. Three other sources of uncertainty in climate models include:

1. sophistication of the model
2. quality and quantity of the data, and
3. complexity of the variables.

Each of these sources of uncertainty is discussed on the next page.

Figure 9.15 Clouds are a challenge for scientists who develop climate models. Clouds can cool the planet by preventing solar radiation from reaching Earth's surface. They also prevent the escape of thermal energy radiated by Earth's surface, which heats the planet.

> **Study Toolkit**
>
> **Identifying Cause and Effect** General circulation models use equations to simulate cause-and-effect relationships in the climate system. Use a cause-and-effect map to describe how the quality and quantity of data affect a climate model.

1. Sophistication of the Model Computers can simulate solutions to the equations that define the model, but the solutions are only approximations. As you can see in the GCM in **Figure 9.14**, each cell of the grid is very large. Neither the weather nor the climate in one of these cells is the same everywhere in that cell. In typical grids, cells can be more than 100 km along each edge. Therefore, any interactions that might affect the climate, such as places where carbon dioxide is added or stored, have to be approximated inside each cell. Every interaction in that 10 000 km^2 area has to be reduced to a single average value, which is assumed to be true throughout that cell.

2. Quality and Quantity of Data A computer model is only as good as the data entered into it. The quality and quantity of data vary for different components of Earth's climate system. For example, direct measurements of carbon dioxide in the atmosphere began about the middle of the 20th century. Reliable records of other greenhouse gases were not collected until later in the 20th century, and accurate measurements of solar radiation have been recorded only since the 1980s. As you learned at the beginning of this section, developments in technology have improved the quality of data, but some factors in the climate system are more difficult to measure than others are.

3. Complexity of Variables Another area of uncertainty concerns how sensitive the climate system is to different factors. For example, we know that greenhouse gases affect temperature, but scientists disagree over how much and how quickly different greenhouse gases may raise global temperature. Scientists also debate the overall effect of complex factors, such as clouds. Clouds, such as the ones in **Figure 9.15**, reflect sunlight back into space and help cool the planet. On the other hand, they also increase the amount of infrared radiation emitted from the atmosphere to Earth's surface, which helps warm the planet. Changes in cloud cover are one of the main uncertainties in predicting future climate change.

Comparing the Accuracy of Climate Models

Suppose you have two models that give different predictions of how climate may change in the future. How can you decide which model is more accurate? One way is to test whether the models can accurately "predict" changes that have already occurred. For example, you can enter climate data from 400 000 to 100 000 years ago, based on ice cores and other evidence. Then, have each model analyze these data and project the climate from 100 000 years ago to the present. The more closely the computer prediction matches the actual measurements from the past 100 000 years, the more confidence you can have in the accuracy of the computer model.

Climate Models Indicate Probabilities, Not Certainty

Another way to assess the reliability of a climate model is to give several different models the same test and then compare the results. For example, **Figure 9.16** shows the results of a test of 19 different climate models. Each model was used to predict the increase in global temperature that would occur if carbon dioxide concentrations increased by 1 percent per year over 80 years. Notice how there is less agreement among the predictions as they move further into the future.

Tests like this one remind us that science cannot make predictions about the future with absolute certainty. Climate models provide probabilities based on our current state of knowledge. All of the model results in **Figure 9.16** agree that temperature will increase. However, they differ about the amount of the increase over time. As models and measurements improve, uncertainties can be reduced and disagreements among scientists may be resolved.

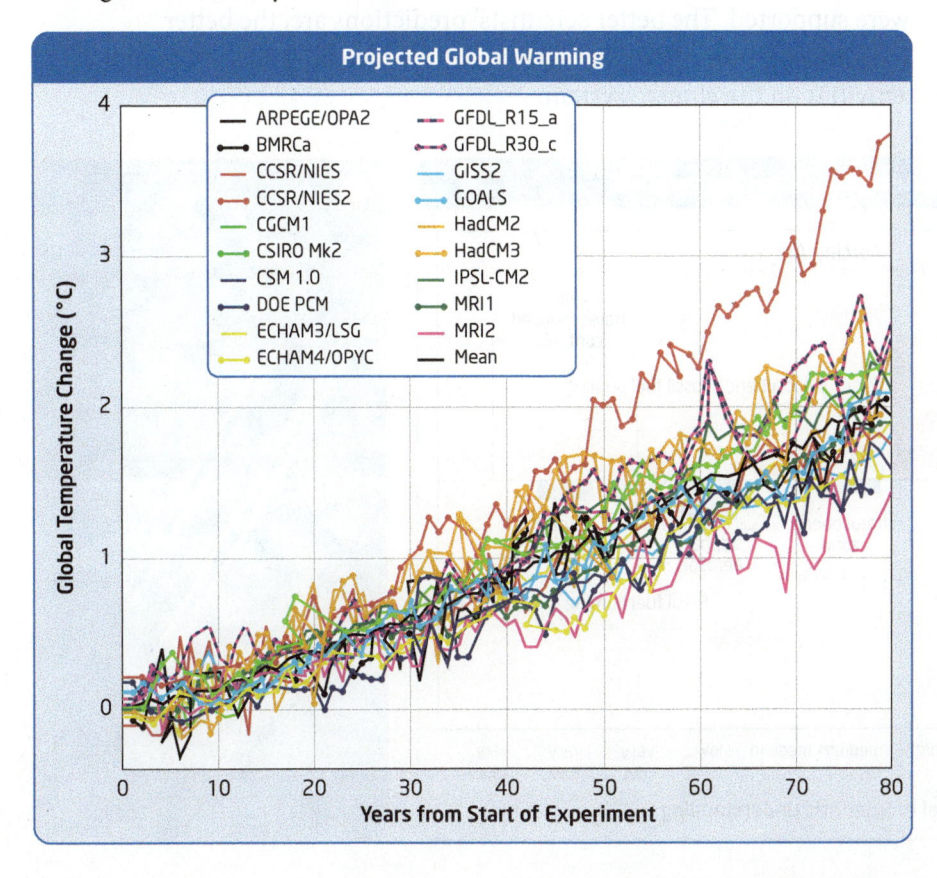

Figure 9.16 This graph shows the responses of 19 different climate models to the same test of climate change. Each acronym in the key represents a different computer model. The models predict how temperature will increase after 80 years of increasing carbon dioxide levels.

forcing agent any substance or process that alters the global energy balance and causes climate to change

Climate Forcing Agents

Anything that alters Earth's energy balance and "forces" the climate to change is known as a **forcing agent**. Different agents have been responsible for climate change at different times throughout Earth's history.

A continuing debate about climate change involves how much of the change being observed today is due to natural causes and how much is anthropogenic. **Figure 9.17** shows how several different forcing agents have contributed to climate change since the 1700s. Although many factors affect the climate in different ways, this model indicates that an increase in greenhouse gases has had a greater impact on current global warming than any other single forcing agent.

Simulating Multiple Factors to Improve Computer Models

Another factor in evaluating models is determining whether all possible answers to the question have been explored. For example, global sea level is rising by about 3 mm each year. Part of this increase comes from the melting of glaciers and polar icecaps, and part comes from the expansion of ocean water through warming. But calculations showed that one third of the measured increase cannot be explained by these two factors alone.

Dr. Richard Peltier, of the University of Toronto's Centre for Global Change Science, suggested that the extra water may result from the drying out of continents or from a higher rate of melting ice in Antarctica than scientists had previously measured. In addition, the melting of ice sheets after the last glacial maximum resulted in uplift of land that was once weighed down by the heavy ice. When all of these additional factors were simulated in a computer model, most of Dr. Peltier's predictions were supported. The better scientists' predictions are, the better recommendations they can make to help reduce the effects of human activities on the climate system.

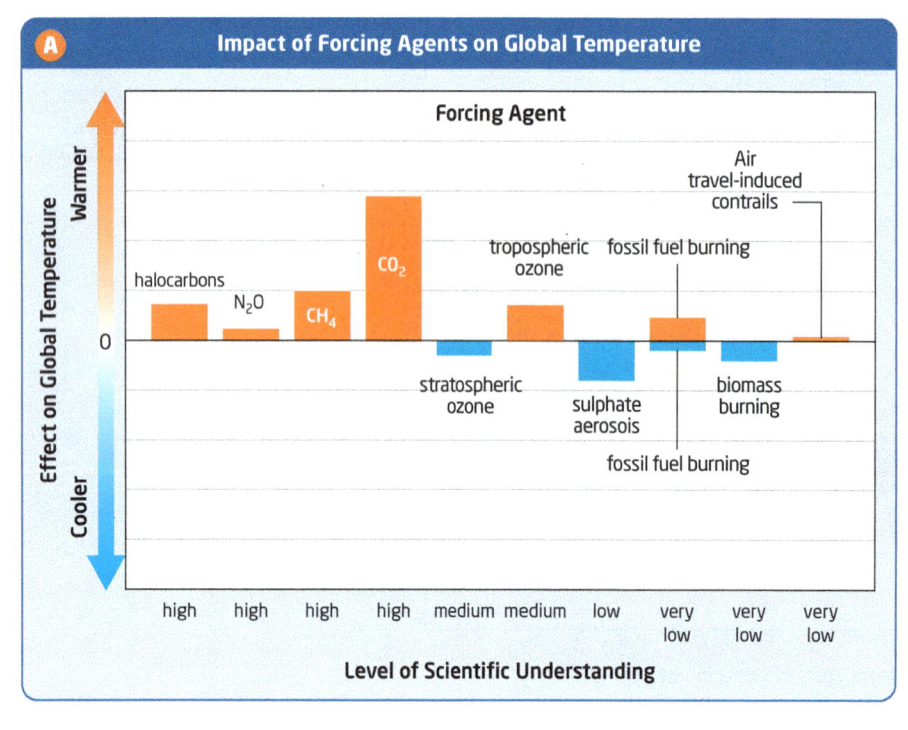

Figure 9.17 The graph in **A** estimates how various forcing agents, such as contrails, have affected global climate from 1750 to the present. Contrails, **B**, are condensed water trails left by airplanes. Bars above the line indicate agents that produce warming. Bars below the line show agents that produce cooling. The height of each bar indicates how much impact each agent has on average global temperature. The bottom of the graph explains how well scientists understand the effects of each forcing agent.

368 NEL • Unit 3 Climate Change

Section 9.2 Review

Section Summary

- Dozens of satellites monitor Earth's climate, to provide scientists with data to analyze changes in the Earth system and to project changes in climate. Each satellite focuses on a different aspect of climate and weather.
- Scientists predict future climates by using computer simulations of Earth.
- General circulation models (GCMs) are three-dimensional models that represent how currents of water and air interact and move around the planet over specified periods of time.
- The predictions of climate models are not 100 percent accurate because of imprecision in the data and difficulties in the calculations.
- The major climate models agree on approximately how much some factors such as greenhouse gases contribute to climate change. However, the effects of other factors, such as clouds, are not as well understood.

Review Questions

K/U 1. What weather features does radar measure?

A 2. The graph on the right shows projected temperature changes made by several computer models. What are the largest and smallest temperature changes predicted by these models? Why might the models have such widely differing projections?

C 3. What are four sources of uncertainty in climate models today? Organize the four sources of uncertainty by using a graphic organizer of your choice. Study Toolkit 4, on pages 565–566, contains instructions for using graphic organizers.

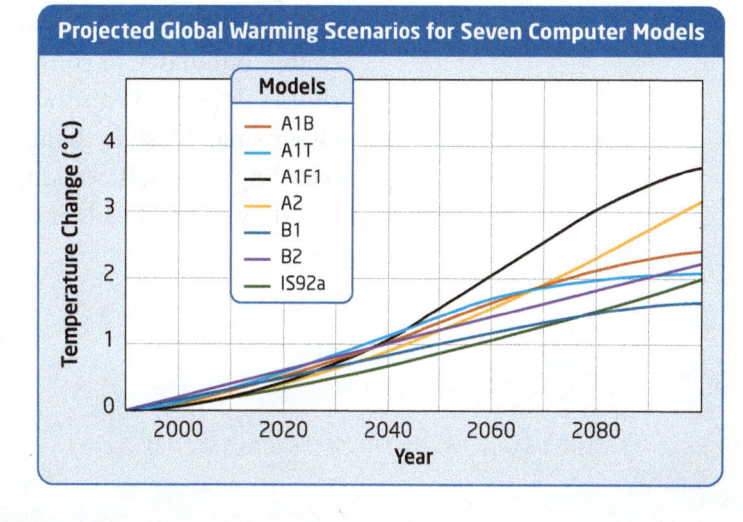

K/U 4. Describe two tests that can be used to determine the reliability of computer models.

T/I 5. Look at **Figure 9.17A**. How does burning fossil fuels cause both warming and cooling of average global temperature?

T/I 6. Given that scientists do not completely understand all of the complexities of climate change, how can they make inferences about what the future climate of Earth will be like?

T/I 7. Why can no climate model ever be 100 percent accurate in predicting the future?

K/U 8. Explain how Dr. Richard Peltier's work shows the importance of analyzing several forcing agents when determining cause and effect in climate change.

Key Terms
bias
carbon footprint
carbon offset

9.3 Taking Action to Slow Climate Change

Scientists do not know how rapidly climate change may occur or how much damage it may cause to ecosystems and human society. However, we do know that human activities affect the climate, and our best choice for the future is to reduce those effects. We can do this as individuals, as a nation, and as an international community.

A changing climate will bring changes in our technologies and personal habits. It will affect the political and economic structures that define our world. For example, a warmer Arctic will have less sea ice. This change will open up sea routes for year-round shipping. The newly available routes may change international trade agreements and influence treaties about fishing grounds and shipping routes.

The first step in taking action to slow climate change is to educate ourselves and each other about factors that cause climate change, including human activities. We must learn to evaluate our everyday activities and determine which activities we can take to slow climate change. It is important to be realistic about the effect that our behaviours have, but a little change can make a big difference. For example, hanging clothes out to dry, as shown in **Figure 9.18**, instead of using an electric clothes dryer prevents the release of 310 kg of carbon dioxide per year. Other small lifestyle changes that can slow climate change include recycling materials, walking or biking instead of driving, and installing low-flow showerheads and toilets in your home.

Figure 9.18 Small lifestyle changes, such as drying clothes on a line instead of using an electric clothes dryer, can result in large reductions in your contribution to climate change.

Educating Yourself About Climate Change

"Scientists Disagree Over Global Warming." "Future Climate Uncertain." You may have seen headlines like these on web sites or in newspapers and magazines, or heard similar claims in the media. Both statements are true. However, non-scientists and scientists often interpret disagreements and uncertainties in different ways.

New data about climate change are added to our knowledge every year. As part of the scientific process, hypotheses are revised and re-tested as new information becomes available. As more and more evidence is published, the scientific community reaches a general agreement or consensus.

Outside of the scientific community, people also have disagreements and uncertainties. People are more likely to disagree over topics that are complex. Although data and hypotheses provide evidence on these topics, people also make decisions based on their beliefs and values.

Making Decisions About Climate Change

The combination of satellites and computers now allows anyone who has access to the Internet to view environmental changes for themselves. Internet sites and their tools allow you to gather information about hurricanes, floods, deserts, sea ice, air pollution, deforestation and reforestation, dust storms, crop growth, forest fires, and many other conditions on Earth. However, understanding the relationship between climate change and human activities is complex. Not all scientists, governments, politicians, or individuals agree on how the scientific data should be interpreted.

The interpretation of scientific and nonscientific information guides how decisions are made at home, at school, in businesses, and at all levels of government. Many different organizations are suggesting many different solutions to a variety of different climate-change issues. How we evaluate the advantages and disadvantages of these solutions is almost as complicated as understanding climate change itself.

Detecting Bias in Information About Climate Change

Magazines and other news sources commonly use dramatic photos and startling headlines to advertise articles about climate change. These photos and headlines are designed to elicit emotional responses from readers and influence opinions. When you read about climate change, it is important to evaluate the fairness and accuracy of the information presented.

Information from different sources commonly contains bias. **Bias** is a tendency toward a particular perspective or point of view that prevents objective assessment of a topic. Biased sources generally present only the information that supports one point of view. The process of detecting and evaluating bias in scientific reports on climate change is not easy. The following questions can help you evaluate sources of information for bias.

- Is the information in a respected scientific journal that is reviewed by professional scientists?
- What is the source of the information? For example, is it based on research at a university, a government department, or a private corporation or institute?
- Does the author of the source have an agenda? For example, is a report trying to raise support for a political party or organization, to influence behaviour, or to sell a product or service?
- Does the report misrepresent information or interpret it in a way that is not supported by evidence?

bias a tendency toward a particular perspective or point of view that prevents objective assessment of a topic

Study Toolkit

Creating a Word Map The illustrations and examples in a word map can help clarify the definition of a term. Create a word map for *bias*.

Calculating Your Carbon Footprint

Most climatologists agree that an increase in greenhouse gases is the largest single cause of current climate change. The main human causes of this increase are activities that produce air pollution and activities (such as cutting down forests) that reduce the ability of natural cycles to absorb greenhouse gases.

Fossil fuels are burned to produce electricity and heat, to power our vehicles for transportation, and to manufacture and transport consumer goods. The burning of fossil fuels releases carbon dioxide into the air, which may lead to climate change. Our net contribution to climate change varies from person to person, business to business, and country to country. To help compare different degrees of impact, researchers developed the concept of a **carbon footprint**. A carbon footprint measures the amount of greenhouse gases produced in units of carbon dioxide. For example, you can calculate how many tonnes of carbon dioxide production you are responsible for in your daily life through such activities as driving or travelling by plane, cooking food, and buying manufactured goods, as shown in **Figure 9.19**. All of these activities involve burning fossil fuels. Many web sites have carbon footprint calculators that let you find out how the carbon footprint of your household compares with that of other families.

Suggested Investigation
Real World Investigation 9-B, Evaluating the "Food Miles" Initiative, on page 384

carbon footprint the effect that human activities have on the environment in terms of the amount of greenhouse gases produced, measured in units of carbon dioxide

Figure 9.19 Canada emits over 630 million tonnes of carbon dioxide per year. Therefore, every Canadian is responsible for releasing an average of about 19.5 tonnes of carbon dioxide annually. That amount is about 30 times more than the amount emitted by the average person in India.

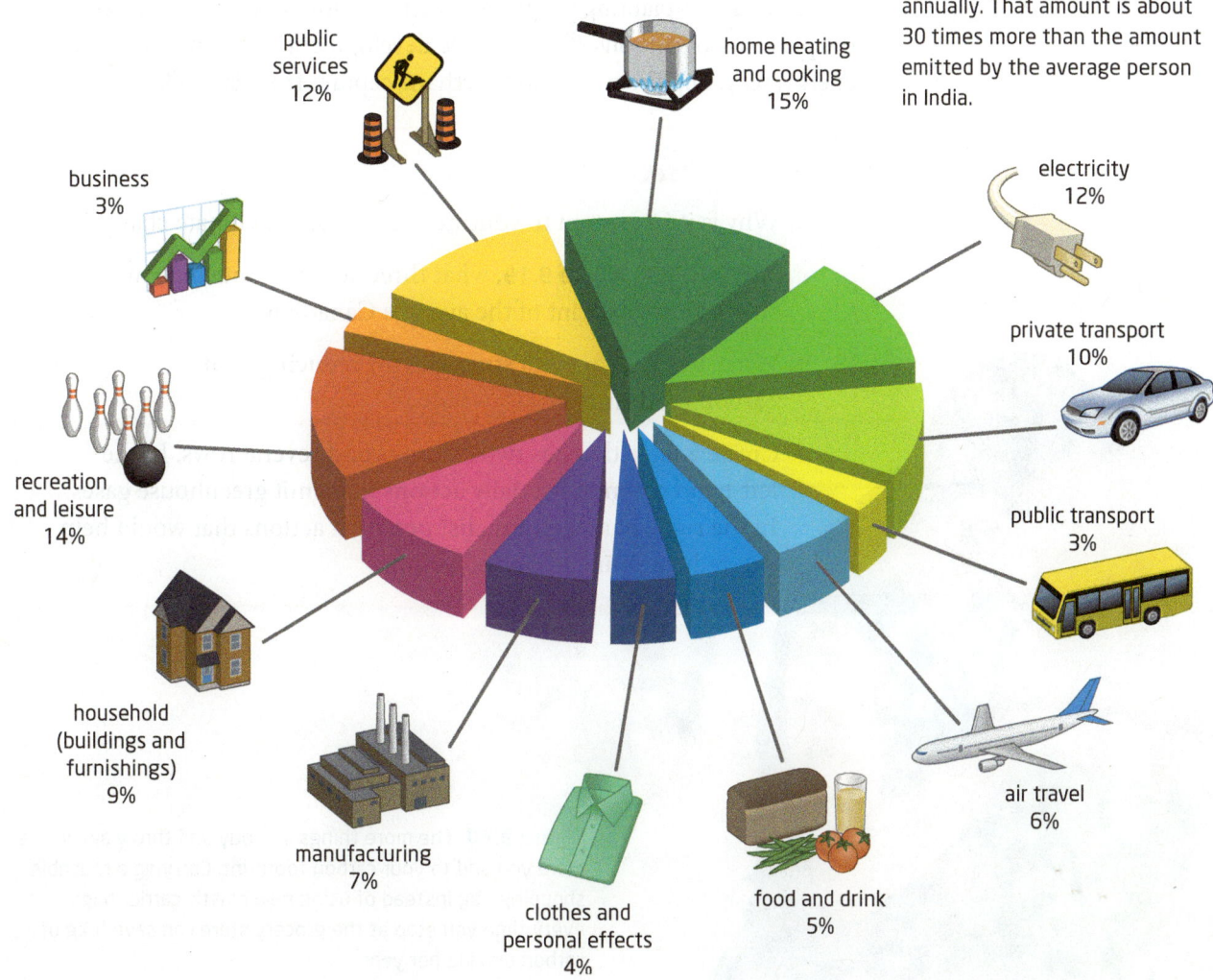

- public services 12%
- home heating and cooking 15%
- electricity 12%
- private transport 10%
- public transport 3%
- air travel 6%
- food and drink 5%
- clothes and personal effects 4%
- manufacturing 7%
- household (buildings and furnishings) 9%
- recreation and leisure 14%
- business 3%

Chapter 9 Addressing Climate Change • NEL 373

carbon offset a means of reducing or avoiding greenhouse gas emissions by purchasing credits to reduce your carbon footprint

Go to **scienceontario** to find out more

Reducing Your Carbon Footprint

People who are skeptical about anthropogenic climate change argue that the carbon footprint is a misleading or unhelpful concept. Some skeptics argue that the influence average individuals have on climate is less significant than the influence that governments and corporations have. They also claim that the calculations of carbon footprints are very crude and inaccurate. However, the combined actions of every person on Earth equal a significant portion of the human contribution to climate change. Therefore, responsibility on the individual level plays an important role in reducing global greenhouse gas emissions.

You can reduce your carbon footprint by choosing activities that reduce or eliminate the need to burn fossil fuels. Simple ways to reduce your carbon footprint include unplugging your mobile phone charger when it's not in use, drinking tap water instead of bottled water when possible, and taking shorter showers to use less heated water. As **Figure 9.20** shows, making a difference doesn't have to be difficult.

You may also choose to purchase **carbon offsets** to minimize your carbon footprint. Carbon offsets are credits that an individual or organization can purchase to compensate for performing a different carbon-dioxide emitting activity. For example, someone who has travelled by airplane may offset the carbon emissions caused by that flight by donating money to a tree-planting program. Other activities that are supported by the purchase of carbon offsets include development of alternative sources of energy, recycling programs, and methane capture from landfills.

Learning Check

1. Why is it important to educate yourself about climate change?
2. According to **Figure 9.19**, what three actions contribute most to the carbon footprint of the average Canadian?
3. What are the two main strategies for reducing your carbon footprint?
4. Create a table that has two columns and several rows. In the left-hand column, list daily actions that emit greenhouse gases. In the right-hand column, list potential actions that would help you reduce your carbon footprint.

Figure 9.20 The more things you buy and throw away, the more you add to your carbon footprint. Carrying a reusable shopping bag instead of using new plastic carrier bags every time you stop at the grocery store can save 5 kg of carbon dioxide per year.

Advocating for Actions to Slow Climate Change

Advocating for awareness and action is another powerful way to affect climate change. For example, as an advocate, you can help educate others and influence how governments and individuals respond to the issue of climate change. The following actions can help you be an effective advocate:

1. identify and join groups or individuals who champion actions that you support
2. learn about the processes by which governments and advocacy groups enact and influence environmental laws
3. set an example by reducing your carbon footprint
4. write letters to corporations and government representatives to encourage them to support initiatives to slow climate change

Activity 9-4

Talking the Talk, Walking the Walk

How much of a difference can a little lifestyle change make in terms of global warming? In this activity, you will choose one action that you can take to slow climate change.

Materials
- Computer with Internet access

Seemingly small actions, like plugging electrical devices into a power strip that is turned off when the devices are not in use, can have a big impact on climate change.

Procedure

1. Choose one of the following actions: washing only full loads of laundry instead of partial loads, drying clothes on a clothesline instead of in an electric dryer, using reusable shopping bags instead of single-use plastic bags, using a power strip to eliminate standby power for electrical devices that are not in use, and listening to the radio instead of watching television.
2. Using the Internet and other sources, identify the daily and annual carbon savings that result from performing each action.
3. Create a plan for making each action part of your daily life. How would your lifestyle have to change in order to implement each action?
4. Choose one action and perform the action for one week.

Questions

1. Calculate the amount of carbon dioxide you prevented from entering the atmosphere by performing that one action for one week.
2. Choose a different action and make a commitment to performing that action every day for a year. Explain which action you chose and why you chose that action.
3. Based on the information provided in **Figure 9.19**, what percentage of your total carbon footprint could you reduce by performing this action?

Figure 9.21 The larger the land area of a country appears in this distorted map, the more greenhouse gases are emitted by that country.

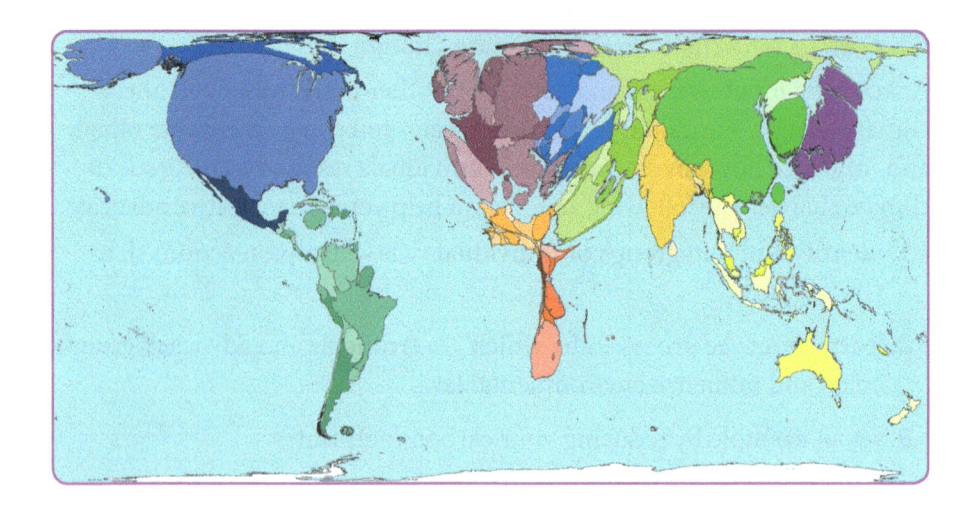

Global Contributions to Climate Change

The map in **Figure 9.21** shows the global warming potential (GWP) of the greenhouse gases emitted by different areas of the world in 2002. Europe, Japan, the United States, and China are disproportionately large because their populations are large and the average lifestyle in those locations expends large amounts of energy. Producing this energy emits much more gas per person and creates more types of greenhouse gases.

On the map, Africa appears smaller than its land area or population would suggest because poverty prevents most people who live there from using electricity or performing activities that would emit greenhouse gases. However, some developing countries contribute to the anthropogenic greenhouse effect by clearing their forests, which removes trees that help absorb carbon dioxide from the atmosphere. Recent studies also indicate that soot, or black carbon, from small cooking stoves in developing countries may be a major contributor to global climate change. In fact, black carbon may be responsible for 18 percent of Earth's warming and as much as half of Arctic warming. Converting to newer stoves that do not release as much soot may have a major positive influence in terms of slowing climate change.

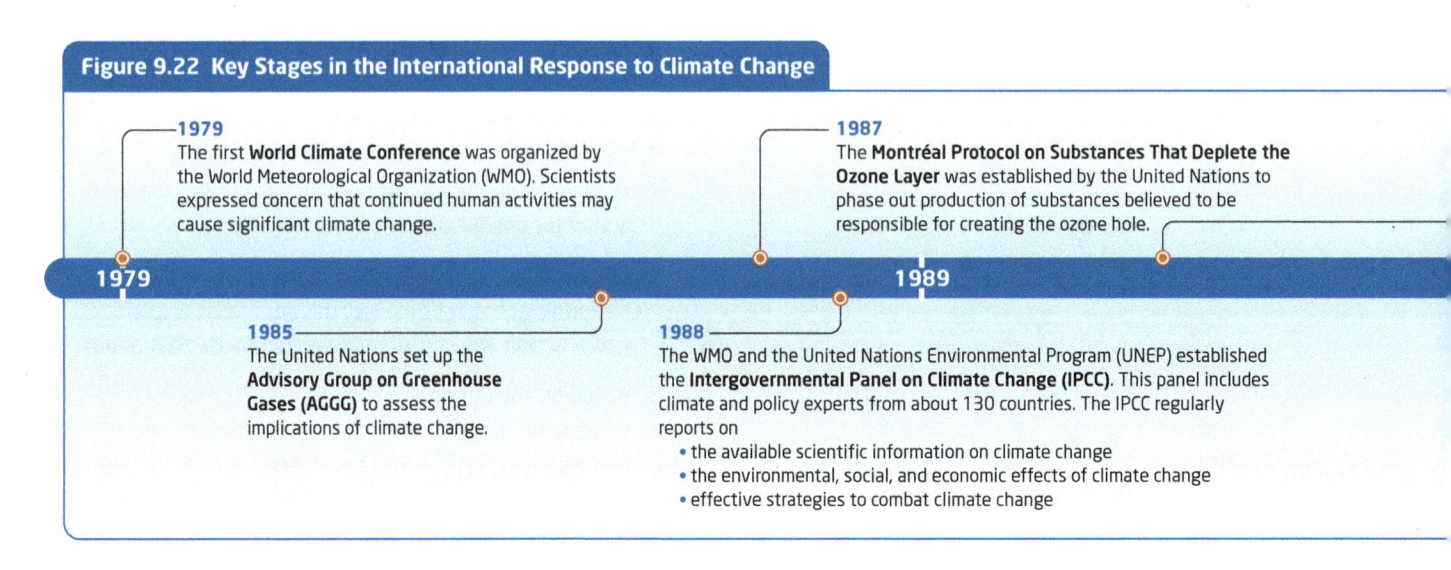

Figure 9.22 Key Stages in the International Response to Climate Change

1979
The first **World Climate Conference** was organized by the World Meteorological Organization (WMO). Scientists expressed concern that continued human activities may cause significant climate change.

1985
The United Nations set up the **Advisory Group on Greenhouse Gases (AGGG)** to assess the implications of climate change.

1987
The **Montréal Protocol on Substances That Deplete the Ozone Layer** was established by the United Nations to phase out production of substances believed to be responsible for creating the ozone hole.

1988
The WMO and the United Nations Environmental Program (UNEP) established the **Intergovernmental Panel on Climate Change (IPCC)**. This panel includes climate and policy experts from about 130 countries. The IPCC regularly reports on
- the available scientific information on climate change
- the environmental, social, and economic effects of climate change
- effective strategies to combat climate change

International Initiatives to Combat Climate Change

The impacts of climate change vary from country to country, depending on location, population, and way of life. However, the climate system is global. Winds and ocean currents do not stop at national borders. Effective solutions to climate change must involve a great deal of international cooperation. **Figure 9.22** summarizes the important steps that have occurred in international cooperation in dealing with climate change.

The Intergovernmental Panel on Climate Change (IPCC)

In 1988, the United Nations Environment Programme and the World Meteorologic Organization formed the Intergovernmental Panel on Climate Change (IPCC). The IPCC is composed of hundreds of scientists from all over the globe. The goals of this panel are to assess the role of human activities in producing climate change and to recommend ways to respond.

The IPCC regularly reports on the available scientific information on climate change; the environmental, social, and economic effects of climate change; and effective strategies to combat climate change. The IPCC also regularly organizes conferences and summits in which delegates from participating governments and organizations, such as Chief Bill Erasmus shown in **Figure 9.23**, meet to discuss new scientific data and policies.

Figure 9.23 In December 2008, Chief Bill Erasmus of the Dene nation in northern Canada attended the United Nations Climate Change Conference in Poland. Erasmus wanted to raise awareness of the effects of climate change on Canada's native species and Aboriginal peoples.

The Kyoto Protocol

In 1997, the Kyoto Protocol was developed. This international treaty was produced as a result of the Earth Summit in Rio de Janiero, Brazil, and acts as a legally binding commitment between nations. The industrialized nations that signed the treaty agreed to reduce their collective emissions of four greenhouse gases and two halocarbons by 5.2 percent compared to the emissions of those gases in 1990. By 2008, 183 nations and the European Union had signed the agreement. At that time, the United States was the only developed country that had not ratified the agreement.

1992
An international treaty called the **United Nations Framework Convention on Climate Change (UNFCCC)** was produced at the Earth Summit held in Rio de Janeiro. Its aim was to stabilize greenhouse gas concentrations in the atmosphere by imposing limits on emissions from individual nations.

1997
The **Kyoto Protocol** was an update of the UNFCCC that commits participating nations to reducing emissions of greenhouse gases to levels specified for each country. The Kyoto Protocol has been signed and approved by 181 countries and the European Union. Together, these countries produce only 60 percent of global greenhouse gas emissions. Participating countries must meet their commitments by December 2012 or face penalties.

2007
The **IPCC Fourth Assessment Report:** Climate Change 2007 concluded that the global climate is warming and that most of the increase in average global temperature since the mid-20th century was due to an increase in anthropogenic greenhouse gas concentrations. It predicted future increases in heat waves and rainfall, and a rise in sea levels.

Figure 9.24 This logo on a product indicates that the product meets high standards of energy efficiency.

Educating and Empowering Consumers

Governments also help individuals combat climate change by passing laws or regulations and by educating consumers to make choices that benefit the environment. Canada's Office of Energy Efficiency (OEE) has implemented a program called the ecoEnergy Efficiency Initiative. One ecoEnergy program provides financial incentives to homeowners and businesses to retrofit older buildings to make them more energy efficient. It also provides helpful tips to the public on buying, driving, and maintaining vehicles to save fuel. In addition, Ontario's Drive Clean program requires all Ontario cars to pass strict emissions inspections.

Imagine that your family wants to buy new light bulbs that use less energy. The task of choosing is made easier by the international ENERGY STAR® symbol, as shown in **Figure 9.24**. The symbol is found on many different energy-efficient products, from CFLs or LED light bulbs to furnaces, refrigerators, and other major appliances. The ENERGY STAR® symbol indicates that a product meets specifications for reduced energy consumption, which helps lower production of greenhouse gas emissions.

STSE Case Study

Reduce, Re-use, Recycle, and Upgrade

Canada's federal government promotes the ENERGY STAR® program, which helps consumers make smart, energy-efficient decisions about items they purchase. The ENERGY STAR® symbol makes identifying products that exceed Canadian federal standards for energy efficiency easy for consumers. The program, run by the Office of Energy Efficiency at Natural Resources Canada, helps consumers choose the most energy-efficient products.

Reducing energy use indirectly reduces greenhouse gas emissions and it saves money for the consumer. The federal, provincial, and municipal governments offer grants and incentives for the purchase of ENERGY STAR® qualified products. For example, the Province of Ontario has a point-of-sale retail sales tax exemption for qualifying energy-efficient products.

However, encouraging consumers to buy new products and throw away the old ones seems to contradict other environmentally friendly messages, including "reduce, re-use, and recycle."

Replacing inefficient products with high-efficiency products is a popular way to conserve energy and benefit the environment. However, this action uses up resources and energy to make these new products. As well, the inefficient products are difficult to dispose of and they cannot be recycled into efficient products. Disposal of inefficient products is a concern because Canada has a limited amount of space in which to dump garbage, especially large appliances.

When consumers replace their old appliances with new energy-efficient appliances, the consumers save energy and money. However, many old appliances end up in landfills, like the refrigerators piled in this dump.

Economic Initiatives to Reduce Greenhouse Gas Emissions

Governments must find ways to support both economic growth and climate change initiatives. How do politicians encourage individuals and corporations to reduce greenhouse gas emissions and encourage the growth of new "eco-friendly" industries? The following two responses have been developed:

Cap-and-Trade Systems In a cap-and-trade system, an authoritative body, most commonly a government, establishes a ceiling (or cap) on how much carbon may be produced. Corporations that produce *less* carbon than their limit may sell or trade their credits to corporations that produce *more* carbon than their limit. Over time, the caps are gradually lowered.

Carbon-Tax Systems In a carbon-tax system, the government levies a tax on either the source of carbon compounds or the emission of greenhouse gases. Under this policy, the price of anything that depends on carbon fuels goes up. As a result, consumers have an incentive to spend their money on alternatives that do not produce carbon emissions. Without the carbon tax, these alternatives are usually more expensive than their carbon-producing counterparts.

Study Toolkit

Identifying Cause and Effect Cap-and-trade systems are designed to reduce the amount of carbon compounds being emitted by industry. Use a cause-and-effect map to explain how a cap-and-trade system works.

Your Turn

1. Consider the ENERGY STAR® program from the viewpoints of an appliance recycler, an appliance manufacturer, and a consumer. Write a statement that describes how each of these interested parties might evaluate the costs and benefits of the ENERGY STAR® program.

2. Make a list of four energy-using products or appliances in your home. Identify whether they are ENERGY STAR® products. For each item, research how much energy it consumes in a month (use an energy calculator, available on-line). Compare your item with another similar model. Look at the price, the energy consumption, and the typical lifespan of the product (time until it needs replacement). Do you think your home is energy efficient? Support your answer with the results of your research.

3. Research an energy-efficiency program from a different region of the world. Write a brief newspaper article that explains how this program compares to Canada's ENERGY STAR® program. Make sure your article identifies at least three costs and three benefits of the other country's energy conservation program.

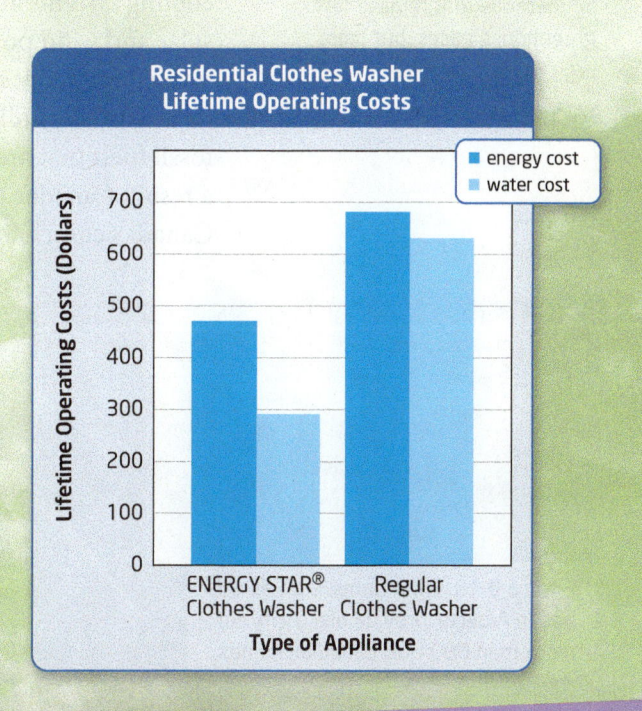

The purchase price of products that meet the ENERGY STAR® standards may be higher than the price of competing products. However, the amount of money saved on utility bills adds up quickly.

Making a Difference

While in high school, Jasmeet Sidhu realized that students at other schools must have knowledge they could share about how to start environmental projects. To help student environmentalists collaborate, she created a forum called PEYA (Peel Environmental Youth Alliance). PEYA has grown to more than 400 members in schools throughout Ontario's Peel Region.

In 2008, Jasmeet blogged for the *Toronto Star* from the United Nations Climate Conference in Poland. For Jasmeet, communicating complex scientific and political issues clearly to the public is important. She plans to work as a journalist and is studying peace and conflict studies at the University of Toronto. Jasmeet has been named one of Canada's Top 20 Under 20 and one of the 100 Most Powerful Women in Canada.

How could you communicate your ideas about climate change in a way that could help make a difference?

Lowering Greenhouse Emissions by Using Alternative Sources of Energy

Approximately 18 percent of the greenhouse gases produced by Canada result from the burning of fossil fuels to generate electricity. Probably the best long-term way to reduce the production of greenhouse gases is to develop sources of energy that produce fewer greenhouse gases or none at all. Canadians already use many of these power sources, including wind, solar, biomass, hydroelectric, tidal, and nuclear power. **Figure 9.25** shows the methods by which Canada's energy is generated.

Converting the existing power-generation infrastructure to a more climate-friendly system, such as the wind farm shown in **Figure 9.26**, will take many years and cost a large amount in both dollars and carbon emissions. However, individuals don't need to wait for major power companies to switch to alternative energy. Geothermal heating and cooling systems are available for most homes, and single-home solar and wind power systems can provide all of the energy needed for many standard households. By switching to these local systems, individuals can reduce the total amount of fossil fuels that are burned for electrical generation. As a result, Canada's total carbon footprint, and therefore Canada's contribution to climate change, can be reduced.

Canada's Electrical Power Generation by Method
- Nuclear 12%
- Fossil fuels 28%
- Hydroelectric 58%
- Wind 1%
- Other 1%

Figure 9.25 Most of Canada's electrical energy is provided by methods that release few greenhouse gases, but more progress can be made.

Figure 9.26 Wind farms, such as this one in Alberta, provide electricity for more than 680 000 Canadian homes.

Section 9.3 Review

Section Summary

- Educating yourself about the facts related to the issue of climate change is important in making informed decisions about how your actions affect climate change.
- Everybody has a carbon footprint, which means that everyone's actions influence the amount of greenhouse gases emitted into the atmosphere. As a result, everybody is responsible for reducing greenhouse gas emissions.
- You can reduce your carbon footprint by performing actions that lower your dependence on burning fossil fuels and by purchasing carbon offsets.
- Governments and international panels are trying to reduce greenhouse gas emissions by passing laws, by educating consumers, and by using economic means to combat climate change.

Review Questions

T/I 1. Why is the source of information important for identifying bias in information?

A 2. How does modern technology affect how people make decisions about climate change?

K/U 3. What is the difference between a carbon offset and a carbon footprint?

K/U 4. List three actions you can take to reduce your carbon footprint.

A 5. The chart on the right shows the "carbon facts" for a cheeseburger. If a person reduced the number of cheeseburgers he or she eats by one burger per week, how many fewer kilograms of carbon dioxide and of methane would his or her actions emit in one year?

K/U 6. What is the IPCC, and what does it do?

K/U 7. Identify three major milestones in the international response to climate change.

C 8. Which system, carbon tax or cap-and-trade, would you recommend for use in Canada? Explain your answer by comparing the advantages and disadvantages of these programs.

Carbon Facts

Product size 1 Cheeseburger (130 g)

Amount Per Serving

Kilograms CO_2 240   Kilograms CH_4 120

Total C: Energy Sources	243 g
Transportation	
Fossil Fuel (Diesel)	120 g
Fossil Fuel (Gasoline)	48 g
Electricity Production	
Fossil Fuel (Natural Gas)	75 g
Fossil Fuel (Coal)	0 g

Total C: Non-Energy Sources	2840 g CO_2E
Cattle digestion	81.0 g
Manure	26.8 g
Other	5.2 g

Sustainable Production Rating	D+

Overall Carbon Code: ORANGE

This chart shows the carbon emissions that result from the production of a single cheeseburger.

Data Analysis Investigation 9-A

Skill Check

Initiating and Planning
✓ Performing and Recording
✓ Analyzing and Interpreting
✓ Communicating

Materials
- calculator

Math Skills
Go to **Math Skills Toolkit 3** for information about how to organize your data into a graph

Understanding Ice-Core Data

As you learned in Section 9.1, the relative amounts of isotopes of oxygen and hydrogen in ice can indicate global temperature in the past. In this investigation, you will investigate how the composition of ice can provide scientists with data about ancient temperatures.

Question

How can analyzing data about oxygen isotopes in ice provide information about past climate?

Organize the Data

Follow these steps to learn how scientists convert information about oxygen isotopes into information about temperature.

1. Construct a graph. Label the *x*-axis "Time (years before present)," and use the range of 0 years to 20 000 years, with an interval of 2000 years. Label the *y*-axis "$^{18}O:^{16}O$ Ratio (parts per thousand)," and use the range of −30 to −45, with an interval of 1. Title the graph "Changes in $^{18}O:^{16}O$ Ratio Over Time."

2. The data in the table below show the ratio of ^{18}O to ^{16}O at eleven points in time. Plot these data on your graph.

Changes in the Oxygen-18 to Oxygen-16 Ratio in Ice Cores from 0 to 20 000 Years Ago

Time (years before present)	Ratio of $^{18}O:^{16}O$ (parts per thousand)	Time (years before present)	Ratio of $^{18}O:^{16}O$ (parts per thousand)
0	−35.19	12 000	−41.38
2000	−35.03	14 000	−39.71
4000	−35.07	16 000	−42.18
6000	−34.96	18 000	−41.69
8000	−34.13	20 000	−43.87
10 000	−35.29		

3. a. What was the average ratio of $^{18}O:^{16}O$ over the last 20 000 years?

   b. Identify years in which the ratio of $^{18}O:^{16}O$ was above average and the ratio was below average.

   c. Compare your graph to the graph of global average temperature below. Does an above-average ratio of $^{18}O:^{16}O$ represent a warmer-than-average global temperature or cooler-than-average global temperature? (**Hint:** remember that you are working with negative numbers.)

Analyze and Interpret

Now that you have seen how scientists use $^{18}O:^{16}O$ ratios to identify warm and cold periods, use that information to evaluate the graphs on this page.

1. How many warm periods and how many cold periods occurred between 0 and 20 000 years ago?

2. How has the average global temperature changed since about 20 000 years ago?

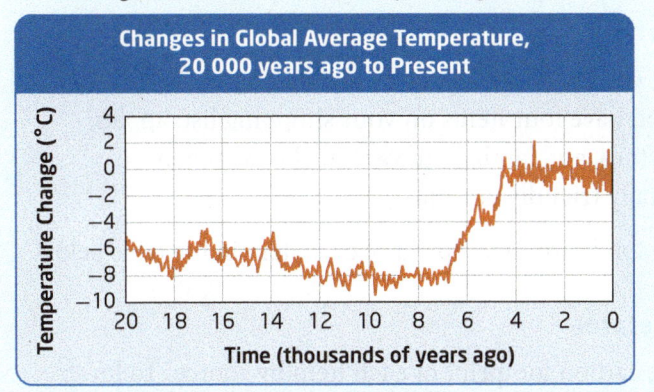

Changes in Global Average Temperature, 20 000 years ago to Present

3. How closely does the plot of carbon dioxide concentration resemble that of methane concentration? of temperature? Describe any patterns you see.

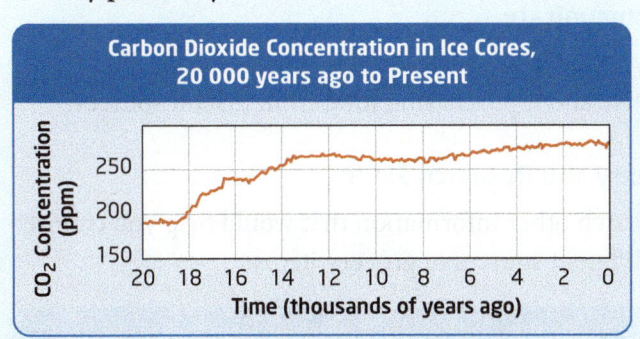

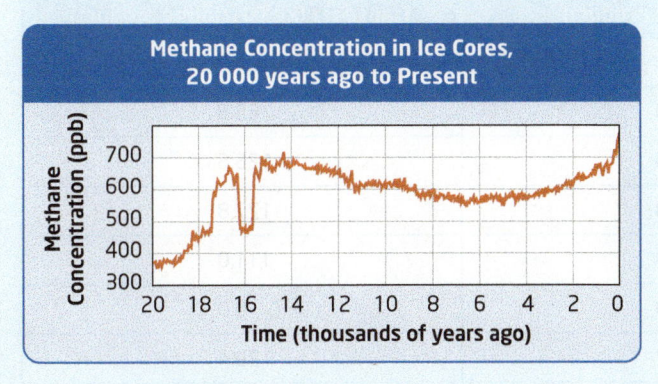

Carbon Dioxide Concentration in Ice Cores, 20 000 years ago to Present

Methane Concentration in Ice Cores, 20 000 years ago to Present

4. The atmospheric carbon dioxide concentration in 2009 was 388 ppm, and the concentration of methane was 1745 ppb. Calculate the rate of change in carbon dioxide and methane concentrations over the last 20 000 years.

Conclude and Communicate

5. How do the ice-core data support the idea that changing concentrations of greenhouse gases are related to global temperature?

6. How accurate do you think the concentrations of oxygen isotopes, methane, and carbon dioxide in ice cores are as a record of temperature? Explain your answer.

7. Create a flowchart that demonstrates how changes in global temperature can be recorded in ice layers.

Extend Your Inquiry and Research Skills

8. **Inquiry** Design a model that shows how scientists use oxygen isotopes to learn about past climates.

9. **Research** The current average temperature at Vostok, Antarctica, is −60°C. Research the estimated temperature of Vostok 20 000 years ago based on ice-core and sediment-core data. Is Vostok colder or warmer today than it was 20 000 years ago?

Real World Investigation 9-B

Skill Check
Initiating and Planning
Performing and Recording
✓ Analyzing and Interpreting
✓ Communicating

Materials
- calculator

Evaluating the "Food Miles" Initiative

A study in the United Kingdom called the "Food Miles" Initiative gathered information about the CO_2 emissions associated with food choices. Use the data to investigate the validity of the slogan "think globally, buy locally."

Question
Are locally-grown items or transported items better for the environment?

Organize the Data

1. Imagine that you are shopping in a supermarket in the United Kingdom. You have four items on your shopping list: apples, onions, tomatoes, and lamb. You want to choose the more environmentally friendly option.

2. Calculate the total carbon footprint of each item in the table below.

Analyze and Interpret

1. Compare the carbon footprint of each item by source. To lower your carbon footprint, which source would you choose for each?

2. What might account for the difference in the emissions related to produce from tropical and temperate sources?

Conclude and Communicate

3. What would you say to advocates of the "think globally, buy locally" initiative about purchasing food from distant sources?

Extend Your Inquiry and Research Skills

4. **Research** Research other information that would help you choose between the different sources of grocery items.

Comparison of Carbon Emissions for Production, Storage, and Transport of Grocery Items in a United Kingdom Supermarket

Food	Source	CO_2 Emissions During Production (kg CO_2/tonne product)	CO_2 Emissions from Storage and/or Transport (kg CO_2/tonne product)
Apples	New Zealand	60.1	124.9
	United Kingdom	186.0	85.8
Onions	New Zealand	58.9	125.6
	United Kingdom	42.3	127.8
Tomatoes	Spain	519.0	111.0
	United Kingdom	2394.0	0.0
Lamb	New Zealand	563.2	129.4
	United Kingdom	2894.1	0.0

Chapter 9 Summary

9.1 Discovering Past Climates
Key Concepts

- Paleoclimatologists reconstruct past climates by using the evidence that climate leaves behind in tree rings, ice, sedimentary rock, and fossils.
- Tree rings can provide evidence about growing conditions, such as temperature and precipitation, during the lifetime of the tree.
- Ice cores can provide information about global temperature and the composition of the atmosphere thousands of years in the past.
- Scientists use chemical analyses of sediment cores from lakes and oceans to reconstruct past conditions of the atmosphere and the hydrosphere.
- Rocks can provide information about the conditions that existed when they formed.
- Fossils are remains of living things. Their distribution and characteristics provide clues about the climate at the time the organisms lived.

9.2 Monitoring and Modelling Climate Change
Key Concepts

- Dozens of satellites monitor Earth's climate to provide scientists with data to analyze changes in the Earth system and to project changes in climate. Each satellite focuses on a different aspect of climate and weather.
- Scientists predict future climates by using computer simulations of Earth.
- General circulation models (GCMs) are three-dimensional models that represent how currents of water and air interact and move around the planet over specified periods of time.
- The predictions of climate models are not 100 percent accurate because of imprecision in the data and difficulties in the calculations.
- The major climate models agree on approximately how much some factors such as greenhouse gases contribute to climate change. However, the effects of other factors, such as clouds, are not as well understood.

9.3 Taking Action to Slow Climate Change
Key Concepts

- Educating yourself about the facts related to the issue of climate change is important in making informed decisions about how your actions affect climate change.
- Everybody has a carbon footprint, which means that everyone's actions influence the amount of greenhouse gases emitted into the atmosphere. As a result, everybody is responsible for reducing greenhouse gas emissions.
- You can reduce your carbon footprint by performing actions that lower your dependence on burning fossil fuels and by purchasing carbon offsets.
- Governments and international panels are trying to reduce greenhouse gas emissions by passing laws, by educating consumers, and by using economic means to combat climate change.

Chapter 9 Review

> **Make Your Own Summary**
>
> Summarize the key concepts of this chapter using a graphic organizer. The Chapter Summary on the previous page will help you identify key concepts. Refer to Study Toolkit 4 on pages 565–566 to help you decide which graphic organizer to use.

Reviewing Key Terms

Match each key term listed below to its definition.

a. paleoclimatologist (9.1)
b. isotope (9.1)
c. ice core (9.1)
d. geostationary (9.2)
e. monitor (9.2)
f. general circulation model (9.2)
g. carbon offset (9.3)
h. carbon footprint (9.3)
i. bias (9.3)

1. refers to a satellite that remains in the same position above Earth
2. a computer model that simulates the global climate system
3. a tendency toward a particular point of view that prevents objective assessment of a topic
4. a long cylinder of ice obtained by drilling into a glacier
5. a way to measure the amount of carbon produced by a person's activities
6. a form of an element that has a different number of neutrons than other atoms of that element
7. to measure something systematically and repeatedly
8. actions or purchased credits that reduce the amount of carbon that individuals emit
9. a scientist who studies the history of Earth's climate system

Knowledge and Understanding K/U

10. Identify four types of evidence that help scientists construct a history of climate change.
11. The diagram below shows two satellites. Which satellite is a polar orbiting satellite and which is a geostationary satellite? Explain your answer.
12. How have satellites changed the ability of scientists to monitor global climate?
13. What is a general circulation model (GCM), and how is it useful to climate scientists?
14. How do scientists refine their climate models?
15. How does the ENERGY STAR® program affect climate change?
16. Identify two laws that international governing bodies have enacted to address the causes or effects of climate change.
17. Compare how a cap-and-trade system works with how a carbon-tax system works.
18. What factors are slowing down a global switch to alternative energy sources? How are governments working to help overcome those factors?
19. How does measuring the mass of water from long ago tell scientists about the temperatures in that era?

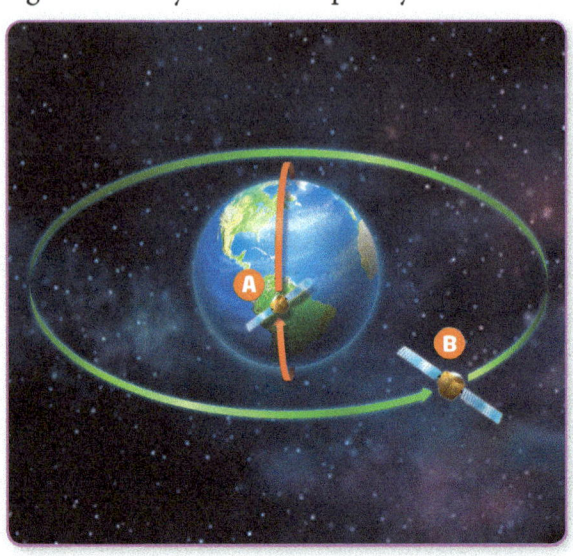

Thinking and Investigation T/I

20. Explain why the sources of weather and climate data are important in assessing whether the climate has changed.

21. Imagine that you are developing a computer model to simulate climate. Identify the natural and anthropogenic variables you would include in your model.

22. What energy source provides most of the electrical energy in Canada? Give this source of energy a grade (A, B, C, D, or F) relative to its effect on the concentration of greenhouse gases in Earth's atmosphere, and justify the grade you gave.

23. The table below describes the relative carbon footprints of ten nations. What ranking does Canada have? How does Canada's contribution to climate change compare to that of the United States? Why do you think Canada is ranked this way relative to the other nations on the list?

Top Ten Carbon-Emitting Nations on Earth 2008

Country	Ranking	CO₂ emissions (millions of tonnes)
United States	1	5957.00
China	2	5323.00
Russia	3	1696.00
Japan	4	1230.00
India	5	1166.00
Germany	6	844.17
Canada	7	631.26
United Kingdom	8	577.17
South Korea	9	499.63
Italy	10	466.64

24. Many factors are known to affect the climate. Why do scientists think that human contribution to greenhouse gases is so significant?

Communication C

25. **BIG IDEAS** Global climate change is influenced by both natural and human factors. Create a short multimedia presentation that illustrates how general circulation models (GCMs) incorporate both natural and anthropogenic factors when predicting future climate changes.

26. **BIG IDEAS** Climate change affects living things and natural systems in a variety of ways. Draw a negative feedback loop that demonstrates how reducing your carbon footprint may have an effect on global warming.

27. **BIG IDEAS** People have the responsibility to assess their impact on climate change and to identify effective courses of action to reduce this impact. Write a brief paragraph that explains the importance of Canada's participation in the Kyoto Protocol.

28. **BIG IDEAS** Earth's climate is dynamic and is the result of interacting systems and processes. Create a poster presentation that explains how a person's carbon footprint can be minimized by using carbon offsets.

Application A

29. What source of evidence would be most useful for determining the climate of Ontario over the past 4000 years?

30. In Japan, the blossoming of the cherry trees is a special day, and records showing the dates on which this event happened go back for centuries. Because the blossoms open after a certain number of days when the temperature is over 5°C, some people have proposed that this record might be one way of tracking temperature changes for Japan over recent centuries. Assess how valuable and reliable these records might be.

31. Why do solar energy and geothermal energy provide so little of Canada's electrical energy?

32. A tree experienced a dry year in which only a little rain fell in the spring, followed by a wet, cool year. Sketch the resulting tree rings.

33. The map in **Figure 9.21** shows only the amount of greenhouse gases actively emitted by various countries. How do you think the map would change if the impact of cutting down forests were calculated into the total?

Science at Work

Canadians in Science

Sheila Watt-Cloutier wants the world to understand the drastic impact that climate change is having on her people, the Inuit of Canada's North. For Sheila, climate change is a human rights issue because it threatens to destroy the Inuit way of life. She is urging nations to decrease their greenhouse gas emissions. She served as president and chair of the Inuit Circumpolar Conference (ICC), an organization representing Inuit in Canada, Alaska, Greenland, and Russia. The ICC persuaded governments to sign a global ban on persistent organic pollutants, which contaminate the Arctic food chain and accumulate in the fat of animals that are important sources of food for Inuit people. Sheila hopes students interested in the environment will look for connections among the many diverse topics related to the environment. She also hopes they will recognize the human stories underlying environmental issues.

Sheila Watt-Cloutier is an Officer of the Order of Canada. She was nominated for the Nobel Peace Prize in 2007 for her work in bringing heightened attention to climate change and global warming.

In Sheila Watt-Cloutier's Words

" Almost every facet of Inuit life has been affected by climate change. Hunting especially has been disturbed. We remain a hunting people of the land, ice, and snow. The process of the hunt teaches our young people to be patient, courageous, bold under pressure, and reflective. They learn to control their impulses, withstand stress, and develop sound judgement and wisdom.

For Inuit people, climate change is an issue related to our right and ability to exist as an Indigenous people. That right is now being challenged and minimized by the unpredictability of our climate. Climate change means that less of our culture in terms of traditional knowledge is being passed down to our young people.

Climate change has been discussed mainly as a scientific, economic, and technological issue, not as a human issue. People have failed to make connections to the human face of the problem. That is all changing now. People everywhere are awakening to the important role of these connections in the web of existence that connects us all through our shared atmosphere. "

Inuit hunters use a blend of modern technology and traditional practices to survive in their northern environment.

Earth Science at Work

The study of climate change contributes to these careers, as well as many more.

Careers in Earth Science include:
- Climate Change Policy Officer
- Oceanographer
- Atmospheric Chemist
- Environmental Technician
- Paleontologist

Meteorologist

Meteorologists study the weather. They collect data from satellites, computer models, radar, and observation stations in order to forecast future weather. Many meteorologists in Canada work for the federal government with Environment Canada.

Ecologist

Ecologists study the relationships among living things and the environment. They might investigate how factors such as temperature, precipitation, or urban development are affecting certain species. They work for governments, research institutions, conservation authorities, environmental consulting firms, and major corporations.

Greenhouse Gas Practitioner

Greenhouse gas practitioners measure, evaluate, and report on emissions from industry and vehicles. They also report on decreases in emissions that occur as a result of new projects launched by companies and other organizations. In addition, they develop plans for monitoring and accounting for emissions.

Go to **scienceontario** to find out more

Over to You

1. Why are ice and snow important to the Inuit way of life?
2. Explain why Sheila Watt-Cloutier believes climate change is a human rights issue.
3. Identify three effects that greenhouse gas emissions have on the Inuit way of life and three effects greenhouse gas emissions have on your life. What changes to your lifestyle can you make to help reduce your contribution to greenhouse gas emissions?
4. Research a career involving climate change that interests you. If you wish, you may choose a career from the list above. **What essential skills would you need for this career?**

Unit 3 Projects

Inquiry Project

Reflecting on Land Use

Over the last few decades that scientists have been making climate predictions, the focus has shifted from avoiding climate change to minimizing it, as well as adapting to it. One suggestion is to change the albedo of Earth's surface by rethinking how we use the land. Since the atmosphere is mostly transparent to visible light, increasing the amount of light that is reflected from the land, and thus reducing the amount that is absorbed by the land, is one way to help reduce the temperature near Earth's surface.

Inquiry Question
How does ground cover affect the amount of solar energy that is absorbed by the land?

Initiate and Plan

1. Identify one specific land use. List three or more materials that the surface of the land could be covered with and still be suitable for the use you identified.

2. Design a process you can follow to expose a small sample of each material to sunlight and measure any change in temperature. List the equipment you will need and the steps you will take to carry out your process. Have your teacher approve your investigation, including any safety precautions.

3. Set up your investigation to test the ability of each material to reflect solar energy and therefore warm the air above it.

4. For each material you test, write a hypothesis describing the results you expect, in absolute terms or relative to the other materials. Explain your hypothesis, based on the physical properties of the material.

Perform and Record

5. Perform your investigation, and record your results.

Analyze and Interpret

1. Compare how effectively each material prevented the surface from warming.

2. What applications might there be for the material that worked most effectively? Keep in mind that the use of the material needs to solve more problems than it creates. For example, replacing black road surfaces with white or reflective surfaces would make it nearly impossible for people to drive on the roads in daylight. On the other hand, planting trees to shade roads and parking lots might be successful.

3. Assess the accuracy of your results. If one of your classmates tried to reproduce your results, how successful would your classmate be? Explain your reasoning.

4. If you had to carry out your investigation again, what would you do differently?

Communicate Your Findings

5. Present your results using both a visual component and a written component.

Assessment Criteria

Once you complete your project, ask yourself these questions. Did you...

- **K/U** provide an accurate description of each ground-cover material, and explain why it would not interfere with the land use?

- **T/I** formulate an appropriate hypothesis about possible changes in temperature for each material?

- **T/I** control appropriate variables and use equipment and materials safely, accurately, and effectively?

- **T/I** analyze and interpret the data for each material you tested to determine whether the evidence supports or contradicts your hypothesis?

- **T/I** identify sources of error that may have limited the accuracy of your process, and suggest improvements to your original design?

- **C** organize and record data accurately, using appropriate visual and written components?

An Issue to Analyze

Dealing with Climate Change

Scientific studies have resulted in some worrying predictions about future climate change. Scientists can only provide probabilities for their predictions, however, and preventing the possible effects of climate change could be very expensive. As a result, there are different opinions about the wisest course of action. A cost-benefit analysis can help you decide what should be done about climate change

> **Issue**
> What actions could be taken to deal with the possible effects of climate change?

Initiate and Plan

1. Make a list of actions and initiatives related to climate change that you have read about in this unit.
2. Research the projected costs and benefits of eight of these actions and initiatives.

Perform and Record

3. Draw a cost-benefit matrix like the one shown below.
4. Choose one action or initiative that would help to reduce the severity of predicted climate change. Place the name of the action or initiative in one of the cells of the cost-benefit matrix, based on the cost of the action or initiative and its perceived benefit. For example, an initiative that would cost a lot but would yield greatly beneficial results would be placed in the "High Benefit, High Cost" quadrant. Any action or initiative requiring technology that is not yet perfected or invented would have a very high cost.
5. Repeat step 4 for each of the other actions and initiatives.

	Low Benefit	High Benefit
High Cost	i. Low Benefit, High Cost	ii. High Benefit, High Cost
Low Cost	iii. Low Benefit, Low Cost	iv. High Benefit, Low Cost

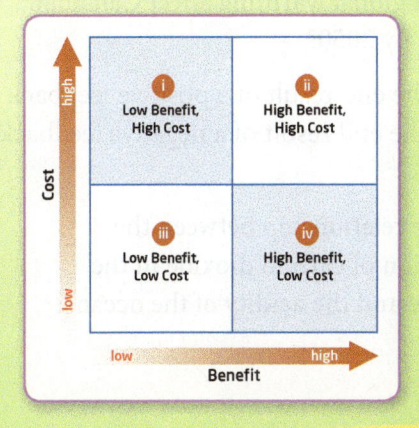

Analyze and Interpret

1. Which actions or initiatives would you recommend, based on their relative costs and benefits? Explain your reasoning.
2. For each action or initiative you recommend, identify two ways that you could contribute to its implementation.
3. Collaborate with your classmates to reach a consensus on the most highly recommended action or initiative. Summarize the reasons for your choice.
4. For your choice, identify the costs and strategies for implementing and enforcing it. Prepare a brief summary that describes the recommendations of your class.

Communicate Your Findings

5. Take what you have learned and decided in this project, and write a persuasive letter to your representative in Parliament (federal or provincial) to express your opinion about Ontario's course of action or inaction regarding climate change.

> **Assessment Criteria**
>
> Once you complete your project, ask yourself these questions. Did you...
>
> - **K/U** make a list of actions and initiatives related to climate change?
> - **A** consider the evidence from your cost-benefit analysis when recommending actions or initiatives?
> - **A** identify two personal contributions you could make to help implement your recommended actions or initiatives?
> - **A** survey the personal opinions of your classmates before choosing one action or initiative?
> - **A** summarize multiple perspectives on the action or initiative, related to cost, implementation, and enforcement?
> - **C** collect information from a variety of sources?
> - **C** organize and communicate the information accurately for the intended audience and purpose?

Unit 3 Review

Connect to the BIG IDEAS

Use this bicycle wheel graphic organizer to connect what you have learned in this unit to the Big Ideas, found on page 263. Draw one bicycle wheel for each Big Idea and write the Big Idea in the centre. Between the spokes of the wheel, briefly describe six examples of that Big Idea.

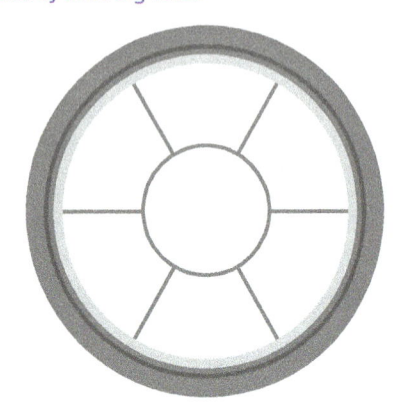

Knowledge and Understanding K/U

1. Which of the following factors affects Earth's climate by changing the albedo of the planet?
   a. the acidity of the oceans
   b. the amount of energy emitted by the Sun
   c. the tilt of Earth's axis
   d. the size of the polar icecaps

2. Which of the following biomes is found in Ontario?
   a. boreal forest
   b. desert
   c. permanent ice
   d. temperate rainforest

3. Which greenhouse gas has the highest global warming potential?
   a. carbon dioxide
   b. chlorofluorocarbons (CFCs)
   c. methane
   d. nitrous oxide

4. Which of the following activities will reduce your carbon footprint?
   a. eating large amounts of meat and dairy products
   b. leaving appliances plugged in when not in use
   c. using compact fluorescent light bulbs
   d. using single-use plastic shopping bags

5. Which of the following tools do scientists use to predict future climate change?
   a. radar
   b. weather satellites
   c. general circulation models
   d. ice cores

6. The diagram below shows a feedback loop in Earth's climate system. Write a short paragraph that describes this feedback loop. Identify it as a positive feedback loop or a negative feedback loop.

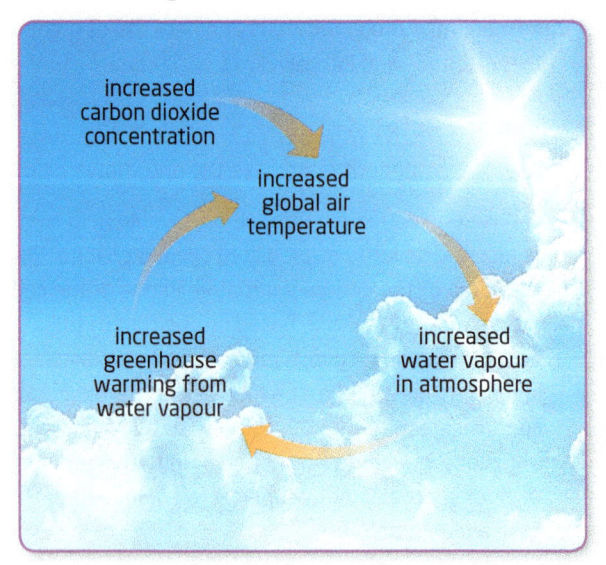

   increased carbon dioxide concentration → increased global air temperature → increased water vapour in atmosphere → increased greenhouse warming from water vapour →

7. How might global warming affect Canadian agriculture by 2050?

8. Compare the end result of a positive feedback loop with the end result of a negative feedback loop.

9. What is the relationship between the concentration of carbon dioxide in the atmosphere and the acidity of the oceans?

10. Explorers have found fossils of ferns, trees, and alligators on islands in the high Arctic. Geologists say that these islands were at the same latitude on the globe when those organisms lived as they are now. What conclusions about climate can scientists draw from the fossils?

11. How do bodies of water affect local temperatures?

12. Global and local climates have changed many times in Earth's history. Name three reasons why people are concerned about the changing climate today.

13. The diagram below shows the temperature profile around an urban area. How do roads and buildings affect local climate?

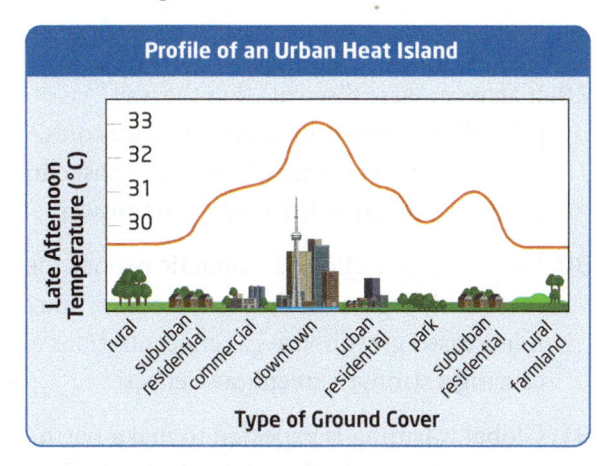

Profile of an Urban Heat Island

14. How do scientists test the accuracy of general circulation models?

15. Explain whether you think a cap-and-trade system is a better way of dealing with increased carbon dioxide emissions than introducing carbon taxes.

Thinking and Investigation T/I

16. One argument against taking action on climate change is that we do not know what changes would have taken place without human intervention, so we cannot know what effect our actions will have on the environment. How can scientists tell which changes are the result of human activities?

17. Research myths and facts about climate change. Which of the myths sound plausible to you? Write a short essay that describes how a specific myth became widespread and explains why this myth is incorrect. Remember to cite all of your references.

18. Some skeptics who claim that anthropogenic climate change is a myth state that carbon dioxide is only a few parts per million in the atmosphere and that it has changed by only a few parts per million in 200 years. They claim that this change is too small to affect the climate. Based on what you have learned in Unit 3, explain why you agree or disagree with the sceptics' claim.

19. The graph below shows the frequency of tropical storms and hurricanes in the North Atlantic Ocean. How does this graph support the idea that Earth's oceans are warming?

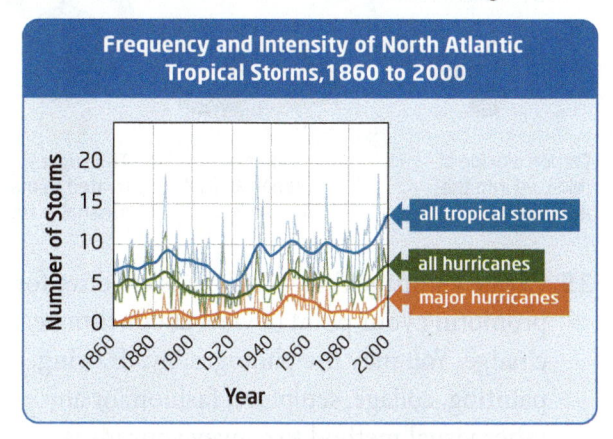

Frequency and Intensity of North Atlantic Tropical Storms, 1860 to 2000

20. Given that the weather is unpredictable within any single week, why do scientists think they can predict climate?

21. Research any new initiatives to monitor Earth's climate that have been developed since the publication of this book. Write a paragraph that outlines these initiatives and their objectives.

22. Imagine that your grandparents lived in the same town in Ontario for the past 80 years. They comment that winters are not like they used to be. Is this statement evidence of a change in weather or in climate? Explain your answer.

23. Identify three sources of bias in weather records. What steps have scientists taken to counteract these biases?

Unit 3 Review

Communication C

24. The following diagram shows how ethanol (a biofuel) is made and used. Analyze the illustration for bias by using the list of questions you learned in Chapter 9. Then create a list of questions you have about the topic described in the diagram. Write a short paragraph that describes any changes you suggest be made to the diagram to clarify the information or to eliminate bias.

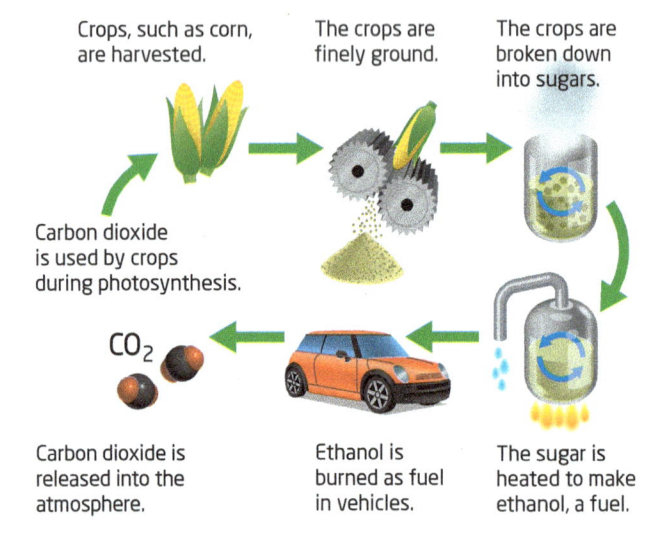

Crops, such as corn, are harvested.
The crops are finely ground.
The crops are broken down into sugars.
Carbon dioxide is used by crops during photosynthesis.
CO_2
Carbon dioxide is released into the atmosphere.
Ethanol is burned as fuel in vehicles.
The sugar is heated to make ethanol, a fuel.

25. Create an image that you think is effective for promoting your point of view about climate change. You may use photography, drawing, painting, collage, sculpture, fashion, or any other visual method to convey your ideas.

26. Write a letter to the editor of your local newspaper outlining five actions that every person can take to lower greenhouse gas emissions in your area. Be sure to include information about how much carbon emissions can be reduced by each action.

27. Summarize the sources and sinks of greenhouse gases by using a graphic organizer of your choice.

28. Think back to the opinion you had when you began this unit about whether humans are responsible for climate change on Earth. Write a paragraph that answers the following questions.
    a. What have you learned that you did not expect?
    b. What have you learned that has supported your opinion?
    c. What have you learned that has challenged your opinion?
    d. What questions have not yet been addressed?
    e. What questions do you have now that you did not have before?
    f. What evidence would cause you to change your opinion?

Application A

29. If an error were discovered in the way paleoclimatologists have evaluated ice cores, would all of their assumptions about past climates have to be discarded? Explain your answer.

30. Why are the Arctic and Antarctic regions the most likely regions of the planet to show warming if increased greenhouse gas concentrations are causing a stronger greenhouse effect?

31. Global warming is expected to make Earth's climate warmer in the winter, hotter in the summer, and drier all year round. What are some adaptations that humans will have to make if these predictions are true?

32. Why would a forestry company be more concerned about the possibility of climate change than a farmer?

33. Hundreds of millions of years ago, carbon dioxide levels were much higher than they are today, but Earth's average temperature was not significantly higher. What factors may have caused these conditions?

34. The winters of 2007 and 2008 were the snowiest in Toronto's history. Explain why these snowfall records do not constitute evidence of climate change.

Literacy Test Prep

Read the selection below and answer the questions that follow it.

Continental Rebound and Sea Level

Some scientists think that global sea level is rising so fast because Antarctic ice is melting faster than they previously thought. Measurements of ice loss in Antarctica may be incorrect due to a factor called rebound, which is illustrated below. During the last ice age, the huge masses of ice that covered parts of the continents pushed down on the land. After the ice melted, the land began to rise again, and it is still rising slowly today. Because measurements of sea level are taken relative to the land, a rise in the land can distort calculations of actual increases in ocean volume.

To determine the impact of continental rebound on sea level, Dr. Richard Peltier of the University of Toronto developed a complex computer model that describes where on Earth land is being uplifted or is subsiding, and by how much. To confirm the predictions of his model, two gravity-measuring satellites were launched into Earth orbit in 2002. They are part of the Gravity Recovery and Climate Experiment (GRACE). The two satellites work together to detect very small variations in gravitational attraction around the planet that indicate where land is growing thicker or thinner. Data collected by the GRACE program have so far confirmed most of the predictions of Dr. Peltier's model.

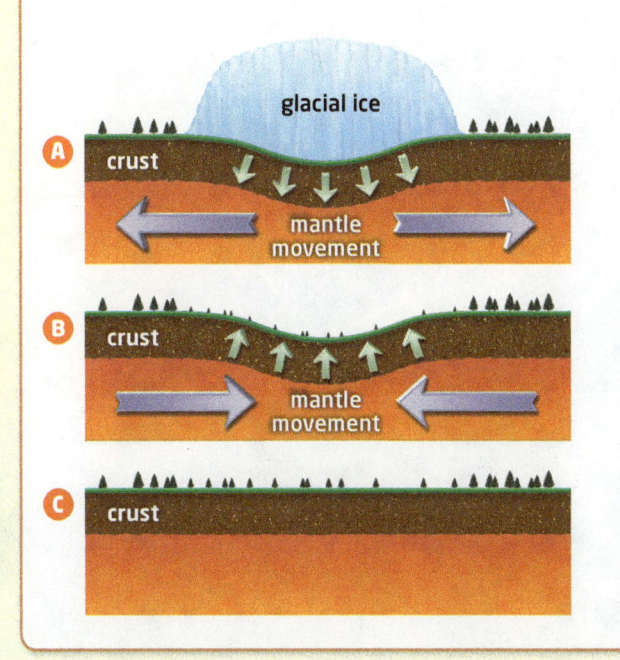

Multiple Choice

In your notebook, record the best or most correct answer.

35. Which of the following statements best summarizes the main point of the first paragraph of the selection?
    a. The movement of the continental crust is causing ice in the Antarctic to melt faster than scientists predicted.
    b. Ocean volume is greater than scientists thought it was because there is so much ice on the continents.
    c. Continental rebound may have caused scientists to incorrectly measure the rate at which Antarctic ice is melting.
    d. The weight of glacial ice is pushing down on the continents and causing sea level to rise.

36. The purpose of the information in the second paragraph is to
    a. encourage the reader to construct a computer model to study sea-level rise
    b. organize information about gravity-measuring satellites
    c. inform the reader about a scientific study on continental rebound
    d. recommend that the reader find additional information about GRACE

37. According to the diagram, what causes the land to uplift?
    a. the weight of the ice
    b. the movement of the mantle
    c. the thickness of the crust
    d. the amount of water in the ocean

Written Answer

38. Write a short essay that explains how important you think the movement of tectonic plates is to the climate change that has been measured in the last 200 years. Use specific details and examples from the selection and from the material you learned in this unit to support your opinion.

UNIT 4
Light and Geometric Optics

BIG IDEAS

- Society has benefited from the development of a range of optical devices and technologies.
- Light has characteristics and properties that can be manipulated with mirrors and lenses for a range of uses.

At one time, it would have been unthinkable for thousands of people to watch a sports event long after sunset. Today, our understanding of the properties of light has led to technologies that allow us to watch a baseball game at night, in a stadium lit up as if it were daytime.

But lighting outdoor spaces, such as stadiums, has drawbacks. It results in light pollution—a wasteful use of energy that disrupts the sleep of humans and the behaviour patterns of animals. Light pollution also interferes with astronomical observations and disconnects city dwellers from the night sky. Turning off the lights would be a solution, but this is often not practical. A more practical way to reduce light pollution is designing lights to illuminate only the intended area.

In this unit, you will learn about the properties of light and how understanding these properties has enabled scientists to develop optical technologies that benefit society.

How can lights be designed to limit light pollution in the surrounding areas?

Chapter 10
Light and Reflection

Chapter 11
Refraction

Chapter 12
Lenses and Lens Technologies

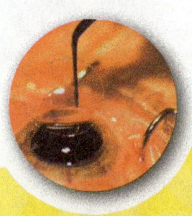

Get Ready for Unit 4

Concept Check

1. Examine the illustration below, and answer the following questions in your notebook.

   a. Identify two sources of natural light and two sources of artificial light.

   b. Name one source of natural light that is not shown in the illustration.

   c. Name three sources of artificial light that are not shown in the illustration.

   d. Identify six objects that reflect light.

2. Light is a form of energy, and it has specific properties. In your notebook, complete each sentence with a word from the box.

   | colours | prism | refracts |
   | light | reflects | straight |

   a. White light is made up of many _____.

   b. A _____ can separate light into colours.

   c. Light travels in a _____ path in one medium.

   d. Light _____ off shiny surfaces.

   e. Light _____ when passing from one medium to another at an oblique angle.

3. In your notebook, match each word listed below with its correct definition.

   i. optical   ii. opaque   iii. transparent
   iv. light   v. translucent

   a. energy that can be detected by the human eye and that makes objects visible

   b. a property of a material that prevents light from being transmitted through the material

   c. a property of a material that allows light to be transmitted through the material but causes sufficient diffusion to prevent clear images from being formed

   d. a property of a material that allows light to be transmitted through the material, producing images that are distinct and clear

   e. related to vision or the transmission of light

Inquiry Check

4. **Interpret** Study the images shown below, which have different types of symmetry.

   vertical symmetry · horizontal symmetry · vertical and horizontal symmetry

   a. Print the letters of the alphabet, in capitals, in your notebook. Identify all the letters that are
      i. vertically symmetrical
      ii. horizontally symmetrical
      iii. both vertically and horizontally symmetrical
   b. Explain how your method for determining vertical symmetry differed from your method for determining horizontal symmetry.

5. **Predict and Perform** Examine the following words:

   MOM DAD

   a. Will these words read correctly from left to right in a mirror? Test your prediction.
   b. What are the distinguishing features of words that read the same in a mirror reflection as they read from left to right on a piece of paper?

Numeracy and Literacy Check

6. **Identify** In the diagram below, identify two lines that
   a. are parallel to each other
   b. are perpendicular to each other
   c. intersect each other

   Write your answers in your notebook.

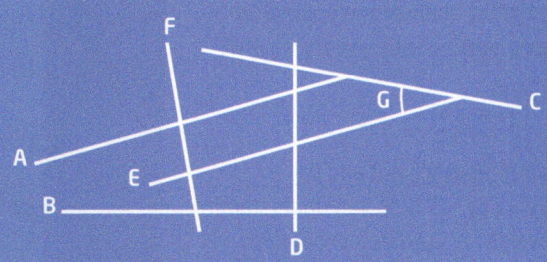

7. **Measure Angles** Use a protractor and a ruler to answer these questions.
   a. What is the measure of ∠G in the diagram?
   b. Draw two lines that have an interior angle of 75°. Label the angle ∠A.

8. **Categorize Words** Put these words into three categories: *image, kaleidoscope, microscope, mirror, reflection, speed, straight, telescope*, and *beam*. Give each category a title, and explain your reasoning.

Looking Ahead to the Unit 4 Projects

At the end of this unit, you will have an opportunity to apply what you have learned in an inquiry or research project. Read the Unit 4 Projects on pages 522-523. Start a project folder now (either paper or electronic). Store ideas, notes, news clippings, website addresses, and lists of materials that might help you to complete your project.

Unit Project
Design a light tunnel to bring natural light to a windowless room.

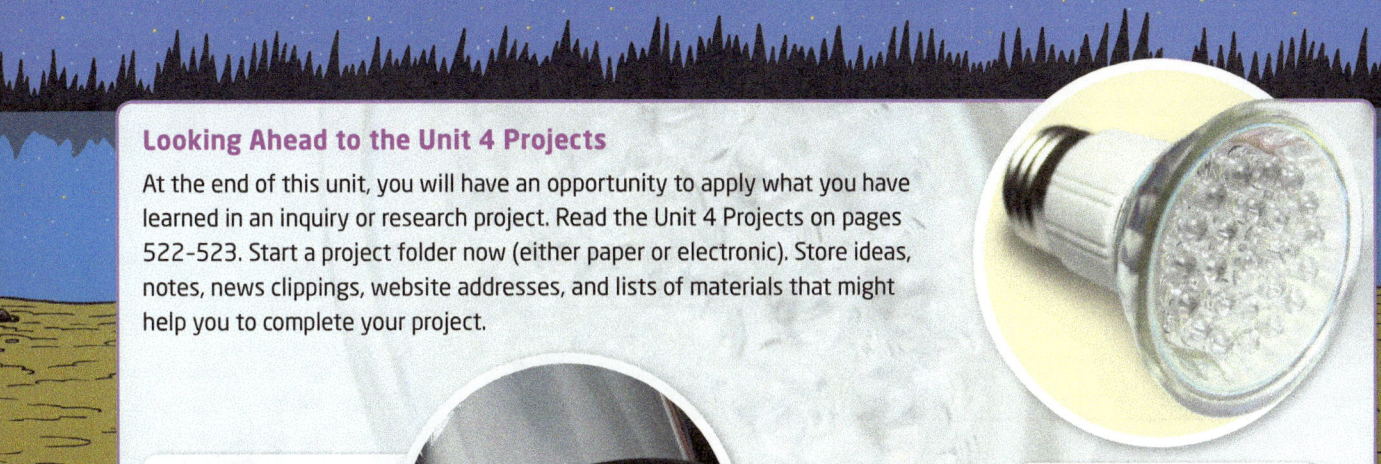

An Issue to Analyze
Analyze the costs and benefits of LED lighting technology.

Chapter 10 Light and Reflection

What You Will Learn

In this chapter, you will learn how to...
- **describe** examples of technologies that use light
- **describe** and **explain** a variety of sources of light
- **explain** how technologies that use light benefit society

Why It Matters

Understanding light and its properties will help you understand how light is used in technologies such as security mirrors, glow sticks, solar ovens, and medical equipment.

Skills You Will Use

In this chapter, you will learn how to...
- **investigate** the laws of reflection using plane and curved mirrors
- **predict**, both quantitatively and qualitatively, the characteristics of images in plane and curved mirrors
- **analyze** a technological device that uses properties of light

The eerie glow that you see in this photograph of the Salton Sea is made by algae that emit light in a process called phosphoresence. The Salton Sea is in California in the United States.

Activity 10-1

Glowing Slime

In this activity, you will make glow-in-the-dark slime using glow-in-the-dark paint powder.

Add the paint powder to the glue solution.

Safety Precautions

- Do not eat the slime.
- Do not inhale the paint powder.

Materials

- two 500 mL measuring cups
- measuring spoons
- glue gel
- tap water
- glow-in-the-dark paint powder
- 4% (saturated) borax solution
- spoon
- resealable plastic bag
- flashlight

Procedure

1. Put on the goggles, apron, and rubber gloves.
2. In a measuring cup, make a glue-gel solution by mixing 15 mL of glue gel with 45 mL of warm water.
3. Stir 1 mL of glow-in-the-dark paint powder into the glue solution. The paint powder will not dissolve, but mix it in well.
4. In a clean measuring cup, mix 30 mL of the glue and paint solution from step 3 with 10 mL of the 4% borax solution.
5. With a spoon, transfer the slime into a resealable plastic bag. Seal the bag.
6. Turn out the lights, and shine a flashlight on the slime.
7. Clean up your work area, and dispose of the materials according to your teacher's instructions.

Questions

1. What happened after you shone the flashlight on the slime?
2. Use your knowledge of electrons to guess what is happening when glow-in-the-dark paint absorbs light.

Chapter 10 Light and Reflection • NEL **401**

Study Toolkit

These strategies will help you use this textbook to develop your understanding of science concepts and skills. To find out more about these and other strategies, refer to the Study Toolkit Overview, which begins on page 560.

Reading Graphic Text

Interpreting Diagrams

A diagram is a drawing that simplifies a concept. It uses symbols to represent objects, directions, and relationships. Reading the labels in a diagram can help you understand these symbols.

To interpret a diagram, first read the title and caption. This will help you understand the main idea. Then consider how each part of the diagram illustrates the main idea. For example, the caption below tells you how a property of light helps you predict shadow characteristics. The diagram illustrates how the shadow of an object changes with distance from a light source. The labels identify the parts of the diagram.

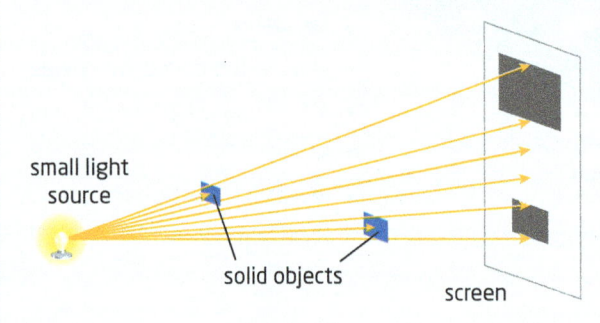

Using the fact that light travels in straight lines, you can predict the size and shape of shadows formed by opaque objects.

Use the Strategy

Examine **Figure 10.8B** on page 407. Read the caption to identify the main idea of the diagram. Explain how each labelled part of the diagram contributes to your understanding of the main idea.

Organizing Your Learning

Comparing and Contrasting

Comparing and contrasting new concepts can help you understand them. **Venn diagrams** and **tables** are two ways that you can graphically organize information. For example, the table below shows the similarities and differences between a real image and a virtual image.

Comparison of a Real Image and a Virtual Image

Type of Image	Differences	Similarities
Real image	A real image is formed when reflected (and refracted) rays meet.	Both images are formed by reflected (and refracted) rays.
Virtual image	The rays that form a virtual image appear to be coming from a specific position, but they are not actually coming from this position.	

Use the Strategy

Read the subsections titled "Chemiluminescence" and "Bioluminescence" on page 407. Make a table to show the similarities and differences between chemiluminescence and bioluminescence.

Word Study

Base Words

Base words are like building blocks or foundations. Knowing the meanings of common base words used in science may help you figure out the meanings of longer words that contain these base words. For example, knowing the meaning of *magnify* (make something appear larger) can help you figure out the meanings of *magnifier* and *magnification*.

Use the Strategy

Think about the meaning of the base word *sphere*. Use it to predict the meaning of *spherical*. Use a dictionary or the Glossary at the end of this textbook to check your predictions.

10.1 Sources and Nature of Light

Key Terms
incandescence
fluorescence
luminescence
phosphorescence
chemiluminescence
bioluminescence
wavelength

The zebrafish in **Figure 10.1** are emitting (giving off) light, similar to the algae shown on page 400. But there are some important differences. First, the algae emit light at the end of the day, after storing energy from the Sun. The fish only emit visible light when they are exposed to ultraviolet light. Second, the algae emit light naturally. The fish are genetically engineered to make them glow. They were developed as a novelty for aquariums. Some environmentalists are concerned that some of these genetically modified fish might escape into streams and ponds and disrupt the populations of natural fish. They believe that laws should be passed to prevent the sale of these fish.

Types of Light Emissions

There are many sources of light. Some sources of light are natural, for example, the Sun. Some sources of light are artificial, such as candles and light bulbs. Notice that these light sources are related to heat. Light from hot objects is made up of many different colours mixed together. This type of light is referred to as "white light." Light, however, can be emitted from sources that are not hot, such as the micro-organisms mentioned earlier and the fish in **Figure 10.1**. These sources of light often emit one main colour of light.

For all light sources, whether natural or artificial, atoms within the materials must absorb some form of energy. After absorbing energy, the atoms are considered to be in an excited state. Then, almost immediately, the excited atoms release the energy. The energy they release is often in the form of light.

Figure 10.1 Researchers implanted a gene from jellyfish into these zebrafish to make them fluorescent. You will learn about fluorescence on page 405.

Figure 10.2 Incandescent light bulbs are usually frosted to make a softer light. A clear bulb is shown here so that you can see the glowing filament.

incandescence light emitted from a material because of the high temperature of the material

Light from the Sun

The most abundant source of light is the Sun. In previous science courses, you may have learned that the hydrogen atoms in the Sun's core have so much energy that when they collide, they sometimes combine, or fuse, to form helium. Such reactions are called *fusion reactions*.

A tremendous amount of energy is released during fusion reactions. This fusion energy is transmitted to the gases on the outer layers of the Sun. When these excited atoms release some of their excess energy, they emit light. Fusion energy is a form of nuclear energy.

Light from Incandescence

For many years, the most common source of light in the home has been the incandescent light bulb. The term **incandescence** [pronounced in-can-DES-ence] means light that is emitted by a very hot object. An incandescent light bulb has a tiny tungsten wire, as shown in **Figure 10.2**, that gets very hot and glows brightly when electric current runs through it. Thus, electrical energy generates the heat that excites the atoms.

An incandescent bulb is inefficient at producing light. Only about 5 percent of the electrical energy used in an incandescent bulb becomes light. The remaining 95 percent is lost as heat. If you were using an incandescent light bulb for heat, it would be 95 percent efficient. Incandescent light bulbs are gradually being replaced by light sources based on newer technologies.

Light from Electric Discharge

Some streetlights, like the one in **Figure 10.3A**, are yellowish. Streetlight bulbs emit light from a heated gas, or vapour, instead of a heated wire. This process is called *electric discharge*. A common form of electric discharge bulb is the sodium vapour bulb. As shown in **Figure 10.3B**, the electric discharge bulb has an electrode at each end. A drop of sodium with a small amount of mercury are placed in the bulb. Most of the air is removed from the bulb, and then some of the sodium and mercury form a vapour in the bulb. An electric current passes through the vapour and excites the atoms. When the excited atoms release their energy, they emit the light that you see as a characteristic yellow.

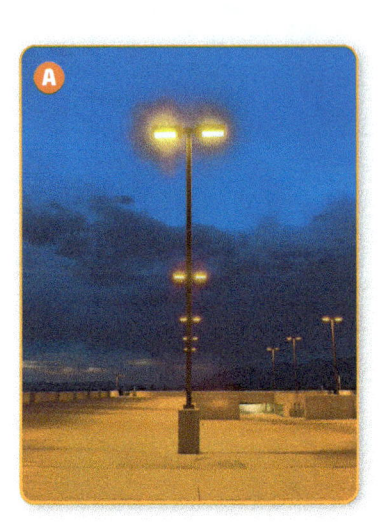

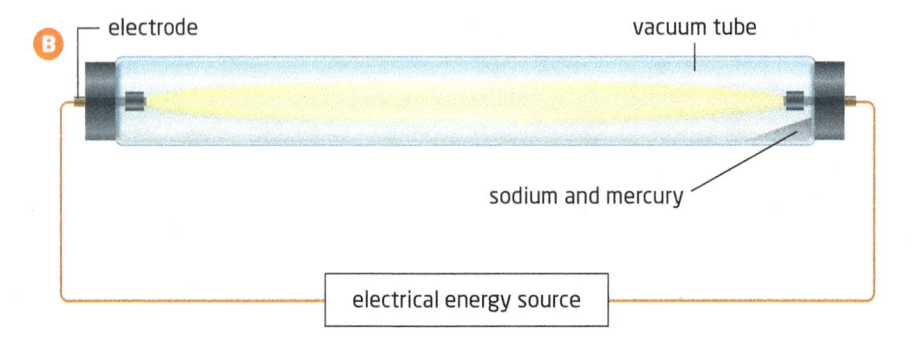

Figure 10.3 A The yellow light that is emitted by many streetlights is produced by excited sodium atoms. **B** Electric charges move rapidly between the electrodes, colliding with the atoms in the vapour and exciting them.

Fluorescence

The long tubular fluorescent bulbs shown in **Figure 10.4A** have been available for many years, and now the compact fluorescent bulbs shown in **Figure 10.4B** are readily available.

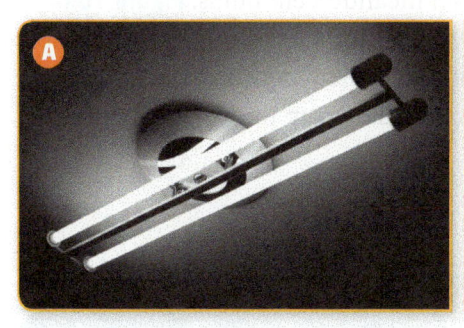

Figure 10.4 A Businesses, industries, and schools have been using the long tubular fluorescent bulbs to light large rooms for a long time. **B** Consumers are now using the newer compact fluorescent bulbs in lamps in their homes.

How a Fluorescent Bulb Works

A fluorescent bulb is an electric discharge tube with an electrode at each end, as shown in **Figure 10.5**. The bulb contains mercury vapour along with an inert gas, such as argon. Recall that argon is one of the noble gases that appear in column 18 of the periodic table.

The inside of a fluorescent bulb is coated with a powdery substance called phosphor. When electrical energy charges the electrodes, they emit electrons. The electrons travel through the gas, from one electrode to the other. As the electrons travel through the gas, they collide with atoms of mercury and excite these atoms. The excited mercury atoms release their excess energy in the form of ultraviolet light, which human eyes cannot see. The energy of the ultraviolet light is absorbed by the phosphor, which emits visible light. The visible light that is emitted in this way is called **fluorescence** [pronounced flor-ES-ence].

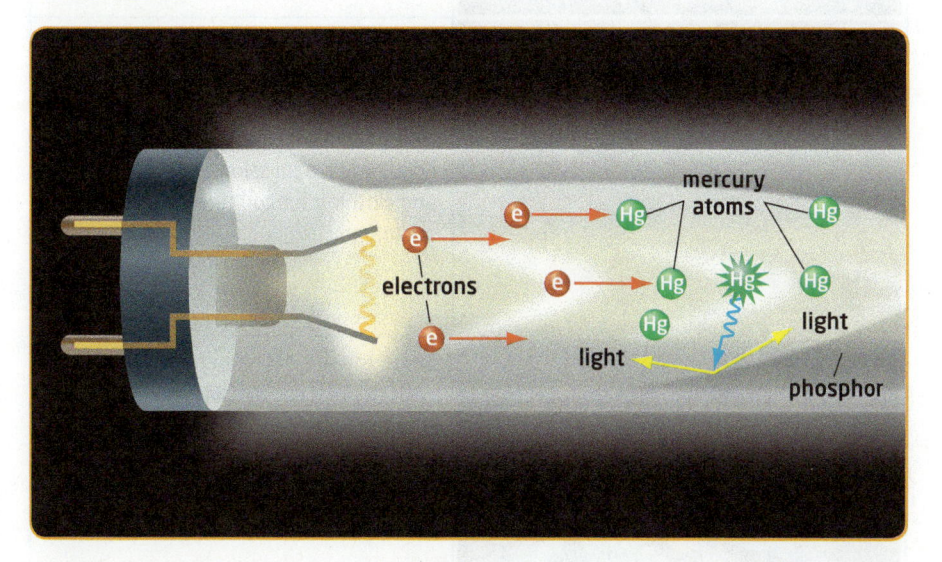

> **Study Toolkit**
>
> **Interpreting Diagrams**
> The caption and labels in **Figure 10.5** can help you understand the source of fluorescence. The labels identify the main parts of the diagram. What does "Hg" stand for?

fluorescence light that is emitted during exposure of the source to ultraviolet light

Figure 10.5 In a fluorescent bulb, the excited mercury atoms emit their excess energy in the form of ultraviolet light. The energy of the ultraviolet light excites atoms in the phosphor lining of the tube, causing them to emit visible light.

Chapter 10 Light and Reflection • NEL

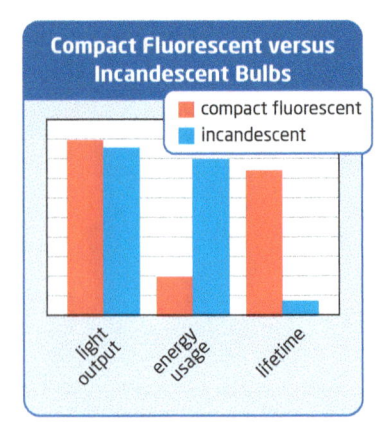

Figure 10.6 Compact fluorescent bulbs are more efficient than incandescent bulbs. Although their purchase price is higher, their lifetime costs are lower because they use less electricity and last longer.

Efficiency of Fluorescent Lighting

Fluorescent lighting is more efficient at producing light than incandescent lighting. For example, a compact fluorescent bulb is 20 percent efficient; that is, 20 percent of the energy it uses is converted into light. Compact fluorescent bulbs last much longer than incandescent bulbs. **Figure 10.6** compares these properties of compact fluorescent and incandescent bulbs. Because of the mercury in fluorescent bulbs, many municipalities accept these bulbs in their hazardous waste centres to keep these bulbs out of landfill.

Uses of Fluorescence

Fluorescent materials are found in many places. **Figure 10.7** shows several.

A Many body fluids contain fluorescent molecules. Forensic scientists use ultraviolet lights at crime scenes to find blood, urine, and semen (all fluorescent).

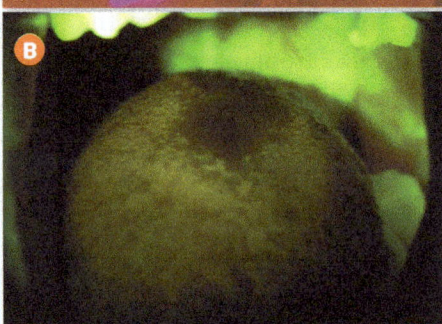

B The tongue's natural fluorescence changes when abnormal tissue is present. A dentist or hygienist can shine a blue light in the mouth and look through a special filter to detect unhealthy oral tissue, which appears as very dark spots.

C Fluorescent materials are used in many types of documents. Banks, businesses, and other organizations have detectors that use ultraviolet lights to check legal documents, admission tickets, currency, and clothing for counterfeit documents and money.

D Some theatre performers use paint with fluorescent dyes. When the theatre is dark and only ultraviolet light is shining on the performers, all the audience can see is the fluorescent light coming from the paint.

Figure 10.7 **A** Forensic investigators can detect fluorescent biological fluids using an ultraviolet lamp. **B** The unhealthy tissue is the dark area. **C** Fluorescent materials are used in some paper currencies. **D** The hands of these performers look like they are floating when you can only see the fluorescent paint.

Types of Luminescence

Luminescence [pronounced loo-mi-NES-ence] is light that is generated without heating the object. The energy used to excite the atoms can come from a variety of sources. Fluorescence is a type of luminescence because the energy used to excite the phosphor in a fluorescent bulb is ultraviolet light. Phosphorescence, chemiluminesence, and bioluminesence are types of luminescence.

Phosphorescence [pronounced fos-for-ES-ence] is similar to fluorescence, except the excited atoms in a phosphorescent material retain the energy for several minutes or even a few hours. Therefore, phosphorescent materials glow long after they have absorbed ultraviolet light. Many glow-in-the-dark objects contain phosphorescent materials.

Chemiluminescence

Chemiluminescence [pronounced CHE-mi-loo-mi-NES-ence] is light that is generated by the energy released in a chemical reaction. The light that you see in glow sticks, such as those in **Figure 10.8A**, is an example of chemiluminescence. **Figure 10.8B** shows how a glow stick works.

> **luminescence** the emission of light by a material or an object that has not been heated; for example, fluorescence
>
> **phosphorescence** light that is emitted due to exposure of the source to ultraviolet light, and that continues to be emitted for some time in the absence of the ultraviolet light
>
> **chemiluminescence** light that is produced by a chemical reaction without a rise in temperature

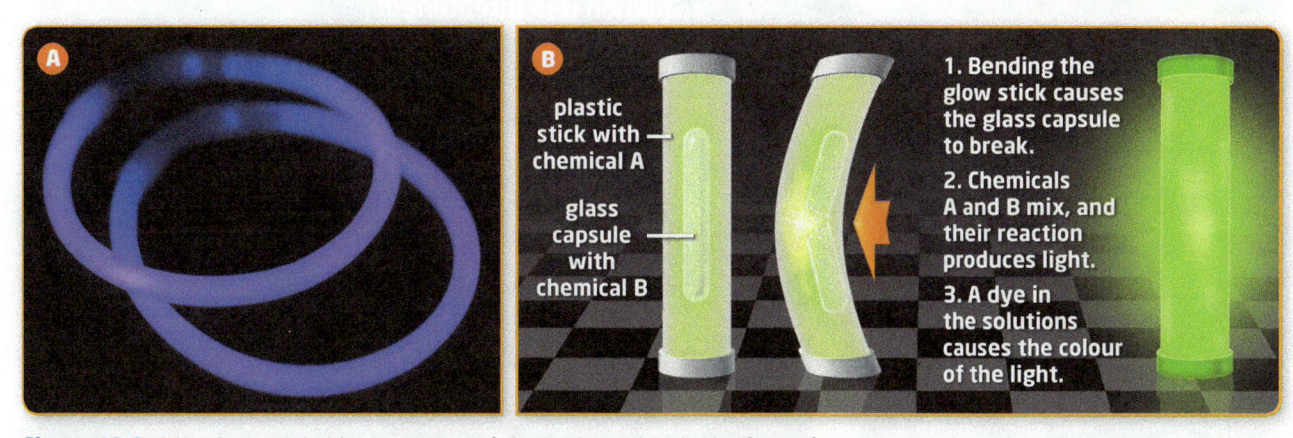

Figure 10.8 A You have probably seen many of these glow sticks in the form of bracelets or necklaces. **B** When chemicals A and B mix, the reaction produces light.

Diagram labels: plastic stick with chemical A; glass capsule with chemical B.
1. Bending the glow stick causes the glass capsule to break.
2. Chemicals A and B mix, and their reaction produces light.
3. A dye in the solutions causes the colour of the light.

Bioluminescence

Bioluminescence [pronounced BIH-OH-loo-mi-NES-ence] is light that is produced by living organisms. Chemical reactions in the living cells produce the light. Bioluminescence is common in marine organisms, as shown in **Figure 10.9** on page 408.

> **bioluminescence** light that is produced by a biochemical reaction in a living organism

> **Learning Check**
>
> 1. What does *excited atom* mean, and what happens after an atom is excited?
> 2. Explain the meaning of *incandescence*.
> 3. Use a diagram to explain how fluorescence works.
> 4. Do you think living organisms should be genetically modified so they can be used for ornamental purposes?

NATIONAL GEOGRAPHIC
VISUALIZING BIOLUMINESCENCE

Figure 10.9

Many marine organisms use bioluminescence as a form of communication. This visible light is produced by a chemical reaction and often confuses predators or attracts mates. Each organism below is shown in its normal and bioluminescent state.

▼ **KRILL** The blue dots shown below the krill are all that are visible when it bioluminesces. The krill may use bioluminescence to confuse predators.

▲ **JELLYFISH** The jellyfish lights up like a neon sign when it is threatened.

◄ **BLACK DRAGONFISH** The black dragonfish lives in the deep ocean where light does not penetrate. It has light organs under its eyes that it uses like a flashlight to search for prey.

▲ **DEEP-SEA SEA STAR** The sea star uses light to warn predators of its unpleasant taste.

The Nature of Light

Light is the only form of energy that can travel like a wave through empty space and through some materials. Light behaves like a special kind of wave, called an *electromagnetic wave*.

Electromagnetic waves are very similar to water waves. Both types of waves involve the movement of energy from one point to another. In water waves, the energy causes water molecules to go up and down, so the shape shown in **Figure 10.10A** is produced. Note that **wavelength** is defined as the distance from one crest (or trough) to the next.

Electromagnetic waves are invisible and can travel through a vacuum. They do not need particles in order to travel. They travel through a vacuum, such as space, at the speed of light (3.00×10^8 m/s). Electromagnetic waves are more complicated than water waves because they involve electric and magnetic fields. But scientists model electromagnetic waves with the same shape as a water wave, as shown in **Figure 10.10B**.

wavelength the distance from one crest (or trough) of a wave to the next crest (or trough)

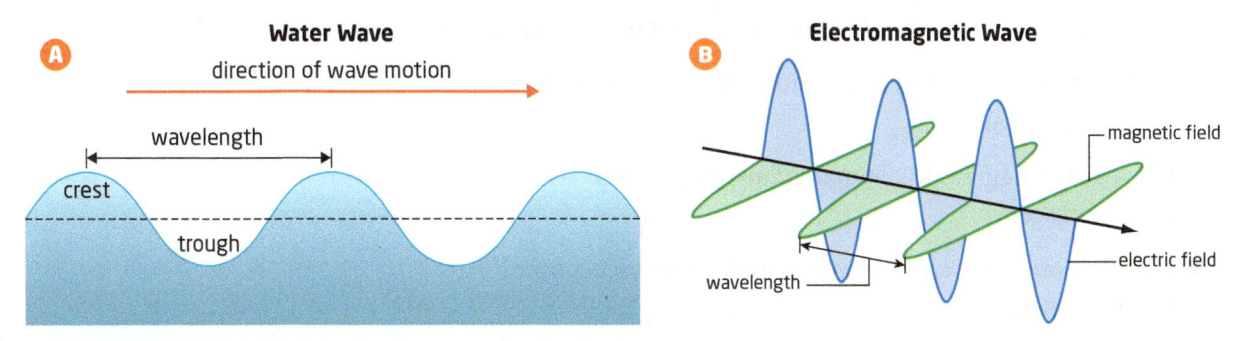

Figure 10.10 Water waves (part **A**) and electromagnetic waves (part **B**) are modelled by the wave patterns shown here.

The Electromagnetic Spectrum

Figure 10.11 shows the electromagnetic spectrum. The *electromagnetic spectrum* is a diagram that illustrates the range, or spectrum, of electromagnetic waves, in order of wavelength or frequency. Notice that the colours of light are just different wavelengths of light. The colour red has the longest wavelength of visible light, which is 700 nm (nm is the symbol for nanometre, or 10^{-9} m). Violet has the shortest wavelength of visible light, which is 400 nm.

Figure 10.11 Notice that visible light makes up only a very small portion of the electromagnetic spectrum. That portion has been expanded in this diagram to show the range of colours.

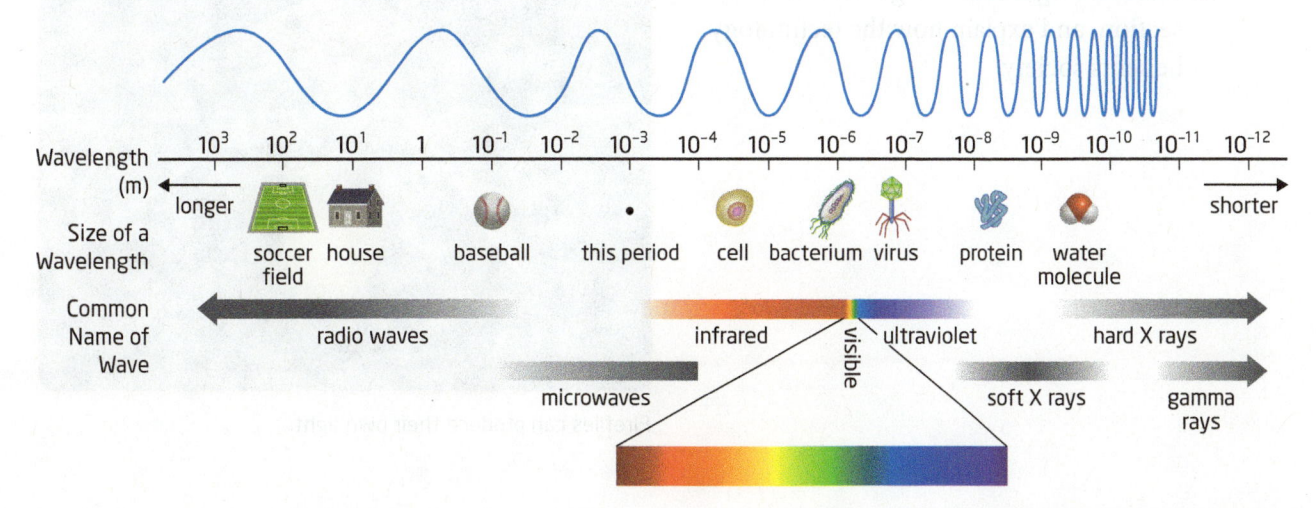

Chapter 10 Light and Reflection •NEL **409**

Section 10.1 Review

Section Summary

- Incandescence is light that is emitted from an object because the object is very hot.
- Luminescence is light that is emitted in the absence of heat. Fluorescence, phosphorescence, chemiluminescence, and bioluminescence are all forms of luminescence.
- Light is transmitted in the form of electromagnetic waves. Visible light makes up only a small part of the electromagnetic spectrum.
- Light is used in many technologies. For example, blue light, with a special filter, is used to detect oral cancer.

Review Questions

C 1. Review **Figure 10.5**. Draw a diagram that shows the steps to convert electrical energy to light in a fluorescent light bulb. Number the steps in your diagram. State what occurs in each step.

K/U 2. State one advantage and one disadvantage of using an incandescent bulb.

K/U 3. Use a Venn diagram to compare phosphorescence and fluorescence.

K/U 4. Describe one difference between chemiluminescence and bioluminescence.

A 5. Examine the firefly in the photograph below. Use your knowledge of light sources to explain what might be happening in the photograph.

K/U 6. Redraw **Figure 10.11** to show the regions of visible and invisible electromagnetic waves. Label the regions in your drawing.

K/U 7. Which region of the electromagnetic spectrum has short wavelengths? Describe some objects that you have learned about that have similar lengths.

A 8. Choose a light technology from this section, and explain how the technology benefits society.

Fireflies can produce their own light.

10.2 Properties of Light and Reflection

All light, regardless of its source, behaves the same. What can you learn about the behaviour of light, including reflection, from the photograph in **Figure 10.12**? **Reflection** is the change in direction of a wave when it reaches a surface and bounces off that surface.

All the light that reaches the eyes of an observer standing beside this lake originally came from the Sun. For example, to see the objects in the photograph, the sunlight had to reflect off every object in the scene.

To see the reflection of the sky, hills, and trees in the lake, the light had to reflect from all of these objects toward the water and then reflect from the surface of the water to your eyes. In the photograph, why do you see only the light that is reflected from the surface of the water and nothing in the water? Why is the reflection from the surface of the water such a clear image of the surroundings?

Rays of Light

Light travels in a straight line as long as it is moving through the same medium. **Medium** is the term for the substance through which light is travelling. This property of light allows you to make predictions about the appearance of objects and, for example, their shadows. You can use a technique called ray tracing to make ray diagrams. A **ray** is a straight line with an arrowhead that shows the direction in which light waves are travelling.

Key Terms

reflection
medium
ray
incident ray
angle of incidence
normal
reflected ray
angle of reflection
plane mirror
virtual image

reflection the change in direction of a light ray when it bounces off a surface

medium the substance through which light travels

ray a straight line with an arrowhead that shows the direction in which light waves are travelling

Figure 10.12 The surface of the water in this photograph is so still that it acts like the surface of a mirror.

Ray Tracing

Figure 10.13 shows how to use rays to predict the location, size, and shape of the shadows of two objects. In this diagram, the source of light is a small light bulb. The light bulb sends out light rays in every direction. You can choose any rays that are travelling in the direction of interest. Draw the rays, and then see where they fall. Note that the smaller object casts the larger shadow, due to its location between the source and the screen.

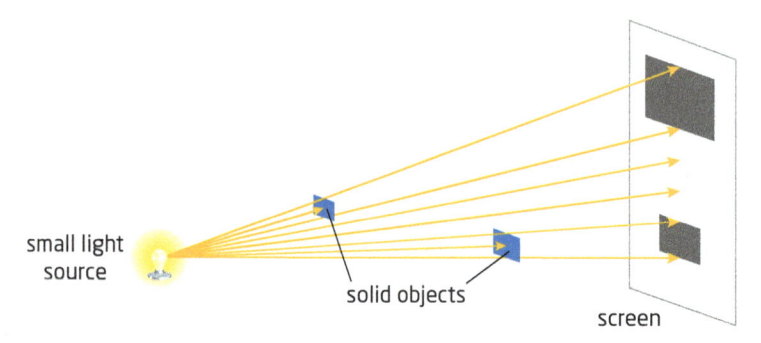

Figure 10.13 Using the fact that light travels in straight lines, you can predict the size and shape of shadows formed by opaque objects.

Fermat's Principle

Fermat's principle predicts the path that light will take after reflecting from a surface or passing through more than one medium. According to *Fermat's principle*, light follows the path that will take the least time. When light reflects from a surface and remains in one medium, its speed is constant. Therefore, the path that takes the least time is the shortest path. Fermat's principle leads to the laws of reflection.

Laws of Reflection

A ray of light coming toward a surface is called an **incident ray**. The **angle of incidence** is measured between the incident ray and a perpendicular line drawn from the point of contact of the incident ray at the surface. This perpendicular line is called the **normal**. The **reflected ray** begins at the point of contact. The **angle of reflection** is measured between the reflected ray and the normal. The incident ray, the normal, and the reflected ray all lie on the same flat surface, or plane.

When you know the angle of incidence, you can predict the angle of reflection because they are the same. The reflected ray always lies on the plane that is defined by the incident ray and the normal. These relationships are called the *laws of reflection*. The laws of reflection apply to light and to all other forms of waves, such as sound waves.

> **incident ray** a ray of light that travels from a light source toward a surface
>
> **angle of incidence** the angle between the incident ray and the normal in a ray diagram
>
> **normal** a line that is perpendicular to a surface where a ray of light meets the surface
>
> **reflected ray** a ray that begins at the point where the incident ray and the normal meet
>
> **angle of reflection** the angle between the reflected ray and the normal in a ray diagram

> **Suggested Investigation**
> Inquiry Investigation 10-B, Studying the Laws of Reflection, on page 440

> **Laws of Reflection**
> 1. The incident ray, the reflected ray, and the normal always lie on the same plane.
> 2. The angle of reflection, $\angle r$, is equal to the angle of incidence, $\angle i$.
> $$\angle r = \angle i$$

Drawing Ray Diagrams

Figure 10.14 illustrates the steps to draw a ray diagram for an incident ray moving toward a mirror. The steps are numbered, so when you read them, start with step 1.

1 Draw the incident ray using a ruler.

2 At the contact point where the incident ray hits the surface, draw a normal by measuring a 90° angle with a protractor.

3 Measure the angle of incidence (*i*) between the incident ray and the normal. Make a mark to indicate the same angle on the other side of the normal. This is the angle of reflection.

4 Draw the reflected ray from the contact point through the mark using a ruler.

5 Label the incident ray, the reflected ray, the angle of incidence (*i*), the angle of reflection (*r*), and the normal.

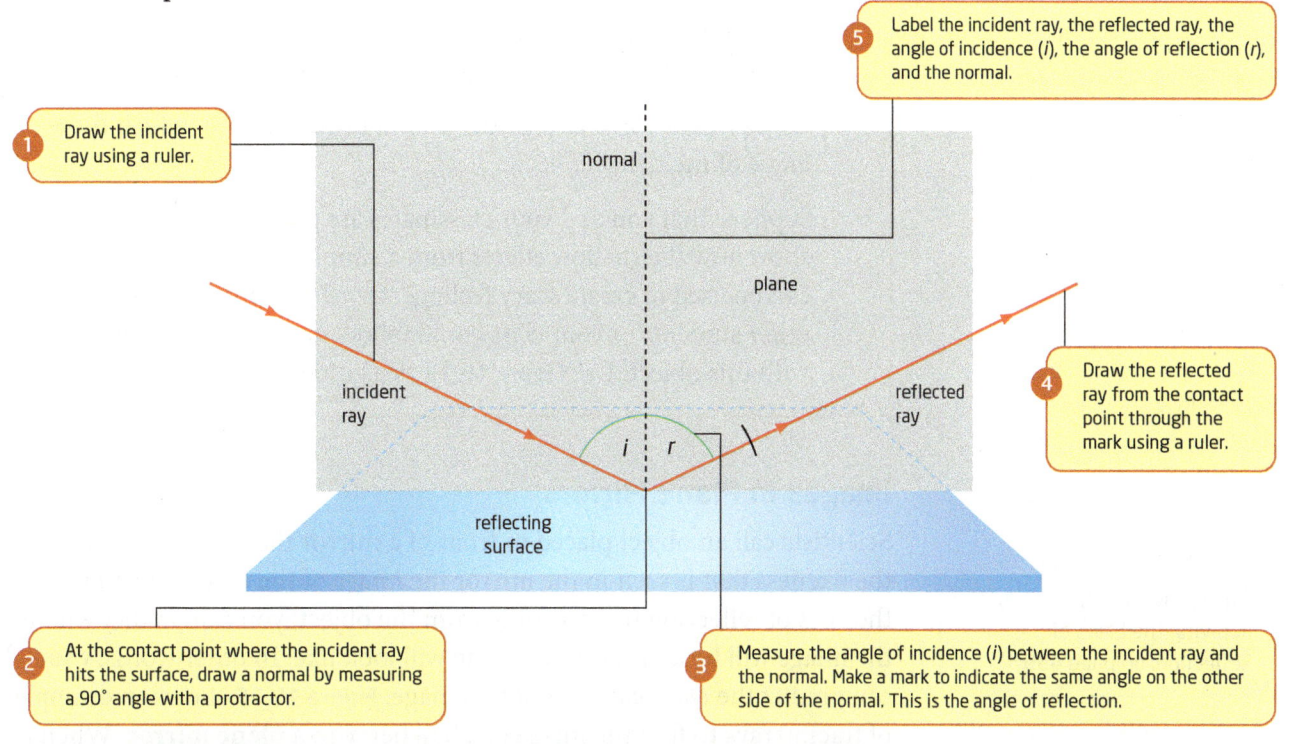

Figure 10.14 Follow the steps illustrated here to learn how to draw a ray diagram for light reflecting off a smooth surface.

Activity 10-2

A Reflection Obstacle Course

Can you use the laws of reflection to hit a target with a light ray? In this activity, you will use two plane (flat) mirrors and a light source to hit the bull's-eye of a target. Then you will use the mirrors and a remote control to turn on a television. Reflection off plane mirrors is discussed on page 414.

Safety Precaution
- Never direct a light source at someone's eyes.

Materials
- targets
- 2 plane (flat) mirrors
- 2 mirror stands
- flashlight
- remote control for a television
- television

Procedure
1. Your teacher will set up different targets at different stations in the classroom, at different heights. One station will have a television and a remote control.
2. Set up two plane mirrors at a target station. Position the mirrors so that you hit the bull's-eye by reflecting the light from the flashlight off the two mirrors.
3. At the station with the television, use the remote control as a source of invisible electromagnetic radiation. Position the mirrors so that you turn on the television by reflecting this invisible source.

Questions
1. How did you have to position the two mirrors to hit the target?
2. How does this activity provide evidence that invisible sources of light also obey the laws of reflection?

> **Learning Check**
>
> 1. Why is the fact that light travels in a straight line critical to the technique of ray tracing?
>
> 2. Using a diagram, explain the laws of reflection. Include the following labels: normal, angle of incidence, angle of reflection.
>
> 3. Using **Figure 10.14** as a guide, draw a ray diagram in which the angle of incidence is 45°.
>
> 4. Suppose that you and your classmates are preparing a project to show how the shadow effects from a simple object, such as a cat, can be used to create scary feelings. Develop a procedure that other students in your class could follow to create these feelings with this object. Use **Figure 10.13** as a guide.

Images in Plane Mirrors

Suggested Investigation
Inquiry Investigation 10-A, Applying the Laws of Reflection, on page 439

plane mirror a mirror with a flat, reflective surface

Scientists call an object placed in front of a mirror the *object*, and they call the likeness that is seen in the mirror the *image* of the object. If you apply the laws of reflection to rays going from the object, you can predict where the image will be and what the image will look like. In other words, you can predict the *characteristics* of the image. **Figure 10.15** shows an example of tracing rays to find the image of a blueberry in a **plane mirror**. When a light shines on the blueberry, it reflects off all the points on the blueberry, in all directions. Rays reflecting off one point on the blueberry are shown in **Figure 10.15**. These rays reach the plane mirror, follow the laws of reflection, and reflect backward. Some of these rays reach the eyes of a person looking at the mirror.

The brain assumes that a light ray travels in a straight line. Therefore, to find out where the eye "sees" the image, extend the rays that reach the eye backward until they meet at a point behind the mirror. These extended rays are shown by the dashed lines in **Figure 10.15**. The point at which the dashed lines meet is the location of one point on the object. By repeating this process for several points on the blueberry, you can find out exactly where the entire image of the blueberry is located.

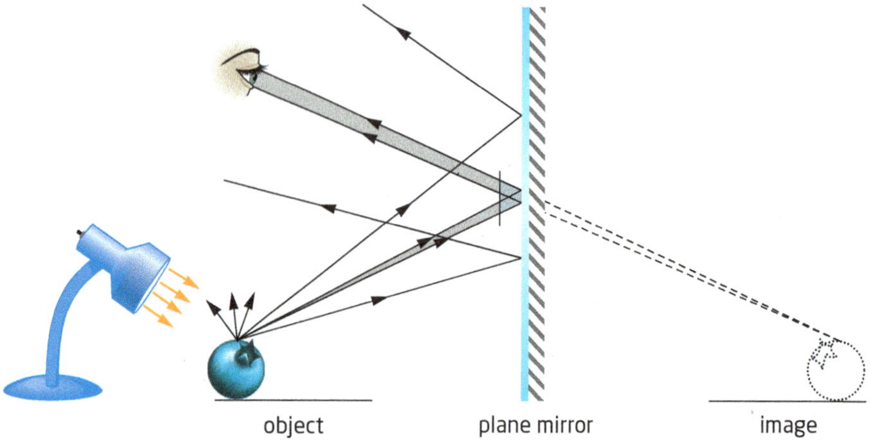

Figure 10.15 No matter where the observer's eye is located, the image will always be in the same place. All the reflected rays can be extended backward and will reach the same point. The dashed lines represent extended rays.

Making a Difference

Pénélope Robinson and Maude Briand-Lemay used their knowledge of mirrors and reflection to double energy production from solar panels on residential roofs.

Residential solar panels are usually installed on the south side of a sloped roof because the south side generally receives more sunlight. Pénélope and Maude's system includes a mirror on a pole placed near the north side of a roof. When the Sun's rays hit the mirror, they are reflected toward solar panels on the north side of the roof.

Pénélope and Maude tested their system. Without the mirror, solar panels on the north side did not collect solar energy. With the mirror, the same amount of energy was collected from solar panels on both sides of the roof.

Pénélope and Maude earned an award for their project at the 2007 Canada Wide Science Fair. They have since registered a patent for their design.

In what other ways could mirrors be used to harness the Sun's energy?

Virtual Images

Notice in **Figure 10.15** that there are no light rays actually going to or coming from the image behind the mirror. Light rays only *appear* to be coming from the image. This type of image is called a **virtual image**. One way to decide whether or not an image is virtual is to imagine putting a screen at the location of the image. If light rays hit the screen and form an image, the image is real and not virtual. If no light rays hit the screen, there is no image on the screen and the image is virtual. You could also say that the image is imaginary because you only imagine that an image forms at this location. If an image is behind a mirror, there is no way that light rays could get there. The image must be virtual. When you study curved mirrors in Sections 10.3 and 10.4, you will learn about "real" images.

virtual image an image formed by rays that appear to be coming from a certain position, but are not actually coming from this position; image does not form a visible projection on a screen

Ray Diagrams and Plane Mirrors

In general, an image has four characteristics:
- its location (closer than, farther than, or the same distance as the object to the mirror)
- orientation (upright or inverted)
- size (same size, larger than, or smaller than the object)
- type (real image or virtual image).

You can predict these characteristics by drawing a ray diagram to locate the image of an object. Follow the steps in **Table 10.1** on the next page to see how to draw a ray diagram for an object placed in front of a plane mirror.

The four characteristics of an image in a plane mirror are the following: An image in a plane mirror is the same size as the object, the same distance from the mirror as the object, and the same orientation as the object. It is also a virtual image.

Figure 10.16 shows how a non-symmetrical object appears in a plane mirror. When you see writing in a plane mirror, the writing *appears* to be backward in the mirror. This is because you write the word and then turn the paper around to face the mirror. The image in the mirror is not *actually* inverted.

Figure 10.16 When you look at writing in a mirror, the writing is difficult to read because it looks like it has been written backward. But it is actually difficult to read because the writing has *not* been inverted. If you wrote the word on a transparent surface, like a piece of plastic wrap, your view of the word on the plastic would match the image in the mirror—the letters on the right stay on the right.

Table 10.1 Locating an Image in a Plane Mirror Using a Ray Diagram

Description	Example
1. Draw a line to represent a mirror. Add hatch marks to show the non-reflecting surface of the mirror. Draw a simple object. The distance between the mirror and the object is called the *object distance*. Label a point at one end of the object "A," and label a point at the other end "B."	
2. Draw an incident ray from point A directly to the mirror at a 90° angle. Because this line is normal to the mirror, the angle of incidence is zero. Therefore, the angle of reflection is also zero. The reflected ray goes directly backward along the same line as the incident ray.	
3. Draw another incident ray from point A at an angle to the mirror. At the point where the incident ray hits the mirror, draw a normal. Measure the angle of incidence with a protractor. Using the knowledge that the angle of reflection is equal to the angle of incidence, draw the reflected ray.	
4. Using a dashed line, extend both reflected rays behind the mirror until they meet. Label this point "A_i" to indicate that it is the image point of the tip of the pencil.	
5. Repeat steps 2 to 4 for point B. Join A_i and B_i using a ruler. The distance between the mirror and the image is called the *image distance*.	

416 NEL • Unit 4 Light and Geometric Optics

Reflection and Stealth Technology

Radar (Radio Detection and Ranging) was invented in 1935 and was used to detect aircraft from the ground during World War II. Military aircraft such as the stealth fighter in **Figure 10.17** need to avoid detection. Two features make the stealth almost invisible to radar. First, the paint used on the aircraft absorbs much of the energy from the radar waves. The base of the paint allows the radar waves to penetrate the surface. Then the radar waves reflect from one particle to the next, losing energy along the way. Although the paint absorbs much of the energy, some radar waves still reflect off the airplane.

The second feature that prevents detection is the shape of the airplane. In **Figure 10.17**, notice that all the surfaces are flat and all the edges are sharp. Most of the incoming radar rays will not hit perpendicular to these surfaces. When the rays reflect from the surfaces of the stealth fighter, most of the reflected rays will not return to the radar antenna. If some of the rays do reflect back to the antenna, it will not be a problem because the signal will be so small that the radar operators will think that the aircraft is a small bird.

Go to **scienceontario** to find out more

The shape of the stealth aircraft ensures that most radar rays will not return to the radar antenna when they are reflected, but will go in other directions.

A radar wave penetrates the base of the paint and then reflects from one particle to another. The paint absorbs most of the energy of the radar wave.

radar wave   reflecting particles

Figure 10.17 The flat sections and sharp corners of a stealth aircraft prevent most of the radio waves from reflecting back toward the radar antenna.

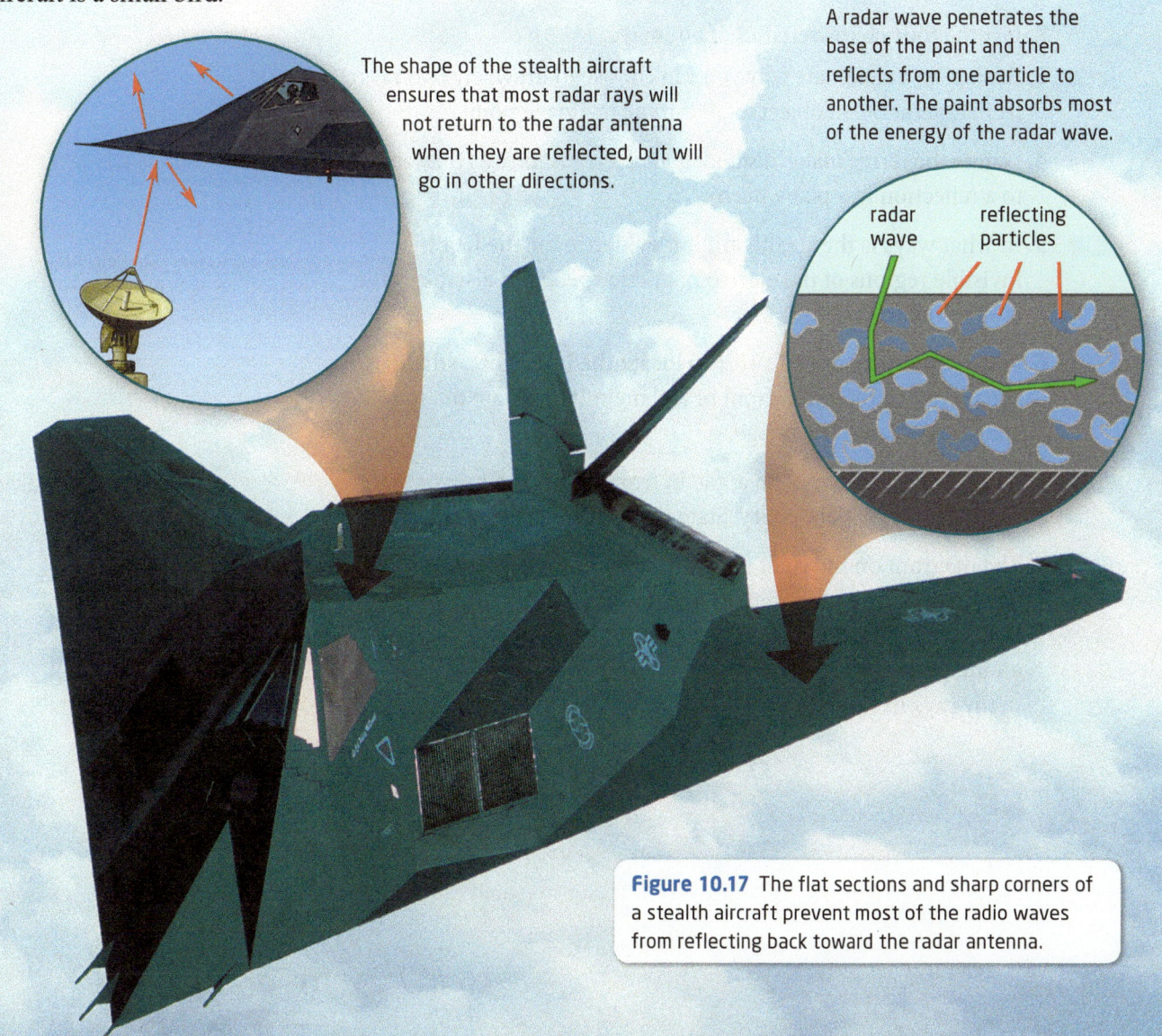

Section 10.2 Review

Section Summary

- A ray is a straight line with an arrowhead that shows the direction in which light is travelling.
- The laws of reflection state that the angle of reflection is equal to the angle of incidence, and that the reflected ray always lies on the plane that is defined by the incident ray and the normal.
- The location of an image in a plane mirror can be found by drawing a ray diagram based on the laws of reflection and tested through inquiry.
- The four characteristics of an image in a plane mirror are the following: the image is the same size as the object, the same distance from the mirror as the object, and the same orientation as the object; the image is a virtual image.

Review Questions

K/U 1. There is a special incident ray that reflects right back on itself.
  a. How would you aim this incident ray to achieve that effect?
  b. What is the angle of incidence of this incident ray?

K/U 2. List the four characteristics of an image.

C 3. Explain to a classmate why you can choose to draw any two rays from a point on an object to determine its image point.

K/U 4. Define the terms *image distance* and *object distance* as they apply to a reflection in a plane mirror.

A 5. In what ways is the stealth aircraft evidence for the fact that invisible regions of the electromagnetic spectrum also obey the laws of reflection?

K/U 6. Follow the steps in **Table 10.1** to locate the image of a small, square object placed in front of a plane mirror. State the four characteristics of the image.

K/U 7. Draw a ray diagram of an apple in front of a plane mirror. Refer to **Figure 10.15** if necessary. State the four image characteristics.

T/I 8. The diagram on the right shows four different objects in front of a mirror. For each object, explain how many image points need to be drawn in order to draw an image of the entire object. For each object, how many rays need to be drawn?

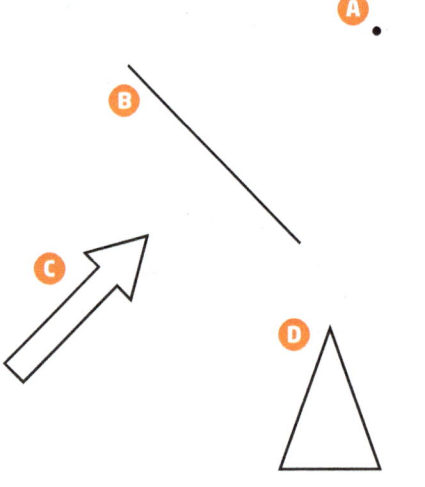

10.3 Images in Concave Mirrors

Key Terms
concave mirror
principal axis
focal point
focal length
real image
magnification
spherical aberration

The giant mirror in **Figure 10.18** is called *Sky Mirror*. It is a piece of art created by artist Anish Kapoor that was on display in New York City in 2006. *Sky Mirror* is more than 10 m in diameter, which makes it nearly three storeys tall. Its reflective surface is made from polished stainless steel, and its mass is about 20 t. As a work of art on the streets of New York, it fascinated crowds of onlookers. The image in the mirror changes as you walk by it.

To people who are interested in the science of optics, *Sky Mirror* is more than a piece of art. You have learned that a plane mirror produces an image that is the same size, shape, and orientation as the object. In a curved mirror, the size of the image is not identical to the size of the object, as demonstrated by *Sky Mirror*. Look carefully at the city scene captured in the photograph of *Sky Mirror*. Look for clues in the image that convince you that *Sky Mirror* cannot be a plane mirror.

By the end of Section 10.3, you will learn that the ray tracing skills you learned earlier can also be used to study the characteristics of images formed by curved mirrors.

Sense of scale
The mass of a small car is about 1300 kg, or about 1.3 t. So the mass of *Sky Mirror* is about the same as 15 small cars.

Figure 10.18 *Sky Mirror* was on display in New York City in 2006.

concave mirror a mirror whose reflecting surface curves inward

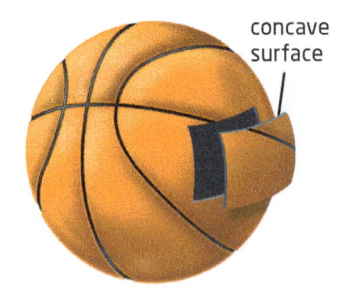

Figure 10.19 The inside surface of a sphere is a concave surface.

principal axis on a concave mirror, the line that passes through the centre of curvature, C, of the mirror and is normal to the centre of the mirror

focal point the point on the principal axis through which reflected rays pass when the incident rays are parallel to and near the principal axis

focal length the distance between the vertex of a mirror and the focal point; half the distance from the vertex to the centre of curvature

Figure 10.20 **A** Think of a curved mirror as a series of small flat mirrors. **B** The incident ray passes through the centre of curvature. **C** The incident ray is near and parallel to the principal axis.

Properties of Concave Mirrors

The portion of *Sky Mirror* you can see in **Figure 10.18** is the inside of a large sphere. One of the most common shapes for a curved mirror is a spherical shape. You can picture a spherical mirror by cutting a section out of a sphere, such as a basketball, as shown in **Figure 10.19**. If you put a mirror surface on the inner surface of the cut-out section, you would have a **concave mirror**.

When you look at objects in a concave mirror, such as the people, buildings, and cars in **Figure 10.18**, the images are distorted. The images are even more distorted toward the edges of the mirror. In the following material, you will learn how to use ray tracing to determine the characteristics of images that are formed near the *centre* of curved mirrors. The optics of images away from the centre of curved mirrors is covered in later studies.

Drawing Ray Diagrams for Concave Mirrors

Recall that when drawing a reflected ray for a plane mirror, you have to measure the angle of incidence between the incident ray and the normal. How do you draw a normal at a point on a curved surface, when all the normal lines will point in different directions? You can apply the same rules of reflection for a plane mirror by thinking of the curved surface as many small, flat mirrors, as shown in **Figure 10.20A**. In **Figure 10.20A**, notice how all the normals meet at a point. This point is called the *centre of curvature, C,* of the mirror. The thick, horizontal normal that touches the centre of the mirror is called the **principal axis**. The principal axis is important because it helps you locate the positions of objects that are placed in front of the mirror. The point at which the principal axis cuts the centre of the mirror is called the *vertex, V*.

In **Figure 10.20B**, the incident ray passes through the centre of curvature. Since the incident ray passes right over the normal, the angle of incidence and the angle of reflection are zero. This means that the incident ray reflects right back on itself.

In **Figure 10.20C**, the incident ray is near and parallel to the principal axis. It also reflects according to the laws of reflection. Notice where it intersects on the principal axis. This point is called the **focal point**, *F*. The geometry of the curved mirror produces two special situations. (1) All rays that are near and parallel to the principal axis will reflect through *F*. The reverse is also true. (2) Any rays that are incident through *F* will reflect off and away from the mirror, parallel to the principal axis. The distance between *F* and the mirror at *V* is called the **focal length**.

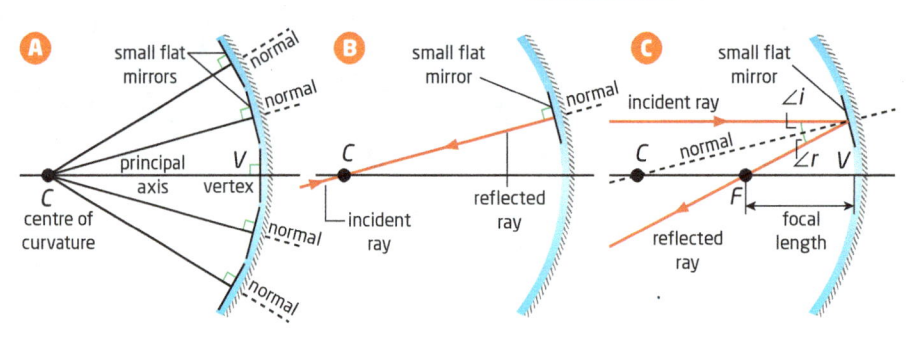

420 NEL • Unit 4 Light and Geometric Optics

Activity 10-3

Reflection from the Concave Surface of a Spoon

In this activity, you will use a simple kitchen tablespoon as a concave mirror.

Materials
- kitchen tablespoon with two shiny, reflective surfaces

Procedure
1. Hold up the inside of the spoon in front of your face. Look at the image of your face.
2. Bring the spoon as close to your face as you can and still see your image. Describe the characteristics of your image in the spoon.
3. Slowly move the spoon away from your face. Observe any changes in your image as the spoon gets farther away. If you can still see your image when the spoon is at arm's length, have someone else move the spoon even farther away. Describe any changes in the image of your face.

Questions
1. How is the image of your face on the inside of the spoon different from your image in a plane mirror?
2. Compare and contrast how lateral inversion happens in a plane mirror and a concave mirror.

Ray Diagrams for Concave Mirrors

When drawing a ray diagram to predict the position of an image, it is helpful to draw the object so that the bottom is on the principal axis. Because the principal axis is normal to the mirror, any ray going toward the mirror along the principal axis will reflect back on itself along the principal axis. Therefore, the bottom of the image will be on the principal axis. You only need to find the image point for the top of the object in order to draw the entire image. By using the special situations described earlier, you can use the laws of reflection to draw two incident rays without measuring angles. Then you can trace back the reflected rays as you did with plane mirrors to locate the image point for the top of the object.

The first ray travels from the top of the object to the mirror, parallel to the principal axis. As you saw in **Figure 10.20C**, the reflected ray will pass through the focal point. If you draw a second ray from the top of the object through the focal point, then the reflected ray will be parallel to the principal axis. A third ray can be drawn through C, the centre of curvature, to the mirror. As mentioned before, any incident ray through C will reflect back on itself because it is directed along a normal to the mirror.

Go to **scienceontario** to find out more

> **Study Toolkit**
>
> **Base Words** Knowing that the base word for *curvature* is *curve* can help you understand the meaning of the word *curvature*.

An Object between the Focal Point and the Mirror

Images in concave mirrors can be very different, depending on where the object is located relative to the focal point. Follow the steps in **Table 10.2** on the next page to draw the image of an object when it is between the focal point and the concave mirror. The focal point is half the distance from the vertex to the centre of curvature. When drawing ray diagrams, be sure to put the focal point at this position.

Table 10.2 Drawing a Ray Diagram for an Object between *F* and a Concave Mirror

Directions	Diagram
1. Draw the principal axis and a curve to represent the concave mirror. • Mark a focal point. • Draw the object so that the bottom is on the principal axis between the focal point and the mirror.	
2. Draw a ray (shown in blue) from the top of the object toward the mirror and parallel to the principal axis. Draw the reflected ray back through the focal point.	
3. If you draw a ray from the top of the object to the focal point, the ray will be going away from the mirror. Instead, start at the focal point and draw a dotted line (shown in green) going toward the top of the object. The dotted line represents the ray coming from the focal point. The actual ray starts at the top of the object and goes toward the mirror. Draw the reflected ray travelling backward, parallel to the principal axis.	
4. Starting at *C*, draw a dotted line (shown in red) to the top of the object. This dotted line represents the ray coming from *C*. The actual ray starts at the top of the object and goes toward the mirror. Draw the reflected ray travelling backward, along the incident ray.	
5. As you can see, the reflected rays are travelling away from each other and will never intersect. Therefore, extend the reflected rays behind the mirror with dashed lines. The point where the reflected rays meet is the top of the image. The bottom of the image is on the principal axis. Draw the image. Notice that the image is larger than the object.	

422 NEL • Unit 4 Light and Geometric Optics

An Object between the Focal Point and the Centre of Curvature

What happens when you put an object between the focal point and *C*? Find out by drawing a ray diagram as described in **Table 10.3**. Note that you use the same three rays, but you get different results than you did when the object was between the mirror and *F*.

When you complete the ray diagram, you will discover that the rays do not have to be extended back behind the mirror. The rays actually meet at the image. Therefore, the image is a **real image** because it would appear on a screen if one were placed at the position of the image.

real image an image that is formed when reflected rays meet

Table 10.3 Drawing a Ray Diagram for an Object between *F* and *C* in Front of a Concave Mirror

Directions	Diagram
1. Draw the principal axis and a curve to represent the concave mirror. • Mark a focal point. • Then mark the point *C* so that it is twice as far from the mirror as the focal point is. • Draw the object so that the bottom is on the principal axis between the focal point and *C*.	
2. Draw a ray (shown in blue) from the top of the object toward the mirror and parallel to the principal axis. Draw the reflected ray back through the focal point.	
3. Draw a ray (shown in green) from the top of the object through the focal point, continuing to the mirror. The reflected ray will travel backward, parallel to the principal axis.	
4. Draw a line (shown in red) from the top of the object toward the mirror, as though it is coming from *C*. The ray will not reach the mirror in the drawing. You know that the reflected ray will travel back along the incident ray. The point where the reflected rays meet is the top of the image. The bottom of the image is on the principal axis. Draw the image.	

An Object beyond the Centre of Curvature

What happens if you put an object farther away from the mirror than C? Find out by drawing a ray diagram, as described in **Table 10.4**. Look for the differences in the characteristics of the image relative to the object compared with previous ray diagrams.

Table 10.4 Drawing a Ray Diagram for an Object beyond *C* in Front of a Concave Mirror

Directions	Diagram
1. Draw the principal axis and a curve to represent the concave mirror. • Mark a focal point. • Then mark *C* so that it is twice as far from the mirror as the focal point. • Draw the object so that the bottom is on the principal axis beyond *C*.	
2. Draw a ray (shown in blue) from the top of the object toward the mirror, parallel to the principal axis. Draw the reflected ray back, through the focal point.	
3. Draw a ray (shown in green) from the top of the object through the focal point, continuing to the mirror. The reflected ray will travel backward, parallel to the principal axis.	
4. Draw a ray (shown in red) from the top of the object through *C*, continuing toward the mirror. Although the line does not reach the mirror in the diagram, draw the reflected ray back along the incident ray. The point where the reflected rays meet is the top of the image. The bottom of the image is on the principal axis. Draw the image.	

> **Learning Check**
>
> 1. An object is between *F* and a concave mirror. Draw a ray diagram to show the characteristics of the image.
>
> 2. An object is in front of a concave mirror between *F* and *C*. Draw a ray diagram to show the characteristics of the image.
>
> 3. The distance from a make-up mirror to *C* (the radius of curvature) is 70 cm. How far from the mirror can a person be and still see an upright, magnified image?
>
> 4. An object is in front of a concave mirror and beyond *C*. Draw a ray diagram to show the characteristics of the image.

Mirror and Magnification Equations

You can also predict the characteristics of an image using two equations: the mirror equation and the magnification equation. The mirror equation allows you to calculate the location of the image. In the magnification equation, the **magnification**, *m*, tells you the size, or height, of the image relative to the object using object and image distances. The magnification equation allows you to find the magnification from the object and image distances. **Figure 10.21** illustrates the variables in the equations.

magnification the change in size of an optically produced image

> **Mirror Equation**
>
> $$\frac{1}{f} = \frac{1}{d_i} + \frac{1}{d_o}$$
>
> The image distance, d_i, is negative if the image is behind the mirror (a virtual image).
>
> **Magnification Equation**
>
> $$m = \frac{h_i}{h_o} = \frac{-d_i}{d_o}$$
>
> The image height, h_i, is negative if the image is inverted relative to the object.

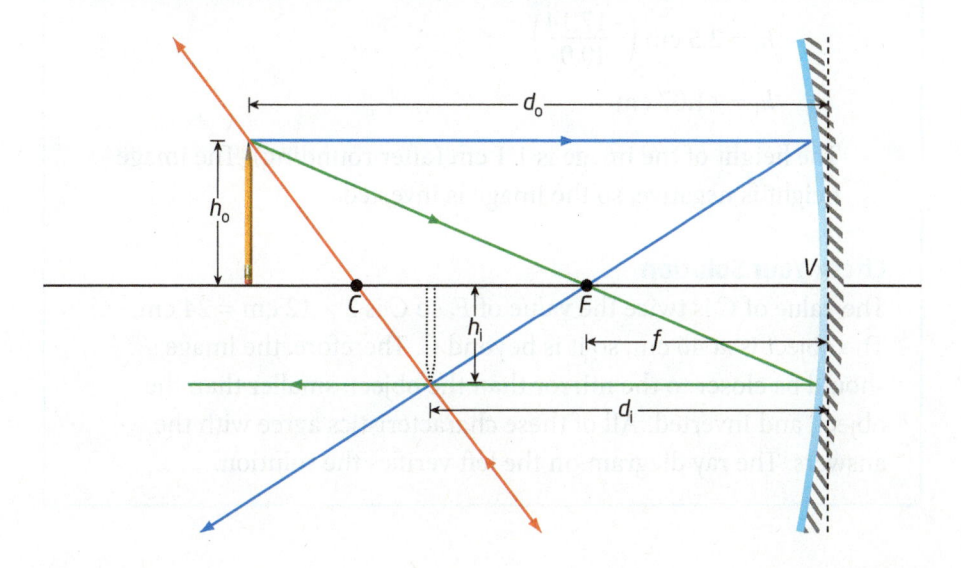

Figure 10.21 Note that *d* represents distance and *h* represents height. The subscripts "o" and "i" indicate whether the symbol represents the object or the image, respectively.

GRASP

Go to **Science Skills Toolkit 11** to learn about an alternative problem solving method.

Hint: Starting with the equation
$\frac{1}{d_i} = \frac{1}{12 \text{ cm}} - \frac{1}{40.0 \text{ cm}}$,
use the [1/x] button to evaluate the second two terms. Put 12 in your calculator, and press the [1/x] button. You will get 0.8333. Now put 40 in your calculator, and press the [1/x] button. You will get 0.025. Your equation has become
$\frac{1}{d_i} = 0.083\,33 - 0.025$
$= 0.058\,333$

Press the [1/x] button again, and the result is $d_i = 17.14$ cm, which rounds to 17 cm.

Sample Problem: Mirror Equations and Concave Surfaces

Problem

A concave mirror has a focal length of 12 cm. An object with a height of 2.5 cm is placed 40.0 cm in front of the mirror.

a. Calculate the image distance.
b. Calculate the image height.

Solution

a. Use the mirror equation to find the image distance.

$$\frac{1}{f} = \frac{1}{d_i} + \frac{1}{d_o}$$

$$\frac{1}{d_i} = \frac{1}{f} - \frac{1}{d_o}$$

$$= \frac{1}{12 \text{ cm}} - \frac{1}{40.0 \text{ cm}}$$

$$= \frac{10}{120 \text{ cm}} - \frac{3}{120 \text{ cm}}$$

$$= \frac{7}{120 \text{ cm}}$$

$$d_i = \frac{120 \text{ cm}}{7}$$

$$= 17.14 \text{ cm}$$

The image is 17 cm (after rounding) from the mirror. The sign is positive, so the image is in front of the mirror.

b. Use the magnification equation to find h_i.

$$\frac{h_i}{h_o} = \frac{-d_i}{d_o}$$

$$\frac{h_i}{2.5 \text{ cm}} = \frac{-17.14}{40.0}$$

$$h_i = 2.5 \text{ cm} \left(\frac{-17.14}{40.0}\right)$$

$$h_i = -1.07 \text{ cm}$$

The height of the image is 1.1 cm (after rounding). The image height is negative, so the image is inverted.

Check Your Solution

The value of C is twice the value of F, so C is 2×12 cm = 24 cm. The object is at 40 cm, so it is beyond C. Therefore, the image should be closer to the mirror than the object, smaller than the object, and inverted. All of these characteristics agree with the answers. The ray diagram on the left verifies the solution.

426 NEL • Unit 4 Light and Geometric Optics

Practice Problems

1. A concave mirror has a focal length of 6.0 cm. An object with a height of 0.60 cm is placed 10.0 cm in front of the mirror.
   a. Calculate the image distance.
   b. Calculate the image height.

2. In the diagram below, the object is between the mirror and *F*. Use the data in the diagram to answer the questions below.
   a. Calculate the image distance.
   b. Calculate the image height.

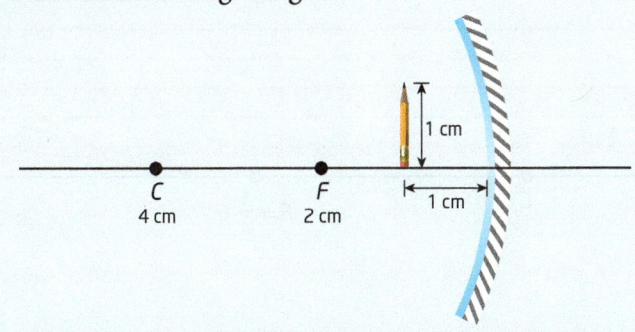

3. In the diagram below, the object is beyond *C*. Use the data in the diagram to answer the questions below.
   a. Calculate the image distance.
   b. Calculate the height of the image.

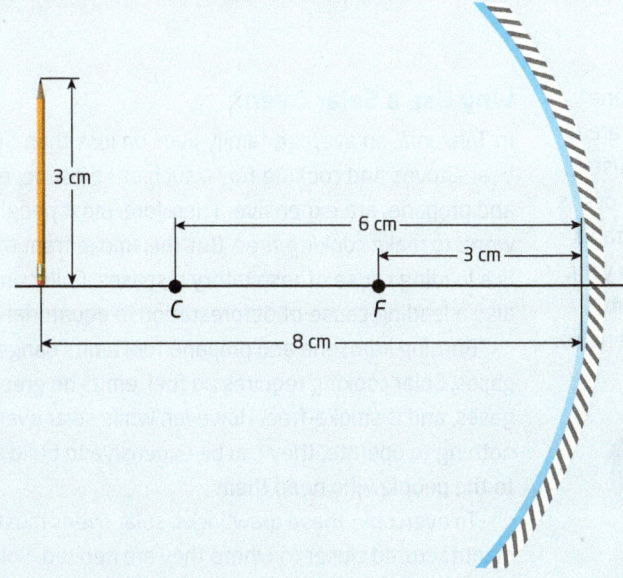

4. A dancer is applying make-up using a concave mirror. The dancer's face is 35 cm in front of the mirror, and the image is 72 cm behind the mirror. Use the mirror equation to calculate the focal length of the mirror.

5. A concave mirror magnifies an object placed 30.0 cm from the mirror by a factor of +3.0. Calculate the radius of curvature of the mirror.

Distortion of Images in Curved Mirrors

Figure 10.22 shows what happens when light rays that are parallel to the principal axis hit a spherical mirror at points that are not within the small centre region of the mirror. In this case, the reflected rays do not meet at the same point. The focal point becomes spread out over a larger area than a point. The same thing happens if you use these rays to try to locate the image point of an object by tracing the rays behind the mirror. The rays will not meet at a point, and the image becomes spread out. This effect is called **spherical aberration**. Scientists have discovered that a concave mirror in the shape of a parabola eliminates spherical aberration.

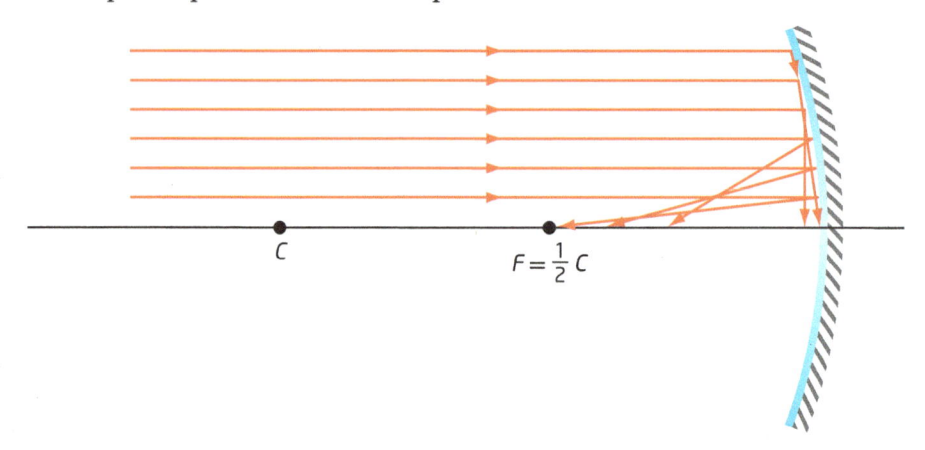

> **spherical aberration**
> irregularities in an image in a curved mirror that result when reflected rays from the outer parts of the mirror do not go through the focal point

Figure 10.22 As the rays get farther from the principal axis, the point at which the reflected rays cross the principal axis moves toward the mirror.

STSE Case Study

Saved by the Sun

In many parts of the world, people burn wood or kerosene to cook their food. But increasingly, people who live in areas that are hot and sunny are using the Sun. Solar ovens use heat from the Sun, which is free, to cook food. So solar ovens can be a big help in countries such as Somalia and Tanzania, where most people live on just a few hundred dollars a year. Solar ovens also work in Canada, and they do not use up electricity or natural gas the way that conventional ovens do.

Why Use a Solar Oven?

In Tanzania, an average family lives on less than $600 a year. Stoves and cooking fuels, such as kerosene, ethanol, and propane, are expensive. Therefore, most people collect wood to make cooking fires. But the smoke from these fires is a leading cause of respiratory diseases. Collecting wood is also a leading cause of deforestation in equatorial areas.

Burning kerosene and propane fuel emits dangerous gases. Solar cooking requires no fuel, emits no greenhouse gases, and is smoke-free. However, while solar ovens cost nothing to operate, they can be expensive to build and ship to the people who need them.

To overcome these drawbacks, solar ovens must be manufactured closer to where they are needed. Solar Circle, a volunteer group based in the United States, is helping to set up a solar oven industry in Tanzania that will use local materials. This local industry will reduce the cost of solar ovens and make it easier for more people to make the switch to solar cooking. Solar cooking, in turn, will protect not only the environment but also people's health.

> Solar ovens can help the environment while improving life for people. Not surprisingly, solar ovens work best in areas that are hot and sunny. These areas are home to most of the world's populations, many of whom are very poor.

Radar Technology and Concave Surfaces

In Section 10.2, you read that radar technology is used to detect aircraft (except the aircraft like the stealth, which need to avoid detection). **Figure 10.23** shows a radar antenna. A radar antenna is basically a concave mirror in the shape of a parabola that can send and receive radio waves. A radio wave generator and detector are located at the focal point of the antenna. A pulse of radio waves that lasts a few thousandths of a second hits the antenna and is sent out toward the sky. For the next few seconds, the antenna acts as a receiver. Any returning radio waves that reach the antenna are directed to the detector at the focal point. Then another pulse is sent out.

focal point

Figure 10.23 A radar antenna acts as a concave mirror for radio waves.

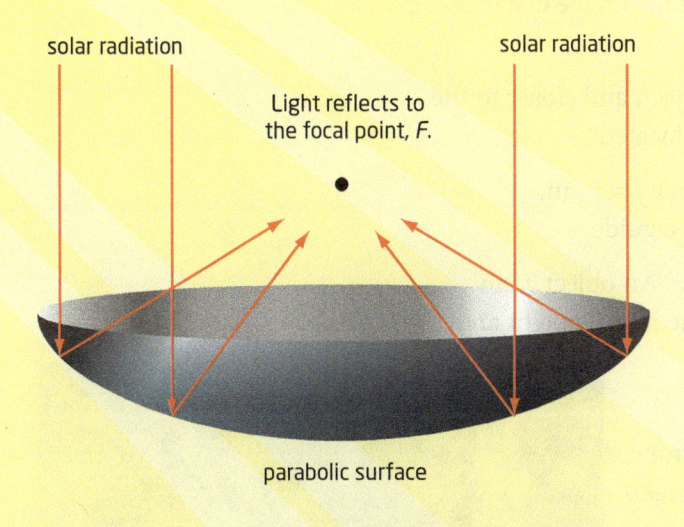

solar radiation   solar radiation

Light reflects to the focal point, *F*.

parabolic surface

The Sun's light rays reflect off the shiny metal (aluminum) dish, similar in shape to the radar dish in **Figure 10.23**. The rays concentrate at the focal point. The light that is concentrated at the focal point is converted to heat. When food is placed at the focal point, it is cooked.

Your Turn

1. List the advantages and disadvantages of using a solar oven.

2. If a $4 canister of propane cooks food for a family for three days, how many days would it take for a $400 solar oven to pay for itself through savings on fuel?

3. Conduct research to find out whether any organizations in Canada are helping to provide people in developing nations with solar ovens. If so, prepare a brief report about these organizations and present it to the class. If not, prepare a brief report that you could submit to a non-governmental organization, promoting the idea of a project to help provide solar ovens. Suggest some ways that students in your school could raise some funds for the project.

Chapter 10 Light and Reflection

Section 10.3 Review

Section Summary

- The reflecting surface of a concave mirror curves inward.
- Rays that travel toward a concave mirror, parallel to and near the principal axis, will reflect and pass through the principal axis at the focal point, F.
- For an object between the focal point and the concave mirror, the virtual, upright image is larger than the object, and the image distance is larger than the object distance.
- For an object between the focal point and the centre of curvature, the real, inverted image is larger than the object, and the image distance is larger than the object distance.
- For an object beyond C, the real, inverted image is smaller than the object, and the image distance is smaller than the object distance.
- You can calculate the image distance and size using the mirror equation, $\frac{1}{f} = \frac{1}{d_i} + \frac{1}{d_o}$, and the magnification equation, $m = \frac{h_i}{h_o} = \frac{-d_i}{d_o}$.
- Spherical aberration is the distortion of an image in a curved mirror that results when reflected rays from the outer parts of the mirror do not go through the focal point.

Review Questions

1. **C** In a diagram, show the relationship between C, the centre of curvature of a concave mirror, and the focal point, F, of the mirror.

2. **K/U** Explain how to draw the three rays that allow you to locate the image of an object in a concave mirror.

3. **K/U** What information does the sign (+ or −) of the image distance give you?

4. **T/I** If an image is inverted, smaller than the object, and closer to the mirror than the object, where is the object located?

5. **K/U** Draw a ray diagram, given the following data: $f = 5$ cm, $d_o = 4$ cm, and $h_o = 3$ cm. Use **Table 10.2** as a guide.

6. **K/U** A concave mirror has a focal length of 5 cm. An object 2 cm high is 11 cm from the mirror. Calculate the image height and image distance. Draw a ray diagram to confirm your solution.

7. **A** Suppose that you are holding a shaving mirror 30 cm from your face and the magnified image of your face is upright. A classmate tells you that the focal length of the mirror is 25 cm. Explain to your classmate why this focal length is not possible.

8. **K/U** Explain the difference between a real image and a virtual image.

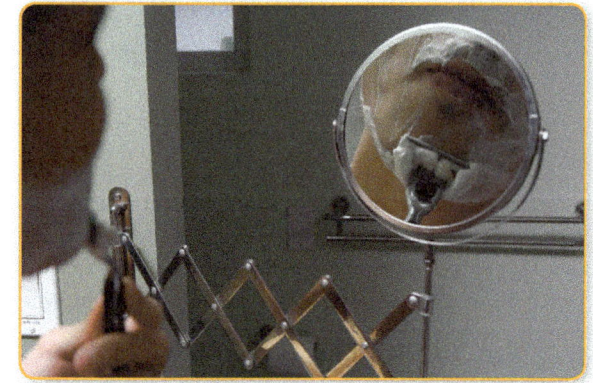

The image in this shaving mirror is magnified and upright.

Key Terms
convex mirror

10.4 Images in Convex Mirrors

The sculpture in **Figure 10.24** is called *Cloud Gate*. Like *Sky Mirror* in Section 10.3, it is a piece of art created by artist Anish Kapoor. It is in the city of Chicago, Illinois, in the United States. *Cloud Gate*'s convex surfaces are made of polished stainless steel, and they act like a **convex mirror**. Convex mirrors bulge, or curve outward. The convex curves reflect the skyline and the clouds. *Cloud Gate* is 10 m high, 20 m long, and has a mass of about 110 t. The 3.6 m high arch allows visitors to touch the surface and see their reflections.

The images in various parts of the sculpture in the photograph are different, but there are some general similarities. Notice that each image is upright and smaller than the object. Also notice that the image near the centre of a convex portion is shaped much like the object. Like an image in a concave mirror, however, the image becomes distorted near the edge of a convex portion.

As you can see, the images that are produced by convex mirrors make them interesting sculptures. In this section, you will learn about some of the practical uses of convex surfaces. You will also learn about the characteristics of images in convex mirrors by drawing ray diagrams.

convex mirror a mirror whose reflecting surface curves outward

Sense of scale
The mass of *Cloud Gate* is about the same mass as 84 small cars.

Figure 10.24 *Cloud Gate*, also called The Bean, is located in Chicago, Illinois.

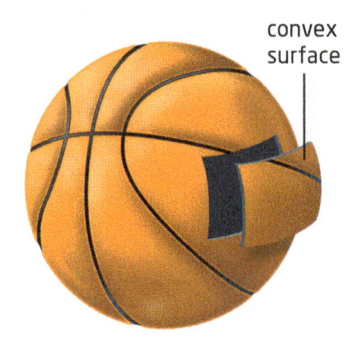

Figure 10.25 The outside surface of a sphere is a convex surface.

Properties of Convex Mirrors

A convex mirror is a spherical mirror, just as a concave mirror is. **Figure 10.25** shows the same diagram of a basketball that you saw in **Figure 10.19**. But if you covered the outside of the cut-out piece with a reflecting surface instead of the inside, you would have a convex mirror. Convex mirrors, like concave mirrors, also have spherical aberration. Only the small centre region of a convex mirror gives images that are not distorted.

Ray Diagrams for Convex Mirrors

Think about the principal axis of a convex mirror in the same way you think about the principal axis of a concave mirror. When you shine rays of light parallel to the principal axis onto a convex mirror, the reflected rays travel out and away from each other, as you can see in **Figure 10.26**. How can a convex mirror have a focal point? Recall how you found the image behind a concave mirror. You extended the reflected rays backward, behind the mirror, until they met. Similarly, the focal point of a convex mirror is behind the mirror.

Suggested Investigation
Inquiry Investigation 10-C, Testing for Real and Virtual Images, on page 442

Figure 10.26 The focal point of a convex mirror is behind the mirror.

Drawing Ray Diagrams for Convex Mirrors

Drawing ray diagrams for convex mirrors is very similar to drawing ray diagrams for concave mirrors. Follow the steps in **Table 10.5** to learn how to draw these ray diagrams.

Study Toolkit

Comparing and Contrasting
A Venn diagram or a table like the one on page 402 can help you clarify the differences between concave and convex mirrors.

Table 10.5 Drawing a Ray Diagram for a Convex Mirror

Directions	Diagram
1. Draw the principal axis and a curve to represent the convex mirror. • Mark a focal point and C. • Draw the object so that the bottom is on the principal axis.	
2. Draw a ray (shown in blue) from the top of the object toward the mirror parallel to the principal axis. Draw the reflected ray back, as though it is coming from the focal point. Draw a dotted line behind the mirror to show that the reflected ray appears to be coming from the focal point.	
3. Draw a ray (shown in green) that is directed toward the focal point, but stop when it reaches the mirror. Draw the reflected ray backward, parallel to the principal axis. Draw a dotted line behind the mirror to show that the incident ray seems to be travelling toward the focal point.	
4. Draw a ray (shown in red) that is directed toward C, but stop when it reaches the mirror. Draw a dotted line behind the mirror to show that the ray seems to be travelling toward C. Draw the reflected ray backward, along the incident ray.	
5. The reflected rays are directed away from each other, so they will never meet. Draw dashed lines to extend the rays backward, behind the mirror, until they meet. This is the top of the image. Draw the image, with the bottom of the image on the principal axis. (Note that the dotted lines are not in this diagram.)	

Chapter 10 Light and Reflection

Activity 10-4

Reflection from the Convex Surface of a Spoon

In this activity, you will use a simple kitchen tablespoon as a convex mirror.

Materials
- kitchen tablespoon with two shiny, reflective surfaces

Procedure
1. Hold up the back of the spoon in front of your face. Look at the image of your face.
2. Bring the spoon as close to your face as you can and still see your image. Describe the characteristics of your image in the spoon.
3. Slowly move the spoon away from your face. Observe any changes in your image as the spoon gets farther away. If you can still see your image when the spoon is at arm's length, have someone else move the spoon farther away. Describe any changes in the image of your face.

Questions
1. How is the image of your face on the back of the spoon different from your image in a plane mirror?
2. Compare and contrast how lateral inversion happens in a plane mirror and a convex mirror.

Learning Check

1. Using a Venn diagram, compare and contrast convex mirrors and concave mirrors.
2. Explain how you would find the focal point of a convex mirror. Use a diagram and **Figure 10.26** as a guide.
3. An object is 3 cm in front of a convex mirror, and the focal length is 4 cm. Draw a ray diagram to show the image characteristics.
4. An object is 1 cm in front of a convex mirror, whose focal length is 3 cm. Draw a ray diagram to show the image characteristics.

Mirror and Magnification Equations

The mirror and magnification equations that are used for concave mirrors are also used for convex mirrors. However, since the focal point is behind the mirror, the focal length, f, for a convex mirror is negative.

Mirror Equation

$$\frac{1}{f} = \frac{1}{d_i} + \frac{1}{d_o}$$

The image distance, d_i, is negative if the image is behind the mirror (a virtual image).

Magnification Equation

$$m = \frac{h_i}{h_o} = \frac{-d_i}{d_o}$$

The image height, h_i, is negative if the image is inverted relative to the object.

Sample Problem: Mirror Equations and Convex Surfaces

Problem

A convex surveillance mirror in a convenience store has a focal length of −0.40 m. A customer, who is 1.7 m tall, is standing 4.5 m in front of the mirror.

a. Calculate the image distance.
b. Calculate the image height.

Solution

a. Use the mirror equation to find the image distance.

$$\frac{1}{f} = \frac{1}{d_i} + \frac{1}{d_o}$$

$$\frac{1}{d_i} = \frac{1}{f} - \frac{1}{d_o}$$

$$= \frac{1}{-0.40 \text{ m}} - \frac{1}{4.5 \text{ m}}$$

$$= \frac{-4.5}{1.8 \text{ m}} - \frac{0.4}{1.8 \text{ m}}$$

$$= \frac{-4.9}{1.8 \text{ m}}$$

$$d_i = \frac{1.8 \text{ m}}{-4.9}$$

$$= -0.367 \text{ m}$$

The image is −0.37 m (after rounding) from the mirror. The sign of the image distance is negative, so the image is behind the mirror and is thus a virtual image.

b. Use the magnification equation to find h_i.

$$\frac{h_i}{h_o} = \frac{-d_i}{d_o}$$

$$h_i = \frac{(h_o)(-d_i)}{d_o}$$

$$= \frac{(1.7 \text{ m})(-(-0.367))}{4.5 \text{ m}}$$

$$= 0.1386 \text{ m}$$

The image height is 0.14 m (after rounding). The image height is positive, so the image is upright.

Check Your Solution

An image in a convex mirror is smaller than the object, virtual, and upright. All of these characteristics agree with the answers. The diagram on the right supports the solution.

GRASP

Go to **Science Skills Toolkit 11** to learn about an alternative problem solving method.

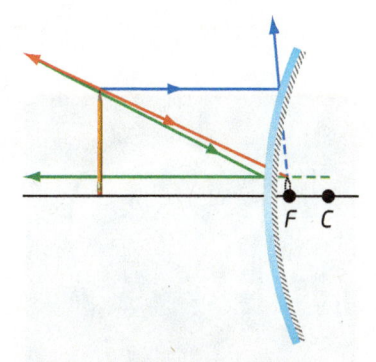

Draw a ray diagram to check your solution.

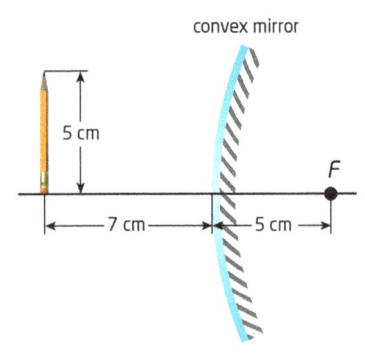

Use this diagram to solve problem 2.

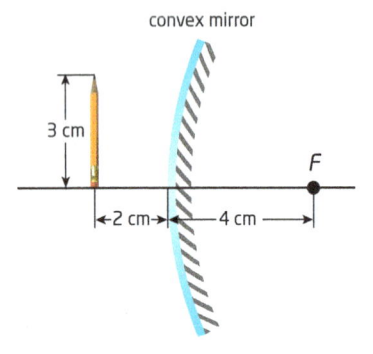

Use this diagram to solve problem 3.

Practice Problems

1. A convex mirror has a focal length of −0.90 m. An object with a height of 0.40 m is 2.5 m from the mirror.
   a. Calculate the image distance.
   b. Calculate the image height.

2. Use the data in the diagram on the left to answer the questions below.
   a. Calculate the image distance.
   b. Calculate the image height of the image.

3. Use the data in the diagram on the left to answer the questions below.
   a. Calculate the image distance.
   b. Calculate the image height.

4. A convex security mirror in a warehouse has a focal length of −0.50 m. A forklift, which is 2.2 m tall, is 6.0 m from the mirror.
   a. Calculate the image distance.
   b. Calculate the image height.

5. A convex security mirror has a focal length of −0.25 m. A person with a height of 1.5 m is 4.0 m from the mirror.
   a. Calculate the image distance.
   b. Calculate the image height.

6. An object 0.4 m tall is placed 2.5 m in front of a convex mirror that has a focal length of −90 cm.
   a. Calculate the image distance.
   b. Calculate the image height.

7. An object 25 cm tall is placed 80 cm in front of a convex mirror that has a radius of curvature of 1.5 m.
   a. Calculate the image distance.
   b. Calculate the image height.

Applications of Convex Surfaces

You have probably seen mirrors like the one in **Figure 10.27** in convenience stores. The image is quite distorted, but this convex security mirror allows a clerk in the store to see a very large area. If the store is small, the clerk can stand at the till and see almost everything in the store. Convex security mirrors are sometimes used on public transportation buses, as well as on roads with sharp curves in some countries.

Figure 10.27 Because this security mirror is convex, it gives the clerk a much wider view of the store than a plane mirror would.

Convex Mirrors at Border Crossings

At truck inspection stations and border crossings, security guards often need to see the underside of large semitrailers and other vehicles. To do this, a convex mirror is attached to the end of a long handle at an angle, as shown in **Figure 10.28**. By moving the mirror just under the side of the vehicle, the security guard can see everything on the bottom of the vehicle.

Figure 10.28 Using a convex mirror on a long handle enables a security guard to see the underside of a vehicle without crawling under it.

Radar Technology and Convex Surfaces

The rounded, aerodynamic surfaces on a typical airplane act like convex mirrors. When a pulse of radio waves hits an airplane, the rays are nearly perpendicular to many areas on the airplane's surface. As shown in **Figure 10.29**, these rays will be reflected almost directly backward. The radar antenna will detect the reflected rays and locate the aircraft.

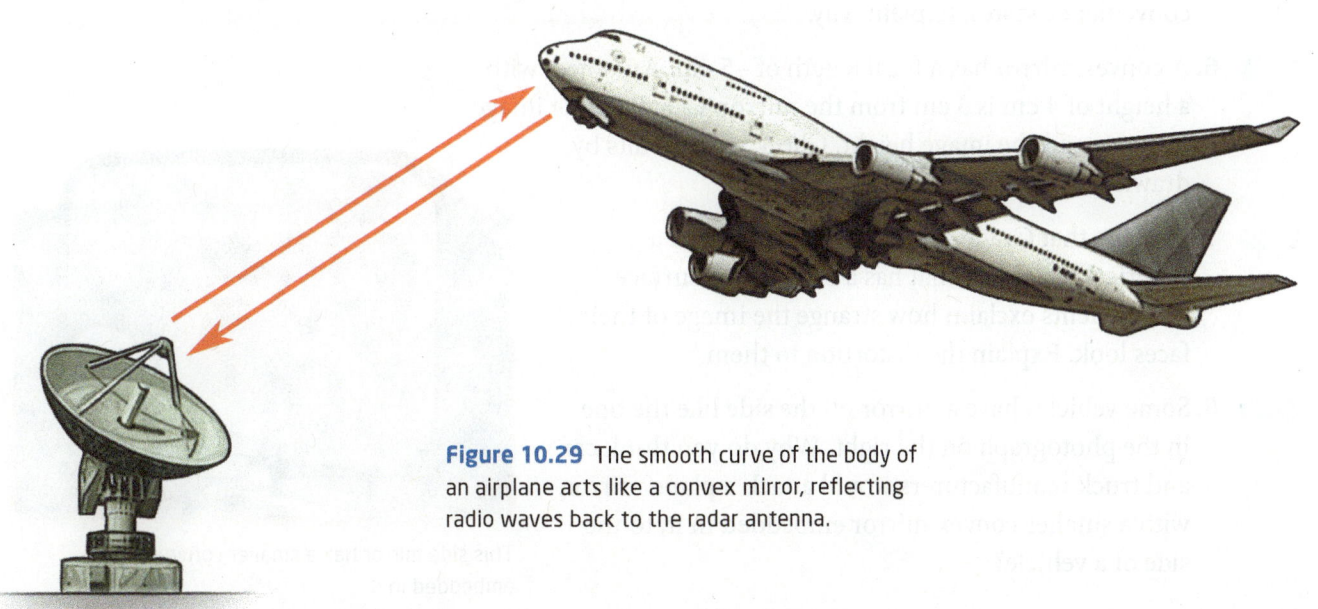

Figure 10.29 The smooth curve of the body of an airplane acts like a convex mirror, reflecting radio waves back to the radar antenna.

Section 10.4 Review

Section Summary

- The reflecting surface of a convex mirror is a mirror that curves outward.
- Rays that travel toward a convex mirror, parallel to and near the principal axis, will reflect back and spread out, away from each other.
- To find F for a convex mirror, extend the reflected rays backward until they appear to meet behind the mirror.
- For an object in a convex mirror, the virtual, upright image is smaller than the object.
- You can predict the location and size of an image in a convex mirror by drawing the bottom of the object on the principal axis and drawing at least two rays that travel from the top of the object toward the mirror.
- You can calculate the image distance and size using the mirror equation, $\frac{1}{f} = \frac{1}{d_i} + \frac{1}{d_o}$, and the magnification equation, $m = \frac{h_i}{h_o} = \frac{-d_i}{d_o}$.
- The focal length of a convex mirror is negative because the F is virtual and behind the mirror.
- There are many practical uses for convex mirrors and surfaces, such as security mirrors and inspection mirrors.

Review Questions

C 1. Using a sketch, show how you would draw a ray diagram for a convex mirror. Use **Table 10.5** as a guide.

K/U 2. The same mirror equations are used for convex mirrors as for concave mirrors. How do you account for the difference in the curvature when using the mirror equations?

K/U 3. Why is the value of the focal length of a convex mirror negative?

T/I 4. When considering the characteristics of a concave mirror, you looked at three different cases. Why would it not be possible to consider three similar cases for a convex mirror?

K/U 5. Convex mirrors are often used as security mirrors in convenience stores. Explain why.

K/U 6. A convex mirror has a focal length of –5 cm. An object with a height of 4 cm is 3 cm from the mirror. Calculate the image distance and the image height. Check your results by drawing a ray diagram.

C 7. Imagine that Grade 7 students are looking at a spherical ornament that has a mirror-like surface. The students exclaim how strange the image of their faces look. Explain the distortion to them.

A 8. Some vehicles have a mirror on the side like the one in the photograph on the right. Why do you think car and truck manufacturers would attach a plane mirror, with a smaller convex mirror embedded in it, to the side of a vehicle?

This side mirror has a smaller convex mirror embedded in it.

Inquiry Investigation 10-A

Skill Check
✓ Initiating and Planning
✓ Performing and Recording
✓ Analyzing and Interpreting
✓ Communicating

Applying the Laws of Reflection

In this investigation, you will make predictions about an image in a plane mirror. Then you will test your predictions using a ray box.

Question

How accurately will you be able to predict the position of an image using a ray diagram?

Prediction

Predict the size and orientation of the reflected image.

Procedure

1. Near the centre of a blank sheet of paper, draw a straight line to represent the surface of a plane mirror. Show which side of the line represents the mirror by drawing hatch marks on the non-reflecting side.

2. Place an object 10 cm from the line. Label one end of the object "A" and the other end "B," as in the diagram below. Trace the object. Remove the object, and draw a ray diagram.

3. Place the plane mirror in its stand on the sheet of paper, so that the reflecting surface is on the line representing the mirror.

4. Use the ray box to shine a single beam of light along each incident ray. Compare the reflected ray you produced with the reflected ray you predicted. If the reflected ray was not close to your predicted ray, sketch the location of the reflected ray.

5. Replace the object on the paper in its outline. Examine the image in the mirror, and compare it with the image you drew. Does your drawing agree with the image in the mirror?

Analyze and Interpret

1. If your predicted incident and reflected rays were not close to the actual reflected rays, explain why they were not close.

Conclude and Communicate

2. How well did your image correspond to the image that you saw in the mirror?

Extend Your Inquiry and Research Skills

3. **Inquiry** Plan and test a method that allows you to make better predictions.

Safety Precautions

- The edges of the mirror may be sharp. Be careful not to cut yourself.
- Be careful not to drop the mirror.

Materials

- blank sheet of paper (letter size)
- pencil
- ruler
- small object (such as a small pencil)
- small plane mirror with support stand
- putty (if mirror stand is unavailable)
- ray box
- protractor

In step 2, arrange your object as shown here.

Inquiry Investigation 10-B

Studying the Laws of Reflection

Skill Check

Initiating and Planning
✓ Performing and Recording
✓ Analyzing and Interpreting
✓ Communicating

When you look in a plane mirror, light reflects off your face in all directions. Some of the light reflects off the mirror into your eyes. This light must follow a consistent pattern because you always see the same image of your face in a mirror. In this investigation, you will be guided through the process of making a ray diagram. When your ray diagram is complete, you will analyze the relationship between incident and reflected rays.

Safety Precautions

- The edges of the mirror may be sharp. Be careful not to cut yourself.
- Be careful not to drop the mirror.

Question

How does light behave when it reflects off a flat surface?

Procedure

1. Near the middle of the blank sheet of paper, draw a straight line to represent the reflecting surface of the plane mirror. Label the line "plane mirror." Show which side of the line represents the mirror by drawing hatch marks on the non-reflecting side.

2. Lay the small object on the paper. Place it about 5 to 10 cm in front of the line that represents the plane mirror. Trace the shape of the object. Label the pointed end "P" and the blunt end "O."

3. Remove the object. Draw two different straight lines from point P to the "plane mirror." On each line, draw an arrowhead pointing toward the mirror. These lines represent the paths of two incident light rays that travel from the object to the mirror.

4. Carefully place the mirror in its stand on the sheet of paper as shown in the photograph below. Make sure that the reflecting surface of the mirror is exactly along the line you drew in step 1.

Materials

- blank sheet of paper (letter size)
- pencil
- ruler
- small object that is shorter than the plane mirror and has a pointed end (for example, a short pencil)
- small plane mirror (about 5 cm × 15 cm) with support stand
- putty (if support stand is unavailable)
- ray box
- protractor

After removing the object, draw the rays.

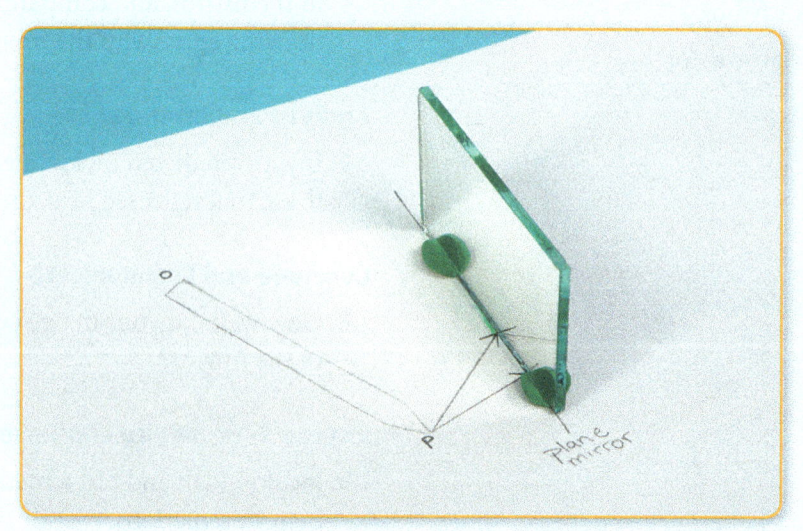

Position the mirror as shown here.

440 NEL • Unit 4 Light and Geometric Optics

5. Use the ray box to shine a thin beam of light along one of the incident rays that you drew from point P. Mark the reflected ray with a series of dots along the path of the reflected light.

6. Remove the mirror and the ray box. Draw a line through the dots, ending at the mirror. Draw an arrowhead pointing away from the mirror to indicate that this line is a reflected ray.

7. At the point where the incident ray and its corresponding reflected ray meet the mirror, draw a line at 90° to the mirror. Label this line as the normal.

8. Measure and record the angle of incidence (the angle between the normal and the incident ray).

9. Measure and record the angle of reflection (the angle between the normal and the reflected ray).

10. Repeat steps 5 to 9 for the second incident ray from point P.

11. If time permits, repeat steps 3 to 9 for point O.

12. Place the mirror and the object back on the sheet of paper. Observe the image of the object and the reflected rays that you drew. From what point do the reflected rays seem to come?

Analyze and Interpret

1. You drew two rays from point P to the mirror. If you had enough time, how many rays could you have drawn between point P and the mirror? (You do not need to draw all the rays. Just think about how many you could have drawn.)

2. How does the angle of reflection compare with the angle of incidence?

3. Extend each reflected ray behind the mirror using a dashed line. Label the point where the two dashed lines meet "P_i." This is the location of the image of point P.

   a. Measure the perpendicular distance between point P (the object) and the mirror.

   b. Measure the perpendicular distance between point P_i (the image) and the mirror.

   c. Compare the distance between the object and the mirror, and the distance between the image and the mirror.

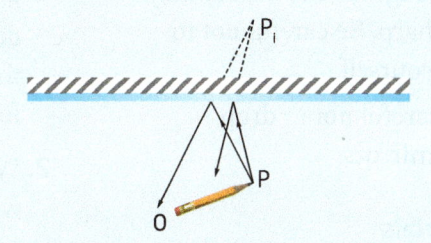

Compare the distance between the object and the mirror, and the distance between the image and the mirror.

Conclude and Communicate

4. Based on your measurements, describe a method for drawing a reflected ray without using a ray box.

5. Based on your measurements, describe a method for locating the image distance for a point placed in front of a plane mirror without tracing back reflected rays.

Extend Your Inquiry and Research Skills

6. **Inquiry** Place a small pointy object in front of two plane mirrors joined to make an angle of 120°. Use ray diagrams to explain why you see two images of the point.

7. **Research** Multiple images are popular in fun houses. Conduct research on multiple images, and explain how the following formula for multiple images works.

$$\text{Number of images} = \frac{360°}{\text{angle between mirrors}} - 1$$

Inquiry Investigation 10-C

Skill Check
✓ Initiating and Planning
✓ Performing and Recording
✓ Analyzing and Interpreting
✓ Communicating

Safety Precautions

- The edges of the mirror may be sharp. Be careful not to cut yourself.
- Be careful not to drop the mirrors.

Materials

- 3 concave mirrors with different curvatures
- flat (plane) mirror
- convex mirror
- white cardboard for screen
- room with a window

This drawing shows the set-up described in step 4.

Testing for Real and Virtual Images

In this investigation, you will test several mirrors and predict which mirrors will form real images on a screen and which mirrors will form virtual images that you can see in the mirror, but not on a screen.

Prediction

Predict which type of mirror will form real images on a screen.

Procedure

1. Create a table to organize your observations. Your table should include room for a labelled sketch of the mirror used and a description of the image you observed. Where applicable, indicate the distance between the mirror and the screen that resulted in a focussed image.

2. Working with a partner, decide who will hold the mirrors and who will hold the cardboard screen.

3. Hold one mirror between 2 and 3 m from the window so that it reflects light onto the cardboard screen about 1 m away.

4. Move the mirror and/or the cardboard screen until light from the window is reflected onto the screen. Adjust the distance between the mirror and the screen, and try to obtain a focussed image of the scene outside the window.

5. Record what you see on the screen. Repeat steps 1 to 4 with the other mirrors, and record what you see.

Analyze and Interpret

1. With which mirrors were you able to obtain a focussed image on the screen?

2. Compare the sizes of the images on the screen with the mirrors that produced the images.

Conclude and Communicate

3. Write a paragraph that explains which kinds of mirrors produce real images and which kinds of mirrors produce virtual images. Include supporting details in your paragraph.

Extend Your Inquiry and Research Skills

4. **Inquiry** Predict the image characteristics of an image produced by a concave mirror that is as large as a person.

Chapter 10 Summary

10.1 Sources and Nature of Light
Key Concepts
- Incandescence is light that is emitted from an object because the object is very hot.
- Luminescence is light that is emitted in the absence of heat. Fluorescence, phosphorescence, chemiluminescence, and bioluminescence are all forms of luminescence.
- Light is transmitted in the form of electromagnetic waves. Visible light makes up only a small part of the electromagnetic spectrum.
- Light is used in many technologies. For example, blue light, with a special filter, can be used to detect oral cancer.

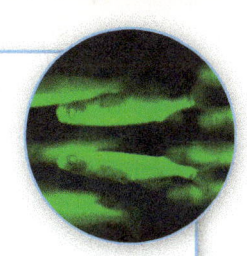

10.2 Properties of Light and Reflection
Key Concepts
- A ray is a straight line with an arrowhead that shows the direction in which light is travelling.
- The laws of reflection state that the angle of reflection is equal to the angle of incidence, and that the reflected ray always lies on the plane that is defined by the incident ray and the normal.
- The location of an image in a plane mirror can be found by drawing a ray diagram based on the laws of reflection and tested through inquiry.
- The four characteristics of an image in a plane mirror are the following: the image is the same size as the object, the same distance from the mirror as the object, and the same orientation as the object; the image is a virtual image.

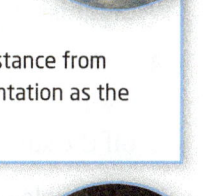

10.3 Images in Concave Mirrors
Key Concepts
- The reflecting surface of a concave mirror curves inward.
- Rays that travel toward a concave mirror, parallel to and near the principal axis, will reflect and pass through the principal axis at the focal point.
- For an object between the focal point and the concave mirror, the virtual, upright image is larger than the object, and the image distance is larger than the object distance.
- For an object between the focal point and the centre of curvature, the real, inverted image is larger than the object, and the image distance is larger than the object distance.
- For an object beyond C, the real, inverted image is smaller than the object, and the image distance is smaller than the object distance.
- You can calculate the image distance and size using the mirror equation, $\frac{1}{f} = \frac{1}{d_i} + \frac{1}{d_o}$, and the magnification equation, $m = \frac{h_i}{h_o} = \frac{-d_i}{d_o}$.
- Spherical aberration is the distortion of an image in a curved mirror that results when reflected rays from the outer parts of the mirror do not go through the focal point.

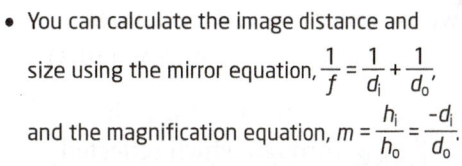

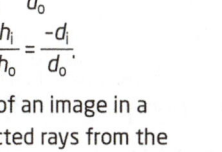

10.4 Images in Convex Mirrors
Key Concepts
- The reflecting surface of a convex mirror curves outward.
- Rays that travel toward a convex mirror, parallel to and near the principal axis, will reflect back and spread out, away from each other.
- To find F for a convex mirror, extend the reflected rays backward until they appear to meet behind the mirror.
- For an object in a convex mirror, the virtual, upright image is smaller than the object.
- You can predict the location and size of an image in a convex mirror by drawing the bottom of the object on the principal axis and drawing at least two rays that travel from the top of the object toward the mirror.
- You can calculate the image distance and size of an image using the mirror equation, $\frac{1}{f} = \frac{1}{d_i} + \frac{1}{d_o}$, and the magnification equation, $m = \frac{h_i}{h_o} = \frac{-d_i}{d_o}$.
- The focal length of a convex mirror is negative because the focal point is virtual and behind the mirror.
- There are many practical uses for convex mirrors and surfaces, such as security mirrors and inspection mirrors.

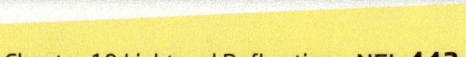

Chapter 10 Review

Make Your Own Summary

Summarize the key concepts of this chapter using a graphic organizer. The Chapter Summary on the previous page will help you identify the key concepts. Refer to Study Toolkit 4 on pages 565-566 to help you decide which graphic organizer to use.

Reviewing Key Terms

1. _____ light is produced by an older type of light bulb. New energy-saving light bulbs are _____ . (10.1)

2. _____ is light produced by living organisms. (10.1)

3. _____ is the change in direction of a wave when it reaches a surface and bounces off the surface. (10.2)

4. The angle of _____ is equal to the angle of _____ . (10.2)

5. When the image distance is negative, the image is _____ . (10.2)

6. A mirror whose reflecting surface curves inward is a _____ mirror. (10.3)

7. The _____ point is the point on the _____ through which reflected rays pass. (10.3)

8. A mirror whose reflecting surface curves outward is a _____ mirror. (10.4)

Knowledge and Understanding K/U

9. Explain the process that produces the light for all sources of light.

10. List the energy transformation steps that occur in an electric discharge tube. That is, what form of energy is transformed into what other form of energy until the energy becomes light?

11. If light is a form of energy, explain how light can be different colours.

12. What is a light ray?

13. What is meant when the image is said to be behind the mirror? What do you call this type of image?

14. Explain how you would find the focal point of a convex mirror.

15. Why does spherical aberration occur?

16. Describe what a convex mirror looks like.

Thinking and Investigation T/I

17. Imagine that the room in the diagram below is dark and has black walls. The air in the room is free from dust and smoke. A very narrow beam of light enters the room in the direction indicated by the ray. If you stay at the position indicated by the eye, can you see the mirror on the opposite wall? Explain why or why not.

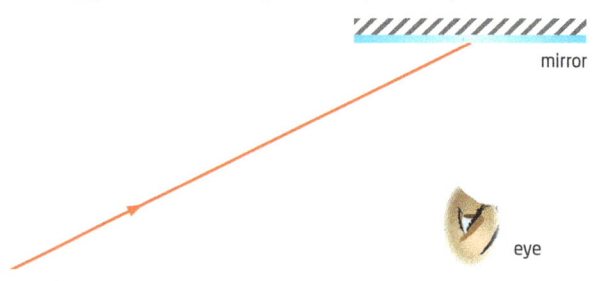

A light ray enters a dark room with black walls.

18. Sometimes, when you sit by a lake in a forest, you can see perfect images of the hills and trees in the lake. Other times, when you are sitting beside the same lake, you cannot see any images in the water. Explain the difference between these two situations.

19. Sometimes, on a sunny day, campers start a campfire using a small mirror to light paper or dry grass. What shape of mirror would they use? What is happening to the sunlight when they do this? Draw a ray diagram to illustrate your answer.

20. A photographer is standing 1.5 m in front of a plane mirror. She wants to take a picture of herself in the mirror. For what distance should she set the focus of her camera to get a clear image?

Communication

21. **BIG IDEAS** Society has benefited from the development of a range of optical devices and technologies. Describe two technologies using light that society has benefited from. Explain how society has benefited from them.

22. **BIG IDEAS** Light has characteristics and properties that can be manipulated with mirrors for a range of uses. Describe a technology involving mirrors that increases the safety of people who use it.

23. Using a diagram or a concept map, describe the processes in the Sun that result in the emission of light from the Sun.

24. Draw a horizontal line, at least 20 cm long, to represent a principal axis. About 3 cm from the right end of the line, draw a curved line through the principal axis to represent a concave mirror. At 5 cm to the left of the concave mirror, draw a dot and label it *F*. At 3 cm to the left of *F*, draw an object that is 2 cm high.
    a. Complete this ray diagram to find the image.
    b. Explain the rationale for each ray that you drew.
    c. Describe the image by stating how far it is from the mirror, how high it is, whether it is real or virtual, and whether it is upright or inverted.

25. How can you tell from a ray diagram whether an image is real or virtual?

Application

26. The famous Chinese magician Foo Ling Yu performs a classic magic trick using a concave mirror with a focal length of 1.6 m. Foo uses the mirror to produce an image of a light bulb that is the same size as the light bulb itself and is at the same location. Explain, in complete sentences, how Foo accomplishes this magic trick. Be specific about the location of the light bulb.

27. The photograph below shows one of several concrete structures in southeast England. These structures were built between 1915 and about 1930. During World War I, airships from mainland Europe bombed England. The English military wanted a way to detect these airships in time to take precautions. From what you have learned about mirrors and the reflection of waves, suggest how these structures were used as early warning systems.

This concrete structure, located in Folkestone, England, served a military purpose in World War I.

28. Choose a career related to optics from this chapter that interests you, and describe why it interests you.

29. The compact fluorescent bulbs are more efficient at producing light than incandescent bulbs, but the fluorescent bulbs are expensive. A newer alternative is to use LED (light-emitting diode) lighting. Until recently, LED lights have also been too expensive. However, researchers in the United Kingdom have produced new, promising technology using gallium nitride (GaN) LED lighting. Research GaN LED lighting using the Internet or other sources, and answer the following questions.
    a. Compare the predicted efficiency of GaN lighting with that of fluorescent bulbs.
    b. How many hours will the new bulbs last?
    c. What are two more advantages of GaN LED lighting compared with fluorescent lighting?
    d. Can LED lights be recycled?
    e. How can this technology benefit society?

Chapter 11 Refraction

What You Will Learn

In this chapter, you will learn how to...

- **explain** refraction and the conditions that are required for partial reflection, partial refraction, and total internal reflection
- **identify** factors that affect the refraction of light as it passes from one medium to another
- **explain** natural effects of refraction, such as apparent depth, mirages, and rainbows, using the ray model of light

Why It Matters

Many modern technologies used in communications and medicine depend on how light behaves when travelling from one substance to another. Also, many of the mysteries of atmospheric phenomena, such as sundogs and rainbows, have been solved by applying our knowledge of how light behaves.

Skills You Will Use

In this chapter, you will learn how to...

- **investigate** the refraction of light and total internal reflection
- **calculate** the velocity of light in a variety of media
- **analyze** how the angles of refraction and incidence change in materials with different indices of refraction

On a cold, crisp day, when the Sun is shining brightly, you might see a halo around the Sun similar to the one shown here. The bright spots beside the Sun are called sundogs. They are created when ice crystals in the air refract the sunlight. Sundogs are just one of the many natural effects of refraction that you will learn about in this chapter.

Activity 11-1

The Re-appearing Coin

For you to see an object, light must reflect from the object and reach your eyes. Sometimes, after reflecting off the object, light will change direction before it reaches your eye, and this will trick your brain. In this activity, you will demonstrate and try to explain this phenomenon.

Safety Precaution
- Be careful not to splash the water on the floor. Wet floors are slippery and dangerous.

Materials
- cup or another container with opaque sides
- coin
- water

Use this diagram for question 1.

Procedure

1. Work with a partner. Place the coin at the bottom of the empty cup, in the middle. Cover one eye with your hand, and look down at the coin with the other eye. Lower your head until the edge of the cup just blocks your view of the coin. Keep your head in this position.

2. Your partner will slowly pour water into the cup. If the coin starts to move, your partner should hold it in place with the end of a pencil. Your partner will continue to pour water into the cup until you can see the coin again.

3. Empty the water in a sink. Be careful not to lose the coin.

4. Change places so that your partner can watch the coin while you pour water into the cup.

Questions

1. Copy the diagram above. Note that the ray in the diagram shows that light from the coin cannot reach your eye if the cup is empty.

2. Sketch a ray diagram to illustrate how light reflects off the coin, travels through the water, and then reaches your eye.

3. How has your brain been tricked by the water?

Study Toolkit

These strategies will help you use this textbook to develop your understanding of science concepts and skills. To find out more about these and other strategies, refer to the Study Toolkit Overview, which begins on page 560.

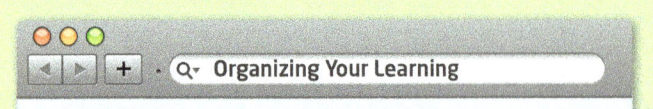

Organizing Your Learning

Summarizing

A summary restates the main ideas of a text concisely, using your own words. It can be in sentence form, paragraph form, point form, or graphic form. The table below shows one way to summarize the "Describing Refraction Using Rays" section on page 451.

Summarizing Text

Section of Text	Main Topic	Main Ideas About the Topic	Supporting Details
page 451, third paragraph	how to describe refraction using rays	1. Use the same terms to describe refraction as you use to describe reflection. 2. Use two new terms: the *refracted ray* and *angle of refraction*.	1. *Incident ray*, *normal*, and *angle of incidence* are all used to describe refraction. 2. Capital *R* is used for refraction, and lower-case *r* is used for reflection.

Summary sentence: The terms used to describe refraction include *incident ray, normal, angle of incidence, refracted ray,* and *angle of refraction* (labelled *R*).

Use the Strategy

Read the first paragraph under "Partial Reflection and Refraction" on page 458. Summarize the paragraph using a table like the one above. Compare your work with that of a partner and revise as necessary.

Reading Effectively

Making Inferences

Making inferences means figuring out the implied meaning of a text. It involves connecting your prior knowledge with information from the text and, often, from visuals. The second paragraph on page 457 says, "The objects outside the area directly above you are not visible because no light from these objects is penetrating the surface of the water." Here is an example of an inference you might make about this information:

- prior knowledge: To see an object, light must reflect from the object and go to my eyes.
- inference: Light is not reflecting from objects to the side and above the water, so I cannot see the objects.

Use the Strategy

Read the first paragraph of Section 11.2 on page 457. Think about your prior knowledge, combine it with the text and the visual on the page, and then make an inference.

Word Study

Multiple Meanings

To reinforce your understanding of a word's multiple meanings, draw a word map like the one on the right. It shows the meaning of *medium* in two different contexts.

Use the Strategy

What does *incident* mean in the context of a police report? in the context of a science chapter about light rays? Draw a word map to show the word's multiple meanings. Use a dictionary if you wish.

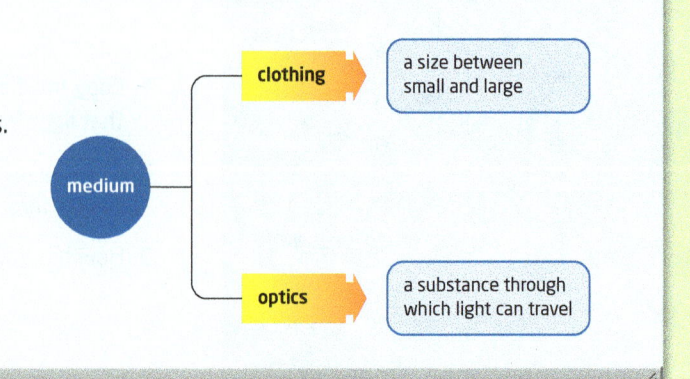

- medium → clothing → a size between small and large
- medium → optics → a substance through which light can travel

11.1 Refraction of Light

Key Terms
refraction
refracted ray
angle of refraction
index of refraction
dispersion

Some aeronautic engineers need to study patterns of moving air so that they can design shapes to reduce air friction. How can they see something that is transparent? The colours in **Figure 11.1** show moving air. As air hits the cone, it gets compressed in different ways. Compressed air has a higher density than uncompressed air. Even though air is transparent, a technique called Schlieren photography uses certain properties of light to create the light and dark regions where changes in density occur. Then, a computer converts the light and dark regions into different colours. All of this is possible because of a property called *refraction*. **Refraction** is a property of light in which the speed of light and its direction of travel change.

refraction the bending of light as it travels, at an angle, from a material with one refractive index to a material with a different refractive index

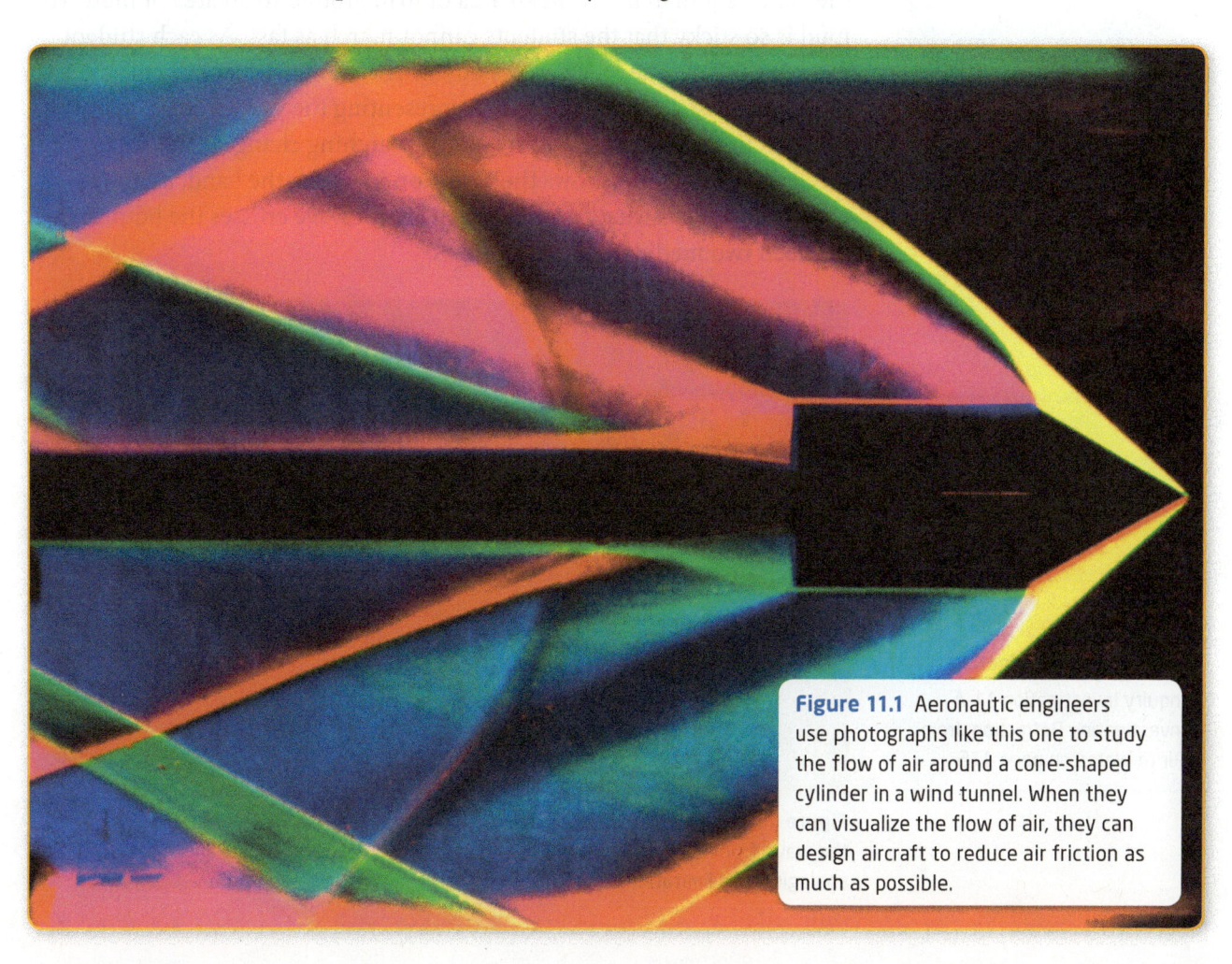

Understanding Refraction

To understand refraction, consider a familiar analogy. What happens if you are riding in a golf cart and you hit some mud or gravel? The front wheels suddenly slow down, but the back wheels keep going and the golf cart twists around. Similarly, when light travels from one medium into a different medium, both its speed and direction may change.

Figure 11.1 Aeronautic engineers use photographs like this one to study the flow of air around a cone-shaped cylinder in a wind tunnel. When they can visualize the flow of air, they can design aircraft to reduce air friction as much as possible.

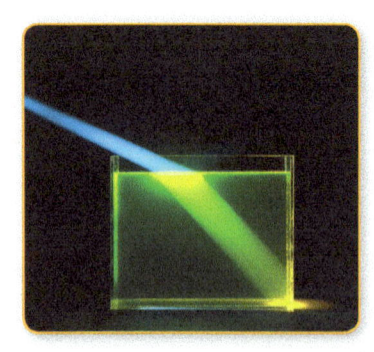

Figure 11.2 Dust particles in the air scatter the light and allow you to see the beam. A fluorescent substance in the water emits a green light, which allows you to see the path of the light beam in the water.

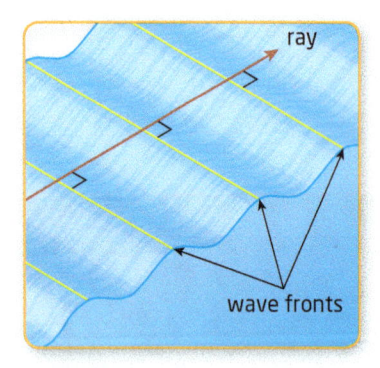

Figure 11.3 All the points on a wave front move together in the direction in which the wave itself is moving.

Suggested Investigation
Inquiry Investigation 11-A, Investigating Refraction, from Air to Water, on page 476

Describing Refraction

As mentioned in Chapter 10, light has many properties. For example, light reflects from smooth surfaces according to the two laws of reflection. There are additional properties of light that are important in describing refraction. Light travels in a straight line and at a constant speed as long as the medium it is travelling in is the same. However, when light travels from one medium to another, for example, from air to water, the light rays refract (bend). Recall that this means that both its direction and speed change. **Figure 11.2** shows how a beam of light refracts as it enters a container of water.

Since light travels as a wave, it is helpful to use the wave model of light along with the concept of a ray to visualize the mechanism that causes light to change direction. To see how the wave model of light and the concept of a ray fit together, look at **Figure 11.3**. Scientists often choose a specific part of a wave to follow and call it a wave front. As you can see in **Figure 11.3**, the crests, or high points, of the waves are *wave fronts*. The ray (red arrow), which shows the direction in which the waves are travelling, is perpendicular to the wave fronts.

To visualize what happens when a wave front reaches the surface between two media—called the *boundary*—imagine each wave front as a row of students in a marching band. **Figure 11.4** shows the movement of the band as it marches from an area of firm ground to an area of mud. The mud is so sticky that the students cannot march as fast. As each student reaches the mud, he or she slows down. The slower students "pull" the line back and cause a bend in the line, representing the wave front. As a result, the direction in which the entire row is marching changes. The larger red arrow in the diagram shows the direction in which the band, as a whole, is moving. This is what happens when a light wave crosses the boundary between two media: its speed changes.

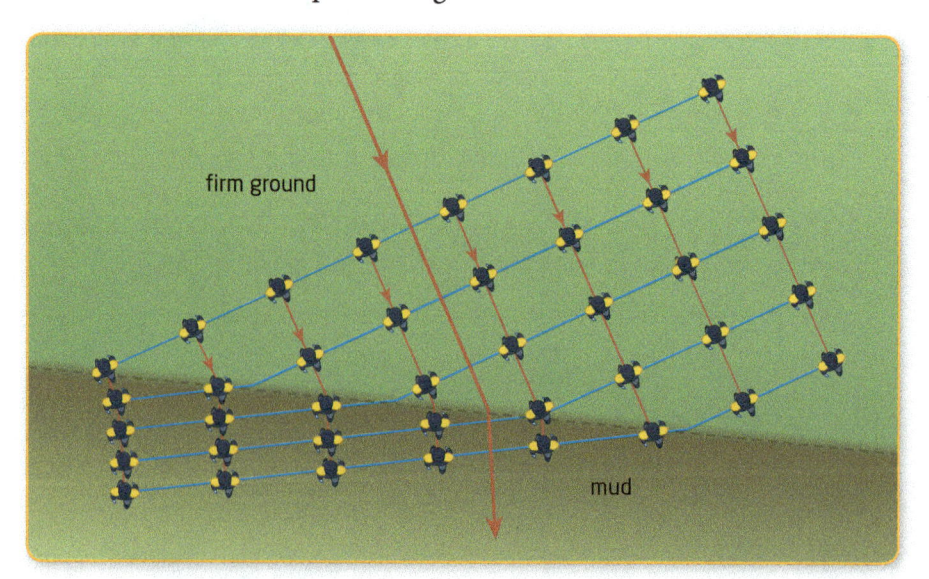

Figure 11.4 Each row of students represents the crest of a wave. When one end of the wave front slows down, the direction of the wave changes. This analogy, like all analogies, has limitations. However, it can help you visualize refraction.

> **Learning Check**
>
> 1. What property of light changes from one medium to another?
> 2. Define the term *refraction*.
> 3. Examine **Figure 11.2**. Explain why light bends when it enters the water. Include a ray diagram with your explanation.
> 4. Think of an analogy, other than a marching band, that helps you understand why light refracts when it goes from one medium to another. Include a sketch to illustrate your analogy.

Fermat's Principle

The exact path of light as it travels from one medium to another can be found by applying Fermat's principle, which says that when light travels from one point to another, it follows the path that will take the least time. In a single medium, the path that takes the least time is a straight line. When travelling from one medium to another, the path that takes the least time is not a straight line.

Compare the dashed line in **Figure 11.5** with the solid, bent line going from point A in air to point B in water. In air, where light travels faster, the solid line is longer than the dashed line. In water, where light travels slower, the solid line is shorter than the dashed line. Light travels a longer distance in air and a shorter distance in water than it would if it followed a straight line. Following the bent path (solid line) takes less time than following the straight path (dashed line).

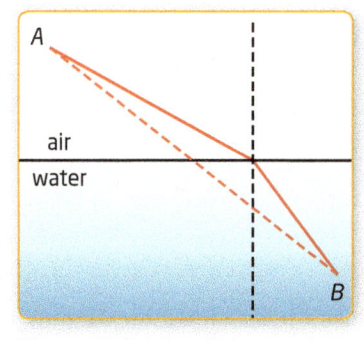

Figure 11.5 When light travels a greater distance in air (where light travels faster) and a shorter distance in water (where light travels slower), the time of travel is minimized.

Describing Refraction Using Rays

Most of the terms used to describe refraction are the same as the terms used to describe reflection. In **Figure 11.6**, notice that in addition to the incident ray and the reflected ray, there is now a third ray called the **refracted ray**. As you can see, the incident ray is divided into two rays—one that reflects and one that refracts. (The word *refract* comes from the Latin word *refringere*, which means to break up). Because there is an additional ray, there is an additional angle to keep track of. The new angle is the **angle of refraction**, shown by the upper-case *R*. The angle of refraction is the angle between the normal and the refracted ray.

refracted ray the ray that is bent upon entering a second medium

angle of refraction the angle between the normal and a refracted ray

Suggested Investigation
Real World Investigation 11-C, Saving Time, on page 478

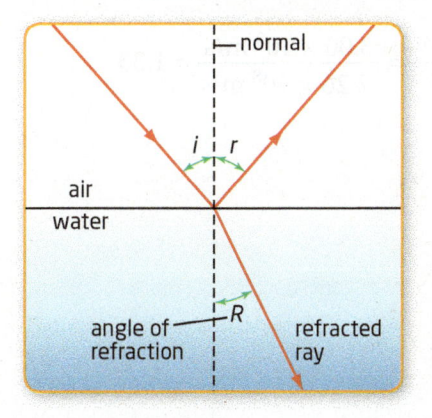

Figure 11.6 Note the new terms: angle of refraction and refracted ray.

Chapter 11 Refraction • NEL 451

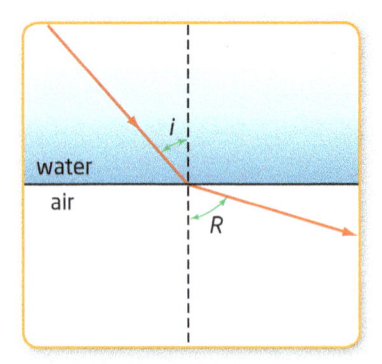

Figure 11.7 Going from water to air, the refracted ray is bent away from the normal.

The Direction of the Refracted Ray

In **Figure 11.6**, a light ray travels from a medium in which its speed is faster (such as air) to a medium in which its speed is slower (such as water). The refracted ray bends toward the normal. However, in **Figure 11.7**, a light ray travels from a medium in which its speed is slower to a medium in which its speed is faster, and the refracted ray bends away from the normal. Note that reflection always occurs. However, when discussing only refraction, the reflected ray will be omitted from the diagrams to focus on the angle of refraction and the refracted ray. Later in the chapter, you will see that the reflected rays are important. For now, as in **Figures 11.6** and **11.7**, only the refracted ray will be drawn.

Index of Refraction

How much a light ray refracts is determined by the extent of the change in the speed of light as it travels from one medium to another. When light passes from one medium to the next and the change in the speed of light becomes greater, the angle of refraction becomes greater.

The speed of light is 3.00×10^8 m/s in a vacuum, such as space, where there is no matter. The speed of light is less than 3.00×10^8 m/s in any other medium. For example, the speed of light in water is 2.26×10^8 m/s. These numbers are extremely large and inconvenient to use for describing relative speeds. Therefore, scientists have devised a much easier system for describing relative speeds.

The **index of refraction** is the ratio of the speed of light in a vacuum to the speed of light in a given medium. The symbol for the index of refraction is n, the symbol for the speed of light in a vacuum is c, and the symbol for the speed of light in any given medium is v. Therefore, you can express the index of refraction in mathematical form as shown below.

index of refraction the ratio of the speed of light in a vacuum to the speed of light in a given medium

Study Toolkit

Multiple Meanings The word *index* has multiple meanings. Drawing a word map like the one on page 448 can reinforce your understanding of a word's multiple meanings.

> **Index of Refraction**
>
> $n = \frac{c}{v}$, where
>
> n is the index of refraction
> c is the speed of light in a vacuum
> v is the speed of light in a medium

For example, the index of refraction of water is in a given medium.

$$\frac{\text{speed of light in a vacuum}}{\text{speed of light in water}} = \frac{3.00 \times 10^8 \text{ m/s}}{2.26 \times 10^8 \text{ m/s}} = 1.33$$

452 NEL • Unit 4 Light and Geometric Optics

Dispersion

In **Figure 11.8A**, white light, which includes all the wavelengths of visible light, is refracting twice: once when it enters the prism and again when it leaves the prism. When the white light leaves the prism, the light is separated into a spectrum of colours. This process is called **dispersion**. This is also illustrated in **Figure 11.8B**. Notice that blue light bends more than red light. So, blue light must travel slower than red light. In fact, each colour of light travels at a slightly different speed in any medium. Only in a vacuum do all the wavelengths of light, and all other forms of electromagnetic waves, travel at the same speed—3.00×10^8 m/s.

dispersion the process of separating colours by refraction

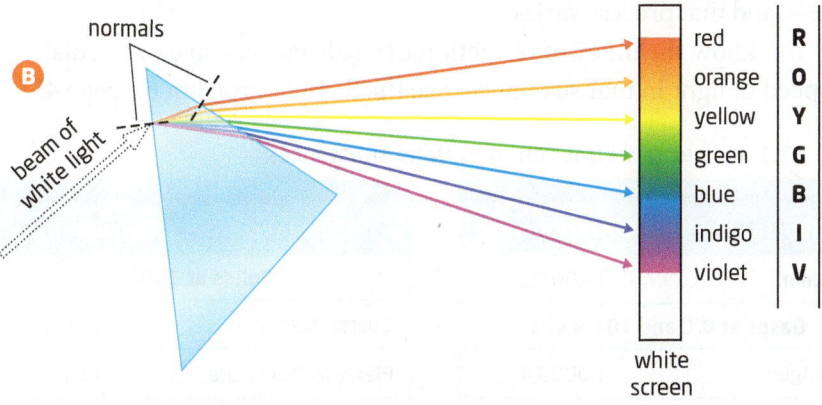

Figure 11.8 A When white light leaves the prism, it is refracted again. Since each colour of light travels at a different speed, each colour of light refracts a different amount. **B** You can remember the order of the colours of light in a spectrum by remembering the name Roy G. Biv, which stands for red, orange, yellow, green, blue, indigo, violet.

YOU CAN CALL ME ROY

Chapter 11 Refraction • NEL   453

> **Sense of scale**
>
> A single aluminum atom is about the size of a nanometre. A nanometre is one billionth of a metre.

> **Suggested Investigation**
>
> Inquiry Investigation 11-B, Analyzing the Index of Refraction, on page 477

Go to **scienceontario** to find out more

Reporting Indices of Refraction

If each colour of light has its own index of refraction, what value do you use as the index of refraction for "light"? Scientists have agreed to use one specific wavelength of light as a standard for reporting. When scientists were first studying indices (plural of *index*) of refraction, one of the easiest pure colours to produce was a yellow with a wavelength of 589 nm (nm is the symbol for nanometre, which is 10^{-9} m). This wavelength of light is emitted from heated sodium vapour. So scientists use yellow as a standard for reporting the index of refraction for light.

When reporting the index of refraction for a gas, remember that gases are affected by both temperature and pressure. Liquids and solids are affected much less by pressure, but they can be affected by temperature. So, in tables of indices of refraction, such as **Table 11.1**, the temperature (in °C) is reported for liquids and solids, but both the temperature and pressure (in kPa) are reported for gases. Notice that the index of refraction is always greater than 1. This is because the speed of light is always higher in a vacuum than in a medium. As the speed of light decreases due to the medium, the index of refraction increases.

The indices of refraction (*n*) for the solids and liquids at 20°C in **Table 11.1** have been measured. Therefore, you can count on the accuracy of the values when you work with the substances at room temperature. All the liquids are clear and colourless. You may recognize the names of some of the substances, such as the liquid carbon disulfide. Carbon disulfide is an example of a solvent. The solid called fused quartz is used in making lenses and mirrors. It is not the same as the mineral with the common name quartz. The three types of glass (crown, crystal, and flint) have different values of *n* because different substances are added in the glass-making process, and that process varies.

If you know the index of refraction of a substance, you can calculate the speed of light in that substance. See the Sample Problem on page 455.

Table 11.1 Indices of Refraction of Various Substances

Substance	Index of Refraction (*n*)
Vacuum	1.000 00
Gases at 0°C and 101.3 kPa	
Hydrogen	1.000 14
Oxygen	1.000 27
Air	1.000 29
Carbon dioxide	1.000 45
Liquids at 20°C	
Water	1.333
Ethyl alcohol	1.362
Glycerol	1.470
Carbon disulfide	1.632

Substance	Index of Refraction (*n*)
Solids at 20°C	
Quartz (fused)	1.46
Plexiglas™ or Lucite™	1.51
Glass (crown)	1.52
Sodium chloride	1.54
Glass (crystal)	1.54
Ruby	1.54
Glass (flint)	1.65
Zircon	1.92
Diamond	2.42

Sample Problem: Calculating the Speed of Light in Different Media

Problem

Calculate the speed of light in fused quartz.

Solution

Look up the index of refraction for fused quartz in **Table 11.1**.

$n = 1.46$

Write the equation that relates the index of refraction to the speed of light in the medium.

$$n = \frac{c}{v}$$

Speed in the medium (v) is the unknown variable, so arrange the equation to solve for v.

$$nv = \frac{c}{\cancel{v}}\cancel{v}$$

$$\frac{\cancel{n}v}{\cancel{n}} = \frac{c}{n}$$

$$v = \frac{c}{n}$$

Insert the values for the index of refraction for fused quartz and the speed of light in a vacuum, and calculate v.

$$v = \frac{3.00 \times 10^8 \text{ m/s}}{1.46}$$

$$= 2.05 \times 10^8 \text{ m/s}$$

The speed of light in fused quartz is 2.05×10^8 m/s.

Check Your Solution

The value for v is smaller than the speed of light in a vacuum, which it must be. The units are metres per second, which they should be for speed.

GRASP

Go to **Science Skills Toolkit 11** to learn about an alternative problem solving method.

Practice Problems

1. Calculate the speed of light in flint glass.

2. Calculate the speed of light in crown glass.

3. a. The speed of light in a solid is 1.24×10^8 m/s. Calculate the index of refraction.
   b. Use **Table 11.1** to identify the substance.

4. The diagrams at the right show the path of light as it passes from air into the three solids in the first three problems. The angle of incidence is the same for all three solids. Examine the index of refraction values in the problems, and identify each solid.

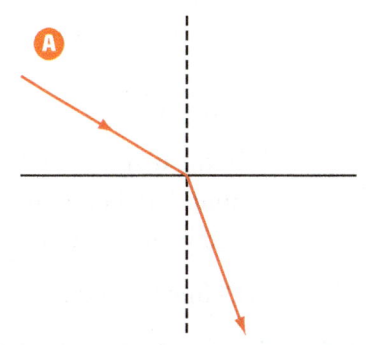

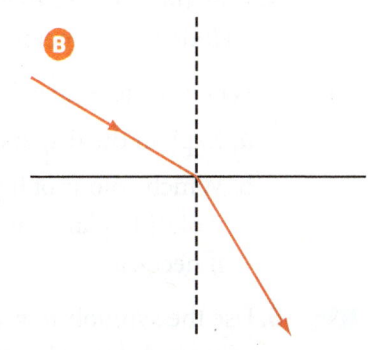

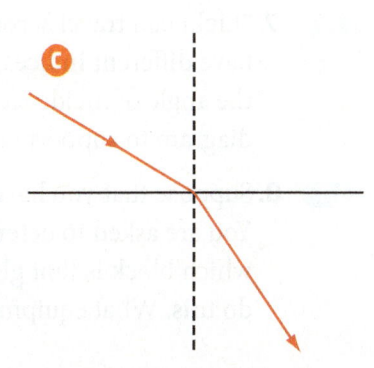

Use these diagrams to answer question 4.

Chapter 11 Refraction • NEL 455

Section 11.1 Review

Section Summary

- Light rays refract when they cross a boundary between media in which the speeds of light are different.
- If a light ray goes from a medium in which its speed is higher (such as air) into a medium in which its speed is lower (such as water), the refracted ray bends toward the normal.
- If a light ray goes from a medium in which its speed is lower (such as water) into a medium in which its speed is higher (such as air), the refracted ray bends away from the normal.
- The index of refraction of a medium is the ratio of the speed of light in a vacuum to the speed of light in the medium $n = \frac{c}{v}$. A ratio greater than 1 results.
- Dispersion is the separation of the various colours of light when white light crosses the boundary between different media at an angle.
- The speed of each wavelength of light is different in any given medium. The speed of all wavelengths of light is 3.00×10^8 m/s in a vacuum.

Review Questions

K/U 1. In the diagram on the right, a light ray is crossing the boundary between air and water. Which medium is air, and which medium is water? Explain your reasoning.

K/U 2. Define the index of refraction.

T/I 3. Calculate the speed of light in glycerol.

K/U 4. Why must a table that lists indices of refraction of gases include the temperature and pressure of the gases?

K/U 5. When white light exits a prism, the light is dispersed.
   a. Explain the dispersion of white light through a prism.
   b. Which colour of light travels faster in glass: yellow or violet? Explain your reasoning. Review **Figure 11.8** if necessary.

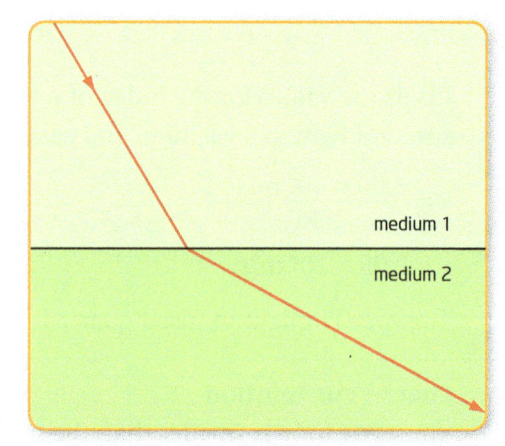

C 6. Use the symbols *n*, *v*, and *c* to show why the index of refraction of any substance is always greater than 1.

A 7. "Light can travel across the boundary between two media that have different indices of refraction without bending." What is the angle of incidence for which this statement is true? Use a diagram to support your answer.

T/I 8. Suppose that you have two blocks of glass that look very similar. You are asked to determine which block is crown glass and which block is flint glass. Describe a method you could use to do this. What equipment would you need?

Use this diagram to answer question 1.

11.2 Partial Refraction and Total Internal Reflection

Key Terms
partial reflection and refraction
critical angle
total internal reflection

If you have never been diving, you might be surprised by what a diver can and cannot see when looking up toward the surface of the water. The photograph in **Figure 11.9** was taken underwater from a diver's perspective. As you can see, only the objects in an area directly above you are clearly visible. The water at the sides is dark, even though the day appears to be clear and bright.

You can analyze **Figure 11.9** based on what you have learned about the refraction of light. To be able to see an object above the water while you are underwater, you know that light must travel from the object to your eyes. The objects outside the area directly above you are not visible because no light from these objects is penetrating the surface of the water. Light is energy so it cannot disappear. If it is not penetrating the water, where is it going? You could find some clues by reviewing **Figure 10.12** on page 411. In **Figure 10.12**, light is reflected from the surface of the water. When light rays reach a boundary between two media, such as air and water, some light is always reflected and some is often refracted. In this section, you will learn about the conditions in which more refraction than reflection occurs and the conditions in which only reflection occurs.

Figure 11.9 When underwater and looking up, you can only see objects in an area directly above you.

Figure 11.10 While looking out of a window, you can often see the reflection of objects inside the room as well as objects that are outside of the window.

partial reflection and refraction a phenomenon in which some of the light that is travelling from one medium into another is reflected and some is refracted at the boundary between the media

Partial Reflection and Refraction

Sometimes, when you look out a window, you see what is outside as well as your own reflection, as shown in **Figure 11.10**. In the photograph, light is obviously coming through the window because you can see objects that are outside. But light is also reflecting off the window because you can see your own reflection. In addition, someone standing outside could see you through the window. As mentioned earlier, some light reflects and some light refracts at a surface between two media that have different indices of refraction, as shown in **Figure 11.11**. This phenomenon is called **partial reflection and refraction**. The amount of reflection compared with the amount of refraction depends on the angle of incidence as well as the relative indices of refraction of the two media.

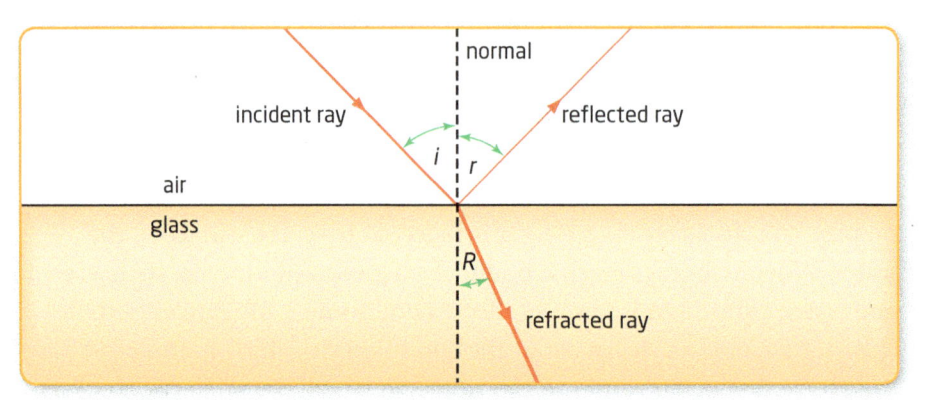

Figure 11.11 Both refraction and reflection occur, but not equally. The amount of each depends on the angle. In this case, more light is refracted than reflected, as indicated by the thickness of the rays.

Consider, first, light travelling from air into water. If the angle of incidence is nearly zero—that is, the light is travelling directly toward the water—most of the light penetrates the surface and very little is reflected. As the angle of incidence increases, more light is reflected at the surface and less light penetrates the surface and is refracted.

You have probably seen evidence of this phenomenon. **Figure 11.12A** shows water with the Sun overhead. You see very little reflection of sunlight because most of the light is penetrating the surface of the water. In **Figure 11.12B**, however, the Sun is close to the horizon, shining light on the water at a large angle of incidence. You can see that much of the light is reflected from the surface of the water.

Figure 11.12 **A** The sunlight is shining on the water, but you do not see any reflection because the Sun is almost directly overhead. **B** When the Sun reflects off the water (for example, at sunset), the reflection of the light can be almost blinding.

Activity 11-2

Investigating Properties of Light

In this activity, you will answer the following questions. How does the angle of incidence of a ray striking a glass surface compare with
(a) the angle of reflection at the surface,
(b) the angle of refraction at the surface, and
(c) the angle of refraction when the ray emerges into air again?

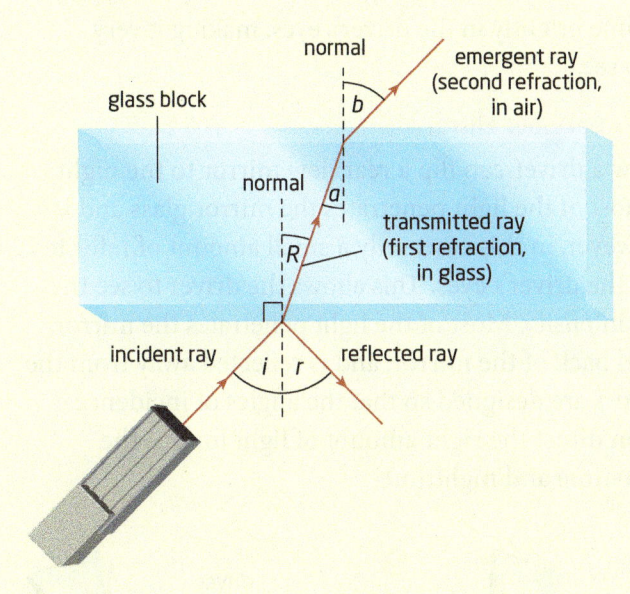

Materials
- glass block
- sheet of paper
- ray box (single slit)
- pencil
- ruler
- protractor

Procedure

1. In your notebook, make a table like the one below to record your observations. Give your table a title.

2. Place the glass block in the centre of the sheet of paper. Carefully draw an outline of the block.

3. Place a single slit in the ray box. Shine the light toward the longest side of the block as shown in the diagram on the left.

4. Make small pencil marks on the incident, reflected, and emergent rays.

5. Remove the block, and use a ruler to connect the dots with a solid line to show the path of the light ray. The light ray should change direction at the outline of the block.

6. Draw a normal at the point where the incident ray enters the block. Draw a second normal where the emergent ray leaves the block. Measure the angles of incidence (i), reflection (r), and refraction (R), as well as the angles labelled a and b in the diagram.

Questions

1. Explain how the reflection you observed in this activity (a) is the same as and (b) is different from the reflection of light at the surface of a plane mirror.

2. In previous activities and investigations, you have not considered a refracted light ray that enters and then continues on through and out the other side of the same medium. Explain how the refracted ray as it enters the medium (a) is the same as and (b) is different from the ray as it leaves.

Incident Ray	Reflected Ray	Transmitted Ray — First Refraction, in Glass		Emergent Ray — Second Refraction, in Air
∠i	∠r	∠R	∠a	∠b

Reflection and Refraction in a Rearview Mirror

The rearview mirror in most cars has a lever that allows the driver to choose how much light from behind the car will reach his or her eyes. During the day, the driver wants to clearly see the traffic that is behind the car. At night, however, the driver does not want to be blinded by headlights.

How a Rearview Mirror Works

As shown in **Figure 11.13A**, rearview mirrors are wedge-shaped and silvered on the back. A lever can quickly flip a rearview mirror from daytime to nighttime positions. Light coming from behind the car hits the mirror at a very small angle of incidence. As a result, most of the light is refracted and reaches the silvered back of the mirror, where it is reflected.

Daytime Setting of a Rearview Mirror

In the daytime, the mirror is positioned as shown in **Figure 11.13B**. The light that has reflected off the back of the mirror is directed to the driver's eyes. Thus, in the daytime, the driver has a clear view of the traffic behind the car. If the mirror was left in this position at night, however, any headlights behind the car would shine brightly in the driver's eyes, making it very difficult for the driver to see.

Nighttime Setting of a Rearview Mirror

Figure 11.13C shows how a driver can flip a rearview mirror to the night setting. At this angle, most of the light penetrates the mirror glass and is refracted as before. However, in this case, only a small amount of reflected light is directed toward the driver's eyes. This allows the driver to see the headlights, but at a low intensity. Most of the light penetrates the mirror, refracts, hits the silvered back of the mirror, and is reflected away from the driver's eyes. Such mirrors are designed so that the angles of incidence, reflection, and refraction direct the right amount of light toward the driver's eyes for both daytime and nighttime.

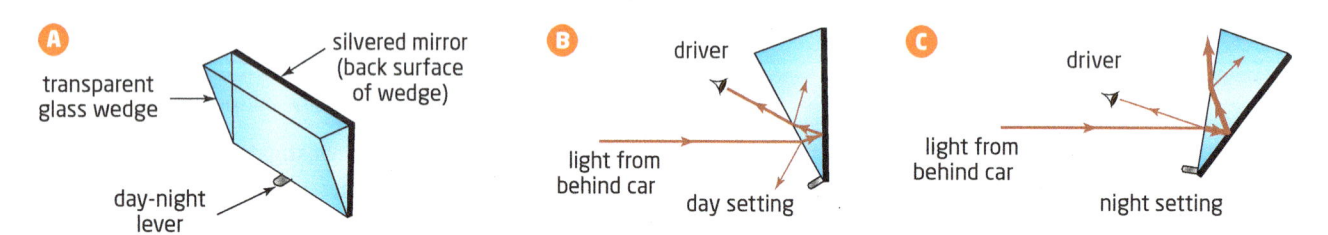

Figure 11.13 **A** A rearview mirror reflects light to the driver's eyes. **B** With the daytime setting, most of the light goes to the driver's eyes. **C** With the nighttime setting, just a small amount of the incoming light goes to the driver's eyes.

Large Angles of Incidence

Now that you understand partial reflection and refraction, you can explain **Figure 11.9** on page 457. Imagine that you are scuba diving and are underwater looking up, as shown in **Figure 11.14**. The light coming from the area directly above you or at a small angle of incidence will penetrate the surface of the water, refract, and be visible to you. But as the angle of incidence of the light increases, more of the light will reflect off the water, and a smaller amount will refract and be visible to you. Nearly all the light that is coming in your direction from large angles of incidence will reflect from the surface and never reach you. Therefore, from below the surface of the water, it looks like light is coming through a hole.

Figure 11.14 When you are underwater, you can only see the light that reaches you from an area directly above. The bottom of the water-air boundary and the sky above look dark because light that is coming from this direction is reflected away and you cannot see it.

Learning Check

1. The term *partial refraction* implies that only part of the light that hits a boundary between two media refracts. What happens to the rest of the light?

2. Explain how a rearview mirror works. Review **Figure 11.13** if necessary. In your explanation, include why many rearview mirrors have two settings.

3. If you were sitting on a riverbank, holding a fishing rod, a fish in the river would probably not be able to see you. Explain why.

4. Describe an example in your everyday life that demonstrates that both reflection and refraction occur at a boundary between two media with different indices of refraction.

Refraction: Water to Air

If you were standing in shallow water at the edge of a clear lake, as in **Figure 11.15**, you would be able to see stones on the bottom of the lake or fish swimming in the water that were very near you. As you look farther away, objects underwater are more difficult to see. At a great enough distance, you cannot see anything below the surface of the water. You know that the water is clear and that there is plenty of light. Why is it not possible to see objects underwater?

Figure 11.15 The water is clear, but you can see objects under the water only when they are close to you.

Chapter 11 Refraction • NEL   461

Suggested Investigation

Inquiry Investigation 11-D, Investigating Total Internal Reflection in Water, on page 480

critical angle the angle of incidence that produces an angle of refraction of 90°

total internal reflection the phenomenon in which incident light is not refracted but is entirely reflected back from the boundary; occurs when light travels from a medium in which its speed is lower to a medium in which its speed is higher

The Critical Angle

For you to see an object underwater, light must hit the object, reflect off it, and travel to your eyes. **Figure 11.16A** shows two separate incident rays travelling toward the boundary between air and water, at relatively small angles of incidence. Because the incident rays are going from water to air, the refracted rays bend away from the normal. As you can see, as the angle of incidence increases, the angle of refraction increases more rapidly.

As the angle of incidence continues to increase, the angle of refraction will eventually reach 90°, as shown in **Figure 11.16B**. At this angle of incidence, the refracted ray lies along the boundary between the two media. No light passes into the second medium, which is air in this example. The angle of incidence that produces a refracted ray at an angle of 90° from the normal is called the **critical angle**, and is symbolized by $\angle c$.

Total Internal Reflection

The size of the critical angle depends on the indices of refraction of the two media. When the angle of incidence is larger than the critical angle, the angle of refraction cannot get any larger because the refracted ray would no longer be in the second medium. So, at angles of incidence that are greater than the critical angle, no refraction occurs. All the light is reflected back into the first medium, as shown in **Figure 11.16C**. This phenomenon is called **total internal reflection**. Note that total internal reflection happens only when light travels from a medium in which its speed is lower to a medium in which its speed is higher.

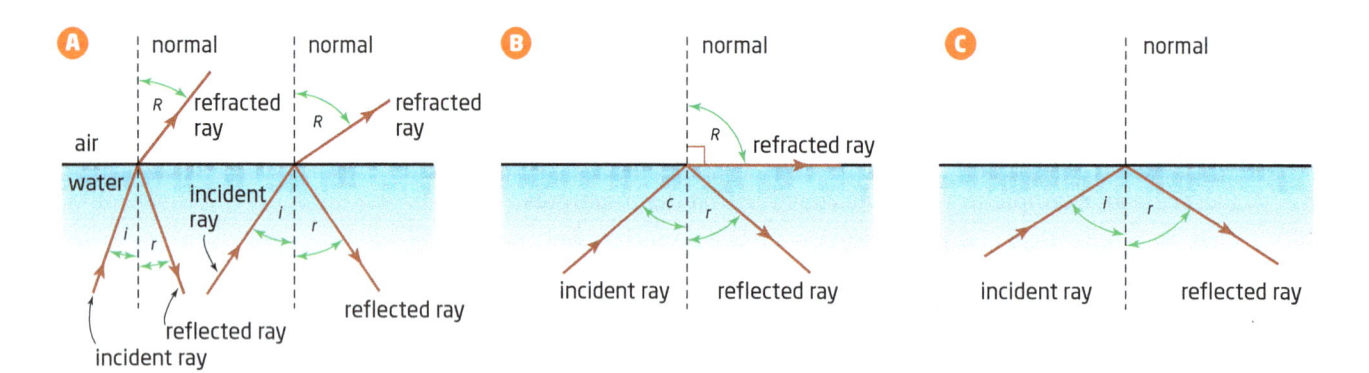

Figure 11.16 A When the angle of incidence is smaller than the critical angle, both refraction and reflection occur at the boundary between the two media. **B** When the angle of refraction reaches 90°, the refracted ray lies along the boundary between the two media. **C** When the angle of incidence is larger than the critical angle, all the light is reflected back into the first medium.

Activity 11-3

The Fountain of Light

What is happening in the diagram on the right? In this activity, you will observe total internal reflection within a stream of water in a darkened room.

Materials

- clear plastic bottle (remove the label if necessary)
- duct tape (about 5 cm)
- thumbtack
- masking tape (about 3 cm)
- water
- bucket (or use a sink)
- flashlight
- scissors

Set up the apparatus as shown here to see the light in the stream of water.

Procedure

1. Place a short piece of duct tape on a part of the bottle that is clear on both sides, about 6 to 8 cm from the bottom of the bottle.

2. Use the thumbtack to make a small hole in the centre of the duct tape. Cover the hole with a small piece of masking tape.

3. Fill the bottle with water. Perform the rest of this activity over a bucket or sink.

4. Have your partner shine the light from a flashlight through the bottle from the side that is opposite the hole. Remove the masking tape, and observe the stream of water as it exits the hole, as well as the height of the water in the bottle as it nears the hole.

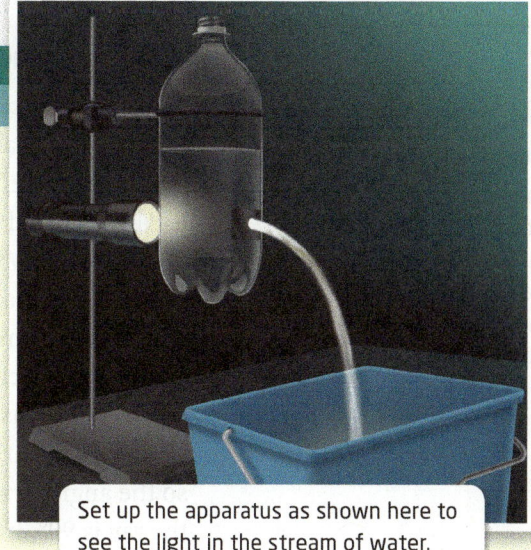

5. Look for the spot where total internal reflection suddenly occurs. Try to measure the critical angle.

6. Empty the water from the bottle. Use the point of the scissors to make the hole larger, and cover the hole with masking tape. Repeat steps 3 to 5.

Questions

1. Total internal reflection occurs when light in water hits the water–air surface at an angle of incidence that is greater than 49°. Compare 49° with your measurement in step 5.

2. When did you observe the greater amount of total internal reflection: when the stream of water fell far from the bottle, or when the stream of water fell close to the bottle? Explain your observation using a diagram.

Making a Difference

Michael Furdyk uses Internet communications technology to make a difference. He is co-founder and director of technology for TakingITGlobal.org, an on-line community for youth interested in positive change. More than five million users from 200 countries have visited TakingITGlobal.org to learn about and engage in global issues, such as education and sustainable development.

Michael started his first computer business when he was 8. At 15, he formed a company called MyDesktop.com with Michael Hayman, an Australian friend. The website had more than 500 000 users monthly, and Michael and his friend eventually sold it. In 2000, Michael co-founded the non-profit TakingITGlobal.org with another friend, Jennifer Corriero.

Michael has advised many organizations on how to engage today's youth. He speaks at conferences around the world and was named one of Teen People's "20 teens that will change the world" in 2000.

How could you use the Internet and other communications technologies to make positive changes in your community?

Study Toolkit

Summarizing It may be helpful to summarize the information in the first three paragraphs on this page in a table like the one on page 448.

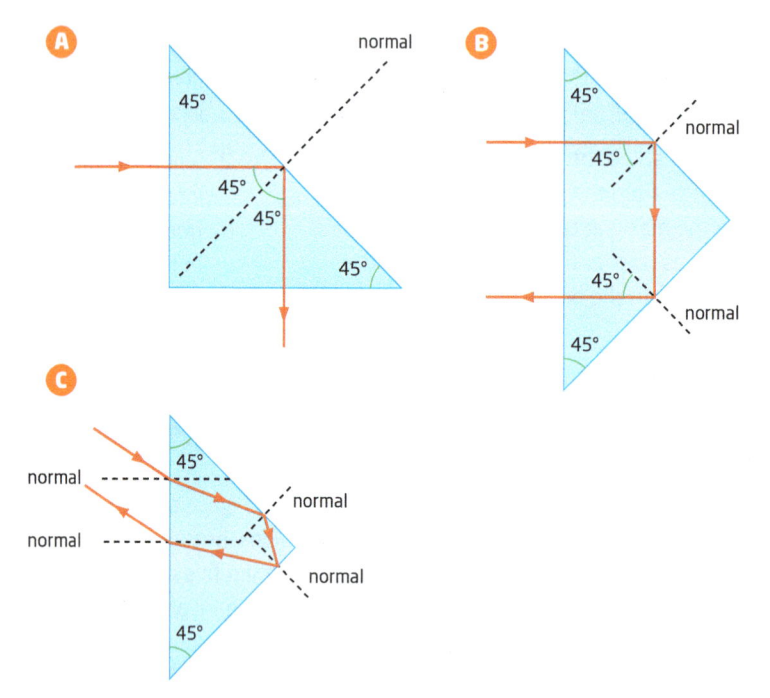

Changing the Direction of a Light Ray

A glass prism can change the direction of light by creating the conditions for total internal reflection. The critical angle between glass and air is less than 45°. Therefore, light hitting an inner surface at exactly 45° will be totally reflected inside the glass.

Figure 11.17A shows how a glass prism that is shaped like an isosceles right triangle can change the direction of a light ray by 90°. When light enters the prism perpendicular to one of the short sides of the prism, the angle of incidence is zero. Thus, there is no refraction at this surface. The light travels straight through the prism to the inside of the long side of the prism. At the long side of the prism, the angle of incidence is 45°, so the angle of reflection is also 45°. The total change in the direction of the ray is 90°. In comparison, when light enters the prism perpendicular to the long side of the prism, as shown in **Figure 11.17B**, it is reflected off both short sides, changing direction by 90° each time. The total change in direction is therefore 180°.

When light enters the long side at any angle, as shown in **Figures 11.17B** and **C**, the reflected light is reflected by 180°, or directly back in the direction that it came from. When the angle of incidence into the prism is not 0°, the light will be refracted. However, after the light has reflected off both inner short sides and then leaves the prism, it will refract at the same angle.

Figure 11.17 **A** The direction of light is changed 90°. **B** The direction of light is changed 180°. **C** Regardless of the angle of incidence at the long side of the prism shown, the refracted and reflected rays will go back in exactly the same direction from which they came.

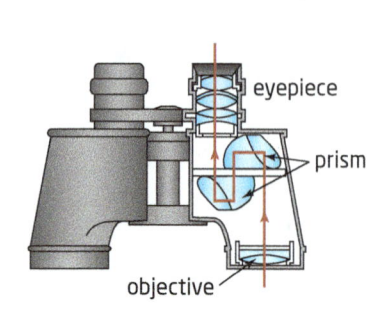

Figure 11.18 The direction of the light is reflected twice in binoculars to make the path of the light longer.

Applications of Total Internal Reflection

Figure 11.18 shows how binoculars use total internal reflection. See how the path of light in the binoculars is lengthened and moved to the side. When you study lenses in Chapter 12, you will find out why the long path length is important.

Retroreflectors

The ability to change the direction of light by 180° has some very useful applications. One of these applications is *retroreflectors*, which look like small plastic prisms. For example, the reflectors on the back of a bicycle are retroreflectors, as shown in **Figure 11.19A**. Regardless of the direction that light from headlights hits the reflectors, the light is always reflected directly back to the car so the driver can see the bicycle, as shown in part **B**.

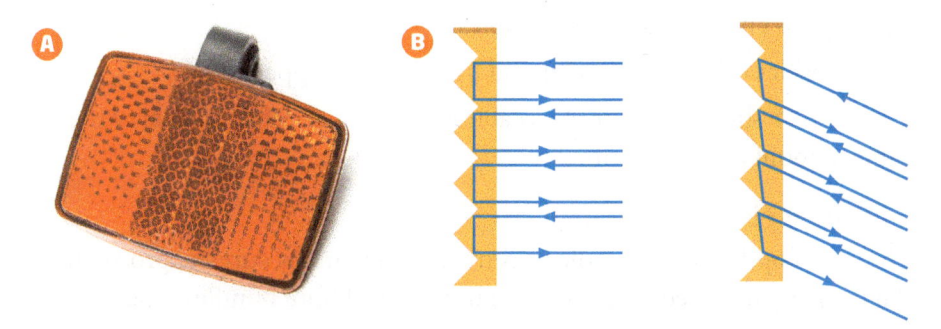

Figure 11.19 A Look closely at this bicycle reflector. You will see small circles or hexagons. **B** Each circle or hexagon is a cut in the plastic. It functions like a prism to reflect light directly back in the direction it came from.

Optical Fibres

Fibre optics has revolutionized all forms of communication, including the Internet. Optical fibres are made from a glass core, which is surrounded by an optical cladding. A *cladding* is a covering, much like a sleeve but completely closed. In this case, the fibre core is made of one type of glass, and the cladding is made of another type of glass. The material that makes up the cladding must have a lower index of refraction than the core to facilitate total internal reflection. See **Figure 11.20A**. When light enters the end of the fibre in a direction that is almost parallel to the axis of the fibre, it hits the boundary between the core and cladding at an angle that is larger than the critical angle, as shown in **Figure 11.20B**. Even when the fibre is bent, the light is totally internally reflected along the entire fibre until it reaches the other end.

Individual fibres are somewhat fragile. Therefore, they are coated for strength and protection. Groups of fibres are then bundled together into a cable, as shown in **Figure 11.20C**. Depending on their use, the cables can be as short as a metre or as long as several kilometres.

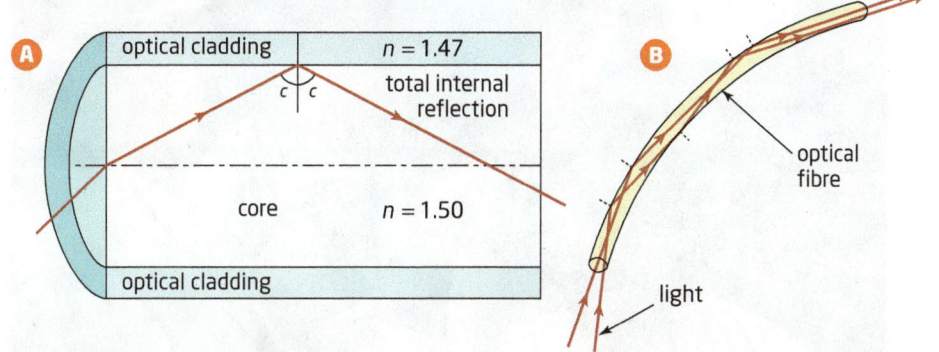

Figure 11.20 A Total internal reflection will occur each time the light hits the boundary between the core and cladding in an optical fibre, regardless of the amount of bending of the fibre. **B** The light is totally internally reflected along the optical fibre until it reaches the other end. **C** A fibre optics cable can carry hundreds of telephone conversations, cable television signals, or data.

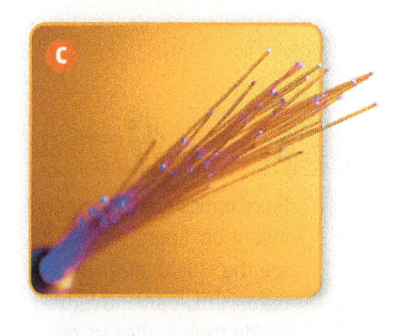

Chapter 11 Refraction • NEL   465

Figure 11.21 The small optical fibres can carry as much information as the large copper cable on the right.

Study Toolkit

Making Inferences Read the text under the heading "Fibre Optics in Telecommunications." What prior knowledge do you have about copper wire cables?

Fibre Optics in Telecommunications

Copper wire cables have been used in the past to carry information. But fibre optic cables are rapidly replacing them. There are three main ways that fibre optics cables are superior to copper wire cables:

- The signals are not affected by electrical storms, as they would be in copper wire cables.
- Fibre optics cables can carry many more signals over long distances, losing less energy than copper cables.
- Fibre optics cables are smaller and lighter than copper cables.

Figure 11.21 shows a fibre optics cable and a copper cable that carry the same amount of information.

Fibre Optics in Medicine

The use of optical fibre bundles has transformed many surgical procedures. An instrument called an endoscope uses optical fibre bundles. The surgeon inserts the endoscope in a small incision. One bundle of optical fibres in the endoscope carries light into the area where the surgery is needed. Another bundle of optical fibres carries an image of the area back to a monitor. The surgeon watches the monitor while manipulating the instrument to complete the surgery. Before this technique was available, a large incision was necessary, making the recovery time several weeks long. Traditional surgery also increases the possibility of infection.

Doctors also use endoscopes to help diagnose problems in their patients. In **Figure 11.22**, the doctor has fed an endoscope down her patient's esophagus and can view the inside of the patient's stomach on a computer monitor. The doctor in the middle, holding the white instrument, is taking a tissue sample from the stomach. By being able to see the inside of the stomach and take a tissue sample, the doctor may be able to diagnose any problems, such as an ulcer or cancer.

Sense of *time*

Fibre optics are not a recent invention. Sponges, which are the oldest multicellular organisms, transmit light inside their bodies using silica structures. The silica structures are basically glass rods.

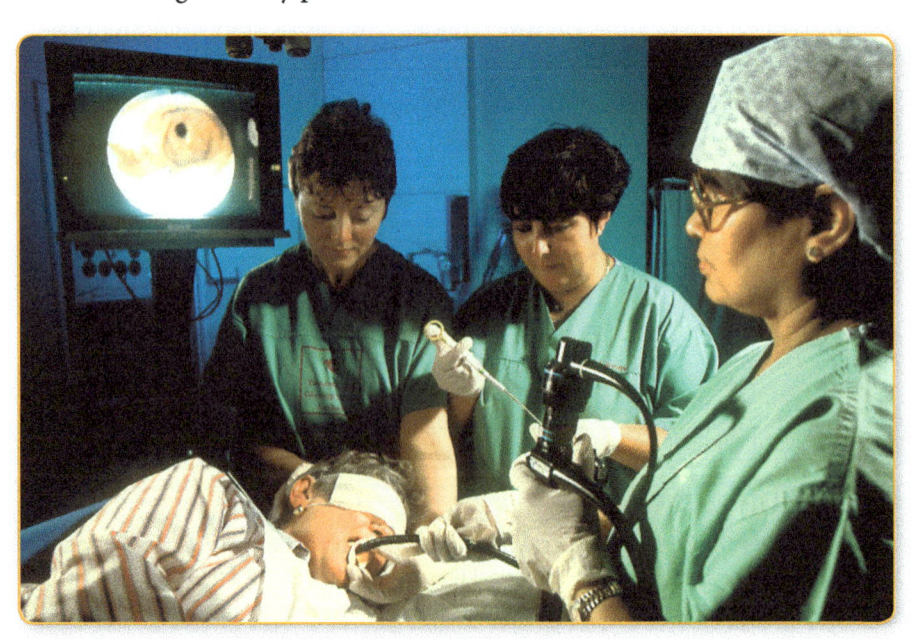

Figure 11.22 The doctor has inserted the flexible, fibre optic end of the endoscope down the patient's throat and is watching the image of the stomach on a monitor.

Section 11.2 Review

Section Summary

- When light strikes a boundary between two transparent media that have different indices of refraction, some light reflects off the boundary and some light refracts through the boundary. This phenomenon is called partial reflection and refraction.

- At a small angle of incidence, more light refracts than reflects. As the angle of incidence increases, more and more light reflects than refracts.

- When light travels from a medium with a higher index of refraction to a medium with a lower index of refraction, the angle of refraction is larger than the angle of incidence. Therefore, an angle of incidence that results in a 90° angle of refraction is eventually reached. This angle of incidence is called the critical angle.

- When the angle of incidence is larger than the critical angle, no refraction occurs. All the light is reflected from the boundary. This phenomenon is called total internal reflection.

- Total internal reflection has many practical applications, such as binoculars, retroreflectors, and optical fibres in telecommunications and in surgical instruments.

Review Questions

C 1. Using diagrams, define the terms *critical angle* and *total internal reflection*.

K/U 2. Under what conditions will nearly all the light that reaches a boundary between two different media be refracted?

K/U 3. What two conditions must exist for total internal reflection to occur?

K/U 4. Describe the structure of optical fibre cables.

A 5. The diagrams on the right show rearview mirrors at two different settings. Which rearview mirror is set for daytime driving, and which is set for nighttime driving? Explain your reasoning. Review **Figure 11.13** if necessary.

T/I 6. Refer to **Figure 11.17**. If the light enters one of the short sides of the prism at an angle of incidence of 40°, will the light change direction by 90°? Explain your answer.

A 7. Evaluate the impact of the development of optical fibres. Which type of application do you think has the greatest impact on our lives?

T/I 8. Diamonds have a large index of refraction of 2.42, and they are cut with many facets. Based on what you know about refraction, explain why cut diamonds sparkle more than any other cut stones.

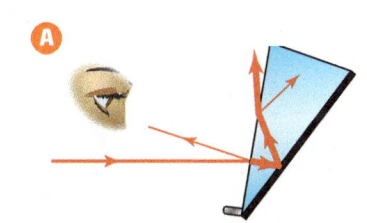

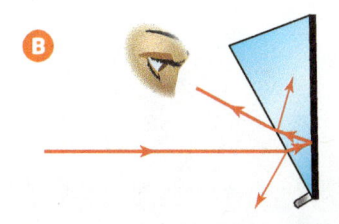

Use these diagrams for question 5.

A facet on a diamond is a small, flat area.

Key Terms
rainbow
apparent depth
shimmering
mirage

11.3 Optical Phenomena in Nature

The double rainbow in **Figure 11.23** is an excellent natural example of the refraction and dispersion of light. Your new understanding of the behaviour of light will allow you to analyze the paths of the light rays that bring this double rainbow to your eyes.

Rainbows

The Sun must be behind you if you are to see a **rainbow**. It must also reflect off something for it to return to your eyes. After a rainstorm, the sky is filled with tiny water droplets. The sunlight reflects off these water droplets.

Now consider the sequence of colours in the two parts of the double rainbow. Red is the top colour of the inner rainbow, but it is the lowest colour of the secondary rainbow. Notice that much more light is coming from the area inside the inner rainbow than the area outside the inner rainbow. All of these factors can be explained by the reflection, refraction, and dispersion of light in raindrops. A secondary rainbow is caused when sunlight reflects twice inside rain droplets. This explains why the secondary bow is less bright, with red at the bottom and blue at the top.

rainbow an arc of colours of the visible spectrum appearing opposite the Sun, caused by reflection, refraction, and dispersion of the Sun's rays as they pass through raindrops

Figure 11.23 Notice how red is at the top of the inner rainbow but at the bottom of the secondary rainbow.

Formation of a Rainbow

A rainbow forms when sunlight enters a water droplet and refracts, reflects off the inner surface of the droplet, and then refracts again when leaving the droplet. The two refractions result in dispersion of the light. Notice in **Figure 11.24A** that within the droplet itself, the different colours cross each other, and then spread out as they leave the droplet.

Compare the colours leaving the single water droplet in **Figure 11.24A** with the colours in the inner rainbow in **Figure 11.23**. Notice that the red light leaving the water droplet is the lowest colour, but red is the top colour in the inner rainbow. Although this seems be a contradiction, it is correct. When you see a rainbow, the colours that you see come from different droplets. Because the red light is directed downward more than the other colours of light, you can only see the red light that is coming from droplets higher in the sky. **Figure 11.24B** shows which colours you see from droplets at different heights in the sky.

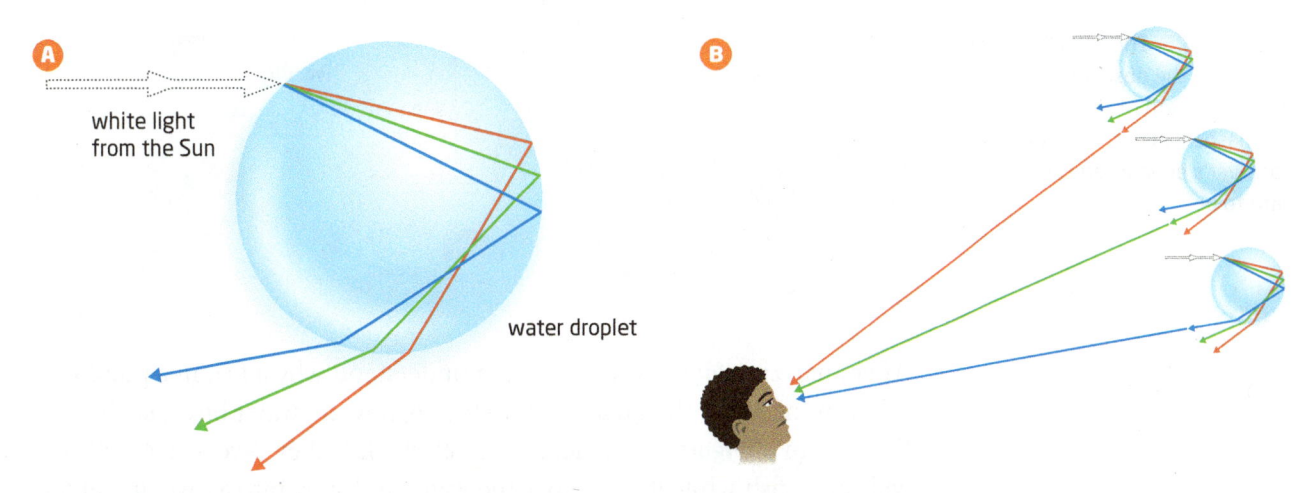

Figure 11.24 **A** The index of refraction is different for each colour of light. When white light leaves a water droplet, refraction causes the colours to disperse. **B** You see the different colours in a rainbow coming from water droplets at different heights in the sky.

Sundogs

At the beginning of this chapter, you saw a photograph of the spectacular atmospheric phenomena known as sundogs, which are bright spots on both sides of the Sun. They are sometimes called "mock suns" for that reason. Their technical name is *parhelia*. Sundogs have something in common with rainbows, but there is a difference. Rainbows are a result from sunlight interacting with water droplets in the atmosphere. Sundogs, however, occur when ice crystals in the atmosphere refract sunlight. The most stunning sundogs occur on cold, clear sunny mornings and evenings, when there are ice crystals in the air, such as in cirrus clouds. (Cirrus clouds are at a high altitude, over 6000 m. They are composed of ice crystals.) Sundogs occur when the Sun is low, near the horizon. These phenomena have been photographed in many provinces and territories of Canada, including Ontario.

Go to **scienceontario** to find out more

The Illusion of Apparent Depth

Just as an image is formed by reflection in a plane or a curved mirror, an image is formed by the refraction of light. Using ray diagrams, you can determine where the refracted image is located when it is viewed from the air. Light rays from the object, like the box at the bottom of the pool in **Figure 11.25**, travel to your eyes. The rays have refracted at the surface of the water. As in Chapter 10, you can draw a ray diagram to locate the image of the object. Locate the image of the box by tracing the rays backward until they meet. Note that the box on the bottom of the pool looks like it is higher and closer to the observer than it actually is. In fact, the bottom of the pool is deeper than it appears to be. The level at which the object or the bottom of the pool appears to be is called the **apparent depth**.

apparent depth an optical effect in which the image of an object appears closer than the object

Figure 11.25 The solid lines from the box to the observer show the actual path of the light rays. The dashed lines show where the observer's brain interprets the path to be.

After analyzing **Figure 11.25**, you can understand why a fish in a pond is lower in the water than it appears to be. So, how do water birds, such as the pelican in **Figure 11.26**, actually catch the fish they dive for? A pelican will spot a fish while flying above the water and start into a dive. It will hit the water forcefully, continue into the water, and catch the fish without difficulty. The pelican has found a way to account for the illusion of apparent depth.

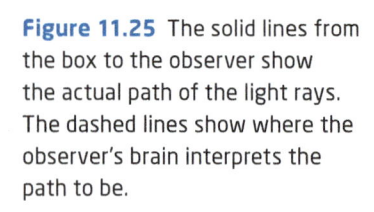

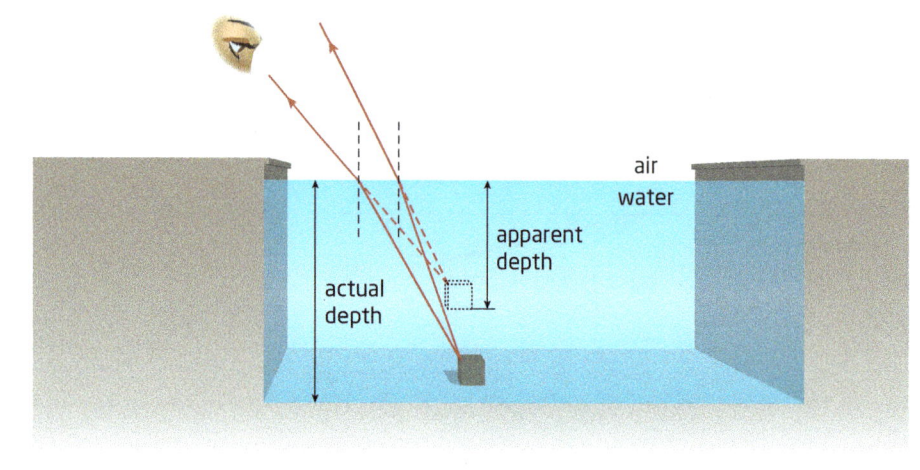

Figure 11.26 Water birds, such as the pelican, dive deeper for a fish than the fish appears in the water to a human observer.

Learning Check

1. Explain why red is at the top of a single rainbow. Review **Figure 11.24**.
2. What is a sundog?
3. If you are trying to spear a fish underwater, should you aim above the fish, below the fish, or at the fish? Use your knowledge of apparent depth to explain.
4. Draw a diagram to show how a double rainbow forms.

Activity 11-4

Apparent Depth

How does the location of an object appear to change when you observe it through a plastic block? In this activity, you will demonstrate the phenomenon of apparent depth.

Materials
- rectangular plastic block
- thick piece of cardboard
- sheet of blank paper
- 5 straight pins
- ruler

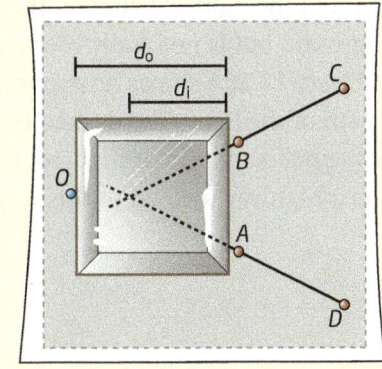

Place the plastic block and pins as shown here.

Procedure
1. Place the cardboard on the desk. Place a sheet of paper on top of the cardboard and the plastic block on the paper.
2. Place a pin at position O shown in the diagram above. The pin should be touching the plastic.
3. Place a pin at positions A and B, as shown in the diagram on the left.
4. Look in the direction shown in the diagram until pin B and the pin at O appear in a straight line. Place pin C so that all three pins appear in a straight line. Similarly, place pin D so that the pins at D, A, and O appear in a straight line.
5. Remove the block, and draw dashed lines to show where the lines CB and DA intersect inside the block at the image of pin O. Measure d_i and d_o.
6. Make a ray diagram to illustrate your observation.
7. Switch places with your partner, and repeat steps 3 and 4.

Questions
1. Where do the rays intersect?
2. Explain your observations.
3. Suppose you used a clear container instead of a plastic block. You then positioned the pins before filling the container with water. Predict how your observations would change compared with your observations above. Test your prediction.

Shimmering and Mirages

Shimmering and mirages are caused by the refraction of light in unevenly heated air. When light travels through air at different temperatures, it refracts because hot air is less dense than cooler air. Because there is no distinct boundary between sections of air at different temperatures, the light does not bend at one specific point. Instead, it travels along a curved path. Also, because air is usually moving, the direction and the amount of the bending are constantly changing.

Shimmering

You can see shimmering in air above any very hot surface. For example, the air above the hood of a car that has been travelling for a long time or hot asphalt being laid can become very hot, due to contact with the hot surface. When you look through the hot air, objects look wavy, as shown in **Figure 11.27**. Objects often look like they are moving, as well. This apparent movement of objects is called **shimmering**.

Figure 11.27 When you look through the hot air around the engine at the distant plane in the middle of the photograph, the distant plane looks wavy.

shimmering the apparent movement of objects in hot air over objects and surfaces

Chapter 11 Refraction • NEL 471

Mirages

A mirage occurs on a much larger scale than shimmering. The most common place to see a mirage is in a very hot desert or on a highway. The sand or paved surface becomes extremely hot after being in sunlight for several hours. The hot ground heats the air just above it, making the lower layer of air much hotter than the higher air. When sunlight reaches the hot air near the ground, the sunlight is refracted upward.

Because you are accustomed to assuming that light travels in a straight line, you interpret the origin of the light as being on the ground. An object that appears to be on the ground but is not really there is called a **mirage** [pronounced mi-RAHJ]. **Figure 11.28A** shows how a mirage forms. The solid line shows the real path of the light. The dashed line shows where the blue light from the sky appears to have originated. **Figure 11.28B** is a photograph of a mirage on a highway formed in this way.

mirage an optical effect caused by the bending of light rays passing through layers of air that have extremely different temperatures

STSE Case Study

Protecting Your Eyes from UV Radiation

You may wear sunglasses for style and protection from the Sun. Whatever the reason, it may surprise you to learn that your sunglasses could be letting through radiation that is harmful to your eyes.

The brightness of light is illustrated in the bar graph on page 473. Sunglasses are tinted to reduce the amount of visible light that reaches your eyes. The tinting, which is applied as a coating on the lens, is made up of light-absorbing molecules. The thicker the coating is, the darker the lens is. The coating does not block ultraviolet (UV) radiation, however.

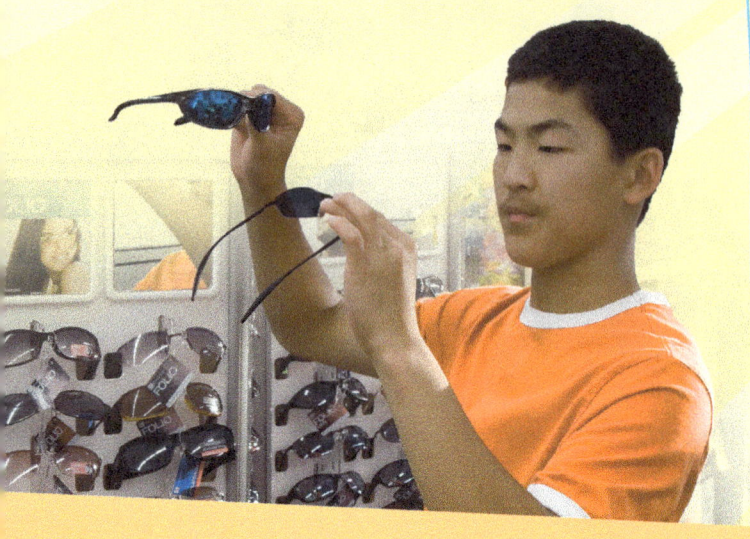

UV Radiation

UV radiation is one of the more energetic types of light in the electromagnetic spectrum. UV radiation causes your skin to tan. If you expose your skin to sunlight for too long, you will get a sunburn. Imagine, therefore, what UV radiation can do to your eyes!

Effects of UV Radiation

- Long-term exposure to UV radiation can damage your eyes.
- Damage from UV radiation cannot be reversed.
- Exposure to UV radiation can contribute to the development of cataracts (a clouding of the natural lens of the eye), cancer, and snow blindness. Snow blindness is a temporary but painful sunburn on the surface of the eyes.

When you buy sunglasses, check the tags to see how much light is blocked. Look for sunglasses that block 99 to 100 percent of UV radiation and 75 to 90 percent of visible light.

Figure 11.28 A The solid, curved line shows the path of light from the sky. The dashed line shows how your brain interprets the scene. **B** The watery area on the road is really a mirage.

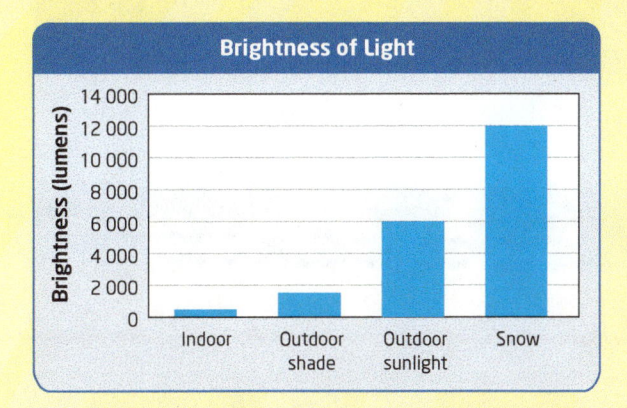

The brightness of light is measured in *lumens*. Your eyes are comfortable up to 4000 lumens. After that, you begin to squint. Sunglasses allow an acceptable amount of light to reach your eyes.

How can you protect your eyes from UV radiation? By simply wearing a cap or a wide-brimmed hat, you can prevent 50 percent of the UV radiation from reaching your eyes. Wearing sunglasses with a special coating will prevent even more UV radiation from reaching your eyes. UV-filtering lenses are coated with special chemicals. These chemicals have a structure that allows visible light to pass through them while reflecting UV radiation away from your eyes.

Wraparound sunglasses offer even more protection because they protect your eyes from UV radiation that enters from the side. Wraparound sunglasses are particularly useful when skiing and when at the beach, where the reflection of sunlight is particularly strong.

Over to You

1. According to the bar graph on the left, how bright is light reflected from snow? Is that level of brightness comfortable for your eyes?

2. Survey your friends and family members to find out how many wear sunglasses and when. What argument could you make to persuade people who do not wear sunglasses to buy a pair to protect their eyes?

3. The lenses of some eyeglasses have features that provide enhanced eye protection. These features include anti-glare coatings, anti-reflective coatings, polarization, and photochromic lenses. Choose one of these features. Research how it protects the eyes. Then design a brochure for an optometrist's office to encourage clients to buy prescription sunglasses that have this feature.

Chapter 11 Refraction • NEL   473

Mirages and Temperature Inversions

Although much less common, a mirage can also be caused by the opposite combination of temperatures. Sometimes, a wind brings warm air over a very cold ocean. This weather condition is called a temperature inversion. Light from an object on the ground starts to travel upward, but it curves and starts back down when it reaches warmer air. The light that reaches an observer can even come from beyond the horizon. When this type of mirage occurs, you think that you are seeing the object in the air. People have seen ships and icebergs, and even buildings from a distant city that appear to be sitting above the ocean.

Depending on the exact paths of the light through the different temperatures of air, part of the object sometimes appears to be upside down. **Figure 11.29** shows a diagram and a mirage in which the object appears to be upright, as well as a diagram and a mirage in which part of the object appears to be upside down.

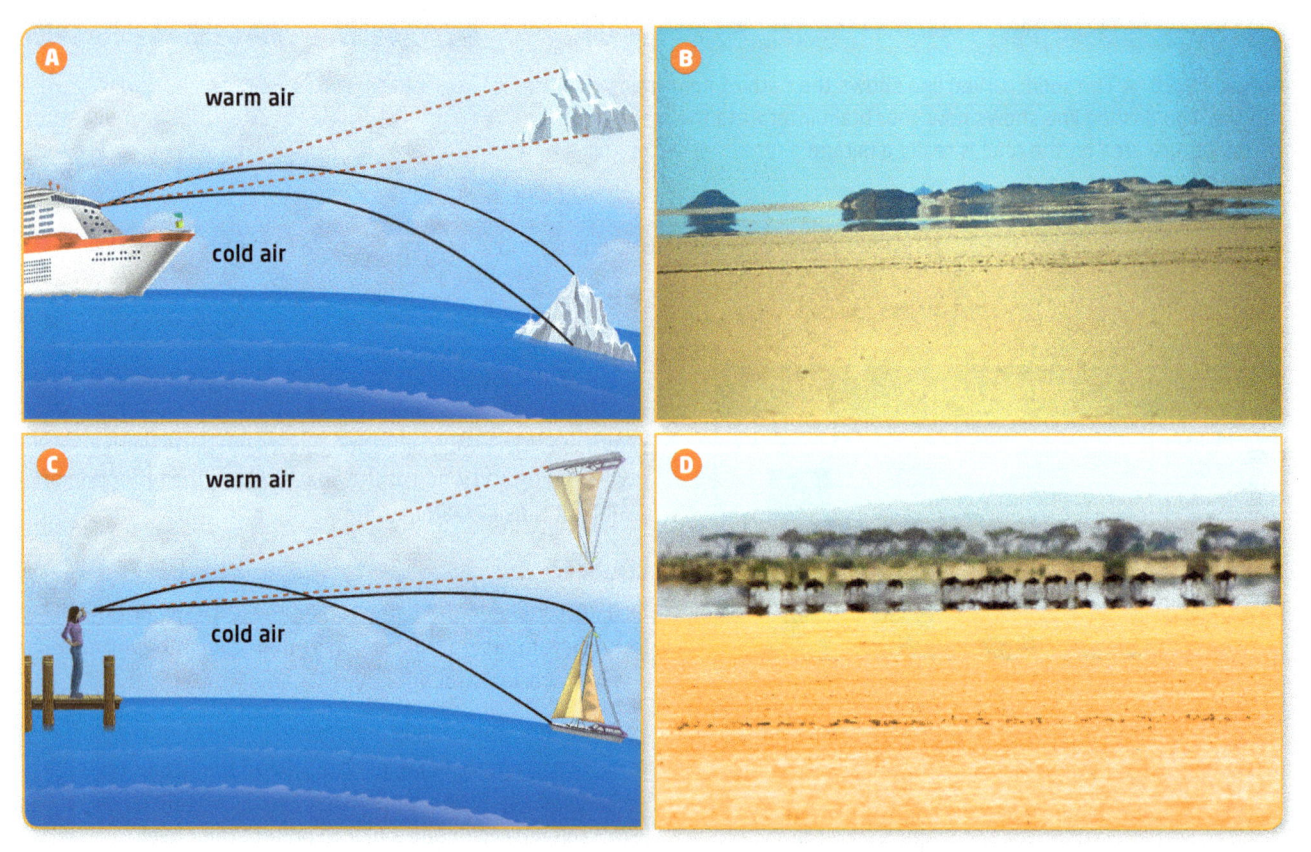

Figure 11.29 **A** The solid, curved lines show the path of light from an object, such as an iceberg. The dashed lines show where the object seems to be. **B** The mountains in this hot desert are a mirage. **C** The curved, solid lines show the path of light from an object, such as a boat. The atmospheric conditions caused the light rays to cross, so the boat appears to be upside down. **D** In this photograph, it looks like the animals are reflected in water, but there is no water. This is a mirage.

Section 11.3 Review

Section Summary

- A rainbow is formed by the refraction and total internal reflection of light and the resulting dispersion of the light by spherical water droplets in the sky.
- As a result of the refraction of light at the surface of water, objects under the water are not where they appear to be when you are looking at them from above the water. The level at which they appear to be is called their apparent depth.
- Shimmering is the apparent movement of objects seen through air that is unevenly heated and moving.
- A mirage is the appearance of water or another object that is not really there. A mirage is caused by light being continuously refracted by layers of air that are at extremely different temperatures.

Review Questions

K/U 1. Under what atmospheric conditions are sundogs likely to appear, and where would they be in the sky?

K/U 2. Use **Figure 11.24B** to explain the sequence of colours that you see in a rainbow.

C 3. Sketch all the conditions that are necessary for you to see a single rainbow. Include the position of the Sun relative to your position.

C 4. Review **Figure 11.25**. Sketch the apparent depth of a fish in a pond when you are looking at the fish from above the water and to the side, at an angle. Explain your sketch.

A 5. An archer fish catches an insect by spitting a stream of water at it to knock it off an overhanging branch. The insect then falls in the water, and the fish eats it. The eyes of the fish remain underwater when it hunts. Only the fish's mouth projects out of the water. Draw a ray diagram based on the photograph on the right to show where the fish must aim to strike the insect.

K/U 6. Explain how understanding the properties of light allows you to explain shimmering images.

K/U 7. What conditions are necessary for a mirage to appear?

C 8. Suppose you are in a hot desert and you see a mirage in which the object is upside down. Sketch the mirage. Show the path that the light rays actually take as well as the path that you assume the light rays take. Refer to **Figure 11.28**.

Use this photograph to answer question 5.

Inquiry Investigation 11-A

Skill Check

Initiating and Planning
✓ Performing and Recording
✓ Analyzing and Interpreting
✓ Communicating

Investigating Refraction, from Air to Water

In this investigation, you will compare the angle of incidence and the angle of refraction when a light ray travels from air into water.

Question

What is the relationship between the angle of incidence and the angle of refraction when light passes from a medium where its speed is greater into a medium where its speed is lower?

Safety Precautions

- Be careful not to spill any water.

Materials

- tap water
- clear, semicircular plastic container
- non-dairy creamer or chalk dust
- stir stick
- ray box
- polar graph paper

Math Skills

Go to **Math Skills Toolkit 3** to learn more about making graphs.

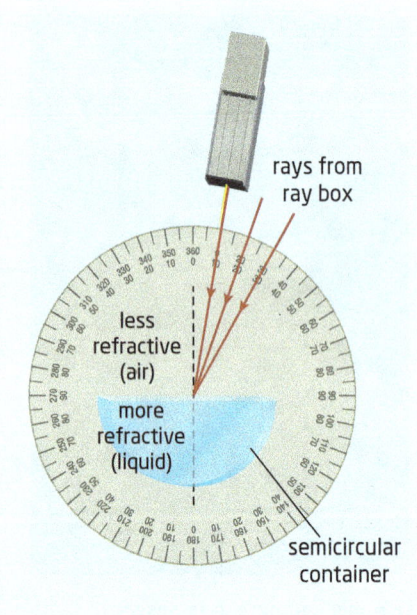

Shine the single beam toward the centre of the semicircular plastic container.

Procedure

1. Design a table or a spreadsheet to record the angle of incidence ($\angle i$) and the angle of refraction ($\angle R$) for eight sets of data. Give your table a title.

2. Put tap water in the container. Dissolve a very small amount of non-dairy creamer in the water. This will make light rays visible in the water.

3. Position the container so that the centre of the flat edge is at the centre of a sheet of polar graph paper. A line joining the 0° to 180° markings should be a normal at the centre of the flat edge of the container.

4. Place a single slit in the ray box. Shine the light ray toward the centre of the container, as shown in the diagram on the left.

5. Shine the light ray along the normal, toward the flat edge of the container, so the angle of incidence is 0°. Record the angle of refraction.

6. Increase the angle of incidence in 10° steps, up to 70°. Record the angle of refraction for each angle of incidence.

Analyze and Interpret

1. Create a graph with the angle of incidence on the *y*-axis and the angle of refraction on the *x*-axis. Give your graph a suitable title. Plot your results, and draw a smooth curve of best fit.

2. Describe and explain the shape of your graph.

Conclude and Communicate

3. Summarize the answer to the investigation question.

Extend Your Inquiry and Research Skills

4. **Research** Research the principle of reversibility. Explain the principle in your own words.

Inquiry Investigation 11-B

Skill Check

Initiating and Planning
✓ Performing and Recording
✓ Analyzing and Interpreting
✓ Communicating

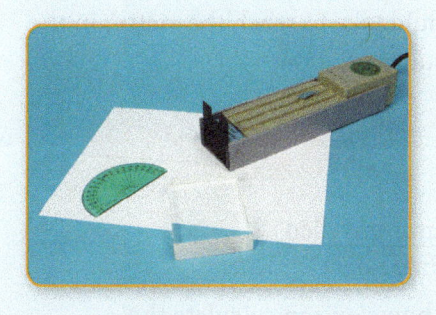

Analyzing the Index of Refraction

In this investigation, you will investigate the refraction of light as it passes through media with different refractive indices and determine whether there is a trend.

Question

How do the angles of refraction and incidence change in media with different indices of refraction?

Safety Precautions

- Be careful not to spill any liquids.
- Ethyl alcohol is volatile. Keep the classroom well ventilated, and keep the container with ethyl alcohol covered.

Materials

- marker
- masking tape
- 4 semicircular plastic containers
- cover for one container
- water
- ethyl alcohol
- glycerol
- glass block
- ray box
- protractor

Procedure

1. Make a table like the one below. Give your table a title.

Material	Angle of Incidence, $\angle i$	Angle of Refraction, $\angle R$	Index of Refraction, n
Air			
Water			
Ethyl alcohol			
Glycerol			
Glass block			

2. Label a semicircular container for each material in the table except for the glass block. Pour water, ethyl alcohol, and glycerol into the containers you labelled for them. Place a cover over the container containing ethyl alcohol.

3. Point a single ray from a ray box into each material listed in your table. Measure and record the angles of incidence and refraction.

4. Refer to **Table 11.1** on page 454. Find the indices of refraction for the materials you tested, and record them in your data table. For the glass block, use the index of refraction for crown glass.

Analyze and Interpret

1. How do the angles of refraction and incidence change in media with different indices of refraction?

Conclude and Communicate

2. Summarize your findings in a statement explaining the trend you observed.

Extend Your Inquiry and Research Skills

3. **Research** Research refractometers. Explain what a refractometer is and how refractometers are useful to society.

Real World Investigation 11-C

Skill Check

Initiating and Planning

✓ Performing and Recording

✓ Analyzing and Interpreting

✓ Communicating

Materials
- calculator

Saving Time

A lifeguard hears cries of distress from someone in the water. To reach the drowning victim as soon as possible, the lifeguard must take one of the three paths shown in the diagram below. Each of the three paths has two parts. First, the lifeguard runs on the sand at 5 m/s. Then the lifeguard swims in the water at 2 m/s. How is the time taken to reach the victim related to the time spent running and the time spent swimming?

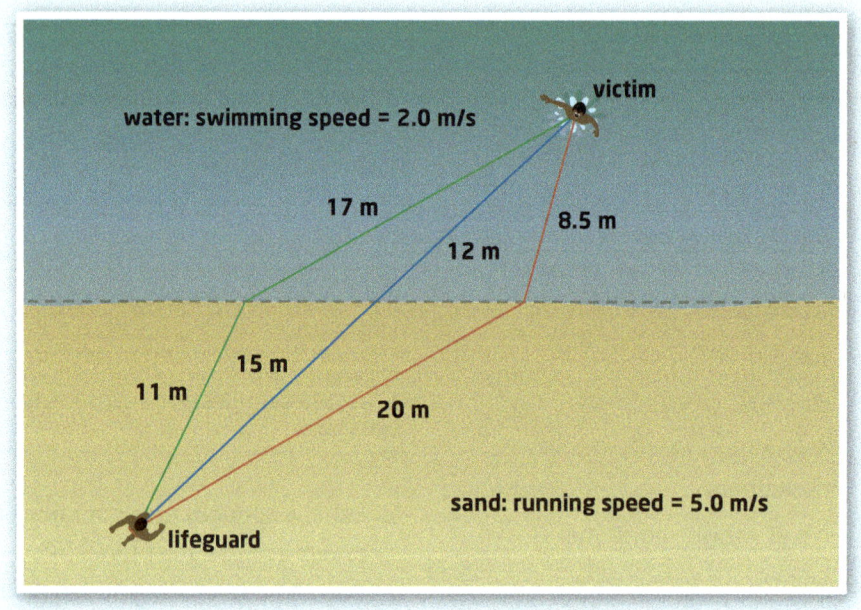

There are three different paths that the lifeguard could take.

Question

How does this analogy illustrate Fermat's principle?

Prediction

Predict which path the lifeguard should take to reach the victim in the shortest amount of time. Explain your prediction.

Organize the Data

1. The formula for speed is

$$\text{speed} = \frac{\text{distance travelled}}{\text{time taken}}$$

Rearrange this formula to show how you can calculate the time taken.

2. Copy the following table into your notebook. Give your table a title. Enter the distance data from the diagram.

Path	Sand Distance (m)	Time Running (s)	Speed (m/s)	Water Distance (m)	Time Swimming (s)	Speed (m/s)	Time to Reach Victim (s)
Green							
Red							
Blue							

3. Calculate the time taken to run and swim along each of the three paths. Show your work, and enter your results in your table.

Analyze and Interpret

4. Which path takes the least time for the lifeguard to rescue the swimmer?

Conclude and Communicate

5. Explain how this analogy illustrates Fermat's principle.

6. Evaluate the analogy.

Extend Your Inquiry and Research Skills

7. **Inquiry** How much time would be lost if the lifeguard chose the blue path, which is a straight line to the victim?

8. **Research** Research the French mathematician Pierre de Fermat (1601–1665), who developed this principle.

A lifeguard has to reach the victim as soon as possible.

Chapter 11 Refraction • NEL 479

Inquiry Investigation 11-D

Investigating Total Internal Reflection in Water

Skill Check

Initiating and Planning
✓ Performing and Recording
✓ Analyzing and Interpreting
✓ Communicating

In this investigation, you will investigate the relationship between the angle of incidence and the angle of refraction when a light ray travels from water into air.

Procedure

1. Design a table or a spreadsheet to record the angle of incidence ($\angle i$), the angle of reflection ($\angle r$), and the angle of refraction ($\angle R$) for several sets of data. Give your table a title.

2. Put tap water in the plastic container. Dissolve a very small amount of non-dairy creamer in the water.

3. Position the container on the polar graph paper, as shown in the diagram on the left. The flat edge of the container must be on the horizontal 90°–90° line, with its centre on the 0°–0° line.

4. Use the ray box to shine a single light ray toward the centre of the straight edge, directly along the normal. Record the angles of incidence, reflection, and refraction.

5. With the light ray directed toward the centre of the straight edge, increase the angle of incidence by increments of 5°. Record the angle of reflection and the angle of refraction. Note the brightness of the reflected and refracted rays relative to each other.

6. When the angle of incidence results in a refracted ray that is close to the flat edge of the container, increase the angle of incidence by increments of 1°. Record the critical angle and your observations when the angle of incidence is greater than the critical angle.

Safety Precautions

- Be careful not to spill any water.

Materials

- tap water
- clear, semicircular plastic container
- non-dairy creamer or chalk dust
- stir stick
- ray box
- polar graph paper

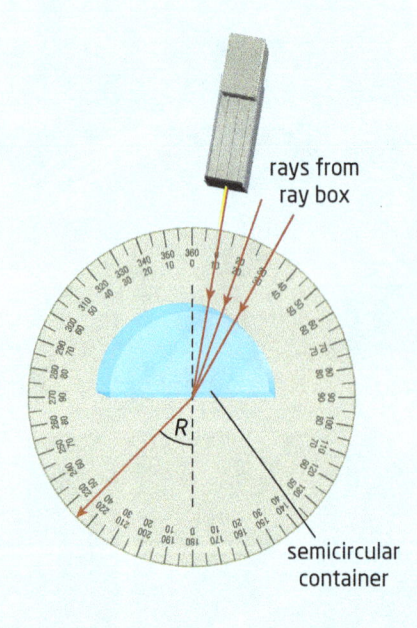

The curved side of the semicircular plastic container must face toward the light source.

Analyze and Interpret

1. Does the incident ray bend when it enters the curved side of the plastic container? Explain your observation.

2. What is the critical angle for light travelling from water into air? What is the angle of refraction at the critical angle?

Conclude and Communicate

3. What happens when the angle of incidence is greater than the critical angle?

Extend Your Inquiry and Research Skills

4. **Inquiry** Design a periscope that uses prisms and total internal reflection.

Chapter 11 Summary

11.1 Refraction of Light

Key Concepts

- Light rays refract when they cross a boundary between media in which the speeds of light are different.
- If a light ray goes from a medium in which its speed is higher (such as air) into a medium in which its speed is lower (such as water), the refracted ray bends toward the normal.
- If a light ray goes from a medium in which its speed is lower (such as water) into a medium in which its speed is higher (such as air), the refracted ray bends away from the normal.
- The index of refraction of a medium is the ratio of the speed of light in a vacuum to the speed of light in the medium. A ratio greater than 1 results.
- Dispersion is the separation of the various colours of light when white light crosses the boundary between different media at an angle.
- The speed of each wavelength of light is different in any given medium. The speed of all wavelengths of light is 3.00×10^8 m/s in a vacuum.

11.2 Partial Refraction and Total Internal Reflection

Key Concepts

- When light strikes a boundary between two transparent media that have different indices of refraction, some light reflects off the boundary and some light refracts through the boundary. This phenomenon is called partial reflection and refraction.
- At a small angle of incidence, more light refracts than reflects. As the angle of incidence increases, more and more light reflects than refracts.
- When light travels from a medium with a higher index of refraction to a medium with a lower index of refraction, the angle of refraction is larger than the angle of incidence. Therefore, an angle of incidence that results in a 90° angle of refraction is eventually reached. This angle of incidence is called the critical angle.
- When the angle of incidence is larger than the critical angle, no refraction occurs. All the light is reflected from the boundary. This phenomenon is called total internal reflection.
- Total internal reflection has many practical applications, such as binoculars, retroreflectors, and optical fibres in telecommunications and in surgical instruments.

11.3 Optical Phenomena in Nature

Key Concepts

- A rainbow is formed by the refraction and total internal reflection of light and the resulting dispersion of the light by spherical water droplets in the sky.
- As a result of the refraction of light at the surface of water, objects under the water are not where they appear to be when you are looking at them from above the water. The level at which they appear to be is called their apparent depth.
- Shimmering is the apparent movement of objects seen through air that is unevenly heated and moving.
- A mirage is the appearance of water or another object that is not really there. A mirage is caused by light being continuously refracted by layers of air that are at extremely different temperatures.

Chapter 11 Review

> **Make Your Own Summary**
>
> Summarize the key concepts of this chapter using a graphic organizer. The Chapter Summary on the previous page will help you identify the key concepts. Refer to Study Toolkit 4 on pages 565-566 to help you decide which graphic organizer to use.

Reviewing Key Terms

1. The ratio of the speed of light in a vacuum to the speed of light in a medium is the _____ of the medium. (11.1)

2. _____ is the separation of white light into its colours. (11.1)

3. The angle of incidence for which the angle of refraction is 90° is called the _____. (11.2)

4. _____ is the apparent movement of objects seen through hot air over objects and surfaces. (11.3)

5. When you think that you are seeing an object but it is not really there, you are seeing a _____. (11.3)

Knowledge and Understanding K/U

6. Explain what happens to a light ray when it goes from air into water at an angle.

7. The speed of each colour (wavelength) of light is different in any given medium. How, then, can a specific index of refraction be reported for a certain substance, such as quartz?

8. Draw a simple diagram of a light ray travelling from one medium into another. Include the following labels: incident ray, normal, refracted ray, angle of incidence, angle of refraction.

9. How would you predict whether an angle of refraction is larger or smaller than the angle of incidence?

10. What information must be included in a table that lists indices of refraction? Why must this information be present?

11. When light crosses the boundary between two substances that have different indices of refraction, what determines the amount of refraction that will occur compared with the amount of reflection?

12. A light ray is travelling from a medium with a larger index of refraction to a medium with a smaller index of refraction. Describe what happens as the angle of incidence gets larger and larger. Include the concept of the critical angle in your discussion.

13. The colours of light can be separated with a prism. What property of light makes this possible?

14. Use a Venn diagram to show the similarities and differences between sundogs and rainbows.

15. Imagine that you are standing in the shallow end of a swimming pool. You look ahead, at the bottom of the pool, and see a coin. Describe the difference between where the coin appears to be and where it actually is.

Thinking and Investigation T/I

16. A clear plastic cube, with exactly the same index of refraction as water, is placed in a container of water. Would you be able to see the plastic cube in the water if you looked at it from an angle? Explain why or why not.

17. Complete the following calculations. Refer to **Table 11.1** on page 454 when necessary.
    a. The speed of light in a solid is 1.96×10^8 m/s. Calculate the index of refraction for the solid.
    b. Calculate the speed of light in diamond.
    c. Calculate the speed of light in ethyl alcohol.
    d. The speed of light in a solid is 1.56×10^8 m/s. Calculate the index of refraction, and identify the solid.

18. Why is a small critical angle desirable for optical fibres? What problems could be caused if the critical angle were increased?

19. The following diagram shows a beaker that contains water and cooking oil. The oil has a higher index of refraction than the water. A light ray is about to enter the cooking oil. Copy the diagram, and show the refracted ray in the oil and then in the water. Ignore the reflected rays.

Use this diagram for question 19.

20. Some of the astronauts who landed on the Moon placed retroreflectors there like the one shown below. What properties of light would you have to know and use if you wanted to determine the exact distance between Earth and the Moon?

This retroreflector is on the Moon.

21. Review Investigation 11-D. The method you used to determine the critical angle of water only works for some liquids. Explain how you could determine the critical angle of a flat piece of glass.

Communication C

22. **BIG IDEAS** Society has benefited from the development of a range of optical devices and technologies. Give two examples.

23. Using a sketch, explain how a rearview mirror can be set for daytime driving and nighttime driving.

24. Using a sketch, explain how a retroreflector can reverse the direction of a light ray.

25. Imagine that you and a friend are hiking across a hot desert. Your friend believes that he sees a pool of water and starts to run toward the water. How could you convince your friend not to exert himself unnecessarily? In your explanation, include a description of the different indices of refraction of the layers of air of different temperatures.

26. In the following diagram, wave fronts are travelling across the boundary between air and water. Explain the significance of the change in the distance between the wave fronts where the light passes from air into water. Draw a similar diagram, but have the light approaching the boundary along a normal, so the angle of incidence is zero. Show and explain what happens when the wave fronts are parallel to the boundary as the light crosses the boundary.

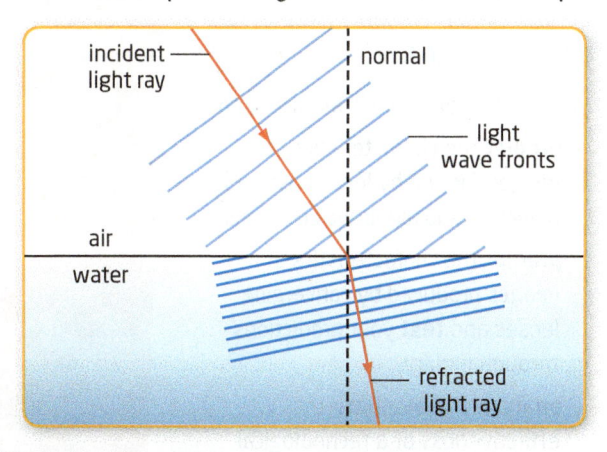

27. Review your observations for Activity 11-1, The Re-appearing Coin, on page 447. Based on what you have learned in this chapter, explain your observations.

Application A

28. Identify two careers related to optics from this chapter.

29. Astronomers can learn a lot about stars by studying the wavelengths of light that are emitted by stars. Some of the early instruments that were used to analyze starlight contained prisms. Explain what you think the function of these prisms is.

Chapter 11 Refraction • NEL 483

Chapter 12 Lenses and Lens Technologies

What You Will Learn

In this chapter, you will learn how to...
- **describe** the characteristics of images formed by lenses
- **identify** ways in which lenses are used in optical instruments, such as microscopes
- **describe** a technological device and a procedure that use the properties of light

Why It Matters

Many everyday devices require lenses, such as eyeglasses. By understanding how lenses work, you will be able to appreciate how they contribute to your everyday life.

Skills You Will Use

In this chapter, you will learn how to...
- **predict** the characteristics of images formed by lenses using ray diagrams and algebraic equations
- **predict** the characteristics of images produced by converging lenses and **test** your predictions through inquiry
- **analyze** and **evaluate** the effectiveness of a technological procedure related to human sight
- **evaluate** the benefits to society of a technological device that uses properties of light

Cataract eye surgery is very common. The doctor removes the clouded lens of the eye and replaces it with a plastic lens. To perfect the procedure, doctors must understand the functions of the eye and artificial and natural lenses.

Activity 12-1

The Disappearing Finger

Your eyes are relatively sensitive to seeing objects and detecting movement at the edge of your vision. Can you determine the sensitivity of your eyes yourself? In this activity, you will estimate your field of view.

While looking at a distant object, cover your right eye with your left hand.

Procedure

1. Look straight ahead, and focus on a distant object.
2. Cover your right eye with your left hand. Extend your right arm sideways.
3. While continuing to stare straight ahead, wiggle the centre finger on your right hand. Keeping your arm outstretched, slowly move your arm forward until you can just see your finger.
4. Keep your head position fixed, and move your left eye toward the wiggling finger. Record your observations.
5. Ask another student to estimate the angle between your head (think of your nose as a normal) and your outstretched arm. Record this angle.
6. Repeat steps 1 to 5, making the appropriate changes, to investigate your vision in your right eye.

Questions

1. Explain the observations you recorded in step 4.
2. When looking ahead, what is your approximate field of view, expressed as an angle?

Chapter 12 Lenses and Lens Technologies • NEL   485

Study Toolkit

These strategies will help you use this textbook to develop your understanding of science concepts and skills. To find out more about these and other strategies, refer to the Study Toolkit Overview, which begins on page 560.

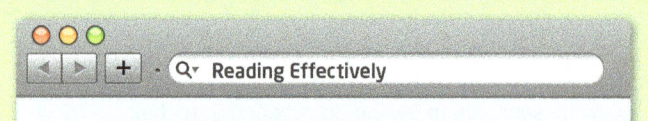

Reading Effectively

Making Connections to Prior Knowledge

You may already know some facts about lenses and the human eye from your own experiences, from reading other texts, or from the media. This prior knowledge can help you understand new information in this chapter. As you read, ask yourself these questions:

- What personal experience does this remind me of? (connect text to self)
  Example: My glasses help things at a distance come into focus.

- What have I read about this before? (connect text to text)
  Example: I read an article about athletes having laser eye surgery.

- What are some new developments in vision correction? (connect text to world)
  Example: On the news, I heard about contact lenses that dispense medication for eye diseases while also correcting vision.

Use the Strategy

Read the first two paragraphs on page 487. Make some connections to your prior knowledge about lenses. Draw a **concept map** to show the connections.

Organizing Your Learning

Using Graphic Organizers

Different graphic organizers can be used for different purposes, as shown in the table below.

Uses for Different Graphic Organizers

Purpose	Possible Graphic Organizers	Pages Where Sample Is Shown
To organize main ideas and supporting details	**Web, chart, spider map**	565–566
To show cause and effect, steps in a process, or a sequence	**Cause-and-effect map, web, flowchart**	565–566
To compare and contrast	**Venn diagram**	566
To analyze a series of numbers or results	**Graph, table**	556, 545

Use the Strategy

Read the text about Galileo's telescope and Kepler's telescope on page 502. Identify the main ideas and record them using a graphic organizer of your choice. Compare your completed graphic organizer with that of a classmate. Which one helps you understand and remember the information better? Why?

Word Study

Word Families

A word family is a group of words that share a common element. For example, the words in the table on the right all have the ending -opia, meaning a condition related to sight. Recognizing word families can help you grasp the meanings of similar words.

Use the Strategy

Make a table like the one on the right. Find three more words in the -opia word family, and add them to the table.

Words Sharing the Ending -opia

Word	Combining Part	Common Element	Definition of the Whole Word
myopia	my	opia	Near-sightedness
hyperopia	hyper	opia	Far-sightedness
presbyopia	presby	opia	Condition in which lenses of the eye become stiff and the muscles can no longer make the lenses change shape

12.1 Characteristics of Lenses

Key Terms
lens
converging lens
diverging lens
chromatic aberration

A **lens** is a transparent object with at least one curved side that causes light to refract. Like mirrors, lenses have surfaces defined as concave and convex, and you can predict characteristics of images produced by lenses, such as in a camera.

You may have focussed a camera while taking pictures and observed the lens moving in and out. This type of focussing is not convenient in applications such as cellphone cameras and instruments such as an endoscope (see page 466). An electronics company has developed a liquid lens, shown in **Figure 12.1**. The lens can change shape and, as you will learn in this section, the shape changes the focal length of the lens. As a result, the liquid lens does not need to move in and out to focus on objects that are nearby or far away.

The liquid lens consists of two liquids sealed in a transparent tube. The liquids have different indices of refraction, and they will not mix together. The shape of the surface between the liquids determines the focal length of the lens. Once the lens is placed in its holder, electrical leads send a potential difference across the tube. The potential difference alters the lens properties such that the shape of the surface between the two fluids changes. The precise shape of the surface, and therefore the focal length of the lens, is controlled by the potential difference.

lens a transparent object with at least one curved side that causes light to refract

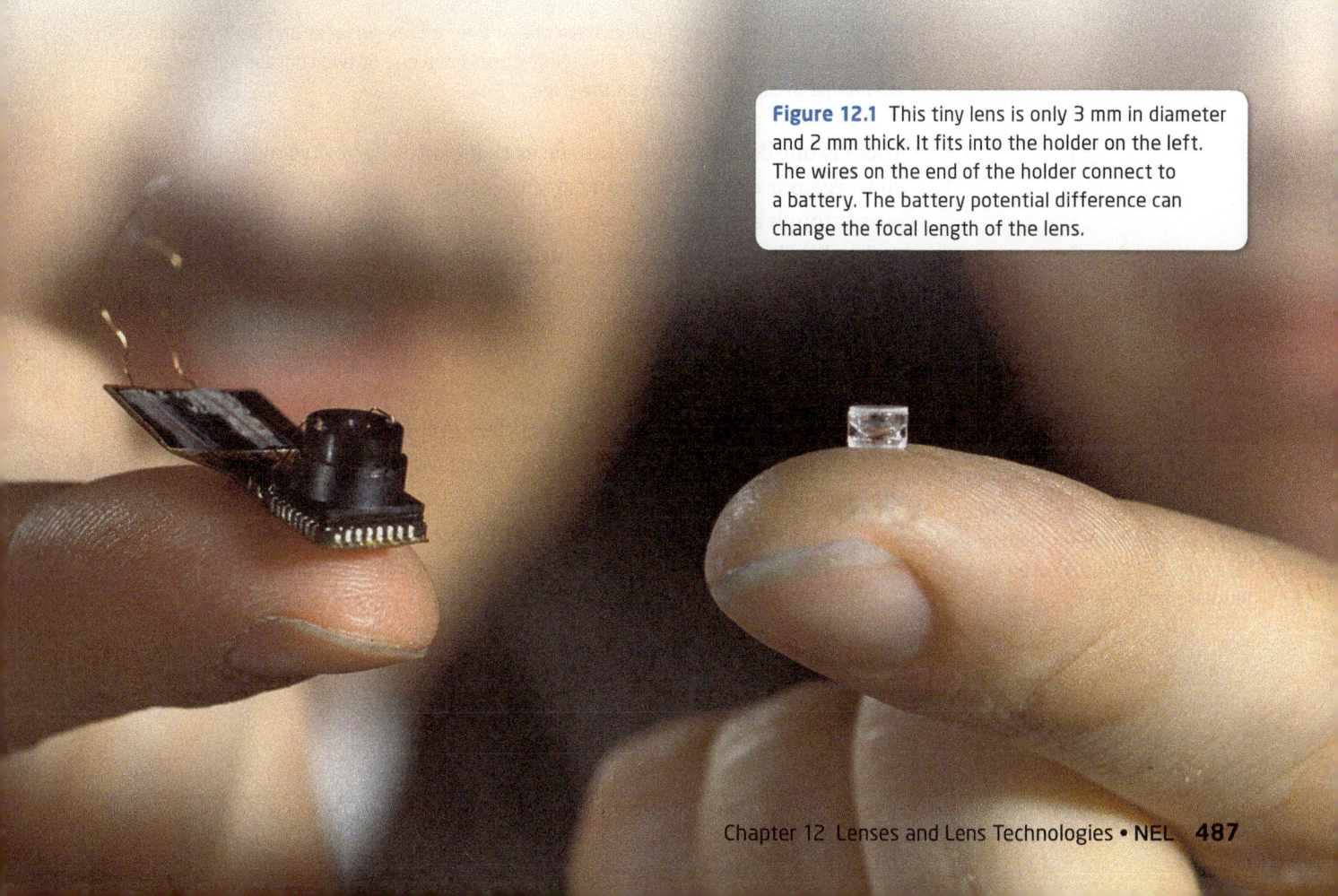

Figure 12.1 This tiny lens is only 3 mm in diameter and 2 mm thick. It fits into the holder on the left. The wires on the end of the holder connect to a battery. The battery potential difference can change the focal length of the lens.

Figure 12.2 Reading stones such as this were used mostly by nuns, monks, and scholars because, around 1000 C.E., they were almost the only people who knew how to read.

Describing Lenses

The first known lenses that were developed to magnify print on a page were "reading stones," like the one shown in **Figure 12.2**. The reader moved the stone across the page and read a few words at a time. As scientists learned more about refraction and lenses, they developed a wide variety of lenses for many applications. To understand the applications, you need to learn some of the basic properties of lenses.

The terms *plane*, *concave*, and *convex* are used to describe lenses as well as mirrors, but lenses have two sides. Either side can be plane, concave, or convex. For example, reading stones have one convex side and one plane side. There are many possible shapes for lenses. Fortunately, you do not have to learn about each individual shape. You need only be concerned with the overall effect that lenses have on parallel rays of light that pass through them. One class of lenses causes parallel light rays to spread away from a common point, or *diverge*. The other class of lenses causes parallel light rays to come together, or *converge*, toward a common point. **Figure 12.3** shows different combinations of surfaces for lenses.

A Converging Lenses   **B** Diverging Lenses

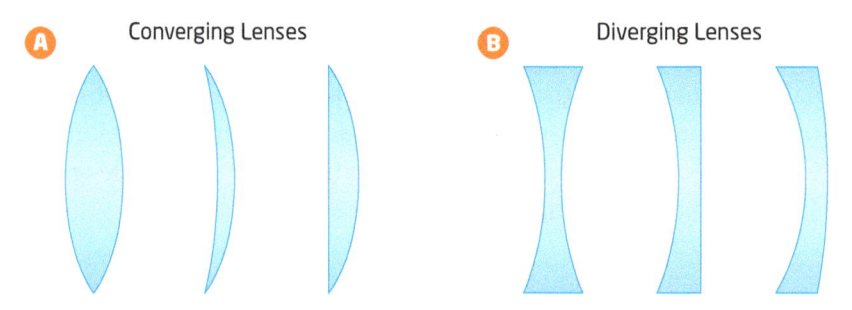

Figure 12.3 A Converging lenses have one or two convex surfaces and are thicker in the centre than on the edges. **B** Diverging lenses have one or two concave surfaces and are thinner in the centre than on the edges.

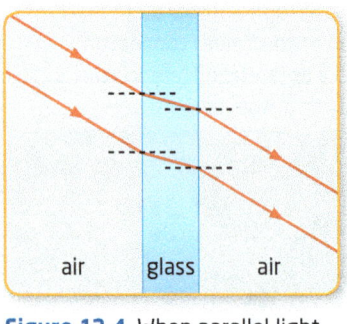

Figure 12.4 When parallel light rays pass through a flat piece of glass like a window pane, the rays shift to the side but do not change their direction relative to each other. This is called lateral displacement.

There is one combination of surfaces that causes light rays to neither converge nor diverge. **Figure 12.4** shows what happens to light rays that pass through a piece of glass that has two plane sides that are parallel to each other, like a window pane. Recall from Chapter 11 that when light travels from a medium with a low refractive index to a medium with a high refractive index, the rays bend toward the normal. Therefore, when light rays enter a piece of glass with a plane surface, the rays bend toward the normal. On the far side of the glass, the rays will bend away from the normal by the same amount that they first bent toward the normal. All rays shift to the side (are laterally displaced), but when they leave the glass, they are travelling in the same direction as when they entered. Because there has been no change in the direction of the rays relative to each other, such a piece of glass (or other transparent material) cannot be considered a lens. However, this information is important to keep in mind when studying lenses.

Converging Lenses

Converge means "to bring together." **Converging lenses** bring parallel light rays toward a common point as shown in **Figure 12.5A**. The shape that most easily illustrates how parallel rays are brought together is a lens that is convex on both sides, or *biconvex*. When rays are incident on the surface on the left side of the lens, they move from a fast medium to a slow medium. Thus, the rays refract toward the normals, causing the rays to converge slightly. When the light rays leave the second surface of the lens, they move from a slow medium to a fast medium, and refract away from the normals. Because of the direction of the normals at this surface, the rays continue to converge.

Diverging Lenses

Diverge means "to spread out in different directions." **Diverging lenses** cause parallel rays to spread away from a common point. A good example of a diverging lens is a lens that is concave on both sides, or *biconcave*. **Figure 12.5B** shows how parallel light rays refract at each surface of a biconcave lens. Note that **Figure 12.5** also shows the axis of symmetry. You may recall from earlier studies that the *axis of symmetry* is a line that divides a shape into two congruent parts that can be matched by folding the shape in half.

> **converging lens** a lens that brings parallel light rays toward a common point

> **Suggested Investigation**
> Inquiry Investigation 12-A, Image Characteristics of a Converging Lens, on page 512

> **diverging lens** a lens that spreads parallel light rays away from a common point

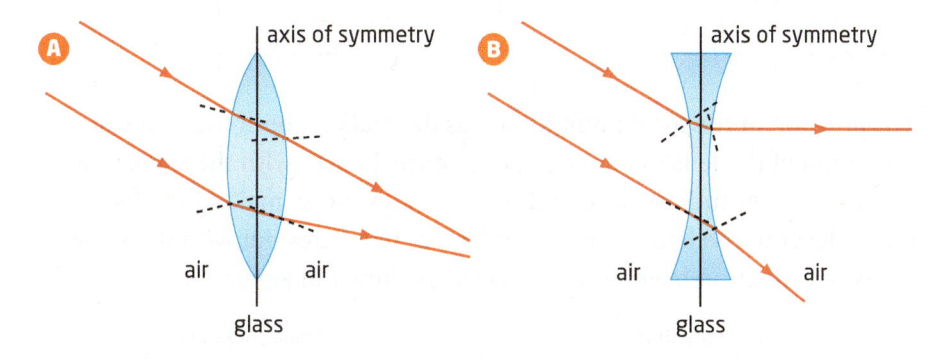

Figure 12.5 In **A**, when parallel rays exit a converging lens, they are travelling toward each other. In **B**, when parallel rays exit a diverging lens, they are travelling away from each other.

Learning Check

1. What properties of a piece of glass or plastic make it a lens?
2. Compare the shapes of converging and diverging lenses in **Figure 12.3**.
   a. What characteristic makes one lens converging and another diverging?
   b. Make a sketch of a converging lens and of a diverging lens. Give both lenses one plane side.
3. Sketch a lens with one convex side and one plane side. Show how two parallel rays would refract as they pass through this lens.
4. Depending on the type of vision correction a person needs, contact lenses can be converging or diverging. However, each of the two sides must have a specific shape because the lens must fit on the surface of the eye. What must be the shape—convex, concave, or plane—of the inside of a contact lens? Explain.

> **Study Toolkit**
>
> **Word Families** *Converging* and *diverging* belong to the same word family. A table like the one on page 486 can help show the meanings of these two words.

Focal Point and Focal Length of Lenses

The principal axis of a lens is a straight line that passes through the centre of the lens, normal to both surfaces of the lens, as with mirrors. When rays that are parallel to the principal axis pass through a converging lens, the rays intersect at a point. As with a concave mirror, this point is called the focal point (F), as shown in **Figure 12.6A**. After parallel rays pass through a diverging lens, the rays diverge. Only by tracing the rays backward do we see that they converge to a point. This point is a virtual focus, as shown in **Figure 12.6B**. Because light can pass through a lens from either side, there are actually two focal points for a lens. These two focal points are the same distance from the centre of the lens. The distance from the centre of the lens to the focal point is the focal length (f).

Figure 12.6 In **A** and **B**, notice that the focal point is symbolized by a capital F, and the focal length is symbolized by a lower-case f. In **B**, the dashed lines indicate that there are no actual rays travelling along these paths.

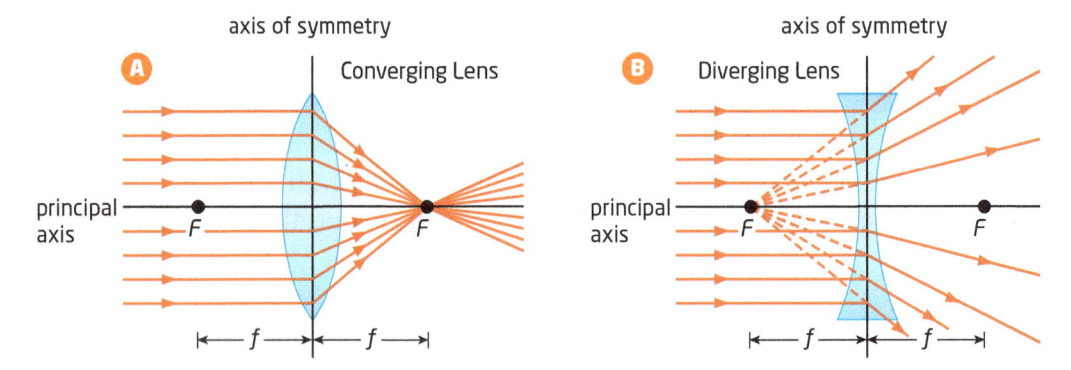

The position of the focal point for a lens depends on both the index of refraction of the lens material and curvature. Lenses with the same shape but with higher indices of refraction bend rays more, making the focal point closer to the lens. Lenses with larger curvatures but with the same index of refraction have the same effect, as shown in **Figure 12.7**.

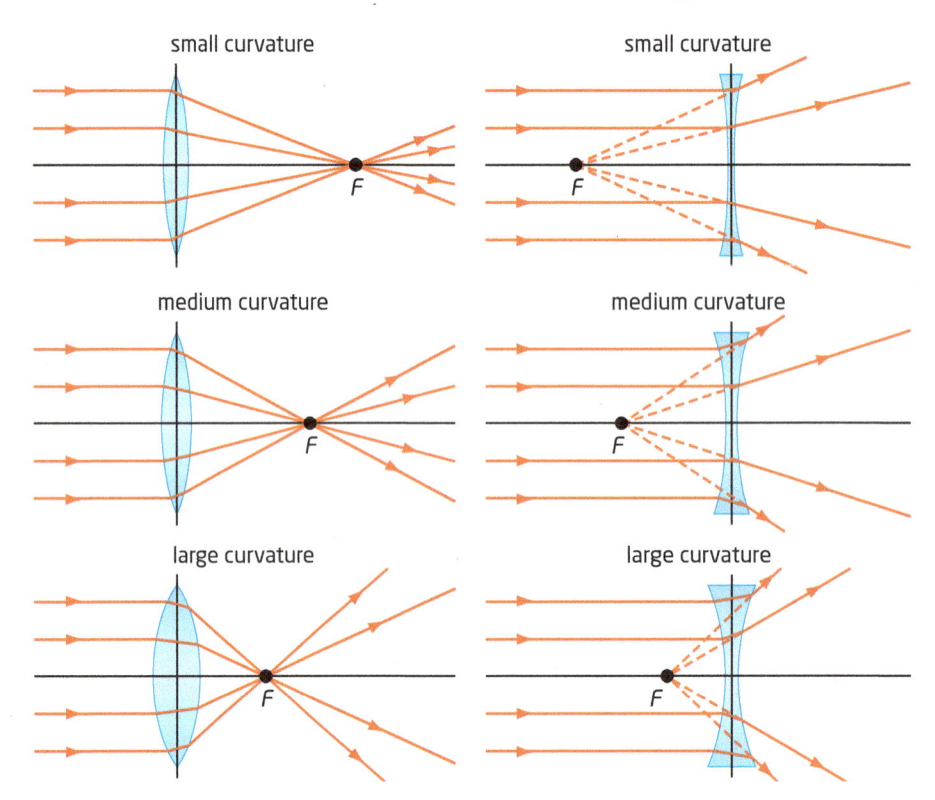

Figure 12.7 If the index of refraction of three different lenses is the same, then the relative focal lengths are determined by the curvature of the lens for both converging and diverging lenses.

Activity 12-2

Hocus Focus

In this activity, you will compare different converging lenses and determine image characteristics and focal lengths.

Materials
- several different converging lenses
- sheet of paper
- metric ruler

Procedure

1. In your notebook, make a table with the headings shown below to record your results. Give your table a title.

Description of Lens	Description of Image	Maximum Thickness of Lens (mm)	Focal Length (cm)

2. Find a location where you can use a distant, bright light source, such as an open window on the far side of the classroom. In one hand, hold a converging lens. In the other hand, hold a sheet of paper to act as a screen.

3. Point the lens toward the light source, and support the paper screen so that the lens is between the screen and the light source. As you look through the lens, move the screen back and forth until you see a focussed image of the light source on the screen.

4. Measure the distance from the centre of the lens to the paper screen. Record this measurement in your table.

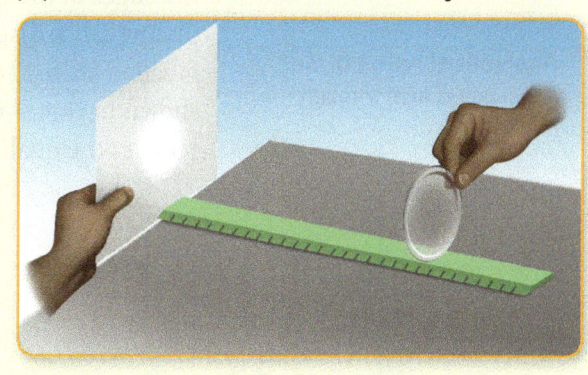

Record the distance from the paper screen to the lens.

5. In your table, describe the image you see on the screen. Describe the lens by noting whether each lens surface is the same shape. Measure the thickness of the lens at its centre.

6. Repeat steps 3 to 5 for other converging lenses.

Questions

1. Write a sentence describing the image formed by a converging lens when the object is far from the lens.

2. How does the thickness of a converging lens affect its focal length?

Effect of Large Lens Curvature

Figure 12.8 shows an image taken with a fish-eye lens. A fish-eye lens has a very short focal length.

Thick and Thin Lenses

Recall from Chapter 10 that spherical aberration occurs when light rays from an object strike a curved mirror far from the principal axis and fail to form a clear image point. Lenses produce spherical aberration for the same reason. If the lenses are very thin, the effect is not noticeable. (The lenses in **Figure 12.6** on page 490 represent the ideal thin lenses.) For thick lens, only light rays that pass through the lens *near the principal axis* meet at the focal point and give a sharp image.

Figure 12.8 A fish-eye lens drastically distorts the image, but it brings a much larger area into view.

Chapter 12 Lenses and Lens Technologies • NEL 491

Chromatic Aberration

Look at **Figure 12.9A**. Rays that are farther from the principal axis of a converging lens do not pass through the focal point. The same condition applies to diverging lenses.

The edges of lenses are similar in shape to prisms, so the edges of lenses disperse the light into colours, as shown in **Figure 12.9B**. Compare the edges of the lens with **Figure 11.8** on page 453 to review the way that prisms cause dispersion. When applied to a lens, this dispersion of light is called **chromatic aberration**. An example of chromatic aberration is shown in **Figure 12.9C**. Spherical and chromatic aberration in thick lenses reduces the quality of images in cameras.

chromatic aberration the dispersion of light through a lens

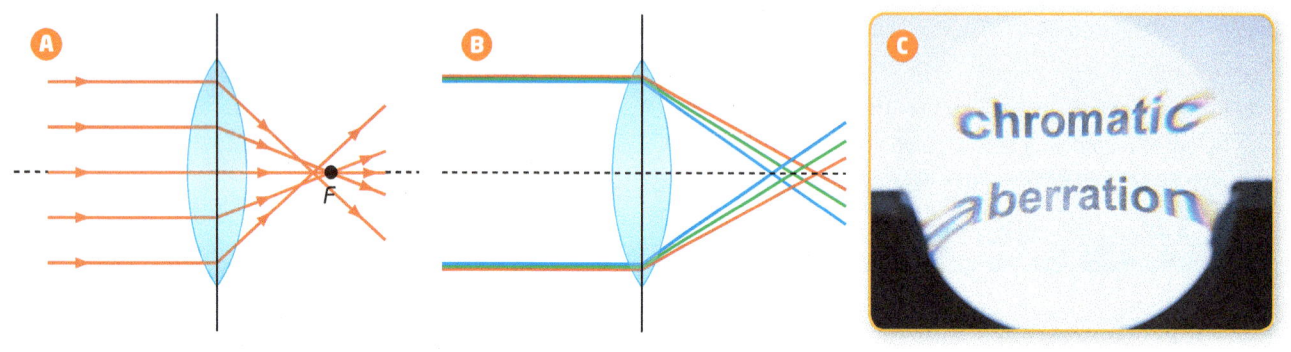

Figure 12.9 In **A**, a single thick lens with spherical surfaces cannot focus all parallel rays at the same point. In **B**, as a result of dispersion, different colours of light are focussed at different points. In **C**, chromatic aberration is most visible along the edges of objects.

Spherical and chromatic aberration can be partially corrected by combining one or more lenses, especially if the lenses are made of materials with different indices of refraction. **Figures 12.10A** and **B** show some combinations of lenses that partially correct for spherical and chromatic aberration. High-quality lenses for expensive cameras usually use a combination of many lenses to reduce aberration as much as possible, as seen in **Figure 12.10C**. Aberrations are not significant if lenses are very thin. When learning about ray diagrams and formulas for lenses, you will consider thin lenses only.

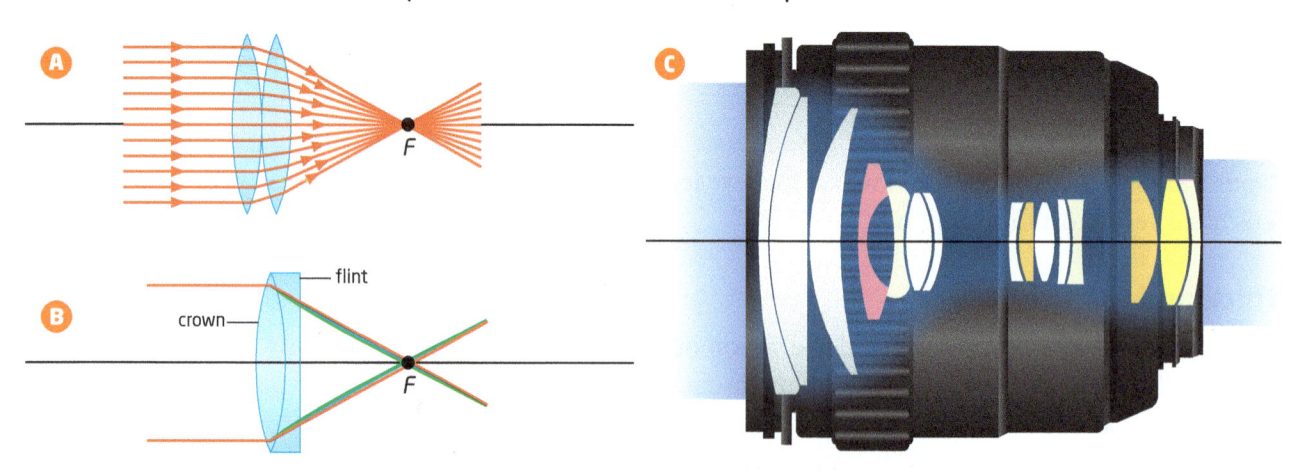

Figure 12.10 Diagram **A** shows that two separate lenses that are thinner than a single lens can reduce spherical aberration. Diagram **B** shows how a combination of lenses made of different types of glass can reduce chromatic aberration. Diagram **C** shows one way to reduce spherical and chromatic aberration in high-quality cameras. As you can see, a combination of many lenses is necessary.

Section 12.1 Review

Section Summary

- Lenses are classified as either converging or diverging, depending on how they affect parallel light rays that refract through them.
- Converging lenses have one or two convex surfaces and are thicker in the centre than on the edges. Diverging lenses have one or two concave surfaces and are thinner in the centre than on the edges.
- The focal point of a converging lens is the point at which parallel rays meet after passing through the lens. The focal point of a diverging lens is the point from which the diverging rays appear to have come after parallel rays have passed through the lens.
- With thick lenses, rays that are farther from the principal axis do not pass through the focal point. This causes spherical aberration.
- Different colours of light have different indices of refraction. Therefore, they focus at different points. This causes chromatic aberration.

Review Questions

1. Why are lenses *not* categorized according to whether their sides are concave, convex, or plane?

2. Define the terms *converging lens* and *diverging lens*. Use a diagram to illustrate your definitions.

3. Classify each of the lenses below as either converging or diverging.

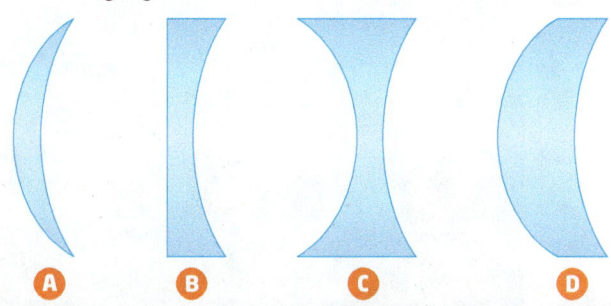

   A   B   C   D

4. Make a sketch that shows how to find the focal point of a diverging lens. Include the focal length of the lens.

5. Why do lenses have two focal points on the principal axis instead of one?

6. The photograph on the right has an aberration. Where is the aberration greatest? Why?

7. Using a diagram, show and explain what chromatic aberration is and why it occurs. Describe how high-quality cameras eliminate chromatic aberration. Refer to **Figure 12.10C**.

8. Explain why spherical aberration affects images formed in mirrors and lenses but chromatic aberration only occurs with lenses.

Key Term

thin lens equation
magnification equation

Go to **scienceontario** to find out more

12.2 Images Formed by Lenses

In **Figure 12.11**, you can see images through two different lenses. In **Figure 12.11A**, the lens has magnified the object and the image appears to be closer than the actual object. In **Figure 12.11B**, the image through the lens is smaller than the object and appears to be farther away than the object.

Using ray diagrams, you can predict the location, orientation, size, and type of image as it appears through a lens. As with mirrors, once the focal point has been identified, three key rays, chosen close to the principal axis, simplify the task of locating an image point produced by the lens.

As shown in **Table 12.1**, a ray that leaves an object parallel to the principal axis converges through the focus on the image side. A second ray that passes through the focus on the object side leaves the lens parallel to the principal axis. It intersects the first ray and forms an image point. If drawn neatly, a third ray through the centre of the lens should pass through the same image point. Note that in **Table 12.1**, the ray diagrams are simplified in two ways. First, partial reflection and refraction is ignored. Second, the refraction that should occur at each surface is replaced with only one bend at the axis of symmetry of the lens, which is represented by a vertical line through the centre of the lens.

Figure 12.11 **A** The image is larger than the object and appears to be closer.
B The image is smaller than the object and appears to be farther away.

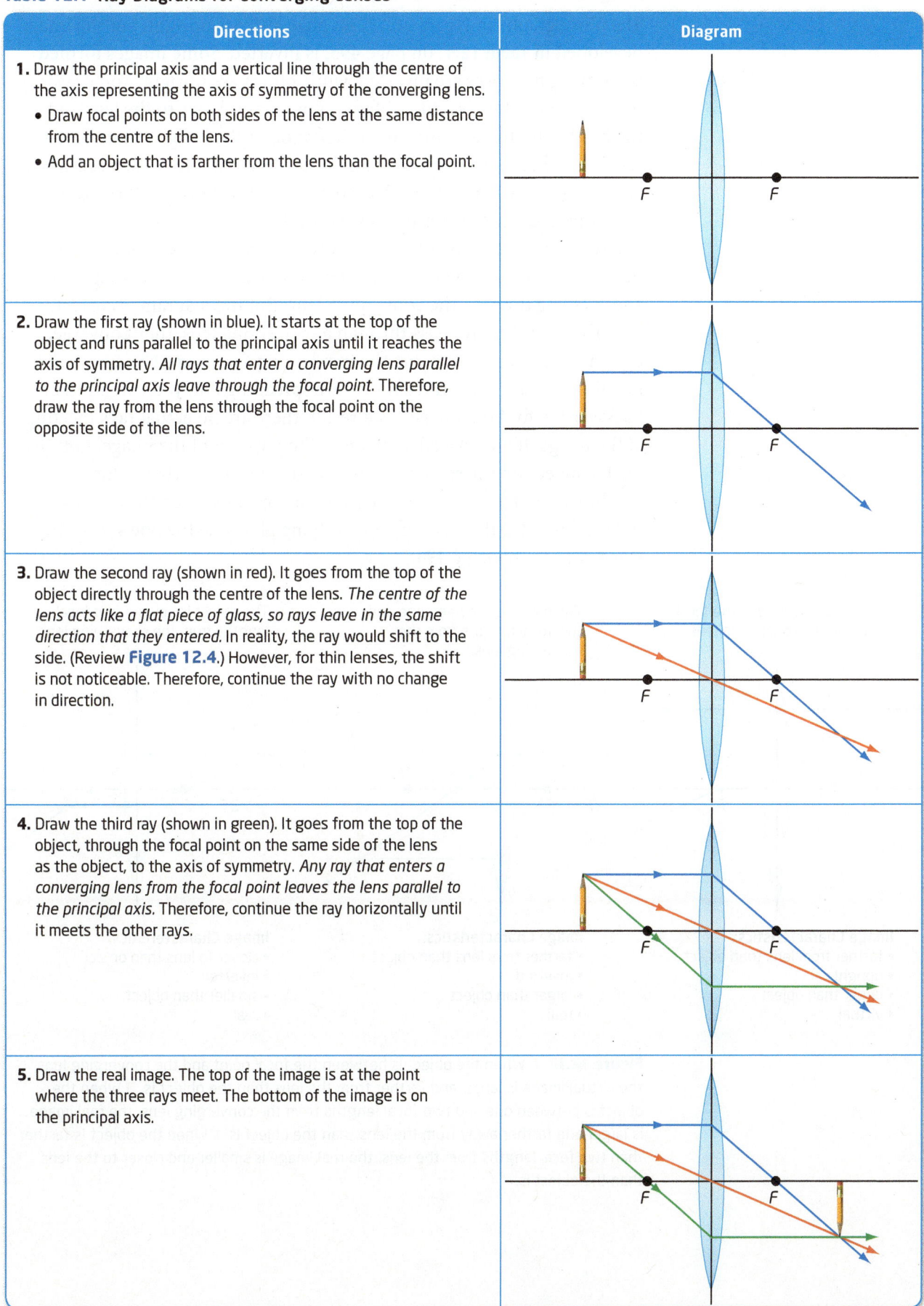

Table 12.1 Ray Diagrams for Converging Lenses

Directions	Diagram
1. Draw the principal axis and a vertical line through the centre of the axis representing the axis of symmetry of the converging lens. • Draw focal points on both sides of the lens at the same distance from the centre of the lens. • Add an object that is farther from the lens than the focal point.	
2. Draw the first ray (shown in blue). It starts at the top of the object and runs parallel to the principal axis until it reaches the axis of symmetry. *All rays that enter a converging lens parallel to the principal axis leave through the focal point.* Therefore, draw the ray from the lens through the focal point on the opposite side of the lens.	
3. Draw the second ray (shown in red). It goes from the top of the object directly through the centre of the lens. *The centre of the lens acts like a flat piece of glass, so rays leave in the same direction that they entered.* In reality, the ray would shift to the side. (Review **Figure 12.4**.) However, for thin lenses, the shift is not noticeable. Therefore, continue the ray with no change in direction.	
4. Draw the third ray (shown in green). It goes from the top of the object, through the focal point on the same side of the lens as the object, to the axis of symmetry. *Any ray that enters a converging lens from the focal point leaves the lens parallel to the principal axis.* Therefore, continue the ray horizontally until it meets the other rays.	
5. Draw the real image. The top of the image is at the point where the three rays meet. The bottom of the image is on the principal axis.	

Chapter 12 Lenses and Lens Technologies

Image Characteristics in Converging Lenses

The photographs in **Figure 12.11**, on page 494, are upright, but the image developed in **Table 12.1**, on page 495, is inverted. Some images formed by converging lenses are inverted, while others are upright. You draw ray diagrams with the object in different positions relative to the lens and the focal point to determine the orientation of the image. **Figure 12.12** shows ray diagrams with objects in locations similar to those used when analyzing images in mirrors. The characteristics of images formed by lenses are the same as those formed by mirrors.

At first glance, some of the features in **Figure 12.12A** might appear to be incorrect for a converging lens. For example, the three rays spread out after passing through the converging lens. But the diagram is correct.

When *parallel* rays pass through a converging lens, they converge, or come together. Notice that the incident rays in **Figure 12.12A** are not parallel. Because the refracted rays are spreading out, you extend them backward to find the image. As a result, there are no actual rays meeting at the image. If you placed a screen in the position of the image, nothing would appear on the screen. Therefore, the image is virtual. This combination of a converging lens and an object between the lens and the focal point is the basis of a magnifying glass like the one shown in **Figure 12.11A**, on page 494.

A The object is between the focal point and the converging lens.

Image Characteristics:
- farther from lens than object
- upright
- larger than object
- virtual

B The object is between one and two focal lengths from the converging lens.

Image Characteristics:
- farther from lens than object
- inverted
- larger than object
- real

C The object is beyond two focal lengths from the converging lens.

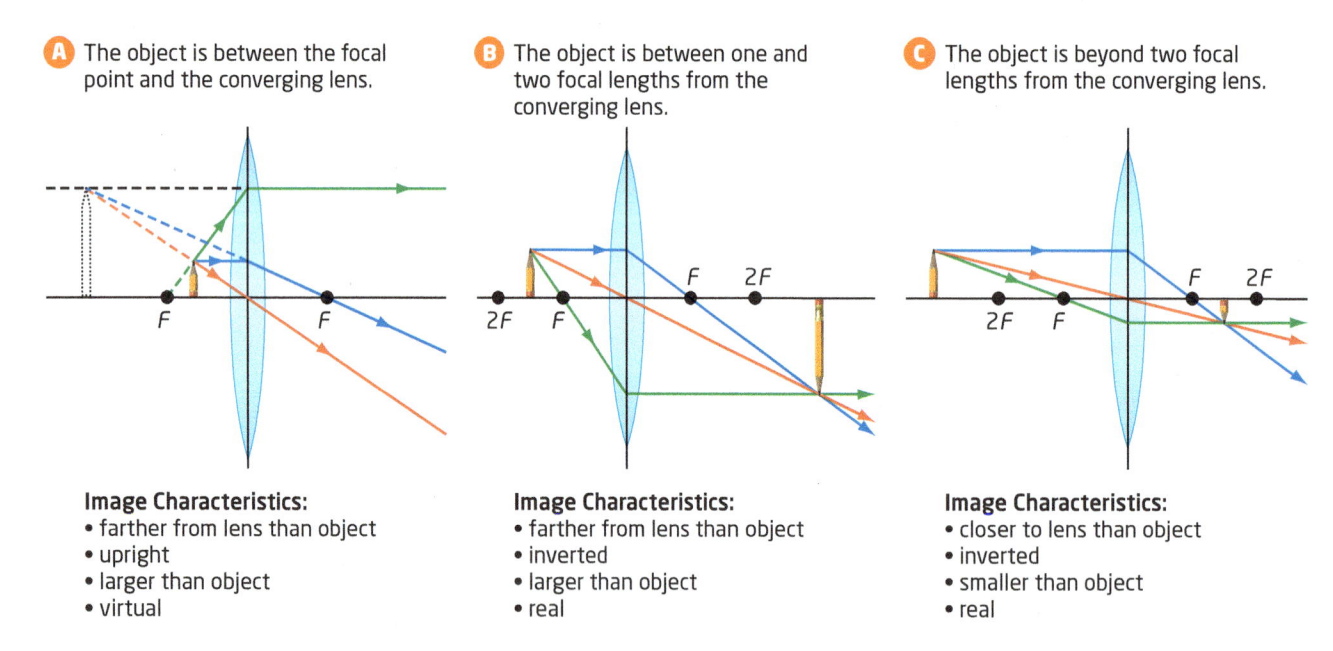

Image Characteristics:
- closer to lens than object
- inverted
- smaller than object
- real

Figure 12.12 A When the object is between the focal point and the converging lens, the virtual image is larger and farther from the lens than the object is. **B** When the object is between one and two focal lengths from the converging lens, the real image is larger and farther away from the lens than the object is. **C** When the object is farther than two focal lengths from the lens, the real image is smaller and closer to the lens than the object is.

Drawing Ray Diagrams for Diverging Lenses

Examine **Table 12.2** to find out how to draw ray diagrams for diverging lenses.

Table 12.2 Ray Diagrams for Diverging Lenses

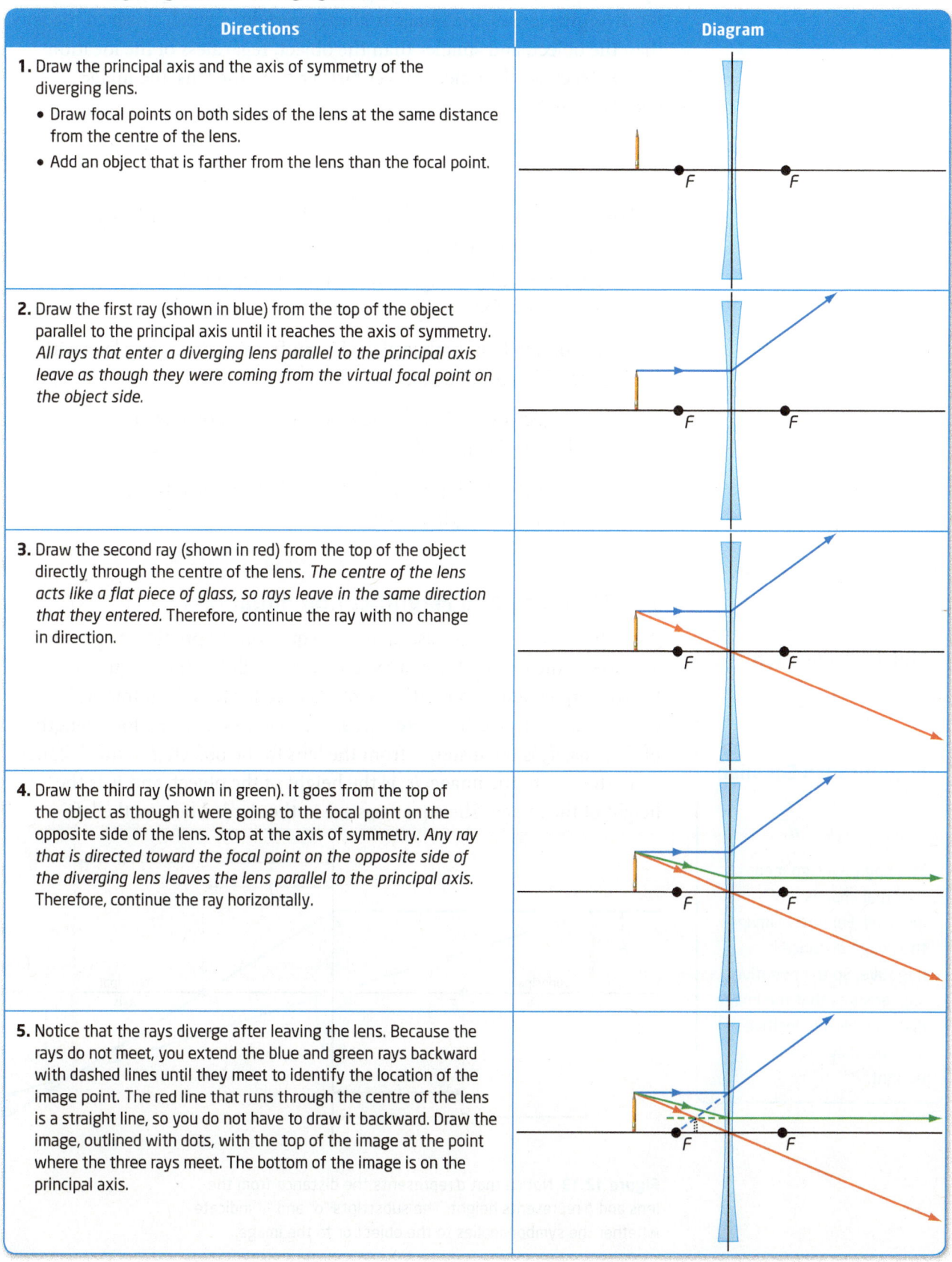

Directions	Diagram
1. Draw the principal axis and the axis of symmetry of the diverging lens. • Draw focal points on both sides of the lens at the same distance from the centre of the lens. • Add an object that is farther from the lens than the focal point.	
2. Draw the first ray (shown in blue) from the top of the object parallel to the principal axis until it reaches the axis of symmetry. *All rays that enter a diverging lens parallel to the principal axis leave as though they were coming from the virtual focal point on the object side.*	
3. Draw the second ray (shown in red) from the top of the object directly through the centre of the lens. *The centre of the lens acts like a flat piece of glass, so rays leave in the same direction that they entered.* Therefore, continue the ray with no change in direction.	
4. Draw the third ray (shown in green). It goes from the top of the object as though it were going to the focal point on the opposite side of the lens. Stop at the axis of symmetry. *Any ray that is directed toward the focal point on the opposite side of the diverging lens leaves the lens parallel to the principal axis.* Therefore, continue the ray horizontally.	
5. Notice that the rays diverge after leaving the lens. Because the rays do not meet, you extend the blue and green rays backward with dashed lines until they meet to identify the location of the image point. The red line that runs through the centre of the lens is a straight line, so you do not have to draw it backward. Draw the image, outlined with dots, with the top of the image at the point where the three rays meet. The bottom of the image is on the principal axis.	

Chapter 12 Lenses and Lens Technologies • NEL 497

Image Characteristics in Diverging Lenses

As you can see in **Figure 12.11B**, on page 494, the image is upright and smaller than the object. This observation agrees with the image developed by the ray diagram for a diverging lens in **Table 12.2**, on page 497. In fact, for diverging lenses, the image is *always* upright, virtual, closer to the lens than the object, and smaller than the object, regardless of the location of the object. As the object moves farther from the lens, the image becomes smaller.

> **Learning Check**
>
> For each situation below, draw a ray diagram and describe the four characteristics of the image.
>
> 1. An object 1.5 cm high is placed 4 cm in front of a converging lens with a focal length of 3 cm.
> 2. An object 1 cm high is placed 5 cm from a converging lens with a focal length of 2 cm.
> 3. An object 1 cm high is placed 4 cm in front of a diverging lens with a focal length of 3 cm.
> 4. An object 1 cm high is placed 5 cm in front of a diverging lens with a focal length of 2 cm.

The Thin Lens and Magnification Equations

As with mirrors, you can use algebraic equations to predict the position and size of the images formed by lenses. You will use these equations for converging lenses only. The symbols used for lens diagrams and equations, illustrated in **Figure 12.13**, are as follows: f is the focal length of the lens, d_o is the distance from the lens to the object, d_i is the distance from the lens to the image, h_o is the height of the object, and h_i is the height of the image. The equations are in the shaded box on the left.

Thin Lens Equation

$$\frac{1}{f} = \frac{1}{d_i} + \frac{1}{d_o}$$

Magnification Equation

$$m = \frac{h_i}{h_o} = \frac{-d_i}{d_o}$$

The negative sign means that real images are inverted. For virtual images, the image distance is negative. So the negative sign ensures that the image distance will be positive and the image will be upright.

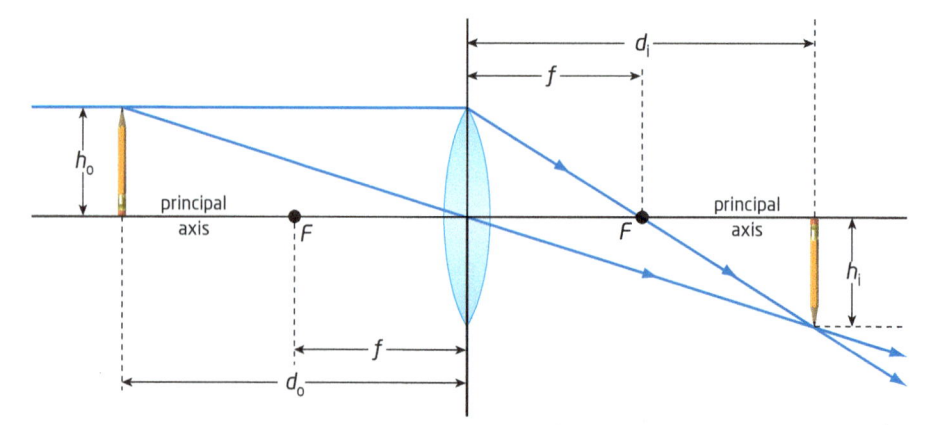

Figure 12.13 Notice that d represents the distance from the lens and h represents height. The subscripts "o" and "i" indicate whether the symbol applies to the object or to the image.

Sample Problem: Using the Thin Lens and Magnification Equations for Converging Lenses

Problem
An object 8.5 cm high is placed 28 cm from a converging lens. The focal length of the lens is 12 cm.

a. Calculate the image distance, d_i.

b. Calculate the image height, h_i.

Solution

a. You know the object distance, $d_o = 28$ cm; the focal length of the lens, $f = 12$ cm; and the object height, $h_o = 8.5$ cm.

Arrange the thin lens equation to solve for d_i. Substitute the known values into the equation, and solve for d_i.

$$\frac{1}{f} = \frac{1}{d_o} + \frac{1}{d_i}$$

$$\frac{1}{d_i} = \frac{1}{f} - \frac{1}{d_o}$$

$$= \frac{1}{12 \text{ cm}} - \frac{1}{28 \text{ cm}} = \frac{7}{84 \text{ cm}} - \frac{3}{84 \text{ cm}}$$

$$= \frac{4}{84 \text{ cm}} = \frac{1}{21 \text{ cm}}$$

$$d_i = 21 \text{ cm}$$

The image is 21 cm from the lens.

b. You know the object distance, $d_o = 28$ cm; the focal length of the lens, $f = 12$ cm; and the object height, $h_o = 8.5$ cm. From part a, you know that the image distance is $d_i = 21$ cm.

Arrange the magnification equation to solve for h_i. Substitute the known values, and solve for h_i.

$$m = \frac{h_i}{h_o} = \frac{-d_i}{d_o}$$

$$\frac{h_i}{h_o} = \frac{-d_i}{d_o}$$

$$h_i = \frac{(-d_i)(h_o)}{d_o} = \frac{(-21 \text{ cm})(8.5 \text{ cm})}{28 \text{ cm}} = -6.375 \text{ cm}$$

The image height is 6.4 cm (after rounding). The negative sign means that the image is inverted.

Check Your Solution
Because the distance from the object to the converging lens is more than two times the focal length, the image should be smaller than the object, inverted, and closer to the lens than the object. The solution confirms these characteristics.

GRASP
Go to **Science Skills Toolkit 11** to learn about an alternative problem solving method.

Hint: Starting with the equation

$$\frac{1}{d_i} = \frac{1}{12 \text{ cm}} - \frac{1}{28 \text{ cm}},$$

use the 1/x button to evaluate the second two terms. Put 12 in your calculator, and press the 1/x button. You will get 0.8333. Now put 28 in your calculator, and press the 1/x button. You will get 0.0357. Your equation has become

$$\frac{1}{d_i} = 0.083\,33 - 0.0357$$

$$= 0.04762$$

Press the 1/x button again, and the result is $d_i = 21$ cm.

Practice Problems

1. A converging lens has a focal length of 12.0 cm. An object 6.30 cm high is placed 54.0 cm from the lens. Calculate the image distance and the image height.

2. An object 7.50 cm high is placed 150 cm from a converging lens that has a focal length of 90.0 cm. Calculate the image distance and the image height.

3. An object that is 4.20 cm high is placed 84.0 cm from a converging lens that has a focal length of 120.0 cm. Calculate the image distance and the image height.

4. A real, inverted image that is 96.0 cm high is formed 144 cm from a converging lens. The object is 36.0 cm from the lens. (**Hint:** Remember that an inverted image is indicated by a negative sign in front of the image height, h_i.) Calculate the focal length and the object height.

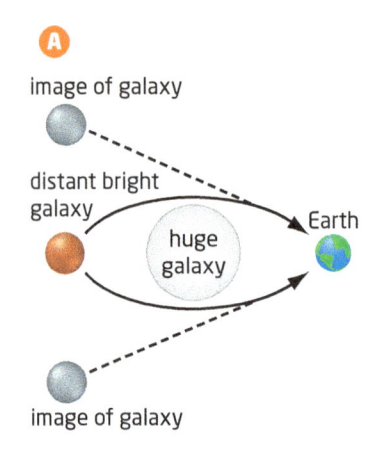

Figure 12.14 A The solid lines show the actual path of the light from the bright galaxy. The dashed lines are the path that the observer on Earth perceives that the light is following. **B** The bright area in the centre is a huge galaxy, and the blue ring is the light from a bright galaxy behind the huge one.

Gravitational Lenses

The famous scientist Albert Einstein proposed that gravity can bend light. According to Einstein's calculations, only a huge galaxy or collection of galaxies is massive enough to bend light enough to observe the effect. According to Einstein, if there were an extremely bright galaxy directly behind a huge galaxy, relative to Earth, the light from the extremely bright galaxy would be bent around the huge galaxy, as illustrated in **Figure 12.14A**. An observer would see the light as a ring around the huge galaxy, like the image in **Figure 12.14B**.

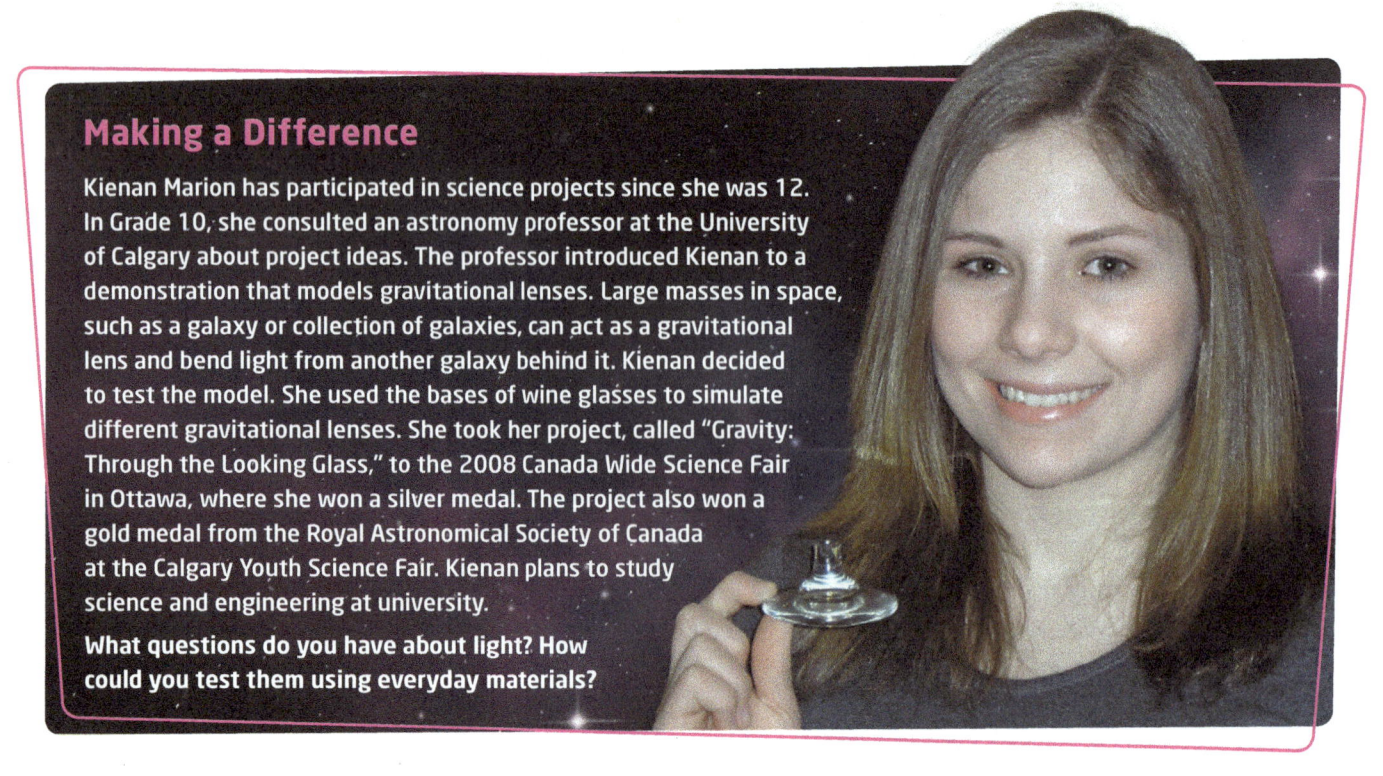

Making a Difference

Kienan Marion has participated in science projects since she was 12. In Grade 10, she consulted an astronomy professor at the University of Calgary about project ideas. The professor introduced Kienan to a demonstration that models gravitational lenses. Large masses in space, such as a galaxy or collection of galaxies, can act as a gravitational lens and bend light from another galaxy behind it. Kienan decided to test the model. She used the bases of wine glasses to simulate different gravitational lenses. She took her project, called "Gravity: Through the Looking Glass," to the 2008 Canada Wide Science Fair in Ottawa, where she won a silver medal. The project also won a gold medal from the Royal Astronomical Society of Canada at the Calgary Youth Science Fair. Kienan plans to study science and engineering at university.

What questions do you have about light? How could you test them using everyday materials?

Section 12.2 Review

Section Summary

- Ray diagrams consisting of three rays can be drawn to determine the characteristics of images formed by lenses.
- When an object is between a converging lens and the focal point, the image is always virtual, upright, and larger than the object.
- When an object is farther from a converging lens than the focal point, the image is always real and inverted.
- When an image is formed by a diverging lens, it is always upright, virtual, smaller than the object, and on the same side as the object.
- Given the focal length of the lens and the size and location of the object, you can use algebraic equations to calculate the characteristics of the image.

Review Questions

1. Copy the table on the right into your notebook. The conditions are for an object in front of a converging lens. Describe and then explain how the rays travel.

2. When an object is between a converging lens and the focal point of the lens, the three rays appear to diverge. Why, then, is the lens considered to be a converging lens?

3. Assume that an image is real, inverted, larger than the object, and farther from the lens than the object.
   a. What type of lens is forming the image?
   b. Where is the object located relative to the lens?

4. Refer to **Figure 12.11B**. Describe the image size and orientation relative to the object. What type of lens formed the image?

5. An object 5.50 cm high is placed 100 cm from a converging lens that has a focal length of 40.0 cm. Calculate the image distance and the image height.

6. Copy the diagram on the right, and complete a ray diagram. Describe the four characteristics of the image.

7. Solve the following problem by using both a ray diagram and algebraic equations. An object that is 3.0 cm high is placed 14 cm from a converging lens that has a focal length of 8.0 cm. Calculate the distance of the image and the image height.

8. What is a gravitational lens?

Ray Diagrams for Converging Lenses

Condition	Where the Ray Goes	Explanation
a. The ray travels parallel to the principal axis until it reaches the converging lens.		
b. The ray travels toward the centre of the lens.		
c. The ray travels through the focal point (or as though it were coming from the focal point) and on to the lens.		

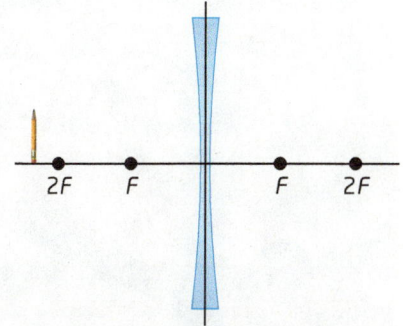

Use this diagram for question 6.

Key Terms

objective lens
eyepiece
cornea
retina
myopia
hyperopia
presbyopia
astigmatism
night-vision device

12.3 Lens Technologies and the Human Eye

In 1608 C.E., Galileo Galilei (1564–1642) heard about the invention of telescopes. Within a year, he was designing and building his own. In 1610 C.E., he discovered four of Jupiter's moons using his homemade telescope, similar to the one shown in **Figure 12.15**. He was also able to see craters on the Moon and the phases of Venus (like phases of the Moon). He made these discoveries before the theory of lenses had been fully developed—a remarkable accomplishment.

However, when Galileo increased the magnification, the field of view—the area that he could see—became smaller. For example, when he looked at the Moon, he could not see the entire Moon. His telescope was also affected by spherical and chromatic aberration.

Telescope Modifications

The famous astronomer Johannes Kepler (1571–1630) modified the design of Galileo's telescope to get greater magnification, but his changes also inverted the image. If he had used it to look at objects on Earth, the inverted image would have been very distracting. However, when studying the skies, the inverted image was not a problem.

Galileo's telescope used two lenses—a converging lens and a diverging lens. He used the converging lens for the objective lens. Light enters the telescope through the **objective lens**. He used the diverging lens for the eyepiece. The observer looks into the **eyepiece**, and light leaves the telescope through the eyepiece.

objective lens the lens through which light enters a telescope

eyepiece the lens in a telescope through which the observer views the object and through which light leaves the telescope

Figure 12.15 Galileo made some remarkable discoveries in astronomy using a telescope like this one.

Ray Diagrams for Telescopes

Figure 12.16 shows a ray diagram for a telescope like Galileo's. Notice that F_1 is the focal point of the objective lens and F_2 is the focal point of the eyepiece. The two lenses are positioned so that the focal points to the right of both lenses are at the same place. Rays (shown in red) from a distant star or planet pass through the objective lens. If the eyepiece lens were not present, the objective lens would focus the image to the far right of the diagram. However, the rays reach the eyepiece before an image is formed. The eyepiece lens refracts the rays (shown in green) and creates a virtual, upright image between the two lenses.

Suggested Investigation
Inquiry Investigation 12-C, Make a Simple Telescope, on page 516

Figure 12.16 In Galileo's telescope, the objective lens alone would produce an inverted image. The eyepiece changes it into an upright image.

A ray diagram of Kepler's telescope is shown in **Figure 12.17**. The two lenses are positioned so that their focal points are at the same point between the lenses. Light from distant stars or planets enters through the objective lens and forms an image between the two lenses. These rays are shown in red. The image formed by the objective lens becomes the object for the eyepiece lens. Light from the first image then passes through the eyepiece lens and forms a virtual image that appears to come from just beyond the objective lens. The rays coming from the first image to the eyepiece are shown in green. The final image is inverted and is larger than the image formed by the objective lens.

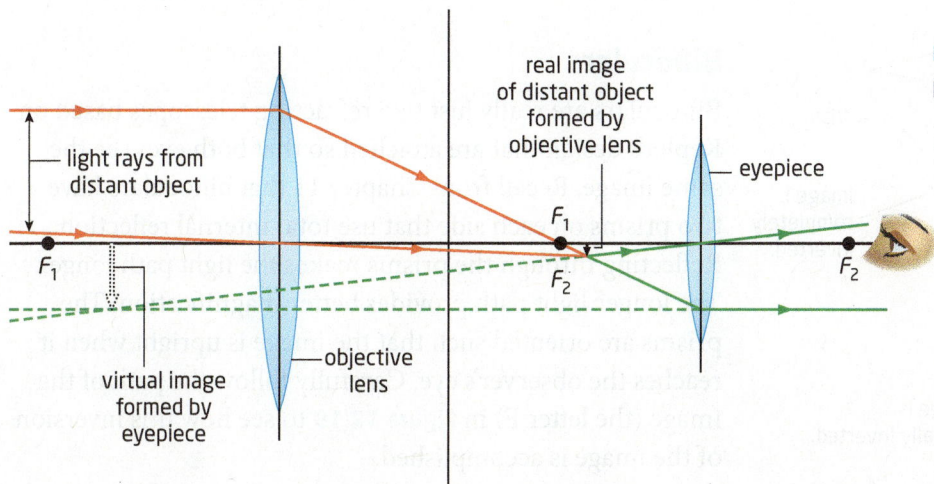

Figure 12.17 Kepler's telescope produces an inverted image.

Chapter 12 Lenses and Lens Technologies • NEL 503

Sense of Value

Sir Isaac Newton's desire to improve telescope design led him to study optics in more detail. In the 1600s, he made ground-breaking contributions to the study of optics and light.

Newton's Innovation

Sir Isaac Newton (1642–1727) was very distracted by the chromatic aberration in Galileo's and Kepler's telescopes. He was able to significantly reduce the chromatic aberration by using a concave mirror as the objective. A ray diagram for Newton's telescope is shown in **Figure 12.18**. Light enters the telescope and travels to the concave mirror objective. The mirror reflects the light toward focal point F_1. Before the rays reach F_1, a flat mirror reflects them to F_2, the focal point of the eyepiece lens. Rays from F_2 pass through the eyepiece, which magnifies the image.

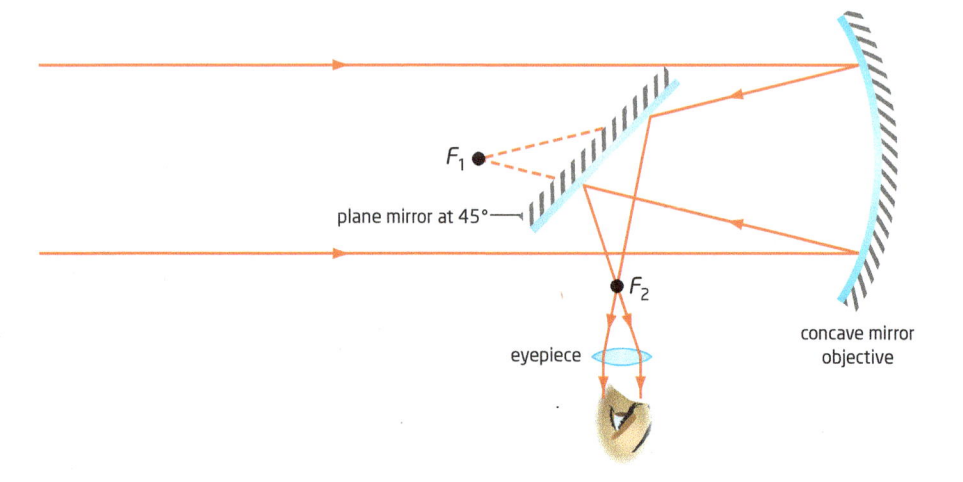

Figure 12.18 The curved mirror in Newton's telescope would form a real image inside the telescope if the flat mirror were not present. The flat mirror reflects the image through a tube to the side of the telescope for viewing.

Modern Telescopes

Although tremendous advances have been made in telescopes, all modern telescopes are based on the designs of Galileo, Kepler, and Newton. Those based on the Galileo and Kepler telescopes are called *refracting telescopes* because they only use lenses. Telescopes based on Newton's design are called *reflecting telescopes* because they also include a mirror.

An important feature of all optical telescopes is the amount of light that they are able to collect. If too little light is collected, a star might be in the field of view but still may not be seen. The only way to allow in more light is to make the objective lens or mirror as large as possible but still maintain a precise shape. A large objective lens is more difficult to make than a large mirror, so most large, modern telescopes are reflecting telescopes.

Figure 12.19 The first prism inverts the image side to side, and the second prism inverts the image up and down.

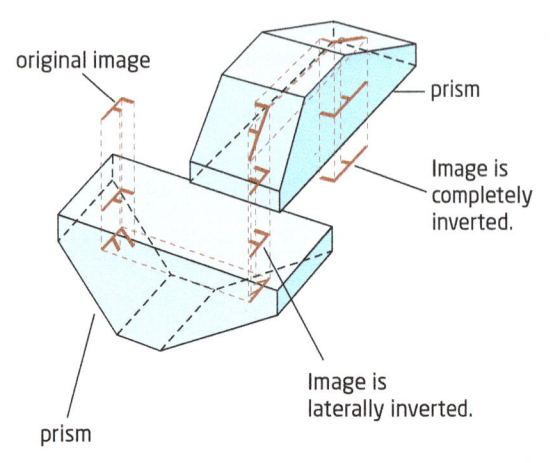

Binoculars

Binoculars are really just two refracting telescopes based on Kepler's design that are attached so that both eyes see the same image. Recall from Chapter 11 that binoculars have two prisms on each side that use total internal reflection. Reflecting through the prisms makes the light path longer. The longer light path provides better magnification. The prisms are oriented such that the image is upright when it reaches the observer's eye. Carefully follow the path of the image (the letter F) in **Figure 12.19** to see how this inversion of the image is accomplished.

Microscopes

As you may know from previous science classes, the purpose of a microscope is to make a tiny specimen larger. The microscope was invented in 1590 by Johannes and Zacharias Jansen, from the Netherlands. At the time, microscopes were used mainly to study plant and animal specimens. Today, microscopes are used in many more applications, such as studying human cells, animal cells, and minerals. Some doctors and medical researchers use microscopes to investigate diseases and even figure out the cause of a person's death.

Ray Diagrams for Microscopes

If you have used a microscope similar to the one in **Figure 12.20** in your classroom, you may remember the objective lenses and the eyepiece, or ocular lens. **Figure 12.21** is a ray diagram for a microscope, but it has been rotated 90° so that it is horizontal. The figure shows the path of light rays from the specimen to the eye of the observer. Rays from the specimen (shown in red) pass through the objective lens, and the refracted rays form an inverted, real image between the lenses. Rays from the image (shown in green) pass through the eyepiece, which again refracts the rays, and then form the final inverted, virtual image.

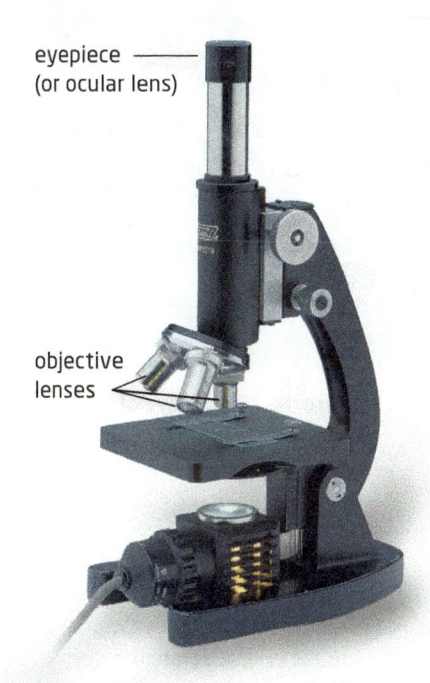

Figure 12.20 You have probably used a classroom microscope similar to this one.

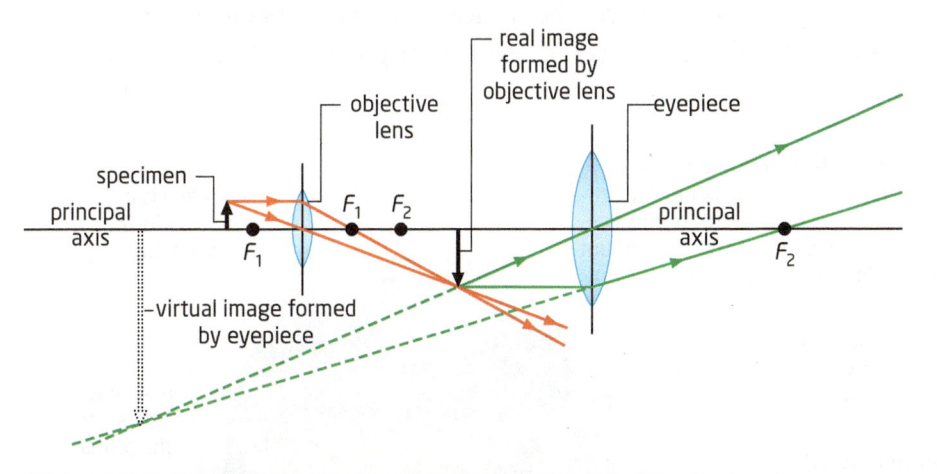

Figure 12.21 You could say that the image produced by the objective lens in a microscope becomes the object for the eyepiece.

> **Study Toolkit**
>
> **Making Connections to Prior Knowledge** What connections to your prior knowledge can you make about microscopes? A concept map can help show the connections.

Learning Check

1. Newton was disturbed by a characteristic of Galileo and Kepler telescopes. What was the problem, and how did he fix it?
2. Using a Venn diagram, compare refracting and reflecting telescopes.
3. Why are most modern telescopes reflecting rather than refracting telescopes?
4. When you think of telescopes, you usually think of studying the stars and planets. Describe a practical application for using telescopes to see objects on Earth.

Sight and the Human Eye

The eye of a colossal squid, shown in **Figure 12.22**, is similar to the human eye except for one characteristic—size. Scientists believe that the eye of a living colossal squid might be as much as 40 cm in diameter, making it larger than a soccer ball. Thus, the squid eye is about 100 times larger than a human eye.

The colossal squid lives in the ocean near Antarctica, at a depth of at least 1000 m. At this depth, there is very little light. A human eye would see total darkness. The size of the eye of the colossal squid allows it to collect much more light, and the squid can therefore see its prey at great depths. In addition, the squid has light organs on each eye that produce light through bioluminescence.

Figure 12.22 The eye of a colossal squid is 100 times larger than the human eye.

The Human Eye

Human sight is a marvellous thing. We can focus on objects at different distances, record images, and detect subtle changes in colour and brightness. The focussing happens at the front of the eye, and everything else happens at the back of the eye and in the brain. **Figure 12.23** describes some features of the human eye. Two important parts of the eye that you will learn about in this section are the cornea and retina. The **cornea** is tissue in front of the eye. The cornea refracts light before it enters the eye. The **retina** is a layer of cells that respond to light and initiate nerve impulses.

cornea tissue that forms a transparent, curved structure in the front of the eye; refracts light before it enters the eye

retina a layer of rod and cone cells that respond to light and initiate nerve impulses; rod cells are very sensitive to light but cannot distinguish between colours; cone cells detect colour

The iris is the coloured tissue that surrounds the pupil. The iris can increase or decrease the size of the pupil to control the amount of light that enters the eye.

The cornea is a transparent, curved structure in front of the eye.

light rays from object

The pupil is an opening. Light enters the eye through the pupil.

lens

ciliary muscle

The retina is a layer of cells that respond to light.

real image formed on the retina

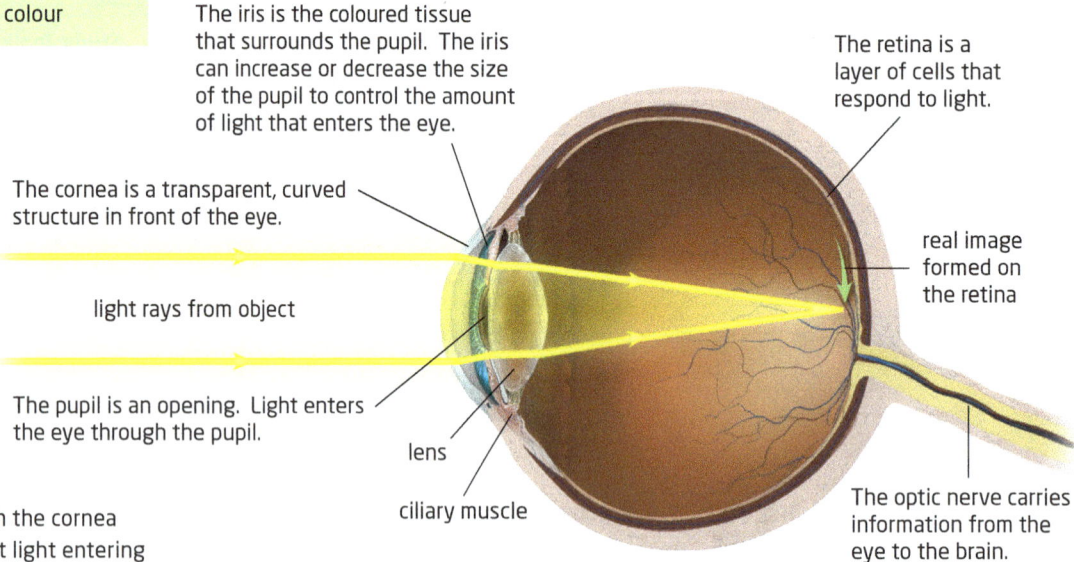

The optic nerve carries information from the eye to the brain.

Figure 12.23 Both the cornea and the lens refract light entering the eye and focus an image on the retina. The cornea causes more refraction than the lens.

How the Human Eye Focusses

Recall from your study of lenses that when an object is moved, the image also moves. In the eye, however, the distance between the retina and the lens is always the same. The cornea refracts the light in the same way regardless of the location of the object. The lens in your eye can change shape and thus refract light to a different extent, allowing it to focus light from both nearby and distant objects on the retina. The ciliary muscles make the lens shorter and thicker.

The Changing Lens

Figure 12.24 shows how the shape of a lens affects the position of the focal length. To focus on a nearby object, the curvature of the lens needs to be greater.

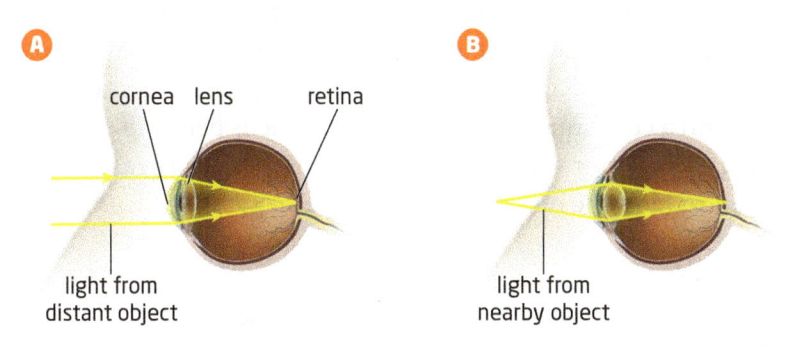

Figure 12.24 In **A**, the relaxed normal eye lens focusses a distant object correctly on the retina. In **B**, the ciliary muscles make the lens shorter and thicker to focus on nearby objects.

Comparing the Eye and the Camera

The camera is designed very much like an eye. **Figure 12.25** compares the human eye to a camera. Both have lenses that focus light on a light-sensitive material. The lens of the eye changes shape in order to focus on objects at different distances. The lens of the camera must be moved in and out to focus on objects at different distances. In the camera, the light-sensitive material is either film or CCDs (charge-coupled devices). In the eye, the retina is the light-sensitive tissue. The camera has an aperture that controls the amount of light that enters the camera. The pupil controls the amount of light that enters the eye.

Correcting Vision Using Lenses

Common causes of poor vision are an incorrect shape of the eyeball, an incorrect shape of the cornea, and hardening of the lens. Each condition can be corrected by eyeglasses or contact lenses. Most can be corrected by laser surgery. Four of these conditions are discussed below.

Myopia

Myopia [pronounced my-OPE-ee-ah] is near-sightedness: the eyes cannot focus on distant objects. **Figure 12.26A** shows parallel light rays coming from a distant object. The cornea and eye lens refract the light and bring the rays together. However, the eyeball is too long, and the image forms in front of the retina. When the rays reach the retina, they have begun to spread out again, and the image is blurry. **Figure 12.26B** shows how a diverging lens spreads out the parallel rays before they reach the eye. The rays that are separating from each other appear to be coming from an object that is closer to the eye. When the eye refracts the light, it is focussed on the retina.

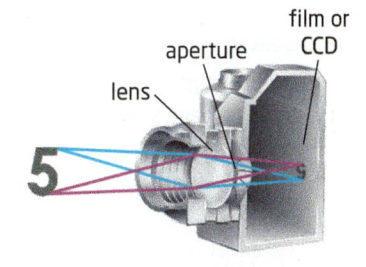

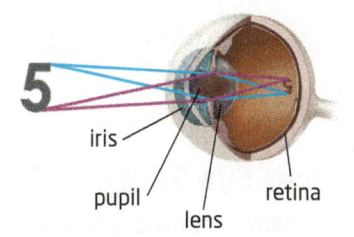

Figure 12.25 Notice that the images in the eye and the camera are upside down. Your brain processes the image it receives from the eye and gives you the sense that it is upright.

myopia near-sightedness; the condition in which the eye cannot focus on distant objects

Figure 12.26 Near-sightedness is caused by an eyeball that is too long. In **A**, the focussed image is in front of the retina instead of on the retina. In **B**, the condition is corrected with diverging lenses in eyeglasses or contact lenses.

Chapter 12 Lenses and Lens Technologies • NEL

Hyperopia

hyperopia far-sightedness; the condition in which the eye cannot focus on nearby objects

Hyperopia [pronounced hi-per-OPE-ee-ah] is far-sightedness. This means that the eyes cannot focus on nearby objects. **Figure 12.27A** shows how light coming from a nearby object is refracted by the cornea and eye lens. In this case, the eyeball is too short. As a result, the rays reach the retina before they meet. The image is so blurry that a far-sighted person cannot read the print on a page. **Figure 12.27B** shows how far-sightedness can be corrected with a converging lens. The corrective lens bends the rays a little, bringing them closer together before they reach the cornea. The lens of the eye then refracts the rays a little more, and the rays are focussed on the retina.

Suggested Investigation
Inquiry Investigation 12-B, I "Speye," on page 514

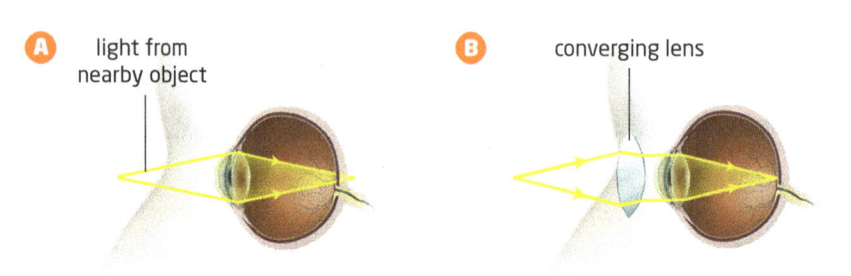

Figure 12.27 In **A**, the eyeball is too short. The person is far-sighted. In **B**, converging lenses, either in eyeglasses or contact lenses, correct hyperopia.

STSE Case Study

Laser Eye Surgery: Shaping Vision

Our ability to see changes over time. As we age, it often deteriorates. Laser eye surgery has revolutionized eye care. It can improve vision, but it is not a risk-free procedure.

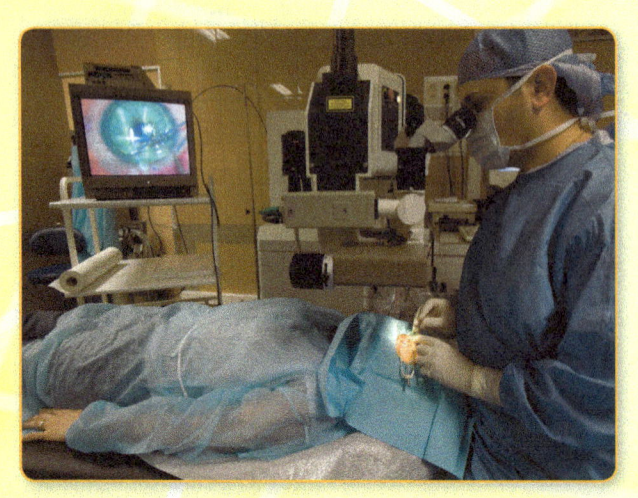

Thousands of Canadians have undergone laser eye surgery to correct vision.

In the 1950s, surgeons began to cut the cornea to alter its shape, changing the way light refracts from the cornea onto the lens and then the retina. Later, procedures advanced with the creation of the excimer laser, a form of ultraviolet laser, patented by Mani Lal Bhaumik. The excimer laser is now the cornerstone of laser eye surgery. Rather than burn tissue, the laser ablates (vaporizes) it.

Risks and Benefits

Most people who have laser eye surgery have positive results—improved vision that needs little or no correction with glasses or contact lenses. However, laser surgery is not for everyone, and any surgery involves risks. The risks for laser surgery include

- dry eyes
- oversensitivity to light
- poor perception of contrast
- double vision and
- perception of ghosted images, starbursts, or halos around light sources

508 NEL • Unit 4 Light and Geometric Optics

Presbyopia

As a person ages, the lenses of the eyes become stiff and the ciliary muscles can no longer make the lenses change shape. The condition is called **presbyopia** [pronounced prez-be-OPE-ee-ah]. Presbyopia is unlike myopia and hyperopia, which are both caused by an incorrect length of the eyeball. People who have presbyopia cannot focus on nearby objects. When people are already near-sighted and they get presbyopia, they cannot focus on either distant or nearby objects. To correct this condition, people wear bifocals, shown in **Figure 12.28.** Bifocals are lenses with two parts. The top part of the lens corrects for near-sightedness, and a small section of the lower part helps the eyes focus on nearby objects. Bifocal contact lenses are also available.

presbyopia the condition in which lenses of the eye become stiff and the ciliary muscles can no longer make the lenses change shape

astigmatism blurred or distorted vision usually caused by an incorrectly shaped cornea

Astigmatism

Astigmatism is blurred or distorted vision that is usually caused by an incorrectly shaped cornea. Instead of being rounded, the cornea is oval. Part of an image might be in focus, but the rest of the image is blurry.

Figure 12.28 The small section at the bottom corrects the near vision, and the rest of the lens corrects for vision at a distance.

People of all ages might think of laser eye surgery as an alternative to wearing glasses or contact lenses. However, a person over age 40 who has laser eye surgery might still need reading glasses afterward—due to presbyopia—and has a higher risk than a younger patient of perceiving starbursts, ghosted images, and halos.

In contrast, a person under age 18 will likely not even be considered for laser eye surgery because eyes have to be stable (unchanging) for at least two years before surgery. There can still be changes in the eye until the age of 18.

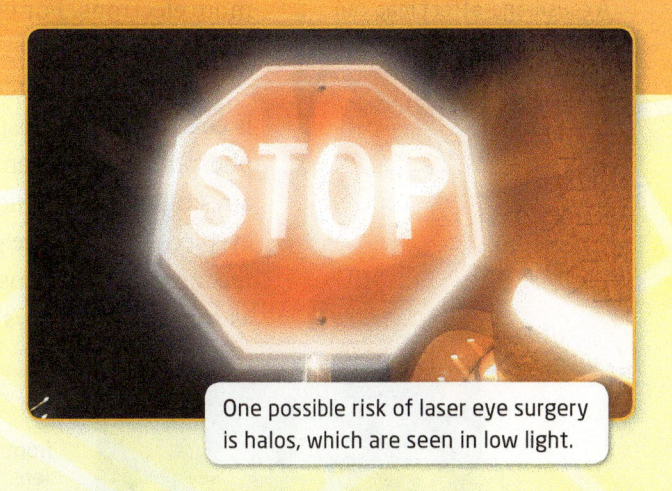

One possible risk of laser eye surgery is halos, which are seen in low light.

Your Turn

1. Do you think the benefits of laser eye surgery outweigh the risks? Explain your answer.
2. Would you enjoy working in a laser eye clinic? Why or why not?
3. Ask some people who have had laser eye surgery what they were told about the procedure and its risks.

Laser Eye Surgery

Before surgery, doctors study the shape and thickness of the cornea to identify the tissue that needs to be removed. During most laser eye surgery, an eye surgeon

- cuts a thin flap in the cornea and pulls it back
- ablates the surface to the desired shape
- replaces the flap

Enhancing Human Vision

The human eye can adapt to a wide range of intensities of light. However, as light becomes extremely dim, a point is reached beyond which the human eye can no longer perceive an image. Usually, the dim light does not cause a problem because we have artificial lighting. However, there are some situations in which it is extremely helpful to be able to see without being seen. Military and law enforcement people as well as people studying wildlife benefit tremendously by using night-vision devices that allow them to see in extremely dim light.

Night-Vision Devices

You may have seen images similar to that in **Figure 12.29A**. This is what a person can see through a **night-vision device**. Night-vision devices use an image-intensifier tube, which is illustrated in **Figure 12.29B**, to enhance vision in dim light.

The front lens of the tube focusses the small amount of light (red dots) available on a plate called a photocathode. The photocathode is sensitive to infrared rays with wavelengths just beyond visible red light. The photocathode emits an electron (yellow dot) at each point that light hits it. A high-voltage power supply attracts the electrons to the next plate, called a microchannel plate. As the name of this plate suggests, there are millions of microscopic holes called microchannels in the plate. As electrons pass through the channels, they collide with the walls, causing the walls to emit more electrons. For every electron that enters the plate, about a thousand leave the plate.

A potential difference then attracts the electrons to the next plate, which is coated with a phosphor. When electrons collide with the phosphor, the phosphor emits green light. The human eye is more sensitive to green than any other colour, which is why the designers chose that colour. Finally, the eyepiece focusses the green light onto the eye of the observer. Alternatively, the image can be transferred to a monitor. With this device, dim light as well as some infrared rays can be intensified enough to make the scene visible.

night-vision device an artificial device that allows people to see when only a very small amount of light is available

Study Toolkit

Using Graphic Organizers
A cause-and-effect map can help clarify the process that allows a night-vision device to make an object visible in dim light.

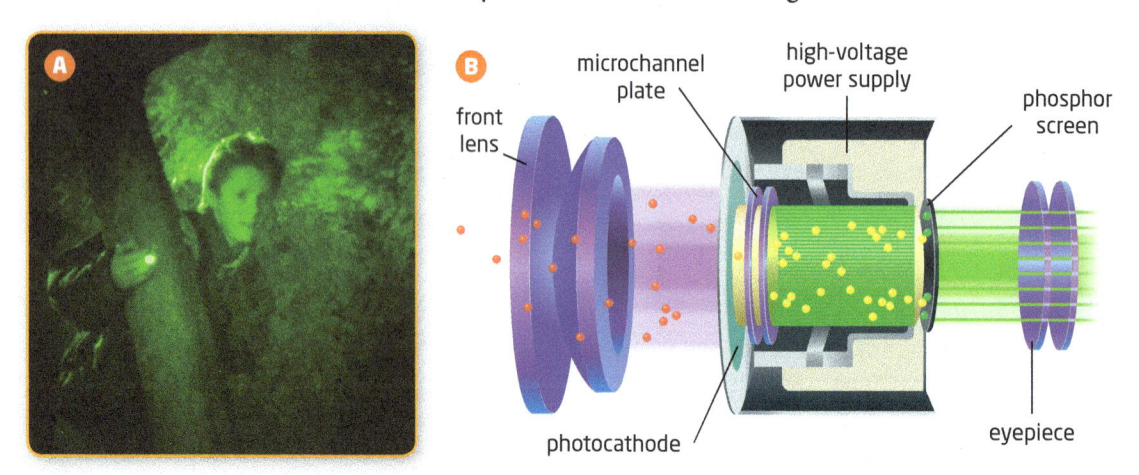

Figure 12.29 **A** Night-vision devices allow you to clearly see images that you could not see with your normal vision. **B** The red dots represent the very small amount of light entering the device. The yellow dots represent electrons.

Section 12.3 Review

Section Summary

- Lenses are used in several technologies. For example, microscopes are used to magnify specimens. Microcsopes are used in many fields.
- The cornea refracts light first. Then the eye lens focusses light once the light enters the eye.
- Myopia (near-sightedness) is caused by an eyeball that is too long. Hyperopia (far-sightedness) is caused by an eyeball that is too short.
- Presbyopia prevents a person from being able to focus up close and is caused by the hardening of the eye lens. Astigmatism causes blurry vision because the cornea is not perfectly round.
- Myopia, hyperopia, presbyopia, and astigmatism can be corrected with eyeglasses, contact lenses, and surgery.
- People in the military and law enforcement and people studying wildlife use night-vision devices to intensify the available light.

Review Questions

C **1.** Use a Venn diagram to compare a telescope with a microscope.

T/I **2.** Use a Venn diagram to compare the liquid lens in **Figure 12.1**, on page 487, with the human eye in **Figure 12.23**, on page 506.

T/I **3.** Suppose that you are examining a fly under a microscope, as shown in the diagram on the right. Copy the diagram into your notebook, and show the fly's approximate image size and location. Use **Figure 12.21** as a reference.

A **4.** Describe two examples of lens technologies that benefit society.

K/U **5.** In the human eye, the distance between the lens and the retina does not change. Explain how the lens can focus images of both distant objects and nearby objects on the retina.

K/U **6.** The following are components of a camera: aperture, film or CCD, ring that moves the lens in and out. Explain what their function is and what part of the eye carries out a similar function.

C **7.** Explain how night-vision devices amplify the amount of available light. Include a simple diagram.

T/I **8.** The diagrams on the right show two eyes. One eye has normal vision and the other eye has defective vision. Identify the eye that has defective vision. Explain why you chose it, what you think the defect is, and how it can be corrected.

Show approximately where the image of the fly will be and its size relative to the fly itself.

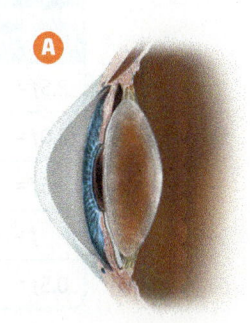

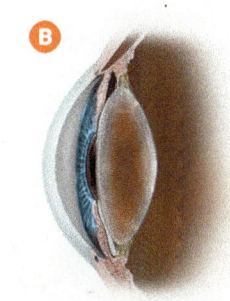

Inquiry Investigation 12-A

Image Characteristics of a Converging Lens

Skill Check

✓ Initiating and Planning
✓ Performing and Recording
✓ Analyzing and Interpreting
✓ Communicating

In this investigation, you will predict the position and characteristics of an image produced by a converging lens. You will then test your predictions.

Question

How can the thin lens equation be used to predict the characteristics of the image formed by a converging lens?

Safety Precautions

- If a candle is used as the light source, handle it with care. Keep flammable materials, such as paper, well away from the candle, and tie back long hair.

Predictions

Draw ray diagrams to make predictions comparing the image size (magnified or smaller), orientation (upright or inverted), and type (real or virtual) formed by a converging lens when the distance between the object and the lens is

a. more than twice the focal length of the lens ($2.5f$)

b. twice the focal length of the lens ($2.0f$)

c. one and a half times farther than the focal length of the lens ($1.5f$)

d. equal to the focal length of the lens (f)

e. less than the focal length of the lens ($0.5f$)

Materials

- screen in a holder
- metric ruler
- support stands
- light source in a holder
- converging lens in a holder

Procedure

1. Copy the following tables into your notebook or into a spreadsheet program.

Data for Converging Lens Investigation

Focal Length, f (cm)
(i) _____ cm (ii) _____ cm (iii) average _____ cm

Observation Data

Object Distance (d_o) (cm)	$\frac{1}{d_o}$ (1 cm)	Image Distance (d_i) (cm)	$\frac{1}{d_i}$ (1 cm)	$\frac{1}{f} = \frac{1}{d_i} + \frac{1}{d_o}$ (1 cm)	Focal Length (f) (cm)	Image Characteristics
$2.5f =$						
$2.0f =$						
$1.5f =$						
$f =$						
$0.5f =$						

Science Skills

Go to **Science Skills Toolkit 2** to learn more about making predictions in an inquiry investigation.

2. Set up the screen, ruler, light source, and converging lens as shown in the diagram below.

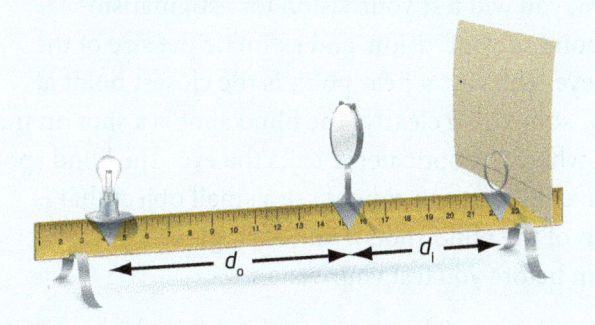

Set up the light source, lens, and paper as shown here.

3. Move the lens back and forth to form a focussed image of the light source (the object) on the screen. The image distance, d_i, is equal to the focal length of the lens. Record this value in (i) in your first table.

4. Turn the lens around and repeat step 3. Record this value in (ii) in your table. (**Note:** The two measurements of the focal length of the lens should not differ by more than 0.5 cm.) Calculate the average focal length of the lens, and record this value in (iii) in your table.

5. Use the average focal length to calculate the following object-to-lens distances (d_o): 2.5f, 2.0f, 1.5f, f, and 0.5f. Record these distances in your second table.

6. Place your object (the light source) so that $d_o = 2.5f$. Move the screen back and forth until you see a sharp, focussed image. Record d_i in your table. Describe the image characteristics: Is the image upright or inverted? Is the image magnified or smaller than the object?

7. Repeat step 6 using $d_o = 2.0f$ and $d_o = 1.5f$.

8. Place the light source at positions corresponding to $d_o = f$ and $d_o = 0.5f$. Record the image characteristics, but do not measure the image distance, d_i.

Analyze and Interpret

1. The thin lens equation is $\frac{1}{f} = \frac{1}{d_i} + \frac{1}{d_o}$.

   a. What happens to the value of $\frac{1}{d_o}$ when the value of d_o is very large?

   b. When d_o is very large, what does the thin lens equation predict for the value of $\frac{1}{f}$?

2. The thin lens equation is given in question 1.

   a. Use the thin lens equation and data for d_o and d_i from the first two rows in your table to calculate the focal length of the lens.

   b. Compare these values with the average value of the focal length you determined in steps 3 and 4.

3. Which position of the object resulted in a very magnified image?

4. Which position of the object resulted in a virtual image?

5. Is there a difference between your experimental results and your predictions? Why or why not?

Conclude and Communicate

6. As the object moves toward the lens, from far away to a position just farther from the lens than its focal length,

   a. How does the position of the image change?

   b. What change occurs in the size of the image?

7. In the images you produced,

   a. In which position(s) was the image upright?

   b. In which position(s) was the image inverted?

8. Which of the object positions that you studied (2.5f, 2f, 1.5f, f, 0.5f) matches the way you use a magnifying glass? Explain.

Extend Your Inquiry and Research Skills

9. **Inquiry** Predict the effect on the image if you cover part of the lens. Test your prediction, and explain your observations.

10. **Research** Research and report history of eyeglasses.

Inquiry Investigation 12-B

Skill Check

Initiating and Planning

✓ Performing and Recording

✓ Analyzing and Interpreting

✓ Communicating

Safety Precautions

- Do not allow anything to touch your eyes.

Materials

- soft measuring tape
- piece of paper

I "Speye"

In this investigation, you will test your vision for astigmatism, measure the near point of your vision, and estimate the size of the blind spot in your eye. The vision near point is the closest point at which you can view something clearly. The blind spot is a spot on the retina, at the point where the optic nerve exits the eye. The blind spot has no light-sensitive cells, so you cannot see a small object that is in the field of vision of the blind spot. If you wear glasses or contact lenses, remove them before you test your vision.

Procedure

Part 1 Checking for Astigmatism

1. Close one eye and look at the diagram below. If some of the lines appear blurred or darker than the others, you may have astigmatism in that eye.

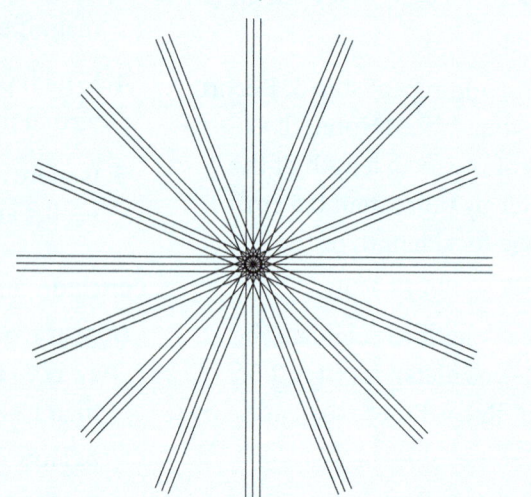

Use this diagram to test for astigmatism.

2. Close the other eye and repeat step 1.

Part 2 Measuring Your Near Point

3. Look at the text on this page. Get your eyes as close to the page as you can, while still seeing the text *clearly*. Your partner can estimate the distance between your eyes and the page by holding a soft measuring tape against the page and well to one side of your eyes. In your notebook, record this value as your near point.

Part 3 Estimating the Size of Your Blind Spot

4. Close one eye and look at the X in the diagram below.

5. Hold the page close to your eye. Then slowly increase the distance between your eye and the page. Stop when you can no longer see the spot.

In the following steps, you will map out a blind spot region for one eye on a piece of paper.

6. Mark a small X in the centre of a sheet of paper. Have your partner help you hold your head so that your eye is 40 cm from the X you marked.

7. Close one eye and stare at the X. Slowly move the tip of your pencil away from the X until the pencil tip disappears from view. Mark the paper with a dot at this point.

8. Repeat step 7, moving your pencil in a different direction to map out an area for your blind spot.

9. The blind spot is typically higher than it is wide. At a distance of 40 cm from your eye, the image on your retina is about 0.044 times the length of an image you can see or, in this case, the blind spot you cannot see.

   a. Measure the maximum height and width of the blind spot you mapped out.

   b. Multiply these values by 0.044 to estimate the dimensions of your blind spot.

Analyze and Interpret

1. What value did you measure for the near point?

2. What are the dimensions of your blind spot? Show your calculations.

Conclude and Communicate

3. Why does a non-spherical cornea or lens result in the blurred vision of astigmatism?

4. Muscles in the eye change the curvature of the lens. At the near point, is the lens relatively thick or relatively thin? Explain your answer.

Extend Your Inquiry and Research Skills

5. **Inquiry** Examine a pair of bifocal lenses. Infer why people who wear bifocals have to move their eyes up and down to see properly.

6. **Research** Research astigmatism.

   a. What forms of treatment are available to correct astigmatism?

   b. Assess the risks and benefits of each treatment to decide which course of treatment you would choose if you were diagnosed with astigmatism.

X

For step 4

Chapter 12 Lenses and Lens Technologies • NEL   515

Inquiry Investigation 12-C

Skill Check

Initiating and Planning
✓ Performing and Recording
✓ Analyzing and Interpreting
✓ Communicating

Make a Simple Telescope

In this investigation, you will use the same principles used by Galileo and Kepler to build two simple telescopes.

Question

How are the Galileo and Kepler telescopes similar, and how are they different?

Safety Precautions

- Do not point the lenses at the Sun.

Materials

- converging lens, large, with a long focal length
- diverging lens, small, with a short focal length
- converging lens, small, with a short focal length

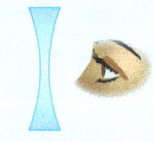

Objective lens   Eyepiece lens

The arrangement of lenses in a Galilean telescope. (This illustration is not to scale.)

Procedure

1. Use a distant bright window or a well-lit building as your object. Hold the small diverging lens very close to your eye. This is the eyepiece of your telescope.

2. The large converging lens is the objective. Hold the objective lens close to the eyepiece, so that light from the object passes through the objective, then the eyepiece.

3. Slowly move the objective lens away from the eyepiece, in the direction of the object. Looking through both lenses, adjust the position of the objective until you can see an image. Describe the characteristics of the image formed by the "Galileo telescope."

4. Now use the small converging lens for the eyepiece and the large converging lens as the objective.

5. Repeat steps 2 and 3, and describe the characteristics of the image formed by the "Kepler telescope."

Analyze and Interpret

1. Compare the image formed by the Galileo telescope with that formed by the Kepler telescope.

2. How does the sharpness of the image change as the magnification increases?

Conclude and Communicate

3. Using a graphic organizer of your choice, compare Galileo's and Kepler's telescopes.

Extend Your Inquiry and Research Skills

4. **Inquiry** Investigate the effects of eyepiece lenses with different focal lengths on the magnifying power of a telescope.

Chapter 12 Summary

12.1 Characteristics of Lenses
Key Concepts

- Lenses are classified as either converging or diverging, depending on how they affect parallel light rays that refract through them.
- Converging lenses have one or two convex surfaces and are thicker in the centre than on the edges. Diverging lenses have one or two concave surfaces and are thinner in the centre than on the edges.
- The focal point of a converging lens is the point at which parallel rays meet after passing through the lens. The focal point of a diverging lens is the point from which the diverging rays appear to have come after parallel rays have passed through the lens.
- With thick lenses, rays that are farther from the principal axis do not pass through the focal point. This causes spherical aberration.
- Different colours of light have different indices of refraction. Therefore, they focus at different points. This causes chromatic aberration.

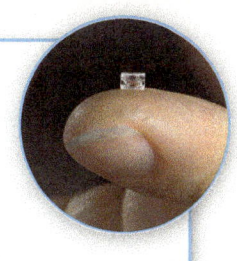

12.2 Images Formed by Lenses
Key Concepts

- Ray diagrams consisting of three rays can be drawn to determine the characteristics of images formed by lenses.
- When an object is between a converging lens and the focal point, the image is always virtual, upright, and larger than the object.
- When an object is farther from a converging lens than the focal point, the image is always real and inverted. If the object is between the focal point and twice the focal point, the image will be larger that the object. If the object is more than twice the distance of the focal point from the mirror, the image will be smaller than the object.
- When an object is at the focal point of a converging lens, its image will be real, inverted, and the same size as the object.
- When an image is formed by a diverging lens, it is always upright, virtual, smaller than the object, and on the same side as the object.
- Given the focal length of the lens and the size and location of the object, you can use algebraic equations to calculate the characteristics of the image.

12.3 Lens Technologies and the Human Eye
Key Concepts

- Lenses are used in several technologies. For example, microscopes are used to magnify specimens. Microscopes are used in many fields.
- The cornea refracts light first. Then the eye lens focusses the light once the light enters the eye.
- Myopia (near-sightedness) is caused by an eyeball that is too long. Hyperopia (far-sightedness) is caused by an eyeball that is too short.
- Presbyopia prevents a person from being able to focus up close and is caused by the hardening of the eye lens. Astigmatism causes blurry vision because the cornea is not perfectly round.
- Myopia, hyperopia, presbyopia, and astigmatism can be corrected with eyeglasses, contact lenses, and surgery.
- People in the military and law enforcement and people studying wildlife use night-vision devices to intensify available light.

Chapter 12 Review

Make Your Own Summary

Summarize the key concepts of this chapter using a graphic organizer. The Chapter Summary on the previous page will help you identify the key concepts. Refer to Study Toolkit 4 on pages 565–566 to help you decide which graphic organizer to use.

Reviewing Key Terms

Match each of these key terms to its definition below.

- **a.** chromatic aberration
- **b.** diverging
- **c.** eyepiece
- **d.** hyperopia
- **e.** presbyopia
- **f.** reflecting
- **g.** retina

1. _____ lenses are thinner in the centre than they are around the edges. (12.1)

2. When viewing a specimen in a microscope, you look through the _____ . (12.3)

3. _____ telescopes use both mirrors and lenses. (12.3)

4. _____ caused problems for Galileo's and Kepler's telescopes. (12.3)

5. The light-sensitive part of the eye is the _____ . (12.3)

6. When people reach 40 to 50 years of age, they nearly always develop _____ . (12.3)

7. When someone's eyes cannot focus on nearby objects, that person has _____ . (12.3)

Knowledge and Understanding K/U

8. What type of lens causes parallel rays to come together after passing through the lens?

9. What happens to parallel rays when they hit a flat piece of glass at an oblique angle with the surface of the glass?

10. Why do lenses have two focal points when mirrors have only one?

11. What two factors determine the focal length of a lens?

12. Define *chromatic aberration*.

13. One type of lens can produce an image that is upright, virtual, and larger than the object. What type of lens is this, and where must the object be located?

14. The rules for drawing ray diagrams and the algebraic equations for lenses specify that they apply only to thin lenses. Explain why the lenses must be thin for these applications.

15. The following two questions are on telescopes.
    a. In what way was Kepler's telescope an improvement over Galileo's telescope?
    b. What was a disadvantage of Kepler's telescope?

16. Copy the table below into your notebook. The conditions are for an object in front of a diverging lens. Describe and then explain how the rays travel.

Ray Diagrams for Diverging Lenses

Condition	Where the Ray Goes	Explanation
a. The ray travels parallel to the principal axis until it reaches the diverging lens.		
b. The ray travels toward the centre of the lens.		
c. The ray travels toward the lens as though it were going to the focal point on the far side of the lens.		

17. Would a night-vision device allow someone to see inside an empty building in complete darkness? Explain.

Thinking and Investigation T/I

18. Copy the diagrams below and complete a ray diagram of the object in each. Describe the four characteristics of each image.

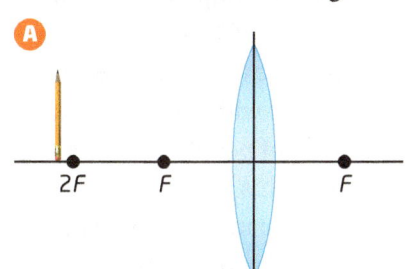

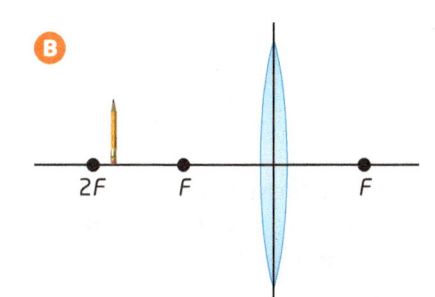

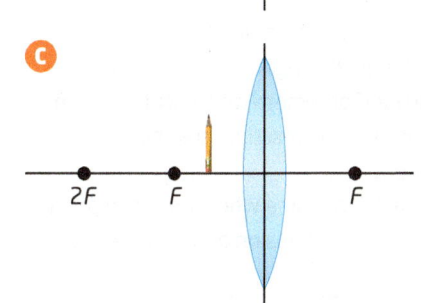

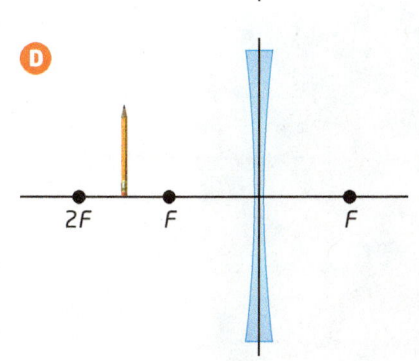

A [Diagram: object beyond 2F, converging lens]

B [Diagram: object between 2F and F, converging lens]

C [Diagram: object between F and lens, converging lens]

D [Diagram: object between 2F and F, diverging lens]

19. A pinhole camera is a box that has a tiny hole in one end and a screen or another type of detector on the inside of the other end, as shown in the diagram below. There is no lens in the hole, but a clear image is created on the screen. Use rays to explain how a pinhole with no lens can form an image that is not blurry.

[Diagram: pinhole camera with tree, image formed on screen inside box]

20. Reducing the aperture of an inexpensive camera reduces the amount of spherical aberration. Explain why this is true.

Communication C

21. Make a sketch of a ray diagram for a hyperopic eye. Explain what causes hyperopia.

22. **BIG IDEAS** Light has characteristics and properties that can be manipulated with mirrors and lenses for a range of uses. Using an example from this chapter, explain how characteristics and properties of lenses can be used to society's benefit.

23. **BIG IDEAS** Society has benefited from the development of a range of optical devices and technologies. Choose an optical device from this chapter, and explain how society has benefited from it.

Application A

24. What do you think would be some advantages of wearing contact lenses over eyeglasses?

25. Describe three situations in which night-vision devices would be advantageous.

26. Suppose that you are an optometrist. Explain the advantages and disadvantages of wearing bifocals to a patient who is over 50 years old.

Chapter 12 Lenses and Lens Technologies • NEL   519

Science at Work

Canadians in Science

The Third World Eye Care Society (TWECS) is a group of Canadian optometrists, opticians, and other volunteers. TWECS collects used eyeglasses from Canadians and provides free eye exams and eyeglasses to people in developing countries. As a volunteer with TWECS, Tuan Trieu has helped restore the vision of hundreds of people. Tuan has travelled with TWECS to the Philippines and to his birthplace, Vietnam.

When he is not volunteering with TWECS, Tuan is an optician in Edmonton. Opticians measure and fit people with prescription eyeglasses and contact lenses.

Optician Tuan Trieu travelled to the Philippines in 2008 with the Third World Eye Care Society. It was not his first trip to the Philippines. Tuan landed in the Philippines as a refugee in 1976 after fleeing Vietnam and before coming to Canada.

In Tuan Trieu's Words

A student interested in becoming an optician should have a good understanding of optics and should like working with people. I enjoy working as an optician because it is challenging. It is rewarding to be able to help people see more clearly.

The most challenging part of a TWECS mission is finding the right prescriptions for the patients. We know the used eyeglasses we give the patients are not as perfect as they would be if optometrists prescribed them. However, we have no choice but to find as close a prescription as possible among the used glasses we have for patients.

The most satisfying moments of our missions come when we can improve a person's vision from complete blurriness to 20/20 vision and then see the smile that results.

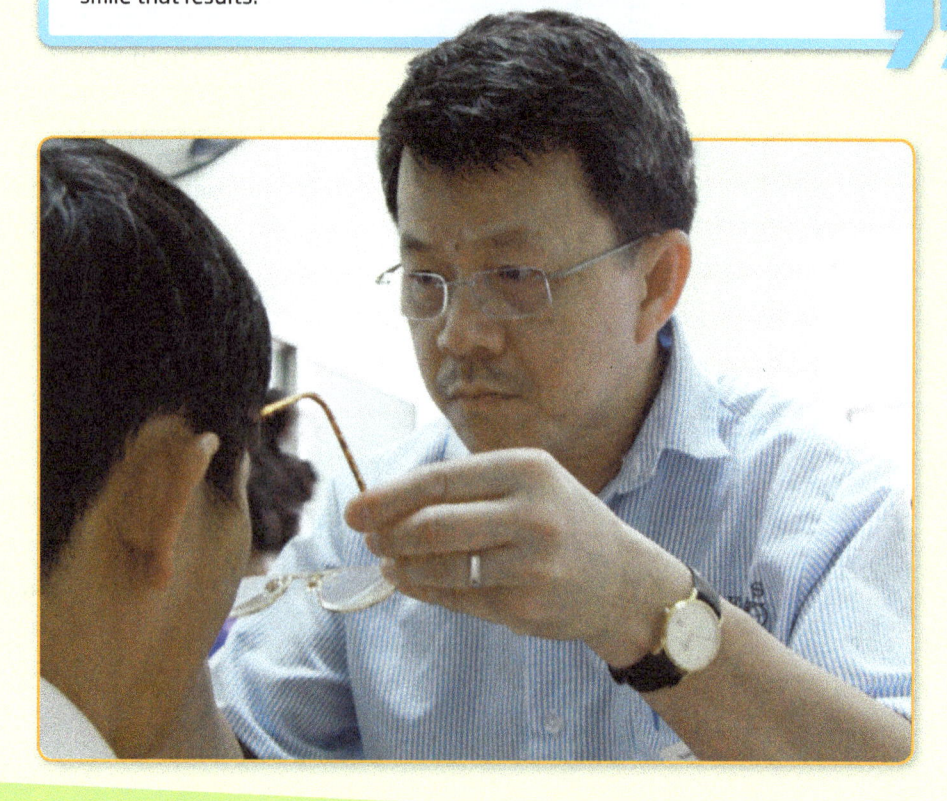

TWECS has sent volunteer teams to Tanzania, Peru, Cambodia, Mexico, India, Malawi, Bolivia, and other countries. This organization has helped restore the vision of more than 30 000 people.

Optics at Work

The study of light and geometric optics contributes to these careers, as well as many more!

- Optical Physicist
- Photographer
- Optometrist
- Physics
- Ophthalmologist
- Fibre Optics Engineer

Lighting Technician
Lighting technicians set up and operate lighting for television, film, and stage productions. They use light fixtures, mirrors, filters, and electronics to create different lighting effects.

Photonics Engineering Technologist
Photonics is the generation, transmission, manipulation, and detection of light. Photonics engineering technologists work in a variety of industries, producing technologies such as light sensors, laser technologies, CDs and DVDs, barcode scanners, and digital cameras.

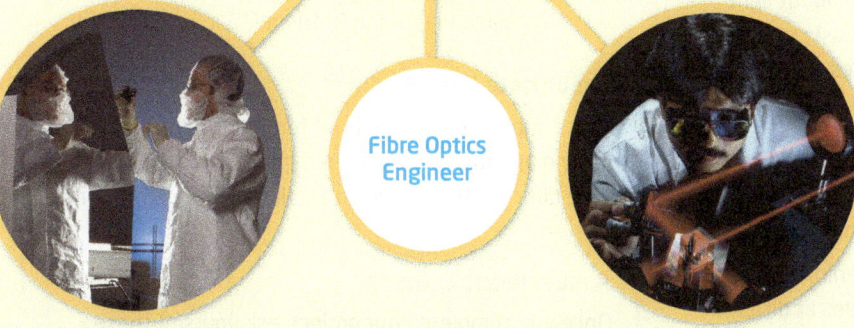

Optics Technician
Optics technicians make lenses for cameras, eyeglasses, microscopes, binoculars, and telescopes. They also create prisms for the aerospace industry. In order to design and manufacture the lenses and prisms needed, optics technicians must have a good knowledge of mathematics and computers.

Go to **scienceontario** to find out more

Over to You

1. Why might TWECS not be able to provide an exact prescription to someone they help in a developing country?

2. If you wear eyeglasses, find out where you can donate your old eyeglasses. Or plan a campaign to get students at your school involved in donating used eyeglasses to a service organization such as TWECS.

3. Photonics is a growing field with many different applications. Choose one application of photonics and conduct research to find out more about the science behind the application.

4. Research a career involving light and geometric optics that interests you. If you wish, you may choose a career from the list above. **What essential skills would you need for this career?**

Unit 4 Projects

Inquiry Project

Design a Light Tunnel

Bringing natural light into a windowless room can be challenging. One way to do this is to construct a light tunnel that redirects light using the properties of lenses and mirrors. For this project, you will take the role of a lighting designer. You have been hired by clients to design a light tunnel that will bring natural light from the roof of their home into a windowless room.

> **Inquiry Question**
> How can mirrors, lenses, and other materials be used to direct natural light through a light tunnel into a windowless room?

Initiate and Plan

1. Make a table to summarize information about light that you will need to consider for this task, such as reflection, refraction, mirrors, and lenses.

2. Design a light tunnel that will
   - allow sunlight through a flat roof, direct the light from the roof through an attic, and disperse the light into the windowless room at the end of the tunnel
   - function morning, afternoon, and evening (sunlight will strike the tunnel at different angles at different times of the day)
   - bend at least three times, with one bend greater than 45°
   - maximize light dispersion into the windowless room

3. Gather materials you can use to create a model of your light tunnel. For example, you may want to use
   - a laser pointer to simulate sunlight
   - acetate, plastic wrap, or a small pane of glass to simulate a window on top of the roof
   - cardboard, paper-towel tubes, shoe boxes, or 2 L soft-drink bottles to make the tunnel
   - empty potato chip bags or another material to simulate a reflective surface on the inside of the tunnel
   - tape
   - mirrors and lenses in various shapes and sizes

4. Make sketches to plan your model, before you begin to assemble it.

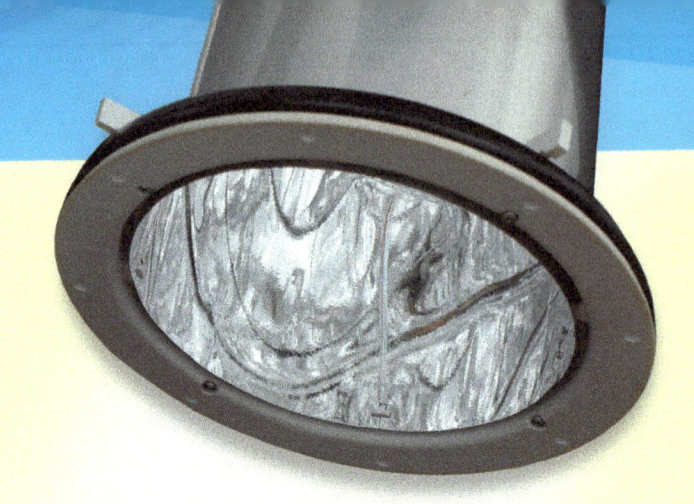

Perform and Record

5. Construct your model to meet the design criteria given in step 2.

6. Draw two well-labelled ray diagrams, showing at least three light rays, to simulate morning and afternoon conditions as the Sun changes position in the sky.

Analyze and Interpret

1. Identify the challenges you had when designing your light tunnel.

2. Which optics components did you find most useful when designing your light tunnel?

Communicate Your Findings

3. Assemble your design brief for your clients. Include your ray diagrams, as well as an explanation of how light will be directed through each section of your light tunnel.

> **Assessment Criteria**
> Once you complete your project, ask yourself these questions. Did you...
> - **K/U** summarize information about reflection, refraction, mirrors, and lenses, as related to this task?
> - **T/I** select appropriate materials to create a model of your light tunnel?
> - **T/I** use the materials in a safe and effective way?
> - **T/I** design your model to meet the criteria provided?
> - **A** identify the challenges you faced when designing your light tunnel?
> - **A** identify the optics components that were most useful in the design of your light tunnel?
> - **C** use appropriate scientific conventions in the ray diagrams for your design brief?
> - **C** use appropriate scientific terminology, for both your audience and your purpose, in the explanation for your design brief?

An Issue to Analyze

LEDs Brighten Up the Darkness

In Canada and many other developed countries, an electrical grid that supplies electricity is taken for granted. In countries with rugged terrain or insufficient development, however, electrical energy is unavailable or very expensive. Consequently, artificial light is produced by burning expensive and difficult-to-obtain fossil fuels in generators, or by burning candles. Fortunately, new light-producing technologies, such as light-emitting diodes (LEDs) require much less electricity to generate light. This feature of LEDs makes them particularly suitable for use in remote or developing communities within the world. Research and analyze the costs and benefits of using LED technology in a remote or developing community.

> **Issue**
> How can LED technology be used to benefit a remote or developing community?

Initiate and Plan

1. Prepare to analyze LED technology from economic, scientific, and social perspectives.

Perform and Record

2. Using human, print, and electronic resources, research responses to the following questions about LED technology:
   - How does LED technology differ from conventional technology?
   - What are the economic costs of using LED lighting technology, compared with the economic costs of using conventional incandescent technology?
   - What scientific challenges prevent the widespread use of LED lighting technology?
   - What are the social implications of LED lighting technology for a remote or developing community?

3. Based on your research, identify the costs and benefits of using LED technology. Organize your research using an appropriate format.

Analyze and Interpret

3. Based on your research, prepare a recommendation that you could present to the town council of a remote or developing community to promote the use of LED technology. Consider responses to the following questions as part of your recommendation:
   - Why is LED technology being used now? Why was it not used in the past?
   - Why are some communities unable to use LEDs for artificial light?
   - What could you (or your school community) do to make it possible for remote or developing communities to use LEDs for artificial lighting?

Communicate Your Findings

2. Select an appropriate format, such as a podcast, poster, or oral presentation, to present your recommendation. Consider both your purpose and your audience.

> **Assessment Criteria**
> Once you complete your project, ask yourself these questions. Did you...
> - **K/U** compare light generated by conventional technology with light generated by LED technology?
> - **A** research the costs and benefits of LED technology from multiple perspectives?
> - **C** organize your research in an appropriate format, using proper academic documentation?
> - **C** select an appropriate format to present your recommendation?

Unit 4 Review

Connect to the BIG IDEAS

Use this bicycle wheel graphic organizer to connect what you have learned in this unit to the Big Ideas, found on page 397. Draw one bicycle wheel for each Big Idea and write the Big Idea in the centre. Between the spokes of the wheel, briefly describe six examples of that Big Idea.

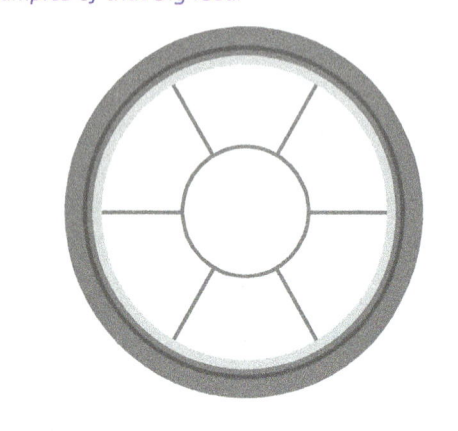

Knowledge and Understanding K/U

1. Which source produces light as a result of the heating of atoms?
   a. fluorescence
   b. incandescence
   c. bioluminescence
   d. chemiluminescence

2. In which of the following mirrors can you always expect an image that is virtual and the same size as the object?
   a. spherical
   b. convex
   c. concave
   d. plane

3. Which of the following optical effects is *not* an effect of refraction?
   a. fluorescence
   b. sun dogs
   c. mirage
   d. shimmering

4. The major difference between Newton's design for telescopes and the designs of his predecessors was the presence of a(n)
   a. objective lens
   b. eyepiece lens
   c. plane mirror
   d. concave mirror

5. Which of the following diseases associated with vision is not the direct result of a change in the shape of the eye lens?
   a. cataracts
   b. near-sightedness
   c. far-sightedness
   d. presbyopia

6. Explain how the production of light is categorized with reference to the type of energy and atoms involved.

7. How is light produced by an incandescent source? Use a diagram in your explanation.

8. Use the diagram below to explain why the image that strikes the retina of an observer's eye is laterally inverted.

The image that strikes the retina is laterally inverted.

9. Explain the cause(s) of spherical aberration in mirrors. Use a diagram in your explanation.

524 NEL • Unit 4 Light and Geometric Optics

10. Explain the difference(s) between partial reflection and refraction of white light that encounters a prism, as shown in the photograph below.

White light entering a prism is partially reflected and refracted.

11. Explain the difference between myopia and hyperopia.

12. In a Venn diagram, illustrate the differences and similarities between a real image and a virtual image.

13. Copy the outline of the concept map shown here in your notebook, and fill in the boxes.

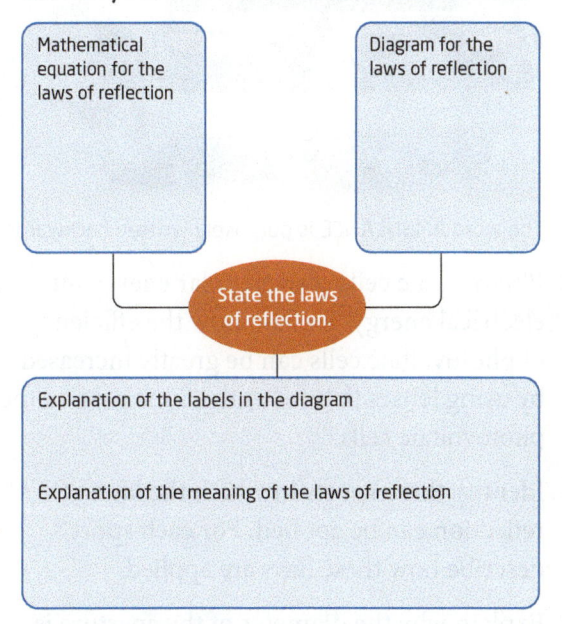

- Mathematical equation for the laws of reflection
- Diagram for the laws of reflection
- State the laws of reflection.
- Explanation of the labels in the diagram
- Explanation of the meaning of the laws of reflection

Thinking and Investigation T/I

14. The image of an object in a mirror is farther from the mirror than the object, larger than the object, real, and inverted. Draw a ray diagram that fits these criteria.

15. How would you determine the difference between the focal lengths of a shiny metal soupspoon and a shiny metal teaspoon? Explain your answer.

16. Copy the diagram below into your notebook. Draw a ray diagram, and calculate the focal length of the concave mirror.

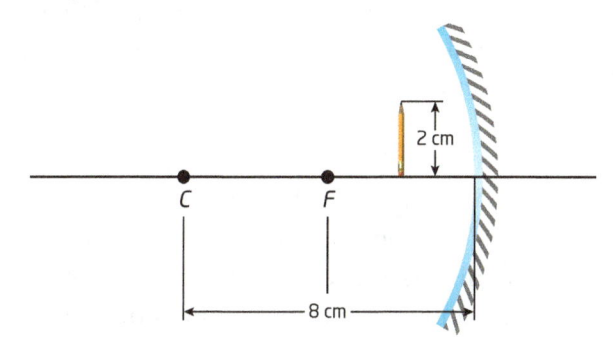

17. Use ray diagrams to explain the difference between real and virtual images in concave spherical mirrors.

18. Use the data in the table below to explain why the speed of light in pure hydrogen is greater than the speed of light in glass.

Indices of Refraction

Substance	Index of Refraction
Hydrogen	1.000 14
Glass (crown)	1.52

19. The objective mirror in the Newtonian telescope in the diagram below has a diameter of 15 cm. Calculate F_1 and F_2.

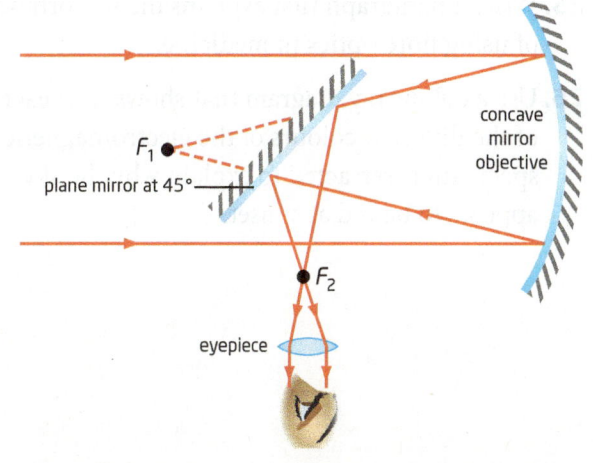

A Newtonian telescope uses a lens and a concave mirror.

Unit 4 Review • NEL 525

Unit 4 Review

20. Explain why the image formed in a camera is inverted and smaller than the object being photographed. Include a ray diagram.

21. While walking on a beach, you find a clear, colourless rock that may be quartz ($n = 1.46$) or a piece of glass ($n = 1.52$). Explain how you could use variations in the angles of refracted light and the index of refraction to determine whether the rock is glass or quartz.

Communication C

22. **BIG IDEAS** Light has characteristics and properties that can be manipulated with mirrors and lenses for a range of uses. Using colour ray diagrams, show how the combination of one or more lenses can decrease chromatic aberration in a camera.

23. **BIG IDEAS** Society has benefited from the development of a range of optical devices and technologies. Use a graphic organizer to compare the causes and treatments of myopia, hyperopia, presbyopia, and astigmatism.

24. Write a public service announcement for a local radio station that might persuade your peers to donate their used eyeglasses to a non-governmental agency that provides used eyeglasses for children in developing countries. Your announcement should be no more than 150 words.

25. Write a paragraph that explains the importance of using fibre optics in medicine.

26. Use a colour ray diagram that shows how each of the different colours of the electromagnetic spectrum is refracted to explain why the sky appears to be red at sunset.

Application A

27. Explain why using compact fluorescent bulbs may be better for the environment than using incandescent bulbs to provide light in your home.

28. Describe how different types of mirrors can be used in the following circumstances.
    a. dental office
    b. variety store
    c. winding roads through a mountainous region

29. In the photograph below, the word AMBULANCE is written backwards. Explain why you think the word is purposely written backwards.

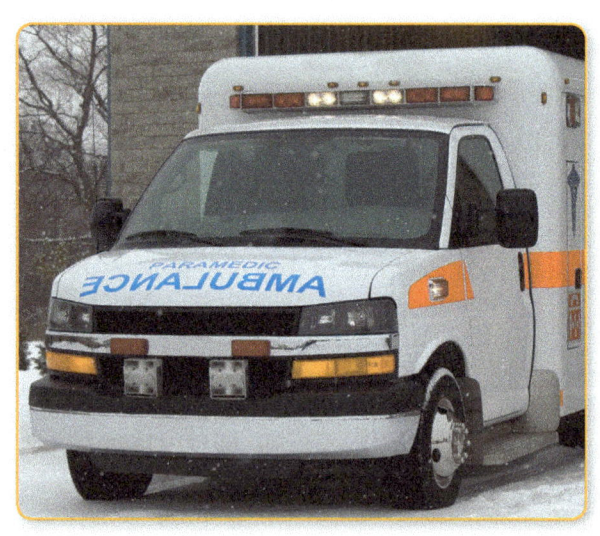

The word AMBULANCE is purposely written backwards.

30. Photovoltaic cells convert solar energy into electrical energy. Explain how the efficiency of photovoltaic cells can be greatly increased by using lenses that focus the Sun's rays on the photovoltaic cells.

31. Identify three sports in which the laws of reflection can be applied. For each sport, describe how these laws are applied.

32. Explain why the diameter of the aperture is important when designing optical instruments. Consider telescopes and cameras. Include references to optical properties, such as aberration and the amount of light transmitted or reflected.

Literacy Test Prep

Read the selection below and answer the questions that follow it.

Liquid Mirror Telescope

A team of researchers at the University of British Columbia, working with teams from Laval University, State University of New York at Stony Brook, and Columbia University, developed and built a reflecting telescope with a liquid mirror. When any liquid is rotated, the surface takes the shape of a perfect parabola. The paraboloid shape focusses all parallel rays to one focal point. A spherical shape can produce spherical aberration.

You might wonder how a mirror precise enough to be used as a telescope can be formed by a liquid. The mirror must be reflective. The researchers use mercury because it is the only metal that is a liquid at room temperature.

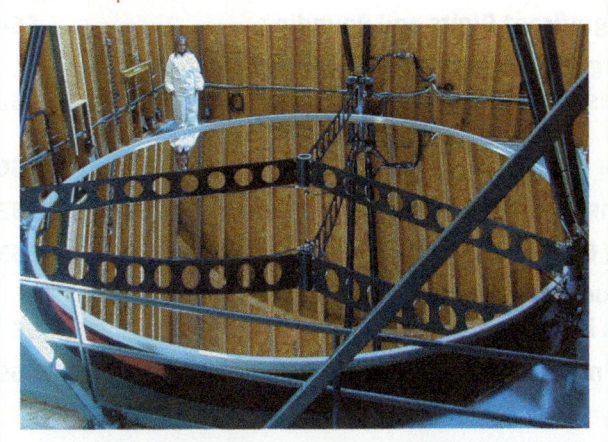

The diameter of the liquid mirror for this reflecting telescope is 6 m. Mercury can be very toxic. People who have to handle the mercury must wear protective clothing, gloves, masks, and goggles.

Advantages and Disadvantages of a Liquid Mirror Telescope Compared with a Solid Mirror Telescope

	Advantages	Disadvantages
Liquid mirror telescope	When a liquid rotates, it forms a paraboloid shape, which is desirable for objective mirrors.	Because it is a liquid, it must be parallel to the ground.
Solid mirror telescope	Does not have to be rotating.	Large mirrors can expand and contract in temperature extremes, which affects their reflecting properties.

Multiple Choice

In your notebook, record the best or most correct answer.

33. In which state of matter is mercury found at room temperature?
    a. solid
    b. liquid
    c. gas
    d. vapour

34. What causes the mercury in the mirror to take a paraboloid shape?
    a. rotation of Earth
    b. rotation of the Sun
    c. rotation of the telescope
    d. rotation of the Moon

35. In the caption of the photograph on the left, "diameter" refers to
    a. the depth of the mercury
    b. the size of the mechanical supports
    c. the size of the opening in the roof
    d. the size of the mirror

36. Which institution was not included in the research teams mentioned in the first paragraph?
    a. State University of New York
    b. University of British Columbia
    c. McMaster University
    d. Laval University

37. Which of the following is a disadvantage of using a liquid mirror?
    a. It has a reflective surface.
    b. It must be parallel to the ground.
    c. Its reflecting properties are affected by high temperature.
    d. Its reflecting properties are affected by low temperature.

Written Answer

38. In a paragraph, explain the advantages and disadvantages of a liquid mirror telescope compared with a telescope that has a solid mirror.

Guide to the Toolkits and Appendices

TOOLKITS

Science Skills Toolkit 1 Analyzing Issues—Science, Technology, Society, and the Environment 529
Science Skills Toolkit 2 Scientific Inquiry 532
Science Skills Toolkit 3 Technological Problem Solving 536
Science Skills Toolkit 4 Estimating and Measuring 538
Science Skills Toolkit 5 Precision and Accuracy 542
Science Skills Toolkit 6 Scientific Drawing 543
Science Skills Toolkit 7 Creating Data Tables 545
Science Skills Toolkit 8 Using a Microscope 546
Science Skills Toolkit 9 Using Models and Analogies in Science 548
Science Skills Toolkit 10 How to Do a Research-Based Project 549
Science Skills Toolkit 11 The GRASP Problem Solving Method 551

Math Skills Toolkit 1 The Metric System and Scientific Notation 552
Math Skills Toolkit 2 Significant Digits and Rounding 554
Math Skills Toolkit 3 Organizing and Communicating Scientific Results with Graphs 556

Study Toolkit Overview 560
Study Toolkit 1 Preparing for Reading: Previewing Text Features 562
Study Toolkit 2 Reading Effectively: Monitoring Comprehension 563
Study Toolkit 3 Word Study: Common Base Words, Prefixes, and Suffixes in Science 564
Study Toolkit 4 Organizing Your Learning: Using Graphic Organizers 565

APPENDICES

Appendix A Chemistry References 567
Appendix B Properties of Common Substances 568
Appendix C Numerical Answers and Answers to Practice Problems 570

Science Skills Toolkit 1

Analyzing Issues—Science, Technology, Society, and the Environment

Can you think of an issue that involves science, technology, society, and the environment? How about the use of salt to de-ice roads in the winter? Roads are safer in winter when they are clear of ice and snow.

However, what if you found out that the salt may eventually reach your drinking water and could have negative effects on aquatic ecosystems? How might you use science and technology to solve this problem?

Suppose your town council is in the process of deciding whether to expand its road salting program. How will you analyze this issue and determine what action to take? The concept map on this page shows a process to help you focus your thinking and stay on track.

A Process for Analyzing Issues

- Identify the issue.
- Gather relevant information.
- Identify all the alternatives.
- Consider each alternative by clarifying its consequences.
- Make a decision.
- Evaluate the decision.
  - The decision is the best alternative based on risks/benefits and, thus, probable consequences.
  - One or more of the steps in the decision-making process were faulty. No action should be taken and the process should be repeated to ensure that the faulty steps are eliminated and replaced by improved thinking.
- Take action and communicate the decision.

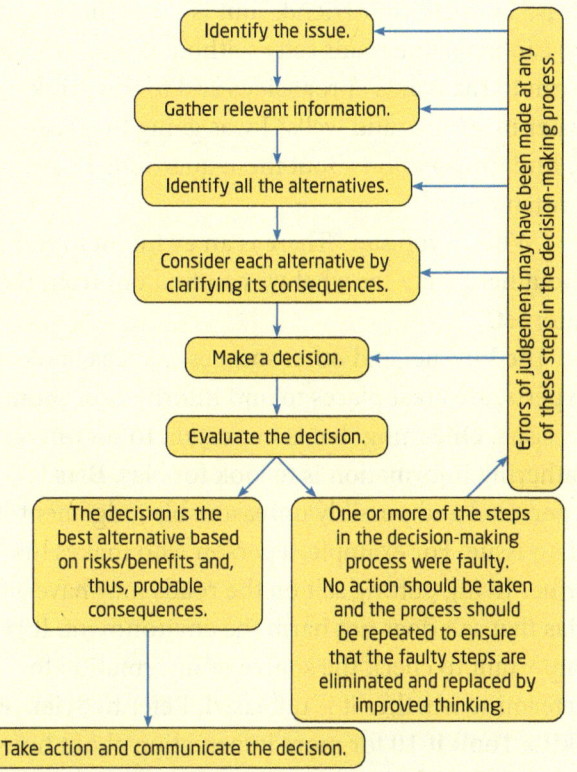

Errors of judgement may have been made at any of these steps in the decision-making process.

Identifying the Issue

Soon after hearing the news about the road salting, you go to your friend's house. You find your friend sitting in front of the computer, composing a letter to the town council. In it, your friend is asking that the salting program not be expanded to your area. "I heard that the salt can damage the environment, but how bad can it be?" you ask. "And, isn't it important to make our roads safer?"

It will be so much easier and safer to get to the arena when the roads are salted.

Salt spray from cars can damage the environment.

Gathering Information

"It is," answers your friend, "but is there some way we can make the roads safer without doing so much harm to the plants at roadsides and to the drinking water in springs and wells? I was going to research to find information about these questions I have written down."

"Whew," you say. "There is an awful lot to think about here. Let's see what we can find out from the Internet."

The Internet and other sources, such as books or experts, are great places to find information about an issue. One thing that is important to do when gathering information is to look for bias. **Bias** is a personal and possibly unreasonable judgement of an issue. For example, a person who makes his or her living putting salt on the roads may have a bias that salt does not harm the environment. It is important to check the source of information to determine whether it is unbiased. Refer to **Science Skills Toolkit 10** for more information about how to research information.

Another important part of gathering information is taking notes so that you can analyze what you have learned. You may read about different viewpoints or solutions and advantages and disadvantages for each one. It is helpful to be able to organize your notes in the form of a graphic organizer such as a concept map, a flowchart, or a Venn diagram. You will find information on using graphic organizers in **Study Toolkit 4** on pages 565–566.

Identifying Alternatives

Your research may lead you to ask new questions about alternative solutions and how successful they might be. For example, you might think about how a combination of salt and sand would work to keep roads clear of ice. Would this be a safer environmental alternative? Answering these questions often leads to more research or possibly doing your own scientific inquiry.

Making a Decision

When you have all of the information that your research can provide, your decision will still involve some very human and personal elements. People have strong feelings about the social and environmental issues that affect them. Something that seems obvious to you might not be so obvious to another person. Even the unbiased scientific evidence you found during your research might not change that person's mind. If you are going to encourage a group to make what you consider a good decision, you have to find ways to persuade the group to think as you do.

Evaluating the Decision

After you have made a decision, it is important to evaluate your decision. Is the decision the best alternative considering the risks and benefits? Have you thought about the possible consequences of the decision and how you might respond to them? If you determine that your decision-making process was faulty—if, for example, you based your decision on information that you later learned was false—you should begin again. If you find that you are comfortable with your decision, the next step is to take action.

Taking Action

Issues rarely have easy answers. People who are affected have differing, valid points of view. It is easier for you to act as an individual, but if you can persuade a group to act, you will have greater influence. In the issue discussed here, you might write a letter to your town council. As a compromise, you might suggest a combination of salt and sand on the roads. Your research can provide you with appropriate statistics. As a group, you could attend a town council meeting or sign a petition to make your views known.

Over time, you can assess the effects of your actions: Are there fewer accidents on the salted/sanded roads? Does less salt end up in the water than when more salt alone is used?

Sometimes taking action involves changing the way you do things. After you have presented your findings to the town council, one of your friends makes you stop and think. "I have noticed you putting a lot of salt out on your sidewalk," your friend says. "You could use a bit of time and muscle power to chip away the ice, but that is not the choice you make." You realize your friend is right—it is not only up to the town council or any other group to act responsibly; it is also up to you and your friends. How easy is it for you to give up an easy way of doing a task in order to make an environmentally responsible decision?

Instant Practice—Analyzing Issues

One way to reduce the generation of greenhouse gases is to reduce energy use. One way to reduce energy use is to replace old appliances with energy-efficient appliances. But isn't it just as wasteful to replace older appliances that still work? Complete the following activity in a group of four.

1. Start by dividing your group into two pairs.
2. One pair will research and record the advantages of replacing an older washing machine with a new, energy-efficient washing machine.
3. The second pair will research and record the disadvantages of replacing an older washing machine with a new, energy-efficient washing machine.
4. The pairs will then regroup, and both sides can present their findings. Record key points in a table for comparison.
5. Determine which pair has the more convincing evidence for its point of view on replacing an old appliance.
6. As a group, research different appliances to learn how older and newer models differ, including advantages and disadvantages of each. What variations in energy efficiency are available? Determine the appliances that it makes the most sense to replace, based on the information you found in steps 2 and 3 above.

Science Skills Toolkit 2

Scientific Inquiry

Scientific inquiry is a process that involves many steps, including making observations, asking questions, performing investigations, and drawing conclusions. These steps may not happen in the same order in each inquiry. There is no universal scientific method. However, one model of the scientific inquiry process is shown here:

The Scientific Inquiry Process

- Observations and curiosity stimulate questions.
- Gather information.
- Identify the problem.
- Form a hypothesis or make a prediction.
- Perform an experiment/investigation.
- Revise prediction or hypothesis. / Analyze data. / Repeat several times.
- Draw conclusions.
- prediction or hypothesis not supported
- prediction or hypothesis supported
- Communicate results.

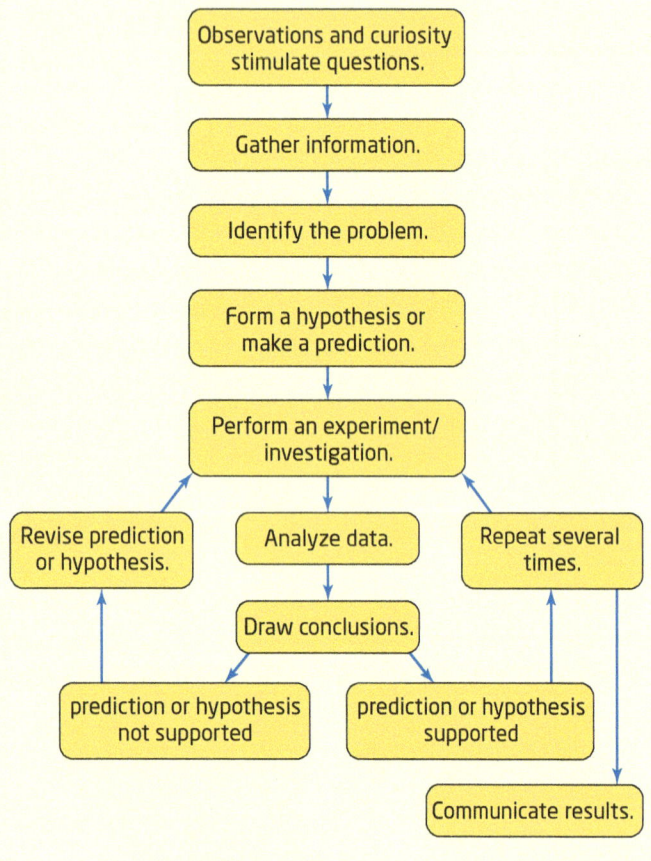

Making Observations and Asking Questions

The rain has stopped, and the Sun is out. You notice that a puddle of water has disappeared from the sidewalk. What happened to that puddle? You could probably quickly answer that question, but how would you prove your answer? You would need to carry out a scientific inquiry.

Gathering Information and Identifying the Problem

First, you might observe what happens to some other puddles. You would watch them closely until they disappeared and record what you observed.

One observation you might make is "The puddle is almost all gone." That would be a **qualitative observation**, an observation in which numbers are not used. A little later, you might also say, "It took five hours for the puddle to disappear completely." You have made a **quantitative observation**, an observation that uses numbers.

Although the two puddles were the same size, one disappeared (evaporated) much more quickly than the other one did. Your quantitative observations tell you that one evaporated in 4 h, whereas the other one took 5 h. Your qualitative observations tell you that the one that evaporated more quickly was in the sun. The one that evaporated more slowly was in the shade. You now have identified one problem to solve: Does water always evaporate more quickly in the sun than in the shade?

Beginning your observations of puddles

Concluding your observations of puddles

Instant Practice—Making Qualitative and Quantitative Observations

Copy the observations below in your notebook. Beside each observation, write "Qual" if you think it is a qualitative observation and "Quan" if you think it is a quantitative observation.

1. a. The reaction in test tube A produced more solid product than the reaction in test tube B.
   b. The reaction in test tube A produced 3.8 g of solid product.
2. a. The solution became warmer.
   b. The solution increased in temperature by 3.5°C.
3. a. The image in the mirror was smaller than the object.
   b. The image in the mirror was inverted.
4. a. At 2:00 P.M., the winds were travelling at 25 km/h.
   b. In the morning, the winds were faster than they were in the evening.
5. a. The solution was clear and blue.
   b. To the beaker was added 20.0 mL of solution.
6. a. The angle of incidence is equal to the angle of reflection.
   b. The angle of incidence is greater than 90°.

Stating a Hypothesis

Now you are ready to make a **hypothesis**, a statement about an idea that you can test, based on your observations. Your test will involve comparing two things to find the relationship between them. You know that the Sun is a source of thermal energy, so you might use that knowledge to make this hypothesis: If a puddle of water is in the sunlight, then the water will evaporate faster than if the puddle is in the shade.

Instant Practice—Stating a Hypothesis

Write a hypothesis for each of the following situations. You may wish to use an "If ... then ..." format. For example, "*If* temperature affects bacterial growth, *then* bacterial culture plates at a higher temperature will have more bacterial colonies than those at a lower temperature."

1. the relationship between temperature and the state of water
2. the relationship between types of atmospheric gases and global warming
3. the way that light is affected by travelling through different media
4. the effect of varying pH on algae growth

Making a Prediction

As you prepare to make your observations, you can make a **prediction**, a forecast about what you expect to observe. In this case, you might predict that puddles A, B, and C will dry up more quickly than puddles X, Y, and Z.

Performing an Investigation

As you know, there are several steps involved in performing a scientific investigation, including identifying variables, designing a fair test, and organizing and analyzing data.

Identifying Variables "But wait a minute," you think, as you look again at your recorded observations. "There was a strong breeze blowing today. What effect might that have had?" The breeze is one factor that could affect evaporation. The Sun is another

Science Skills Toolkit 2 • NEL 533

factor that could affect evaporation. Scientists think about every possible factor that could affect tests they conduct. These factors are called **variables**. It is important to test only one variable at a time.

You need to control your variables. This means that you change only one variable at a time. The variable that you change is called the **independent variable** (also called the manipulated variable). In this case, the independent variable is the condition under which you observe the puddle (one variable would be adding thermal energy; another would be moving air across it).

According to your hypothesis, adding thermal energy will change the time it takes for the puddle to evaporate. The time in this case is called the **dependent variable** (also called the responding variable).

Often, experiments have a **control**. This is a test that you carry out with no variables, so that you can observe whether your independent variable does indeed cause a change. Look at the illustration below to see some examples of variables.

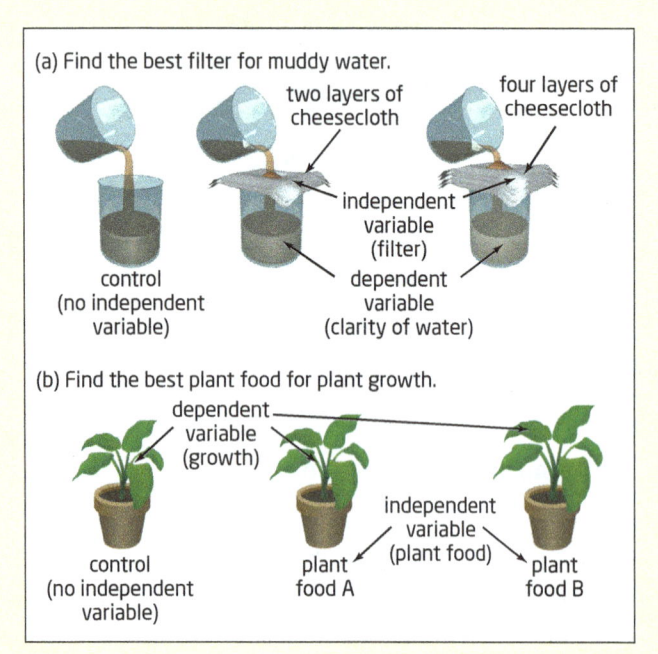

> **Instant Practice—Identifying Variables**
> For each of the following questions, state your control, your independent variable, and your dependent variable.
> 1. Does light travel the same way through different substances?
> 2. Does adding compost to soil promote vegetable growth?
> 3. How effective are various kinds of mosquito repellent?

Controlling Variables for a Fair Test If you consider more than one variable in a test, you are not conducting a **fair test** (one that is valid and unbiased), and your results will not be useful. You will not know whether the breeze or the Sun made the water evaporate.

(a) Find the best filter for muddy water.
- control (no independent variable)
- two layers of cheesecloth
- four layers of cheesecloth
- independent variable (filter)
- dependent variable (clarity of water)

(b) Find the best plant food for plant growth.
- dependent variable (growth)
- control (no independent variable)
- plant food A
- plant food B
- independent variable (plant food)

As you have been reading, a question may have occurred to you: How is it possible to do a fair test on puddles? How can you be sure that they are the same size? In situations such as this one, scientists often use **models**. A model can be a mental picture, a diagram, a working model, or even a mathematical expression. To make sure your test is fair, you can prepare model puddles that you know are all exactly the same. **Science Skills Toolkit 9** gives you more information on using models.

Before you begin your investigation, review safety procedures and identify what safety equipment you may need. Refer to page xiv in this textbook for more information on safety.

Recording and Organizing Data Another step in performing an investigation is recording and organizing your data. Often, you can record your data in a table like the one shown below. Refer to **Science Skills Toolkit 7** for more information on making tables.

Puddle Evaporation Times

Puddle	Evaporation Time (min)
A	37
B	34
C	42
X	100
Y	122
Z	118

Analyzing and Presenting Data After recording your data, the next step is to present your data in a format so that you can analyze it. Often, scientists make a graph, such as the bar graph below. For more information on constructing graphs, refer to **Math Skills Toolkit 3**.

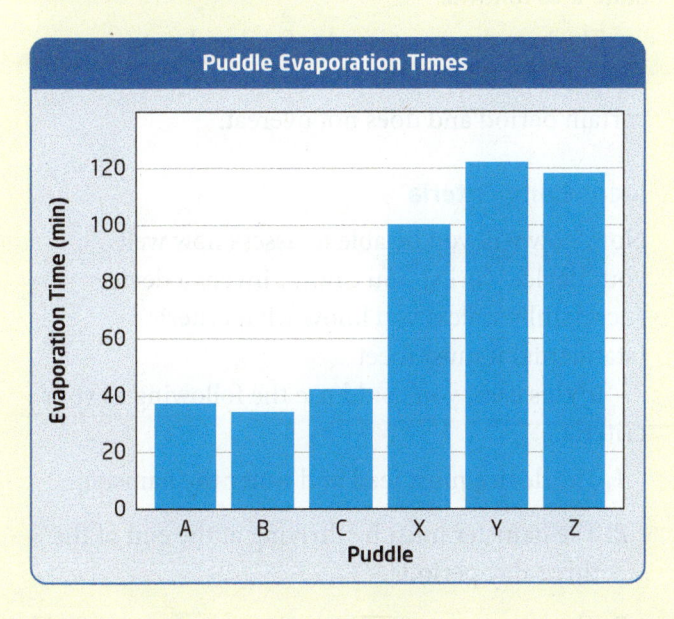

Forming a Conclusion

Many investigations are much more complex than the one described here, and there are many more possibilities for error. That is why it is so important to record careful qualitative and quantitative observations.

After you have completed all your observations, you are ready to analyze your data and draw a **conclusion**. A conclusion is a statement that indicates whether your results support or do not support your hypothesis. If you had hypothesized that the addition of thermal energy would have no effect on the evaporation of water, your results would not support your hypothesis. A hypothesis gives you a place to start and helps you design your experiment. If your results do not support your hypothesis, you use what you have learned in the experiment to come up with a new hypothesis to test.

Scientists often set up experiments without knowing what will happen. Sometimes they deliberately set out to prove that something will *not* happen.

Eventually, when a hypothesis has been thoroughly tested and nearly all scientists agree that the results support the hypothesis, it becomes a **theory**. For example, you will learn about cell theory, which describes the structure of living things, in Unit 1 of this textbook.

Science Skills Toolkit 3

Technological Problem Solving

Technology is the use of scientific knowledge, as well as everyday experience, to solve practical problems. Have you ever used a pencil to flip something out of a tight spot where your fingers could not reach? Have you ever used a stone to hammer bases or goal posts into the ground? Then you have used technology. You may not know why your pencil works as a lever or the physics behind levers, but your everyday experiences tell you how to use a lever successfully.

A Process for Technological Problem Solving

People turn to technology to solve problems. One problem-solving model is shown below.

Solving a Technological Problem

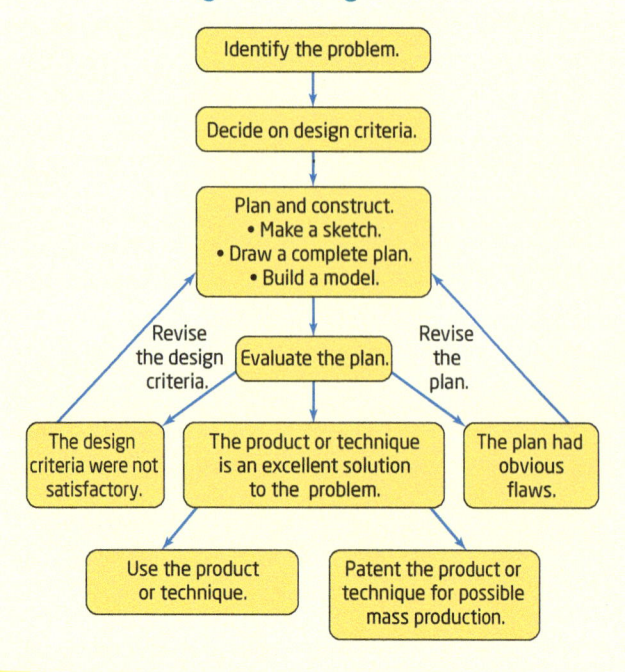

- Identify the problem.
- Decide on design criteria.
- Plan and construct.
  - Make a sketch.
  - Draw a complete plan.
  - Build a model.
- Evaluate the plan.
  - Revise the design criteria.
  - Revise the plan.
- The design criteria were not satisfactory.
- The product or technique is an excellent solution to the problem.
- The plan had obvious flaws.
- Use the product or technique.
- Patent the product or technique for possible mass production.

Identifying the Problem

When you used that pencil to move the small item you could not reach, you did so because you needed to move that item. In other words, you had identified a problem that needed to be solved. Clearly identifying a problem is a good first step in finding a solution. In the case of the lever, the solution was right before your eyes, but finding a solution is not always quite so simple.

Suppose school is soon to close for a 16-day winter holiday. Your science class has a hamster whose life stages the class observes. Student volunteers will take the hamster home and care for it over the holiday. However, there is a three-day period when no one will be available to feed the hamster. Leaving extra food in the cage is not an option because the hamster will eat it all at once. What devices could you invent to solve this problem?

First, you need to identify the exact nature of the problem you have to solve. You could state it as follows.

The hamster must receive food and water on a regular basis so that it remains healthy over a certain period and does not overeat.

Identifying Criteria

Now, how will you be able to assess how well your device works? You cannot invent a device successfully unless you know what criteria (standards) it must meet.

In this case, you could use the following as your criteria.

1. The device must feed and water the hamster.
2. The hamster must be thriving at the end of the three-day period.
3. The hamster must not appear to be "overstuffed."

How could you come up with such a device? On your own, you might not. If you work with a team, however, each of you will have useful ideas to contribute.

Planning and Constructing

You will probably come up with some good ideas on your own. Like all other scientists, though, you will want to use information and devices that others have developed. Do some research and share your findings with your group. Can you modify someone else's idea? With your group, brainstorm some possible designs. How would the designs work? What materials would they require? How difficult would they be to build? How many parts are there that could stop working during the three-day period? Make a clear, labelled drawing of each design, with an explanation of how it would work.

Examine all of your suggested designs carefully. Which do you think would work best? Why? Be prepared to share your choice and your reasons with your group. Listen carefully to what others have to say. Do you still feel yours is the best choice, or do you want to change your mind? When the group votes on the design that will be built, be prepared to co-operate fully, even if the group's choice is not your choice.

Get your teacher's approval of the drawing of the design your group wants to build. Then gather your materials and build a **prototype** (a model) of your design. Experiment with your design to answer some questions you might have about it. For example, should the food and water be provided at the same time? Until you try it out, you may be unsure if it is possible (or even a good idea) for your invention to deliver both food and water at the same time. Keep careful, objective records of each of your tests and of any changes you make to your design.

You might find, too, that your invention fails in a particular way. Perhaps it always leaks at a certain point where two parts are joined. Perhaps the food and water are not kept separate. Perhaps you notice a more efficient way to design your device as you watch it operate. Make any adjustments and test them so that your device works in the best and most efficient way possible.

Evaluating

When you are satisfied with your device, you can demonstrate it and observe devices constructed by other groups. Evaluate each design in terms of how well it meets the design criteria. Think about the ideas other groups tried out and why they work better than (or not as well as) yours. What would you do differently if you were to redesign your device?

Instant Practice—Technological Problem Solving

Suppose that you have collected an ice core sample that you want to store and keep frozen for at least a day. You do not have access to a source of electricity, and you do not have a ready-made refrigeration or insulating device.

1. Identify the problem. What is the exact nature of the challenge you face?
2. State at least three criteria that your solution must satisfy.
3. Design a device to solve the problem. Make a labelled sketch to show your proposed design.
4. Ask a friend to propose alterations or improvements to your design.
5. With the approval of your teacher, build your device and test it.
6. Evaluate the success of your device. Propose improvements.

Science Skills Toolkit 4

Estimating and Measuring

Estimating

How long will it take you to read this page? How heavy is this textbook? You could probably answer these questions by **estimating**—making an informed judgement about a measurement. An estimate gives you an idea of a particular quantity but is not an exact measurement.

For example, suppose you wanted to know how many ants live in a local park. Counting every ant would be very time-consuming. What you can do is count the number of ants in a typical square-metre area. Then, multiply the number of ants by the number of square metres in the total area you are investigating. This will give you an estimate of the total population of ants in that area.

Measuring Length and Area

You can use a metre stick or a ruler to measure short distances. These tools are usually marked in centimetres and/or millimetres. Use a ruler to measure the length in millimetres between points A and C, C and E, E and B, and A and D below. Convert your measurements to centimetres and then to metres.

A •   • B

   • C   • E   • D

To calculate an area, you can use length measurements. For example, for a square or a rectangle, you can find the area by multiplying the length by the width.

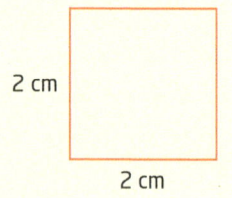

2 cm
2 cm

Area of square is 2 cm × 2 cm = 4 cm^2

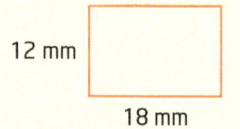

12 mm
18 mm

Area of rectangle is 18 mm × 12 mm = 216 mm^2

Make sure you always use the same units—if you mix up centimetres and millimetres, your calculations will be wrong. Remember to ask yourself if your answer is reasonable (you could make an estimate to consider this).

> **Instant Practice—Estimating and Measuring**
>
> Imagine that all rulers in the school have vanished. The only measurement tool that you now have is a toothpick.
>
> 1. Estimate the length and width of your textbook in toothpick units. Compare your estimates with a classmate's estimates.
>
> 2. Measure the length and width of your textbook with your toothpick. How close was your estimate to the actual measurement?
>
> 3. If you had a much larger area to measure, such as the floor of your classroom, what could you use instead of toothpicks to measure the area? (Be creative!)
>
> 4. What is your estimate of the number of units you chose (in question 3) for the width of your classroom?

Measuring Volume

The **volume** of an object is the amount of space that the object occupies. There are several ways of measuring volume, depending on the kind of object you want to measure.

As you can see in Diagram A below, the volume of a regularly shaped solid object can be measured directly. You can calculate the volume of a cube by multiplying its sides, as shown on the left in Diagram A. You can calculate the volume of a rectangular solid by multiplying its length × width × height, as shown on the right in Diagram A.

A

$2 \text{ cm} \times 2 \text{ cm} \times 2 \text{ cm} = 8 \text{ cm}^3$ $4 \text{ cm} \times 6 \text{ cm} \times 2 \text{ cm} = 48 \text{ cm}^3$

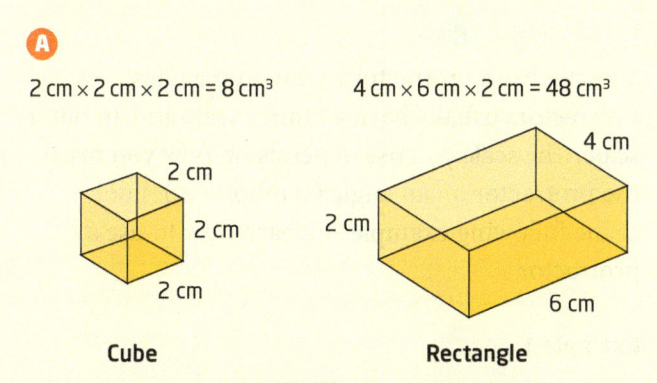

Cube   Rectangle

Measuring the volume of a regularly shaped solid

If all the sides of a solid object are measured in millimetres (mm), the volume will be in cubic millimetres (mm^3). If all the sides are measured in centimetres (cm), the volume will be in cubic centimetres (cm^3). The units for measuring the volume of a solid are called cubic units.

The units used to measure the volume of liquids are called capacity units. The basic unit of volume for liquids is the litre (L). Recall that 1 L = 1000 mL.

Cubic units and capacity units are interchangeable. For example,

$1 \text{ cm}^3 = 1 \text{ mL}$
$1 \text{ dm}^3 = 1 \text{ L}$
$1 \text{ m}^3 = 1 \text{ kL}$

The volume of a liquid can be measured directly, as shown in Diagram B below. Make sure you measure to the bottom of the **meniscus**, the slight curve where the liquid touches the sides of the container. To measure accurately, make sure your eye is at the same level as the bottom of the meniscus.

B

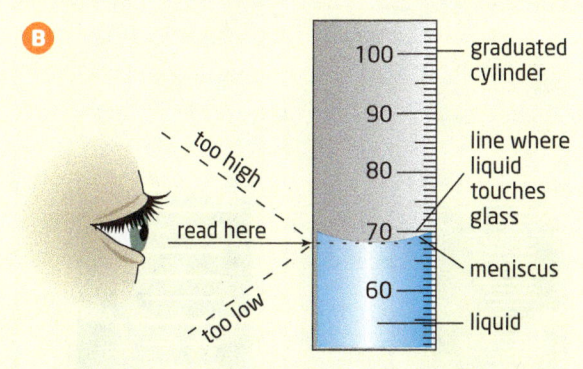

Measuring the volume of a liquid

The volume of an irregularly shaped solid object, however, must be measured indirectly, as shown in Diagram C below. This is done by determining the volume of a liquid it will displace.

C

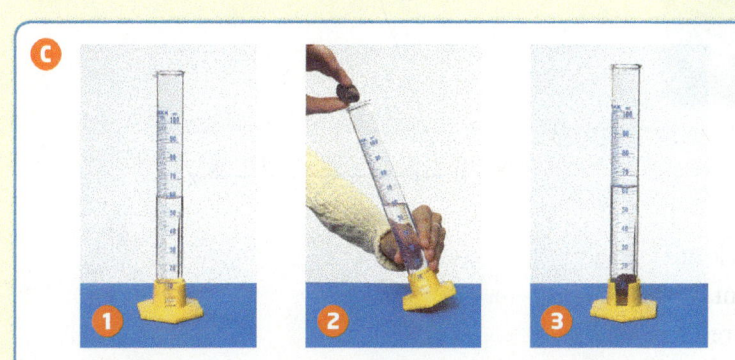

1. Record the volume of the liquid.
2. Carefully lower the object into the cylinder containing the liquid. Record the volume again.
3. The volume of the object is equal to the difference between the two volumes of the liquid. The equation below the photographs shows you how to calculate this volume.

Measuring the volume of an irregularly shaped solid
volume of object = volume of water with object − original volume of water
= 85 mL − 60 mL
= 25 mL

Science Skills Toolkit 4 • NEL   539

Instant Practice—Measuring Volume

Determine the volume of liquids present in the three graduated cylinders shown here.

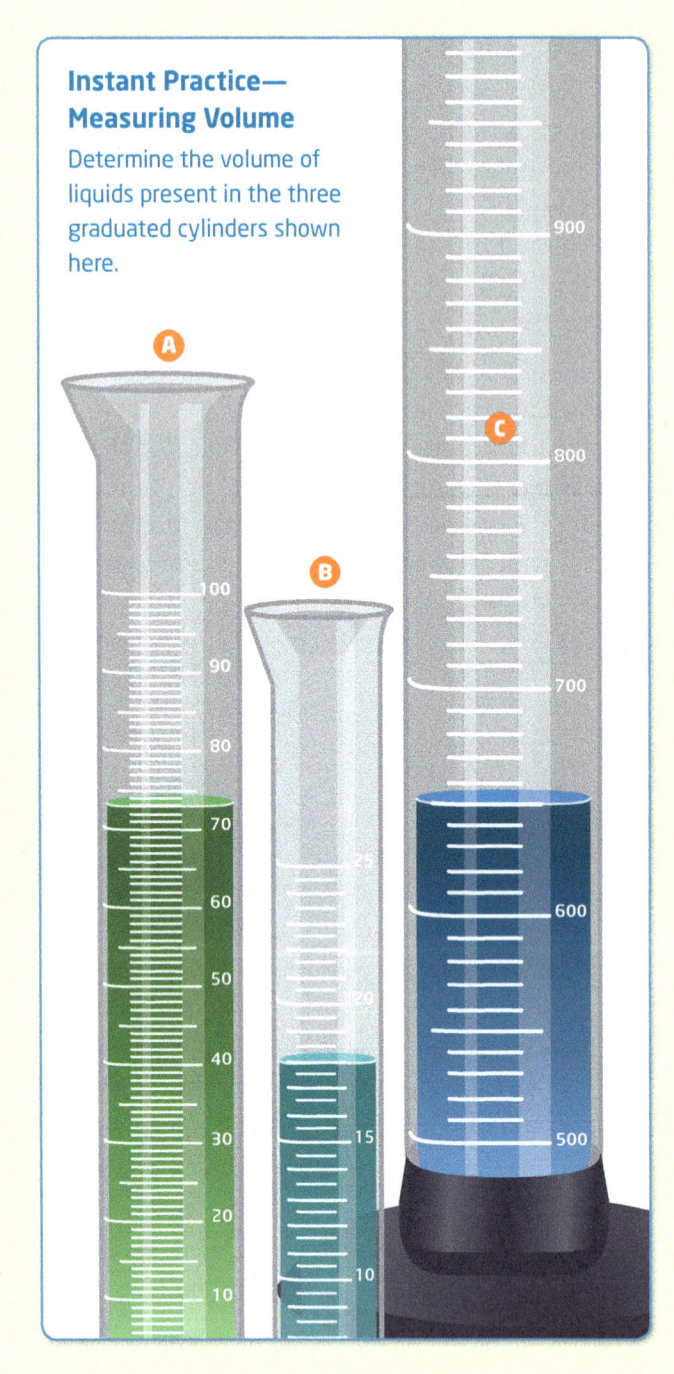

How can you find the mass of a certain quantity of a substance, such as table salt, that you have added to a beaker? First, find the mass of the beaker. Next, pour the salt into the beaker and find the mass of the beaker and salt together. To find the mass of the salt, simply subtract the beaker's mass from the combined mass of the beaker and salt.

Instant Practice—Measuring Mass

Use the following information to determine the mass of the table salt. The mass of a beaker is 160 g. The mass of the table salt and beaker together is 230 g.

Measuring Angles

You can use a protractor to measure angles. Protractors usually have an inner scale and an outer scale. The scale you use depends on how you place the protractor on an angle (symbol = ∠). Look at the following examples to learn how to use a protractor.

Example 1

What is the measure of ∠XYZ?

Solution

Place the centre of the protractor on point Y. YX crosses 0° on the inner scale. YZ crosses 70° on the inner scale. So ∠XYZ is equal to 70°.

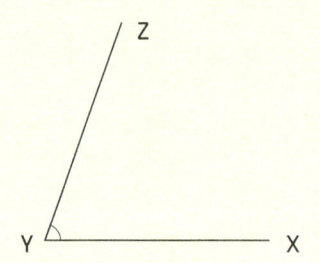

Measuring Mass

Is your backpack heavier than your friend's backpack? You can check by holding a backpack in each hand. The **mass** of an object is the amount of matter in a substance or object. Mass is measured in milligrams, grams, kilograms, and tonnes. You need a balance for measuring mass.

Example 2

Draw ∠ABC = 155°.

Solution

First, draw a straight line, AB. Place the centre of the protractor on B and line up AB with 0° on the outer scale. Mark C at 155° on the outer scale. Join BC. The angle you have drawn, ∠ABC, is equal to 155°.

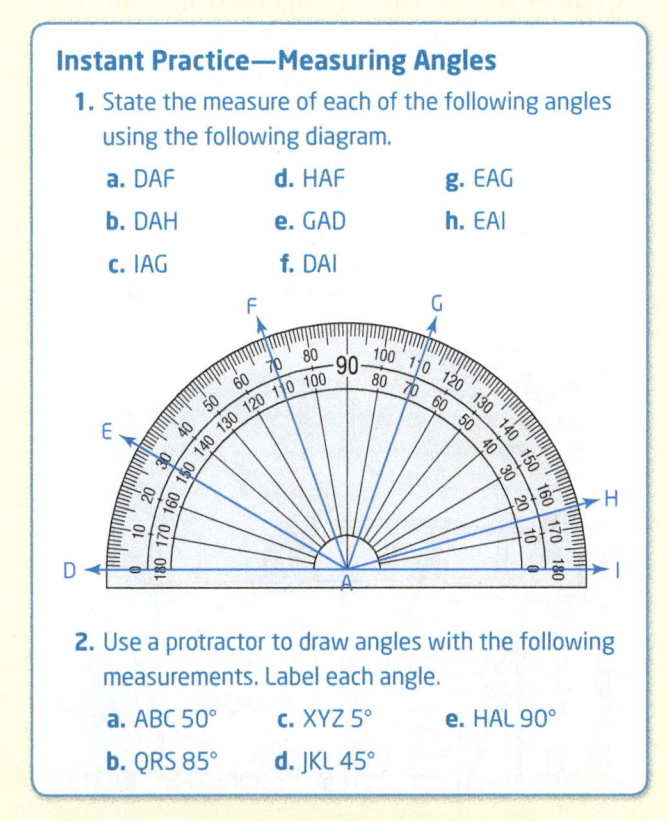

> **Instant Practice—Measuring Angles**
>
> 1. State the measure of each of the following angles using the following diagram.
>
>   a. DAF   d. HAF   g. EAG
>   b. DAH   e. GAD   h. EAI
>   c. IAG   f. DAI
>
> 2. Use a protractor to draw angles with the following measurements. Label each angle.
>
>   a. ABC 50°   c. XYZ 5°   e. HAL 90°
>   b. QRS 85°   d. JKL 45°

Measuring Temperature

Temperature is a measure of the thermal energy of the particles of a substance. In the very simplest terms, you can think of temperature as a measure of how hot or how cold something is. The temperature of a material is measured with a thermometer.

For most scientific work, temperature is measured on the Celsius scale. On this scale, the freezing point of water is zero degrees (0°C) and the boiling point of water is 100 degrees (100°C). Between these points, the scale is divided into 100 equal divisions. Each division represents one degree Celsius. On the Celsius scale, average human body temperature is 37°C, and a typical room temperature may be between 20°C and 25°C.

The SI unit of temperature is the kelvin (K). Zero on the Kelvin scale (0 K) is the coldest possible temperature. This temperature is also known as absolute zero. It is equivalent to −273°C, which is about 273 degrees below the freezing point of water. Notice that degree symbols are not used with the Kelvin scale.

Most laboratory thermometers are marked only with the Celsius scale. Because the divisions on the two scales are the same size, the Kelvin temperature can be found by adding 273 to the Celsius reading. This means that on the Kelvin scale, water freezes at 273 K and boils at 373 K.

Tips for Using a Thermometer

When using a thermometer to measure the temperature of a substance, here are three important tips to remember.

- Handle the thermometer extremely carefully. It is made of glass and can break easily.
- Do not use the thermometer as a stirring rod.
- Do not let the bulb of the thermometer touch the walls of the container.

Science Skills Toolkit 5

Precision and Accuracy

No measuring device can give an absolutely exact measure. So how do scientists describe how close an instrument comes to measuring the true result?

Precision Quantitative data from any measuring device are uncertain. You can describe this uncertainty in terms of precision and accuracy. The term **precision** describes both the exactness of a measuring device and the range of values in a set of measurements.

The precision of a measuring instrument is usually half the smallest division on its scale. For example, the bottom ruler below is graduated in centimetres, so it is precise to ± 0.5 cm. The length of the object above the ruler would be reported as 9.0 ± 0.5 cm, because it is closer to 9 cm than to 8 cm, and the uncertainty must be included in the measurement. The top ruler below is graduated in millimetres, so it is precise to ± 0.05 cm. The length of the object below the ruler would be reported as 8.7 ± 0.05 cm.

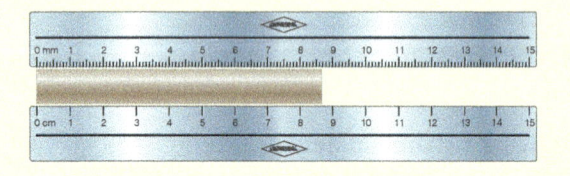

A precise measuring device will give nearly the same result every time it is used to measure the same object. Consider the following measurements of a 50 g weight on a balance. Both give the same average mass, but Scale B is more precise because it has a smaller range of measured values (± 0.3 versus ± 0.5).

Measurements of Mass on Two Scales

	Scale A Mass (g)	Scale B Mass (g)
Trial 1	49.9	49.9
Trial 2	49.8	50.2
Trial 3	50.3	49.9
Average	50.0	50.0
Range	± 0.5	± 0.3

Accuracy How close a measurement or calculation comes to the true value is described as **accuracy**. To improve accuracy, scientific measurements are often repeated and combined mathematically. The average measurements in the table on this page are more accurate than any of the individual measurements.

The darts in diagram A below are very precise, but they are not accurate because they did not hit the bull's-eye. The darts in diagram B are neither precise nor accurate. However, the darts in diagram C are both precise and accurate.

A precise but not accurate

B neither precise nor accurate

C precise and accurate

Instant Practice—Precision and Accuracy

1. A student measures the temperature of ice water four times, and each time gets a result of 10.0°C. Is the thermometer precise and accurate? Explain your answer.

2. Two students collected data on the mass of a substance for an experiment. Each student used a different scale to measure the mass of the substance over three trials. Student A had a range of measurements that was ±0.06 g. Student B had a range of measurements that was ±0.11 g. Which student had the more precise scale?

Science Skills Toolkit 6

Scientific Drawing

Have you ever used a drawing to explain something that was too difficult to explain in words? A clear drawing can often assist or replace words in a scientific explanation. In science, drawings are especially important when you are trying to explain difficult concepts or describe something that contains a lot of detail. It is important to make scientific drawings clear, neat, and accurate.

Examine the drawing shown below. It is taken from a student's lab report on an experiment to test the expansion of air in a balloon. The student's written description of results included an explanation of how the particle model can explain what happens to the balloon when the bottle is placed in hot water and in ice water. As you can see, the clear diagrams of the results can support or even replace many words of explanation. While your drawing itself is important, it is also important to label it clearly. If you are comparing and contrasting two objects, label each object and use labels to indicate the points of comparison between them.

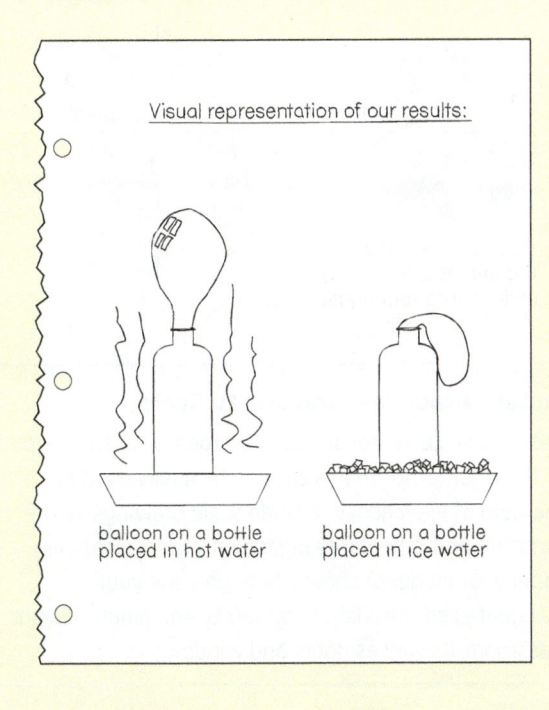

Making a Scientific Drawing

Follow these steps to make an effective scientific drawing.

1. Use unlined paper and a sharp pencil with an eraser.

2. Give yourself plenty of space on the paper. You need to make sure that your drawing will be large enough to show all necessary details. You also need to allow space for labels. Labels identify parts of the object you are drawing. Place all of your labels to the right of your drawing, unless there are so many labels that your drawing looks cluttered.

3. Carefully study the object that you will be drawing. Make sure you know what you need to include.

4. Draw only what you see, and keep your drawing simple. Do not try to indicate parts of the object that are not visible from the angle of observation. If you think it is important to show another part of the object, do a second drawing, and indicate the angle from which each drawing is viewed.

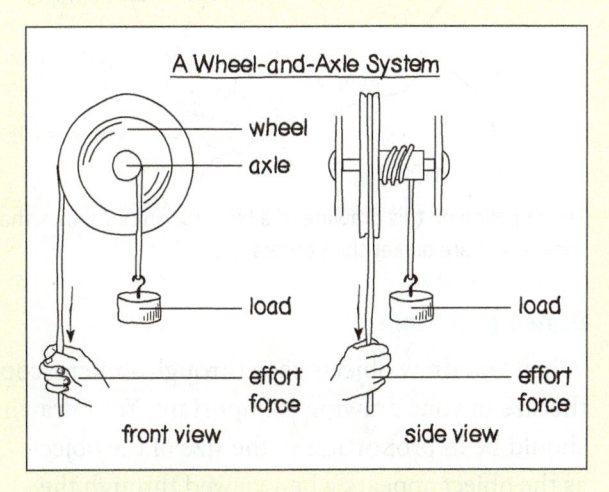

5. Shading or colouring is not usually used in scientific drawings. If you want to indicate a darker area, you can use stippling (a series of dots). You can use double lines to indicate thick parts of the object.

6. If you do use colour, try to be as accurate as you can and choose colours that are as close as possible to the colours in the object you are observing.

7. Label your drawing carefully and completely, using lower-case (small) letters. Think about what you would need to know if you were looking at the object for the first time. Remember to place all your labels to the right of the drawing, if possible. Use a ruler to draw a horizontal line from the label to the part you are identifying. Make sure that none of your label lines cross.

8. Give your drawing a title. The drawing of a human skin cell shown below is from a student's notebook. This student used stippling to show darker areas, horizontal label lines for the cell parts viewed, and a title—all elements of an excellent final drawing.

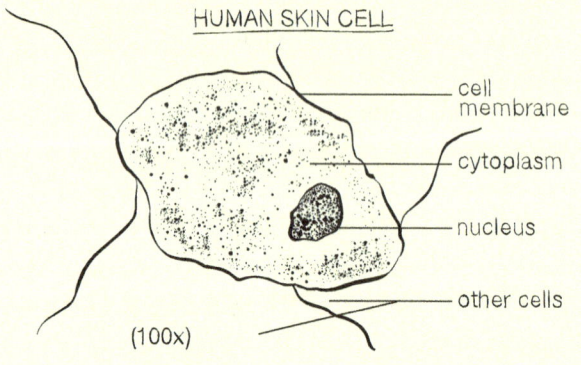

HUMAN SKIN CELL
— cell membrane
— cytoplasm
— nucleus
— other cells
(100x)

The stippling on this drawing of a human skin cell shows that some areas are darker than others.

Drawing to Scale

When you draw objects seen through a microscope, the size of your drawing is important. Your drawing should be in proportion to the size of the object as the object appears when viewed through the microscope. This type of drawing is called a **scale drawing**. A scale drawing allows you to compare the sizes of different objects and to estimate the actual size of the object being viewed. Here are some steps to follow when making scale drawings of magnified objects.

1. Use a mathematical compass to draw an accurate circle in your notebook. The size of the circle does not matter. The circle represents the microscope's field of view.

2. Imagine the circle is divided into four equal sections (see the diagram below). Use a pencil and a ruler to draw these sections in your circle, as shown below.

3. Using low or medium power, locate an object under the microscope. Imagine that the field of view is also divided into four equal sections.

4. Observe how much of the field of view is taken up by the object. Note the location of the object in the field of view.

5. Draw the object in the circle. Position the object in about the same part of the circle as it appears in the field of view. Draw the object so that it takes up about the same amount of space within the circle as it takes up in the field of view, as shown in the diagram.

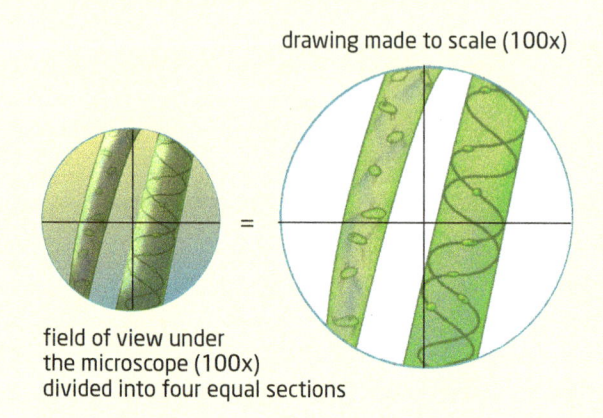

drawing made to scale (100x)

field of view under the microscope (100x) divided into four equal sections

Instant Practice—Drawing to Scale

Design a scale model of your classroom. Use the shape of the floor rather than a circle, which was used for the field of view above. Include scale drawings of the furniture and other large objects in your classroom. Label your model to show where you and your classmates sit. Also label any safety equipment in your classroom, as well as doors and windows.

Science Skills Toolkit 7

Creating Data Tables

Scientific investigation is about collecting information to help you answer a question. In many cases, you will develop an hypothesis and collect data to see if your hypothesis is supported. An important part of any successful investigation includes recording and organizing your data. Often, scientists create tables in which to record data.

Planning to Record Your Data Suppose you are doing an investigation on the water quality of a stream that runs near your school. You will take samples of the numbers and types of organisms at three different locations along the stream. You need to decide how to record and organize your data. Begin by making a list of what you need to record. For this experiment, you will need to record the sample site, the pH of the water at each sample site, the types of organisms found at each sample site, and how many of each type of organism you collected.

Creating Your Data Table Your data table must allow you to record your data neatly. To do this you need to create

- headings to show what you are recording
- columns and rows that you will fill with data
- enough cells to record all the data
- a title for the table

In this investigation, you will find multiple organisms at each site, so you must make space for multiple recordings at each site. This means every row representing a sample site will have at least three rows associated with it for the different organisms.

If you think you might need extra space, create a special section. In this investigation, leave space at the bottom of your table, in case you find more than three organisms at a sample site. Remember, if you use the extra rows, make sure you identify which sample site the extra data are from. Your data table might look like the one at the top of this page.

Observations Made at Three Sample Stream Sites

headings show what is being recorded

columns and rows contain data

Sample Site	pH	Type of Organism	Number of Organisms
1		beetle	3
		snail	1
		dragonfly larva	8
2		beetle	6
		dragonfly larva	7
3		snail	5
		leech	1
		dragonfly larva	2

extra rows to collect data in case you need to add observations

Instant Practice—Creating Data Tables

1. You are interested in how weeds grow in a garden. You decide to collect data from your garden every week for a month. You will identify the weeds and count how many there are of each type of weed. Design and draw a data table that you could use to record your data.

2. Many investigations have several different experimental treatments. Copy the following data table into your notebook and fill in the missing title and headings. The investigation tests the effect of increased fertilizer on plant height. There are four plants, and measurements are being taken every two days.

Day 1	Plant 1	5 mL	
	Plant 2	10 mL	10 cm
		15 mL	
		20 mL	

Science Skills Toolkit 8

Using a Microscope

The light microscope is an optical instrument that greatly increases our powers of observation by magnifying objects that are usually too small to be seen with the unaided eye. The microscope you will use is called a compound light microscope because it uses a series of lenses (rather than only one, as in a magnifying glass) and it uses light to view the object.

A microscope is a delicate instrument, so you must use proper procedure and care. This *Science Skills Toolkit* reviews the skills that you will need to use a microscope effectively. Before you use your microscope, you need to know the parts of a microscope and their functions.

A Eyepiece (or Ocular Lens)
You look through the eyepiece. It has a lens that magnifies the object, usually by 10 times (10×). The magnifying power is engraved on the side of the eyepiece.

B Tube
The tube holds the eyepiece and the objective lenses at the proper working distance from each other.

C Revolving Nosepiece
This rotating disk holds two or more objective lenses. Turn it to change lenses. Each lens clicks into place.

D Objective Lenses
The objective lenses magnify the object. Each lens has a different power of magnification, such as 4×, 10×, and 40×. (Your microscope may instead have 10×, 40×, and 100× objective lenses.) The objective lenses are referred to as low, medium, and high power. The magnifying power is engraved on the side of each objective lens. Be sure you can identify each lens.

E Arm
The arm connects the base and the tube. Use the arm for carrying the microscope.

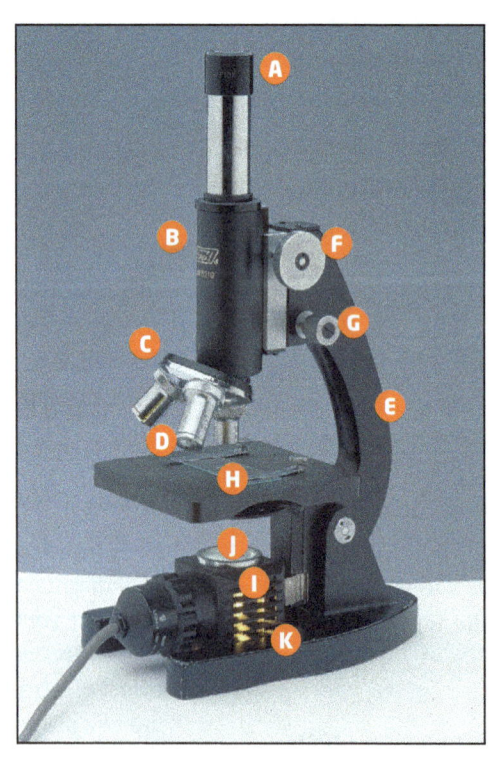

K Light Source
Shining a light through the object being viewed makes it easier to see the details. If your microscope has a mirror instead of a light, adjust the mirror to direct light through the lenses. CAUTION: Use an electric light, not sunlight, as the light source for focussing your mirror.

F Coarse-adjustment Knob
The coarse-adjustment knob moves the tube up and down to bring the object into focus. Use it only with the low-power objective lens.

G Fine-adjustment Knob
Use the fine-adjustment knob with medium- and high-power magnification to bring the object into sharper focus.

H Stage
The stage supports the microscope slide. Stage clips hold the slide in position. An opening in the centre of the stage allows light from the light source to pass through the slide.

I Condenser Lens
The condenser lens directs light to the object being viewed.

J Diaphragm
The diaphragm controls the amount of light reaching the object being viewed.

Troubleshooting

You may encounter difficulties when using your microscope. The following list details the more common problems and how you can deal with them.

- *You cannot see anything.* Make sure the microscope is plugged in and the light is turned on. If the microscope has no light, adjust your mirror.
- *Are you having trouble finding anything on the slide?* Be patient. Make sure the object being viewed is in the middle of the stage opening. While watching from the side, lower the low-power objective as far as it will go. Then look through the ocular lens and slowly raise the objective lens using the coarse-adjustment knob.
- *Are you having trouble focussing, or is the image very faint?* Try closing the diaphragm slightly. Some objects are almost transparent. If there is too much light, a specimen may be difficult to see or will appear "washed out."
- *Do you see lines and specks floating across the slide?* These are probably structures in the fluid of your eyeball that you see when you move your eyes. Do not worry; this is normal.
- *Do you see a double image?* Check that the objective lens is properly clicked into place.
- *Do you close one eye while you look through the microscope with the other eye?* You might try keeping both eyes open. This will help prevent eye fatigue. It also lets you sketch an object while you are looking at it.
- Always place the part of the slide you are interested in at the centre of the field of view before changing to a higher-power objective lens. Otherwise, when you turn to medium and high power, you may not see the object you were viewing under low power.

Instant Practice—Applying Stains

When working with microscopic specimens, it is often difficult to observe the structures in the specimens clearly. You can use various stains to colour the structures you want to see. Common stains that are used for biological specimens are

- iodine, for staining starch
- crystal violet, for staining bacterial cell walls
- methylene blue, for observing nuclei in cheek cells

Suppose that you want to observe the stages of mitosis in an onion root tip.

1. Slice off the root tips from a green onion, or from a yellow onion that has been allowed to grow in water for a few days.
2. Cut off the root tips. Place them in a small amount of 1 M HCl(aq) for a few minutes to stop mitosis. CAUTION: HCl(aq) is a strong acid. Follow the safety rules for working with acids.
3. Slice a very thin section of the onion root tip, and place it on a microscope slide.
4. Add several drops of a stain, such as 1% toluidine blue, to the root tip section. Leave the stain on the section for several minutes.
5. Blot off the extra stain with a paper towel. Add a few drops of water to the section to remove the extra stain, and then blot off the water. Repeat, if necessary. There should not be a lot of stain left on the section.
6. Add one drop of water. Place a cover slip on the microscope slide, edge first. Carefully lower the cover slip over the section.
7. If the section is too thick, carefully apply gentle pressure to flatten the section.
8. Place the slide on a microscope. Use the low power for your first observation.

Science Skills Toolkit 9

Using Models and Analogies in Science

Scientists often use models and analogies to help communicate their ideas to other scientists or to students.

Using Models

When you think of a model, you might think of a toy such as a model airplane. Is a model airplane similar to a scientific model? If building a model airplane helps you learn about flight, then you could say it is a scientific model.

In science, a model is anything that helps you better understand a scientific concept. A model can be a picture, a mental image, a structure, or even a mathematical formula. Sometimes, you need a model because the objects you are studying are too small to see with the unaided eye. You may have learned about the particle model of matter, for example, which is a model that states that all matter is made of tiny, invisible particles. Sometimes a model is useful because the objects you are studying are extremely large—the planets in our solar system, for example. In other cases, the object may be hidden from view, like the interior of Earth or the inside of a living organism. A mathematical model can show you how to perform a calculation.

Scientists often use models to test an idea, to find out if an hypothesis is supported, and to plan new experiments in order to learn more about the subject they are studying. Sometimes, scientists discover so much new information that they have to modify their models. Examine the model shown in the photograph below. How can this model help you learn about science?

You can learn about day and night by using a globe and a flashlight to model Earth and the Sun.

> **Instant Practice—Using Models**
> Describe how you could use a model to help you explain the following concept to a Grade 8 student: Two hydrogen molecules react with one oxygen molecule to form two water molecules.

Using Analogies

An analogy is a comparison between two things that have some characteristic in common. Scientists use analogies to help explain difficult concepts. For example, scientists sometimes refer to plants as the lungs of Earth. Recall that plants take in carbon dioxide (CO_2) from the atmosphere to use during photosynthesis. Plants then release the oxygen (O_2) produced by photosynthesis back into the atmosphere.

In a sense, the plants are "breathing" for Earth. When animals breathe, they take oxygen into their lungs and give off carbon dioxide.

> **Instant Practice—Using Analogies**
> Use an analogy to help you explain the functions of the various parts of a cell.

Science Skills Toolkit 10

How to Do a Research-Based Project

Imagine if your teacher simply stated that he or she wanted you to complete a research-based project on endangered species. This is a really big topic, and it is now your job to decide which smaller aspect of the topic you will research. One way to approach a research project is to break it up into four stages—exploring, investigating, processing, and creating.

Explore—Pick a Topic and Ask Questions

You need to start by finding out some general things about endangered species. Make a list of questions as you conduct your initial research, such as, What factors cause species to become endangered? Why does it matter? What types of species are endangered? Suppose, in the course of your research, you decided to learn more about polar bears. A good research question about polar bears would be, Why are polar bears endangered? An even better question could be, What can I do to help prevent polar bear extinction? Both of these questions are deep and can be subdivided into many subtopics.

Investigate—Research Your Topic

When putting together a research project, it is important to find reliable sources to help you answer your question. Before you decide to use a source that you find, you should consider whether it is reliable or whether it shows any bias.

Sources of Information There are many sources of information. For example, you can use a print resource, such as an encyclopedia from the reference section of the library.

Another approach is to go on-line and check the Internet. When you use the Internet, be careful about which sites you choose to search for information. You need to be able to determine the validity of a website before you trust the information you find on it. To do this, check that the author is identified, a recent publication date is given, and the source of facts or quotations is identified. It is also important that the website is published by a well-known company or organization.

You may also want to contact an expert on your topic. A credible expert has credentials showing his or her expertise in an area. For example, an expert may be a doctor or have a master's degree. Alternatively, an expert could have many years of experience in a specific career or field of study.

No matter which sources you use, it is your responsibility to be a critical consumer of information and to find trustworthy sources for your research.

You should also ask yourself if the sources you are using are primary or secondary.

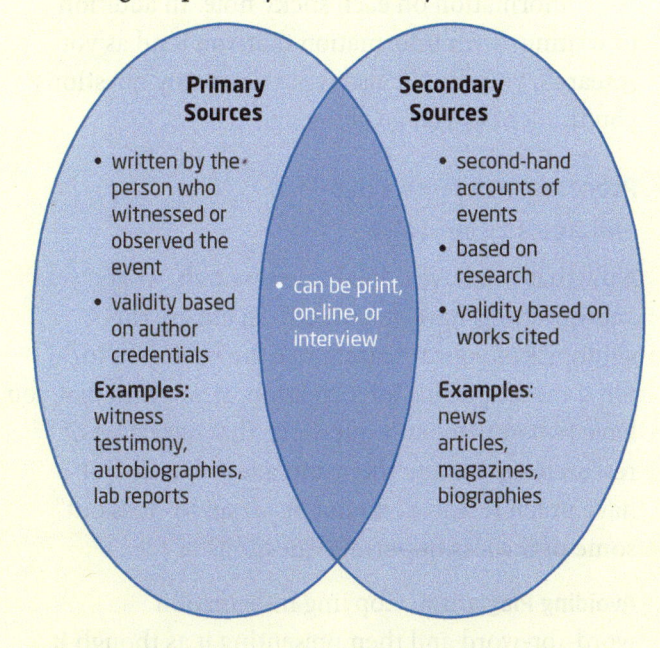

Primary Sources
- written by the person who witnessed or observed the event
- validity based on author credentials

Examples: witness testimony, autobiographies, lab reports

- can be print, on-line, or interview

Secondary Sources
- second-hand accounts of events
- based on research
- validity based on works cited

Examples: news articles, magazines, biographies

Reliability and Bias Two other things to check for in a source are reliability and bias. To check for reliability, try to find the same "fact" in two other sources. But keep in mind that even if you cannot find the same idea somewhere else, the source may still be reliable if it is a research paper or if it was written by an author with strong credentials. To check for bias, look for judgemental statements. Does the author tend to favour one side of an issue more than another? Are all sides of an issue treated equally? A good source shows little bias.

Source	Information	Reliability	Bias	Questions I Have
The Canadian Encyclopedia website	Polar bears inhabit ice and coastlines of arctic seas.	• author: Brian Knudsen • secondary source • has links to external sites that are reliable	only lists facts	• Why do they live on ice? • Why don't they move south?
Polar Bears International website	shrinking sea ice habitat	• date at bottom of page 2009 • non-profit organization	designed to save the polar bear	• Why is the ice shrinking?

Recording Information As you find information, jot it down on sticky notes or use a chart similar to the one shown above. Sticky notes are useful because you can move them around, group similar ideas together, and reorganize your ideas easily. Using a different colour for each sub-question is even better! Remember to write the source of your information on each sticky note. In addition to writing down information that you find as you research, you should also write down any questions you think of as you go along.

Process—Ask More Questions and Revise Your Work

Now that you have done some research, what sub-questions have you asked? These are the subtopics of your research. Use the subtopics to find more specific information. If you find that you have two or three sub-questions that have a lot of research supporting them and a few that do not have much research, do not be afraid to "toss out" some of the less important questions or ideas.

Avoiding Plagiarism Copying information word-for-word and then presenting it as though it is your own work is called *plagiarism*. When you refer to your notes to write your project, put the information in your own words. It is also important to give credit to the original source of an idea.

Recording Source Information Research papers always include a bibliography—a list of relevant information sources the authors consulted while preparing them. Bibliographic entries give the author, title, and facts of publication for each information source. Sometimes, you may want to give the exact source of information within the paper. This is done using footnotes. *Footnotes* identify the exact source (including page number) of quotations and ideas. Ask your teacher how you should prepare your list of works cited and your footnotes.

Create—Present Your Work

Before you choose a format for your final project, consider whether your researched information has answered the question you originally asked. If you have not answered this question, you need to either refine your original question or do some more research! You also need to consider who the audience is for your project. How you format your final project will be very different if it is meant for a Grade 2 class compared to the president of a company or a government official. You could present your project as a computer slide presentation, a graphic novel, a video, or a research paper.

> **Instant Practice**
>
> 1. Describe the steps you should follow when preparing a project on the topic of acid precipitation.
>
> 2. The following example is not an effective question on which to base a research project: "What is the pH range of acid precipitation?" Modify the question to make it an effective research question.
>
> 3. Assume that the target audience for your project is a group of Grade 6 students from a local elementary school. How would you need to modify your project for this target audience? What would be the best format to use to present your project to your audience?

Science Skills Toolkit 11

The GRASP Problem Solving Method

Solving any problem is easier when you establish a logical, step-by-step procedure. One useful method for solving numerical problems includes five basic steps: **G**iven, **R**equired, **A**nalysis, **S**olution, and **P**araphrase. You can easily remember these steps because the first letter of each word spells the word **GRASP**.

Example of the GRASP Problem Solving Method

A concave mirror has a focal length of 12 cm. An object with a height of 2.5 cm is placed 40.0 cm in front of the mirror.
  a. Calculate the image distance.
  b. Calculate the image height.

Given—Organize the given data.

focal length, $f = 12$ cm
object height, $h_o = 2.5$ cm
object distance, $d_o = 40.0$ cm

Required—Identify what information the problem requires you to find.

image distance, d_i (cm)
image height, h_i (cm)

Analysis—Decide how to solve the problem.

The units are consistent, so no conversions are required. The mirror equation and the magnification equation are needed.

$$\frac{1}{f} = \frac{1}{d_i} + \frac{1}{d_o} \quad \text{and} \quad \frac{h_i}{h_o} = \frac{-d_i}{d_o}$$

Solution—Solve the problem.

a. Use the mirror equation to find d_i.

$$\frac{1}{d_i} = \frac{1}{f} - \frac{1}{d_o}$$
$$= \frac{1}{12 \text{ cm}} - \frac{1}{40.0 \text{ cm}}$$
$$= \frac{10}{120 \text{ cm}} - \frac{3}{120 \text{ cm}} = \frac{7}{120 \text{ cm}}$$
$$d_i = \frac{120 \text{ cm}}{7} = 17.14 \text{ cm}$$

b. Use the magnification equation to find h_i.

$$\frac{h_i}{h_o} = \frac{-d_i}{d_o}$$
$$\frac{h_i}{2.5 \text{ cm}} = \frac{-17.14 \text{ cm}}{40.0 \text{ cm}}$$
$$h_i = 2.5 \text{ cm} \left(\frac{-17.14 \text{ cm}}{40.0 \text{ cm}}\right)$$
$$h_i = -1.07 \text{ cm}$$

Paraphrase—Restate the solution and check your answer.

Restate The image is 17 cm (after rounding) from the mirror. The sign is positive, so the image is in front of the mirror. The height of the image is 1.1 cm (after rounding). The image height is negative, so the image is inverted.

Check The value of C is twice the value of F, so C is 2×12 cm = 24 cm. The object is at 40 cm, so it is beyond C. Therefore, the image should be closer to the mirror than the object, smaller than the object, and inverted. All of these characteristics agree with the answers. The ray diagram below verifies the solution.

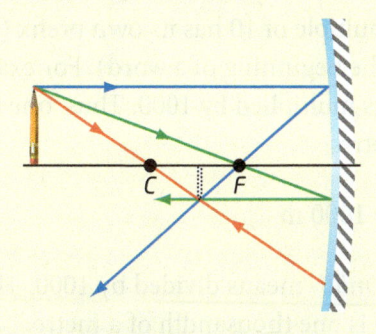

Instant Practice—Using GRASP

Use the GRASP method to solve the following problems.

1. A concave mirror has a focal length of 6.0 cm. An object with a height of 0.60 cm is placed 10.0 cm in front of the mirror.
   a. Calculate the image distance.
   b. Calculate the image height.

2. A concave mirror has a focal length of 3.0 cm. An object with a height of 0.8 cm is placed 1.5 cm in front of the mirror.
   a. Calculate the image distance.
   b. Calculate the image height.

Math Skills Toolkit 1

The Metric System and Scientific Notation

Throughout history, people have developed systems of numbering and measurement. When different groups of people began to communicate with each other, they discovered that their systems and units of measurement were different. Some groups within societies created their own unique systems of measurement.

Today, scientists around the world use the metric system of numbers and units. The metric system is the official system of measurement in Canada.

The Metric System

The metric system is based on multiples of 10. For example, the basic unit of length is the metre. All larger units of length are expressed in units based on metres multiplied by 10, 100, 1000, or more. Smaller units of length are expressed in units based on metres divided by 10, 100, 1000, or more.

Each multiple of 10 has its own prefix (a syllable joined to the beginning of a word). For example, *kilo-* means multiplied by 1000. Thus, one kilometre is 1000 metres.

1 km = 1000 m

The prefix *milli-* means divided by 1000. Thus, one millimetre is one thousandth of a metre.

1 mm = $\frac{1}{1000}$ m

In the metric system, the same prefixes are used for nearly all types of measurements, such as mass, weight, area, and energy. A table of the most common metric prefixes is given at the top of the next column.

Commonly Used Metric Prefixes

Prefix	Symbol	Relationship to the Base Unit
giga-	G	10^9 = 1 000 000 000
mega-	M	10^6 = 1 000 000
kilo-	k	10^3 = 1000
hecto-	h	10^2 = 100
deca-	da	10^1 = 10
—	—	10^0 = 1
deci-	d	10^{-1} = 0.1
centi-	c	10^{-2} = 0.01
milli-	m	10^{-3} = 0.001
micro-	μ	10^{-6} = 0.000 001
nano-	n	10^{-9} = 0.000 000 001

Example

There are 250 g of cereal in a package. Express this mass in kilograms.

Solution

$$1 \text{ kg} = 1000 \text{ g}$$
$$250 \text{ g} \times 4 = 1000 \text{ g}$$
$$\frac{1000}{4} \text{ g} = 250 \text{ g}$$
$$\frac{1}{4} \text{ kg} = 0.25 \text{ kg}$$

Instant Practice—Using Metric Measurements

1. A hummingbird has a mass of 3.5 g. Express its mass in mg.
2. For an experiment, you need to measure 350 mL of dilute acetic acid. Express the volume in L.
3. A bald eagle has a wingspan up to 2.3 m. Express the length in cm.
4. A student added 0.0025 L of food colouring to water. Express the volume in mL.

Exponents of Scientific Notation

An exponent is the symbol or number denoting the power to which another number or symbol is to be raised. The exponent shows the number of repeated multiplications of the base. In 10^2, the exponent is 2 and the base is 10. So 10^2 means 10×10.

Powers of 10

	Standard Form	Exponential Form
Ten thousands	10 000	10^4
Thousands	1000	10^3
Hundreds	100	10^2
Tens	10	10^1
Ones	1	10^0
Tenths	0.1	10^{-1}
Hundredths	0.01	10^{-2}
Thousandths	0.001	10^{-3}
Ten thousandths	0.0001	10^{-4}

Why use exponents? Consider this. Mercury is about 58 000 000 km from the Sun. If a zero were accidentally added to this number, the distance would appear to be 10 times larger than it actually is. To avoid mistakes when writing many zeros, scientists express very large and very small numbers in scientific notation.

Example 1

Mercury is about 58 000 000 km from the Sun. Write 58 000 000 in scientific notation.

Solution

In scientific notation, a number has the form $x \times 10^n$, where x is greater than or equal to 1 but less than 10, and 10^n is a power of 10.

58 000 000. ← The decimal point starts here. Move the decimal point 7 places to the left.
= 5.8 × 10 000 000
= 5.8×10^7

When you move the decimal point to the left, the exponent of 10 is positive. The number of places you move the decimal point is the number in the exponent.

Example 2

The electron in a hydrogen atom is, on average, 0.000 000 000 053 m from the nucleus. Write 0.000 000 000 053 in scientific notation.

Solution

To write the number in the form $x \times 10^n$, move the decimal point to the right until there is one non-zero number to the left of the decimal point.

The decimal point starts here. 0.000 000 000 053
Move the decimal point 11 places to the right.
= 5.3 × 0.000 000 000 01
= 5.3×10^{-11}

When you move the decimal point to the right, the exponent of 10 is negative. The number of places you move the decimal point is the number in the exponent.

Instant Practice—Scientific Notation

1. Express each of the following in scientific notation.
   a. The approximate number of stars in our galaxy, the Milky Way:
      400 000 000 000 stars
   b. The approximate distance of the Andromeda Galaxy from Earth:
      23 000 000 000 000 000 000 km
   c. The estimated distance across the universe:
      800 000 000 000 000 000 000 km
   d. The approximate mass of a proton:
      0.000 000 000 000 000 000 000 0017 g

2. Change the following to standard form.
   a. 9.8×10^5 m
   b. 2.3×10^9 kg
   c. 5.5×10^{-5} L
   d. 6.5×10^{-10} s

Math Skills Toolkit 2

Significant Digits and Rounding

You might think that a measurement can be an exact quantity. But in fact, whenever you take a measurement, you are only making an estimate. **Accuracy** is the difference between a measurement and its true value. No measuring device is 100 percent accurate. For example, the illustration below shows a ruler measuring the length of a rod. The ruler can give a quite accurate reading, as it is divided into millimetre marks. But the end of the rod falls between two marks. There is still uncertainty in the measurement.

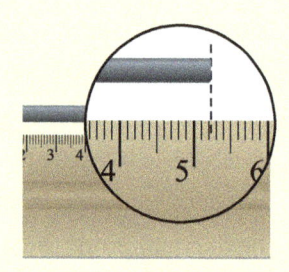

Significant Digits

Significant digits are used to represent the amount of uncertainty in a measurement. The significant digits in a measured quantity include all the certain digits plus the first uncertain digit. In the example above, the length of the rod is between 5.2 cm and 5.3 cm. We must estimate the distance between the 2 mm and 3 mm marks. Suppose we estimate the length to be 5.23 cm. The first two digits (5 and 2) are certain (we can see those marks), but the last digit (0.03) was estimated. The measurement 5.23 cm has three significant digits.

Determining the Number of Significant Digits

The following rules will help you determine the number of significant digits in a given measurement.

1. All non-zero digits (1–9) are considered significant.

   Examples:
   - 123 m – three significant digits
   - 23.56 km – four significant digits

2. Zeros between non-zero digits are also significant.

   Examples:
   - 1207 m – four significant digits
   - 120.5 km/h – four significant digits

3. Any zero that follows a non-zero digit *and* is to the right of the decimal point is significant.

   Examples:
   - 12.50 m/s^2 – four significant digits
   - 6.0 km – two significant digits

4. Zeros used to indicate the position of the decimal are not significant. These zeros are sometimes called spacers.

   Examples:
   - 500 km – one significant digit (the decimal point is assumed to be after the final zero)
   - 0.325 m – three significant digits
   - 0.000 34 km – two significant digits

5. All counting numbers have an infinite number of significant digits.

   Examples:
   - 6 apples – infinite number of significant digits
   - 125 people – infinite number of significant digits

554 NEL • Math Skills Toolkit 2

Instant Practice

Determine the number of significant digits in each measurement.

a. 25 g
b. 584 mL
c. 0.003 56 km
d. 505.2 m
e. 1.030 L
f. 12 000 cm
g. 0.0070 kg

Using Significant Digits in Mathematical Operations

When you use measured values in mathematical operations, the calculated answer cannot be more certain than the measurements on which it is based. Often the answer on your calculator will have to be rounded to the correct number of significant digits.

Rules for Rounding

1. When the first digit to be dropped is less than 5, the preceding digit is not changed.

   Example:
   6.723 m rounded to two significant digits is 6.7 m. The digit after the 7 is less than 5, so the 7 does not change.

2. When the first digit to be dropped is 5 or greater, the preceding digit is increased by one.

   Example:
   7.237 m rounded to three significant digits is 7.24 m. The digit after the 3 is greater than 5, so the 3 is increased by one.

Adding or Subtracting Measurements

Perform the mathematical operation, and then round off the answer to the value having the fewest decimal places.

Example:
Add the following measured lengths and express the answer to the correct number of significant digits.

x = 2.3 cm + 6.47 cm + 13.689 cm
  = 22.459 cm
  = 22.5 cm

Since 2.3 cm has only one decimal place, the answer can have only one decimal place.

Multiplying or Dividing Measurements

Perform the mathematical operation, and then round off the answer to the least number of significant digits of the data values.

Example:
Multiply the following measured lengths and express the answer to the correct number of significant digits.

x = (2.342 m)(0.063 m)(306 m)
  = 45.149 076 m^3
  = 45 m^3

Since 0.063 m has only two significant digits, the final answer must also have two significant digits.

Instant Practice

Perform the following calculations, rounding off your answer to the correct number of significant digits.

a. (2.475 m) + (3.5 m) + (4.65 m)
b. (47 g) − (12.27 g) − (8.384 g)
c. (15.3 cm) × (0.2265 cm)
d. (12.34 km) / (0.50 h)
e. (12 mL) × (3.56 mL) / (4.060 mL)

Math Skills Toolkit 3

Organizing and Communicating Scientific Results with Graphs

In your investigations, you will collect information, often in numerical form. To analyze and report the information, you will need a clear, concise way to organize and communicate the data.

A graph is a visual way to present data. A graph can help you to see patterns and relationships among the data. The type of graph you choose depends on the type of data you have and how you want to present them. You can use line graphs, bar graphs, and pie graphs (pie charts).

The instructions given here describe how to make graphs using paper and pencil. Computer software provides another way to generate graphs. Whether you make them on paper or on the computer, however, the graphs you make should have the features described in the following pages.

Drawing a Line Graph

A line graph is used to show the relationship between two variables. The following example will demonstrate how to draw a line graph from a data table.

Example

Suppose you have conducted a survey to find out how many students in your school are recycling drink containers. Out of 65 students that you surveyed, 28 are recycling cans and bottles. To find out if more recycling bins would encourage students to recycle cans and bottles, you add one recycling bin per week at different locations around the school. In follow-up surveys, you obtain the data shown in **Table 1**. Compare the steps in the procedure with the graph on the next page to learn how to make a line graph to display your findings.

Table 1 Students Using Recycling Bins

Number of Recycling Bins	Number of Students Using Recycling Bins
1	28
2	36
3	48
4	60

Procedure

1. With a ruler, draw an *x*-axis and a *y*-axis on a piece of graph paper. (The horizontal line is the *x*-axis, and the vertical line is the *y*-axis.)

2. To label the axes, write "Number of Recycling Bins" along the *x*-axis and "Number of Students Using Recycling Bins" along the *y*-axis.

3. Now you have to decide what scale to use. You are working with two numbers (number of students and number of bins). You need to show how many students use the existing bin and how many would recycle if there were a second, a third, and a fourth bin. The scale on the *x*-axis will go from 0 to 4. There are 65 students, so you might want to use intervals of 5 for the *y*-axis. That means that every space on your *y*-axis represents 5 students. Use a tick mark at major intervals on your scale, as shown in the graph on the next page.

4. You want to make sure you will be able to read your graph when it is complete, so make sure your intervals on the *x*-axis are large enough.

5. To plot your graph, gently move a pencil up the *y*-axis until you reach a point just below 30 (you are representing 28 students). Now move along the line on the graph paper until you reach the vertical line that represents the first recycling bin. Place a dot at this point (1 bin, 28 students). Repeat this process for all of the data.

6. If it is possible, draw a line that connects all of the points on your graph. This might not be possible. Scientific investigations often involve quantities that do not change smoothly. On a graph, this means that you should draw a smooth curve (or straight line) that most closely fits the general shape outlined by the points. This is called a **line of best fit**. A best-fit line often passes through many of the points, but sometimes it goes between points. Think of the dots on your graph as clues about where the perfect smooth curve (or straight line) should go. A line of best fit shows the trend of the data. It can be extended beyond the first and last points to indicate what might happen.

7. Give your graph a title. Based on these data, what is the relationship between the number of students using recycling bins and the number of recycling bins?

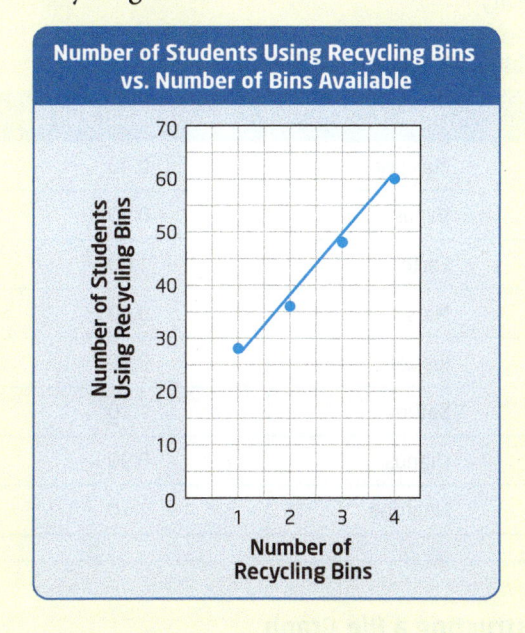

Instant Practice—Line Graph

The level of ozone in Earth's upper atmosphere is measured in Dobson units (all the ozone present in a column of air above a particular point). Using the information in the table below, create a line graph showing what happened to the amount of ozone over Antarctica during a period of 40 years.

Table 2 Ozone Levels in Earth's Upper Atmosphere

Year	Total Ozone (DU)
1960	300
1965	280
1970	280
1975	275
1980	225
1985	200
1990	160
1995	110
2000	105

Constructing a Bar Graph

Bar graphs help you to compare a numerical quantity with some other category at a glance. The second category may or may not be a numerical quantity. It could be places, items, organisms, or groups, for example.

Example

To learn how to make a bar graph to display the data in **Table 3** on the next page, examine the graph in the column next to the table as you read the steps that follow. The data show the area in square kilometres of principal Ontario lakes, not including the Great Lakes.

Table 3 Area Covered by Principal Ontario Lakes

Lake	Area (km^2)
Big Trout Lake	661
Lac Seul	1657
Lake Abitibi	931
Lake Nipigon	4848
Lake Nipissing	832
Lake of the Woods	3150
Lake Simcoe	744
Lake St. Clair	490
Rainy Lake	741

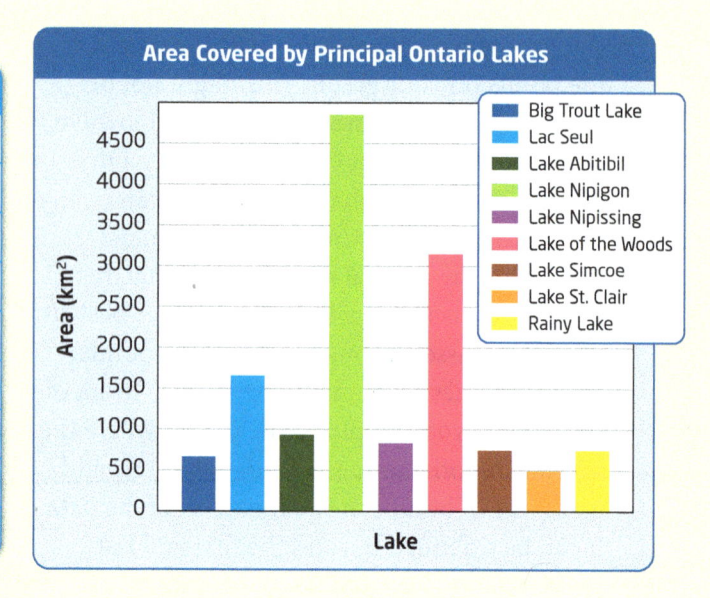

Procedure

1. Draw your *x*-axis and *y*-axis on a sheet of graph paper. Label the *x*-axis "Ontario Lakes" and the *y*-axis "Area (km^2)."

2. Look at the data carefully in order to select an appropriate scale. Write the scale of your *y*-axis.

3. Decide on a width for the bars that will be large enough to make the graph easy to read. Leave the same amount of space between each bar.

4. Using Big Trout Lake and 661 as the first pair of data, move along the *x*-axis the width of your first bar, then go up the *y*-axis to 661. Use a pencil and ruler to draw in the first bar lightly. Repeat this process for the other pairs of data.

5. When you have drawn all of the bars, add labels on the *x*-axis to identify the bars. Alternatively, use colour to distinguish among them.

6. If you are using colour to distinguish among the bars, you will need to make a legend or key to explain the meaning of the colours. Write a title for your graph.

Instant Practice—Bar Graph

Make a vertical bar graph using the following table of each planet's gravitational force in relation to Earth's gravity.

Table 4 Gravitational Pull of Planets

Planet	Gravitational Pull (*g*)
Mercury	0.40
Venus	0.90
Earth	1.00
Mars	0.40
Jupiter	2.50
Saturn	1.10
Uranus	0.90
Neptune	1.10

Constructing a Pie Graph

A pie graph (sometimes called a pie chart) uses a circle divided into sections (like pieces of pie) to show the data. Each section represents a percentage of the whole. All sections together represent all (100 percent) of the data.

Example

To learn how to make a pie graph from the data in Table 5, study the corresponding pie graph on the right as you read the following steps.

Table 5 Birds Breeding in Canada

Type of Bird	Number of Species	Percent of Total	Degrees in Section
Ducks	36	9.0	32
Birds of prey	19	4.8	17
Shorebirds	71	17.7	64
Owls	14	3.5	13
Perching birds	180	45.0	162
Other	80	20.0	72

Procedure

1. Use a mathematical compass to make a large circle on a piece of paper. Make a dot in the centre of the circle.

2. Determine the percent of the total number of species that each type of bird represents by using the following formula.

$$\text{Percent of total} = \frac{\text{Number of species within the type}}{\text{Total number of species}} \times 100\%$$

For example, the percent of all species of birds that are ducks is

$$\text{Percent that are ducks} = \frac{36 \text{ species of ducks}}{400 \text{ species}} \times 100\% = 9.0\%$$

3. To determine the number of degrees in the section that represents each type of bird, use the following formula.

$$\text{Degrees in "piece of pie"} = \frac{\text{Percent for a type of bird}}{100\%} \times 360°$$

Round your answer to the nearest whole number. For example, the section for ducks is

$$\text{Degrees for ducks} = \frac{9.0\%}{100\%} \times 360° = 32.4° \text{ or } 32°$$

4. Draw a straight line from the centre to the edge of the circle. Use your protractor to measure 32° from this line. Make a mark, then use your mark to draw a second line 32° from the first line.

5. Repeat steps 2 to 4 for the remaining types of birds.

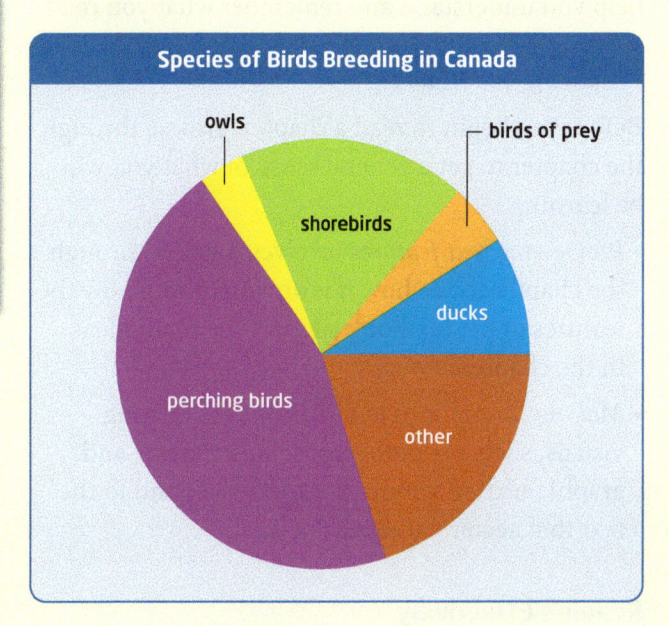

Species of Birds Breeding in Canada

Instant Practice—Pie Graph

Use the following data on total energy (oil, gas, electricity, etc.) consumption for 2004 to develop a pie graph to visualize energy consumption in the world.

Table 6 World Energy Consumption in 2004

Area in the World	Consumption (quadrillion btu)
North America	120.62
Central and South America	22.54
Europe	85.65
Eurasia	45.18
Middle East	21.14
Africa	13.71
Eastern Asia and Oceania	137.61

Math Skills Toolkit 3 • NEL   559

Study Toolkit Overview

At the beginning of every chapter, you will find a Study Toolkit page. Each Study Toolkit page features three of the many helpful study strategies that are described below. Using these strategies can help you understand and remember what you read.

Preparing for Reading

Before you begin to read a chapter, browse through the chapter to get a general sense of what you will be learning.

- *Previewing text features* involves flipping through the chapter to see how it is organized and how the features of the textbook support the main ideas in the chapter.
- *Making connections to visuals* means relating visuals, such as photographs, illustrations, and graphic text, to your own experiences and to the text that accompanies each visual.

Reading Effectively

While you are reading, you can apply these strategies to help you understand what you are reading:

- *Asking questions* helps you engage actively in reading the text and gives you a purpose for continuing to read.
- *Identifying the main idea and details* helps you figure out what is the most important information in the text you are reading. You can also use this strategy after reading, to help you organize what you have learned.
- *Making connections to prior knowledge* helps you relate what you already know to what you are learning.

- *Making inferences* helps you figure out the meaning of the text by combining information in the text with what you already know and by "reading between the lines."
- *Monitoring comprehension* ensures that you stop from time to time as you are reading to ask yourself whether you have understood what you have read.
- *Skim, scan, or study* helps you alter your reading speed based on your purpose for reading.
- *Visualizing* helps you transform a chunk of text into an image in your mind to help you understand and remember details and comparisons in the text.

Reading Graphic Text

Reading tables, graphs, and diagrams is different from reading text. The three strategies below can help you identify elements that are specific to each type of graphic text so you can interpret what the graphic text represents:

- *Interpreting diagrams* requires you to read and understand the parts of the diagram and then relate the parts to each other and to the concepts explained in the text.
- *Interpreting graphs* requires you to understand the organization and functions of the parts of a graph, such as axes, points, and lines. It also requires you to pay attention to the graph's title and caption.
- *Interpreting tables* requires you to examine data that have been organized in rows and columns with explanatory headings. Keep in mind that the title of a table gives information about the table's purpose and meaning.

- *Interpreting cross sections* requires you to examine a drawing that shows the insides of an object, as though it has been sliced open either horizontally or vertically through its centre. It requires you to visualize the object in three dimensions. You also need to pay attention to the title or caption that accompanies the drawing.

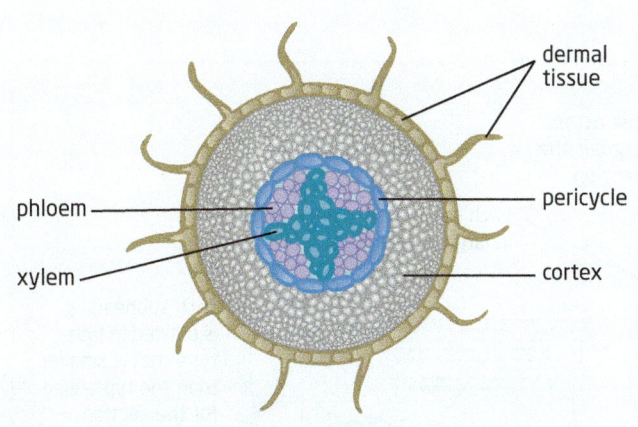

This cross section shows the structure of a typical root of a plant. You will learn more about the structure of roots in Chapter 2.

Word Study

Science textbooks include many words that may be unfamiliar to you. Use the following strategies to help you determine the meanings of new words:

- Identify the *base word*. The base word is the main part of the word, which is distinct from a prefix, suffix, or combining part.
- Examine the smaller words that make up *compound words*.
- *Create a word map* to analyze a word beyond its definition—for example, by identifying its opposites and by listing synonyms for the word.
- Consider the *multiple meanings* of a word when it appears in different contexts.
- Identify the *word parts* that combine to form multisyllabic words. The names of compounds, for example, hydrofluoric acid, are formed by combining the word part *hydro* indicating hydrogen and *fluor* (indicating fluorine) and the ending *-ic acid*.
- Analyze *word families* to understand relationships among words that have common parts, such as the same base.
- Look up *word origins* in a dictionary to deepen your understanding of a word.

Organizing Your Learning

Taking notes in class is only the first step in understanding a new concept. You may want to organize what you have learned in a way that helps you remember key concepts and helps you study for tests.

- *Comparing and contrasting* involves identifying the similarities and differences between two concepts or things.
- *Identifying cause and effect* helps you understand why and how events occur, as well as their consequences.
- *Making study notes* means identifying the most important information and recording it in a way that makes sense to you.
- *Summarizing* involves stating the main ideas of a paragraph or a section of text in your own words. You can summarize text using a list, a drawing, point-form notes, a table, or a graphic organizer.
- *Using graphic organizers* helps you to organize information in a visual format.
- *Synthesizing* is the process of combining information from a variety of sources with prior knowledge to gain a new understanding of a topic.

On the following pages, you will find more information about some of the strategies listed above.

Study Toolkit 1

Preparing for Reading: Previewing Text Features

Before you begin reading a textbook, become familiar with the book's overall structure and features. If you look at the Table of Contents on page v, you will see that this textbook is divided into four *units*. Each unit is divided into three *chapters*. Each chapter is subdivided into numbered *sections*.

As well as the Table of Contents, this textbook has many other features designed to help you find your way while reading. Examine the sample pages below. They include several text features that will help you understand the content.

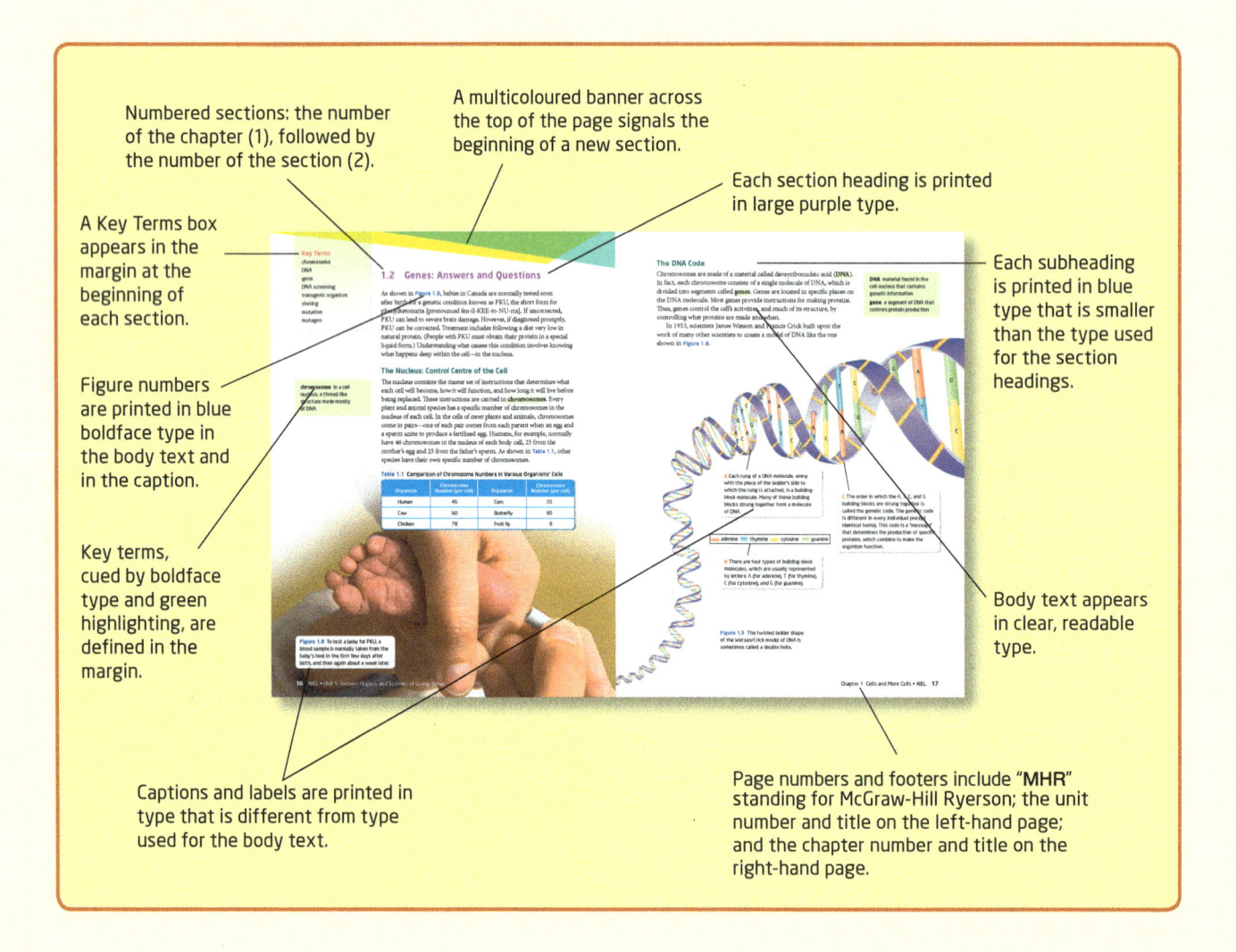

Numbered sections: the number of the chapter (1), followed by the number of the section (2).

A multicoloured banner across the top of the page signals the beginning of a new section.

Each section heading is printed in large purple type.

A Key Terms box appears in the margin at the beginning of each section.

Each subheading is printed in blue type that is smaller than the type used for the section headings.

Figure numbers are printed in blue boldface type in the body text and in the caption.

Key terms, cued by boldface type and green highlighting, are defined in the margin.

Body text appears in clear, readable type.

Captions and labels are printed in type that is different from type used for the body text.

Page numbers and footers include "MHR" standing for McGraw-Hill Ryerson; the unit number and title on the left-hand page; and the chapter number and title on the right-hand page.

Instant Practice

1. Describe two ways to identify the key terms in a section.
2. Describe two ways to learn more about a visual in this textbook.

562 NEL • Study Toolkit 1

Study Toolkit 2

Reading Effectively: Monitoring Comprehension

When you are reading text that contains new ideas and new key terms, stop after each chunk of text to make sure that you understand what you have just read. An effective way to do this is to use the steps in the following flowchart.

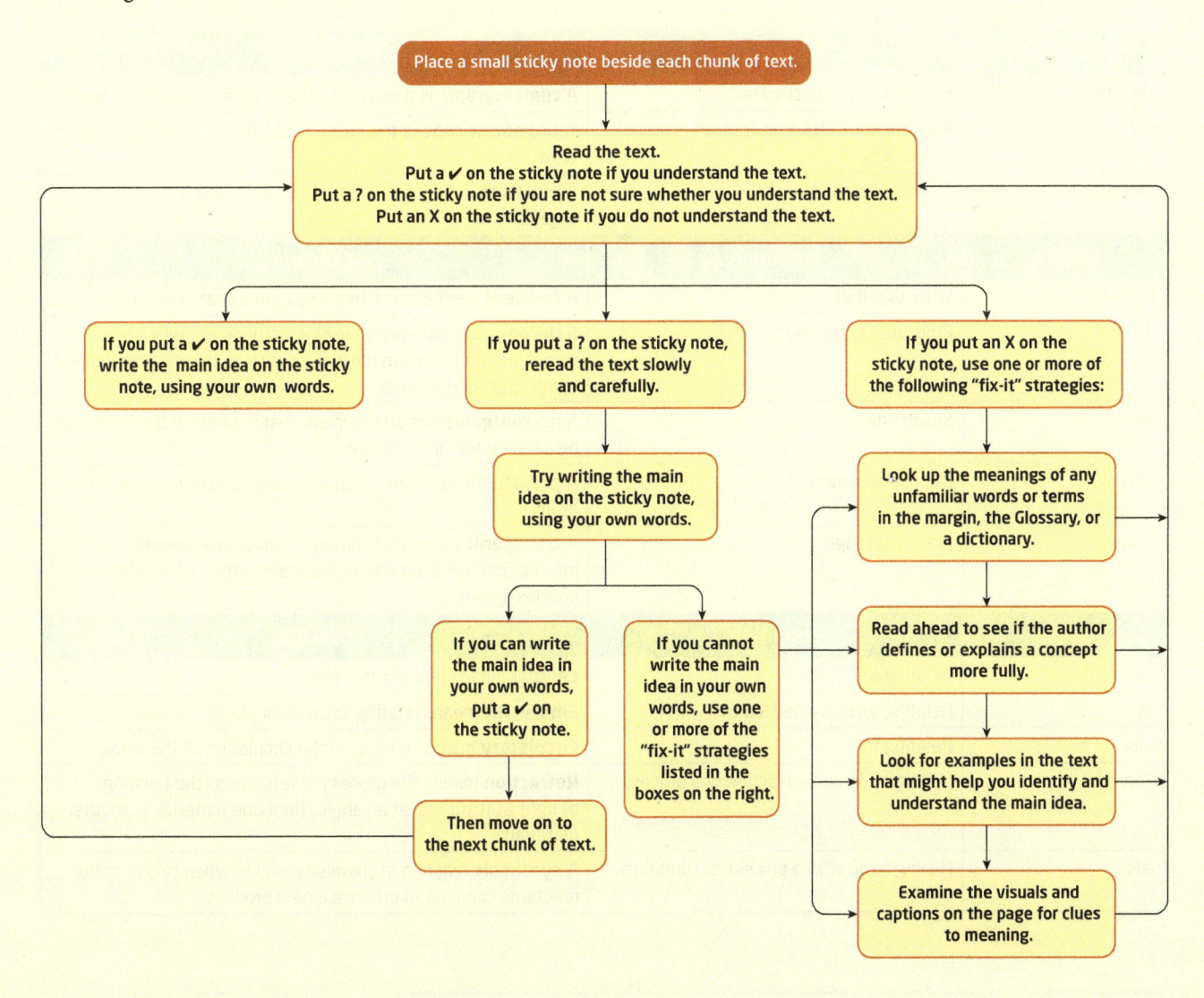

```
Place a small sticky note beside each chunk of text.
                        ↓
Read the text.
Put a ✓ on the sticky note if you understand the text.
Put a ? on the sticky note if you are not sure whether you understand the text.
Put an X on the sticky note if you do not understand the text.
```

- **If you put a ✓ on the sticky note,** write the main idea on the sticky note, using your own words.

- **If you put a ? on the sticky note,** reread the text slowly and carefully.
  - Try writing the main idea on the sticky note, using your own words.
    - If you can write the main idea in your own words, put a ✓ on the sticky note.
    - If you cannot write the main idea in your own words, use one or more of the "fix-it" strategies listed in the boxes on the right.
  - Then move on to the next chunk of text.

- **If you put an X on the sticky note,** use one or more of the following "fix-it" strategies:
  - Look up the meanings of any unfamiliar words or terms in the margin, the Glossary, or a dictionary.
  - Read ahead to see if the author defines or explains a concept more fully.
  - Look for examples in the text that might help you identify and understand the main idea.
  - Examine the visuals and captions on the page for clues to meaning.

Instant Practice

1. Make a list of steps you could follow if you were not sure that you had understood a section of text. Number your steps.

2. Make a bulleted list of the four "fix-it" strategies, using your own words. Post your list for easy reference.

Study Toolkit 3

Word Study: Common Base Words, Prefixes, and Suffixes in Science

Understanding how words are put together can help you figure out their meanings. The list below includes some common *base words* that are used in science. Also listed are some common *prefixes* and *suffixes*, which change the meaning of a base word when they are combined with the base word.

Base Word	Definition	Example
climate	Having to do with climate	A **climatograph** is a graph of climate data for a specific region.
gene	A segment of DNA that controls protein production	Your **genetic code** is the order in which your genes are strung together.
mutate	To change or alter	A **mutation** in biology means a change in the DNA of an organism.

Prefix	Definition	Example
co-	With; together	A **covalent** bond forms when two atoms share electrons.
de-	From; away from; out of	A **decomposition** reaction in chemistry occurs when a compound breaks down (decomposes) into two or more simpler compounds or elements.
micro-	Small; tiny	A **microorganism** is an organism that is so small that it cannot be seen by the unaided eye.
poly-	Much; many; more than one	A **polyatomic** ion is an ion that is composed of more than one atom.
trans-	Across; through	A **transgenic** organism is an organism whose genetic information has been altered by the insertion of another species' genes.

Suffix	Definition	Example
-ar	Relating to	**Cellular** means relating to a cell.
-ic	Relating to; characterized by	**Embryonic** means relating to an embryo.
-ory	Relating to	**Circulatory** means relating to the circulation of the blood.
-ion	Having to do with an action or a process	**Refraction** means the process of refracting (the bending of light as it travels, at an angle, from one material to another material).
-sis	Having to do with a process or condition	A **synthesis** reaction in chemistry occurs when two or more reactants combine to produce a new product.

Instant Practice

1. Use the table to predict the meaning of *hydrochloric*.
2. Think of a word that begins with one of the prefixes listed above. (You can browse through this textbook or a dictionary to find a word, if you wish.) Explain the meaning of your word. Compare your word and definition with words and definitions that your classmates suggest.

Study Toolkit 4

Organizing Your Learning: Using Graphic Organizers

When deciding which type of graphic organizer to use, consider your purpose: to brainstorm, to show relationships among ideas, to summarize a section of text, to record research notes, or to review what you have learned before writing a test. Several different graphic organizers are shown on these two pages.

Main Idea Web

A *main idea web* shows a main idea and several supporting details. The main idea is written in the centre of the web, and each detail is written at the end of a line going from the centre.

- Fluorescent materials are in currency, legal documents, and admission tickets.
- Many body fluids are fluorescent.
- Some body tissues, such as those in the tongue, are fluorescent.
- Fluorescent materials are in clothing, costumes, and stage props.

Centre: Fluorescent materials are found in many places.

Spider Map

A *spider map* shows a main idea and several ideas associated with the main idea. It does not show the relationships among the ideas. A spider map is useful when you are brainstorming or taking notes.

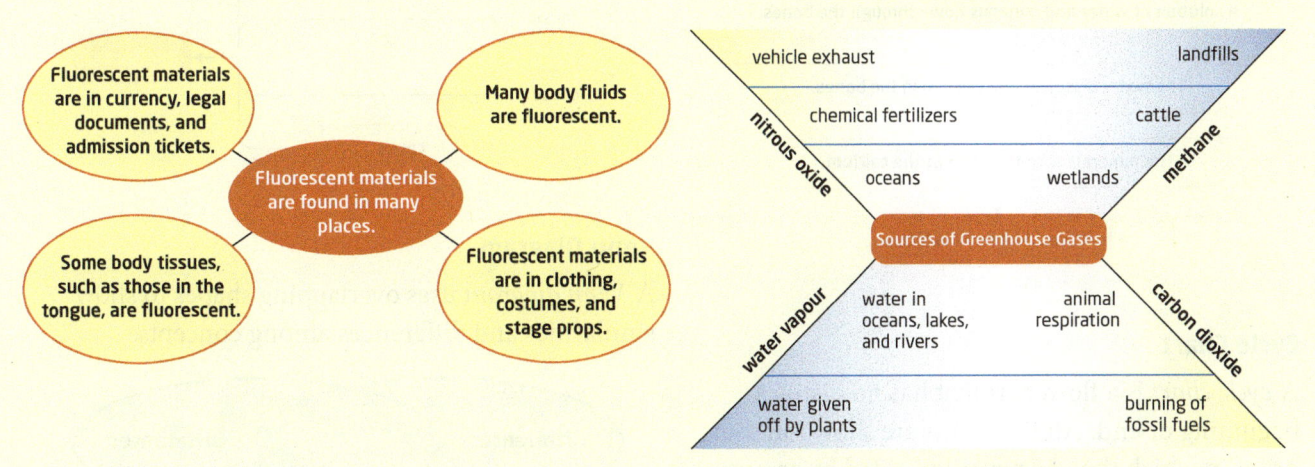

Sources of Greenhouse Gases:
- nitrous oxide: vehicle exhaust, chemical fertilizers, oceans
- methane: landfills, cattle, wetlands
- water vapour: water in oceans, lakes, and rivers; water given off by plants
- carbon dioxide: animal respiration, burning of fossil fuels

Concept Map

A *concept map* uses shapes and lines to show how ideas are related. Each idea, or concept, is written inside a circle, a square, a rectangle, or another shape. Words that explain how the concepts are related are written on the lines that connect the shapes.

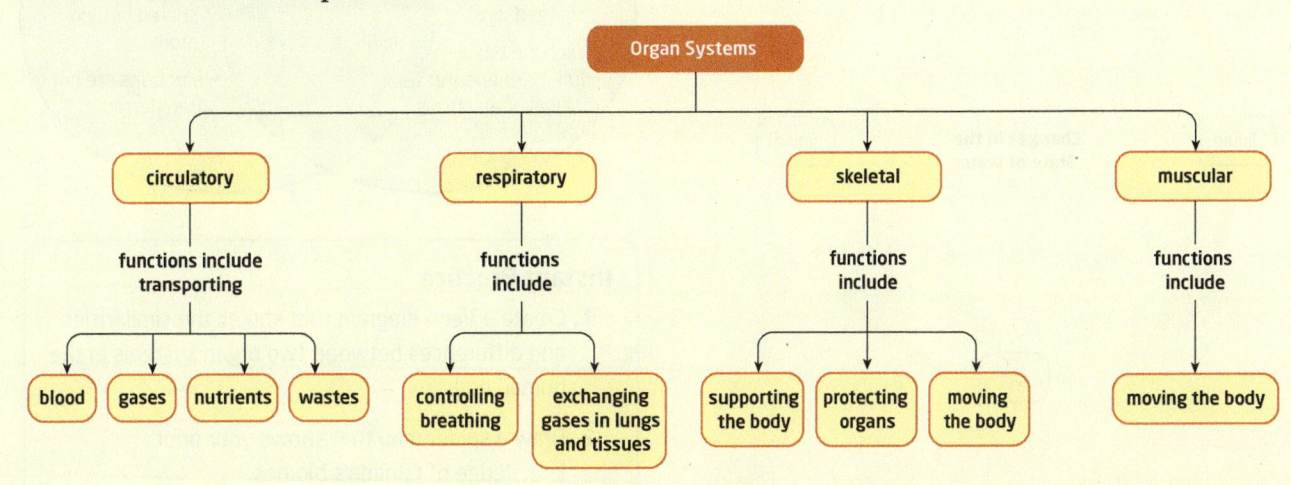

Organ Systems:
- circulatory — functions include transporting: blood, gases, nutrients, wastes
- respiratory — functions include: controlling breathing, exchanging gases in lungs and tissues
- skeletal — functions include: supporting the body, protecting organs, moving the body
- muscular — functions include: moving the body

Study Toolkit 4 • NEL 565

Flowchart

A *flowchart* shows a sequence of events or the steps in a process. A flowchart starts with the first event or step. An arrow leads to the next event or step, and so on, until the final outcome. All the events or steps are shown in the order in which they occur.

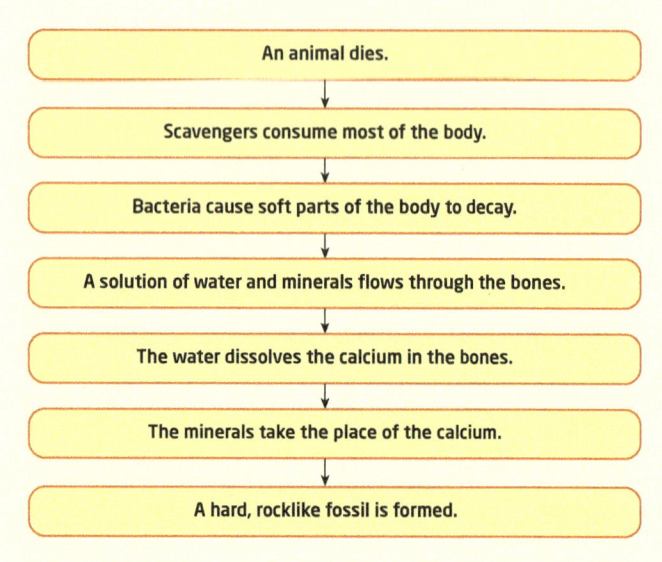

- An animal dies.
- Scavengers consume most of the body.
- Bacteria cause soft parts of the body to decay.
- A solution of water and minerals flows through the bones.
- The water dissolves the calcium in the bones.
- The minerals take the place of the calcium.
- A hard, rocklike fossil is formed.

Cycle Chart

A *cycle chart* is a flowchart that has no distinct beginning or end. All the events are shown in the order in which they occur, as indicated by arrows, but there is no first or last event. Instead, the events occur again and again in a continuous cycle.

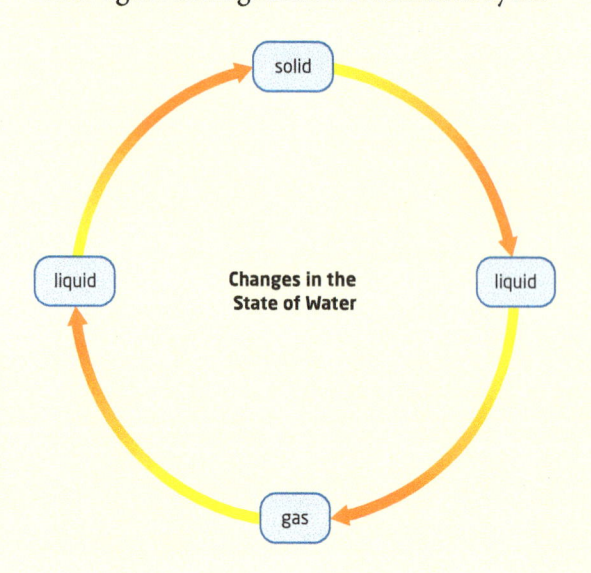

Changes in the State of Water: solid → liquid → gas → liquid → solid

Cause-and-Effect Map

The first *cause-and-effect map* below shows one cause that results in several effects. The second map shows one effect that has several causes.

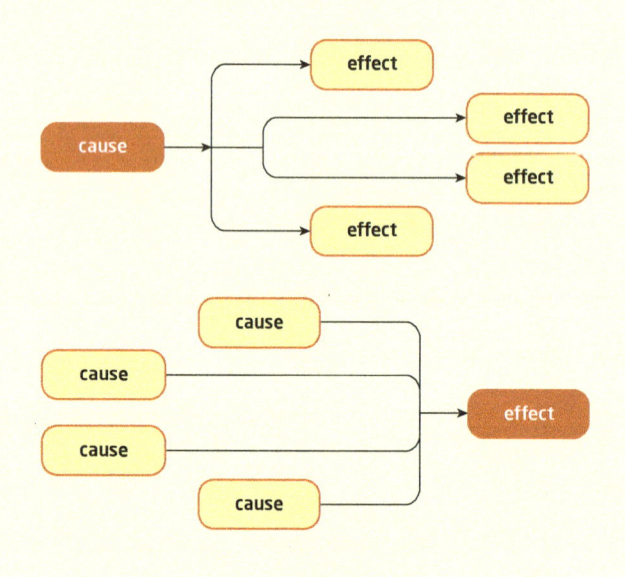

Venn Diagram

A *Venn diagram* uses overlapping shapes to show similarities and differences among concepts.

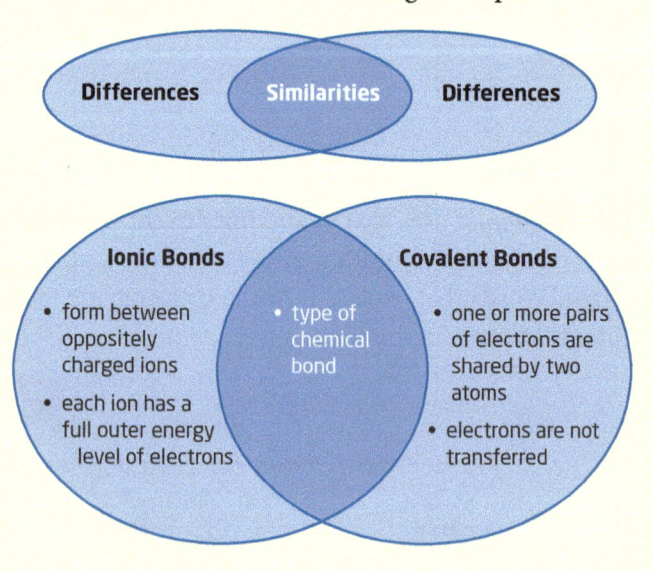

Ionic Bonds
- form between oppositely charged ions
- each ion has a full outer energy level of electrons

Similarities
- type of chemical bond

Covalent Bonds
- one or more pairs of electrons are shared by two atoms
- electrons are not transferred

Instant Practice

1. Create a Venn diagram that shows the similarities and differences between two organ systems in the human body.

2. Draw a spider map that shows your prior knowledge of Canada's biomes.

Appendix A

Chemistry References

Names, Formulas, and Charges of Some Polyatomic Ions

Name	Formula
Acetate	CH_3COO^-
Ammonium	NH_4^+
Carbonate	CO_3^{2-}
Chlorate	ClO_3^-
Chlorite	ClO_2^-
Chromate	CrO_4^{2-}
Cyanide	CN^-
Dichromate	$Cr_2O_7^{2-}$
Hydrogen carbonate, bicarbonate	HCO_3^-
Hydrogen sulfate, bisulfate	HSO_4^-
Hydrogen sulfide, bisulfide	HS^-
Hydrogen sulfite, bisulfite	HSO_3^-
Hydroxide	OH^-
Hypochlorite	ClO^-
Nitrate	NO_3^-
Nitrite	NO_2^-
Perchlorate	ClO_4^-
Permanganate	MnO_4^-
Phosphate	PO_4^{3-}
Phosphite	PO_3^{3-}
Sulfate	SO_4^{2-}
Sulfite	SO_3^{2-}

Electron Arrangements of the First 20 Elements

Atom			Ion		
H	1 p	1	H^+	1 p	0
			H^-	1 p	2
He	2 p	2	He	Does not form an ion	
Li	3 p	2, 1	Li^+	3 p	2
Be	4 p	2, 2	Be^{2+}	4 p	2
B	5 p	2, 3	B^{3+}	5 p	2
C	6 p	2, 4	C^{4-}	6 p	2, 8
N	7 p	2, 5	N^{3-}	7 p	2, 8
O	8 p	2, 6	O^{2-}	8 p	2, 8
F	9 p	2, 7	F^-	9 p	2, 8
Ne	10 p	2, 8	Ne	Does not form an ion	
Na	11 p	2, 8, 1	Na^+	11 p	2, 8
Mg	12 p	2, 8, 2	Mg^{2+}	12 p	2, 8
Al	13 p	2, 8, 3	Al^{3+}	13 p	2, 8
Si	14 p	2, 8, 4	Si^{4-}	14 p	2, 8, 8
P	15 p	2, 8, 5	P^{3-}	15 p	2, 8, 8
S	16 p	2, 8, 6	S^{2-}	16 p	2, 8, 8
Cl	17 p	2, 8, 7	Cl^-	17 p	2, 8, 8
Ar	18 p	2, 8, 8	Ar	Does not form an ion	
K	19 p	2, 8, 8, 1	K^+	19 p	2, 8, 8
Ca	20 p	2, 8, 8, 2	Ca^{2+}	20 p	2, 8, 8

Acid-Base Indicators

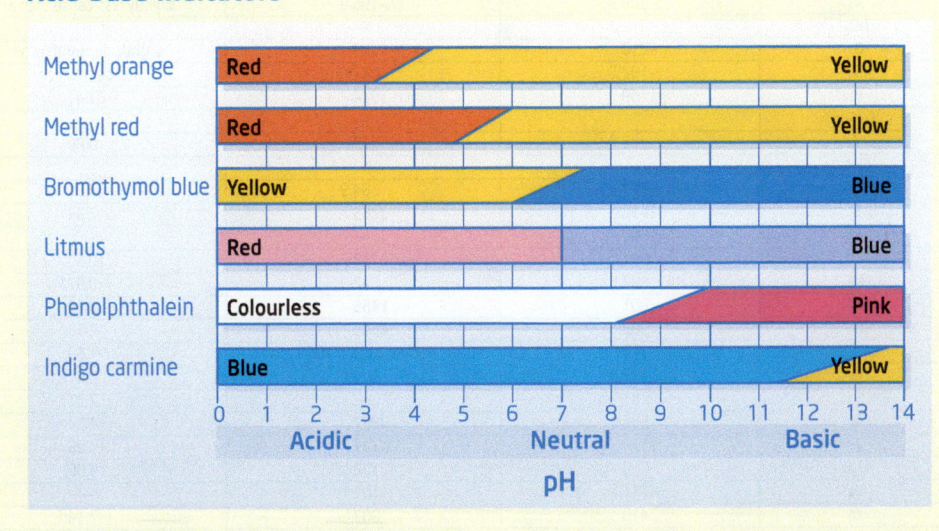

Indicator	Acidic colour	Basic colour	Transition pH range
Methyl orange	Red	Yellow	~3–5
Methyl red	Red	Yellow	~4–6
Bromothymol blue	Yellow	Blue	~6–8
Litmus	Red	Blue	~5–8
Phenolphthalein	Colourless	Pink	~8–10
Indigo carmine	Blue	Yellow	~11–13

pH scale: 0–6 Acidic, 7 Neutral, 8–14 Basic

Appendix B

Properties of Common Substances

KEY TO SYMBOLS:
Common names of substances are enclosed in parentheses.
(*) water solution of a pure substance   (e) element   (c) compound

Name	Formula	Melting Point (°C)	Boiling Point (°C)	Density (g/cm³ or g/mL)
acetic acid (vinegar) (c)	CH_3COOH	16.6	118.1	—
aluminum (e)	Al	659.7	2519	2.7
ammonia (c)	NH_3	−77.8	−33.4	less dense than air
ammonium nitrate (c)	NH_4NO_3	169.6	210	1.73
argon (e)	Ar	−189	−185	denser than air
arsenic (e)	As	—	—	5.727 (grey), 4.25 (black), 2.0 (yellow)
barium (e)	Ba	727	1897	3.62
beryllium (e)	Be	1280	2471	1.85
boron (e)	B	2075	4000	2.37 (brown), 2.34 (yellow)
bromine (e)	Br_2	−7.2	58.8	3.12
calcium (e)	Ca	845	1484	1.55
calcium carbonate (limestone) (c)	$CaCO_3$	decomposes at 900°C	—	2.93
calcium hydroxide (slaked lime) (c)	$Ca(OH)_2$	decomposes at 522°C	—	2.24
calcium oxide (lime) (c)	CaO	2580	2850	3.3
carbon (diamond) (e)	C	3500	3930	3.51
carbon (graphite) (e)	C	4492	4492	2.25
carbon dioxide (c)	CO_2	—	—	—
chlorine (e)	Cl_2	−101.6	−34.6	denser than air
copper (e)	Cu	1084	2562	8.95
copper(II) nitrate (c)	$Cu(NO_3)_2$	—	—	—
copper(II) sulfate (bluestone) (c)	$CuSO_4 \cdot 5H_2O$	decomposes at 150°C	—	2.28
ethanol (ethyl alcohol) (c)	C_2H_5OH	−114.5	78.4	0.789
fluorine (e)	F_2	−270	−188	—
gold (e)	Au	1063	2856	19.3
glucose (c)	$C_6H_{12}O_6$	146	decomposes before it boils	1.54
helium (e)	He	−272.2	−268.93	—
hematite (c)	Fe_2O_3	1565	—	5.24
hydrochloric acid (*)	HCl	varies	varies	varies
hydrogen (e)	H_2	−259	−253	much less dense than air
hydrogen peroxide (c)	H_2O_2	−0.4	150.2	1.45
iodine (e)	I_2	114	184	4.95
iron (e)	Fe	1535	2861	7.86
lead (e)	Pb	327.4	1750	11.34
lithium (e)	Li	179	1340	0.534
magnesium (e)	Mg	651	1107	1.74
magnesium chloride (c)	$MgCl_2$	708	1412	2.3
magnetite (c)	Fe_3O_4	—	—	5.18
mercury (e)	Hg	−38.9	356.6	13.6
methane (c)	CH_4	−182.5	−161.5	—
neon (e)	Ne	−248	−246	—
nickel (e)	Ni	1455	2913	8.90
nitrogen (e)	N_2	−209.9	−195.8	slightly less dense than air
nitrogen dioxide (c)	NO_2	—	—	—
oxygen (e)	O_2	−218	−183	slightly denser than air
ozone (e)	O_3	−192.5	−112	denser than air
platinum (e)	Pt	1769	3824	21.41
polyethylene (polythene) (c)	$(C_2H_4)_n$	—	—	—
potassium (e)	K	63.5	759	0.86
propane (c)	C_3H_8	—	−42.17	—
selenium (e)	Se	217	684.9	4.81
silicon (e)	Si	1410	3265	2.33
silicon dioxide (silica) (c)	SiO_2	1600	—	—
silver (e)	Ag	961	2162	10.5
sodium (e)	Na	97.5	892	0.971
sodium chloride (table salt) (c)	NaCl	801	1465	2.16
sodium fluoride (c)	NaF	988	1695	2.56
sucrose (sugar) (c)	$C_{12}H_{22}O_{11}$	170	decomposes at 186°C	1.59
sulfur (brimstone) (e)	S_8	112.8	444.6	2.07
tin (e)	Sn	231.9	2602	7.31
titanium (e)	Ti	1666	3287	4.5
uranium (e)	U	1130	4131	19.05
water (c)	H_2O	0	100	1.00
xenon (e)	Xe	−111.9	−107.1	—
zinc (e)	Zn	419	907	7.14

DEFINITIONS:
deliquescent: able to absorb water from the air to form a concentrated solution
sublime: to form a vapour directly from a solid

Appearance (at room temperature: 20°C)	Comments
colourless liquid with pungent smell	used in the manufacture of cellulose ethanoate; vinegar is a 5 to 7 percent solution in water
silver-white metal	used in aircraft, cooking utensils, and electrical apparatus
very soluble gas with pungent smell	used as refrigerant and in manufacture of resins, explosives, and fertilizers
white, soluble, crystalline salt	used in explosives and as a fertilizer
inert gas	used in electric lights
grey, black, or yellow solid	used in semiconductors and alloys; compounds are very poisonous and are used in medicine and as pesticides
silver-white solid	used in X-ray diagnosis
hard, white metal	used for corrosion-resistant alloys
brown, amphorous powder or yellow crystals	used for hardening steel and for producing enamels and glasses
red-brown liquid	used to make certain pain-relieving drugs; liquid causes severe chemical burns; vapour is harmful to lungs
soft, white metal that tarnishes easily	very abundant; essential to life
white solid	main ingredient in chalk and marble
white solid	aqueous solution used to test for CO_2
white solid	used in cement and for marking lines on playing fields
colourless, solid crystals	very hard; used for drilling through rock
grey-black solid	very soft; used in lubricants, pencil leads, and electrical apparatus
colourless gas with a faint tingling smell and taste	does not support combustion and is denser than air; used in fire extinguishers and as a refrigerant at −78.5°C
green gas	poisonous; used to kill harmful organisms in water
shiny, reddish solid	soft metal; good conductor of heat
blue, solid crystals	used in pesticides
colourless liquid	derived from fermentation of sugar; used as solvent or fuel; found in wine
greenish yellow gas	similar to chlorine
shiny, yellow solid	very soft metal; highly resistant to tarnishing
white solid	simple sugar; human body converts most sugars and starches to glucose
nonflammable inert gas	used as refrigerant; provides inert atmosphere for welding; used to fill air ships and balloons
rusty red colour	found in iron ore and rusted iron
colourless liquid	corrosive acid; properties vary according to concentration
colourless gas	highly flammable; liquid form used as rocket fuel
colourless liquid	thick and syrupy when pure; an antiseptic
violet-black, solid crystals	crystals sublime readily to form poisonous violet vapour
shiny, silver solid	rusts readily; soft when pure
shiny, blue-white solid	soft metal; forms poisonous compounds
silver-white metal (least dense solid known)	used in alloys; its salts have various medical uses
light, silvery-white metal that tarnishes easily in air	used in alloys and photography; compounds used in medicine; essential to life
white, deliquescent substance	
shiny, black, crystalline solid	strongly magnetic
shiny, silvery liquid	only liquid metal; forms poisonous compounds
odourless, flammable gas formed from decaying organic matter	main constituent in natural gas
colourless, odourless gas	discharge of electricity at low pressures through neon produces an intense orange-red glow
silvery-white, magnetic metal that resists corrosion	used for nickel plating and coinage, in alloys, and as a catalyst
colourless gas	will not burn or support burning; makes up 80 percent of air
brown gas	causes reddish-brown colour in smog
colourless gas	must be present for burning to take place; makes up 20 percent of air
bluish gas	used for purifying air and water and in bleaching; atmospheric layer blocks most of the Sun's ultraviolet light
silver-white solid	used in jewellery; alloyed with cobalt, used in pacemakers
tough, waxy, thermoplastic material	polymer of ethylene; used as insulating material; flexible and chemically resistant
silvery-white, soft, highly reactive, alkali metal	essential to all life; found in all living matter; salts used in fertilizers
colourless gas	flammable; used as fuel
non-metal resembling sulfur; silvery-grey, crystalline solid	used in manufacture of rubber and ruby glass; used in photoelectric cells and semiconductors
steel-grey metalloid similar to carbon in its chemical properties	used in pure form in semiconductors and alloys and in the form of silicates in glass
hard, granular powder; insoluble in water	main constituent of sand; used in clocks and watches as quartz
shiny, white solid	soft metal; best-known conductor of electricity
soft, silvery-white metal; very reactive	used in preparation of organic compounds, as coolant, and in some types of nuclear reactors
white, crystalline solid	used to season or preserve foods
colourless, crystalline substance	used in water fluoridation and as an insecticide
white solid	made from sugar cane or sugar beets
yellow solid	used to make dyes, pesticides, and other chemicals
shiny, slightly yellow solid	soft metal; rust resistant
lustrous white solid	alloys are widely used in the aerospace industry
metallic grey solid	used as a nuclear fuel (usually converted into plutonium)
colourless liquid	good solvent for non-greasy matter
inert gas	used in fluorescent tubes and light bulbs
hard, bluish-white metal	used in alloys such as brass and galvanized iron

Appendix C

Numerical Answers and Answers to Practice Problems

Unit 1

Section 1.2 Review page 28
6. 25 093.75 min or 418.23 h or 17.43 days

Section 1.3 Review page 39
5. 20 (or 10 in each daughter cell)

Chapter 1 Review page 53
23. a. interphase, 631; prophase, 100; metaphase, 15.4; anaphase, 15.4; telophase, 38.5

Unit 1 Review pages 128-131
1. d 2. d 3. c 4. c 5. b
21. 65 536
38. a 39. c 40. b 41. c 42. a

Unit 2

Section 4.3 Review page 168
3. a. 2Fe, 6I
   b. 3Ca, 6O, 6H
   c. 3Ca, 6N, 18O
   d. 3N, 12H, 3Cl, 12O
7. a. not balanced; Al; $2Al(s) + 3F_2(g) \rightarrow 2AlF_3(s)$
   b. not balanced; H and O; $Ca(OH)_2(aq) + 2HCl(aq) \rightarrow CaCl_2(aq) + 2H_2O(\ell)$
   c. balanced
   d. not balanced; K, N, O; $K_2SO_4(aq) + 2AgNO_3(aq) \rightarrow Ag_2SO_4(s) + 2KNO_3(aq)$
8. chemical equation: $2Na(s) + 2H_2O(\ell) \rightarrow H_2(g) + 2NaOH(aq)$

Chapter 4 Review pages 174-175
8. a. 3; tri-
   b. 8; octa-
11. a. 4H, 2O, 2Na, 2F
    b. 6Br, 2Fe, 6I
    c. 1Pb, 2N, 6O, 2Na, 2I
    d. 6K, 2P, 20O, 6N, 24H, 3S
12. a. $Mg_3N_2(s) \rightarrow 3Mg(s) + N_2(g)$
    b. $4Mn(s) + 3O_2(g) \rightarrow 2Mn_2O_3(s)$
    c. $CO_2(g) + 4H_2(g) \rightarrow CH_4(g) + 2H_2O(g)$
    d. $2PbO(s) \rightarrow 2Pb(s) + O_2(g)$
    e. $2C_2H_6(g) + 7O_2(g) \rightarrow 4CO_2(g) + 6H_2O(g)$
    f. $Cu(s) + 2AgNO_3(aq) \rightarrow 2Ag(s) + Cu(NO_3)_2(aq)$
    g. $C_3H_8(g) + 5O_2(g) \rightarrow 3CO_2(g) + 4H_2O(g)$
    h. $3PbCl_4(aq) + 4K_3PO_4(aq) \rightarrow 12KCl(aq) + Pb_3(PO_4)_4(s)$
13. a. chemical equation: $N_2(g) + 3H_2(g) \rightarrow 2NH_3(g)$
    b. chemical equation: $CaCO_3(s) \rightarrow CaO(s) + CO_2(g)$
    c. chemical equation: $2Al(s) + O_2(g) \rightarrow Al_2O_3(s)$
    d. chemical equation: $6H_2O(\ell) + 6CO_2(g) \rightarrow C_6H_{12}O_6(s) + 6O_2(g)$
    e. chemical equation: $CaCl_2(aq) + 2K(s) \rightarrow 2KCl(aq) + Ca(s)$
    f. chemical equation: $BaSO_4(aq) + 2NaOH(aq) \rightarrow Na_2SO_4(aq) + Ba(OH)_2(s)$
    g. chemical equation: $TiCl_4(g) + 2Mg(\ell) \rightarrow Ti(s) + 2MgCl_2(\ell)$
16. a. $2NH_3 \rightarrow N_2 + 3H_2$; Nitrogen is diatomic ($N_2$).
    b. $C + O_2 \rightarrow CO_2$; Atoms are already balanced.
20. b. $2Mg(s) + O_2(g) \rightarrow 2MgO(s)$
    c. 16 g of oxygen; According to the law of conservation of mass, if the total mass of the product is 40 g, then the combined mass of the reactants (magnesium and oxygen) must also be 40 g; 40 g – 24 g = 16 g

Section 5.1 Review page 189
3. $4Fe(s) + 3O_2(g) \rightarrow 2Fe_2O_3(s)$
5. $2H_2O \rightarrow 2H_2(g) + O_2(g)$
7. a. $2Ca(s) + O_2(g) \rightarrow 2CaO(s)$; synthesis
   b. $8Ca(s) + S_8(s) \rightarrow 8CaS(s)$; synthesis
   c. $2CsCl(s) \rightarrow 2Cs(s) + Cl_2(g)$; decomposition
8. a. $3Mg(s) + N_2(g) \rightarrow Mg_3N_2(s)$; synthesis reaction
   b. $2K_2O(s) \rightarrow 4K(s) + O_2(g)$; decomposition reaction
   c. $2Na(s) + Br_2(\ell) \rightarrow 2NaBr(s)$; synthesis reaction

Section 5.2 Review page 198
2. a. $Ca(s) + 2AgNO_3(aq) \rightarrow 2Ag(s) + Ca(NO_3)_2(aq)$
   b. No reaction
   c. $2Al(s) + 6HCl(aq) \rightarrow 2AlCl_3(aq) + 3H_2(g)$
6. a. single; $Cl_2(g) + 2CsBr(aq) \rightarrow Br_2 + 2CsCl$
   b. double; $2AgNO_3(aq) + Na_2CrO_4(aq) \rightarrow Ag_2CrO_4 + 2NaNO_3$
   c. double; $MgCl_2(aq) + 2AgNO_3(aq) \rightarrow 2AgCl + Mg(NO_3)_2$
   d. single; $F_2(g) + 2NaI(aq) \rightarrow I_2 + 2NaF$
7. single displacement; $2Al(s) + 3CuSO_4(aq) \rightarrow Al_2(SO_4)_3(aq) + 3Cu(s)$; copper

Chapter 5 Review pages 214-215
9. $2H_2(\ell) + O_2(\ell) \rightarrow 2H_2O(g)$; synthesis
12. a. $Li(s) + NaCl(aq) \rightarrow LiCl(aq) + Na(s)$
    b. $2Al(s) + 3Cu(NO_3)_2(aq) \rightarrow 3Cu(s) + 2Al(NO_3)_3(aq)$
    c. No reaction
14. a. $Cl_2(g) + CaBr_2(aq) \rightarrow CaCl_2 + Br_2$
    b. $6Li(s) + N_2(g) \rightarrow 2Li_3N$
    c. $AgNO_3(aq) + NaCl(aq) \rightarrow AgCl + NaNO_3$
    d. $PbO_2(s) \rightarrow Pb + O_2$
    e. $3Fe(ClO_4)_2(aq) + 2Al(s) \rightarrow 2Al(ClO_4)_3 + 3Fe$
    f. $Ba(NO_3)_2(aq) + MgSO_4(aq) \rightarrow Mg(NO_3)_2 + BaSO_4$
    g. $BaCl_2(aq) + Na_2CrO_4(aq) \rightarrow 2NaCl + BaCrO_4$
    h. $4Rb(s) + O_2(g) \rightarrow 2Rb_2O$
    i. No reaction
    j. $8Mg(s) + S_8(s) \rightarrow 8MgS$

Section 6.1 Review page 228
7. a. $HClO_3(aq) \rightarrow H^+(aq) + ClO_3^-(aq)$; acid
   b. $KOH(aq) \rightarrow K^+(aq) + OH^-(aq)$; base

Section 6.3 Review page 246
1. $H_2SO_4 + 2KOH \rightarrow 2H_2O + K_2SO_4$; potassium sulfate, K_2SO_4

Chapter 6 Review pages 252-253
16. a. $2HBr(aq) + Ca(OH)_2(aq) \rightarrow CaBr_2(aq) + 2H_2O(\ell)$
    b. $2LiOH(aq) + H_2SO_3(aq) \rightarrow Li_2SO_3(aq) + 2H_2O(\ell)$
    c. $3Mg(OH)_2(aq) + 2H_3PO_4(aq) \rightarrow Mg_3(PO_4)_2(aq) + 6H_2O(\ell)$
18.

Indicator	Colour	pH Estimate
Methyl orange	yellow	3.2 - 4.4
Bromothymol blue	yellow	< 6.0
Phenolphthalein	pink	> 8.2

28. b. 100 times

Unit 2 Review pages 258-262
1. b 2. c 3. b 4. a 5. d
7. a. synthesis; $S_8(s) + 8O_2(g) \rightarrow 8SO_2(g)$
   b. decomposition; $2HF(g) \rightarrow H_2(g) + F_2(g)$
   c. double displacement or neutralization; $H_2SO_4(aq) + 2NaOH(aq) \rightarrow Na_2SO_4(aq) + 2HNO(\ell)$
   d. double displacement; $Fe(NO_3)_3(aq) + 3KOH(aq) \rightarrow FeOH_3(s) + 3KNO_3(aq)$
   e. single displacement; $2Al(s) + 3CuCl_2(aq) \rightarrow 2AlCl_3(aq) + 3Cu(s)$
8. a. chemical equation: $4Na(s) + O_2(g) \rightarrow 2Na_2O(s)$
   b. chemical equation: $Mg(s) + CuCl_2(aq) \rightarrow Cu(s) + MgCl_2(aq)$
   c. chemical equation: $MgCO_3(s) \rightarrow MgO(s) + CO_2(g)$

d. chemical equation: $CrCl_3(aq) + 3KOH(aq) \rightarrow 3KCl(aq) + Cr(OH)_3(s)$
   e. chemical equation: $2Al(s) + 3H_2SO_4(aq) \rightarrow 3H_2(g) + Al_2(SO_4)_3(aq)$
10. a. 4   b. 13   c. 6
14. a. $2CO + O_2 \rightarrow 2CO_2$
23. b. double displacement; $Hg(NO_3)_2 + Na_2SO_4 \rightarrow 2NaNO_3 + HgSO_4$
29. b   30. d   31. a   32. a   33. c

Unit 3

Section 8.3 Review   page 338
8. 110% increase

Section 9.3 Review   page 381
5. 12 480 kg/year of CO_2; 6240 kg/year of CH_4

Unit 3 Review   pages 392-396
1. d   2. a   3. b   4. c   5. c
35. c   36. c   37. b

Unit 4

Section 10.3 Review   page 430
6. $h_i = -1.67$ cm; $d_i = 9.167$ cm

Section 10.4 Review   page 438
6. $h_i = 2.5$ cm; $d_i = -1.875$ cm

Chapter 10 Review   pages 444-445
20. 3 m
24. c. $h_i = 3.3$ cm; $d_i = 13.3$ cm

Section 11.1 Review   page 456
3. 2.04×10^8 m/s
7. 0°

Chapter 11 Review   pages 482-483
13. a. 1.53
    b. 1.24×10^8 m/s
    c. 2.20×10^8 m/s
    d. 1.92

Section 12.2 Review   page 501
5. $h_i = -3.67$ cm; $d_i = 66.7$ cm
7. $h_i = 4.0$ cm; $d_i = 19$ cm

Unit 4 Review   pages 524-527
1. b   2. d   3. a   4. d   5. a
19. $F_1 = F_2 = 3.75$ cm
33. b   34. c   35. a   36. c   37. b

Answers to Practice Problems

Chapter 4   page 157
1. a. NF_3
   b. PBr_3
   c. NH_3
   d. SF_2
   e. P_2O_6
   f. CCl_4

Chapter 4   page 165
1. a. chemical equation: $2Mg(s) + O_2(g) \rightarrow 2MgO(s)$
   b. chemical equation: $4Fe(s) + 3O_2(g) \rightarrow 2Fe_2O_3(s)$
   c. chemical equation: $N_2(g) + 3Br_2(g) \rightarrow 2NBr_3(g)$
2. $CH_4(g) + 2O_2(g) \rightarrow CO_2(g) + 2H_2O(g)$

Chapter 5   page 184
1. a. $3Ca(s) + N_2(g) \rightarrow Ca_3N_2(s)$
   b. $4K(s) + O_2(g) \rightarrow 2K_2O(s)$
   c. $12Cs(s) + P_4(s) \rightarrow 4Cs_3P(s)$
   d. $2Al(s) + 3F_2(g) \rightarrow 2AlF_3(s)$
2. $H_2(g) + Cl_2(g) \rightarrow 2HCl(g)$

Chapter 5   page 187
1. a. $2AuCl_3(s) \rightarrow 2Au(s) + 3Cl_2(g)$
   b. $MgF_2(s) \rightarrow Mg(s) + F_2(g)$
   c. $2Li_2O(s) \rightarrow 4Li(s) + O_2(g)$
   d. $2CsCl(s) \rightarrow 2Cs(s) + Cl_2(g)$
2. $2Cr_2O_3(s) \rightarrow 4Cr(s) + 3O_2(g)$
3. $2NaN_3(s) \rightarrow 2Na(s) + 3N_2(g)$

Chapter 5   page 193
1. a. $3SnCl_4(aq) + 4Al(s) \rightarrow 3Sn(s) + 4AlCl_3(aq)$
   b. $CuF_2(aq) + Mg(s) \rightarrow MgF_2(aq) + Cu(s)$
   c. No reaction
   d. $Au(NO_3)_3(aq) + 3Ag(s) \rightarrow 3AgNO_3(aq) + Au(s)$
   e. $2Al(s) + Fe_2O_3(s) \rightarrow Al_2O_3 + 2Fe(s)$
   f. $2Li(s) + 2HCl(aq) \rightarrow 2LiCl(aq) + H_2(g)$
2. $CuSO_4(aq) + Mg(s) \rightarrow MgSO_4(aq) + Cu(s)$

Chapter 5   page 196
1. a. $Pb(NO_3)_2(aq) + 2KI(aq) \rightarrow PbI_2 + 2KNO_3$
   b. $SrCl_2(aq) + Pb(NO_3)_2(aq) \rightarrow PbCl_2 + Sr(NO_3)_2$
   c. $AlCl_3(aq) + 3CuNO_3(aq) \rightarrow 3CuCl + Al(NO_3)_3$
   d. $KCl(aq) + AgNO3(aq) \rightarrow KNO_3 + AgCl$
   e. $CaI_2(aq) + Na_2CO_3(aq) \rightarrow CaCO_3 + 2NaI$
2. $2K_3PO_4(aq) + 3MgI_2(aq) \rightarrow Mg_3(PO_4)_2 + 6KI$

Chapter 6   page 224
1. HBr; Br^-; bromide ion
2. a. HCl
   b. HNO_3
   c. HF
   d. H_2SO_4

Chapter 6   page 227
1. $NaOH(aq)$; Na^+, sodium ion
2. a. $Ca(OH)_2$
   b. $Al(OH)_3$
   c. $Be(OH)_2$
   d. $LiOH$
   e. $Mn(OH)_2$
   f. $Ni(OH)_2$

Chapter 10   page 427
1. a. 15 cm
   b. −0.9 cm
2. a. −2 cm
   b. 2 cm
3. a. 4.8 cm
   b. −1.8 cm
4. 68 cm
5. 90 cm

Chapter 10   page 436
1. a. −0.66 m
   b. 0.11 m
2. a. −2.92 cm
   b. 2.08 cm
3. a. −1.33 cm
   b. 2.00 cm
4. a. −0.46 m
   b. 0.17 m
5. a. −0.24 m
   b. 0.088 m
6. a. −0.7 cm
   b. 11 cm
7. a. −39 cm
   b. 12 cm

Chapter 11   page 455
1. 1.82×10^8 m/s
2. 1.97×10^8 m/s
3. a. 2.42   b. diamond
4. A: Diamond; B: Flint; C: Crown

Chapter 12   page 500
1. $d_i = 15.4$ cm; $h_i = -1.80$ cm
2. $d_i = 225$ cm; $h_i = -11.3$ cm
3. $d_i = -280$ cm; $h_i = 14.0$ cm
4. $f = 28.8$ cm; $h_o = 24.0$ cm

Glossary

How to Use This Glossary

This Glossary provides the definitions of the key terms that are shown in boldface type in the text. Definitions for other important terms are included as well. The Glossary entries also show the sections where you can find the boldface words. A pronunciation guide, using the key below, appears in square brackets after selected words.

a = mask, back
ae = same, day
ah = car, farther
aw = dawn, hot
e = met, less

ee = leaf, clean
i = simple, this
ih = idea, life
oh = home, loan
oo = food, boot

u = wonder, Sun
uh = taken, travel
uhr = insert, turn

A

acid a compound that produces hydrogen ions, H⁺(aq), when dissolved in water (6.1)

activity series a list of elements organized according to their chemical reactivity; the most reactive element appears at the top and the least reactive element appears at the bottom (5.2)

aerosols tiny particles, such as dust, salt, and ash, that are suspended in the atmosphere and that scatter and reflect solar radiation (7.1)

albedo [al-BEE-doh] the fraction of incident light or electromagnetic radiation that is reflected by the surface of an object, such as from Earth back into space (for example, the extent of an object's ability to reflect sunlight) (7.1)

alveoli [al-VEE-oh-lih] the tiny air sacs in the lungs where gas exchange occurs (3.2)

anaphase the phase of mitosis in which the centromere splits apart and the chromatids are pulled to opposite sides of the cell by the spindle fibres (1.3)

angle of incidence (∠i) the angle between the incident ray and the normal in a ray diagram (10.2)

angle of reflection (∠r) the angle between the reflected ray and the normal in a ray diagram (10.2)

angle of refraction (∠R) the angle between the normal and a refracted ray (11.1)

anion [AN-ih-uhn] a negatively charged ion (4.1)

antacid a substance capable of neutralizing an acid (6.3)

anthropogenic [an-thruh-puh-JEN-ik] relating to or resulting from the influence of humans (7.1)

anthropogenic greenhouse effect the increased capacity of the atmosphere to absorb and prevent the escape of thermal energy because of an increase in greenhouse gases introduced by human activity (8.2)

antibodies specialized, disease-fighting proteins used by the immune system to bind specific antigens; some are always present in the body, while others are produced in response to antigens (3.3)

antigen any material that stimulates an immune response in the body (3.3)

aorta the main blood vessel carrying oxygenated blood from the heart to branch arteries that lead to the rest of the body (3.2)

apparent depth an effect observed in water in which the image of an underwater object appears closer to the surface than the object actually is (11.3)

astigmatism blurred or distorted vision usually caused by an incorrectly shaped cornea (12.3)

atmosphere a layer of gases that surrounds a planet or moon (7.1)

axis of symmetry a line that divides a shape into two congruent parts that can be matched by folding the shape in half (12.1)

B

balanced chemical equation a skeleton equation with coefficients added to balance the number of atoms (4.3)

base A compound that forms hydroxide ions, OH⁻(aq), when dissolved in water (6.1)

bias [BIH-uhs] a tendency toward a particular perspective or point of view that prevents objective assessment of a topic (9.3)

biconcave a lens that is concave on both sides (12.1)

biconvex a lens that is convex on both sides (12.1)

binary acid an acid composed of hydrogen and a non-metal (6.1)

binary ionic compound A compound composed of a metal cation and a non-metal anion (4.1)

binary molecular compound a compound composed of two non-metals joined by one or more covalent bonds (4.2)

biogeochemical cycle a natural process that exchanges matter and energy between the abiotic environment to living things and back to the abiotic environment (8.3)

bioluminescence [BIH-oh-loo-muh-NES-uhns] light that is produced by a biochemical reaction in a living organism (10.1)

biome the largest division of the biosphere; includes large regions that have similar biotic components (such as plants and animals) and similar abiotic components (such as temperature and amount of precipitation) (7.2)

biophotonics all procedures and devices that use various light technologies to work with living systems, including humans (3.3)

blood clot a clumping of blood cells within a vessel (3.2)

boundary the surface between two media (11.1)

bronchi the two tubes branching from the trachea where air passes into the lungs (3.2)

bronchioles [BRONG-kee-olz] the numerous smaller tubes branching from the bronchi (3.2)

C

cancer cells with abnormal genetic material that are dividing uncontrollably and can spread to other body parts (1.4)

cancer screening tests used to detect cancer cells at an early stage of the disease so that it can be treated more effectively (3.3)

carbon footprint the effect that human activities have on the environment in terms of the amount of greenhouse gases produced, measured in units of carbon dioxide (9.3)

carbon offset a means of reducing or avoiding greenhouse gas emissions in order to achieve carbon neutrality, either by performing actions that remove greenhouse gases from the atmosphere or by purchasing credits to negate a carbon footprint (9.3)

catalyst a substance that increases the rate of a reaction and is regenerated at the end of the reaction (5.3)

cation [KAT-ih-uhn] a positively charged ion (4.1)

cell the smallest unit that can perform the functions of life (1.1)

cell cycle a continuous sequence of cell growth and division, including the stages of interphase, mitosis, and cytokinesis (1.4)

cell cycle checkpoints a point in the life of a cell when proteins determine whether cell division should or should not occur (1.4)

cell differentiation a stage of development of a living organism during which specialized cells form (2.1)

cell division the process by which a parent cell divides into two daughter cells (1.3)

cell plate a structure that helps to form the cell wall in the process of plant cell cytokinesis (1.3)

cell specialization the process by which cells develop from similar cells into those that have specific functions within a multicellular organism (2.1)

chemical equation a representation of what happens to the reactants and products during a chemical change (4.3)

chemical reaction a process in which new substances with new properties are formed (4.3)

chemiluminescence [kem-uh-loo-muh-NES-uhns] light that is produced by a chemical reaction (10.1)

chlorofluorocarbon (CFC) a human-made chemical compound that contains chlorine, fluorine, and carbon; when released into the atmosphere, it may cause depletion of the ozone layer (8.2)

chromatic aberration the dispersion of light through a lens (12.1)

chromosome in a cell nucleus, a thread-like structure made mostly of DNA (1.2)

cilia [SIL-ee-ah] microscopic, hair-like projections on epithelial cells that may secrete mucus and help to keep foreign particles out of the body (3.2)

cladding covering that surrounds the glass core of an optical fibre (11.2)

climate the characteristic pattern of weather conditions within a region, including temperature, wind velocity, precipitation, and other features, averaged over a long period of time (7.1)

climate model a mathematical or computer program that describes, simulates, and predicts the interactions of Earth's atmosphere, oceans, land surface, and ice to simulate past, present, and future climate conditions (9.2)

climate zones large regions of Earth's surface that share similar weather conditions (7.2)

climatograph a graph of climate data for a specific region; the data are usually obtained over 30 years from observations made at local weather stations (7.2)

cloning the process of creating identical genetic copies of an organism (1.2)

closed system a system in which energy enters and leaves the system but matter does not cross the system's boundary (8.1)

coefficient a number placed in front of a chemical formula in a balanced chemical equation (4.3)

concave mirror a mirror whose reflecting surface curves inward (10.3)

concentration the amount of a particular substance in a specific amount of another substance; also, the amount of dissolved substance contained per unit of volume of solvent (8.2)

converge to bring together (12.1)

converging lens a lens that brings parallel light rays toward a common point (12.1)

convex mirror a mirror whose reflecting surface curves outward (10.4)

cornea tissue that forms a transparent, curved structure in the front of the eye; refracts light before it enters the eye (12.3)

covalent compound See molecular compound

crest the highest point of a wave (10.1)

critical angle (∠c) the angle of incidence that produces an angle of refraction of 90° (11.2)

cross-over method a method for determining the formula of an ionic compound (4.1)

Glossary • NEL 573

crystal lattice a repeating pattern of ions arranged in three dimensions (4.1)

cytokinesis [sih-toh-ki-NEE-sis] following mitosis, the separation of the two nuclei and cell contents into two daughter cells (1.3)

cytoplasm [SIH-toh-pla-zum] the cytosol and organelles contained by the cell membrane (1.1)

D

dead zones areas in Earth's oceans, lakes, and rivers where growth of algae results in the removal of oxygen from the water, which causes fish and other animals to die (8.3)

decomposition reaction a chemical reaction in which a compound breaks down (decomposes) into two or more simpler compounds or elements (5.1)

deforestation the destruction of the world's forests through direct human activity, such as logging or slash-and-burn clearing for agriculture and grazing, and through the indirect effects of climate change, pollution, and acid precipitation (7.3)

dermal tissue the outermost protective layer of a plant (2.1)

desertification the process by which land slowly dries out until little or no vegetation can survive and the land becomes a desert (7.3)

dispersion the process of separating colours by refraction (11.1)

diverge to spread out in different directions (12.1)

diverging lens a lens that spreads parallel light rays away from a common point (12.1)

DNA material found in the cell nucleus that contains genetic information (1.2)

DNA replication the process by which DNA is copied, creating sister chromatids joined at the centromere (1.3)

DNA screening the process of testing individuals to determine whether they have the gene or genes associated with certain genetic disorders (1.2)

double displacement reaction a chemical reaction in which the positive ions of two different compounds exchange places; results in the formation of two new compounds, one of which may be a precipitate (5.2)

duodenum the first metre of the small intestine, where most digestion occurs (3.2)

E

ecoregion a subdivision of an ecozone that is characterized by local landforms such as plains, lakes, mountains, and rivers (7.2)

ecozone a division of Earth's surface that has developed over a long period of time and is separated from neighbouring ecozones by a geological feature such as an ocean, desert, or mountain range (7.2)

electric discharge the process of emitting light by heating a gas, or vapour, instead of a wire with an electric current (10.1)

electromagnetic radiation energy that travels as waves that move outward in all directions from a source; includes infrared radiation, ultraviolet radiation, radio waves, X rays, gamma rays, and visible light (8.1)

electromagnetic spectrum the entire range of electromagnetic waves in order of wavelength and/or frequency (10.1)

embryonic stem cell [em-bree-AWN-ik stem cell] an unspecialized cell that can become any one of an organism's body cells (3.1)

endoscopy a technique for looking inside the body that involves inserting a tiny light and camera attached to a flexible tube into a body opening, such as the mouth or a small incision (3.2)

energy budget a description of the total energy exchange within a system; a summary of how energy from the Sun enters, moves through, and leaves the Earth system (8.1)

esophagus a muscular tube between the pharynx and the stomach (3.2)

eyepiece the lens in a telescope through which the observer views the object and through which light leaves the telescope (12.3)

F

feedback loop a process in which part of a system's output is returned, or fed back, to the input (8.1)

Fermat's principle light follows the path that will take the least time when travelling from one point to another (10.2)

fluorescence [flor-ESS-uhns] light that is emitted during exposure of the source to ultraviolet light (10.1)

focal length the distance between the vertex of a mirror and the focal point; half the distance from the vertex to the centre of curvature (10.3)

focal point the point on the principal axis through which reflected rays pass when the incident rays are parallel to and near the principal axis (10.3)

forcing agent any substance or process that alters the global energy balance and causes climate to change (9.2)

fossil the traces or remains of a once-living organism (9.1)

frequency the number of crests (or troughs) in a wave that pass a given point in one second (10.1)

fusion reaction a reaction that release large amounts of energy when atoms collide with so much energy that they fuse together; for example, hydrogen's fusion into helium in the Sun's core (10.1)

G

gall [GAWL] an abnormal growth of plant tissue caused by insects or micro-organisms (2.1)

gastric juices digestive secretions from the stomach wall composed of hydrochloric acid and pepsin (3.2)

gene a segment of DNA that controls protein production (1.2)

general circulation model (GCM) a complex computer program that uses mathematical equations to describe the physical processes of the atmosphere and to manipulate the variables that affect how the natural climate system works (9.2)

geostationary a satellite that travels around Earth's equator at a speed that matches the speed of Earth's rotation, so that the satellite remains in the same position relative to Earth's surface (9.2)

global carbon budget the relative amounts of carbon in different parts of the carbon cycle; also an accounting of the exchanges (incomes and losses) of carbon between the stores of the carbon cycle (8.3)

global warming an increase in global average temperature (7.3)

global warming potential (GWP) the ability of a substance to warm the atmosphere by absorbing thermal energy (8.2)

greenhouse effect the natural warming caused when gases in Earth's atmosphere absorb thermal energy that is radiated by the Sun and Earth (7.1)

greenhouse gas a gas in Earth's atmosphere that absorbs and prevents the escape of radiation as thermal energy; examples include carbon dioxide and methane (8.2)

ground tissue most of the inner tissues of a plant, including palisade cells, mesophyll cells, and other specialized cells (2.1)

H

halocarbons a large group of chemicals formed from carbon and one or more halogens, such as chlorine, fluorine, or iodine (8.2)

heart attack death of or damage to heart muscle tissue caused by insufficient blood supply (3.2)

hydrosphere the collective mass of water found on, under, and over the surface of Earth in the form of liquid water, ice, and water vapour (7.1)

hydroxide a chemical compound containing hydrogen and oxygen (4.1)

hyperopia [hi-per-OPE-ee-ah] far-sightedness; the condition in which the eye cannot focus on nearby objects (12.3)

I

ice core a long cylinder of ice obtained by drilling into a glacier (9.1)

incandescence [in-can-DESS-uhns] light emitted from a material because of the high temperature of the material (10.1)

incident ray a ray of light that travels from a light source toward a surface (10.2)

index of refraction the ratio of the speed of light in a vacuum to the speed of light in a given medium (11.1)

indicator a chemical that changes colour in response to changes in the concentration of hydrogen ions or hydroxide ions (6.2)

Industrial Revolution a period in the late 1700s that saw a rapid increase in the rate at which new machines were invented and new methods of transportation and manufacturing were adopted (7.1)

interphase periods of growth in the life of a cell; consists of two growth stages and a stage of DNA replication (1.4)

ion a charged particle formed from the loss or gain of one or more electrons (4.1)

ionic compound a compound composed of oppositely charged ions (4.1)

isotope any of two or more forms of an element that have the same number of protons but a different number of neutrons (for example, deuterium is an isotope of hydrogen) (9.1)

J

jet stream high-altitude winds that travel long distances at very high speeds (7.1)

K

Köppen climate classification system a method of identifying and describing climates based on observable features such as temperature ranges and rates of precipitation (7.2)

L

large intestine organ divided into the colon, rectum, and anus, where water, salt, and vitamins are absorbed, and feces are formed and eliminated (3.2)

law of conservation of mass the mass of products produced by a chemical reaction is always equal to the mass of the reactants (4.3)

laws of reflection 1. The incident ray, reflected ray, and the normal always lie in the same plane. 2. The angle of incidence is equal to the angle of reflection. (10.2)

leaching a technique used to extract metals by dissolving the metal in an aqueous solution (5.3)

lens a transparent object with at least one curved side that causes light to bend (12.1)

liming the application of basic materials, typically lime-based, to renew acidified lakes and regions (6.3)

luminescence [loo-mi-NESS-uhns] the emission of light by a material or an object that has not been heated; for example, fluorescence (10.1)

M

magnification the change in size of an optically produced image (10.3)

magnification equation an algebraic formula used to predict the size of an image formed by a thin converging lens (12.2)

$$m = \frac{h_i}{h_o} = \frac{-d_i}{d_o}$$

medical imaging technology techniques used to form an image of a body's internal cells, tissues, and organs (3.2)

medium substance through which light travels (10.2)

meristematic stem cell [MER-es-te-MA-tik stem cell] an unspecialized cell found in plants that gives rise to a specific specialized cell (2.1)

metaphase the phase of mitosis in which the chromosomes are aligned across the centre of the cell (1.3)

micrograph a photograph taken with a microscope (1.1)

microscopy the science of using microscopes to view samples or objects (1.1)

mirage an optical effect caused by the bending of light rays passing through layers of air that have very different temperatures (11.3)

mitosis [mih-TOH-sis] the process by which the duplicated contents of the cell's nucleus divide into two equal parts (1.3)

molecular compound a compound formed when atoms of two or more different elements share electrons (4.2)

molecule A neutral particle composed of two or more atoms joined together by covalent bonds (4.2)

monitor to measure conditions systematically and repeatedly in order to track changes (9.2)

mucus [MYOO-cuhss] protective secretions from the stomach wall that prevent the stomach lining from breaking down (3.2)

multivalent metal [muhl-ti-VAE-luhnt MET-uhl] a metal that can form different ions (4.1)

mutagen a substance or factor that can cause a mutation in DNA (1.2)

mutation a change in the DNA of an organism (1.2)

myopia [my-OPE-ee-ah] near-sightedness; the condition in which the eye cannot focus on distant objects (12.3)

N

negative feedback loop a feedback loop in which each process acts to decrease the effects of the initial process or event and helps maintain equilibrium (8.1)

neutralization the reaction of an acid and a base to produce a salt and water (6.3)

night-vision device an artificial device that allows people to see when only a very small amount of light is available (12.3)

nitrogen fixation the process by which atmospheric nitrogen is changed into forms that can be used by plants and other organisms (8.3)

normal a line constructed to be perpendicular to a surface where a ray of light meets the surface (10.2)

nucleus [NOO-klee-us] the organelle that controls the cell's activities (1.1)

O

objective lens the lens through which light enters a telescope (12.3)

open system a system in which energy and matter cross the system's boundary (8.1)

organ a combination of several types of tissue working together to perform a specific function (2.1)

organelle a specialized structure in a cell (1.1)

oxoacid an acid composed of hydrogen, oxygen, and another element (6.1)

ozone a greenhouse gas that is composed of three atoms of oxygen; it is commonly found in a concentrated layer in the stratosphere (8.2)

P

paleoclimatologist a scientist who studies past climates on Earth (9.1)

partial reflection and refraction a phenomenon in which some of the light that is travelling from one medium into another is reflected and some is refracted at the boundary between the media (11.2)

parts per million (ppm) a unit of measurement that indicates the number of parts of a substance per million parts of another substance; for example, for salt water, 1000 ppm of salt means 1000 parts salt in 1 000 000 parts of pure water (8.2)

pathogen a disease-causing agent, such as a virus, bacteria, or fungus (3.3)

peroxide a chemical compound containing two oxygens covalently bonded together (4.1)

pH indicator A substance that changes colour to show the concentration of hydrogen ions (H^+) or hydroxide ions (OH^-) in a solution (6.2)

pH scale a numerical scale ranging from 0 to 14 that is used to classify aqueous solutions as acidic, basic, or neutral (6.2)

phagocyte a cell that engulfs and digests waste material and invading micro-organisms (3.3)

phloem [FLOH-um] vascular tissue that transports sap carrying the sugars produced through photosynthesis from the leaves to the rest of the plant (2.1)

phosphorescence [foss-for-ESS-uhns] light that is emitted due to exposure of the source to ultraviolet light, and that continues to be emitted for some time in the absence of the ultraviolet light (10.1)

photosynthesis the process by which carbon dioxide enters the leaves of plants and reacts with water in the presence of sunlight to produce glucose and oxygen (2.1)

plane mirror a mirror with a flat, reflective surface (10.2)

pluripotent stem cell an unspecialized cell that can develop into many, but not all, of an organism's types of body cells (3.1)

polyatomic ion an ion that is composed of more than one atom (4.1)

positive feedback loop a feedback loop in which each process acts to increase the effects of the initial process or event and results in a change in the system (8.1)

potential an ability that may or may not be developed (1.3)

precession a change in the direction of the axis of rotation of Earth; also known as wobble (7.1)

precipitate an insoluble solid formed in a chemical reaction (5.1)

presbyopia [prez-bee-OPE-ee-ah] the condition in which lenses of the eye become stiff and the ciliary muscles can no longer make the lenses change shape (12.3)

prevailing winds air currents that blow in fairly constant directions around the world (7.1)

principal axis the line that passes through the centre of curvature, C, of a mirror or lens and is normal to the axis of symmetry (10.3)

product a pure substance that is formed in a chemical change; the properties of the product are different from the properties of the reactants (4.3)

prophase the phase of mitosis in which sister chromatids condense and the chromosomes become visible (1.3)

public health strategy a co-ordinated effort to track, research, and reduce the incidence of specific health problems in a population (3.3)

pulmonary artery vessel that carries deoxygenated blood from the heart to the lungs (3.2)

R

rainbow an arc of colours of the visible spectrum appearing opposite the Sun, caused by reflection, refraction, and dispersion of the Sun's rays as they pass through raindrops (11.3)

ray a straight line with an arrowhead that shows the direction in which a light ray is travelling (10.2)

reactant a pure substance that undergoes a chemical change (4.3)

real image an image that is formed when reflected rays meet (10.3)

reflected ray a ray that begins at the point where the incident ray and the normal meet (10.2)

reflecting telescope a telescope that uses a combination of mirrors and lenses (12.3)

reflection the change in direction of a light ray when it bounces off a surface (10.2)

refracted ray the ray that is bent upon entering a second medium (11.1)

refracting telescope a telescope that uses lenses only (12.3)

refraction the bending of light as it travels, at an angle, from a material with one refractive index to a material with a different refractive index (11.1)

retina a layer of rod and cone cells that respond to light and initiate nerve impulses; rod cells are very sensitive to light but cannot distinguish between colours; cone cells detect colour (12.3)

retroreflector a material that reflects light back to its source (11.2)

root system a system that takes in water and minerals from the soil and transports them to the shoot system (2.2)

S

sedimentary rock a type of rock formed by the deposition of sediment (9.1)

shatter cones rare rock formations that form from meteorite impacts (6.3)

shimmering the apparent movement of objects in hot air over objects and surfaces (11.3)

shoot system a system that supports the plant, performs photosynthesis, and transports sap (2.2)

single displacement reaction a chemical reaction in which one element takes the place of another element in a compound (5.2)

sink a process or reservoir that removes greenhouse gases from the atmosphere (8.2)

skeleton equation a word equation in which the words are replaced by chemical formulas (4.3)

small intestine organ between the stomach and the large intestine, where most digestion occurs (3.2)

smog a form of air pollution produced by the reaction of sunlight with chemical compounds, such as hydrocarbons and nitrogen oxides, in the air (8.3)

source a process that adds greenhouse gases to the atmosphere (8.2)

specific heat capacity the amount of thermal energy that must be added to or removed from a substance to raise or lower the temperature of 1 g of the substance by 1°C (7.1)

spherical relating to a sphere or to the properties of a sphere (10.3)

spherical aberration irregularities in an image in a curved mirror that result when reflected rays from the outer parts of the mirror do not go through the focal point (10.3)

sphincter a circular muscle that contracts and relaxes to control the passage of substances (3.2)

stable octet an atom with a full outer energy level of electrons (8.1)

stem cell an unspecialized cell that can produce various types of specialized cells (3.1)

store a part of a biogeochemical cycle in which matter or energy accumulates; also called a reservoir (8.3)

stroke loss of brain function caused by an interruption of blood flow (and therefore oxygen supply) to the brain (3.2)

synthesis reaction a chemical reaction in which two or more reactants combine to produce a new product (5.1)

system a group of interdependent parts that work together to form a single, functioning whole (8.1); in biology, a group of tissues and organs that perform specific functions (2.2)

T

tectonic plate a piece of Earth's outer shell (the lithosphere) that moves around on the slowly flowing, underlying rock layer (the asthenosphere) (7.1)

telophase the phase of mitosis in which two daughter nuclei are formed (1.3)

ternary compound a compound composed of three different elements (4.1)

thermohaline circulation a three-dimensional pattern of ocean circulation driven by wind, heat, and salinity that is an important component of the ocean-atmosphere climate system (8.1)

thin lens equation an algebraic formula used to predict the position of an image formed by a thin converging lens (12.2)
$$\frac{1}{f} = \frac{1}{d_o} + \frac{1}{d_i}$$

tissue a cluster of similar cells that share the same specialized structure and function (2.1)

total internal reflection the phenomenon in which incident light is not refracted but is entirely reflected back from the boundary; occurs when light travels from a medium in which its speed is lower to a medium in which its speed is higher (11.2)

totipotent stem cell [toh-tee-POH-tent stem cell] an unspecialized cell that can develop into any one of an organism's body cells (3.1)

trachea [TRAE-kee-uh] the main tube through which air passes from the mouth into the bronchi (3.2)

transgenic organism an organism whose genetic information has been altered with the insertion of genes from another species (1.2)

transpiration the evaporation of water from leaves (2.2)

trough [TRAWF] the lowest point of a wave (10.1)

tumour an abnormal clump or group of cells (1.4)

V

vaccination the process of giving a vaccine by mouth or injection to provide active immunity against a disease (3.3)

valence electron an electron in the outermost occupied energy level (4.1)

valve flexible flap of tissue that ensures one-way flow of blood (3.2)

vascular tissue structures that transport sap and provide vertical support for the plant's body (2.1)

virtual image an image formed by rays that appear to be coming from a certain position, but are not actually coming from that position; image does not form a visible projection on a screen (10.2)

W

wave front the crest, or high point, of a wave (11.1)

wavelength the distance from one crest (or trough) of a wave to the next crest (or trough) (10.1)

weather the condition of the atmosphere in a specific place at a specific time (7.1)

wind the movement of air from an area of high pressure to an area of low pressure (7.1)

word equation an equation in which the products and reactants in a chemical reaction are represented by words (4.3)

X

xylem [ZIH-lum] vascular tissue that conducts water and minerals from the roots to the leaves (2.1)

Index

Boldface numbers correspond to **key terms** in the text.
Terms that occur in figures (*f*) and tables (*t*) are also indicated.

A

abnormal development, 87, 87*f*
absorption of solar radiation, 320*f*, 320*t*
acetic acid, 220, 221*f*
acid leaching, 344–245
acid precipitation, 236, 236*f*, 239–243, 242*f*, 243*f*
acid spills, 238, 238*f*
acid-base indicators, 231–234, 231*f*, 232*f*, 233*f*, 234*f*
acidified lakes, 240–241, 241*t*, 243, 243*f*
acids, 219–227, **220**
　detecting, 217
　in foods, 219, 220
　formulas, writing, 224
　in nature, 221*f*
　neutralizing, 237–238
　pH scale, 230, 230*f*
　properties, 234*t*
　reactions, 236–245
Activities
　acid-base detection, 217
　acidity and coral reefs, 293
　air pollution and lakes, 244
　apparent depth, 471
　carbon stores, 336
　cell structure of a leaf, 62
　chemical reactions, 137, 177, 188, 194
　climate change, 267, 349, 375
　climatograph, making, 281
　concave mirror, 421
　conservation of mass, 177
　converging lenses, comparing, 491
　convex mirror, 434
　coral reefs and acidity, 293
　decomposition reaction, 188
　electron sharing, 143
　field of view, 485
　genetic testing, ethics of, 21
　global warming, 329, 375
　glowing slime, making, 401
　internal reflection of light, 463
　ionic compounds, modelling, 143
　ions and acids, matching, 225
　law of reflection, 413
　light, properties of, 459
　matter and energy, flow of, 309
　message transfer, cell to cell, 5
　mitosis, modelling, 36
　molecular compounds, modelling, 154
　non-metal reactivity, 194
　phloem function, 71
　plant growth, observing, 55
　properties of light, 459
　pulse rate, 101
　refraction, 447
　skin cloning, 83
　solar energy heating Earth, 315
　synthesis reaction, 188
　tissue characteristics, 89
　toxic material removal, 200
　tree rings, analyzing, 352
　universal indicator, 232
　volcanic eruptions, effects of, 276
　water vapour movement, simulating, 365
activity series, **192**–194, 192*f*
adenine, 17*f*
adhesion, of water, 74
adipose tissue, 89*t*
aerosols (from volcanoes), 276
AIDS, 112–113
air bags, 136, 187*f*
air pollution, 244
albedo, 268, **275**, 312–313
　changing, 321, 390
　energy budget, 321, 321*f*
　feedback loops, 312, 312*f*, 313, 313*f*, 325
aluminum carbonate, 149*t*
aluminum chloride, 143, 143*f*
aluminum fluoride, 145*t*
aluminum sulfide, 144*f*
alveoli, 104, 104*f*, 106
ammonia, 165, 165*f*, 182, 182*f*, 205, 337
ammonium, 148, 148*t*, 337
ammonium sulfate, 149*t*, 166
amniocentesis, 19, 109
amoeba, 85, 85*f*
amylase, 97
anaphase, **35**, 35*f*, 56
angioplasty, 102, 103*f*
angle of incidence, **412**
　different materials, through, 477
　and glass surfaces, 458, 461*f*, 459
　large, 460–461, 461*f*
　and mirrors, 413*f*, 416, 420, 420*f*, 460, 460*f*
　prism, through, 464, 464*f*
　small, 462, 462*f*
　and water, 458, 458*f*, 462, 462*f*, 476, 480
angle of reflection, **412**, 413*f*
angle of refraction, **452**, 452*f*
　different materials, through, 477
　and glass surfaces, 459
　and water, 451, 451*f*, 452, 452*f*, 462, 462*f*, 476, 480
animal cells, 46*f*
　cytokinesis, 37, 37*f*
　mitosis, 34–35*f*, 37, 37*f* 48–49, 48*f*, 49*f*
　organelles, 10*f*, 11, 12, 12*f*, 14, 85, 85*f*
　specialization, 85–87
anions, **140**
　in displacement reactions, 194, 195, 196
　forming ionic compounds, 140
　naming ionic compounds, 142, 147, 147*t*, 148, 223
　writing chemical formulas, 144, 145*t*, 149, 227
ant stings, 221
antacids, 150, 225, 225*f*, 237
anthropogenic, **277**
anthropogenic climate change, 277, 368, 368*f*, 374
anthropogenic greenhouse effect, **329**, 344, 376, 377*f*
antibodies, 110, 111
antigen, 110, 111
anus, 97*f*, 99
aorta, 99*f*, 100, 100*f*
apparent depth, **470**, 471
Aqua (satellite), 362*f*, 363, 363*f*
aqueous solutions, 162*t*
　acids, 220, 230
　bases, 226, 230
　classifying, 230
　conductivity of, 220, 226
　displacement reactions, 191, 191*f*, 193, 195, 195*f*, 212–213
　gold in, 202–203, 202*f*
argon, 405
Aristotle, 279
arteries, 104*f*, 116*f*
　aorta, 99*f*, 100, 100*f*
　blocked, 102, 102*f*, 103*f*, 131
　in closed circulatory system, 101
　and heart disease, 102
　pulmonary, 100, 100*f*
arteriosclerosis, 102, 116*f*
astatine, 194
asthma, 294
astigmatism, **509**
atmosphere, **269**
　carbon cycle, 334, 335*f*, 336
　carbon dioxide, 323, 324, 324*f*, 325, 325*f*, 334, 335*f*, 336
　climate, 273–274, 273*f*, 274*f*
　composition, 324*f*
　concentration of gases, 323, 323*t*, 324
　feedback loops, 312–313, 312*f*, 313*f*, 315
　solar energy, 273, 273*f*, 311
　water vapour, 273, 325
Atmospheric Infrared Sounder (AIRS), 363
atom economy, 167*f*
Aura (satellite), 362, 362*f*, 363*f*
auxin, 59, 59*f*
axis of symmetry, 490, 490*f*, 494, 495*t*, 496*f*, 497*t*, 498*f*
　converging lenses, 489, 489*f*, 490, 490*f*, 495*t*, 496*f*, 498*t*
　diverging lenses, 489, 489*f*, 490, 490*f*, 497*f*

B

bacteria, 7, 23*t*, 27
baking soda, 137, 150, 225
balanced chemical equation, 161, 179, 181, 182, 187
barium X rays, 95, 95*f*
bases, 219, **225**–227
　indicators, 231–234, 231*f*, 232*f*, 233*f*, 234*f*
　neutralizing, 237
　pH scale, 230, 230*f*
Basrur, Dr. Sheela, 112*f*
Beverly Swamp, 298*f*
bias, **372**
biconcave lens, 489
Bild-Enkin, Simon, 242
bile, 98*f*
binary acids, **222**
binary ionic compounds, **142**, 144–145, 184
binary molecular compounds, **154**–157, 154*t*, 155*t*, 156*t*
binoculars, 464, 464*f*, 504, 504*f*
bioclimate profiles, 286
biogeochemical cycle, **333**
bioluminescence, **407**, 408*f*
biomes, **283**, 283*f*, 284, 284*f*, 297–298, 297*f*
biophotonics, **108**, 109*f*
black dragonfish, 408*f*
bladder, 99, 99*f*
bleach and ammonia, 205, 205*f*
blood, 89*t*, 99, 100–102, 104
blood cells, red, 7, 7*f*, 11*f*, 26*f*, 104, 104*f*
blood clots, 102, 102*f*
blood vessels, 83*f*, 99
Bodnar, BJ, 292
bogs, 298
Bohr-Rutherford water model, 153, 153*f*
bone, 89*t*
boreal forest, 283*f*, 284*f*
Boreal Forest ecozone, 303*f*
Boreal Shield ecoregions, 287*f*
boundary, 450
breast cancer, 21
Briand-Lemay, Maude, 415
brightfield/darkfield microscope, 8*f*
"broken telephone" game, 5

Index • NEL 579

bromine, 142*t*, 155*t*, 164, 181
bromine monochloride, 155*t*
bromothymol blue, 218, 233*f*, 233*t*
bronchiole, 103*f*, 104, 104*f*
bronchus/bronchi, 103*f*, 104
buds, 59, 59*f*
butterfly, number of chromosomes, 16*t*

C

calcium carbonate, 148, 148*f*, 150, 162, 188, 242
calcium hydroxide, 149, 149*f*, 226*t*
calcium oxide, 139, 145
camera lenses, 487, 492, 492*f*, 507, 507*f*, 521
Canada-U.S. Air Quality Agreement, 241
Canada-Wide Acid Rain Strategy, 239
cancer, 42–44, 43*f*, 50, 67, 114, 114*f*
cancer screening, **114**
cap-and-trade system, 379
capillaries, 102, 102*f*, 104*f*
car exhaust and environment, 200
carbon cycle, 334, 335*f*, 336
carbon dioxide, 103, 153*f*, 154, 162, 180
　atmosphere, 323, 324, 324*f*, 325, 325*f*, 329*t* 334, 335*f*, 336
　cellular respiration, 14, 14*f*, 63
　climate, 354–355, 355*f*, 367
　global warming potential, 330*t*
carbon footprint, **373**–374
carbon monoxide, 176
carbon offsets, **374**
carbon sinks, 325, 325*f*
carbon stores, 336
carbon-tax systems, 379
carbonate, 148, 148*t*
carbonic acid, 162, 221*f*, 223*t*
cardiac muscle, 88*t*
Case Studies
　acid precipitation, 240–241
　cloning animals, 24–25
　energy efficiency, 378–379
　green medicines, 166–167
　hydrogen fuel, 182–183
　laser eye surgery, 508–509
　ocean's forests, overheating, 312–313
　phytoplankton, 312–313
　solar ovens, 428–429
　UV radiation, 472–473
　vaccinations, 110–111
　Walkerton water tragedy, 294–295
　wheat rust, 66–67
CAT scan, 94*t*

catalyst, **201**
catalytic converters, 201, 201*f*
cataract eye surgery, 484
cations, **140**, 142*f*, 144, 145*t*, 149*t*
cause and effect, identifying, 178, 350
cause-and-effect maps, 350, 486
cell cycle, 40–44, 40*f*, 41*f*
cell cycle checkpoints, **41**, 41*f*
cell differentiation, **57**, 57*f*, 86, 86*f*
cell division, 29, **30**, 37, 37*f* 40*f*
cell membrane, 12*f*, 13*f*, 30, 31, 31*f*
cell plate, **38**
cell specialization, **57**–59, 57*f*, 85–87
cell theory, 11
cell wall, 13*f*
cells, **7**, 29–38
　animal, 12, 12*f*, 14, 34–35*f*, 37, 37*f*, 48–49, 48*f*, 49*f*, 85–87
　average life span, 40*t*
　cancer, 42–44, 43*f*, 50, 67, 114, 114*f*
　cellular respiration, 14, 14*f*, 63
　chemical concentrations, 30, 31
　cytokinesis, **32**, 37–38, 37*f*, 38*f*, 40, 40*f*
　daughter, 29, 32, 33, 35*f*, 37, 37*f*, 38*f*, 40, 40*f*, 43*f*
　death, 42
　division, 29, 29*f*, 40, 40*f*
　glucose, 12*f*, 13*f*, 14
　membrane, 12*f*, 13*f*, 30–31, 31*f*
　mitosis, 34–35*f*, 37, 37*f*, 48–49, 48*f*, 49*f*
　organelles, 10, 10*f*, 11, 12–14, 12*f*, 13*f*, 85, 85*f*
　osmosis, 30, 31, 31*f*, 73, 73*f*
　parent, 29, 33, 34–35*f*, 37, 37*f*, 38, 38*f*
　permeability of membranes, 31
　plant, 38*f*, 57
　red blood, 7, 7*f*, 11*f*, 26*f*, 104, 104*f*
　reproduction, 29, 29*f*, 34–35*f*, 37, 37*f*, 48–49, 48*f*, 49*f*
　sickle, 26, 26*f*
　size, 30, 32, 32*f*
　structure, 7, 10, 10*f*
　suicide, 42
　walls, 38
　water, 14
　white blood, 11*f*, 89, 110, 110*f*, 111
　see also tissue
cellular respiration, 14, 14*f*, 63
centre of curvature, 421, 420, 420*f*, 423, 423*f*, 424, 424*f*
centromere, 33*f*, 34*f*, 35*f*, 56
centrosome, 33, 34*f*, 35*f*,
CERES, 321

chemical equations, **161**, 163–165
chemical reactions, 137, **160**, 199
　car exhaust, 200–201, 200*f*, 201*f*
　decomposition reactions, 179, **185**–188, 185*f*, 186*f*, 197*t*
　displacement reactions, 190–197
　evidence of 180, 180*f*, 207
　in household cleaning products, 204–205, 204*f*, 205*f*
　gold, recovering, 202–203, 202*f*
　pools, cleaning and disinfecting, 203, 203*f*
　synthesis reactions, **181**–183, 181*f*, 182*f*, 183*f*, 197*t*
chemiluminescence, **407**, 407*f*
chicken, number of chromosomes, 16*t*
chlor-alkali process, 226, 226*f*
chloric acid, 223*t*
chloride, 142*t*
chlorination, 203
chlorine, 164, 203
chlorofluorocarbons (CFCs), **328**, 329*t*, 330*t*
chlorophyll, 63*f*
chloroplasts, 13*f*, 14, 57*f*, 61, 63, 63*f*
chromatic aberration, **492**, 492*f*, 502, 504
chromatids, 33, 33*f*, 34*f*, 35*f*, 56
chromosomes, **16**–17, 16*t*, 19, 23*t*, 29, 29*f*, 56
　cytokinesis, 37
　DNA, 17, 32–34
　mitosis, 34–35
　number, 16, 16*f*
cilia, 103
cigarette smoking, 105, 105*f*
circulatory system, 95*f*, 96, 96*f*, 100–102, 100*f*, 102*f*
citric acid, 137, 219, 219*f*, 220
cladding, 465
climate, **266**, **269**
　atmosphere, 273–274, 273*f*
　classifying, 266, 282, 282*t*
　describing, 279–288
　health effects, 294
　human activity, 277
　solar radiation, 270
　tectonic plates, 275–276
　volcanic activity, 276
　zones, 279, 279*f*, 284–285*f*
climate change, 266*f*, 267, 290, 348, 349
　carbon cycle, 334–335
　factors affecting, 269–277
　greenhouse gases, 323–331
　melting sea ice, 266, 291–292, 290*f*, 291*f*, 317
　modelling, 364–368
　monitoring, 360–363

nitrogen cycle, 337–339
oceans, affecting, 293*t*, 316–317, 318–319*f*, 341–342
past patterns, 351–358
taking action, 370–380
vegetation, affecting, 286, 288, 397–398
climate model, **364**–368
climate zones in Canada, 284*f*
climatograph, 268, **280**, 280*f*, 281, 284–285*f*
cloning, **24**–25, 24*f*, 25*f*, 82, 83
closed circulatory system, 101
closed system (climate), 311
Cloud Gate, 431, 431*f*
Clout, Jerri, 113
coefficient, **161**
cohesion, 74
colon, 97*f*, 99
columnar epithelia, 88*t*
comprehension, 178
concave mirrors, 419–429, **420**, 420*f*
concentration, **323**, 323*t*
concrete, 188
conduction, 314*t*, 315, 315*f*
cone cells, 506
connective tissue, 88, 89*t*
conservation of mass, 159–167
continental rebound, 395
convection, 314*t*, 315, 315*f*
converging lenses, 488, 488*f*, **489**–490, 489*f*, 490*f*, 495*t*, 496, 496*f*, 499
convex mirrors, **431**–437, 432*f*, 433*t*, 436*f*, 437*f*
copper(I) nitride, 147*t*
copper(I) oxide, 146, 146*f*
copper(II) nitrate, 191, 191*f*
copper(II) oxide, 146, 146*f*
corn, number of chromosomes, 16*t*
cornea, **506**, 506*f*, 507*f*
corrosion, 179, 179*f*
cortex, 65, 65*f*
covalent compounds, 153
cow, number of chromosomes, 16*t*
Crick, Francis, 17
critical angle, 462, 462*f*
cross sections, interpreting, 56
cryptosporidiosis, 294
crystal lattices, 144, 144*f*
CT scans, 94, 94*f*, 94*t*
cuticle, 60*f*, 61
cyanide, 202, 203
cystic fibrosis, 21
cytokinesis, **32**, 37–38, 37*f*, 38*f*, 40, 40*f*
cytoplasm, **11**, 12*f*, 13*f*, 85
cytosine, 17*f*
cytoskeleton, 12*f*, 13*f*, 34*f*
cytosol, 11

580 NEL • Index

D

Dalton, John, 160
dandelions, 65f
daughter cells
  animal cells, 37, 37f
  cell division, 29, 40, 40f
  cytokinesis, 32, 33, 35f, 37, 37f, 43f
  DNA replication, 33
  mitosis, 32, 33, 35f, 37, 37f, 43f, 85
  plant cells, 38f
  single-celled organisms, 29
  telophase, 35f
dead zones, 338
decomposition reactions, 179, **185**–188, 185f, 186f, 197t
decomposition of water, 185
deep-sea sea star, 408f
deforestation, 297f, **298**
deoxyribonucleic acid (DNA), **17**–21, 17f, 18f, 32–34, 38
dermal tissue, 56, 58, 58f, 61, 65f
desert, 283f, 285
desertification, **296**
diagrams, interpreting, 402
diaphragm, 103f
diatomic molecules, 164f
diffusion across cell membranes, 30–31, 31f
digestive system, 84, 96–99, 96f, 97f, 237, 237f
digestive vacuoles, 85
dihydrogen monoxide, 152, 152f
dinitrogen pentoxide, 157
dinitrogen tetroxide, 155, 155t
diseases, 112–114
disinfecting pools, 203, 203f
dispersion, **453**, 453f
displacement reactions, 190–197
dissociation, 226
distortion, 428, 428f
disulfur dinitride, 156t
Diumering, Adrienne, 166
diverging lenses, 488, 488f, **489**, 489f, 490, 490f, 497, 497f, 497t
DNA, **17**–21, 17f, 18f, 32–34, 38
DNA screening, **19**–21
Dolly (cloned sheep), 25
double displacement reactions, 176, **195**–197, 195f, 197t
double helix, 17f
Down syndrome, 19, 19f, 21
Drive Clean program, 378
droughts, 296, 296f
drug research, ethical issues, 21–22
duodenum, 97f, 98, 98f

E

E. coli, 23t, 99f, 110f, 294
Earth, 270–272, 271f, 272f
  orbit, 270, 271, 271f, 270f
  tilt of axis, 271, 271f, 272, 272f
Earth observing system (EOS), 362
Eastern Canada Acid Rain program, 239
ecoregions, **286**, 287
ecozones, **286**, 287
Einstein, Albert, 500
El Niño, 317, 318f, 319f, 341–342, 362
electric discharge, 404, 404f, 405
electromagnetic radiation, **314**
electromagnetic spectrum, 409, 409f
electromagnetic waves, 409, 409f
embryonic stem cells, **91**
endocrine system, 96f
endodermis, 56, 65, 65f, 73f
endoplasmic reticulum, 12f, 13f
endoscope, 466, 466f, 487
endoscopy, 95, 95f, 108, 108f
energy budget, **320**, 321, 321f
Energy Star®, 378–379
energy transfer, 315, 316
environment, 87, 139, 176, 199, 200
environmental clean-up, 167f
enzymes, 18, 19, 97, 98
epidermal cells, 58f, 60f
epidermis, 83f
epiglottis, 103f
epithelial tissue, 88, 88t, 104
Erasmus, Bill, 377, 377f
esophagus, 97, 97f
etching, 222f
ethical issues in drug research, 22
ethylene, 68, 68f
European Project for Ice Coring in Antarctica, 352
excretory system, 96f, 99, 99f
explosions as decomposition reactions, 186, 186f
extinction, 297
eyepiece, **502**, 503
eyes, 492, 492f, 506–510

F

far-sightedness, 486, 508, 508f
fat (adipose tissue), 89t
fat deposits, 83f
feedback loops, **312**, 315
fens, 298
Fermat's principle, 412, 451
fertilization, 68
fibre optics, 465, 465f, 466, 466f
fibrous roots, 65, 65f
field of view (eyes), 485
fire retardants, 166
fish-eye lenses, 491, 491f
flow of air, 449, 449f
flowers, 60, 60f, 68, 70f
fluorescence, 403f, **405**–406, 405f, 406f
fluorescence microscope, 8f
fluoride, 142t
fluorine, 164, 181
focal length, **420**, 490, 490f
focal point, **420**, 421
  converging lenses, 490, 490f, 495t, 496, 496f
  convex mirror, 432, 432f
  diverging lenses, 490, 490f, 497t, 498
follicles, 84
"Food Miles" Initiative, 384
food preservation, 197, 197f
forcing agent, **368**, 368f
forest fires, 54
formic acid, 221
fossil fuels, 200f, 335f
fossils, **357**, 357f
fruit, 70f
fruit fly, number of chromosomes, 16t
fungicides, 66
Furdyk, Michael, 463
fusion reactions, 404

G

Galilei, Galileo, 502
gall bladder, 97f, 98, 98f
galls, **67**, 67f
gamma rays, 409f
gas, 162t
gas exchange systems, 105
gastric juices, 95, 97
gene therapy, 27
general circulation model (GCM), **364**, 364f, 366, 367
genes, 16, **17**–27, 18f
genetic engineering, 4
genetic screening, 19–21
genetically modified organisms (GMOs), 22–23, 23t
geostationary, **361**
Gerber Daisy, 60f
germs, 7
giardiasis, 294
gills, 105, 105f
glacial ice, 291
glacial lakes and sediment cores, 356
glaciation, 269f
global carbon budget, **334**
global climate, 317
global warming, **290**, 313f, 317, 324
global warming potential, **330**, 376, 376f
glow sticks, 400, 407, 407f
glowing slime, making, 401
glucose
  in animal cells, 12f, 14
  in plant cells, 13f, 14, 60, 63, 75, 75f, 180
gold mining, 202
Golgi body, 12f, 13f, 38
granum, 63, 63f
graph, 486
graphic organizer, 218, 486
grass-pink orchids, 298
grassland, 283f, 285
gravitational lenses, 500, 500f
Great Lakes Wetlands Conservation Action Plan, 298
great ocean conveyor belt, 316f

green medicines, 166–167
greenhouse effect, 152, **273**, 273f, 277, 308
greenhouse gases, 276, 308, 323–331, 373f, 379, 380, 380f
Greenland Ice Core Project, 352
ground tissue, 58, 58f
growth hormone, 23t
guanine, 17f
guard cells, 60f, 61, 61f

H

Haber, Fritz, 182
Haber process, 182
Haber-Bosch process, 337
hair follicle, 83f
hairs, 83f
halocarbons, 328
halogens, activity series, 194
hantavirus, 294, 294f
hard X rays, 409f
Hayman, Michael, 463
Hazardous Household Product Symbols (HHPS), 204, 204t
health and climate, 294
heart, 100, 100f
heart attack, 102, 131
heart disease, 102
heat reservoir, 275
helium, 140
hemoglobin, 104
high blood pressure, 102
HIV/AIDS, 112
Hooke, Robert, 10, 46
hormones in plants, 68
Hudson Plains ecozone, 287f, 303t
human, number of chromosomes, 16t
human papilloma virus (HPV), 44
Huntington disease, 20, 21, 22
hurricanes, 296
hydrangea flowers, 221, 221f
hydrobromic acid, 218, 222t
hydrochloric acid, 97, 218, 220, 220f, 222, 222t
hydrofluoric acid, 218, 222, 222f, 222t
hydrogen, 162t, 164, 181, 192f, 454t
hydrogen fuel cells, 176, 182–183
Hydrogen Highway, 176
hydrogen peroxide, 161
Hydrogen Village, 176, 183
hydroiodic acid, 222t
hydroponics, 72f
hydrosphere, **274**
hydroxide, 148, 148t
hydroxide ions, 226
hydroxyapatite, 170
hyperopia, 486, **508**, 508f
hypertension, 102
hypochlorous acid, 229

Index • NEL **581**

I

ice, sea, 266, 291–292, 290f, 291f, 317
ice cores, **352**–355, 353f, 355
ice sheets, 269f
Igliniit Project, 291
image distance, 416t
images, 402, 484
    concave mirrors, 419–429
    converging lens, 496, 496f
    diverging lenses, 497
    lens magnification, 494, 494f
    plane mirrors, 414
immune system, 96f
incandescence, **404**, 404f
incandescent bulbs, 331, 404, 404f
incident ray, **412**, 413f, 420, 421, 458f
index of refraction, **452**, 454, 454t, 490
indicators in pH scale, 229–234
indigo carmine, 233f, 233t
induced pluripotent stem cells, 91, 91f
Industrial Revolution, 240, 277, 329t
infectious diseases, 110
inference, 268, 448
infrared, 409f
infrared radiation, 314
inheritance, 27
insulin, 23t
integumentary system, 96f
Intergovernmental Panel on Climate Change (IPCC), 269, 376, 376f, 377
International Union of Pure and Applied Chemistry (IUPAC), 142, 222
interphase, **40**, 40f
intestine, 97f
Inuit Circumpolar Council, 291
Investigations
    acid neutralization, 250
    acids and bases, exposure to, 247
    astigmatism, 514–515
    cancer report, 50
    cell structures, 46–47
    chemical change, evidence of, 207
    climate change and vegetation, 304
    converging lens, 512, 513
    decomposition reactions, 208, 209
    displacement reactions, 210–211
    ecoregions of Canada, 302–303
    El Niño and La Niña, effects of, 341–342
    Fermat's principle, 478–479
    "Food Miles" Initiative, 384
    frog dissection, 117–118
    greenhouse effect, modelling, 344
    heart disease, risk factors for, 116
    heat absorption of soil and water, 300–301, 343
    ice core data, understanding, 382–383
    index of refraction, 477
    internal reflection, 463, 480
    laws of reflection, 439–441
    mass of reactant and product, 172
    metal activity, 212
    mitosis, 48–49
    paper recycling pollutants, 169
    pH of lakes near Sudbury, 248–249
    real or virtual images, 442
    refraction, air to water, 476
    smoking rates, 119–120
    synthesis reactions, 208, 209
    telescope, making a simple, 516
    toothpaste effectiveness, 170–171
    total internal reflection, 480
    transpiration in plants, 77
    water transport in plants, 78
iodine, 164, 181
ionic compounds, 136, 139–150, 187
ionization, 220
ions, 140, 142t
iris (of eyes), 506
iron, 179
iron(II) oxide, 147
iron(III) oxide, 179
isotopes, 354

J

Jansen, Johannes and Zacharias, 505
jellyfish, 408f
jet streams, 274
Jupiter, 502

K

kangaroos, 326, 326f
Kapoor, Anish, 419
karotype, 19, 29f
Kepler, Johannes, 502
kidneys, 99, 99f, 102
Koppen climate classification system, 282, 282t
Koppen, Wladimir, 282
krill, 408f
Kyoto Protocol, 377

L

La Niña, 317, 318f, 319f, 341–342
Lake Temagami ecoregion, 286
lakes as heat reservoirs, 275
large intestine, 99
larynx, 103f
laser eye surgery, 109, 109f, 508–509
lateral bud, 59, 59f
latitude, 272, 272f
Lavoisier, Antoine, 160, 160f
Lavoisier, Marie-Anne, 160f
law of conservation of mass, 136, 160, 161
laws of reflection, 412, 420, 421
leaching, **202**, 203
leaves, 60–63, 60f, 61f, 63f, 70f
Leeuwenhoek microscope, 8f
lenses, 484, **487**
    axis of symmetry, 489
    biconcave, 489
    camera, 487, 492, 492f, 507, 507f, 521
    chromatic aberration, 492, 492f
    converging lenses, 489, 489f, 490, 490f, 495t, 496f, 498f
    curvature, 490, 490f, 491, 491f
    distortion, 428, 428f
    diverging lenses, 489, 489f, 490, 490f, 497f
    in eyes, 492, 492f, 506–510
    focal length, 420, 490, 490
    gravitational, 500, 500f
    images formed, 494–500, 494f
    index of refraction, 452, 454, 454t, 490
    liquid, 487, 487f
    magnification equation for, 498
    spherical aberrations, 491
    thick, 491–492, 491f, 492f
    thin, 492f, 498–499, 498f
    see also focal point, reflection, refraction
light, 449–454, 484
    colour of, 454
    concave mirrors, 419–429, **420**, 420f
    convex mirrors, **431**–437, 432f, 433t, 436f, 437f
    dispersion, 453, 453f
    distortion, 428
    electromagnetic spectrum, 409, 409f
    emissions, types of, 413–404
    fluorescence, 415–406, 405f, 406f
    luminescence, 407, 407f, 408f
    mirages, 472–474, 473f, 474f
    nature of, 409, 409f
    optical phenomena, 468–473
    plane mirror images, 414–415, 409f, 409f, 409f
    rainbows, 468–470, 468f, 470f
    rays, 411–416, 420–424, 451–452, 457–466
    reflection, 412, 413, 414f, 415f, 416f
    shimmering, 471, 471f
    speed of, 452–455
    ultraviolet, 405, 405f
    see also refraction
lily cell, 13f
limestone, 188
liming, **243**, 243f
liquid, 162t
liquid lenses, 487, 487f
litmus, 231, 231f
liver, 97f, 98, 98f
London School of Economics, 328
Lorenz, Edward, 365
luminescence, **407**
lungs, 102, 103f
lyme disease, 294

M

magnesium chloride, 144f, 145
magnesium hydroxide, 150, 226
magnesium nitride, 145t
magnetic resonance imaging (MRI), 94t
magnification, 402, **425**
magnification equation, 425, 434, 498, 499
malaria, 294
Malpighi, Marcello, 71
maple sap, 75, 75f
Marion, Kienan, 500
marshes, 298
mass, conversion of, 177
Material Safety Data Sheets (MSDS), 203
McCulloch, Dr. Ernest, 91
medical imaging technology, **93**, 93f
medical sonography, 94t
medical technology, 82
medium, 411, 448
mercury as vapour, 405
mercury(II) oxide, 160
mercury mirror telescope, 527
meristematic cells, **58**, 58f, 59, 59f
mesophyll tissue, 60f, 61
metalloids, 141t
metals, 140, 141t
    acid leaching, 244
    activity series, 176
    corrosion, 179f
    multivalent, 146
    reactivity series, 192, 192f
    single displacement reactions, 191, 193
    toxic, clean-up, 245
metaphase, **34**, 34f
meteorite impact, 190, 190f, 236
methane, 154, 326, 329t, 330t
methyl orange, 218, 233, 233f, 233t
methyl red, 218, 233, 233f, 233t
micrograph, **10**, 10f, 11f
microscopes, 7, 8–9f, 484, 505, 505f

microscopy, **7**
microvilli, 98, 102
microwaves, 409
Migratory Bird Sanctuaries, 298
Milankovic, Milutin, 271
mining, 190, 202
mirages, 471, **472**, 473f, 474, 474f
mirror equation, 425, 426, 434, 435
mitochondrion, 12f, 13f, 14, 61
mitosis, **32**, 33–38, 34–35f, 40f, 56
mixed-wood forest, 302f, 303t
"mock suns" (sun dogs), 446, 469
molecular compounds, 136, 152–157, **153**
    binary, **154**–157, 154t, 155t, 156t
molecules, **153**
monitoring, **360**
Moon, 502
mortar, 188
Mount Pinatubo, 325, 325f
Mount St. Helens, 276f
mountain pine beetle, 298, 298f
MRI scan, 94t
mucus, 97, 103
multivalent metals, 145, 147, 147f
muscle tissue, 88, 88t
muscular system, 96f, 106, 106f
mutagens, **27**
mutations, **26**, 27, 27f
mycorrhizal fungus, 66
myopia, 486, **507**, 507f

N

nasal cavity, 103
National Wildlife Areas, 298
near-sightedness. See myopia
negative feedback loop, 313, 313f, 321
nerve endings, 83f
nervous system, 96f
nervous tissue, 88, 89t
nettle stings, 221
neutralization, **237**
Newton, Sir Isaac, 504
nickel, mining, 190
nickel(II) sulfide, 190
night-vision device, **510**, 510f
nitric acid, 223
nitride, 142t
nitrogen, 164, 181, 273
nitrogen cycle, 337–339, 338f
nitrogen dioxide, 155, 155f, 176, 183, 183f, 201
nitrogen fixation, **337**, 337f
nitrogen monoxide, 176, 183, 201
nitrous oxide, 327, 329t, 330t
noble gases, 140
non-metals, 140, 141t, 142t, 194
normal, **412**, 413f, 420
North American Waterfowl Management Plan, 298
northern flying squirrel, 298f

nuclear membrane, 10f
nuclear pores, 10f
nucleolus, 10f
nucleus, **10**, 10f, 11f, 12f, 13f, 16
nutrients, 61

O

object distance, 416t
objective lens, **502**, 503
oceans
    acidity, 292, 293t
    carbon cycle, 335f
    climate change affecting, 293t, 297, 297f
    currents and wind, 274, 274f
    energy transfer, 316, 316t, 317
    heat retention and reflection, 274–275
    human activities disrupting, 333, 333t
    salinity, 316–317
    thermohaline circulation, 316–317
    water density, 316–317
octane, 157
Office of Energy Efficiency (OEE), 378
oil gland, 83f
Oke, Isdin, 68
open circulatory system, 101
open system (climate), 311
optical fibres, 465
organ transplants, 4
organelles, **10**
    animal, 10f, 11, 12, 12f, 14, 85, 85f
    plant, 12, 13f, 14, 63, 63f
organs, **58**, 60
    human, 93–106
    plant, 58–68
osmosis, 30, 31, 31f, 73, 73f
oxide, 142t
oxoacids, **223**, 223t
oxygen, 14, 164, 180, 181, 273, 454t
ozone, **327**, 327f, 328, 328f

P

paleoclimatologists, 350, **351**, 357
palisade tissue, 60f, 61
pancreas, 97f, 98, 98f
PAP smears, 114, 114f
Papanicolaou, Dr. George, 114
paper manufacturing, 139, 139f
paramecium, 8f, 9f, 29f
Paranjothy, Ted, 44
parent cells, 29, 33, 34–35f, 37, 37f, 38, 38f
parhelia, 469
partial reflection and refraction, **458**
Partington, P.J., 328
parts per million (ppm), **323**, 323t
pathogens, 110

Peltier, Dr. Richard, 368, 395
pepsin, 97
pericycle, 56, 65, 65f
periodic table, 140, 141t
Perkins, Colin, 68
permafrost, 268
permanent embryos, 58
permanent ice, 284f
permeability, 31
peroxide, 148, 148t
pesticide run-off, 205
pH indicator, **231**–234, 232f
pH of lakes, 240–241, 241t, 243
pH meter, 218, 231, 231f
pH probe, 218, 231
pH scale, 216, 229–234, 232f, **230**, 230f
phagocytes, 110
pharynx, 97, 97f
phase-contrast microscope, 9f
phenolphthalein, 233f, 233t
phenylalanine, 19
phenylketonuria, 16, 19, 21
phloem, 56, 60f, 64, 64f, 65f, 71, 73f
phosphide, 142t
phosphorescence, 400, 400f, **407**
phosphoric acid, 223, 223t
phosphorus trichloride, 156, 156f
photography chemicals, 196
photosynthesis, 70, 71, 180
    chloroplasts used for, 13f, 58f, 60f, 61, 63f
    glucose production, 60, 63, 75, 75f
    sucrose production, 75, 75f
photosynthetic cell, 58f
Physicians for a Smoke-Free Canada, 119
phytoplankton, 312–313
pitcher plant, 72
PKU test, 22
plague, 294
plane mirrors, 414–415, 409f, 409f, 409f
plant cells and cytokinesis, 37
plant galls, 67
plants
    buds, 59, 59f, 75
    chloroplasts, 13f, 58f, 60f, 61, 63f
    cytokinesis, 38, 38f
    flowers, 60, 60f, 66f, 68, 68f
    galls, 67, 67f
    glucose production, 60, 63, 75, 75f
    growing up, 59
    hormones, 68
    hydroponics, 72f
    leaves, 60–63, 60f, 61f, 63f, 74, 74f
    meristematic cells, 58, 58f, 59, 59f
    organelles, 12, 13f, 14, 63, 63f
    organs, 54, 57, 60
    phloem, 56, 60f, 64, 64f, 65f, 71, 73f

roots, 59, 59f, 60, 60f, 65, 65f, 70, 70f
rust, 66, 66f
specialized cells, 57–59
stems, 60, 60f, 64, 64f
sucrose production, 75, 75f
tissues, 58–65
transpiration, 61, 74, 74f, 77
viruses, 66, 66f
water, absorbing, 61, 63, 63f, 65, 72–74, 72f, 73f, 74f, 78
xylem, 56, 58f 60f, 64, 64f, 65f, 71, 73f
pluripotent stem cells, 90, 90f
polar bears, 291, 291f
polar ice cover, 291
polar zone, 279, 279f
pollen, 68
pollutants from synthesis reactions, 183, 183f
pollution, 200f, 216f
polyatomic ions, **148**, 148t, 149, 149t
positive feedback loop, 312, 312f, 324
potassium bromide, 144f
potassium chromate, 195
ppm (parts per million), **323**, 323t
precession of Earth, 271, 271f
precipitate, **178**, **180**, 180f
precipitation
    acid, 236, 236f, 239–243, 242f, 243f
    in biomes, 283, 284–285f
    changing levels of, 288, 295–296, 295f, 296f
    climatographs, 280, 280f, 284–285f
    wind affecting, 274, 274f, 295–296, 295f, 296f
prenatal care, 19, 109
presbyopia, 486, **509**
prevailing winds, 274, 274f
preventive health care, 109
principal axis, **420**, 421
    concave mirror, 420
    converging lenses, 490, 490f, 495t
    diverging lenses, 490, 490f, 497f, 497t
prisms, 453f, 464, 464f
products, **160**
    decomposition reactions, 184–188
    double displacement reactions, 195–196
    state, 162f, 162t
    synthesis reaction, 181–183
properties of acids and bases, 234t
prophase, **34**, 34f, 56
proteins, 12, 12f, 13f, 17, 17f, 18, 19
public health, 58
Public Health Agency of Canada, 113

Index • NEL 583

public health strategy, **109**
pulmonary artery, 100
pulse rate, 101
pupils (of eyes), 506

Q

quartz, index of refraction, 454*t*
Quick Scatterometer, 362

R

radar, 417, 417*f*
   concave surfaces, 429, 429*f*
   convex surfaces, 437, 437*f*
radiation, 314*t*, 315*f*
radio waves, 409
rainbows, 446, **468**, 468*f*, 469, 469*f*
ray diagrams
   apparent depth, 470*f*
   concave mirrors, 420*t*, 422*t*, 423*t*, 424*t*, 428*t*
   converging lenses, 495*t*
   convex mirrors, 432, 433*t*
   diverging lenses, 497*t*
   mirages, 473*f*, 474*f*
   reflected light, 458*f*, 459*f*, 461*f*, 462*f*, 464*f*, 465*f*
   refracted light, 450*f*, 451*f*, 452*f*, 453*f*, 458*f*, 459*f*, 461*f*, 462*f*
   rainbows, 470*f*, 472*f*
   telescopes, 503, 503*f*
ray model of light, 446
rays (of light), **411**–416, 412*f*, 413*f*, 416*t*, 420–424, 451–452, 457–466
reactants, 138, 160, 162*t*, 176, 181, 185
reading stones, 488*f*
real image, 402, 423
rebreather, 162, 162*f*
rectum, 97*f*, 99
recycling, 139, 331
red blood cells, 7*f*, 11*f*, 26*f*, 104*f*
reflected rays, **412**, 413*f*, 420, 458*f*
   see also reflection
reflecting telescopes, 504, 504*f*
reflection, **411**–437
   concave mirrors, 419–429
   convex mirrors, 431–437
   critical angle, 462
   and distortion, 428, 428*f*
   Fermat's principle, 412
   fibre optics, 465–466, 465*f*, 466*f*
   focal point, 420–424, 422*t*, 423*t*, 424*t*
   internal, total, 457, 463
   laws of, 400, 412, 420, 421
   partial, 458–461, 458*f*, 460*f*, 461*f*
   in plane mirrors, 414–415, 414*f*, 415*f*, 416*t*
   radar technology, 429, 429*f*
   ray diagrams, 458*f*, 459*f*, 461*f*, 462*f*, 464*f*, 465*f*
   rearview mirror, 459, 460
   retroreflectors, 465, 465*f*
   and solar ovens, 428–429
   of solar radiation, 320–321, 320*f*, 320*t*
   and stealth technology, 417, 417*f*
   total internal, 457, 462–466
refracted rays, **452**, 452*f*, 458*f*
   see also refraction
refracting telescopes, 504
refraction, 446–447, **449**–466
   apparent depth, 470, 470*f*
   boundary, reaching the, 450, 450*f*, 457, 457*f*, 458
   changing direction of light ray, 464, 464*f*
   critical angle, **462**
   describing, 450, 450*f*, 451
   dispersion, 453, 453*f*
   effects of, 468
   Fermat's principle, 451
   indices of, 452, 454, 454*t*
   in lenses, 488–489, 490
   mirages, 472–474, 473*f*, 474*f*
   partial reflection and, 458–461, 458*f*, 460*f*, 461*f*
   prisms, 453, 453*f*, 464, 464*f*
   rainbows, 468–470, 468*f*, 470*f*
   ray diagrams, 450*f*, 451*f*, 452*f*, 453*f*, 458*f*, 459*f*, 461*f*, 462*f*
   rearview mirror, 459–460, 460*f*
   shimmering, 471, 471*f*
   sundogs, 446, 469
   water to air, 461–462, 461*f*, 462*f*
regeneration, 90
Rembrandt tulips, 66, 66*f*
reproductive system, 96*f*
respiratory system, 96*f*, 103, 103*f*
retina, **506**
retroreflectors, 465, 465*f*
ribosomes, 10*f*, 12*f*, 13*f*
Robinson, Penelope, 415
rod cells, 506
Roman Numerals, 147*t*
root hairs, 73
root pressure and xylem, 73
root system, 70, 70*f*
roots, 59, 59*f*, 60, 60*f*, 65, 65*f*, 70, 70
rust, 179
rust, wheat, 66–67

S

safety in the lab, xiv–xvii
salamanders, 90
saliva, 97
salivary glands, 97*f*
salmon, 23*t*
Salton Sea, 400
SARS, 112, 112*f*
satellites, 361–363, 362*f*
scanning electron microscope, 9*f*
scrubbers, 242
scurvy, 108
sea ice, melting, 266, 291–292, 290*f*, 291*f*, 317
sea level, rising, 292, 292*f*
security mirrors, 436–437, 436*f*, 437*f*
sediment cores, 356, 356*f*
sedimentary rocks, 356, 356*f*
selective breeding, 66
shatter cones, 236
shimmering, **471**, 471*f*
shoot system, **70**, 70*f*
Siamese cats, 86, 86*f*
sickle cell anemia, 26, 26*f*
Sidhu, Jasmeet, 380
sight, 484, 506
silver chromate, 195
silver nitrate, 191, 195, 196
Singh, Nikhita, 205
single displacement reactions, 176, **191**, 197*t*
   metals, 191, 191*f*, 193
   non-metals, 194
single-celled organisms
   amoeba, 85, 85*f*
   paramecium, 8*f*, 9*f*, 29*f*
   reproduction in, 29
sink, **324**
skeletal muscle, 88*t*
skeletal system, 96*f*
skeleton equations, 161, 165
skin, 82
skin epithelia, 88*t*
Sky Mirror, 419, 419*f*, 420
small intestine, 97*f*, 98
smallpox, 109
Smith, Robert Angus, 240
smog, 155, 155*f*, 339
smoking, 105, 105*f*
smooth muscle, 88*t*
snow and albedo, 275
soap, 219, 225, 225*f*
sodium, reaction with water, 159, 159*f*
sodium azide, 187, 187*f*
sodium bicarbonate, 150, 166
sodium carbonate, 139
sodium chloride, 142*f*, 142*t*, 143, 144, 150, 162*t*, 454*t*
sodium fluoride, 170
sodium hydroxide, 162, 226, 226*f*
sodium hypochlorite, 229
sodium vapour bulb, 404, 404*f*
soft X rays, 409*f*
soil erosion, 152
solar activity and climate, 270
solar cycle, 270
solar ovens, 428–429
solar panels, 415
solar radiation, 314–315, 315*f*, 320*f*, 320*t*
solid, 162*t*
Sorenson, Soren, 230

specialized cells, 57–59
species and extinction, 297
specific heat capacity, 275
spectrum, 453
sphere, 402
spherical aberrations, **428**, 428*f*, 492, 502
sphincter, 96*f*, 98
spider maps, **138**, 486
spina bifida, 21
spindle fibres, 34*f*, 35*f*
spongy parenchyma cells, 60*f*
stable octet, 140, 143
starfish, 90
state and reactants, 162, 162*t*
steel, 179
stem, 58, 60, 60*f*, 64, 70*f*
stem cells, **90**, 91, 91*f*
Steward, Fredrick, 24*f*
stoma, 61, 61*f*
stomach, 97*f*, 98*f*, 237, 237*f*
stomata, 60*f*, 61
store, 333
storms, 296
striations, 88
stroke, 102
Study Toolkit
   asking questions, 84
   base words, 138, 402
   comparing and contrasting, 56, 402
   creating a word map, 178, 350
   identifying cause and effect, 178, 350
   identifying main ideas and details, 138, 350
   interpreting climatographs, 268
   interpreting cross sections, 56
   interpreting diagrams, 402
   interpreting tables, 218
   making connections to prior knowledge, 486
   making connections to visuals, 310
   making inferences, 268, 448
   making study notes, 84
   monitoring comprehension, 178
   multiple meanings, 56, 448
   previewing text features, 6
   skim, scan, or study, 138
   summarizing, 448
   synthesizing, 310
   using graphic organizers, 218, 486
   visualizing, 6
   word families, 6, 486
   word origins, 84, 268
   word parts, 218, 310
sucrose, 75
Sudbury, 236, 236*f*, 239, 244
Sudbury Basin, 190, 190*f*
sulfide, 142*t*
sulfur dioxide, 239, 242

in food preservation, 197, 197f
sulfur oxides, 242
sulfuric acid, 223, 223t
sulfurous acid, 223
summary, 448
Sun, 270, 404
sunblock, 150, 150f
sundogs, 446, 469
sunscreen, 150, 150f
sunspots, 270, 270f
surgical lasers, 108
swamps, 298, 298f
sweat glands and pores, 83, 83f
synthesis and ammonia, 182f
synthesis reactions, **181**–183, 181f, 182f, 183f, 197t
synthesizing, 310
synthetic elements, 141t
systems, **70**, **311**
    human body, 95–106, 96f
    plant organs, 70–75

T

table salt, 142f, 142t, 150
tables, interpreting, 218
tailings, 245, 245f
taproots, 65, 65f
tectonic, 268
tectonic plates, **275**–276
telescopes, 484, 502–504, 502f, 503f, 504f, 516
telophase, 35, 35f
temperate deciduous forest, 283f, 285
temperate rainforest, 283f, 285
temperate zone, 279f
temperature, 280, 280f, 283
temperature inversions, 474, 474f
terminal bud, 59, 59f
ternary compound, **148**
Terra (satellite), 362, 362f
Terrestrial ecozones, 287f
thermal energy, 314t
thermohaline circulation, **316**–317
thick lenses, 491–492, 491f, 492f
thin lenses, 492f, 498–499, 498f
thylakoid, 63, 63f
thymine, 17f
Till, Dr. James, 91
tin(IV) sulfide, 147t
tissue, **58**
    adipose, 89t
    characteristics, 89
    connective, 88, 89t
    dermal, 56, 58, 58f, 61, 65f
    epithelial, 88, 88t, 104
    ground, 58, 58f
    mesophyll, 60f, 61
    muscle, 88, 88t
    nervous, 88, 89t
    palisade, 60f, 61
    plants, 58–65
    spongy parenchyma, 60f
    types of, 88

    vascular, 58, 58f
    see also cells
tobacco mosaic virus, 66, 66f
tongue, 97f
toothpaste, 150, 170–171
total internal reflection, **462**
totipotent stem cells, 90, 90f
toxic material removal, 200
trachea, 103f, 104
trade winds, 274f
transgenic organisms, **22**–23, 23t
transgenic therapy, 66–67
transmission electron microscope, 9f
transpiration, **61**, 74, 74f, 77
tree rings, 351, 351f, 352
trinitrotoluene, 186, 186f
tropical rainforest, 283f
tropical storms, 296
tropical zone, 279, 279f
trough, 409
tubules, 33, 34f
tumours (cancerous), **42**, 43f
tundra, 268, 283f, 284f

U

ultrasound, 84, 94t, 109, 109f
ultraviolet, 409f
ultraviolet light, 405, 405f
ultraviolet (UV) radiation, 472, 473
univalent metals, 184
universal indicator of pH scale, 232, 232f
upwelling, 317
ureters, 99f
urethra, 99f
UV radiation, 472–473

V

vaccinations, **109**–111
vacuoles, 12f, 13f, 57f
valence electrons, **140**, 140f
valves, 100
van Leeuwenhoek, Anton, 46
vascular bundle, 60f, 64
vascular tissue, 58, 58f
veins, 61, 100, 100f, 104f
velocity of light, 446
vena cava, 99f
Venn diagrams, 56, 267, 402, 486
ventricle, 100f
Venus, 502
Venus flytrap, 72
vertex of concave mirror, 420
vesicles, 12f, 13f, 38, 38f
villi, 98, 98f, 102
vinegar, 219, 220, 221f
virtual images, 402, **415**
viruses, 7, 66–67, 66f
vision, 507, 510, 510f
visualizing, 6
vitamin C, 108
volcanic activity, 276

W

Walkerton water tragedy, 294–295
water
    adhesion, 74
    angle of incidence, 458, 458f, 462, 462f, 476, 480
    angle of refraction, 451, 451f, 452, 452f, 462, 462f, 476, 480
    atmosphere, 273, 325
    Bohr-Rutherford model, 153, 153f
    in cells, 14
    cohesion, 74
    decomposition of, 185
    density, 316–317
    dihydrogen monoxide, 152, 152f
    greenhouse gases, 324
    heat absorption of soil and, 300–301, 343
    index of refraction, 454t
    models, 153, 153f, 154
    pH, 241
    plants absorbing, 61, 63, 63f, 65, 72–74, 72f, 73f, 74f, 78
    pollution, 338
    reaction with sodium, 159, 159f
    refraction, air to water, 476
    refraction, water to air, 461–462, 461f, 462f
    state, 162t
    test kit, 229f
    vapour, 273, 324, 325, 365
    Walkerton tragedy, 294–295
    see also oceans
water test kit, 229f
Watson, James, 17
wave fronts, 450, 450f
wavelength, **409**, 409f
weather
    changing patterns, 269, 295–296
    droughts, 296, 296f
    prevailing winds, 274, 274f
    storms, 296
    see also precipitation
West Nile virus, 113, 113f
westerly winds, 274f
wetlands, shrinking, 298
Wexler, Nancy, 20, 20f
whales, 85f
wheat rust, 66–67
whip scorpion, 221
white blood cells, 11f, 89, 110, 110f, 111
white light, 403
WHMIS symbols, xvii
whooping cough, 111
wind farms, 380f
winds, 273, 273f, 274, 274f, 295–296, 295f, 296f
word equations, 161, 165
word families, 6

word maps, 178, 350
World Conservation Society (WCS), 291

X

X rays, 94, 94t, 95, 95f, 409f
xylem
    and cohesion (of water), 74
    and energy stores, 71
    in leaves, 60, 60f, 61, 71, 74, 74f
    Malpighi's experiment, 71
    maple sap, transporting, 75, 75f
    nutrients, transporting, 71, 72, 72f, 73, 73f
    pressure in, 73
    in roots, 65, 65f, 71, 73, 73f
    sap, 75, 75f
    in stems, 64, 64f
    transpiration, function in, 74, 74f
    vascular bundles, 61, 64, 64f
    water, transporting, 58f, 61, 64, 71–74, 72f, 73f, 74f

Y

yarrow, 65f
"Year Without a Summer", 276

Z

zebra fish and fluorescence, 403f
zero-emission in paper manufacturing, 139
zinc and gold mining, 202
zinc oxide, 150, 150f

Credits

Photo Credits

COV: (tr) ©Markus Gann/iStockphoto; COV: (bl) ©Henrik Jonsson/iStockphoto; COV: (cr) ©Joel Simon/Digital Vision/Getty Images; COV: (cl) ©Magictorch/Getty Images; COV: (br) ©Steven Puetzer/Getty Images; iv-v: (b) ©Joe Bator/CORBIS; v: (tr) ©Reuters/CORBIS; v: (cr) ©Joe Bator/CORBIS; v: (br) ©PHOTOTAKE Inc./Alamy; vi: (tl) ©Romilly Lockyer/Getty Images; vi: (cl) ©WENN/Newscom; vi: (bl) ©Daryl Benson/Masterfile; vi-vii: (b) ©Daryl Benson/Masterfile; vii: (tr) ©Gordon Wiltsie/National Geographic/Getty Images; vii: (cr) ©REUTERS/Marcos Brindicci; vii: (br) ©CP Photo/Ian Barrett; viii: (tl) ©AP Photo/Imperial Valley Press, Kevin Marty; viii: (cl) ©John Poirier/Alamy; viii: (bl) ©Antonia Reeve/Photo Researchers, Inc.; viii-ix: (b) ©John Poirier/Alamy; xiv: (br) ©Michael Thompson/iStockphoto; xv: (tr) ©Stockbyte/Punchstock; xv: (bl) ©John Clines/iStockphoto; xvi: (bl) ©SW Productions/Getty Images; 000–001: (c) ©Alexander Tsiaras/Photo Researchers, Inc.; 001: (cl) ©Michael Mahovlich/Masterfile; 002: (bl) ©John Walsh/Photo Researchers, Inc.; 002: (c) ©Gary Meszaros/Photo Researchers, Inc.; 002: (cr) ©Martin Shields/Alamy; 002–003: (bkgd) ©Steve Gschmeissner/SPL/Photo Researchers, Inc.; 003: (bl) ©Corbis Premium RF/Alamy; 003: (br) ©Courtesy of The Organ Donation and Transplant Association of Canada; 004–005: (c) ©Reuters/CORBIS; 005: (c) © Yvonne Chamberlain/iStock Photo; 007: (b) ©Micro Discovery/Corbis; 010: (br) ©Dr. Dennis Kunkel/Visuals Unlimited/Getty Images; 011: (tl) ©Eric Grave / Photo Researchers, Inc.; 011: (tr) ©Steve Gschmeissner/SPL/Photo Researchers, Inc.; 012: (bl) ©Alfred Pasieka / Photo Researchers, Inc.; 013: (cr) ©PHOTOTAKE Inc./Alamy; 016: (b) ©Picture Partners/Alamy; 019: (br) ©moodboard/Alamy; 020: (br) ©Acey Harper/Time Life Pictures/Getty Images; 021: (br) ©Purestock/Getty Images; 022: (tl) ©Gorilla Photo Agency Ltd/Alamy; 023: (tr) ©Volker Steger / Photo Researchers, Inc.; 023: (cr) ©Jim West/Alamy; 023: (br) ©STEVE RINGMAN/SEATTLE TIMES/Newscom; 024: (b) ©Radius Images/Alamy; 025: (b) ©Colin McPherson/epa/Corbis; 026: (b) ©Eye of Science/Photo Researchers, Inc.; 027: (tr) ©Science Source/Photo Researchers, Inc.; 027: (br) ©Gilbert S. Grant / Photo Researchers, Inc.; 029: (cr) ©James Cavallini / Photo Researchers, Inc.; 029: (b) ©WaterFrame/Alamy; 030: (br) ©Edward Kinsman / Photo Researchers, Inc.; 033: (br) ©Adrian T Sumner/Stone/Getty Images; 034: (cr) ©Dr. Alexey Khodjakov / Photo Researchers, Inc.; 034: (bl) ©Dr. Alexey Khodjakov / Photo Researchers, Inc.; 035: (tr) ©Dr. Alexey Khodjakov / Photo Researchers, Inc.; 035: (br) ©Dr Alexey Khodjakov / Photo Researchers, Inc.; 037: (b) ©Dr Gopal Murti / Photo Researchers, Inc.; 038: (cl) ©Ed Reschke / Peter Arnold Inc.; 039: (br) ©Ed Reschke / Peter Arnold Inc.; 042: (br) ©Biophoto Associates / Photo Researchers, Inc.; 044: (bl) ©Courtesy of Jamie Busman; 045: (tr) ©Martin Dohrn / Photo Researchers, Inc.; 045: (cr) ©uli nusko/Alamy; 045: (r) ©The McGraw-Hill Companies, Inc./Photo and dissection by Christine Eckel; 045: (br) ©Carlos Santa Maria/iStockphoto; 045: (b) ©Michael Abbey / Photo Researchers, Inc.; 046: (tr) ©PHOTOTAKE Inc./Alamy; 046: (br) ©Ed Reschke / Peter Arnold Inc.; 048: (tl) ©Michael Abbey / Photo Researchers, Inc.; 048: (tr) ©Eye of Science / Photo Researchers, Inc.; 048: (bl) ©Michael Abbey / Photo Researchers, Inc.; 048: (br) ©Eye of Science / Photo Researchers, Inc.; 049: (tl) ©Michael Abbey / Photo Researchers, Inc.; 049: (tr) ©Eye of Science / Photo Researchers, Inc.; 049: (bl) ©Michael Abbey / Photo Researchers, Inc.; 049: (br) ©Eye of Science / Photo Researchers, Inc.; 051: (tr) ©Micro Discovery/Corbis; 051: (b) ©Picture Partners/Alamy; 051: (cr) ©James Cavallini/Photo Researchers, Inc.; 051: (br) ©Biophoto Associates / Photo Researchers, Inc.; 054–055: (c) ©Joe Bator/CORBIS; 057: (cr) ©Biophoto Associates/Photo Researchers, Inc.; 057: (br) ©John Durham/Photo Researchers, Inc.; 057: (bl) ©Lloyd Sutton/Alamy; 060: (tl) ©The McGraw-Hill Companies Inc./Ken Cavanagh Photographer; 061: (br) ©Dr. Jeremy Burgess/Photo Researchers, Inc.; 062: (tr) ©Lee W. Wilcox; 063: (cr) ©ISM/Phototake; 064: (cr) ©Ed Reschke/Peter Arnold Inc.; 065: (tr) ©C Squared Studios/Getty Images; 065: (bl) ©John Kaprielian/Photo Researchers, Inc.; 065: (bc) ©TH Foto-Werbung/Photo Researchers, Inc.; 066: (cr) ©Jack Dykinga/USDA; 066: (tl) ©Budd Titlow/Visuals Unlimited; 066: (br) ©Nigel Cattlin/Photo Researchers, Inc.; 067: (cr) ©Robert L. Calentine/Visuals Unlimited; 067: (bl) ©Microfield Scientific Ltd/Photo Researchers, Inc.; 068: (tl) ©SZE FEI WONG/iStockphoto; 068: (c) ©Nigel Cattlin/Alamy; 068: (cr) ©Dorothea Mirwald/iStockphoto; 068: (bl) ©Courtesy of Isdin Oke; 069: (br) ©Lynn Betss, courtesy of USDA Natural Resources Conservation Service; 070: (c) ©J.A. Kraulis/All Canada Photos; 072: (cr) ©David Kay/iStockphoto; 073: (tr) ©Dennis Drenner/Visuals Unlimited; 077: (bl) ©Günay Mutlu/iStockphoto; 079: (tr) ©Lloyd Sutton/Alamy; 079: (cr) ©J.A. Kraulis/All Canada Photos; 082–083: (c) ©PHOTOTAKE Inc./Alamy; 085: (cl) ©Melba Photo Agency/PunchStock; 085: (b) ©David B Fleetham/Photolibrary; 086: (t) ©Photodisc/Getty Images; 086: (b) ©Jerome Wexler/Photo Researchers, Inc.; 087: (cl) ©AP Photo/Craig Line; 088: (tr) ©Dr. Gladden Willis/Visuals Unlimited, Inc.; 088: (t) ©John D. Cunningham/Visuals Unlimited; 088: (bl) ©Biophoto Associates/Photo Researchers, Inc.; 088: (c) ©Dr. Gladden Willis/Visuals Unlimited, Inc.; 088: (b) ©Biology Media/Photo Researchers, Inc.; 089: (t) ©Purestock/Getty Images; 089: (tr) ©Eric V. Grave/Photo Researchers, Inc.; 089: (br) ©Dr. Alvin Telser/Visuals Unlimited, Inc.; 089: (b) ©Martin M. Rotker/Photo Researchers, Inc.; 091: (tr) ©RAJAU/PHANIE/Photo Researchers, Inc.; 091: (bl) ©Toronto Star/ZUMA Press; 092: (tl) ©Dr. Gladden Willis/Visuals Unlimited, Inc.; 092: (tr) ©John D. Cunningham/Visuals Unlimited, Inc.; 092: (bl) ©Purestock/Getty Images; 092: (br) ©Martin M. Rotker/Photo Researchers, Inc.; 093: (b) ©Organica/Alamy; 093: (cl) ©Mehau Kulyk/Photo Researchers, Inc.; 094: (cr) ©Scott Camazine/Photo Researchers, Inc.; 094: (t) ©nicholas belton/iStockphoto; 094: (tl) ©PHOTOTAKE Inc./Alamy; 094: (c) ©Zephyr/Photo Researchers, Inc.; 094: (b) ©Simon Fraser/Royal Victoria Infirmary, Newcastle upon Tyne/Photo Researchers, Inc.; 095: (cl) ©Simon Fraser/Photo Researchers, Inc.; 095: (cr) ©David M. Martin, M. D./Photo Researchers, Inc.; 099: (tr) ©Steve Gschmeissner/Photo Researchers, Inc.; 101: (br) ©Karl Weatherly/Photodisc/Getty Images; 105: (c) ©St Bartholomew's Hospital/Photo Researchers, Inc.; 108: (b) ©Nicolas Edwige/Photo Researchers, Inc.; 109: (cr) ©B. SLAVEN/Custom Medical Stock Photo; 109: (tl) ©PHOTOTAKE Inc./Alamy; 110: (tl) ©Eye of Science/Photo Researchers, Inc.; 110: (bc) ©Ian Hooton / Photo Researchers, Inc.; 110–111: (bkgd) ©Matthew Chambers/iStockphoto; 111: (br) ©PHOTOTAKE Inc./Alamy; 112: (cr) ©CP PHOTO/Frank Gunn; 112: (cl) ©CP PHOTO/Toronto Star - Andrew Stawicki; 113: (b) ©Roger Eritja/Alamy; 113: (tl) ©Courtesy of Jerri Clout; 113: (cr) ©Dale Taylor/iStockphoto; 114: (br) ©Dr. Isabelle Cartier/ISM/Phototake, Inc.; 115: (t) ©James Benet/iStockphoto; 115: (c) ©Medicimage/Phototake Inc.; 115: (b) ©zilli/iStockphoto; 116: (bl) ©James Cavallini/BSIP/Phototake Inc.; 116: (tl) ©CNRI/Photo Researchers, Inc.; 119: (cl) ©CP Photo/Steve White; 120: (b) ©Chris Schmidt/iStockphoto; 121: (tr) ©Melba Photo Agency/PunchStock; 121: (cr) ©Organica/Alamy; 121: (b) ©B. SLAVEN/Custom Medical Stock Photo; 124: (tl) ©Photo courtesy of National Research Council Canada; 124: (bkgd) ©PHOTOTAKE Inc./Alamy; 125: (tr) ©AP Photo/Yves Logghe; 125: (br) ©Mauro Fermariello/Photo Researchers, Inc.; 125: (bl) ©Mark Kostich/iStockphoto; 126: (b) ©Corbis Premium RF/Alamy; 127: (bkgd) ©Steve Gschmeissner/SPL/Photo Researchers, Inc.; 127: (br) ©Courtesy of The Organ Donation and Transplant Association of Canada; 129: (bl) ©Dr. Fred Hossler/Visuals Unlimited, Inc.; 129: (br) ©Microfield Scientific Ltd./Photo Researchers, Inc.; 129: (tl) ©Perennou Nuridsany/Photo Researchers, Inc.; 129: (tr) ©Jennifer C. Waters/Photo Researchers, Inc.; 131: (cl) ©Ian Hooton/Photo Researchers, Inc.; 132–133: (c) ©Photos 12/Alamy; 133: (cl) ©Don Johnston/Photolibrary; 134: (bl) ©Biophoto Associates/Photo Researchers, Inc.; 134: (c) ©Biophoto Associates/Photo Researchers, Inc.; 134: (cr) ©George Whitely/Photo Researchers, Inc.; 135: (bkgd) ©Arno Massee/iStockphoto; 135: (bl) ©Arno Massee/iStockphoto; 135: (br) ©AP Photo/Paul Sancya; 136–137: (c) ©Romilly Lockyer/Getty Images; 139: (b) ©Thomas Kitchin & Victoria Hurst/Getty Images; 142: (b) ©The McGraw-Hill Companies, Inc./Stephen Frisch, photographer; 146: (br) ©Martyn F. Chillmaid/Photo Researchers, Inc.; 148: (bl) ©Jules Frazier/Getty Images; 149: (cl) ©Mehmet Ali Cida/iStockphoto; 151: (br) ©phil morley/iStockphoto; 152: (bl) ©Stockbyte/Getty Images; 153: (br) ©Dirk Rietschel/iStockphoto; 155: (bl) ©Stockbyte/Getty Images; 156: (tl) ©Zirafek/iStockphoto; 157: (cr) ©Zsolt Biczó/iStockphoto; 159: (b) ©E. R. Degginger/Photo Researchers, Inc.; 160: (bl) ©Bettmann/CORBIS; 161: (tl) ©Charles D. Winters/Photo Researchers, Inc.; 161: (tc) ©Charles D. Winters/Photo Researchers, Inc.; 162: (bl) ©Mark Conlin/Alamy; 165: (tr) ©mitch achiron/iStockphoto; 166: (tl) ©Courtesy of Adrienne Duimering; 167: (br) ©Photodisc/Getty Images; 167: (tr) ©AP Photo/Mike Derer; 168: (cr) ©Charles D. Winters/Photo Researchers, Inc.; 173: (cr) ©Getty Images; 173: (tr) ©Thomas Kitchin & Victoria Hurst/Getty Images; 173: (br) ©E. R. Degginger/Photo Researchers, Inc.; 174: (bl) ©Ivanov Valeriy/iStockphoto; 174: (bc) ©Comstock Images / Alamy; 176–177: (c) ©WENN/Newscom; 179: (b) ©Time & Life Pictures/Getty Images; 180: (tl) ©Dennis DeSilva/iStockphoto; 180: (tr) ©Charles D. Winters/Photo Researchers, Inc.; 180: (bl) ©Scott Newbern/iStockphoto; 180: (br) ©Bryan Myhr/iStockphoto; 181: (br) ©Digital Vision Ltd./SuperStock; 182: (b) ©Courtesy of BC Transit; 182: (cl) ©Grant Heilman Photography/Alamy; 183: (tr) ©matthew guillory/Alamy; 183: (cr) ©Courtesy of Hydrogen Village; 184: (bl) ©Charles D. Winters/Photo

Researchers, Inc.; 185: (br) ©Charles D. Winters/Photo Researchers, Inc.; 186: (cr) ©Doug Steley B/Alamy; 187: (br) ©CC Studio/Photo Researchers, Inc.; 188: (bl) ©Gavin Newman/Alamy; 189: (cr) ©Daniel Jones/iStockphoto; 190: (b) ©Thomas Kitchin & Victoria Hurst/All Canada Photos; 191: (br) ©Charles D. Winters/Photo Researchers, Inc.; 192: (bc) ©Charles D. Winters/Photo Researchers, Inc.; 192: (br) ©Charles D. Winters/Photo Researchers, Inc.; 193: (br) ©Andrew Lambert Photography/Photo Researchers, Inc.; 195: (br) ©Charles D. Winters/Photo Researchers, Inc.; 197: (tr) ©parrus/iStockphoto; 198: (br) ©Charles D. Winters/Photo Researchers, Inc.; 199: (br) ©Julie Dermansky/Photo Researchers, Inc.; 200: (bl) ©David Parsons/iStockphoto; 201: (bc) ©Astrid & Hanns-Frieder Michler/Photo Researchers, Inc.; 201: (br) ©Astrid & Hanns-Frieder Michler/Photo Researchers, Inc.; 202: (b) ©JUPITERIMAGES/Creatas/Alamy; 202: (tl) ©Christoph Ermel/iStockphoto; 203: (bl) ©Spencer Grant/PhotoEdit Inc.; 205: (br) ©Courtesy of Nikhita Singh; 212: (bl) ©Andrew Lambert Photography/Photo Researchers, Inc.; 213: (tr) ©Time & Life Pictures/Getty Images; 213: (cr) ©Thomas Kitchin & Victoria Hurst/All Canada Photos; 213: (br) ©Julie Dermansky/Photo Researchers, Inc.; 215: (tc) ©Charles D. Winters/Photo Researchers, Inc.; 216–217: (c) ©Daryl Benson/Masterfile; 219: (b) ©Hilary Brodey/iStockphoto; 220: (bc) ©sciencephotos/Alamy; 221: (tc) ©Nature's Images/Photo Researchers, Inc.; 221: (cl) ©David Hogan/iStockphoto; 221: (bc) ©Eric Delmar/iStockphoto; 221: (br) ©Stephen Dalton/Photo Researchers, Inc.; 221: (cr) ©vera bogaerts/iStockphoto; 222: (br) ©Niall McDiarmid/Alamy; 228: (cr) ©Ints Tomsons/iStockphoto; 229: (b) ©luxxtek/iStockphoto; 231: (cr) ©Charles D. Winters/Photo Researchers, Inc.; 231: (bl) ©Andrew Lambert Photography / Photo Researchers, Inc.; 232: (tr) ©Andrew Lambert Photography/Photo Researchers, Inc.; 232: (cl) ©Sabine Kappel/iStockphoto; 234: (tl) ©dobri dobrinov/iStockphoto; 235: (cr) ©Charles D. Winters/Photo Researchers, Inc.; 236: (b) ©Paul A. Souders/CORBIS; 236: (br) ©Don Johnston/Alamy; 237: (br) ©Eye of Science/Photo Researchers, Inc.; 238: (br) ©CP PHOTO/Northern News/Rick Owen; 240: (tl) ©Thomas Sparks/iStockphoto; 240: (br) ©Mary Evans Picture Library/Alamy; 241: (bl) ©Ron Smid/First Light; 241: (tr) ©Rich Phalin/iStockphoto; 242: (tr) ©Courtesy of Simon Bild-Enkin; 243: (cl) ©MARK EDWARDS/Peter Arnold Inc.; 245: (tr) ©Brian Milne/First Light; 249: (bl) ©NASA; 251: (tr) ©Hilary Brodey/iStockphoto; 251: (cr) ©luxxtek/iStockphoto; 251: (br) ©Paul A. Souders/CORBIS; 253: (bl) ©Andrew Lambert Photograph/Photo Researchers, Inc.; 254: (tl) ©Courtesy Dalia Bagby; 254: (b) ©Courtesy of Dalia Bagby; 255: (tr) ©Peter Close/iStockphoto; 255: (br) ©Blend Images/Alamy; 255: (bl) ©simonmcconico/iStockphoto; 256: (b) ©Arno Massee/iStockphoto; 257: (tr) ©AP Photo/Paul Sancya; 264–265: (c) ©Paul Souders/Photodisc/Getty Images; 265: (bc) ©eb33/iStockphoto; 265: (cl) ©Car Culture/Getty Images; 266–267: (c) ©Gordon Wiltsie/National Geographic/Getty Images; 269: (b) ©NASA; 274: (bl) ©NASA Goddard Space Flight Center; 275: (bl) ©Gordon Wood/Alamy; 276: (tl) ©U.S. Geological Survey; 276: (b) © hougaard malan/iStock Photo; 277: (bl) ©Dennis MacDonald/Alamy; 280: (b) © hywit dimyadi/iStock Photo; 282: (b) ©F. Jourdan/Photo Researchers, Inc.; 283: (t) ©Ryerson Clark/iStockphoto; 284: (c) ©Photodisc Collection/Getty Images; 284: (b) ©Fred McConnaughey / Photo Researchers, Inc.; 285: (t) ©Pixtal/age fotostock; 285: (tc) ©Doug Sherman/Geofile; 285: (bc) © Don Wilkie/iStock Photo; 285: (b) ©Kaj R. Svensson / Photo Researchers, Inc.; 287: (b) ©Janusz Wrobel/Alamy; 290: (b) ©Digital Vision/Getty Images; 291: (b) ©Jeff Vanuga/Corbis; 292: (tl) ©Students on Ice; 294: (tl) ©Courtesy of the Center for Disease Control; 294: (br) ©Nature Picture Library/Alamy; 294: (bc) ©Hybrid Medical Animation / Photo Researchers, Inc.; 295: (cr) ©john t. fowler/Alamy; 296: (br) ©Lucas Oleniuk/The Toronto Star/First Light; 296: (tl) ©CP Photo/Jeff McIntosh; 298: (tl) ©Tracy Ferrero/Alamy; 298: (b) © Arpad Benedek/iStock Photo; 302: (b) ©Brigitte Smith/iStockphoto; 305: (tr) ©Dennis MacDonald/Alamy; 305: (cr) ©Photodisc Collection/Getty Images; 305: (br) ©Digital Vision/Getty Images; 308–309: (c) ©REUTERS/Marcos Brindicci; 310: (c) ©Janusz Wrobel/Alamy; 312: (cr) ©Jacques Descloitres, MODIS Land Rapid Response Team, NASA/GSFC; 312: (bc) ©Steve Gschmeissner / Photo Researchers, Inc.; 314: (tr) ©Zia Soleil/Getty Images; 314: (cl) ©Alena Root/iStockphoto; 314: (br) ©Howard Sandler/iStockphoto; 317: (tr) ©Frank & Joyce Burek/Getty Images; 321: (tl) ©NASA; 321: (tr) ©NASA; 323: (b) ©Arco Images GmbH/Alamy; 325: (tr) ©wonganan sukcharoenkana/iStockphoto; 325: (bl) ©InterNetwork Media/Getty Images; 326: (b) ©John Carnemolla/Corbis; 327: (bl) ©NASA; 327: (br) ©NASA; 328: (c) ©Janusz Wrobel/Alamy; 328: (b) ©Courtesy of P.J. Partington; 331: (tr) ©Phillip Jones/iStockphoto; 331: (b) ©Barbara Stitzer/PhotoEdit Inc.; 335: (tr) ©Royalty-Free/CORBIS; 335: (tl) ©Royalty-Free/CORBIS; 335: (br) ©Creatas/PunchStock; 335: (c) ©Photodisc Collection/Getty Images; 335:

(bl) ©Alex L. Fradkin/Stockbyte/Getty Images; 337: (bl) ©Marinko Tarlac/iStockphoto; 337: (bc) ©Wally Eberhart/Visuals Unlimited ; 345: (cr) ©Phillip Jones/iStockphoto; 345: (br) ©Marinko Tarlac/iStockphoto; 348–349: (c) ©CP Photo/Ian Barrett; 351: (b) ©esemelwe/iStockphoto; 352: (cr) ©Siede Preis/Getty Images; 353: (tl) ©Lonnie ThompsonByrd Polar Research Center, The Ohio State University/NOAA; 353: (tr) ©AP Photo/University of Alaska, Fairbanks, Matt Nolan; 356: (tl) ©William Crawford, Integrated Ocean Drilling Program/Texas A&M University; 356: (cr) ©Steven P. Lynch; 357: (b) ©British Antarctic Survey/Photo Researchers, Inc.; 360: (b) ©Michael Dwyer / Alamy; 363: (cr) ©NASA - Goddard Space Flight Center Scientific Visualization Studio; 363: (cl) ©NASA; 366: (t) ©Eric Michaud/iStockphoto; 368: (br) ©Luca di Filippo/iStockphoto; 370: (b) ©Scott Barrow/Solus-Veer/Corbis; 374: (bl) ©Randy Faris/Corbis; 375: (bl) ©Feng Yu/iStockphoto; 376: (tr) ©Courtesy Worldmapper; 377: (cr) ©CP Photo/AP Photo/Alik Keplic; 378: (tl) ©The ENERGY STAR® mark is administered and promoted in Canada by Natural Resources Canada and is registered in Canada by the United States Environmental Protection Agency.; 378: (bl) ©Phil Noble/PA Wire URN:6018697 (Press Association via AP Images); 380: (tr) ©Courtesy of Jenna Muirhead; 380: (b) ©Paul Giamou/iStockphoto; 385: (tr) ©esemelwe/iStockphoto; 385: (cr) ©Michael Dwyer / Alamy; 385: (br) ©Scott Barrow/Solus-Veer/Corbis; 388: (tl) ©Courtesy of Sheila Watt-Cloutier; 388: (b) ©Chris Anderson/Aurora/Getty Images; 389: (tr) ©RIA Novosti / Photo Researchers, Inc.; 389: (br) ©Greenshoots Communications / Alamy; 389: (bl) ©Hank Morgan/Photo Researchers, Inc.; 390: (bl) ©eb33/iStockphoto; 396–397: (c) ©Allan Baxter/Digital Vision/Getty Images; 397: (cl) ©chris scredon/iStockphoto; 399: (bkgd) ©dirkr/iStockphoto; 399: (bl) ©Lyroky/Alamy; 399: (br) ©dirkr/iStockphoto; 400–401: (c) ©AP Photo/Imperial Valley Press, Kevin Marty; 403: (b) ©SAM YEH/AFP/Getty Images; 404: (tl) ©Ragnar Schmuck/fStop/Getty Images; 404: (bl) ©A. T. Willett/Alamy; 405: (tl) ©JoLin/iStockphoto; 405: (tc) ©Robert Payne/iStockphoto; 406: (t) ©Mauro Fermariello/SPL/Photo Researchers, Inc.; 406: (tc) ©Courtesy of British Columbia Oral Cancer Prevention Program; 406: (b) ©Jon Fox Photo/Brand X Pictures/age fotostock; 406: (bc) ©Andreas Reh/iStockphoto; 407: (cl) ©Junko Yokoyama/Photodisc/Getty Images; 410: (br) ©Darwin Dale/Photo Researchers, Inc.; 411: (b) ©ELIZABETH QUILLIAM/iStockphoto; 415: (tr) ©Courtesy of Penelope Robinson; 415: (br) ©GIPhotostock / Photo Researchers, Inc.; 417: (b) ©The Flight Collection/Alamy; 419: (b) ©Mario Tama/Getty Images; 428: (bl) ©Orjan F. Ellingvag/Dagens Naringsliv/Corbis; 429: (tr) ©NASA; 430: (br) ©Eyecandy Images/Photolibrary; 431: (b) ©The McGraw-Hill Companies, Inc./Jill Braaten, photographer; 436: (bl) ©Kayte M. Deioma/PhotoEdit Inc.; 437: (tl) ©AP Photo/Glenn Beil; 438: (br) ©Marissa Henrikson/iStockphoto; 443: (cr) ©Mario Tama/Getty Images; 443: (br) ©The McGraw-Hill Companies, Inc./Jill Braaten, photographer; 443: (tr) ©SAM YEH/AFP/Getty Images; 443: (r) ©ELIZABETH QUILLIAM/iStockphoto; 445: (cr) ©white-windmill/Alamy; 446–447: (c) ©John Poirier/Alamy; 449: (b) ©Gary S. Settles/Photo Researchers, Inc.; 450: (tl) ©1989 Richard Megna, Fundamental Photographs, NYC; 453: (cl) ©Getty Images; 457: (b) ©Miguel Angelo Silva/iStockphoto; 458: (tl) ©Tomaz Levstek/iStockphoto; 458: (bl) ©ngirish/iStockphoto; 458: (br) ©Jeroen Peys/iStockphoto; 461: (br) ©Damir Spanic/iStockphoto; 463: (br) ©Courtesy of Michael Furdyk; 465: (tl) ©Tatjana Brila/iStockphoto; 465: (br) ©Sergey Kashkin/iStockphoto; 466: (tl) ©Spencer Grant/Photo Researchers, Inc.; 466: (br) ©Deep Light Productions/Photo Researchers, Inc.; 467: (br) ©Achim Prill/iStockphoto; 468: (b) ©Forest Woodward/iStockphoto; 470: (bl) ©Larry Hennessy/iStockphoto; 471: (br) ©Patrick Lynch/Alamy; 472: (bl) ©John Morrison/PhotoEdit Inc.; 473: (tr) ©Jeremy Woodhouse/Getty Images; 474: (tr) ©Damien Lovegrove/Photo Researchers, Inc.; 474: (br) ©Maximilian Weinzierl/Alamy; 475: (br) ©G. I. Bernard/Photo Researchers, Inc.; 479: (br) ©Macduff Everton/Getty Images; 481: (tr) ©Gary S. Settles/Photo Researchers, Inc.; 481: (c) ©Miguel Angelo Silva/iStockphoto; 481: (br) ©Forest Woodward/iStockphoto; 483: (cl) ©NASA; 484–485: (c) ©Antonia Reeve/Photo Researchers, Inc.; 487: (b) ©Philips; 488: (tl) ©Optisches Museum Jena der Ernst-Abbe-StiftungMuseumspädagogik/Öffentlichkeitsarbeit; 491: (br) ©PhotoLink/Getty Images; 492: (cr) ©Andrew Lambert Photography/Photo Researchers, Inc.; 493: (br) ©Gabe Palmer/Alamy; 494: (bl) ©Andrew Lambert Photography/Photo Researchers, Inc.; 494: (br) ©E. R. Degginger/Photo Researchers, Inc.; 500: (cl) ©NASA, ESA, A. Bolton (Harvard-Smithsonian CfA) and the SLACS Team; 500: (br) ©Courtesy of Kienan Marion; 502: (b) ©Jim Sugar/CORBIS; 506: (tl) ©Christian Darkin/Photo Researchers, Inc.; 508: (bl) ©Olivier Voisin/Photo Researchers, Inc.; 509: (br) ©Sandorah/Pixtal/age fotostock; 509: (cr) ©Rod Lorance/Alamy; 510: (bl) ©SPL/Photo Researchers, Inc.; 517: (tr) ©Philips; 517: (cr) ©Andrew Lambert Photography/Photo

Researchers, Inc.; 517: (br) ©Jim Sugar/CORBIS; 520: (tl) ©Courtesy of Tuan Trieu; 520: (b) ©Courtesy of Third World Eye Care Society, Photo by Jason Keel; 521: (tr) ©Michael Newman/PhotoEdit; 521: (bl) ©Northrop Grumman/NASA; 521: (br) ©Geoff Tompkinson/Photo Researchers, Inc.; 522: (tr) ©Lyroky/Alamy; 523: (br) ©dirkr/iStockphoto; 525: (tl) ©Getty Images; 526: (cr) ©David Wilson/iStockphoto; 527: (cl) ©Courtesy Paul Hickson (UBC)/NASA

Illustration Credits

2-3: Phil Wilson; 14: Deborah Crowle; 18: Deborah Crowle; 24: Deborah Crowle; 37: Deborah Crowle; 38: Deborah Crowle; 58: Deborah Crowle; 59: Deborah Crowle; 63: Deborah Crowle; 71: Neil Stewart; 74 tree: Ralph Voltz; 75: Ralph Voltz; 81: Deborah Crowle; 83: Deborah Crowle; 90: Deborah Crowle; 97: Dave Mazierski; 117: David Wysotski; 118: David Wysotski; 130: Deborah Crowle; 131: Neil Stewart; 144: Deborah Crowle; 150: Charlene Chua; 153: Deborah Crowle; 158: Deborah Crowle; 160: Malcolm Cullen; 194: Steve Attoe; 204: Ralph Voltz; 205: Ralph Voltz; 245: Deborah Crowle; 264–265: Dave Whamond; 269: Joe LeMonnier; 271: Argosy Publishing; 287: Joe LeMonnier; 288: Joe LeMonnier; 292: Joe LeMonnier; 295: Joe LeMonnier; 304: Joe LeMonnier; 306: Argosy Publishing; 311: Ralph Voltz; 313: Neil Stewart; 315: Cynthia Watada; 316: Joe LeMonnier; 320: Cynthia Watada; 335: Deborah Crowle; 346: Cynthia Watada; 349: Joe LeMonnier; 354: Deborah Crowle; 362: Argosy Publishing; 364: Joe LeMonnier; 371: Dave Whamond; 372: Dave Whamond; 373: Deborah Crowle; 386: Argosy Publishing; 393: Deborah Crowle; 394: Deborah Crowle; 395: Rob Schuster; 398–399: James Yamasaki; 404: Argosy Publishing; 405: Argosy Publishing; 407: Rob Schuster; 409: Deborah Crowle; 412: Deborah Crowle; 417: Tad Majewski; 420: Rob Schuster; 432: Rob Schuster; 437: Tad Majewski; 442: Deborah Crowle; 447: Cynthia Watada; 450: Deborah Crowle; 453: bottom left: Neil Stewart; bottom right: Dave Whamond; 459: Deborah Crowle; 461: Deborah Crowle; 463: Ralph Voltz; 469: Neil Stewart; 470: Deborah Crowle; 471: Cynthia Watada; 473: Rob Schuster; 474: Rob Schuster; 476: Deborah Crowle; 478: Deborah Crowle; 480: Deborah Crowle; 483: Cynthia Watada; 485: Charlene Chua; 491: Ralph Voltz; 500: Argosy Publishing; 506: Argosy Publishing; 507: Argosy Publishing; 508: Argosy Publishing; 510: Argosy Publishing; 511: Argosy Publishing; 513: Argosy Publishing; 529–537: Steve Attoe; 542: Dave Whamond; 548: Dave Whamond; 570–571: Argosy Publishing